League Express

LEAGUE
Publications Ltd

RUGBY LEAGUE
2017-2018
New order?

League Publications Ltd

First published in Great Britain in 2017 by
League Publications Ltd, Wellington House, Briggate, Brighouse, West Yorkshire HD6 1DN

Copyright © League Publications Ltd

A CIP catalogue record for this book is available from the British Library
ISBN 978-1-901347-36-4

Designed and Typeset by League Publications Limited
Printed by H Charlesworth & Co Ltd, Wakefield

Contributing Editor
Tim Butcher

Statistics, production and design
Daniel Spencer

Contributors
Thomas Alderson
Malcolm Andrews
Jack Asbery
Patrick Baines
Marc Bazeley
Peter Bird
Aaron Bower
Martin Butcher
Phil Caplan
Josh Chapman
Tom Coates
John Cox
Joseph Crabtree
John Davidson
Simon Davies
Alex Davis
John Drake
Daniel Fowler
Ian Golden
Ryan Gould
Adam Grey
Tim Griffiths
Michael Hale
Sean Hayes
Ian Henshaw
Phil Hodgson
Ash Hope
Mike Hyde
Andrew Jackson
Chris Jackson

Ian Judson
Connor Kelly
Steve Kilmartin
David Kuzio
Lorraine Marsden
Paddy McAteer
Keith McGhie
Joe Mills
Michael Park
Dave Parkinson
Huw Richards
Ian Rigg
Andrew Robson
Martyn Sadler
David Saffer
Matthew Shaw
Steve Slater
James Stott
Mitchell Tierney
Callum Walker
Gareth Walker
John Walsh
Jordan Weir
Adam Whiteside
Ricky Wilby
Chris Wilson
Gavin Wilson
Ian Wilson
Peter Wilson
Jack Wynne

Pictures
Steve Gaunt
Matthew Merrick
Magi Haroun
Richard Land
Craig Milner
Steve Jones
Bill Watkinson
Dean Williams
Paul Clayton
Richard Long
NRL Imagery
Peter Morley
Bernard Platt
Neville Wright
Bob Brough
David Greaves
Simon Hall
Brian King
Steve McCormick
Jackie Meredith
Bernard Rieu
Melanie Allatt
Neko Grouch
Ian Lovell
Gareth Lyons
Paul McCarthy
Lewis Mitchell
Dave Murgatroyd
Prime Photos
John Rushworth
Ken Sparks
Marc Taylor
Mal Walker

Main cover picture
Craig Milner

CONTENTS

ACKNOWLEDGEMENTS

The League Express Yearbook 2017-2018 is the 22nd of League Publications Ltd's annual series of Rugby League Yearbooks.

In compiling this historical record of the Rugby League year, we rely on the hard work and dedication of all the contributors to *Rugby Leaguer & Rugby League Express*, *Rugby League World* magazine and the totalrl.com website. Without their efforts this yearbook would not be possible.

We are able to include some wonderful action photography provided by, in particular Steve Gaunt of Touchline Pics, Matthew Merrick, Magi Haroun, Richard Land and Craig Milner.

Thanks also to the Rugby Football League for their help during the year and to the historians and statisticians at clubs who help us resolve any anomalies.

Acknowledgement also to the Rothmans Yearbook 1999, compiled by our late friend Ray Fletcher, the British Rugby Records Book from London Publications, and to the club officials, and some supporters, who helped us verify records.

The comprehensive statistical review was put together meticulously, as always, by Daniel Spencer, who also designed the book.

Special thanks to Matthew Shaw, Lorraine Marsden and Malcolm Andrews, who respectively wrote the Championship, League 1 and NRL sections.

Thanks also to Opta Sportdata, who compiled the Opta Index Analysis in our statistical section.

TIM BUTCHER
Contributing Editor

INTRODUCTION

As seasons go, Super League XXII will surely go down as one of the best.

For those who wanted to see a year of unpredictability end with a new name engraved on the Super League trophy, it might not have finished perfectly, with old-hands Leeds Rhinos registering their eighth Grand Final win over the team that had dominated the competition, in at times, breathtaking fashion. But even then, the disappointing performance of Castleford Tigers on that October day was the result of a dramatic twist of fate that no-one could have predicted. And let's face it, for Leeds fans it was a wonderful way to say farewell to two more of their greatest players in Danny McGuire and Rob Burrow.

It would be reasonable to say that the year began under a cloud. England's failure to get into the previous year's Four Nations final didn't help and there were ongoing worries at several clubs, including the once all-conquering Bradford Bulls. Players who had added panache to Super League, in James Segeyaro and Chris Sandow, had refused to come back from Australia and there was a rumbling disquiet about the way England coach Wayne Bennett, 12,000 miles away, was approaching his job. The cancellation of an England training camp in Dubai in January seemed symptomatic of a lack of clarity and coordination within the Rugby Football League.

But by the second week in February, the doom and gloom had disappeared into the ether. The World Club Series, reduced from three games to two this year, lifted everybody within the British game with the 2016 Grand Finalists Warrington and Wigan beating their NRL opponents, Brisbane and NRL Premiers Cronulla respectively, by some margin, the Warriors to become World Club Champions for the first time since 1994.

Overnight the game had a collective spring in its step, although the Wolves and the Warriors surprisingly both went on to have moderate seasons by their standards, failing to make even the play-offs, with Warrington safely seeing out their year in the Qualifiers.

Neutral supporters didn't worry too much about that, as clubs that had been also-rans in years gone by started to look like top dogs.

Salford Red Devils spent the bulk of the season in the top four, and some weeks in second, while Wakefield Trinity were within an inch of making the play-offs and, despite not quite getting there, finished their season on a great high.

And then there was Castleford. Seasoned observers had noted their pre-season promise and as the season unfolded it became apparent eventual coach of the year Daryl Powell had assembled and developed a squad that could play at a high level, with humiliating consequences for more than one big-name club.

One of those was the Rhinos. But that was at the start of March. Leeds, as reigning Champions in 2016, had experienced their own humbling downfall by not making the top-eight. Some thought that 66-10 reverse could have been a continuation of that decline. In the light of that, the euphoria after their Grand Final win in October was more than understandable.

The Tigers' suffering over those last three days of the season could be seen as rough justice after a stellar season that ended with the club topping the table for the first

Jake Webster celebrates with jubilant Castleford fans, on the night the Tigers won the League Leaders Shield

time in its 91-year existence. The night they beat Wakefield at home to be presented with the League Leaders Shield was a marvellous occasion. Had key man Zak Hardaker not been suspended two days before Old Trafford, who knows how it might have ended.

The other major trophy winner was Hull FC, who retained the Challenge Cup with an 18-14 win over Wigan, in a game they at one stage looked like winning comfortably until a late Wigan fightback that produced one of the most exciting finishes to a Wembley final.

And of the rest, St Helens had a slow start to the year but finished like a train, seconds away from causing a major upset in their Super 8s semi-final at Castleford on what was undoubtedly the most dramatic finish of the year, if not of the decade. Huddersfield Giants' season followed a similar pattern, though they couldn't make the play-offs despite a late charge.

Widnes Vikings finished bottom of the table, starting the season after the sudden departure of key man Kevin Brown to Warrington and with their two halfbacks injured and unavailable. But they managed secure their Super League status in the Qualifiers with a tense 12-10 win in Perpignan.

Catalans saved their bacon on the last day of their season with a win at Leigh in the Million Pound Game, with the Centurions relegated after only one season. In no way were Leigh easy beats in 2017 though, picking up some valuable scalps along the way, most notably their first competitive win over neighbours Wigan in 33 years.

Introduction

Hull Kingston Rovers bounced straight back after an outstanding season built on the unswaying support of their fan base, which contributed to their full-time operation and turned out in greater numbers than in Super League.

And Rugby League extended its horizons once more with the entry of Toronto Wolfpack, who secured promotion from League 1 with relative ease, assembling a high-quality squad while paying for the travel and accommodation costs for the rest of the teams in the division.

It's one of Rugby League's most colourful stories and there's plenty more in this year's Yearbook. We hope you enjoy reliving the 2017 season.

TIM BUTCHER
Contributing Editor

The 22nd League Express Yearbook contains the full story of the domestic year, the Australian NRL season and match facts for all Super League, Challenge Cup games involving professional teams, Championship and League 1 games. Every player who has played Super League is also listed along with those players to have made their debuts this year. We have also selected five individuals who we judge to have made the biggest impact on Rugby League in 2017. There are scoring and attendance records for every club. The 2016 Four Nations tournament is also detailed.

League Publications publishes the weekly newspaper Rugby Leaguer & Rugby League Express, as well as the monthly glossy magazine Rugby League World and the UK's most popular League website 'totalrl.com'.

* Because of print deadlines, full details of the 2017 World Cup will be included in next year's edition.

1
THE 2017 SEASON

DECEMBER 2016
Club v Country

England's lacklustre Four Nations campaign left British Rugby League in a state of mild depression. Not only had new coach Wayne Bennett not managed to get England into the final but the Rugby Football League admitted after Australia had beaten New Zealand comfortably at Anfield that there had been shortcomings in the tournament's organisation. One of them had been staging a double header at Coventry on Saturday 5th November that finished late on the traditional Bonfire night evening.

Bennett's major target was winning the World Cup to be staged Down Under at the end of 2017, one which had universal approval. Despite that, a club v country argument was already brewing. Bennett was planning to name a group of players in December that would head to Dubai in January as part of a warm-weather training camp.

St Helens coach Keiron Cunningham slammed the England coach in the pages of League Express. Cunningham was fuming that more pressure and workload was being placed onto the shoulders of elite players and that clubs' pre-season preparations would be severely disrupted. And he reckoned the RFL was as culpable as Bennett for agreeing to his demanding plans, even though it transpired that the governing body was to compensate clubs financially. Bennett insisted he still had support from Super League coaches and remained positive about England's World Cup chances.

Three days before Christmas, the trip was cancelled by the Rugby Football League. A statement read: 'The England coaching staff and RFL have reflected on all views and concluded the plans now in place would not deliver what was initially expected.'

As the year stumbled to a close, the domestic game was throwing up problems too, the most headline-grabbing that four-time Super League Champions Bradford Bulls had entered administration for the third time in four years. The Bulls, relegated in 2014, had set their stall on a return to Super League but had failed to even reach the Qualifiers in 2016.

The club's holding company, Bradford Bulls Northern Ltd, was understood to be carrying debts of close to £1 million, the bulk of it owed to HMRC.

Despite a queue of six potential buyers reportedly lining up to take the Bulls out of administration the saga ran on and on. Former Bulls Chairman Mark Moore, with help from Supporters Direct, was amongst the interested parties.

The future of York City Knights was in the balance for even longer, the League 1 (third tier) side having folded in July because of financial difficulties. The Knights had faced a battle over playing venues and lost revenue for the past few years. They had been evicted from the Huntington Stadium in 2014 with the promise of a new community stadium to be shared with the city's soccer club.

When the fixtures for the 2017 season were published, the City Knights were not included. But at the start of December it was announced the club had been taken over by a consortium headed by former London Skolars general manager Jon Flatman. The RFL reinstated York into League 1 and re-issued the fixture list. But the club was still awaiting confirmation that a new deal could be struck to remain at the soccer club's Bootham Crescent ground as part of the City of York Council's community stadium plan.

Championship Sheffield Eagles was another club in trouble. Since 2013, with the closure and demolition of their Don Valley Stadium home, the Eagles, not for the first time in their history, had been nomadic, with their home games in 2016 played at Sheffield Hallam University's sports ground. And that in a year when the club had upgraded to a full-time squad with the promised aid of a financial backer, who had pulled out before the start of the season.

The Eagles, who had punched afar above their weight as a part-time Championship club, had a disappointing campaign and were at one point in danger of being relegated to League 1. By the end of the season they were in danger of folding when another prospective investor pulled out, with a new stadium still in doubt. But by Christmas, coach and stalwart Mark Aston had resumed the CEO role and begun to assemble a playing squad, with Wakefield's Belle Vue stadium set to be the Eagles home for 2017.

Meanwhile, Castleford, Warrington and Leeds were reflecting on the sudden departure of star players.

Tigers winger Denny Solomona, who had set a new Super League tries-in-a-season record in 2016, failed to report for the start of pre-season training in early November. Solomona had been training with rugby union outfit Sale for a number of weeks.

Solomona's cross-code transfer was expected to be announced by the rugby union side, though the Tigers remained defiant they had not agreed to sell the player. The Tigers began legal proceedings against Solomona, Sale and the player's agent, Andy Clarke, after the player walked out on the remaining two years of his contract. The Sale coach claimed Solomona had been fired by Castleford.

Leeds Rhinos' playing fortunes had been turned around with the late-season arrival of hooker James Segeyaro and they duly tied him up on a two-year contract. But after he returned to Australia for the off-season, the Papua New Guinean openly spoke of his desire to walk out of his contract. Segeyaro, who told the Brisbane Courier Mail that he did not want to return to the UK for the sake of his 'happiness', was linked with a return to the NRL, with current Premiers Cronulla Sharks.

The Rhinos remained adamant they would not negotiate a release for the 26-year-old, insisting that the hooker was in 'good condition' and would report back to training on January 3rd.

Warrington didn't put up a fight and were hunting a replacement for departed scrum-half Chris Sandow after they confirmed the Australian would not be returning to England to fulfil the remainder of his contract, although the club said in a statement they would be retaining his registration until further notice.

Tony Smith refused to rule out a move for Ben Barba, granted a release by Cronulla in order to enter rehabilitation after testing positive for cocaine use shortly after his side's Grand Final triumph over Melbourne Storm.

But in early December, the Wolves tempted Widnes captain and England Four Nations stand-off Kevin Brown on a two-year deal, paying the Vikings a six-figure transfer fee. Widnes had rejected overtures from both Cronulla and St Helens in the previous 18 months for their influential captain

Hull FC snapped up another star halfback. Head coach Lee Radford admitted he had no hesitation in signing Albert Kelly after the enigmatic halfback joined the club on a one-year deal. Kelly, 25, made the controversial switch across the city after leaving relegated Hull Kingston Rovers, where he was suspended by the club during their doomed 2016 Qualifiers campaign when he reported back late after being granted time off.

Radford also revealed that the decision was made to let forward Frank Pritchard return to the NRL with a year left on his contract because he couldn't guarantee him a starting berth.

Wakefield, who dropped the 'Wildcats' nickname during the off-season, also saw the sudden departure of a key player, French prop Mickael Simon, who agreed to re-join

13

his former club Catalans Dragons. Huddersfield Giants prop Craig Huby was lined up by Trinity as a replacement. Hull KR's Australian prop Mitch Allgood also joined Trinity.

Huby was part of an ongoing clearout at Huddersfield, with new coach Rick Stone's pursuit of Newcastle fullback Jake Mamo finally set to pay off, with Joe Wardle going to the Knights with immediate effect. Eorl Crabtree revealed he was happy to continue his playing career but retired to free up salary cap space at the Giants. The long-serving one-club forward brought an end to his 16 seasons in Giants colours, taking up a new role as club ambassador.

The year ended with a series of festive friendlies, with winger Tom Johnstone scoring a hat-trick in Wakefield's 30-6 win at Leeds in the Boxing Day Wetherby Whaler Festive Challenge; Castleford proving far too strong for a youthful Hull FC side, winning at home by 42-10 on the same day and the day after, Warrington Wolves recording a 28-18 win at Widnes.

JANUARY
Bulls fight

Hull FC dominated the 2016 League Express Readers' Poll, with hooker Danny Houghton winning the highest accolade of Player of the Year, captain Gareth Ellis topping the poll as Mature Player of the Year and Captain of the Year, while Lee Radford was the Super League Coach of the Year. And the club itself was voted Club of the Year, narrowly edging out Leigh Centurions into second place. Houghton gained 51 per cent of almost 1,000 votes to win the poll, beating Albert Goldthorpe Medal winner Luke Gale of Castleford into second place. Wakefield Trinity winger Tom Johnstone was voted 2016's Young Player of the Year.

Retired Sky commentator Mike Stephenson was awarded the MBE in the 2017 New Year's Honours list, along with Tim Adams. Stevo's honour was for services to Rugby League and Sports Broadcasting while Adams was awarded his MBE for services to Rugby League and Horseracing. He was Chairman of Sheffield Eagles when they won the Challenge Cup in 1998 and Chairman of the RFL's Benevolent Fund since its inception.

Royal patronage also caused a stir in the pages of League Express after the Queen's grandson Prince Harry replaced her as patron of the Rugby Football League. Former Wakefield MP David Hinchliffe, who was the founding secretary of the Parliamentary Rugby League Group from 1988 until he stood down from the House of Commons in 2005, strongly criticised the appointment of the prince, a regular at high-profile rugby union matches but as yet to show any interest in Rugby League.

There were bigger and more immediate matters to deal with as the new year opened with the news that Bradford Bulls were to be placed into liquidation, after financial administrators turned down a bid from a consortium headed by former New Zealand Rugby League Chairman Andrew Chalmers, with the club carrying debts of about £1 million and facing a further £1m shortfall. The Rugby Football League nonetheless confirmed that a new Bradford side could compete in the second-tier Championship, with the kick-off a month away. The Bulls were scheduled to play at Hull Kingston Rovers on February 5th and any new club would start the season with a 12-point deduction.

The Chief Executive of Rotherham Titans rugby union club, Richard Lamb and his partner Damian Irvine, the former CEO of the NRL's Cronulla Sharks, were still keen to buy the club.

Two weeks later, the RFL agreed to allow a new Bulls club to be operated by a new company - Bradford Bulls 2017 Limited - wholly owned by Chalmers through his New Zealand-based company Orcas Rugby League Limited and ex-Wigan coach Graham Lowe.

Weeks of criticism followed the decision to put the Bulls straight back into the second tier rather than place the new company into League 1.

January

Lamb launched a scathing attack on the Rugby Football League, calling the governing body the most 'amateurish' he'd come across. His plan had included creating a fans' trust, which would have allowed supporters the opportunity to play a part in the club's future. 'The whole process has been an absolute shambles,' said Lamb.

The new Bulls were beaten 28-10 in Luke Robinson's testimonial match by Huddersfield Giants, but with a team largely comprising youth players they more than held their own against a Giants side with eight Super League regulars in the starting 13. Acting head coach Leigh Beattie was holding the reins for new coach, former Manly legend Geoff Toovey.

The episode had left Bradford's players as free agents and several were snapped up by Super League clubs.

Former Hull KR stalwart centre Kris Welham signed a two-year deal at Salford, with Bulls product, second-rower Tom Olbison joining Widnes Vikings and James Clare signing for promoted Leigh. Huddersfield Giants had already signed Lee Gaskell, Dale Ferguson and Paul Clough and they now added Alex Mellor and Adam O'Brien.

Another new Huddersfield signing, Jake Mamo, was in doubt for the start of the Super League season as he recovered from injury and waited for his UK visa. Mamo signed a two-year deal to join the Giants from the Newcastle Knights but the Australian fullback was recovering from a broken bone in his leg, which he suffered when struck by a scooter on holiday in Bali.

Coach Rick Stone also signed giant forward Shannon Wakeman from NSW Cup side Illawarra Cutters as a direct replacement for Craig Huby, who signed for Wakefield Trinity.

St Helens' signing from relegated Hull KR, prop Adam Walker was voted Scotland's 2016 Player of the Year and received the Dave Valentine Award, after standing out in the 2016 Four Nations.

But Saints' biggest signing, their former junior Matty Smith was out for the start of a season after breaking his leg just before the half-time hooter in their 16-0 Karalius Cup victory over Widnes Vikings.

Salford head coach Ian Watson had begun scouring the transfer market in Australia following Daniel Vidot's departure from the club. The former Brisbane Broncos winger was granted an early release from his contract after expressing a desire to return Down Under. The Red Devils landed the services of the former Dally M and Australia international Todd Carney on a one-year deal following the stand-off's departure from Catalans Dragons at the end of the previous year.

The Red Devils were due to face their former Director of Rugby Tim Sheens at an Employment Tribunal in early February, with the former Australian national coach claiming in excess of £50,000 in alleged unpaid wages. Sheens became the club's Director of Rugby in June 2015, but was unveiled as Hull KR's new coach for the 2017 season on 9th September 2016, three weeks before Hull KR and Salford met in the Million Pound Game at the Lightstream Stadium. Sheens stood down from his role with the Red Devils prior to that game to avoid a conflict of interest.

Wakefield Trinity parted company with hooker Scott Moore after agreeing to end his contract by mutual consent.

Leeds Rhinos signed Manly hooker Matt Parcell to replace departed forward James Segeyaro, who controversially walked out on Leeds to return to

LADBROKES CHALLENGE CUP - ROUND 1

Saturday 28th January 2017

Aberdeen Warriors 8 Pilkington Recs 62
Egremont Rangers 24 The Army 14
Featherstone Lions 29 Distington 28
Fryston Warriors 33 Normanton Knights 10
Leigh Miners Rangers 12 Wigan St Patricks 16
London Chargers 116 Bridgend Blue Bulls 0
RAF 12 York Acorn 30
Royal Navy 34 Myton Warriors 38
Siddal 16 Milford Marlins 4
Thatto Heath Crusaders 30 Skirlaugh 10
Thornhill Trojans 32 Castleford Lock Lane 18
University of Hull 12 Rochdale Mayfield 22
Wath Brow Hornets 4 Haydock 17
West Bowling 0 Kells 12
West Hull 24 Hull Dockers 10
Wests Warriors 40 British Police 224

LADBROKES CHALLENGE CUP - ROUND 2

Saturday 11th February 2017

Featherstone Lions 0 Wests Warriors 26
Haydock 30 Thornhill Trojans 20
Kells 14 Rochdale Mayfield 16 *(aet)*
London Chargers 12 Fryston Warriors 40
Myton Warriors 18 York Acorn 4
Pilkington Recs 10 Siddal 32
Wigan St Patricks 18 Egremont Rangers 28

Saturday 18th February 2017

West Hull 18 Thatto Heath Crusaders 16

Australia late in 2016, despite being contracted to the club.

Parcell made his first appearance in a Rhinos shirt in the Ryan Hall Testimonial game, a 30-4 win over Hull KR, with Hall kicking a touchline conversion for Leeds' last try of the evening.

Hull KR, gearing up for a tilt at an immediate return to Super League for 2018, had early in January recorded a 40-16 friendly win at rivals Hull FC. Hull FC also lost a friendly by 18-6 at Salford two weeks before the league kick-off and on the same day Castleford won 22-6 at St Helens.

The Tigers handed on-loan Leeds fullback Zak Hardaker, who spent the last part of 2016 on loan at the Penrith Panthers after leaving the Rhinos, the number one shirt for the upcoming Super League season.

Tigers prop Andy Lynch set his sights on becoming Super League's most capped player in 2017. Since making his debut for Castleford in 1999, Lynch had made 433 Super League appearances, 21 fewer than current record holder Kevin Sinfield, who held the record of 454.

Widnes coach Denis Betts solved the leadership problem of replacing departed skipper Kevin Brown by naming Chris Houston, who joined Widnes from Newcastle Knights at the end of 2015, and Joe Mellor as co-captains.

And on Sunday 22nd January, new League 1 team Toronto Wolfpack, coached by former Leigh coach Paul Rowley, made their professional debut in a 26-20 friendly defeat at Hull FC.

FEBRUARY
Top of the World

Round 1

St Helens came from behind to edge out Leeds Rhinos 6-4 in a bruising and nail-biting Thursday night Super League opener at Langtree Park, re-named the Totally Wicked Stadium for 2017.

Leeds were just in front at the break after enjoying a lion's share of possession, with centre Joel Moon having shown his strength in the 22nd minute by brushing off Saints' new centre Ryan Morgan to touch down in the corner. Liam Sutcliffe couldn't convert from the touchline.

There was only one try in the second half too and it proved crucial as Theo Fages capped off a memorable all-round performance to score the winner on 43 minutes, dummying and going over to the left of the sticks. Crucially Mark Percival kicked the extra two points.

Four minutes later the Rhinos looked to have taken the lead again after Kallum Watkins got on the outside of Percival to sprint down the touch line. The supporting Sutcliffe took his pass on the inside and hared for the right corner, but a superb cover tackle from Tommy Makinson, who raced from the far wing, saw him slide the halfback into touch.

As well as scoring the winning try, French halfback Fages made 42 tackles as the Rhinos targeted him all game.

Another youngster, Leeds fullback Ashton Golding had a great game, holding up Dominique Peyroux, Makinson and outstanding Alex Walmsley.

Saints were without new signing Matty Smith after he broke his leg in pre-season, meaning a debut for Academy product Danny Richardson in the halves. Coach Keiron Cunningham also handed debuts to Morgan, who'd started the previous season with Parramatta and ended it with Melbourne, Tommy Lee, signed from Salford, and Luke Douglas from the Gold Coast Titans. There was no place for former Hull KR prop Adam Walker.

The Rhinos had hooker Matt Parcell on debut following his move from Manly, while Rob Burrow made his 500th career appearance as he partnered Sutcliffe in the halves. Danny McGuire was a late withdrawal for the Rhinos because of a quad injury as he joined Brett Delaney, Brett Ferres and Keith Galloway on the sidelines.

> There were five rule changes brought in for the start of Super League XXII. The two major changes were that the tackle made after a 20-metre restart would be a zero tackle and a 40/20 kick would be rewarded not with a scrum but a tap ten metres in. There was to be a stricter ruling of markers not being square and players outside a scrum would have to stand at least ten metres back, instead of five. The ball would be deemed dead only if it touched the line or the ground beyond, preventing players from making a moving ball dead by putting a foot out before touching it.

Friday's TV game was a different beast altogether when Leigh played their first Super League game since 2005. But they couldn't live with Castleford as the Tigers made a statement of intent with a 44-16 victory at the Mend-a-Hose Jungle.

The Centurions, who had not won at Castleford since 1987, gave as good as they got in a scoreless opening quarter and had the better of the closing stages, at least in terms of scoring, after having trailed 44-4 on 62 minutes. But in the middle segment the Tigers ran riot, particularly in a sizzling spell before the break.

Leigh sorely missed captain and hooker Micky Higham, out with a calf injury, but Castleford were on fire. The Tigers' flamboyant style was on show when winger Greg Eden tried to jink clear of a posse of defenders in his own in-goal area before firing a pass to Zak Hardaker, who then raced 10 metres into the field of play.

Reigning Albert Goldthorpe Medal winner Luke Gale scored two tries and landed eight goals from as many attempts – several from the touchline - in a 24-point contribution, equalling the club record in a Super League game.

For the record, Ryan Hampshire, who had spent a year on loan at Castleford in 2016 and signed from Wigan, scored Leigh's first try in their second spell in Super League in the 47th minute, but by that stage the Tigers led 32-0.

On the same night, Huddersfield showed glimpses of their old selves and gave an indication that their poor 2016 campaign was behind them with a 28-16 win at Widnes. Danny Brough caused chaos with his kicking game, while the forward pack, led by the outstanding Sebastine Ikahihifo, dominated as the Giants led 24-6 going into the last ten minutes.

The Vikings' two off-season signings, Tom Armstrong from Leigh and Tom Olbison from Bradford, both made debuts. With Kevin Brown's departure to Warrington Wolves and Joe Mellor injured, Widnes boss Denis Betts opted for Chris Bridge alongside Tom Gilmore in the halves.

Huddersfield coach Rick Stone handed debuts to four players and they all played a key part in the victory. Lee Gaskell was solid at fullback and distributed the ball well in attack, Paul Clough and Shannon Wakeman put in good shifts in the pack and Dale Ferguson was man of the match as he excelled on the left side on his first appearance since returning to the Giants. They were expecting to be without backrower Tom Symonds for eight weeks after he sustained a knee injury.

On the Saturday, Catalans claimed a 20-12 win over Warrington in Perpignan.

The Dragons' plans were thrown into disarray 24 hours prior to the kick-off when it was announced Tony Gigot had received a two-year suspension from the French Rugby League Federation, even though he had tested negative for illegal substances. The Federation alleged that Gigot had attempted to bribe the tester into not going through with the test. The Dragons were expected to appeal the decision.

It was a gritty and determined showing from the Dragons, epitomised by former Australia forward Greg Bird, making, along with prop Mickael Simon, a second Catalans debut. There were also debuts for former Manly centre Brayden Wiliame, who played at fullback, Roosters and one-time Hull FC prop Sam Moa and former St Helens scrum-half Luke Walsh. Centre Iain Thornley didn't play despite the Dragons settling a long-running wrangle with Hull KR about his off-season transfer only days before.

Warrington were without Stefan Ratchford, Ben Westwood and Chris Hill, while new signing Brown was also out injured. Mike Cooper made his second club debut after re-signing from St George and there were debuts for former Wigan prop Dominic Crosby, Academy product Harvey Livett and Andre Savelio, signed from St Helens, who had a fine game, putting Warrington into the lead with a try in the ninth minute.

Bird's try on 48 minutes gave the home side the lead for the first time and despite Rhys Evans' try, after a great tip-on from Ashton Sims, pulling the Wolves back to 14-12, Wiliame's try on the hooter sealed the win. Catalans winger Fouad Yaha was set for several weeks on the sidelines after suffering knee ligament damage.

February

Wigan made a comfortable start to their title defence with a 26-16 Sunday afternoon victory over Salford at the AJ Bell Stadium.

Two tries from Oliver Gildart in a dominant left-side attack helped the Warriors to a 26-0 interval lead. Gildart's winger, Joe Burgess, back from a year in the NRL with the Roosters and South Sydney, George Williams and Joel Tomkins also got first-half tries, with new signing from Catalans Morgan Escaré kicking the goals.

The Red Devils rallied in the second half to create some optimism for the new campaign, hooker from York Kris Brining, Junior Sa'u and Michael Dobson touching down for the hosts.

The Red Devils were still waiting for the green light to fly Todd Carney into the UK after announcing his signing in January on a one-year deal. They had however agreed a severance payment with former Director of Rugby Tim Sheens who had left at the end of 2016 to join Hull Kingston Rovers.

Snow and rain on the Sunday afternoon in west Yorkshire created a mudbath at Belle Vue, known in 2017 as the Beaumont Legal Stadium, as new signing from Huddersfield Jake Connor's late try, who had come off the bench due to an injury for fullback Jamie Shaul, and three goals from the boot of Marc Sneyd, proved to be enough for Hull FC to record a 12-8 victory over Wakefield.

The re-signed Scott Grix's try early in the second half looked likely to have got Wakefield in a winning position but Connor was the first to Sneyd's spilled chip to the Wakefield line. There was an exciting finish as Trinity attacked from deep and Fetuli Talanoa hacked the ball dead just before Grix touched down.

Hull had Albert Kelly on debut, although he was subsequently banned for a game for a high tackle on Matty Ashurst, along with Connor and Josh Griffin. Grix and Kyle Wood made second debuts for Wakefield after signing from Huddersfield. Former Giants prop Craig Huby was also on debut, as was Canberra halfback Sam Williams.

A crowd of over 8,800 at the renamed KCOM Craven Park saw Hull Kingston Rovers secure a 54-24 victory over the reborn Bradford Bulls in the first round of the Kingstone Press Championship, which had kicked off the weekend before Super League. There was a tribute to the Hull KR President, former player and coach Colin Hutton, who had died at the age of 90.

World Club Challenge

Wigan coach Shaun Wane declared it time for Super League to 'pat ourselves on the back' after the Warriors completed a series whitewash in the World Club Series as Wigan became World Champions for the fourth time after a 22-6 Sunday-afternoon victory against Cronulla. The Warriors backed up Warrington's win against Brisbane on the Saturday night as Super League ended its drought in the series - reduced from three games to two this year - with its first ever wins in the competition's expanded format.

Wigan won their first World Club Challenge since 1994 with a dogged 22-6 win over the reigning NRL Premiers Cronulla. They played superbly in defence, particularly in the first half, although they had a couple of lucky escapes when the video referee disallowed tries to Luke Lewis - with offside winger Jesse Ramien technically within the ten metres but playing no part - and Kurt Capewell, judged to have brushed the touch-in-goal line as he grounded the ball.

Wigan's Liam Farrell halted by Cronulla's Andrew Fifita and Jayden Brailey

It took Wigan only four minutes to break the deadlock. Hat-trick hero Joe Burgess, after a season of making little impact in the NRL, scored a balletic try in the left corner. His second in the 23rd minute may not have been quite as spectacular but it was a lovely step inside to finish. And his third a minute from time completed a wonderful afternoon when he raced onto George Williams' deft kick into the in-goal.

Williams was a rock in attack and defence, with every one of his teammates also giving their all. New signing Morgan Escaré was a revelation, with his contributions just after half-time doing much to secure the result. First he stood up to huge prop Sam Tagataese when he ran free down the middle and obviously fancied his chances of running through the former Catalans fullback.

Minutes later he was scooping up a loose ball during a Wigan attack and cleverly working the ball to Oliver Gildart, who shrugged off Jack Bird for Wigan's third try. Escaré even converted from the touchline. Cronulla's only score came from a Ramien try just before the hour mark and James Maloney's conversion.

DACIA WORLD CLUB CHALLENGE

Sunday 19th February 2017

WIGAN WARRIORS 22 CRONULLA SHARKS 6

WARRIORS: 22 Morgan Escare; 21 Lewis Tierney; 3 Anthony Gelling; 4 Oliver Gildart; 5 Joe Burgess; 6 George Williams; 7 Thomas Leuluai; 8 Frank-Paul Nuuausala; 16 Sam Powell; 10 Ben Flower; 14 John Bateman; 12 Liam Farrell; 13 Sean O'Loughlin (C). Subs (all used): 11 Joel Tomkins; 15 Tony Clubb; 17 Taulima Tautai; 19 Ryan Sutton.
Tries: Burgess (4, 23, 79), Gildart (45);
Goals: Escare 2/3, Powell 1/1.
SHARKS: 1 Gerard Beale; 2 Jesse Ramien; 3 Jack Bird; 4 Ricky Leutele; 5 Kurt Capewell; 6 James Maloney; 7 Chad Townsend; 8 Andrew Fifita; 14 Jayden Brailey; 10 Matt Prior; 11 Luke Lewis; 12 Wade Graham; 13 Paul Gallen (C). Subs (all used): 9 Fa'amanu Brown; 15 Chris Heighington; 16 Jason Bukuya; 17 Sam Tagataese.
Try: Ramien (59); **Goals:** Maloney 1/1.
Rugby Leaguer & League Express Men of the Match:
Warriors: George Williams; *Sharks:* Paul Gallen.
Penalty count: 12-6; **Half-time:** 10-0; **Referee:** Robert Hicks;
Attendance: 21,011 *(at DW Stadium).*

Warrington, despite the absence of Chris Hill, Ben Currie and Stefan Ratchford, set up the World Club weekend on the Saturday night with a 27-18 win over Brisbane Broncos.

With debutant Kevin Brown pulling the strings from stand-off and Mike Cooper setting an outstanding lead up front, the Wolves raced into an improbable 20-0 lead in fine style.

But then, arguably just as impressively, they stood firm when the Broncos mounted their expected response, standing toe-to-toe with their NRL opponents - literally at times - in what was an enthralling encounter.

Brisbane never recovered from having Ben Hunt's first kick charged down in the opening set by the non-stop Joe Westerman. Hunt saved himself in the short-term to haul down Westerman but on the very next play Brown dummied over from the play-the-ball with his first touch in a Wolves shirt. The crowd exploded into life and it set the tone for the rest of the night.

Ryan Atkins, Matty Russell and Tom Lineham helped the hosts into a 20-0 lead. Declan Patton added 11 points with the boot, while Corey Oates, James Roberts and David Mead replied for Brisbane.

DACIA WORLD CLUB SERIES

Saturday 18th February 2017

WARRINGTON WOLVES 27 BRISBANE BRONCOS 18

WOLVES: 7 Kurt Gidley (C); 5 Matthew Russell; 3 Rhys Evans; 4 Ryan Atkins; 2 Tom Lineham; 6 Kevin Brown (D); 22 Declan Patton; 14 Mike Cooper; 9 Daryl Clark; 10 Ashton Sims; 12 Jack Hughes; 18 Andre Savelio; 13 Joe Westerman. Subs (all used): 15 Brad Dwyer; 23 Joe Philbin; 28 Harvey Livett; 34 Ben Westwood. **Tries:** Brown (2), Atkins (14), Russell (18), Lineham (39); **Goals:** Patton 5/6; **Field goal:** Patton (63).
BRONCOS: 1 Darius Boyd (C); 2 Corey Oates; 3 James Roberts; 4 Jordan Kahu; 5 David Mead; 6 Anthony Milford; 7 Ben Hunt; 8 Joe Ofahengaue; 9 Andrew McCullough; 10 Herman Ese'ese; 11 Sam Thaiday; 12 Matt Gillett; 13 Josh McGuire. Subs (all used): 14 Alex Glenn; 15 Tevita Pangai; 16 Jai Arrow; 18 George Fai. **Tries:** Oates (25), Roberts (44), Mead (72); **Goals:** Kahu 3/3.
Rugby Leaguer & League Express Men of the Match:
Wolves: Kevin Brown; *Broncos:* Andrew McCullough.
Penalty count: 8-6; **Half-time:** 24-6; **Referee:** Phil Bentham; **Attendance:** 12,082 *(at Halliwell Jones Stadium)*.

Round 11

With the World Club Series taking centre stage on what should have been round two, the previous year's bottom four teams brought forward their round eleven games to allow them to enter the Challenge Cup.

Salford gained their first victory of the new season with a thrilling 30-20 Thursday night triumph over the Giants at the John Smith's Stadium, in which Gareth O'Brien scored 22 points. The fullback scored two of his side's four tries and kicked seven goals from as many attempts.

O'Brien gave the Red Devils the lead with a ninth-minute penalty but Huddersfield scored the first try of the game through England winger Jermaine McGillvary.

The Red Devils won the second quarter, with centre Junior Sa'u taking O'Brien's pass to scythe through for a 22nd minute try and O'Brien adding a penalty on the stroke of half-time to extend his side's lead to 10-4. It was 16-4 just after the restart thanks to a try from O'Brien but two tries in three minutes from centre Alex Mellor, a close-season signing from Bradford, saw the Giants come back to 14-16.

O'Brien cut through for his second try in the 63rd minute before adding his fifth goal to make it 22-14. But Huddersfield, with Sebastine Ikahihifo almost unplayable at times, gave themselves a chance with a 69th minute try through Ukuma Ta'ai, who stormed to the line after a superb popped pass from Brough.

Then came the game's true turning point. With minutes left, Brough carved open Salford with an inside pass to the onrushing Ryan Hinchcliffe, but his wayward pass was intercepted by Sa'u who raced back up the field. Then Josh Jones showed supreme strength and determination to bounce off six tiring Huddersfield defenders to score the decisive try, before O'Brien's late penalty goal got Salford up and running with the two points.

The game included a ridiculous ploy which had featured in several games of dummy-halves deliberately passing a ball into a prostrate defender at the ruck, even if he was not interfering with play. Salford centre Jones actually passed the ball forward but still won a penalty.

In the week following, Rugby Football League Head of Match Officials Steve Ganson wrote to all Head Coaches that a player would be guilty of misconduct if he behaved in any way contrary to the true spirit of the game.

The night after Salford's win, Leeds eked out a 17-14 victory over newly promoted Leigh Centurions in a tight game at Leigh Sports Village.

Leeds were hit with the late withdrawal of prop Mitch Garbutt because of illness, which resulted in Anthony Mullally starting and Josh Walters moving to the bench, while Leigh coach Neil Jukes made five changes from the Centurions' defeat at Castleford, notably with Ben Reynolds replacing Martyn Ridyard at stand-off, although captain Micky Higham was still not fit to play. And Leigh were set to be without Liam Hood for several weeks after the hooker suffered a broken jaw in an off-field incident.

Leigh led 8-0 after a lightning start but they were gradually clawed back. Matty Dawson opened the scoring after four minutes and fullback Mitch Brown added a second three minutes later following an offload close to the line by Reynolds, who couldn't convert either.

But Adam Cuthbertson crashed through for a try in the 12th minute - shortly after he entered the action from the bench - and winger Ryan Hall added another two minutes later.

Jimmy Keinhorst, a replacement for the injured Joel Moon, forced his way over for Leeds' third try eight minutes before the break. Liam Sutcliffe was able to convert only one of his side's tries but he slotted a 40-metre field goal on the stroke of half-time to open up a two-score lead at 15-8.

Sutcliffe added another two points on the hour mark before Leigh blew the game wide open on 67 minutes when Ben Crooks forced his way over for his side's third try, with Reynolds converting. Crooks was denied a second by the video referee before second-rower Atelea Vea was hauled down superbly by Keinhorst a foot short of the line on the last tackle.

Round 2

Catalans Dragons made it two from two with a 16-14 win at Hull FC in the Thursday TV game. It was a game littered with errors and a high penalty count, but no less exciting. There was high drama from start to finish in a contest that saw the lead change hands five times, with the boot of Luke Walsh being the eventual difference between two sides that didn't give an inch physically throughout.

Eventually it came down to superior game management and leadership from Dragons halves Walsh and Richie Myler, with the class of NRL import Greg Bird rising to the fore again. Despite being sin-binned in the first half, he more than made amends, having involvement in everything the Catalans did well and making a key break in the build-up to his side's only try. Walsh kicked six from six, with his final penalty on 67 minutes giving the final margin of victory.

A first half dominated by the forwards ended with the hosts taking an 8-4 lead thanks to Carlos Tuimavave's try off a superb one-handed inside pass from Sika Manu.

Within 60 seconds of the second-half restart the lead changed again as Bird broke up the middle and combined with Thomas Bosc to send in Myler. On the hour mark, Hull were two in front when Liam Watts wrenched the ball out of Krisnan Inu's grasp and crashed over the line for a try converted by Marc Sneyd. But a Walsh penalty after a late tackle by Scott Taylor levelled the scores.

And Watts was then penalised for a spear tackle on Jason Baitieri - he was subsequently banned for four games - allowing Walsh to win the game.

The Friday TV game was scheduled to be Wigan versus Widnes but on the Thursday Skysports announced it had been postponed and that they would cover Warrington-Castleford instead. That was the game that most viewers wanted to see anyway.

However the next morning, the day of the game, the Wigan-Widnes fixture was switched and the game went ahead, without the presence of the TV cameras, at the Select Security Stadium.

Wigan were to be investigated by the Rugby Football League over the postponement, thought to be in breach of the sport's operational rules by calling off the game without consulting both the RFL and Widnes. Wigan Chairman Ian Lenagan said that the pitch could not sustain two games of sport that weekend due to 'intermittent standing water on the pitch and the further forecasted bad weather'. But images that materialised on social media over the weekend appeared to show Wigan Athletic, the stadium's co-tenants, watering the pitch at half-time on the Saturday during their game with Nottingham Forest.

In July it emerged that Wigan had been fined £2,000 for the postponement, although Lenagan revealed that the RFL had tried to fine the Warriors £50,000 but that was overturned by the Independent Appeals Tribunal.

The Vikings received praise for the way they responded to put the reversed fixture on with just a few hours' notice. They had initially sought clarity over whether they could claim the two competition points and not play the game. The Vikings were given a financial contribution as compensation from Wigan in return for hosting the game.

On the night, the Warriors produced an amazing second half comeback to win 28-26. The first half was end-to-end, with the Vikings edging it 18-12 thanks to tries from Lloyd White, Danny Craven and Tom Armstrong, while Thomas Leuluai and Oliver Gildart crossed for the Champions.

The second half was a half of two halves with Widnes in full control as they led 26-12 at one stage. It looked like Wigan were going to lose for the first time this season but an amazing comeback, led by captain Sean O'Loughlin, saw them score 16-unanswered points in the final 20 minutes to take the spoils.

The same night, the Headingley faithful breathed a collective sigh of relief when sub Liam Sutcliffe combined with Rob Burrow to seal a 20-14 victory against Salford. Level at 14-all with barely three minutes remaining, the industrious Stevie Ward's offload on half way to birthday boy Adam Cuthbertson was clearly forward. But the dextrous Aussie then produced a wonderful flipped offload to Burrow, the scrum-half turning the ball back inside to Sutcliffe, who romped between the posts, with Burrow adding his fourth goal from seven shots to secure the points.

'I don't know how two touch judges and a referee can miss it,' said an unusually agitated Red Devils coach Ian Watson.

Watson was also unhappy that the RFL Disciplinary Committee had controversially suspended Salford winger Justin Carney for two matches for making contact with referee James Child in the Red Devils' clash with Huddersfield. The referee had appeared to walk up close to Carney, who raised his forearm, apparently to prevent a collision.

Youngsters Sam Wood, Alex Mellor and Kruise Leeming excelled in the Giants' 24-16 victory over Wakefield at the John Smith's Stadium, also on the Friday night.

With new captain Leroy Cudjoe out, Wood came into the centres for only his fifth Super League game and crossed twice in the first seven minutes. Despite that early 8-0 lead the Giants were left trailing 8-16 at the break after Liam Finn fought his way over and Ben Jones-Bishop scored two tries. But a late scoring spree, inspired by Ukuma Ta'ai and Danny Brough, saved their bacon.

The last try that sealed it was a beauty as Brough ran back to collect a loose offload, shot through a gap and, as he was closed down, sent a perfect kick to the touchline for Jermaine McGillvary to collect and race over.

But even that was bettered by Jones-Bishop's effort on 25 minutes for which he ran the length of the field, turning defenders inside out en route for the try line. Jones-Bishop left the field in the 70th minute with a broken nose after being felled in a tackle involving Ta'ai. The incident was not penalised but put on report and Ta'ai was banned for one game the following Tuesday.

There was a major surprise when the Centurions made history on the Friday night with their first Super League win at Leigh Sports Village, beating St Helens 24-16.

The building blocks to victory came during an outstanding first half-hour from the Centurions. Tries from former Saint Atelea Vea, Gareth Hock and Jamie Acton put Leigh 18-4 up at the break, with Saints' only first-half try an acrobatic effort from Adam Swift.

A second-half score from James Roby gave Saints hope before returning captain Micky Higham's try with 13 minutes remaining ensured Leigh's first Super League win over Saints, Alex Walmsley getting St Helens' third try. James Green was sin-binned for the hosts after a shoulder charge on Walmsley but there was still no way through for Saints.

Media reports Down Under claimed that St Helens had made a mammoth offer to Cronulla skipper Paul Gallen to play his final two seasons in Super League.

The round was completed by Friday night as no Super League game ended with a margin greater than eight points. After 27 minutes the TV game looked like breaking the pattern as visitors Castleford led at Warrington by 22-6 following four blistering tries in eight minutes.

With Zak Hardaker producing the kind of performance that won him a Man of Steel award in 2015 and double Albert Goldthorpe Medal winner Luke Gale orchestrating from scrum-half, the Tigers looked unbeatable in that period.

After the euphoria of the win over Brisbane, the Wolves did well to steady the ship, Andre Savelio's second try in the 71st minute getting them back to within two points before a superbly worked Greg Eden try took Castleford home by 30-22.

BETFRED SUPER LEAGUE
Sunday 26th February

	P	W	D	L	F	A	D	Pts
Castleford Tigers	2	2	0	0	74	38	36	4
Wigan Warriors	2	2	0	0	54	42	12	4
Catalans Dragons	2	2	0	0	36	26	10	4
Huddersfield Giants	3	2	0	1	72	62	10	4
Leeds Rhinos	3	2	0	1	41	34	7	4
Hull FC	2	1	0	1	26	24	2	2
Salford Red Devils	3	1	0	2	60	66	-6	2
St Helens	2	1	0	1	22	28	-6	2
Leigh Centurions	3	1	0	2	54	77	-23	2
Wakefield Trinity	2	0	0	2	24	36	-12	0
Widnes Vikings	2	0	0	2	42	56	-14	0
Warrington Wolves	2	0	0	2	34	50	-16	0

MARCH
Wolves lose their bite

Round 3

A sell-out Thursday-night crowd at the Mend-A-Hose Jungle saw Castleford remain at the top of the table following a stunning 66-10 win against local rivals Leeds.

The Tigers were playing Rugby League at its best and were unstoppable for much of the televised clash. Rhinos coach Brian McDermott, reflecting on a game in which the Tigers scored twelve tries, with wingers Greg Eden and Greg Minikin both claiming hat-tricks, said: 'We weren't actually all that bad in the first half, but Castleford were white hot. Their first try summed it up. We'd spent all week working on stopping them scoring that kind of try – and they scored that kind of try. In my 21 years in Super League as a player and as a coach I can't recall a more clinical performance.'

Leeds' cause wasn't helped by the withdrawal on the day because of illness of halfback Rob Burrow, while second-rower Carl Ablett was suspended following a collision with referee Chris Campbell against Salford the previous week. Jamie Jones-Buchanan, Stevie Ward and Tom Briscoe were also absentees.

Castleford had their own problems, with Rangi Chase having been suspended for a game by the Tigers for an undisclosed internal issue, while fellow halfback Ben Roberts remained ruled out by injury.

But with Paul McShane stepping in at stand-off to forge an effective partnership with another Rhinos reject in scrum-half Luke Gale, Castleford maintained their scintillating early-season form, with fullback Zak Hardaker, on loan from Leeds, coming into the line from deep to highly-telling effect, and Minikin and Eden duly prospering on the flanks.

Gale registered 22 points and moved top of the early Albert Goldthorpe Medal standings.

The Rhinos' defeat eclipsed the 68-14 loss to Wigan in 1996 as their biggest-margin defeat in the summer era.

Champions Wigan were the only other team left on maximum points when they beat Leigh 20-0 the following night in the 'Battle of the Borough'.

A torrential downpour, before and during the game, ensured it was not a free-flowing contest, but it didn't lack excitement. The only score in the first half came when the brilliant George Williams confused Leigh with a deft kick behind the defensive line and good work from Lewis Tierney and Willie Isa eventually set Anthony Gelling up for the try.

The second half, again, was a battle of the middles in a real blood-and-thunder affair. But it was two moments of brilliance from Williams, first scoring a try himself before creating Gelling's second, that saw the Warriors come out on top.

Youngster Liam Marshall acquitted himself well, coming in on the wing for his debut, while Oliver Gildart missed out with a shoulder knock, with Joe Burgess moving into the centre.

Curtis Naughton was called up for his Leigh debut to replace Adam Higson on the wing, while Lachlan Burr made his debut off the bench.

The Wolves were still point-less after a 24-14 Saturday-afternoon defeat at Salford, who themselves were playing some fine football, with scrum-half Michael Dobson outstanding. Warrington led at the end of a tight first half, with tries from Declan Patton and Jack Hughes cancelling out efforts from Junior Sa'u and George Griffin.

Kris Brining's touchdown from dummy-half put the Red Devils in front before Warrington levelled at 14-14 through Jack Johnson's score. But Gareth O'Brien struck a penalty goal five minutes after, and Sa'u won it seven minutes from time when he crossed for the second time from a grubber kick.

In Perpignan, Widnes Vikings came back from 14-0 down late in the first half to secure a 14-14 draw in a game played in torrential rain and mud.

The Catalans were without Sam Moa, Julian Bousquet and Jason Baitieri but were 12-0 up by the 12th minute through Brayden Wiliame and Richie Myler tries, both converted by Luke Walsh, who extended the lead with a penalty goal.

But tries to Patrick Ah Van and Tom Olbison either side of half-time gave the Vikings - themselves missing Alex Gerrard, Joe Mellor and Tom Gilmore - a real foothold. And when in the 73rd minute Hanbury pounced on a grubber in the right corner from Aaron Heremaia, the fullback had the chance to win the game with the conversion - but he couldn't nail it.

On the Friday Marc Sneyd scored a hat-trick and kicked eight goals as Hull FC won 48-8 at injury-hit Huddersfield Giants. The Airlie Birds led 24-0 at the break through a brace from Sneyd and tries from Fetuli Talanoa and Albert Kelly. Kelly scored his second after the restart and Josh Griffin and Carlos Tuimavave got tries before Sneyd crossed for his third.

Sam Wood and Oliver Roberts got consolation scores for the Giants in the second half.

And on the same night, Wakefield got off the mark with a 16-12 win at St Helens in another rain-affected game.

Trinity were good value for their 10-0 lead until just before half-time when Saints centre Ryan Morgan forced his way over. Two second-half tries from Mark Percival looked as though Saints had muscled their way to a 12-10 win.

But six minutes from the end, Sam Williams put in a measured grubber under the posts and as Jacob Miller raced to ground it he was fouled by young half Danny Richardson. Referee James Child ruled no try but sent it upstairs where the video ref ruled a penalty try should be awarded.

Round 4

Winger Liam Marshall collected a memorable four tries as Wigan piled on the misery for point-less Warrington in the Thursday night TV game at the Halliwell Jones Stadium.

The final scoreline of 38-16 was a reflection of the Warriors' dominance, despite them missing nine frontline players, with former Wigan junior Liam Forsyth, back from a spell in rugby union with Bath, making his debut along with young ex-Catalans prop Romain Navarrete. Trainee accountant Marshall, who was making just his second top-flight start, scored two tries in either half as the Warriors chalked up a fourth straight league win to go alongside their World Club Challenge triumph.

The Wolves were badly missing their captain Chris Hill up front, alongside key strike players like Ben Currie and Stefan Ratchford.

Liam Farrell was outstanding on the left edge that terrorised the Wolves and yielded five tries, four of them to the excellent Marshall, a week after his debut against Leigh.

Morgan Escaré looked like the shrewdest signing of the winter, halfbacks Thomas Leuluai and George Williams both contributed significantly, and captain Sean O'Loughlin was outstanding.

Tony Smith chose to leave out Declan Patton at halfback and instead started with 20-year-old Harvey Livett alongside Kevin Brown. But the Wolves looked off their game all round as they remained rooted to the bottom of the table.

Meanwhile Wigan forward John Bateman underwent shoulder surgery. Bateman had only made one appearance for the Warriors so far in 2017 in their World Club Challenge victory over Cronulla in February.

At the end of the weekend Wigan remained joint top with Castleford, whose perfect start to the season continued with a comprehensive 34-0 win at Widnes on the Sunday.

The heavy rain couldn't stop the Tigers' spectacular, expansive play that had yielded four wins from their first four games. Defeated Vikings coach Denis Betts said after the game: 'You find it hard not to clap because there's some fantastic stuff.'

Castleford had to show grit and toughness in defence during the opening 20 minutes. At that point, Widnes were well on top and hammering the Castleford line as the Tigers looked out-of-sorts early on.

But they dug in and within 13 minutes they had put four tries on the board, raced into a 22-0 lead and put themselves into a winning position. The league's top scorers, Greg Eden and Greg Minikin finished with two tries each.

The Vikings remained without a win, with co-captain Joe Mellor yet to appear in 2017 after off-season surgery and another first-choice halfback Tom Gilmore still out with an ankle injury.

Before the game, Widnes staged a minute's applause for one of their club legends, paying tribute to their former captain Mick Adams, who passed away the previous Thursday at the age of 65. Adams played in four Challenge Cup winning teams and scored 68 tries in more than 400 appearances.

Another side doing it tough was St Helens, who lost for the third week running on the Friday night, by 24-14 at Hull FC, who came into the game buoyed by the milestones of head coach Lee Radford's 100th game in charge as well as reigning Man of Steel Danny Houghton's 250th Super League appearance.

There was high drama and controversy again as Hull had Jansin Turgut sin-binned before Saints fell foul of a rare eight-point try. Alex Walmsley was deemed to have fouled Carlos Tuimavave in the act of scoring a crucial try that firmly swung the game back in Hull's favour after Saints had managed to wrestle back the lead.

The first half ended 8-6 to Saints as a Dominique Peyroux try and Mark Percival goals cancelled out Albert Kelly's converted opener. Two Marc Sneyd penalties after the break gave Hull the lead, but Percival's penalty after Turgut's departure and his try three minutes later had Saints 14-10 up.

Tuimavave's eight-pointer on 69 minutes swung it and Kelly's second try in the last minute ended the contest. Walmsley escaped a ban with an EGP while Turgut got two matches.

Leigh Centurions notched their second Super League win of the season, hammering Huddersfield at home by 30-0. Adam Higson and Jamie Acton tries, both converted by Ben Reynolds, got Leigh clear in the first half.

Harrison Hansen, Reynolds and Sam Hopkins all went over after the break, while continuing to hold out the Giants, Danny Tickle leading a terrific defensive effort.

On the same Friday night, Leeds scored 40 point for the first time since August 2015 when they defeated unbeaten Catalans Dragons 46-10 at Headingley.

It came on the back of a record defeat at Castleford the week before and after an open letter to supporters from chief executive Gary Hetherington warning that changes could be made if performances didn't improve within a month.

The Rhinos were grateful for the return of Carl Ablett and Rob Burrow, while some positional changes also seemed to spice up the attack, with 22-point Liam Sutcliffe operating in the back row and Joel Moon spending a significant part of the game at stand-off.

Catalans forward Greg Bird was ruled out for six to eight weeks with a broken thumb, although he played on. Winger Jodie Broughton was also injured, suffering a torn bicep, and he also underwent surgery, likely to be sidelined for at least four months.

Bird was also the victim of a late elbow to the back of the head from Brad Singleton, which left him needing seven stitches. The incident wasn't spotted by match officials but Singleton later pleaded guilty to the offence and was banned for six games.

On the Sunday afternoon, Wakefield snatched victory from the jaws of defeat with a nail-biting 24-22 win over a shattered Salford at the Beaumont Legal Stadium.

In a see-sawing affair that saw the game twice turned on its head in the second half, Reece Lyne's second try and a Sam Williams conversion with 62 seconds left saved Trinity's bacon. But the Red Devils got the ball back from a short kick-off and, right on full-time, Ben Murdoch-Masila got over the try-line but lost the ball as he went to ground it.

The home team dominated possession and the penalty count, but were behind by 10 points with 11 minutes left until Bill Tupou and Lyne struck to sensationally steal the two points.

Utility forward Dean Hadley made his Trinity debut after arriving on an initial one-month loan deal from Hull FC, although that was extended and he played all season at Wakefield.

Round 5

Leigh backed up their big win over Huddersfield with another committed performance to beat mis-firing Warrington 22-8 in the Thursday TV game at the Leigh Sports Village.

Gareth Hock produced a performance reminiscent of his Great Britain days and finished with two tries as the Wolves equalled their worst ever start to a Super League season, despite the return of captain Chris Hill for his first appearance of the season.

Tries from Hock and Ben Crooks gave Leigh a 12-2 half-time lead. Adam Higson and Hock extended the advantage to 20-2 after the break before Tom Lineham crossed to give Wolves faint hope. Ben Reynolds had missed three conversions but his late penalty goal sealed it.

Lineham had earlier spent ten minutes in the sin bin for elbowing Ryan Hampshire in the face as the Leigh fullback pulled him back whilst chasing a loose ball. Lineham was later banned for two games.

The following night, Wigan dropped their first point of the season after a 16-all draw with Huddersfield at the DW Stadium.

The Giants, who were never behind, led 14-10 at the break, with both teams crossing for two tries apiece, the first coming from nothing for Huddersfield with Lee Gaskell going over from a metre out after Jermaine McGillvary was hauled down following a 95-metre interception.

Morgan Escaré and young fullback Darnell McIntosh then traded four pointers, before youngster Tom Davies crossed on debut to put Wigan just two points adrift. Danny Brough's penalty goal then ensured the lead was four at the interval.

Wigan, who had 15 men for over 70 minutes after Sean O'Loughlin and Jack Wells were injured in the first ten minutes, scored the only try of the second half through Anthony Gelling, with Escaré and Brough kicking a penalty apiece. But no one could produce that one piece of magic to earn the win, Sam Powell and Brough both missing late field-goal attempts.

March

The Warriors were missing Liam Farrell, who had suffered a calf strain at an England training camp earlier in the week.

On the Sunday, Huddersfield head coach Rick Stone rubbished an article in The Sun on Sunday that claimed Brough had played his final game for the club following an alleged dispute between player and coach.

At the end of the weekend Wigan were clear at the top of the table after Castleford Tigers' 100 per cent start ended when they lost at Salford 13-12. On another Sunday afternoon of wind and rain, Gareth O'Brien stepped up in the 76th minute to pot the winning field goal.

When Luke Gale touched down his own kick to make it 6-0 after five minutes, it looked like it was going to be business as usual. But Castleford could not unlock the Red Devils' line again in the first half and in return they were being careless in possession.

For a while they held Salford at bay but the pressure told on the half-hour mark when Ben Murdoch-Masila charged over on the angle. O'Brien missed the conversion. However, right on half-time, just as it looked as though the two sides would go in at 6-4, there was a huge moment.

For a split second, Castleford came alive with ball in hand. The ball went through the hands at a rate of knots before Michael Shenton sent Greg Eden careering away to the line. But the pass was pulled back, adjudged to be forward.

However, Castleford did extend the lead three minutes after half-time when Greg Minikin showed strength to force his way over the line - after Junior Sa'u had spilled in midfield - taking Justin Carney and O'Brien over the line with him.

But Murdoch-Masila got his second try on 54 minutes for O'Brien's conversion to make it 12-10. After Castleford conceded a penalty on their own line, O'Brien levelled it up before kicking the field goal with four minutes left.

Todd Carney was named on the bench for Salford but didn't get on to make his debut.

Widnes head coach Denis Betts conceded his side were 'in a hole' following their 32-12 Friday-night defeat at Hull FC.

After being in the contest for much of the first half, the Vikings had no answer to the Airlie Bird juggernaut in the second as the home side, once again inspired by Albert Kelly, notched up three tries in a blistering thirteen-minute spel. Kelly was on great form, collecting another two tries.

On the same night, Leeds confirmed they had recovered from the mauling at Castleford barely two weeks earlier by beating Wakefield at home 38-14.

A couple of hours before a derby that had been deemed too close to call beforehand, Leeds released an expected statement that they had reached a financial agreement to sever James Segeyaro's two-year contract on which the Papuan hooker reneged.

The Rhinos had already reinvested, paying Manly a fee to release Matt Parcell. Parcell, renowned for his speed out of dummy-half, starred with a try, two assists, two offloads and a stunning covering tackle to help down disappointing Trinity, who failed to show their best form. They did provide the try of the game from their winger Tom Johnstone, who showed the Leeds cover a clean pair of heels when Wakefield were still in the game in the first half hour.

Props Adam Cuthbertson and Mitch Garbutt thrived on the momentum that Parcell provided.

St Helens forward Kyle Amor called on supporters to get rid of the negativity surrounding the club and on the Saturday Saints produced a superb 28-24 win over the Catalans in Perpignan.

Saints looked to be heading for their fourth defeat in a row, down 24-22 after a nip-and-tuck game until a piece of magic from Perpignan-born Theo Fages sent Jack Owens over to score the match-winning try eight minutes from time. The French international produced a miraculous back-of-the-hand offload as he was tackled to send in Owens and Mark Percival added the conversion.

Dragons president Bernard Guasch slammed the performance of referee Robert Hicks, angered to see tries ruled out for both Richie Myler (obstruction) and Thomas Bosc (forward pass).

Round 6

Wakefield came back from the dead in the Thursday-night TV game, overcoming a 12-point deficit to keep Leigh still without a win away from home.

The 28-24 home victory looked highly unlikely as the Centurions carried on where they had left off the week before to seemingly be in control at half-time, leading 24-12. But it was not to be, as tenacious Trinity fought their way back through three tries without reply to steal the spoils.

For Wakefield there were strong second-half performances from David Fifita, Craig Huby, Tinirau Arona and Keegan Hirst, who was finally making his Super League debut after his winter move from neighbours Batley and having played two games on dual-registration for Dewsbury. Tom Johnstone scored another sparkling try to start the comeback and Ben Jones-Bishop scored his 100th career try 14 minutes from the end to give Wakefield the lead for the conclusive time, catching a smart kick from Sam Williams to just about get over in Matt Dawson's tackle. Dawson himself had earlier in the half had a try disallowed for a forward pass.

Trinity chairman Michael Carter had earlier in the week denied accusations he was set to sell the club's Super League franchise, insisting the fight for their new stadium in nearby Newmarket was still alive.

The next night, Hull FC became the first team to beat Wigan since the previous September, hanging on for a 22-20 victory at the DW Stadium, in a game that looked over just after half-time.

The injury-hit Warriors looked down and out as Hull blew them away with three tries in a nine-minute period in the first half as they took their chances to lead 0-18 with Steve Michaels, Albert Kelly and Jake Connor all touching down.

A try from Jamie Shaul put Hull 22 points in front at the start of the second half to seemingly put the game out of reach for the Warriors but they showed great fighting spirit to almost snatch a late victory.

Liam Forsyth grabbed his first try for the club, while George Williams, Tom Davies and Liam Marshall all went over to set up a grandstand finish. But Hull managed to hang on after Morgan Escaré was unable to convert Marshall's try from the touchline.

St Helens coach Keiron Cunningham paid tribute to scrum-half Matty Smith after he made a winning return to the club in Friday's 31-6 home victory over Warrington.

The Saints Academy product, who rejoined the club from Wigan during the winter after having last played for Saints in 2010, had been forced to sit out the first five matches of the campaign after breaking his leg in pre-season.

The previous week's win against the Catalans had clearly boosted Keiron Cunningham's team's confidence and they moved onto another level again against the Wolves, controlling the game for long periods.

Warrington, who had Stefan Ratchford returning for his first game of the season, briefly rallied after trailing 18-0 at the break but, with Smith in control, Mark Percival excellent out wide and Alex Walmsley a tower of strength up front, Saints eventually eased to an impressive win.

The Wolves remained bottom of Super League as the only pointless team in the competition after their sixth straight defeat of the campaign.

A third consecutive victory - by 28-12 at Huddersfield - made the Rhinos the early pacesetters alongside Hull FC.

March

Much of the pre-match build-up had centred around Danny Brough, who would start the game for the Giants after reports that he had played his final game for the club following an alleged bust-up with coach Rick Stone.

The club mocked the reports. However, the Scotland captain's main involvement resulted in a second-half sin-binning after an altercation with Leeds forward Carl Ablett. Huddersfield had scored just six tries in their last four matches. Adam Cuthbertson's early season form continued with a big effort down the middle.

Widnes Vikings failed in a bid to bring Castleford halfback Rangi Chase to the Select Security Stadium to cover the absence of Joe Mellor and Tom Gilmore.

On the Friday they suffered a sixth successive game without a victory, the 46-10 home defeat by Salford a real humbling.

In the week, head coach Ian Watson had agreed a new three-year deal with the Red Devils, with Junior Sa'u, Ben Murdoch-Masila, Weller Hauraki and Lama Tasi also agreeing to stay into 2018 and beyond.

They celebrated in style with a nine-try demolition of the Vikings. The home fans booed their side at half time as they trailed 30-0, with Tasi the first of six different try scorers in the first half.

After the break, Corey Thompson grabbed a Widnes try before Michael Dobson and Robert Lui added to the visitors' lead. Debutant Todd Carney then came off the bench to help set Gareth O'Brien up for Salford's ninth try.

On the Sunday afternoon, Greg Eden scored twice to move ahead of injured team-mate Greg Minikin in the try-scoring tables, taking his tally to 10 during the 43-26 home win against Catalans.

Castleford were determined to show that the previous week's defeat at Salford was an anomaly. But they were staring down the barrel of a 14-point deficit after just eleven minutes after Iain Thornley and Richie Myler tries and three Luke Walsh goals.

But Catalans ultimately had no answer to what the Tigers would throw at them over the remaining 70 minutes or so and by half-time, that bright start had quickly faded and they found themselves eight points behind. With Castleford's array of attacking brilliance, it never really felt as if they would be able to turn that deficit around.

They got back to 22-20 but Michael Shenton's try just after the hour mark ensured there would be no way back for Catalans.

* That weekend Hull KR scrum-half Jamie Ellis equalled the world record of 41 set by Liam Finn - set at Featherstone in 2012 - for consecutive goal-kicks after landing his first four efforts against Halifax. Ellis could have taken the record outright 13 minutes from the end of his side's 28-14 victory.

* The RFL was awarded £10.75 million by Sport England for the next four years - a reduction in funding of 38 per cent from the last cycle.

BETFRED SUPER LEAGUE
Sunday 26th March

	P	W	D	L	F	A	D	Pts
Castleford Tigers	6	5	0	1	229	87	142	10
Hull FC	6	5	0	1	152	78	74	10
Leeds Rhinos	7	5	0	2	163	136	27	10
Wigan Warriors	6	4	1	1	148	96	52	9
Salford Red Devils	7	4	0	3	165	126	39	8
St Helens	6	3	0	3	107	98	9	6
Leigh Centurions	7	3	0	4	130	133	-3	6
Wakefield Trinity	6	3	0	3	106	132	-26	6
Catalans Dragons	6	2	1	3	110	157	-47	5
Huddersfield Giants	7	2	1	4	108	184	-76	5
Widnes Vikings	6	0	1	5	78	182	-104	1
Warrington Wolves	6	0	0	6	78	165	-87	0

APRIL
Raising the cap

Round 7

The 2016 Super League runners-up, Warrington, avoided a seventh consecutive defeat since the start of the 2017 campaign, earning their first point with a 22-22 home draw against Hull FC on the first Saturday of April.

The Wolves fought back from 22-8 down and Hull coach Lee Radford insisted that in the end it was a point gained for his side, even though they lost ground on leaders Castleford and Leeds.

Warrington were inspired by virtuoso performances from the likes of Daryl Clark and Ben Westwood, running in 14 points in the final half-hour without reply to get their points tally up and running. And it could easily have been converted into a win in a dramatic final few minutes, both Stefan Ratchford and Kurt Gidley missing with late field-goal attempts.

Albert Kelly, a standout in the early part of the season, broke the early deadlock with a magnificent individual try. Warrington briefly hit back with the first of Matty Russell's three tries to make it 6-4, but from there, the Wolves began to implode.

They conceded two further tries before the break, both of them while in great attacking positions. Kevin Brown's stray pass was picked off by Jake Connor, who went the distance. Then they received a penalty and on the first tackle Ratchford spilled the ball. Hull countered and Jamie Shaul finished a scintillating long-range move. Boos rang out around the Halliwell Jones Stadium.

But Warrington rallied, and reduced the deficit with Russell's second try after the break, which was another well-taken finish in the corner, to make it 20-8 after Sneyd had added a penalty.

Rhys Evans had a try disallowed before Clark's return from the bench proved to be the catalyst for the momentum to turn, as the hooker charged over from close range. When Josh Bowden dropped the ball under pressure, Russell's hat-trick reduced the gap to two before Kurt Gidley knocked over a penalty to set up a thrilling finale.

Leeds and Castleford were both a point clear in the table after Friday-night wins.

In the TV game, the Rhinos made it four wins in a row after a 26-18 home victory against Wigan, with the outcome uncertain until three minutes from time when Carl Ablett, in his 250th Super League game, powered onto Joel Moon's pass and through three defenders. Ablett was a standout. He produced a wonderful pass to send Kallum Watkins clear for Ryan Hall's 21st-minute try, plucked out two vital interceptions lurking round the back, made 28 tackles that left a mark and generally got under the skin of his opponents. His running battle with Frank-Paul Nuuausala was a battle within a battle to savour.

Watkins set up Hall's try and spectacularly scored another to celebrate his 200th appearance in a Rhinos shirt. His 53rd minute effort came after Nick Gregson was ruled to have made a double movement as he crossed, with video referee Phil Bentham overturning the on-field call, with the score at 16-12 in Leeds' favour.

Wigan's poor completion rate in the second half cost them dear. The highlight for them was George Williams' two breathtaking first-half tries, exhibiting speed, balance and poise out of the top drawer. Williams, at the age of 22, was being chased by several NRL clubs, with Parramatta being reportedly at the front of the queue.

Brett Ferres was sin-binned in the 39th minute for a crusher tackle on Oliver Gildart, just back from injury. The Wigan centre was re-introduced but then was immediately withdrawn after the break. Ferres copped a six-match ban the following Tuesday.

Castleford coach Daryl Powell described the Tigers' home 52-16 win over the Giants as a 'mixed bag'. The league leaders were some way off their fluent best against a Giants team that had not won in their last five outings and which missed suspended halfback Danny Brough. Luke Gale, celebrating his 250th career appearance, and winger Joel Monaghan both scored second-half hat-tricks in the ten-try victory.

Wigan's defeat at Headingley left Salford in fourth spot after the Red Devils beat St Helens at home 22-14 in the Thursday-night TV game.

Halves Robert Lui's running and Michael Dobson's kicking had Saints pinned in their own half for much of the first half. Gareth O'Brien nudged the Red Devils ahead with a penalty goal in the 23rd minute and the lead was extended to 8-0 when Craig Kopczak came off the bench to cross from Kris Brining's flat pass under the sticks.

Salford took command in the 43rd minute with a pulsating try. After defending a set on their line, Todd Carney offloaded on half way to Mark Flanagan, who in return provided a great pass to allow Kopczak through a gap. He charged to within ten metres of the line before passing left to Dobson to score. O'Brien's conversion gave Salford a commanding 14-0 lead.

Saints, who had lost halfback Theo Fages in the opening two minutes of the game with concussion, rallied. Two tries in seven minutes, from Alex Walmsley and Ryan Morgan, cut the deficit to four points.

After that, Salford's defence on their own line was unrelenting and, despite Lui being sin-binned for delaying a restart, they sealed the game with five minutes to go. Morgan made a calamitous mistake off Todd Carney's kick and the halfback picked up the loose ball to free Dobson for the crucial score. Lomax, returned from injury, scored in the final two minutes following a fantastic run and offload from Mark Percival, but it was too late for Saints.

There was a major blowout in Perpignan on the Saturday as Wakefield flew in and out on the same day and registered a 38-18 win at the Stade Gilbert Brutus. Trinity's wingers had a field day, with Ben Jones-Bishop registering a hat-trick and Tom Johnstone scoring a brace.

A fourth defeat in a row and fifth game without a win saw the Catalans, still without the injured Greg Bird and Jodie Broughton while Brayden Wiliame withdrew before the game late on with a calf complaint, rooted in the bottom four. Wakefield were impressive all game and moved into sixth place on the ladder.

Widnes gained their first victory in the 2017 season on the Saturday afternoon, a gutsy display against Leigh at a sun-drenched Leigh Sports Village resulting in a deserved 37-24 win. A hat-trick of tries to Danny Craven and a stellar performance from fellow halfback Tom Gilmore, playing his first match since the opening game of the season, were enough for Widnes to finally to break their losing run.

Round 8

In the first week of April, the 12 Super League clubs voted 7-5 in favour, Castleford, Huddersfield, St Helens, Wakefield and Widnes voted against, of an incremental increase in the finite salary cap and an increase of the number of marquee players to two per club.

The cap was to rise from £1.825m in 2017 to £1.9m in 2018, £2m in 2019 and £2.1m in 2020 while club-trained marquee players would be deemed to have a salary cap value of £75k and all other marquee players of £150k.

There was also to be a new dispensation for new and returning players. New players, targetting rugby union players, would have a salary cap value of zero in year one and 50 per cent in year two. For a returning talent pool player, one who had not played Rugby League in the preceding five years (for reasons other than as a result of a disciplinary sanction or criminal conviction) a club's salary cap value would be reduced by 50 per cent in his first full season and by 25 per cent in his second full season. A player had to be over 19 on 31st August prior to the start of the season.

All players outside a club's Top 25 paid players who were age eligible to play at under-21s level in the relevant season and were paid £20k or less, were to be excluded from a club's salary cap.

Super League chief Roger Draper conceded that the changes were unlikely to attract the world's best players from the NRL, with the focus on retaining home-grown players.

Senior officials at some clubs were upset that the new regulations would favour the richer clubs and that the most even Super League in recent years could be the last. Dispensations and exemptions could, in theory, lead to every club spending £500,000 more on players every year. Investment by clubs in Academy rugby was also predicted to suffer with clubs likely to divert the money into their first-team squads.

In the following week George Williams became Wigan's second marquee player alongside Sam Tomkins after agreeing a four-year contract.

One of the clubs against the cap increase, Castleford, were the new favourites to win the 2017 Super League title after their 27-10 win over Wigan at the DW Stadium on the Thursday.

The Warriors dominated the opening 20 minutes as they camped out on the Tigers' line but they were unable to score and were made to pay dearly later in the half. Castleford grabbed the opening try on 24 minutes when Jake Webster crashed through off Ben Roberts' flat pass before Luke Gale raced clear following an offload by Jesse Sene-Lefao and subsequent break from Zak Hardaker to see the Tigers cross twice in three minutes.

Wigan were 14-0 down after Gale slotted over a penalty but they went into the break in better shape after Morgan Escaré showed some pace to cross for 14-4 at half-time.

But the Tigers extended their lead three minutes after the turnaround with Sene-Lefao shrugging off two defenders and racing over from 15 metres to put them 16 points in front. Wigan threw everything at the Tigers in the second half but it took them until the 73rd minute to break through as Escaré went over for his second, backing up a break down the right by young winger Jack Davies. But Greg Eden assured a Tigers victory with a 90-metre interception before Gale kicked a field goal.

Warrington's first win of the season the following night - a 25-14 home success over Leeds - saw the Tigers stand alone at the top of the Super League table with seven wins from eight matches.

Declan Patton played a key role on his return as Warrington finally climbed off the foot of Super League. Stand-off Patton had been left out of the side in the wake of the away defeat at Salford at the beginning of March but, with Kevin Brown ruled out with concussion, he took his chance with both hands. Patton provided a kicking game, along with Kurt Gidley, that helped the Wolves force a remarkable seven goal-line drop-outs.

Ryan Atkins scored two tries and Tom Lineham one down Patton's left edge, while Gidley's second-half effort was crucial after quickfire scores to Matt Parcell and Joel Moon had hinted at a Rhinos comeback.

Ben Westwood was shown a yellow card after a high tackle on Liam Sutcliffe in the opening set, which resulted in the young halfback missing the remainder of the game. Westwood was subsequently banned for four games. Leeds suffered their own blow with

April

Carl Ablett sidelined by a knee injury.

With the Easter weekend looming, all the other games were played on the Friday night.

Salford moved into second spot on points difference after an astounding 54-18 win at Hull FC. Hull, still missing Danny Houghton with a calf injury suffered in the win at Wigan, had been the best defensive side over the first seven rounds but they were pulled apart from all directions as Salford scored tries from all over the field.

Robert Lui, Michael Dobson and Gareth O'Brien were in outstanding form and were far too good. Amazingly the home side led 8-0 until the 12th minute.

Wakefield Trinity recorded a 30-4 home victory over Widnes to go above Wigan into fifth after five wins in six games. Boom winger Tom Johnstone, touted by some Super League coaches as England's new winger, grabbed his sixth try in four games. Trinity prop David Fifita played almost an hour in total, continually punishing the Vikings with forceful drives and morale-sapping offloads.

Tony Gigot made a surprise return in the Dragons' 37-26 victory at Leigh which moved them above the Centurions into eighth place. And the fullback gained three Albert Goldthorpe Medal points for his performance.

The French international was banned by the French Federation for 'inappropriate behaviour' towards an anti-doping officer following a routine test during the France national team's training camp ahead of the previous October's Test match with England. Gigot, 26, did not fail the test, but was still suspended for his behaviour and subsequently missed Catalans' first seven games of the season. However, the Dragons successfully appealed the decision, with the ban being reduced to three months, allowing the 26-year-old to resume playing immediately.

The Dragons were not so fortunate with prop forward Luke Burgess, who ruptured anterior cruciate ligaments in his right knee, and loose forward Jason Baitieri, who broke a wrist.

Injury-hit Huddersfield Giants, after five games without a victory, battled back to earn a 14-all draw at St Helens.

Despite being mediocre for the majority of the game, Saints appeared to have it wrapped up after a 12-minute spell saw them score 14 points just before half-time. After a poor opening 20 minutes, the introduction of Adam Walker and Kyle Amor resulted in momentum turning the way of the hosts, who scored three tries in 12 minutes, two from Theo Fages and Adam Swift scoring straight from a scrum.

At 14-0 the game was not secure and Huddersfield ensured a nervy finish when young fullback Darnell McIntosh bagged a try as he powered over from Danny Brough's pass. Ten minutes later Brough's grubber towards the posts was dropped by Fages and McIntosh raced on to the loose ball to score. Brough's conversion cut the deficit to four.

The Saints faithful had their worst fears realised when Huddersfield drew level. Brough's cross-field kick was dropped by Tommy Makinson and young Giants centre Sam Wood pounced to score in the corner. Brough had the chance to give Huddersfield the lead with the touchline conversion but he pulled it wide.

There was still time for late drama in the final three minutes, Matty Smith and Brough both missing field-goal attempts.

St Helens coach Keiron Cunningham was relieved of his duties the following Monday after two years in charge. Cunningham had a 58 per cent win rate at St Helens, with 43 victories, 30 losses and one draw from 74 games.

Round 9

Wigan ended a four-game winless run on a rainy Good Friday lunchtime with a convincing 29-18 home win over 12-man St Helens, to make it eight successive Good Friday victories over their fierce rivals.

Wigan's Liam Marshall goes airbourne to score in the Warriors' Good Friday win against St Helens

The Super League Champions had failed to win since beating Warrington in March. Since then they had drawn with Huddersfield and tasted three successive defeats against Hull, Leeds and Castleford.

There was much controversy after referee Ben Thaler sent Kyle Amor off 13 minutes into the game. The Saints prop was given his marching orders after Thaler deemed he had hit Wigan winger Liam Marshall high, though television replays showed the first contact was on the ball. Amor's offence was deemed sending-off sufficient the following Wednesday. 'It just wasn't a red card,' said one of Saints' three acting coaches, Jamahl Lolesi, in temporary charge with Sean Long and Derek Traynor.

Wigan led 8-2 at the break as they went on to dominate the rest of the first half with a try from Joe Burgess and two goals from Morgan Escaré. The opening 19 minutes of the second half saw Saints give it a real go, with tries from Ryan Morgan and on-debut, 20-year-old Welsh winger Regan Grace, but not surprisingly they tired and three tries in seven minutes from Marshall, Burgess and Liam Farrell saw the Warriors bounce back in style. Michael McIlorum came onto the field after 32 minutes to a great reception from the Wigan fans, back from a 14-month injury absence after breaking and dislocating an ankle against Brisbane in the World Club Series in February 2016.

England centre Mark Percival was set to remain with the Saints until the end of 2021 after signing a new four-year contract that week.

Wigan moved back into the top four after Hull conceded over 50 points at the KCOM Stadium for the second time in eight days as they were convincingly despatched by Leeds Rhinos, by 52-24.

The Rhinos consolidated their place in the top four with three tries in six minutes in a first half of ruthless attacking play. At the spearhead was Joel Moon, who was virtually unplayable in the opening 40 minutes when his step, ghost and glide brought

37

him two touchdowns, until he was forced back from stand-off to centre in the second half. After the break, Kallum Watkins took over, his menacing, bludgeoning runs creating havoc.

Castleford Tigers remained clear at the head of the table after overcoming Wakefield by 42-24 in a potential banana-skin of a fixture, Trinity having gone into the Adam Watene Trophy game with three successive victories behind them.

The Tigers were 36-12 ahead at the break and seemingly on course for yet another half-century of points on their own patch but improved commitment by Wakefield denied them that.

Castleford scored six first-half tries, with Jake Webster and Grant Millington crossing twice, after David Fifita gave Wakefield an early lead. Fifita completed his double in the second half to add to Trinity's second from Bill Tupou in the opening 40 minutes. Greg Eden's 12th try of the season ensured a fourth straight Tigers win. Ben Jones-Bishop's spectacular late airborne score, one of several the winger scored for Trinity that season, was immaterial to the outcome.

Luke Gale escaped a ban with an early guilty plea (EGP) after being charged with contact with the referee.

Salford stayed in second with their fifth win in a row, but it was close in a 12-6 home win over Leigh Centurions. Michael Dobson was in charge in the second half after the sides were level, 6-all, at the break, moving the Centurions around with a superb kicking game that yielded four second-half goal-line drop-outs. Gareth O'Brien's converted try on 66 minutes nudged Salford in front.

Leigh fullback Gregg McNally was cited for contact with referee Jack Smith and took a two-match EGP.

On the Thursday night, Warrington offered evidence of their improvement as they registered a 19-10 win at Widnes to secure back-to-back Super League wins.

Stefan Marsh gave the Vikings a perfect start by scoring inside two minutes following a Warrington mistake but the Wolves hit back with tries from Tom Lineham, Jack Hughes and Joe Philbin, plus Declan Patton's field goal, to lead 17-4 at half-time. Charly Runciman pulled one back but Patton's late penalty made it three games unbeaten for Warrington.

Widnes co-captain Chris Houston went into the weekend facing a five-match suspension after being charged for a collision with referee Phil Bentham. The RFL Disciplinary ruled the collision accidental and Houston not guilty.

The Easter weekend had actually begun on the Wednesday night in Huddersfield, where Catalans continued their revival with a 29-22 win. Fullback Jake Mamo scored on his long-awaited debut having recovered from a broken foot, although the Giants suffered a seventh straight game without victory.

The Dragons' display was far from impressive, but they were dangerous with the ball as Tony Gigot once again put in a superb display following his return from a three-month suspension, while centres Krisnan Inu and Brayden Wiliame were a constant threat.

The margin of the defeat was small but Huddersfield never gave themselves a chance after Aaron Murphy opened the scoring early on in the first half. Their performance was riddled with errors and ill-discipline and in the end the sheer weight of possession against them counted.

Danny Brough was sin-binned on 50 minutes. Without him on the pitch the Catalans scored as they utilised their one-man advantage, with Vincent Duport scoring in the left corner for a 24-10 lead. And when Brough did return to the field, his night went from bad to worse when his pass was pounced on by Luke Walsh, who raced 20 metres to score a try that finished the Giants off. Brough copped a one-match ban for foul and abusive language towards a match official.

Round 10

Castleford were pulled back to the chasing pack on Easter Monday as St Helens won a tight encounter 26-22 at the Totally Wicked Stadium.

The Tigers, who welcomed back their captain Michael Shenton into the centre, with Greg Minikin switching back to the wing, opened the scoring after seven minutes when Tommy Makinson was unable to gather Paul McShane's kick into the in-goal and Greg Eden was on hand to touch down, with Luke Gale adding the goal.

Gale extended the Tigers' lead when he kicked a penalty for offside. But Saints replied when Matty Fleming did well to score in the corner in the face of a challenge from Shenton. Mark Percival's goal made it 6-8 and Saints were in again two minutes later when Luke Douglas stretched out to score under the posts, with Percival's goal giving Saints the lead for the first time. And on 35 minutes Percival touched down Theo Fages' grubber into the in-goal, converting the try and then adding a penalty to give Saints a half-time lead of 20-8.

That margin was reduced to six points early in the second half with a Ben Roberts try, converted by Gale. Saints forced several goal-line drop-outs but couldn't convert them into points before Eden scored his second from a great passing movement on 59 minutes. Gale couldn't convert and the score stood at 20-18.

Saints got some breathing space, however, when winger Regan Grace scored his second try in as many matches, with Percival again converting and, although the Tigers scored a try on the hooter with Roberts' second, Saints had inflicted the Tigers' second defeat of the Super League season.

Leeds resisted a second-half comeback from Widnes Vikings to move joint top with Castleford with a 42-22 win at Headingley.

The Rhinos' saw the return of Ash Handley, who deputised at fullback after Ashton Golding and Liam Sutcliffe failed late fitness tests following injuries picked up on Good Friday against Hull. Vikings coach Denis Betts, meanwhile, made a whole host of changes to his team, with the notable inclusions being youngsters Owen Farnworth and Liam Walsh, both making their Super League debuts.

Early tries from Kallum Watkins, Matt Parcell and Joel Moon saw Leeds take an 18-0 lead in as many minutes and from there the Rhinos never looked in danger, despite Widnes showing more resistance in the second half. After Leeds' strong start, Widnes' Tom Gilmore converted his own try to bring Widnes onto the board midway through the half but Moon's second try and Tom Briscoe's effort gave the Rhinos a 30-6 half-time lead.

The game looked over but the Vikings weren't giving up as Gilmore went over for his second before Chris Houston and Corey Thompson cut the deficit to just eight points. But Watkins and Parcell completed their respective braces, with the former kicking seven from seven goals, to earn Leeds the two points.

Salford, on the back of a five-match winning run, missed their chance to go joint top, losing 38-6 at Catalans, having come into the game with two days less rest than their opponents. And the Red Devils' task was made more difficult with the loss of first Logan Tomkins (concussion) and then Junior Sa'u (adductor) through injury.

Catalans had now won three games in a row following their 38-18 home defeat to Wakefield Trinity that forced crisis talks at the club and reportedly saw coach Laurent Frayssinous given three games to save his job. Tony Gigot had revitalised the Catalans since his return and he was outstanding once again.

The Dragons built a 14-0 half-time lead with two tries by Vincent Duport, both converted by Luke Walsh, who also added a penalty. And they extended their lead in the second half when Richie Myler's last-tackle kick to the right corner was taken above his head by Krisnan Inu, allowing him to run around towards the posts to touch down. Walsh added the goal but Salford were handed a lifeline when another Catalans kick to the right was plucked out of the air by Justin Carney, who raced 100 metres to score. Gareth

O'Brien added the conversion to narrow the Catalans lead.

A Walsh kick downfield sat up, evaded O'Brien and bounced perfectly into the hands of the chasing Myler, who touched down to seal the win. Walsh added the conversion and the Catalans added two more tries from Tony Gigot, who intercepted Robert Lui's pass and raced seventy metres to score in the right corner, with Duport adding his third, which came after Walsh kicked two field goals.

Wigan held off a determined challenge from Wakefield Trinity to gain a hard-earned 16-10 victory at the Beaumont Legal Stadium.

Wigan took an early lead with a try from skipper Sean O'Loughlin, who took advantage of some poor line defence from Wakefield. Morgan Escaré converted and Wakefield quickly replied when Scott Grix touched down an Ashley Gibson grubber into Wigan's in-goal. Liam Finn couldn't convert but he did add a penalty to level the scores on 24 minutes.

Escaré then produced the highlight of the first half with a brilliant try created by a George Williams pass and great footwork from the French star, who converted his own try. But Wakefield replied again when Ben Jones-Bishop went over in the corner after great passing by Wakefield, although Finn couldn't add the goal and the half-time score had Wigan 12-10 ahead.

The second half was a tightly contested affair, with Sam Powell held up over the line, Kyle Wood held up just short at the other end and Romain Navarrete unable to ground the ball under the Wakefield posts. But the stalemate was finally broken when Williams gave an overhead pass to Liam Marshall in the 78th minute, for the young winger, who made four clean breaks in total, to score in the corner and clinch the points for Wigan.

Hull FC boosted their top four hopes with a four-try, 24-10 victory at Leigh Centurions.

Lee Radford's side lacked several key stars for the clash, including Josh Griffin and Fetuli Talanoa, who were replaced by Jake Connor and Carlos Tuimavave. Leigh, meanwhile, welcomed back halfback Josh Drinkwater and he replaced Martyn Ridyard, while Dave Thompson came in for Adam Higson on the wing to make his debut.

Neither team could get over the line early in the game but, in the second quarter, Hull took what was to be a decisive lead. Liam Watts went over for the opening score before Tuimavave and Albert Kelly added further tries, with Marc Sneyd's boot helping the visitors to an 18-0 half-time lead.

Tuimavave went over for his second try as the game approached the final quarter but the Centurions rallied to finish strongly. Liam Hood's converted try brought them onto the board before Ryan Hampshire got Leigh into double figures late on. But it wasn't enough to stop the Leythers suffering a fifth straight Super League defeat.

Warrington just held off a strong challenge from Huddersfield Giants at the Halliwell Jones Stadium, winning 26-24 thanks to Giants goalkicker Danny Brough being unable to convert a late try in the corner by Jermaine McGillvary.

Harvey Livett, in at centre for the absent Ryan Atkins, scored for the Wolves after three minutes, but the Giants replied almost immediately when Darnell McIntosh touched down. Both conversions were missed.

Warrington took the lead for a second time when Daryl Clark scored on 12 minutes after some fine interplay with Kurt Gidley, with Declan Patton converting for a six-point lead. The Giants replied again, however, when Jake Mamo supported a Sam Wood break to touch down on 17 minutes, with Brough adding the conversion. And Brough gave the Giants the lead for the first time with a penalty when a Giants player was tackled off the ball. But the Wolves snatched the lead back before half-time with a Gidley try, goaled by Patton, to make it 16-12 at the break.

The Giants were back in front on 46 minutes, however, when Brough dived over from dummy-half and converted his own try moments after he had kicked a superb 40/20.

And he added a penalty on 60 minutes when Chris Hill was caught offside.

The Wolves then pulled level with a try to Rhys Evans that was unconverted, with the score standing at 20-20 with 15 minutes remaining. Four minutes later they were ahead when Toby King touched down a Patton kick and Patton added the goal.

But in a frantic finish McGillvary scored in the corner following a scrum. But Brough was unable to claim a draw with his attempted conversion from the touchline.

Round 11

Round 11 featured only four games to allow the previous year's bottom four teams to enter the fifth round of the Challenge Cup.

One of those clubs was 2015 Champions Leeds, whose revival after a year of struggle had them joint top. So Castleford had the chance to move two points clear but missed it after losing 26-24 at battling Hull FC on the Sunday.

That outcome looked unlikely when Hull prop Liam Watts was shown a red card 22 minutes into an absorbing encounter. Watts was dismissed for a high tackle on Luke Gale, who left the field and did not return after a concussion assessment.

A Scott Taylor try and two from Mahe Fonua helped Hull take an early 18-0 lead before Watts was sent off. There was an inevitable Tigers fightback and they went in 20-14 behind at the break through Greg Minikin, Ben Roberts and Michael Shenton scores. Roberts missed the first two conversions, with Paul McShane potting the third. With Marc Sneyd kicking all three of his efforts, and a penalty goal, that was ultimately the difference.

Roberts crossed again after another Sneyd penalty goal but Carlos Tuimavave's 63rd-minute try in the corner gave Hull back-to-back victories. Boom second-rower Mike McMeeken scored a consolation on the hooter for the Tigers.

Albert Kelly was man of the match, days after Hull ended speculation surrounding his future by tying him down to a one-year contract extension. A number of NRL clubs had been linked with a move for the 26-year-old star.

Watts was suspended for two games, reduced on appeal to one match.

With Castleford suffering back-to-back defeats, four teams were now split by just a solitary point at the Super League summit, with Hull among them.

Wigan had also ominously climbed back into the mix after a profitable Easter, a 42-22 home win over Catalans Dragons seeing them level with Hull.

The Warriors looked in cruise control after 20 minutes as they led 16-0 thanks to two breakaway tries from Tom Davies and a well-worked one from Joe Burgess. But the Dragons refused to give in and mounted their fightback as Fouad Yaha was awarded a try in the corner, before two towering bombs caused havoc in the Wigan ranks and Tony Gigot and Louis Anderson both scored to turn a 16-0 deficit into a 16-16 half-time score.

Despite conceding early in the second half through gamestar Liam Forsyth, the Dragons took the lead for the first time in the 47th minute through Louis Anderson. That was as good as it got for the visitors. Forsyth and Burgess both went over for their second tries, while Liam Marshall and Liam Farrell both got in on the act as the Warriors finally saw off a determined Dragons side.

Wigan halfback Thomas Leuluai faced a spell on the sidelines after he suffered a broken jaw.

In the Friday night TV game, Widnes Vikings got their first home win of the season, by 16-14, in a tense encounter against derby rivals St Helens.

Two tries from Patrick Ah Van and a controlled display from halfback Tom Gilmore led the way, while St Helens could only rue their missed chances. The scores were level at 12-all at the break with Theo Fages and Matty Smith crossing for Saints and Joe Mellor and Ah Van going over for Widnes.

Saints took the lead three minutes after the break when Mark Percival kicked a penalty. But the Vikings eventually made their pressure tell when Ah Van crashed over nine minutes from time.

In a rare Saturday afternoon TV game, there was an even closer finish as Warrington continued their rehabilitation with a last-gasp 22-20 home win over Wakefield, their fourth win in a row.

Three scores down during the second half, Warrington produced another second-half revival, racking up three unanswered tries, including one to Tom Lineham in the 78th minute to steal the win in the most heartbreaking fashion for a Wakefield team that was tenacious and competitive throughout.

Warrington were without the suspended Daryl Clark and Ben Westwood, whilst Max Jowitt made his first appearance of the season for Trinity, with Scott Grix being rested alongside a number of other absent players on both sides as the Easter schedule took its toll on both squads. Prop Mitch Allgood was out after he broke his hand during the Easter Monday defeat to Wigan.

Wakefield made a dream start with two tries in two minutes to take an early 12-0 lead, Kyle Wood kicking ahead for Ashley Gibson to touch down before Jacob Miller broke from deep and the supporting Mason Caton-Brown was on hand to take the stand-off's pass and score under the posts.

Declan Patton and Stefan Ratchford combined to send centre Atkins off on an 80-metre run from deep to get Wire on the scoreboard with a converted try, before Finn's penalty earned a 14-6 interval lead.

Trinity still looked to be on their way to a comfortable victory when winger Tom Johnstone scored a long-range interception try early in the second half. But tries by Chris Hill, who led the revival, and Kevin Brown set up a frantic finish capped by Lineham's spectacular winning dive for the corner.

Challenge Cup Round 5

Championship part-timers Swinton Lions produced the shock of the year as they dumped Huddersfield Giants out of the Challenge Cup at the John Smith's Stadium by 28-24, as Luke Waterworth scored the winning try from dummy-half with just four minutes remaining.

Triumphant head coach John Duffy only had one session with his players in the build-up to their victory over Huddersfield as only 15 members of his squad were fit enough to train. As a result, Duffy was forced to draft in three new faces to make up the numbers in his squad, with Wigan under 19 players Caine Barnes and Josh Woods making their debuts alongside Liam Carberry, who had not played a game for seven months.

The Giants had 19-year-old Izaac Farrell, son of former Huddersfield, Sheffield and Leeds prop Anthony Farrell on debut at scrum-half, with Ryan Brierley set to join Toronto Wolfpack.

Swinton became the second Championship team to defeat Super League opposition as Hull Kingston Rovers beat Leigh Centurions 23-10 at the Leigh Sports Village less than 24 hours earlier.

The Robins were running away with the Championship and this was an early pointer to their promotion credentials. Early tries by Ryan Shaw and George Lawler were cancelled out by Lachlan Burr and Curtis Naughton, before James Greenwood's converted late first-half try earned Rovers a 16-10 lead. Former Leigh scrum-half Jamie Ellis kicked a field goal in the 71st minute and winger Shaw's last-gasp converted try rounded it off.

As eye-catching debuts go, 17-year old Leeds fullback Jack Walker's was right up there, a 16-minute first-half hat-trick at Headingley announcing his arrival on the scene, as the Rhinos cruised past Doncaster 64-28 into the sixth round.

Despite playing for nearly an hour with twelve men, Salford Red Devils inflicted a first competitive defeat, by 29-22, on Toronto Wolfpack in a feisty encounter.

The Wolfpack had taken League 1 by storm so far in 2017 and had crossed for a total of 310 points in their previous five matches.

There was big fallout after the game. With Toronto leading 16-12 on 27 minutes, Salford winger Justin Carney was shown a red card for dissent by referee Jack Smith. Gareth O'Brien, Robert Lui and Michael Dobson marshalled the remainder of the tie superbly, despite being a man short, as Toronto eventually ran out of steam.

Ten days later Carney was banned for eight matches for verbal abuse based on race and colour towards Wolfpack prop Ryan Bailey.

Barrow became the only League 1 side to make it into the last 16, running in 10 tries in a 50-28 win at York, powerful winger Luke Cresswell's personal tally of four tries ensuring their progression.

Championship challengers Featherstone marked the 50th anniversary of their 1967 Challenge Cup win over Barrow with a 30-4 home win over Oldham; Halifax won 36-12 at Whitehaven and a golden-point field goal from Lewis Fairhurst sealed a dramatic 23-22 home derby win for Dewsbury over Batley.

Round 12

Huddersfield, five days after their Challenge Cup humiliation against Swinton, turned the table on its head on the last Thursday of April by beating high-flying Leeds 31-12 at Headingley.

Without a victory in nine games, Huddersfield's clinical dismantling of the Rhinos - it was 19-0 in the second half - maintained their decent away record, whilst inflicting a first home defeat of the season on their hosts.

The vastly understrength Giants played the grimy conditions perfectly and their ultimately comprehensive win was a triumph of collectivism. Reinstated skipper Danny Brough signalled his worth and intent on a rainy backdrop when kicking was always going to determine the outcome with a 40/20 at the end of the very first set.

Leeds missed suspended Brett Ferres and still-out with a knee injury Carl Ablett but Jack Walker impressed on his Super League debut, a week after scoring a hat-trick in the Cup win over Doncaster.

The Giants players dedicated the impressive victory to the Davy family following the death of owner Ken's wife the day before.

The Rhinos fell from second to fourth spot, with Hull FC and Salford both winning.

Hull's 34-10 success over the Wolves in the Friday night TV game was one of their best displays of the season, despite missing captain Gareth Ellis and Man of Steel Danny Houghton, as well as the suspended Liam Watts.

It was a comprehensive win in the end but the decision of the video-referee Ben Thaler to rule out a try for Jack Hughes in the first minute of the second half, after the on-field referee had awarded it but gone upstairs to check its legality, was a crucial turnaround. The dummy runner Joe Philbin, who had set up position with a storming long run out of defence, was adjudged to have obstructed a defender.

After that decision, Hull went downfield and two Marc Sneyd kicks won goal-line drop-outs before Jamie Shaul scored from a Jake Connor pass and Sneyd's goal made it 20-10. Sneyd then kicked a penalty and a 40/20, which paved the way for Albert Kelly's first try. And that clinched the game for Hull, with Connor, a pre-season signing from Huddersfield, showing his value for the black and whites.

There had been controversy earlier, with the decision of the referee James Child to show Sika Manu a yellow card, rather than a red one, for a chicken-wing tackle on Warrington centre Ryan Atkins in the 22nd minute. Manu was subsequently banned for two matches.

The game marked the hundredth anniversary of the death of Hull FC legend Jack Harrison, who was posthumously awarded the Victoria Cross for his services in the First World War.

The Red Devils beat Widnes at home on the Sunday by 30-10. Salford, who had not tasted defeat at home since losing to Wigan on the opening weekend of the season, never looked in any real danger and led 12-0 at the interval thanks to tries from Ben Murdoch-Masila and Greg Johnson.

The Vikings improved after the break and only trailed by eight going into the final 15 minutes thanks to tries from Tom Gilmore and Patrick Ah Van. But the Red Devils showed their dominance by scoring 18 second-half points, including the outstanding Murdoch-Masila's second bulldozing try.

On the same afternoon Wakefield snapped a three-game losing streak with a comprehensive 30-10 home victory over Catalans, who welcomed the return of Greg Bird. But an undisciplined Dragons side had three players yellow-carded in a poor showing from the French club.

Wakefield lost Tom Johnstone and Anthony England to injury but still managed to cross for six tries in a team performance highlighted by a hat-trick to Mason Caton-Brown. Johnstone's knee injury proved worse than first thought and he was out for the season.

On Friday night, Leigh's 28-6 defeat at St Helens extended their winless run in all competitions to seven matches, despite them leading 6-0 until the 20th minute. But once Saints had established a 12-point lead after 50 minutes they always looked at ease, with Alex Walmsley in commanding form on his 150th career appearance.

Jamie Acton had rumbled through for the opener early on but tries from Mark Percival and Theo Fages established Saints' six-point lead at the break. Ryan Morgan, Regan Grace and Alex Walmsley tries finished Leigh hopes.

There was a huge result on the Saturday night as Castleford held on to pole position with a 54-4 home win over Wigan. After stuttering to two successive defeats, the Tigers produced a nine-try special in the battle of the sides seeking to leap-frog Friday-night winners Hull to the top of the table.

The Warriors' cause, already hindered by the absence of halfback Thomas Leuluai with a broken jaw, was also hampered by injuries during the game to centre Anthony Gelling (knee), stand-off George Williams (knee, ruling him out of England's game with Samoa on the following Saturday), prop Ben Flower (snapped Achilles tendon) and substitute Taulima Tautai (neck), while loose forward Sean O'Loughlin was affected by a groin strain.

Tigers scrum-half Luke Gale, who was only cleared to play in the morning after having sustained concussion six days earlier at Hull, was a key figure in the victory, orchestrating many of Castleford's attacks and scoring a try and eight goals. Captain and centre Michael Shenton had his best game since returning from a year out through injury in 2016, regularly making real inroads, while second rower and England call-up, Basingstoke-born Mike McMeeken hit a new high. McMeeken's try late in the first half, a brilliant stepping effort from 40 metres, stretched

BETFRED SUPER LEAGUE
Sunday 30th April

	P	W	D	L	F	A	D	Pts
Castleford Tigers	12	9	0	3	450	193	257	18
Hull FC	12	8	1	3	300	250	50	17
Salford Red Devils	12	8	0	4	289	212	77	16
Leeds Rhinos	12	8	0	4	309	256	53	16
Wigan Warriors	12	7	1	4	267	253	14	15
Wakefield Trinity	12	6	0	6	258	244	14	12
St Helens	12	5	1	6	221	207	14	11
Catalans Dragons	12	5	1	6	264	321	-57	11
Warrington Wolves	12	4	1	7	202	289	-87	9
Huddersfield Giants	12	3	2	7	215	317	-102	8
Leigh Centurions	12	3	0	9	202	271	-69	6
Widnes Vikings	12	2	1	9	177	341	-164	5

Castleford's lead to 22 points, from which Wigan clearly wouldn't recover.

MAY
Red Devils rise up

Round 13

With England playing a warm-up match against Samoa Down Under on the first weekend of May, several teams had to field under-strength sides in round 13 of Super League.

One such was Castleford Tigers who, for the first time this year, were made to win tough, emerging from a see-saw Thursday-night clash at Huddersfield 26-21 victors to retain their position at the top of Super League.

The Tigers were without their England contingent of Luke Gale, Zak Hardaker and Mike McMeeken, plus injured Oliver Holmes and Ben Roberts - as well as losing Rangi Chase midway through the game with an injury. The Giants had Jermaine McGillvary on international duty.

Joel Monaghan's eighth-minute try in the left corner from typically slick crossfield passing put the Tigers ahead but Jake Mamo went over twice to put the Giants 12-6 in front. Castleford levelled with a try from Greg Minikin before Mamo's third converted try made it 18-12 to the home side at the break.

Greg Eden's try converted by Paul McShane seven minutes after the break made it 18-all and for an exciting last 25 minutes.

A Danny Brough field goal gave the Giants a one-point lead for 12 minutes before McShane kicked a penalty to give Castleford a one-point lead.

That was reversed when Brough kicked a penalty controversially awarded when Jake Webster was penalised for stripping the ball from Sebastine Ikahihifo, who had raced clear. It was a 50/50 call but to rub salt into Tigers' wounds, referee Ben Thaler sin-binned Webster.

But then Brough was yellow-carded himself for a cannonball tackle on Grant Millington and the penalty gave Castleford the position for Jesse Sene-Lefao to barge over from close range.

The game was still in the balance right until Mamo's pass to the left fell into touch on the hooter.

Brough got a one-game ban for the cannonball and another game for an earlier crusher on Jake Webster.

The following Monday Castleford were in court after they failed to reach an out-of-court settlement with Denny Solomona and his agent over the winger's departure to Sale rugby union club. The only progress made was that a date was set for the case to be heard at the end of the year.

Back on the field, there was a shake-up in the chasing pack on the following night when Salford recorded their first win at Wigan in 20 years with a 31-16 success.

The Red Devils dominated the opening half and were unlucky not to be further than 16-0 in front as they looked dangerous every time they entered Wigan's half. Tries from Kris Welham, Niall Evalds and Ben Murdoch-Masila put Salford in full control at the break, while Liam Farrell wasted Wigan's only real chance as he dropped the ball with the line at his mercy.

May

Salford looked like cruising to victory after two quick-fire second-half tries from Evalds and Greg Johnson as they led 28-0 with over 30 minutes remaining. Tries to Wigan from Tom Davies, Ryan Sutton and Lewis Tierney made the scoreline look more respectable, but all the damage was done in the first 50 minutes.

The Warriors were without a 14 first-teamers, with Anthony Gelling, George Williams, Ben Flower, Sean O'Loughlin, Michael McIlorum and Morgan Escaré all missing from the side that had been defeated at Castleford.

Youngster Josh Woods was handed his debut at stand-off alongside Sam Powell, while Josh Ganson made his first start at hooker following his debut from the bench at Castleford. Lewis Tierney was named at fullback after missing the last nine matches as the Warriors named 13 home-grown players in their team. The Warriors' injury crisis was aggravated during the game, with Powell not returning for the second half.

Salford were far from full-strength themselves, with Mark Flanagan joining Lee Mossop, Todd Carney, Weller Hauraki and George Griffin, and the suspended Justin Carney, on the sidelines. But the win moved them into third, two points behind Castleford and three points ahead of fifth-placed Wigan.

On the same night at the Halliwell Jones Stadium, Warrington produced a remarkable turnaround to sweep aside St Helens by 40-18.

The Wolves overturned a 14-0 deficit on the half hour with a blistering spell in the middle of the game, scoring 36 points without reply in a 29-minute period.

It was too much for a St Helens side in need of the arrival of new coach Justin Holbrook, whose appointment had been announced that week. The Sydney Roosters assistant and Junior Kangaroos coach was awaiting visa clearance.

Saints lost skipper Jon Wilkin in the warm-up with a hamstring strain that forced a last-minute re-shuffle but were in the lead after just 41 seconds. After retaining the kick-off when a wicked bounce deceived Harvey Livett, Tommy Makinson and Jake Spedding combined superbly to give Adam Swift enough space to finish in the corner.

Makinson added a touchline conversion and a 12th-minute penalty for Kurt Gidley's high tackle on Kyle Amor and Saints extended their lead before the half-hour mark. Warrington had seen both Brad Dwyer and Tom Lineham held up over the line before Theo Fages' smart wide pass allowed Ryan Morgan to run over Gidley and score. Makinson's goal made it 14-0 and St Helens looked well in control.

But by half-time the gap was just two points as the Wolves roared back. After a Swift mistake, Declan Patton's short ball saw the excellent Benjamin Jullien crash over. Five minutes later it was a similar scenario with Gidley providing the assist for Mike Cooper, and two Livett goals made it 12-14 at the break.

Livett then stepped forward with two crucial contributions at the start of the second half. First he showed tremendous skill to pick up a loose ball on the run following a Fages error and a clean pair of heels to sprint away and score. Then Livett produced an excellent short ball for Rhys Evans to scythe through and make it 24-12.

The onslaught continued, with the Wolves taking advantage of every Saints slip-up. When Makinson spilled the ball on halfway it was Lineham who collected to race clear and finish.

Then came the try of the night, as Evans produced a brilliant run down the right before the Wolves quickly transferred the ball to the left on the next play, with Livett and Ashton Sims combining for Ryan Atkins to touch down.

Dominique Peyroux grabbed a consolation score but the last word rightly went to the Wolves as Atkins collected his second in the last minute.

Leeds remained level in third after a 30-24 win over Catalans Dragons in a warm and windy Perpignan.

The Rhinos came back from ten points down with a quarter of an hour remaining, despite missing Ryan Hall and Kallum Watkins in the backline, both on England duty, while Brett Ferres was also serving the last game of his suspension.

For the Catalans, Jodie Broughton, Krisnan Inu, Justin Horo and Jason Baitieri all missed the game with injury, while halfback Luke Walsh was suspended for one game for dissent in the loss at Wakefield.

Catalans had lost the influential Greg Bird at half-time in their match at Headingley earlier in the season. This time around, the Australian World Cup winner lasted only five minutes as he left the field with a facial injury after attempting to tackle Tom Briscoe.

Adam Cuthbertson produced a great performance for the Rhinos, with his try in the 65th minute starting the comeback from 22-12 down that Danny McGuire completed with his four-pointer on 76 minutes.

On the same evening, Leigh fell to an eighth straight defeat as they went down 40-26 to Wakefield Trinity at the Leigh Sports Village.

Wakefield coach Chris Chester described it as a bizarre game as his side led 20-0 after 15 minutes, only to see Curtis Naughton's converted try on 50 minutes give Leigh a 26-22 lead, which lasted seven minutes as Joe Arundel's six-pointer made it 28-26.

The 63rd minute brought a disallowed try for Leigh, a sin-binning for Danny Tickle blatantly delaying the restart and a superbly worked try from Mason Caton-Brown tipping the game in Wakefield's favour.

Trinity moved three points clear of St Helens in sixth but were set to lose Hull loanee Dean Hadley after he suffered a broken jaw.

In the only Sunday game, Hull FC stayed within a point of the Tigers after a fourth successive win, by 33-22 at Widnes. It was one of the comebacks of the season as they were 22-0 down just before half-time.

The Vikings looked set for only a third win of the season when tries from Chris Houston, Rhys Hanbury and two from Patrick Ah Van opened up a big lead. But Jansin Turgut got a try back for Hull after a half-break by Jamie Shaul 30 seconds before half-time. And fullback Shaul got two of Hull's five unanswered second-half tries, with Carlos Tuimavave, Albert Kelly and Danny Washbrook also crossing.

* In a warm-up for the 2017 World Cup on Saturday 6th May, England recorded a convincing 30-10 win over Samoa at Campbelltown Stadium in Sydney.

Challenge Cup Round 6

Castleford Tigers versus St Helens was chosen as the Saturday BBC game in the expectation of a close encounter. But that didn't unfold as the Tigers continued their blistering form with a 53-10 humiliation of one of the three teams that had managed to beat them so far this year.

The Tigers, who began explosively, had seen the momentum go St Helens' way by the half-hour, the visitors having clawed their way back from 10-0 down - through Michael Shenton and Jake Webster tries inside the first 11 minutes - to be only 10-4 adrift after a try by centre Ryan Morgan, who rose high to collect scrum-half Matty Smith's pinpoint kick. And Saints might well have restored parity on 22 minutes after fullback Tommy Makinson's surge from behind his own posts, followed by a penalty, to help establish the position from which second row Zeb Taia powered to the line.

Referee Phil Bentham, passing the final decision to video referee Robert Hicks, felt that Taia had been held just short and Hicks found no evidence to decide otherwise. And the Tigers made the most of the let-off with four scintillating touchdowns to establish a tie-defining 31-4 lead by the break.

The first, after Greg Eden had been tackled in the air by visiting winger Adam Swift, went to centre Jake Webster, who celebrated a one-year contract extension by beating young Saints winger Regan Grace to a lofted kick by substitute Ben Roberts, who made a telling impact in a 20-minute cameo appearance.

That score, on 32 minutes, was followed immediately by a touchdown for hooker Paul McShane after a race down the touchline by Eden had been thwarted by a fine cover tackle by James Roby, the hooker being one of the few Saints players to emerge from the tie with any real credit.

But Castleford moved the ball swiftly across field and, after Webster had been held short, four defenders were unable to prevent McShane getting the ball down on the try-line.

The Tigers were back on the rampage again straight from the kick-off. Roberts, who was back in the side after a game's absence with a groin strain, broke through and kicked to the corner, with winger Greg Minikin following up for a roof-raising score.

Castleford went in at the break in buoyant mood when Luke Gale potted a field goal and then sent substitute Nathan Massey crashing over from short range, Gale adding the goal for a 31-4 interval advantage.

Eden had a second-half hat-trick and Minikin ran 70 metres for another try, while Luke Douglas scored St Helens' consolation.

Rangi Chase wasn't selected, the subject of an internal investigation at the Tigers after allegedly being ejected from the ground at Featherstone Rovers' Challenge Cup tie with Halifax the previous Thursday.

Featherstone had won that game 24-12. Ben Heaton's try put the visitors ahead before John Davies and Scott Turner went over to help give Featherstone a 13-6 half-time lead.

Turner grabbed his second try before Ben Johnston jinked his way through to reduce the deficit for Halifax. But Anthony Thackeray kicked his second field goal of the night and Josh Hardcastle's try made the game safe.

On the Friday night there was another all-Super League clash as Cup holders Hull FC out-classed a weakened Catalans side 62-0.

Albert Kelly, surprisingly not among the scorers, was untouchable at times, playing off the back of excellent go-forward from the Hull pack, led by the outstanding Liam Watts. And they were complemented by Jamie Shaul, who was instrumental in the win. Celebrating his 100th career appearance, the lightning fullback produced several assists as well as recording two for himself.

Warrington got the better of Widnes on the Sunday by 34-20. Kevin Brown ultimately proved to be the difference in a game which see-sawed throughout and was never properly settled until three Warrington tries in the final eleven minutes. Matty Russell's try seven minutes from time put daylight between the teams for the first time.

Salford recovered from a 14-0 deficit to book their quarter-final place with a 24-14 home win over Hull KR in an absorbing Million Pound rematch on the Friday night.

Championship leaders Hull Kingston Rovers, who had been relegated by Ian Watson's side in the previous year's showdown, looked every inch a Super League team in taking what looked a commanding advantage with two opportunist Shaun Lunt tries.

But, after responding before the break with a Ryan Lannon try, the Red Devils then dominated the second half, two quick tries from Craig Kopczak and Kris Brining turning the game around to give Salford a four-point advantage.

Ben Murdoch-Masila scored Salford's fourth try on 72 minutes, while Michael Dobson made it four out of four conversions.

Three other ties involving Super League teams against lower league opposition went to form.

Barrow, the only remaining League 1 (third tier) side, lost 72-10 against the Rhinos at Headingley, Joel Moon getting a first-half hat-trick; Wigan Warriors didn't have it all their own way as Championship Swinton Lions played some enterprising rugby at Heywood Road but progressed with a 42-12 win; and Mason Caton-Brown scored four tries in Wakefield's 54-6 win at Dewsbury.

Round 14 - Magic Weekend

The Magic Weekend was played for the third consecutive year in Newcastle as 65,407 fans attended St James' Park over two days, down slightly on the previous year's total of 68,276.

In the first game on the Saturday, Wakefield moved to within two points of fourth-placed Leeds and above sixth-placed Wigan on points difference with a controlled 34-12 win over thinly stretched Widnes, who remained bottom.

The Vikings had seen the arrivals of loan trio Jack Johnson and Sam Wilde from Warrington for a month each and, perhaps most notably, Rangi Chase from Castleford until the end of the season. But they were unable to get enough preparation for the game, with Chase in particular looking uncomfortable.

The Vikings defended admirably in the first quarter but the opening score eventually came through Scott Grix in the 19th minute. In Widnes's first real attack, a loose pass from Chase was raced onto by Ben Jones-Bishop and the winger galloped downfield towards the line. Incredibly, young winger Ryan Ince somehow hunted down the Wakefield speedster to provide a spectacular try-saver. But Grix was over soon after from dummy-half, a yard from the line.

Reece Lyne went over untouched from a delayed Jacob Miller pass and, from a scrum in the 33rd minute, Miller's pass to the left gave Grix a clear passage to the line. Wakefield had a comfortable 16-0 lead.

Two minutes after the restart Jones-Bishop was the beneficiary of a flowing right-edge attack before he finished one-handed and mid-air in the corner.

Widnes then scored a fine try of their own in the 46th minute. Young centre Ed Chamberlain's superb offload down the right edge sent Ince towards the line and he brilliantly stepped inside and away from Grix to score by the posts, taking the score to 22-6.

But Wakefield ruthlessly finished the game off. Liam Finn kicked a penalty to extend the lead to 18 and they added two further tries to add gloss to the scoreline. Jones-Bishop's excellent campaign continued with a second try after further good play opened a sliver of space for him in which he tiptoed to the line.

Chase then had another moment to forget with six minutes remaining, with his loose dummy-half pass on his own '20' going to no-one. Matty Ashurst was more than happy to accept the opportunity and score.

Widnes did wrap up proceedings with a try, with Hep Cahill barging over from close range.

One highlight for the Vikings was the performance of local product Ince, 20, who that week had signed a one-year contract extension until the end of the 2018 season. Utility back Lloyd Roby, 18, and twin prop forwards Jay and Ted Chapelhow also signed new contracts.

Miller and David Fifita had both agreed new contracts with Wakefield that week.

Saints' new coach Justin Holbrook arrived in the UK on the Thursday and took his first session with his new charges the day after as they tried to bounce back from the

Challenge Cup humiliation of the previous week.

He could only sit and smile as Saints defied the form book to stun high-flying Hull FC with a sensational 45-0 success.

Alex Walmsley was in unstoppable form and plunged over from close range for the opening score after 15 minutes before Ryan Morgan met a towering kick to cross. Morgan Knowles pounced on a Steve Michaels error from a high kick and Matty Smith made it 19-0 at half-time with a field goal.

Walmsley's second-half try was followed by Louie McCarthy-Scarsbrook and Tommy Makinson tries, before Regan Grace's exciting double finished the scoring.

Makinson's try came on his 150th Saints appearance and was rated the best try of the weekend, claiming and returning a high kick, pushing off Carlos Tuimavave, sidestepping Albert Kelly and storming 95-metres upfield to touch down despite a fantastic chase and grasp by Danny Houghton.

Ben Barba was the main talking point of the day after flying into the country with his time in French rugby union with Toulon seemingly at an end after his 12-game NRL suspension for a positive test for cocaine.

St Helens were favourites for his signature, with Warrington also interested.

The Wolves were in the last game of the Saturday, with Wigan, that ended in a 24-all draw that excited the fans but didn't make either coach happy.

For long periods it looked like Wigan's injury-hit side would pull off another commendable result against the odds. But a magnificent Warrington fightback, a shade or two of controversy and a last-gasp finish led to one of the most enthralling games seen at Magic Weekend.

Warrington had never led throughout a topsy-turvy game until the 76th minute, when former Wigan man Jack Hughes seemingly broke the Warriors' hearts with a well-taken try to round off a great second-half comeback from the Wolves.

But in the final minute, Joe Burgess scored a sensational try, collecting a Sean O'Loughlin bomb cleanly to grab a share of the spoils. Goalkicker, young halfback Josh Woods had left the field early with an injury and George Williams was wide with the difficult conversion that would have won the game.

Young winger Liam Marshall finished with a try hat-trick to add to the four he scored against the Wolves in round four. Both he and fellow winger Tom Davies had signed contracts to the end of the 2020 season. Liam Farrell signed a five-year deal; Taulima Tautai a three-year contract and Joel Tomkins to the end of the 2019 season.

Adam O'Brien's first try for Huddersfield sealed one of Magic Weekend's more forgettable contests in the opening game of day two, as the Giants left it late to record an 18-10 win over Catalans. The former Bradford hooker stole over from dummy-half three minutes after Sam Rapira had given the Giants the lead for the first time.

The Dragons opened the scoring with a superb effort from Richie Myler in the fourth minute - the game's best moment by quite a distance. Myler took an offload from Julian Bousquet on half-way before exchanging passes with Iain Thornley and finishing out wide.

Bousquet thought he had extended the lead soon afterwards when he touched down after the Giants failed to deal with a spiralling Luke Walsh kick, only for the try to be disallowed as Myler was offside.

And Huddersfield then responded, with Lee Gaskell taking a smart pass from Kruise Leeming to crash over from close range. But for the vast majority of the half both sides struggled to find any kind of fluidity.

The Giants did draw level shortly before the hooter when Martyn Ridyard, on loan from Leigh, kicked a penalty awarded for a Rémi Casty high tackle on Alex Mellor.

But they fell behind eight minutes after the restart when the hard-working Thornley took Tony Gigot's pass and dummied over in the left-hand corner.

Greg Bird looked to have extended the lead to two scores for the first time on 65 minutes when he reached out to score after collecting a Walsh kick, only for Myler to infringe in the build-up, obstructing the defending Gaskell.

But even without suspended Danny Brough, Huddersfield had the direction to get Rapira and O'Brien into close positions for the winning scores.

A fifth defeat on the row sent the Dragons into the bottom four and cost coach Laurent Frayssinous his job.

Salford jumped a point clear of Hull into second spot with a 36-22 win over Leigh. The defeat was Leigh's eighth in a row in Super League and ninth consecutive, combined with the loss to Hull KR in the Challenge Cup.

Not for the first time, ill-discipline proved their undoing, with Adam Higson sent off in the 55th minute, with the game in the balance, for a dangerous high tackle on Gareth O'Brien. Referee James Child had little choice but to give the winger a red card and he received a five-match ban the following Wednesday.

The dismissal came after Leigh had cut Salford's lead to just six points with a fine try from Ben Crooks but the Red Devils scored off the next play after the dismissal and then closed out the match with another try.

For the Red Devils, there were braces from both Ben Murdoch-Masila and Greg Johnson

Centre Matty Fleming marked his Centurions debut - having arrived five days earlier on loan from St Helens - in fine style, scoring the Centurions' maiden Magic Weekend try.

In the closing game of the weekend, Castleford needed another purple patch to see off Leeds in a game which, level at the break, was threatening to go either way. And they found it with the kind of breathtaking play that had become their 2017 trademark.

Left winger Greg Eden scored a second-half hat-trick to set up a 29-18 win. The second came courtesy of the pass of the weekend as Michael Shenton fired a bullet pass out of the back of his hands as he was knocked to the ground. His other assists were excellent too.

Eden's treble and Tom Holmes' long-range interception try put Castleford 28-6 up after 64 minutes. Joel Moon and Liam Sutcliffe then went over for Leeds but that couldn't stop the Tigers going two points clear at the top of the table.

Round 15

A second weekend of double fixtures had been scheduled for the end of May Bank Holiday weekend to accommodate an England pre-season training camp in preparation for that year's World Cup. The camp never took place after pressure from Super League clubs but the pressure on Super League players to play twice over the weekend remained, to almost universal opposition within the game.

The weekend opened with a pulsating contest between St Helens and Wigan on the Thursday night, which home team Saints edged 22-19 after a dramatic 77th-minute try from Mark Percival.

With Wigan having taken a 19-18 lead five minutes earlier with a Thomas Leuluai field goal and Jon Wilkin having missed a one-point attempt to try and level the scores, Matty Smith's superbly judged bomb saw Percival take the ball out of the hands of Lewis Tierney and plunge over in the corner.

Smith had already created two more St Helens tries with his inch-perfect kicks. The first one was taken by Ryan Morgan, who out-jumped Liam Marshall for a try in the corner. And Saints' second try came when Zeb Taia touched down Smith's perfectly weighted grubber.

Battling Wigan, who led 14-6 after half an hour, had gone four games without a win in the league as they remained without a whole host of senior players, losing Joel Tomkins in the warm-up, as well as centre Liam Forsyth in the first half.

51

May

St Helens were to consult with the Rugby Football League for absolute clarification over when marquee signing Ben Barba, whose capture until the end of the 2019 season had been announced that week, could make his debut for the club. There was the significant stumbling block of the 12-game ban imposed on him by the NRL for cocaine use.

Saints' win moved them four points clear of the bottom four but neighbours Warrington were still in the mix after a 40-0 hammering at Leeds the following night.

The Wolves, who many had tipped for a return to Old Trafford again, produced mistake-induced, often panic-stricken football, resorting, under that self-inflicted pressure, to try and score off every play.

On the other hand the Rhinos scored seven tries, the pick of the bunch the final score from Rob Burrow as he scorched clear from dummy-half on a trademark scoot, evading a high challenge and then rounding Stefan Ratchford. Form hooker Matt Parcell scored a hat-trick whilst maintaining his position as the competition's top tackler.

That week Leeds had secured the services of promising 20-year-old fullback Ashton Golding on a new five-year deal.

The Rhinos went above Hull FC into third spot as the Airlie Birds fell to their second successive defeat, this time at home to Leigh by 26-22.

The Centurions deservedly notched their first win in ten games. The writing was on the wall early for the hosts, who fielded a number of youngsters, including a debut for Nick Rawsthorne, as they were punished for another slow start and were generally out-enthused by a desperate Leigh side in a display littered with errors and poor execution.

Halfback Josh Drinkwater grew into the game and steered the Centurions around brilliantly as his kicks led to three of Leigh's five tries. Atelea Vea's second try took the Centurions out to a two-score lead going into the final quarter, which Hull never looked likely to peg back.

Huddersfield were the better team at the Beaumont Legal Stadium but lost 28-26 to Wakefield Trinity, themselves moving clear into fifth spot.

The Giants led for large parts of the game after having gone behind early to an acrobatic Ben Jones-Bishop try. Jones-Bishop scored the winning try too on 71 minutes, taking Sam Williams' superb long pass to level with a try in the right corner. Williams's touchline conversion gave Trinity a two-point lead which proved conclusive.

Trinity had swooped for former Hull KR and Huddersfield Giants prop Adam Walker, after Saints signed Ben Barba, while former St Helens and Salford utility Jordan Turner joined the Giants on a long-term deal after he was released by NRL side Canberra.

Salford, with stand-off Robert Lui in imposing mood, were electric on an emotional night at the AJ Bell Stadium, running in nine tries in a 50-12 success over Catalans, condemning the Dragons to a sixth successive defeat.

Red Devils owner Marwan Koukash had waived admission fees, asking instead for donations to support the families of victims of the previous Monday night's suicide bomb attack at the Manchester Arena which had killed over 20 people.

Interim Dragons coaches Jerome Guisset and Michael Monaghan took charge but things didn't start well for the Dragons when skipper Rémi Casty was sent to the bin on three minutes for a late challenge on Gareth O'Brien. By half-time it was 28-0, despite the sin-binning of Salford debutant James Hasson, the Ireland international signed from Parramatta.

Salford remained second but they were all still chasing Castleford at the top of the table after their hard-fought 32-22 home win over injury-hit Widnes.

Widnes, who lacked Joe Mellor, Rhys Hanbury, Chris Bridge, Patrick Ah Van, Tom Gilmore, Jack Buchanan, Chris Houston, Matt Whitley and Gil Dudson, with recent loan signing from Castleford Rangi Chase contractually unable to play against his parent club, tackled heroically and aggressively and the Tigers' usually well-oiled machine serially misfired - even if Castleford winger Greg Eden scored a third successive hat-trick on his

100th career appearance.

It was the first time the Tigers hadn't scored 40 points at home this season as the Vikings led 22-10 after 50 minutes and went into the last six minutes 22-20 ahead. But then Luke Gale and Michael Shenton combined to send Eden sizzling down the flank for his third score. Matt Cook's try two minutes from time helped seal a flattering win for the Tigers.

Round 16

Catalans Dragons, who had reportedly made Tony Smith their number one target to take their vacant head coaching role following the departure of Laurent Frayssinous, moved out of the Super League bottom four with a tense 23-18 home win over Hull FC.

Sam Moa, who had an outstanding game, went over to give the hosts an early lead but Albert Kelly levelled proceedings midway through the first half after Moa had been sin-binned. Luke Walsh kicked a penalty goal to put Catalans back in front before adding a field goal to open up a 9-6 half-time lead.

Nick Rawsthorne crossed after the restart with Jake Connor's conversion seeing Hull back in front. Rawsthorne scored again with the final ten minutes fast approaching but Fouad Yaha touched down to make it a one-point deficit after Walsh's conversion.

And Tony Gigot went over just three minutes later to steal the win for the Dragons in dramatic fashion before Liam Watts was red-carded for a high challenge on Rémi Casty in the dying moments. He got a one-match ban the following Wednesday.

Warrington's 38-12 home defeat by Salford dropped them into the Super League bottom four.

Niall Evalds recorded a hat-trick as the Red Devils, with Todd Carney outstanding, cruised past the Wolves for their seventh successive win to stay within two points of league leaders Castleford.

Jake Bibby, Evalds and Junior Sa'u put Salford in cruise control within 25 minutes, as they started the game in the same vein as they finished the previous Friday's demolition of Catalans.

Warrington's task was made even harder shortly before the break as Benjamin Jullien was sin-binned for preventing a quick restart. The Wolves' twelve men did cut the deficit through Brad Dwyer but Sa'u went over for his second to give the Red Devils a 22-6 half-time lead.

Evalds continued Salford's dominance by completing his brace before making it a hat-trick shortly afterwards. Kevin Brown then saw an effort ruled out but Tom Lineham brought the Wolves into double figures with 15 minutes remaining. However, the Red Devils deservedly had the final say through Kris Brining.

Salford were four points clear in second after Widnes Vikings overturned an early ten-point deficit to stun Leeds Rhinos 28-20 at the Select Security Stadium, their third win of the season.

Having been prevented from playing against his parent club Castleford three days earlier, on-loan halfback Rangi Chase sparked a Widnes fightback from 4-0 down as he impressed on his home debut. Rhys Hanbury cancelled out Ash Handley's early score but Leeds soon got the ascendancy through Kallum Watkins' and Stevie Ward's touchdowns.

Chase gave a superb show-and-go and pass for Ryan Ince to score his first try and Chase's towering kick was batted back by Charly Runciman into the arms of Corey Thompson for Widnes's third.

Aaron Heremaia went over the line midway through the second half to put Widnes ahead for the first time, before Adam Cuthbertson crossed at the other end. That was to be the Rhinos' final score, however, as Ince and Thompson completed their respective braces in the last ten minutes.

Hull's defeat in Perpignan saw Wakefield climb into the top four after Bill Tupou, playing on the right wing, scored a first-half hat-trick as Trinity came from 20-0 down to seal a remarkable 42-30 win at Wigan Warriors.

Wigan raced into a commanding position in the first 20 minutes through a debut James Worthington try and further efforts from Lewis Tierney, Liam Marshall and Tommy Leuluai. But Tupou grabbed a quick-fire hat-trick and Mason Caton-Brown crossed as Wakefield completed a stunning comeback to lead 22-20 at half-time.

Danny Kirmond touched down as Trinity continued their remarkable revival early in the second half, with Anthony England's try and three more goals from Liam Finn opening up a 16-point lead. The Warriors finally responded to 36 unanswered points through Worthington's second but Jacob Miller soon brought Wakefield up to the 40-point mark.

Marshall went over for his second late in the closing stages but it was too little as Wakefield opened up a four-point gap on their hosts in the table.

It was a win at a cost for Wakefield as stand-off Miller suffered a broken leg, while on-debut Adam Walker suffered a medial rupture and Tinirau Arona tore a hamstring.

Greg Eden made it four hat-tricks in a row as Castleford eased past Leigh Centurions 38-0 at Leigh Sports Village.

Jesse Sene-Lefao touched down for two tries to put Castleford in control with just over 20 minutes played. The first try was spectacular. Having been released down the left wing by Luke Gale, the Samoan international then kicked in-field to find Gale, who in return offloaded to the former Cronulla man to open the scoring.

Eden then scored three tries in five pulsating minutes to continue his blistering run of form, putting the Tigers into a 28-0 half-time lead, effectively securing the victory. The Centurions had been unlucky when the video referee ruled out a try by Eloi Pelissier

Eden touched down his fourth shortly after the re-start to close further on Denny Solomona's Super League try-scoring record, with Eden's total now moving to 25 Super League touchdowns.

Jamie Acton saw his effort ruled out with Leigh still scoreless before Gale was held up at the other end. Jake Webster crashed over two tackles later to finish the scoring.

Huddersfield were allowed to postpone their home game with St Helens because the town's soccer club was playing in a play-off game at Wembley. In the light of the fixture demands of the weekend, both of their next opponents voiced loud objections.

BETFRED SUPER LEAGUE
Monday 29th May

	P	W	D	L	F	A	D	Pts
Castleford Tigers	16	13	0	3	575	254	321	26
Salford Red Devils	16	12	0	4	444	274	170	24
Leeds Rhinos	16	10	0	6	417	337	80	20
Wakefield Trinity	16	10	0	6	402	338	64	20
Hull FC	16	9	1	6	373	366	7	19
Wigan Warriors	16	7	2	7	356	372	-16	16
St Helens	15	7	1	7	306	266	40	15
Catalans Dragons	16	6	1	9	333	437	-104	13
Warrington Wolves	16	5	2	9	278	409	-131	12
Huddersfield Giants	15	4	2	9	280	381	-101	10
Leigh Centurions	16	4	0	12	276	407	-131	8
Widnes Vikings	16	3	1	12	261	460	-199	7

* Barrow Raiders, in the first game of the Summer Bash at Blackpool on the last Saturday of May, won the first major silverware of the season as they defeated North Wales Crusaders 38-32 to win the League 1 Cup.

JUNE
Tiger Tiger

Round 17

Another weekend of double fixtures had taken its toll on most clubs and the first round of Super League played in June was almost universally acclaimed as sub standard.

Nevertheless there were some significant results, not least the startling 44-4 home win by Huddersfield over Warrington on the Sunday.

The Giants, alongside St Helens, had played one game over the Bank Holiday weekend when everyone else in Super League played two and Wolves coach Tony Smith was amongst the most outspoken about the issue. He insisted it had an impact in their heavy defeat but admitted he was still disappointed with his side's performance.

Warrington were second best throughout and couldn't have had too many complaints if their hosts, who leapfrogged them to move within a point of eighth-placed Catalans Dragons, had put a half-century of points on them.

Kevin Penny was given a start at fullback for Warrington while Giants coach Rick Stone threw new signing Jordan Turner straight into the side, with playmaker Danny Brough returning from his two-game ban.

Ryan Hinchcliffe was brilliant throughout for the Giants and was heavily involved in most scores, even if he didn't cross himself. Paul Clough's 44th-minute try ended any chances of an unlikely Warrington comeback.

Rangi Chase was in scintillating form as Widnes made it back-to-back wins for the first time in 2017 and moved off the bottom of the Super League ladder with a 26-6 home success over Catalans.

Chase showed glimpses of his 2011 Man of Steel and Albert Goldthorpe Medal form as he formed a great partnership with Aaron Heremaia and Rhys Hanbury. The Dragons found themselves down to twelve men on four separate occasions during the 80 minutes as the discipline from both teams left a lot to be desired.

Chris Bridge and Iain Thornley were sent off for ten minutes inside the opening five minutes for fighting and it was a battle that continued for the rest of the game, while Richie Myler was also binned in the first half as the Vikings ran in two tries to one, with Jack Buchanan and Hanbury putting the home side in front 12-6. Jordan Dezaria and Sam Moa saw yellow in the second half as Corey Thompson's try just after half-time knocked the stuffing out of the Dragons. Young forward Dezaria later took a two-game ban on an EGP for dangerous contact.

Greg Bird was likely to be missing for a long spell after sustaining a knee injury.

Adam Cuthbertson insisted the sport's administrators should find a way to ensure the game was consistently played at a high standard following Leeds' low-key 22-14 home win over Leigh on the Friday. Three games in eight days for both sides, near constantly drizzling rain and a plethora of penalties ruined the spectacle.

The Rhinos had Cuthbertson again to thank for the victory. The Aussie prop was a menace every time he sought involvement, which produced two tries and a desperate tackle from Antoni Maria to prevent a third. His second touchdown in the 57th minute established a 12-point lead that, whilst never comfortable, proved to be enough.

Hull FC coach Lee Radford launched a scathing attack on the RFL's attitude to player welfare, labelling it as 'not paramount' in the governing body's current thinking. Radford pulled no punches after his side's 39-26 home win over Wigan Warriors on the Saturday, branding the so-called 'second Easter' that saw his side in action twice over the Bank Holiday weekend, and again just five days later, as 'ridiculous'.

Steve Michaels scored a pair of tries as Hull FC dominated the Super League Champions. A big first half-hour from the injury-hit Black and Whites saw them race into a 24-point lead against a Warriors side also still shorn of a number of key players. And, despite some second-half resistance, Hull never looked likely to allow Wigan to get back on terms.

Perhaps summing up the Warriors' day, their late flurry of points actually resulted in both teams scoring six tries but Wigan's wayward goal-kicking and poor discipline saw them finish a distant second.

Mark Minichiello underlined why he had been persuaded to sign for another year at Hull with a powerful display both with and without the ball.

At the AJ Bell Stadium on the Sunday, Mason Caton-Brown came back to haunt his old club as his hat-trick helped Wakefield on their way to a seventh consecutive victory, by 34-24, ending Salford's seven-game winning streak in the process.

Despite holding a healthy 16-6 lead at the break, Wakefield were made to work for their advantage as they defended superbly in the face of large spells of Salford dominance.

A try on the stroke of half-time gave Salford hope, though, and they kicked on after the break to establish an 18-16 lead by the hour mark. And there was plenty of drama inside the final ten minutes as the lead changed hands on two occasions. Eventually, it was Wakefield who prevailed with a late try from young second-rower James Batchelor sealing Trinity's 11th win in 17 games.

Castleford coach Daryl Powell labelled the demands being made on players by the RFL as '...wrong. It's just plain wrong'.

In both a show of defiance to the sport's organisers amidst growing fixture congestion and a desire to keep his men fit for the full season, Powell opted to rest some of his key players for the home game with St Helens, with Luke Gale, Adam Milner, Matt Cook, Michael Shenton, Zak Hardaker and Grant Millington all missing out. In came fringe players such as Jy Hitchcox, Kevin Larroyer and Alex Foster, with debuts for Kieran Gill and Jake Trueman.

The fresher-looking Saints led 12-4 at half-time through Mark Percival and Louie McCarthy-Scarsbrook tries against one for Gill, who suffered a season-ending leg injury in the process of scoring. But the Tigers kept them out all second half and a converted Mike McMeeken try on 59 minutes and Tom Holmes' 71st-minute chase of Greg Minikin's kick ahead, again converted by Paul McShane, completed a 16-12 win. 'It's one of the biggest wins I've been involved in,' Powell said.

Round 18

Leigh Centurions created another landmark on the Thursday night as they beat local rivals Wigan at home in a competitive fixture for the first time in 33 years, and in some style by 50-34.

A late Wigan flurry, which produced tries by Joe Burgess and Josh Ganson, made the scoreline more respectable but it was hard watching for the Warriors fans. Ben Reynolds' nine goals marked a Super League record for the Centurions, who moved above Widnes into 11th.

Leigh went in 20-14 ahead at the break thanks to tries from Ryan Hampshire, Danny Tickle and Lachlan Burr. Liam Marshall, Josh Ganson and George Williams had replied for Warriors and they reduced the deficit to two points three minutes after half-time with a try from the returning Oliver Gildart.

But Mitch Brown, Liam Hood, who scored two from close range, Cory Paterson and Matty Dawson tries gave Leigh their biggest ever Super League win.

After two consecutive wins, Widnes found themselves back at the bottom of the table 24 hours after Leigh's win as St Helens jumped above Wigan with a 26-10 home win over the Vikings.

Saints led 10-0 at half-time through a Mark Percival try, which he converted, and another to flying wingman Regan Grace. Another emerging winger, Ryan Ince, pulled one back after the break but Alex Walmsley replied and Ryan Morgan's 61st minute try finally took the starch out of the Vikings.

On the same night at the AJ Bell Stadium, Hull FC swept aside a high-flying Salford side sitting second in the ladder by 34-10.

Hull were avenging a 50-point drubbing from the reverse fixture and playing in memory of their club legend Arthur Bunting, who passed away the previous week. They were too good for Salford from start to finish, despite missing six key players.

Two-try Albert Kelly was at his brilliant best, particularly in the first half, and was supported well by Jake Connor, finding his feet in the absence of Marc Sneyd, as Hull overwhelmed the hosts with four unanswered tries in a blistering first half.

Jamie Shaul's length-of-the-field try on the hour mark was the straw that broke the camel's back as Hull ended a Salford period of pressure and dominance.

On the Saturday, Huddersfield moved into the top eight for the first time in 2017 with a superb 56-12 win over Catalans Dragons in Perpignan, with fullback Jake Mamo giving an outstanding performance to score four tries.

Catalans president Bernard Guasch revealed after the game that a new coach would be in place within the next week, which was a clear attempt to stop the rot as the Catalans slid towards the Qualifiers. League Express revealed that former England head coach Steve McNamara had landed the job.

On the same night, Leeds drew level second with Salford with an 18-16 win at Wakefield that ended Trinity's winning run at seven games.

Trinity began encouragingly, with the latest of Mason Caton-Brown's spectacular length-of-the-field breakaway tries plus a well-worked score from Kyle Wood giving them a 10-0 lead with barely eleven minutes on the clock.

But the Rhinos, at virtually full strength with Rob Burrow the only notable absentee, hit back though two quick-fire tries from Stevie Ward and the first of a brace from Tom Briscoe, to trail by just two points at the break.

Then, after the generally impressive Scott Grix bombed a gilt-edged chance early in the second half, Joel Moon-inspired Leeds again struck twice in quick succession, either side of the hour mark to take control.

Former Leeds winger Ben Jones-Bishop - who that week had signed a new three-year contract at Bell Vue - grabbed a score back for Wakefield to ensure an interesting last seven minutes, but Leeds clung on for their third win in four games.

Trinity, already without injured skipper Danny Kirmond and Craig Huby and long-term casualties Tom Johnstone, Jacob Miller, Tinirau Arona and Jon Molloy, also lost powerhouse Australian prop David Fifita to a first-half knee problem.

And in the only Sunday game, Greg Eden scored five more tries to extend Super League leaders Castleford's advantage at the summit to six points with a 36-16 home victory over a beleaguered Warrington Wolves.

Eden's hat-trick try before half-time snuffed out any hopes for Warrington.

June

Challenge Cup Quarter-finals

Salford were the first in the hat for the Challenge Cup semi-finals after their comfortable 30-6 Thursday-night, home win over Wakefield. The Red Devils controlled the game from start to finish against a weakened Trinity side that rarely appeared to be in the battle.

From the outset, Salford's drive to win the match was there for all to see. Their forwards carried the ball with intent, with Lama Tasi, Craig Kopczak and Ben Murdoch-Masila punching holes in Wakefield's lacklustre defence time and time again, halves Michael Dobson and Robert Lui making hay, despite the absence of fullback Gareth O'Brien.

Trinity were without props David Fifita, Mitch Allgood and Tinirau Arona, as well as long-term absentees Jacob Miller and Tom Johnstone, then hindered by the late pull-outs of top scorer Ben Jones-Bishop and captain Danny Kirmond. They then lost wing Bill Tupou to a hamstring injury in the warm-up and were down to their last 17 players, new prop Adam Walker having to cut short his rehabilitation from a knee injury.

Ryan Lannon, Murdoch-Masila and Niall Evalds all scored tries to give Salford a deserved 20-0 half-time lead. Greg Johnson and Craig Kopczak added further tries to book the Red Devils' place in the last four, before Liam Finn's late consolation for Wakefield.

The following night, Leeds had little trouble disposing of the last Championship team standing, Featherstone, by 58-0 at Headingley.

By the time Rovers touched the ball in anger after 14 minutes, they were 18 points down, hard pressed to stop the rampaging, angled runs of Stevie Ward and the relentless charges of Keith Galloway which sapped their energy, or get a hand on dictating halves Joel Moon and Danny McGuire.

Things got more competitive the next day as Wigan edged a thriller at Warrington 27-26, Sam Tomkins ending a nine-month injury nightmare by kicking the winning field goal seven minutes from time.

The game, in scorching conditions, had ebbed and flowed throughout as the Warriors, bolstered by the return of six first-team stars, including England International John Bateman and the first appearance after ten months out injured for marquee man Tomkins, enjoyed periods of dominance in both halves to rack up substantial leads before being pegged back by the plucky Wolves. The home side lost influential halfback Kevin Brown in the warm-up but almost snatched it, going within inches of winning and then levelling the game as they finished with a flourish.

The final three minutes in particular were intensely dramatic.

After Kurt Gidley's late try had given the Wire one final flicker of hope, Joe Burgess's brain explosion to kick the restart out on the full had Wigan fans covering their eyes as Stefan Ratchford stepped up to attempt a winning penalty goal from half-way.

His effort drifted wide but the drama continued when Warrington won a goal-line drop-out. But they were unable to compose themselves enough to get the game-levelling field goal - Declan Patton's well-struck attempt from 11 metres out somehow going wide.

The final game of the round on the Sunday was a high-quality affair at the KCOM Stadium, holders Hull FC recording a 32-24 win over form team Castleford.

Hull handled the hot conditions better than their opponents and were worthy winners on the day. The Tigers had taken the lead after first fighting back from a 12-0 deficit courtesy of tries from Ben Roberts and Zak Hardaker to level the game at 12-all, after Carlos Tuimavave and Fetuli Talanoa had put Hull ahead.

Two penalties from the boot of Jake Connor either side of half-time - he would kick two more in the second half - then made it 16-12 before Roberts' second, a wonderful solo effort to touch down, seemingly put Castleford in control.

Given their form of protecting leads in 2017, the Tigers immediately were the favourites. Instead, they started offloading and knocking on at will, with Hull doing the basics almost to perfection.

First, Mahe Fonua touched down in the corner with brute strength to extend Hull's lead to eight after a Connor penalty had earlier levelled the scores, before the try of the game put the seal on Hull's progression to the final four.

It came when a wonderful break downfield caught the tiring Tigers out, with Jamie Shaul eventually finishing to secure victory. By the time Greg Minikin's consolation arrived seven minutes from time, Hull fans were already celebrating.

That week, Castleford reached an out-of-court settlement with Sale Sharks for a fee in excess of £200,000 plus costs after their signing of Denny Solomona at the end of the 2016 season.

Round 16

In the game postponed from Spring Bank Holiday Monday, Huddersfield shrugged off injuries to two key players to claim a third successive win - by 24-16 at home to St Helens - and climb to seventh in Super League.

Influential fullback Jake Mamo, a four-try scorer in France, limped off the pitch and down the tunnel before half-time and it turned out to be his last game of the season because of damaged foot ligaments. The Giants then lost Kruise Leeming to a jaw problem in the second half but deservedly came through to claim a fourth win in five and maintain their push for the Super 8s.

Leroy Cudjoe and Martin Ridyard put Huddersfield into a 12-0 lead. However, Saints recovered from a patchy start to reduce the gap to two points with scores either side of half-time from Luke Thompson and Mark Percival.

Huddersfield's Adam O'Brien and St Helens prop Kyle Amor both crossed before former Saints man Lee Gaskell touched down for the hosts late on as on-loan from Leigh Martyn Ridyard, alongside halves partner Danny Brough, ran the show.

Round 19

Castleford opened up a seven-point gap at the top of Super League after a 23-12 defeat of Leeds at Headingley.

Fullback Zak Hardaker was again in scintillating form, scoring a solo try and producing a magnificent performance against his parent club. The following Monday, the Tigers announced that Hardaker had signed a four-and-a-half year contract to the end of 2021, with a £150,000 transfer fee going to the Rhinos.

It was much different to the meeting between the two clubs at Castleford at the start of March, when the Tigers had annihilated the Rhinos 66-10. This time Leeds went into the lead when Ben Roberts collected a grubber in his in-goal and passed wide, almost straight into the arms of Ash Handley, who touched down.

Back came the Tigers. Ryan Hall, again at centre, lost possession running the ball out of his own quarter and, although Paul McShane and Greg Millington looked to have spilt possession, Luke Gale, Hardaker and Greg Minikin spread the ball for Greg Eden to find the corner for his 34th try of the campaign in 21 games.

Danny McGuire's foul-mouthed protestations saw him yellow-carded by Robert Hicks - he later received a one-match ban - before the try was confirmed, with Gale landing a superb touchline conversion to level the scores and a subsequent Gale penalty goal was all that separated them at half-time.

After six minutes of Castleford winning the second-half territorial battle, Hardaker

59

pounced on the back of a Jy Hitchcox run, leaving defenders trailing on a glorious 70-metre run and standing up Liam Sutcliffe with a mesmerising change of pace.

Six minutes later came the decisive try, Gale's long pass freeing Minikin who snaffled the ball to Eden. His clever footballing skills got it back to Gale, whose wonderfully measured kick to the in-goal found scorer Millington in the clear.

Adam Cuthbertson got a try back before Jamie Jones-Buchanan and Adam Milner squared up after a tackle, with Gale kicking the resulting penalty for a shoulder by the Leeds player before landing a late one-pointer to rub salt in the wound.

Second-placed Salford also lost as St Helens produced one of the best comebacks of the year, overturning a 16-point deficit at Totally Wicked Stadium with seven minutes remaining to defeat the Red Devils 25-24.

Matty Smith sealed an astonishing late surge from St Helens, that featured three unanswered tries - from James Roby, Regan Grace and Jonny Lomax - that saw them come back from 24-8 down on 73 minutes to win with a field goal after the final hooter sounded. The dramatic play came after the otherwise excellent Robert Lui kicked forward, Louie McCarthy-Scarsbrook fielded and passed quickly for the former Salford halfback Smith to nail the one point from forty metres. It was tough luck on the Red Devils, who were chasing their first win in St Helens for 37 years.

Smith had put Saints ahead with the first try of the match before Niall Evalds capitalised on a defensive error to level the scores on the brink of half-time. Greg Johnson and Robert Lui crossed for Salford shortly after the break before Evalds added another to put the visitors in that commanding position within sight of the final whistle.

Hull FC climbed into second, courtesy of their 40-18 home win over Wakefield. Astoundingly, with such a one-sided scoreline, Trinity regarded this as a game that got away.

The game swung around one incident on 59 minutes. With Wakefield 18-10 up and in full control, Kyle Wood collected a Marc Sneyd chip through to the line and looked to find his speed men out wide. If he had, winger Mason Caton-Brown would have been in at the other end and Wakefield's lead might have been unassailable. But Wood's pass went straight to Jake Connor, who scored a gift-wrapped try which was converted by Sneyd.

From there, the home side never looked back, scoring a further 24 unanswered points as Trinity completely collapsed. For Hull, Liam Watts and Sika Manu, in particular, were outstanding in the middle and provided the springboard for Hull to overcome Wakefield's tenacious pack. And fullback Jamie Shaul was at the top of his game, contributing two more opportunistic tries.

Wigan were on their worst league run since 1903 after their 19-19 draw at Huddersfield on the Friday night extended their winless league streak to eight matches.

The Giants had twice shared the spoils with the Warriors this season, after a 16-16 draw at the DW Stadium on March 19th and the clubs remained locked together on 17 points in seventh and eighth places in the table.

Tries from Leroy Cudjoe and Lee Gaskell put the Giants ahead, with Danny Brough adding a field goal for a 13-0 lead. But John Bateman and Liam Marshall replied for a 13-12 half-time scoreline. Huddersfield's one-point lead was wiped out three minutes after the break as Marshall grabbed his second try of the night.

Jermaine McGillvary's 64th minute try converted by Brough swung the game back in the Giants' favour but George Williams' 68th-minute field goal was the last score of a thrilling game.

Williams was just short with a drop-goal attempt from 60 metres with four minutes remaining, while Tommy Leuluai's attempt in the last minute drifted just wide.

Despite Wigan's winless run, coach Shaun Wane still believed the Warriors could successfully defend their Super League crown, although their top eight spot was still far from secure, with the World Champions now just three points above ninth-placed Warrington with four games to go.

Matty Smith celebrates landing the winning field goal in St Helens' incredible comeback win against Salford

The Wolves reduced the gap on the Saturday afternoon with a 24-16 home victory against Catalans, who had new coach Steve McNamara in charge for the first time.

After Jodie Broughton's early opening try for Catalans, Benjamin Jullien and Ryan Atkins scores put Wolves on top, before Richie Myler restored parity. A late Kurt Gidley penalty goal gave the Wolves a 12-10 lead at the break.

Atkins and Myler exchanged second-half tries as the Dragons enforced a nervy finish. But Andre Savelio's score a minute from time ensured Wire ended their six-game winless run and kept up hopes that a late-season revival might sneak them into the Super 8s.

Rangi Chase was again influential on the Thursday as Widnes picked up their third win in four games to keep their top-eight hopes alive, after a convincing 36-10 home victory over Leigh lifted them off the bottom of Super League.

The Vikings' victory was based on a dominant first half that saw them lead 20-0 at the break and a strong final quarter after the Centurions had mounted an unlikely comeback. There was a man-of-the-match performance from veteran backrower Chris Houston, who finished with two tries and a double for winger Corey Thompson, including a gamebreaking long-range interception effort just after the hour mark.

Bottom now, Leigh were gearing up for another Qualifiers campaign and had announced they had signed Australian halfback Daniel Mortimer from Cronulla Sharks on an immediate contract until the end of 2019. Warrington centre Rhys Evans, sidelined for the rest of the current campaign through injury, was also recruited on a three-year deal.

BETFRED SUPER LEAGUE
Sunday 25th June

	P	W	D	L	F	A	D	Pts
Castleford Tigers	19	16	0	3	650	294	356	32
Hull FC	19	12	1	6	486	420	66	25
Salford Red Devils	19	12	0	7	502	367	135	24
Leeds Rhinos	19	12	0	7	469	390	79	24
Wakefield Trinity	19	11	0	8	470	420	50	22
St Helens	19	9	1	9	385	340	45	19
Huddersfield Giants	19	7	3	9	423	432	-9	17
Wigan Warriors	19	7	3	9	435	480	-45	17
Warrington Wolves	19	6	2	11	322	505	-183	14
Catalans Dragons	19	6	1	12	367	543	-176	13
Widnes Vikings	19	5	1	13	333	502	-169	11
Leigh Centurions	19	5	0	14	350	499	-149	10

JULY
Catalans in peril

Round 20

First took on second in the Friday-night game of round 20 and leaders Castleford beat Hull FC for the first time in 2017, by 24-22.

It was a close-run thing in the end at the Mend-A-Hose Jungle after the Tigers had led 22-4 on 50 minutes. In the final analysis the Tigers, who scored three tries to Hull's four after the visitors registered three unanswered touchdowns in the last 14 minutes, owed their ninth successive Super League win to scrum-half Luke Gale, who landed six goals from as many attempts and scored an opportunist try.

The Tigers looked well in command when a turning point came shortly before the hour mark, when the Tigers were 18 points clear. Gale attempted a field goal from 15 metres in front of the Hull posts but his effort barely reached shoulder height. The ball bounced off a defender, however, and into the in-goal area, where visiting stand-off Albert Kelly collected and cleared his line.

Tigers centre Jake Webster clattered him to the ground and the ball came loose in what appeared to be a forward direction. Referee Chris Kendall, however, ruled a scrum with a Hull feed and put Webster on report. He took a one-game ban on an Early Guilty Plea the following Tuesday.

From that point, Hull dominated territorially as Marc Sneyd, who had previously been relatively quiet, came more into the game, with his superb kicking skills helping force the last four of his side's five goal-line drop-outs.

Sika Manu had a try disallowed by video but Mahe Fonua scored his second before opposite winger Feleti Talanoa scored two magnificent tries in the left corner. Sneyd converted all three and, with three minutes to go, Hull looked capable of winning. But a last-gasp raid on the left came to nothing when, after collecting a chip by Sneyd, Talanoa passed the ball forward to Jamie Shaul as the hooter sounded.

The defeat meant Hull FC dropped to fourth, Salford and Leeds both registering wins.

The Rhinos had done it tough the night before, edging St Helens by 24-22 at Headingley. With Jamie Jones-Buchanan (use of shoulder) and Danny McGuire (foul language to referee) both suspended for a game from the Castleford defeat and Rob Burrow injured, young halfback Jordan Lilley returned from his spell at Championship Bradford to guide Leeds.

Eighteen year-old Leeds fullback Jack Walker, in his third start and fourth appearance, stood head and shoulders above the more experienced players around him, plucking a variety of peppered, testing kicks out of the air, producing some stunning try-saving tackles and using his speed to clear the lines in a near faultless and brave display.

Saints' chances were damaged by the withdrawal of Matty Smith in the sixth minute with a nasty eye injury, when caught in unfriendly fire from teammate Jon Wilkin. In his absence, Theo Fages impressed. Wilkin later spent ten minutes in the sin bin for a crusher on Mitch Garbutt. He took one match on an EGP the following week. Mark Percival was also missing, suspended for one game after being found guilty of 'other contrary behaviour; after he'd kicked the ball in frustration the week before and it accidentally hit the referee.

Joel Moon was the key for Leeds at stand-off, improvising and elusive in equal measure, leaving defenders in two minds, scoring a try and assisting in two others.

The Rhinos had confirmed that week that Richie Myler was to move to Headingley from Catalans on a three-year contract from the 2018 season.

Salford went back into second, a place above the Rhinos on points difference, after a 36-20 home win over form side Huddersfield.

For the Red Devils, Michael Dobson was deadly with boot while Robert Lui - fresh from signing a new contract with the club - was menacing and, on occasions, untouchable. Ben Murdoch-Masila was again a force to be reckoned with, while there were also fine cameos from fellow packmen Josh Jones and Craig Kopczak.

Leroy Cudjoe gave the Giants an early lead before tries in quick succession by Junior Sa'u, Lui and Kris Welham put Salford in control. Aaron Murphy reduced the arrears before the break.

After the turnaround Gareth O'Brien touched down for the hosts, Sa'u scored his second and Greg Johnson and Murdoch-Masila ended the contest at 36-10. Kruise Leeming and Darnell McIntosh scored late consolations for the visitors, who slipped to eighth in the table.

Salford had confirmed that former New Zealand winger Manu Vatuvei was to join them for the rest of this and the 2018 season.

Wakefield Trinity ended a three-game losing streak by defeating Warrington 26-12 at home, a result that kept them within touching distance of the top four. The Wolves' top-eight hopes were by contrast hanging by a thread.

A converted Brad Dwyer try gave the Wolves a brief advantage in the first half after Liam Finn edged the hosts ahead with the first of two penalties.

Peta Hiku, the New Zealand international and new Warrington arrival from NRL side Penrith, started on his debut and went closest to adding a second for the visitors. That came after Trinity reclaimed the lead through Bill Tupou, with Ben Jones-Bishop's try then putting them 14-6 up.

Second-half tries from Kyle Wood and Mason Caton-Brown, interspersed by a Chris Hill score, sealed the win.

Reece Lyne was placed on report following an incident that saw Wolves youngster Will Dagger stretchered off the field, while Keegan Hirst was sin-binned for dangerous contact on Daryl Clark. Hirst escaped a ban with an EGP but Lyne got two matches, failing with an appeal. Dagger was taken to hospital with what was feared to be a serious neck injury but was discharged from hospital after X-rays.

Also on the Saturday, Catalans snatched a 40-36 victory from the jaws of defeat with a Julian Bousquet try 13 seconds from time to defeat Leigh in Perpignan.

The Centurions never trailed throughout the game except for those final 13 seconds and dominated the majority of proceedings, leading 18-0 and 28-12 at different stages. A penalty goal from Ben Reynolds, who had a fine game for Leigh, looked to have settled the result but the Dragons wouldn't be beaten.

There was plenty of fallout at the following Tuesday's disciplinary meeting centred on a 45th minute flare-up between Ben Crooks and Greg Bird. They both got one-game bans for punching, while Dragons pair Fouad Yaha (one game) and Ben Garcia (two) were suspended for running in and punching.

Leigh prop Jamie Acton was in bigger trouble. He was caught on camera picking up and then letting go of Greg Bird after he had been laid out in a collision in back play. A special hearing at Red Hall was delayed twice and eventually took place on July 18th. Acton was banned for nine games for Grade F Other Contrary Behaviour.

On the Sunday, Wigan won their first league game since April 23rd to keep their top-four hopes alive with a 28-12 home win over Widnes

The build-up was all about the return of Tony Clubb following the removal of one of his kidneys. He came off the bench midway through the first half and was a key figure in the Warriors getting the victory.

Clubb grabbed Wigan's second try of the game after skipper Sean O'Loughlin had put his side in front, while Lewis Tierney also went over as the Warriors looked to have full control.

Widnes, missing Rangi Chase, who had been suspended for striking with the shoulder in the win over Leigh, gave themselves a glimmer of hope at the end of the first half as Lloyd White managed to collect a kick through and score to reduce the deficit to ten points.

White scored a great try from nothing to put Widnes just four points behind in the second half, before Joe Burgess scored two late tries for the Warriors to end their poor run of results and move up a spot in the ladder.

Round 21

A Luke Gale field goal in the dying minutes was enough to complete a remarkable Thursday-night Castleford comeback at Wakefield's Beaumont Legal Stadium and continue their relentless charge towards the League Leaders' Shield.

In a terrific game on a warm, humid evening, Trinity led 16-0 at half-time against the Super League leaders, as well as 24-18 with nine minutes remaining, before eventually losing 25-24 to their local rivals.

The Tigers struggled before the break thanks to Trinity's well-organised defence, with their best chance coming when Jake Webster spilled the ball as he dived over the line. Greg Eden also had a try ruled out by the video referee, who ruled that Ben Jones-Bishop had been obstructed as he tried to regather a loose ball. A Jones-Bishop breakaway try and a burrowing effort from Kyle Wood, plus two conversions and two penalties from Liam Finn gave Wakefield a big advantage.

But three minutes after the turnaround, it was Eden capitalising on a lost ball to race 90 metres and score a momentum-turning try and Castleford looked their old selves as converted tries to Grant Millington and Mike McMeeken gave them a two-point lead.

Trinity looked shot but, somehow, returning David Fifita got the ball down on the Cas tryline and Finn's conversion and penalty on 74 minutes saw them lead 24-18. But Gale then dropped off Webster on the right for the equalising score before snapping the vital one-pointer with a minute to go.

Friday night's TV game wasn't quite as exciting but St Helens fans weren't too concerned as their side beat Hull FC at home by 19-12.

The game was decided by one of the season's outstanding moments of skill, produced by Saints' England centre Mark Percival.

Seven minutes from the end of a rain-affected game that featured 39 handling errors from both teams and led to criticism of the match balls currently in use, Saints were clinging on to a 14-12 lead when Theo Fages posted a chip to the left corner.

Percival was in no position to ground the ball as he caught the kick and Hull fullback Jamie Shaul tackled him in the air, heading quickly into touch-in-goal. But somehow he managed to twist his body and plant the ball down one-handed.

Danny Richardson, back in the side for the injured Matty Smith, kicked a field goal to seal it three minutes from time.

Shaul had scored to put Hull ahead on 25 minutes off a Josh Griffin break but Saints led at half-time thanks to James Roby's try from dummy-half and a penalty from Percival. Percival went over in the 47th minute after a break from Fages, before Mahe Fonua crossed on 64 minutes and Marc Sneyd kicked his second conversion to reduce the visitors' deficit.

St Helens were now only four points behind fourth-placed Hull.

On the same night Warrington thrashed Leigh at home by 50-10, leaving the Wolves still with a technical chance of catching Huddersfield in eighth spot, the Giants themselves enjoying a big home win, by 40-0 over Widnes, to stay three points clear.

At the Halliwell Jones Stadium, Stefan Ratchford was dazzling in attack, producing the final pass for a number of tries and added six goals for good measure. And left winger Tom Lineham finished with a four-try haul.

Both sides had Aussies on debut, Ben Pomeroy scoring for the Wolves, the former Catalans centre having finished his season with Lezignan. And halfback Daniel Mortimer was joined by another mid-season Leigh signing in Tongan international stand-off Samisoni Langi.

At the John Smith's Stadium, the Giants handed a home debut to new signing Jordan Rankin as they led the Vikings 18-0 after 16 minutes with tries from Shannon Wakeman, Jermaine McGillvary and Ryan Hinchcliffe.

Adam O'Brien and Darnell McIntosh crossed either side of half-time to extend the lead to 30 points. And McGillvary and Ukuma Ta'ai went over late on as the hosts moved four points clear of ninth-placed Catalans, who the next night lost at home to Wigan, making a Qualifiers place almost certain.

Rangi Chase was absent, on the second week of his two-game ban, but that week had joined the Vikings on a permanent two-year contract.

Assistant John Winder was in charge for the Warriors' 32-10 win in Perpignan, with Shaun Wane back in England having undergone a hip operation on the Saturday morning.

Wigan led just 8-4 at the break and then trailed early in the second half after Vincent Duport's second try, before Joe Burgess completed a hat-trick alongside George Williams and Sam Tomkins tries, his first since his return from long-term injury.

In the only Sunday game, Leeds went clear of Salford into second spot after beating the Red Devils at the AJ Bell Stadium by 50-24.

Salford took an early lead thanks to young halfback Josh Wood but the Rhinos' emphatic response, centred around Danny McGuire, Joel Moon and Matt Parcell, was devastating. Ryan Hall scored the first of seven tries in a first-half burst of 36-unanswered points. Tom Briscoe's second just before half-time conclusively ended the contest.

The following Tuesday, Danny McGuire announced he would be leaving the Rhinos at the end of the season after a 16-year playing career with his hometown club.

Round 22

England international Ben Currie ended a ten-month injury nightmare in the Thursday TV game. And Currie marked his return to action following an anterior cruciate ligament knee injury by scoring the winning try in the Wolves' 16-10 win at Wigan.

It was the first time in four attempts in 2017 that Warrington had beaten the Warriors and though it came too late to save them from the Qualifiers, it severely dented the reigning Champions' hopes of reaching the top four this season.

The Warriors led 10-8 at half-time thanks to tries from Oliver Gildart and John Bateman, while Benjamin Jullien and Ryan Atkins crossed for the Wolves.

The second half was a blood and thunder affair with the emphasis on defence. For large spells Wigan dominated but they found it increasingly difficult to break the Wolves line. It took a try from a Declan Patton grubber by Currie followed by two Stefan Ratchford penalties to win it but victory for Huddersfield on Friday night meant the Wolves couldn't finish in the top eight.

Sean O'Loughlin was named in a Wigan team for a 400th time, becoming only the eleventh player to reach that milestone.

That week the Wolves announced Andre Savelio would leave them at the end of the season to join NRL club Brisbane Broncos.

Hull dropped out of the play-off places following a 10-7 defeat at Leeds on the Friday night, their third successive loss.

The Rhinos had to play 68 minutes with 15 men after Stevie Ward suffered concussion and the luckless Keith Galloway again ruptured an Achilles tendon.

There was an exciting finish to a defence-orientated clash that Hull led 7-0 at the break thanks to a sixth-minute Scott Taylor try from dummy-half converted by Marc Sneyd, who added a field goal on the half-time hooter. By the end Leeds were desperately clinging on to a three-point lead courtesy of Ryan Hall and Jack Walker tries, the latter goaled by Jordan Lilley.

Hull, who had already had late efforts by Josh Griffin and Mahe Fonua ruled out in the right corner, launched a final assault down the same route.

Danny Houghton, Marc Sneyd, Jake Connor and Griffin again freed the bullocking Fonua on a course for the corner. But Jimmy Keinhorst, back after 15 weeks out with a hand ligament injury, saved the Rhinos by forcing him into touch, with the hooter sounding immediately afterwards.

Wakefield Trinity were 36-8 winners at Widnes to move into fourth ahead of Hull FC.

Trinity's forwards were too much for Widnes to handle all night, even though the Vikings led 6-0 early on thanks to Joe Mellor's try. David Fifita, in particular, was immense. In the backs, Bill Tupou caused endless problems in attack, combining excellently with winger Mason Caton-Brown, with both finishing with try-braces.

Super League's top try-scorer Greg Eden suffered a serious shoulder injury in Castleford's 38-14 home victory over Salford.

Eden injured his shoulder diving in for his second touchdown, which was his 37th of the season in Cup and League, although his replacement off the bench, the highly-experienced Joel Monaghan, also crossed twice

Tigers' scrum-half Luke Gale was involved in all but one of his side's six tries and landed seven goals from eight attempts, as well as a 40/20.

Huddersfield's 26-4 home victory over Leigh secured their top-eight spot, completing a remarkable turnaround after the Giants looked like certainties for the Qualifiers around the Easter period.

With Martyn Ridyard ineligible to play against his parent club, Lee Gaskell moved into the halves and ended with two tries. Leigh captain Micky Higham made his 500th career appearance in the defeat.

St Helens had also turned their season around, with James Roby on fire in the 46-28 home win against Catalans on the Sunday.

It was a close-run thing until the last seven minutes. The Dragons took the lead three times in the first half thanks to tries from Justin Horo, Luke Walsh and Tony Gigot. However, scores from Theo Fages, Alex Walmsley and Louie McCarthy-Scarsbrook gave Saints a 20-18 lead at the interval.

Horo's second try put the Dragons back in front but a penalty from Mark Percival and a converted Jonny Lomax try edged the home team ahead. Then Luke Walsh's goal after Richie Myler's try moved the French side back to within two points.

In a whirlwind finish, Saints crossed three times in the final seven minutes, through Percival, Luke Thompson and Ryan Morgan.

Catalans were gearing up for the Qualifiers and gave debuts to season-long loan signings from Wigan, their former prop Romain Navarrete and winger Lewis Tierney.

Round 23

The surprise packet of 2017, Wakefield Trinity, blew their bid to make the top four after the last regular-season round - and Salford were the beneficiaries ahead of the Super 8s. The Red Devils were left to sweat after their 25-0 defeat at Leigh Centurions on the Friday put Trinity in the driving seat for the top four, which guaranteed four rather than three home games in the top-eight play-offs.

A win on the Sunday at home to St Helens would have put Wakefield third at the expense of Hull FC and left Salford in fifth and if they avoided defeat by 15 points or more they would finish fourth.

However rejuvenated Saints won 41-16, leaving Wakefield fifth and denying them a first top-four finish since 1981.

In the continued absence of Matty Smith at scrum-half, the Danny Richardson-Theo Fages halfback pairing got another outing and again showed up extremely well, with James Roby back to his best at hooker.

Saints led 24-6 at half-time and though Wakefield came back to 26-16 after the break, Louie McCarthy-Scarsbrook's try in the 70th minute killed off home hopes of a revival.

Wakefield were still talking up their chances in the Super 8s and signed Ireland international prop forward James Hasson from Salford to the end of the season and Newcastle Knights hooker Tyler Randell on a two-year deal. Prop Mitch Allgood was heading back to Australia after an injury-riddled season.

Salford's performance at Leigh on the Friday night could have been described as lacklustre, the weekend before their Challenge Cup semi-final with Wigan. Leigh had motivation of their own, Widnes's defeat to Warrington the night before giving them a chance to climb off the foot of the final table.

They did that with style and 25-0 was a fair reflection. Gregg McNally lit the game up with his two tries and recent signing, Tonga stand-off Samisoni Langi was a force out wide too. Forward Lachlan Burr was hungry for work on both sides of the ball and was the outstanding forward.

Warrington's 22-6 home win over a below-strength Widnes closed their disappointing league campaign. The Wolves recovered from a 4-6 interval deficit to ease to victory after the break, aided by considerable contributions from centre pairing Peta Hiku and Ryan Atkins. Winger Matty Russell scored two well-taken tries

Both sides were already condemned to the Qualifiers, where their points total would be wiped to zero, and the game was never likely to live up to the slogan of 'every minute matters'. The Vikings but were solid and structured in the first half before seeing the game move away from them with two tries created by the boot of Declan Patton in the third quarter.

On the Friday night, Wigan ran in seven unanswered tries at the DW Stadium to steamroll a heavily weakened Leeds Rhinos side 34-0 and keep their top-four dream alive.

Leeds were down to the bare bones, with players injured and rested ahead of their Challenge Cup semi-final against Hull FC on the following Saturday. They put out a team with two 17-year-olds and five 18-year-olds. Harry Newman was one of three Leeds debutants, the others were Alex Sutcliffe and Harvey Whiteley. Winger Newman was the first player born in the year 2000 to play in Super League.

In wet conditions, the Warriors dominated the opening 40 minutes without being brilliant, as Leeds struggled to get into Wigan's half and the home side should have held a more comfortable lead than 14-0.

They led thanks to two tries in four minutes from Michael McIlorum and Sam Tomkins, while Willie Isa had two attempts chalked off by video referee James Child before George Williams crossed for their third try before half-time.

The second half was all Wigan and the scoreline was kept down by Williams' relative lack of success kicking goals, with two from six before Sam Powell converted their last try. Oliver Gildart scored two tries in five minutes and he had Williams to thank for both of them, although he did repay the favour later on after Tom Davies had also crossed.

On the same night, Hull FC snapped their three-game losing streak with a hard fought 14-10 home win over the resurgent Huddersfield Giants, securing a top-four finish as well as seeing the successful and long awaited return of inspirational captain Gareth

Ellis from injury. The former Leeds Rhinos and West Tigers star had endured a frustrating season and took the field after over three months on the sidelines with a sternum injury. Man of the match Ellis visibly lifted his Hull side, coming up with a try-assist and good metres in two spells on the field.

The game was tough, tight and a real arm-wrestle, particularly in the second half, with the majority of the points scored in the first as Hull raced out to a twelve-point lead after an explosive opening quarter, only to be pegged back at half-time. Marc Sneyd's penalty goal five minutes from time was the only score of the second half.

Castleford finished the regular season ten points clear at the top of the table. The Tigers defeated Catalans Dragons 32-24 in Perpignan on the Saturday, with the injured Greg Eden's replacement, Jy Hitchcox, scoring two spectacular tries. Eden's shoulder injury suffered the week before against Salford had been revealed to be not as bad as first feared. He was now expected to miss four weeks of action.

Catalans led 18-16 at half-time and the Tigers scored two late tries to secure the win, despite being down to eleven men at one point in the second half following the sin-binnings of Kevin Larroyer (unsportsmanlike behaviour) and Mike McMeeken (holding down in the tackle).

With the Catalans already condemned to the Qualifiers, new coach Steve McNamara insisted his side were heading in the right direction.

BETFRED SUPER LEAGUE
Sunday 23rd July

	P	W	D	L	F	A	D	Pts
Castleford Tigers	23	20	0	3	769	378	391	40
Leeds Rhinos	23	15	0	8	553	477	76	30
Hull FC	23	13	1	9	541	483	58	27
Salford Red Devils	23	13	0	10	576	500	76	26
Wakefield Trinity	23	13	0	10	572	506	66	26
St Helens	23	12	1	10	513	420	93	25
Wigan Warriors	23	10	3	10	539	518	21	23
Huddersfield Giants	23	9	3	11	519	486	33	21
Warrington Wolves	23	9	2	12	422	557	-135	20
Catalans Dragons	23	7	1	15	469	689	-220	15
Leigh Centurions	23	6	0	17	425	615	-190	12
Widnes Vikings	23	5	1	17	359	628	-269	11

KINGSTONE PRESS CHAMPIONSHIP
Sunday 23rd July

	P	W	D	L	F	A	D	Pts
Hull Kingston Rovers	23	19	1	3	850	385	465	39
London Broncos	23	18	0	5	832	410	422	36
Halifax	23	16	0	7	567	357	210	32
Featherstone Rovers	23	15	1	7	687	421	266	31
Toulouse Olympique	23	15	0	8	720	466	254	30
Batley Bulldogs	23	11	0	12	549	663	-114	22
Sheffield Eagles	23	10	0	13	568	785	-217	20
Dewsbury Rams	23	8	0	15	388	736	-348	16
Rochdale Hornets	23	7	1	15	457	680	-223	15
Swinton Lions	23	6	0	17	477	648	-171	12
Oldham	23	5	1	17	410	735	-325	11
Bradford Bulls *	23	6	0	17	500	719	-219	0

* Twelve points deducted for entering administration

Challenge Cup Semi-finals

At the end of a week when it was announced that Hull FC and Wigan were to play a regular-season league game in Australia in 2018, in Wollongong on 10th February, the two clubs qualified to play in the Challenge Cup Final at Wembley in 2017.

Hull recorded a convincing 43-24 victory over Leeds Rhinos in the Saturday clash at Doncaster's Keepmoat Stadium, while the Warriors defeated Salford Red Devils 27-14 at Warrington's Halliwell Jones Stadium on the Sunday.

Holders Hull put in one of their best performances of recent times at a packed stadium against a team that had held an advantage over them - their last win against the Rhinos had been by 24-19 at home on 12th September, 2014.

Albert Kelly returned from injury and looked a class apart when he scored a try of his own and when he laid two tries on a plate for others. He was also strong defensively

Jamie Shaul tackled by Joel Moon as Hull FC sweep past Leeds to reach Wembley

as he, alongside Marc Sneyd, controlled the game for Hull.

Leeds winger Tom Briscoe was mercilessly targeted by Sneyd's kicking game allowing Hull winger Fetuli Talanoa the momentum to torment the former Hull player into making several errors.

The Rhinos played their part in a high-quality contest, notching some eye-catching tries of their own. Ryan Hall scored two brilliantly taken first-half tries, whilst skipper Danny McGuire combined with Kallum Watkins to constantly threaten Hull's defence, culminating in a quality second-half try.

However, there was no questioning Hull's superiority as Leeds struggled to stay in the contest after the break despite a late consolation try in the final few minutes.

After taking a slender 18-12 lead into half-time, Lee Radford's side went up a gear in the second half, racking up four well-worked tries to completely overwhelm Leeds.

Michael McIlorum dives past Michael Dobson as Wigan see off Salford in the Challenge Cup semi-final

Wigan saw off a considerable challenge from the Red Devils the day after, by 27-14.

It looked like it would be a comfortable afternoon's work for the Warriors when, following a rip-roaring opening 15 minutes, converted tries from Oliver Gildart and Willie Isa made it 12-0 in the blink of an eye.

Salford handed debuts to Manu Vatuvei and Tyrone McCarthy and while all eyes were on the former, it was the latter who impressed when he arrived from the bench. He gave the Red Devils an undoubted lift when he came on and he scored one of the two back-to-back tries that made it a level game soon after his arrival, the first coming when Greg Johnson finished off a slick Red Devils play.

Salford actually ended the half in front. McCarthy nearly got his second before being pulled back by Sam Tomkins, which earned the fullback a yellow card and gave Michael Dobson an easy opportunity to make it 14-12.

The second half was a brutal, professional and truly Wigan-like display. They thought they had gone ahead when Joe Burgess finished a scintillating move three minutes after half-time, only to be denied by a wonderful tackle from Niall Evalds that forced Burgess to lose his grip on the ball, with video-referee Ben Thaler taking a long time to decide that he hadn't grounded.

However, a penalty from the boot of George Williams levelled it up soon afterwards. And, while he would miss with a repeat attempt three minutes later, it wasn't long before Wigan went ahead.

Michael McIlorum's return from the bench gave the Warriors a huge lift and when Burgess broke again down the left he had the wherewithal to kick back inside for the hooker to collect and dive over unchallenged. Advantage Wigan, just as an extraordinary storm began to rain down from the skies.

Sam Tomkins had kicked the decisive field goal in the quarter-final win against Warrington and he repeated the trick with 14 minutes left to open up a two-score lead which, despite plenty of effort from Salford, they never really looked like overhauling.

Anthony Gelling's sin bin for interference didn't even allow Salford any more points and the Warriors finished with a flourish on the hooter as Gildart's second secured a return to Wembley for Wigan once again.

AUGUST
Robins bobbin'

Super League Super 8s - Round 1

Castleford finished the regular season with a ten-point lead at the top of the table but that lead was cut as St Helens laid down a marker of their title credentials in the opening game of the Super 8s, with James Roby inspiring an impressive first home defeat of the season on the runaway leaders.

Saints' pack got the better of their opponents in the Thursday TV game with a 26-12 win, with props Luke Thompson and Alex Walmsley again prominent. Jonny Lomax and Theo Fages both produced touches of class in attack and there was an assured second-half return from Matty Smith from his bad eyelid injury, with a concussion to Danny Richardson allowing him to provide a vital kicking game in the second half.

St Helens went ahead when Zeb Taia burst past Zak Hardaker's challenge to go over and Mark Percival added the extras, before converting a penalty five minutes later. Kyle Amor had a score disallowed for a knock-on, while the Tigers were denied a try for offside. Smith's field-goal attempt for the hosts fell well short on the stroke of half-time as St Helens went to the break with an eight-nil lead.

After half-time, Adam Milner scored under the posts from close range and Luke Gale's conversion reduced the deficit to two points but St Helens surged back when Lomax's short pass set up Roby for his fifth Super League try in the past six matches - and then Lomax pounced on a bobbling ball from Smith's low kick.

Joel Monaghan's one-handed dive in the right corner gave the Tigers a ray of hope, before Roby powered over from close range to secure a convincing victory.

Wigan suffered a 32-16 defeat at second-placed Leeds on the Friday night, with the result further denting their hopes of defending their Super League crown as they slipped into eighth, four points adrift of fourth-placed Saints.

Stevie Ward, with his first Rhinos hat-trick, set a magnificent lead, running strongly off Danny McGuire passes and leading the home tackle count with 40. Ashton Golding, with the added competition of the even younger Jack Walker for the fullback spot, also had a fine game.

Adam Cuthbertson was on top form, his seven offloads almost as many as Wigan managed in total. McGuire's sensational short ball to send Ward in for his second try with 12 minutes to go and make it 26-10 settled the game.

Salford slumped to a fifth straight league defeat on the same night, as Hull FC stayed third with a 32-18 home win, leaving the Red Devils outside the top four.

The sides were level at half-time at 14-all but Hull were able to go up the gears once again to shock the Red Devils with three quickfire tries after the break, effectively ending the game as a contest.

Scrum-half Marc Sneyd, backrower Mark Minichiello and prop Josh Bowden all missed the game after the three of them suffered minor injuries in the Challenge Cup semi-final defeat of Leeds. But Jake Connor got his chance at halfback and laid on three tries and scored one himself, adding six goals for good measure. Manu Vatuvei scored two tries for Salford in his first Super League game.

Huddersfield Giants still had hopes of a play-off finish and were now just four points adrift of fourth-placed St Helens following their 36-6 home win over Wakefield. They were boosted by the return of Jordan Turner from injury, while Shannon Wakeman and Ukuma Ta'ai also came back into the starting 13 as Danny Brough dictated the game throughout, adding six goals and a try for good measure. Leroy Cudjoe's 61st-minute try opened up an unassailable 20-point lead for Huddersfield.

It was easily Wakefield's worst performance of the year as they made error after error and after the game it emerged that recently signed prop Adam Walker had been suspended after testing positive for cocaine.

Super 8s, The Qualifiers - Round 1

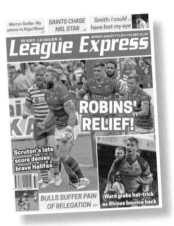

Denis Betts' plans for Widnes's opening Qualifiers match at home to Warrington were in disarray when he discovered the news just over 24 hours before kick-off that Rangi Chase had also tested positive for cocaine.

Widnes suspended Chase, who had recently signed a two-year contract, with immediate effect and his career now appeared over. Danny Craven stepped in at the last minute to replace Chase and his performance earned praise from Betts.

The Wolves won the game 28-14 after the Vikings led from the 31st through to the 63rd minute and showed great spirit throughout. Stefan Ratchford was in brilliant form, at his elusive best in attack and solid as a rock in defence. The key moment came in the 68th minute. After a Ratchford try saver at one end, Warrington broke out of their own half on the next set and Matty Russell finished a brilliant counter attack that gave the Wolves an eight-point advantage heading into the last ten minutes.

Catalans Dragons also had problems with drug testers as Tony Gigot, was re-suspended for two years for 'inappropriate conduct' towards a French Anti-Doping official, although he had not tested positive at that or subsequent tests. After initially having his suspension reduced to three months earlier in the year following an appeal, the French Anti-Doping authorities had won their appeal over that reduction and the initial two-year ban stood.

On the Saturday, the Dragons got the fright of their life when they struggled to beat Championship London Broncos at home, eventually emerging 20-18 winners.

Former Catalans halfback William Barthau could have had a hat-trick as the Broncos flirted with victory but he lost possession twice when looking to touch down over the line following his seventh-minute opener. Luke Walsh's conversion of Louis Anderson's 67th minute try proved to be the gamebreaker and secured the Dragons the two points.

Ben Crooks and Gareth Hock both missed Leigh's first Qualifiers match at Featherstone Rovers on the Saturday with leg injuries as the Centurions eased to a 38-12 win.

The game's outstanding player was Aussie halfback Daniel Mortimer, who twice stamped his authority within the first seven minutes, first with a well-timed pass to put Atelea Vea through and clever anticipation to take the return pass and score and then a teasing grubber that evaded three defenders to sit up kindly for Gregg McNally. Josh Drinkwater's try on 59 minutes killed off any chance of a Featherstone fightback.

Hull KR opened their Qualifiers campaign with a nerve-jangling 26-22 victory over fellow Championship side Halifax at KCOM Craven Park. The relief that received top performer Nick Scruton's 72nd-minute, match-winning try summed up just how hard Halifax - who led 22-14 after Ben Heaton's fourth try on 52 minutes - had pushed the big-spending, heavily-fancied Robins

Super League Super 8s - Round 2

Super League XXII was turning out to be the most unpredictable season to date as the top eight shuffled around yet again.

Following a convincing 38-6 home victory against Leeds on the Thursday night, coupled with results elsewhere, Wakefield Trinity sat fourth on the table with just five games of the season remaining.

It was Wakefield's first ever Super 8s win at the ninth attempt as, with the game in the balance at 6-6 in the 25th minute, Trinity, led by mercurial hooker Kyle Wood, stepped up a series of gears to blow away their second-placed neighbours with 32-unanswered points.

Leeds were buoyant, coming off the back of a great win against Wembley-bound Wigan the previous week and having Rob Burrow on the bench for his first appearance since June.

But the Rhinos never really got going. Joe Arundel scored for Wakefield early on before Adam Cuthbertson crossed to put the visitors level. Ben Jones-Bishop put Wakefield in front again while Scott Grix added the hosts' third almost straight from the restart, a scintillating move from deep started by dummy-half Wood.

Jacob Miller, back for his first game since breaking his leg at Wigan in May, scored just before half-time while Matty Ashurst and Bill Tupou wrapped up the win for Trinity in a second half they dominated.

St Helens dropped out of the four and, after their 8-6 victory at a rain-soaked Totally Wicked Stadium on the Friday night, Hull now sat in third place, four points ahead of Saints.

Marc Sneyd converted his own try in the 34th minute to level Regan Grace's score in the opening minutes goaled by Mark Percival. And Sneyd's penalty goal from half way just after the hour mark were the only points of the second half.

Saints coach Justin Holbrook aimed some criticism at the balls used in Super League after the game which was played in almost continuous rain. 'It was one of the worst games of Rugby League I've been involved in and I feel sorry for everyone that had to watch that,' he said.

On the same wet night, Wigan leap-frogged Huddersfield at the bottom of the table with an 18-4 home win over the Giants, who had drawn their previous two matches with the Warriors.

The Giants took an early lead when Jermaine McGillvary picked up a loose ball from a Danny Brough kick, before Wigan hit back through Anthony Gelling.

It looked like it was going to be all square at half-time until George Williams' kick through was touched down by Liam Farrell for the Champions to lead 10-4.

For large periods of the second half it seemed like only two points from the boot of Sam Powell were going to be posted, before man of the match Sam Tomkins rubbed salt in Huddersfield's wounds with a late try.

Castleford re-opened a ten-point gap at the top after a 23-4 win at Salford as Zak Hardaker's first-half double left them singing in the rain and all but mathematically sure of the League Leaders' Shield.

Hardaker showed two moments of class and awareness to score his tries and he played a key role in his side's fourth from Jy Hitchcox. In between, the excellent Paul McShane also touched down. Manu Vatuvei's growing influence on the Salford left wing continued with his side's only try

August

Super 8s, The Qualifiers - Round 2

Hull KR were indebted to skipper Shaun Lunt as they held on to win 20-16 at Leigh Sports Village. The hooker, brought on as replacement midway through the first half, scored two tries to edge the contest in Rovers' favour, although the main talking point came from the game-winning touchdown, with Leigh contending that Nick Scruton had not played the ball correctly.

Robins coach Tim Sheens admitted his side 'got lucky' and it was a cruel way to decide the game, although with Leigh receiving three penalties in the final minute there was plenty to keep both sets of fans involved through to the final hooter.

Rovers restricted Leigh to two tries, from Daniel Mortimer and Atelea Vea and ran in three themselves, with winger Ryan Shaw bagging their second. Jamie Ellis and Josh Drinkwater kicked four goals each.

Warrington also made it two from two with a comprehensive 52-24 home win over Catalans on the Saturday, with young halfback Declan Patton scoring 20 points from a try and eight goals, while his kicking game played a large part. The game was over by half-time, Warrington's dominance seeing them lead 30-6 at half-time.

Back-from-injury Ben Westwood made his 400th appearance for the Wolves.

The day after, Halifax winger Ben Heaton scored another two tries to add to his four the previous week at Hull KR but that couldn't prevent Widnes registering a 36-12 win at the Shay. Widnes scored seven tries to Halifax's two and, having forced the hosts to do an immense amount of defensive work in the first 40 minutes, Richard Marshall's side inevitably tired, with Widnes running out comfortable winners to register their first win of the Qualifiers.

Lloyd White was the standout for Widnes as Joe Mellor's late try killed off any hopes of a Halifax comeback.

Also on the Sunday, London Broncos and Featherstone produced an astounding 32-all draw at Ealing Trailfinders.

It was a resilient performance from Rovers, as they trailed 14-0 after the first quarter and then by 32-22 with just over ten minutes of the game left. Featherstone's second response began when the tireless John Davies drove to the line and Kyle Briggs swept up his offload to send Luke Briscoe over in the corner. Ian Hardman missed the kick but Fev were back within six points.

London could, and probably should, have ended it with nine minutes to go as they in turn pressed, setting up what seemed an obvious field-goal opportunity. Rovers did not waste the reprieve, pressing hard in the final minutes. Twice Briggs launched huge kicks which London struggled to clear. The second fell into Fev hands and was worked rapidly to the left, where Chris Ulugia dived joyously to score.

But that would have been no more than a consolation had Hardman, who had missed an eminently kickable goal in the first half, not been bang on target from the touchline.

Super League Super 8s - Round 3

Castleford Tigers secured top spot for the first time in their 91-year history and, with it, the League Leaders' Shield with a 45-20 home victory against Wakefield.

The Tigers were made to do it the hard way by their local rivals in front of a sell-out Thursday-night crowd but, as had often been the case in 2017, Cas proved too good.

Trinity were well in the game as Mason Caton-Brown crashed over from dummy-half, leaving the score 18-10 at the break. When Danny Kirmond cut the deficit further after crossing from a smart blindside play, it looked like Wakefield may just spoil the party.

But Castleford, who had Junior Moors back from a knee injury suffered in June, opened a two-score cushion through Greg Eden, himself back from a shoulder injury, with Super League's leading scorer racing home after a pinpoint looping pass from Luke Gale left Ben Jones-Bishop helplessly grasping at thin air. Three minutes later, another Castleford raid down their right flank reaped rewards. Zak Hardaker provided the overlap and, although his pass looking for Greg Minikin was snuffed out by Bill Tupou he could only palm the ball towards the try line, where Jake Webster had the simplest of finishes.

Webster bagged his hat-trick try as he powered through the defence from Ben Roberts' sublime flat ball and the popular centre soon sent the fans into further delirium as he got a fourth from Mike McMeeken's offload, which came a few minutes after Gale had landed a field goal.

Max Jowitt dampened the celebrations minimally when he scored for Trinity but normal service was resumed two minutes later as Hardaker scored again, superbly supporting Roberts after his sidestep breached the Wakefield defence.

The celebrations continued for over an hour at The Jungle.

Wakefield stayed in fourth because of St Helens' 16-14 loss at Headingley on the Friday night. The game will be remembered as the last before the old South Stand was demolished, rather than for its quality, with both sides unable to find any fluency, hookers James Roby and Matt Parcell the two stand-out players on the night.

Kallum Watkins' penalty goal in the 69th minute established a two-score lead for the only time and it was just enough for Leeds.

Hull FC captain Gareth Ellis announced he would be retiring at the end of the season after he turned down the opportunity to play on with the Airlie Birds in 2018, instead moving into an off-field role with the club. He was probably convinced he had made the right call after his side were humbled 46-18 at home by the Giants, stand-off Lee Gaskell scoring three tries and having a hand in numerous others through the hands and with the boot.

And that after Ellis opened the scoring in what was his 450th career appearance. Young prop Tyler Dickinson's converted try on 51 minutes gave the Giants an 18-point lead and from that point Hull didn't look like recovering.

Wigan kept their Super League semi-final dreams alive with a convincing 42-6 home win against Salford. The Warriors produced one of their best halves of the season as they ran in five unanswered tries, with Joe Burgess grabbing a brace, as they dominated the Red Devils to lead 26-0 at the break.

The Champions again bossed the second half with tries from George Williams and Frank-Paul Nuuausala securing the victory, although the Red Devils avoided the humiliation of being nilled, as Niall Evalds crossed late on.

Super 8s, The Qualifiers - Round 3

After suffering a potentially damaging defeat to Hull Kingston Rovers a week earlier, Leigh Centurions gave an impressive performance to comfortably account for Catalans Dragons 30-6 in warm and sunny Perpignan.

The omens for Catalans didn't look good as Paul Aiton hobbled off with a calf injury in the third minute and the Centurions opened the scoring a minute later when a penalty gifted Leigh good attacking field position before on-loan Lewis Tierney allowed

Josh Drinkwater's kick to bounce and the loose ball was knocked back to Adam Higson by Samisoni Langi. Ben Reynolds added the conversion.

It was 24-0 by the hour mark as Catalans spilled most of the possession they gained, with Leigh having another four scores denied by the video referee, Brayden Wiliame and Cory Paterson exchanging tries in the last ten minutes.

Widnes built on their professional display at Halifax with a comprehensive 58-10 home victory over Featherstone Rovers to boost their Qualifiers campaign. Chris Bridge, in his last season before retiring, and the outstanding Rhys Hanbury both scored hat-tricks.

Warrington and Hull KR both maintained their hundred per cent records to set them fair for Super League in 2018.

The Wolves' 22-8 home win over Halifax on the Saturday looked like it was comfortable enough. It was anything but. For all but the last ten or 15 minutes the visitors went toe to toe with their illustrious hosts before predictably running short of steam.

Not until the third Wolves try from Matty Russell in the 66th minute was swiftly followed by a Declan Patton penalty to extend the lead to eight points did Halifax look unlikely to come back into it. And the Wolves had a lot to thank captain Chris Hill for, not for the first time that year. He was almost outshone by Halifax's local winger Chester Butler, drafted in amid an injury crisis, who scored both their tries.

BETFRED SUPER LEAGUE - SUPER 8s								
Sunday 20th August								
	P	W	D	L	F	A	D	Pts
Castleford Tigers	26	22	0	4	849	428	421	44
Leeds Rhinos	26	17	0	9	607	545	62	34
Hull FC	26	15	1	10	599	553	46	31
Wakefield Trinity	26	14	0	12	636	593	43	28
St Helens	26	13	1	12	559	456	103	27
Wigan Warriors	26	12	3	11	615	560	55	27
Salford Red Devils	26	13	0	13	604	597	7	26
Huddersfield Giants	26	11	3	12	605	528	77	25

SUPER 8s - THE QUALIFIERS								
Sunday 20th August								
	P	W	D	L	F	A	D	Pts
Warrington Wolves	3	3	0	0	102	46	56	6
Hull Kingston Rovers	3	3	0	0	81	68	13	6
Widnes Vikings	3	2	0	1	108	50	58	4
Leigh Centurions	3	2	0	1	84	38	46	4
Catalans Dragons	3	1	0	2	50	100	-50	2
London Broncos	3	0	1	2	80	87	-7	1
Featherstone Rovers	3	0	1	2	54	128	-74	1
Halifax	3	0	0	3	42	84	-42	0

On the Sunday, London Broncos pushed Hull KR with a thrilling fightback in the closing moments at KCOM Craven Park but, in the end, Rovers had enough to hold them at arm's length and emerge with a 35-30 win. Jamie Ellis's penalty, his seventh goal, which made it 35-20, gave London too much to do. They were left to reflect on a frustrating first 40 minutes in which they trailed 25-8 and were effectively out of the contest, though they convincingly won the second half.

Challenge Cup Final

Twelve months on from laying their Wembley hoodoo to rest with their first win at Wembley stadium, Hull FC were more convincing in retaining the Challenge Cup with an 18-14 win over Wigan.

The holders dominated for much of the game but a late Wigan comeback made for the most exciting finish to a Wembley final in living memory, the Warriors having a try that would have levelled the scores disallowed two minutes from time.

Hull halfback Marc Sneyd became only the second man to retain the Lance Todd Trophy as the Challenge Cup Final man of the match since the award's 1946 inauguration. While the first to do so, Paul Wellens,

Hull FC's Fetuli Talanoa bursts past Wigan's John Bateman during the Challenge Cup Final

shared the award with his St Helens teammate Leon Pryce in 2007, Sneyd had won both of his outright. Sneyd was head and shoulders above anybody else on the field with only one other player, Hull winger Mahe Fonua, attracting any votes from the assembled media.

Sneyd's 40/20 on 48 minutes and touchline conversion to Mahe Fonua's second try that followed gave Hull an 18-10 lead, enough to ward off the late comeback. Sneyd had already done plenty of damage to Wigan before then. His cross-field kicking had the Warriors defenders at sixes and sevens all afternoon.

After watching his team concede an early try to John Bateman from a bouncing high Thomas Leuluai kick collected by Anthony Gelling, Sneyd's kicking game soon caused mayhem among Wigan's edge defence. Their first try came from a precise kick that put Liam Marshall under extreme pressure on his own line, with Fetuli Talanoa out-jumping him to level the scores.

Sneyd was forcing Wigan to drop out too and, moments after Joe Burgess tapped behind another excellent kick, the scrum-half repeated the high-kick trick to allow Fonua to touch down, following an expert flick-back by Albert Kelly.

At 12-6, Hull appeared to be assuming control of the game. But Wigan rallied well after that setback, applying more and more pressure on the Hull line. Eventually, they got their reward when George Williams danced close to the line and put Oliver Gildart through a gap to touch down.

But, crucially, Williams missed the conversion to leave Hull two ahead at the break.

Sneyd's devastating kicking game should have yielded a third try soon after the break but Josh Griffin spilled the ball in the act of scoring to let Wigan off the hook.

But after Sneyd's booming 40/20, which was reminiscent of the one that turned the game in Hull's favour the previous year, Hull wouldn't let Wigan off again.

This time it was Kelly who was chief architect, wriggling his arms free and hurling the ball wide for Fonua to claim his second try in incredible fashion, with a wonderful winger's finish in the corner.

The Warriors fought back. It took them until the 73rd minute to score but they felt they should have had some reward earlier for a Tony Clubb try that was chalked off.

Clubb, some felt, had the ball stripped by Hull defender Carlos Tuimavave before eventually touching down but it was judged by the video referee as a knock-on.

But Joe Burgess set up a thrilling finale by rampaging over from a great cut-out pass from Liam Farrell with seven minutes to go. Suddenly, Hull's lead was just four points and when slick hands to the left again sent Burgess streaking away it looked like George Williams would have a difficult conversion to win the Cup for Wigan for a twentieth time.

But as one end of Wembley went crazy, referee Phil Bentham kept his cool and rightly pulled the try back for a forward pass in the build-up.

The game ended with Talanoa racing away from an incomplete tackle in his own 40-metre area and sending Liam Watts towards the posts before Marshall and Bateman cut him down.

Cue mass celebrations from the army of black and white fans packed into Wembley.

LADBROKES CHALLENGE CUP FINAL

Saturday 26th August 2017

HULL FC 18 WIGAN WARRIORS 14

HULL FC: 1 Jamie Shaul; 2 Mahe Fonua; 4 Josh Griffin; 3 Carlos Tuimavave; 5 Fetuli Talanoa; 6 Albert Kelly; 7 Marc Sneyd; 8 Scott Taylor; 9 Danny Houghton; 10 Liam Watts; 21 Sika Manu; 12 Mark Minichiello; 13 Gareth Ellis (C). Subs (all used): 14 Jake Connor; 22 Josh Bowden; 15 Chris Green; 17 Danny Washbrook.
Tries: Talanoa (13), Fonua (20, 49); **Goals:** Sneyd 3/3.
WARRIORS: 1 Sam Tomkins; 35 Liam Marshall; 3 Anthony Gelling; 4 Oliver Gildart; 5 Joe Burgess; 6 George Williams; 7 Thomas Leuluai; 8 Frank-Paul Nuuausala; 9 Michael McIlorum; 15 Tony Clubb; 12 Liam Farrell; 14 John Bateman; 13 Sean O'Loughlin (C). Subs (all used): 20 Willie Isa; 16 Sam Powell; 19 Ryan Sutton; 17 Taulima Tautai.
Tries: Bateman (5), Gildart (33), Burgess (73);
Goals: Williams 1/3.
Rugby Leaguer & League Express Men of the Match:
Hull FC: Marc Sneyd; *Warriors:* Sean O'Loughlin.
Penalty count: 6-7; **Half-time:** 12-10; **Referee:** Phil Bentham;
Attendance: 68,525 *(at Wembley Stadium).*

SEPTEMBER
Top of the class Cas

Super League Super 8s - Round 4

Superstar fullback Ben Barba made his long-awaited debut for St Helens on the first Friday night of September. Barba scored a controversial try during Saints' 26-16 home defeat to Wigan - his first game of Rugby League for ten months after the end of his 12-game ban by the NRL for cocaine use.

It was a fine way for Wigan to rebound from their Wembley defeat the week before, keeping them within one point of the top four and seemingly set to finish the season with a bang.

With captain Sean O'Loughlin in imperious form, two tries from Oliver Gildart within the opening five minutes - the second from a sloppy Barba pass - and three goals from George Williams fired Wigan into an early lead before Barba pulled one back for Saints, although he looked to have lost control of the ball before grounding. Despite that, Wigan were 14-4 to the good at half-time.

Tries from Anthony Gelling and Williams extended Wigan's lead in the second half before Zeb Taia and Tommy Makinson scores brought Saints back into it. A penalty goal from Williams late on sealed the 26-16 victory.

The loss left St Helens three points outside the top four with three games still to play, with a make-or-break visit to fourth-placed Wakefield Trinity the following Thursday night to come.

After a 38-26 Thursday-night defeat at Leeds, Cup-winners Hull FC, widely expected to make the top four with ease alongside the Rhinos and Castleford, were now just two points clear of the fifth-placed Warriors, who they were due to face the week after in a huge Challenge Cup final rematch.

The win guaranteed the Rhinos' play-off place, on a surreal night in front of the deserted, due-to-be demolished Headingley South Stand.

It was a scrappy game and Kallum Watkins' penalty ten minutes from time to re-establish a two-score lead finally extinguished the gallant Hull fight.
Leeds scored four tries in the first half, with the standout player Rob Burrow - who was only in the line-up after Joel Moon pulled out in the warm-up with a groin injury.

Burrow was penalised for a head-butt on Jake Connor as he tackled him and was banned for one game the following Tuesday. Hull skipper Gareth Ellis got the same punishment after being sin-binned for a crusher tackle on Stevie Ward.

Having confirmed their position at the top of the table for the first time in their 91-year existence, it would have been easy for Castleford to take their foot off the gas. But, despite a first-half scare, Castleford's class told in the end as the Tigers crucially kept their momentum with a 24-16 win at Huddersfield.

Jake Webster put the visitors ahead but Huddersfield turned it around to lead 12-6 at half-time thanks to tries from Oliver Roberts and Paul Clough. The Tigers scored two early second-half tries through Ben Roberts and Greg Eden. Darnell McIntosh scored a consolation for the Giants but they were now five points adrift of the top four and out of the play-off reckoning.

Wakefield were back in the mix after a 43-18 win at fading Salford, the Red Devils suffering an eighth Super League defeat in a row, leaving Trinity within one point of Hull FC in third place.

Trinity gave a debut to Tyler Randell, signed for the next two years from Newcastle Knights, and the Australian hooker repaid the club by scoring two outstanding show-and-go tries.

Back-to-back tries to start the second half through Randell and Bill Tupou establish a massive 36-12 lead that the Red Devils never looked like clawing back.

Super 8s, The Qualifiers - Round 4

Widnes's Super League survival took a significant step with a 24-8 Sunday afternoon win at Leigh.

The Centurions' cause wasn't helped by the injury withdrawal of recent Aussie recruit Daniel Mortimer after just four minutes. Mortimer came off just as Widnes were opening the scoring through Lloyd White, one of two tries which helped establish a commanding 14-0 lead at the break.

The Vikings lost Rhys Hanbury to a groin injury just before the break and when Danny Walker went off with a knee problem, the reshuffle allowed Leigh the opportunity to score via James Clare - making his debut after a serious knee injury suffered just after signing from Bradford at the start of the year.

But Cory Paterson spilled on the first set after the restart before Joe Mellor linked up superbly with stand-in fullback Corey Thompson, as he scythed through the Leigh line to devastating effect, with Chris Bridge converting to open up a 16-point lead.

Matty Dawson scored with 14 minutes left to raise faint hopes but two more Bridge penalties secured a crucial win for the Vikings.

Catalans steadied their Qualifiers campaign with a professional 24-0 win at Halifax. But at a cost. Greg Bird was sin-binned on 25 minutes for an horrendous-looking spear tackle on Ben Heaton. The following Tuesday Bird was banned for four games by the RFL Disciplinary but had the sentence reduced on appeal to three, meaning if needed he would be available for the Million Pound Game.

Hull KR's march straight back into Super League took another giant stride when they recorded a 30-18 win at Featherstone.

Featherstone shocked the Robins with an excellent early converted try from left winger Kyran Johnson and were on the way to scoring again with the same move. But a loose pass saw Hull KR winger Ryan Shaw pick up the ball and race away to level the scores. By half-time it was 18-6 after Danny Addy and Jamie Ellis tries but Frankie Mariano scored a try and would have levelled with another but for a superb Adam Quinlan tackle.

But Featherstone lost their discipline and five minutes later the game was sealed when Thomas Minns raced over off Chris Atkin's neat pass before star man Andrew Heffernan wrapped up Hull KR's scoring.

Warrington were already within touching distance of safety after their thrilling 40-38 win at London Broncos.

Either side of half-time, particularly in the third quarter, the Wolves totally dominated, befitting last season's League Leaders and beaten Grand Finalists, scoring seven tries between the 29th and 65th minutes. But they were overrun by the Broncos at the beginning and end of the match. London, who had scored the first three tries of the evening, followed with the last three to leave Warrington hanging on as their lead dwindled from 20 points to two in the final eight minutes.

Broncos stand-off Jarrod Sammut was at his box-of-tricks best, scoring three tries and kicking five goals for 22 points in total.

Super League Super 8s - Round 5

Suddenly, reigning Champions Wigan were in a top-four play-off spot after a season in which at times it looked like they would not even make the Super 8s.

The Warriors ended the weekend in third spot after leapfrogging both Wakefield and Hull FC, who they beat on the Friday night at KCOM Stadium 30-22, thanks to two late tries from Anthony Gelling and John Bateman.

It was a controversial win. Hull prop Liam Watts was sent off on 22 minutes, with the prop forward adjudged to have led with the elbow in a tackle by Warriors hooker Michael McIlorum. It was Watts' third red card of the season. On this occasion Watts looked to have been victim of a harsh decision, though McIlorum left the field concussed.

The following Monday Watts was found to have no charge to answer but that was no consolation to Hull, whose play-off place was now looking less than certain.

Hull almost snatched an unlikely win with three quick-fire tries in the second half, all assisted by the brilliant Albert Kelly. However, the Warriors, led by their tireless leader Sean O'Loughlin, having given up a 14-point advantage to fall two points behind, regained control of the game at the vital time with those two late tries.

It meant Hull had to beat Wakefield at home the following week to keep their place in the top four.

St Helens were poised to take the place of any team that faltered. In the Thursday-night TV game they had to win at Wakefield to stay in with a chance and they did that in dramatic circumstances, Jonny Lomax scoring the winning try with two minutes remaining.

The arrival of Ben Barba and the absence of Ryan Morgan meant fullback Lomax played centre for a game Saints won 18-16 thanks to his dramatic late try.

For 76 minutes Trinity looked in control despite the sin-binning of Dean Hadley early in the second half. The game then turned when Liam Finn hit an upright with a penalty goal attempt that would have made it 16-10 to the home side. For some reason Wakefield didn't chase the kick and after Saints regained possession they upped the tempo of the game.

After a series of ambitious offloads, they worked the ball left where centre Mark Percival kicked hopefully down the line. Scott Grix, who had played a huge part in Wakefield's stellar season, took his time picking it up and Lomax was on the loose ball like a flash. Percival's conversion kept Saints' season alive.

St Helens owed much to prop Alex Walmsley for his go-forward. He set up a try in the 63rd minute for Theo Fages and then, almost immediately, rushed off to hospital before the end of the game to be with his wife who was in labour.

After eight straight losses, Salford ended any semi-final hopes that Huddersfield may have harboured and kept their own slim hopes alive in emphatic fashion, defeating the Giants at home 52-14.

Robert Lui was the star performer, creating havoc with his passing, kicking and running game. After only two minutes of the second half, Manu Vatuvei's try ended any chance of a Giants comeback.

In the first versus second clash Castleford notched an eighth successive win over the Rhinos, and inflicted a fourth defeat on them, this time by 38-24, in as many meetings between the sides this year.

The Tigers, who were 30-6 ahead at the interval and had been in white-hot form for much of the first half, lost their way a little in the second half.

Hull's defeat to Wigan on the same night meant the Rhinos were guaranteed to finish second and enjoy a home semi-final.

September
Super 8s, The Qualifiers - Round 5

Hull Kingston Rovers secured a return to Super League at the first attempt, following a nail-biting 12-6 victory against top-flight Widnes on the Saturday.

The appointment of former Australia coach Tim Sheens as head coach had paid off big style, with crowds at KCOM Craven Park up on the previous year in Super League.

The Vikings came up short, failing to register any points after Hep Cahill's 22-minute try which had put them 6-2 in front and their remaining fixtures against London Broncos and Catalans were now must-win to secure a top-three finish.

When former St Helens prop Mose Masoe, signed near the end of the season, produced a wonderful offload right on the stroke of half-time to send Thomas Minns over for a try converted by Jamie Ellis, it shifted the balance of power back in the hosts' favour.

The gamebreaker came with ten minutes left and with the Vikings pressing. Widnes had numbers out wide after a superb break by Chris Houston. All Matt Whitley had to do was find a teammate to enable the Vikings to level it up. Instead, he found Ryan Shaw, who raced the length of the field to send the 8,000-strong contingent of Rovers fans into meltdown.

Warrington Wolves' Super League future was secured on the same afternoon as they came from behind on three separate occasions to edge past unlucky Leigh Centurions, 32-30. Harvey Livett's penalty with just over ten minutes left proved to be the difference between the two sides.

Peta Hiku caused Leigh endless problems at the end of a week it was announced he would be leaving to join New Zealand Warriors at the end of the season.

The following day the Wolves confirmed that Tony Smith was to leave the club at the end of the season too. Since joining as head coach in March 2009, Smith had won two League Leaders' Shield titles, three Challenge Cups and taken the Wolves to the Grand Final on three occasions.

Later on Saturday Catalans kept their top-three chances alive with an unconvincing 26-12 home win over Featherstone.

Luke Walsh had a hand in almost everything good the Catalans did in attack as Sam Moa's try 13 minutes from time gave the Dragons a match-clinching 14-point advantage.

London Broncos won for the first time in the Qualifiers, beating Halifax 36-14 at home, and kept up their hopes of promotion via the Million Pound Game. They scored their points in two bursts of three tries in each half, with Elliot Kear's pace doing much of the damage. Winger Rhys Williams' try just after the sin-binning of Rob Worrincy and Jarrod Sammut for fighting left Halifax with a mountain they looked unlikely to climb.

Super League Super 8s - Round 6

With Castleford and Leeds' top two positions secured, four clubs remained in the contest for the other two play-off spots after the penultimate Super 8s round.

Hull FC jumped back into third on the Thursday night, with a thrilling 19-18 home win over Wakefield, who slipped from fifth to sixth, but still had a chance of making fourth if last-round results went their way.

Trinity looked likely to win for long periods but, for the second successive week, they suffered another defeat in the dying minutes. In a game that had absolutely everything in terms of excitement and drama, a video-referee referral to rule that Liam Finn's last-second field-goal attempt had shaved the wrong side of the left upright denied Wakefield a draw that could have salvaged their semi-final ambitions.

It was a special night for the Airlie Birds, with Gareth Ellis, Mahe Fonua and Steve Michaels all playing their final game in a Hull shirt on home soil. They certainly didn't disappoint the fans, with both Fonua and Ellis grabbing crucial tries on their KCOM Stadium farewell.

Wakefield bossed the first half, Joe Arundel and Jacob Miller scoring tries before Fonua scored his and David Fifita burst over the line, only to be bundled touch in-goal by five Hull defenders.

Jamie Shaul was sin-binned just before the break for a professional foul on Miller after a long-range break and Liam Finn kicked a penalty goal.

After half-time, Wakefield opened the second half with plenty of energy and innovation but couldn't score from a tremendous Joe Arundel break.

Trinity's missed chance came back to bite them minutes later when Marc Sneyd stepped his way through to score a terrific solo try, despite the best efforts of Mason Caton-Brown, who almost held the scrum-half up. The Hull halfback converted his own try to bring the scores level.

The pressure on Trinity was beginning to tell and Hull went in front through a barnstorming try by Ellis. Sneyd tagged on a field goal to seemingly put the game to bed.

However, Trinity set up a grandstand finish with a converted Caton-Brown try with minutes remaining, but the highest drama was yet to come.

With 18 seconds left on the clock, Wakefield set up for the game-levelling field goal, but Finn shaved the outside of the upright and Hull celebrated a remarkable win.

St Helens moved into fourth with a 40-16 home thrashing of Huddersfield on the Friday night, with Ben Barba playing a starring role. Jonny Lomax played at centre the week before against Wakefield but moved back into the halves, playing alongside youngster Danny Richardson, keeping Matty Smith out of the side. Mark Percival's try just before the break put Saints 24-6 ahead at a time when the game already looked done and dusted.

Wigan's play-off march, which had gained momentum over recent weeks, stuttered when they suffered a 38-20 defeat to a weakened Castleford side at DW Stadium on the Sunday.

Tigers starman Luke Gale, who had already secured the Albert Goldthorpe Medal for the third time, had been forced to undergo an appendix operation that week. Coach Daryl Powell gave 18-year-old Jake Trueman, signed from Bradford in January, his first start.

It was the stuff dreams are made of. Trueman scored a first-half hat-trick as the Tigers racked up a 20-0 lead at half-time. He also set up Greg Eden's 38th Super League try of the season before scoring his three - the third a sensational solo effort.

The Warriors got themselves back into the game in the second half, but they couldn't resist a late Castleford surge. Michael Shenton's try with ten minutes remaining killed off Wigan's comeback.

Leeds had an ideal preparation on the Friday night going into the semi-finals, not conceding a try in their 44-2 rout of Salford. The return of Joel Moon and the jet-heeled Rob Burrow, who played the full 80 minutes, gave the Rhinos greater fluency and variation in attack and their defensive resolve never faltered.

Salford, along with Huddersfield, were now out of the equation.

September
Super 8s, The Qualifiers - Round 6

Catalans secured a place in the Million Pound Game at worst as they came back from the dead on the Friday night to win 20-19 at promoted Hull KR.

An early Richie Myler try and two goals from the boot of his influential halfback partner Luke Walsh had given Catalans an eight-point half-time lead. But despite their much-changed side training just once in the lead-up to the game, Rovers roared back with three tries in the space of ten second-half minutes to stun the Dragons. A Chris Atkin field goal increased Rovers' lead to 19-8 with 14 minutes to play.

However, former Robin Iain Thornley crossed with nine minutes to play to give the Catalans a lifeline and, after Walsh landed the tricky conversion to set up a grandstand finish, Brayden Wiliame went over for a try, again improved from wide out by Walsh.

There was still time for Atkin to miss a long-range penalty and slice a hurried field-goal attempt wide.

That week, Thomas Bosc had announced he was to retire at the end of the season. The 34-year-old was the last remaining member of the Dragons' inaugural Super League squad.

Leigh's participation in the Million Pound Game was assured on the same night with a 40-6 home win over Halifax.

After successive losses to Widnes and Warrington, they turned on the style against a workmanlike Halifax, with Mitch Brown scoring a hat-trick and James Clare notching two tries.

Warrington recorded a 68-0 hammering of Championship Featherstone at Post Office Road, known in 2017 as the LD Nutrition Stadium. The Wolves were totally dominant from start to finish as they made it six Qualifiers wins from six, Peta Hiku scoring a try hat-trick. Harvey Livett scored two tries amongst 28 points, while Jack Hughes and Jack Johnson also picked up a brace apiece.

The Wolves played brilliantly but Tony Smith, rather than praise his side, was far more concerned to discuss the flaws in the Qualifiers system and called for a return to licensing.

Widnes warmed up for the Super League survival shoot-out at Catalans the following Saturday with a comfortable, if at times chaotic 38-16 home win over London. The two points saw Widnes go third in the Qualifiers table and there was now 101 points difference between them and fourth-placed Catalans Dragons.

Defeat ended the Broncos' hopes of making the Million Pound Game in disappointing fashion, after an encouraging opening quickly turned to a fractured and frustrating display.

The Vikings were worthy winners, recovering from an early 6-0 deficit with halfback Joe Mellor and fullback Danny Craven both scoring twice. The only real negative was a hamstring injury sustained by Lloyd White when taking a second-half conversion, which would rule him out of the World Cup with Wales.

Super League Super 8s - Round 7

The battle for the top-four play-offs in the first two seasons of the Super 8s had been less than exciting. But the third instalment in 2017 made up for that, with four clubs able to secure the last two places in the top four going into the 30th round.

One of those, St Helens, made sure of their place on the Thursday night with an eventually resounding 30-4 win at Salford.

Two first-half incidents were the major talking points. Man of the match Alex Walmsley scored his first try to put Saints into a 10-4 lead on the half-hour mark. But just minutes later he was involved in a tackle with Salford forward Jordan Walne, when, carrying the ball, his elbow clashed with Walne's head. Referee James Child put the collision on report and Walne left the field for a head test. He didn't return to the action.

Tempers flared following the incident. Almost immediately, in the 36th minute, Salford youngster Ryan Lannon was sent off for a late and high challenge on Theo Fages after he had kicked the ball. The following week Lannon received a three-match suspension, while Walmsley was not charged.

With the Red Devils down to 12 men, Zeb Taia's try in the 64th minute put Saints into a comfortable 18-4 lead and the game was out of reach for Salford.

A week later Salford Red Devils owner Marwan Koukash announced he was to hand over control of the Super League club to a community trust.

Hull FC had the chance to secure third spot on the Friday night at League Leaders Castleford and they took it with both hands, coming away with a 48-16 victory.

The result was rarely in doubt, despite a spirited second-half comeback from the under-strength Tigers, for whom London product Tuoyo Egodo, playing on the wing, scored a hat-trick on debut.

Albert Kelly scored the opening try and created a hat-trick for Jake Connor, who excelled at right centre. Hull also had an excellent performance from fullback Jamie Shaul, who scored two outstanding individual tries. But arguably their best performer was up front in Liam Watts, who continued his fine recent form since his controversial red card against Wigan.

Hull's reward was a semi-final trip to Leeds the following Friday night.

The Saturday-afternoon TV game which could have been a straight shootout for fourth place was not quite a dead rubber. Wigan had to win by at least 91 points at Wakefield to overtake St Helens in fourth. But a 32-0 defeat meant Trinity overtook them into fifth place, securing their joint-highest finish since 1981.

Wakefield played with great flair and capitalised on an error-ridden Warriors' display. Wigan were reduced to twelve men in the first half when Joel Tomkins was sin-binned for a dangerous tackle, while Wakefield scored two converted tries in the first half and added three more after the interval, with their chief architect Liam Finn adding six goals.

In a match with no bearing on league positions, Danny McGuire ran the show and scored two classy tries in a 36-12 Leeds win at Huddersfield.

Super 8s, The Qualifiers - Round 7

Widnes secured their place in the 2018 Super League with their first ever win in Perpignan, producing a major defensive effort to secure a tight 12-10 victory over relegation-threatened Catalans.

The result condemned the Catalans to the Million Pound Game the following Saturday and they would have to travel to Leigh to secure their status.

It was 4-4 at the break after two penalties each, before two second-half tries from Widnes winger Corey Thompson and centre Stefan Marsh. Julian Bousquet's 71st-minute converted try narrowed the gap to two points.

The Catalans had the opportunity to take the lead with five minutes remaining when Luke Walsh and Richie Myler combined to send Lewis Tierney away down the left. With the tryline in sight Tierney pinned his ears back and went for glory, only for Marsh to appear from nowhere to haul the on-loan fullback to the ground, forcing him to lose possession.

With time running down, the home side had two more opportunities in the final minutes to level the game with two late penalties. A draw would have seen them host Leigh, but those goal opportunities were turned down.

At the fourteenth attempt, Featherstone won a Qualifiers game, emerging 26-20 victors at Halifax, who were trying to achieve the same feat. Misi Taulapapa's try in the 65th minute looked to have killed the game off but tries to Rob Worrincy and Ben Heaton set up a nervy finale. In the end only goal kicks, Ian Hardman kicking five from five, separated the two sides. Ben Heaton and Richard Moore were red-carded after a last-minute fracas. Both got sending off sufficient.

Ben Reynolds controlled the Friday night game at London Broncos as Leigh warmed up for the Million Pound Game with a 41-4 win, nineteen points in the last ten minutes ending the Broncos season on a disappointing note.

On the Saturday afternoon, Warrington Wolves ended Tony Smith's nine-year tenure at the club on a high with a 46-24 victory over Hull Kingston Rovers to make it seven wins out of seven in the Super 8s Qualifiers. It looked an unlikely outcome when Ryan Shaw's 27th minute try put Rovers into an 18-4 lead. But Andre Savelio scored two tries in his last game

BETFRED SUPER LEAGUE - SUPER 8s
Final table - Sunday 24th September

	P	W	D	L	F	A	D	Pts
Castleford Tigers	30	25	0	5	965	536	429	50
Leeds Rhinos	30	20	0	10	749	623	126	40
Hull FC	30	17	1	12	714	655	59	35
St Helens	30	16	1	13	663	518	145	33
Wakefield Trinity	30	16	0	14	745	648	97	32
Wigan Warriors	30	14	3	13	691	668	23	31
Salford Red Devils	30	14	0	16	680	728	-48	28
Huddersfield Giants	30	11	3	16	663	680	-17	25

SUPER 8s - THE QUALIFIERS
Final table - Sunday 24th September

	P	W	D	L	F	A	D	Pts
Warrington Wolves	7	7	0	0	288	138	150	14
Widnes Vikings	7	5	0	2	188	96	92	10
Hull Kingston Rovers	7	5	0	2	166	158	8	10
Leigh Centurions	7	4	0	3	203	104	99	8
Catalans Dragons	7	4	0	3	130	143	-13	8
London Broncos	7	1	1	5	174	220	-46	3
Featherstone Rovers	7	1	1	5	110	272	-162	3
Halifax	7	0	0	7	82	210	-128	0

before heading to Brisbane Broncos and Peta Hiku's try with eleven minutes left took Warrington's lead to 12 points. From that point onwards, there looked to be no way back for Rovers.

Super League Semi-finals

The first Super 8s semi-final provided one of the great sporting spectacles of 2017 as Castleford booked their ticket at Old Trafford in the eighth minute of golden-point time.

Luke Gale's 40-metre field goal gave the Tigers a 23-22 victory over St Helens, who, with a minute and a half left of normal time themselves looked destined for the Grand Final, Ryan Morgan scoring Saints' fifth try from a brilliant James Roby break and long, wide precision pass.

But the Tigers won back the short kick-off and at the end of the last set of the game, Michael Shenton was obstructed by Morgan when he was chasing a grubber to the Saints line. Just 16 days after having appendix

surgery, Gale held his nerve to kick a penalty goal from wide out after the hooter to take the game to golden-point territory for the first time in Super League play-offs.

Saints fought all the way, with some outstanding performances of their own, particularly from Ben Barba, scoring five tries to Castleford's three, Barba having a key role in several of them. But Mark Percival could only convert one of those five tries, while Luke Gale kicked three conversions and two penalties, and then applied the coup de grace with the superbly taken field goal to win the match.

Zak Hardaker crossed for Castleford's opening try after 48 seconds but scores from Regan Grace, with a spectacular somersault dive in the left corner, and Morgan Knowles gave Saints a 10-8 half-time lead.

After weathering a spell of St Helens pressure, Castleford went ten points up with

Luke Gale scores during Castleford's heartstopping semi-final win against St Helens

tries from Gale, as he backed up after sending Greg Eden down the left wing, and Adam Milner, before the thrilling climax.

Tommy Makinson and Percival tries brought the visitors back within two points and Morgan's try brought tears from many Tigers fans. But after Gale's double whammy, dismay turned to euphoria with the realisation their side had reached the Grand Final for the first time.

There was plenty of excitement the next night at Headingley too as Leeds bounced back from their disappointing 2016 season by beating Hull FC 18-16 in another excellent semi-final. Rhinos coach Brian McDermott was unable to speak in front of the TV cameras post-match, such was the emotion.

In the opening 20 minutes, when Leeds built a 12-point lead, Hull KR-bound captain Danny McGuire, making his 450th career appearance, was imperious, shuffling and dealing with masterful effect.

But after Hull had clawed back the deficit, Liam Sutcliffe ensured the return to Manchester for the tenth time with a majestic try just after the hour. Kallum Watkins landed the goal from wide out, maintaining a perfect record with the boot, after the usually accurate Marc Sneyd had missed following Mahe Fonua's try 18 minutes before - a key moment in the contest.

Stevie Ward and Anthony Mullally gave Leeds a deserved 12-0 lead after 17 minutes. Ward showed astonishing presence of mind to keep his arm off the grass to secure a grounding which was confirmed by video referee Robert Hicks, who rightly overturned the on-field decision.

Then when Liam Watts surrendered possession on halfway, Watkins and Moon made haste and McGuire's last-tackle skip and spin set up Mullally to make the line and claim a score with his first touch.

But Josh Bowden made an instant impact from the bench, setting the position for Houghton to send Ellis barrelling through Jack Walker on the 27-minute mark, with Sneyd's conversion cutting Leeds' lead to 12-6. McGuire missed with a long-range field-goal attempt on the half-time hooter.

The Black and Whites, through Houghton and Sika Manu, made the early running in the second half. Ellis put in a typical charge and Sneyd's crosskick came off Ryan Hall's fingers. From the scrum, Ellis, Sneyd, Chris Green, Albert Kelly and Jake Connor, with a beautiful one-handed flick pass, put Fonua over out wide, but Sneyd was wayward with the goal attempt.

Hull twice reverted to kicking early but when Sneyd put the ball high on a last-tackle play and Jamie Shaul gathered, it all nearly went wrong when his pass was intercepted by Mitch Garbutt, who found Walker in support.

Ellis did magnificently to shepherd the young fullback's run. But then, after 56 minutes, Josh Griffin defused a McGuire kick, Connor and Mark Minichiello raided and, on the last, Sneyd's crosskick was sensationally tipped on by Connor for Manu to cross. Sneyd goaled and Hull had the lead for the first time.

But Walker and Burrow instigated the key move and Brad Singleton, with a pass, and Ryan Hall, linking from temporary fullback, released Sutcliffe, who turned inside Albert Kelly and held off Shaul in a superb run to glory. Watkins' goal set up a showdown with Castleford Tigers.

Hull captain Gareth Ellis's career came to an end as he moved into the role as the club's football manager but there was one last hurrah to come for McGuire and Rob Burrow, who was due to retire at the end of the season.

The only negative for Leeds was the sight of Ward leaving the field clutching a dislocated shoulder.

Million Pound Game

Around a thousand fans turned up at Perpignan airport on the Saturday night of the Million Pound Game to welcome home Catalans Dragons after a dramatic 26-10 victory at Leigh that afternoon secured the French club's Super League survival. The Centurions were relegated after one season.

The final scoreline suggested a polished, convincing Dragons performance. It was anything but that for the opening 40 minutes. In attack they were blunt, with Iain Thornley's try five minutes before half-time the only thing they had to show for a frustrating half.

A penalty count of 9-3 against Leigh in the second half was the catalyst for the Catalans scoring 22-unanswered points in the final 30 minutes.

Leigh were ahead after seven minutes when, following a scrum close to the Catalans' line, some superb handling sent Matty Dawson over in the corner to make it 6-0. But despite more opportunities to extend the lead, a combination of frustration in attack from Leigh and great defending from Catalans kept the lead to just six points.

Greg Bird, returning from suspension, was everywhere in defence, denying Leigh half-breaks on two separate occasions. And when Catalans hit back through Thornley's try on 35 minutes, it left the scoreline at a very nervy 6-4 in Leigh's favour at the break.

Leigh began the second 40 minutes well and quickly scored more points when, after a repeat set, a magnificent pass from Josh Drinkwater missed out two Leigh attackers and put James Clare in unmarked in the corner.

Six points ahead, Leigh appeared in complete control. With Catalans' confidence in question following a difficult season, the Centurions were becoming increasing favourites to survive.

But the Dragons' response was magnificent. Their first try of the half came when a brilliant team move saw Richie Myler - in his final game for Catalans before moving to Leeds - put Lewis Tierney away for a try, though Luke Walsh again missed the conversion to keep Catalans behind.

However, Walsh did not make the same mistake from a penalty four minutes after, a trick he would repeat three minutes later too to put the Dragons ahead for the first time.

After another penalty helped the Catalans into prime attacking position again, the Dragons made Leigh pay when Tierney claimed his second. This time, Walsh made no mistake with the conversion to open up an eight-point lead.

Another penalty allowed Walsh to turn the lead from eight to 10, before a Walsh offload sent Fouad Yaha charging to the line to seal the Dragons' Super League safety.

OCTOBER
Record-breaking Rhinos

Super League Grand Final

Leeds Rhinos were worthy Champions once again after a 24-6 win over League Leaders Castleford on a cold, wet night in Manchester.

Rhinos captain Danny McGuire, due to extend his career at Hull KR the next year, won his second Harry Sunderland Trophy, controlling the game expertly and scoring two tries and two field goals. The Leeds skipper's defensive input was also huge, keeping a tight hold of Tigers centre Michael Shenton and in the 30th minute making the tackle that stymied Castleford's inevitable comeback, desperately diving at Greg Eden as he went in for a try and knocking the ball from his grasp.

Fullback Jack Walker became the youngest player, at 18 years and 60 days, to play in a Grand Final-winning team and he looked as though he had played in all of Leeds' eight Grand Final wins, such was his composure.

The player he replaced for that youngest player record, Stevie Ward, had his own cameo, recovering Lazarus-like from a shoulder dislocated in the semi-final win over Hull to take his part and he played strongly for the whole eighty minutes.

Tigers coach Daryl Powell remarked post-game that his side, which had dominated Super League all season, had reserved the worst for last. Cas certainly didn't do themselves justice, despite the huge mitigating factor of Zak Hardaker's absence. His suspension by the club, after news came through that he had failed a drugs test after the Super 8s win over Leeds, came only two days before the biggest date in the club's history.

It was a cold wet night and that didn't help the handling or the spectacle. The Tigers made eight handling errors in each half of the game, ranging from loose carries and sloppy play the balls to dropping passes cold.

After Walker kicked off the game there was little indication of what would unfold. The Tigers had the better of the opening minutes. At the end of the first set Ben Roberts kicked and Walker was dumped hard by Oliver Holmes. McGuire put his first kick dead under pressure from Luke Gale and, after Castleford turned down the chance for an easy two points when Brad Singleton was penalised for lying in the ruck, McGuire was first to drop on Gale's grubber to the line.

When Tom Briscoe took Gale's first bomb assuredly, fewer than six minutes had elapsed but it turned out to have great significance, as the Rhinos back three of Briscoe, Ryan Hall and Walker went on to be faultless under those kicks and Ben Roberts' short kicking game near the line proved to be ineffective apart from one instance.

Stand-in fullback Eden coped well in the first half and took McGuire's first bomb with ease but then Adam Milner dropped a pass cold on halfway. It wasn't too damaging as Ward couldn't hold McGuire's short ball and Shenton sent Eden away on a 50-metre break although he lost control of the ball in Liam Sutcliffe's covering tackle.

It was a free play and Cas were soon back on the attack, moving forward with real pace. With the Leeds defence going backwards, Paul McShane tried to scoop up the ball one handed at dummy half and his knock on was a key moment.

Instead of the Tigers taking a lead they had probably earned, the Rhinos struck first.

There was a hint of good fortune in gaining the field position. McGuire's wayward bomb went straight across the pitch. Hall tried to volley the ball down field but sliced it straight into the arms of Sutcliffe, who was stood next to him.

BETFRED SUPER LEAGUE - GRAND FINAL

Saturday 7th October 2017

CASTLEFORD TIGERS 6 LEEDS RHINOS 24

TIGERS: 5 Greg Eden; 2 Greg Minikin; 3 Jake Webster; 4 Michael Shenton (C); 25 Jy Hitchcox; 16 Ben Roberts; 7 Luke Gale; 14 Nathan Massey; 9 Paul McShane; 15 Jesse Sene-Lefao; 11 Oliver Holmes; 12 Mike McMeeken; 13 Adam Milner. Subs (all used): 10 Grant Millington; 17 Junior Moors; 18 Matt Cook; 34 Alex Foster. **Try:** Foster (79); **Goals:** Gale 1/1.
RHINOS: 31 Jack Walker; 2 Tom Briscoe; 3 Kallum Watkins; 14 Liam Sutcliffe; 5 Ryan Hall; 4 Joel Moon; 6 Danny McGuire (C); 16 Brad Singleton; 9 Matt Parcell; 17 Mitch Garbutt; 13 Stevie Ward; 11 Jamie Jones-Buchanan; 10 Adam Cuthbertson. Subs (all used): 20 Anthony Mullally; 12 Carl Ablett; 7 Rob Burrow; 19 Brett Ferres. **Tries:** Briscoe (11, 59), McGuire (51, 70); **Goals:** Watkins 3/4; **Field goals:** McGuire (40, 77).
Rugby Leaguer & League Express Men of the Match: *Tigers:* Matt Cook; *Rhinos:* Danny McGuire. **Penalty count:** 5-1; **Half-time:** 0-7; **Referee:** James Child; **Attendance:** 72,827 *(at Old Trafford, Manchester).*

Sutcliffe's hopeful grubber was collected and fumbled behind his own line by Greg Minikin and Jamie Jones-Buchanan and Singleton were on hand to force the GLDO.

Sutcliffe was almost through from Walker's quick pass and, at the end of the set, McGuire's kick to right corner was superbly taken by Briscoe in an aerial challenge from Jy Hitchcox and Shenton. The grounding was confirmed by the video referee and Kallum Watkins kicked a good conversion for a 6-0 lead. From then on there was an extra spring in Leeds' step.

Another mistake, this time Shenton losing the ball in Mitch Garbutt's tackle 30 metres out, the referee ruling loose carry, almost proved calamitous. McGuire this time grubbered right into in-goal and Watkins was through to dive on the ball in a flash. James Child thought it was a try but the slo-mo suggested an improper grounding and the video ref ruled it out.

It was just about all Leeds but when Watkins spilled the ball the momentum swung back to the Tigers.

Gale's next bomb was taken by Walker on his own line but the chasing Roberts was shepherded by Briscoe. Two easy points were spurned and it looked a good decision when the ball was worked left and Eden at last found a gap. It was a try until McGuire's flailing arm knocked the ball from Eden's grasp.

The tide was still with Castleford as Carl Ablett lost possession trying to play the ball. Roberts produced his effective grubber that Walker scooped dead and Millington had a tilt at the line but Junior Moors' short pass was harshly ruled forward.

It mattered not as Hall lost the ball straight from the scrum and, after Ablett was penalised for a ball strip on Jake Webster, the Tigers thought they had broken the dam, Hitchcox racing onto and grounding Gale's grubber. Mr Child asked for an obstruction to be checked and video evidence showed Gale had run behind Holmes just before launching his kick.

It was effectively Cas's last hurrah. Leeds finished the half strongly. Holmes lost the ball 25 metres out and McGuire's impromptu grubber was chased and grounded by Briscoe, the try ruled out by the video ref again, this time for a light push in the back by Briscoe on McShane.

There was just time for McGuire to pot a one-point drop goal after Parcell's 30-metre break from the base of the scrum and, although 7-0 wasn't that big a lead, Cas needed to up their game significantly after the break.

They did pep themselves up in the early minutes of the second half and McGuire's

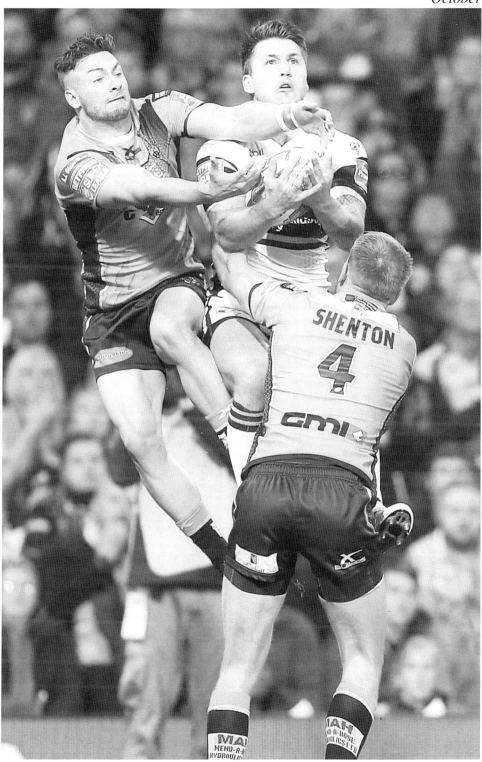

Tom Briscoe beats Michael Shenton and Jy Hitchcox to a high ball during Leeds' Super League Grand Final victory

kick straight into touch from dummy half might have been a sign of a change. But Moors dropped the ball on the second tackle as the game fell into its first-half pattern. A tame Roberts grubber and later a chip into the hands of Hall to the line were part of the same trend.

On 51 minutes the contest was just about done after Eden dropped Moon's bomb and McGuire picked up to dive over. The video referee couldn't find any problem and, though Watkins missed the kick, Leeds were under a wet sail.

Another Moon bomb taken on the full by Hall ended with McGuire's grubber trapping Webster in-goal. Walker made a fine run after picking up Brett Ferres's offload from the floor and Parcell was carried over the line by the Cas defence. But it was all too much as Moon ghosted through the right centre and sent Briscoe into the corner with a forward looking pass. Watkins kicked a beauty from the touchline

It was certainly done and dusted after Rob Burrow's grubber was fumbled by Mike McMeeken under the posts and McGuire tapped ahead to chase through for his second try.

Eden had a try ruled out at the other end with the video showing Hitchcox had stepped onto the touchline a millisecond before flinging the ball back in-field, before McGuire potted another field goal.

And Castleford were just over a minute away from becoming the first team to be nilled in 20 years of Grand Finals before they kept the ball alive in a frenzy and McShane hacked ahead for Alex Foster to score in the left corner. Gale's conversion was probably the most insignificant last act of a major showpiece. For this was Leeds Rhinos' day.

It capped off an era as they said goodbye to two more of the major players in their Millennial wonder years in McGuire and Burrow, who had called time on his playing career.

2
CHAMPIONSHIP
& LEAGUE 1 2017

CHAMPIONSHIP SEASON
Rovers return

After a decade away, **HULL KINGSTON ROVERS** were back in the Championship after the most pain-staking relegation in the Million Pound Game.

Their response, however, could not have been better.

After an off-season of heightened activity to keep spirits high, there was a strong sense of optimism going into the campaign.

The Championship itself was relatively straightforward. The only blemishes on their record were against Toulouse who did the double over the Robins, and Halifax on the final day.

The real business, in truth, started in the Qualifiers for Tim Sheens's side. However, there was a great sense of scepticism going in, after a number of underwhelming displays.

They did little to convince anyone thereafter, as they scraped past Halifax.

However, a season-defining victory over Leigh followed as Rovers won 20-16, and from there further wins over London, Featherstone and Widnes secured their place back in Super League.

Should the Super 8s structure remain, the Robins are the blueprint for any relegated side.

After shocking everyone in 2016, **LONDON BRONCOS'** challenge was to handle the expectations now firmly rested on their shoulders. They did so excellently.

Albeit, they were early fears the Broncos weren't going to live up to the hype.

The Broncos struggled for form, scraping to victories over Swinton and Oldham in the early rounds before subsequently losing four games in five matches.

However, a victory over Toulouse over Easter turned their season around as they went on an outstanding ten-match winning streak, with the highlight coming in a two-week period. First, they hammered Featherstone at the Summer Bash, and a week later they dissected Halifax, another of their top four rivals.

They comfortably finished second in the end, and they were being tipped to put on a serious promotion challenge.

Sadly, that never materialised, as they suffered a number of agonising defeats.

Despite outplaying Catalans, Andrew Henderson's side just lost in France 20-18, and then lost 40-38 to Warrington Wolves a few rounds later.

It killed their hopes of reaching the Million Pound Game, although they secured healthy central funding.

Times of change are approaching with Henderson moving to Warrington as their assistant coach, with former Leeds prop Danny Ward being announced as his successor.

Hull KR's Jordan Abdull races past Featherstone's Ian Hardman

One of the success stories of 2017 came at The Shay, where **HALIFAX** regained their place among the top four of the Championship.

They did so against all the odds. The playing budget was cut, which led to the departure of popular forward Dane Manning to Batley, while Toulouse's inclusion in the competition left them competing with yet another full-time team.

At first, it appeared a return to the Qualifiers wouldn't be realistic. Four defeats in their opening seven league games left them playing catch up. Seven straight league wins helped them do just that but three defeats in their next five games, to top four rivals Toulouse and London plus a shock defeat to Swinton, appeared to leave their hopes in tatters.

But Toulouse were struggling too, so when Halifax travelled to France at the start of July, they still had a realistic hope. However, with the French club, Featherstone and Hull Kingston Rovers in their final three games, it was a mammoth task.

Yet Marshall's men rallied and conquered all before them, winning in France, cruising to victory at Featherstone before defeating the Robins 28-6 on the final day to secure their top four spot.

They failed to win in the Qualifiers, but that only minimally took the gloss of a strong campaign.

Championship Season

It was a season of slight progress for **FEATHERSTONE ROVERS**, who bettered 2016's finish by placing seventh in the Super 8s Qualifiers.

But that only tells half the story.

A promising start to the year saw Fev always look likely to finish in the top four, however, that didn't earn Jon Sharp a new deal when his contract expired midway through the season, with owner Mark Campbell unimpressed with their brand of rugby.

John Duffy, the Swinton head coach, came in to take his place following the Lions' eye-catching offensive displays, and ultimately managed one victory from his first eight games, a final-day win over Halifax to secure seventh place and an estimated £50,000 of additional funding.

In the Challenge Cup, the Rovers progressed to the quarter-finals stage where they bowed out against Leeds, while they also earned a draw against Hull Kingston Rovers during the regular season.

A home defeat to Rochdale was a low point.

The unknown quantity of the 2017 season, nobody really knew what to expect from Sylvain Houles' **TOULOUSE OLYMPIQUE** side as they entered the second tier.

At first, it appeared they would adopt a stigma attached to French counterparts Catalans, as they won handsomely at home, but struggled on the road.

That changed, however, as back-to-back away wins against Halifax and Featherstone launched them into the top four and seemingly on their way to the Qualifiers.

For so long, it appeared that would be the case. They inflicted defeat on Hull Kingston Rovers for the first time over Easter before victory over Halifax at the Summer Bash further strengthened their grip on a place in the top four.

However, an injury to key halfback, the Cook Islands international Johnathon Ford, caught up with them.

An end of season collapse saw them lose four consecutive matches, which subsequently cost them their top four place.

Although they ended the regular season superbly, defeating the Robins again and then Featherstone through a last-gasp Kuni Minga try, it wasn't enough to secure a top-four berth.

Instead, they won the Championship Shield, defeating Sheffield in the final.

After their heroics of the year before, it was always going to be difficult for **BATLEY BULLDOGS** to maintain the lofty standards set in 2016.

That challenge was made undeniably harder with the departure of John Kear, who was replaced by rookie coach, the former Bradford and Leeds hooker Matt Diskin.

A transitional period looked inevitable, and that proved to be the case as the Bulldogs failed to find consistency in their new, expansive style of play.

When they were on form, the Bulldogs were irresistible. They devoured Sheffield 70-12 in June, scored 62 against Swinton at the start of August and hit the half-century on two other occasions.

But they struggled greatly against top-half teams, managing just one win from ten against the top five sides, and they were dispatched comfortably on the most part.

In the end, they lost in the Championship Shield semi-finals to Sheffield.

A frustrating year, but one that gives the Bulldogs faithful reason to believe they could be on the cusp of something bigger.

continued on page 113

PERSONALITIES OF 2017

Eric Perez

...ere is only one realistic contender for the category of ...ost exotic Rugby League story of 2017'.

On 13th October 2014, Rugby League Express ...orted in its news pages that the Rugby Football ...gue had received an application from Rugby League ...ada to enter a team based in Toronto into League ...om the 2016 season. Behind the plan was a bloke ...led Eric Perez.

Perez was confident that the globalisation of ...gby League competitions was the future, having ...t seen the game on TV while on a business trip ...irmingham. 'We are proposing to create the first ...nscontinental sports team - the first North American ...e in a European league. It will open up markets that ...re unthinkable recently,' Perez told League Express.

Most people thought he was nuts. The history of ... game has been littered with dreamers whose plans, ...e of them anywhere near as ambitious as this one,

came to nought. Perez even offered to fly opposition teams out to Toronto for home games on a Thursday, play on Saturday and then fly them back on Sunday, all expenses paid, as well as being confident the team would draw significant crowds.

Perez isn't nuts. The pipedream became a reality in 2017.

Former Bradford, Wigan and Great Britain coach Brian Noble became director of rugby and he and head coach, former Leigh coach, Paul Rowley assembled a high-quality squad good enough to win promotion at a canter. Crowds have averaged just under 7,000.

The transatlantic dream of Eric Perez won't end with the irresistible rise of Toronto Wolfpack. He firmly believes there will be up to six more North American teams in the next ten years. After the adventure that was Toronto Wolfpack in 2017, who could really doubt him?

Marc Sneyd
Hull F.C.

Players make their mark by winning one Lance Todd Trophy as man of the match in the Challenge Cup Final. When they do it twice, and in consecutive years, they have truly established their place in the history of the sport.

In Hull FC's first win at Wembley in 2016, Sneyd had won the game's most revered individual accolade by a close shave from captain Danny Houghton. But in 2017 he was an outright winner of the poll of Rugby League Writers present at the game. Hull's 18-14 win over Wigan not only confirmed that the Airlie Birds were back among the game's elite, but halfback Marc Sneyd was the player for the big occasion.

Sneyd became the second player to retain the Lance Todd Trophy since its 1946 inauguration but the first to do it outright. Paul Wellens shared the award with his St Helens teammate Leon Pryce in 2007 before winning it again the year after.

In this year's final, from start to finish, Sneyd's kicking game caused Wigan a heap of problems. After Hull conceded an early try, Sneyd's kicks created tries for wingers Fetuli Talanoa and Mahe Fonua. After half-time, another score went begging when Josh Griffin spilled another Sneyd kick, shortly before a perfect 40/20 led to a crucial try for Fonua. Sneyd's goalkicking was perfect and in the end it was his two kicks that separated the sides.

Sneyd has become the most oft-sung name coming from the stands. Not only do his own supporters drone his name every time he lands a goal, opposition fans have taken to mimic the chant whenever he misses. You might hear the name again in the very near future.

Danny McGuire
Leeds Rhinos

...dings are only ...ritten like this in ...ollywood. When ...anny McGuire ...d his long-time ...ppo' Rob Burrow ...oth held the Super ...ague Trophy aloft ... Old Trafford on ...aturday October ...h, it was a perfect ...ay for the pair to say farewell to the massed Leeds ...hinos supporters packed into the East Stand.

Burrow retired after the game, with McGuire ...ading for promoted Hull Kingston Rovers, where ... was due to link up with former teammate and now ...obins football manager Jamie Peacock.

The Rhinos' eighth Grand Final win was probably ...eir most remarkable in the light of their 2016 ...mpaign, when, as reigning Champions they failed ...en to make the top-eight split and were forced to ...ay out their year in the Qualifiers. The departure of ...e retired Kevin Sinfield and Peacock was the start ... a slow decline in some observers eyes. A 66-10 ...mbling at Castleford at the start of March this year ...trenched the view.

To most people's bewilderment coach Brian ...Dermott said at the time that he thought his team ...uld still win the Grand Final. Some of the few people ...ho believed him were his players, with McGuire at ...e forefront of the Rhinos' second-placed finish. As ...e season wore on he became more energised and ...ished it, and his 17-season Leeds career, off with ...wo-try, two-field-goal Harry Sunderland Trophy ...atch-winning performance at Old Trafford.

There's no way around it, it will just not be the ...me without Danny McGuire and Rob Burrow in the ...ue and Amber any more.

Shaun Lunt
Hull Kingston Rovers

When Hull Kingston Rovers were relegated, in the most cruel manner possible, at the end of the 2016 season, the first player to commit himself to the great old club was Shaun Lunt. 'As far as I'm concerned, I was part of the team that got the club relegated and I want to be part of the team that gets the club promoted back up to Super League again,' said Lunt at the time.

The hooker was good to his word and at the end of the Robins' wonder 2017 season, he had led his side back into Super League and was crowned Kingstone Press Championship Player of the Year.

No Million Pound Game this year for Rovers, whose fans have played a big part in the club's renaissance. Wins against two of their four Super League opponents were enough to secure a third-place finish in the Qualifiers. The first of those two wins, at Leigh, showed Lunt at his typical best, as he scored two trademark tries from dummy-half to edge Hull KR home.

Shaun Lunt's career has zig-zagged after being offloaded from the Academy at Castleford. He had to learn his trade with his local club Workington Town, where he perfected the art of winning his sides games from dummy half. He won the National League Two Young Player of the Year award two years in a row (2006 and 2007) with Workington before getting an opportunity at Super League Huddersfield.

Lunt started to make a name for himself under Nathan Brown at the Giants in 2009 but suffered more than his fair share of injuries. He went out on two loan spells while at the John Smith's Stadium, the first in 2012 when he spent the second half of the year at Leeds Rhinos, playing a big part off the bench in Leeds' Grand Final win against Warrington.

His second spell on loan also came up trumps when he joined Hull KR in 2015, eventually signing for them a permanent deal at the end of that season.

Whenever Lunt moves into dummy-half close to the line defences must panic. They know what he is going to do, but stopping him is another matter. Super League opponents beware.

Luke Gale
Castleford Tigers

e road to stardom is often long and winding and it
take a special kind of personality to make it to the

One such is the Steve Prescott Man of Steel of
7, Castleford halfback Luke Gale, who was the
hpin of the League Leaders, considered by many as
most complete side ever to grace Super League.

The Super 8s semi-final against St Helens
nmed up Gale and Castleford's year. With the game
t about lost, Gale's difficult tricky penalty goal sent
game into extra time. It was written in the stars
t Gale should go on to score the golden point, 16 days
from undergoing emergency appendix surgery.

Gale was released by Leeds in 2007 after being at
dingley all through his scholarship and Academy
rs and he signed for third-tier Doncaster. It was quite
eason for the Dons, coached by Ellery Hanley, as they
n promotion from National League Two, with Gale
king off with the competition's player of the year
ard.

It was enough for then Harlequins coach Brian
Dermott to give Gale a chance in the top flight and
layed 72 games for the London club before his
ase was negotiated by Bradford Bulls ahead of the
2 season. When the Bulls were relegated in 2014
e joined the Tigers. The link-up with 2017 coach of
year Daryl Powell proved to be Gale's biggest break
e collected the Albert Goldthorpe Medal in three
secutive years as the Tigers rose higher and higher.

2017 SEASON REVIEW

DACIA RUGBY LEAGUE **WORLD CLUB SERIES**

WIGAN WARRIORS ....
CRONULLA SHARKS ....

ABOVE: Wigan celebrate victory against Cronulla

BELOW LEFT: Oliver Gildart heads for the tryline

ABOVE: Warrington's Ben Westwood in action during a memorable World Club Series win against Brisbane

DACIA MAGIC WEEKEND

RIGHT: St Helens' Louie McCarthy-Scarsbrook celebrates scoring against Hull FC

LEFT: Warrington's Mike Cooper halted by Wigan's Ryan Sutton and Frank-Paul Nuuausala

RIGHT: Castleford's Greg Eden dives past Leeds' Ryan Hall for a try

ABOVE: Wakefield's Kyle Wood takes on Widnes' Alex Gerrard

RIGHT: Trinity fans enjoy the Magic Weekend occasion

RIGHT: Wakefield's Scott Grix races past Wigan's Oliver Gildart to score

BELOW RIGHT: Salford's Manu Vatuvei closes down St Helens' Ben Barba

SUPER LEAGUE AWARDS

STEVE PRESCOTT MBE MAN OF STEEL
Luke Gale (Castleford Tigers)

YOUNG PLAYER OF THE YEAR
Oliver Gildart (Wigan Warriors)

COACH OF THE YEAR
Daryl Powell (Castleford Tigers)

CLUB OF THE YEAR
Castleford Tigers

TOP TRY SCORER
Greg Eden (Castleford Tigers) (38)

TOP METRE MAKER
Alex Walmsley (St Helens) (4256)

TOP TACKLER
Danny Houghton (Hull FC) (1123)

(totals include regular season & Super 8s only)

SUPER LEAGUE DREAM TEAM
(previous selections in italics)

1. Zak Hardaker (Castleford Tigers) *2014, 2015*
2. Greg Eden (Castleford Tigers) *Debut*
3. Michael Shenton (Castleford Tigers) *2014, 2015*
4. Mark Percival (St Helens) *Debut*
5. Mahe Fonua (Hull FC) *2016*
6. Albert Kelly (Hull FC) *Debut*
7. Luke Gale (Castleford Tigers) *2015, 2016*
8. Grant Millington (Castleford Tigers) *Debut*
9. Matt Parcell (Leeds Rhinos) *Debut*
10. Sebastine Ikahihifo (Huddersfield Giants) *Debut*
11. Ben Murdoch-Masila (Salford Red Devils) *Debut*
12. Mike McMeeken (Castleford Tigers) *Debut*
13. Sean O'Loughlin (Wigan Warriors)
2010, 2011, 2012, 2013, 2014

ALBERT GOLDTHORPE MEDAL
Luke Gale (Castleford Tigers)

ALBERT GOLDTHORPE ROOKIE OF THE YEAR
Liam Marshall (Wigan Warriors)

BELOW: Luke Gale - 2017 Man of Steel; Oliver Gildart - 2017 Young Player of the

BELOW: The 2017 Super League Dream Team

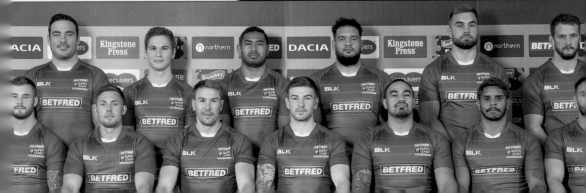

BELOW: The Castleford squad celebrate finishing top of the league for the first time in the club's history

BETFRED SUPER LEAGUE LEAGUE LEADERS 2017

RIGHT: Leeds' Ashton Golding drives forward against Huddersfield

BETFRED SUPER LEAGUE SUPER 8s

RIGHT: Castleford's hat-trick hero Jake Trueman mobbed after scoring against Wigan

LEFT: Luke Gale celebrates with Zak Hardaker after kicking Castleford's golden point semi-final winner against St Helens

BELOW: Gareth Ellis, in the last game of his career, bursts past Kallum Watkins as Leeds reach Old Trafford at the expense of Hull FC

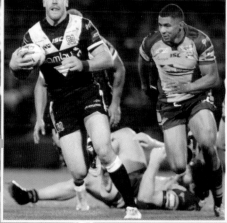

Ladbrokes CHALLENGE CUP

ABOVE: Sam Powell slumps in defeat as Gareth Ellis leads the celebrations on the final hooter

LEFT: Hull lift the Challenge Cup for the second successive year

ABOVE: Fireworks as Leeds lift the Super League trophy for the eighth time

RIGHT: Departing Rhinos legends Danny McGuire and Rob Burrow celebrate with coach Brian McDermott

BELOW: Harry Sunderland Trophy winner Danny McGuire lands the first of his field goals on the stroke of half-time

BETFRED SUPER LEAGUE
GRAND FINAL

MELBOURNE STORM........................34
NORTH QUEENSLAND COWBOYS.......6

BELOW: Cooper Cronk, Cameron Smith and Billy Slater celebrate with the Storm's fans

RIGHT: Billy Slater makes a break on the way to scoring

BELOW: Melbourne's Tohu Harris looks for a way through the Cowboys' defence

NRL
TELSTRA
PREMIERSHIP

GRAND FINAL
SYDNEY 2017

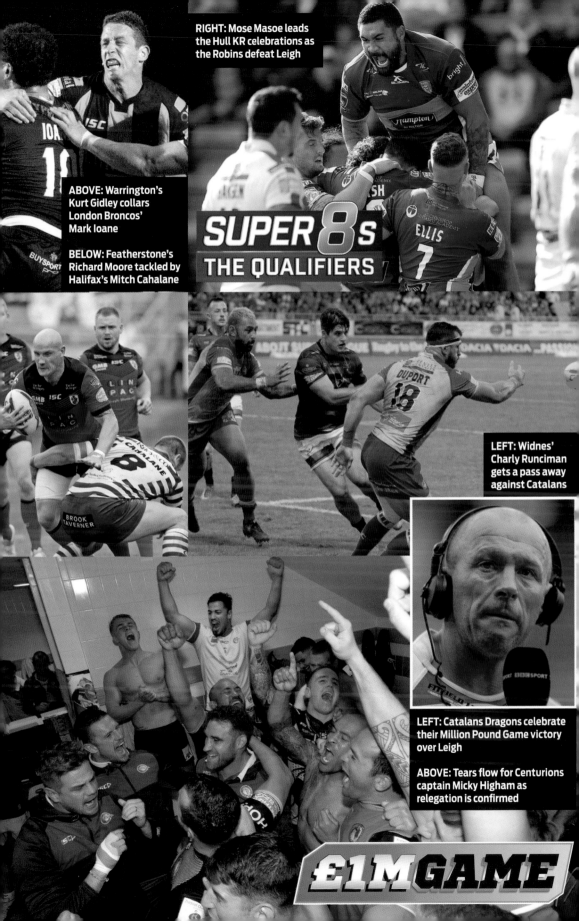

RIGHT: Mose Masoe leads the Hull KR celebrations as the Robins defeat Leigh

ABOVE: Warrington's Kurt Gidley collars London Broncos' Mark Ioane

BELOW: Featherstone's Richard Moore tackled by Halifax's Mitch Cahalane

SUPER 8s
THE QUALIFIERS

LEFT: Widnes' Charly Runciman gets a pass away against Catalans

LEFT: Catalans Dragons celebrate their Million Pound Game victory over Leigh

ABOVE: Tears flow for Centurions captain Micky Higham as relegation is confirmed

£1M GAME

LEFT: London Broncos' Rhys Williams takes on Rochdale's Jordan Case

BELOW: Swinto[n] Jack Murphy touches down against Oldha[m]

RIGHT: Featherstone's John Davies driven back by Batley's Joel Farrell

LEFT: Halifax's Will Sharp tries to shake off the attentions of Bradford's Kevin Larroyer

BELOW: A distraught Damian Sironen reflects on Bradford's relegation

BELOW: Hull KR lift the Championship League Leaders' Shield

KINGSTONE PRESS CHAMPIONSHIP
LEAGUE LEADERS 2017

BELOW: Craig Hall leads the Toronto celebrations following the Wolfpack's League 1 title win

Kingstone Press
LEAGUE 1

Kingstone Press
LEAGUE 1
SHIELD

ABOVE: Hunslet show off the League 1 Shield

LEFT: Barrow's Tom Walker, Nathan Mossop and Declan Hulme with the League 1 Cup

BELOW: Barrow celebrate earning promotion to the Championship after a tense win against Whitehaven

Kingstone Press
AMPIONSHIP SHIELD FINAL

ABOVE: Toulouse celebrate Championship Shield Final victory over Sheffield

Kingstone Press
LEAGUE 1 PROMOTION FINAL

RIGHT: England's Sam Burgess breaks through against Scotland

Ladbrokes RUGBY LEAGUE FOUR NATIONS

BELOW: Scotland celebrate Ben Hellewell's try in a thrilling draw with New Zealand

ABOVE: Valentine Holmes held short of the Kiw

AUSTRALIA..34
NEW ZEALAND 8

ABOVE: Johnathan Thurston presents a young fan with his headguard

RIGHT: Australia show their delight at their Four Nations triumph

continued from page 96

If ever there was a more inconsistent side than that of **SHEFFIELD EAGLES'** class of 2017, the head coach would probably have resigned in frustration.

A bizarre season ended in the comfort of mid-table, however that only begins to tell the tale of Sheffield's season.

In truth, seeing the Eagles emerge at the start of the campaign was a relief to some, as pressures on the club's resources had at one stage appeared to leave the club's status in danger.

A return to part-time rugby resulted in an overhaul of the club's playing roster, and that was evident in the opening stages of the season.

Despite an impressive win over Toulouse, it was the club's only win in their opening seven games. During that period, they conceded a concerning 281 points, an average of over 40 points per game.

But the beginning of April saw their fortunes change. After coach Mark Aston questioned their desire, Sheffield won four of their next five matches and started climbing the table.

Still, there would be plenty of hiccups along the way.

A 54-0 hammering at the hands of Halifax was followed by an embarrassing 70-12 defeat to Batley. However, they would then recover and continue to pick up wins against those alongside them in the bottom half.

By the time the Super 8s arrived Sheffield were safe, and in the end they reached the Championship Shield final, where they lost out to Toulouse.

Was this the greatest managerial turnaround we've ever seen?

DEWSBURY RAMS had been backed by most to be relegated in 2017, and those predictions looked correct as they endured a dismal start to the campaign, losing their opening eight matches.

Long-standing coach Glenn Morrison was sent on his way and in came former coach Neil Kelly.

That's when things changed.

They got up and running with victory over fierce rivals Batley, but it was their second victory over the Bulldogs, a scrappy 13-12 win at the Summer Bash, that rejuvenated the Rams.

Dewsbury's Aaron Brown gets a pass away against Sheffield

Championship Season

With the arrival of Gareth Moore from Halifax, Dewsbury won five of their final six regular season matches to steer them well clear of relegation.

Three further wins followed to give hope they could win the Championship Shield, although their season fizzled out from there.

Nevertheless, most people associated with the club would have snapped your hand off for a Championship Shield appearance back in April.

2017 was a year of consolidation for **ROCHDALE HORNETS** as they secured an impressive ninth-placed finish in their first year back in the second-tier.

They raced out of the blocks in superb style, topping the table after the first two weeks. A 46-0 annihilation of Dewsbury on the opening day got them off to a flying start before they went to Odsal and picked up a famous victory over Bradford.

A narrow defeat to Hull Kingston Rovers followed, however it triggered a tough spell for the club as they managed just one win in their next 13 matches, albeit it was a superb one, as they defeated Featherstone 10-9 on the road.

They returned to winning ways at the Summer Bash after coming from behind against Oldham, and despite a few scares along the way, the relegation zone was at arm's length for most of the season.

In the end, they finished three points clear of safety, although their season did end on a negative note as they were trounced 74-12 by Bradford.

SWINTON LIONS' second year in the Championship saw them labelled as dark horses following an impressive recruitment drive.

What unfolded was completely different.

A stack of injuries at the start of the season, including a season-ending blow to new recruit Matt Sarsfield, contributed to a slow start to the season.

Nevertheless, they produced the shock of the season as they defeated Huddersfield Giants in the Challenge Cup.

But their league form was a concern, and behind the scenes, financial issues were growing that resulted in the club's immediate and long-term future looking in danger.

Swinton's Ben Austin scores despite the challenge of Oldham's Richard Lepori

The club was forced to sell star player Chris Atkin to Hull Kingston Rovers while head coach John Duffy would leave to take up a new role at Featherstone Rovers.

It left the Lions in a mess. However, the club managed to see off a number of winding-up orders and keep the club afloat until the end of the season.

But players were leaving and new recruits were brought in from all angles, including the amateur game.

It appeared relegation would be a probability for the Lions, however, their resiliense was there for all to see. They picked up pivotal victories over Halifax and Bradford at the end of the regular campaign and ultimately secured their Championship status with a 29-6 win over Oldham at the start of September.

It was a year of what could have been for **OLDHAM**, who ended up losing their Championship status as they finished 11th.

Sadly, the Roughyeds ended the season with only themselves to blame, as they threw away points on an all too regular basis.

Narrow defeats to high-fliers London, Featherstone and Halifax were encouraging as much as frustrating and gave Scott Naylor much to build on despite the fact they should have left those encounters with league points.

However, it was their inconsistent displays against the teams around them that ultimately saw the damage done.

The most obvious collapse in their season came at the Summer Bash against local rivals Rochdale.

Naylor's men were excellent in the first-half and led 26-8. However, not for the first time, they put in a performance of complete contrast in the second period and lost 38-28.

Sadly, it was a pattern that continued and ultimately resulted in the Roughyeds going down.

Where do you start with **BRADFORD BULLS'** 2017 campaign?

In truth, the damage was done to the Bulls way before the first hooter of the season had sounded. The old entity of the club was liquidated and in its place, a new club rose from the ashes.

But with that came a twelve point penalty, that left the Bulls climbing a mountain from the start.

Still optimism loomed. Five wins from their opening nine games left the Bulls in a strong position and a great escape appeared likely.

However, defeat on Good Friday to local rivals Halifax started a nine-match winless run, and by the time they ended that losing streak against Oldham in June, relegation was almost inevitable.

Five defeats that followed ensured relegation to League 1. A prospect completely unfathomable just ten years earlier, was now a very painful reality.

CHAMPIONSHIP AWARDS

PLAYER OF THE YEAR
Shaun Lunt
(Hull Kingston Rovers)

YOUNG PLAYER OF THE YEAR
James Bentley (Bradford Bulls)

COACH OF THE YEAR
Andrew Henderson
(London Broncos)

CLUB OF THE YEAR
Hull Kingston Rovers

Andrew
Henderson

LEAGUE 1 SEASON
A Transatlantic Tale

TORONTO WOLFPACK took League 1 by storm in their debut campaign in the ever-expanding and, in 2017, worldwide competition, strolling to promotion and delivering their promise to pay for all their opponents' travel and accommodation costs.

The Wolfpack pulled together a squad of experienced former Super League and Championship players who all delivered on the Trans-Atlantic stage. It is no surprise the crowds, better than many Championship and some Super League clubs, kept coming back for more. And who could blame them when they were being treated to free-flowing, high scoring entertainment on a weekly basis.

Paul Rowley's men got the better of those teams who faced a four-day trip to Canada, winning all their games at the Lamport Stadium and only dropped league points in the UK when they lost at York City Knights and drew with Keighley Cougars in the Super 8s phase the season.

Their Challenge Cup campaign also saw them beat Championship opposition in London Broncos, before succumbing after tight game at Salford Red Devils in round five.

Liam Kay, Craig Hall, Jonny Pownall, Quentin Laulu-Togagae and Blake Wallace were among the league's top try scorers, bagging an incredible 109 between them. Hall added 162 goals across 22 games to finish as the game's overall top points scorer with 420.

A change in the league structure meant Toronto didn't need to endure a play-off campaign to get promotion, instead going straight up to the Championship, courtesy of a four-point lead over second-place Barrow Raiders.

Whether they can continue their quest for Super League in 2018 remains to be seen but with the signings of Ashton Sims and Joe Westerman from Warrington Wolves confirmed, a second successive promotion isn't beyond them.

BARROW RAIDERS went one step further than the previous year by finally sealing a return to the Championship.

The club's 2016 campaign had ended with a disappointing defeat to Toulouse in the play-off final but there was no repeat of that this time around as the Raiders saw off Cumbrian rivals Whitehaven 10-6 in the Promotion Final.

Three years of hard work from Paul Crarey and everyone else at Barrow has finally paid off and they would now be the sole Cumbria representative in the second tier of the game.

Add to that a narrow 38-32 win over North Wales Crusaders in the League 1 Cup Final in Blackpool and 2017 was a highly successful year for the Raiders, especially as the fixtures did not fall kindly for them and saw them face trips to big guns Toronto, Doncaster and York.

What was even more incredible about that Cup win was that it came just four days after the squad returned from their first of two trips to Toronto and just a fortnight after facing Super League Leeds Rhinos in the Challenge Cup. That Cup fixture also saw Barrow forced to play a midweek rearranged fixture against Keighley Cougars.

Unlike 12 months earlier when only a late surge saw them scrape into the play-offs, Barrow looked like serious promotion contenders right from the start of the season, racking up 160 points in their opening three fixtures and conceding just 14.

The winter signing of halfback/hooker Lewis Charnock from St Helens not only showed the club's intent, but also proved an astute acquisition, as a he went on to score 14 tries and 81 goals in 30 games.

WHITEHAVEN came agonisingly close to an immediate return to the Championship but a successful penalty kick just before the hour mark and a late try saw Barrow Raiders condemn their Cumbrian neighbours to another year in League 1.

Whitehaven's incredible semi-final the weekend before took just too much out of them and they didn't quite have enough to claw the game back when Barrow went in front.

That semi-final against York City Knights was probably the most nail-biting match of the season. It wasn't until Steve Roper knocked over a field goal after 105 minutes of action that the two sides could be separated.

Whilst the Barrow defeat will have been hard to take, one big positive for the club will have been the success of Carl Forster in his first season as a head coach.

As the youngest coach in the professional game, Forster took on a big challenge when he took the coaching reins at the start of the year whilst also continuing to play. Forster guided his team to become one of the most consistent teams in the league and the other team other than Toronto to beat Barrow in a regular-season game.

Whitehaven' form helped earn Forster the League 1 Coach of the Year accolade and he also played a big role up front on the field along with fellow prop Glenn Riley, with Papuan halfback Dion Aiye taking a starring role towards the end of the season.

YORK CITY KNIGHTS came a long way in 2017. To go from almost folding as a club, to attracting 2,602 spectators to witness them becoming the only side to defeat the all-conquering Toronto Wolfpack is quite some turn around.

When Jon Flatman and his consortium took over the club in December 2016, coach James Ford had little time to get a squad together for the season ahead. But he did, and by bringing in a host of hungry new faces eager to show what they could do, Ford had a squad all eager to work for each other and do what was needed to get the club back on track.

Whilst not many people would have expected to make the play-offs because of their troublesome winter, Ford knows that their final finishing spot was a just reward.

When the City Knights won only one of their opening four games - a narrow 26-24 victory over South Wales Ironmen - some might have suspected their turbulent off season was catching up with them. But once a largely new-look squad settled down, form suddenly improved and they made the top five with two games to spare, with back-rower Joe Batchelor a standout.

If they can avoid the heavy turnaround of players that stunted them at the start of this year, coupled with the acquisition of former Super League fullback Ben Cockayne, York can be confident of making a strong push for promotion in 2018.

NEWCASTLE THUNDER were perhaps the League's biggest surprise packet of the year, although it didn't look that way in May, when a run of five defeats saw Thunder sitting 12th in the table.

That poor form cost Australian coach Michael Mantelli, who had guided the club to League 1 Shield glory the previous season, his job.

Former player and club favourite Jason Payne stepped in to take charge on an interim basis knowing he would need to change things round quickly if the club were to have any chance of making the top eight once the league split just two months later.

Payne led to side to six wins from seven games to seal that eighth spot that had previously looked unlikely.

But the revival didn't end there and three victories in the first six Super 8s games meant Thunder went into the final game against York needing a win, coupled with defeats for Barrow and Keighley, to sneak into the play-offs. That is exactly how the weekend panned out, and despite the season ending in a disappointing 60-0 play-off defeat to Barrow, Payne had shown the club enough to earn himself the head coach role on a two-year deal.

Among Thunder's star performers, fullback Lewis Young picked up the League 1 Player of the Year award.

DONCASTER saw three different coaches take the reins in a season of mixed performances and results.

The club parted company with Gary Thornton in May after league defeats to Toronto Wolfpack and York City Knights, along with a heavy Challenge Cup defeat to Leeds Rhinos and a draw at home with London Skolars, threatened to derail a season that had started with three straight wins.

Up stepped former player Peter Green to take temporary charge, and to put on a plying shirt again, until Thornton's replacement could be found. Green fared slightly better and the club found some form under him, picking up three wins and a draw in his four matches in charge alongside Rhys Lovegrove and Pete Bell.

Then on June 13th, former Hull FC halfback Richard Horne was announced as the new head coach but mixed fortunes meant Doncaster missed the play-off cut.

Horne went on to pick up four wins and a draw in his 12 games in charge. But they got the closest of any side on their visit to Toronto on the last day of the season, leading early on before succumbing to the star-studded Wolfpack by 26-14.

Kieran Cross and Russ Spiers were the two most consistent squad members, with Cross being the club's top-tryscorer. With an off-season behind him, it will be interesting to see if former Great Britain star Horne can help Doncaster kick on in 2018.

KEIGHLEY COUGARS, an early season tip to be challenging for promotion, will no doubt have been left disappointed after a frustrating season under new coach Craig Lingard.

Consistency was a major issue for the club early in the year, with strong performances one week not always backed up the next. Although it improved as the season progressed, it is something the club will not be able to afford to have happen again if Lingard is to steer the club back into the Championship over the next two seasons and complete the three-year plan he took into the job.

Back-to-back away defeats to Whitehaven and Newcastle quickly dampened any celebrations following a draw against Toronto and ultimately cost them a play-off place. And while their season ended with defeat at Barrow, they were able to send two club favourites out on a high as their home campaign came to a close with a 28-6 win over Workington Town.

That game was a farewell to Cougar Park for hooker James Feather and prop Neil Cherryholme, who both retired from he game at the end of the season.

Meanwhile Keighley's hold on the League 1 Cup came to an end with a second round defeat at the hands of eventual winners Barrow.

WORKINGTON TOWN went into their first season in League 1 with a new look squad and a new coach in Australian Dave Clark. While all the changes would take some getting used to, Clark said at the start of the year that he wouldn't use that as an excuse for anything less than 100 per cent effort each week.

Whilst it was a tough season for them, Town still managed to make the top eight, which was the ultimate aim for the season. That meant that anything else they achieved that season would be seen as a bonus but, after that, they only picked up win against Newcastle Thunder and a one-point victory over Doncaster as the season petered out.

Although they beat Whitehaven in the opening League 1 Cup game, Town lost both Cumbrian league derbies. They didn't fare much better against Barrow Raiders and those results in particular will have been hard to swallow.

It could well be a similar story in 2018, with Clark having parted company with the club and experienced players Phil Joseph and Kris Coward already announcing that they are moving on.

But the post-season announcement that former Great Britain star Leon Pryce would take up the role of head coach will boost the hopes of Town fans going into 2018.

HUNSLET may have been left disappointed at narrowly missing out on a spot in the League 1 Super 8s but that did allow them to pick up some silverware.

A week after facing London Skolars at the South Leeds Stadium to decide who took home advantage in the League 1 Shield final, the sides met again in the trophy showdown.

Hunslet, who at the start of the year had dropped the Hawks moniker, won both games against the Skolars to take the Shield won by Newcastle Thunder 12 months earlier.

The club will be hoping that the success at the end of the season can be a springboard to better fortunes next year but in 2017, for the club and the fans, it was good to taste a bit of success after a third change of coach in two years. Hooker George Flanagan ended the year by picking up two club player of the year awards.

Matt Bramald, who took over from Barry Eaton in 2016, left ahead of the season and was replaced by James Coyle. But a 24-22 defeat against Oxford in May saw his time at the club come to an end, eventually being replaced by Gary Thornton, who had left Doncaster just weeks before. Under Thornton Hunslet picked up 10 wins in 14 games.

That form impressed enough to earn Thornton an extension to his contract for 2018.

LONDON SKOLARS went into the season looking to learn from past mistakes after failing to win a single game in the Super 8s the previous year.

With coach Jermaine Coleman admitting they had previously focussed all their energy on getting into the top-eight split and then not knowing how to handle it once there, he was keen to make amends in 2017.

Defeats to Toronto and Newcastle in the opening two weekends of the season meant they were playing catch up with their top-eight challengers from early on and then injuries to key players for crucial games also had an impact.

But they never gave up, and prior to their two defeats to Hunslet in the final two games, Skolars enjoyed a run of eight straight victories, their best run of wins since turning professional in 2003.

NORTH WALES CRUSADERS went into the season with a clean slate and a new look after more financial troubles had blighted the club the previous year.

Working on a much tighter budget than previously, the club brought in Mike Grady to steady the ship and he brought together a group of players with experience but also a willingness to put in the hard work and dig in when it mattered.

Given what had gone before the season started, not many will have predicted a top eight or a Shield Final position, but the fact the club were so disappointed to miss out on the latter by just two points shows how far they came under Grady's guidance.

A lack of consistency often frustrated Grady, who also saw numerous injuries affect his squad all year, but with many of this year's players already re-signing for 2018 a more positive year could be in the pipeline.

GLOUCESTERSHIRE ALL GOLDS once again used mainly locally-based players as they equalled the previous season's 12th place finished.

But most importantly, 12 victories in all competitions meant 2017 was the club's most successful season to date. Their previous best record was nine wins in 2015.

Many of those wins were helped by hooker Steve Parry and winger Mo Agoro, who led the way with 23 and 20 tries respectively.

Add to that the fact that four of the club's players were involved in the Student World Cup in July and that several first team players were set to be involved in the senior tournament, all was looking positive in the South West.

The year ended with confirmation of a merger with Oxford and the new club relocating to Bristol in time for the 2019 season.

OXFORD looked on course to enjoy their best ever season at one stage mid-way through the year. As well as making the League 1 Cup semi-final, impressive wins over York City Knights and Hunslet among others had left the Blues level on points with Workington Town and Keighley Cougars in seventh and eighth place in the table.

But the run of injuries that followed put even more pressure on the already young and inexperienced squad. That showed with a run of heavy defeats in which they shipped over 400 points in the final eight matches before the split.

Mixed form in the Shield saw the club finish 13th in what proved to be their final year as a club, before becoming part of the new Bristol-based club in 2019.

COVENTRY BEARS improved on last season's four wins with five victories in 2017. But the increased competitiveness of League 1 actually saw them finish lower in the league this time round.

Wins over Oxford, Hemel, twice, North Wales Crusaders and South Wales Ironmen will have pleased coach Tom Tsang, as will some of the performances they put in against teams that finished much higher then them.

Once again, the season didn't get off to the best of starts, leaving the Challenge Cup and the League 1 Cup at the first hurdle to fellow League 1 opposition in Hunslet and Oxford respectively.

After changing his squad much more than he would have liked ahead of 2017, Tsang will be hoping to avoid the same disturbance this time round so the club celebrate 20 years of development with their most promising season yet.

HEMEL STAGS' move up north to base themselves at Dewsbury Rams did not have the desired effect as they once again struggled at the wrong end of the table.

A large turnaround of players, which included a number of Yorkshire-based amateur players, saw the squad took time to settle and get to know each other, meaning they had to wait until July to pick up their first win at the expense of South Wales Ironmen.

They once again beat the Welsh side and Oxford in the League 1 Shield to avoid finishing bottom.

The season, and all the travelling involved, proved too much for long-serving coach Troy Perkins, who announced he was leaving the club for family reasons. The impact he has had over the previous decade will still be felt under the new leadership set up of player-coach Mitch Stringer and first team coaches Tim Farnden and Jack Howieson.

SOUTH WALES IRONMEN are no more after just one season under that identity. Any hopes they had about the previous year's rebrand proved unfounded as they faced another year of financial hardship, which manifested itself in a bottom-of-the-table finish and several faces moving on mid-season.

The club picked up just five points all year, beating Coventry Bears and Gloucestershire All Golds, as well as drawing against Oxford.

These points and other games in which they pushed their opponents all the way were some achievement as there were several games in which the Ironmen were unable to field the full 17 players and had to rely strongly at times on local community players.

2018 will see another new owner at the helm of the newly titled West Wales Raiders and a new home of Stebonheath Park in Llanelli.

LEAGUE 1 FINALS
Into the Furness

Barrow Raiders won the League 1 Cup in Blackpool but they were made to work hard for their 38-32 win by North Wales Crusaders.

Few tipped a tight game for the Summer Bash opener but North Wales could have very easily been lifting the trophy come the final hooter.

It took a late Danny Morrow try to eventually seal the game for the third-tier high-flyers in a thrilling representation of League 1 Rugby League which saw the Raiders come from ten points behind to claim victory.

Winning coach Paul Crarey admitted he was happy to take an ugly win at the end of a month where they had played Toronto Wolfpack and Leeds Rhinos, in the Challenge Cup, away from home.

LEAGUE 1 CUP FINAL

Saturday 27th May 2017

BARROW RAIDERS 38 NORTH WALES CRUSADERS 32

RAIDERS: 1 Ryan Fieldhouse; 5 Shane Toal; 3 Declan Hulme; 45 Tom Loxam; 24 Luke Cresswell; 6 Jamie Dallimore; 7 Lewis Charnock; 8 Joe Bullock; 9 Nathan Mossop; 10 Oliver Wilkes; 18 Danny Morrow; 11 Dan Toal; 13 Martin Aspinwall. Subs (all used): 14 Dan Abram; 17 Tom Walker; 21 James Duerden; 16 Andrew Dawson.
Tries: Mossop (2), Cresswell (30), Hulme (34), Morrow (37, 75), S Toal (64), Bullock (67); **Goals:** Charnock 2/5, Dallimore 3/3.
CRUSADERS: 1 Tommy Johnson; 2 Corey Lee; 11 Alex Thompson; 28 Callum Mulkeen; 5 Dale Bloomfield; 26 Jack Hansen; 7 Ryan Smith; 8 Jonny Walker; 14 James Dandy; 10 Alex Davidson; 17 Kenny Baker; 24 Jack Houghton; 16 Luke Warburton. Subs (all used): 27 Aaron Moore; 19 Dan Price; 20 Andy Unsworth; 31 Blake Turner.
Tries: Houghton (10), Bloomfield (21), Hansen (45), Mulkeen (54), Smith (56); **Goals:** Johnson 6/6.
Rugby Leaguer & League Express Men of the Match:
Raiders: Danny Morrow; *Crusaders:* Ryan Smith.
Penalty count: 9-9; **Half-time:** 20-12; **Referee:** Steve Race.
(at Bloomfield Road, Blackpool).

Barrow were the overwhelming favourites and they lived up to that title in the opening stages as Nathan Mossop somehow managed to get the ball down when it looked like the defence had dealt with the hooker. Lewis Charnock converted.

Having received a penalty straight from the kick-off, Charnock very nearly went over himself moments later, but he couldn't finish off his own grubber kick.

North Wales responded well, however, as Alex Thompson brought them close to the line before Jack Houghton took a short pass to crash over and Tommy Johnson's goal levelled the game.

Morrow was held up over the line as Barrow looked to re-take the lead.

The Raiders continued to push for the lead and looked set to do so with men over on the right wing, but Dale Bloomfield intercepted Charnock's intended pass and raced the length of the field to put North Wales in front, with Johnson adding his second goal.

Barrow's pressure told ten minutes later, however, as a kick bounced up nicely for Luke Cresswell to cross in the corner before Charnock's touchline conversion made it 12-12.

Dan Abram and Charnock both made strong breaks through the middle before the former became the second Barrow player to be held up.

Their dominance told with five minutes remaining in the half as Declan Hulme fell onto Ryan Fieldhouse's short pass and over the line, but Charnock's kick fell well wide.

Barrow were soon over for another score, however, as Morrow collected Jamie Dallimore's pass to dive over in the corner before they nearly added another try in almost the same position, but the hooter sounded as they had just earned a fresh set of six

Barrow's Danny Morrow beats North Wales' Tommy Johnson to score during the League 1 Cup Final

tackles from ten metres away.

Crarey's team started the second half on top but, rather than fall further behind, North Wales got themselves right back in contention as Jack Hanson strolled under the posts and Johnson slotted the simple conversion from just in front.

Barrow regained possession from the kick-off and looked set to threaten, but Moore and Alex Davidson forced a knock-on.

Fieldhouse and Abram combined as they went close again, but the latter couldn't keep hold of the ball five metres out.

But it was North Wales who re-took the lead for the first time in 20 minutes. A sweeping move saw the ball go from left to right and Callum Mulkeen powerfully finished it off, despite multiple defenders being in attendance, with Johnson converting once again.

Remarkably, the so-called underdogs then extended their lead moments after collecting their opponents' attempted short kick-off. They marched upfield after receiving a penalty and Ryan Smith made a break from 20 metres and raced under the posts, with Johnson making it a 10-point margin.

Barrow weren't done yet, however, as they moved back to within a score as the game entered the final quarter with Shane Toal acrobatically finishing in the corner after a break down the right wing.

Joe Bullock then spotted a gap and powered over from close range and Dallimore knocked over the conversion to tie the game at 30-all going into the final ten minutes.

Moore nearly put North Wales back in front from dummy-half at the other end, but although he didn't score, his efforts earned a penalty, which Johnson coolly slotted from straight in front.

Dallimore was then stopped illegally on an attempted chip and chase 20 metres out from the line, with the stand-off sending the resulting penalty through the sticks to level the game once again.

And it was the Raiders who snatched the win late on as Morrow dummied and fell over the line to complete his brace and confirm League 1 Cup glory.

Barrow won their way back to the Championship after a three-year absence thanks to a spectacular try from free-scoring winger Shane Toal.

His second touchdown of the game was all that separated the Cumbrian rivals in a nail-biting play-off final watched by a bumper Craven Park crowd of 3,128.

With the sides locked at 6-6, Toal outsprinted the Whitehaven cover defence to score in the corner and set up a frantic final ten minutes.

Haven ran out of time and luck – they felt aggrieved at having a late Steve Roper effort ruled out for a knock-on – and it was party time for the home supporters.

KINGSTONE PRESS LEAGUE 1 - PROMOTION FINAL

Sunday 1st October 2017

BARROW RAIDERS 10 WHITEHAVEN 6

RAIDERS: 1 Ryan Fieldhouse; 2 Brett Carter; 33 Eze Harper; 3 Declan Hulme; 5 Shane Toal; 6 Jamie Dallimore; 7 Lewis Charnock; 8 Joe Bullock; 15 Karl Ashall; 10 Oliver Wilkes; 12 Jarrad Stack; 22 Bradd Crellin; 13 Martin Aspinwall. Subs (all used): 9 Nathan Mossop; 17 Tom Walker; 11 Dan Toal; 21 James Duerden.
Tries: S Toal (10, 71); **Goals:** Dallimore 1/3.
WHITEHAVEN: 1 Elliott Miller; 2 Craig Calvert; 4 Jessie Joe Parker; 3 Chris Taylor; 5 Jordan Burns; 15 Dion Aiye; 7 Paul Crook; 8 Marc Shackley; 14 James Tilley; 10 Carl Forster; 13 Karl Olstrum; 12 Scott McAvoy; 6 Steve Roper. Subs: 9 James Newton; 16 Connor Holliday (not used); 17 Tommy Holland; 19 Glenn Riley.
Try: Aiye (45); **Goals:** Crook 1/1.
Rugby Leaguer & League Express Men of the Match:
Raiders: Shane Toal; *Whitehaven:* James Newton.
Penalty count: 10-10; **Half-time:** 4-0; **Referee:** Scott Mikalauskas; **Attendance:** 3,128.

The conditions dictated against open rugby but it was no less tense and dramatic for that. There were moments when tension and passion got the better of the players, but it was nothing more than the crowd expected from a derby between two sides who had a win apiece in their two previous meetings this year.

Two early penalties put Whitehaven in a promising position, but Barrow's defensive wall held out.

With the rewards so high it was hardly surprising that tension was quick to build and the first flare-up came after just seven minutes as Chris Taylor upended Eze Harper.

Barrow chose to keep up the pressure by running the ball and were rewarded with the opening try after ten minutes.

Joe Bullock set up the move which brought fullback Ryan Fieldhouse into the line, and his long pass found top tryscorer Toal, who went over in the corner.

Tom Walker dumps Glenn Riley during Barrow's Promotion Final victory against Whitehaven

League 1 Finals

The wet conditions led to a string of handling errors by both sides and the Barrow line came under pressure when Declan Hulme knocked on behind his own line.

Five minutes into the second half, Whitehaven went in front.

A short kick through from dangerman Newton wasn't cleared in the scramble that followed and Dion Aiye got the score, Paul Crook's goal nudging his side ahead.

Prompted by James Newton and Aiye, Whitehaven started to find the gaps and thought they had increased their lead when fullback Elliot Miller went over, only for the touchdown to be ruled out for obstruction.

Barrow needed a spark to get themselves back into the hunt and it eventually came from playmaker-in-chief Jamie Dallimore, who put Whitehaven back with his accurate kicking.

It was Dallimore's boot that pulled the home side level on 57 minutes. Jarrad Stack was poleaxed by a high tackle and the Barrow man took the two points on offer.

There was no let-up in the penalty count as both sides tested the patience of referee Scott Mikalauskas, and Barrow were pinned behind their own line by some clever kicking by Crook.

Another forward pass ruled out a Brett Carter effort in the corner and from the restart, Whitehaven were able to take the safety-first option to clear the danger.

Yet another penalty – the 20th of the game – gave Barrow the chance to go in front, but Dallimore's 40-yard effort bounced off a post and into the safety of a Whitehaven defender's clutches.

But the reprieve was short, and within a minute, the home side went in front in spectacular style. Bullock began the move that sent Declan Hulme away and he fed the speedy Toal, who outran the cover defence.

Dallimore missed the kick so the gap remained at four points. It was a nerve-jangling time for both sets of fans, and the Whitehaven contingent thought their side had levelled when Roper raced in only to be pulled back by that knock-on ruling.

LEAGUE 1 AWARDS

PLAYER OF THE YEAR
Craig Hall (Toronto Wolfpack)

YOUNG PLAYER OF THE YEAR
Lewis Young
(Newcastle Thunder)

COACH OF THE YEAR
Carl Forster (Whitehaven)

CLUB OF THE YEAR
Toronto Wolfpack

Lewis Young

4
INTERNATIONAL YEAR

2017 INTERNATIONALS
England make hay

England won a mid-season Test against Samoa by 30-10 at Campbelltown Sports Stadium on the first Saturday of May in an encouraging performance that gave fans reasons to be optimistic ahead of the World Cup at the end of the year.

There was some controversy around coach Wayne Bennett's decision to call up two Australians and the subsequent selection of Chris McQueen and Chris Heighington ahead of Scott Taylor and Alex Walmsley, who made the trip Down Under.

Add to that Mark Percival's exclusion at the expense of Stefan Ratchford, the Warrington utility who wasn't even selected in the original 20-man squad, and anything but a positive performance would have seen Bennett come in for heavy criticism.

But his selection was completely vindicated as England put in a strong display against a Samoa side blessed with talent and fifth in the world rankings.

Ratchford and Kevin Brown were among those who impressed and it was hard to pick out one player who didn't prove his worth.

After a disappointing Four Nations campaign in 2016 it was vital that England responded with a good performance and that they did, particularly in the opening 40 minutes as they raced into a 14-0 lead.

Although the second half was not quite as polished as the first, it was still strong enough to suggest that progress was being made in the camp.

A 14-0 lead at the break was a fair reward after a complete performance brimming with skill, resilience and unity.

The starting front row of Sam Burgess and James Graham set the tone for what would follow as they took the upper hand and allowed Josh Hodgson to shine around the ruck.

Mike McMeeken was also comfortable on the international stage on his debut.

TEST MATCH

Saturday 6th May 2017

SAMOA 10 ENGLAND 30

SAMOA: 1 Peter Mata'utia (Newcastle Knights); 2 Ken Maumalo (New Zealand Warriors); 3 Joseph Leilua (Canberra Raiders); 4 Tim Lafai (St George Illawarra Dragons); 5 Antonio Winterstein (North Queensland Cowboys); 6 Anthony Milford (Brisbane Broncos) (C); 7 Fa'amanu Brown (Cronulla Sharks); 8 Sam Kasiano (Canterbury Bulldogs); 9 Pita Godinet (Manly Sea Eagles); 10 Junior Paulo (Canberra Raiders); 11 Sione Mata'utia (Newcastle Knights); 12 Leeson Ah Mau (St George Illawarra Dragons); 13 Josh McGuire (Brisbane Broncos). Subs (all used): 14 John Asiata (North Queensland Cowboys); 15 Suaia Matagi (Parramatta Eels); 16 Sauaso Sue (Wests Tigers); 17 Herman Ese'ese (Brisbane Broncos).
Tries: Leilua (44), Milford (66); **Goals:** Milford 1/2.
ENGLAND: 1 Stefan Ratchford (Warrington Wolves); 2 Jermaine McGillvary (Huddersfield Giants); 3 Kallum Watkins (Leeds Rhinos); 4 Zak Hardaker (Castleford Tigers); 5 Ryan Hall (Leeds Rhinos); 6 Kevin Brown (Warrington Wolves); 7 Luke Gale (Castleford Tigers); 8 James Graham (Canterbury Bulldogs); 9 Josh Hodgson (Canberra Raiders); 10 Sam Burgess (South Sydney Rabbitohs); 11 Elliott Whitehead (Canberra Raiders); 12 Mike McMeeken (Castleford Tigers) (D); 13 Sean O'Loughlin (Wigan Warriors) (C). Subs (all used): 14 Chris Hill (Warrington Wolves); 15 Chris Heighington (Cronulla Sharks); 16 Chris McQueen (Gold Coast Titans) (D); 17 Tom Burgess (South Sydney Rabbitohs).
Tries: Hall (3), Ratchford (38), Hodgson (52), Graham (74), McGillvary (80); **Goals:** Gale 5/6.
Rugby Leaguer & League Express Men of the Match:
Samoa: Sam Kasiano; *England:* Sam Burgess.
Penalty count: 5-8; **Half-time:** 0-14; **Referee:** Gerard Sutton (Australia); **Attendance:** 18,271 (at Campbelltown Sports Stadium, Sydney).

England's Jermaine McGillvary breaks through the Samoa defence

A promising start was rewarded with points when Ryan Hall's impressive try record for England continued, bagging his 34th try in as many appearances.

England forced Samoa into relinquishing possession with a superb tackle by Elliott Whitehead. From there Sean O'Loughlin, captaining the side once again after missing the Four Nations, found Hall with a scoring pass.

Luke Gale converted and, soon afterwards, he extended the lead further with a penalty as Samoa started to become frustrated with England's defence showing no weakness.

But offensively England were potent too. Without Gareth Widdop and George Williams, Gale and Brown were handed the opportunity to impress in the halves and they did so with creativity and excitement.

It was Gale who provided the pass for the second try of the match. A move to the left edge resulted in Gale putting Ratchford through a gap after a well-timed run. He subsequently produced a brilliant side-step to round the fullback and score by the posts. Gale's conversion made it 14-0 at the break.

Samoa showed much more intent in the second half. Canberra centre Joey Leilua showed great strength to work his way to the line despite the presence of several England defenders, giving Samoa a glimmer of hope four minutes in.

But England weathered the storm and hit back with a try of their own ten minutes later. It was the two halfbacks who combined again - Brown sending Gale through a gap before he found the supporting Hodgson to score under the sticks.

That gave England a 20-6 lead going into the final quarter but Samoa were still in the contest and when Brisbane halfback Anthony Milford scored, exploiting England's uncharacteristically stretched defence, the lead was just ten points going into the closing stages of the game.

But England snuffed out thoughts of a comeback with six minutes to go. Brown was afforded plenty of space, and he picked out Graham, who clattered his way through a couple of defenders to secure victory for England.

There was still time for one final try, as Huddersfield winger Jermaine McGillvary latched on to a superb kick into space by Brown to wrap up proceedings and bring an end to a very satisfactory evening for England.

PACIFIC TRI-SERIES

Saturday 14th October 2017
Papua New Guinea 10 Fiji 0
Australia 20 Papua New Guinea 4
Australia 18 Fiji 0
(all played in Suva, 40 minute games)

WOMEN'S INTERNATIONALS

Friday 5th May 2017
Australia 16 New Zealand 4
(at Canberra Stadium)
Wednesday 21st June 2017
France 16 England 26
(at Stade de la Mer, Perpignan)
Saturday 24th June 2017
France 8 England 14
(at Stade de la Mer, Perpignan)

NORDIC CUP

Saturday 17th June 2017
Norway 38 Sweden 18
(at Bislett Stadium, Oslo)
Saturday 19th August 2017
Denmark 24 Norway 46
(in Kalundborg)

Australia imposed a 30-12 thrashing of New Zealand on the first Friday night of May, in a five tries to two hammering in Canberra.

It continued New Zealand's abysmal record in the mid-season ANZAC Tests, with 17 losses in 18 encounters.

On the back of last year's dominant Four Nations victory, it confirmed the position of Mal Meninga's side as red-hot favourites for the end-of-season World Cup.

Australia had the game wrapped up at half-time after charging to a 24-0 lead. Their first try came when Josh Dugan jumped to catch Johnathan Thurston's kick on twelve minutes, with Thurston converting, as he did all the Kangaroo tries.

The second came when the Kiwis moved the ball to the left Blake Ferguson intercepted Shan Johnson's and ran 90 metres to touch down.

Jordan Rapana touched down for the Kiwis but the try was disallowed because of a forward pass from Johnson, before a great run from Sam Thaiday led to the Kangaroos' third try from Will Chambers.

Ferguson thought he had scored the fourth try but it was turned down because he had a foot in touch, before former Welsh international Tyson Frizell was more successful, touching down a Thurston kick that rebounded off the post protector.

And when Cooper Cronk passed blindly behind his back for 23-year-old prop Jake Trbojevic to score four minutes after the resumption in the second half, the Australians were cruising at 30-nil.

They then took their foot off the accelerator to allow a couple of consolation tries to the Kiwis later in the half.

The Kiwis finally touched down when Simon Mannering scored on 56 minutes for Jordan Kahu to add the goal. Roger Tuivasa-Sheck added a second try, with Kahu again goaling.

The Australians seemed to lift for what was the 50th Test appearance of captain Cameron Smith. Only the legendary Darren Lockyer had played more and it was fitting that on the eve of the Test Lockyer should present his successor with the latter's historic Test shirt.

In yet another record, Smith posted his 27th appearance as skipper, equalling the tally of the man they dubbed "The Little Master", Clive Churchill (and again second only to Lockyer).

ANZAC TEST

Friday 5th May 2017

AUSTRALIA 30 NEW ZEALAND 12

AUSTRALIA: 1 Darius Boyd (Brisbane Broncos); 2 Valentine Holmes (Cronulla Sharks); 3 Will Chambers (Melbourne Storm); 4 Josh Dugan (St George Illawarra Dragons); 5 Blake Ferguson (Sydney Roosters); 6 Johnathan Thurston (North Queensland Cowboys); 7 Cooper Cronk (Melbourne Storm); 8 Andrew Fifita (Cronulla Sharks); 9 Cameron Smith (Melbourne Storm) (C); 10 David Klemmer (Canterbury Bulldogs); 11 Boyd Cordner (Sydney Roosters); 12 Matt Gillett (Brisbane Broncos); 13 Trent Merrin (Penrith Panthers). Subs (all used): 14 Michael Morgan (North Queensland Cowboys); 15 Jake Trbojevic (Manly Sea Eagles); 16 Tyson Frizell (St George Illawarra Dragons); 17 Sam Thaiday (Brisbane Broncos). **Tries:** Dugan (12), Ferguson (17), Chambers (28), Frizell (35), Trbojevic (44); **Goals:** Thurston 5/5.
NEW ZEALAND: 1 Roger Tuivasa-Sheck (New Zealand Warriors); 2 Dallin Watene-Zelezniak (Penrith Panthers); 3 Jordan Kahu (Brisbane Broncos); 4 Dean Whare (Penrith Panthers); 5 Jordan Rapana (Canberra Raiders); 6 Kieran Foran (New Zealand Warriors); 7 Shaun Johnson (New Zealand Warriors); 8 Jesse Bromwich (Melbourne Storm) (C); 9 Issac Luke (New Zealand Warriors); 10 Russell Packer (St George Illawarra Dragons); 11 Kevin Proctor (Gold Coast Titans); 12 Simon Mannering (New Zealand Warriors); 13 Jason Taumalolo (North Queensland Cowboys). Subs (all used): 14 Adam Blair (Brisbane Broncos); 15 Martin Taupau (Manly Sea Eagles); 16 Kenny Bromwich (Melbourne Storm); 17 Kodi Nikorima (Brisbane Broncos). **Tries:** Mannering (55), Tuivasa-Sheck (64); **Goals:** Kahu 2/2.
Rugby Leaguer & League Express Men of the Match:
Australia: Matt Gillett; *New Zealand:* Jesse Bromwich.
Half-time: 24-0; **Referee:** Matt Cecchin (Australia); **Attendance:** 18,535 *(at GIO Stadium, Canberra)*.

OTHER INTERNATIONALS

Wednesday 2nd November 2016 South Africa 0 44 Niue 44 *(in Pretoria)*	*Saturday 9th September 2017* Netherlands 28 Sweden 24 *(at Bok de Korverweg, Amsterdam)*
Saturday 4th November 2016 Hungary 50 Uruguay 4 El Salvador 12 Thailand 32 *(both at Hillier Oval, Sydney)* Malta 44 Philippines 26 *(at Cabramatta)*	*Sunday 8th October 2017* Italy 24 Malta 24 *(at Marconi Stadium, Sydney)*
	Friday 13th October 2017 France 34 Jamaica 12 *(at Stade Gilbert Brutus, Perpignan)*
Saturday 6th May 2017 Fiji 24 Tonga 26 Papua New Guinea 32 Cook Islands 22 *(both at Campbelltown, Sydney)* Malta 4 Lebanon 24 *(at Cabramatta)*	*Saturday 14th October 2017* Wales Dragonhearts 34 Germany 38 *(at Glamorgan Wanderers)*
	2017 Colonial Cup *Saturday 22nd July 2017* USA 48 Jamaica 6 *(at Hodges Stadium, Jacksonville)*
Saturday 3rd June 2017 Lebanon 6 Italy 4 *(in Beirut)*	*Saturday 26th August 2017* Jamaica 28 Canada 14 *(in Kingston, Jamaica)*
Saturday 10th June 2017 Italy 94 Spain 4 *(in Saluzzo)*	*Saturday 16th September 2017* Canada 18 USA 36 *(at Lamport Stadium, Toronto)*
Saturday 22nd July 2017 Hungary 6 Czech Republic 26 *(at KFKI Pálya, Budapest)*	**Balkan Championship** *Friday 6th October 2017* Greece 68 Bulgaria 8 *Sunday 8th October 2017* Serbia 50 Bulgaria 20
Saturday 26th August 2017 Germany 18 Netherlands 30 *(in Osnabrück)*	Serbia 50 Greece 8 *(all at Rakovica, Belgrade)*

SEASON DOWN UNDER
Storm show dominance

At the very least the Storm side which swept to the Premiership in 2017 is certainly one of greatest on record. In their ranks they could boast three Golden Boot laureates, Billy Slater, Cooper Cronk and Cameron Smith and several other Test match stars from Australia or New Zealand. They lost only four games all season, once against the Gold Coast by just two points and another against the Roosters by one in golden point extra-time. The Men in Purple were particularly dominant in the final fortnight of the season. After a close encounter with the Parramatta Eels in the first weekend of the play-offs they hammered Brisbane 30-0 in Melbourne to reach their second straight Grand Final, against North Queensland. The Cowboys had scraped into the finals by the skin of their teeth, thanks to a shock loss to the Bulldogs by the Dragons in the last round of the regular season but then, despite a growing injury toll, proceeded to eliminate Cronulla, Parramatta, and Sydney Roosters in successive weeks.

There were just a few short of 80,000 fans at Sydney's Olympic stadium for the Grand Final. And in years to come every last one of them will be looking back in awe at the display by Melbourne. The perfect storm? Quite possibly!

The Melbournites led 18-0 at half-time and went on to win 34-6. The Cowboys were the fans' sentimental favourites in what was only the third decider without a team from the traditional home of the sport in Australia, Sydney. But as Golden Boot winner from Melbourne, Cronk noted: 'There are no fairytales in Rugby League. You work hard and hope the results go your way.'

They certainly went Melbourne's way.

The match rung down the curtain on the era of the 'The Three Musketeers', Cronk, Slater, and Smith, after 231 appearances in 14 seasons together in Storm colours. Cronk had decided to quit Melbourne to move to Sydney to be with his partner, Fox Sports television reporter Tarah Rushton. But Smith will continue his record-breaking career and Slater is expected to follow suit to help mentor the Storm's up-and-coming young stars.

Cronk explained: 'The Melbourne Storm makes you bigger than you are.' Slater returned to the fray this season after being sidelined through a shoulder injury sustained in early 2015. He was a stand-out winner of the Clive Churchill Medal as Man of the Match, wiping away tears as the medal was hung over his head: 'There has been a lot of hard work ... a lot of hard work,' he said. 'We have been doing it all year. So we knew we could win.'

The Storm looked strong from the kick-off. Jesse Bromwich made an instant break after less than three minutes of action and, in the tackle that stopped any chance of a try, Cowboys' prop Shaun Fenson was laid low by a break to his left leg. Origin forward Coen Hess was quickly rushed off the bench as his replacement. As Fensom was driven off the pitch in pain he gave the thumbs up to fans as if to say 'I'm okay'. What a salute of confidence in the Cowboys!

After 19 minutes without a score, it all changed when Storm winger Josh Addo-Carr, after a leap for a bomb by several players, raced 95 metre to score his 22nd try of the season.

What talent there is among the Melbourne stars. Cronk straightened the attack, Slater was on his shoulder and sent Tongan hardman Felise Kaufusi through a yawning gap to score. Then it was Smith to Slater, who touched down to send the Storm to half-time ahead 18-0.

Early after the resumption, Michael Morgan put his halfback partner Te Marie Martin over for the Cowboys' only try of the night.That was as good as it got for the Cowboys. Smith orchestrated a try for loose forward Dale Finucane before Addo-Carr set up former Sharks excitement machine Curtis Scott before scoring a second try himself.

This year's Grand Final was arguably the most controversial in the history of the game in Australia. Scheduled as the voters were involved in a postal plebiscite on same-sex marriage, the NRL chiefs shocked everyone by choosing to headline the pre-game entertainment with American rap artist Macklemore, known for a gay marriage anthem Same Love. The NRL stood by Macklemore, with chief executive Todd Greenberg saying it was 'one of the bravest decisions we've made'.

Here's how the sides fared in 2017:

MELBOURNE STORM (Premiers/Minor Premiers)
Top pointscorer: Cameron Smith (192)*; Top tryscorers:* Josh Addo-Carr/Suliasi Vunivalu (23)

Melbourne Storm stamped themselves as the finest club of the current era with a dominant season in which they were beaten only four times and inflicted a crushing defeat of the Cowboys in the Grand Final. They scored some 715 points, 357 more than their rivals in the 27 encounters in which they were involved. They touched down for more tries than any other club, and conceded fewer.

Of course, the Grand Final rang down the curtain on the greatest club, Origin and Test 'spine' in decades - Slater, Cronk and Smith, with Cronk moving to Sydney for personal reasons.

Skipper Smith had arguably the finest season of his career, setting a number of Australian records. His 23 appearances took his senior NRL tally to 358, a Premiership record, topping the previous best of 355 by Brisbane's Darren Lockyer. Smith extended his lead with the greatest number of Origin appearances to 42. And he became the first player in Australian history to kick 1,000 goals in club games. He reached 50 Test appearances for Australia in the Trans-Tasman encounter in May. This tally is second only to Lockyer's 59.

Slater's dramatic return to the big league after two shoulder reconstructions sidelined him for almost two years saw him back in the Queensland Origin and was chosen in the Australian side for the end-of-season World Cup. He won his second Clive Churchill Medal as Man of the Match in the Grand Final.

Smith, Cronk and centre Will Chambers all played for Australia in the ANZAC Test against a Kiwis side containing their Melbourne teammates Jesse and Kenny Bromwich. The Storm were well represented in the World Cup with no less than seven stars in the green and gold – Smith, Slater, Cronk, Chambers, stand-off Cameron Munster and forwards Jordan McLean and Felise Kaufusi.

NORTH QUEENSLAND COWBOYS (Runners-up)
Top pointscorer: Ethan Lowe (102); *Top tryscorer:* Kyle Feldt (15)

The Cowboys were subjected to the mother of all hidings in the Grand Final ... but there is no doubting the spirit that got them to the season's decider. They had an incredible run of injuries including those that forced a premature end to the hopes of co-captains Johnathan Thurston and Matt Scott.

A shoulder injury cost Thurston a significant milestone. He finished the season with a total of 299 senior NRL appearances – and will reach the magic 300 when the Cowboys play Cronulla in their first game in 2018.

The North Queenslanders only just scraped into the play-offs in eighth place but a series of gritty displays then saw them overcome the reigning Premiers Cronulla (in controversial circumstances), a revitalised Parramatta and finally Sydney Roosters to earn the chance of taking on Melbourne in the Grand Final.

Much of their success can be attributed to State of Origin stand-off Michael Morgan, who willingly accepted the added responsibility after the loss of Thurston. He took his game to a new level, dictating the attack from behind the ruck and producing a kicking game of which JT would have been proud.

Coach Green was careful when talking about individual players: 'If I single out anyone it probably doesn't do the whole story justice. It was great to see so many up. There are plenty of young guys who did a great job for us.'

And some of them not so young!

'Scott Bolton was outstanding all year and he was playing busted,' said Green. Former Dally M Medal winner Jason Taumalolo was outstanding, filling the void in the pack left by Scott. He averaged 206 metres in torrid runs per match, more than any other player in the NRL and broke no less than 130 tackles in those charges. Only one other forward, Souths' Angus Crichton (117), managed to top the century.

Morgan was chosen in Australia's World Cup squad, stand-off Te Marie Martin for New Zealand, and Taumalolo for Tonga,

SYDNEY ROOSTERS (3rd)

Top pointscorer: Michael Gordon (172); *Top tryscorer:* Latrell Mitchell (15)

What a difference a year makes. In 2016 the Roosters had finished in front of only one club, the hapless Newcastle Knights. But 12 months later they ranked second on the NRL Ladder after the regular season was concluded before narrowly sneaking past Brisbane in the opening week of the finals. The Sydneysiders only failed on the penultimate weekend, beaten by a gallant North Queensland Cowboys' outfit.

The co-captain Boyd Cordner was outstanding. He ran some 2755 metres (at an average of 153 per appearance) and made around 30 tackles per match. His inspirational displays from the Tricolours saw him take over as NSW State of Origin skipper – and there is no doubt that once Cameron Smith retires, Cordner will be waiting in the wings to assume the captaincy of the Australian Test side. He was ably supported in the pack by Kiwis international Jared Waerea-Hargreaves, who played in every Roosters' game – a welcome relief after two injury-plagued seasons.

Luke Keary came from South Sydney and was a perfect match for Mitchell Pearce in the halves. Another off-season signing, 33-year-old fullback Michael Gordon from Parramatta, was worth his weight in gold, especially with his goalkicking, booting 72 with a success rate of around 80 per cent.

After a stellar debut season in 2016, rookie utility back Latrell Mitchell was dropped to the Roosters feeder cub, the Wyong Roos, early this year. It was the wake-up call the youngster needed as he came back with a vengeance to top the Roosters' tryscoring lists for the second straight year. He also made a total of 18 line-breaks and no less than 102 tackle busts.

Cordner made the Australian World Cup squad, Waerea-Hargreaves was in the Kiwis' line-up, winger Daniel Tupou and backrower Sio Siua Taukeiaho played for Mate Ma'a Tonga and forwards Kane Evans and Eloni Vunakece for Fiji Bati.

BRISBANE BRONCOS (4th)
Top pointscorer: Jordan Kahu (187); *Top tryscorer:* Corey Oates (16)

Brisbane Broncos defied the critics and made their way into the play-offs for the third straight year since coach Wayne Bennett returned to the fold. But a rash of injuries put paid to any genuine Premiership hopes. After going down to Sydney Roosters by just two points the Broncos regrouped to bundle Penrith Panthers out of the finals series before Melbourne produced the perfect Storm to lash them 30-nil in their preliminary final.

Arguably the most telling injury was to hooker Andrew McCullough in July, when he tore ligaments in a clash with Parramatta. This forced the Broncos to experiment with several different names in the playmaker's role. Eventually they settled on 'the six million dollar man' Ben Hunt, their scrum-half who is off to the Dragons next year. As Test star Josh McGuire explained: 'I thought Ben Hunt did a phenomenal job. But when McCullough is there it means you don't have to carry an extra hooker or utility on the bench in case the starting hooker gets tired. That gives our big guys an extra interchange.'

Then the Broncos lost inspirational skipper Darius Boyd at the back end of the season. A hamstring tear forced him to miss the first two weeks of the finals and when he was an 11th-hour inclusion for the preliminary final his lack of mobility had him caught out of position several times. He was one of the first players to drop out of Australia's challenge for the World Cup.

Exciting centre James 'Jimmy the Jet' Roberts showed some of the best form of his career, scoring 18 tries and breaking 108 tackles in scintillating bursts, that netted him an average of 125 metres per game.

Boyd may have missed the World Cup. But there were still nine Broncos involved – Hunt, McGuire and Matt Gillett (Australia), the Kiwis Kodi Nikorima and captain Adam Blair, Joe Ofahengaue and Tevita Pangai Jnr (both Tonga), David Mead (Papua New Guinea) and Korbin Sims (Fiji).

PARRAMATTA EELS (5th)
Top pointscorer: Clint Gutherson (142); *Top tryscorer:* Semi Radradra (22)

The Eels put the horrors of 2016 and a slow start to this year (winning just two of their opening six encounters) behind them. A spirited revival, in which they won nine of their final 10 matches of the regular season, saw them end an eight-year finals' drought and claim their first top-four finish since 2005. They showed guts in a two-point loss to Melbourne Storm in the opening weekend of the play-offs, but then crashed out a week later, beaten 24-16 by the Cowboys. 'I am disappointed we didn't go out on our terms,' said coach Brad Arthur. 'The Cowboys taught us a lesson in what semi-finals football is all about. But we did a great job in getting as far as we did.'

There could be some excuses for Parramatta, especially injuries to some of the key players such as Clint Gutherson, Bevan French, Beau Scott, Corey Norman, Isaac De Gois (forced into premature retirement) and his replacement at No 9, Kaysa Pritchard. But they made a useful mid-season signing from Wests Tigers, halfback Mitchell Moses, who helped set up 10 tries and assisted in 14 line-breaks by teammates in his 16 appearances.

Fijian winger Semi Radradra said farewell to Rugby League and headed for French rugby union with yet another stellar season, scoring 22 tries. This brought his tally to 82 in his 94 games for the Eels. He will be sorely missed in 2018.

Eleven senior Eels players were chosen in the squads for the end-of-season World Cup – Toa Samoa's skipper Frank Pritchard and hard-working international teammates Suaia Matagi and Ben Nakubuwai for Fiji, Michael Jennings, Manu Ma'u and Peni Terepo for Mate Ma'a Tonga, Daniel Alvaro and Nathan Brown with the Italian Azzurri, as well as Moses and Parramatta captain Tim Mannah with Lebanon.

Season Down Under

PENRITH PANTHERS (6th)

Top pointscorer: Nathan Cleary (228); *Top tryscorer:* Nathan Cleary (11)

Penrith started the year as competition favourites after their great finish to 2016 and their wealth of talented young players. But the inexperience told, with the youngsters plagued by internal dissent that saw them win only two of their first nine matches.

Coach Andrew Griffin refused to give up on his young players, who managed to stop the rot, with the Panthers winning 11 of their next 13 encounters. This was achieved despite the fact that they had to cope without some key stars in captain Matt Moylan, international winger Josh Mansour, Four Nations loose forward Trent Merrin and veteran hooker Peter Wallace at various stages of the season.

Moylan was in the headlines for all the wrong reasons. First he and threequarters Waqa Blake and Peta Hiku were dropped for breaking a team curfew after a match against the Storm in Melbourne. Then there were rumours of Moylan falling out with Griffin and wanting to join another club. He was given time away from rugby to deal with some personal issues. But Panthers chiefs say he will remain at Penrith next season.

At 19 years of age, scrum-half Nathan Cleary became the youngest leading Premiership pointscorer since the great Souths' winger Harold Horder, way back in 1913. Cleary was also the competition's most reliable goalkicker, booting 92 from 102 attempts, at an incredibly successful strike rate, some 10 per cent more than in his rookie season of 2016.

Meanwhile, the Panthers NSW Cup side won the State Championships by thrashing their Queensland Cup counterparts, the Papua New Guinea Hunters 42-18. The Holden Cup (Under-20s) side reached the penultimate weekend of the season. And with the likes of Cleary, exciting rookie Dylan Edwards and Dally M Interchange Player of the Year Reagan Campbell-Gillard making real impacts, the future at the foot of the Blue Mountains looks rosy.

Mansour and Campbell-Gillard were chosen in Australia's World Cup squad and threequarters Dallin Watene-Zelezniak and Dean Whare for the Kiwis. Among the Cup minnows the Fiji Bati laid claim to 22-year-old prop Viliame Kikau and Mate Ma'a Tonga to hooker Sione Katoa.

CRONULLA SHARKS (7th)

Top pointscorer: James Maloney (161); *Top tryscorer:* Sosaia Seki (13)

Back-to-back Premierships continued to elude the champion sides. Cronulla was able to reach the finals series, but fifth on the ladder meant it was sudden death in the first round of the play-offs. And they lost after a contentious refereeing decision right on full-time gave North Queensland the chance to level the scores and take the game into extra time, where the Cowboys snapped the winning field goal. Coach Shane Flanagan was later fined $30,000 – three times the normal penalty – for a scathing attack on the referees.

Cronulla never really recovered from the departure of Ben Barba. Initially he was banned because of a drug offence, then he moved to French rugby union side Toulon, and finally to St Helens in Super League. Utility back Valentine Holmes was capable at fullback but lacked the dazzling attack of Barba.

The Sharks also suffered from the retirement of hooker Michael Ennis after a 15-year career in which he appeared in four Grand Finals. His replacement, Australian Schoolboys star Jayden Brailey, had a great debut year. Flanagan noted: 'Jayden did a tremendous job. But as a first-year player there was always going to be a big difference.' It will be interesting in the coming years as his younger brother Blayke Brailey, starred for Cronulla's Under-20s' outfit and is destined for a great future in the senior ranks. Ironically, he also is a hooker.

The evergreen skipper Paul Gallen, without the burden of Test and Origin rugby, was outstanding once again in a year in which he reached the 300-game milestone. Holmes, James Maloney and second-rower Wade Graham were chosen in Australia's World Cup squad, while centre Gerard Beale was snapped up by New Zealand and Chris Heighington by England. Ricky Leutele was chosen for Samoa, while Andrew Fifita, after playing for Australia in the ANZAC Test switched to Tonga for the World Cup. Holmes, Fifita and Maloney turned out for the Prime Minister's XIII in their 48-8 romp against a below-strength Papua New Guinea Kumuls.

MANLY SEA EAGLES (8th)
Top pointscorer: Dylan Walker (108); *Top tryscorer:* Akuila Uate (14)

The Manly Sea Eagles players were left shaking their heads in disbelief. Back in the play-offs after two seasons in the wilderness, they lasted only one match, beaten 22-10 by Penrith, the very same side they had thrashed 28-12 the previous weekend.

It was a controversial victory and Manly's coach Trent Barrett was livid, with the NRL slapping a $20,000 fine on him for a rant against the match officials: 'To have our season ended by two video referee calls which in my opinion were incorrect, is extremely hard to take. There's a massive problem with the system. It's crazy and it's cost us our season.'

It was a topsy-turvy year for the Sea Eagles, with some solid wins – 30-8 over the Cowboys, 36-0 against the Bulldogs, 46-8 over the Rabbitohs and 35-18 against the Sharks – punctuated by a couple of hammerings by the Dragons and a 40-6 drubbing by Melbourne.

Nevertheless there was some coming of age among a few of the Sea Eagles. Captain Dale Cherry-Evans produced his best season on record, highlighted by 50 tackle-breaks and the setting up of 20 tries for teammates. The Fijian flyer Akuila Uate saw his career rejuvenated after some disappointing form at Newcastle, running in 14 tries. Former Wigan and Hull KR star Blake Green added some stability in the halves. Frank Winterstein was a revelation on his return from a spell in rugby union. Hooker Api Koroisau orchestrated play around the rucks. The virtually unknown Brian Kelly was revelation in his rookie year and fellow centre Dylan Walker appreciated his switch from fullback.

The Trbojevic brothers excelled – the 20-year-old fullback Tom and forward Jake, three years his senior. Tom scored a hat-trick for the Prime Minister's XIII in their 48-8 victory over Papua New Guinea. Jake played in the ANZAC Test against the Kiwis and both were chosen in the World Cup squad.

The Sea Eagles are positive about their future after their Holden Cup side finished a giant-killing run from eighth place in the play-offs by snatching a breathtaking 20-18 Grand Final over Parramatta as the full-time siren sounded.

ST GEORGE ILLAWARRA DRAGONS (9th)
Top pointscorer: Gareth Widdop (191); *Top tryscorer:* Jason Nightingale (16)

What a disappointing end to the season it was for St George Illawarra. After leading the early race after winning six of their first seven outings, they came crashing back to earth, losing 11 of their last 17 matches, including a shock defeat at the hands of the Bulldogs on the final day of the regular season costing the Dragons eighth spot in the play-offs.

'We're shattered not to be playing finals footy,' said coach Paul McGregor in what must rank as the understatement of the season.

After struggling to score sufficient points in recent years, the Dragons clicked into top gear in many matches. England Four Nations half Gareth Widdop led the charge with the best attacking year of his NRL career. Like fine, old wine, veteran Kiwi winger Jason Nightingale continued to get better with each passing year, leading the tryscoring for the side with 16 touchdowns. Even evergreen prop Paul Vaughan got into the act, his eight tries being the most by any front-rower in the Premiership.

Centre Josh Dugan made the Australian line-up for both the ANZAC Test against New Zealand and the World Cup. He was joined by former Wales World Cup forward Tyson Frizell, who averaged 110 metres per appearance in terrifying runs and crunched opponents with an average of 30 tackles. Reformed prop Russell Packer was a mountain on strength in the pack and Jack de Belin regularly topped 150 metres in bullocking bursts.

They will be joined by England prop James Graham and the Broncos Ben Hunt next season, the latter joining Widdop in a formidable halfback pairing. There is also the exciting fullback Matt Dufty who made his senior debut late in 2017.

Other Dragons to figure in the World Cup were Nightingale and Packer (both New Zealand), centre Tim Lafai (Samoa), and Vaughan (Italy).

CANBERRA RAIDERS (10th)
Top pointscorer: Jarrod Croker (190); *Top tryscorer:* Jordan Rapana (21)

Canberra Raiders were among the great underachievers of 2017. They were expected to make a bold charge for Premiership honours. Instead they fell from grace and couldn't even make the play-offs. They were particularly found wanting in the close encounters, winning just two of their 10 games decided by six or fewer points. That's where the men are separated from the boys.

There were, however, a few positives as far as individuals were concerned. Captain Jarrod Croker became only the third Raiders player (after Jason Croker, with 120, and Brett Mullins, 105) to score a century of tries. Jarrod Croker finished the season with a career tally of 107.

Kiwis Four Nations winger Jordan Rapana followed up his 23 tries from 27 games in 2016 with another 21 from 23 this year. And on the other flank Nick Cotric was named Dally M Rookie of the Year, touching down 16 times in his 24 appearances. 'To play every game this year is just surreal – I'm still pinching myself,' said the exciting 20-year-old former Australian Schoolboy representative.

The disappointing season was reflected in the Raiders' sparse representation in the World Cup squads. Josh Hodgson and Elliott Whitehead were there for England, and Rapana and forward Joe Tapine for New Zealand. Others included Joey Leilua, Josh Papalii and Junior Paulo (all Samoa), and Kurt Baptiste (Papua New Guinea).

CANTERBURY BULLDOGS (11th)
Top pointscorer: Kerrod Holland (80); *Top tryscorer:* Marcelo Montoya (12)

Television scriptwriters could not have written a better soap opera than the one acted out at Belmore, as the Bulldogs imploded in 2017.

The adage that the first step by a coach towards his ultimate demise is him signing his first contract proved true. Canterbury failed to reach the play-offs for the first time since Des Hasler moved from Manly in 2012. And even the promise of a contract extension, trumpeted by the Bulldogs hierarchy in April, couldn't save him. And at the end of the season he had been replaced by one of Canterbury's favourite sons, former international and later NSW Under-20s coach Dean Pay.

Maybe the board should have sacked themselves. They had overspent both in 2017 and even more for 2018, expecting a huge increase in the salary cap. And when it didn't come to fruition, they had to start unloading players left, right and centre. They had already signed Test players Aaron Woods from Wests Tigers, Keiran Foran (New Zealand) and Nu Brown (Samoa) for next season. To make room they watched long-serving stand-off Josh Reynolds head for the Tigers, inspirational captain James Graham to the Dragons and Sam Kasiano to Melbourne. And popular hooker Michael Lichaa only stayed after Pay took over and saw him as a key figure in any Canterbury resurgence.

'When you've got guys who have been at the club and with whom everyone loves playing, when they about to leave it unsettles you,' said prop Aiden Tolman. 'That's not an excuse. It happens every year. It's part of the game. But it is something we didn't deal with properly this year.'

On the pitch the internal turmoil manifested itself. The Bulldogs scored only 360 points, the fewest in their past 27 seasons. Some players could hold their heads high. Rookie winger Marcelo Montoya made a real impact, and earned himself a three-year contract extension. And Adam Elliott stamped himself as a star of the future. His fellow second-rowers David Klemmer and Josh Jackson never threw in the towel. Klemmer played in the ANZAC Test and was included in Australia's World Cup squad. Fullback Will Hopoate was named skipper of Mate Ma'a Tonga, Lichaa pulled on the Lebanon Cedars' shirt and Montoya took his place for the Fiji Bati.

SOUTH SYDNEY RABBITOHS (12th)
Top pointscorer: Adam Reynolds (144); *Top tryscorer:* Alex Johnston (22)

Three years after taking out the Premiership, Souths Rabbitohs were struggling to get away from the foot of the NRL Ladder. They were shocked 18-34 by Wests Tigers in their opening game of 2018 (losing marquee player Greg Inglis with a season-ending injury in the process) and never looked like getting the momentum to get them back among the genuine contenders.

Coach Michael Maguire paid the price, shown the door after six years at the helm (to be replaced by his assistant, Anthony Seibold, a protégé of the Storm's Craig Bellamy).

Seibold can approach his new job with some positives from 2017 – not the least being the form of former Australian Four Nations utility Alex Johnston. Johnston scored 22 tries this season, including a mind-boggling five against Penrith in July. And former schoolboy rugby union star Angus Crichton was an eye-catcher in the back row. It won't be long before he is wearing the green and gold for Australia.

England dual-international Sam Burgess never gave up and was rewarded with the accolade of South's best. It was Burgess's third Player of the Year award, having won the George Piggins Medal previously in 2014 and 2016.

Sam Burgess and his brother Tom were both included in England's World Cup squad, hooker Robbie Farah was the captain of Lebanon and Zane Musgrave represented Samoa.

NEW ZEALAND WARRIORS (13th)
Top pointscorer: Shaun Johnson (108); *Top tryscorer:* David Fusitu'a (12)

Once again the Warriors promised so much, but delivered so little, with a nine-match losing streak at the end of the season ensuring the Auckland club's worst result since 2004. They won just one of 13 games away from Mt Smart Stadium, unacceptable if a side is going to give the Premiership title a nudge.

Coach Stephen Kearney had no answers: 'It was disappointing ... that's putting it as simple as I can. We put ourselves in the position to win games, but we couldn't finish off our opponents.'

A few of the Warriors gave their all, notably internationals Simon Mannering, Roger Tuivasa-Sheck, David Fusitu'a and James Gavet. But overall the rest of the side would have received the thumbs down from all but the most avid of supporters.

Mannering and Tuivasa-Shcck joined half Shaun Johnson in the Kiwis World Cup squad, while others got a chance to atone with other nations – Bunty Afoa, Sam Lisone, Ken Maumalo and Jazz Tevaga (all Samoa), together with Ata Hingano and Solomone Kata (who joined Fusitu'a in Tongan colours).

WESTS TIGERS (14th)

Top pointscorer: Tui Lolohea (92); *Top tryscorer:* Kevin Naiqama (9)

What a horror season for the club merged from two of the pioneers of the sport in Australia. Coach Jason Taylor was sacked three games into the season after two massive losses (36-2 to Penrith and 46-6 to Canberra). He was replaced by Ivan Cleary – but it was too late to persuade three of the Tigers' stars – home-grown pin-ups Aaron Woods, James Tedesco and Mitchell Moses – to stay.

Moses went to Parramatta mid-season. Of the other pair 'Teddy' announced he had accepted a lucrative offer from the Roosters, while captain Woods was going to play for Canterbury in 2018. Tedesco's decision was a cruel blow as he finished the year with more tackle breaks than any other player in the NRL – an incredible 175.

As veteran Chris Lawrence, who became equal top try-scorer for the club (his 76 matching Benji Marshall's tally) noted: 'It's the most bizarre season I've had.'

The Tigers won only three home games, the fewest of any season in their history. Nevertheless under Cleary the Tigers seemed to show there could well be light at the end of the tunnel with some solid performances in the closing rounds against top sides Sea Eagles, Roosters and Cowboys. With some clever signings for 2018, including some 'never-take-a-backwards-step' forwards, the dreadful days could be a thing of the past.

Woods and Tedesco made the Prime Minister's XIII line-up for the annual clash with Papua New Guinea. Woods played in the ANZAC Test and the World Cup. Tedesco represented Italy in the World Cup, Kevin Naiqama captained Fiji, Player of the Year Elijah Taylor pulled on the Kiwis shirt, and Moses was with the Lebanon Cedars,

GOLD COAST TITANS (15th)

Top pointscorer: Ash Taylor (96); *Top tryscorer:* Anthony Don (12)

It was a season to forget for the Titans. A huge injury toll, uncertainty about who would eventually own the club and a dreadful start to proceedings (six losses in the first seven matches) said it all.

Coach Neil Henry was sacked and it was a long time before the powers-that-be decided on a replacement – the rookie Garth Brennan. He is an ex-policeman of 18 years experience in handling young offenders and more lately coach of the Penrith Panthers' side which won the NSW Cup before humbling the Papua New Guinea Hunters in the State Championship on NRL Grand Final day. He noted: 'I am a development coach. That's where I get my enjoyment ... seeing these young kids represent their home club. It means more to the player when they make their debut for the area in which they grew up.'

He comes in after a season in which the Titans' marquee player Jarryd Hayne continued to disappoint. Brennan says he is well equipped as a man-manager – and one of his first tasks is to see what makes Hayne tick. Another is to retain playmaker Ash Taylor, who 18 months ago sought him out as a possible mentor. Taylor's form was one of the few bright spots for the Titans in 2017. Despite the Titans' lowly position on the ladder (with fewer wins than in any other season since joining the big league), Taylor set up more tries for teammates than another other player in the NRL.

The club provided just two players for the World Cup – Hayne (Fiji), and Konrad Hurrell (Tonga).

NEWCASTLE KNIGHTS (16th)

Top pointscorer: Trent Hodkinson (97); *Top tryscorer:* Nathan Ross (10)

It was the third wooden spoon for Newcastle. But the Knights, under coach Nathan Brown, are full of hope for the future. And with the most faithful following of fans in the NRL, who can blame them?

SEASON DOWN UNDER - ROUND-UP

NRL PREMIERSHIP FINALS SERIES

QUALIFYING FINALS
Friday 8th September 2017

Sydney Roosters 24 ....Brisbane Broncos 22

Saturday 9th September 2017

Melbourne Storm 18 ....Parramatta Eels 16

ELIMINATION FINALS
Saturday 9th September 2017

Manly Sea Eagles 10 .... Penrith Panthers 22
(at Allianz Stadium, Sydney)

Sunday 10th September 2017

Cronulla Sharks 14 ....North Queensland Cowboys 15
(at Allianz Stadium, Sydney)

SEMI-FINALS
Friday 15th September 2017

Brisbane Broncos 13.......................................Penrith Panthers 6

Saturday 16th September 2017

Parramatta Eels 16...........................North Queensland Cowboys 24

PRELIMINARY FINALS
Friday 22nd September 2017

Melbourne Storm 30 .... Brisbane Broncos 0

Saturday 23rd September 2017

Sydney Roosters 16 ....North Queensland Cowboys 29

NRL GRAND FINAL

Sunday 1st October 2017

MELBOURNE STORM 34 NORTH QUEENSLAND COWBOYS 6

STORM: 1 Billy Slater; 2 Suliasi Vunivalu; 3 Will Chambers; 4 Curtis Scott; 5 Josh Addo-Carr; 6 Cameron Munster; 7 Cooper Cronk; 8 Jesse Bromwich; 9 Cameron Smith (C); 10 Jordan McLean; 11 Felise Kaufusi; 12 Tohu Harris; 13 Dale Finucane. Subs (all used): 14 Kenny Bromwich; 15 Nelson Asofa-Solomona; 16 Tim Glasby; 17 Slade Griffin.
Tries: Addo-Carr (19, 72), Kaufusi (27), Slater (31), Finucane (63), Scott (67); **Goals:** Smith 5/6.
COWBOYS: 1 Lachlan Coote; 2 Kyle Feldt; 3 Justin O'Neill; 4 Kane Linnett; 5 Antonio Winterstein; 6 Te Maire Martin; 7 Michael Morgan; 17 Shaun Fensom; 9 Jake Granville; 10 Scott Bolton; 11 Gavin Cooper (C); 12 Ethan Lowe; 13 Jason Taumalolo. Subs (all used): 8 John Asiata; 14 Ben Hampton; 15 Coen Hess; 16 Corey Jensen.
Try: Martin (48); **Goals:** Lowe 1/1.
Clive Churchill Medal: Billy Slater (Melbourne Storm).
Rugby Leaguer & League Express Men of the Match:
Storm: Billy Slater; *Cowboys:* Gavin Cooper.
Half-time: 18-0; **Referees:** Matt Cecchin & Gerard Sutton.
Attendance: 79,722 *(at ANZ Stadium, Sydney).*

NRL PREMIERSHIP - FINAL TABLE

	P	W	D	L	B	F	A	D	Pts
Melbourne Storm	24	20	0	4	2	633	336	297	44
Sydney Roosters	24	17	0	7	2	500	428	72	38
Brisbane Broncos	24	16	0	8	2	597	433	164	36
Parramatta Eels	24	16	0	8	2	496	457	39	36
Cronulla Sharks	24	15	0	9	2	476	417	69	34
Manly Sea Eagles	24	14	0	10	2	552	512	40	32
Penrith Panthers	24	13	0	11	2	504	459	45	30
North Queensland Cowboys	24	13	0	11	2	467	443	24	30
St George Illawarra Dragons	24	12	0	12	2	533	450	83	28
Canberra Raiders	24	11	0	13	2	558	497	61	26
Canterbury Bulldogs	24	10	0	14	2	360	455	-95	24
South Sydney Rabbitohs	24	9	0	15	2	464	564	-100	22
New Zealand Warriors	24	7	0	17	2	444	595	-151	18
Wests Tigers	24	7	0	17	2	413	571	-158	18
Gold Coast Titans	24	7	0	17	2	448	638	-190	18
Newcastle Knights	24	5	0	19	2	428	648	-220	14

LEADING POINTSCORERS

Nathan Cleary	Penrith Panthers	228
Cameron Smith	Melbourne Storm	192
Gareth Widdop	St George Illawarra Dragons	191
Jarrod Croker	Canberra Raiders	190
Jordan Kahu	Brisbane Broncos	187

TOP TRYSCORERS

Josh Addo-Carr	Melbourne Storm	23
Suliasi Vunivalu	Melbourne Storm	23
Semi Radradra	Parramatta Eels	22
Alex Johnston	South Sydney Rabbitohs	22
Jordan Rapana	Canberra Raiders	21

HOLDEN CUP GRAND FINAL *(Under-20s)*
Sunday 1st October 2017

Manly Sea Eagles 20 ....Parramatta Eels 18
(at ANZ Stadium, Sydney)

STATE CHAMPIONSHIP *(Winners of Queensland and NSW Cups)*
Sunday 1st October 2017

Papua New Guinea Hunters 18 ....Penrith Panthers 42
(at ANZ Stadium, Sydney)

DALLY M AWARDS

Dally M Medal (Player of the Year):
Cameron Smith (Melbourne Storm)
Provan Summons Medal (People's Choice):
Clinton Gutherson (Parramatta Eels)
Coach of the Year: Craig Bellamy (Melbourne Storm)
Captain of the Year: Cameron Smith (Melbourne Storm)
Rookie of the Year: Nick Cotric (Canberra Raiders)
Holden Cup (Under-20s) Player of the Year:
Jake Clifford (North Queensland Cowboys)
Female Player of the Year:
Simaima Taufa (Australia & New South Wales)

An average home attendance of 15,619 is one that the leading Premiership sides would envy. And the Knights' final game of the season, against the Sharks, drew no less than 20,535.

As Super League fans know, Brown's coaching credentials are impeccable – now he has to get just that little piece of luck to succeed in the NRL. Success will be on the back of several 'no-names'. But one of those little-known figures, Mitch Barnett showed how it could be done. The 21-year-old prop Daniel Saifiti is another, averaging some 160 metres in stirring runs in his most recent seven appearances.

The Knights have lost Test centre Dane Gagai, but have some wonderful recruits including Aiden Guerra and Connor Watson (Roosters), Herman Ese'ese and Tautau Moga (Broncos) and the wonderful youngster Kalyn Ponga (Cowboys).

Gagai played for Australia this year. He wore the green and gold at the World Cup, with Peter Mata'utia playing for Samoa.

Season Down Under
STATE OF ORIGIN

The Queensland Maroons won their eleventh State of Origin series in twelve years, winning the series 2-1 with a dominant 22-6 win in the decider in Brisbane.

After New South Wales' performance in Origin I, when they administered one of the most comprehensive defeats - by 28-4 - ever handed to Queensland, Sydney critics were boasting how it was the start of a new Blues dynasty.

But after Johnathan Thurston kept Maroons hopes alive with a touchline conversion that gave them an 18-16 win in Sydney, there was no end to the Queensland dynasty in sight, with the emergence of a new breed of young stars.

Much to the annoyance of members of the Sydney media, who almost unanimously had been tipping a victory for the Blues, the Queenslanders gave New South Wales a hammering in the Brisbane re-match.

The Maroons were without such revered injured international figures as Johnathan Thurston, Greg Inglis, Matt Scott and Darius Boyd but their replacements were unfazed.

They were led by 22-year-old Cameron Munster, who took over Thurston's role as the Maroons' No 6.

And young Maroons winger Dane Gagai from Newcastle was outstanding, named winner of the Wally Lewis Medal as Man of the Series.

The decider drew an Australian television audience of almost 4.18 million, the largest for any sporting event in 2017.

In game 1, New South Wales administered one of the most comprehensive defeats - by 28-4 - ever handed to Queensland in the history of State of Origin.

The game was played at a tremendous pace with the ball almost constantly in play for the whole first half, with virtually no handling errors from either side.

The Blues led 12-4 at the interval after a first half of almost mistake-free football. But in the second half, with Cronulla forward Andrew Fifita reminding many supporters of the great Artie Beetson, they cut loose to score another 16 points without reply by the outgunned Maroons, who suddenly were looking like a team that had passed its sell-by date.

Fifita's superb charges set up James Maloney's try in the seventh minute and the Mitchell Pearce try in the 40th. Queensland simply had no answer for his power, strength, speed and offloads, and to his size and footwork. He ran for 183 metres and made eleven tackle busts. And when he took a break, Queensland then had to deal with a rampant David Klemmer coming off the bench, running for another 172 metres.

The Blues were relentless and Queensland finished the night battered and bruised and well beaten. Their defence in the second half was crucial, with both Josh Dugan and James Tedesco making try-saving tackles to deny Aidan Guerra and Matt Gillett respectively.

STATE OF ORIGIN - GAME I

Wednesday 31st May 2017

QUEENSLAND 4 NEW SOUTH WALES 28

QUEENSLAND: 1 Darius Boyd (Brisbane Broncos); 2 Corey Oates (Brisbane Broncos); 3 Will Chambers (Melbourne Storm); 4 Justin O'Neill (North Queensland Cowboys); 5 Dane Gagai (Newcastle Knights); 6 Anthony Milford (Brisbane Broncos); 7 Cooper Cronk (Melbourne Storm); 8 Dylan Napa (Sydney Roosters); 9 Cameron Smith (Melbourne Storm) (C); 10 Nate Myles (Manly Sea Eagles); 11 Josh Papalii (Canberra Raiders); 12 Matt Gillett (Brisbane Broncos); 13 Josh McGuire (Brisbane Broncos). Subs (all used): 14 Michael Morgan (North Queensland Cowboys); 15 Sam Thaiday (Brisbane Broncos); 16 Aidan Guerra (Sydney Roosters); 17 Jacob Lillyman (New Zealand Warriors).
Try: Oates (35); **Goals:** Smith 0/1.
NEW SOUTH WALES: 1 James Tedesco (Wests Tigers); 2 Blake Ferguson (Sydney Roosters); 3 Josh Dugan (St George Illawarra Dragons); 4 Jarryd Hayne (Gold Coast Titans); 5 Brett Morris (Canterbury Bulldogs); 6 James Maloney (Cronulla Sharks); 7 Mitchell Pearce (Sydney Roosters); 8 Aaron Woods (Wests Tigers); 9 Nathan Peats (Gold Coast Titans); 10 Andrew Fifita (Cronulla Sharks); 11 Josh Jackson (Canterbury Bulldogs); 12 Boyd Cordner (Sydney Roosters) (C); 13 Tyson Frizell (St George Illawarra Dragons). Subs (all used): 14 David Klemmer (Canterbury Bulldogs); 15 Wade Graham (Cronulla Sharks); 16 Jake Trbojevic (Manly Sea Eagles); 17 Jack Bird (Cronulla Sharks).
Tries: Maloney (6), Pearce (40), Tedesco (52), Fifita (55), Hayne (60); **Goals:** Maloney 4/5.
Rugby Leaguer & League Express Men of the Match:
Queensland: Cooper Cronk; *New South Wales:* Andrew Fifita.
Half-time: 4-12; **Referees:** Matt Cecchin & Gerard Sutton; **Attendance:** 50,390 *(at Suncorp Stadium, Brisbane).*

NSW put the game to bed early in the second half. James Tedesco scored the first try after the interval, forcing his way over the line brilliantly, despite the attention of several Queensland defenders.

Fifita then scored himself, taking advantage of the most crucial mistake of the night, a dropped ball from Justin O'Neill just five metres from his own line, to score the easiest try of the night before Jarryd Hayne sliced through the Queensland defence to score in his first Origin appearance since 2014, pushing the scoreline to 28-4.

Debutant hooker Nathan Peats was another Blue to excel, on the field for 80 minutes and getting through an enormous amount of work against his opposite number, Cameron Smith.

For the Queenslanders, Smith and Cooper Cronk always looked capable of pulling something out of the fire, but they were simply outplayed on the night.

Corey Oates was the other star for Queensland, defusing a series of NSW bombs in the first half and taking Cronk's bomb in the 35th minute to score the Maroons' only try.

It was the first time since 2009 that the Blues had scored 28 points, and their biggest winning margin since the 32-10 scoreline in 2005.

The 24-point loss was Queensland's heaviest ever at home in the Origin era. The previous worst was the 22-point loss in 2005.

After New South Wales' dominant performance in Origin I, misguided Sydney critics were boasting how it was the start of a new Blues' Dynasty.

And when the Maroons trailed 16-6 at the interval in the second encounter, at Homebush, these very same commentators had wide smiles that suggested: 'We told you so!'.

But you write off legendary players at your peril. The Blues failed to score a point in the second spell and lost the game at the death by 18-16.

The Maroons had a long list of legendary players. Johnathan Thurston, carrying what proved to be a season-ending injury to his right shoulder for most of the match; Billy Slater, back in the interstate fray after an absence of 735 days; Cameron Smith (in his 40th Origin appearance), Cooper Cronk (20th) and Darius Boyd (27th). And they pulled off a miracle win with a try in the final minute of the action and a JT conversion from wide out on the right flank in the last couple of seconds.

The Blues thrived on quick play-the-balls early in the action. But when the Maroons had possession they sent the ball wide to their flanks.

It was there that Queensland scored first, with debutant Valentine Holmes diving though the air to touch down in the left corner after some superb lead-up work by Boyd, in the unfamiliar role as a centre.

It was a milestone - the 600th try in Origin history.

It didn't faze the New South Welshmen, who struck back almost immediately with a try to Gold Coast centre Jarryd Hayne. And James Maloney's conversion levelled the scores.

STATE OF ORIGIN - GAME II

Wednesday 21st June 2017

NEW SOUTH WALES 16 QUEENSLAND 18

NEW SOUTH WALES: 1 James Tedesco (Wests Tigers); 2 Blake Ferguson (Sydney Roosters); 3 Josh Dugan (St George Illawarra Dragons); 4 Jarryd Hayne (Gold Coast Titans); 5 Brett Morris (Canterbury Bulldogs); 6 James Maloney (Cronulla Sharks); 7 Mitchell Pearce (Sydney Roosters); 8 Aaron Woods (Wests Tigers); 9 Nathan Peats (Gold Coast Titans); 10 Andrew Fifita (Cronulla Sharks); 11 Josh Jackson (Canterbury Bulldogs); 12 Boyd Cordner (Sydney Roosters) (C); 13 Tyson Frizell (St George Illawarra Dragons). Subs (all used): 14 David Klemmer (Canterbury Bulldogs); 15 Wade Graham (Cronulla Sharks); 16 Jake Trbojevic (Manly Sea Eagles); 17 Jack Bird (Cronulla Sharks).
Tries: Hayne (14), Morris (24), Pearce (25); **Goals:** Maloney 2/3.
QUEENSLAND: 1 Billy Slater (Melbourne Storm); 2 Valentine Holmes (Cronulla Sharks); 3 Will Chambers (Melbourne Storm); 4 Darius Boyd (Brisbane Broncos); 5 Dane Gagai (Newcastle Knights); 6 Johnathan Thurston (North Queensland Cowboys); 7 Cooper Cronk (Melbourne Storm); 8 Dylan Napa (Sydney Roosters); 9 Cameron Smith (Melbourne Storm) (C); 10 Jarrod Wallace (Gold Coast Titans); 11 Gavin Cooper (North Queensland Cowboys); 12 Matt Gillett (Brisbane Broncos); 13 Josh McGuire (Brisbane Broncos). Subs (all used): 14 Michael Morgan (North Queensland Cowboys); 15 Josh Papalii (Canberra Raiders); 16 Coen Hess (North Queensland Cowboys); 17 Tim Glasby (Melbourne Storm).
Tries: Holmes (9), Gagai (52, 79); **Goals:** Thurston 3/3.
Rugby Leaguer & League Express Men of the Match:
New South Wales: Jake Trbojevic; *Queensland:* Johnathan Thurston.
Half-time: 16-6; **Referees:** Matt Cecchin & Gerard Sutton;
Attendance: 82,259 *(at ANZ Stadium, Sydney).*

Midway through the half, the Blues scored two tries within the space of as many minutes, from Brett Morris and Mitchell Pearce, to stretch the lead to ten points.

That's the way it remained until half-time with two NSW try-saving tackles in the closing seconds, with young Manly prop Jake Trobojevic grassing Cooper Cronk centimetres from the stripe before Josh Dugan held up Michael Morgan over the tryline.

It was State of Origin Rugby League at its very best!

The Queenslanders got back into the equation twelve minutes after the interval with a wonderful passing rush involving Josh McGuire, Cronk and Will Chambers for Dane Gagai to score a vital try.

However, they had to wait until the closing minute to pull the match out of the fire. Constant pressure eventually told in the closing minutes as Michael Morgan flicked out a pass and Gagai crashed over for his second try. Thurston had already kicked two conversions from wide out and he made no mistake with this one either as the Maroons kept alive their hopes of winning the series outright.

In the decider back in Brisbane, the Queenslanders gave New South Wales a 22-6 drubbing. And the final score was really no reflection of the one-sided display.

The Maroons were without such revered international figures as Johnathan Thurston, Greg Inglis, Matt Scott and Darius Boyd. But their replacements were unfazed, stepping up a rung to show they were more than ready to carry the hopes of Queensland in the future.

They were led by 22-year-old Cameron Munster, who took over Thurston's role as the Maroons' No 6. And he was ably supported by the next generation of Maroons, including Man of the Series Dane Gagai, hat-trick hero Valentine Holmes and forwards Dylan Napa, Josh McGuire and Coen Hess, as well as veterans Smith, Cooper Cronk and Billy Slater.

Slater proved why he should have been playing in the first Origin clash with another five-star effort.

STATE OF ORIGIN - GAME III

Wednesday 12th July 2017

QUEENSLAND 22 NEW SOUTH WALES 6

QUEENSLAND: 1 Billy Slater (Melbourne Storm); 2 Valentine Holmes (Cronulla Sharks); 3 Will Chambers (Melbourne Storm); 4 Michael Morgan (North Queensland Cowboys); 5 Dane Gagai (Newcastle Knights); 6 Cameron Munster (Melbourne Storm); 7 Cooper Cronk (Melbourne Storm); 8 Dylan Napa (Sydney Roosters); 9 Cameron Smith (Melbourne Storm) (C); 10 Jarrod Wallace (Gold Coast Titans); 11 Gavin Cooper (North Queensland Cowboys); 12 Matt Gillett (Brisbane Broncos); 13 Josh McGuire (Brisbane Broncos). Subs (all used): 14 Ben Hunt (Brisbane Broncos); 15 Josh Papalii (Canberra Raiders); 16 Coen Hess (North Queensland Cowboys); 17 Tim Glasby (Melbourne Storm).
Tries: Holmes (15, 26, 60), Wallace (66); **Goals:** Smith 3/5.
NEW SOUTH WALES: 1 James Tedesco (Wests Tigers); 2 Brett Morris (Canterbury Bulldogs); 3 Josh Dugan (St George Illawarra Dragons); 4 Jarryd Hayne (Gold Coast Titans); 5 Blake Ferguson (Sydney Roosters); 6 James Maloney (Cronulla Sharks); 7 Mitchell Pearce (Sydney Roosters); 8 Aaron Woods (Wests Tigers); 9 Nathan Peats (Gold Coast Titans); 10 Andrew Fifita (Cronulla Sharks); 11 Boyd Cordner (Sydney Roosters) (C); 12 Josh Jackson (Canterbury Bulldogs); 13 Tyson Frizell (St George Illawarra Dragons). Subs (all used): 14 David Klemmer (Canterbury Bulldogs); 15 Wade Graham (Cronulla Sharks); 16 Jake Trbojevic (Manly Sea Eagles); 17 Jack Bird (Cronulla Sharks).
Try: Dugan (47); **Goals:** Maloney 1/1.
Rugby Leaguer & League Express Men of the Match:
Queensland: Cameron Smith; *New South Wales:* David Klemmer.
Half-time: 12-0; **Referees:** Matt Cecchin & Gerard Sutton;
Attendance: 52,540 *(at Suncorp Stadium, Brisbane).*

Wally Lewis Medal (Man of the Series): Dane Gagai (Queensland).

There was great organisation from the Queensland attack early in the action, resulting in the first of the three tries to Holmes before the evergreen Cronk was denied one because the video bunker ruled he had lost the ball as he slid across the stripe.

But it wasn't too long before Cronk put in a superb low, flat kick across the pitch. It landed right on the chest of Holmes, who was in for his second try of the evening.

And right on half-time Holmes was almost in for a third, but the final pass was ruled to have been forward.

Early in the second spell some brilliance by Josh Dugan brought the Blues back into the equation with a wonderful try.

But it was a brief respite as Munster set up two quick Queensland tries, including the third to Holmes, to give the Maroons their winning 22-6 lead.

Smith called Thurston up onto the podium to help him lift the Origin shield, calling him the greatest player ever to pull on a Maroon shirt.

2016 FOUR NATIONS
Australia back on top

Australia won the 2016 Four Nations tournament staged in England and sponsored by bookmakers Ladbrokes. The Kangaroos, coached by former playing legend Mal Meninga, beat New Zealand 34-8 at Anfield to not only re-gain the Four Nations crown they lost to the Kiwis in 2014, but also to return to the top of the Rugby League International Federation world rankings. The final at Liverpool FC's soccer ground attracted a crowd of 40,042 fans despite England not qualifying. England, coached for the first time by Australian Wayne Bennett, lost to both Australia and New Zealand, who were held to a draw in their third game by surprise packets Scotland.

Australia, fielding a side without Johnathan Thurston and Greg Inglis, made relatively light work of Scotland, who were down 30-0 on 35 minutes, at Hull KR's KC Lightstream Stadium on the last Friday of October.

Australia coach Mal Meninga was left facing a selection dilemma, with Penrith fullback Matt Moylan putting on a magnificent performance on debut in place of the rested Darius Boyd. On the wings, Blake Ferguson and Josh Mansour were given the nod over Cronulla flier Valentine Holmes and both impressed in try-scoring performances. And James Maloney, a key in Cronulla's 2016 NRL Premiership-winning season, scored 18 points in an impressive display at stand-off.

Some of the Bravehearts' Super League contingent showed their quality. Adam Walker, booed throughout by the vociferous Hull Kingston Rovers contingent in attendance following his move to St Helens, was exceptional. Danny Brough did a great job with his kicking game, while Huddersfield team-mate Ryan Brierley scored Scotland's first ever try against the green and golds.

Scotland started the game well but Australia's forwards soon had them on the back foot. Ferguson was the first scorer and, shortly after, Cameron Smith's stunning reverse kick bamboozled Scotland and Cooper Cronk touched down to score.

Cronk then turned provider as he combined with Moylan to send Maloney to the line, before Cronk scored once again as the impressive Tyson Frizell ran rampant down the left edge. That made the score 22-0 after just 15 minutes but Scotland ensured

FOUR NATIONS - GAME ONE

Friday 28th October 2016

AUSTRALIA 54 SCOTLAND 12

AUSTRALIA: 1 Matt Moylan (Penrith Panthers); 5 Blake Ferguson (Sydney Roosters); 4 Josh Dugan (St George Illawarra Dragons); 3 Justin O'Neill (North Queensland Cowboys); 2 Josh Mansour (Penrith Panthers); 6 James Maloney (Cronulla Sharks); 7 Cooper Cronk (Melbourne Storm); 8 Aaron Woods (Wests Tigers); 9 Cameron Smith (Melbourne Storm) (C); 10 David Klemmer (Canterbury Bulldogs); 11 Sam Thaiday (Brisbane Broncos); 12 Tyson Frizell (St George Illawarra Dragons); 13 Jake Trbojevic (Manly Sea Eagles). Subs (all used): 14 Jake Friend (Sydney Roosters); 15 Shannon Boyd (Canberra Raiders); 16 Trent Merrin (Penrith Panthers); 17 Michael Morgan (North Queensland Cowboys).
Tries: Ferguson (6), Cronk (10, 15), Maloney (13), Mansour (26, 35), Dugan (44), Frizell (66), Morgan (68), Trbojevic (80); **Goals:** Maloney 7/10.
SCOTLAND: 1 Lachlan Coote (North Queensland Cowboys); 2 Lewis Tierney (Wigan Warriors); 3 Euan Aitken (St George Illawarra Dragons); 4 Kane Linnett (North Queensland Cowboys); 5 Matthew Russell (Warrington Wolves); 6 Danny Brough (Huddersfield Giants) (C); 7 Ryan Brierley (Huddersfield Giants); 8 Adam Walker (Hull Kingston Rovers); 9 Liam Hood (Leigh Centurions); 10 Luke Douglas (Gold Coast Titans); 11 Danny Addy (Bradford Bulls); 12 Dale Ferguson (Bradford Bulls); 13 Ben Kavanagh (Bradford Bulls). Subs (all used): 14 Ben Hellewell (London Broncos); 15 Sheldon Powe-Hobbs (Northern Pride); 16 Sam Brooks (Widnes Vikings); 17 Billy McConnachie (Ipswich Jets).
Tries: Brierley (38), Kavanagh (58); **Goals:** Brough 2/2.
Rugby Leaguer & League Express Men of the Match:
Australia: Matt Moylan; *Scotland:* Adam Walker.
Penalty count: 4-4; **Half-time:** 30-6; **Referee:** Ben Thaler (England); **Attendance:** 5,337 *(at KCOM Lightstream Stadium, Hull).*

thereafter that they wouldn't be humiliated, with a gutsy display epitomised by Liam Hood's thunderous tackle on Moylan.

That tackle did little to disrupt Moylan's performance, however, with the Panthers fullback twice playing a key role to put club-mate Mansour over for tries in the 26th and 35th minute.

Scotland deservedly got on the scoreboard through Brierley, who instinctively raced on to Brough's deflected kick to score by the posts, leaving Australia 30-6 ahead at the break.

Australia, with Smith withdrawn, extended their lead in the 44th minute through Josh Dugan, before the offloading Walker's smart pass at the line allowed Ben Kavanagh to score.

Australia took over twenty minutes to add another try, albeit they did score twice in as many minutes. Frizell got a deserved try as he crashed over the line on the left edge before Michael Morgan scored from the following set after another break.

In the end, Australia broke the half-century with the final action. Against a tiring Scotland side, Jake Trbojevic found a gap to score from close range, with Maloney's seventh goal from ten attempts ending the rout.

Shaun Johnson proved to be the scourge of England again, this time with not one as in the 2013 World Cup semi-final, but two telling plays.

The first came in the moments after half-time when, with England pressing and looking to overturn the two-point half-time lead the Kiwis had established, Johnson plucked a Gareth Widdop pass out of mid-air to race the length of the field and score. Had he not snaffled that pass, John Bateman seemed certain to score a try.

Then on 65 minutes, with the game level at 16-all thanks to an admirable England fightback, Johnson seized the moment once again, kicking a short-range field goal.

England had plenty of pressure to overturn that one-point deficit but they didn't have the composure to win the game, that after totally dominating the Kiwis for the first 25 minutes of the game but only having two penalty goals from the boot of Widdop to show for their efforts.

FOUR NATIONS - GAME TWO

Saturday 29th October 2016

ENGLAND 16 NEW ZEALAND 17

ENGLAND: 1 Jonny Lomax (St Helens); 2 Jermaine McGillvary (Huddersfield Giants); 3 Kallum Watkins (Leeds Rhinos); 4 Dan Sarginson (Wigan Warriors); 5 Ryan Hall (Leeds Rhinos); 6 Gareth Widdop (St George Illawarra Dragons); 7 Luke Gale (Castleford Tigers); 8 Chris Hill (Warrington Wolves); 9 Josh Hodgson (Canberra Raiders); 10 James Graham (Canterbury Bulldogs); 11 John Bateman (Wigan Warriors); 12 Elliott Whitehead (Canberra Raiders); 13 Sam Burgess (South Sydney Rabbitohs) (C). Subs (all used): 14 Tom Burgess (South Sydney Rabbitohs); 15 George Burgess (South Sydney Rabbitohs); 16 Mike Cooper (St George Illawarra Dragons); 17 Daryl Clark (Warrington Wolves).
Tries: McGillvary (48), Hall (60); **Goals:** Widdop 4/4.
NEW ZEALAND: 1 Jordan Kahu (Brisbane Broncos); 5 Jordan Rapana (Canberra Raiders); 4 Shaun Kenny-Dowall (Sydney Roosters); 3 Solomon Kata (New Zealand Warriors); 2 Jason Nightingale (St George Illawarra Dragons); 6 Thomas Leuluai (New Zealand Warriors); 7 Shaun Johnson (New Zealand Warriors); 8 Jesse Bromwich (Melbourne Storm) (C); 9 Issac Luke (New Zealand Warriors); 10 Jared Waerea-Hargreaves (Sydney Roosters); 11 Kevin Proctor (Melbourne Storm); 12 Tohu Harris (Melbourne Storm); 13 Jason Taumalolo (North Queensland Cowboys). Subs (all used): 14 Lewis Brown (Manly Sea Eagles); 15 Martin Taupau (Manly Sea Eagles); 16 Manu Ma'u (Parramatta Eels); 17 Adam Blair (Brisbane Broncos).
Tries: Rapana (35, 55), Johnson (42); **Goals:** Kahu 2/4;
Field goal: Johnson (65).
Rugby Leaguer & League Express Men of the Match:
England: Jermaine McGillvary; *New Zealand:* Shaun Johnson.
Penalty count: 6-8; **Half-time:** 4-6; **Referee:** Robert Hicks (England); **Attendance:** 24,070 *(at John Smith's Stadium, Huddersfield)*.

In that early spell, Jermaine McGillvary was held up close to the line, Dan Sarginson wasted the chance to put Ryan Hall over unchallenged in the corner and James Graham was denied a try by the video referee for a double-movement.

It proved costly. The Kiwis converted a penalty of their own from Jordan Kahu and when Widdop kicked the resulting kick-off out on the full it piled the pressure on the hosts. Johnson forced England to drop out on two consecutive occasions - he did it six times in all throughout the afternoon - before playing a crucial role in the sweeping move which opened up just enough space for Jordan Rapana to touch down in the right corner. Though Kahu hooked the conversion attempt wide, the Kiwis had somehow opened up a half-time lead.

And that lead was quickly extended on 42 minutes thanks to Johnson's interception

England's Sam Burgess brought down by New Zealand's Adam Blair

try. Within six minutes the gap was reduced when McGillvary touched down on the right. But Rapana's second try seven minutes later pushed the gap back out to six.

Crucially, another missed conversion from Kahu left it as a one-score game and when Widdop's improvisation allowed Hall just enough room to squeeze over in the corner, Widdop nailed the touchline conversion to spark wild celebrations inside the John Smith's Stadium.

Suddenly, England looked the more likely. Their energy levels were up and they were on the hunt for more points. But in a rare moment of possession in the England end, Johnson struck once again with the decisive one-pointer.

In the first game of a Saturday afternoon double header at the Ricoh Arena in Coventry, England laboured their way to a 38-12 win after falling behind in the opening half-hour against Scotland.

145

England were colourless in the opening 30 minutes before eventually coming to life and running in seven tries to pick up their first win of the Four Nations.

Led by Danny Brough, the Bravehearts gave a fantastic account of themselves, taking a deserved 8-0 lead through Kane Linnett and Matty Russell tries, before things started to unravel.

Ill-discipline cost them dear, with Brough's sin-binning just prior to the hour mark the tipping point, effectively killing off any chance they had of a grand comeback, although Dale Ferguson's try ten minutes from time epitomised the never-say-die attitude of the Bravehearts.

England finally got into the game, surging forwards into the Scotland end and, after a penalty gave them yet more opportunity to strike, they did so when Luke Gale's flat pass sent Elliott Whitehead over from close range, with Gale's conversion narrowing the gap to two.

That was perhaps the most England deserved following a lack-lustre half from the host nation, but they managed to get their noses in front when the Gale-Whitehead partnership bore further fruit soon after, this time with Gale's delicate kick finding its way into the arms of the Canberra forward for try number two.

After the break, recalled stand-off George Williams grew more and more lively. First he dummied his way across the Scotland line. Then his pass sent St Helens centre Mark Percival over before he put in a superb kick for Ryan Hall to collect and make it 30 tries in 30 England appearances.

Brough's yellow card for a professional foul then allowed England to get on the front foot again and, after Jonny Lomax's smart pass put Jermaine McGillvary over, a bustling break down the middle by Sam Burgess saw Gale claim his first international try.

After Ferguson's try, the last word went to England - in a somewhat unusual manner. Penalty number 16 on the hooter sparked a debate about whether to go for goal and take a guaranteed two points to boost the points difference column, but as the referee pointed to the sticks, captain Sam Burgess overruled the decision.

So England pressed on, were duly awarded penalty number 17 and again refused the easy two points, finally crossing when more neat play from Williams allowed Wigan team-mate Liam Farrell to touch down, with Gale's conversion turning four points into six.

FOUR NATIONS - GAME THREE

Saturday 5th November 2016

ENGLAND 38 SCOTLAND 12

ENGLAND: 1 Jonny Lomax (St Helens); 2 Jermaine McGillvary (Huddersfield Giants); 3 Kallum Watkins (Leeds Rhinos); 4 Mark Percival (St Helens); 5 Ryan Hall (Leeds Rhinos); 6 George Williams (Wigan Warriors); 7 Luke Gale (Castleford Tigers); 8 Chris Hill (Warrington Wolves); 9 Josh Hodgson (Canberra Raiders); 10 Scott Taylor (Hull FC); 11 Liam Farrell (Wigan Warriors); 12 Elliott Whitehead (Canberra Raiders); 13 Sam Burgess (South Sydney Rabbitohs) (C). Subs (all used): 14 Tom Burgess (South Sydney Rabbitohs); 15 George Burgess (South Sydney Rabbitohs); 16 Mike Cooper (St George Illawarra Dragons); 17 Daryl Clark (Warrington Wolves).
Tries: Whitehead (28, 34), Percival (49), Hall (55), McGillvary (58), Gale (64), Farrell (80); **Goals:** Gale 5/7.
SCOTLAND: 1 Lachlan Coote (North Queensland Cowboys); 2 Lewis Tierney (Wigan Warriors); 3 Euan Aitken (St George Illawarra Dragons); 4 Kane Linnett (North Queensland Cowboys); 5 Matthew Russell (Warrington Wolves); 6 Danny Brough (Huddersfield Giants) (C); 7 Danny Addy (Bradford Bulls); 8 Adam Walker (Hull Kingston Rovers); 9 Liam Hood (Leigh Centurions); 10 Luke Douglas (Gold Coast Titans); 11 Ben Hellewell (London Broncos); 12 Dale Ferguson (Bradford Bulls); 13 Ben Kavanagh (Bradford Bulls). Subs (all used): 14 Tyler Cassel (Wests Tigers); 15 Frankie Mariano (Castleford Tigers); 16 Callum Phillips (Workington Town); 17 Sam Brooks (Widnes Vikings).
Tries: Linnett (6), Russell (24), Ferguson (70); **Goals:** Brough 0/3.
Sin bin: Brough (58) - professional foul.
Rugby Leaguer & League Express Men of the Match:
England: George Williams; *Scotland:* Danny Brough.
Penalty count: 17-7; **Half-time:** 12-8; **Referee:** Gerard Sutton (Australia).

FOUR NATIONS - GAME FOUR

Saturday 5th November 2016

AUSTRALIA 14 NEW ZEALAND 8

AUSTRALIA: 1 Darius Boyd (Brisbane Broncos); 5 Blake Ferguson (Sydney Roosters); 4 Justin O'Neill (North Queensland Cowboys); 3 Greg Inglis (South Sydney Rabbitohs); 2 Valentine Holmes (Cronulla Sharks); 7 Johnathan Thurston (North Queensland Cowboys); 6 Michael Morgan (North Queensland Cowboys); 8 Matt Scott (North Queensland Cowboys); 9 Cameron Smith (Melbourne Storm) (C); 10 Aaron Woods (Wests Tigers); 11 Boyd Cordner (Sydney Roosters); 12 Matt Gillett (Brisbane Broncos); 13 Trent Merrin (Penrith Panthers). Subs (all used): 14 Shannon Boyd (Canberra Raiders); 15 James Maloney (Cronulla Sharks); 16 David Klemmer (Canterbury Bulldogs); 17 Sam Thaiday (Brisbane Broncos).
Tries: Ferguson (9), Thurston (13); **Goals:** Thurston 3/4.
NEW ZEALAND: 1 Jordan Kahu (Brisbane Broncos); 5 Jordan Rapana (Canberra Raiders); 3 Solomone Kata (New Zealand Warriors); 4 Shaun Kenny-Dowall (Sydney Roosters); 2 Gerard Beale (Cronulla Sharks); 6 Thomas Leuluai (New Zealand Warriors); 7 Shaun Johnson (New Zealand Warriors); 8 Jesse Bromwich (Melbourne Storm) (C); 9 Issac Luke (New Zealand Warriors); 17 Greg Eastwood (Canterbury Bulldogs); 11 Kevin Proctor (Melbourne Storm); 12 Tohu Harris (Melbourne Storm); 13 Jason Taumalolo (North Queensland Cowboys). Subs (all used): 10 Adam Blair (Brisbane Broncos); 14 Lewis Brown (Manly Sea Eagles); 15 Martin Taupau (Manly Sea Eagles); 16 Manu Ma'u (Parramatta Eels).
Tries: Kata (48), Rapana (76); **Goals:** Johnson 0/2.
Rugby Leaguer & League Express Men of the Match:
Australia: Blake Ferguson; *New Zealand:* Shaun Johnson.
Penalty count: 7-4; **Half-time:** 10-0; **Referee:** Ben Cummins (Australia).

Attendance: 21,009 *(at Ricoh Arena, Coventry)*
(Games three and four played as a double-header)

Australia accounted for New Zealand 14-8 in the second game of the Coventry double-header, which ended in thrilling fashion.

With five minutes to go, the result looked done and dusted, with Australia comfortable 14-4 in front and the Kiwis having showed little in attack. But a flash of brilliance from New Zealand scrum-half Shaun Johnson in the 76th minute threatened an unlikely turnaround.

Johnson, whose kicking game had created the win over England the week before but had been controlled well by Australia, produced an amazing midfield chip over the top out of his own half. He regathered and passed in one movement to Shaun Kenny-Dowall who sent Jordan Rapana in the right corner.

Johnson's conversion attempt missed but, suddenly, the Kiwis were only six points behind and full of energy. And it could so easily have been a draw as, with one last thrilling attack in the final seconds, Johnson dashed for the line down the right from first receiver and looked to have pinched it. But the video referee rightly ruled he had been prevented from grounding the ball by the desperate tackle of Johnathan Thurston, Greg Inglis and Darius Boyd.

A draw would have been rough justice on an Australia side that had dominated most of the game, albeit hard-won dominance over a Kiwi side that had competed hard.

Australia took control early on. With sustained possession on the Kiwi line they attacked right, with Michael Morgan firing a perfect cut-out pass to man of the match Blake Ferguson, who stepped inside to crash over in the ninth minute. Thurston couldn't convert from the sideline but it didn't take the Kangaroos long to notch their second try. In the eleventh minute Valentine Holmes was almost in as he raced away down the left flank. Two minutes later again the green and gold spun the ball to the right.

Morgan, starting in the halves alongside Thurston with Cooper Cronk rested, ran to the right and released Ferguson with an inside pass. The winger then found Thurston in support on his inside and the halfback barged over to score, this time nailing the conversion for 10-0.

If the first 40 minutes was a show of Aussie dominance, the second 40 was a different story. It took just eight minutes for the Kiwis to come back into the game. Left centre Solomone Kata made a short-side run from dummy-half and the hulking centre was too strong from short range. Johnson couldn't add the goal.

In the 61st minute, after Thurston had stretched the lead with an easy penalty goal, Ferguson got over the line for what would have been his second try but he was denied by the touch judge for a forward pass.

With ten minutes to go Australia added another two points from the boot of Thurston and they appeared to have the game sewn up. They had, but the brilliance of Johnson produced a memorable finish.

Scotland became the first tier-two nation to take a point from one of the big three in a Four Nations tournament. They relished the wintry conditions at Workington, rolled up their sleeves and produced one of the greatest performances in international Rugby League history.

Playing with numerous pain-killing injections in an injured heel, Scotland captain Danny Brough was at the centre of many of the game's key moments, while North Queensland fullback Lachlan Coote was magnificent in defence and attack.

In icy, driving rain, defences were on top early in the game and it took 23 minutes for the first score, for the Kiwis against the run of play. Issac Luke fed the mercurial Shaun Johnson and his short ball released a marauding Tohu Harris to send debutant winger David Fusitu'a to the line. Luke converted to put the Kiwis six ahead.

Within three minutes the Scots posted a try of their own when Coote dabbed an inch-perfect grubber kick into the in-goal area for Lewis Tierney to touch down inches

Euan Aitken dives over for a last-gasp try as Scotland share the spoils with the Kiwis

from the sideline. Brough missed the wide conversion and New Zealand led, perhaps undeservedly, at the break by 6-4.

Brough opened the second half with a 40/20 while, at the other end, Matty Russell produced one of the tackles of the tournament in preventing the Kiwi fullback, Dallin Watene-Zelezniak, from touching down when a try seemed a formality.

When Fusitu'a fielded a raking Scottish kick, he was bundled into touch by four enthusiastic chasers, led by the impressive Tierney. Minutes later, Joseph Tapine and Danny Addy sparked an all-in brawl by swinging punches at each other.

FOUR NATIONS - GAME FIVE

Friday 11th November 2016

SCOTLAND 18 NEW ZEALAND 18

SCOTLAND: 1 Lachlan Coote (North Queensland Cowboys); 2 Lewis Tierney (Wigan Warriors); 3 Euan Aitken (St George Illawarra Dragons); 4 Kane Linnett (North Queensland Cowboys); 5 Matthew Russell (Warrington Wolves); 6 Danny Brough (Huddersfield Giants) (C); 7 Danny Addy (Bradford Bulls); 8 Adam Walker (Hull Kingston Rovers); 9 Liam Hood (Leigh Centurions); 10 Luke Douglas (Gold Coast Titans); 11 Ben Hellewell (London Broncos); 12 Dale Ferguson (Bradford Bulls); 13 Ben Kavanagh (Bradford Bulls). Subs (all used): 14 Ryan Brierley (Huddersfield Giants); 15 Frankie Mariano (Castleford Tigers); 16 Brett Phillips (Workington Town); 17 Billy McConnachie (Ipswich Jets).
Tries: Tierney (27), Hellewell (67), Aitken (79); **Goals:** Brough 3/4.
NEW ZEALAND: 1 Dallin Watene-Zelezniak (Penrith Panthers); 5 David Fusitu'a (New Zealand Warriors); 4 Gerard Beale (Cronulla Sharks); 3 Solomone Kata (New Zealand Warriors); 2 Jason Nightingale (St George Illawarra Dragons); 6 Thomas Leuluai (New Zealand Warriors); 7 Shaun Johnson (New Zealand Warriors); 8 Jesse Bromwich (Melbourne Storm) (C); 9 Issac Luke (New Zealand Warriors); 10 Adam Blair (Brisbane Broncos); 11 Manu Ma'u (Parramatta Eels); 12 Tohu Harris (Melbourne Storm); 13 Greg Eastwood (Canterbury Bulldogs). Subs (all used): 14 Te Maire Martin (Penrith Panthers); 15 Martin Taupau (Manly Sea Eagles); 16 James Fisher-Harris (Penrith Panthers); 17 Joseph Tapine (Canberra Raiders).
Tries: Fusitu'a (24, 54), Beale (73, 76); **Goals:** Luke 1/4.
Rugby Leaguer & League Express Men of the Match:
Scotland: Lachlan Coote; *New Zealand:* Tohu Harris.
Penalty count: 10-5; **Half-time:** 4-6; **Referee:** Ben Cummins (Australia);
Attendance: 6,628 *(at Zebra Claims Stadium, Workington).*

That may have woken the tourists up, because they scored with their next possession, in the 55th minute, when Johnson found Watene-Zelezniak who put Fusitu'a away for his second try. Luke's conversion attempt was off target, so the gap was still one score at 10-4.

Shortly afterwards the Kiwis were disrupted by the loss of stand-off Thomas Leuluai, who left the field holding his broken jaw after a collision.

It looked all over when Johnson skipped away but Coote gathered his kick. Three tackles later, Brough kicked inventively across field inside his own half for Tierney, who offloaded to Euan Aitken. With the Kiwis on the back foot, Tierney was sent clear and he passed back on the inside to Ben Hellewell, who brought the house down by dummying Watene-Zelezniak en route to the line.

With 13 minutes left, Brough's

conversion levelled the scores. And Scotland went straight back from the kick-off, allowing the excellent Liam Hood to win a penalty, which Brough sent between the posts.

The last ten minutes were absolutely sensational.

The Kiwis forced a goal-line drop-out and when Greg Eastwood broke through he offloaded to Johnson who sent Gerard Beale to the line with a superb long pass. Luke missed the goal, but at 14-12 Scotland were behind again.

And when Beale touched down on the same blade of grass three minutes later, after some superb handling from the Kiwis, the game seemed up. But another missed goal from Luke meant the margin was still only six points at 18-12.

In desperation, Brough sent the kick-off short and his side won the ball back after Beale was unable to collect.

Luke Douglas and Brett Phillips drove Scotland forward and, on the last tackle, Brough and Addy moved the ball to the left, where Aitken dummied the cover and scythed over to score a try that sent the crowd into hysteria.

Scotland were a conversion away from drawing with New Zealand and Brough, despite his injury, curled the ball sweetly between the posts.

Australia eliminated England, who needed to avoid defeat to reach the final but came up with a sub-standard Test performance at the London (formerly Olympic) Stadium.

England led 6-2 at the half-hour mark after a try from Jermaine McGillvary but Australia dominated territory there-on in, thanks in the main to a brilliant show from scrum-half Cooper Cronk.

For England Kevin Brown was drafted in as part of a third halfback pairing in as many games, partnering Gareth Widdop, with hooker Daryl Clark missing out at the expense of George Williams, who dropped to the bench after starting against Scotland in Coventry.

In the early exchanges, England acquitted themselves fairly well but the halves struggled to exert any sort of influence on the game, best summed up by Widdop failing to find touch after England won an early penalty, before Sam Burgess was handed the task of kicking on the last tackle.

FOUR NATIONS - GAME SIX

Sunday 13th November 2016

ENGLAND 18 AUSTRALIA 36

ENGLAND: 1 Jonny Lomax (St Helens); 2 Jermaine McGillvary (Huddersfield Giants); 3 Kallum Watkins (Leeds Rhinos); 4 Mark Percival (St Helens); 5 Ryan Hall (Leeds Rhinos); 6 Kevin Brown (Widnes Vikings); 7 Gareth Widdop (St George Illawarra Dragons); 8 Chris Hill (Warrington Wolves); 9 Josh Hodgson (Canberra Raiders); 10 James Graham (Canterbury Bulldogs); 11 John Bateman (Wigan Warriors); 12 Elliott Whitehead (Canberra Raiders); 13 Sam Burgess (South Sydney Rabbitohs) (C). Subs (all used): 14 Tom Burgess (South Sydney Rabbitohs); 15 George Burgess (South Sydney Rabbitohs); 16 Mike Cooper (St George Illawarra Dragons); 17 George Williams (Wigan Warriors).
Tries: McGillvary (25), Widdop (67), Hall (76); **Goals:** Widdop 3/4.
AUSTRALIA: 1 Darius Boyd (Brisbane Broncos); 5 Blake Ferguson (Sydney Roosters); 3 Greg Inglis (South Sydney Rabbitohs); 4 Josh Dugan (St George Illawarra Dragons); 2 Valentine Holmes (Cronulla Sharks); 6 Johnathan Thurston (North Queensland Cowboys); 7 Cooper Cronk (Melbourne Storm); 8 Matt Scott (North Queensland Cowboys); 9 Cameron Smith (Melbourne Storm) (C); 10 Aaron Woods (Wests Tigers); 11 Boyd Cordner (Sydney Roosters); 12 Matt Gillett (Brisbane Broncos); 13 Trent Merrin (Penrith Panthers). Subs (all used): 14 David Klemmer (Canterbury Bulldogs); 15 Michael Morgan (North Queensland Cowboys); 16 Tyson Frizell (St George Illawarra Dragons); 17 Sam Thaiday (Brisbane Broncos).
Tries: Ferguson (36), Inglis (48), Scott (55), Dugan (58), Gillett (72), Holmes (78); **Goals:** Thurston 6/8.
Rugby Leaguer & League Express Men of the Match:
England: Jonny Lomax; *Australia:* Cooper Cronk.
Penalty count: 10-8; **Half-time:** 6-10; **Referee:** Robert Hicks (England); **Attendance:** 35,569 *(at London Stadium).*

Widdop at least recovered enough to kick England ahead on eleven minutes when he converted a penalty. Johnathan Thurston responded in kind seven minutes later before some brilliant play from Jonny Lomax provided the inch-perfect cut-out pass for Jermaine McGillvary to cross for his third try in as many games.

But as the pressure from the Australians began to grow as half-time approached, England began to pile it on themselves even further. When Mark Percival shot out of the line as Australia attacked, the Kangaroos swooped as Blake Ferguson dived over after an expert flick pass from Darius Boyd, with Thurston converting for a two-point lead.

Josh Hodgson missed touch with a penalty in the dying seconds of the half, and a lack of discipline from Sam Burgess in front of his own posts allowed Thurston to make it a four-point lead.

A ten-minute blitz shortly after the break ended the contest. First, Greg Inglis made

149

a mockery of England's defending at the scrum when he charged over on the short side.

Then Matt Scott carried the entire England front row over the line with him to touch down, before Josh Dugan added his name to an ever-increasing scorers list when Cronk busted down the right. With Thurston converting all three, England were suddenly behind by 22.

England rallied in the final quarter. Widdop stretched out to touch down, and Ryan Hall made it 31 tries in 31 games, but those scores were sandwiched either side of further Australian tries.

Matt Gillett touched down with eight minutes remaining and the final word went fittingly to Australia, as Valentine Holmes acrobatically touched down for yet another Kangaroos try.

Australia returned to the top of the world rankings with a masterclass at Anfield and a fourth win of 2016 against New Zealand.

For the opening 40 minutes the Kangaroos were untouchable; inspired by their experienced triumvirate of Johnathan Thurston, Cameron Smith and Cooper Cronk, the Aussies ran in four tries of the highest quality to kill off any lingering hopes the Kiwis had of a comeback.

New Zealand's lack of quality halfbacks was exposed once again. Thomas Leuluai's broken jaw meant that second-rower Tohu Harris started at stand-off and his inexperience in that role was ruthlessly exploited in Australia's first meaningful attack. They struck from the base of the scrum in the third minute as Darius Boyd's inch-perfect pass found Blake Ferguson on the fly and the form winger touched down to make it 4-0.

New Zealand responded. Their enterprising play in attack almost brought

FOUR NATIONS - FINAL

Sunday 20th November 2016

AUSTRALIA 34 NEW ZEALAND 8

AUSTRALIA: 1 Darius Boyd (Brisbane Broncos); 2 Blake Ferguson (Sydney Roosters); 4 Josh Dugan (St George Illawarra Dragons); 3 Greg Inglis (South Sydney Rabbitohs); 5 Valentine Holmes (Cronulla Sharks); 6 Johnathan Thurston (North Queensland Cowboys); 7 Cooper Cronk (Melbourne Storm); 8 Matt Scott (North Queensland Cowboys); 9 Cameron Smith (Melbourne Storm) (C); 10 Aaron Woods (Wests Tigers); 11 Boyd Cordner (Sydney Roosters); 12 Matt Gillett (Brisbane Broncos); 13 Trent Merrin (Penrith Panthers). Subs (all used): 14 Michael Morgan (North Queensland Cowboys); 15 David Klemmer (Canterbury Bulldogs); 16 Tyson Frizell (St George Illawarra Dragons); 17 Shannon Boyd (Canberra Raiders). **Tries:** Ferguson (2), Dugan (15, 33), Merrin (21), D Boyd (45), Cordner (74); **Goals:** Thurston 5/8.
NEW ZEALAND: 1 Jordan Kahu (Brisbane Broncos); 5 Jordan Rapana (Canberra Raiders); 3 Solomone Kata (New Zealand Warriors); 4 Shaun Kenny-Dowall (Sydney Roosters); 2 David Fusitu'a (New Zealand Warriors); 6 Tohu Harris (Melbourne Storm); 7 Shaun Johnson (New Zealand Warriors); 8 Jesse Bromwich (Melbourne Storm) (C); 9 Issac Luke (New Zealand Warriors); 10 Adam Blair (Brisbane Broncos); 11 Kevin Proctor (Melbourne Storm); 12 Manu Ma'u (Parramatta Eels); 13 Jason Taumalolo (North Queensland Cowboys). Subs (all used): 14 Lewis Brown (Manly Sea Eagles); 15 Martin Taupau (Manly Sea Eagles); 16 Greg Eastwood (Canterbury Bulldogs); 17 Joseph Tapine (Canberra Raiders). **Tries:** Kahu (56, 68); **Goals:** Kahu 0/2.
Rugby Leaguer & League Express Men of the Match:
Australia: Darius Boyd; *New Zealand:* Adam Blair.
Penalty count: 7-10; **Half-time:** 24-0; **Referee:** Ben Cummins (Australia); **Attendance:** 40,042 *(at Anfield, Liverpool).*

them a reward on a couple of occasions. And they should have been level when Jordan Rapana broke from his own half and the supporting Shaun Kenny-Dowall sent Shaun Johnson away. But Johnson couldn't find Harris with his pass thanks to the scramble of Greg Inglis and Valentine Holmes and Holmes' subsequent scoop up and surge down towards the Kop yielded a reward.

It was a lesson in how to punish your opponents; within seconds of Holmes gathering the ball, Josh Dugan had danced his way over for another Australia try.

Again the Kiwis coughed up possession, again Australia made them pay. This time hooker Issac Luke was the guilty party, with Trent Merrin bullocking his way over from close range off Smith's short pass for try number three.

That try had come either side of two penalty goals from Thurston.

And there was still time for try number four before the break as Dugan scampered through for another. Boyd's effort five minutes after the break emphasised the real gulf in class between the teams.

New Zealand didn't stop fighting or throwing the ball around. Eventually, it gained them a reward via two tries for Jordan Kahu - but the Aussies always had control.

And they were afforded the final say of the 2016 season as Boyd Cordner charged over.

Shannon Boyd halted during Australia's Four Nations Final win against New Zealand

England beat a much-improved France by 40-6 in a warm-up game in Avignon a week before the start of the Four Nations in Wayne Bennett's first game in charge.

England trailed 6-0 briefly in the opening half-hour after Eloi Pelissier's try from dummy-half and were still only 22-6 ahead on 67 minutes. Late flurries of tries at the end of both halves saw them comfortably home, with Ryan Hall taking his record for his country to 28 tries in 28 games with a well-taken first-half double.

Bennett handed debuts to five players - Jonny Lomax, Mark Percival, Luke Gale, Stefan Ratchford and Scott Taylor - and each had their moments, with Taylor particularly impressive in the front row.

Fellow forwards, NRL-based Tom Burgess, Elliott Whitehead and Josh Hodgson caught the eye too, with Kevin Brown impressing in the final half-hour after emerging off the bench.

TEST MATCH

Saturday 22nd October 2016

FRANCE 6 ENGLAND 40

FRANCE: 1 Tony Gigot (Catalans Dragons); 5 Olivier Arnaud (Avignon); 3 Benjamin Garcia (Catalans Dragons); 4 Vincent Duport (Catalans Dragons); 2 Mathias Pala (unattached); 6 Stan Robin (Catalans Dragons); 7 William Barthau (London Broncos); 8 Romain Navarrete (Catalans Dragons); 9 Alrix Da Costa (Catalans Dragons); 10 Remi Casty (Catalans Dragons) (C); 11 Mickael Simon (Wakefield Trinity Wildcats); 12 Benjamin Jullien (Warrington Wolves); 13 Julian Bousquet (Catalans Dragons). Subs (all used): 14 Eloi Pelissier (Catalans Dragons); 15 Mickael Goudemand (Avignon); 16 Gadwin Springer (Castleford Tigers); 17 Kevin Larroyer (Hull Kingston Rovers).
Try: Pelissier (19); **Goals:** Gigot 1/1.
Sin bin: Pelissier (71) - dangerous challenge on Graham.
ENGLAND: 1 Jonny Lomax (St Helens); 2 Jermaine McGillvary (Huddersfield Giants); 3 Kallum Watkins (Leeds Rhinos); 4 Mark Percival (St Helens); 5 Ryan Hall (Leeds Rhinos); 6 Gareth Widdop (St George Illawarra Dragons); 7 Luke Gale (Castleford Tigers); 8 James Graham (Canterbury Bulldogs) (C); 9 Josh Hodgson (Canberra Raiders); 10 Scott Taylor (Hull FC); 11 Elliott Whitehead (Canberra Raiders); 12 Mike Cooper (St George Illawarra Dragons); 13 Tom Burgess (South Sydney Rabbitohs). Subs (all used): 14 George Burgess (South Sydney Rabbitohs); 15 Kevin Brown (Widnes Vikings); 16 Stefan Ratchford (Warrington Wolves); 17 Daryl Clark (Warrington Wolves).
Tries: Hall (26, 40), Clark (30), T Burgess (35), Brown (68), McGillvary (71), Widdop (76); **Goals:** Widdop 6/7.
Rugby Leaguer & League Express Men of the Match:
France: Tony Gigot; *England:* Josh Hodgson.
Penalty count: 6-12; **Half-time:** 6-22; **Referee:** Phil Bentham (England); **Attendance:** 14,267 *(at Parc des Sports, Avignon).*

151

2017 WORLD CUP QUALIFIERS - EUROPE

POOL A

Saturday 15th October 2016

WALES 50 SERBIA 0

WALES: Elliot Kear; Regan Grace; Andrew Gay; Christiaan Roets; Rhys Williams; Courtney Davies; Ollie Olds; Gil Dudson; Lloyd White; Craig Kopczak; Rhodri Lloyd; Joe Burke; Phil Joseph. Subs (all used): Steve Parry; Jake Emmitt; Anthony Walker; Matty Fozard.
Tries: Williams (12, 19), Grace (28, 56), Olds (33, 69), Davies (46), Gay (52), Dudson (76); **Goals:** White 4/6, Davies 3/3.
SERBIA: Vladislav Dedic; Joshua Marjanovic; Milos Calilc; Stevan Stevanovic; Pero Madzarevic; Daniel Burke; Dalibor Vukanovic; David Andjelic; Vojislav Dedic; Jordan Grant; Chad Grant; Jason Muranka; Stefan Nedeljkovic. Subs (all used): Ilija Radan; James Mirceski; Reece Grkinic; Dzavid Jasari.
Sin bin: Madzarevic (51) - tripping.
Half-time: 20-0; **Referee:** Chris Campbell (England); **Attendance:** 902
(at Parc Stebonheath, Llanelli).

Saturday 22nd October 2016

SERBIA 14 ITALY 62

SERBIA: Vojislav Dedic; Milos Zogovic; Milos Calilc; Stevan Stevanovic; Joshua Marjanovic; Daniel Burke; Dalibor Vukanovic; Ilija Radan; Reece Grkinic; Jordan Grant; James Mirceski; Jason Muranka; Chad Grant. Subs (all used): David Andjelic; Miodrag Tomic; Vlado Kusic; Vladislav Dedic.
Tries: Marjanovic (68, 79), Burke (73); **Goals:** Burke 0/1, Vojislav Dedic 1/2.
ITALY: Mason Cerruto; Christopher Centrone; Justin Castellaro; Mirco Bergamasco; Richard Lepori; Terry Campese; Ryan Ghietti; Shannon Wakeman; Dean Parata; Gavin Hiscox; Jayden Walker; Brenden Santi; Joel Reithmuller. Subs (all used): Col Wilkie; Christophe Calegari; Kieran Quabba; Gioele Celerino.
Tries: Lepori (4, 10, 12, 46), Cerruto (17, 35, 49, 71), Wakeman (22), Santi (45), Campese (58), Calegari (62); **Goals:** Bergamasco 7/11, Campese 0/1.
Half-time: 0-32; **Referee:** James Child (England); **Attendance:** 1,037
(at Makis Stadium, Belgrade).

Saturday 29th October 2016

ITALY 14 WALES 20

ITALY: Christopher Centrone; Justin Castellaro; Christophe Calegari; Mirco Bergamasco; Richard Lepori; Terry Campese; Ryan Ghietti; Shannon Wakeman; Dean Parata; Gavin Hiscox; Jayden Walker; Brenden Santi; Joel Reithmuller. Subs (all used): Mason Cerruto; Col Wilkie; Kieran Quabba; Gioele Celerino.
Tries: Wilkie (26), Castellaro (30); **Goals:** Campese 3/3.
WALES: Elliot Kear; Rhys Williams; Ben Morris; Andrew Gay; Dai Evans; Courtney Davies; Lloyd White; Gil Dudson; Steve Parry; Craig Kopczak; Rhodri Lloyd; Matty Fozard; Phil Joseph. Subs (all used): Joe Burke; Anthony Walker; Sam Hopkins; Danny Ansell.
Tries: Morris (16, 58), Walker (37), Gay (53); **Goals:** Davies 2/4.
Half-time: 14-10; **Referee:** Chris Campbell (England); **Attendance:** 500
(at Stadio Brianteo, Monza).

POOL B

Saturday 15th October 2016

RUSSIA 40 SPAIN 6

RUSSIA: Nikolai Zagoskin; Vadim Buryak; Kirill Kosharin; Leonid Kalinin; Dmitry Bratko; Aleksandr Lysokon; Denis Tiulenev; Sergei Konstantinov; Petr Botnarash; Ivan Troitskii; Mikhail Burlutskii; Andrey Kuznetsov; Viacheslav Eremin. Subs (all used): Igor Chuprin; Maksim Suchkov; Vladimir Vlasyuk; Sergey Gaponov.
Tries: Burlutskii (12), Zagoskin (14), Kosharin (33), Lysokon (44), Bratko (54), Chuprin (76), Buryak (79); **Goals:** Lysokon 4/5, Bratko 1/1, Burlutskii 1/1.
SPAIN: Daniel Garcia; Clement Laguerre; Antonio Puerta; Alex Doutres; Chris Lopez; Ivan Ordaz; Miguel Charters-Blanco; Luis Thorp; Gonzalo Morro; Adria Alonso; Cedric Bringuier; Matt Dulley; Aitor Davila. Subs (all used): Andrew Pilkington; Leandre Torres; Kevin Aparicio; Juan Pablo Rango.
Try: Rango (69); **Goals:** Garcia 1/1.
Half-time: 18-0; **Referee:** Jack Smith (England); **Attendance:** 427
(at Fili Stadium, Moscow).

Saturday 22nd October 2016

SPAIN 6 IRELAND 46

SPAIN: Daniel Garcia; Clement Laguerre; Antonio Puerta; Alex Doutres; Chris Lopez; Ivan Ordaz; Miguel Charters-Blanco; Luis Thorp; Nicolas Munoz; Joel Laynez; Leandre Torres; Cedric Bringuier; Kevin Aparicio. Subs (all used): Andrew Pilkington; Aitor Davila; Matt Dulley; Adria Alonso.
Try: Charters-Blanco (62); **Goals:** Garcia 1/1.
Sin bin: Bringuier (65) - punching.
IRELAND: Shannon McDonnell; Casey Dunne; Stuart Littler; Oliver Roberts; Alan McMahon; Scott Grix; Liam Finn; James Hasson; Joe Keyes; Luke Ambler; Dave Allen; Will Hope; George King. Subs (all used): Haydn Peacock; Matty Hadden; James Kelly; Gareth Gill.
Tries: Roberts (2), Dunne (5, 52), Littler (29, 74), Hasson (39), Peacock (56), G King (66), Grix (77); **Goals:** Finn 5/9.
Half time: 0-22; **Referee:** Patrice Benausse (France); **Attendance:** 323
(at Polideportivo Quatre Carrares, Valencia).

Sunday 30th October 2016

IRELAND 70 RUSSIA 16

IRELAND: Shannon McDonnell; Alan McMahon; Stuart Littler; Toby King; Casey Dunne; Scott Grix; Liam Finn; George King; Joe Keyes; Will Hope; Dave Allen; Oliver Roberts. Subs (all used): Joe Philbin; Matty Hadden; James Kelly; Gareth Gill.
Tries: Hope (7), Dunne (10), McMahon (13, 36), Grix (23, 62), T King (32), McDonnell (38), Roberts (46, 72), G King (59), Kelly (64), Littler (69); **Goals:** Finn 8/11, Littler 1/2.
RUSSIA: Viacheslav Eremin; Vadim Buryak; Kirill Kosharin; Leonid Kalinin; Dmitry Bratko; Aleksandr Lysokon; Denis Tiulenev; Sergei Konstantinov; Petr Botnarash; Ivan Troitskii; Andrey Kuznetsov; Mikhail Burlutskii; Nikolai Zagoskin. Subs (all used): Vadim Fedchuk; Vladimir Vlasyuk; Maksim Tsynkovich; Maksim Suchkov.
Tries: Eremin (4), Kalinin (26), Buryak (79); **Goals:** Lysokon 2/3.
Half-time: 38-12; **Referee:** Chris Kendall (England); **Attendance:** 867
(at Carlisle Grounds, Bray).

PLAY-OFF

Friday 4th November 2016

ITALY 76 RUSSIA 0

ITALY: Mason Cerruto; Christopher Centrone; Justin Castellaro; Col Wilkie; Richard Lepori; Terry Campese; Ryan Ghietti; Shannon Wakeman; Dean Parata; Gavin Hiscox; Jayden Walker; Brenden Santi; Joel Reithmuller. Subs (all used): Joseph Tramontana; Ryan Tramonte; Guiseppe Pagani; Gioele Celerino.
Tries: Cerruto (3, 20), Lepori (6, 28), Wilkie (9, 45), Santi (17), Wakeman (24), Centrone (31), Celerino (38), Castellaro (43, 49), Walker (62), Campese (70); **Goals:** Campese 10/14.
RUSSIA: Maksim Suchkov; Vadim Buryak; Nikolai Zagoskin; Leonid Kalinin; Maksim Tsynkovich; Aleksandr Lysokon; Denis Tiulenev; Vadim Fedchuk; Vladimir Vlasyuk; Ivan Troitskii; Mikhail Burlutskii; Andrey Kuznetsov; Viacheslav Eremin. Subs (all used, only three named): Igor Chuprin; Dmitry Bratko; Sergei Konstantinov.
Half-time: 46-0; **Referee:** Chris Campbell (England); **Attendance:** 450
(at Leigh Sports Village).

WARM-UP GAME

Friday 21st October 2016

WALES 16 JAMAICA 16

WALES: Elliot Kear; Ian Newbury; Andrew Gay; Christiaan Roets; Dai Evans; Courtney Davies; Lloyd White; Gil Dudson; Steve Parry; Anthony Walker; Rhodri Lloyd; Ben Morris; Joe Burke. Subs (all used): Rhys Williams; Matty Fozard; Morgan Evans; Connor Farrer.
Tries: Lloyd (11), Davies (30), White (67); **Goals:** White 0/2, Davies 2/2.
JAMAICA: Wayne Reittie; Richie Barnett; Alex Brown; Lewis Bowman; Aaron Jones-Bishop; Jy-mel Coleman; Danny Thomas; Jode Sheriffe; Joel Farrell; Jordan Andrade; Danny Bravo; Mo Agoro; Corey Hanson. Subs (all used): Keenen Tomlinson; Kadeem Williams; Jamel Goodall; Ross Peltier.
Tries: Jones-Bishop (23, 37, 78); **Goals:** Coleman 2/4.
Sin bin: Hanson (65) - high tackle.
Half-time: 8-12; **Referee:** Joe Cobb (England); **Attendance:** 1,378
(at Belle Vue, Wakefield).

5
STATISTICAL REVIEW

SUPER LEAGUE PLAYERS
1996-2017

Super League Players 1996-2017

PLAYER	CLUB	YEAR	APP	TRIES	GOALS	FG	PTS
Jordan Abdull	Hull	2014-16	22(12)	5	7	0	34
Carl Ablett	Leeds	2004, 2006-17	223(37)	62	0	0	248
	London	2005	3(2)	0	0	0	0
Darren Abram	Oldham	1996-97	25(2)	11	0	0	44
Mitch Achurch	Leeds	2013-16	25(50)	14	0	0	56
Jamie Acton	Leigh	2017	11(4)	4	0	0	16
Brad Adams	Bradford	2014	1(1)	0	0	0	0
Darren Adams	Paris	1996	9(1)	1	0	0	4
Guy Adams	Huddersfield	1998	1(2)	0	0	0	0
Luke Adamson	Salford	2006-07, 2009-12	73(39)	11	1	0	46
Matt Adamson	Leeds	2002-04	54(8)	9	0	0	36
Phil Adamson	St Helens	1999	(1)	0	0	0	0
Toby Adamson	Salford	2010	(1)	0	0	0	0
Danny Addy	Bradford	2010-14	49(42)	13	7	0	66
Ade Adebisi	London	2004	(1)	0	0	0	0
Patrick Ah Van	Widnes	2012-17	89	68	54	0	380
	Bradford	2011	26	9	87	0	210
Jamie Ainscough	Wigan	2002-03	30(2)	18	0	0	72
Shaun Ainscough	Bradford	2011-12	27	15	0	0	60
	Wigan	2009-10	12	13	0	0	52
	Castleford	2010	7	4	0	0	16
Glen Air	London	1998-2001	57(13)	27	0	1	109
Paul Aiton	Catalans	2016-17	28(6)	3	0	0	12
	Leeds	2014-15	36(6)	2	0	0	8
	Wakefield	2012-13	43(2)	7	0	0	28
Makali Aizue	Hull KR	2007-09	18(32)	4	0	0	16
Darren Albert	St Helens	2002-05	105	77	0	0	308
Lucas Albert	Catalans	2015-17	15(1)	4	2	0	20
Paul Alcock	Widnes	2003, 2005	1(7)	1	0	0	4
Neil Alexander	Salford	1998	(1)	0	0	0	0
Malcolm Alker	Salford	1997-2002, 2004-07, 2009-10	271(2)	40	0	1	161
Danny Allan	Leeds	2008-09	2(5)	0	0	0	0
Chris Allen	Castleford	1996	(1)	0	0	0	0
Dave Allen	Widnes	2012-14	50(13)	5	0	0	20
	Wigan	2003, 2005	6(15)	2	0	0	8
Gavin Allen	London	1996	10	0	0	0	0
John Allen	Workington	1996	20(1)	6	0	0	24
Ray Allen	London	1996	5(3)	3	0	0	12
Mitch Allgood	Wakefield	2017	6(2)	0	0	0	0
	Hull KR	2015-16	27(2)	5	0	0	20
Richard Allwood	Gateshead	1999	(4)	0	0	0	0
Sean Allwood	Gateshead	1999	3(17)	1	0	0	4
David Alstead	Warrington	2000-02	23(10)	3	0	0	12
Luke Ambler	Harlequins	2011	5(17)	1	0	0	4
	Leeds	2010	1(8)	1	0	0	4
Asa Amone	Halifax	1996-97	32(7)	10	0	0	40
Kyle Amor	St Helens	2014-17	75(26)	13	0	0	52
	Wakefield	2011-13	51(23)	9	0	0	36
	Leeds	2010	(3)	0	0	0	0
Thibaut Ancely	Catalans	2011	(2)	0	0	0	0
Grant Anderson	Castleford	1996-97	15(6)	3	0	0	12
Louis Anderson	Catalans	2012-17	82(29)	31	0	0	124
	Warrington	2008-11	92	18	0	0	72
Paul Anderson	St Helens	2005-06	48(5)	7	1	0	30
	Bradford	1997-2004	74(104)	30	0	0	120
	Halifax	1996	5(1)	1	0	0	4
Paul Anderson	Sheffield	1999	3(7)	1	0	0	4
	St Helens	1996-98	2(28)	4	1	0	18
Scott Anderson	Wakefield	2014-16	25(18)	2	0	0	8
Vinnie Anderson	Salford	2011-12	33(3)	14	0	0	56
	Warrington	2007-10	57(19)	22	0	0	88
	St Helens	2005-06	28(14)	17	0	0	68
Phil Anderton	St Helens	2004	1	0	0	0	0
Chris Annakin	Wakefield	2013-17	3(48)	1	0	0	4
Eric Anselme	Leeds	2008	2(2)	2	0	0	8
	Halifax	1997	(2)	0	0	0	0
Mark Applegarth	Wakefield	2004-07	20(5)	3	0	0	12
Graham Appo	Warrington	2002-05	60(13)	35	80	0	300
	Huddersfield	2001	7	4	0	0	16
Anthony Armour	London	2005	11(7)	1	0	0	4
Colin Armstrong	Workington	1996	11(2)	1	0	0	4
Tom Armstrong	Widnes	2017	11	1	0	0	4
	St Helens	2009-11	10(5)	9	0	0	36
Richard Armswood	Workington	1996	5(1)	1	0	0	4
Danny Arnold	Salford	2001-02	26(13)	13	0	0	52
	Huddersfield	1998-2000	55(7)	26	0	0	104
	Castleford	2000	(4)	0	0	0	0
	St Helens	1996-97	40(1)	33	0	0	132
Tinirau Arona	Wakefield	2016-17	38(18)	1	0	0	4
Joe Arundel	Wakefield	2015-17	53(7)	14	4	0	64
	Bradford	2014	9(3)	5	0	0	20
	Hull	2013-14	16	7	1	0	30
	Castleford	2008, 2010-12	35(4)	14	2	0	60
Craig Ashall	St Helens	2006	1	1	0	0	4
Nathan Ashe	St Helens	2011-13	6(4)	0	0	0	0
Chris Ashton	Wigan	2005-07	44(2)	25	2	0	104
Matty Ashurst	Wakefield	2015-17	56(3)	11	0	0	44
	Salford	2012-14	65(7)	11	0	0	44
	St Helens	2009-11	12(39)	8	0	0	32
Jack Ashworth	St Helens	2015-16	4(3)	2	0	0	8
Roy Asotasi	Warrington	2014-15	16(37)	5	1	0	22
Peter Aspinall	Huddersfield	2013	1(1)	0	0	0	0
Martin Aspinwall	Hull	2012	12(15)	0	0	0	0
	Castleford	2011	12(6)	2	0	0	8
	Huddersfield	2006-10	72(8)	22	0	0	88
	Wigan	2001-05	85(13)	27	0	0	108
Mark Aston	Sheffield	1996-99	67(6)	6	243	6	516
Paul Atcheson	Widnes	2002-04	16(35)	4	0	0	16
	St Helens	1998-2000	58(4)	18	0	0	72
	Oldham	1996-97	40	21	0	0	84
David Atkins	Huddersfield	2001	26(1)	4	0	0	16
Jordan Atkins	London	2014	13(1)	4	0	0	16
Ryan Atkins	Warrington	2010-17	206(1)	126	0	0	504
	Wakefield	2006-09	86(2)	45	0	0	180
Josh Atkinson	Castleford	2012	2	0	0	0	0
Brad Attwood	Halifax	2003	(3)	0	0	0	0
Warren Ayres	Salford	1999	2(9)	1	2	0	8
Jerome Azema	Paris	1997	(1)	0	0	0	0
Marcus Bai	Bradford	2006	24	9	0	0	36
	Leeds	2004-05	57	42	0	0	168
David Baildon	Hull	1998-99	26(2)	4	0	0	16
Jean-Philippe Baile	Catalans	2008-14	62(16)	23	0	0	92
Andy Bailey	Hull	2004-05	2(8)	1	0	0	4
Chris Bailey	Huddersfield	2014-15	17(17)	5	0	0	20
	London	2012-13	41	14	0	0	56
	Harlequins	2011	24	3	0	0	12
Julian Bailey	Huddersfield	2003-04	47	13	0	0	52
Phil Bailey	Wigan	2007-10	84(4)	13	0	0	52
Ricky Bailey	St Helens	2015, 2017	2	0	0	0	0
Ryan Bailey	Warrington	2016	1(11)	0	0	0	0
	Castleford	2015	3(2)	0	0	0	0
	Hull KR	2015	(1)	1	0	0	4
	Leeds	2002-14	171(102)	17	0	0	68
Jason Baitieri	Catalans	2011-17	120(35)	17	0	0	68
Simon Baldwin	Salford	2004-06	20(29)	3	0	0	12
	Sheffield	1999	7(15)	2	0	0	8
	Halifax	1996-98	16(15)	16	0	1	65
Jordan Baldwinson	Leeds	2013, 2016-17	4(9)	1	0	0	4
	Bradford	2014	2(4)	0	0	0	0
Rob Ball	Wigan	1998-2000	3(4)	0	0	0	0
Paul Ballard	Celtic	2009	2	0	0	0	0
	Widnes	2005	3(1)	2	0	0	8
Darren Bamford	Salford	2005	2(1)	0	0	0	0
Michael Banks	Bradford	1998	(1)	0	0	0	0
Steve Bannister	Harlequins	2007	(6)	0	0	0	0
	St Helens	2006-07	(3)	0	0	0	0
Frederic Banquet	Paris	1996	16(2)	7	4	0	36
Ben Barba	St Helens	2017	5	3	0	0	12
Lee Bardauskas	Castleford	1996-97	(2)	0	0	0	0
Craig Barker	Workington	1996	(2)	0	0	0	0
Dwayne Barker	Harlequins	2008	5(5)	1	0	0	4
	London	2004	3	1	0	0	4
	Hull	2003	(1)	0	0	0	0
Mark Barlow	Wakefield	2002	(1)	0	0	0	0
Danny Barnes	Halifax	1999	2	0	0	0	0
Richie Barnett	Salford	2007	7	4	0	0	16
	Warrington	2006-07	26(10)	15	0	0	60
	Hull	2004-05	21(5)	21	0	0	84
	Widnes	2005	4	2	0	0	8
Richie Barnett	Hull	2003-04	31(1)	17	0	0	68
	London	2001-02	31(4)	13	0	0	52
David Barnhill	Leeds	2000	20(8)	5	0	0	20
Trent Barrett	Wigan	2007-08	53(1)	22	0	4	92
Paul Barrow	Warrington	1996-97	1(10)	1	0	0	4
Scott Barrow	St Helens	1997-2000	9(13)	1	0	0	4
Steve Barrow	Salford	2000	2	0	0	0	0
	Hull	1998-99	4(17)	1	0	0	4
	Wigan	1996	(8)	3	0	0	12
William Barthau	Catalans	2010, 2012-14	13(3)	2	15	0	38
Ben Barton	Huddersfield	1998	1(6)	1	0	0	4
Danny Barton	Salford	2001	1	0	0	0	0
Wayne Bartrim	Castleford	2002-03	41(2)	9	157	0	350
Greg Barwick	London	1996-97	30(4)	21	110	2	306
David Bastian	Halifax	1996	(2)	0	0	0	0
James Batchelor	Wakefield	2016-17	2(10)	2	0	0	8
Ashley Bateman	Celtic	2009	1	0	0	0	0
John Bateman	Wigan	2014-17	83(8)	27	0	0	108
	Bradford	2011-13	25(5)	7	0	0	28
David Bates	Castleford	2001-02	(4)	0	0	0	0
	Warrington	2001	1(2)	0	0	0	0

PLAYER	CLUB	YEAR	APP	TRIES	GOALS	FG	PTS
Sam Bates	Bradford	2014	(2)	0	0	0	0
Nathan Batty	Wakefield	2001	1(1)	0	0	0	0
Andreas Bauer	Hull KR	2007	10(2)	5	0	0	20
Russell Bawden	London	1996-97, 2002-04	50(49)	15	0	0	60
Neil Baxter	Salford	2001	1	0	0	0	0
Neil Baynes	Salford	1999-2002, 2004	84(19)	10	0	0	40
	Wigan	1996-98	(10)	1	0	0	4
Chris Beasley	Celtic	2009	15(5)	2	0	0	8
Chris Beattie	Catalans	2006	22(5)	3	0	0	12
Richard Beaumont	Hull KR	2011-13	1(16)	1	0	0	4
Robbie Beazley	London	1997-99	48(15)	13	0	0	52
Robbie Beckett	Halifax	2002	27	15	0	0	60
Matty Beharrell	Hull KR	2013	1	0	0	0	0
Dean Bell	Leeds	1996	1	1	0	0	4
Ian Bell	Hull	2003	(1)	0	0	0	0
Mark Bell	Wigan	1998	22	12	0	0	48
Paul Bell	Leeds	2000	1	0	0	0	0
Steven Bell	Catalans	2009-10	43	14	0	0	56
Troy Bellamy	Paris	1997	5(10)	0	0	0	0
Adrian Belle	Huddersfield	1998	10(2)	0	0	0	0
	Oldham	1996	19	8	0	0	32
Lambert Belmas	Catalans	2017	2(1)	0	0	0	0
Jamie Benn	Castleford	1998, 2000	3(8)	1	15	0	34
Andy Bennett	Warrington	1996	6(5)	1	0	0	4
Mike Bennett	St Helens	2000-08	74(70)	15	0	0	60
Andrew Bentley	Catalans	2007-10	9(15)	1	0	0	4
John Bentley	Huddersfield	1999	13(4)	3	0	0	12
	Halifax	1996, 1998	22(3)	24	0	0	96
Kane Bentley	Catalans	2007-10	11(19)	5	0	0	20
Phil Bergman	Paris	1997	20(1)	14	0	0	56
Shaun Berrigan	Hull	2008-10	60(8)	12	0	0	48
Joe Berry	Huddersfield	1998-99	25(14)	3	0	0	12
David Berthezene	Salford	2007	9(1)	0	0	0	0
	Catalans	2006-07	5(14)	0	0	0	0
Colin Best	Hull	2003-04	57	34	0	0	136
Roger Best	London	1997-98	1(5)	1	0	0	4
Bob Beswick	Wigan	2004-05	5(14)	2	0	0	8
Monty Betham	Wakefield	2006	26	2	0	0	8
Mike Bethwaite	Workington	1996	17(3)	1	0	0	4
Denis Betts	Wigan	1998-2001	82(24)	33	0	0	132
Cliff Beverley	Salford	2004-05	47(1)	14	0	0	56
Kyle Bibb	Wakefield	2008-10	1(24)	0	0	0	0
	Harlequins	2010	(2)	0	0	0	0
	Hull KR	2009	(2)	0	0	0	0
Jake Bibby	Salford	2016-17	19(2)	6	0	0	24
Adam Bibey	Widnes	2004	(1)	0	0	0	0
Ricky Bibey	Wakefield	2007-09	32(25)	1	0	0	4
	St Helens	2004	4(14)	0	0	0	0
	Wigan	2001-03	5(29)	0	0	0	0
Chris Birchall	Halifax	2002-03	24(22)	4	0	0	16
	Bradford	2000	(1)	0	0	0	0
Deon Bird	Castleford	2006	17(6)	5	0	0	20
	Widnes	2003-04	39(6)	9	0	0	36
	Wakefield	2002	10(1)	1	0	0	4
	Hull	2000-02	37(22)	20	0	0	80
	Gateshead	1999	19(3)	13	0	0	52
	Paris	1996-97	30	12	2	0	52
Greg Bird	Catalans	2009, 2017	31(3)	6	3	0	30
Mike Bishay	London	2013-14	7(11)	2	2	0	12
Nathan Blacklock	Hull	2005-06	44(3)	33	0	0	132
Ben Blackmore	Huddersfield	2013-14	3	4	0	0	16
	Castleford	2012	1	0	0	0	0
Richie Blackmore	Leeds	1997-2000	63	25	0	0	100
Anthony Blackwood	Crusaders	2010	1	0	0	0	0
	Celtic	2009	25	5	0	0	20
Jack Blagbrough	Huddersfield	2013	(1)	0	0	0	0
Maurice Blair	Hull KR	2015-16	41(2)	9	1	0	38
Luke Blake	Wakefield	2009	(2)	0	0	0	0
Matthew Blake	Wakefield	2003-04	1(5)	0	0	0	0
Steve Blakeley	Salford	1997-2002	103(5)	26	241	2	588
	Warrington	2000	4(3)	1	9	0	22
Richard Blakeway	Castleford	2002-04	1(14)	0	0	0	0
Damien Blanch	Catalans	2011-13	70	42	0	0	168
	Wakefield	2008-10	44(3)	31	0	0	124
	Castleford	2006	3(2)	0	0	0	0
Matt Blaymire	Wakefield	2007-11	96(3)	26	0	1	105
Ian Blease	Salford	1997	(1)	0	0	0	0
Jamie Bloem	Huddersfield	2003	18(4)	3	11	0	34
	Halifax	1998-2002	82(25)	25	100	2	302
Vea Bloomfield	Paris	1996	4(14)	3	0	0	12
Matty Blythe	Warrington	2007-12, 2017	30(28)	12	0	0	48
	Bradford	2013-14	24(6)	8	0	0	32
Ben Bolger	London	2012	2(7)	1	0	0	4
	Harlequins	2010-11	4(15)	0	0	0	0

PLAYER	CLUB	YEAR	APP	TRIES	GOALS	FG	PTS
Pascal Bomati	Paris	1996	17(1)	10	0	0	40
Simon Booth	Hull	1998-99	15(9)	2	0	0	8
	St Helens	1996-97	10(4)	1	0	0	4
Steve Booth	Huddersfield	1998-99	16(4)	2	3	0	14
Alan Boothroyd	Halifax	1997	2(3)	0	0	0	0
Thomas Bosc	Catalans	2006-17	199(21)	48	483	12	1170
John Boslem	Paris	1996	(5)	0	0	0	0
Liam Bostock	St Helens	2004	1	0	0	0	0
Liam Botham	Wigan	2005	5	0	0	0	0
	Leeds	2003-05	2(11)	4	0	0	16
	London	2004	6(2)	3	7	0	26
Frano Botica	Castleford	1996	21	5	84	2	190
Matthew Bottom	Leigh	2005	(1)	0	0	0	0
Hadj Boudebza	Paris	1996	(2)	0	0	0	0
John Boudebza	Hull KR	2015-16	13(17)	2	0	0	8
David Boughton	Huddersfield	1999	26(1)	4	0	0	16
Julian Bousquet	Catalans	2012-17	35(74)	11	0	0	44
David Bouveng	Halifax	1997-99	66(2)	19	0	0	76
Josh Bowden	Hull	2012-17	47(61)	11	0	0	44
Matt Bowen	Wigan	2014-15	43	21	31	0	146
Tony Bowes	Huddersfield	1998	3(2)	0	0	0	0
Radney Bowker	London	2004	3	1	0	0	4
	St Helens	2001	(1)	0	0	0	0
David Boyle	Bradford	1999-2000	36(13)	15	0	1	61
Ryan Boyle	Castleford	2006, 2008-09, 2013-16	12(60)	5	0	0	20
	Salford	2010-13	57(14)	3	0	0	12
Andy Bracek	Crusaders	2011	(2)	0	0	0	0
	Warrington	2005-08	7(49)	7	0	0	28
	St Helens	2004	(1)	0	0	0	0
David Bradbury	Hudds-Sheff	2000	21(2)	1	0	0	4
	Salford	1997-99	23(10)	6	0	0	24
	Oldham	1996-97	19(6)	9	0	0	36
John Braddish	St Helens	2001-02	1(1)	0	3	0	6
Graeme Bradley	Bradford	1996-98	62(1)	29	0	0	116
Nick Bradley-Qalilawa	Harlequins	2006	27	6	0	0	24
	London	2005	28	19	0	0	76
Darren Bradstreet	London	1999-2000	1(3)	0	0	0	0
Dominic Brambani	Castleford	2004	2(2)	0	0	0	0
Joe Bretherton	Wigan	2016-17	2(13)	1	0	0	4
Liam Bretherton	Wigan	1999	(5)	2	0	0	8
	Warrington	1997	(2)	0	0	0	0
Johnny Brewer	Halifax	1996	4(2)	2	0	0	8
Chris Bridge	Widnes	2016-17	28(1)	4	11	0	38
	Warrington	2005-15	186(17)	89	248	1	853
	Bradford	2003-04	2(14)	4	6	0	28
Danny Bridge	Bradford	2014	4(4)	0	0	0	0
	Warrington	2013	(2)	0	0	0	0
Ryan Brierley	Huddersfield	2016-17	19(1)	6	2	0	28
Lee Briers	Warrington	1997-2013	365(12)	130	810	70	2210
	St Helens	1997	3	0	11	0	22
Carl Briggs	Salford	1999	8(5)	3	0	1	13
	Halifax	1996	5(3)	1	0	0	4
Kyle Briggs	Bradford	2011	6	4	0	0	16
	Harlequins	2011	3	0	0	0	0
Mike Briggs	Widnes	2002	1(2)	1	0	0	4
Kriss Brining	Salford	2017	2(20)	4	0	0	16
Luke Briscoe	Leeds	2014, 2016	5(4)	2	0	0	8
	Wakefield	2014	2	0	0	0	0
Shaun Briscoe	Widnes	2012-13	11(2)	4	0	0	16
	Hull KR	2008-11	92	27	0	0	108
	Hull	2004-07	83(9)	50	0	0	200
	Wigan	2002-03	23(5)	11	0	0	44
Tom Briscoe	Leeds	2014-17	78	33	0	0	132
	Hull	2008-13	131(3)	83	0	0	332
Darren Britt	St Helens	2002-03	41	3	0	0	12
Gary Broadbent	Salford	1997-2002	117(2)	22	0	0	88
Paul Broadbent	Wakefield	2002	16(5)	0	0	0	0
	Hull	2000-01	40(9)	3	0	0	12
	Halifax	1999	26(1)	2	0	0	8
	Sheffield	1996-98	63(1)	6	0	0	24
Andrew Brocklehurst	Salford	2004-07	34(23)	5	0	0	20
	London	2004	12(6)	2	0	0	8
	Halifax	2001-03	37(8)	2	0	0	8
Justin Brooker	Wakefield	2001	25	9	0	0	36
	Bradford	2000	17(4)	11	0	0	44
Sam Brooks	Widnes	2016-17	1(3)	1	0	0	4
Danny Brough	Huddersfield	2010-17	198(4)	44	659	18	1512
	Wakefield	2008-10	50(1)	14	174	4	408
	Castleford	2006	10	1	31	2	68
	Hull	2005-06	25(12)	3	85	1	183
Jodie Broughton	Catalans	2016-17	33	21	0	0	84
	Huddersfield	2014-15	30	16	0	0	64
	Salford	2010-13	93	53	0	0	212
	Hull	2008-09	9(3)	6	0	0	24

Super League Players 1996-2017

PLAYER	CLUB	YEAR	APP	TRIES	GOALS	FG	PTS
Alex Brown	Hull KR	2013	16	9	0	0	36
	Huddersfield	2009	1	0	0	0	0
Darren Brown	Salford	1999-2001	47(9)	11	6	0	56
Gavin Brown	Leeds	1996-97	5(2)	1	2	0	8
Kevin Brown	Warrington	2017	12(1)	2	0	0	8
	Widnes	2013-16	80	37	1	1	151
	Huddersfield	2006-12	156	43	0	1	173
	Wigan	2003-06	46(18)	27	0	0	108
Lee Brown	Hull	1999	(1)	0	0	0	0
Michael Brown	Huddersfield	2008	(1)	0	0	0	0
Michael Brown	London	1996	(2)	0	0	0	0
Mitch Brown	Leigh	2017	21	4	0	0	16
Todd Brown	Paris	1996	8(1)	2	0	0	8
Adrian Brunker	Wakefield	1999	17	6	0	0	24
Lamont Bryan	Harlequins	2008-11	9(22)	2	0	0	8
Justin Bryant	Paris	1996	4(1)	0	0	0	0
	London	1996	7(8)	1	0	0	4
Mark Bryant	London	2012-13	16(36)	3	1	0	14
	Crusaders	2010-11	42(8)	1	0	0	4
	Celtic	2009	23(3)	0	0	0	0
Austin Buchanan	Wakefield	2005-06	6	2	0	0	8
	London	2003	3(1)	2	0	0	8
Jack Buchanan	Widnes	2016-17	29(2)	2	0	0	8
Danny Buderus	Leeds	2009-11	57(14)	14	0	0	56
Neil Budworth	Celtic	2009	8(19)	0	0	0	0
	Harlequins	2006	2(19)	0	0	0	0
	London	2002-05	59(11)	4	1	0	18
James Bunyan	Huddersfield	1998-99	8(7)	2	0	0	8
Andy Burgess	Salford	1997	3(12)	0	0	0	0
Joe Burgess	Wigan	2013-15, 2017	73	63	0	0	252
Luke Burgess	Catalans	2017	3(2)	0	0	0	0
	Leeds	2008-11	10(63)	6	0	0	24
	Harlequins	2007	(3)	0	0	0	0
Sam Burgess	Bradford	2006-09	46(34)	14	5	0	66
Tom Burgess	Bradford	2011-12	1(41)	3	0	0	12
Greg Burke	Widnes	2016-17	10(9)	0	0	0	0
	Wigan	2013-14, 2016	13(26)	1	0	0	4
	Hull KR	2015	9(5)	0	0	0	0
	Bradford	2014	(1)	0	0	0	0
Joe Burke	Crusaders	2011	(1)	0	0	0	0
Mike Burnett	Harlequins	2011	16(4)	1	0	0	4
	Hull	2008-10	13(21)	3	0	0	12
Darren Burns	Warrington	2002-04	66(6)	19	0	0	76
Gary Burns	Oldham	1996	6	1	0	0	4
Paul Burns	Workington	1996	5(2)	1	0	0	4
Travis Burns	St Helens	2015-16	27(2)	4	28	0	72
	Hull KR	2013-14	46	8	81	2	196
Lachlan Burr	Leigh	2017	5(14)	1	0	0	4
Rob Burrow	Leeds	2001-17	313(116)	168	131	5	939
Dean Busby	Warrington	1999-2002	34(34)	7	0	0	28
	Hull	1998	8(6)	0	0	0	0
	St Helens	1996-98	1(7)	0	0	0	0
Tom Bush	Leeds	2010	3(1)	1	0	0	4
Ikram Butt	London	1996	5(1)	0	0	0	0
Shane Byrne	Huddersfield	1998-99	1(5)	0	0	0	0
Todd Byrne	Hull	2008-09	20	4	0	0	16
Didier Cabestany	Paris	1996-97	20(6)	2	0	0	8
Hep Cahill	Widnes	2012-17	102(8)	4	0	0	16
	Crusaders	2011	16	2	0	0	8
Joel Caine	Salford	2004	24	8	13	0	58
	London	2003	6	4	1	0	18
Mark Calderwood	Harlequins	2011	13	2	0	0	8
	Hull	2009-10	23	6	0	0	24
	Wigan	2006-08	64	23	0	0	92
	Leeds	2001-05	117(9)	88	0	0	352
Mike Callan	Warrington	2002	(4)	0	0	0	0
Matt Calland	Huddersfield	2003	2	0	0	0	0
	Hull	1999	1	0	0	0	0
	Bradford	1996-98	44(5)	24	0	0	96
Dean Callaway	London	1999-2000	26(24)	12	0	0	48
Laurent Cambres	Paris	1996	(1)	0	0	0	0
Chris Campbell	Warrington	2000	7(1)	2	0	0	8
Liam Campbell	Wakefield	2005	(1)	0	0	0	0
Logan Campbell	Hull	1998-99, 2001	70(13)	14	0	0	56
	Castleford	2000	14(2)	3	0	0	12
	Workington	1996	7(1)	1	0	0	4
Terry Campese	Hull KR	2015-16	19(1)	2	4	0	16
Blake Cannova	Widnes	2002	(1)	0	0	0	0
Phil Cantillon	Widnes	2002-03	27(21)	18	0	0	72
	Leeds	1997	(1)	0	0	0	0
Liam Carberry	Widnes	2014-15	2(5)	0	0	0	0
Damien Cardace	Catalans	2012, 2014-15	23	14	0	0	56
Daryl Cardiss	Warrington	2003-04	23(2)	3	4	0	20
	Halifax	1999-2003	91(8)	39	4	0	164
	Wigan	1996-98	12(6)	4	0	0	16
Dale Cardoza	Warrington	2002	5	1	0	0	4
	Halifax	2001	3	1	0	0	4
	Huddersfield	2000-01	20(9)	11	0	0	44
	Sheffield	1998-99	11(7)	3	0	0	12
Paul Carige	Salford	1999	24(1)	7	0	0	28
Dane Carlaw	Catalans	2008-10	58(15)	9	0	0	36
Keal Carlile	Hull KR	2012-15	6(28)	1	0	0	4
	Huddersfield	2009, 2011	2(1)	1	0	0	4
	Bradford	2008	(1)	0	0	0	0
Jim Carlton	Huddersfield	1999	3(11)	2	0	0	8
George Carmont	Wigan	2008-12	136	71	0	0	284
Brian Carney	Warrington	2009	4	2	0	0	8
	Wigan	2001-05	91(10)	42	1	0	170
	Hull	2000	13(3)	7	0	0	28
	Gateshead	1999	3(2)	2	0	0	8
Justin Carney	Salford	2016-17	28	12	0	0	48
	Castleford	2013-15	58	56	0	0	224
Martin Carney	Warrington	1997	(1)	0	0	0	0
Todd Carney	Salford	2017	9(5)	0	7	0	14
	Catalans	2015-16	32	9	4	1	45
Omari Caro	Hull KR	2013-14	21	20	0	0	80
	London	2012	11	4	0	0	16
Paul Carr	Sheffield	1996-98	45(5)	15	0	0	60
Bernard Carroll	London	1996	2(1)	1	0	0	4
Mark Carroll	London	1998	15(3)	1	0	0	4
Tonie Carroll	Leeds	2001-02	42(2)	30	0	0	120
Darren Carter	Workington	1996	10(3)	0	1	0	2
Steve Carter	Widnes	2002	14(7)	4	0	0	16
John Cartwright	Salford	1997	9	0	0	0	0
Garreth Carvell	Castleford	2014	1(4)	1	0	0	4
	Hull	2001-08, 2014	75(84)	22	0	0	88
	Warrington	2009-13	77(40)	13	0	0	52
	Leeds	1997-2000	(4)	0	0	0	0
	Gateshead	1999	4(4)	1	0	0	4
Garen Casey	Salford	1999	13(5)	3	23	0	58
Ray Cashmere	Salford	2009-11	63(3)	5	0	0	20
Mick Cassidy	Widnes	2005	24	0	0	0	0
	Wigan	1996-2004	184(36)	30	0	0	120
Remi Casty	Catalans	2006-13, 2015-17	145(92)	22	0	0	88
Ned Catic	Castleford	2008	7(7)	3	0	0	12
	Wakefield	2006-07	17(29)	4	0	0	16
Mason Caton-Brown	Wakefield	2017	20	17	0	0	68
	Salford	2014-16	28	10	0	0	40
	London	2013-14	19	15	0	0	60
Joe Cator	Hull KR	2016	(2)	0	0	0	0
Chris Causey	Warrington	1997-99	(18)	1	0	0	4
Jason Cayless	St Helens	2006-09	62(9)	7	0	0	28
Arnaud Cervello	Paris	1996	4	4	0	0	16
Marshall Chalk	Celtic	2009	13	4	0	0	16
Ed Chamberlain	Widnes	2016-17	6(1)	0	5	0	10
Gary Chambers	Warrington	1996-2000	65(28)	2	0	0	8
Pierre Chamorin	Paris	1996-97	27(3)	8	3	0	38
Alex Chan	Catalans	2006-08	59(19)	11	0	0	44
Jason Chan	Hull KR	2014	5(1)	3	0	0	12
	Huddersfield	2014	46(12)	9	0	0	36
	Crusaders	2010-11	48(1)	10	0	0	40
	Celtic	2009	17(6)	3	0	0	12
Joe Chandler	Leeds	2008	(1)	0	0	0	0
Michael Channing	Castleford	2013-15	27(2)	8	0	0	32
	London	2012-13	15(3)	2	0	0	8
Jay Chapelhow	Widnes	2016-17	9(12)	0	0	0	0
Ted Chapelhow	Widnes	2016-17	1(7)	0	0	0	0
Chris Chapman	Leeds	1999	(1)	0	0	0	0
Damien Chapman	London	1998	6(2)	3	4	1	21
David Chapman	Castleford	1996-98	24(6)	8	0	0	32
Jaymes Chapman	Halifax	2002-03	5(8)	1	0	0	4
Richard Chapman	Sheffield	1996	1	2	0	0	8
Chris Charles	Salford	2004-06	59(16)	6	140	0	304
	Castleford	2001	1(4)	1	0	0	4
Olivier Charles	Catalans	2007	2	2	0	0	8
Josh Charnley	Wigan	2010-16	151(2)	141	77	0	718
	Hull KR	2010	5	5	0	0	20
Lewis Charnock	St Helens	2013, 2015	4(1)	2	6	0	20
Rangi Chase	Widnes	2017	6	0	0	0	0
	Castleford	2009-13, 2016-17	122(12)	39	0	3	159
	Salford	2014-15	37	10	13	2	68
Andy Cheetham	Huddersfield	1998-99	30	11	0	0	44
Kris Chesney	London	1998	1(2)	0	0	0	0
Chris Chester	Hull KR	2007-08	28(6)	4	0	0	16
	Hull	2002-06	67(25)	13	0	0	52
	Wigan	1999-2001	21(22)	5	0	0	20
	Halifax	1996-99	47(14)	16	15	1	95

158

PLAYER	CLUB	YEAR	APP	TRIES	GOALS	FG	PTS
Lee Chilton	Workington	1996	10(3)	6	0	0	24
Dane Chisholm	Hull KR	2015	1	0	0	0	0
Gary Christie	Bradford	1996-97	4(7)	1	0	0	4
James Clare	Castleford	2012-15	33	21	0	0	84
Daryl Clark	Warrington	2015-17	66(9)	18	0	0	72
	Castleford	2011-14	34(51)	31	0	0	124
Dean Clark	Leeds	1996	11(2)	3	0	0	12
Des Clark	St Helens	1999	4	0	0	0	0
	Halifax	1998-99	35(13)	6	0	0	24
Greg Clarke	Halifax	1997	1(1)	0	0	0	0
John Clarke	Oldham	1996-97	27(4)	5	0	0	20
Jon Clarke	Widnes	2012-14	59(1)	5	0	0	20
	Warrington	2001-11	217(25)	56	2	0	228
	London	2000-01	19(11)	2	0	0	8
	Wigan	1997-99	13(10)	3	0	0	12
Chris Clarkson	Hull KR	2016	20	1	0	0	4
	Widnes	2015	17(1)	4	0	0	16
	Leeds	2010-14	61(39)	9	0	0	36
Adam Clay	Salford	2011	2	3	0	0	12
Ryan Clayton	Castleford	2004,					
		2008-10	36(24)	5	0	0	20
	Salford	2006	3(8)	2	0	0	8
	Huddersfield	2005	4(6)	0	0	0	0
	Halifax	2000,					
		2002-03	28(12)	6	0	0	24
Gavin Clinch	Salford	2004	21(1)	1	0	1	5
	Halifax	1998-99,					
		2001-02	88(2)	26	45	5	199
	Hudds-Sheff	2000	18(2)	5	0	1	21
	Wigan	1999	10(2)	4	12	0	40
Joel Clinton	Hull KR	2010-12	42(14)	2	0	0	8
John Clough	Salford	2004-06	1(16)	0	0	0	0
Paul Clough	Huddersfield	2017	8(22)	2	0	0	8
	Widnes	2014	4(8)	1	0	0	4
	St Helens	2005-13	53(113)	16	0	0	64
Tony Clubb	Wigan	2014-17	28(51)	11	0	0	44
	London	2012-13	24(8)	7	0	0	28
	Harlequins	2006-11	100(11)	29	0	0	116
Bradley Clyde	Leeds	2001	7(5)	1	0	0	4
Michael Coady	Leeds	2010	1	0	0	0	0
Evan Cochrane	London	1996	5(1)	1	0	0	4
Ben Cockayne	Hull KR	2007-11,					
		2014-16	125(30)	38	18	0	188
	Wakefield	2012-13	54	28	2	0	116
Liam Colbon	Hull	2014	8	1	0	0	4
	London	2012-13	22	5	0	0	20
	Hull KR	2009-11	51	20	0	0	80
	Wigan	2004-05,					
		2007-08	37(14)	15	0	0	60
Anthony Colella	Huddersfield	2003	5(1)	2	0	0	8
Liam Coleman	Leigh	2005	1(4)	0	0	0	0
Andy Coley	Wigan	2008-11	100(10)	8	0	0	32
	Salford	2001-02,					
		2004-07	112(34)	34	0	0	136
Richard Colley	Bradford	2004	1	0	0	0	0
Steve Collins	Hull	2000	28	17	0	0	68
Wayne Collins	Gateshead	1999	20(4)	13	0	0	52
	Leeds	1997	21	3	0	0	12
Dean Collis	Wakefield	2012-15	64	28	0	0	112
Aurelien Cologni	Catalans	2006	4(1)	3	0	0	12
Gary Connolly	Widnes	2005	20	4	1	0	18
	Wigan	1996-2002,					
		2004	168(10)	70	5	0	290
	Leeds	2003-04	27	6	0	0	24
Jake Connor	Hull	2017	21(7)	10	20	0	80
	Huddersfield	2013-16	47(1)	21	2	0	88
Nathan Conroy	Bradford	2013-14	(4)	0	0	0	0
Matt Cook	Castleford	2008,					
		2015-17	16(53)	7	0	0	28
	London	2012-14	50(7)	8	0	0	32
	Hull KR	2010-11	9(16)	7	0	0	28
	Bradford	2005-09	11(52)	4	0	0	16
Mick Cook	Sheffield	1996	9(10)	2	0	0	8
Paul Cook	Huddersfield	1998-99	11(6)	2	13	0	34
	Bradford	1996-97	14(8)	7	38	1	105
Peter Cook	St Helens	2004	(1)	0	0	0	0
Paul Cooke	Wakefield	2010	16(1)	2	36	1	85
	Hull KR	2007-10	54(5)	8	76	2	186
	Hull	1999-2007	177(27)	32	333	4	798
Ben Cooper	Leigh	2005	25(1)	5	0	0	20
	Huddersfield	2000-01,					
		2003-04	28(12)	3	0	0	12
Mike Cooper	Warrington	2006-13,					
		2017	47(88)	7	0	0	28
	Castleford	2010	1(5)	2	0	0	8
Ged Corcoran	Halifax	2003	1(11)	0	0	0	0
Wayne Corcoran	Halifax	2003	4(2)	0	0	0	0
Jamie Cording	Huddersfield	2011-13	4(21)	5	0	0	20
Josh Cordoba	Hull	2009	8	1	0	0	4
Mark Corvo	Salford	2002	7(5)	0	0	0	0
Neville Costigan	Hull KR	2014	24	3	0	0	12
Brandon Costin	Huddersfield	2001,					
		2003-04	69	42	93	3	357
	Bradford	2002	20(1)	8	0	0	32
Wes Cotton	London	1997-98	12	3	0	0	12
Phil Coussons	Salford	1997	7(2)	3	0	0	12
Alex Couttet	Paris	1997	1	0	0	0	0
Nick Couttet	Paris	1997	1	0	0	0	0
Jamie Coventry	Castleford	1996	1	0	0	0	0
Jimmy Cowan	Oldham	1996-97	2(8)	0	0	0	0
Will Cowell	Warrington	1998-2000	6(8)	1	0	0	4
Neil Cowie	Wigan	1996-2001	116(27)	10	0	1	41
Danny Cowling	Wakefield	2012-13	2	0	0	0	0
Jordan Cox	Warrington	2016	(16)	0	0	0	0
	Hull KR	2011-15	17(44)	4	0	0	16
	Huddersfield	2015	(2)	0	0	0	0
Mark Cox	London	2003	(3)	0	0	0	0
James Coyle	Wigan	2005	2(3)	1	0	0	4
Thomas Coyle	Wigan	2008	2(1)	0	0	0	0
Eorl Crabtree	Huddersfield	2001,					
		2003-16	180(167)	52	0	0	208
Andy Craig	Halifax	1999	13(7)	1	3	0	10
	Wigan	1996	5(5)	2	0	0	8
Owen Craigie	Widnes	2005	15	7	0	2	30
Scott Cram	London	1999-2002	65(7)	4	0	0	16
Danny Craven	Widnes	2012-15, 2017	38(15)	10	5	2	52
Steve Craven	Hull	1998-2003	53(42)	4	0	0	16
Nicky Crellin	Workington	1996	(2)	0	0	0	0
Jason Critchley	Wakefield	2000	7(1)	4	0	0	16
	Castleford	1997-98	27(3)	11	0	0	44
Jason Croker	Catalans	2007-09	56(2)	11	0	1	45
Martin Crompton	Salford	1998-2000	30(6)	11	6	2	58
	Oldham	1996-97	36(1)	16	0	3	67
Paul Crook	Widnes	2005	2(2)	0	5	1	11
Paul Crook	Oldham	1996	4(9)	0	3	0	6
Jason Crookes	Hull	2013-14	15(1)	5	0	0	20
	Bradford	2009-12	25(1)	7	0	0	28
Ben Crooks	Leigh	2017	19	6	0	0	24
	Castleford	2016	24(2)	5	1	0	22
	Hull	2012-14	42(3)	30	23	0	166
Lee Crooks	Castleford	1996-97	27(2)	2	14	0	36
Dominic Crosby	Warrington	2017	(6)	0	0	0	0
	Wigan	2012-16	57(35)	6	0	0	24
Alan Cross	St Helens	1997	(2)	0	0	0	0
Ben Cross	Widnes	2012-13	27(1)	2	0	0	8
	Wigan	2011	(4)	0	0	0	0
	Leeds	2011	1(9)	0	0	0	0
Steve Crossley	Castleford	2015	(6)	0	0	0	0
	Bradford	2010-11	(9)	1	0	0	4
Garret Crossman	Hull KR	2008	8(18)	0	0	0	0
Steve Crouch	Castleford	2004	4(1)	2	0	0	8
Kevin Crouthers	Warrington	2001-03	12(1)	4	0	0	16
	London	2000	6(4)	1	0	0	4
	Wakefield	1999	4(1)	1	0	0	4
	Bradford	1997-98	3(9)	2	0	0	8
Jordan Crowther	Wakefield	2014-17	3(10)	1	0	0	4
Matt Crowther	Hull	2001-03	48	20	166	0	412
	Hudds-Sheff	2000	10(4)	5	22	0	64
	Sheffield	1996-99	43(4)	22	10	0	108
Heath Cruckshank	Halifax	2003	19(1)	0	0	0	0
	St Helens	2001	1(12)	0	0	0	0
Leroy Cudjoe	Huddersfield	2008-17	239(1)	98	57	1	507
Paul Cullen	Warrington	1996	19	3	0	0	12
Francis Cummins	Leeds	1996-2005	217(13)	120	26	2	534
James Cunningham	Hull	2012, 2014-15	(9)	0	0	0	0
	London	2014	10(7)	2	0	0	8
Keiron Cunningham	St Helens	1996-2010	357(24)	138	0	0	552
Liam Cunningham	Hull	2010	(1)	0	0	0	0
Ben Currie	Warrington	2012-17	76(31)	49	0	0	196
Andy Currier	Warrington	1996-97	(2)	1	0	0	4
Peter Cusack	Hull	2008-10	34(22)	3	0	0	12
Adam Cuthbertson	Leeds	2015-17	64(16)	23	0	0	92
Alrix Da Costa	Catalans	2016-17	5(17)	0	0	0	0
Will Dagger	Warrington	2017	3	0	0	0	0
Joe Dakuitoga	Sheffield	1996	6(3)	1	0	0	4
Matty Dale	Hull	2006, 2008	7(1)	1	0	0	4
	Wakefield	2008	1(1)	0	0	0	0
Brett Dallas	Wigan	2000-06	156	89	0	0	356
Mark Dalle Cort	Celtic	2009	23	4	0	0	16
Paul Darbyshire	Warrington	1997	(6)	0	0	0	0

Super League Players 1996-2017

PLAYER	CLUB	YEAR	APP	TRIES	GOALS	FG	PTS
James Davey	Wakefield	2009-11	3(14)	1	0	0	4
Maea David	Hull	1998	1	0	0	0	0
Alex Davidson	Salford	2011, 2013	(3)	0	0	0	0
Paul Davidson	Halifax	2001-03	22(30)	10	0	0	40
	London	2000	6(10)	4	0	0	16
	St Helens	1998-99	27(16)	7	0	0	28
	Oldham	1996-97	17(18)	14	0	1	57
Ben Davies	Castleford	2011, 2013	3(4)	2	0	0	8
	Widnes	2012-13	10(15)	3	0	0	12
	Wigan	2010	(5)	0	0	0	0
Gareth Davies	Warrington	1996-97	1(6)	0	0	0	0
Geraint Davies	Celtic	2009	(7)	0	0	0	0
John Davies	Castleford	2010-12	1(6)	1	0	0	4
Jordan Davies	Salford	2013	2(3)	0	0	0	0
Macauley Davies	Wigan	2016	(1)	0	0	0	0
Olly Davies	St Helens	2016	(1)	0	0	0	0
Tom Davies	Wigan	2017	22	13	0	0	52
Wes Davies	Wigan	1998-2001	22(22)	11	0	0	44
Brad Davis	Castleford	1997-2000, 2004, 2006	102(3)	31	43	10	220
	Wakefield	2001-03	51(12)	15	22	5	109
Matty Dawson	Leigh	2017	23	12	0	0	48
	St Helens	2014-16	46(1)	15	0	0	60
	Huddersfield	2012-13	4	0	0	0	0
Brad Day	Castleford	2014	(1)	0	0	0	0
Matt Daylight	Hull	2000	17(1)	7	0	0	28
	Gateshead	1999	30	25	0	0	100
Michael De Vere	Huddersfield	2005-06	36	6	74	0	172
Paul Deacon	Wigan	2010-11	32(11)	4	14	0	44
	Bradford	1998-2009	258(43)	72	1029	23	2369
	Oldham	1997	(2)	0	0	0	0
Chris Dean	Widnes	2012-17	105(6)	20	0	0	80
	Wakefield	2011	20	8	0	0	32
	St Helens	2007-10	18(3)	9	0	0	36
Craig Dean	Halifax	1996-97	25(11)	12	1	1	51
Gareth Dean	London	2002	(4)	0	0	0	0
Yacine Dekkiche	Hudds-Sheff	2000	11(3)	3	0	0	12
Brett Delaney	Leeds	2010-17	139(27)	23	0	0	92
Jason Demetriou	Wakefield	2004-10	174(3)	50	2	0	204
	Widnes	2002-03	47(1)	15	1	0	62
Martin Dermott	Warrington	1997	1	0	0	0	0
David Despin	Paris	1996	(1)	0	0	0	0
Fabien Devecchi	Paris	1996-97	17(10)	2	0	0	8
Paul Devlin	Widnes	2002-04	32	16	0	0	64
Jordan Dezaria	Catalans	2016-17	3(2)	0	0	0	0
Stuart Dickens	Salford	2005	4(5)	0	4	0	8
Tyler Dickinson	Huddersfield	2016-17	(11)	1	0	0	4
Matt Diskin	Bradford	2011-14	64(16)	11	0	0	44
	Leeds	2001-10	195(37)	40	0	0	160
Andrew Dixon	Salford	2013-14	34(2)	8	0	0	32
	St Helens	2009-12	19(41)	12	0	0	48
Kieran Dixon	Hull KR	2015-16	23(4)	21	9	0	102
	London	2012-14	49(1)	32	2	0	132
Kirk Dixon	Castleford	2008-14	143(2)	63	267	0	786
	Hull	2004-06	13(4)	7	4	0	36
Paul Dixon	Sheffield	1996-97	5(9)	1	0	0	4
Nabil Djalout	Catalans	2017	1	0	0	0	0
Gareth Dobson	Castleford	1998-2000	(10)	0	0	0	0
Michael Dobson	Salford	2015-17	58(1)	14	77	1	211
	Hull KR	2008-13	142	51	500	11	1215
	Wigan	2006	14	5	61	0	142
	Catalans	2006	10	4	31	1	79
Michael Docherty	Hull	2000-01	(6)	0	0	0	0
Mitchell Dodds	Warrington	2016	(2)	0	0	0	0
Erjon Dollapi	London	2013-14	(18)	4	0	0	16
Sid Domic	Hull	2006-07	39(4)	15	0	0	60
	Wakefield	2004-05	48	30	0	0	120
	Warrington	2002-03	41(4)	17	0	0	68
Scott Donald	Leeds	2006-10	131	77	0	0	308
James Donaldson	Hull KR	2015-16	8(19)	2	0	0	8
	Bradford	2009-14	38(35)	4	0	0	16
Glen Donkin	Hull	2002-03	(10)	1	0	0	4
Stuart Donlan	Castleford	2008	20	8	0	0	32
	Huddersfield	2004-06	59(3)	15	0	0	60
	Halifax	2001-03	65(2)	22	0	0	88
Jason Donohue	Bradford	1996	(4)	0	0	0	0
Jeremy Donougher	Bradford	1996-99	40(21)	13	0	0	52
Justin Dooley	London	2000-01	37(18)	2	0	0	8
Dane Dorahy	Halifax	2003	20	7	45	0	118
	Wakefield	2000-01	16(2)	4	19	1	55
Jamie Doran	Wigan	2014	(2)	0	0	0	0
Luke Dorn	Castleford	2008, 2014-16	78(2)	60	0	0	240
	London	2005, 2012-13	58(8)	42	0	0	168
	Harlequins	2006, 2009-11	83(1)	57	0	0	228
	Salford	2007	19(8)	11	0	0	44

PLAYER	CLUB	YEAR	APP	TRIES	GOALS	FG	PTS
Brandon Douglas	Castleford	2016	(1)	0	0	0	0
Luke Douglas	St Helens	2017	17(9)	1	0	0	4
Ewan Dowes	Hull	2003-11	169(51)	10	0	0	40
	Leeds	2001-03	1(9)	0	0	0	0
Jack Downs	Hull	2015-17	2(11)	0	0	0	0
Adam Doyle	Warrington	1998	9(3)	4	0	0	16
Rod Doyle	Sheffield	1997-99	52(10)	10	0	0	40
Brad Drew	Huddersfield	2005-07, 2010	78(13)	18	13	1	99
	Wakefield	2008-09	27(9)	7	14	1	57
Josh Drinkwater	Leigh	2017	19	1	12	1	29
	London	2014	23(1)	5	54	0	128
Damien Driscoll	Salford	2001	23(1)	1	0	0	4
James Duckworth	London	2014	3	0	0	0	0
	Leeds	2013	2	1	0	0	4
Gil Dudson	Widnes	2015-17	51(10)	1	0	0	4
	Wigan	2012-14	26(16)	2	0	0	8
	Crusaders	2011	3(7)	0	0	0	0
	Celtic	2009	(1)	0	0	0	0
Jason Duffy	Leigh	2005	3(1)	0	0	0	0
John Duffy	Leigh	2005	21	6	0	0	24
	Salford	2000	3(11)	0	1	1	3
	Warrington	1997-99	12(12)	0	0	0	0
Tony Duggan	Celtic	2009	4	3	0	0	12
Andrew Duncan	London	1997	2(4)	2	0	0	8
	Warrington	1997	(1)	0	0	0	0
Andrew Dunemann	Salford	2006	25	1	0	2	6
	Leeds	2003-05	76(4)	11	0	2	46
	Halifax	1999-2002	68	19	0	1	77
Matt Dunford	London	1997-98	18(20)	3	0	1	13
Vincent Duport	Catalans	2007-09, 2011-17	152(15)	74	0	0	296
Jamie Durbin	Widnes	2005	1	0	0	0	0
	Warrington	2003	(1)	0	0	0	0
Scott Dureau	Catalans	2011-15	88(1)	29	315	10	756
James Durkin	Paris	1997	(5)	0	0	0	0
Bernard Dwyer	Bradford	1996-2000	65(10)	14	0	0	56
Brad Dwyer	Warrington	2012-17	12(63)	11	0	0	44
	Huddersfield	2013	(6)	0	0	0	0
Luke Dyer	Crusaders	2010	23(1)	5	0	0	20
	Celtic	2009	21	6	0	0	24
	Hull KR	2007	26	13	0	0	52
	Castleford	2006	17(2)	5	0	0	20
Adam Dykes	Hull	2008	12	1	0	2	6
Jim Dymock	London	2001-04	94(1)	15	0	1	61
Leo Dynevor	London	1996	8(11)	5	7	0	34
Jason Eade	Paris	1997	9	4	0	0	16
Michael Eagar	Hull	2004-05	12	4	0	0	16
	Castleford	1999-2003	130(2)	60	0	0	240
	Warrington	1998	21	6	0	0	24
Kyle Eastmond	St Helens	2007-11	46(20)	35	117	3	377
Greg Eastwood	Leeds	2010	5(12)	1	0	0	4
Barry Eaton	Widnes	2002	25	2	49	4	110
	Castleford	2000	1(4)	0	3	0	6
Greg Ebrill	Salford	2002	15(6)	1	0	0	4
Cliff Eccles	Salford	1997-98	30(5)	1	0	0	4
Chris Eckersley	Warrington	1996	1	0	0	0	0
Greg Eden	Castleford	2011, 2017	31	39	0	0	156
	Hull KR	2013-14	37	23	0	0	92
	Salford	2014	4	1	0	0	4
	Huddersfield	2012	24	8	0	0	32
Steve Edmed	Sheffield	1997	15(1)	0	0	0	0
Mark Edmondson	Salford	2007	10(2)	0	0	0	0
	St Helens	1999-2005	27(75)	10	0	0	40
Diccon Edwards	Castleford	1996-97	10(5)	1	0	0	4
Grant Edwards	Castleford	2006	(2)	0	0	0	0
Max Edwards	Harlequins	2010	1	0	0	0	0
Peter Edwards	Salford	1997-98	35(2)	4	0	0	16
Shaun Edwards	London	1997-2000	32(8)	16	1	0	66
	Bradford	1998	8(2)	4	0	0	16
	Wigan	1996	17(3)	12	1	0	50
Tuoyo Egodo	Castleford	2017	1	3	0	0	12
Danny Ekis	Halifax	2001	(1)	0	0	0	0
Abi Ekoku	Bradford	1997-98	21(4)	6	0	0	24
	Halifax	1996	15(1)	5	0	0	20
Shane Elford	Huddersfield	2007-08	26(1)	7	0	0	28
Olivier Elima	Catalans	2008-10, 2013-16	99(35)	34	0	0	136
	Bradford	2011-12	37(3)	12	0	0	48
	Wakefield	2003-07	40(47)	13	0	0	52
	Castleford	2002	(1)	1	0	0	4
Abderazak Elkhalouki	Paris	1997	(1)	0	0	0	0
George Elliott	Leeds	2011	1	0	0	0	0
Andy Ellis	Wakefield	2012	10	0	0	0	0
	Harlequins	2010-11	26(11)	8	0	0	32

PLAYER	CLUB	YEAR	APP	TRIES	GOALS	FG	PTS
Gareth Ellis	Hull	2013-17	82(5)	19	0	0	76
	Leeds	2005-08	109	24	1	0	98
	Wakefield	1999-2004	86(17)	21	2	0	88
Jamie Ellis	Huddersfield	2015-16	37(3)	14	31	3	121
	Castleford	2012-14	36(8)	10	80	1	201
	Hull	2012	4(5)	1	0	0	4
	St Helens	2009	1(2)	0	1	0	2
Danny Ellison	Castleford	1998-99	7(16)	6	0	0	24
	Wigan	1996-97	15(1)	13	0	0	52
Andrew Emelio	Widnes	2005	22(2)	8	0	0	32
Jake Emmitt	Salford	2013	5(10)	0	0	0	0
	Castleford	2011-13	32(17)	0	0	0	0
	St Helens	2008-10	1(16)	1	0	0	4
Anthony England	Wakefield	2016-17	33(7)	1	0	0	4
	Warrington	2014-15	12(21)	3	0	0	12
Matty English	Huddersfield	2017	(1)	0	0	0	0
Patrick Entat	Paris	1996	22	2	0	0	8
Jason Erba	Sheffield	1997	1(4)	0	0	0	0
Morgan Escare	Wigan	2017	12	4	30	1	77
	Catalans	2013-16	83	58	1	2	236
Ryan Esders	Harlequins	2009-10	9(11)	3	0	0	12
	Hull KR	2009	(1)	0	0	0	0
Sonny Esslemont	Hull KR	2014-15	(5)	0	0	0	0
Niall Evalds	Salford	2013-17	60(10)	48	0	0	192
Ben Evans	Warrington	2014-15	3(16)	2	0	0	8
	Bradford	2013	3(12)	1	0	0	4
James Evans	Castleford	2009-10	26(1)	13	0	0	52
	Bradford	2007-08	43(5)	20	0	0	80
	Wakefield	2006	6	3	0	0	12
	Huddersfield	2004-06	51	22	0	0	88
Paul Evans	Paris	1997	18	8	0	0	32
Rhys Evans	Warrington	2010-17	87(7)	37	0	0	148
Wayne Evans	London	2002	11(6)	2	0	0	8
Toby Everett	London	2014	(2)	0	0	0	0
Richie Eyres	Warrington	1997	2(5)	0	0	0	0
	Sheffield	1997	2(3)	0	0	0	0
Henry Fa'afili	Warrington	2004-07	90(1)	70	0	0	280
David Fa'alogo	Huddersfield	2010-12	38(16)	13	0	0	52
Sala Fa'alogo	Widnes	2004-05	8(15)	2	0	0	8
Richard Fa'aoso	Castleford	2006	10(15)	5	0	0	20
Maurie Fa'asavalu	St Helens	2004-10	5(137)	29	0	0	116
Bolouagi Fagborun	Huddersfield	2004-06	4(2)	1	0	0	4
Theo Fages	St Helens	2016-17	41(5)	15	0	0	60
	Salford	2013-15	57(5)	18	4	0	80
Esene Faimalo	Salford	1997-99	23(25)	2	0	0	8
	Leeds	1996	3(3)	0	0	0	0
Joe Faimalo	Salford	1998-2000	23(47)	7	0	0	28
	Oldham	1996-97	37(5)	7	0	0	28
Jacob Fairbank	Huddersfield	2011-15	12(3)	0	0	0	0
	Wakefield	2014	1(3)	0	0	0	0
	London	2013	4(1)	1	0	0	4
	Bradford	2013	(2)	0	0	0	0
Karl Fairbank	Bradford	1996	17(2)	4	0	0	16
David Fairleigh	St Helens	2001	26(1)	8	0	0	32
David Faiumu	Huddersfield	2008-14	38(108)	13	0	0	52
Jamal Fakir	Bradford	2014	5(8)	1	0	0	4
	Catalans	2006-14	55(100)	13	0	0	52
Jim Fallon	Leeds	1996	10	5	0	0	20
Beau Falloon	Leeds	2016	8(2)	0	0	0	0
Owen Farnworth	Widnes	2017	1	0	0	0	0
Ben Farrar	London	2014	22	1	0	0	4
	Catalans	2011	13	3	0	0	12
Danny Farrar	Warrington	1998-2000	76	13	0	0	52
Andy Farrell	Wigan	1996-2004	230	77	1026	16	2376
Anthony Farrell	Widnes	2002-03	24(22)	4	1	0	18
	Leeds	1997-2001	99(23)	18	0	0	72
	Sheffield	1996	14(5)	5	0	0	20
Connor Farrell	Widnes	2016	3(9)	3	0	0	12
	Wigan	2014-15	1(8)	1	0	0	4
Craig Farrell	Hull	2000-01	1(3)	0	0	0	0
Liam Farrell	Wigan	2010-17	138(47)	71	0	0	284
Brad Fash	Hull	2015, 2017	(28)	0	0	0	0
Abraham Fatnowna	London	1997-98	7(2)	2	0	0	8
	Workington	1996	5	2	0	0	8
Sione Faumuina	Castleford	2009	18	1	0	0	4
	Hull	2005	3	1	0	0	4
Vince Fawcett	Wakefield	1999	13(1)	2	0	0	8
	Warrington	1998	4(7)	1	0	0	4
	Oldham	1997	5	3	0	0	12
Danny Fearon	Huddersfield	2001	(1)	0	0	0	0
	Halifax	1999-2000	5(6)	0	0	0	0
Chris Feather	Castleford	2009	1(23)	0	0	0	0
	Bradford	2007-08	7(20)	1	0	0	4
	Leeds	2003-04, 2006	16(35)	6	0	0	24
	Wakefield	2001-02, 2004-05	29(32)	9	0	0	36

PLAYER	CLUB	YEAR	APP	TRIES	GOALS	FG	PTS
Dom Feaunati	Leigh	2005	4	1	0	0	4
	St Helens	2004	10(7)	7	0	0	28
Adel Fellous	Hull	2008	1(2)	0	0	0	0
	Catalans	2006-07	16(22)	4	0	0	16
Luke Felsch	Hull	2000-01	46(6)	7	0	0	28
	Gateshead	1999	28(1)	2	0	0	8
Leon Felton	Warrington	2002	4(2)	0	0	0	0
	St Helens	2001	1(1)	0	0	0	0
Dale Ferguson	Huddersfield	2011-13, 2017	51(18)	15	0	0	60
	Bradford	2014	3(3)	0	0	0	0
	Hull KR	2013	3(1)	1	0	0	4
	Wakefield	2007-11	40(14)	12	0	0	48
Brett Ferres	Leeds	2016-17	23(6)	5	0	0	20
	Huddersfield	2012-15	72	27	0	0	108
	Castleford	2009-12	78(5)	26	0	0	104
	Wakefield	2007-08	36(2)	6	5	0	34
	Bradford	2005-06	18(17)	11	2	0	48
David Ferriol	Catalans	2007-12	72(55)	8	0	0	32
Jason Ferris	Leigh	2005	4	1	0	0	4
Callum Field	Wigan	2017	(4)	0	0	0	0
Jamie Field	Wakefield	1999-2006	133(59)	19	0	0	76
	Huddersfield	1998	15(5)	0	0	0	0
	Leeds	1996-97	3(11)	0	0	0	0
Mark Field	Wakefield	2003-07	28(7)	3	0	0	12
Jamie Fielden	London	2003	(1)	0	0	0	0
	Huddersfield	1998-2000	4(8)	0	0	0	0
Stuart Fielden	Huddersfield	2013	8(1)	0	0	0	0
	Wigan	2006-12	105(24)	2	0	0	8
	Bradford	1998-2006	142(78)	41	0	0	164
David Fifita	Wakefield	2016-17	18(21)	4	0	0	16
Lafaele Filipo	Workington	1996	15(4)	3	0	0	12
Salesi Finau	Warrington	1996-97	16(15)	8	0	0	32
Brett Finch	Wigan	2011-12	49(3)	16	0	0	64
Vinny Finigan	Bradford	2010	4(1)	4	0	0	16
Liam Finn	Wakefield	2004, 2016-17	57(4)	3	180	0	372
	Castleford	2014-15	45(2)	8	5	2	44
	Halifax	2002-03	16(5)	2	30	1	69
Lee Finnerty	Halifax	2003	18(2)	5	2	0	24
Phil Finney	Warrington	1998	1	0	0	0	0
Simon Finnigan	Widnes	2003-05, 2012	56(24)	21	0	0	84
	Huddersfield	2009-10	22(5)	6	0	0	24
	Bradford	2008	14(13)	8	0	0	32
	Salford	2006-07	50	17	0	0	68
Matt Firth	Halifax	2000-01	12(2)	0	0	0	0
Andy Fisher	Wakefield	1999-2000	31(8)	4	0	0	16
Ben Fisher	London	2013	8(12)	1	0	0	4
	Catalans	2012	9(5)	1	0	0	4
	Hull KR	2007-11	78(46)	18	0	0	72
Craig Fitzgibbon	Hull	2010-11	42(1)	9	8	0	52
Daniel Fitzhenry	Hull KR	2008-09	36(11)	14	0	0	56
Karl Fitzpatrick	Salford	2004-07, 2009-10	89(11)	33	2	0	136
Conor Fitzsimmons	Castleford	2016	(2)	0	0	0	0
Mark Flanagan	Salford	2016-17	34(5)	4	0	0	16
	St Helens	2012-15	40(39)	9	0	0	36
	Wigan	2009	3(7)	1	0	0	4
Chris Flannery	St Helens	2007-12	108(11)	32	0	0	128
Darren Fleary	Leigh	2005	24	1	0	0	4
	Huddersfield	2003-04	43(8)	4	0	0	16
	Leeds	1997-2002	98(9)	3	0	0	12
Daniel Fleming	Castleford	2013-14	(15)	1	0	0	4
Greg Fleming	London	1999-2001	64(1)	40	2	0	164
Matty Fleming	Leigh	2017	5	1	0	0	4
	St Helens	2015-17	17	7	0	0	28
Adam Fletcher	Castleford	2006, 2008	16(7)	11	0	0	44
Bryan Fletcher	Wigan	2006-07	42	14	0	0	56
Richard Fletcher	Castleford	2006	13(5)	3	4	0	20
	Hull	1999-2004	11(56)	5	0	0	20
Greg Florimo	Halifax	2000	26	6	4	0	32
	Wigan	1999	18(2)	7	1	0	30
Ben Flower	Wigan	2012-17	92(24)	16	0	0	64
	Crusaders	2010-11	10(23)	2	0	0	8
	Celtic	2009	2(15)	0	0	0	0
Jason Flowers	Salford	2004	6(1)	0	0	0	0
	Halifax	2002	24(4)	4	0	0	16
	Castleford	1996-2001	119(19)	33	0	1	133
Stuart Flowers	Castleford	1996	(3)	0	0	0	0
Adrian Flynn	Castleford	1996-97	19(2)	10	0	0	40
Paddy Flynn	Castleford	2016	9(1)	6	0	0	24
	Widnes	2012-15	72	41	0	0	164
Wayne Flynn	Sheffield	1997	3(5)	0	0	0	0
Adam Fogerty	Warrington	1998	4	0	0	0	0
	St Helens	1996	13	1	0	0	4

Super League Players 1996-2017

PLAYER	CLUB	YEAR	APP	TRIES	GOALS	FG	PTS
Mahe Fonua	Hull	2016-17	50	25	0	0	100
Liam Foran	Salford	2013	10(3)	1	0	0	4
Carl Forber	Leigh	2005	4	1	0	0	4
	St Helens	2004	1(1)	0	6	0	12
Paul Forber	Salford	1997-98	19(12)	4	0	0	16
Byron Ford	Hull KR	2007	13	6	0	0	24
James Ford	Castleford	2009	3(5)	1	0	0	4
Mike Ford	Castleford	1997-98	25(12)	5	0	3	23
	Warrington	1996	3	0	0	0	0
Jim Forshaw	Salford	1999	(1)	0	0	0	0
Mike Forshaw	Warrington	2004	20(1)	5	0	0	20
	Bradford	1997-2003	162(7)	32	0	0	128
	Leeds	1996	11(3)	5	0	0	20
Carl Forster	Salford	2015-16	5(7)	1	0	0	4
	St Helens	2011-12, 2014	(4)	0	0	0	0
	London	2014	2(3)	0	0	0	0
Mark Forster	Warrington	1996-2000	102(1)	40	0	0	160
Liam Forsyth	Wigan	2017	10(2)	3	0	0	12
Alex Foster	Castleford	2017	11(7)	2	0	0	8
	London	2014	20	3	0	0	12
	Leeds	2013	(8)	1	0	0	4
David Foster	Halifax	2000-01	4(9)	0	0	0	0
Jamie Foster	Huddersfield	2016	3	2	5	0	18
	Bradford	2013-14	32	12	111	0	270
	Hull	2012	9	5	45	0	110
	St Helens	2010-12	44(3)	30	201	0	522
Peter Fox	Wakefield	2007, 2012-14	85	44	0	0	176
	Hull KR	2008-11	95	52	0	0	208
Matty Fozard	St Helens	2014	1	0	0	0	0
Nick Fozzard	Castleford	2011	7(10)	0	0	0	0
	St Helens	2004-08, 2010	100(25)	7	0	0	28
	Hull KR	2009	18(4)	1	0	0	4
	Warrington	2002-03	43(11)	2	0	0	8
	Huddersfield	1998-2000	24(8)	2	0	0	8
	Leeds	1996-97	6(16)	3	0	0	12
David Fraisse	Workington	1996	8	0	0	0	0
Daniel Frame	Widnes	2002-05	100(6)	24	0	0	96
Paul Franze	Castleford	2006	2(1)	0	0	0	0
Laurent Frayssinous	Catalans	2006	14(2)	3	32	0	76
Andrew Frew	Halifax	2003	17	5	0	0	20
	Wakefield	2002	21	8	0	0	32
	Huddersfield	2001	26	15	0	0	60
Dale Fritz	Castleford	1999-2003	120(4)	9	0	0	36
Gareth Frodsham	St Helens	2008-09	1(9)	0	0	0	0
Liam Fulton	Huddersfield	2009	12(3)	4	0	0	16
David Furner	Leeds	2003-04	45	8	23	0	78
	Wigan	2001-02	51(2)	21	13	0	110
David Furness	Castleford	1996	(1)	0	0	0	0
Matt Gafa	Harlequins	2006-09	81	26	16	0	136
Luke Gale	Castleford	2015-17	85	31	354	11	843
	Bradford	2012-14	56(2)	13	108	4	272
	Harlequins	2009-11	56(12)	18	86	3	247
Ben Galea	Hull	2013	12(2)	3	0	0	12
	Hull KR	2008-12	115(2)	33	0	0	132
Danny Galea	Widnes	2014-15	38(4)	5	0	0	20
Tommy Gallagher	Hull KR	2007	1(7)	0	0	0	0
	Widnes	2004	(6)	0	0	0	0
	London	2003	1(9)	1	0	0	4
Keith Galloway	Leeds	2016-17	28(4)	1	0	0	4
Mark Gamson	Sheffield	1996	3	0	0	0	0
Jim Gannon	Hull KR	2007	7(16)	1	0	0	4
	Huddersfield	2003-06	79(14)	11	0	0	44
	Halifax	1999-2002	83(4)	14	0	0	56
Josh Ganson	Wigan	2017	13(2)	2	0	0	8
Mitch Garbutt	Leeds	2015-17	29(23)	6	0	0	24
Steve Garces	Salford	2001	(1)	0	0	0	0
Benjamin Garcia	Catalans	2013-17	32(42)	12	0	0	48
Jean-Marc Garcia	Sheffield	1996-97	35(3)	22	0	0	88
Ade Gardner	Hull KR	2014	18	7	0	0	28
	St Helens	2002-13	236(12)	146	0	0	584
Matt Gardner	Harlequins	2009	6(3)	2	0	0	8
	Huddersfield	2006-07	22(3)	7	0	0	28
	Castleford	2004	1	1	0	0	4
Steve Gartland	Oldham	1996	1(1)	0	1	0	2
Daniel Gartner	Bradford	2001-03	74(1)	26	0	0	104
Dean Gaskell	Warrington	2002-05	58(1)	10	0	0	40
Lee Gaskell	Huddersfield	2017	26	12	0	0	48
	Bradford	2014	21	5	0	0	20
	Salford	2013	17	8	2	0	36
	St Helens	2010-13	33(9)	14	12	1	81
George Gatis	Huddersfield	2008	5(5)	1	0	0	4
Richard Gay	Castleford	1996-2002	94(16)	39	0	0	156
Andrew Gee	Warrington	2000-01	33(1)	4	0	0	16
Matty Gee	Salford	2015	(2)	0	0	0	0

PLAYER	CLUB	YEAR	APP	TRIES	GOALS	FG	PTS
Anthony Gelling	Wigan	2012-17	101(1)	52	0	0	208
Stanley Gene	Hull KR	2007-09	37(17)	9	0	0	36
	Bradford	2006	5(16)	8	0	0	32
	Huddersfield	2001, 2003-05	70(6)	27	0	0	108
	Hull	2000-01	5(23)	6	0	0	24
Steve Georgallis	Warrington	2001	5(1)	2	0	0	8
Luke George	Bradford	2014	9(1)	3	0	0	12
	Huddersfield	2012-13	28(2)	18	0	0	72
	Hull KR	2013	4	2	0	0	8
	Wakefield	2007-11	38(3)	24	0	0	96
Shaun Geritas	Warrington	1997	(5)	1	0	0	4
Alex Gerrard	Widnes	2012-17	41(38)	3	0	0	12
Anthony Gibbons	Leeds	1996	9(4)	2	0	1	9
David Gibbons	Leeds	1996	3(4)	2	0	0	8
Scott Gibbs	St Helens	1996	9	3	0	0	12
Ashley Gibson	Wakefield	2016-17	9	4	0	0	16
	Castleford	2014-15	27	9	0	0	36
	Salford	2010-13	77(4)	41	0	0	164
	Leeds	2005-09	25(7)	13	9	0	70
Damian Gibson	Castleford	2003-04	40(3)	5	0	0	20
	Salford	2002	28	3	0	0	12
	Halifax	1998-2001	104(1)	39	0	0	156
	Leeds	1997	18	3	0	0	12
Kurt Gidley	Warrington	2016-17	44	11	97	0	238
Matt Gidley	St Helens	2007-10	105	40	6	0	172
Tony Gigot	Catalans	2010-11, 2015-17	70(13)	29	25	1	167
	London	2014	2	0	4	0	8
Ian Gildart	Oldham	1996-97	31(7)	0	0	0	0
Oliver Gildart	Wigan	2015-17	47(2)	25	0	0	100
	Salford	2015	3	1	0	0	4
Chris Giles	Widnes	2003-04	35	12	0	0	48
	St Helens	2002	(1)	0	0	0	0
Kieran Gill	Castleford	2017	1	1	0	0	4
Peter Gill	London	1996-99	75(6)	20	0	0	80
Carl Gillespie	Halifax	1996-99	47(36)	13	0	0	52
Michael Gillett	London	2001-02	23(21)	12	2	0	52
Simon Gillies	Warrington	1999	28	6	0	0	24
Tom Gilmore	Widnes	2012-17	25(1)	9	18	3	75
Lee Gilmour	Wakefield	2014	10(3)	2	0	0	8
	Castleford	2013	10(2)	0	0	0	0
	Huddersfield	2010-12	71(1)	17	0	0	68
	St Helens	2004-09	149(3)	41	0	0	164
	Bradford	2001-03	44(31)	20	0	0	80
	Wigan	1997-2000	44(39)	22	0	0	88
Marc Glanville	Leeds	1998-99	43(3)	5	0	0	20
Eddie Glaze	Castleford	1996	1	0	0	0	0
Paul Gleadhill	Leeds	1996	4	0	0	0	0
Ben Gledhill	Salford	2012-13	3(10)	1	0	0	4
	Wakefield	2010-11	(16)	0	0	0	0
Mark Gleeson	Warrington	2000-08	38(102)	12	0	0	48
Martin Gleeson	Salford	2013-14	26(1)	4	0	0	16
	Hull	2011	6	4	0	0	16
	Wigan	2009-11	46(1)	19	0	0	76
	Warrington	2005-09	110(1)	44	0	0	176
	St Helens	2002-04	56(1)	25	0	0	100
	Huddersfield	1999-2001	47(9)	18	0	0	72
Sean Gleeson	Hull KR	2013	6	0	0	0	0
	Salford	2011-12	35	14	0	0	56
	Wakefield	2007-10	67(6)	20	0	0	80
	Wigan	2005-06	3(3)	0	0	0	0
Jon Goddard	Hull KR	2007	20	2	0	0	8
	Castleford	2000-01	(2)	0	0	0	0
Richard Goddard	Castleford	1996-97	11(3)	2	10	0	28
Brad Godden	Leeds	1998-99	47	15	0	0	60
Pita Godinet	Wakefield	2014-15	18(19)	10	0	0	40
Wayne Godwin	Salford	2011-13, 2015	43(8)	6	0	0	24
	Bradford	2008-10	16(44)	9	0	0	36
	Hull	2007	3(13)	1	0	0	4
	Wigan	2005-06	9(38)	6	0	0	24
	Castleford	2001-04	30(33)	18	56	0	184
Jason Golden	London	2012	7(2)	1	0	0	4
	Harlequins	2009-11	34(12)	3	0	0	12
	Wakefield	2007-08	26(5)	1	0	0	4
Marvin Golden	Widnes	2003	4	1	0	0	4
	London	2001	17(2)	1	0	0	4
	Halifax	2000	20(2)	5	0	0	20
	Leeds	1996-99	43(11)	19	0	0	76
Ashton Golding	Leeds	2014-17	30(4)	4	14	0	44
Brett Goldspink	Halifax	2000-02	64(5)	2	0	0	8
	Wigan	1999	6(16)	1	0	0	4
	St Helens	1998	19(4)	2	0	0	8
	Oldham	1997	13(2)	0	0	0	0
Lee Gomersall	Hull KR	2008	1	0	0	0	0
Luke Goodwin	London	1998	9(2)	3	1	1	15
	Oldham	1997	16(4)	10	17	2	76

PLAYER	CLUB	YEAR	APP	TRIES	GOALS	FG	PTS
Grant Gore	Widnes	2012-15	6(11)	1	0	0	4
Aaron Gorrell	Catalans	2007-08	23	6	14	0	52
Andy Gorski	Salford	2001-02	(2)	0	0	0	0
Cyrille Gossard	Catalans	2006-12	54(30)	5	0	0	20
Bobbie Goulding	Salford	2001-02	31(1)	2	56	4	124
	Wakefield	2000	12	3	25	3	65
	Huddersfield	1998-99	27(1)	3	65	4	146
	St Helens	1996-98	42(2)	9	210	4	460
Bobbie Goulding (Jnr)							
	Wakefield	2013	1(2)	0	1	0	2
Darrell Goulding	Hull KR	2015	8	1	0	0	4
	Wigan	2005-14	129(24)	68	0	0	272
	Salford	2009	9	5	0	0	20
Mick Govin	Leigh	2005	5(6)	4	0	0	16
Craig Gower	London	2012-13	40	7	24	0	76
David Gower	Salford	2006-07	(16)	0	0	0	0
Regan Grace	St Helens	2017	23	11	0	0	44
Shane Grady	London	2013	5(4)	1	2	0	8
James Graham	St Helens	2003-11	132(63)	47	0	0	188
Nathan Graham	Bradford	1996-98	17(28)	4	0	1	17
Nick Graham	Wigan	2003	13(1)	2	0	0	8
Dalton Grant	Crusaders	2011	(1)	0	0	0	0
Jon Grayshon	Harlequins	2007-09	10(32)	4	0	0	16
	Huddersfield	2003-06	7(43)	5	0	0	20
Blake Green	Wigan	2013-14	42(1)	15	0	0	60
	Hull KR	2011-12	35	14	0	0	56
Brett Green	Gateshead	1999	10(2)	0	0	0	0
Chris Green	Hull	2012-17	19(79)	6	0	0	24
James Green	Leigh	2017	4(5)	0	0	0	0
	Hull KR	2012-16	8(64)	3	0	0	12
Toby Green	Huddersfield	2001	3(1)	1	0	0	4
Craig Greenhill	Castleford	2004	21(4)	1	0	0	4
	Hull	2002-03	56	3	2	0	16
Clint Greenshields	Catalans	2007-12	137	81	0	0	324
Brandon Greenwood							
	Halifax	1996	1	0	0	0	0
Gareth Greenwood	Huddersfield	2003	(1)	0	0	0	0
	Halifax	2002	1	0	0	0	0
James Greenwood	Hull KR	2015-16	13(13)	4	0	0	16
	Salford	2015	1(1)	1	0	0	4
	Wigan	2013, 2015	(2)	0	0	0	0
	London	2014	10(5)	3	0	0	12
Joe Greenwood	St Helens	2012-17	40(28)	26	0	0	104
Lee Greenwood	Huddersfield	2005	7	3	0	0	12
	London	2004-05	30(2)	19	0	0	76
	Halifax	2000-03	38(2)	17	0	0	68
	Sheffield	1999	1(1)	0	0	0	0
Nick Gregson	Wigan	2016-17	5(9)	1	0	0	4
James Grehan	Castleford	2012	2(2)	0	0	0	0
Maxime Greseque	Wakefield	2007	2(1)	0	0	0	0
Mathieu Griffi	Catalans	2006-08	1(25)	0	0	0	0
Darrell Griffin	Salford	2013-15	31(27)	1	0	0	4
	Leeds	2012	8(19)	2	0	0	8
	Huddersfield	2007-11	65(60)	13	0	0	52
	Wakefield	2003-06	55(37)	9	3	0	42
George Griffin	Salford	2015-17	43(15)	9	0	0	36
	Wakefield	2015	5	0	0	0	0
	London	2014	(19)	1	0	0	4
	Hull KR	2012-13	11(7)	0	0	0	0
Josh Griffin	Hull	2017	21(5)	2	0	0	8
	Salford	2014-16	42	23	77	0	246
	Castleford	2012	20	13	1	0	54
	Wakefield	2011	17	5	21	0	62
	Huddersfield	2009	2	0	0	0	0
Jonathan Griffiths	Paris	1996	(4)	1	0	0	4
Andrew Grima	Workington	1996	2(9)	2	0	0	8
Tony Grimaldi	Hull	2000-01	56(1)	14	0	0	56
	Gateshead	1999	27(2)	10	0	0	40
Danny Grimley	Sheffield	1996	4(1)	1	0	0	4
Scott Grix	Wakefield	2008-09, 2017	66(3)	27	0	0	108
	Huddersfield	2010-16	137(11)	52	32	0	272
Simon Grix	Warrington	2006-14	133(25)	42	0	0	168
	Halifax	2003	2(4)	0	0	0	0
Brett Grogan	Gateshead	1999	14(7)	3	0	0	12
Brent Grose	Warrington	2003-07	134(1)	55	0	0	220
David Guasch	Catalans	2010	1	0	0	0	0
Joan Guasch	Catalans	2014-15	(6)	0	0	0	0
Renaud Guigue	Catalans	2006	14(4)	3	0	0	12
Jerome Guisset	Catalans	2006-10	102(23)	9	0	0	36
	Wigan	2005	20(2)	3	0	0	12
	Warrington	2000-04	59(65)	21	0	0	84
Awen Guttenbeil	Castleford	2008	19	4	0	0	16
Reece Guy	Oldham	1996	3(4)	0	0	0	0
Josh Guzdek	Hull KR	2013, 2015	2	1	0	0	4
Tom Haberecht	Castleford	2008	2(2)	1	0	0	4
Dean Hadley	Wakefield	2017	14(7)	2	0	0	8
	Hull	2013-16	27(19)	6	0	0	24
Gareth Haggerty	Harlequins	2008-09	8(28)	6	0	0	24
	Salford	2004-07	1(93)	15	0	0	60
	Widnes	2002	1(2)	1	0	0	4
Kurt Haggerty	Widnes	2012	6(8)	2	0	0	8
Andy Haigh	St Helens	1996-98	20(16)	11	0	0	44
Scott Hale	St Helens	2011	(3)	1	0	0	4
Michael Haley	Leeds	2008	(1)	0	0	0	0
Carl Hall	Leeds	1996	7(2)	3	0	0	12
Craig Hall	Wakefield	2015-16	35	14	30	0	116
	Hull KR	2011-14	74(3)	38	41	2	236
	Hull	2007-10	59(9)	39	11	0	178
Glenn Hall	Bradford	2010	7(18)	2	0	0	8
Martin Hall	Halifax	1998	2(10)	4	0	0	0
	Hull	1999	7	0	0	0	0
	Castleford	1998	4	0	0	0	0
	Wigan	1996-97	31(5)	7	6	0	40
Ryan Hall	Leeds	2007-17	258(3)	187	0	0	748
Steve Hall	Widnes	2004	1	0	0	0	0
	London	2002-03	35(3)	10	0	0	40
	St Helens	1999-2001	36(22)	19	0	0	76
Graeme Hallas	Huddersfield	2001	1	0	0	0	0
	Hull	1998-99	30(10)	6	39	1	103
	Halifax	1996	11(4)	5	0	0	20
Sam Hallas	Leeds	2016	(2)	0	0	0	0
Macauley Hallett	Hull KR	2014	2	3	0	0	12
Dave Halley	Bradford	2007-10	63(12)	20	0	0	80
	Wakefield	2009	5	4	0	0	16
Danny Halliwell	Salford	2007	2(3)	0	0	0	0
	Leigh	2005	5	3	0	0	12
	Halifax	2000-03	17(8)	4	0	0	16
	Warrington	2002	9(1)	8	0	0	32
	Wakefield	2002	3	0	0	0	0
Colum Halpenny	Wakefield	2003-06	103(1)	36	0	0	144
	Halifax	2002	22	12	0	0	48
Jon Hamer	Bradford	1996	(1)	0	0	0	0
Andrew Hamilton	London	1997, 2003	1(20)	3	0	0	12
John Hamilton	St Helens	1998	3	0	0	0	0
Karle Hammond	Halifax	2002	10(2)	2	14	0	36
	Salford	2001	2(3)	1	0	0	4
	London	1999-2000	47	23	2	3	99
	St Helens	1996-98	58(8)	28	0	4	116
Ryan Hampshire	Leigh	2017	12(1)	3	0	0	12
	Castleford	2016	19(2)	8	0	0	32
	Wigan	2013-15	20(5)	8	24	0	80
Rhys Hanbury	Widnes	2012-17	135	68	99	1	471
	Crusaders	2010-11	26(1)	14	0	0	56
Anthony Hancock	Paris	1997	8(6)	1	0	0	4
Michael Hancock	Salford	2001-02	12(24)	7	0	0	28
Jordan Hand	Wakefield	2015	(2)	0	0	0	0
	St Helens	2013-14	(3)	0	0	0	0
Gareth Handford	Castleford	2001	7(2)	0	0	0	0
	Bradford	2000	1(1)	0	0	0	0
Paul Handforth	Castleford	2006	2(15)	2	1	0	10
	Wakefield	2000-04	17(44)	10	13	0	66
Ash Handley	Leeds	2014-17	42(3)	19	0	0	76
Paddy Handley	Leeds	1996	1(1)	2	0	0	8
Dean Hanger	Warrington	1999	7(11)	3	0	0	12
	Huddersfield	1998	20(1)	5	0	0	20
Josh Hannay	Celtic	2009	17	2	24	0	56
Harrison Hansen	Leigh	2017	12(1)	1	0	0	4
	Salford	2014-15	41(2)	7	0	0	28
	Wigan	2004-13	155(62)	39	0	0	156
Lee Hansen	Wigan	1997	10(5)	0	0	0	0
Shontayne Hape	Bradford	2003-08	123(2)	79	0	0	316
Lionel Harbin	Wakefield	2001	(1)	0	0	0	0
Zak Hardaker	Castleford	2017	28	12	1	0	50
	Leeds	2011-16	135	57	43	1	315
Ian Hardman	Hull KR	2007	18	4	0	0	16
	St Helens	2003-07	32(11)	9	5	0	46
Jeff Hardy	Hudds-Sheff	2000	20(5)	6	0	1	25
	Sheffield	1999	22(4)	7	0	0	28
Spencer Hargrave	Castleford	1996-99	(6)	0	0	0	0
Bryn Hargreaves	Bradford	2011-12	45(5)	1	0	0	4
	St Helens	2007-10	53(44)	7	0	0	28
	Wigan	2004-06	16(12)	1	0	0	4
Lee Harland	Castleford	1996-2004	148(35)	20	0	0	80
Neil Harmon	Halifax	2003	13(3)	0	0	0	0
	Salford	2001	6(5)	0	0	0	0
	Bradford	1998-2000	15(13)	2	0	0	8
	Huddersfield	1998	12	1	0	0	4
	Leeds	1996	10	1	0	0	4
Ben Harris	Bradford	2005-07	70(4)	24	0	0	96
Iestyn Harris	Bradford	2004-08	109(11)	35	87	2	316
	Leeds	1997-2001	111(7)	57	490	6	1214
	Warrington	1996	16	4	63	2	144

Super League Players 1996-2017

PLAYER	CLUB	YEAR	APP	TRIES	GOALS	FG	PTS
Ben Harrison	Wakefield	2016	3	0	0	0	0
	Warrington	2007-15	125(59)	14	0	0	56
Karl Harrison	Hull	1999	26	2	0	0	8
	Halifax	1996-98	60(2)	2	0	0	8
Andrew Hart	London	2004	12(1)	2	0	0	8
Tim Hartley	Harlequins	2006	2	1	0	0	4
	Salford	2004-05	6(7)	5	0	0	20
Carlos Hassan	Bradford	1996	6(4)	2	0	0	8
Phil Hassan	Wakefield	2002	9(1)	0	0	0	0
	Halifax	2000-01	25(4)	3	0	0	12
	Salford	1998	15	2	0	0	8
	Leeds	1996-97	38(4)	12	0	0	48
James Hasson	Wakefield	2017	(4)	0	0	0	0
	Salford	2017	4(1)	0	0	0	0
Tom Haughey	Castleford	2006	1(3)	1	0	0	4
	London	2003-04	10(8)	1	0	0	4
	Wakefield	2001-02	5(11)	0	0	0	0
Simon Haughton	Wigan	1996-2002	63(46)	32	0	0	128
Solomon Haumono							
	Harlequins	2006	10(9)	6	0	0	24
	London	2005	24(5)	8	0	0	32
Weller Hauraki	Salford	2015-17	34(10)	5	0	0	20
	Castleford	2013-14	50(2)	9	0	0	36
	Leeds	2011-12	18(17)	6	0	0	24
	Crusaders	2010	26(1)	11	0	0	44
Richie Hawkyard	Bradford	2007	1(2)	1	0	0	4
Andy Hay	Widnes	2003-04	50(2)	7	0	0	28
	Leeds	1997-2002	112(27)	43	0	0	172
	Sheffield	1996-97	17(3)	5	0	0	20
Adam Hayes	Hudds-Sheff	2000	2(1)	0	0	0	0
Joey Hayes	Salford	1999	9	2	0	0	8
	St Helens	1996-98	11(6)	7	0	0	28
James Haynes	Hull KR	2009	1	0	0	0	0
Mathew Head	Hull	2007	9(1)	1	0	1	5
Mitch Healey	Castleford	2001-03	68(1)	10	16	0	72
Daniel Heckenberg	Harlequins	2006-09	31(39)	4	0	0	16
Chris Heil	Hull KR	2012-13	4	2	0	0	8
Ricky Helliwell	Salford	1997-99	(2)	0	0	0	0
Tom Hemingway	Huddersfield	2005-09	7(7)	1	17	0	38
Bryan Henare	St Helens	2000-01	4(12)	1	0	0	4
Richard Henare	Warrington	1996-97	28(2)	24	0	0	96
Andrew Henderson							
	Castleford	2006, 2008	44(11)	4	0	0	16
Ian Henderson	Catalans	2011-15	118(9)	12	0	0	48
	Bradford	2005-07	33(37)	13	0	0	52
Kevin Henderson	Wakefield	2005-11	52(68)	9	0	0	36
	Leigh	2005	(1)	0	0	0	0
Adam Henry	Bradford	2014	23(1)	5	0	0	20
Mark Henry	Salford	2009-11	67	22	0	0	88
Brad Hepi	Castleford	1999, 2001	9(21)	3	0	0	12
	Salford	2000	3(5)	0	0	0	0
	Hull	1998	15(1)	3	0	0	12
Tyla Hepi	Hull KR	2013	(4)	0	0	0	0
Jon Hepworth	Castleford	2003-04	19(23)	7	8	0	44
	Leeds	2003	(1)	0	0	0	0
	London	2002	(2)	0	0	0	0
Marc Herbert	Bradford	2011	20	4	2	0	20
Aaron Heremaia	Widnes	2015-17	26(39)	6	0	0	24
	Hull	2012-14	27(37)	12	0	0	48
Maxime Herold	London	2014	(2)	0	0	0	0
Ian Herron	Hull	2000	9	1	17	0	38
	Gateshead	1999	25	4	105	0	226
Jason Hetherington							
	London	2001-02	37	9	0	0	36
Gareth Hewitt	Salford	1999	2(1)	0	0	0	0
Andrew Hick	Hull	2000	9(9)	1	0	0	4
	Gateshead	1999	12(5)	2	0	0	8
Jarrad Hickey	Wakefield	2011	(8)	2	0	0	8
Chris Hicks	Warrington	2008-10	72	56	119	0	462
Paul Hicks	Wakefield	1999	(1)	0	0	0	0
Darren Higgins	London	1998	5(6)	2	0	0	8
Iain Higgins	London	1997-98	1(7)	2	0	0	8
Liam Higgins	Wakefield	2011	4(12)	0	0	0	0
	Castleford	2008-10	42(32)	2	0	0	8
	Hull	2003-06	1(34)	0	0	0	0
Jack Higginson	Wigan	2016	2(1)	1	0	0	4
Micky Higham	Leigh	2017	11(1)	2	0	0	8
	Warrington	2009-15	73(78)	34	0	0	136
	Wigan	2006-08	61(28)	13	0	0	52
	St Helens	2001-05	43(56)	32	0	0	128
Chris Highton	Warrington	1997	1(1)	0	0	0	0
David Highton	London	2004-05	21(24)	2	0	0	8
	Salford	2002	4(5)	2	0	0	8
	Warrington	1998-2001	18(14)	2	0	0	8
Paul Highton	Salford	1998-2002, 2004-07	114(80)	14	0	0	56
	Halifax	1996-97	12(18)	2	0	0	8
Adam Higson	Leigh	2017	13	2	0	0	8
Peta Hiku	Warrington	2017	4	1	0	0	4
Andy Hill	Huddersfield	1999	(4)	0	0	0	0
	Castleford	1999	4(4)	0	0	0	0
Chris Hill	Warrington	2012-17	155(10)	21	0	0	84
	Leigh	2005	(1)	0	0	0	0
Danny Hill	Wigan	2006-07	1(10)	0	0	0	0
	Hull KR	2007	2	0	0	0	0
	Hull	2004-06	4(6)	0	0	0	0
Howard Hill	Oldham	1996-97	22(12)	4	0	0	16
John Hill	St Helens	2003	(1)	0	0	0	0
	Halifax	2003	1(2)	0	0	0	0
	Warrington	2001-02	(4)	0	0	0	0
Scott Hill	Harlequins	2007-08	41(2)	13	0	0	52
Mark Hilton	Warrington	1996-2000, 2002-06	141(40)	7	0	0	28
Ryan Hinchcliffe	Huddersfield	2016-17	49(3)	7	0	0	28
Ian Hindmarsh	Catalans	2006	25	3	0	0	12
Keegan Hirst	Wakefield	2017	3(18)	1	0	0	4
Jy Hitchcox	Castleford	2016-17	17(1)	10	0	0	40
Brendan Hlad	Castleford	2008	(3)	0	0	0	0
Andy Hobson	Widnes	2004	5(13)	0	0	0	0
	Halifax	1998-2003	51(85)	8	0	0	32
Gareth Hock	Leigh	2017	12(1)	3	0	0	12
	Salford	2014-15	15(1)	4	0	0	16
	Widnes	2013	15(2)	9	1	0	38
	Wigan	2003-09, 2011-12	126(43)	38	0	0	152
Tommy Hodgkinson							
	St Helens	2006	(1)	0	0	0	0
Andy Hodgson	Wakefield	1999	14(2)	2	1	0	10
	Bradford	1997-98	8(2)	4	0	0	16
Brett Hodgson	Warrington	2011-13	66	33	268	1	669
	Huddersfield	2009-10	45	13	166	0	384
David Hodgson	Hull KR	2012-14	51	31	0	0	124
	Huddersfield	2008-11	84	59	0	0	236
	Salford	2005-07	81	30	47	0	214
	Wigan	2000-04	90(19)	43	0	0	172
	Halifax	1999	10(3)	5	0	0	20
Elliot Hodgson	Huddersfield	2009	1	0	0	0	0
Josh Hodgson	Hull KR	2010-14	98(29)	35	0	0	140
	Hull	2009	(2)	0	0	0	0
Ryan Hoffman	Wigan	2011	28(1)	11	0	0	44
Darren Hogg	London	1996	(1)	0	0	0	0
Michael Hogue	Paris	1997	5(7)	0	0	0	0
Lance Hohaia	St Helens	2012-15	67(9)	21	0	1	85
Chris Holden	Warrington	1996-97	2(1)	0	0	0	0
Daniel Holdsworth	Hull	2013	19	2	28	2	66
	Salford	2010-12	71	18	183	1	439
Stephen Holgate	Halifax	2000	1(10)	0	0	0	0
	Hull	1999	1	0	0	0	0
	Wigan	1997-98	11(26)	2	0	0	8
	Workington	1996	19	3	0	0	12
Stephen Holker	Hull KR	2015-16	(4)	0	0	0	0
Martyn Holland	Wakefield	2000-03	52(3)	6	0	0	24
Oliver Holmes	Castleford	2010-17	120(23)	23	0	0	92
Tim Holmes	Widnes	2004-05	15(4)	0	0	0	0
Tom Holmes	Castleford	2015-17	7(8)	3	0	0	12
Graham Holroyd	Huddersfield	2003	3(5)	0	0	0	0
	Salford	2000-02	40(11)	8	75	5	187
	Halifax	1999	24(2)	3	74	5	165
	Leeds	1996-98	40(26)	22	101	8	298
Dallas Hood	Wakefield	2003-04	18(9)	1	0	0	4
Liam Hood	Leigh	2017	8(5)	3	0	0	12
	Salford	2015	2(15)	0	0	0	0
	Leeds	2012	1(4)	3	0	0	12
Jason Hooper	St Helens	2003-07	89(6)	35	30	0	200
Will Hope	Salford	2013	1(2)	0	0	0	0
Lee Hopkins	Harlequins	2006-07	44(3)	11	0	0	44
	London	2005	29	6	0	0	24
Sam Hopkins	Leigh	2017	3(17)	6	0	0	24
Sean Hoppe	St Helens	1999-2002	69(16)	32	0	0	128
Graeme Horne	Hull KR	2012-16	81(18)	21	0	0	84
	Huddersfield	2010-11	23(17)	11	0	0	44
	Hull	2003-09	49(74)	24	0	0	96
Richard Horne	Hull	1999-2014	341(16)	115	12	6	490
Justin Horo	Catalans	2016-17	34(1)	12	0	0	48
John Hough	Warrington	1996-97	9	2	0	0	8
Danny Houghton	Hull	2007-17	223(47)	36	0	0	144
Sylvain Houles	Wakefield	2003, 2005	8(1)	1	0	0	4
	London	2001-02	17(10)	11	0	0	44
	Hudds-Sheff	2000	5(2)	1	0	0	4
Chris Houston	Widnes	2016-17	47(1)	5	0	0	20
Harvey Howard	Wigan	2001-02	25(27)	1	0	0	4
	Bradford	1998	4(2)	1	0	0	4
	Leeds	1996	8	0	0	0	0

PLAYER	CLUB	YEAR	APP	TRIES	GOALS	FG	PTS
Kim Howard	London	1997	4(5)	0	0	0	0
Stuart Howarth	Wakefield	2011, 2015-16	30(5)	4	0	0	16
	Hull	2015	2(3)	0	0	0	0
	Salford	2012-14	25(12)	1	0	0	4
	St Helens	2013	14(1)	0	0	0	0
Stuart Howarth	Workington	1996	(2)	0	0	0	0
David Howell	London	2012-13	24	5	0	0	20
	Harlequins	2008-11	76	26	0	0	104
Phil Howlett	Bradford	1999	5(1)	2	0	0	8
Craig Huby	Wakefield	2017	15(12)	2	0	0	8
	Huddersfield	2015-16	37(2)	2	0	0	8
	Castleford	2003-04, 2006, 2008-14	130(57)	27	41	0	190
Ryan Hudson	Castleford	2002-04, 2009-12	138(12)	31	0	0	124
	Huddersfield	1998-99, 2007-08	51(22)	10	0	0	40
	Wakefield	2000-01	42(9)	11	0	1	45
Adam Hughes	Widnes	2002-05	89(2)	45	51	0	282
	Halifax	2001	8(8)	8	0	0	32
	Wakefield	1999-2000	43(3)	21	34	0	152
	Leeds	1996-97	4(5)	4	0	0	16
Ian Hughes	Sheffield	1996	9(8)	4	0	0	16
Jack Hughes	Warrington	2016-17	50	9	0	0	36
	Huddersfield	2015	30(1)	5	0	0	20
	Wigan	2011-14	31(33)	9	0	0	36
Mark Hughes	Catalans	2006	23	9	0	0	36
Steffan Hughes	London	1999-2001	1(13)	1	0	0	4
David Hulme	Salford	1997-99	53(1)	5	0	0	20
	Leeds	1996	8(1)	2	0	0	8
Declan Hulme	Widnes	2013-15	5	2	0	0	8
Paul Hulme	Warrington	1996-97	23(1)	2	0	0	8
Gary Hulse	Widnes	2005	12(5)	2	0	0	8
	Warrington	2001-04	20(28)	8	0	1	33
Alan Hunte	Salford	2002	19(2)	9	0	0	36
	Warrington	1999-2001	83	49	0	0	196
	Hull	1998	21	7	0	0	28
	St Helens	1996-97	30(2)	28	0	0	112
Alex Hurst	London	2013	8(2)	2	0	0	8
Kieran Hyde	Wakefield	2010-11	11	4	4	0	24
Nick Hyde	Paris	1997	5(5)	1	0	0	4
Chaz l'Anson	Hull KR	2007-10	17(13)	3	0	0	12
Sebastine Ikahihifo							
	Huddersfield	2016-17	29(3)	0	0	0	0
Ryan Ince	Widnes	2016-17	10	6	0	0	24
Krisnan Inu	Catalans	2015-17	39	11	3	0	50
Andy Ireland	Hull	1998-99	22(15)	0	0	0	0
	Bradford	1996	1	0	0	0	0
Kevin Iro	St Helens	1999-2001	76	39	0	0	156
	Leeds	1996	16	9	0	0	36
Willie Isa	Wigan	2016-17	43(12)	3	0	0	12
	Widnes	2012-15	44(33)	3	0	0	12
	Castleford	2011	7(2)	6	0	0	24
Andrew Isherwood	Wigan	1998-99	(5)	0	0	0	0
Olu Iwenofu	London	2000-01	2(1)	0	0	0	0
Chico Jackson	Hull	1999	(4)	0	0	0	0
Lee Jackson	Hull	2001-02	37(9)	12	1	0	50
	Leeds	1999-2000	28(24)	7	0	0	28
Michael Jackson	Sheffield	1998-99	17(17)	2	0	0	8
	Halifax	1996-97	27(6)	11	0	0	44
Paul Jackson	Castleford	2003-04, 2010-12	44(30)	5	0	0	20
	Huddersfield	1998, 2005-09	50(73)	4	0	0	16
	Wakefield	1999-2002	57(42)	2	0	0	8
Rob Jackson	Leigh	2005	20(3)	5	0	0	20
	London	2002-04	26(14)	9	0	0	36
Wayne Jackson	Halifax	1996-97	17(5)	2	0	0	8
Aled James	Crusaders	2011	1	0	0	0	0
	Celtic	2009	3(3)	0	0	0	0
	Widnes	2003	3	0	0	0	0
Andy James	Halifax	1996	(4)	0	0	0	0
Jordan James	Wigan	2006, 2014	3(18)	4	0	0	16
	Salford	2012-13	1(40)	6	0	0	24
	Crusaders	2010-11	5(24)	3	0	0	12
	Celtic	2009	17(4)	1	0	0	4
Matt James	Wakefield	2012	(4)	0	0	0	0
	Harlequins	2010	(2)	0	0	0	0
	Bradford	2006-09	1(23)	0	0	0	0
Pascal Jampy	Catalans	2006	4(7)	0	0	0	0
	Paris	1996-97	3(2)	0	0	0	0
Adam Janowski	Harlequins	2008	(1)	0	0	0	0
Ben Jeffries	Bradford	2008-09, 2011-12	76(3)	20	0	0	80
	Wakefield	2003-07, 2010-11	151(10)	70	20	6	326
Mick Jenkins	Hull	2000	24	2	0	0	8
	Gateshead	1999	16	3	0	0	12
Ed Jennings	London	1998-99	1(2)	0	0	0	0
Rod Jensen	Huddersfield	2007-08	26(3)	13	0	0	52
Anthony Jerram	Warrington	2007	(2)	0	0	0	0
Lee Jewitt	Castleford	2014-16	22(12)	0	0	0	0
	Salford	2007, 2009-13	32(62)	4	0	0	16
	Wigan	2005	(2)	0	0	0	0
Isaac John	Wakefield	2012	13	1	19	0	42
Andrew Johns	Warrington	2005	3	1	12	1	29
Matthew Johns	Wigan	2001	24	3	0	1	13
Andy Johnson	Salford	2004-05	8(26)	7	0	0	28
	Castleford	2002-03	32(16)	11	0	0	44
	London	2000-01	24(21)	12	0	0	48
	Huddersfield	1999	5	1	0	0	4
	Wigan	1996-99	24(20)	19	0	0	76
Bruce Johnson	Widnes	2004-05	(4)	0	0	0	0
Dallas Johnson	Catalans	2010	26	1	0	0	4
Greg Johnson	Salford	2014-17	72	31	1	0	126
	Wakefield	2011	12	2	0	0	8
Jack Johnson	Warrington	2015-17	13	4	0	0	16
	Widnes	2017	3	1	0	0	4
Jason Johnson	St Helens	1997-99	2	0	0	0	0
Josh Johnson	Huddersfield	2013-16	14(17)	0	0	0	0
Mark Johnson	Salford	1999-2000	22(9)	16	0	0	64
	Hull	1998	10(1)	4	0	0	16
	Workington	1996	12	4	0	0	16
Nick Johnson	Hull KR	2012	1	0	0	0	0
Nick Johnson	London	2003	(1)	0	0	0	0
Paul Johnson	Crusaders	2011	6(4)	0	0	0	0
	Wakefield	2010	12(3)	4	0	0	16
	Warrington	2007-09	37(9)	17	0	0	68
	Bradford	2004-06	46(8)	19	0	0	76
	Wigan	1996-2003	74(46)	54	0	0	216
Paul Johnson	Widnes	2014	5(11)	0	0	0	0
	Hull	2013	3(16)	0	0	0	0
	Wakefield	2011-12	25(21)	6	0	0	24
	St Helens	2010	(2)	0	0	0	0
Richard Johnson	Bradford	2008	(2)	0	0	0	0
Ben Johnston	Castleford	2012	2	0	0	0	0
Jordan Johnstone	Widnes	2016-17	12(6)	1	0	0	4
Tom Johnstone	Wakefield	2015-17	44	30	0	0	120
Ben Jones	Harlequins	2010	(2)	0	0	0	0
Chris Jones	Leigh	2005	1(1)	0	0	0	0
Danny Jones	Halifax	2003	1	0	0	0	0
David Jones	Oldham	1997	14(1)	5	0	0	20
Josh Jones	Salford	2016-17	45(3)	9	0	0	36
	St Helens	2012-15	88(9)	22	0	0	88
Mark Jones	Warrington	1996	8(11)	2	0	0	8
Phil Jones	Leigh	2005	16	8	31	0	94
	Salford	1999-2001	14(7)	6	25	0	74
Stacey Jones	Catalans	2006-07	39	11	43	3	133
Stephen Jones	Huddersfield	2005	(1)	0	0	0	0
Stuart Jones	Castleford	2009-12	69(27)	14	0	0	56
	Huddersfield	2004-08	96(22)	17	0	0	68
	St Helens	2003	(18)	2	0	0	8
	Wigan	2002	5(3)	1	0	0	4
Ben Jones-Bishop	Wakefield	2016-17	46	30	0	0	120
	Salford	2015	17	12	0	0	48
	Leeds	2008-09, 2011-14	70(2)	46	0	0	184
	Harlequins	2010	10	10	0	0	40
Jamie Jones-Buchanan	Leeds	1999-2017	276(69)	67	0	0	268
Tim Jonkers	Wigan	2006	3(1)	0	0	0	0
	Salford	2004-06	5(11)	0	0	0	0
	St Helens	1999-2004	41(64)	12	0	0	48
Darren Jordan	Wakefield	2003	1	0	0	0	0
Josh Jordan-Roberts	Leeds	2017	(1)	0	0	0	0
Phil Joseph	Salford	2016	(12)	0	0	0	0
	Widnes	2013-15	11(38)	1	0	0	4
	Bradford	2012	(6)	0	0	0	0
	Huddersfield	2004	7(6)	0	0	0	0
Max Jowitt	Wakefield	2014-17	25(1)	6	0	0	24
Warren Jowitt	Hull	2003	(2)	0	0	0	0
	Salford	2001-02	17(4)	2	0	0	8
	Wakefield	2000	19(3)	8	0	0	32
	Bradford	1996-99	13(25)	5	0	0	20
Chris Joynt	St Helens	1996-2004	201(14)	68	0	0	272
Benjamin Jullien	Warrington	2016-17	19(7)	4	0	0	16
Gregory Kacala	Paris	1996	7	1	0	0	4
Andy Kain	Castleford	2004, 2006	9(7)	3	10	0	32
Antonio Kaufusi	Huddersfield	2014	15(2)	1	0	0	4
	Bradford	2014	4	0	0	0	0
	London	2012-13	44(5)	5	0	0	20

PLAYER	CLUB	YEAR	APP	TRIES	GOALS	FG	PTS
Mal Kaufusi	London	2004	1(3)	0	0	0	0
Ben Kavanagh	Wakefield	2015	6(3)	0	0	0	0
	Widnes	2012-15	18(33)	0	0	0	0
Liam Kay	Wakefield	2012-13	4	4	0	0	16
Ben Kaye	Harlequins	2009-10	2(13)	0	0	0	0
	Leeds	2008	2(2)	1	0	0	4
Elliot Kear	Bradford	2012-14	53(2)	17	0	0	68
	Crusaders	2010-11	16(1)	4	0	0	16
	Celtic	2009	3	0	0	0	0
Brett Kearney	Bradford	2010-14	107	55	0	0	220
Stephen Kearney	Hull	2005	22(2)	5	0	0	20
Damon Keating	Wakefield	2002	7(17)	1	0	0	4
Kris Keating	Hull KR	2014	23	5	0	0	20
Shaun Keating	London	1996	1(3)	0	0	0	0
Mark Keenan	Workington	1996	3(4)	1	0	0	4
Jimmy Keinhorst	Leeds	2012-17	42(22)	22	0	0	88
	Wakefield	2014	7	1	0	0	4
Albert Kelly	Hull	2017	25	19	0	1	77
	Hull KR	2015-16	37	21	3	0	90
Tony Kemp	Wakefield	1999-2000	15(5)	2	0	1	9
	Leeds	1996-98	23(2)	5	0	2	22
Damien Kennedy	London	2003	5(11)	1	0	0	4
Ian Kenny	St Helens	2004	(1)	0	0	0	0
Sean Kenny	Salford	2016	(4)	0	0	0	0
Jason Kent	Leigh	2005	23	1	0	0	4
Liam Kent	Hull	2012-13	1(5)	0	0	0	0
Shane Kenward	Wakefield	1999	28	6	0	0	24
	Salford	1998	1	0	0	0	0
Jason Keough	Paris	1997	2	1	0	0	4
Keiran Kerr	Widnes	2005	6	2	0	0	8
Martin Ketteridge	Halifax	1996	7(5)	0	0	0	0
Ronnie Kettlewell	Warrington	1996	(1)	0	0	0	0
Joe Keyes	London	2014	7	5	0	0	20
Younes Khattabi	Catalans	2006-08	24(4)	10	0	0	40
David Kidwell	Warrington	2001-02	14(12)	9	0	0	36
Andrew King	London	2003	23(1)	15	0	0	60
Dave King	Huddersfield	1998-99	11(17)	2	0	0	8
George King	Warrington	2014-17	7(54)	1	0	0	4
James King	Leigh	2005	5(7)	0	0	0	0
Kevin King	Wakefield	2005	8(1)	2	0	0	8
	Castleford	2004	(1)	0	0	0	0
Matt King	Warrington	2008-11	91	58	0	0	232
Paul King	Wakefield	2010-11	10(19)	0	0	1	1
	Hull	1999-2009	136(93)	20	0	1	81
Toby King	Warrington	2014-17	22(6)	4	0	0	16
Andy Kirk	Wakefield	2005	6(3)	1	0	0	4
	Salford	2004	20	5	0	0	20
	Leeds	2001-02	4(4)	0	0	0	0
Ian Kirke	Wakefield	2015	2(2)	1	0	0	4
	Leeds	2006-14	52(132)	10	0	0	40
John Kirkpatrick	London	2004-05	18(1)	5	0	0	20
	St Helens	2001-03	10(11)	10	0	0	40
	Halifax	2003	4	1	0	0	4
Danny Kirmond	Wakefield	2010, 2012-17	123(7)	41	0	0	164
	Huddersfield	2008-11	18(31)	9	0	0	36
Wayne Kitchin	Workington	1996	11(6)	3	17	1	47
Sione Kite	Widnes	2012	6(8)	1	0	0	4
Ian Knott	Leigh	2005	8(1)	2	0	0	8
	Wakefield	2002-03	34(5)	7	79	0	186
	Warrington	1996-2001	68(41)	24	18	0	132
Matt Knowles	Wigan	1996	(3)	0	0	0	0
Michael Knowles	Castleford	2006	(1)	0	0	0	0
Morgan Knowles	St Helens	2016-17	20(31)	7	0	0	28
Phil Knowles	Salford	1997	1	0	0	0	0
Simon Knox	Halifax	1999	(6)	0	0	0	0
	Salford	1998	1(1)	0	0	0	0
	Bradford	1996-98	9(19)	7	0	0	28
Toa Kohe-Love	Warrington	1996-2001, 2005-06	166(3)	90	0	0	360
	Bradford	2004	1(1)	0	0	0	0
	Hull	2002-03	42	19	0	0	76
Paul Koloi	Wigan	1997	1(2)	1	0	0	4
Craig Kopczak	Salford	2016-17	33(17)	10	0	0	40
	Huddersfield	2013-15	48(37)	6	0	0	24
	Bradford	2006-12	32(83)	10	0	0	40
Michael Korkidas	Wakefield	2003-06, 2009-11	133(36)	15	0	0	60
	Huddersfield	2009	4(1)	1	0	0	4
	Castleford	2008	15(6)	1	0	0	4
	Salford	2007	26(1)	1	0	0	4
Nick Kouparitsas	Harlequins	2011	2(13)	1	0	0	4
Olsi Krasniqi	Salford	2015-17	8(29)	1	0	0	4
	London	2012-14	28(34)	3	0	0	12
	Harlequins	2010-11	3(20)	1	0	0	4
David Krause	London	1996-97	22(1)	7	0	0	28
Ben Kusto	Huddersfield	2001	21(4)	9	0	1	37
Anthony Laffranchi							
	St Helens	2012-14	50(18)	19	0	0	76
James Laithwaite	Warrington	2013-15	23(22)	1	0	0	4
	Hull KR	2012	1(2)	1	0	0	4
Adrian Lam	Wigan	2001-04	105(2)	40	1	9	171
Callum Lancaster	Hull	2014-16	7	9	0	0	36
Mark Lane	Paris	1996	(2)	0	0	0	0
Allan Langer	Warrington	2000-01	47	13	4	0	60
Kevin Langer	London	1996	12(4)	2	0	0	8
Junior Langi	Salford	2005-06	27(7)	7	0	0	28
Samisoni Langi	Leigh	2017	3	1	0	0	4
Chris Langley	Huddersfield	2000-01	18(1)	3	0	0	12
Gareth Langley	St Helens	2006	1	1	3	0	10
Jamie Langley	Hull KR	2014	6(5)	1	0	0	4
	Bradford	2002-13	182(57)	36	0	0	144
Ryan Lannon	Salford	2015-17	11(19)	3	0	0	12
Kevin Larroyer	Castleford	2017	2(4)	0	0	0	0
	Hull KR	2014-16	34(13)	9	0	0	36
	Catalans	2012-13	9(10)	6	0	0	24
Andy Last	Hull	1999-2005	16(10)	4	0	0	16
Sam Latus	Hull KR	2010-13	34(3)	13	0	0	52
Epalahame Lauaki	Wigan	2012-13	14(16)	2	0	0	8
	Hull	2009-11	3(50)	4	0	0	16
Dale Laughton	Warrington	2002	15(1)	0	0	0	0
	Huddersfield	2000-01	36(2)	4	0	0	16
	Sheffield	1996-98	48(22)	5	0	0	20
Ali Lauitiiti	Wakefield	2012-15	46(31)	16	0	0	64
	Leeds	2004-11	64(117)	58	0	0	232
Jason Laurence	Salford	1997	1	0	0	0	0
Graham Law	Wakefield	1999-2002	34(30)	6	40	0	104
Neil Law	Wakefield	1999-2002	83	39	0	0	156
	Sheffield	1998	1(1)	1	0	0	4
Dean Lawford	Widnes	2003-04	17(1)	5	2	4	28
	Halifax	2001	1(1)	0	0	0	0
	Leeds	1997-2000	15(8)	2	3	0	14
	Huddersfield	1999	6(1)	0	6	1	13
	Sheffield	1996	9(5)	2	1	1	11
George Lawler	Hull KR	2016	12(5)	1	0	0	4
Johnny Lawless	Halifax	2001-03	73(1)	10	0	0	40
	Hudds-Sheff	2000	19(6)	3	0	0	12
	Sheffield	1996-99	76(4)	11	0	0	44
Michael Lawrence	Huddersfield	2007-17	173(37)	45	0	0	180
Adam Lawton	Widnes	2013-14	2(10)	5	0	0	20
Charlie Leaeno	Wakefield	2010	7(3)	2	0	0	8
Mark Leafa	Castleford	2008	5(9)	1	0	0	4
	Leigh	2005	28	2	0	0	8
Leroy Leapai	London	1996	2	0	0	0	0
Jim Leatham	Hull	1998-99	20(18)	4	0	0	16
	Leeds	1997	(1)	0	0	0	0
Andy Leathem	Warrington	1999	2(8)	0	0	0	0
	St Helens	1996-98	20(1)	1	0	0	4
Danny Lee	Gateshead	1999	16(2)	0	0	0	0
Jason Lee	Halifax	2001	10(1)	2	0	0	8
Mark Lee	Salford	1997-2000	25(11)	1	0	4	8
Robert Lee	Hull	1999	4(3)	0	0	0	0
Tommy Lee	St Helens	2017	9(9)	0	0	0	0
	Salford	2014-16	37(5)	4	0	0	16
	London	2013	16(4)	2	0	0	8
	Huddersfield	2012	11(7)	3	0	0	12
	Wakefield	2011	25	6	0	0	24
	Crusaders	2010	3(9)	0	0	0	0
	Hull	2005-09	44(27)	6	0	0	24
Kruise Leeming	Huddersfield	2013-17	29(37)	6	0	0	24
Matty Lees	St Helens	2017	(1)	0	0	0	0
Matthew Leigh	Salford	2000	(6)	0	0	0	0
Chris Leikvoll	Warrington	2004-07	72(18)	4	0	0	16
Jim Lenihan	Huddersfield	1999	19(1)	10	0	0	40
Mark Lennon	Celtic	2009	10(3)	1	8	0	20
	Hull KR	2007	11(4)	5	7	0	34
	Castleford	2001-03	30(21)	10	21	0	82
Tevita Leo-Latu	Wakefield	2006-10	28(49)	10	0	0	40
Gary Lester	Hull	1998-99	46	17	0	0	68
Stuart Lester	Wigan	1997	1(3)	0	0	0	0
Heath L'Estrange	Bradford	2010-13	56(35)	7	0	0	28
Afi Leuila	Oldham	1996-97	17(3)	2	0	0	8
Kylie Leuluai	Leeds	2007-15	182(45)	20	0	0	80
Macgraff Leuluai	Widnes	2012-17	50(52)	5	0	0	20
Phil Leuluai	Salford	2007, 2009-10	7(47)	3	0	0	12
Thomas Leuluai	Wigan	2007-12, 2017	194(1)	54	0	1	217
	Harlequins	2006	15(2)	6	0	0	24
	London	2005	20	13	0	0	52
Simon Lewis	Castleford	2001	4	3	0	0	12
Paul Leyland	St Helens	2006	1	0	0	0	0
Jon Liddell	Leeds	2001	1	0	0	0	0
Jason Lidden	Castleford	1997	15(1)	7	0	0	28

PLAYER	CLUB	YEAR	APP	TRIES	GOALS	FG	PTS
Jordan Lilley	Leeds	2015-17	18(11)	2	37	0	82
Danny Lima	Wakefield	2007	(3)	0	0	0	0
	Salford	2006	7(2)	0	0	0	0
	Warrington	2004-06	15(47)	9	0	0	36
Jeff Lima	Catalans	2014-15	37(7)	3	1	0	14
	Wigan	2011-12	24(29)	4	0	0	16
Tom Lineham	Warrington	2016-17	40	31	0	0	124
	Hull	2012-15	61(1)	50	0	0	200
Jez Litten	Hull	2017	(3)	0	0	0	0
Harry Little	London	2013	2	0	0	0	0
Craig Littler	St Helens	2006	1	1	0	0	4
Stuart Littler	Salford	1998-2002, 2004-07, 2009-10	217(30)	65	0	0	260
Harvey Livett	Warrington	2017	4(6)	2	8	0	24
Peter Livett	Workington	1996	3(1)	0	0	0	0
Rhodri Lloyd	Wigan	2012-13, 2015	3(4)	0	0	0	0
	Widnes	2014	(4)	0	0	0	0
	London	2013	2	0	0	0	0
Kevin Locke	Wakefield	2015	3	0	0	0	0
	Salford	2014-15	13	6	11	0	46
Jack Logan	Hull	2014-16	21	9	0	0	36
Scott Logan	Wigan	2006	10(11)	0	0	0	0
	Hull	2001-03	27(20)	5	0	0	20
Jamahl Lolesi	Huddersfield	2007-10	75(9)	27	0	0	108
Filimone Lolohea	Harlequins	2006	3(6)	0	0	0	0
	London	2005	8(15)	0	0	0	0
David Lomax	Huddersfield	2000-01	45(9)	4	0	0	16
	Paris	1997	19(2)	1	0	0	4
Jonny Lomax	St Helens	2009-17	145(24)	66	84	2	434
Dave Long	London	1999	(1)	0	0	0	0
Karl Long	London	2003	(1)	0	0	0	0
	Widnes	2002	4	1	0	0	4
Sean Long	Hull	2010-11	22	6	0	0	24
	St Helens	1997-2009	263(8)	126	826	20	2176
	Wigan	1996-97	1(5)	0	0	0	0
Davide Longo	Bradford	1996	1(3)	0	0	0	0
Gary Lord	Oldham	1996-97	28(12)	3	0	0	12
Paul Loughlin	Huddersfield	1998-99	34(2)	4	4	0	24
	Bradford	1996-97	36(4)	15	8	0	76
Rhys Lovegrove	Hull KR	2007-14	75(74)	19	0	0	76
Karl Lovell	Hudds-Sheff	2000	14	5	0	0	20
	Sheffield	1999	22(4)	8	0	0	32
Will Lovell	London	2012-14	16(16)	4	0	0	16
James Lowes	Bradford	1996-2003	205	84	2	2	342
Laurent Lucchese	Paris	1996	13(5)	2	0	0	8
Robert Lui	Salford	2016-17	45(3)	14	2	0	60
Zebastian Luisi	Harlequins	2006-07	23(2)	4	0	0	16
	London	2004-05	21(1)	7	0	0	28
Keith Lulia	Bradford	2012-13	50	19	0	0	76
Shaun Lunt	Hull KR	2015-16	20(5)	10	0	0	40
	Huddersfield	2009-15	73(39)	60	0	0	240
	Leeds	2012	10(9)	7	0	0	28
Peter Lupton	Crusaders	2010-11	37(9)	10	0	0	40
	Celtic	2009	16(4)	4	0	0	16
	Castleford	2006, 2008	40	11	0	0	44
	Hull	2003-06	19(26)	10	3	0	46
	London	2000-02	10(15)	2	2	0	12
Andy Lynch	Castleford	1999-2004, 2014-17	157(54)	17	0	0	68
	Hull	2012-13	39(14)	3	0	0	12
	Bradford	2005-11	159(29)	46	0	0	184
Reece Lyne	Wakefield	2013-17	92(1)	33	0	0	132
	Hull	2010-11	11(1)	2	0	0	8
Jamie Lyon	St Helens	2005-06	54(1)	39	172	0	500
Iliess Macani	London	2013-14	12(3)	4	0	0	16
Duncan MacGillivray	Wakefield	2004-08	75(18)	6	0	0	24
Brad Mackay	Bradford	2000	24(2)	8	0	0	32
Graham Mackay	Hull	2002	27	18	24	0	120
	Bradford	2001	16(3)	12	1	0	50
	Leeds	2000	12(8)	10	2	0	44
Keiron Maddocks	Leigh	2005	1(3)	0	0	0	0
Steve Maden	Leigh	2005	23	9	0	0	36
	Warrington	2002	3	0	0	0	0
Mateaki Mafi	Warrington	1996-97	7(8)	7	0	0	28
Shaun Magennis	St Helens	2010-12	7(19)	3	0	0	12
Brendan Magnus	London	2000	3	1	0	0	4
Mark Maguire	London	1996-97	11(4)	7	13	0	54
Adam Maher	Hull	2000-03	88(4)	24	0	0	96
	Gateshead	1999	21(5)	3	0	0	12
Lee Maher	Leeds	1996	4(1)	0	0	0	0
Will Maher	Castleford	2014-17	1(24)	1	0	0	4
Shaun Mahony	Paris	1997	5	0	0	0	0
Hutch Maiava	Hull	2007	(19)	1	0	0	4
David Maiden	Hull	2000-01	32(10)	11	0	0	44
	Gateshead	1999	5(16)	8	0	0	32
Craig Makin	Salford	1999-2001	24(20)	2	0	0	8
Tom Makinson	St Helens	2011-17	150(5)	86	102	0	548
Brady Malam	Wigan	2000	5(20)	1	0	0	4
Dominic Maloney	Hull	2009	(7)	0	0	0	0
Francis Maloney	Castleford	1998-99, 2003-04	71(7)	24	33	3	165
	Salford	2001-02	45(1)	26	5	0	114
	Wakefield	2000	11	1	1	0	6
	Oldham	1996-97	39(2)	12	91	2	232
Jake Mamo	Huddersfield	2017	9	12	0	0	48
Dominic Manfredi	Wigan	2013-16	52	47	0	0	188
	Salford	2014	1	2	0	0	8
George Mann	Warrington	1997	14(5)	1	0	0	4
	Leeds	1996	11(4)	2	0	0	8
Dane Manning	Leeds	2009	(1)	0	0	0	0
Josh Mantellato	Hull KR	2015-16	26	16	88	0	240
Misili Manu	Widnes	2005	1	0	0	0	0
Sika Manu	Hull	2016-17	53(2)	6	0	0	24
Willie Manu	St Helens	2013-14	35(11)	9	0	0	36
	Hull	2007-12	133(18)	33	0	0	132
	Castleford	2006	19(4)	9	0	0	36
Manase Manuokafoa	Widnes	2015-17	3(54)	3	0	0	12
	Bradford	2012-16	49(21)	3	0	0	12
Darren Mapp	Celtic	2009	9(2)	1	0	0	4
David March	Wakefield	1999-2007	164(23)	34	126	0	388
Paul March	Wakefield	1999-2001, 2007	42(31)	17	23	0	114
	Huddersfield	2003-06	71(19)	17	36	1	141
Nick Mardon	London	1997-98	14	2	0	0	8
Thibaut Margalet	Catalans	2013-17	1(17)	0	0	0	0
Remy Marginet	Catalans	2011	2	0	9	0	18
Antoni Maria	Leigh	2017	2(6)	0	0	0	0
	Catalans	2012-16	4(33)	0	0	0	0
Frankie Mariano	Castleford	2014-16	14(21)	8	0	0	32
	Wakefield	2011-13	41(12)	20	0	0	80
	Hull KR	2010	(3)	0	0	0	0
Oliver Marns	Halifax	1996-2002	54(19)	23	0	0	92
Paul Marquet	Warrington	2002	23(2)	0	0	0	0
Callum Marriott	Salford	2011	(1)	0	0	0	0
Iain Marsh	Salford	1998-2001	1(4)	0	0	0	0
Lee Marsh	Salford	2001-02	3(4)	0	0	0	0
Matthew Marsh	Hull KR	2015-16	13(2)	3	0	0	12
Stefan Marsh	Widnes	2012-17	106	52	17	0	242
	Wigan	2010-11	12	3	0	0	12
Liam Marshall	Wigan	2017	21	21	5	0	94
Richard Marshall	Leigh	2005	4(16)	0	0	0	0
	London	2002-03	33(11)	1	0	0	4
	Huddersfield	2000-01	35(14)	1	0	0	4
	Halifax	1996-99	38(34)	2	0	0	8
Charlie Martin	Castleford	2013	(6)	0	0	0	0
Jason Martin	Paris	1997	15(2)	3	0	0	12
Scott Martin	Salford	1997-99	32(18)	8	0	0	32
Tony Martin	Hull	2012	10	1	0	0	4
	Crusaders	2010-11	40(1)	14	1	0	58
	Wakefield	2008-09	33	10	33	0	106
	London	1996-97, 2001-03	97(1)	36	170	1	485
Mick Martindale	Halifax	1996	(4)	0	0	0	0
Sebastien Martins	Catalans	2006, 2009-11	(21)	2	0	0	8
Tommy Martyn	St Helens	1996-2003	125(20)	87	63	12	486
Dean Marwood	Workington	1996	9(6)	0	22	0	44
Martin Masella	Warrington	2001	10(14)	5	0	0	20
	Warrington	2000	14(8)	4	0	0	16
	Leeds	1997-1999	59(5)	1	0	0	4
Colin Maskill	Castleford	1996	8	1	1	0	6
Mose Masoe	St Helens	2014-15	17(39)	10	0	0	40
Keith Mason	Castleford	2006, 2013	11(6)	0	0	0	0
	Huddersfield	2006-12	118(14)	4	0	0	16
	St Helens	2003-05	33(23)	4	0	0	16
	Wakefield	2000-01	5(17)	0	0	0	0
Nathan Mason	Huddersfield	2013, 2015-17	3(26)	3	0	0	12
Willie Mason	Catalans	2016	6(8)	1	0	0	4
	Hull KR	2011	6	1	0	0	4
Samy Masselot	Wakefield	2011	(1)	0	0	0	0
Nathan Massey	Castleford	2008-17	105(55)	8	0	0	32
Nesiasi Mataitonga	London	2014	11(1)	1	0	0	4
Vila Matautia	St Helens	1996-2001	31(68)	9	0	0	36
Feleti Mateo	London	2005	4(10)	1	0	0	4
Barrie-Jon Mather	Castleford	1998, 2000-02	50(12)	21	0	0	84
Richard Mathers	Wakefield	2012-14	71	24	0	0	96
	Castleford	2011	21(1)	7	0	0	28
	Warrington	2002, 2009-10	42(3)	11	0	0	44
	Wigan	2008-09	23(1)	2	0	0	8
	Leeds	2002-06	85(2)	26	0	0	104

Super League Players 1996-2017

PLAYER	CLUB	YEAR	APP	TRIES	GOALS	FG	PTS
Jamie Mathiou	Leeds	1997-2001	31(82)	3	0	0	12
Masi Matongo	Hull	2015, 2017	(10)	0	0	0	0
Terry Matterson	London	1996-98	46	15	90	6	246
Vic Mauro	Salford	2013	1(7)	1	0	0	4
Luke May	Harlequins	2009-10	(3)	0	0	0	0
Casey Mayberry	Halifax	2000	1(1)	0	0	0	0
Chris Maye	Halifax	2003	3(4)	0	0	0	0
Judah Mazive	Wakefield	2016	2	1	0	0	4
Joe Mbu	Harlequins	2006-09	33(20)	3	0	0	12
	London	2003-05	29(19)	4	0	0	16
Danny McAllister	Gateshead	1999	3(3)	1	0	0	4
	Sheffield	1996-97	33(7)	10	0	0	40
John McAtee	St Helens	1996	2(1)	0	0	0	0
Nathan McAvoy	Bradford	1998-2002, 2007	83(31)	46	0	0	184
	Wigan	2006	15(2)	5	0	0	20
	Salford	1997-98, 2004-05	57(4)	18	0	0	72
Tyrone McCarthy	Salford	2017	6	2	0	0	8
	Hull KR	2015	20(1)	4	0	0	16
	Warrington	2009-13	12(24)	2	0	0	8
	Wakefield	2011	2(5)	1	0	0	4
Louie McCarthy-Scarsbrook							
	St Helens	2011-17	117(82)	41	0	0	164
	Harlequins	2006-10	41(50)	17	0	0	68
Dave McConnell	London	2003	(4)	0	0	0	0
	St Helens	2001-02	3(2)	4	0	0	16
Robbie McCormack							
	Wigan	1998	24	2	0	0	8
Steve McCurrie	Leigh	2005	7(3)	1	0	0	4
	Widnes	2002-04	55(22)	10	0	0	40
	Warrington	1998-2001	69(26)	31	0	0	124
Barrie McDermott	Leeds	1996-2005	163(69)	28	0	0	112
Brian McDermott	Bradford	1996-2002	138(32)	33	0	0	132
Ryan McDonald	Widnes	2002-03	6(4)	0	0	0	0
Wayne McDonald	Huddersfield	2005-06	11(23)	1	0	0	4
	Wigan	2005	(4)	0	0	0	0
	Leeds	2002-05	34(47)	14	0	0	56
	St Helens	2001	7(11)	4	0	0	16
	Hull	2000	5(8)	4	0	0	16
	Wakefield	1999	9(17)	8	0	0	32
Shannon McDonnell							
	St Helens	2014-16	28	15	0	0	60
	Hull	2013	19	2	0	0	8
	Hull KR	2012	21	6	0	0	24
Craig McDowell	Huddersfield	2003	(1)	0	0	0	0
	Warrington	2002	(1)	0	0	0	0
	Bradford	2000	(1)	0	0	0	0
Wes McGibbon	Halifax	1999	1	0	0	0	0
Jermaine McGillvary							
	Huddersfield	2010-17	186	133	0	0	532
Dean McGilvray	Salford	2009-10	14	4	0	0	16
	St Helens	2006-08	5(1)	1	0	0	4
Billy McGinty	Workington	1996	1	0	0	0	0
Ryan McGoldrick	Salford	2013	19(1)	3	0	1	13
	Hull	2012	8	1	0	0	4
	Castleford	2006, 2008-12	129(5)	24	11	0	118
Kevin McGuinness	Salford	2004-07	63(3)	11	0	0	44
Casey McGuire	Catalans	2007-10	87(4)	27	0	0	108
Danny McGuire	Leeds	2001-17	331(39)	238	0	6	958
Gary McGuirk	Workington	1996	(4)	0	0	0	0
Michael McIlorum	Wigan	2007-17	156(54)	22	0	0	88
Darnell McIntosh	Huddersfield	2017	22(1)	12	0	0	48
Richard McKell	Castleford	1997-98	22(7)	2	0	0	8
Chris McKenna	Bradford	2006-07	40(7)	7	0	0	28
	Leeds	2003-05	65(4)	18	0	0	72
Phil McKenzie	Workington	1996	4	0	0	0	0
Chris McKinney	Oldham	1996-97	4(9)	2	0	0	8
Wade McKinnon	Hull	2012	10	4	0	0	16
Mark McLinden	Harlequins	2006-08	46(1)	20	0	1	81
	London	2005	22(3)	8	0	0	32
Mike McMeeken	Castleford	2015-17	62(8)	15	0	0	60
	London	2012-14	25(9)	5	0	0	20
Shayne McMenemy							
	Hull	2003-07	80(8)	12	0	0	48
	Halifax	2001-03	63	11	0	0	44
Andy McNally	London	2004	5(3)	0	0	0	0
	Castleford	2001, 2003	2(5)	1	0	0	4
Gregg McNally	Leigh	2017	9	3	0	0	12
	Huddersfield	2011	1	0	6	0	12
Steve McNamara	Huddersfield	2001, 2003	41(9)	3	134	1	281
	Wakefield	2000	15(2)	2	32	0	72
	Bradford	1996-99	90(3)	14	348	7	759
Paul McNicholas	Hull	2004-05	28(12)	4	0	0	16
Neil McPherson	Salford	1997	(1)	0	0	0	0
Shannan McPherson							
	Salford	2012-14	20(11)	0	0	0	0
Duncan McRae	London	1996	11(2)	3	0	1	13
Paul McShane	Castleford	2015-17	48(19)	9	17	0	70
	Wakefield	2014-15	39(9)	5	0	0	20
	Leeds	2009-13	17(38)	12	0	0	48
	Widnes	2012	6(5)	3	4	0	20
	Hull	2010	(4)	0	0	0	0
Derek McVey	St Helens	1996-97	28(4)	6	1	0	26
Dallas Mead	Warrington	1997	2	0	0	0	0
Robbie Mears	Leigh	2005	8(6)	0	0	0	0
	Leeds	2001	23	6	0	0	24
Paul Medley	Bradford	1996-98	6(35)	9	0	0	36
Francis Meli	Salford	2014	16	11	0	0	44
	St Helens	2006-13	194(1)	122	0	0	488
Vince Mellars	Wakefield	2012-13	21(5)	4	0	0	16
	Crusaders	2010-11	46	17	0	0	68
Chris Melling	London	2012-13	25(12)	5	2	0	24
	Harlequins	2007-11	100(11)	33	6	0	144
	Wigan	2004-05	8(2)	1	3	0	10
Alex Mellor	Huddersfield	2017	22(5)	3	0	0	12
	Bradford	2013-14	(10)	0	0	0	0
Joe Mellor	Widnes	2012-17	113(1)	42	0	1	169
	Wigan	2012	1(1)	1	0	0	4
	Harlequins	2011	(1)	0	0	0	0
Paul Mellor	Castleford	2003-04	36(3)	18	0	0	72
James Mendeika	London	2013	4(2)	2	0	0	8
Craig Menkins	Paris	1997	4(5)	0	0	0	0
Luke Menzies	Hull KR	2008	(1)	0	0	0	0
Steve Menzies	Catalans	2011-13	61(6)	30	0	0	120
	Bradford	2009-10	52(1)	24	1	0	98
Gary Mercer	Castleford	2002	(1)	0	0	0	0
	Leeds	1996-97, 2001	40(2)	9	0	0	36
	Warrington	2001	18	2	0	0	8
	Halifax	1998-2001	73(2)	16	0	0	64
Tony Mestrov	London	1996-97, 2001	59(8)	4	0	0	16
	Wigan	1998-2000	39(39)	3	0	0	12
Keiran Meyer	London	1996	4	1	0	0	4
Brad Meyers	Bradford	2005-06	40(11)	13	0	0	52
Steve Michaels	Hull	2015-17	68(1)	26	0	0	104
Gary Middlehurst	Widnes	2004	(2)	0	0	0	0
Simon Middleton	Castleford	1996-97	19(3)	8	0	0	32
Constantine Mika	Hull KR	2012-13	45(4)	9	0	0	36
Daryl Millard	Catalans	2011-14	91	38	1	0	154
	Wakefield	2010-11	21(1)	11	0	0	44
Shane Millard	Wigan	2007	19(6)	3	0	0	12
	Leeds	2006	6(21)	3	0	0	12
	Widnes	2003-05	69	23	0	0	92
	London	1998-2001	72(14)	11	1	0	46
Jack Miller	Huddersfield	2013	1	0	1	0	2
Jacob Miller	Wakefield	2015-17	67(3)	29	17	2	152
	Hull	2013-14	20	6	9	0	42
Grant Millington	Castleford	2012-17	106(45)	24	0	0	96
David Mills	Harlequins	2006-07, 2010	25(32)	2	0	0	8
	Hull KR	2008-09	20(11)	1	0	0	4
	Widnes	2002-05	17(77)	8	0	0	32
Lewis Mills	Celtic	2009	(4)	0	0	0	0
Adam Milner	Castleford	2010-17	122(51)	28	0	0	112
Lee Milner	Halifax	1999	(1)	0	0	0	0
Elliot Minchella	Leeds	2013-16	(6)	1	0	0	4
Mark Minichiello	Hull	2015-17	74(3)	17	0	0	68
Greg Minikin	Castleford	2016-17	42(1)	25	0	0	100
Thomas Minns	Hull KR	2016	14(1)	10	0	0	40
	London	2014	23	6	0	0	24
	Leeds	2013	2(1)	1	0	0	4
John Minto	London	1996	13	4	0	0	16
Lee Mitchell	Castleford	2012	13(10)	2	0	0	8
	Warrington	2007-11	8(27)	4	0	0	16
	Harlequins	2011	11(1)	1	0	0	4
Sam Moa	Catalans	2017	21	4	0	0	16
	Hull	2009-12	29(44)	6	0	0	24
Martin Moana	Salford	2004	6(3)	1	0	0	4
	Halifax	1996-2001, 2003	126(22)	62	0	1	249
	Wakefield	2002	19(2)	10	0	0	40
	Huddersfield	2001	3(3)	2	0	0	8
Adam Mogg	Catalans	2007-10	74	19	0	1	77
Jon Molloy	Wakefield	2013-16	25(18)	5	0	0	20
	Huddersfield	2011-12	2(1)	0	0	0	0
Steve Molloy	Huddersfield	2000-01	26(20)	3	0	0	12
	Sheffield	1998-99	32(17)	3	0	0	12
Chris Molyneux	Huddersfield	2000-01	1(18)	0	0	0	0
	Sheffield	1999	1(2)	0	0	0	0

PLAYER	CLUB	YEAR	APP	TRIES	GOALS	FG	PTS
Joel Monaghan	Castleford	2016-17	29(3)	13	0	0	52
	Warrington	2011-15	127	125	2	0	504
Michael Monaghan							
	Warrington	2008-14	143(28)	31	0	4	128
Joel Moon	Leeds	2013-17	118(1)	56	0	0	224
	Salford	2012	17	9	0	0	36
Adrian Moore	Huddersfield	1998-99	1(4)	0	0	0	0
Danny Moore	London	2000	7	0	0	0	0
	Wigan	1998-99	49(3)	18	0	0	72
Gareth Moore	Wakefield	2011	5	1	14	1	33
Jason Moore	Workington	1996	(5)	0	0	0	0
Richard Moore	Wakefield	2007-10, 2014	52(57)	10	0	0	40
	Leeds	2012-13	3(27)	1	0	0	4
	Crusaders	2011	11(10)	1	0	0	4
	Leigh	2005	2(5)	0	0	0	0
	Bradford	2002-04	1(26)	0	0	0	0
	London	2002, 2004	5(9)	2	0	0	8
Scott Moore	Wakefield	2015-16	12(2)	0	0	0	0
	Castleford	2008, 2015	24(6)	2	0	0	8
	London	2014	26	3	0	0	12
	Huddersfield	2009, 2012	29(7)	9	0	0	36
	Widnes	2012	3(3)	0	0	0	0
	St Helens	2004-07, 2010-11	29(37)	9	0	0	36
Junior Moors	Castleford	2015-17	32(34)	7	0	0	28
Dennis Moran	Wigan	2005-06	39	17	1	1	71
	London	2001-04	107(2)	74	2	5	305
Kieran Moran	Hull KR	2016	(5)	0	0	0	0
Ryan Moran	St Helens	2017	27	11	0	0	44
Willie Morganson	Sheffield	1997-98	18(12)	5	3	0	26
Paul Moriarty	Halifax	1996	3(2)	0	0	0	0
Adrian Morley	Salford	2014-15	31(14)	2	0	0	8
	Warrington	2007-13	135(21)	8	0	0	32
	Bradford	2005	2(4)	0	0	0	0
	Leeds	1996-2000	95(14)	25	0	0	100
Chris Morley	Salford	1999	3(5)	0	0	0	0
	Warrington	1998	2(8)	0	0	0	0
	St Helens	1996-97	21(16)	4	0	0	16
Frazer Morris	Wakefield	2016	(1)	0	0	0	0
Glenn Morrison	Wakefield	2010-11	43(1)	9	0	0	36
	Bradford	2007-09	48(2)	19	0	0	76
Iain Morrison	Hull KR	2007	5(6)	1	0	0	4
	Huddersfield	2003-05	11(23)	0	0	0	0
	London	2001	(1)	0	0	0	0
Daniel Mortimer	Leigh	2017	3	0	0	0	0
Dale Morton	Wakefield	2009-11	22(3)	8	5	0	42
Gareth Morton	Hull KR	2007	7(4)	3	23	0	58
	Leeds	2001-02	1(1)	0	0	0	0
Lee Mossop	Salford	2017	9	0	0	0	0
	Wigan	2008-13, 2015-16	80(65)	11	0	0	44
	Huddersfield	2009	1(4)	1	0	0	4
Aaron Moule	Salford	2006-07	45	17	0	0	68
	Widnes	2004-05	29	12	0	0	48
Bradley Moules	Wakefield	2016	(1)	0	0	0	0
Wilfried Moulinec	Paris	1996	1	0	0	0	0
Gregory Mounis	Catalans	2006-16	149(105)	27	19	0	146
Mark Moxon	Huddersfield	1998-2001	20(5)	1	0	1	5
Rob Mulhern	Hull KR	2016	8(11)	1	0	0	4
	Leeds	2014-15	(5)	0	0	0	0
Anthony Mullally	Leeds	2016-17	6(39)	8	0	0	32
	Wakefield	2015	(2)	0	0	0	0
	Huddersfield	2013-15	12(24)	5	0	0	20
	Bradford	2014	1(5)	0	0	0	0
	Widnes	2012	(9)	0	0	0	0
Jake Mullaney	Salford	2014	12	2	24	0	56
Brett Mullins	Leeds	2001	5(3)	1	0	0	4
Damian Munro	Widnes	2002	8(2)	1	0	0	4
	Halifax	1996-97	9(6)	8	0	0	32
Matt Munro	Oldham	1996-97	26(5)	8	0	0	32
Ben Murdoch-Masila							
	Salford	2016-17	46(1)	15	0	0	60
Craig Murdock	Salford	2000	(2)	0	0	0	0
	Hull	1998-99	21(6)	8	0	2	34
	Wigan	1996-98	18(17)	14	0	0	56
Aaron Murphy	Huddersfield	2012-17	126	63	0	0	252
	Wakefield	2008-11	57(2)	12	0	0	48
Jack Murphy	Wigan	2012, 2014	3	1	0	0	4
	Salford	2013	10	3	1	0	14
Jamie Murphy	Crusaders	2011	(2)	0	0	0	0
Jobe Murphy	Bradford	2013	(4)	0	0	0	0
Justin Murphy	Catalans	2006-08	59	49	0	0	196
	Widnes	2004	5	1	0	0	4
Daniel Murray	Salford	2017	3(4)	0	0	0	0
Doc Murray	Warrington	1997	(2)	0	0	0	0
	Wigan	1997	6(2)	0	0	0	0
Scott Murrell	Hull KR	2007-12	114(24)	24	26	1	149
	Leeds	2005	(1)	0	0	0	0
	London	2004	3(3)	2	0	0	8
David Mycoe	Sheffield	1996-97	12(13)	1	0	0	4
Richie Myler	Catalans	2016-17	40	21	2	0	88
	Warrington	2010-15	127(4)	69	1	1	279
	Salford	2009	18	11	0	0	44
Rob Myler	Oldham	1996-97	19(2)	6	0	0	24
Stephen Myler	Salford	2006	1	0	15	0	34
	Widnes	2003-05	35(14)	8	74	0	180
Vinny Myler	Salford	2004	(4)	0	0	0	0
	Bradford	2003	(1)	0	0	0	0
Matt Nable	London	1997	2(2)	1	0	0	4
Brad Nairn	Workington	1996	14	4	0	0	16
Frank Napoli	London	2000	14(6)	2	0	0	8
Carlo Napolitano	Salford	2000	(3)	1	0	0	4
Stephen Nash	Castleford	2012	3(4)	0	0	0	0
	Salford	2007, 2009	2(18)	1	0	0	4
	Widnes	2005	4(1)	0	0	0	0
Curtis Naughton	Leigh	2017	5	3	0	0	12
	Hull	2015-16	26	13	1	0	54
	Bradford	2013	1	0	0	0	0
Romain Navarrete	Catalans	2016-17	1(12)	0	0	0	0
	Wigan	2017	(9)	0	0	0	0
Jim Naylor	Halifax	2000	7(6)	2	0	0	8
Scott Naylor	Salford	1997-98, 2004	30(1)	9	0	0	36
	Bradford	1999-2003	127(1)	51	0	0	204
Adam Neal	Salford	2010-13	17(28)	0	0	0	0
Mike Neal	Salford	1998	(1)	0	0	0	0
	Oldham	1996-97	6(4)	3	0	0	12
Jonathan Neill	Huddersfield	1998-99	20(11)	0	0	0	0
	St Helens	1996	1	0	0	0	0
Chris Nero	Salford	2011-13	31(16)	7	0	0	28
	Bradford	2008-10	65(5)	24	0	0	96
	Huddersfield	2004-07	97(8)	38	0	0	152
Jason Netherton	Hull KR	2007-14	60(74)	4	0	0	16
	London	2003-04	6	0	0	0	0
	Halifax	2002	2(3)	0	0	0	0
	Leeds	2001	(3)	0	0	0	0
Kirk Netherton	Castleford	2009-10	5(23)	3	0	0	12
	Hull KR	2007-08	9(15)	2	0	0	8
Paul Newlove	Castleford	2004	5	1	0	0	4
	St Helens	1996-2003	162	106	0	0	424
Richard Newlove	Wakefield	2003	17(5)	8	0	0	32
Harry Newman	Leeds	2017	1	0	0	0	0
Clint Newton	Hull KR	2008-11	90(3)	37	0	0	148
Terry Newton	Wakefield	2010	(2)	0	0	0	0
	Bradford	2006-09	83(6)	26	0	0	104
	Wigan	2000-05	157(9)	62	0	0	248
	Leeds	1996-1999	55(14)	4	0	0	16
Gene Ngamu	Huddersfield	1999-2000	29(2)	9	67	0	170
Danny Nicklas	Hull	2010, 2012	2(8)	0	0	0	0
Sonny Nickle	St Helens	1999-2002	86(18)	14	0	0	56
	Bradford	1996-98	25(16)	9	0	0	36
Jason Nicol	Salford	2000-02	52(7)	11	0	0	44
Tawera Nikau	Warrington	2000-01	51	7	0	0	28
Rob Nolan	Hull	1998-99	20(11)	6	0	0	24
Paul Noone	Harlequins	2006	5(2)	0	0	0	0
	Warrington	2000-05	60(59)	12	20	0	88
Chris Norman	Halifax	2003	13(3)	2	0	0	8
Paul Norman	Oldham	1996	(1)	0	0	0	0
Andy Northey	St Helens	1996-97	8(17)	2	0	0	8
Danny Nutley	Castleford	2006	28	3	0	0	12
	Warrington	1998-2001	94(1)	3	0	0	12
Tony Nuttall	Oldham	1996-97	1(7)	0	0	0	0
Frank-Paul Nuuausala							
	Wigan	2016-17	34(7)	2	0	0	8
Will Oakes	Hull KR	2016	1	0	0	0	0
Adam O'Brien	Huddersfield	2017	1(15)	3	0	0	12
	Bradford	2011-14	12(29)	6	0	0	24
Clinton O'Brien	Wakefield	2003	(2)	0	0	0	0
Gareth O'Brien	Salford	2016-17	45(3)	11	96	2	238
	Warrington	2011-15	48(3)	16	69	3	205
	St Helens	2013	7	0	25	0	50
	Castleford	2013	2	0	0	1	1
	Widnes	2012	4	0	15	0	30
Sam Obst	Hull	2011	17(6)	6	0	0	24
	Wakefield	2005-11	100(28)	40	7	0	174
Jamie O'Callaghan	London	2012-14	44(2)	4	0	0	16
	Harlequins	2008-11	54(3)	12	0	0	48
Eamon O'Carroll	Widnes	2012-17	58(11)	3	0	0	12
	Hull	2012	1(9)	0	0	0	0
	Wigan	2006-11	2(59)	3	0	0	12
Matt O'Connor	Paris	1997	11(4)	1	26	2	58
Terry O'Connor	Widnes	2005	25	2	0	0	8
	Wigan	1996-2004	177(45)	9	0	0	36

Super League Players 1996-2017

PLAYER	CLUB	YEAR	APP	TRIES	GOALS	FG	PTS
Jarrod O'Doherty	Huddersfield	2003	26	3	0	0	12
David O'Donnell	Paris	1997	21	3	0	0	12
Luke O'Donnell	Huddersfield	2011-13	22(2)	2	0	0	8
Martin Offiah	Salford	2000-01	41	20	0	2	82
	London	1996-99	29(3)	21	0	0	84
	Wigan	1996	8	7	0	0	28
Mark O'Halloran	London	2004-05	34(3)	10	0	0	40
Ryan O'Hara	Hull KR	2012	8(7)	1	0	0	4
	Crusaders	2010-11	41(8)	3	0	0	12
	Celtic	2009	27	3	0	0	12
Hefin O'Hare	Huddersfield	2001, 2003-05	72(10)	27	0	0	108
Edwin Okanga-Ajwang	Salford	2013	2	0	0	0	0
Hitro Okesene	Hull	1998	21(1)	0	0	0	0
Anderson Okiwe	Sheffield	1997	1	0	0	0	0
Tom Olbison	Widnes	2017	6(12)	1	0	0	4
	Bradford	2009-14	55(26)	11	0	0	44
Michael Oldfield	Catalans	2014-15	41	28	0	0	112
Mikolaj Oledzki	Leeds	2017	(2)	0	0	0	0
Jamie Olejnik	Paris	1997	11	8	0	0	32
Aaron Ollett	Hull KR	2013-15	5(16)	1	0	0	4
Kevin O'Loughlin	Halifax	1997-98	2(4)	0	0	0	0
	St Helens	1997	(3)	0	0	0	0
Sean O'Loughlin	Wigan	2002-17	336(22)	69	3	2	284
Mark O'Meley	Hull	2010-13	70(13)	13	0	0	52
Jules O'Neill	Widnes	2003-05	57(3)	14	158	7	379
	Wakefield	2005	10(2)	2	4	0	16
	Wigan	2002-03	29(1)	12	72	0	192
Julian O'Neill	Widnes	2002-05	57(39)	3	0	0	12
	Wakefield	2001	24(1)	2	0	0	8
	St Helens	1997-2000	95(8)	5	0	0	20
Mark O'Neill	Hull KR	2007	17	5	0	0	20
	Leeds	2006	1(8)	0	0	0	0
Steve O'Neill	Gateshead	1999	1(1)	0	0	0	0
Tom O'Reilly	Warrington	2001-02	8(6)	1	0	0	4
Matt Orford	Bradford	2010	12	3	31	2	76
Jack Ormondroyd	Leeds	2017	2(3)	0	0	0	0
Gene Ormsby	Huddersfield	2016-17	8	4	0	0	16
	Warrington	2014-16	37	26	0	0	104
Chris Orr	Huddersfield	1998	19(3)	2	0	0	8
Danny Orr	Castleford	1997-2003, 2011-12	197(23)	75	308	3	919
	Harlequins	2007-10	90(4)	13	96	0	244
	Wigan	2004-06	66(2)	18	12	0	96
Gareth Owen	Salford	2010, 2012-13	4(32)	6	0	0	24
Nick Owen	Leigh	2005	8(1)	1	11	0	26
Richard Owen	Wakefield	2014-15	29(1)	9	0	0	36
	Castleford	2008-14	109(3)	57	0	0	228
Jack Owens	St Helens	2016-17	31	8	14	0	60
	Widnes	2012-15	53(1)	26	103	0	310
Lopini Paea	Wakefield	2015	1(3)	0	0	0	0
	Catalans	2011-14	41(41)	9	0	0	36
Mickey Paea	Hull	2014-15	44(5)	3	0	0	12
	Hull KR	2012-13	34(17)	5	0	0	20
Mathias Pala	Catalans	2011-15	28(1)	4	0	0	16
Iafeta Palea'aesina	Hull	2014-16	(47)	1	0	0	4
	Salford	2011-12	4(37)	3	0	0	12
	Wigan	2006-10	55(77)	16	0	0	64
Jason Palmada	Workington	1996	12	2	0	0	8
Junior Paramore	Castleford	1996	5(5)	3	0	0	12
Matt Parcell	Leeds	2017	29(2)	17	0	0	68
Paul Parker	Hull	1999-2002	23(18)	9	0	0	36
Rob Parker	Castleford	2011	4(2)	2	0	0	8
	Salford	2009-11	23(14)	4	0	0	16
	Warrington	2006-08	10(56)	6	0	0	24
	Bradford	2000, 2002-05	19(76)	14	0	0	56
	London	2001	9	1	0	0	4
Wayne Parker	Halifax	1996-97	12(1)	0	0	0	0
Ian Parry	Warrington	2001	(1)	0	0	0	0
Jules Parry	Paris	1996	10(2)	0	0	0	0
Regis Pastre-Courtine	Paris	1996	4(3)	4	0	0	16
Cory Paterson	Leigh	2017	13	2	0	0	8
	Salford	2015	14(1)	7	6	0	40
	Hull KR	2013	15	7	0	0	28
Andrew Patmore	Oldham	1996	8(5)	3	0	0	12
Larne Patrick	Castleford	2016-17	14(7)	1	0	0	4
	Huddersfield	2009-14, 2016	30(107)	30	0	0	120
	Wigan	2015	7(20)	4	0	0	16
Luke Patten	Salford	2011-12	53	16	0	0	64
Declan Patton	Warrington	2015-17	32(2)	6	47	4	122
Henry Paul	Harlequins	2006-08	60(1)	8	94	2	222
	Bradford	1999-2001	81(5)	29	350	6	822
	Wigan	1996-98	60	37	23	0	194
Junior Paul	London	1996	3	1	0	0	4
Robbie Paul	Salford	2009	2(24)	2	0	0	8
	Huddersfield	2006-07	44(8)	7	0	0	28
	Bradford	1996-2005	198(31)	121	3	0	490
Jason Payne	Castleford	2006	1(1)	0	0	0	0
Danny Peacock	Bradford	1997-99	32(2)	15	0	0	60
Jamie Peacock	Leeds	2006-15	234(16)	24	0	0	96
	Bradford	1999-2005	163(25)	38	0	0	152
Martin Pearson	Wakefield	2001	21(1)	3	60	3	135
	Halifax	1997-98, 2000	55(6)	24	181	0	458
	Sheffield	1999	17(6)	9	36	2	110
Jacques Pech	Paris	1996	16	0	0	0	0
Mike Pechey	Warrington	1998	6(3)	2	0	0	8
Bill Peden	London	2003	21(3)	7	0	0	28
Adam Peek	Crusaders	2010-11	5(22)	1	0	0	4
	Celtic	2009	5(12)	3	0	0	12
Eloi Pelissier	Leigh	2017	4(16)	0	0	0	0
	Catalans	2011-16	38(104)	23	0	1	93
Dimitri Pelo	Catalans	2007-10	79	37	0	0	148
Sean Penkywicz	Huddersfield	2004-05	21(11)	7	0	0	28
	Halifax	2000-03	29(27)	8	0	0	32
Julian Penni	Salford	1998-99	4	0	0	0	0
Kevin Penny	Warrington	2006-09, 2014-17	83(1)	52	0	0	208
	Wakefield	2011	5	1	0	0	4
	Harlequins	2010	5	3	0	0	12
Lee Penny	Warrington	1996-2003	140(5)	54	0	0	216
Paul Penrice	Workington	1996	11(2)	2	0	0	8
Chris Percival	Widnes	2002-03	26	6	0	0	24
Mark Percival	St Helens	2013-17	91(2)	45	205	0	590
Apollo Perelini	St Helens	1996-2000	103(16)	27	0	0	108
Ugo Perez	Catalans	2015, 2017	1(5)	0	0	0	0
Mark Perrett	Halifax	1996-97	15(4)	4	0	0	16
Josh Perry	St Helens	2011-13	32(9)	2	0	0	8
Shane Perry	Catalans	2009	8(8)	1	0	0	4
Adam Peters	Paris	1997	16(3)	0	0	0	0
Dominic Peters	London	1998-2003	58(11)	12	0	0	48
Mike Peters	Warrington	2000	2(12)	1	0	0	4
	Halifax	2000	1	0	0	0	0
Willie Peters	Widnes	2004	9	3	0	2	14
	Wigan	2000	29	15	5	6	76
	Gateshead	1999	27	11	1	6	52
Dave Petersen	Hull KR	2012	2(2)	1	0	0	4
Matt Petersen	Wakefield	2008-09	14	3	0	0	12
Adrian Petrie	Workington	1996	(1)	0	0	0	0
Eddy Pettybourne	Wigan	2014	1(15)	0	0	0	0
Dominique Peyroux	St Helens	2016-17	29(15)	4	0	0	16
Cameron Phelps	Widnes	2012-15	66(1)	23	2	0	96
	Hull	2011	19	2	0	0	8
	Wigan	2008-10	43(1)	14	4	0	64
Joe Philbin	Warrington	2014-17	10(33)	5	0	0	20
Rowland Phillips	Workington	1996	22	1	0	0	4
Nathan Picchi	Leeds	1996	(1)	0	0	0	0
Ian Pickavance	Hull	1999	4(2)	2	0	0	8
	Huddersfield	1999	3(14)	0	0	0	0
	St Helens	1996-98	12(44)	6	0	0	24
James Pickering	Castleford	1999	1(19)	0	0	0	0
Steve Pickersgill	Widnes	2012-15	27(8)	1	0	0	4
	Warrington	2005-09	1(36)	0	0	0	0
Nick Pinkney	Salford	2000-02	64	29	0	0	116
	Halifax	1999	26(2)	13	0	0	52
	Sheffield	1997-98	33	10	0	0	40
Mikhail Piskunov	Paris	1996	1(1)	1	0	0	4
Darryl Pitt	London	1996	2(16)	4	0	1	17
Jay Pitts	Bradford	2014	15(1)	3	0	0	12
	Hull	2012-16	18(30)	1	0	0	4
	Leeds	2009-12	10(15)	1	0	0	4
	Wakefield	2008-09	9(8)	2	0	0	8
Andy Platt	Salford	1997-98	20(3)	1	0	0	4
Michael Platt	Salford	2001-02, 2014	4(1)	1	0	0	4
	Bradford	2007-13	121(6)	44	0	0	176
	Castleford	2006	26	7	0	0	28
Willie Poching	Leeds	2002-06	58(73)	44	0	0	176
	Wakefield	1999-2001	65(4)	20	0	0	80
Ben Pomeroy	Warrington	2017	2	1	0	0	4
	Catalans	2014-15	44	10	0	0	40
Quentin Pongia	Wigan	2003-04	15(10)	0	0	0	0
Justin Poore	Hull KR	2014	7	0	0	0	0
	Wakefield	2013	23	1	0	0	4
Dan Potter	Widnes	2002-03	34(2)	6	0	0	24
	London	2001	1(3)	1	0	0	4
Craig Pouchet	Hull	1999-2002	31(5)	5	0	0	20
Andy Powell	Wigan	2013	2(3)	1	0	0	4

PLAYER	CLUB	YEAR	APP	TRIES	GOALS	FG	PTS
Bryn Powell	Salford	2004	1(1)	0	0	0	0
Daio Powell	Sheffield	1999	13(1)	2	0	0	8
	Halifax	1997-98	30(3)	17	0	0	68
Daryl Powell	Leeds	1998-2000	49(30)	12	0	2	50
Sam Powell	Wigan	2012-17	71(46)	17	0	2	70
Karl Pratt	Bradford	2003-05	35(19)	18	0	0	72
	Leeds	1999-2002	62(12)	33	0	0	132
Paul Prescott	Wigan	2004-13	49(75)	4	0	0	16
Steve Prescott	Hull	1998-99, 2001-03	99	46	191	3	569
	Wakefield	2000	22(1)	3	13	0	38
	St Helens	1996-97	32	15	17	0	94
Lee Prest	Workington	1996	(1)	0	0	0	0
Gareth Price	Salford	2002	(2)	0	0	0	0
	London	2002	2(2)	3	0	0	12
	St Helens	1999	(11)	2	0	0	8
Gary Price	Wakefield	1999-2001	55(13)	11	0	0	44
Richard Price	Sheffield	1996	1(2)	0	0	0	0
Tony Priddle	Paris	1997	11(7)	3	0	0	12
Frank Pritchard	Hull	2016	10(13)	4	0	0	16
Karl Pryce	Bradford	2003-06, 2012	47(19)	46	1	0	186
	Harlequins	2011	11(7)	12	0	0	48
	Wigan	2009-10	11(2)	12	0	0	48
Leon Pryce	Hull	2015-16	32(2)	8	0	0	32
	Catalans	2012-14	72(2)	15	0	0	60
	St Helens	2006-11	133(3)	64	0	0	256
	Bradford	1998-2005	159(29)	86	0	0	344
Waine Pryce	Wakefield	2007	10(2)	4	0	0	16
	Castleford	2000-06	97(12)	49	0	0	196
Tony Puletua	Hull KR	2015	7	0	0	0	0
	Salford	2014	16(9)	3	0	0	12
	St Helens	2009-13	108(18)	39	0	0	156
Andrew Purcell	Castleford	2000	15(5)	3	0	0	12
	Hull	1999	27	4	0	0	16
Rob Purdham	Harlequins	2006-11	112(3)	18	131	1	335
	London	2002-05	53(15)	16	2	1	69
Adrian Purtell	Bradford	2012-14	45(1)	16	0	0	64
Luke Quigley	Catalans	2007	16(1)	1	0	0	4
Adam Quinlan	St Helens	2015	11	6	0	0	24
Damien Quinn	Celtic	2009	20(1)	4	12	0	40
Scott Quinnell	Wigan	1996	6(3)	1	0	0	4
Florian Quintilla	Catalans	2008-09	1(4)	0	0	0	0
Lee Radford	Hull	1998, 2006-12	138(30)	23	1	0	94
	Bradford	1999-2005	79(65)	18	12	0	96
Kris Radlinski	Wigan	1996-2000	236(1)	134	1	0	538
Sebastien Raguin	Catalans	2007-12	103(22)	28	0	0	112
Adrian Rainey	Castleford	2002	4(7)	1	0	0	4
Andy Raleigh	Wakefield	2012-14	42(21)	9	0	0	36
	Huddersfield	2006-11	74(46)	13	0	0	52
Jean-Luc Ramondou							
	Paris	1996	1(1)	1	0	0	4
Chad Randall	London	2012-13	29(9)	4	0	0	16
	Harlequins	2006-11	141(2)	37	0	1	149
Craig Randall	Halifax	1999	8(11)	4	0	0	16
	Salford	1997-98	12(18)	4	0	0	16
Tyler Randell	Wakefield	2017	3	2	0	0	8
Jordan Rankin	Huddersfield	2017	11	1	5	0	14
	Hull	2014-15	41(6)	20	43	0	166
Scott Ranson	Oldham	1996-97	19(2)	7	0	0	28
Aaron Raper	Castleford	1999-2001	48(4)	4	2	1	24
Sam Rapira	Huddersfield	2016-17	29(19)	3	0	0	12
Steve Rapira	Salford	2014	5(13)	0	0	0	0
Stefan Ratchford	Warrington	2012-17	143(10)	52	164	2	538
	Salford	2007, 2009-11	65(5)	23	20	0	132
Mike Ratu	Hull KR	2010	5	1	0	0	4
	Leeds	2007, 2009	1(5)	1	0	0	4
Paul Rauhihi	Warrington	2006-09	67(20)	10	0	0	40
Ben Rauter	Wakefield	2001	15(6)	4	0	0	16
Nick Rawsthorne	Leigh	2017	1	1	0	0	4
	Hull	2017	3	2	2	0	12
Gareth Raynor	Bradford	2011	18	4	0	0	16
	Crusaders	2010	7	4	0	0	16
	Hull	2001-09	186	102	0	0	408
	Leeds	2000	(3)	0	0	0	0
Tony Rea	London	1996	22	4	0	0	16
Stuart Reardon	Crusaders	2011	25	11	0	0	44
	Bradford	2003-05, 2010	78(11)	37	0	0	148
	Warrington	2006-08	48	12	0	0	48
	Salford	2002	7(1)	3	0	0	12
Mark Reber	Wigan	1999-2000	9(9)	5	0	0	20
Alan Reddicliffe	Warrington	2001	1	0	0	0	0
Tahi Reihana	Bradford	1997-98	17(21)	0	0	0	0
Paul Reilly	Wakefield	2008	5(2)	1	0	0	4
	Huddersfield	1999-2001, 2003-07	150(8)	35	1	0	142
Robert Relf	Widnes	2002-04	68(2)	5	0	0	20
Steve Renouf	Wigan	2000-01	55	40	0	0	160
Steele Retchless	London	1998-2004	177(6)	13	0	0	52
Ben Reynolds	Leigh	2017	16	6	48	0	120
	Castleford	2013-14	1(3)	0	0	0	0
Scott Rhodes	Hull	2000	2	0	0	0	0
Phillipe Ricard	Paris	1996-97	2	0	0	0	0
Andy Rice	Huddersfield	2000-01	2(13)	1	0	0	4
Basil Richards	Huddersfield	1998-99	28(17)	1	0	0	4
Craig Richards	Oldham	1996	1	0	0	0	0
Greg Richards	Leigh	2017	(1)	0	0	0	0
	St Helens	2013-17	19(49)	1	0	0	4
Pat Richards	Catalans	2016	19	9	69	0	174
	Wigan	2006-13	199	147	759	4	2110
Andy Richardson	Hudds-Sheff	2000	(2)	0	0	0	0
Danny Richardson	St Helens	2017	11(2)	2	0	2	10
Sean Richardson	Widnes	2002	2(18)	1	0	0	4
	Wakefield	1999	5(1)	0	0	0	0
	Castleford	1996-97	3(8)	1	0	0	4
Mark Riddell	Wigan	2009-10	45(11)	5	2	0	24
Martyn Ridyard	Huddersfield	2017	7	1	26	0	56
	Leigh	2017	4	0	2	0	4
Neil Rigby	St Helens	2006	(1)	0	0	0	0
Shane Rigon	Bradford	2001	14(11)	12	0	0	48
Craig Rika	Halifax	1996	2	0	0	0	0
Chris Riley	Wakefield	2014-15	44	16	0	0	64
	Warrington	2005-14	146(10)	102	0	0	408
	Harlequins	2011	3	2	0	0	8
Glenn Riley	Warrington	2013-14	(15)	0	0	0	0
Peter Riley	Workington	1996	7(5)	0	0	0	0
Julien Rinaldi	London	2012	4(16)	1	0	0	4
	Wakefield	2002, 2010-11	27(9)	6	0	0	24
	Bradford	2009	(7)	1	0	0	4
	Harlequins	2007-08	4(43)	9	0	0	36
	Catalans	2006	16(6)	3	1	0	14
Dean Ripley	Castleford	2004	3(4)	1	0	0	4
Leroy Rivett	Warrington	2002	9	1	0	0	4
	Hudds-Sheff	2000	5(1)	1	0	0	4
	Leeds	1996-2000	39(15)	21	0	0	84
Jason Roach	Warrington	1998-99	29(7)	15	0	0	60
	Castleford	1997	7	4	0	0	16
Ben Roarty	Castleford	2006	11(6)	2	0	0	8
	Huddersfield	2003-05	52	5	0	0	20
Amos Roberts	Wigan	2009-11	47(2)	27	5	0	118
Ben Roberts	Castleford	2015-17	46(11)	20	0	2	82
Mark Roberts	Wigan	2003	(3)	0	0	0	0
Oliver Roberts	Huddersfield	2016-17	22(25)	7	0	0	28
	Bradford	2013-14	(5)	0	0	0	0
Robert Roberts	Huddersfield	2001	(1)	0	0	0	0
	Halifax	2000	(3)	0	0	0	0
	Hull	1999	24(2)	4	13	4	46
Michael Robertson	London	2012-13	35	17	0	0	68
Stan Robin	Catalans	2015-16	5(2)	1	0	0	4
Chad Robinson	Harlequins	2009	13(1)	2	0	0	8
Connor Robinson	Hull KR	2014-15	(2)	0	0	0	0
Craig Robinson	Wakefield	2005	(1)	0	0	0	0
Jason Robinson	Wigan	1996-2000	126(1)	87	0	1	349
Jeremy Robinson	Paris	1997	10(3)	1	21	0	46
John Robinson	Widnes	2003-04	7	1	0	0	4
Luke Robinson	Huddersfield	2008-15	191(18)	45	4	0	188
	Salford	2005-07	79	28	10	2	134
	Wigan	2002-04	17(25)	9	6	1	49
	Castleford	2004	9	4	3	0	22
Will Robinson	Hull	2000	22	4	0	0	16
	Gateshead	1999	28	9	0	0	36
Ash Robson	Castleford	2015	3	1	0	0	4
James Roby	St Helens	2004-17	239(122)	89	1	0	358
Mike Roby	St Helens	2004	(1)	0	0	0	0
Carl Roden	Warrington	1997	1	0	0	0	0
Shane Rodney	London	2012-13	28	3	12	0	36
Matt Rodwell	Warrington	2002	10	3	0	0	12
Darren Rogers	Castleford	1999-2004	162(1)	81	0	0	324
	Salford	1997-98	42	16	0	0	64
Arthur Romano	Catalans	2017	2	0	0	0	0
Jamie Rooney	Wakefield	2003-09	113(7)	60	321	21	903
	Castleford	2001	2(1)	0	6	0	12
Jonathan Roper	Castleford	2001	13	7	12	0	52
	Salford	2000	1(4)	1	3	0	10
	London	2000	4	0	0	0	0
	Warrington	1996-2000	75(8)	33	71	0	274
Scott Roskell	London	1996-97	30(2)	16	0	0	64
Steve Rosolen	London	1996-98	25(9)	10	0	0	40
Adam Ross	London	1996	(1)	0	0	0	0

Super League Players 1996-2017

PLAYER	CLUB	YEAR	APP	TRIES	GOALS	FG	PTS
Paul Round	Castleford	1996	(3)	0	0	0	0
Steve Rowlands	Widnes	2004-05	18(3)	2	15	0	38
	St Helens	2003	(1)	0	0	0	0
Paul Rowley	Leigh	2005	15(7)	3	0	0	12
	Huddersfield	2001	24	3	0	0	12
	Halifax	1996-2000	107(3)	27	1	3	113
Nigel Roy	London	2001-04	100	39	0	0	156
Nicky Royle	Widnes	2004	13	7	0	0	28
Shad Royston	Bradford	2011	17(1)	10	0	0	40
Chris Rudd	Warrington	1996-98	31(17)	10	16	0	72
Sean Rudder	Catalans	2006	22(1)	6	0	0	24
	Castleford	2004	9(3)	2	0	0	8
Charly Runciman	Widnes	2016-17	48	7	0	0	28
James Rushforth	Halifax	1997	(4)	0	0	0	0
Danny Russell	Huddersfield	1998-2000	50(13)	8	0	0	32
Ian Russell	Oldham	1997	1(3)	1	0	0	4
	Paris	1996	3	0	0	0	0
Matthew Russell	Warrington	2014-17	74(4)	22	0	0	88
	Hull	2012	6	0	0	0	0
	Wigan	2012	2	3	0	0	12
Richard Russell	Castleford	1996-98	37(4)	2	0	0	8
Robert Russell	Salford	1998-99	2(1)	0	1	0	2
Sean Rutgerson	Salford	2004-06	60(9)	4	0	0	16
Chris Ryan	London	1998-99	44(3)	17	10	0	88
Matt Ryan	Wakefield	2014-15	28(12)	7	0	0	28
Sean Ryan	Castleford	2004	11(5)	2	0	0	8
	Hull	2002-03	53	8	0	0	32
Justin Ryder	Wakefield	2004	19(3)	11	0	0	44
Jason Ryles	Catalans	2009	19(2)	2	0	0	8
Setaimata Sa	Widnes	2016	7(5)	3	0	0	12
	Hull	2014-15	18(6)	6	0	0	24
	Catalans	2010-12	58(5)	21	0	0	84
Teddy Sadaoui	Catalans	2006	7	0	0	0	0
Liam Salter	Hull KR	2012-16	71	16	0	0	64
Matt Salter	London	1997-99	14(34)	0	0	0	0
Ben Sammut	Hull	2000	20	4	67	0	150
	Gateshead	1999	26(2)	6	17	0	58
Jarrod Sammut	Wakefield	2014-15	19(1)	9	52	0	140
	Bradford	2012-13	35(3)	28	47	1	207
	Crusaders	2010-11	17(16)	17	0	0	68
Dean Sampson	Castleford	1996-2003	124(28)	24	0	0	96
Paul Sampson	London	2004	1(2)	1	0	0	4
	Wakefield	2000	17	8	0	0	32
Lee Sanderson	London	2004	1(5)	1	7	0	18
Chris Sandow	Warrington	2015-16	27(1)	11	26	1	97
Jason Sands	Paris	1996-97	28	0	0	0	0
Mitchell Sargent	Castleford	2008-10	37(21)	6	0	0	24
Dan Sarginson	Wigan	2014-16	71(1)	21	0	0	84
	London	2012-13	35(1)	10	0	0	40
	Harlequins	2011	8	5	0	0	20
Matt Sarsfield	Salford	2016	2(2)	1	0	0	4
Junior Sa'u	Salford	2014-17	85	38	0	0	152
Andre Savelio	Warrington	2017	3(14)	4	0	0	16
	Castleford	2016	6(1)	1	0	0	4
	St Helens	2014-16	12(25)	2	0	0	8
Lokeni Savelio	Halifax	2000	2(11)	0	0	0	0
	Salford	1997-98	18(20)	0	0	0	0
Tom Saxton	Salford	2007	5	0	0	0	0
	Wakefield	2006	9(6)	2	0	0	8
	Hull	2005	19(8)	3	0	0	12
	Castleford	2002-04	37(12)	11	0	0	44
Jonathan Scales	Halifax	2000	1	0	0	0	0
	Bradford	1996-98	46(4)	24	0	0	96
Andrew Schick	Castleford	1996-98	45(13)	10	0	0	40
Clinton Schifcofske	Crusaders	2010-11	44	5	115	0	250
Garry Schofield	Huddersfield	1998	(2)	0	0	0	0
Gary Schubert	Workington	1996	(1)	0	0	0	0
Matt Schultz	Hull	1998-99	23(9)	2	0	0	8
	Leeds	1996	2(4)	0	0	0	0
John Schuster	Halifax	1996-97	31	9	127	3	293
Nick Scruton	Wakefield	2014-16	62(3)	9	0	0	36
	Bradford	2009-14	70(27)	5	0	0	20
	Leeds	2002, 2004-08	11(53)	3	0	0	12
	Hull	2004	2(16)	3	0	0	12
Danny Sculthorpe	Huddersfield	2009	5(8)	0	0	0	0
	Wakefield	2007-09	14(28)	1	0	0	4
	Castleford	2006	18(1)	4	0	1	17
	Wigan	2002-05	13(49)	7	0	0	28
Paul Sculthorpe	St Helens	1998-2008	223(4)	94	356	7	1095
	Warrington	1996-97	40	6	0	0	24
Mick Seaby	London	1997	3(2)	1	0	0	4
Danny Seal	Halifax	1996-99	8(17)	3	0	0	12
Matt Seers	Wakefield	2003	11(1)	2	0	0	8
James Segeyaro	Leeds	2016	3	1	0	0	4
Paul Seguier	Catalans	2016-17	(7)	0	0	0	0
Anthony Seibold	London	1999-2000	33(19)	5	0	0	20
Jesse Sene-Lefao	Castleford	2017	25(7)	6	0	0	24
Keith Senior	Leeds	1999-2011	319(2)	159	0	0	636
	Sheffield	1996-99	90(2)	40	0	0	160
Fili Seru	Hull	1998-99	37(1)	13	0	0	52
Anthony Seuseu	Halifax	2003	1(11)	1	0	0	4
Jerry Seuseu	Wigan	2005-06	29(9)	1	0	0	4
Brett Seymour	Hull	2012-13	26(1)	7	0	0	28
Will Sharp	Hull	2011-12	27(8)	10	0	0	40
	Harlequins	2008-10	65(1)	19	0	0	76
Jamie Shaul	Hull	2013-17	104	62	0	0	248
Darren Shaw	Salford	2002	5(9)	1	0	0	4
	London	1996, 2002	22(8)	3	0	0	12
	Castleford	2000-01	50(6)	1	0	0	4
	Sheffield	1998-99	51(1)	3	0	1	13
Mick Shaw	Halifax	1999	5	1	0	0	4
	Leeds	1996	12(2)	7	0	0	28
Ryan Shaw	Hull KR	2016	6(1)	4	6	0	28
	London	2013	2	1	2	0	8
Phil Shead	Paris	1996	3(2)	0	0	0	0
Richard Sheil	St Helens	1997	(1)	0	0	0	0
Kelly Shelford	Warrington	1996-97	25(3)	4	0	2	18
Kyle Shelford	Wigan	2016	(1)	0	0	0	0
Michael Shenton	Castleford	2004, 2006, 2008-10, 2013-17	204(2)	89	0	0	356
	St Helens	2011-12	51	15	0	0	60
Ryan Sheridan	Castleford	2004	2	0	0	0	0
	Widnes	2003	14(3)	2	0	0	8
	Leeds	1997-2002	123(7)	46	0	1	185
	Sheffield	1996	9(3)	5	0	1	21
Louis Sheriff	Hull KR	2011-12	8	3	0	0	12
Rikki Sheriffe	Bradford	2009-10	51	14	0	0	56
	Harlequins	2006-08	35(1)	16	0	0	64
	Halifax	2003	6(1)	3	0	0	12
Ian Sherratt	Oldham	1996	5(3)	1	0	0	4
Brent Sherwin	Catalans	2010	12	1	0	1	5
	Castleford	2008-10	48(1)	4	0	3	19
Peter Shiels	St Helens	2001-02	44(3)	11	0	0	44
Gary Shillabeer	Huddersfield	1999	(2)	0	0	0	0
Mark Shipway	Salford	2004-05	30(12)	3	0	0	12
Jake Shorrocks	Wigan	2016-17	2(11)	0	8	0	16
Ian Sibbit	Bradford	2011-12	11(7)	0	0	0	0
	Salford	2005-07, 2009-10	64(17)	11	0	0	44
	Warrington	1999-2001, 2003-04	63(18)	24	0	0	96
Mark Sibson	Huddersfield	1999	2	2	0	0	8
Adam Sidlow	Bradford	2013-14	20(22)	8	0	0	32
	Salford	2009-12	34(44)	14	0	0	56
Harry Siejka	Wakefield	2014	6(3)	1	0	0	4
Jordan Sigismeau	Catalans	2015-16	11	3	0	0	12
Jon Simms	St Helens	2002	(1)	0	0	0	0
Craig Simon	Hull	2000	23(2)	8	0	0	32
	Gateshead	1999	25(4)	6	0	0	24
Mickael Simon	Catalans	2010-14, 2017	26(56)	3	0	0	12
	Wakefield	2015-16	15(22)	3	0	0	12
Darren Simpson	Huddersfield	1998-99	17(1)	5	0	0	20
Jamie Simpson	Huddersfield	2011	8(1)	0	0	0	0
Jared Simpson	Huddersfield	2015-17	7	2	0	0	8
Robbie Simpson	London	1999	6(7)	0	0	0	0
Ashton Sims	Warrington	2015-17	69(11)	5	0	0	20
Kevin Sinfield	Leeds	1997-2015	425(29)	70	1566	31	3443
Matt Sing	Hull	2007-08	41	14	0	0	56
Wayne Sing	Paris	1997	18(1)	2	0	0	8
Brad Singleton	Leeds	2011-17	68(45)	14	0	0	56
	Wakefield	2013	(1)	0	0	0	0
Fata Sini	Salford	1997	22	7	0	0	28
Ken Sio	Hull KR	2015-16	42	23	13	0	118
Michael Sio	Wakefield	2015-17	25(14)	6	0	0	24
John Skandalis	Huddersfield	2007-08	37(5)	4	0	0	16
Dylan Skee	Harlequins	2008-09	(3)	0	0	0	0
Ben Skerrett	Castleford	2003	(1)	0	0	0	0
Kelvin Skerrett	Halifax	1997-99	31(6)	2	0	0	8
	Wigan	1996	1(8)	0	0	0	0
Troy Slattery	Wakefield	2002-03	33(5)	4	0	0	16
	Huddersfield	1999	3	1	0	0	4
Mick Slicker	Huddersfield	2001, 2003-05	17(48)	2	0	0	8
	Sheffield	1999	(3)	1	0	0	4
	Halifax	1997	2(5)	0	0	0	0
Nick Slyney	London	2014	20(4)	3	0	0	12
Ian Smales	Castleford	1996-97	10(8)	5	0	0	20
Aaron Smith	Castleford	2006	(2)	0	0	0	0
	Bradford	2003-04	12(1)	0	0	0	0
Andy Smith	Harlequins	2007	6(3)	3	0	0	12
	Bradford	2004-06	9(9)	4	0	0	16
	Salford	2005	4	1	0	0	4

172

Super League Players 1996-2017

PLAYER	CLUB	YEAR	APP	TRIES	GOALS	FG	PTS
Byron Smith	Castleford	2004	(9)	0	0	0	0
	Halifax	2003	6(1)	0	0	0	0
Cameron Smith	Leeds	2016-17	(2)	0	0	0	0
Chris Smith	Hull	2001-02	12	3	0	0	12
	St Helens	1998-2000	62(9)	26	0	0	104
	Castleford	1996-97	36(1)	12	0	0	48
Craig Smith	Wigan	2002-04	77(3)	10	0	0	40
Damien Smith	St Helens	1998	21(1)	8	0	0	32
Daniel Smith	Huddersfield	2015-17	3(23)	2	0	0	8
	Wakefield	2014-15	21(15)	6	0	0	24
Danny Smith	Paris	1996	10(2)	1	15	0	34
	London	1996	2(1)	1	0	0	4
Darren Smith	St Helens	2003	25(1)	14	0	0	56
Gary Smith	Castleford	2001	(1)	0	0	0	0
Hudson Smith	Bradford	2000	8(22)	2	0	0	8
	Salford	1999	23(2)	5	0	0	20
James Smith	Salford	2000	23(3)	6	0	0	24
Jamie Smith	Hull	1998-99	24(6)	6	12	0	48
	Workington	1996	5(3)	0	1	0	2
Jason Smith	Hull	2001-04	61(3)	17	0	1	69
Jeremy Smith	Wakefield	2011	9(1)	1	0	0	4
	Salford	2009-10	27(17)	2	0	0	8
Kris Smith	London	2001	(1)	0	0	0	0
	Halifax	2001	(1)	0	0	0	0
Lee Smith	Wakefield	2012-13, 2015	30(4)	16	54	2	174
	Leeds	2005-12	125(10)	60	34	1	309
Leigh Smith	Workington	1996	9	4	0	0	16
Mark Smith	Widnes	2005	12(15)	4	0	0	16
	Wigan	1999-2004	35(77)	8	0	0	32
Martyn Smith	Harlequins	2010	(2)	0	0	0	0
Matty Smith	St Helens	2006-08, 2010, 2017	35(5)	5	10	4	44
	Wigan	2012-16	122(3)	17	279	25	651
	Salford	2010-12	67(4)	13	6	1	65
	Celtic	2009	15(1)	3	2	1	17
Michael Smith	Hull KR	2007	(3)	1	0	0	4
	Castleford	1998, 2001-04	86(33)	32	0	0	128
	Hull	1999	12(6)	3	0	0	12
Morgan Smith	Warrington	2016-17	(11)	1	1	0	6
Paul Smith	Huddersfield	2004-06	52(17)	13	0	0	52
Paul Smith	Warrington	2001	(1)	0	0	0	0
	Castleford	1997-2000	6(37)	3	0	0	12
Paul Smith	London	1997	7(1)	2	0	0	8
Peter Smith	Oldham	1996	2	0	0	0	0
Richard Smith	Wakefield	2001	8(1)	1	0	0	4
	Salford	1997	(1)	1	0	0	4
Tim Smith	Wakefield	2012-15	79	11	0	0	44
	Salford	2014	12	2	7	0	22
	Wigan	2008-09	13(8)	2	0	0	8
Tony Smith	Hull	2001-03	43(5)	26	0	0	104
	Wigan	1997-2000	66(5)	46	0	0	184
	Castleford	1996-97	18(2)	10	0	0	40
Tony Smith	Workington	1996	9	1	0	0	4
Tyrone Smith	Harlequins	2006-07	49(3)	13	0	0	52
	London	2005	20(4)	11	0	0	44
Rob Smyth	Leigh	2005	15(1)	4	0	0	16
	Warrington	2000-03	65	35	20	0	180
	London	1998-2000	32(2)	9	15	0	66
	Wigan	1996	11(5)	16	0	0	64
Marc Sneyd	Hull	2015-17	82	14	287	14	644
	Castleford	2014	25(1)	6	100	2	226
	Salford	2010-13	33(12)	4	61	3	141
Steve Snitch	Castleford	2010-12	38(18)	10	0	0	40
	Wakefield	2002-05, 2009	33(55)	9	0	0	36
	Huddersfield	2006-08	24(35)	12	0	0	48
Bright Sodje	Wakefield	2000	15	4	0	0	16
	Sheffield	1996-99	54	34	0	0	136
Iosia Soliola	St Helens	2010-14	83(24)	27	0	0	108
David Solomona	Warrington	2010-12	8(49)	16	1	0	66
	Bradford	2007-09	44(9)	19	0	0	76
	Wakefield	2004-06	73(3)	26	0	0	104
Denny Solomona	Castleford	2015-16	42	58	0	0	232
	London	2014	19(1)	8	0	0	32
Alfred Songoro	Wakefield	1999	8(5)	4	0	0	16
Romain Sort	Paris	1997	(1)	0	0	0	0
Paul Southern	Salford	1997-2002	79(33)	6	13	0	50
	St Helens	2002	1(1)	0	0	0	0
Steve Southern	Wakefield	2012	7(8)	3	0	0	12
Cain Southernwood	Bradford	2010	2	0	0	0	0
Roy Southernwood	Wakefield	1999	1	0	0	0	0
	Halifax	1996	2	0	0	0	0
Jason Southwell	Huddersfield	2004	(1)	0	0	0	0
Waisale Sovatabua	Wakefield	2001-03	44(3)	19	0	0	76
	Hudds-Sheff	2000	23(1)	8	0	0	32
	Sheffield	1996-99	56(17)	19	0	1	77
Jamie Soward	London	2013	6(1)	4	21	0	58
Yusef Sozi	London	2000-01	(5)	0	0	0	0
Scott Spaven	Hull KR	2010	(2)	0	0	0	0
Andy Speak	Castleford	2001	4(4)	0	0	0	0
	Wakefield	2000	6(5)	2	0	0	8
	Leeds	1999	4	1	0	0	4
Dom Speakman	St Helens	2013	(1)	0	0	0	0
Tim Spears	Castleford	2003	(3)	0	0	0	0
Jake Spedding	St Helens	2016-17	3	0	0	0	0
Ady Spencer	London	1996-99	8(36)	5	0	0	20
Jack Spencer	Salford	2009-11	(7)	0	0	0	0
Tom Spencer	Wigan	2012-13	(7)	0	0	0	0
Rob Spicer	Wakefield	2002-05	28(18)	4	0	0	16
Russ Spiers	Wakefield	2011	(2)	0	0	0	0
Gadwin Springer	Castleford	2015-17	15(35)	3	0	0	12
	Catalans	2014-15	(3)	1	0	0	4
Stuart Spruce	Widnes	2002-03	45(4)	19	0	0	76
	Bradford	1996-2001	107(2)	57	0	0	228
Lee St Hilaire	Castleford	1997	4(2)	0	0	0	0
Marcus St Hilaire	Bradford	2006-07	34(1)	12	0	0	48
	Huddersfield	2003-05	72(2)	30	0	0	120
	Leeds	1996-2002	59(33)	31	0	0	124
Cyril Stacul	Catalans	2007-12	61(1)	18	0	0	72
Dylan Stainton	Workington	1996	2(3)	0	0	0	0
Mark Stamper	Workington	1996	(1)	0	0	0	0
John Stankevitch	Widnes	2005	17(5)	0	0	0	0
	St Helens	2000-04	74(40)	25	0	0	100
Gareth Stanley	Bradford	2000	1	1	0	0	4
Craig Stapleton	Salford	2009	24	2	0	0	8
	Leigh	2005	27(1)	4	0	0	16
Graham Steadman	Castleford	1996-97	11(17)	5	0	0	20
Jon Steel	Hull KR	2007-08	18	6	0	0	24
Jamie Stenhouse	Warrington	2000-01	9(3)	3	0	0	12
Gareth Stephens	Sheffield	1997-99	23(6)	2	0	0	8
David Stephenson	Hull	1998	11(7)	3	0	0	12
	Oldham	1997	10(8)	2	0	0	8
Francis Stephenson	London	2002-05	42(34)	5	0	0	20
	Wigan	2001	2(9)	0	0	0	0
	Wakefield	1999-2000	50(1)	6	0	0	24
Paul Sterling	Leeds	1997-2000	79(12)	50	0	0	200
Paul Stevens	Oldham	1996	2(1)	0	0	0	0
	London	1996	(1)	0	0	0	0
Warren Stevens	Leigh	2005	4(14)	1	0	0	4
	Warrington	1996-99, 2002-05	17(66)	1	0	0	4
	Salford	2001	(8)	0	0	0	0
Anthony Stewart	Harlequins	2006	4	0	0	0	0
	Salford	2004-06	51(2)	15	0	0	60
	St Helens	1997-2003	93(23)	44	0	0	176
Glenn Stewart	Leigh	2017	15	0	0	0	0
	Catalans	2016	28	3	0	0	12
Troy Stone	Widnes	2002	18(6)	1	0	0	4
	Huddersfield	2001	12(1)	1	0	0	4
James Stosic	Wakefield	2009	8(10)	1	0	0	4
Lynton Stott	Wakefield	1999	21	4	6	1	29
	Sheffield	1996-98	40(4)	15	0	0	60
Mitchell Stringer	Salford	2005-06	12(4)	0	0	0	0
	London	2004-05	10(9)	0	0	0	0
Graham Strutton	London	1996	9(1)	2	0	0	8
Matt Sturm	Leigh	2005	8(19)	3	0	0	12
	Warrington	2002-04	1(18)	0	0	0	0
	Huddersfield	1998-99	46	8	0	0	32
Anthony Sullivan	St Helens	1996-2001	137(2)	105	0	0	420
Michael Sullivan	Warrington	2006-07	21(16)	8	1	0	34
Phil Sumner	Warrington	1996	(5)	0	0	0	0
Alex Sutcliffe	Leeds	2017	1	0	0	0	0
Liam Sutcliffe	Leeds	2013-17	75(27)	36	111	1	367
	Bradford	2014	3(1)	1	0	0	4
Ryan Sutton	Wigan	2014-17	34(45)	4	0	0	16
Simon Svabic	Salford	1998-2000	13(5)	3	19	0	50
Luke Swain	Salford	2009-10	54	3	0	0	12
Richard Swain	Hull	2004-07	89	5	0	0	20
Anthony Swann	Warrington	2001	3	1	0	0	4
Logan Swann	Warrington	2005-06	49(1)	17	0	0	68
	Bradford	2004	25	6	0	0	24
Willie Swann	Warrington	1996-99	25(2)	6	0	0	24
Adam Swift	St Helens	2012-17	102	70	0	0	280
Nathan Sykes	Castleford	1996-2004	158(52)	3	0	0	12
Paul Sykes	Wakefield	2012-14	59(1)	12	135	6	324
	Bradford	1999-2002, 2008-12	99(4)	35	64	2	270
	Harlequins	2006-07	31(2)	15	47	1	155
	London	2001-05	95(1)	26	219	3	545

173

Super League Players 1996-2017

PLAYER	CLUB	YEAR	APP	TRIES	GOALS	FG	PTS
Wayne Sykes	London	1999	(2)	0	0	0	0
Tom Symonds	Huddersfield	2016-17	6	3	0	0	12
Ukuma Ta'ai	Huddersfield	2013-17	78(42)	35	0	0	140
Semi Tadulala	Wakefield	2004-07, 2011	92	37	0	0	148
	Bradford	2008-09	49	30	0	0	120
Whetu Taewa	Sheffield	1997-98	33(7)	8	0	0	32
Zeb Taia	St Helens	2017	28(1)	6	0	0	24
	Catalans	2013-15	75	35	0	0	140
Alan Tait	Leeds	1996	3(3)	1	0	0	4
Fetuli Talanoa	Hull	2014-17	92(1)	40	0	0	160
Willie Talau	Salford	2009-10	22	4	0	0	16
	St Helens	2003-08	130(1)	50	0	0	200
Ian Talbot	Wakefield	1999	9(5)	2	31	0	70
	Wigan	1997	3	1	0	0	4
Albert Talipeau	Wakefield	2004	2(3)	0	0	0	0
Gael Tallec	Halifax	2000	5(19)	3	0	0	12
	Castleford	1998-99	19(21)	3	0	0	12
	Wigan	1996-97	8(12)	3	0	0	12
Joe Tamani	Bradford	1996	11(3)	4	0	0	16
Ryan Tandy	Hull KR	2007	8(4)	2	0	0	8
Andrew Tangata-Toa	Huddersfield	1999	15	2	0	0	8
David Tangata-Toa	Celtic	2009	1(18)	4	0	0	16
	Hull KR	2007	(17)	3	0	0	12
Jordan Tansey	Huddersfield	2016	2	1	1	0	6
	Wakefield	2015	4	1	0	0	4
	Castleford	2013-15	44(1)	15	0	0	60
	Crusaders	2011	14(4)	5	0	0	20
	Hull	2009-10	30	9	0	0	36
	Leeds	2006-08	18(32)	19	3	0	82
Lama Tasi	Salford	2014-15, 2017	44(16)	4	0	0	16
	St Helens	2016	9(8)	0	0	0	0
Kris Tassell	Wakefield	2002	24	10	0	0	40
	Salford	2000-01	35(10)	12	0	0	48
Shem Tatupu	Wigan	1996	(3)	0	0	0	0
Tony Tatupu	Wakefield	2000-01	20	2	0	0	8
	Warrington	1997	21(1)	6	0	0	24
Taulima Tautai	Wigan	2015-17	7(77)	2	0	0	8
	Wakefield	2013-14	6(19)	2	0	0	8
Dave Taylor	Catalans	2016	20(4)	8	0	0	32
James Taylor	Leigh	2005	(4)	0	0	0	0
Joe Taylor	Paris	1997	9(5)	2	0	0	8
Lawrence Taylor	Sheffield	1996	(1)	0	0	0	0
Scott Taylor	Hull	2016-17	50(4)	7	0	0	28
	Salford	2015	23	5	0	0	20
	Wigan	2013-14	18(29)	6	0	0	24
	Hull KR	2009-12	21(29)	8	0	0	32
Frederic Teixido	Sheffield	1999	(4)	0	0	0	0
	Paris	1996-97	2(3)	1	0	0	4
Lionel Teixido	Catalans	2006-07	11(13)	3	0	0	12
Karl Temata	London	2005, 2012	1(8)	1	0	0	4
	Harlequins	2006-11	94(22)	7	0	0	28
Jason Temu	Hull	1998	13(2)	1	0	0	4
	Oldham	1996-97	25(3)	1	0	0	4
Paul Terry	London	1997	(1)	0	0	0	0
Anthony Thackeray	Castleford	2008	3(6)	0	0	0	0
	Hull	2007	2	0	0	0	0
Jamie Thackray	Crusaders	2010	1(16)	2	0	0	8
	Hull	2005-06, 2008-09	37(45)	6	0	0	24
	Leeds	2006-07	5(27)	7	0	0	28
	Castleford	2003-04	7(11)	3	0	0	12
	Halifax	2000-02	10(38)	3	0	0	12
Adam Thaler	Castleford	2002	(1)	0	0	0	0
Gareth Thomas	Crusaders	2010-11	27(1)	6	0	0	24
Giles Thomas	London	1997-99	1(2)	0	0	0	0
Oscar Thomas	London	2014	4(2)	0	1	0	2
Rob Thomas	Harlequins	2011	(2)	0	0	0	0
Steve Thomas	London	2004	4(2)	0	0	0	0
	Warrington	2001	2	0	0	0	0
Alex Thompson	Warrington	2009	(1)	1	0	0	4
Alex Thompson	Sheffield	1997	4(11)	0	0	0	0
Bobby Thompson	Salford	1999	28	5	2	0	24
Corey Thompson	Widnes	2016-17	48	36	9	0	162
David Thompson	Leigh	2017	0	0	0	0	0
	Hull KR	2016	1	0	0	0	0
Jordan Thompson	Hull	2014-17	25(71)	11	0	0	44
	Castleford	2009-13	47(24)	25	0	0	100
Luke Thompson	St Helens	2013-17	39(54)	11	0	0	44
Sam Thompson	Harlequins	2009	(2)	0	0	0	0
	St Helens	2008	(5)	0	0	0	0
Chris Thorman	Hull	2009	19(2)	1	0	0	4
	Huddersfield	2000-01, 2005-08	126(20)	51	320	3	847
	London	2003	26(1)	7	81	1	191
	Sheffield	1999	5(13)	2	8	1	25

PLAYER	CLUB	YEAR	APP	TRIES	GOALS	FG	PTS
Tony Thorniley	Warrington	1997	(5)	0	0	0	0
Andy Thornley	Salford	2009	(1)	1	0	0	4
Iain Thornley	Catalans	2017	18	4	0	0	16
	Hull KR	2016	21	10	0	0	40
	Wigan	2012-14	40	25	0	0	100
Danny Tickle	Leigh	2017	10(13)	4	0	0	16
	Castleford	2016	6(3)	0	1	0	2
	Widnes	2014-15	33(1)	3	88	0	188
	Hull	2007-13	159(5)	45	528	1	1237
	Wigan	2002-06	94(36)	34	200	2	538
	Halifax	2000-02	25(17)	10	91	2	224
Kris Tickle	Warrington	2001	(1)	0	0	0	0
Lewis Tierney	Catalans	2017	2	0	0	0	0
	Wigan	2013-17	35	17	0	0	68
James Tilley	St Helens	2013-14	(3)	0	0	0	0
Dane Tilse	Hull KR	2015-16	29(1)	1	0	0	4
John Timu	London	1998-2000	57(3)	11	0	0	44
Kerrod Toby	London	1997	2(2)	0	0	0	0
Tulsen Tollett	London	1996-2001	105(5)	38	49	1	251
Joel Tomkins	Wigan	2005-11, 2014-17	154(45)	57	0	0	228
Logan Tomkins	Salford	2014-17	57(17)	5	0	0	20
	Wigan	2012-15	9(32)	1	0	0	4
Sam Tomkins	Wigan	2009-13, 2016-17	149(6)	118	29	1	531
Glen Tomlinson	Wakefield	1999-2000	41(5)	8	0	0	32
	Hull	1998	5	1	0	0	4
	Bradford	1996-97	27(13)	12	0	0	48
Willie Tonga	Leigh	2017	3	0	0	0	0
	Catalans	2015	18	6	0	0	24
Ryan Tongia	Wakefield	2011	4	2	0	0	8
Ian Tonks	Castleford	1996-2001	32(50)	11	13	0	70
Tony Tonks	Huddersfield	2012	(1)	0	0	0	0
Motu Tony	Wakefield	2011-12	7(3)	1	0	0	4
	Hull	2005-09	76(20)	25	0	0	100
	Castleford	2004	8(1)	1	0	0	4
Mark Tookey	Harlequins	2006	12(14)	1	0	0	4
	London	2005	13(14)	5	0	0	20
	Castleford	2004	2(8)	1	0	0	4
Clinton Toopi	Leeds	2006-08	40(3)	9	0	0	36
David Tootill	Harlequins	2008	(4)	0	0	0	0
Paul Topping	Oldham	1996-97	23(10)	1	19	0	42
Patrick Torreilles	Paris	1996	9(1)	1	25	0	54
Albert Torrens	Huddersfield	2006	7	5	0	0	20
Mat Toshack	London	1998-2004	120(21)	24	0	0	96
Julien Touxagas	Catalans	2006-11	14(45)	4	0	0	16
Darren Treacy	Salford	2002	24(1)	6	1	0	26
Dean Treister	Hull	2003	16(1)	3	0	0	12
Rocky Trimarchi	Crusaders	2010	16(8)	0	0	0	0
Steve Trindall	London	2003-05	40(20)	3	0	0	12
Shane Tronc	Wakefield	2010	8(3)	2	0	0	8
Kyle Trout	Wakefield	2012-15	6(17)	3	0	0	12
George Truelove	Wakefield	2002	2	1	0	0	4
	London	2000	5	1	0	0	4
Jake Trueman	Castleford	2017	2(1)	3	0	0	12
Va'aiga Tuigamala	Wigan	1996	21	10	3	0	46
Fereti Tuilagi	St Helens	1999-2000	43(15)	21	0	0	84
	Halifax	1996-98	55(3)	27	0	0	108
Carlos Tuimavave	Hull	2016-17	46(1)	19	0	0	76
Evarn Tuimavave	Hull KR	2013	11(12)	2	0	0	8
Sateki Tuipulotu	Leeds	1996	6(3)	1	2	0	8
Anthony Tupou	Wakefield	2016	12(9)	4	0	0	16
Bill Tupou	Wakefield	2015-17	40(3)	16	0	0	64
Tame Tupou	Bradford	2007-08	10(7)	8	0	0	32
Jansin Turgut	Hull	2015-17	7(16)	2	0	0	8
Neil Turley	Leigh	2005	6(3)	2	20	1	49
Darren Turner	Huddersfield	2000-01, 2003-04	42(13)	13	0	0	52
	Sheffield	1996-99	41(29)	15	0	0	60
Ian Turner	Paris	1996	1(1)	1	0	0	4
Jordan Turner	Huddersfield	2017	9	1	0	0	4
	St Helens	2013-16	106(4)	44	13	3	205
	Hull	2010-12	62(5)	28	0	0	112
	Salford	2006-07, 2009	22(10)	4	1	0	18
Chris Tuson	Hull	2014	10(1)	0	0	0	0
	Wigan	2008, 2010-13	24(49)	13	0	0	52
	Castleford	2010	3(5)	0	0	0	0
Gregory Tutard	Paris	1996	1(1)	0	0	0	0
Brendon Tuuta	Warrington	1998	18(2)	4	0	0	16
	Castleford	1996-97	41(1)	3	0	0	12
Steve Tyrer	Salford	2010	20	6	9	0	42
	Celtic	2009	8	2	5	0	18
	St Helens	2006-08	17(3)	12	42	0	132
Bobby Tyson-Wilson	Hull	2015	(1)	0	0	0	0

174

PLAYER	CLUB	YEAR	APP	TRIES	GOALS	FG	PTS
Harry Tyson-Wilson							
	Hull	2014	(1)	0	0	0	0
Wayne Ulugia	Hull KR	2014	3	1	0	0	4
Mike Umaga	Halifax	1996-97	38(1)	16	5	0	74
Kava Utoikamanu	Paris	1996	6(3)	0	0	0	0
Frederic Vaccari	Catalans	2010-11,					
		2013-14	50	26	0	0	104
David Vaealiki	Wigan	2005-07	67(1)	17	0	0	68
Joe Vagana	Bradford	2001-08	176(44)	17	0	0	68
Nigel Vagana	Warrington	1997	20	17	0	0	68
Tevita Vaikona	Bradford	1998-2004	145(2)	89	0	0	356
Lesley Vainikolo	Bradford	2002-07	132(4)	136	1	0	546
Eric Van Brussell	Paris	1996	2	0	0	0	0
Jace Van Dijk	Celtic	2009	19	1	1	0	6
Richard Varkulis	Warrington	2004	4(1)	3	0	0	12
Marcus Vassilakopoulos							
	Sheffield	1997-99	15(11)	3	10	2	34
	Leeds	1996-97	1(3)	0	0	0	0
Manu Vatuvei	Salford	2017	7	5	0	0	20
Atelea Vea	Leigh	2017	19(1)	5	0	0	20
	St Helens	2015-16	19(17)	10	0	0	40
	London	2014	19(3)	2	0	0	8
Josh Veivers	Salford	2012	5	2	0	0	8
	Wakefield	2011	10(2)	2	22	0	52
Phil Veivers	Huddersfield	1998	7(6)	1	0	0	4
	St Helens	1996	(1)	1	0	0	4
Michael Vella	Hull KR	2007-11	111(5)	13	0	0	52
Bruno Verges	Catalans	2006	25	6	0	0	24
Eric Vergniol	Paris	1996	14(1)	6	0	0	24
Gray Viane	Salford	2007	9	2	0	0	8
	Castleford	2006	20(7)	14	0	0	56
	Widnes	2005	20	13	0	0	52
	St Helens	2004	4	1	0	0	4
Joe Vickery	Leeds	2013	9	1	0	0	4
Daniel Vidot	Salford	2016	5(1)	5	0	0	20
Adrian Vowles	Castleford	1997-2001,					
		2003	125(1)	29	1	1	119
	Wakefield	2002-03	24(3)	6	1	0	26
	Leeds	2002	14(3)	2	0	0	8
Michael Wainwright							
	Castleford	2008-10	70	22	0	0	88
	Wakefield	2004-05	21(10)	8	0	0	32
Mike Wainwright	Salford	2000-02,					
		2007	75(3)	9	0	0	36
	Warrington	1996-99,					
		2003-07	168(14)	23	0	0	92
Shannon Wakeman							
	Huddersfield	2017	16(11)	2	0	0	8
Adam Walker	Wakefield	2017	5(1)	0	0	0	0
	St Helens	2017	(9)	1	0	0	4
	Hull KR	2013-16	60(27)	6	0	0	24
	Huddersfield	2010-12	1(5)	0	0	0	0
Alex Walker	London	2014	1	0	0	0	0
Anthony Walker	Wakefield	2015-17	1(11)	1	0	0	4
	St Helens	2013-14	9(7)	2	0	0	8
Ben Walker	Leeds	2002	23(1)	8	100	0	232
Brad Walker	Widnes	2016-17	2(2)	0	0	0	0
Chev Walker	Bradford	2011-14	44(22)	5	0	0	20
	Hull KR	2008-09	24(7)	5	0	0	20
	Leeds	1999-2006	142(19)	77	0	0	308
Chris Walker	Catalans	2010	11	6	2	0	28
Danny Walker	Widnes	2017	(6)	0	0	0	0
Jack Walker	Leeds	2017	9(1)	2	0	0	8
Jonathan Walker	Hull KR	2014	2(6)	0	0	0	0
	Castleford	2010-13	17(31)	4	0	0	16
Jonny Walker	Wigan	2010	(1)	0	0	0	0
Matt Walker	Huddersfield	2001	3(6)	0	0	0	0
Anthony Wall	Paris	1997	9	3	3	0	18
Jon Wallace	London	2014	4(12)	0	0	0	0
Mark Wallace	Workington	1996	14(1)	3	0	0	12
Alex Walmsley	St Helens	2013-17	72(66)	23	0	0	92
Adam Walne	Salford	2012-17	15(50)	2	0	0	8
Jordan Walne	Salford	2013-17	20(32)	3	0	0	12
Joe Walsh	Huddersfield	2009	1(1)	1	0	0	4
	Harlequins	2007-08	1(4)	0	0	0	0
Liam Walsh	Widnes	2017	(1)	0	0	0	0
Luke Walsh	Catalans	2017	21	2	69	4	150
	St Helens	2014-16	56(2)	14	188	9	441
Lucas Walshaw	Wakefield	2011-14	15(6)	3	0	0	12
Josh Walters	Leeds	2014-17	10(26)	7	0	0	28
Kerrod Walters	Gateshead	1999	10(12)	2	1	0	10
Kevin Walters	Warrington	2001	1	0	0	0	0
Jason Walton	Wakefield	2016	7(8)	0	0	0	0
	Salford	2009,					
		2014-15	7(19)	1	0	0	4
Barry Ward	St Helens	2002-03	20(30)	4	0	0	16

PLAYER	CLUB	YEAR	APP	TRIES	GOALS	FG	PTS
Danny Ward	Harlequins	2008-11	89(7)	4	0	0	16
	Hull KR	2007	11(9)	0	0	0	0
	Castleford	2006	18(7)	2	0	0	8
	Leeds	1999-2005	70(48)	9	0	1	37
Robbie Ward	Leeds	2014-15	5(3)	1	0	0	4
Stevie Ward	Leeds	2012-17	70(26)	18	0	0	72
Joe Wardill	Hull KR	2016	6(1)	1	0	0	4
Joe Wardle	Huddersfield	2011-16	125	58	0	0	232
	Bradford	2010	1(1)	0	0	0	0
Phil Waring	Salford	1997-99	6(8)	2	0	0	8
Brett Warton	London	1999-2001	49(7)	14	133	0	322
Kyle Warren	Castleford	2002	13(14)	3	0	0	12
Danny Washbrook	Hull	2005-11,					
		2016-17	116(62)	18	0	0	72
	Wakefield	2012-15	93(8)	12	0	0	48
Adam Watene	Wakefield	2006-08	45(8)	5	0	0	20
	Bradford	2006	(4)	0	0	0	0
Frank Watene	Wakefield	1999-2001	24(37)	6	0	0	24
Trent Waterhouse	Warrington	2012-14	65(5)	15	0	0	60
Luke Waterworth	Wigan	2016	1	0	0	0	0
Kallum Watkins	Leeds	2008-17	184(7)	101	51	0	506
Dave Watson	Sheffield	1998-99	41(4)	4	0	0	16
Ian Watson	Salford	1997, 2002	24(17)	8	3	5	43
	Workington	1996	4(1)	1	15	0	34
Kris Watson	Warrington	1996	11(2)	2	0	0	8
Anthony Watts	Widnes	2012	(1)	0	0	0	0
Brad Watts	Widnes	2005	6	3	0	0	12
Liam Watts	Hull	2012-17	114(18)	9	0	0	36
	Hull KR	2008,					
		2010-12	31(26)	6	0	0	24
Michael Watts	Warrington	2002	3	0	0	0	0
Brent Webb	Catalans	2013-14	10	2	0	0	8
	Leeds	2007-12	137(1)	73	0	0	292
Jason Webber	Salford	2000	25(1)	10	0	0	40
Ian Webster	St Helens	2006	1	0	0	0	0
Jake Webster	Castleford	2013-17	82(9)	40	0	0	160
	Hull KR	2008-12	95(1)	34	7	0	150
James Webster	Hull	2008	1	0	0	0	0
	Hull KR	2007-08	36	2	0	2	10
Pat Weisner	Hull KR	2007	(2)	0	0	0	0
	Harlequins	2006	10(6)	3	0	0	12
Taylor Welch	Warrington	2008	1	0	0	0	0
Kris Welham	Salford	2017	25	11	0	0	44
	Hull KR	2007-15	164(2)	90	1	0	362
Paul Wellens	St Helens	1998-2015	399(40)	199	34	1	865
Calvin Wellington	St Helens	2016	1	0	0	0	0
Jack Wells	Wigan	2016-17	4(11)	1	0	0	4
Jon Wells	Harlequins	2006-09	66	10	0	0	40
	London	2004-05	42(2)	19	0	0	76
	Wakefield	2003	22(1)	1	0	0	4
	Castleford	1996-2002	114(14)	49	0	0	196
Dwayne West	St Helens	2000-02	8(16)	6	0	0	24
	Wigan	1999	1(1)	0	0	0	0
Joe Westerman	Warrington	2016-17	45(1)	12	0	0	48
	Hull	2011-16	110(10)	26	52	1	209
	Castleford	2008-10	68(7)	29	151	0	418
Craig Weston	Widnes	2002, 2004	23(9)	2	1	2	12
	Huddersfield	1998-99	46(1)	15	15	0	90
Dayne Weston	Leigh	2017	6(5)	1	0	0	4
Ben Westwood	Warrington	2002-17	333(21)	111	64	0	572
	Wakefield	1999-2002	31(7)	8	1	0	34
Michael Weyman	Hull KR	2014	22(1)	7	0	0	28
Andrew Whalley	Workington	1996	(2)	0	0	0	0
Paul Whatuira	Huddersfield	2008-10	59	23	0	0	92
Scott Wheeldon	Castleford	2014-15	14(23)	5	0	0	20
	London	2012-13	27(4)	3	0	0	12
	Hull KR	2009-12	30(42)	4	0	0	16
	Hull	2006-08	2(60)	4	0	0	16
Gary Wheeler	Warrington	2015-16	6(4)	4	0	0	16
	St Helens	2008-14	48(10)	17	13	0	94
Matt Whitaker	Castleford	2006	8(2)	0	0	0	0
	Widnes	2004-05	10(20)	9	0	0	36
	Huddersfield	2003-04	3(14)	0	0	0	0
Ben White	Leeds	2014	1	0	0	0	0
David White	Wakefield	2000	(1)	0	0	0	0
Josh White	Salford	1998	18(3)	5	5	1	31
	London	1997	14(2)	8	1	0	33
Lloyd White	Widnes	2012-17	70(42)	27	24	1	157
	Crusaders	2010-11	13(11)	8	0	0	32
	Celtic	2009	6	1	0	0	4
Paul White	Salford	2009	1	1	0	0	4
	Wakefield	2006-07	24(12)	12	0	0	48
	Huddersfield	2003-05	11(32)	17	16	0	100
Elliott Whitehead	Catalans	2013-15	64(1)	30	0	0	120
	Bradford	2009-13	90(10)	30	0	0	120
Harvey Whiteley	Leeds	2017	(1)	0	0	0	0

175

PLAYER	CLUB	YEAR	APP	TRIES	GOALS	FG	PTS
Richard Whiting	Hull	2004-15	163(72)	69	19	2	316
Matt Whitley	Widnes	2015-17	30(25)	9	0	0	36
Emmerson Whittel	Bradford	2014	(1)	0	0	0	0
Danny Whittle	Warrington	1998	(2)	0	0	0	0
David Whittle	St Helens	2002	1(2)	0	0	0	0
	Warrington	2001	1(2)	0	0	0	0
Jon Whittle	Wakefield	2006	8(2)	3	0	0	12
	Widnes	2005	13	2	0	0	8
	Wigan	2003	1	0	0	0	0
Joel Wicks	London	2013-14	3(10)	0	0	0	0
Dean Widders	Castleford	2009-11	25(32)	23	0	0	92
Stephen Wild	Salford	2011-13	71	4	0	0	16
	Huddersfield	2006-10	116(2)	33	0	0	132
	Wigan	2001-05	67(20)	24	0	0	96
Sam Wilde	Widnes	2017	2	0	0	0	0
	Warrington	2015-17	3(15)	1	0	0	4
Matty Wildie	Wakefield	2010-14	13(26)	3	0	0	12
Brayden Wiliame	Catalans	2017	11	6	0	0	24
Oliver Wilkes	Wakefield	2008-09, 2012-13	55(47)	10	0	0	40
	Harlequins	2010-11	39(13)	4	0	0	16
	Wigan	2006	1(5)	0	0	0	0
	Leigh	2005	13(1)	1	0	0	4
	Huddersfield	2000-01	1(6)	0	0	0	0
	Sheffield	1998	(1)	0	0	0	0
Jon Wilkin	St Helens	2003-17	324(28)	77	0	2	310
Alex Wilkinson	Hull	2003-04	11(4)	1	0	0	4
	Huddersfield	2003	8	4	0	0	16
	London	2002	5(1)	0	0	0	0
	Bradford	2000-01	3(3)	1	0	0	4
Bart Williams	London	1998	5(3)	1	0	0	4
Connor Williams	Salford	2016	(1)	0	0	0	0
Daley Williams	Salford	2006-07	9(2)	4	0	0	16
Danny Williams	Harlequins	2006	9(13)	4	0	0	16
	London	2005	1(16)	0	0	0	0
Danny Williams	Bradford	2014	7	2	0	0	8
	Salford	2011-14	54	31	0	0	124
	Leeds	2006, 2008	13(2)	7	0	0	28
	Hull	2008	3	0	0	0	0
Dave Williams	Harlequins	2008-11	1(17)	0	0	0	0
Desi Williams	Wigan	2004	2	0	0	0	0
George Williams	Wigan	2013-17	91(13)	34	51	1	239
Jonny Williams	London	2004	(4)	0	0	0	0
Lee Williams	Crusaders	2011	1(7)	0	0	0	0
Rhys Williams	Warrington	2010-13	23(1)	15	0	0	60
	Salford	2013	4	0	0	0	0
	Castleford	2012	8	4	0	0	16
	Crusaders	2011	6	3	0	0	12
Sam Williams	Wakefield	2017	17(5)	4	26	0	68
	Catalans	2014	11(1)	4	21	0	58
Luke Williamson	Harlequins	2009-10	39	6	0	0	24
John Wilshere	Salford	2006-07, 2009	72(2)	32	142	0	412
	Leigh	2005	26	8	6	0	44
	Warrington	2004	5	2	0	0	8
Craig Wilson	Hull	2000	2(16)	1	0	1	5
	Gateshead	1999	17(11)	5	0	1	21
George Wilson	Paris	1996	7(2)	3	0	0	12
John Wilson	Catalans	2006-08	69	23	0	0	92
Richard Wilson	Hull	1998-99	(13)	0	0	0	0
Scott Wilson	Warrington	1998-99	23(2)	6	0	0	24
Johan Windley	Hull	1999	2(2)	1	0	0	4
Paul Wingfield	Warrington	1997	5(3)	6	1	0	26
Frank Winterstein	Widnes	2012-13	37(9)	16	0	0	64
	Crusaders	2010-11	26(19)	4	0	0	16
	Wakefield	2009	(5)	0	0	0	0
Lincoln Withers	Hull KR	2012-13	18(22)	10	0	0	40
	Crusaders	2010-11	47	4	0	0	16
	Celtic	2009	21	6	0	0	24
Michael Withers	Wigan	2007	6(1)	1	0	0	4
	Bradford	1999-2006	156(6)	94	15	4	410
Michael Witt	London	2012-13	37	10	89	1	219
	Crusaders	2010-11	39	13	47	4	150
Jeff Wittenberg	Huddersfield	1998	18(1)	1	0	0	4
	Bradford	1997	8(9)	4	0	0	16
Josh Wood	Salford	2015-17	5(6)	1	0	0	4
Kyle Wood	Wakefield	2012-13, 2017	28(41)	12	0	0	48
	Huddersfield	2011, 2013-16	39(33)	7	0	0	28
	Castleford	2010	1(4)	0	0	0	0
Martin Wood	Sheffield	1997-98	24(11)	4	18	2	54
Mikey Wood	Huddersfield	2016-17	1(1)	0	0	0	0
Nathan Wood	Warrington	2002-05	90	38	0	3	155
	Wakefield	2002	11	2	0	0	8
Paul Wood	Warrington	2000-14	138(171)	40	0	0	160
Phil Wood	Widnes	2004	2(1)	0	0	0	0
Sam Wood	Bradford	2013-14	7(1)	0	0	0	0

PLAYER	CLUB	YEAR	APP	TRIES	GOALS	FG	PTS
Sam Wood	Huddersfield	2016-17	12	5	0	0	20
James Woodburn-Hall	London	2013-14	9(4)	2	0	0	8
Darren Woods	Widnes	2005	(1)	0	0	0	0
David Woods	Halifax	2002	18(2)	8	0	0	32
Josh Woods	Wigan	2017	2	0	3	0	6
Simon Worrall	Leeds	2008-09	5(16)	1	0	0	4
Michael Worrincy	Bradford	2009-10	12(34)	12	0	0	48
	Harlequins	2006-08	20(12)	10	0	0	40
Rob Worrincy	Castleford	2004	1	0	0	0	0
James Worthington	Wigan	2017	1	2	0	0	8
Troy Wozniak	Widnes	2004	13(7)	1	0	0	4
Matthew Wray	Wakefield	2002-03	13(3)	2	0	0	8
David Wrench	Wakefield	2002-06	28(52)	6	0	0	24
	Leeds	1999-2001	7(17)	0	0	0	0
Callum Wright	Wigan	2014	(2)	0	0	0	0
Craig Wright	Castleford	2000	1(9)	0	0	0	0
Nigel Wright	Huddersfield	1999	4(6)	1	0	0	4
	Wigan	1996-97	5(5)	2	0	1	9
Ricky Wright	Sheffield	1997-99	2(13)	0	0	0	0
Vincent Wulf	Paris	1996	13(4)	4	0	0	16
Andrew Wynyard	London	1999-2000	34(6)	4	0	0	16
Bagdad Yaha	Paris	1996	4(4)	2	4	0	16
Fouad Yaha	Catalans	2015-17	41	18	0	0	72
Malakai Yasa	Sheffield	1996	1(3)	0	0	0	0
Andy Yates	Wakefield	2016	(7)	0	0	0	0
	Leeds	2015	(9)	1	0	0	4
Kirk Yeaman	Hull	2001-16	321(18)	159	0	0	636
Grant Young	London	1998-99	22(2)	2	0	0	8
Nick Youngquest	Castleford	2011-12	37	28	0	0	112
	Crusaders	2010	26(1)	9	0	0	36
Ronel Zenon	Paris	1996	(4)	0	0	0	0
Nick Zisti	Bradford	1999	6(1)	0	0	0	0
Freddie Zitter	Catalans	2006	1	0	0	0	0

All totals in 'Super League Players 1996-2017' include play-off games & Super League Super 8s from 2015. 2015-2017 Super 8s (Qualifiers) not included.

NEW FACES - Players making their Super League debuts in 2017

PLAYER	CLUB	DEBUT vs	ROUND	DATE
Jamie Acton	Leigh	Leeds (h)	11	17/2/17
		(club debut: Barrow (a), ChR2, 23/2/14)		
Ben Barba	St Helens	Wigan (h)	S84	1/9/17
Lambert Belmas	Catalans	Huddersfield (a)	9	12/4/17
Kriss Brining	Salford	Wigan (h)	1	11/2/17
Mitch Brown	Leigh	Castleford (a)	1	10/2/17
		(club debut: London Broncos (h), S8-QR1, 6/8/16)		
Lachlan Burr	Leigh	Wigan (a)	3	3/3/17
Will Dagger	Warrington	Castleford (a)	18	11/6/17
Tom Davies	Wigan	Huddersfield (h)	5	19/3/17
Nabil Djalout	Catalans	Huddersfield (h)	18	10/6/17
Luke Douglas	St Helens	Leeds (h)	1	9/2/17
Tuoyo Egodo	Castleford	Hull (h)	S87	22/9/17
Matty English	Huddersfield	Leeds (a)	12	27/4/17
		(club debut: Swinton (h), CCR5, 23/4/17)		
Owen Farnworth	Widnes	Leeds (a)	10	17/4/17
Callum Field	Wigan	Warrington (MW)	14	20/5/17
		(club debut: Swinton (a), CCR6, 14/5/17)		
Liam Forsyth	Wigan	Warrington (a)	4	9/3/17
Josh Ganson	Wigan	Castleford (a)	12	29/4/17
Kieran Gill	Castleford	St Helens (h)	17	4/6/17
Regan Grace	St Helens	Wigan (a)	9	14/4/17
James Hasson	Salford	Catalans (h)	15	26/5/17
Adam Higson	Leigh	Castleford (a)	1	10/2/17
		(club debut: Celtic Crusaders (h), NL1R9, 8/6/08)		
Peta Hiku	Warrington	Wakefield (a)	20	1/7/17
Keegan Hirst	Wakefield	Leigh (h)	6	23/3/17
Sam Hopkins	Leigh	Leeds (h)	11	17/2/17
		(club debut: Hull Dockers (h), CCR3, 6/3/11)		
Josh Jordan-Roberts				
	Leeds	Wigan (a)	23	21/7/17
		(club debut: Leigh (h), S8-QR7, 22/9/16)		
Samisoni Langi	Leigh	Warrington (a)	21	7/7/17
Matty Lees	St Helens	Wakefield (a)	S85	7/9/17
Jez Litten	Hull	Warrington (a)	7	1/4/17
Harvey Livett	Warrington	Catalans (a)	1	11/2/17
Jake Mamo	Huddersfield	Catalans (h)	9	12/4/17
Liam Marshall	Wigan	Leigh (h)	3	3/3/17
Darnell McIntosh	Huddersfield	Hull (h)	3	2/3/17
Ryan Morgan	St Helens	Leeds (h)	1	9/2/17
Daniel Mortimer	Leigh	Warrington (a)	21	7/7/17
Daniel Murray	Salford	Widnes (h)	12	30/4/17
Harry Newman	Leeds	Wigan (a)	23	21/7/17
Mikolaj Oledzki	Leeds	Catalans (a)	13	6/5/17
		(club debut: Doncaster (h), CCR5, 21/4/17)		
Jack Ormondroyd	Leeds	Leigh (a)	11	17/2/17
Matt Parcell	Leeds	St Helens (a)	1	9/2/17
Tyler Randell	Wakefield	Salford (a)	S84	1/9/17
Nick Rawsthorne	Hull	Leigh (h)	15	26/5/17
Danny Richardson	St Helens	Leeds (h)	1	9/2/17
Martyn Ridyard	Leigh	Castleford (a)	1	10/2/17
		(club debut: London Skolars (h), NRCR2, 15/2/09)		
Arthur Romano	Catalans	Hull (h)	16	29/5/17
		(club debut: Hull (a), CCR6, 12/5/17)		
Jesse Sene-Lefao	Castleford	Leigh (h)	1	10/2/17
Alex Sutcliffe	Leeds	Wigan (a)	23	21/7/17
Jake Trueman	Castleford	St Helens (h)	17	4/6/17
Manu Vatuvei	Salford	Hull (a)	S81	4/8/17
		(club debut: Wigan, CCSF, 30/7/17)		
Shannon Wakeman				
	Huddersfield	Widnes (a)	1	10/2/17
Danny Walker	Widnes	Leigh (a)	7	1/4/17
Jack Walker	Leeds	Huddersfield (h)	12	27/4/17
		(club debut: Doncaster (h), CCR5, 21/4/17)		
Liam Walsh	Widnes	Leeds (a)	10	17/4/17
Dayne Weston	Leigh	Castleford (a)	1	10/2/17
		(club debut: Batley (a), ChR1, 7/2/16)		
Harvey Whiteley	Leeds	Wigan (a)	23	21/7/17
Brayden Wiliame	Catalans	Warrington (h)	1	11/2/17
Josh Woods	Wigan	Salford (h)	13	5/5/17
James Worthington				
	Wigan	Wakefield (h)	16	29/5/17

Players making their club debuts in other competitions in 2017

PLAYER	CLUB	DEBUT vs	ROUND	DATE
James Clare	Leigh	Widnes (h)	S8-QR4	3/9/17
Izaac Farrell	Huddersfield	Swinton (h)	CCR5	23/4/17
Matthieu Khedimi	Catalans	Hull (a)	CCR6	12/5/17
Lloyd Roby	Widnes	Warrington (a)	CCR6	14/5/17

OLD FACES - Players making their Super League debuts for new clubs in 2017

PLAYER	CLUB	DEBUT vs	ROUND	DATE
Mitch Allgood	Wakefield	Salford (h)	4	12/3/17
Tom Armstrong	Widnes	Huddersfield (h)	1	10/2/17
Greg Bird	Catalans	Warrington (h) (D2)	1	11/2/17
Matty Blythe	Warrington	Salford (a) (D2)	1	4/3/17
Kevin Brown	Warrington	Castleford (h)	2	24/2/17
		(club debut: Brisbane (h), WCS, 18/2/17)		
Joe Burgess	Wigan	Salford (a) (D2)	1	11/2/17
Luke Burgess	Catalans	Widnes (h)	3	4/3/17
Todd Carney	Salford	Widnes (a)	6	24/3/17
Mason Caton-Brown				
	Wakefield	St Helens (a)	3	3/3/17
Rangi Chase	Widnes	Wakefield (MW)	14	20/5/17
Paul Clough	Huddersfield	Widnes (a)	1	10/2/17
Jake Connor	Hull	Wakefield (a)	1	12/2/17
Mike Cooper	Warrington	Catalans (a) (D2)	1	11/2/17
Ben Crooks	Leigh	Castleford (a)	1	10/2/17
Dominic Crosby	Warrington	Catalans (a)	1	11/2/17
Matty Dawson	Leigh	Castleford (a)	1	10/2/17
		(club debut: Dewsbury (h), ChR23, 24/7/16)		
Josh Drinkwater	Leigh	Castleford (a)	1	10/2/17
		(club debut: Swinton (a), ChR14, 22/5/16)		
Greg Eden	Castleford	Leigh (h) (D2)	1	10/2/17
Morgan Escare	Wigan	Salford (a)	1	11/2/17
Dale Ferguson	Huddersfield	Widnes (a) (D2)	1	10/2/17
Matty Fleming	Leigh	Salford (MW)	14	21/5/17
Alex Foster	Castleford	Huddersfield (a)	13	4/5/17
Lee Gaskell	Huddersfield	Widnes (a)	1	10/2/17
James Green	Leigh	Castleford (a)	1	10/2/17
Josh Griffin	Hull	Wakefield (a)	1	12/2/17
Scott Grix	Wakefield	Hull (h) (D2)	1	12/2/17
Dean Hadley	Wakefield	Salford (h)	4	12/3/17
Ryan Hampshire	Leigh	Castleford (a)	1	10/2/17
Harrison Hansen	Leigh	Castleford (a)	1	10/2/17
		(club debut: Batley (a), ChR1, 7/2/16)		
Zak Hardaker	Castleford	Leigh (h)	1	10/2/17
James Hasson	Wakefield	St Helens (h)	23	23/7/17
Micky Higham	Leigh	St Helens (h)	2	24/2/17
		(club debut: Barrow (a), CCR4, 14/2/99;		
		second debut: Featherstone, SB, 24/5/15)		
Gareth Hock	Leigh	Castleford (a)	1	10/2/17
		(club debut: Workington (h), ChR8, 6/4/17)		
Liam Hood	Leigh	Castleford (a)	1	10/2/17
		(club debut: Halifax (a), ChR6, 13/3/16)		
Craig Huby	Wakefield	Hull (h)	1	12/2/17
Jack Johnson	Widnes	Wakefield (MW)	14	20/5/17
Albert Kelly	Hull	Wakefield (a)	1	12/2/17
Kevin Larroyer	Castleford	Leigh (a)	16	29/5/17
Tommy Lee	St Helens	Leeds (h)	1	9/2/17

PLAYER	CLUB	DEBUT vs	ROUND	DATE
Thomas Leuluai	Wigan	Salford (a) (D2)	1	11/2/17
Antoni Maria	Leigh	Leeds (h)	11	17/2/17
Tyrone McCarthy	Salford	Hull (a)	S81	4/8/17
		(club debut: Wigan, CCSF, 30/7/17)		
Gregg McNally	Leigh	Catalans (h)	8	7/4/17
		(club debut: Barrow (h), NRCR1, 12/2/12)		
Alex Mellor	Huddersfield	Widnes (a)	1	10/2/17
Sam Moa	Catalans	Warrington (h)	1	11/2/17
Lee Mossop	Salford	Wigan (h)	1	11/2/17
Curtis Naughton	Leigh	Wigan (a)	3	3/3/17
Romain Navarrete	Wigan	Warrington (a)	4	9/3/17
	Catalans	St Helens (a) (D2)	22	16/7/17
Adam O'Brien	Huddersfield	Leeds (a)	12	27/4/17
		(club debut: Swinton (h), CCR5, 23/4/17)		
Tom Olbison	Widnes	Huddersfield (h)	1	10/2/17
Cory Paterson	Leigh	Castleford (a)	1	10/2/17
		(club debut: Bradford (a), ChR4, 28/2/16)		
Eloi Pelissier	Leigh	Castleford (a)	1	10/2/17
Ben Pomeroy	Warrington	Leigh (h)	21	7/7/17
Jordan Rankin	Huddersfield	Salford (a)	20	2/7/17
Nick Rawsthorne	Leigh	Widnes (a)	19	22/6/17
Ben Reynolds	Leigh	Leeds (h)	1	10/2/17
		(club debut: Halifax (h), ChR12, 10/5/15)		
Greg Richards	Leigh	Salford (h)	23	21/7/17
Martyn Ridyard	Huddersfield	Catalans (MW)	14	21/5/17
Andre Savelio	Warrington	Catalans (a)	1	11/2/17
Mickael Simon	Catalans	Warrington (h) (D2)	1	11/2/17
Matty Smith	St Helens	Warrington (h) (D2)	6	24/3/17
Glenn Stewart	Leigh	Castleford (a)	1	10/2/17
Zeb Taia	St Helens	Wakefield (h)	3	3/3/17
Lama Tasi	Salford	Wigan (h) (D2)	1	11/2/17
David Thompson	Leigh	Hull (h)	10	17/4/17
Iain Thornley	Catalans	Hull (a)	2	23/2/17
Danny Tickle	Leigh	Castleford (a)	1	10/2/17
		(club debut: Dewsbury (h), ChR23, 24/7/16)		
Lewis Tierney	Catalans	St Helens (a)	22	16/7/17
Willie Tonga	Leigh	Leeds (h)	11	17/2/17
		(club debut: Swinton (h), ChR7, 24/3/16)		
Jordan Turner	Huddersfield	Warrington (h)	17	4/6/17
Atelea Vea	Leigh	Castleford (a)	1	10/2/17
Adam Walker	St Helens	Wakefield (h)	3	3/3/17
	Wakefield	Wigan (a)	16	29/5/17
Luke Walsh	Catalans	Warrington (h)	1	11/2/17
Kris Welham	Salford	Huddersfield (a)	11	16/2/17
Sam Wilde	Widnes	Wakefield (MW)	14	20/5/17
Sam Williams	Wakefield	Hull (h)	1	12/2/17
Kyle Wood	Wakefield	Hull (h) (D2)	1	12/2/17

SUPER LEAGUE XXII
Club by Club

---

14 October 2016 - Junior Moors signs new two-year deal to end of 2019. Tom Holmes and Will Maher join Batley on loan for 2017.

19 October 2016 - London Broncos outside back Tuoyo Egodo and Oxford forward Daniel Igbinedion sign two-year contracts.

20 October 2016 - Cronulla forward Jesse Sene-Lefao signs two-year contract.

7 November 2016 - Ben Crooks moves to Leigh on one-year loan deal.

8 November 2016 - Zak Hardaker joins on one-year loan deal from Leeds for undisclosed fee, with Tigers holding option for permanent signing at end of 2017 season.

13 December 2016 - Denny Solomona signs for Sale rugby union club with two years left on contract.

24 January 2017 - Tuoyo Egodo joins Kieran Gill at Oldham on loan with 24-hour recall clause.

25 January 2017 - 17-year-old Bradford halfback Jake Trueman joins on two-year contract.

29 January 2017 - 22-6 win at St Helens in last pre-season game.

10 February 2017 - 44-16 televised home victory over promoted Leigh in round one. Paul McShane takes one game on EGP for dangerous tackle.

15 February 2017 - French second-rower Kevin Larroyer signs one-year contract with club option for two more years.

16 February 2017 - French Guiana-born prop Gadwin Springer signs two-year contract extension to end of 2019. Back-rower Alex Foster arrives on trial.

24 February 2017 - four tries in nine first-half minutes sets up 30-22 win at Warrington.

2 March 2017 - Greg Eden and Greg Minikin both score hat-tricks in 66-10 home rout of Leeds.

12 March 2017 - Gregs Minikin and Eden score two tries each in 34-0 win at Widnes.

19 March 2017 - late field goal means first defeat of season, by 13-12 at Salford.

26 March 2017 - Tigers come back from early 14-0 deficit to go back to top of league with 43-26 home win over Catalans.

31 March 2017 - Luke Gale scores second-half hat-trick in 52-16 home demolition of Huddersfield.

6 April 2017 - Tigers move two points clear at top of table with 27-10 win at Wigan.

14 April 2017 - 42-24 home Good Friday win over Wakefield.

17 April 2017 - 26-22 Easter Monday defeat at St Helens.

23 April 2017 - 26-24 defeat at Hull FC after 22nd minute high tackle puts Luke Gale out of game.

KEY DATES

29 April 2017 - 54-4 home win over Wigan keeps Tigers top of table.

4 May 2017 - Jesse Sene-Lefao try five minutes from time steals 26-21 win at Huddersfield with Luke Gale, Zak Hardaker and Mike McMeeken away on England duty.

13 May 2017 - Greg Eden scores hat-trick in 53-10 home, sixth round Challenge Cup win over St Helens.

15 May 2017 - Rangi Chase joins Widnes on loan for rest of season.

21 May 2017 - Greg Eden scores second-half hat-trick in 29-18 Magic Weekend win over Leeds.

26 May 2017 - Greg Eden scores third successive hat-trick in 32-22 come-from-behind home win over Widnes.

29 May 2017 - Greg Eden scores four tries, including five-minute hat-trick, in 38-0 win at Leigh.

4 June 2017 - debutant Kieran Gill scores try and suffers season-ending knee injury as key players, including Greg Eden, rested in late 16-12 home win over St Helens. Jake Trueman also makes debut.

7 June 2017 - Kieran Gill signs contract for 2018 with option for club of further two years.

9 June 2017 - Alex Foster signs new two-year contract to end of 2019.

10 June 2017 - Andy Lynch announces retirement at season end.

11 June 2017 - Greg Eden scores five tries in 36-16 home win over Warrington. Junior Moors suffers knee injury.

16 June 2017 - out-of-court settlement sees Sale pay Tigers £200,000 compensation and legal costs for signing of Denny Solomona.

18 June 2017 - 32-24 Challenge Cup quarter-final defeat at Hull FC.

23 June 2017 - 23-12 win at Leeds extends lead at top of table to seven points.

27 June 2017 - on-loan Zak Hardaker signs four-and-a-half year contract to end of 2021, with £150,000 transfer fee going to Leeds.

29 June 2017 - prop Daniel Igbinedion leaves for Featherstone.

30 June 2017 - 24-22 home win over Hull FC.

5 July 2017 - Mike McMeeken extends contract by two years to end of 2020.

6 July 2017 - last-minute Luke Gale field goal secures 25-24 win at Wakefield.

14 July 2017 - Greg Eden injures shoulder scoring his second try in 38-14 home win over Salford.

22 July 2017 - Jy Hitchcox scores try double in last regular-season round 32-24 win at Catalans.

17 August 2017 - Greg Eden back from injury in 45-20 home win over Wakefield that secures League Leaders Shield.

21 August 2017 - former Huddersfield utility Joe Wardle signs for 2018 on three-year contract from Newcastle Knights.

23 August 2017 - Grant Millington signs new three-year deal to end of 2020.

9 September 2017 - halfback Tom Holmes to be released to join Featherstone.

12 September 2017 - Luke Gale undergoes appendix operation.

17 September 2017 - Jake Trueman scores hat-trick in 38-20 win at Wigan.

22 September 2017 - Tuoyo Egodo scores hat-trick on debut in 48-16 home defeat by Hull FC.

22 September 2017 - Papuan winger Garry Lo joins from Sheffield on two-year contract.

25 September 2017 - last second penalty goal and golden-point field goal from Luke Gale ensures 23-22 home semi-final win over St Helens.

3 October 2017 - Luke Gale crowned Steve Prescott Man of Steel.

5 October 2017 - Zak Hardaker suspended for 'breach of club rules', later confirmed as positive doping test.

7 October 2017 - 24-6 defeat to Leeds Rhinos in Super League Grand Final.

CLUB RECORDS
Highest score: 106-0 v Rochdale, 9/9/2007 **Highest score against:** 12-76 v Leeds, 14/8/2009 **Record attendance:** 25,449 v Hunslet, 9/3/35

MATCH RECORDS
Tries: 5 Derek Foster v Hunslet, 10/11/72 John Joyner v Millom, 16/9/73 Steve Fenton v Dewsbury, 27/1/78 Ian French v Hunslet, 9/2/86 St John Ellis v Whitehaven, 10/12/89 Greg Eden v Warrington, 11/6/2017 **Goals:** 17 Sammy Lloyd v Millom, 16/9/73 **Points:** 43 Sammy Lloyd v Millom, 16/9/73

SEASON RECORDS
Tries: 42 Denny Solomona 2016 **Goals:** 158 Sammy Lloyd 1976-77 **Points:** 355 Luke Gale 2017

CAREER RECORDS
Tries: 206 Alan Hardisty 1958-71 **Goals:** 875 Albert Lunn 1951-63 **Points:** 1,870 Albert Lunn 1951-63 **Appearances:** 613 John Joyner 1973-92

CASTLEFORD TIGERS

DATE	FIXTURE	RESULT	SCORERS	LGE	ATT
10/2/17	Leigh (h)	W44-16	t:Gale(2),Sene-Lefao,Minikin(2),Moors,Eden g:Gale(8)	1st	8,722
24/2/17	Warrington (a)	W22-30	t:Sene-Lefao,Hardaker,Eden(2),Gale,Minikin g:Gale(3)	1st	11,374
2/3/17	Leeds (h)	W66-10	t:Eden(3),Minikin(3),McMeeken,Hardaker,McShane,Webster,Gale,Shenton g:Gale(9)	1st	11,500
12/3/17	Widnes (a)	W0-34	t:Minikin(2),Shenton,Eden(2),Cook g:Gale(5)	1st	6,396
19/3/17	Salford (a)	L13-12	t:Gale,Minikin g:Gale(2)	2nd	5,221
26/3/17	Catalans Dragons (h)	W43-26	t:Hardaker,Millington,Monaghan,Eden(2),Moors,Shenton g:Gale(7) fg:Gale	1st	8,126
31/3/17	Huddersfield (h)	W52-16	t:Roberts,Webster,McMeeken,Gale(3),Milner,Monaghan(3) g:Gale(6)	1st	8,035
6/4/17	Wigan (a)	W10-27	t:Webster,Gale,Sene-Lefao,Eden g:Gale(5) fg:Gale	1st	12,423
14/4/17	Wakefield (h)	W42-24	t:Roberts,Webster(2),O Holmes,Millington(2),Eden g:Gale(7)	1st	10,349
17/4/17	St Helens (a)	L26-22	t:Eden(2),Roberts g:Gale(3)	1st	12,499
23/4/17	Hull FC (a)	L26-24	t:Minikin,Roberts(2),Shenton,McMeeken g:McShane(2)	1st	12,801
29/4/17	Wigan (h)	W54-4	t:Milner,Shenton,Cook,McMeeken,Minikin(2),Gale,Millington,Webster g:Gale(8),McShane	1st	9,333
4/5/17	Huddersfield (a)	W21-26	t:Monaghan,Minikin,Eden,Sene-Lefao g:McShane(5)	1st	5,566
13/5/17	St Helens (h) (CCR6)	W53-10	t:Shenton,Webster(2),McShane,Minikin(2),Massey,Eden(3) g:Gale(6) fg:Gale	N/A	5,216
21/5/17	Leeds (MW) ●	W29-18	t:Gale,Eden(3),T Holmes g:Gale(4) fg:Gale	1st	N/A
26/5/17	Widnes (h)	W32-22	t:Eden(3),Springer,Minikin,Cook g:Gale(4)	1st	7,648
29/5/17	Leigh (a)	W0-38	t:Sene-Lefao(2),Eden(4),Webster g:Gale(5)	1st	5,905
4/6/17	St Helens (h)	W16-12	t:Gill,McMeeken,T Holmes g:McShane(2)	1st	8,515
11/6/17	Warrington (h)	W36-16	t:Eden(5),Minikin,McMeeken g:Gale(4)	1st	8,577
18/6/17	Hull FC (a) (CCQF)	L32-24	t:Roberts(2),Hardaker,Minikin g:Gale(4)	N/A	11,944
23/6/17	Leeds (a)	W12-23	t:Eden,Hardaker,Millington g:Gale(5) fg:Gale	1st	18,029
30/6/17	Hull FC (h)	W24-22	t:Gale,McMeeken,Hardaker g:Gale(6)	1st	8,371
6/7/17	Wakefield (a)	W24-25	t:Eden,Millington,McMeeken,Webster g:Gale(4) fg:Gale	1st	6,430
14/7/17	Salford (h)	W38-14	t:Eden(2),Roberts,Monaghan(2),Hardaker g:Gale(7)	1st	7,094
22/7/17	Catalans Dragons (a)	W24-32	t:Hitchcox(2),Hardaker,Minikin,McShane g:Gale(5),Hardaker	1st	8,657
3/8/17	St Helens (h) (S8)	L12-26	t:Milner,Monaghan g:Gale(2)	1st	6,849
11/8/17	Salford (h) (S8)	W4-23	t:Hardaker(2),McShane,Hitchcox g:Gale(3) fg:Gale	1st	2,811
17/8/17	Wakefield (h) (S8)	W45-20	t:Hardaker(2),McMeeken,Webster(4),Eden g:Gale(6) fg:Gale	1st	11,235
1/9/17	Huddersfield (a) (S8)	W16-24	t:Webster,Roberts,Eden,Gale g:Gale(4)	1st	6,284
8/9/17	Leeds (h) (S8)	W38-24	t:Eden,Roberts(2),Webster,Foster,Minikin g:Gale(7)	1st	9,557
17/9/17	Wigan (a) (S8)	W20-38	t:Eden,Trueman(3),Minikin(2),Shenton g:McShane(5)	1st	15,706
22/9/17	Hull FC (h) (S8)	L16-48	t:Egodo(3) g:McShane(2)	1st	7,974
28/9/17	St Helens (h) (SF)	W23-22 (aet)	t:Hardaker,Gale,Milner g:Gale(5) fg:Gale	N/A	11,235
7/10/17	Leeds (GF) ●●	L6-24	t:Foster g:Gale	N/A	72,827

● Played at St James' Park, Newcastle
●● Played at Old Trafford, Manchester

		APP		TRIES		GOALS		FG		PTS	
	D.O.B.	ALL	SL	ALL	SL	ALL	SL	ALL	SL	ALL	SL
Rangi Chase	11/4/86	3(5)	3(5)	0	0	0	0	0	0	0	0
Matt Cook	14/11/86	3(20)	3(19)	3	3	0	0	0	0	12	12
Greg Eden	14/11/90	31	29	41	38	0	0	0	0	164	152
Tuoyo Egodo	16/2/97	1	1	3	3	0	0	0	0	12	12
Alex Foster	25/9/93	11(8)	11(7)	2	2	0	0	0	0	8	8
Luke Gale	22/6/88	30	28	14	14	145	135	9	8	355	334
Kieran Gill	4/12/95	1	1	1	1	0	0	0	0	4	4
Zak Hardaker	17/10/91	30	28	13	12	1	1	0	0	54	50
Jy Hitchcox	18/8/89	9(1)	9(1)	3	3	0	0	0	0	12	12
Oliver Holmes	7/8/92	7(3)	7(3)	1	1	0	0	0	0	4	4
Tom Holmes	2/3/96	4(4)	3(4)	2	2	0	0	0	0	8	8
Kevin Larroyer	19/6/89	2(5)	2(4)	0	0	0	0	0	0	0	0
Andy Lynch	20/10/79	16(5)	14(5)	0	0	0	0	0	0	0	0
Will Maher	4/11/95	(1)	(1)	0	0	0	0	0	0	0	0
Nathan Massey	11/7/89	27(3)	26(2)	1	0	0	0	0	0	4	0
Mike McMeeken	10/5/94	31(1)	29(1)	9	9	0	0	0	0	36	36
Paul McShane	19/11/89	33	31	4	3	17	17	0	0	50	46
Grant Millington	1/11/86	19(11)	18(10)	6	6	0	0	0	0	24	24
Adam Milner	19/12/91	22(7)	20(7)	4	4	0	0	0	0	16	16
Greg Minikin	29/3/95	29	27	22	19	0	0	0	0	88	76
Joel Monaghan	22/4/82	13(3)	13(3)	8	8	0	0	0	0	32	32
Junior Moors	30/7/86	3(20)	3(19)	2	2	0	0	0	0	8	8
Larne Patrick	3/11/88	(7)	(6)	0	0	0	0	0	0	0	0
Ben Roberts	8/7/85	25(4)	24(3)	12	10	0	0	0	0	48	40
Jesse Sene-Lefao	8/12/89	27(7)	25(7)	6	6	0	0	0	0	24	24
Michael Shenton	22/7/86	28	26	7	6	0	0	0	0	28	24
Gadwin Springer	4/4/93	7(13)	7(13)	1	1	0	0	0	0	4	4
Jake Trueman	16/2/99	2(1)	2(1)	3	3	0	0	0	0	12	12
Jake Webster	29/10/83	28	26	16	14	0	0	0	0	64	56

'SL' totals include Super 8s, semi-final & Grand Final; 'All' totals also include Challenge Cup

Luke Gale

LEAGUE RECORD
P30-W25-D0-L5
(1st, SL/Grand Final Runners-Up)
F965, A536, Diff+429
50 points.

CHALLENGE CUP
Quarter Finalists

ATTENDANCES
Best - v Leeds (SL - 11,500)
Worst - v St Helens (CC - 5,216)
Total (SL/S8s/SF only) - 143,120
Average (SL/S8s/SF only) - 8,945
(Up by 1,487 on 2016)

17 October 2016 - Iain Thornley joins from Hull KR on two-year contract.

18 October 2016 - prop Luke Burgess joins on two-year deal from Salford.

25 October 2016 - Rod Howe joins as head of conditioning on contract to 2019.

27 October 2016 - Luke Walsh signs from St Helens on one-year contract.

8 November 2016 - Fiji International Brayden Wiliame signs from Manly on two-year contract .

18 November 2016 - Mickael Simon returns from Wakefield on two-year contract.

9 December 2016 - prop Paul Séguier and hooker Alrix Da Costa sign full-time contracts.

21 January 2017 - 22-6 pre-season defeat at Toulouse.

28 January 2017 - 26-22 pre-season home defeat by Wigan.

17 February 2017 - Dragons reveal Tony Gigot is banned for two years by French Federation for "inappropriate behaviour" towards an anti-doping officer at national team training camp the previous October. Club promises appeal.

23 February 2017 - Luke Walsh kicks five penalties and a conversion in 16-14 win at Hull FC. Jason Baitieri banned for one game for contact with match official.

4 March 2017 - late Widnes try means 14-14 home draw in rain-affected game and first point of season lost.

10 March 2017 - 46-10 defeat at Leeds ends unbeaten start to season. Greg Bird breaks thumb and Jodie Broughton tears biceps.

18 March 2017 - late try means 28-24 home defeat by St Helens.

26 March 2017 - 43-26 defeat at Castleford after leading 14-0.

7 April 2017 - Tony Gigot suspension reduced to three months following appeal against FFR XIII anti-doping department decision.

7 April 2017 - Tony Gigot scores try as 37-26 win at Leigh ends five-game win-less run. Jason Baitieri ruled out for long spell with broken wrist. Luke Burgess damages ACL.

11 April 2017 - Sam Moa avoids suspension with EGP for raising knee into contact in win at Leigh.

17 April 2017 - Vincent Duport scores hat-trick as 38-6 home win ends Salford's five-match winning run.

30 April 2017 - Greg Bird returns in 30-10 defeat at Wakefield. Three Dragons sin-binned.

2 May 2017 - Luke Walsh banned for one game for abusing in-goal official.

6 May 2017 - Greg Bird suffers eye injury five minutes into 30-24 home defeat by Leeds.

9 May 2017 - Vincent Duport avoids suspension for contrary behaviour with EGP.

KEY DATES

12 May 2017 - 62-0 Challenge Cup sixth-round elimination at Hull FC.

21 May 2017 - 18-10 Magic Weekend defeat to Huddersfield.

22 May 2017 - coach Laurent Frayssinous leaves. Assistants Jérôme Guisset and Michael Monaghan and General Manager Alex Chan take over on interim basis.

23 May 2017 - Greg Bird banned for one game for standing on opponent.

29 May 2017 - two tries in last nine minutes as 23-18 home win over Hull FC ends six-match losing run.

31 May 2017 - Julian Bousquet banned for one game for high tackle; Sam Moa escapes with fine for punching, both in win over Hull. Krisnan Inu avoids suspension for dangerous contact at Salford with EGP.

4 June 2017 - 26-6 defeat at Widnes.

6 June 2017 - Jordan Dezaria banned for two matches for dangerous contact after EGP.

10 June 2017 - 56-12 home defeat to Huddersfield.

19 June 2017 - Steve McNamara announced as new coach on three-and-a-half year contract.

22 June 2017 - young halfback Louis Jouffret joins Championship club Toulouse on dual-registration.

24 June 2017 - Steve McNamara takes charge for first time and Iain Thornley tears pectoral in 24-16 defeat at Warrington.

27 June 2017 - Richie Myler to join Leeds at season end.

27 June 2017 - Tony Gigot found not guilty of using aggressive body language against match official.

1 July 2017 - last-minute Julian Bousquet try ensures 40-36 home win over Leigh.

4 July 2017 - Greg Bird suspended for one game for punching; Fouad Yaha gets one game and Ben Garcia two games for running and punching.

13 July 2017 - Romain Navarrete and Lewis Tierney join on loan from Wigan until end of season.

16 July 2017 - Romain Navarrete and Lewis Tierney make debuts in 46-28 defeat at St Helens.

24 July 2017 - 32-24 home defeat to Castleford ends regular season.

3 August 2017 - Tony Gigot banned for two years by French Federation for "inappropriate behaviour" towards an anti-doping officer at national team training camp the previous October.

5 August 2017 - 20-18 home victory over London in first Super 8s Qualifiers tie.

12 August 2017 - 52-24 defeat at Warrington.

19 August 2017 - 30-6 home defeat by Leigh.

3 September 2017 - Greg Bird and Vincent Duport sin-binned in 24-0 win at Halifax.

6 September 2017 - Greg Bird banned for four games for dangerous tackle, reduced to three games on appeal.

6 September 2017 - assistant coach Jérôme Guisset to leave at season end.

9 September 2017 - 26-12 home win over Featherstone. Louis Anderson escapes ban for punching with EGP.

13 September 2017 - Thomas Bosc to retire at end of season.

15 September 2017 - Iain Thornley and Brayden Wiliame score late tries to snatch 20-19 win at Hull KR.

20 September 2017 - Justin Horo to join Wakefield at end of season.

23 September 2017 - 12-10 home defeat by Widnes means trip to Leigh for Million Pound Game.

30 September 2017 - Super League status secured as Lewis Tierney scores two tries in 26-10 win at Leigh.

10 October 2017 - loose forward Thibault Margolet signs new two-year contract.

CATALANS DRAGONS

DATE	FIXTURE	RESULT	SCORERS	LGE	ATT
11/2/17	Warrington (h)	W20-12	t:Myler,Bird,Wiliame g:Walsh(4)	4th	8,842
23/2/17	Hull FC (a)	W14-16	t:Myler g:Walsh(6)	3rd	13,544
4/3/17	Widnes (h)	D14-14	t:Wiliame,Myler g:Walsh(3)	3rd	7,254
10/3/17	Leeds (a)	L46-10	t:Wiliame,Bousquet g:Walsh	5th	13,208
18/3/17	St Helens (h)	L24-28	t:Bosc,Bousquet,Thornley,Aiton g:Walsh(4)	7th	8,158
26/3/17	Castleford (a)	L43-26	t:Thornley,Myler,Anderson,Duport g:Walsh(5)	9th	8,126
1/4/17	Wakefield (h)	L18-38	t:Garcia,Inu,Yaha g:Walsh(3)	9th	7,931
7/4/17	Leigh (a)	W26-37	t:Thornley,Wiliame,Inu,Anderson,Myler,Gigot g:Walsh(6) fg:Walsh	8th	5,612
12/4/17	Huddersfield (a)	W22-29	t:Gigot,Wiliame,Myler,Duport,Walsh g:Walsh(4) fg:Gigot	7th	4,973
17/4/17	Salford (h)	W38-6	t:Duport(3),Inu,Myler,Gigot g:Walsh(5),Gigot fg:Walsh(2)	6th	10,804
23/4/17	Wigan (a)	L42-22	t:Yaha,Gigot,Anderson(2) g:Walsh(3)	6th	11,637
30/4/17	Wakefield (a)	L30-10	t:Duport,Yaha g:Walsh	8th	4,017
6/5/17	Leeds (h)	L24-30	t:Anderson,Bousquet,Wiliame,Casty g:Gigot(4)	8th	8,759
12/5/17	Hull FC (a) (CCR6)	L62-0		N/A	6,470
21/5/17	Huddersfield (MW) ●	L10-18	t:Myler,Thornley g:Walsh	9th	N/A
26/5/17	Salford (a)	L50-12	t:Duport,Yaha g:Walsh(2)	9th	4,957
29/5/17	Hull FC (h)	W23-18	t:Moa,Yaha,Gigot g:Walsh(5) fg:Walsh	8th	8,439
4/6/17	Widnes (a)	L26-6	t:Moa g:Walsh	8th	4,253
10/6/17	Huddersfield (h)	L12-56	t:Gigot,Moa g:Walsh(2)	9th	9,169
24/6/17	Warrington (a)	L24-16	t:Broughton,Myler(2) g:Walsh(2)	10th	9,798
1/7/17	Leigh (h)	W40-36	t:Broughton,Simon,Yaha,Duport,Moa,Horo,Bousquet g:Walsh(6)	9th	8,728
8/7/17	Wigan (h)	L10-32	t:Duport(2) g:Walsh	10th	9,810
16/7/17	St Helens (a)	L46-28	t:Horo(2),Walsh,Gigot,Myler g:Walsh(4)	10th	10,024
22/7/17	Castleford (h)	L24-32	t:Albert,Gigot,Yaha,Duport g:Gigot(4)	10th	8,657
5/8/17	London Broncos (h) (S8-Q)	W20-18	t:Myler,Wiliame,Anderson g:Walsh(4)	4th(S8-Q)	7,102
12/8/17	Warrington (a) (S8-Q)	L52-24	t:Casty,Inu(2),Tierney g:Walsh(4)	5th(S8-Q)	8,595
19/8/17	Leigh (h) (S8-Q)	L6-30	t:Wiliame g:Inu	5th(S8-Q)	6,632
3/9/17	Halifax (a) (S8-Q)	W0-24	t:Anderson,Myler,Wiliame,Yaha g:Walsh(4)	5th(S8-Q)	1,853
9/9/17	Featherstone (h) (S8-Q)	W26-12	t:Inu,Wiliame,Garcia,Moa g:Walsh(2),Inu(3)	4th(S8-Q)	8,649
15/9/17	Hull KR (a) (S8-Q)	W19-20	t:Myler,Thornley,Wiliame g:Walsh(4)	4th(S8-Q)	7,405
23/9/17	Widnes (h) (S8-Q)	L10-12	t:Bousquet g:Walsh(3)	5th(S8-Q)	10,245
30/9/17	Leigh (a) (MPG)	W10-26	t:Thornley,Tierney(2),Yaha g:Walsh(5)	N/A	6,888

● Played at St James' Park, Newcastle

		APP		TRIES		GOALS		FG		PTS	
	D.O.B.	ALL	SL	ALL	SL	ALL	SL	ALL	SL	ALL	SL
Paul Aiton	29/5/85	28	22	1	1	0	0	0	0	4	4
Lucas Albert	4/7/98	4(6)	3(1)	1	1	0	0	0	0	4	4
Louis Anderson	27/6/85	18(6)	10(6)	7	5	0	0	0	0	28	20
Jason Baitieri	2/7/89	6(14)	6(6)	0	0	0	0	0	0	0	0
Lambert Belmas	11/8/97	3(1)	2(1)	0	0	0	0	0	0	0	0
Greg Bird	10/2/84	15(2)	11(1)	1	1	0	0	0	0	4	4
Thomas Bosc	5/8/83	6(5)	6(5)	1	1	0	0	0	0	4	4
Julian Bousquet	18/7/91	10(20)	6(15)	5	4	0	0	0	0	20	16
Jodie Broughton	9/1/88	7	7	2	2	0	0	0	0	8	8
Luke Burgess	20/2/87	3(2)	3(2)	0	0	0	0	0	0	0	0
Remi Casty	5/2/85	27(1)	21(1)	2	1	0	0	0	0	8	4
Alrix Da Costa	2/10/97	4(14)	1(14)	0	0	0	0	0	0	0	0
Jordan Dezaria	6/11/96	3(1)	3(1)	0	0	0	0	0	0	0	0
Nabil Djalout	28/3/89	1	1	0	0	0	0	0	0	0	0
Vincent Duport	15/12/87	28(1)	19(1)	11	11	0	0	0	0	44	44
Benjamin Garcia	5/4/93	20(5)	15(2)	2	1	0	0	0	0	8	4
Tony Gigot	27/12/90	16	16	8	8	9	9	1	1	51	51
Justin Horo	7/9/86	19	11	3	3	0	0	0	0	12	12
Krisnan Inu	17/3/87	25	18	6	3	4	0	0	0	32	12
Matthieu Khedimi	15/1/97	(1)	0	0	0	0	0	0	0	0	0
Thibaut Margalet	3/1/93	1(18)	1(11)	0	0	0	0	0	0	0	0
Sam Moa	14/6/86	30	21	5	4	0	0	0	0	20	16
Richie Myler	21/5/90	31	22	14	11	0	0	0	0	56	44
Romain Navarrete	30/6/94	1(3)	1(1)	0	0	0	0	0	0	0	0
Ugo Perez	30/11/94	2(3)	1(3)	0	0	0	0	0	0	0	0
Arthur Romano	17/8/97	3	2	0	0	0	0	0	0	0	0
Paul Seguier	8/9/97	(5)	(4)	0	0	0	0	0	0	0	0
Mickael Simon	2/4/87	1(17)	1(16)	1	1	0	0	0	0	4	4
Iain Thornley	11/9/91	23	18	6	4	0	0	0	0	24	16
Lewis Tierney	20/10/94	10	2	3	0	0	0	0	0	12	0
Luke Walsh	12/5/87	30	21	2	2	95	69	4	4	202	150
Brayden Wiliame	17/12/92	19	11	11	6	0	0	0	0	44	24
Fouad Yaha	19/8/96	22(1)	17	9	7	0	0	0	0	36	28

'SL' totals include regular season only; 'All' totals also include Super 8s (Qualifiers) & Challenge Cup

Richie Myler

LEAGUE RECORD
SL: P23-W7-D1-L15 (10th)
F469, A689, Diff-220, 15 points.

S8-Q: P7-W4-D0-L3 (5th)
F130, A143, Diff-13, 8 points.
(Winners, Million Pound Game)

CHALLENGE CUP
Round Six

ATTENDANCES
Best - v Salford (SL - 10,804)
Worst - v Leigh (S8 - 6,632)
Total (SL/S8s only) - 129,179
Average (SL/S8s only) - 8,612
(Down by 736 on 2016)

183

3 November 2016 - Kyle Wood leaves for Wakefield; prop Josh Johnson turns down contract offer.

7 November 2016 - Eorl Crabtree announces retirement after 423-game Giants career.

11 November 2016 - Paul Clough joins from Bradford on two-year deal.

14 November 2016 - stand-off Lee Gaskell joins from Bradford on four-year contract.

28 November 2016 - Scotland second-rower Dale Ferguson signs from Bradford on two-year deal.

3 December 2016 - Craig Huby joins Wakefield half way into four-year contract.

19 December 2016 - Newcastle Knights fullback Jake Mamo joins on two-year deal; Joe Wardle heads in opposite direction.

22 December 2016 - Illawarra Cutters prop Shannon Wakeman joins on two-year contract.

7 January 2017 - 23-year-old Bradford hooker Adam O'Brien signs three-year contract.

16 January 2017 - 21-year-old hooker Kruise Leeming extends contract to end of 2020 season.

2 February 2017 - Leroy Cudjoe named as new club captain.

10 February 2017 - 28-16 win at Widnes in round one.

16 February 2017 - 30-20 home defeat by Salford in brought-forward round 11 game.

24 February 2017 - Sam Wood gets two tries in 24-16 home, round-two win over Wakefield. Ukuma Ta'ai takes EGP for high tackle and banned for one match.

2 March 2017 - fullback Darnell McIntosh makes debut as injury-depleted side suffers 48-8 home defeat to Hull FC.

10 March 2017 - 30-0 defeat at Leigh. Sebastine Ikahifo avoids suspension with EGP for punching.

19 March 2017 - battling 16-all draw at Wigan.

24 March 2017 - Danny Brough sin-binned in 28-12 home defeat by Leeds.

28 March 2017 - Danny Brough suspended for one match for punching.

31 March 2017 - 52-16 hammering at top of the table Castleford.

7 April 2017 - Darnell McIntosh scores two tries in 14-14 draw at St Helens.

KEY DATES

12 April 2017 - Jake Mamo makes man-of-the-match debut in 29-22 home defeat by Catalans.

17 April 2017 - 26-24 Easter Monday defeat at Warrington after leading 20-16 on the hour mark.

20 April 2017 - Ryan Brierley moves to League 1 Toronto Wolfpack for undisclosed transfer fee.

20 April 2017 - utility back Jared Simpson signs contract extension to end of 2018 season.

23 April 2017 - humiliating 28-24 home defeat to Championship side Swinton means Challenge Cup exit.

27 April 2017 - Giants players dedicate 31-12 win at Leeds to Jennifer Davy, wife of club owner Ken Davy, who died suddenly the day before.

4 May 2017 - Jake Mamo scores hat-trick in 26-21 defeat at home to Castleford.

9 May 2017 - Danny Brough picks up two-one match suspensions for dangerous contact.

13 May 2017 - halfback Martyn Ridyard joins on month's loan from Leigh.

21 May 2017 - late Sam Rapira and Adam O'Brien tries seal 18-10 Magic Weekend win over Catalans.

26 May 2017 - Jordan Turner signs from Canberra Raiders on three-and-a-half year contract with immediate effect.

26 May 2017 - late 28-26 defeat at Wakefield.

29 May 2017 - home game with St Helens postponed because of soccer club's involvement in a play-off game at Wembley.

4 June 2017 - Jordan Turner scores try on debut in convincing 44-4 home win over Warrington.

10 June 2017 - Jake Mamo scores four tries in 56-12 win at Catalans.

16 June 2017 - Jake Mamo injures foot which ends his season as 24-16 home win over St Helens lifts Giants out of bottom four.

16 June 2017 - utility-back Jordan Rankin joins from Wests Tigers with immediate effect to end of season.

23 June 2017 - 19-all home draw with Wigan.

2 July 2017 - four-match unbeaten run ends with 36-20 defeat at Salford.

7 July 2017 - 40-0 round 21 home win over Widnes all but secures top-eight spot.

14 July 2017 - 26-4 home win over Leigh secures top-eight place.

18 July 2017 - Salford prop Adam Walne signs for 2018 from Salford.

4 August 2017 - 36-6 home win over Wakefield in Super 8s opener.

11 August 2017 - 18-4 defeat at Wigan damages hopes of top-four play-off.

18 August 2017 - Lee Gaskell scores hat-trick in 46-18 win at Hull.

31 August 2017 - Jordan Rankin signs permanent three-year contract.

1 September 2017 - 24-16 home defeat by Castleford ends play-off chances.

6 September 2017 - Sam Rapira to leave at end of season to join Toulouse.

8 September 2017 - young prop Tyler Dickinson signs new two-year contract.

22 September 2017 - 36-12 home defeat to Leeds ends season.

12 October 2017 - utility Colton Roche joins from Bradford on two-year deal.

CLUB RECORDS

Highest score:
142-4 v Blackpool, 26/11/94
Highest score against:
12-94 v Castleford, 18/9/88
Record attendance:
32,912 v Wigan, 4/3/50 *(Fartown)*
15,629 v Leeds, 10/2/2008
*(McAlpine/Galpharm/
John Smith's Stadium)*

MATCH RECORDS

Tries:
10 Lionel Cooper v Keighley, 17/11/51
Goals: 18 Major Holland
v Swinton Park, 28/2/1914
Points: 39 Major Holland
v Swinton Park, 28/2/1914

SEASON RECORDS

Tries: 80 Albert Rosenfeld 1913-14
Goals: 156 *(inc 2fg)* Danny Brough 2013
Points: 346 Danny Brough 2013

CAREER RECORDS

Tries: 420 Lionel Cooper 1947-55
Goals: 958 Frank Dyson 1949-63
Points: 2,072 Frank Dyson 1949-63
Appearances: 485 Douglas Clark 1909-29

HUDDERSFIELD GIANTS

DATE	FIXTURE	RESULT	SCORERS	LGE	ATT
10/2/17	Widnes (a)	W16-28	t:McGillvary(2),Gaskell,Symonds,Murphy,Cudjoe g:Brough(2)	2nd	5,031
16/2/17	Salford (h)	L20-30	t:McGillvary,Mellor(2),Ta'ai g:Brough(2)	5th	6,017
24/2/17	Wakefield (h)	W24-16	t:S Wood(2),Ta'ai,Roberts,McGillvary g:Brough(2)	4th	6,337
2/3/17	Hull FC (h)	L8-48	t:S Wood,Roberts	6th	5,176
10/3/17	Leigh (a)	L30-0		9th	6,001
19/3/17	Wigan (a)	D16-16	t:Gaskell,McIntosh g:Brough(4)	8th	12,704
24/3/17	Leeds (h)	L12-28	t:Ta'ai,McGillvary g:Brough(2)	10th	8,666
31/3/17	Castleford (a)	L52-16	t:Hinchcliffe,Brierley,Gaskell g:Brierley(2)	10th	8,035
7/4/17	St Helens (a)	D14-14	t:McIntosh(2),S Wood g:Brough	10th	9,080
12/4/17	Catalans Dragons (h)	L22-29	t:Murphy,Mamo,McGillvary,S Wood g:Brough(3)	10th	4,973
17/4/17	Warrington (a)	L26-24	t:McIntosh,Mamo,Brough,McGillvary g:Brough(4)	11th	10,111
23/4/17	Swinton (h) (CCR5)	L24-28	t:Murphy,S Wood,McIntosh,Roberts g:Farrell(4)	N/A	1,298
27/4/17	Leeds (a)	W12-31	t:Mamo,Leeming,Ferguson,McIntosh,Roberts g:Brough(5) fg:Brough	10th	13,169
4/5/17	Castleford (h)	L21-26	t:Mamo(3) g:Brough(4) fg:Brough	10th	5,566
21/5/17	Catalans Dragons (MW) ●	W10-18	t:Gaskell,Rapira,O'Brien g:Ridyard(3)	10th	N/A
26/5/17	Wakefield (a)	L28-26	t:Mamo,McGillvary,Gaskell,Ferguson g:Ridyard(5)	10th	4,642
4/6/17	Warrington (h)	W44-4	t:Roberts,McGillvary(2),Murphy(2),Clough,Turner,Mamo g:Brough(6)	9th	5,362
10/6/17	Catalans Dragons (a)	W12-56	t:Murphy,Wakeman,Brough(2),Mamo(4),McGillvary(2) g:Brough,Ridyard(7)	8th	9,169
16/6/17	St Helens (h)	W24-16	t:Cudjoe,Ridyard,O'Brien,Gaskell g:Brough(4)	7th	5,660
23/6/17	Wigan (h)	D19-19	t:Cudjoe,Gaskell,McGillvary g:Ridyard(2),Brough(2) fg:Brough	7th	5,718
2/7/17	Salford (a)	L36-20	t:Cudjoe,Murphy,Leeming,McIntosh g:Brough(2)	8th	3,718
7/7/17	Widnes (h)	W40-0	t:Wakeman,McGillvary(2),Hinchcliffe,O'Brien,McIntosh,Ta'ai g:Ridyard(6)	8th	5,253
14/7/17	Leigh (h)	W26-4	t:Gaskell(2),Ta'ai,Cudjoe g:Brough(5)	7th	5,535
21/7/17	Hull FC (a)	L14-10	t:McIntosh,McGillvary g:Brough	8th	11,467
4/8/17	Wakefield (h) (S8)	W36-6	t:Brough,McIntosh,Hinchcliffe,Cudjoe,McGillvary,Smith g:Brough(6)	7th	5,429
11/8/17	Wigan (a) (S8)	L18-4	t:McGillvary	8th	10,619
18/8/17	Hull FC (h) (S8)	W18-46	t:McIntosh(2),Gaskell(3),Mellor,Dickinson,Leeming g:Brough(4),Rankin(3)	8th	10,535
1/9/17	Castleford (h) (S8)	L16-24	t:Roberts,Clough,McIntosh g:Rankin(2)	8th	6,284
9/9/17	Salford (a) (S8)	L52-14	t:McGillvary,Roberts,Hinchcliffe g:Brough	8th	1,405
15/9/17	St Helens (a) (S8)	L40-16	t:Roberts,Hinchcliffe,Rankin g:Brough(2)	8th	9,419
22/9/17	Leeds (h) (S8)	L12-36	t:Lawrence,Hinchcliffe g:Brough(2)	8th	6,247

● Played at St James' Park, Newcastle

	D.O.B.	APP ALL	APP SL	TRIES ALL	TRIES SL	GOALS ALL	GOALS SL	FG ALL	FG SL	PTS ALL	PTS SL
Ryan Brierley	12/3/92	6	6	1	1	2	2	0	0	8	8
Danny Brough	15/1/83	27	27	4	4	61	61	3	3	141	141
Paul Clough	27/9/87	8(22)	8(22)	2	2	0	0	0	0	8	8
Leroy Cudjoe	7/4/88	18	18	6	6	0	0	0	0	24	24
Tyler Dickinson	18/8/96	1(10)	(10)	1	1	0	0	0	0	4	4
Matty English	14/11/97	(2)	(1)	0	0	0	0	0	0	0	0
Izaac Farrell	30/1/98	1	0	0	0	4	0	0	0	8	0
Dale Ferguson	13/4/88	17	17	2	2	0	0	0	0	8	8
Lee Gaskell	28/10/90	27	26	12	12	0	0	0	0	48	48
Ryan Hinchcliffe	7/10/84	28(2)	28(2)	6	6	0	0	0	0	24	24
Sebastine Ikahihifo	27/1/91	28(1)	28	0	0	0	0	0	0	0	0
Michael Lawrence	12/4/90	4(4)	4(4)	1	1	0	0	0	0	4	4
Kruise Leeming	7/9/95	24(7)	23(7)	3	3	0	0	0	0	12	12
Jake Mamo	6/6/94	9	9	12	12	0	0	0	0	48	48
Nathan Mason	8/9/93	1(8)	(8)	0	0	0	0	0	0	0	0
Jermaine McGillvary	16/5/88	26	26	19	19	0	0	0	0	76	76
Darnell McIntosh	5/7/97	23(1)	22(1)	13	12	0	0	0	0	52	48
Alex Mellor	24/9/94	23(5)	22(5)	3	3	0	0	0	0	12	12
Aaron Murphy	26/11/88	19	18	7	6	0	0	0	0	28	24
Adam O'Brien	11/7/93	1(16)	1(15)	3	3	0	0	0	0	12	12
Gene Ormsby	12/9/92	4	4	0	0	0	0	0	0	0	0
Jordan Rankin	17/12/91	11	11	1	1	5	5	0	0	14	14
Sam Rapira	8/4/87	15(11)	14(11)	1	1	0	0	0	0	4	4
Martyn Ridyard	25/7/86	7	7	1	1	26	26	0	0	56	56
Oliver Roberts	24/12/94	19(7)	18(7)	8	7	0	0	0	0	32	28
Jared Simpson	4/1/96	2	1	0	0	0	0	0	0	0	0
Daniel Smith	20/3/93	2(12)	1(12)	1	1	0	0	0	0	4	4
Tom Symonds	17/2/89	2	2	1	1	0	0	0	0	4	4
Ukuma Ta'ai	17/1/87	15(4)	15(4)	5	5	0	0	0	0	20	20
Jordan Turner	9/1/89	9	9	1	1	0	0	0	0	4	4
Shannon Wakeman	15/2/90	16(12)	16(11)	2	2	0	0	0	0	8	8
Mikey Wood	18/4/96	1	1	0	0	0	0	0	0	0	0
Sam Wood	11/6/97	9	8	6	5	0	0	0	0	24	20

'SL' totals include Super 8s; 'All' totals also include Challenge Cup

Kruise Leeming

LEAGUE RECORD
P30-W11-D3-L16
(8th, SL)
F663, A680, Diff-17
25 points.

CHALLENGE CUP
Round Five

ATTENDANCES
Best - v Leeds (SL - 8,666)
Worst - v Swinton (CC - 1,298)
Total (SL/S8s only) - 82,223
Average (SL/S8s only) - 5,873
(Up by 602 on 2016)

185

11 November 2016 - Jordan Abdull moves to Hull KR on season-long loan.

11 November 2016 - Albert Kelly signs from Hull KR on one-year deal. Steve Michaels signs new one-year deal.

17 November 2016 - Frank Pritchard signs for Parramatta.

28 November 2016 - Jamie Shaul signs contract extension to end of 2020.

8 January 2017 - 40-16 home defeat to Hull KR in Clive Sullivan Trophy match.

22 January 2017 - 26-20 home friendly win over Toronto Wolfpack in historic clash.

29 January 2017 - 18-6 pre-season defeat at Salford.

7 February 2017 - Curtis Naughton joins Leigh on season-long loan.

12 February 2017 - 12-8 round-one win at Wakefield in sleet and mud. Albert Kelly gets one-match ban for high tackle.

20 February 2017 - Marc Sneyd signs two-year contract extension to end of 2019.

23 February 2017 - 16-14 home defeat by Catalans. Liam Watts pleads guilty to dangerous throw and banned for four matches.

2 March 2017 - Marc Sneyd scores three tries and eight goals in 48-8 victory at Huddersfield.

4 March 2017 - Dean Hadley joins Wakefield on month's loan.

10 March 2017 - coach Lee Radford's 100th match in charge ends in hard-fought 24-14 home win over St Helens. Jansin Turgut pleads guilty to striking with elbow/forearm and suspended for two matches.

17 March 2017 - Liam Watts signs two-year extension to end of 2020. Jordan Abdull signs until end of 2019.

17 March 2017 - Albert Kelly scores two tries in 32-12 home win over Widnes.

24 March 2017 - 22-20 win at Wigan ends their winning run and moves Hull FC to joint top of table.

2 April 2017 - Dean Hadley loan deal at Wakefield extended by a month.

7 April 2017 - early 8-0 lead ends in 54-18 home hammering by Salford.

14 April 2017 - 52-24 Good Friday home defeat by Leeds.

17 April 2017 - Carlos Tuimavave scores two tries in 24-10 Easter Monday win at Leigh.

19 April 2017 - Albert Kelly ends speculation of NRL return by extending contract to end of 2018.

23 April 2017 - Liam Watts sent off on 22 minutes as Hull led 18-0 before battling 26-24 win over league leaders Castleford.

25 April 2017 - Liam Watts banned for two games for high tackle on Luke Gale, reduced to one match on appeal.

HULL F.C.

Est. 1865

KEY DATES

28 April 2017 - Mahe Fonua stars in 34-10 home win over Warrington. Sika Manu banned for two games after sin-binning for chicken-wing tackle on Ryan Atkins.

7 May 2017 - Jamie Shaul scores two tries as Hull overcome 22-point deficit at Widnes to win 33-22.

12 May 2017 - winger Steve Michaels scores hat-trick in 62-0 home, Challenge Cup sixth-round crushing of Catalans.

20 May 2017 - 45-0 hammering by St Helens at Magic Weekend.

22 May 2017 - Mahe Fonua to join Wests Tigers at end of season.

26 May 2017 - 26-22 home defeat to Leigh, who end eight-match losing run.

29 May 2017 - Liam Watts dismissed for high tackle two minutes from end of 23-18 defeat at Catalans and banned for one game

2 June 2017 - forward Mark Minichiello signs new contract for 2018.

3 June 2017 - three-match losing run ends with convincing 39-26 home win over Wigan.

7 June 2017 - 1983 Championship-winning coach Arthur Bunting dies.

9 June 2017 - 34-10 win at second-placed Salford moves Hull into top four.

13 June 2017 - assistant coach Richard Horne appointed as new head coach at dual registration partner club Doncaster.

14 June 2017 - Danny Washbrook, Fetuli Talanoa (both one year) and Jordan Thompson (two years) sign new contracts.

18 June 2017 - 32-24 home win over Castleford secures Challenge Cup semi-final place.

19 June 2017 - young winger Nick Rawsthorne joins Leigh on one-month's loan.

23 June 2017 - 40-18 home win over fifth-placed Wakefield moves Hull back into second spot.

29 June 2017 - Nick Rawsthorne signs two-year contract.

30 June 2017 - two late Feluti Talanoa tries not enough to prevent 24-22 defeat at leaders Castleford.

7 July 2017 - 19-12 defeat at St Helens leaves Hull in fourth spot.

14 July 2017 - 10-7 defeat at Leeds.

21 July 2017 - 14-10 home win over Huddersfield ends regular season.

29 July 2017 - commanding 43-24 Challenge Cup semi-final win over Leeds at Keepmoat Stadium, Doncaster.

31 July 2017 - prop Mickey Paea to return from Newcastle in 2018, joined by Parramatta winger Bureta Faraimo, both on two-year deals.

4 August 2017 - 32-18 home win over Salford in Super 8s opener.

11 August 2017 - late 50-metre Marc Sneyd penalty secures 8-6 win at St Helens,

16 August 2017 - captain Gareth Ellis announces he is to retire at end of season.

18 August 2017 - 46-18 home defeat by Huddersfield.

26 August 2017 - Marc Sneyd wins Lance Todd Trophy for second successive year in 18-14 Challenge Cup final win over Wigan.

31 August 2017 - 38-26 defeat at Leeds.

6 September 2017 - Steve Michaels to return to Australia after three seasons.

8 September 2017 - Liam Watts sent off in 22nd minute of 30-22 home defeat by Wigan.

11 September 2017 - Liam Watts gets sending off sufficient after no charge for leading with elbow.

14 September 2017 - Marc Sneyd field goal secures 19-18 home win over Wakefield.

22 September 2017 - Jake Connor scores hat-trick in 48-16 win at Castleford that secures semi-final berth.

29 September 2017 - 18-16 defeat at Leeds in semi-final.

6 October 2017 - Jordan Thompson signs for Leigh.

CLUB RECORDS
Highest score: 88-0 v Sheffield, 2/3/2003
Highest score against: 18-76 v Huddersfield, 19/9/2013
Record attendance: 28,798 v Leeds, 7/3/36 *(The Boulevard)* 23,004 v Hull KR, 2/9/2007 *(KC Stadium)*

MATCH RECORDS
Tries: 7 Clive Sullivan v Doncaster, 15/4/68
Goals: 14 Jim Kennedy v Rochdale, 7/4/21 Sammy Lloyd v Oldham, 10/9/78 Matt Crowther v Sheffield, 2/3/2003
Points: 36 Jim Kennedy v Keighley, 29/1/21

SEASON RECORDS
Tries: 52 Jack Harrison 1914-15
Goals: 170 Sammy Lloyd 1978-79
Points: 369 Sammy Lloyd 1978-79

CAREER RECORDS
Tries: 250 Clive Sullivan 1961-74; 1981-85
Goals: 687 Joe Oliver 1928-37; 1943-45
Points: 1,842 Joe Oliver 1928-37; 1943-45
Appearances: 500 Edward Rogers 1906-25

HULL F.C.

DATE	FIXTURE	RESULT	SCORERS	LGE	ATT
12/2/17	Wakefield (a)	W8-12	t:Connor g:Sneyd(4)	5th	7,027
23/2/17	Catalans Dragons (h)	L14-16	t:Tuimavave,Watts g:Sneyd(3)	6th	13,544
2/3/17	Huddersfield (a)	W8-48	t:Talanoa,Sneyd(3),Kelly(2),Griffin,Tuimavave g:Sneyd(8)	4th	5,176
10/3/17	St Helens (h)	W24-14	t:Kelly(2),Tuimavave g:Sneyd(6)	3rd	11,587
17/3/17	Widnes (h)	W32-12	t:Kelly(2),Fonua,Houghton,Shaul g:Sneyd(6)	3rd	10,814
24/3/17	Wigan (a)	W20-22	t:Michaels,Kelly,Connor,Shaul g:Sneyd(3)	2nd	12,319
1/4/17	Warrington (a)	D22-22	t:Kelly,Connor,Shaul g:Sneyd(5)	3rd	10,676
7/4/17	Salford (h)	L18-54	t:Michaels(2),Shaul g:Sneyd(2),Connor	4th	11,016
14/4/17	Leeds (h)	L24-52	t:Michaels,Taylor,Shaul,Minichiello g:Sneyd(4)	5th	15,487
17/4/17	Leigh (a)	W10-24	t:Watts,Tuimavave(2),Kelly g:Sneyd(4)	5th	6,296
23/4/17	Castleford (h)	W26-24	t:Taylor,Fonua(2),Tuimavave g:Sneyd(5)	4th	12,801
28/4/17	Warrington (h)	W34-10	t:Connor,Fonua,Shaul,Kelly(2) g:Sneyd(7)	2nd	10,734
7/5/17	Widnes (a)	W22-33	t:Turgut,Shaul(2),Tuimavave,Kelly,Washbrook g:Sneyd(4) fg:Sneyd	2nd	5,082
12/5/17	Catalans Dragons (h) (CCR6)	W62-0	t:Michaels(3),Griffin,Fonua,Watts,Taylor,Turgut,Thompson,Shaul(2), Connor g:Sneyd(2),Connor(5)	N/A	6,470
20/5/17	St Helens (MW) ●	L0-45		3rd	N/A
26/5/17	Leigh (h)	L22-26	t:Shaul(2),Tuimavave,Kelly g:Sneyd(3)	4th	10,222
29/5/17	Catalans Dragons (a)	L23-18	t:Kelly,Rawsthorne(2) g:Connor(3)	5th	8,439
3/6/17	Wigan (h)	W39-26	t:Michaels(2),Minichiello,Houghton,Shaul,Kelly g:Connor(5),Rawsthorne(2) fg:Kelly	5th	10,333
9/6/17	Salford (a)	W10-34	t:Talanoa,Kelly(2),Washbrook,Tuimavave,Shaul g:Connor(5)	4th	2,678
18/6/17	Castleford (h) (CCQF)	W32-24	t:Tuimavave,Talanoa,Fonua,Shaul g:Connor(8)	N/A	11,944
23/6/17	Wakefield (h)	W40-18	t:Shaul(2),Talanoa,Connor,Sneyd,Fonua,Turgut g:Sneyd(6)	2nd	10,895
30/6/17	Castleford (a)	L24-22	t:Fonua(2),Talanoa(2) g:Sneyd(3)	4th	8,371
7/7/17	St Helens (a)	L19-12	t:Shaul,Fonua g:Sneyd(2)	4th	9,910
14/7/17	Leeds (a)	L10-7	t:Taylor g:Sneyd fg:Sneyd	5th	16,938
21/7/17	Huddersfield (h)	W14-10	t:Minichiello,Bowden g:Sneyd(3)	3rd	11,467
29/7/17	Leeds (CCSF) ●●	W43-24	t:Kelly,Tuimavave(2),Green,Watts,Shaul,Taylor g:Sneyd(7) fg:Sneyd	N/A	14,526
4/8/17	Salford (h) (S8)	W32-18	t:Kelly,Tuimavave(2),Talanoa,Connor g:Connor(6)	3rd	10,239
11/8/17	St Helens (a) (S8)	W6-8	t:Sneyd g:Sneyd(2)	3rd	10,338
18/8/17	Huddersfield (h) (S8)	L18-46	t:Ellis,Connor,Griffin g:Sneyd(3)	3rd	10,535
26/8/17	Wigan (CCF) ●●●	W18-14	t:Talanoa,Fonua(2) g:Sneyd(3)	N/A	68,525
31/8/17	Leeds (a) (S8)	L38-26	t:Michaels,Taylor,Washbrook,Bowden g:Sneyd(5)	3rd	13,219
8/9/17	Wigan (h) (S8)	L22-30	t:Fonua(2),Manu,Sneyd g:Sneyd(3)	4th	11,291
14/9/17	Wakefield (h) (S8)	W19-18	t:Fonua,Sneyd,Ellis g:Sneyd(3) fg:Sneyd	3rd	10,924
22/9/17	Castleford (a) (S8)	W16-48	t:Kelly,Connor(3),Houghton,Shaul(2),Tuimavave g:Sneyd(8)	3rd	7,974
29/9/17	Leeds (a) (SF)	L18-16	t:Ellis,Fonua,Manu g:Sneyd(2)	N/A	12,500

● *Played at St James' Park, Newcastle*
●● *Played at Keepmoat Stadium, Doncaster*
●●● *Played at Wembley Stadium*

		APP		TRIES		GOALS		FG		PTS	
	D.O.B.	ALL	SL	ALL	SL	ALL	SL	ALL	SL	ALL	SL
Josh Bowden	14/1/92	17(11)	16(8)	2	2	0	0	0	0	8	8
Jake Connor	18/10/94	23(9)	21(7)	11	10	33	20	0	0	110	80
Jack Downs	10/11/95	(6)	(6)	0	0	0	0	0	0	0	0
Gareth Ellis	3/5/81	15(3)	13(3)	3	3	0	0	0	0	12	12
Brad Fash	24/1/96	(23)	(21)	0	0	0	0	0	0	0	0
Mahe Fonua	24/12/92	30	26	16	12	0	0	0	0	64	48
Chris Green	3/1/90	6(17)	5(15)	1	0	0	0	0	0	4	0
Josh Griffin	9/5/90	24(5)	21(5)	3	2	0	0	0	0	12	8
Danny Houghton	25/9/88	28	24	3	3	0	0	0	0	12	12
Albert Kelly	21/3/91	29	25	20	19	0	0	1	1	81	77
Jez Litten	10/3/98	(3)	(3)	0	0	0	0	0	0	0	0
Sika Manu	22/1/87	31(1)	28(1)	2	2	0	0	0	0	8	8
Masi Matongo	15/5/96	(9)	(9)	0	0	0	0	0	0	0	0
Steve Michaels	13/1/87	21(1)	19(1)	10	7	0	0	0	0	40	28
Mark Minichiello	30/1/82	30	26	3	3	0	0	0	0	12	12
Nick Rawsthorne	30/9/95	3	3	2	2	2	2	0	0	12	12
Jamie Shaul	1/7/92	33	29	21	17	0	0	0	0	84	68
Marc Sneyd	9/2/91	30	27	7	7	117	105	4	3	266	241
Fetuli Talanoa	23/11/87	21	18	8	6	0	0	0	0	32	24
Scott Taylor	27/2/91	25(3)	22(2)	6	4	0	0	0	0	24	16
Jordan Thompson	4/9/91	11(17)	11(15)	1	0	0	0	0	0	4	0
Carlos Tuimavave	10/1/92	28	25	15	12	0	0	0	0	60	48
Jansin Turgut	8/3/96	8(12)	7(11)	3	2	0	0	0	0	12	8
Danny Washbrook	18/9/85	16(18)	15(15)	3	3	0	0	0	0	12	12
Liam Watts	8/7/90	26(2)	22(2)	4	2	0	0	0	0	16	8

'SL' totals include Super 8s & semi-final; 'All' totals also include Challenge Cup

Jamie Shaul

LEAGUE RECORD
P30-W17-D1-L12
(3rd, SL/Semi-Finalists)
F714, A655, Diff+59
35 points.

CHALLENGE CUP
Winners

ATTENDANCES
Best - v Leeds (SL - 15,487)
Worst - v Catalans Dragons
(CC - 6,470)
Total (SL/S8s only) - 171,889
Average (SL/S8s only) - 11,459
(Down by 131 on 2016)

187

KEY DATES

4 November 2016 - halfback Cory Aston signs from Sheffield on two-year contract.

8 November 2016 - Zak Hardaker joins Castleford on one-year loan deal, with Tigers holding option for permanent signing at end of 2017 season.

23 November 2016 - Rhinos maintain James Segeyaro will remain at the club despite reports he is reluctant to return from Australia.

5 December 2016 - Rhinos place valuation of £250,000 on James Segeyaro and consider legal proceedings after he reneges on two-year contract.

21 December 2016 - 24-year-old hooker Matt Parcell signs from Manly on three-year contract for undisclosed fee.

26 December 2016 - 30-6 home defeat by Wakefield in Wetherby Whaler Challenge.

2 February 2017 - halfback Jordan Lilley, hooker Sam Hallas, backrower Josh Jordan-Roberts and prop Mikolaj Oledzki join Bradford on month's loan.

9 February 2017 - round-one 6-4 defeat at St Helens.

17 February 2017 - 17-14 win after trailing 8-0 at Leigh in brought-forward round 11 game.

24 February 2017 - Liam Sutcliffe scores late try to secure 20-14 round-two home win over Salford. Carl Ablett banned for one game for contact with match official.

2 March 2017 - 66-10 hammering at Castleford.

10 March 2017 - stunning 46-10 win at Headingley ends Catalans' unbeaten start to season. Brad Singleton pleads guilty to striking Greg Bird with elbow and suspended for six matches.

17 March 2017 - Leeds reach financial settlement with James Segeyaro, who joins Cronulla.

17 March 2017 - hooker Matt Parcell stars in 38-14 home win over Wakefield.

24 March 2017 - 28-12 win at Huddersfield moves Rhinos into second spot.

31 March 2017 - Kallum Watkins scores try on 200th club appearance in 26-18 home win over Wigan.

7 April 2017 - Liam Sutcliffe concussed in first minute - Ben Westwood sin-binned - as 25-14 defeat at Warrington ends four-match winning run. Carl Ablett suffers knee injury.

14 April 2017 - commanding 52-24 Good Friday win at Hull FC.

17 April 2017 - Kallum Watkins scores two tries and seven goals in 42-22 Easter Monday win over Widnes.

21 April 2017 - debutant 17-year-old fullback Jack Walker scores hat-trick in 64-28 Challenge Cup fifth-round home win over Doncaster.

27 April 2017 - 31-12 home defeat to Huddersfield.

6 May 2017 - late Danny McGuire try secures 30-24 comeback win at Catalans.

14 May 2017 - 72-10 home victory over Barrow in Challenge Cup sixth round.

21 May 2017 - 29-18 defeat to Castleford at Magic Weekend.

23 May 2017 - fullback Ashton Golding signs new five-year deal to end of 2021 season.

26 May 2017 - Matt Parcell scores hat-trick in 40-0 home rout of Warrington.

29 May 2017 - 28-20 Bank Holiday Monday defeat at Widnes.

3 June 2017 - Adam Cuthbertson scores two tries in 22-14 home win over Leigh.

10 June 2017 - Tom Briscoe scores two tries in 18-16 victory at Wakefield as Rhinos move back to third spot. Jamie Jones-Buchanan gets one game for dangerous contact.

16 June 2017 - 58-0 home hammering of Championship Featherstone in Challenge Cup quarter-final.

23 June 2017 - 23-12 home defeat by Castleford. Captain Danny McGuire banned for one game for swearing at official. Jamie Jones-Buchanan gets one game for use of shoulder.

27 June 2017 - Catalans Dragons halfback Richie Myler signs on three-year contract from 2018 to end of 2020 season.

29 June 2017 - halfback Jordan Lilley plays first Super League game of season in 24-22 home victory over St Helens.

7 July 2017 - Jordan Lilley signs new three-year contract to end of 2020.

9 July 2017 - Rhinos move clear in second spot with 50-24 win at third-placed Salford.

11 July 2017 - Danny McGuire announces 2017 will be final season with Leeds.

14 July 2017 - Jack Walker scores winner in 10-7 home win over Hull FC.

19 July 2017 - Rob Burrow announces he will retire at end of season.

21 July 2017 - team missing 13 regulars loses 34-0 at Wigan. Harry Newman, Alex Sutcliffe and Harvey Whiteley all make debuts.

21 July 2017 - hooker Brad Dwyer signs from Warrington for 2018 on two-year contract.

29 July 2017 - 43-24 Challenge Cup semi-final defeat by Hull FC at Keepmoat Stadium, Doncaster.

3 August 2107 - Jack Walker, three years, and Alex Sutcliffe, four years, sign new contracts.

4 August 2107 - Stevie Ward scores hat-trick in 32-16 home win over Wigan

13 August 2107 - Jordan Baldwinson signs for Wakefield from 2018.

18 August 2107 - Ryan Hall makes 300th club appearance in 16-14 home win over St Helens, in the last game before demolition of South Stand.

31 August 2107 - semi-final spot secured with 38-26 home win over Hull FC.

8 September 2017 - second league spot and home-play off tie confirmed despite 38-24 defeat at Castleford.

27 September 2017 - Gold Coast Titans prop Nathaniel Peteru signs three-year contract.

29 September 2017 - 18-16 home win over Hull FC secures tenth Grand Final.

7 October 2017 - two-try Danny McGuire wins Harry Sunderland Trophy after 24-6 win over Castleford secures eighth Super League Grand Final win.

CLUB RECORDS
Highest score: 106-10 v Swinton, 11/2/2001 **Highest score against:** 6-74 v Wigan, 20/5/92 **Record attendance:** 40,175 v Bradford, 21/5/47

MATCH RECORDS
Tries: 8 Fred Webster v Coventry, 12/4/1913 Eric Harris v Bradford, 14/9/31 **Goals:** 17 Iestyn Harris v Swinton, 11/2/2001 **Points:** 42 Iestyn Harris v Huddersfield, 16/7/99

SEASON RECORDS
Tries: 63 Eric Harris 1935-36 **Goals:** 173 *(inc 5fg)* Kevin Sinfield 2012 **Points:** 431 Lewis Jones 1956-57

CAREER RECORDS
Tries: 391 Eric Harris 1930-39 **Goals:** 1,831 *(inc 39fg)* Kevin Sinfield 1997-2015 **Points:** 3,967 Kevin Sinfield 1997-2015 **Appearances:** 625 John Holmes 1968-89

LEEDS RHINOS

DATE	FIXTURE	RESULT	SCORERS	LGE	ATT
9/2/17	St Helens (a)	L6-4	t:Moon	7th	12,208
17/2/17	Leigh (a)	W14-17	t:Cuthbertson,Hall,Keinhorst g:L Sutcliffe(2) fg:L Sutcliffe	7th	6,692
24/2/17	Salford (h)	W20-14	t:Hall,Keinhorst,L Sutcliffe g:Burrow(4)	5th	14,575
2/3/17	Castleford (a)	L66-10	t:Mullally,Moon g:L Sutcliffe	7th	11,500
10/3/17	Catalans Dragons (h)	W46-10	t:Cuthbertson(2),Parcell,Keinhorst,Burrow,McGuire,L Sutcliffe g:L Sutcliffe(9)	4th	13,208
17/3/17	Wakefield (h)	W38-14	t:Watkins(2),Mullally,Hall,Cuthbertson,Parcell g:Golding(7)	4th	14,411
24/3/17	Huddersfield (a)	W12-28	t:Briscoe,Hall,Ablett,Parcell,Baldwinson g:Golding(2),L Sutcliffe(2)	3rd	8,666
31/3/17	Wigan (h)	W26-18	t:Hall,Moon,Watkins,Ablett g:Golding(5)	2nd	17,030
7/4/17	Warrington (a)	L25-14	t:Briscoe,Parcell,Moon g:Watkins	3rd	10,035
14/4/17	Hull FC (a)	W24-52	t:McGuire,Hall,Parcell,Moon(2),Watkins,Garbutt,Mullally g:L Sutcliffe(9),Burrow	3rd	15,487
17/4/17	Widnes (h)	W42-22	t:Watkins(2),Parcell(2),Moon(2),Briscoe g:Watkins(7)	2nd	15,408
21/4/17	Doncaster (h) (CCR5)	W64-28	t:Handley,Burrow(2),Garbutt(2),McGuire,Walker(3),Lilley,Oledzki,Moon g:Watkins(6),Lilley(2)	N/A	5,097
27/4/17	Huddersfield (h)	L12-31	t:Parcell,Moon g:Watkins(2)	4th	13,169
6/5/17	Catalans Dragons (a)	W24-30	t:L Sutcliffe,Ward,Cuthbertson,Burrow,McGuire g:L Sutcliffe(5)	4th	8,759
14/5/17	Barrow (h) (CCR6)	W72-10	t:Moon(3),Parcell(2),Handley(2),Hall,Ward,L Sutcliffe,Burrow(2),Galloway g:L Sutcliffe(10)	N/A	5,226
21/5/17	Castleford (MW) ●	L29-18	t:Watkins,Moon,L Sutcliffe g:L Sutcliffe(3)	4th	N/A
26/5/17	Warrington (h)	W40-0	t:Parcell(3),L Sutcliffe,Jones-Buchanan,Moon,Burrow g:L Sutcliffe(6)	3rd	14,974
29/5/17	Widnes (a)	L28-20	t:Handley,Watkins,Ward,Cuthbertson g:L Sutcliffe(2)	3rd	5,518
2/6/17	Leigh (h)	W22-14	t:Cuthbertson(2),Briscoe,Moon g:L Sutcliffe(3)	3rd	13,445
10/6/17	Wakefield (a)	W16-18	t:Ward,Briscoe(2),Moon g:L Sutcliffe	3rd	7,183
16/6/17	Featherstone (h) (CCQF)	W58-0	t:Ward,Ferres,Moon,Handley(2),Ablett,L Sutcliffe,Singleton(2),Hall g:L Sutcliffe(9)	N/A	6,181
23/6/17	Castleford (h)	L12-23	t:Handley,Cuthbertson g:L Sutcliffe(2)	4th	18,029
29/6/17	St Helens (h)	W24-22	t:Moon,Ward,Watkins,Hall g:Lilley(4)	3rd	13,262
9/7/17	Salford (a)	W24-50	t:Hall,Briscoe(2),Watkins,Parcell,Moon,Jones-Buchanan,Mullally,Walker g:Watkins(3),Lilley(2)	2nd	5,056
14/7/17	Hull FC (h)	W10-7	t:Hall,Walker g:Lilley	2nd	16,938
21/7/17	Wigan (a)	L34-0		2nd	15,119
29/7/17	Hull FC (CCSF) ●●	L43-24	t:Hall(2),Watkins,Golding g:Watkins(3),Lilley	N/A	14,526
4/8/17	Wigan (h) (S8)	W32-16	t:Ward(3),Golding(2),Parcell g:Watkins(4)	2nd	13,579
10/8/17	Wakefield (a) (S8)	L38-6	t:Cuthbertson g:Watkins	2nd	5,607
18/8/17	St Helens (h) (S8)	W16-14	t:Hall,Cuthbertson g:Watkins(4)	2nd	16,326
31/8/17	Hull FC (h) (S8)	W38-26	t:Burrow,Singleton,L Sutcliffe,Garbutt,Cuthbertson,Parcell g:Watkins(7)	2nd	13,219
8/9/17	Castleford (a) (S8)	L38-24	t:Watkins,Jones-Buchanan,Parcell,Garbutt g:Watkins(4)	2nd	9,557
15/9/17	Salford (h) (S8)	W44-2	t:L Sutcliffe,McGuire,Briscoe,Parcell(2),Cuthbertson,Mullally,Ferres g:Watkins(6)	2nd	13,094
22/9/17	Huddersfield (a) (S8)	W12-36	t:Watkins,McGuire(2),Keinhorst,Mullally,Burrow g:Watkins(6)	2nd	6,247
29/9/17	Hull FC (h) (SF)	W18-15	t:Ward,Mullally,L Sutcliffe g:Watkins(3)	N/A	12,500
7/10/17	Castleford (GF) ●●●	W6-24	t:Briscoe(2),McGuire(2) g:Watkins(3) fg:McGuire(2)	N/A	72,827

● Played at St James' Park, Newcastle ●● Played at Keepmoat Stadium, Doncaster ●●● Played at Old Trafford, Manchester

		APP		TRIES		GOALS		FG		PTS	
	D.O.B.	ALL	SL	ALL	SL	ALL	SL	ALL	SL	ALL	SL
Carl Ablett	19/12/85	20(4)	18(4)	3	2	0	0	0	0	12	8
Jordan Baldwinson	10/11/94	5(7)	4(6)	1	1	0	0	0	0	4	4
Tom Briscoe	19/3/90	34	31	11	11	0	0	0	0	44	44
Rob Burrow	26/9/82	10(14)	9(13)	9	5	5	5	0	0	46	30
Adam Cuthbertson	24/2/85	29(6)	27(4)	13	13	0	0	0	0	52	52
Brett Delaney	26/10/85	6(11)	6(11)	0	0	0	0	0	0	0	0
Brett Ferres	17/4/86	10(5)	8(4)	2	1	0	0	0	0	8	4
Keith Galloway	2/9/85	10(3)	7(3)	1	0	0	0	0	0	4	0
Mitch Garbutt	18/4/89	13(13)	12(11)	5	3	0	0	0	0	20	12
Ashton Golding	4/9/96	22	20	3	2	14	14	0	0	40	36
Ryan Hall	27/11/87	34	30	14	10	0	0	0	0	56	40
Sam Hallas	18/10/96	(1)	0	0	0	0	0	0	0	0	0
Ash Handley	16/2/96	9(3)	6(3)	7	2	0	0	0	0	28	8
Jamie Jones-Buchanan	1/8/81	28(2)	27(1)	3	3	0	0	0	0	12	12
Josh Jordan-Roberts	26/8/98	(1)	(1)	0	0	0	0	0	0	0	0
Jimmy Keinhorst	14/7/90	12(4)	11(4)	4	4	0	0	0	0	16	16
Jordan Lilley	4/9/96	4(5)	3(4)	1	0	12	9	0	0	28	18
Danny McGuire	6/12/82	31(1)	27(1)	9	8	0	0	2	2	38	34
Joel Moon	20/5/88	31(1)	27(1)	20	15	0	0	0	0	80	60
Anthony Mullally	28/6/91	6(28)	6(25)	7	7	0	0	0	0	28	28
Harry Newman	19/2/00	1	1	0	0	0	0	0	0	0	0
Mikolaj Oledzki	8/11/98	(3)	(2)	1	0	0	0	0	0	4	0
Jack Ormondroyd	7/11/91	2(4)	2(3)	0	0	0	0	0	0	0	0
Matt Parcell	30/10/92	32(2)	29(2)	19	17	0	0	0	0	76	68
Brad Singleton	29/10/92	27(1)	23(1)	3	1	0	0	0	0	12	4
Cameron Smith	7/11/98	(1)	(1)	0	0	0	0	0	0	0	0
Alex Sutcliffe	21/1/99	1	1	0	0	0	0	0	0	0	0
Liam Sutcliffe	25/11/94	24(4)	22(4)	10	8	64	45	1	1	169	123
Jack Walker	8/8/99	10(2)	9(1)	5	2	0	0	0	0	20	8
Josh Walters	23/12/94	2(7)	1(7)	0	0	0	0	0	0	0	0
Stevie Ward	17/11/93	23(3)	20(3)	10	8	0	0	0	0	40	32
Kallum Watkins	12/3/91	32	29	13	12	60	51	0	0	172	150
Harvey Whiteley	26/9/98	(1)	(1)	0	0	0	0	0	0	0	0

'SL' totals include Super 8s, semi-final & Grand Final; 'All' totals also include Challenge Cup

Joel Moon

LEAGUE RECORD
P30-W20-D0-L10
(2nd, SL/Grand Final Winners, Champions)
F749, A623, Diff+126
40 points.

CHALLENGE CUP
Semi-Finalists

ATTENDANCES
Best - v Castleford (SL - 18,029)
Worst - v Doncaster (CC - 5,097)
Total (SL/S8s/SF only) - 233,167
Average (SL/S8s/SF only) - 14,573
(Down by 905 on 2016)

25 September 2016 - former Australian international forward Glenn Stewart signs from Catalans on two-year contract from 2017.

3 October 2016 - French international hooker Eloi Pelissier signs from Catalans on two-year contract from 2017.

4 October 2016 - threequarter Dave Thompson signs from Warrington on two-year contract until end November 2018.

5 October 2016 - back-row forward Atelea Vea signs from St Helens on two-year contract.

6 October 2016 - Hull KR prop James Green joins on two-year contract.

3 November 2016 - Wigan utility back Ryan Hampshire joins on two-year contract.

7 November 2016 - Ben Crooks joins from Castleford on one-year loan deal.

22 November 2016 - assistant coach Paul Cooke signs new contract to end of 2018.

19 January 2017 - Australian forward Lachlan Burr signs one-year contract with further two-year option after liquidation of Bradford Bulls.

7 February 2017 - Curtis Naughton joins from Hull FC on season-long loan.

10 February 2017 - 44-16 televised defeat at Castleford in round one.

17 February 2017 - 17-14 home defeat by Leeds after leading 8-0 in brought-forward round 11 game.

24 February 2017 - 24-16 home win over St Helens in round two.

3 March 2017 - 20-0 defeat at Wigan in 'Battle of the Borough'.

10 March 2017 - astounding 30-0 home win over Huddersfield.

16 March 2017 - Gareth Hock scores two tries in 22-8 home win over Warrington.

23 March 2017 - 28-24 defeat at Wakefield despite leading 24-12 at half-time.

1 April 2017 - 37-24 home defeat to win-less Widnes.

7 April 2017 - 37-26 home defeat to Catalans as Centurions slip out of top-eight.

14 April 2017 - 12-6 Good Friday defeat at high-flying Salford.

17 April 2017 - 24-10 home Easter Monday defeat by Hull FC is fifth successive league loss.

22 April 2017 - 23-10 home Challenge Cup defeat to runaway Championship leaders Hull KR.

28 April 2017 - 28-6 defeat at St Helens is seventh straight loss.

KEY DATES

6 May 2017 - despite coming back from 20-0 down to lead, 40-26 home defeat by Wakefield is eighth consecutive defeat.

13 May 2017 - Martyn Ridyard joins Huddersfield on month's loan.

18 May 2017 - St Helens centre Matty Fleming joins on one-month loan.

21 May 2017 - Adam Higson sent off after 55 minutes of 36-22 Magic Weekend defeat by Salford.

23 May 2017 - Adam Higson suspended for five matches for late, high tackle on Gareth O'Brien.

26 May 2017 - eight-game losing streak in Super League ended with 26-22 win at Hull FC.

29 May 2017 - 38-0 Bank Holiday Monday home defeat to leaders Castleford.

3 June 2017 - 22-14 defeat at Leeds.

8 June 2017 - 50-34 home win is first over Wigan since 1984.

12 June 2017 - NZ international Bryson Goodwin to join from South Sydney on two-year contract at end of season.

19 June 2017 - young Hull FC winger Nick Rawsthorne joins on one-month's loan.

20 June 2017 - Warrington centre Rhys Evans signs for 2018 on three-year deal.

21 June 2017 - Willie Tonga leaves by mutual agreement less than half way into two-year contract.

22 June 2017 - Martyn Ridyard loan spell at Huddersfield extended to end of season.

22 June 2017 - 36-10 defeat at Widnes sends Centurions to bottom of table.

23 June 2017 - Tonga international Samisoni Langi joins on contract until end of season with further club option after that.

25 June 2017 - Cronulla halfback Daniel Mortimer joins with immediate effect until end of 2019 season. Sam Hopkins signs new three-year contract to end of 2020.

1 July 2017 - last-second try means 40-36 defeat at Catalans. Ben Crooks suspended for one match for punching. Jamie Acton faces eight-match ban for 'other contrary behaviour'.

6 July 2017 - chairman Derek Beaumont fined £2,000 for comments after round 16 home defeat by Castleford.

7 July 2017 - 50-10 hammering at Warrington.

14 July 2017 - Mickey Higham makes 500th career appearance in 26-4 defeat at Huddersfield.

17 July 2017 - Greg Richards signs from St Helens with immediate effect to end of 2018 with option for further year.

21 July 2017 - 25-0 home win over Salford lifts Leigh into 11th placed finish.

5 August 2017 - 38-12 win at Featherstone opens Super 8s Qualifiers campaign.

12 August 2017 - late try means 20-16 home defeat to Hull KR.

19 August 2017 - Cory Paterson stars in 30-6 win at Catalans.

3 September 2017 - 24-8 home defeat by Widnes.

9 September 2017 - 32-30 defeat at Warrington means Million Pound Game involvement at best.

15 September 2017 - Mitch Brown scores hat-trick in 40-6 home win over Halifax.

30 September 2017 - 26-10 home defeat to Catalans in Million Pound Game.

2 October 2017 - yet-to-arrive Bryson Goodwin signed by Warrington for large transfer fee.

5 October 2017 - Ben Reynolds signs new three-year contract to end of 2020.

6 October 2017 - Jordan Thompson signs from Hull on two-year contract.

CLUB RECORDS
Highest score: 92-2 v Keighley, 30/4/86
Highest score against:
4-94 v Workington, 26/2/95
Record attendance:
31,326 v St Helens, 14/3/53 *(Hilton Park)*;
10,556 v Batley, 17/9/16
(Leigh Sports Village)

MATCH RECORDS
Tries: 6 Jack Wood v York, 4/10/47;
Neil Turley v Workington, 31/1/2001
Goals: 15 Mick Stacey v Doncaster, 28/3/76
Points: 42 Neil Turley v Chorley, 4/4/2004

SEASON RECORDS
Tries: 55 Neil Turley 2001
Goals: 187 Neil Turley 2004
Points: 468 Neil Turley 2004

CAREER RECORDS
Tries: 189 Mick Martyn 1954-67
Goals: 1,043 Jimmy Ledgard 1948-58
Points:
2,492 John Woods 1976-85; 1990-92
Appearances: 503 Albert Worrall 1920-38

LEIGH CENTURIONS

DATE	FIXTURE	RESULT	SCORERS	LGE	ATT
10/2/17	Castleford (a)	L44-16	t:Hampshire,Dawson,Tickle g:Ridyard(2)	12th	8,722
17/2/17	Leeds (h)	L14-17	t:Dawson,Brown,Crooks g:Reynolds	12th	6,692
24/2/17	St Helens (h)	W24-16	t:Vea,Hock,Acton,Higham g:Reynolds(4)	9th	9,012
3/3/17	Wigan (a)	L20-0		10th	15,699
10/3/17	Huddersfield (h)	W30-0	t:Higson,Acton,Hansen,Reynolds,Hopkins g:Reynolds(5)	8th	6,001
16/3/17	Warrington (h)	W22-8	t:Hock(2),Crooks,Higson g:Reynolds(3)	6th	7,011
23/3/17	Wakefield (a)	L28-24	t:Reynolds,Higham,Hopkins,Crooks g:Reynolds(4)	7th	4,592
1/4/17	Widnes (h)	L24-37	t:Tickle,Crooks(2),Hopkins g:Reynolds(4)	8th	6,196
7/4/17	Catalans Dragons (h)	L26-37	t:Naughton,Weston,McNally,Hopkins g:Reynolds(5)	9th	5,612
14/4/17	Salford (a)	L12-6	t:Brown g:Reynolds	9th	5,834
17/4/17	Hull FC (h)	L10-24	t:Hood,Hampshire g:Reynolds	10th	6,296
22/4/17	Hull KR (h) (CCR5)	L10-23	t:Burr,Naughton g:Reynolds	N/A	3,818
28/4/17	St Helens (a)	L28-6	t:Acton g:Reynolds	11th	10,268
6/5/17	Wakefield (h)	L26-40	t:Naughton(2),Acton,Dawson(2) g:Drinkwater(3)	11th	4,938
21/5/17	Salford (MW) ●	L22-36	t:Fleming,Brown,Crooks,Dawson g:Drinkwater(3)	11th	N/A
26/5/17	Hull FC (a)	W22-26	t:Dawson(2),Vea(2),Reynolds g:Reynolds(3)	11th	10,222
29/5/17	Castleford (h)	L0-38		11th	5,905
2/6/17	Leeds (a)	L22-14	t:Dawson(2),Paterson g:Drinkwater	12th	13,445
8/6/17	Wigan (h)	W50-34	t:Hampshire,Tickle,Burr,Brown,Hood(2),Paterson,Dawson g:Reynolds(9)	11th	7,080
22/6/17	Widnes (a)	L36-10	t:Rawsthorne,Vea g:Drinkwater	12th	5,604
1/7/17	Catalans Dragons (a)	L40-36	t:Dawson,Tickle,Reynolds(2),Hopkins(2) g:Reynolds(6)	12th	8,728
7/7/17	Warrington (a)	L50-10	t:Reynolds,Dawson g:Reynolds	12th	10,597
14/7/17	Huddersfield (a)	L26-4	t:Drinkwater	12th	5,535
21/7/17	Salford (h)	W25-0	t:McNally(2),Vea,Langi g:Drinkwater(4) fg:Drinkwater	11th	7,002
5/8/17	Featherstone (a) (S8-Q)	W12-38	t:Mortimer,McNally(2),Brown,Hood,Dawson,Drinkwater g:Drinkwater(5)	1st(S8-Q)	2,679
12/8/17	Hull KR (h) (S8-Q)	L16-20	t:Mortimer,Vea g:Drinkwater(4)	3rd(S8-Q)	5,335
19/8/17	Catalans Dragons (a) (S8-Q)	W6-30	t:Higson(2),Paterson(2),Drinkwater g:Reynolds(5)	4th(S8-Q)	6,632
3/9/17	Widnes (h) (S8-Q)	L8-24	t:Clare,Dawson	4th(S8-Q)	6,209
9/9/17	Warrington (a) (S8-Q)	L32-30	t:Clare,Hood,Maria,Vea,Burr g:Drinkwater(5)	5th(S8-Q)	9,787
15/9/17	Halifax (h) (S8-Q)	W40-6	t:Clare(2),Reynolds,Brown(3),Hansen,McNally g:Reynolds(2),Drinkwater(2)	5th(S8-Q)	4,341
22/9/17	London Broncos (a) (S8-Q)	W4-41	t:Fleming,Hansen,Hopkins,Clare,Reynolds,Drinkwater,Maria g:Reynolds(6) fg:Drinkwater	4th(S8-Q)	1,234
30/9/17	Catalans Dragons (h) (MPG)	L10-26	t:Dawson,Clare g:Reynolds	N/A	6,888

● *Played at St James' Park, Newcastle*

		APP		TRIES		GOALS		FG		PTS	
	D.O.B.	ALL	SL	ALL	SL	ALL	SL	ALL	SL	ALL	SL
Jamie Acton	4/4/92	12(4)	11(4)	4	4	0	0	0	0	16	16
Mitch Brown	7/11/87	26	21	8	4	0	0	0	0	32	16
Lachlan Burr	27/9/92	13(15)	5(14)	3	1	0	0	0	0	12	4
James Clare	13/4/91	5	0	6	0	0	0	0	0	24	0
Ben Crooks	15/6/93	23	19	6	6	0	0	0	0	24	24
Matty Dawson	2/10/90	31	23	15	12	0	0	0	0	60	48
Josh Drinkwater	15/6/92	28	19	4	1	28	12	2	1	74	29
Matty Fleming	13/1/96	9(1)	5	2	1	0	0	0	0	8	4
James Green	29/11/90	4(5)	4(5)	0	0	0	0	0	0	0	0
Ryan Hampshire	29/12/94	15(1)	12(1)	3	3	0	0	0	0	12	12
Harrison Hansen	26/10/85	24(6)	19(2)	3	1	0	0	0	0	12	4
Micky Higham	18/9/80	14(3)	11(1)	2	2	0	0	0	0	8	8
Adam Higson	19/5/87	15	13	4	2	0	0	0	0	16	8
Gareth Hock	5/9/83	12(1)	12(1)	3	3	0	0	0	0	12	12
Liam Hood	6/1/92	12(8)	8(5)	5	3	0	0	0	0	20	12
Sam Hopkins	17/2/90	3(23)	3(17)	7	6	0	0	0	0	28	24
Samisoni Langi	11/6/93	9	3	1	1	0	0	0	0	4	4
Antoni Maria	21/3/87	9(6)	2(6)	2	0	0	0	0	0	8	0
Gregg McNally	2/1/91	15	9	6	3	0	0	0	0	24	12
Daniel Mortimer	13/6/89	7	3	2	0	0	0	0	0	8	0
Curtis Naughton	25/2/95	6	5	4	3	0	0	0	0	16	12
Cory Paterson	14/7/87	20	13	4	2	0	0	0	0	16	8
Eloi Pelissier	18/6/91	4(20)	4(16)	0	0	0	0	0	0	0	0
Nick Rawsthorne	30/9/95	1	1	1	1	0	0	0	0	4	4
Ben Reynolds	15/1/94	22	16	8	6	63	48	0	0	158	120
Greg Richards	12/7/95	(9)	(1)	0	0	0	0	0	0	0	0
Martyn Ridyard	25/7/86	5	4	0	0	2	2	0	0	4	4
Glenn Stewart	11/1/84	20(4)	15	0	0	0	0	0	0	0	0
David Thompson	13/9/95	1	1	0	0	0	0	0	0	0	0
Danny Tickle	10/3/83	15(16)	10(13)	4	4	0	0	0	0	16	16
Willie Tonga	8/7/83	3	3	0	0	0	0	0	0	0	0
Atelea Vea	27/11/86	26(1)	19(1)	7	5	0	0	0	0	28	20
Dayne Weston	15/12/86	7(5)	6(5)	1	1	0	0	0	0	4	4

'SL' totals include regular season only; 'All' totals also include Super 8s (Qualifiers) & Challenge Cup

Matty Dawson

LEAGUE RECORD
SL: P23-W6-D0-L17 (11th)
F425, A615, Diff-190, 12 points.

S8-Q: P7-W4-D0-L3 (4th)
F203, A104, Diff+99, 8 points.
(Losers, Million Pound Game)

CHALLENGE CUP
Round Five

ATTENDANCES
Best - v St Helens (SL - 9,012)
Worst - v Hull KR (CC - 3,818)
Total (SL/S8s only) - 94,518
Average (SL/S8s only) - 6,301
(Up by 2,041 on 2016, Championship)

191

31 October 2016 - former player Ian Blease appointed new CEO.

3 November 2016 - Wigan prop Lee Mossop signs on unspecified deal.

8 November 2016 - Logan Tomkins extends contract to end of 2017.

5 January 2017 - former Hull KR centre Kris Welham joins on two-year contract after liquidation of Bradford Bulls.

15 January 2017 - Josh Jones breaks hand and Ben Murdoch-Masila suffers knee ligament damage in 44-18 pre-season win over Rochdale Hornets.

20 January 2017 - halfback Todd Carney signs for 2017 season.

29 January 2017 - 18-6 pre-season home win over Hull FC.

11 February 2017 - 26-16 round-one home defeat by Wigan.

16 February 2017 - Gareth O'Brien scores seven goals from as many attempts in 30-20 win at Huddersfield in brought-forward round 11 game. Justin Carney banned for two games for making contact with referee.

23 February 2017 - Red Devils fined £10,000, with £7,500 suspended and £3,000 fine added from previous suspended breach after crowd problems in 2016 at Huddersfield, after crowd trouble at Craven Park in Million Pound Game at Hull KR.

24 February 2017 - controversial late try means 20-14 round-two defeat at Leeds.

1 March 2017 - Gareth O'Brien signs new three-year contract to end of 2020.

4 March 2017 - Junior Sa'u scores two tries in 24-14 Saturday afternoon home win over Warrington.

12 March 2017 - Ben Murdoch-Masila drops ball in act of scoring last-second winner, meaning dramatic 24-22 defeat at Wakefield. Lama Tasi takes EGP one-game suspension for dangerous tackle.

19 March 2017 - late Gareth O'Brien field goal inflicts first defeat of season on Castleford, at home by 13-12.

23 March 2017 - coach Ian Watson signs new contract to end of 2020. Ben Murdoch-Masila signs three-year extension.

24 March 2017 - Todd Carney impresses on debut in 46-10 win at win-less Widnes.

30 March 2017 - Michael Dobson scores two tries in 22-14 home win over St Helens.

7 April 2017 - dominant 54-18 win at Hull FC is fourth in a row.

14 April 2017 - Gareth O'Brien scores try 12 minutes from time to secure 12-6 home Good Friday win over Leigh.

17 April 2017 - 38-6 Easter Monday defeat at Catalans ends five-match winning run.

KEY DATES

23 April 2017 - Justin Carney sent off for verbal abuse in 29-22 fifth round home Challenge Cup win over Toronto.

23 April 2017 - halfback Josh Wood signs new two-year contract.

26 April 2017 - Lee Mossop signs new three-year contract.

28 April 2017 - Josh Jones signs new two-year contract extension.

30 April 2017 - Ben Murdoch-Masila scores two tries in impressive 30-10 victory over Widnes.

2 May 2017 - Justin Carney banned for eight games after pleading guilty to racial abuse in Cup win over Toronto.

5 May 2017 - 31-16 victory is first win at Wigan in 20 years.

12 May 2017 - Challenge Cup progress into quarter-finals with 24-14 home victory over Hull KR.

18 May 2017 - Justin Carney joins Hull KR with immediate effect.

21 May 2017 - Ben Murdoch-Masila and Greg Johnson both score twice as 36-22 Magic Weekend win over Leigh moves Red Devils into second spot.

26 May 2017 - 50-12 home win over Catalans as free admission offered in exchange for donation to fund set up to help victims of Manchester Arena bomb attack of previous Monday.

29 May 2017 - winger Niall Evalds scores hat-trick in 38-12 win at Warrington.

4 June 2017 - seven-match winning run ends with 34-24 home defeat by Wakefield.

5 June 2017 - Mark Flanagan signs new contract to end of 2019.

7 June 2017 - Logan Tomkins and Greg Johnson sign new unspecified contracts.

15 June 2017 - 30-6 home win over Wakefield secures first Challenge Cup semi-final in 19 years.

23 June 2017 - Matty Smith field goal on full-time means 25-24 defeat at St Helens after leading 24-8 with eight minutes to go.

26 June 2017 - Robert Lui signs new two-year contract. Niall Evalds signs new unspecified long-term contract.

2 July 2017 - 36-20 home win over Huddersfield moves Red Devils into second spot.

9 July 2017 - 50-24 home defeat to Leeds.

10 July 2017 - winger Manu Vatuvei signs from NZ Warriors with immediate effect until end of 2018 season.

21 July 2017 - 25-0 defeat at Leigh sees Red Devils finish in fourth spot.

30 July 2017 - 27-14 Challenge Cup semi-final defeat to Wigan at Halliwell Jones Stadium, Warrington.

2 August 2017 - Mark Flanagan, shoulder, and Lama Tasi, knee, ruled out for season.

4 August 2017 - 32-18 defeat at Hull FC in first game of Super 8s.

11 August 2017 - 23-4 defeat at Castleford.

18 August 2017 - Michael Dobson suffers thumb injury in 42-6 defeat at Wigan.

31 August 2017 - Michael Dobson announces he is to retire and return to Australia at end of season.

1 September 2017 - 43-18 home defeat by Wakefield.

6 September 2017 - Albanian prop Olsi Krasniqi to leave at end of season and signs for Toronto.

9 September 2017 - eight-match losing run ends with 52-14 home win over Huddersfield.

16 September 2017 - play-off chances end with 44-2 defeat at Leeds.

16 September 2017 - Todd Carney to leave club at end of season.

3 October 2017 - forward Gavin Bennion signs from Rochdale.

CLUB RECORDS

Highest score:
100-12 v Gateshead, 23/3/2003
Highest score against:
16-96 v Bradford, 25/6/2000
Record attendance:
26,470 v Warrington, 13/2/37
(The Willows)
7,102 v Wakefield, 16/2/2014
(AJ Bell Stadium)

MATCH RECORDS

Tries:
6 Frank Miles v Lees, 5/3/1898
Ernest Bone v Goole, 29/3/1902
Jack Hilton v Leigh, 7/10/39
Goals:
14 Steve Blakeley v Gateshead, 23/3/2003
Points:
39 Jim Lomas v Liverpool City, 2/2/1907

SEASON RECORDS

Tries: 46 Keith Fielding 1973-74
Goals: 221 David Watkins 1972-73
Points: 493 David Watkins 1972-73

CAREER RECORDS

Tries: 297 Maurice Richards 1969-83
Goals: 1,241 David Watkins 1967-79
Points: 2,907 David Watkins 1967-79
Appearances:
498 Maurice Richards 1969-83

SALFORD RED DEVILS

DATE	FIXTURE	RESULT	SCORERS	LGE	ATT
11/2/17	Wigan (h)	L16-26	t:Brining,Sa'u,Dobson g:O'Brien(2)	10th	6,527
16/2/17	Huddersfield (a)	W20-30	t:Sa'u,O'Brien(2),Jones g:O'Brien(7)	8th	6,017
24/2/17	Leeds (a)	L20-14	t:O'Brien,Welham,Tomkins g:O'Brien	7th	14,575
4/3/17	Warrington (h)	W24-14	t:Sa'u(2),Griffin,Brining g:O'Brien(4)	5th	5,492
12/3/17	Wakefield (a)	L24-22	t:Murdoch-Masila,Welham,Johnson,Griffin g:O'Brien(3)	6th	4,964
19/3/17	Castleford (h)	W13-12	t:Murdoch-Masila(2) g:O'Brien(2) fg:O'Brien	5th	5,221
24/3/17	Widnes (a)	W10-46	t:Tasi,Johnson,Griffin,Murdoch-Masila,Welham,J Carney,Dobson,Lui, O'Brien g:O'Brien(2),Dobson(3)	5th	5,565
30/3/17	St Helens (h)	W22-14	t:Kopczak,Dobson(2) g:Dobson(4),O'Brien	4th	3,686
7/4/17	Hull FC (a)	W18-54	t:Lui,Johnson(2),Kopczak(2),Sa'u,J Carney,Dobson,Griffin, Murdoch-Masila g:Dobson(3),O'Brien(4)	4th	11,016
14/4/17	Leigh (h)	W12-6	t:Welham,O'Brien g:O'Brien,Dobson	2nd	5,834
17/4/17	Catalans Dragons (a)	L38-6	t:J Carney g:O'Brien	3rd	10,804
23/4/17	Toronto (h) (CCR5)	W29-22	t:Welham,Johnson(2),Dobson,O'Brien g:Dobson(3),O'Brien fg:O'Brien	N/A	1,318
30/4/17	Widnes (h)	W30-10	t:Murdoch-Masila(2),Johnson,Evalds,Bibby g:Dobson(5)	3rd	3,127
5/5/17	Wigan (h)	W16-31	t:Welham,Evalds(2),Murdoch-Masila,Johnson g:Dobson(4),O'Brien fg:O'Brien	3rd	11,861
12/5/17	Hull KR (h) (CCR6)	W24-14	t:Lannon,Kopczak,Brining,Murdoch-Masila g:Dobson(4)	N/A	3,100
21/5/17	Leigh (MW) ●	W22-36	t:Murdoch-Masila(2),Welham,Johnson(2),Evalds g:O'Brien,Dobson(5)	2nd	N/A
26/5/17	Catalans Dragons (h)	W50-12	t:O'Brien,Jones,Welham,Evalds,Lannon,Brining,Lui,Krasniqi,Flanagan g:Dobson(7)	2nd	4,957
29/5/17	Warrington (a)	W12-38	t:Bibby,Evalds(3),Sa'u(2),Brining g:O'Brien(5)	2nd	10,684
4/6/17	Wakefield (h)	L24-34	t:Bibby(2),Kopczak,Tasi g:Dobson(4)	2nd	3,277
9/6/17	Hull FC (h)	L10-34	t:Evalds,Hauraki g:Dobson	2nd	2,678
15/6/17	Wakefield (h) (CCQF)	W30-6	t:Lannon,Murdoch-Masila,Evalds,Johnson,Kopczak g:Dobson(5)	N/A	2,808
23/6/17	St Helens (a)	L25-24	t:Evalds(2),Johnson,Lui g:T Carney(4)	3rd	10,001
2/7/17	Huddersfield (h)	W36-20	t:Sa'u(2),Lui,Welham,O'Brien,Johnson,Murdoch-Masila g:Dobson(4)	2nd	3,718
9/7/17	Leeds (h)	L24-50	t:Wood,Murdoch-Masila(2),Dobson g:Dobson(4)	3rd	5,056
14/7/17	Castleford (a)	L38-14	t:O'Brien,Welham,Bibby g:Dobson	3rd	7,094
21/7/17	Leigh (a)	L25-0		4th	7,002
30/7/17	Wigan (CCSF) ●●	L14-27	t:Johnson,McCarthy g:Dobson(3)	N/A	10,796
4/8/17	Hull FC (a) (S8)	L32-18	t:Vatuvei(2),Evalds,Lui g:Lui	5th	10,239
11/8/17	Castleford (h) (S8)	L4-23	t:Vatuvei	6th	2,811
18/8/17	Wigan (a) (S8)	L42-6	t:Evalds g:O'Brien	7th	11,229
1/9/17	Wakefield (h) (S8)	L18-43	t:Kopczak,Johnson,McCarthy g:T Carney(3)	7th	2,489
9/9/17	Huddersfield (h) (S8)	W52-14	t:Welham(2),McCarthy,Vatuvei(2),Evalds,Bibby,Murdoch-Masila,Jones g:O'Brien(8)	7th	1,405
15/9/17	Leeds (a) (S8)	L44-2	g:O'Brien	7th	13,094
21/9/17	St Helens (h) (S8)	L4-30	t:Evalds	7th	2,840

● *Played at St James' Park, Newcastle*
●● *Played at Halliwell Jones Stadium, Warrington*

APP TRIES GOALS FG PTS

	D.O.B.	ALL	SL	ALL	SL	ALL	SL	ALL	SL	ALL	SL
Jake Bibby	17/6/96	17	16	6	6	0	0	0	0	24	24
Kriss Brining	16/11/93	2(23)	2(20)	5	4	0	0	0	0	20	16
Justin Carney	16/6/88	10	9	3	3	0	0	0	0	12	12
Todd Carney	2/6/86	10(6)	9(5)	0	0	7	7	0	0	14	14
Michael Dobson	29/5/86	26	22	7	6	61	46	0	0	150	116
Niall Evalds	26/8/93	23	20	16	15	0	0	0	0	64	60
Mark Flanagan	4/12/87	17(2)	15(2)	1	1	0	0	0	0	4	4
George Griffin	26/6/92	12(13)	11(11)	4	4	0	0	0	0	16	16
James Hasson	1/5/92	4(1)	4(1)	0	0	0	0	0	0	0	0
Weller Hauraki	18/2/85	15(4)	14(2)	1	1	0	0	0	0	4	4
Greg Johnson	20/2/90	28	24	15	11	0	0	0	0	60	44
Josh Jones	12/5/93	25(3)	22(3)	3	3	0	0	0	0	12	12
Craig Kopczak	20/12/86	13(19)	11(17)	7	5	0	0	0	0	28	20
Olsi Krasniqi	26/6/92	9(18)	8(16)	1	1	0	0	0	0	4	4
Ryan Lannon	11/1/96	9(10)	7(10)	3	1	0	0	0	0	12	4
Robert Lui	23/2/90	29(3)	26(3)	6	6	1	1	0	0	26	26
Tyrone McCarthy	21/4/88	6(1)	6	3	2	0	0	0	0	12	8
Lee Mossop	17/1/89	11	9	0	0	0	0	0	0	0	0
Ben Murdoch-Masila	7/2/91	27(1)	23(1)	16	14	0	0	0	0	64	56
Daniel Murray	21/3/96	3(4)	3(4)	0	0	0	0	0	0	0	0
Gareth O'Brien	31/10/91	24(5)	23(3)	9	8	46	45	3	2	131	124
Junior Sa'u	18/4/87	24	21	9	9	0	0	0	0	36	36
Lama Tasi	3/5/90	21(5)	17(5)	2	2	0	0	0	0	8	8
Logan Tomkins	1/8/91	29	26	1	1	0	0	0	0	4	4
Manu Vatuvei	4/3/86	8	7	5	5	0	0	0	0	20	20
Adam Walne	3/10/90	8(9)	8(8)	0	0	0	0	0	0	0	0
Jordan Walne	28/12/92	(4)	(4)	0	0	0	0	0	0	0	0
Kris Welham	12/5/87	29	25	12	11	0	0	0	0	48	44
Josh Wood	15/11/95	3(4)	2(4)	1	1	0	0	0	0	4	4

'SL' totals include Super 8s; 'All' totals also include Challenge Cup

Ben Murdoch-Masila

LEAGUE RECORD
P30-W14-D0-L16
(7th, SL)
F680, A728, Diff-48
28 points.

CHALLENGE CUP
Semi-Finalists

ATTENDANCES
Best - v Wigan (SL - 6,527)
Worst - v Toronto (CC - 1,318)
Total (SL/S8s only) - 59,118
Average (SL/S8s only) - 3,941
(Up by 713 on 2016)

19 October 2016 - utility Tommy Lee joins from Salford on two-year contract.

27 October 2016 - Luke Walsh leaves for Catalans.

10 November 2016 - Jonah Cunningham, son of coach Keiron, one of seven academy players handed full-time contracts.

14 November 2016 - Jon Wilkin signs new two-year deal. Kyle Amor pens new three-year contract.

22 January 2017 - Matty Smith breaks leg in 16-0 home pre-season win over Widnes. Manase Manuokafoa banned for two games.

29 January 2017 - 22-6 home defeat to Castleford in last pre-season game.

9 February 2017 - round-one 6-4 home win over Leeds.

20 February 2017 - second-rower Joe Greenwood moves to Gold Coast Titans in swap deal for Zeb Taia, signed to end of 2019.

24 February 2017 - 24-16 defeat at Leigh in round two.

3 March 2017 - late Jacob Miller penalty try means 16-12 home defeat to Wakefield.

10 March 2017 - hard-fought 24-14 defeat at Hull FC is third in a row. Alex Walmsley avoids suspension with EGP for light contact with knees that conceded eight-point try.

18 March 2017 - late Jack Owens try ends three-match losing run with 28-24 win at Catalans.

24 March 2017 - Matty Smith makes second club debut and masterminds 31-6 home win over Warrington.

30 March 2017 - 22-14 defeat at Salford.

5 April 2017 - winger Adam Swift signs new two-year contract.

7 April 2017 - 14-all home draw with struggling Huddersfield.

10 April 2017 - coach Keiron Cunningham sacked.

13 April 2017 - Mark Percival signs new contract until end of 2021 season.

14 April 2017 - Kyle Amor sent of after 13 minutes of 29-18 Good Friday defeat at Wigan. Welsh youngster Regan Grace scores on debut.

17 April 2017 - 26-22 home Easter Monday home win over league leaders Castleford.

21 April 2017 - 16-14 defeat at bottom club Widnes.

25 April 2017 - Kyle Amor gets sending off sufficient for high tackle on Wigan winger Liam Marshall.

28 April 2017 - 28-6 home win over Leigh.

KEY DATES

3 May 2017 - Justin Holbrook, assistant at Sydney Roosters appointed new head coach on two-and-a-half-year contract.

5 May 2017 - despite leading 14-0 at 25 minutes, 40-18 defeat at Warrington.

13 May 2017 - 53-10 humiliation in sixth round of Challenge Cup at Castleford.

18 May 2017 - centre Matty Fleming joins Leigh on one-month loan.

20 May 2017 - new coach Justin Holbrook arrives in time for 45-0 hammering of Hull FC at Magic Weekend.

24 May 2017 - Ben Barba, currently suspended for 12 games, signs on two-and-a-half year deal after fruitless spell in French rugby union.

25 May 2017 - prop Adam Walker joins Wakefield with immediate effect.

25 May 2017 - two tries in final quarter from centre Mark Percival seals dramatic 22-19 home win over Wigan.

30 May 2017 - rising star Regan Grace signs new two-and-a-half year contract to end of 2019.

4 June 2017 - late 16-12 defeat at Castleford.

10 June 2017 - Mark Percival scores 500th Saints point in 26-10 home win over Widnes.

16 June 2017 - 24-16 defeat at Huddersfield.

23 June 2017 - dual registration announced with Sheffield Eagles.

23 June 2017 - Matty Smith field goal after final hooter seals 25-24 home comeback win over Salford. Mark Percival banned for one game for bouncing ball that hits referee.

26 June 2017 - Jonny Lomax signs new contract to end of 2019 season.

28 June 2017 - tribunal decides Ben Barba NRL 12-match ban stands, ruling him out until last week in August.

29 June 2017 - Matty Smith suffers eye injury minutes into 24-22 defeat at Leeds. Jon Wilkin takes one match on EGP for crusher tackle.

7 July 2017 - Mark Percival scores 14 points in 19-12 home win over Hull FC as top-eight spot is secured.

16 July 2017 - Mark Percival scores 22 points in 46-28 home win over Catalans.

17 July 2017 - prop Greg Richards moves to Leigh.

23 July 2017 - 41-16 win at Wakefield in last round of regular season.

3 August 2017 - 26-12 win in Super 8s opener inflicts first home defeat of year on leaders Castleford

11 August 2017 - 50-metre Marc Sneyd penalty means 8-6 home defeat to Hull FC.

14 August 2017 - 19-year-old back-rower James Bentley signs from Bradford on three-year contract.

18 August 2017 - 16-14 defeat at Leeds.

1 September 2017 - marquee signing Ben Barba scores try on debut in 26-16 home defeat by Wigan.

6 September 2017 - Tommy Makinson signs new contract to end of 2021.

7 September 2017 - Luke Thompson signs new contract to end of 2020.

7 September 2017 - Matty Smith dropped as last-gasp Jonny Lomax try secures 18-16 win at Wakefield to keep play-off hopes alive.

15 September 2017 - 40-16 home win over Huddersfield moves Saints into fourth.

21 September 2017 - 30-4 win at Salford secures semi-final spot.

28 September 2017 - 23-22 golden-point semi-final defeat at Castleford.

3 October 2017 - halfback Danny Richardson signs new three-year contract to end of 2020 with option for further year.

CLUB RECORDS
Highest score: 112-0 v Carlisle, 14/9/86 **Highest score against:** 6-78 v Warrington, 12/4/1909 **Record attendance:** 35,695 v Wigan, 26/12/49 *(Knowsley Road)* 17,980 v Wigan, 6/4/2012 v Wigan, 18/4/2014 v South Sydney, 22/2/2015 *(Langtree Park)*
MATCH RECORDS
Tries: 6 Alf Ellaby v Barrow, 5/3/32 Steve Llewellyn v Castleford, 3/3/56 Steve Llewellyn v Liverpool, 20/8/56 Tom van Vollenhoven v Wakefield, 21/12/57 Tom van Vollenhoven v Blackpool, 23/4/62 Frank Myler v Maryport, 1/9/69 Shane Cooper v Hull, 17/2/88 **Goals:** 16 Paul Loughlin v Carlisle, 14/9/86 **Points:** 40 Paul Loughlin v Carlisle, 14/9/86
SEASON RECORDS
Tries: 62 Tom van Vollenhoven 1958-59 **Goals:** 214 Kel Coslett 1971-72 **Points:** 452 Kel Coslett 1971-72
CAREER RECORDS
Tries: 392 Tom van Vollenhoven 1957-68 **Goals:** 1,639 Kel Coslett 1962-76 **Points:** 3,413 Kel Coslett 1962-76 **Appearances:** 531 Kel Coslett 1962-76

ST HELENS

DATE	FIXTURE	RESULT	SCORERS	LGE	ATT
9/2/17	Leeds (h)	W6-4	t:Fages g:Percival	6th	12,208
24/2/17	Leigh (a)	L24-16	t:Swift,Roby,Walmsley g:Percival(2)	8th	9,012
3/3/17	Wakefield (h)	L12-16	t:Morgan,Percival(2)	9th	9,040
10/3/17	Hull FC (a)	L24-14	t:Peyroux,Percival g:Percival(3)	10th	11,587
18/3/17	Catalans Dragons (a)	W24-28	t:Swift,Percival,Morgan,Walker,Owens g:Percival(4)	9th	8,158
24/3/17	Warrington (h)	W31-6	t:Taia,Owens,Swift(2),Walmsley g:Percival(5) fg:Smith	6th	11,598
30/3/17	Salford (a)	L22-14	t:Walmsley,Morgan,Lomax g:Percival	7th	3,686
7/4/17	Huddersfield (h)	D14-14	t:Fages(2),Swift g:Percival	7th	9,080
14/4/17	Wigan (a)	L29-18	t:Knowles,Grace,Makinson g:Percival(3)	8th	23,390
17/4/17	Castleford (h)	W26-22	t:Fleming,Douglas,Percival,Grace g:Percival(5)	8th	12,499
21/4/17	Widnes (a)	L16-14	t:Fages,Smith g:Percival(3)	8th	6,171
28/4/17	Leigh (h)	W28-6	t:Percival,Fages,Morgan,Grace,Walmsley g:Percival(4)	7th	10,268
5/5/17	Warrington (a)	L40-18	t:Swift,Morgan,Peyroux g:Makinson(3)	7th	11,681
13/5/17	Castleford (a) (CCR6)	L53-10	t:Morgan,Douglas g:Percival	N/A	5,216
20/5/17	Hull FC (MW) ●	W0-45	t:Walmsley(2),Morgan,Knowles,McCarthy-Scarsbrook,Makinson,Grace(2) g:Percival(6) fg:Smith	7th	N/A
25/5/17	Wigan (h)	W22-19	t:Morgan,Taia,Percival(2) g:Percival(3)	7th	13,138
4/6/17	Castleford (a)	L16-12	t:Percival,McCarthy-Scarsbrook g:Makinson(2)	7th	8,515
9/6/17	Widnes (h)	W26-10	t:Percival,Grace,Walmsley,Morgan,Fages g:Percival(3)	6th	10,474
16/6/17	Huddersfield (a)	L24-16	t:Thompson,Percival,Amor g:Percival(2)	6th	5,660
23/6/17	Salford (h)	W25-24	t:Smith,Roby,Grace,Lomax g:Percival(4) fg:Smith	6th	10,001
29/6/17	Leeds (a)	L24-22	t:Swift,Makinson,Roby,Walmsley g:Makinson(3)	6th	13,262
7/7/17	Hull FC (h)	W19-12	t:Roby,Percival(2) g:Percival(3) fg:Richardson	6th	9,910
16/7/17	Catalans Dragons (h)	W46-28	t:Fages,Walmsley,McCarthy-Scarsbrook,Lomax,Percival,Thompson,Morgan g:Percival(9)	6th	10,024
23/7/17	Wakefield (a)	W16-41	t:Richardson,Roby,Makinson,Grace,McCarthy-Scarsbrook,Taia g:Percival(8) fg:Richardson	6th	5,820
3/8/17	Castleford (a) (S8)	W12-26	t:Taia,Roby(2),Lomax g:Percival(5)	4th	6,849
11/8/17	Hull FC (h) (S8)	L6-8	t:Grace g:Percival	5th	10,338
18/8/17	Leeds (a) (S8)	L16-14	t:Lomax,Richardson g:Percival(3)	5th	16,326
1/9/17	Wigan (h) (S8)	L16-26	t:Barba,Taia,Makinson g:Percival(2)	6th	15,248
7/9/17	Wakefield (a) (S8)	W16-18	t:McCarthy-Scarsbrook,Fages,Lomax g:Percival(3)	6th	4,837
15/9/17	Huddersfield (h) (S8)	W40-16	t:Lomax(2),Grace,Percival,Barba,Morgan,McCarthy-Scarsbrook g:Percival(6)	4th	9,419
21/9/17	Salford (a) (S8)	W4-30	t:Percival,Walmsley(2),Taia,Barba g:Percival(5)	4th	2,840
28/9/17	Castleford (a) (SF)	L23-22 *(aet)*	t:Grace,Knowles,Makinson,Percival,Morgan g:Percival	N/A	11,235

● *Played at St James' Park, Newcastle*

		APP		TRIES		GOALS		FG		PTS	
	D.O.B.	ALL	SL	ALL	SL	ALL	SL	ALL	SL	ALL	SL
Kyle Amor	26/5/87	15(11)	15(10)	1	1	0	0	0	0	4	4
Ricky Bailey	25/4/97	1	1	0	0	0	0	0	0	0	0
Ben Barba	13/6/89	5	5	3	3	0	0	0	0	12	12
Luke Douglas	12/5/86	18(9)	17(9)	2	1	0	0	0	0	8	4
Theo Fages	23/8/94	28(2)	27(2)	8	8	0	0	0	0	32	32
Matty Fleming	13/1/96	2	2	1	1	0	0	0	0	4	4
Regan Grace	12/12/96	24	23	11	11	0	0	0	0	44	44
Joe Greenwood	2/4/93	1		0		0		0		0	
Morgan Knowles	5/11/96	16(14)	15(14)	3	3	0	0	0	0	12	12
Tommy Lee	1/2/88	9(9)	9(9)	0	0	0	0	0	0	0	0
Matty Lees	4/2/98	(1)	(1)	0	0	0	0	0	0	0	0
Jonny Lomax	4/9/90	19	19	8	8	0	0	0	0	32	32
Tom Makinson	10/10/91	31	30	6	6	8	8	0	0	40	40
Louie McCarthy-Scarsbrook	14/1/86	9(21)	9(20)	6	6	0	0	0	0	24	24
Ryan Morgan	4/5/90	28	27	12	11	0	0	0	0	48	44
Jack Owens	3/6/94	5	5	2	2	0	0	0	0	8	8
Mark Percival	29/5/94	30	29	17	17	97	96	0	0	262	260
Dominique Peyroux	21/1/89	9(15)	9(15)	2	2	0	0	0	0	8	8
Greg Richards	12/7/95	1(2)	1(1)	0	0	0	0	0	0	0	0
Danny Richardson	2/9/96	11(2)	11(2)	2	2	0	0	2	2	10	10
James Roby	22/11/85	23(4)	22(4)	7	7	0	0	0	0	28	28
Matty Smith	23/7/87	19(3)	18(3)	2	2	0	0	3	3	11	11
Jake Spedding	26/9/96	1	1	0	0	0	0	0	0	0	0
Adam Swift	20/2/93	18	17	7	7	0	0	0	0	28	28
Zeb Taia	11/10/84	29(1)	28(1)	6	6	0	0	0	0	24	24
Luke Thompson	27/4/95	18(9)	17(9)	2	2	0	0	0	0	8	8
Adam Walker	20/2/91	(9)	(9)	1	1	0	0	0	0	4	4
Alex Walmsley	10/4/90	15(16)	14(16)	11	11	0	0	0	0	44	44
Jon Wilkin	11/1/83	29(1)	29	0	0	0	0	0	0	0	0

'SL' totals include Super 8s & semi-final; 'All' totals also include Challenge Cup

Mark Percival

LEAGUE RECORD
P30-W16-D1-L13
(4th, SL/Semi-Finalists)
F663, A518, Diff+145
33 points.

CHALLENGE CUP
Round Six

ATTENDANCES
Best - v Wigan (S8 - 15,248)
Worst - v Wakefield (SL - 9,040)
Total (SL/S8s only) - 153,245
Average (SL/S8s only) - 10,946
(Up by 235 on 2016)

30 October 2016 - prop David Fifita takes up second-year contract option.

6 November 2016 - halfback Kyle Wood returns from Huddersfield on two-year deal.

18 November 2016 - prop Mickael Simon leaves to re-join Catalans.

3 December 2016 - prop Craig Huby signs from Huddersfield on three-year deal.

16 December 2016 - homesick Anthony Tupou released half way through two-year contract.

26 December 2016 - 30-6 win at Leeds in Wetherby Whaler Challenge.

9 January 2017 - Scott Moore released by mutual consent.

18 January 2017 - prop Anthony England, who joined Trinity on two-year deal at end of 2015, extends contract to end of 2019 season with mutual option for another year.

12 February 2017 - 12-8 round-one home defeat by Hull FC in sleet and mud.

24 February 2017 - 24-16 round-two defeat at Huddersfield after leading 16-6 at half-time.

3 March 2017 - late Jacob Miller penalty try earns 16-12 win at St Helens. Mason Caton-Brown scores impressive winger's try on debut.

4 March 2017 - Reece Lyne signs two-year contract extension to end of 2019. Dean Hadley joins one month's loan from Hull FC.

12 March 2017 - late Reece Lyne try and touchline Sam Williams conversion seals dramatic 24-22 home win over Salford. Lyne tears medial ligaments in last second and Anthony England undergoes foot surgery.

17 March 2017 - Tom Johnstone scores two tries in 38-14 defeat at Leeds. Danny Kirmond sin-binned and subsequently fined for late tackle on Rob Burrow.

23 March 2017 - 28-24 home win over Leigh despite trailing 24-12 at half-time.

28 March 2017 - coach Chris Chester signs two-year contract extension to end of 2019.

28 March 2017 - young fullback Luke Hooley signs two-and-a half year contract.

1 April 2017 - Ben Jones-Bishop scores hat-trick in 38-18 win at Catalans.

2 April 2017 - Dean Hadley loan deal extended by a month.

7 April 2017 - commanding 30-4 home win over Widnes.

14 April 2017 - 42-24 Good Friday defeat at Castleford ends three-match winning run.

17 April 2017 - late 16-10 Easter Monday defeat at home to Wigan.

19 April 2017 - 17-year-old winger Lee Kershaw signs first professional contract.

22 April 2017 - last-minute 22-20 defeat at Warrington.

KEY DATES

24 April 2017 - halfback Liam Finn signs contract extension to end of 2018.

30 April 2017 - Tom Johnstone suffers season-ending knee injury as Mason Caton-Brown scores hat-trick in 30-10 home win over Catalans.

6 May 2017 - 40-26 win at Leigh after giving up 20-0 first-half lead.

12 May 2017 - Mason Caton-Brown scores hat-trick in 54-6 sixth round Challenge Cup win at Dewsbury.

19 May 2017 - Jacob Miller signs new two-year contract; prop David Fifita signs new two year contract to end of 2019 with option of additional year.

20 May 2017 - 34-12 Magic Weekend win over Widnes.

25 May 2017 - prop Adam Walker joins two-and-a-half year deal from St Helens.

26 May 2017 - Ben Jones-Bishop scores late try and Sam Williams kicks touchline goal to secure 28-26 home win over Huddersfield.

26 May 2017 - centre Joe Arundel signs new two-year deal until end of 2019.

29 May 2017 - Bill Tupou scores hat-trick as 20-0 deficit at Wigan ends in 42-30 win. Adam Walker suffers knee injury on debut; Jacob Miller breaks leg and Tinirau Arona tears hamstring.

4 June 2017 - Mason Caton-Brown scores hat-trick as winning run extended to seven games with 34-24 win at Salford.

5 June 2017 - Ben Jones-Bishop turns down interest from Catalans and Hull FC to sign new three-year contract to end of 2020.

10 June 2017 - seven-match winning run ends with 18-16 home defeat by Leeds.

15 June 2017 - 30-6 defeat at Salford means Challenge Cup quarter-final exit.

24 June 2017 - 40-18 defeat at Hull FC after leading 12-10 at half-time.

1 July 2017 - 26-12 home win over Warrington mathematically secures top-eight spot.

4 July 2017 - Reece Lyne banned for two games for dangerous contact and loses appeal.

6 July 2017 - late field goal means 25-24 home defeat to leaders Castleford.

14 July 2017 - Mason Caton-Brown and Bill Tupou each score two tries in 36-8 win at Widnes.

15 July 2017 - prop James Hasson joins from Salford to end of season.

23 July 2017 - 41-16 home defeat to St Helens in last round of regular season drops Trinity into fifth.

23 July 2017 - Newcastle Knights hooker Tyler Randell joins on two-year contract.

4 August 2017 - prop Adam Walker suspended after testing positive for cocaine.

4 August 2017 - 36-6 defeat at Huddersfield in Super 8s opener.

8 August 2017 - football manager John Kear signs new one-year contract.

8 August 2017 - young backrower Jordan Crowther signs one-year extension to end of 2018.

11 August 2017 - Jacob Miller returns from broken leg injury in 38-6 home win over Leeds.

13 August 2017 - prop Jordan Baldwinson signs from Leeds on two-year contract to end of 2018.

17 August 2017 - Bill Tupou signs new three-year deal to end of 2020.

17 August 2017 - 45-20 defeat at Castleford.

2 September 2017 - Tyler Randell scores two tries on debut in 43-18 win at Salford.

6 September 2017 - Chris Annakin signs new contract to end of 2019.

7 September 2017 - late try consigns Trinity to 18-16 home defeat by St Helens.

15 September 2017 - last second Liam Finn field-goal attempt shaves outside of post in 19-18 defeat at Hull FC.

20 September 2017 - backrower Justin Horo signs from Catalans on two-year deal.

21 September 2017 - new council backed plan to build new stadium at Belle Vue unveiled.

23 September 2017 - 32-0 home win over Wigan ends season.

CLUB RECORDS

Highest score:
90-12 v Highfield, 27/10/92
Highest score against:
0-86 v Castleford, 17/4/95
Record attendance:
30,676 v Huddersfield, 26/2/21

MATCH RECORDS

Tries:
7 Fred Smith v Keighley, 25/4/59
Keith Slater v Hunslet, 6/2/71
Goals:
13 Mark Conway v Highfield, 27/10/92
Points:
36 Jamie Rooney v Chorley, 27/2/2004

SEASON RECORDS

Tries: 38 Fred Smith 1959-60
David Smith 1973-74
Goals: 163 Neil Fox 1961-62
Points: 407 Neil Fox 1961-62

CAREER RECORDS

Tries: 272 Neil Fox 1956-74
Goals: 1,836 Neil Fox 1956-74
Points: 4,488 Neil Fox 1956-74
Appearances:
605 Harry Wilkinson 1930-49

WAKEFIELD TRINITY

DATE	FIXTURE	RESULT	SCORERS	LGE	ATT
12/2/17	Hull FC (h)	L8-12	t:Grix g:Williams(2)	8th	7,027
24/2/17	Huddersfield (a)	L24-16	t:Finn,Jones-Bishop(2) g:Williams(2)	10th	6,337
3/3/17	St Helens (a)	W12-16	t:Caton-Brown,Miller g:Williams(4)	8th	9,040
12/3/17	Salford (h)	W24-22	t:Lyne(2),Miller,Tupou g:Williams(4)	7th	4,964
17/3/17	Leeds (a)	L38-14	t:Johnstone(2),Fifita g:Williams	10th	14,411
23/3/17	Leigh (h)	W28-24	t:Arundel,Grix,Johnstone,Miller,Jones-Bishop g:Williams(4)	8th	4,592
1/4/17	Catalans Dragons (a)	W18-38	t:Jones-Bishop(3),Johnstone(2),Arundel,Ashurst g:Williams(5)	6th	7,931
7/4/17	Widnes (h)	W30-4	t:Tupou,Johnstone,Hadley(2),Grix,Huby g:Finn(3)	5th	4,214
14/4/17	Castleford (a)	L42-24	t:Fifita(2),Tupou,Jones-Bishop g:Williams(3),Finn	6th	10,349
17/4/17	Wigan (h)	L10-16	t:Grix,Jones-Bishop g:Finn	7th	4,640
22/4/17	Warrington (a)	L22-20	t:Gibson,Caton-Brown,Johnstone g:Finn(4)	7th	9,152
30/4/17	Catalans Dragons (h)	W30-10	t:Caton-Brown(3),Jones-Bishop(2),Huby g:Finn(3)	6th	4,017
6/5/17	Leigh (a)	W26-40	t:Miller,Kirmond(2),Lyne,Arundel,Caton-Brown g:Finn(8)	6th	4,938
12/5/17	Dewsbury (a) (CCR6)	W6-54	t:Caton-Brown(4),Ashurst,Williams,Tupou(2),Gibson g:Finn(9)	N/A	2,125
20/5/17	Widnes (MW) ●	W34-12	t:Grix(2),Lyne,Jones-Bishop(2),Ashurst g:Finn(5)	5th	N/A
26/5/17	Huddersfield (h)	W28-26	t:Jones-Bishop(2),Lyne(2),Kirmond g:Finn(3),Williams	5th	4,642
29/5/17	Wigan (a)	W30-42	t:Tupou(3),Caton-Brown,Kirmond,England,Miller g:Finn(7)	4th	13,110
4/6/17	Salford (a)	W24-34	t:Caton-Brown(3),Lyne(2),Batchelor g:Finn(5)	4th	3,277
10/6/17	Leeds (h)	L16-18	t:Caton-Brown,Wood,Jones-Bishop g:Finn(2)	5th	7,183
15/6/17	Salford (a) (CCQF)	L30-6	t:Finn g:Finn	N/A	2,808
23/6/17	Hull FC (a)	L40-18	t:Batchelor,Williams,Lyne g:Finn(3)	5th	10,895
1/7/17	Warrington (a)	W26-12	t:Tupou,Jones-Bishop,Wood,Caton-Brown g:Finn(5)	5th	4,829
6/7/17	Castleford (h)	L24-25	t:Jones-Bishop,Wood,Fifita g:Finn(6)	5th	6,430
14/7/17	Widnes (a)	W8-36	t:Caton-Brown(2),Tupou(2),Williams,Arona g:Finn(6)	4th	4,977
23/7/17	St Helens (h)	L16-41	t:Ashurst,Grix,Caton-Brown g:Finn(2)	5th	5,820
4/8/17	Huddersfield (a) (S8)	L36-6	t:Williams g:Finn	7th	5,429
10/8/17	Leeds (h) (S8)	W38-6	t:Arundel,Jones-Bishop,Grix,Miller,Ashurst,Tupou g:Finn(7)	4th	5,607
17/8/17	Castleford (a) (S8)	L45-20	t:Jones-Bishop,Caton-Brown,Kirmond,Jowitt g:Finn(2)	4th	11,235
1/9/17	Salford (a) (S8)	W18-43	t:Miller(2),Arundel,Randell(2),Tupou g:Finn(9) fg:Miller	4th	2,489
7/9/17	St Helens (h) (S8)	L16-18	t:Tupou(2) g:Finn(4)	5th	4,837
14/9/17	Hull FC (a) (S8)	L19-18	t:Arundel,Miller,Caton-Brown g:Finn(3)	6th	10,924
23/9/17	Wigan (h) (S8)	W32-0	t:Jones-Bishop,Miller,Williams,Grix,Hirst g:Finn(6)	5th	5,165

● *Played at St James' Park, Newcastle*

APP TRIES GOALS FG PTS

		APP		TRIES		GOALS		FG		PTS	
	D.O.B.	ALL	SL	ALL	SL	ALL	SL	ALL	SL	ALL	SL
Mitch Allgood	27/4/89	6(2)	6(2)	0	0	0	0	0	0	0	0
Chris Annakin	30/1/91	(13)	(12)	0	0	0	0	0	0	0	0
Tinirau Arona	8/5/89	23(6)	23(5)	1	1	0	0	0	0	4	4
Joe Arundel	22/8/91	19(3)	17(3)	6	6	0	0	0	0	24	24
Matty Ashurst	1/11/89	31	29	5	4	0	0	0	0	20	16
James Batchelor	9/4/98	3(7)	2(7)	2	2	0	0	0	0	8	8
Mason Caton-Brown	24/5/93	22	20	21	17	0	0	0	0	84	68
Jordan Crowther	19/2/97	1(2)	(1)	0	0	0	0	0	0	0	0
Anthony England	19/10/86	20(6)	18(6)	1	1	0	0	0	0	4	4
David Fifita	28/6/89	14(15)	13(15)	4	4	0	0	0	0	16	16
Liam Finn	2/11/83	28(3)	26(3)	2	1	106	96	0	0	220	196
Ashley Gibson	25/9/86	6	4	2	1	0	0	0	0	8	4
Scott Grix	1/5/84	29	27	9	9	0	0	0	0	36	36
Dean Hadley	5/8/92	15(7)	14(7)	2	2	0	0	0	0	8	8
James Hasson	1/5/92	(4)	(4)	0	0	0	0	0	0	0	0
Keegan Hirst	13/12/88	3(20)	3(18)	1	1	0	0	0	0	4	4
Craig Huby	21/5/86	15(13)	15(12)	2	2	0	0	0	0	8	8
Tom Johnstone	13/8/95	12	12	7	7	0	0	0	0	28	28
Ben Jones-Bishop	24/8/88	27	27	20	20	0	0	0	0	80	80
Max Jowitt	6/5/97	3	3	1	1	0	0	0	0	4	4
Danny Kirmond	11/11/85	19(3)	19(3)	5	5	0	0	0	0	20	20
Reece Lyne	2/12/92	18(1)	17(1)	9	9	0	0	0	0	36	36
Jacob Miller	22/8/92	19(3)	19(3)	10	10	0	0	1	1	41	41
Tyler Randell	31/8/92	3	3	2	2	0	0	0	0	8	8
Michael Sio	16/5/93	6(3)	5(2)	0	0	0	0	0	0	0	0
Bill Tupou	2/7/90	24(2)	23(2)	15	13	0	0	0	0	60	52
Adam Walker	20/2/91	6(1)	5(1)	0	0	0	0	0	0	0	0
Anthony Walker	28/12/91	(5)	(4)	0	0	0	0	0	0	0	0
Sam Williams	18/3/91	19(5)	17(5)	5	4	26	26	0	0	72	68
Kyle Wood	18/6/89	25(4)	23(4)	3	3	0	0	0	0	12	12

'SL' totals include Super 8s; 'All' totals also include Challenge Cup

Mason Caton-Brown

LEAGUE RECORD
P30-W16-D0-L14
(5th, SL)
F745, A648, Diff+97
32 points.

CHALLENGE CUP
Quarter Finalists

ATTENDANCES
Best - v Leeds (SL - 7,183)
Worst - v Catalans Dragons
(SL - 4,017)
Total (SL/S8s only) - 73,967
Average (SL/S8s only) - 5,283
(Up by 291 on 2016)

26 October 2016 - Ryan Atkins and Matty Russell agree new deals until November 2019, Declan Patton until November 2018 and Benjamin Jullien for 2017.

9 November 2016 - Karl Fitzpatrick appointed new CEO.

12 November 2016 - Chris Hill signs new contract until November 2021. Ben Currie signs deal to November 2020.

17 November 2016 - Stefan Ratchford injures knee in training for England and will miss start of season.

21 November 2016 - Chris Sandow announces he will not return from Australia to fulfil rest of contract for 2017 season.

9 December 2016 - Widnes halfback Kevin Brown joins on two-year contract.

18 January 2017 - hooker Daryl Clark extends contract by four years to end of 2020 season.

12 February 2017 - 20-12 round-one defeat at Catalans.

18 February 2017 - Kevin Brown scores on debut in stunning 27-18 World Series win over Brisbane.

24 February 2017 - 30-22 home round-two defeat by Castleford.

4 March 2017 - 24-14 Saturday afternoon defeat at Salford.

9 March 2017 - 38-16 home hammering by Wigan makes it four defeats in first four league games.

16 March 2017 - Chris Hill makes first start of season in 22-8 defeat at Leigh. Tom Lineham banned for two games for lashing out with elbow.

24 March 2017 - Stefan Ratchford makes first appearance of season but 31-6 loss at St Helens is sixth league defeat in a row.

1 April 2017 - Matty Russell scores hat-trick as fightback, home 22-all draw with Hull FC ends six-match losing run since start of season.

6 April 2017 - 20-year old winger Taylor Prell signs from Yorkshire Carnegie on two-year contract.

7 April 2017 - Ryan Atkins gets two tries in first win of year, by 25-14 at home to Leeds.

11 April 2017 - Ben Westwood banned for four matches for high shot on Leeds' Liam Sutcliffe.

13 April 2017 - 19-10 win at Widnes makes it two in a row.

17 April 2017 - nail-biting 26-24 home win over Huddersfield.

22 April 2017 - Tom Lineham scores try two minutes from time to secure 22-20 win over Wakefield.

28 April 2017 - 34-10 defeat at Hull FC.

5 May 2017 - 14-0 deficit on 25 minutes turned into 40-18 home win over St Helens.

KEY DATES

14 May 2017 - Kevin Brown hat-trick in 34-20 home Challenge Cup sixth-round win over Widnes.

15 May 2017 - back-rower Sam Wilde and utility back Jack Johnson go on four-week loans to Widnes.

20 May 2017 - last-minute Joe Burgess try means 24-all Magic Weekend draw with Wigan.

24 May 2017 - Stefan Ratchford signs new two-year contract extension to November 2020

26 May 2017 - 40-0 defeat at Leeds.

29 May 2017 - 38-12 Bank Holiday Monday defeat by Salford.

4 June 2017 - 44-4 defeat at Huddersfield.

11 June 2017 - Matty Blythe fractures leg in 36-16 defeat at Castleford

17 June 2017 - 27-26 home defeat by Wigan means Challenge Cup quarter-final exit.

19 June 2017 - Penrith centre Peta Hiku signs with immediate effect until end of 2019.

20 June 2017 - Rhys Evans leaves to join Leigh Centurions.

24 June 2017 - 24-16 home win over Catalans moves Wolves into ninth spot.

28 June 2017 - Kurt Gidley announces he will retire at end of season.

1 July 2017 - Peta Hiku makes debut in 26-12 defeat at Wakefield.

7 July 2017 - Tom Lineham scores four tries in 50-10 home win over Leigh. Ben Westwood banned for three games for dangerous throw.

11 July 2017 - Andre Savelio to join Brisbane Broncos on two-year contract at end of season.

13 July 2017 - Ben Currie scores try on return from 10-month injury lay-off in 16-10 win at Wigan.

19 July 2017 - backrower Sam Wilde joins London Broncos on loan to end of season.

20 July 2017 - Matty Russell scores two tries in 22-6 final regular round home win over Widnes.

21 July 2017 - hooker Brad Dwyer signs for Leeds for 2018.

4 August 2017 - 28-14 win at Widnes in opening Qualifiers game.

12 August 2017 - Declan Patton scores 20 points in 52-24 home win over Catalans.

19 August 2017 - hard-fought 22-8 home win over Halifax.

23 August 2017 - prop Sitaleki Akauola signs for 2018 from Penrith Panthers on two-year deal

1 September 2017 - Sam Wilde to join Widnes in 2018.

2 September 2017 - 40-38 win at London Broncos after trailing 14-0.

6 September 2017 - Ben Westwood extends contract to end of 2018.

9 September 2017 - home 32-20 win over Leigh guarantees Super League place in 2018.

10 September 2017 - coach Tony Smith to leave at end of season.

12 September 2017 - prop Ashton Sims to join Toronto.

12 September 2017 - Matty Blythe and Kevin Penny to leave club.

23 September 2017 - 46-24 home win over promoted Hull KR means 100 per cent record in Qualifiers.

1 October 2017 - Joe Westerman transfers to Toronto Wolfpack for 130,000 fee.

2 October 2017 - South Sydney centre Bryson Goodwin signs two-year deal, with relegated Leigh getting a transfer fee.

5 October 2017 - coach Richard Agar released to take up offer in NRL.

6 October 2017 - Cronulla assistant Steve Price appointed head coach on two-year contract.

CLUB RECORDS

Highest score:
112-0 v Swinton, 20/5/2011
Highest score against:
12-84 v Bradford, 9/9/2001
Record attendance:
34,404 v Wigan, 22/1/49 *(Wilderspool)*
15,008 v Widnes, 25/3/2016
(Halliwell Jones Stadium)

MATCH RECORDS

Tries:
7 Brian Bevan v Leigh, 29/3/48
Brian Bevan v Bramley, 22/4/53
Goals:
16 Lee Briers v Swinton, 20/5/2011
Points:
44 Lee Briers v Swinton, 20/5/2011

SEASON RECORDS

Tries: 66 Brian Bevan 1952-53
Goals: 170 Steve Hesford 1978-79
Points: 363 Harry Bath 1952-53

CAREER RECORDS

Tries: 740 Brian Bevan 1945-62
Goals: 1,159 Steve Hesford 1975-85
Points: 2,586 Lee Briers 1997-2013
Appearances: 620 Brian Bevan 1945-62

WARRINGTON WOLVES

DATE	FIXTURE	RESULT	SCORERS	LGE	ATT
11/2/17	Catalans Dragons (a)	L20-12	t:Savelio,Evans g:Patton(2)	9th	8,842
18/2/17	Brisbane (h) (WCS)	W27-18	t:Brown,Atkins,Russell,Lineham g:Patton(5) fg:Patton	N/A	12,082
24/2/17	Castleford (h)	L22-30	t:Savelio(2),Lineham(2) g:Patton(2),Livett	12th	11,374
4/3/17	Salford (a)	L24-14	t:Patton,Hughes,Johnson g:Patton	12th	5,492
9/3/17	Wigan (h)	L16-38	t:Atkins,Evans,Lineham g:Gidley(2)	12th	11,250
16/3/17	Leigh (a)	L22-8	t:Lineham g:Gidley,Livett	12th	7,011
24/3/17	St Helens (a)	L31-6	t:Gidley g:Ratchford	12th	11,598
1/4/17	Hull FC (h)	D22-22	t:Russell(3),Clark g:Gidley(3)	12th	10,676
7/4/17	Leeds (h)	W25-14	t:Atkins(2),Lineham,Gidley g:Patton(4) fg:Patton	11th	10,035
13/4/17	Widnes (h)	W10-19	t:Lineham,Hughes,Philbin g:Patton(3) fg:Patton	11th	8,279
17/4/17	Huddersfield (h)	W26-24	t:Livett,Clark,Gidley,Evans,T King g:Patton(3)	9th	10,111
22/4/17	Wakefield (h)	W22-20	t:Atkins,Hill,Brown,Lineham g:Patton(3)	9th	9,152
28/4/17	Hull FC (a)	L34-10	t:Russell,Westerman g:Patton	9th	10,734
5/5/17	St Helens (h)	W40-18	t:Jullien,Cooper,Livett,Evans,Lineham,Atkins(2) g:Livett(6)	9th	11,681
14/5/17	Widnes (h) (CCR6)	W34-20	t:Atkins,Brown(3),Russell,Hill g:Ratchford(5)	N/A	5,971
20/5/17	Wigan (MW) ●	D24-24	t:Clark,Ratchford,Lineham,Hughes g:Ratchford(4)	8th	N/A
26/5/17	Leeds (a)	L40-0		8th	14,974
29/5/17	Salford (h)	L12-38	t:Dwyer,Lineham g:Patton(2)	9th	10,684
4/6/17	Huddersfield (a)	L44-4	t:Lineham	10th	5,362
11/6/17	Castleford (a)	L36-16	t:Lineham,Westerman,Hughes g:Patton(2)	10th	8,577
17/6/17	Wigan (h) (CCQF)	L26-27	t:Atkins(2),Savelio,Gidley g:Patton(5)	N/A	7,312
24/6/17	Catalans Dragons (h)	W24-16	t:Jullien,Atkins(2),Savelio g:Gidley(4)	10th	9,798
1/7/17	Wakefield (a)	L26-12	t:Dwyer,Hill g:Ratchford(2)	10th	4,829
7/7/17	Leigh (h)	W50-10	t:Atkins,Sims,Lineham(4),Pomeroy,Hughes,Patton g:Ratchford(6),Westwood	9th	10,597
13/7/17	Wigan (a)	W10-16	t:Jullien,Atkins,Currie g:Ratchford(2)	9th	12,790
20/7/17	Widnes (h)	W22-6	t:Russell(2),Hiku,Brown g:Ratchford(3)	9th	9,895
4/8/17	Widnes (a) (S8-Q)	W14-28	t:Hughes,Lineham,Patton,Russell,Hiku g:Patton(4)	2nd(S8-Q)	6,202
12/8/17	Catalans Dragons (h) (S8-Q)	W52-24	t:Ratchford(2),Russell,Patton,Atkins(2),Lineham(2),Hiku g:Patton(8)	1st(S8-Q)	8,595
19/8/17	Halifax (h) (S8-Q)	W22-8	t:Hiku,Hill,Russell,Savelio g:Patton(3)	1st(S8-Q)	8,353
2/9/17	London Broncos (a) (S8-Q)	W38-40	t:Lineham,G King,Hiku,Brown(2),Patton,Westwood g:Patton(6)	1st(S8-Q)	1,577
9/9/17	Leigh (h) (S8-Q)	W32-30	t:Russell,Westwood,Gidley,Brown,Hiku,Hill g:Patton(2),Livett(2)	1st(S8-Q)	9,787
17/9/17	Featherstone (a) (S8-Q)	W0-68	t:Hiku(3),Ratchford,Livett(2),Hughes(2),Pomeroy,Savelio,Johnson(2) g:Livett(10)	1st(S8-Q)	2,441
23/9/17	Hull KR (h) (S8-Q)	W46-24	t:Pomeroy(2),Ratchford,Dwyer,Savelio(2),Hiku,Currie,Livett g:Livett(5)	1st(S8-Q)	10,466

● *Played at St James' Park, Newcastle*

		APP		TRIES		GOALS		FG		PTS	
	D.O.B.	ALL	SL	ALL	SL	ALL	SL	ALL	SL	ALL	SL
Ryan Atkins	7/10/85	27	20	16	10	0	0	0	0	64	40
Matty Blythe	20/11/88	2(1)	2(1)	0	0	0	0	0	0	0	0
Kevin Brown	2/10/84	21(1)	12(1)	9	2	0	0	0	0	36	8
Daryl Clark	10/2/93	22(2)	16(2)	3	3	0	0	0	0	12	12
Mike Cooper	15/9/88	24(2)	18(1)	1	1	0	0	0	0	4	4
Dominic Crosby	11/12/90	(7)	(6)	0	0	0	0	0	0	0	0
Ben Currie	15/7/94	2(2)	(2)	2	1	0	0	0	0	8	4
Will Dagger	21/2/99	4	3	0	0	0	0	0	0	0	0
Brad Dwyer	28/4/93	6(18)	6(13)	3	2	0	0	0	0	12	8
Rhys Evans	30/10/92	11(3)	10(3)	4	4	0	0	0	0	16	16
Kurt Gidley	7/6/82	24(1)	18	5	3	10	10	0	0	40	32
Peta Hiku	4/12/92	11	4	10	1	0	0	0	0	40	4
Chris Hill	3/11/87	25	17	5	2	0	0	0	0	20	8
Jack Hughes	4/1/92	33	23	8	5	0	0	0	0	32	20
Jack Johnson	25/4/96	6(1)	6	3	1	0	0	0	0	12	4
Benjamin Jullien	1/3/95	22(1)	15	3	3	0	0	0	0	12	12
George King	24/2/95	1(18)	1(11)	1	0	0	0	0	0	4	0
Toby King	9/7/96	6	6	1	1	0	0	0	0	4	4
Tom Lineham	21/9/91	27	19	21	16	0	0	0	0	84	64
Harvey Livett	4/1/97	7(7)	4(6)	5	2	25	8	0	0	70	24
Declan Patton	23/5/95	24(1)	16(1)	5	2	56	23	3	2	135	56
Kevin Penny	3/10/87	4	4	0	0	0	0	0	0	0	0
Joe Philbin	16/11/94	5(22)	4(15)	1	1	0	0	0	0	4	4
Ben Pomeroy	10/1/84	4	2	4	1	0	0	0	0	16	4
Stefan Ratchford	19/7/88	25	16	5	1	23	18	0	0	66	40
Matthew Russell	6/6/93	24	15	12	6	0	0	0	0	48	24
Andre Savelio	21/3/95	4(22)	3(14)	9	4	0	0	0	0	36	16
Ashton Sims	26/2/85	25(7)	15(7)	1	1	0	0	0	0	4	4
Morgan Smith	30/4/98	2(9)	(5)	0	0	0	0	0	0	0	0
Joe Westerman	15/11/89	18(1)	16	2	2	0	0	0	0	8	8
Ben Westwood	25/7/81	13(3)	8(2)	2	0	1	1	0	0	10	2
Sam Wilde	8/9/95	(3)	(2)	0	0	0	0	0	0	0	0

'SL' totals include regular season only; 'All' totals also include Super 8s (Qualifiers), Challenge Cup & World Club Series

Jack Hughes

LEAGUE RECORD
SL: P23-W9-D2-L12 (9th)
F422, A557, Diff-135, 20 points.

S8-Q: P7-W7-D0-L0 (1st)
F288, A138, Diff+150, 14 points.

CHALLENGE CUP
Quarter Finalists

ATTENDANCES
Best - v Brisbane (WCS - 12,082)
Worst - v Widnes (CC - 5,971)
Total (SL/S8s only) - 152,454
Average (SL/S8s only) - 10,164
(Down by 931 on 2016)

17 October 2016 - Paddy Flynn and Setaimata Sa's contracts not renewed.

9 December 2016 - Kevin Brown signs for Warrington.

5 January 2017 - forward Tom Olbison signs for 2017 with option for 2018 after Bradford enter liquidation.

24 January 2017 - Chris Houston and Joe Mellor named as co-captains, Aaron Heremaia and Tom Gilmore vice-captains, after poll of players and coaches. Mellor to miss season start with knee injury.

10 February 2017 - 28-16 home defeat by Huddersfield in round one.

22 February 2017 - Tom Gilmore ruled out for two months with ankle injury suffered in defeat to Giants.

24 February 2017 - four tries conceded in last 20 minutes mean 28-26 defeat to Wigan in round-two game switched to Select Security Stadium at short notice.

4 March 2017 - Rhys Hanbury try eight minutes from time sees Vikings hit back from 14-0 deficit to snatch 14-14 draw and first point of season at Catalans.

10 March 2017 - news emerges of death at age 65 of former Widnes great Mick Adams.

12 March 2017 - minute's applause held before 34-0 home hammering by Castleford. Danny Craven avoids suspension with EGP for contact with match official.

17 March 2017 - 32-12 defeat at Hull FC.

24 March 2017 - 46-10 home defeat by Salford.

1 April 2017 - Danny Craven scores hat-trick in first win of season, by 37-24 at Leigh.

7 April 2017 - 30-4 defeat at Wakefield.

13 April 2017 - 19-10 home defeat by Warrington.

17 April 2017 - 42-22 defeat at Leeds.

21 April 2017 - Patrick Ah Van scores two tries in first home win of season, by 16-14 over St Helens.

30 April 2017 - 30-10 defeat at Salford.

4 May 2017 - winger Corey Thompson activates NRL 'Opt Out' clause in contract and will return Down Under for 2018 season.

7 May 2017 - 22-0 lead just before half-time turns to 33-22 home defeat to Hull.

14 May 2017 - Kevin Brown hat-trick means 34-20 Challenge Cup sixth-round defeat at Warrington.

15 May 2017 - Rangi Chase joins on loan from Castleford for rest of season.

WIDNES VIKINGS
KEY DATES

15 May 2017 - back-rower Sam Wilde and utility back Jack Johnson arrive on four-week loans from Warrington.

19 May 2017 - props Jay and Ted Chapelhow sign contracts until end of 2019 season.

20 May 2017 - Rangi Chase makes mistake-ridden debut in 34-12 Magic Weekend defeat by Wakefield.

26 May 2017 - Rangi Chase unable to play against old club as 22-10 lead ends in 32-22 defeat at Castleford.

29 May 2017 - rookie winger Ryan Ince scores two tries in 28-20 home Bank Holiday Monday win over Leeds.

4 June 2017 - 26-6 home win over Catalans lifts Vikings off foot of table.

7 June 2017 - Danny Craven signs new contract for 2018 season. Chris Bridge to retire at end of current season.

10 June 2017 - 26-10 defeat at St Helens sends Vikings to bottom of table.

16 June 2017 - halfback Jordan Johnstone signs new contract to end of 2019 season.

22 June 2017 - 36-10 home win over Leigh sees Vikings leapfrog Centurions into 11th spot. Rangi Chase gets two-match ban for shoulder charge.

2 July 2017 - two late Wigan tries mean 28-12 defeat at Wigan.

6 July 2017 - prop Alex Gerrard signs new contract for 2018.

6 July 2017 - on-loan from Castleford Rangi Chase signs two-year contract. Teenage hooker Danny Walker signs four-year deal.

7 July 2017 - 40-0 defeat at Huddersfield.

11 July 2017 - Chris Houston signs new contract for 2018.

14 July 2017 - 36-8 home defeat by Wakefield.

17 July 2017 - forward Tom Olbison extends contract to end of 2018. Assistant coach Brett Hodgson to leave and join Wests Tigers.

3 August 2017 - Rangi Chase suspended by club after testing positive for cocaine.

4 August 2017 - 28-14 home defeat by Warrington in opening Qualifiers game.

7 August 2017 - prop Eamon O'Carroll retires aged 30 after suffering nerve injury in Wakefield defeat.

13 August 2017 - Corey Thompson scores two second-half tries in 36-12 win at Halifax.

20 August 2017 - Chris Bridge and Rhys Hanbury score hat-tricks in 58-10 home win over Featherstone.

1 September 2017 - Sam Wilde signs from Warrington for 2018 on two-year deal.

3 September 2017 - 24-8 win at Leigh is third in a row.

9 September 2017 - 12-6 defeat at Hull KR secures promotion for Championship side.

11 September 2017 - forward Will Rogers signs for 2018 from St George Illawarra on two-year deal.

16 September 2017 - Danny Craven and Joe Mellor score braces in 38-16 home win over London Broncos.

21 September 2017 - Francis Cummins appointed assistant coach.

23 September 2017 - 12-10 win at Catalans means third-placed finish in Qualifiers.

25 September 2017 - Ed Chamberlain signs contract for 2018.

CLUB RECORDS
Highest score:
90-4 v Doncaster, 10/6/2007
Highest score against:
6-76 v Catalans Dragons, 31/3/2012
Record attendance:
24,205 v St Helens, 16/2/61

MATCH RECORDS
Tries: 7 Phil Cantillon v York, 18/2/2001
Goals: 14 Mark Hewitt v Oldham, 25/7/99
Tim Hartley v Saddleworth, 7/3/2009
Points:
38 Gavin Dodd v Doncaster, 10/6/2007

SEASON RECORDS
Tries: 58 Martin Offiah 1988-89
Goals: 161 Mick Nanyn 2007
Points: 434 Mick Nanyn 2007

CAREER RECORDS
Tries: 234 Mal Aspey 1964-80
Goals: 1,083 Ray Dutton 1966-78
Points: 2,195 Ray Dutton 1966-78
Appearances: 591 Keith Elwell 1970-86

WIDNES VIKINGS

DATE	FIXTURE	RESULT	SCORERS	LGE	ATT
10/2/17	Huddersfield (h)	L16-28	t:Runciman,Marsh,Hanbury g:Hanbury(2)	11th	5,031
24/2/17	Wigan (h)	L26-28	t:White,Craven,Armstrong,Marsh g:Hanbury(5)	11th	6,561
4/3/17	Catalans Dragons (a)	D14-14	t:Ah Van,Olbison,Hanbury g:Hanbury	11th	7,254
12/3/17	Castleford (h)	L0-34		11th	6,396
17/3/17	Hull FC (a)	L32-12	t:Heremaia,White g:White(2)	11th	10,814
24/3/17	Salford (h)	L10-46	t:Thompson,Hanbury g:Bridge	11th	5,565
1/4/17	Leigh (a)	W24-37	t:Bridge,Craven(3),Brooks,Runciman g:Gilmore(6) fg:Gilmore	11th	6,196
7/4/17	Wakefield (a)	L30-4	t:Thompson	12th	4,214
13/4/17	Warrington (h)	L10-19	t:Marsh,Runciman g:Bridge	12th	8,279
17/4/17	Leeds (a)	L42-22	t:Gilmore(2),Houston,Thompson g:Gilmore(3)	12th	15,408
21/4/17	St Helens (h)	W16-14	t:Mellor,Ah Van(2) g:Gilmore(2)	12th	6,171
30/4/17	Salford (a)	L30-10	t:Gilmore,Ah Van g:Gilmore	12th	3,127
7/5/17	Hull FC (h)	L22-33	t:Houston,Hanbury,Ah Van(2) g:Gilmore(3)	12th	5,082
14/5/17	Warrington (a) (CCR6)	L34-20	t:Burke,J Chapelhow,Ah Van g:Ah Van(4)	N/A	5,971
20/5/17	Wakefield (MW) ●	L34-12	t:Ince,Cahill g:Chamberlain(2)	12th	N/A
26/5/17	Castleford (a)	L32-22	t:Ince,Johnson,Thompson,Johnstone g:Chamberlain(3)	12th	7,648
29/5/17	Leeds (h)	W28-20	t:Hanbury,Ince(2),Thompson(2),Heremaia g:Bridge(2)	12th	5,518
4/6/17	Catalans Dragons (h)	W26-6	t:Buchanan(2),Hanbury,Thompson g:Hanbury(2),Thompson(3)	11th	4,253
9/6/17	St Helens (a)	L26-10	t:Ince,Craven g:Craven	12th	10,474
22/6/17	Leigh (h)	W36-10	t:Bridge,Houston(2),Thompson(2),Ince,Whitley g:Bridge(3),Craven	11th	5,604
2/7/17	Wigan (a)	L28-12	t:White(2) g:White(2)	11th	12,758
7/7/17	Huddersfield (a)	L40-0		11th	5,253
14/7/17	Wakefield (h)	L8-36	t:Mellor g:Marsh(2)	11th	4,977
20/7/17	Warrington (h)	L22-6	t:Mellor g:Marsh	12th	9,895
4/8/17	Warrington (h) (S8-Q)	L14-28	t:Buchanan,Mellor g:White(3)	7th(S8-Q)	6,202
13/8/17	Halifax (h) (S8-Q)	W12-36	t:Bridge,White,Runciman,Thompson(2),Mellor,Craven g:White(4)	4th(S8-Q)	2,291
20/8/17	Featherstone (h) (S8-Q)	W58-10	t:Hanbury(3),Runciman(2),Bridge(3),Marsh(2),Mellor g:White(5),Craven,Hanbury	3rd(S8-Q)	4,373
3/9/17	Leigh (a) (S8-Q)	W8-24	t:White,Gerrard,Thompson g:Hanbury(3),Bridge(3)	3rd(S8-Q)	6,209
9/9/17	Hull KR (a) (S8-Q)	L12-6	t:Cahill g:White	3rd(S8-Q)	8,227
16/9/17	London Broncos (h) (S8-Q)	W38-16	t:Whitley,White,Craven(2),Runciman,Mellor(2) g:White(3),Gilmore(2)	3rd(S8-Q)	4,199
23/9/17	Catalans Dragons (a) (S8-Q)	W10-12	t:Thompson,Marsh g:Gilmore(2)	2nd(S8-Q)	10,245

● Played at St James' Park, Newcastle

		APP		TRIES		GOALS		FG		PTS	
	D.O.B.	ALL	SL	ALL	SL	ALL	SL	ALL	SL	ALL	SL
Patrick Ah Van	17/3/88	6	5	7	6	4	0	0	0	36	24
Tom Armstrong	12/9/89	11	11	1	1	0	0	0	0	4	4
Chris Bridge	5/7/84	19(1)	15(1)	6	2	10	7	0	0	44	22
Sam Brooks	29/9/93	1(1)	1(1)	1	1	0	0	0	0	4	4
Jack Buchanan	10/4/92	25	17	3	2	0	0	0	0	12	8
Greg Burke	12/2/93	5(9)	2(8)	1	0	0	0	0	0	4	0
Hep Cahill	15/10/86	19(6)	13(4)	2	1	0	0	0	0	8	4
Ed Chamberlain	8/2/96	4	3	0	0	5	5	0	0	10	10
Jay Chapelhow	21/9/95	8(9)	8(6)	1	0	0	0	0	0	4	0
Ted Chapelhow	21/9/95	1(6)	1(6)	0	0	0	0	0	0	0	0
Rangi Chase	11/4/86	6	6	0	0	0	0	0	0	0	0
Danny Craven	21/11/91	18(1)	11(1)	8	5	3	2	0	0	38	24
Chris Dean	17/1/88	5(1)	4(1)	0	0	0	0	0	0	0	0
Gil Dudson	16/6/90	26(1)	18(1)	0	0	0	0	0	0	0	0
Owen Farnworth	11/2/99	1	1	0	0	0	0	0	0	0	0
Alex Gerrard	5/11/91	3(12)	3(7)	1	1	0	0	0	0	4	0
Tom Gilmore	2/2/94	10	8	3	3	19	15	1	1	51	43
Rhys Hanbury	27/8/85	18	13	9	6	14	10	0	0	64	44
Aaron Heremaia	19/9/82	12(6)	10(6)	2	2	0	0	0	0	8	8
Chris Houston	15/2/85	28	21	4	4	0	0	0	0	16	16
Ryan Ince	16/9/96	12	9	6	6	0	0	0	0	24	24
Jack Johnson	25/4/96	3	3	1	1	0	0	0	0	4	4
Jordan Johnstone	24/5/97	13(6)	12(4)	1	1	0	0	0	0	4	4
Macgraff Leuluai	9/2/90	2(5)	2(5)	0	0	0	0	0	0	0	0
Manase Manuokafoa	24/3/85	(14)	(9)	0	0	0	0	0	0	0	0
Stefan Marsh	3/9/90	23	16	6	3	3	3	0	0	30	18
Joe Mellor	28/11/90	17(1)	9(1)	8	3	0	0	0	0	32	12
Eamon O'Carroll	13/6/87	(7)	(6)	0	0	0	0	0	0	0	0
Tom Olbison	20/3/91	7(19)	6(12)	1	1	0	0	0	0	4	4
Lloyd Roby	3/1/99	1	0	0	0	0	0	0	0	0	0
Charly Runciman	22/7/93	31	23	7	3	0	0	0	0	28	12
Corey Thompson	15/5/90	24	18	13	9	3	3	0	0	58	42
Brad Walker	30/1/98	2(1)	2(1)	0	0	0	0	0	0	0	0
Danny Walker	29/6/99	(12)	(6)	0	0	0	0	0	0	0	0
Liam Walsh	12/9/98	1(1)	1(1)	0	0	0	0	0	0	0	0
Lloyd White	9/8/88	16(2)	10(2)	7	4	20	4	0	0	68	24
Matt Whitley	20/1/96	23(3)	16(3)	2	1	0	0	0	0	8	4
Sam Wilde	8/9/95	2	2	0	0	0	0	0	0	0	0

Charly Runciman

LEAGUE RECORD
SL: P23-W5-D1-L17 (12th)
F359, A628, Diff-269, 11 points.

S8-Q: P7-W5-D0-L2 (2nd)
F188, A96, Diff+92, 10 points.

CHALLENGE CUP
Round Six

ATTENDANCES
Best - v Warrington (SL - 8,279)
Worst - v London Broncos
(S8 - 4,199)
Total (SL/S8s only) - 78,211
Average (SL/S8s only) - 5,587
(Up by 116 on 2016)

'SL' totals include regular season only; 'All' totals also include Super 8s (Qualifiers) & Challenge Cup

18 October 2016 - prop Dom Crosby signs for Widnes.

3 November 2016 - Lee Mossop leaves for Salford.

28 January 2017 - 26-22 pre-season win at Catalans.

11 February 2017 - Oliver Gildart scores try-double in 26-16 round-one win at Salford.

19 February 2017 - Joe Burgess scores try-hat-trick in stunning 22-6 World Club Championship win over Cronulla.

24 February 2017 - four tries in last 20 minutes secure 28-26 win at Widnes in game switched to Select Security Stadium at short notice.

3 March 2017 - Anthony Gelling scores two tries in 20-0 home win over Leigh in 'Battle of the Borough'.

9 March 2017 - Liam Marshall marks second appearance by scoring four of the Warriors' seven tries in clinical 38-16 rout at winless Warrington.

10 March 2017 - John Bateman undergoes shoulder surgery.

13 March 2017 - Liam Farrell suffers calf strain in England training camp.

19 March 2017 - 16-all home draw with Huddersfield is first point of season dropped. Sean O'Loughlin leaves field on eight minutes with calf injury. Winger Tom Davies scores try on debut.

24 March 2017 - second-half fightback just falls short in 22-20 home defeat to Hull FC.

28 March 2017 - Sam Tomkins' recovery from foot injury suffers setback.

31 March 2017 - Oliver Gildart injures back in comeback in 26-18 defeat at Leeds. Leeds forward Brett Ferres suspended for six games for crusher tackle.

6 April 2017 - 27-10 home defeat by Castleford.

12 April 2017 - George Williams signs new four-year marquee player deal until 2020, with an option for 2021.

14 April 2017 - Morgan Escaré signs new contract to end of 2020 season.

14 April 2017 - hooker Michael McIlorum back after 14 months in 29-18 home Good Friday win over St Helens, who have Kyle Amor sent off on 13 minutes.

17 April 2017 - late Liam Marshall try secures 16-10 Easter Monday win at Wakefield.

18 April 2017 - Tony Clubb undergoes kidney surgery and Jake Shorrocks out for season with knee injury.

KEY DATES

23 April 2017 - Joe Burgess, Liam Forsyth and Tom Davies score two tries each in 42-22 home win over Catalans. Thomas Leuluai breaks jaw.

29 April 2017 - 54-4 humbling at Castleford. Michael McIlorum banned for one game on EGP for standing on Jake Webster. George Williams ruled out of England's Samoa Test with knee injury. Josh Ganson makes debut.

5 May 2017 - 14 first-team players unavailable as Josh Woods makes debut at stand-off in 31-16 home defeat to Salford.

14 May 2017 - Joe Burgess scores two tries in 42-12 Challenge Cup sixth round win at Swinton.

19 May 2017 - young wingers Liam Marshall and Tom Davies sign new contracts to end of 2020. Liam Farrell signs five-year deal to end of 2022. Connor Farrell joins Swinton on loan.

20 May 2017 - last-minute Joe Burgess try earns 24-all Magic Weekend draw with Warrington.

25 May 2017 - last-gasp 22-19 defeat at St Helens.

29 May 2017 - early 20-0 lead ends in 42-30 home defeat to Wakefield.

3 June 2017 - 39-26 defeat at Hull FC is sixth game without win.

8 June 2017 - 50-34 defeat at Leigh sees Wigan sink to eighth spot.

17 June 2017 - Sam Tomkins field goal seven minutes from time is difference in 27-26 Challenge Cup quarter-final win at Warrington.

23 June 2017 - long-range George Williams field goal secures 19-all draw at Huddersfield.

2 July 2017 - Joe Burgess scores two late tries as eight-match winless league streak ends with 28-12 home win over Widnes. Tony Clubb scores try on return from having kidney removed.

8 July 2017 - coach Shaun Wane misses trip because of hip operation as 32-10 win at Catalans secures top-eight spot.

13 July 2017 - Romain Navarrete and Lewis Tierney join Catalans on loan until end of season.

13 July 2017 - 16-10 home defeat by Warrington in Sean O'Loughlin's 400th Wigan appearance.

21 July 2017 - George Williams and Oliver Gildart both score two tries in emphatic 34-0 home victory over weakened Leeds.

30 July 2017 - 27-14 Challenge Cup semi-final win over Salford at Halliwell Jones Stadium, Warrington.

11 August 2017 - hard-fought 18-4 Super 8s home win over Huddersfield keeps alive top-four hopes.

18 August 2017 - Warriors moves within one point of top four after 42-6 home win over Salford.

26 August 2017 - 18-14 Challenge Cup final defeat to Hull FC.

1 September 2017 - 26-16 win at St Helens keeps Wigan within one point of semi-final spot.

8 September 2017 - late Anthony Gelling and John Bateman tries earn 30-22 win at 12-man Hull FC.

17 September 2017 - 38-20 home defeat to Castleford leaves play-off chances in balance.

23 September 2017 - 32-0 defeat at Wakefield means sixth-place finish.

2 October 2017 - Sean O'Loughlin signs new one-year contract for 2018.

CLUB RECORDS

Highest score:
116-0 v Flimby & Fothergill, 14/2/25
Highest score against:
0-75 v St Helens, 26/6/2005
Record attendance:
47,747 v St Helens, 27/3/59 *(Central Park)*
25,004 v St Helens, 25/3/2005
(JJB/DW Stadium)

MATCH RECORDS

Tries: 10 Martin Offiah v Leeds, 10/5/92
Shaun Edwards v Swinton, 29/9/92
Goals: 22 Jim Sullivan
v Flimby & Fothergill, 14/2/25
Points: 44 Jim Sullivan
v Flimby & Fothergill, 14/2/25

SEASON RECORDS

Tries: 62 Johnny Ring 1925-26
Goals: 186 Frano Botica 1994-95
Points: 462 Pat Richards 2010

CAREER RECORDS

Tries: 478 Billy Boston 1953-68
Goals: 2,317 Jim Sullivan 1921-46
Points: 4,883 Jim Sullivan 1921-46
Appearances: 774 Jim Sullivan 1921-46

WIGAN WARRIORS

DATE	FIXTURE	RESULT	SCORERS	LGE	ATT
11/2/17	Salford (a)	W16-26	t:Gildart(2),Burgess,Williams,J Tomkins g:Escare(3)	3rd	6,527
19/2/17	Cronulla (h) (WCC)	W22-6	t:Burgess(3),Gildart g:Escare(2),Powell	N/A	21,011
24/2/17	Widnes (a)	W26-28	t:Leuluai,Gildart(2),Burgess(2),Tierney g:Escare(2)	2nd	6,561
3/3/17	Leigh (h)	W20-0	t:Gelling(2),Williams g:Escare(4)	2nd	15,699
9/3/17	Warrington (a)	W16-38	t:Marshall(4),Gelling,Farrell,Wells g:Escare(5)	2nd	11,250
19/3/17	Huddersfield (h)	D16-16	t:Escare,Davies,Gelling g:Escare(2)	1st	12,704
24/3/17	Hull FC (a)	L20-22	t:Forsyth,Williams,Davies,Marshall g:Escare(2)	4th	12,319
31/3/17	Leeds (a)	L26-18	t:Williams(2),Marshall g:Escare(3)	5th	17,030
6/4/17	Castleford (h)	L10-27	t:Escare(2) g:Escare	6th	12,423
14/4/17	St Helens (h)	W29-18	t:Burgess(2),Marshall(2),Farrell g:Escare(4) fg:Escare	4th	23,390
17/4/17	Wakefield (a)	W10-16	t:O'Loughlin,Escare,Marshall g:Escare(2)	4th	4,640
23/4/17	Catalans Dragons (h)	W42-22	t:Davies(2),Burgess(2),Forsyth(2),Marshall,Farrell g:Escare(2),Powell(3)	3rd	11,637
29/4/17	Castleford (a)	L54-4	t:Powell	5th	9,333
5/5/17	Salford (h)	L16-31	t:Davies,Sutton,Tierney g:Woods(2)	5th	11,861
14/5/17	Swinton (a) (CCR6)	W12-42	t:J Tomkins,Farrell,Burgess(2),Marshall,Davies,Ganson,Gregson g:Marshall(5)	N/A	2,003
20/5/17	Warrington (MW) ●	D24-24	t:Marshall(3),Burgess g:Woods,Williams(3)	6th	N/A
25/5/17	St Helens (a)	L22-19	t:Davies,Tierney,Burgess g:Williams(3) fg:Leuluai	6th	13,138
29/5/17	Wakefield (h)	L30-42	t:Worthington(2),Tierney,Marshall(2),Leuluai g:Williams(2),Marshall	6th	13,110
3/6/17	Hull FC (a)	L39-26	t:Davies(2),Marshall(2),Tierney,Burgess g:Marshall	6th	10,333
8/6/17	Leigh (a)	L50-34	t:Marshall,Ganson(2),Williams,Gildart,Nuuausala,Burgess g:Marshall(3)	7th	7,080
17/6/17	Warrington (a) (CCQF)	W26-27	t:Burgess(2),Marshall,Bateman g:Williams(5) fg:S Tomkins	N/A	7,312
23/6/17	Huddersfield (a)	D19-19	t:Bateman,Marshall(2) g:Williams(3) fg:Williams	8th	5,718
2/7/17	Widnes (h)	W28-12	t:O'Loughlin,Clubb,Tierney,Burgess(2) g:Williams(4)	7th	12,758
8/7/17	Catalans Dragons (a)	W10-32	t:Burgess(3),Williams,S Tomkins g:Williams(6)	7th	9,810
13/7/17	Warrington (h)	L10-16	t:Gildart,Bateman g:Williams	8th	12,790
21/7/17	Leeds (h)	W34-0	t:McIlrorum,S Tomkins,Williams(2),Gildart(2),Davies g:Williams(2),Powell	7th	15,119
30/7/17	Salford (CCSF) ●●	W14-27	t:Gildart(2),Isa,McIlrorum g:Williams(5) fg:S Tomkins	N/A	10,796
4/8/17	Leeds (a) (S8)	L32-16	t:Davies(2),S Tomkins g:Williams(2)	8th	13,579
11/8/17	Huddersfield (h) (S8)	W18-4	t:Gelling,Farrell,S Tomkins g:Powell(2),S Tomkins	7th	10,619
18/8/17	Salford (h) (S8)	W42-6	t:O'Loughlin,Burgess(2),Farrell,Powell,Williams,Nuuausala,Marshall g:Williams(5)	6th	11,229
26/8/17	Hull FC (CCF) ●●●	L18-14	t:Bateman,Gildart,Burgess g:Williams	N/A	68,525
1/9/17	St Helens (a) (S8)	W16-26	t:Gildart(2),Gelling,Williams g:Williams(5)	5th	15,248
8/9/17	Hull FC (h) (S8)	W22-30	t:Gildart,Gelling(2),Davies,Bateman g:Williams(5)	3rd	11,291
17/9/17	Castleford (a) (S8)	L20-38	t:Davies,S Tomkins,Leuluai,Isa g:Williams(2)	5th	15,706
23/9/17	Wakefield (a) (S8)	L32-0		6th	5,165

● *Played at St James' Park, Newcastle* ●● *Played at Halliwell Jones Stadium, Warrington* ●●● *Played at Wembley Stadium*

APP TRIES GOALS FG PTS

	D.O.B.	ALL	SL	ALL	SL	ALL	SL	ALL	SL	ALL	SL
John Bateman	30/9/93	16	12	5	3	0	0	0	0	20	12
Joe Bretherton	5/10/95	(4)	(4)	0	0	0	0	0	0	0	0
Joe Burgess	14/10/94	26	21	26	18	0	0	0	0	104	72
Tony Clubb	12/6/87	8(14)	7(12)	1	1	0	0	0	0	4	4
Tom Davies	11/1/97	24	22	14	13	0	0	0	0	56	52
Morgan Escare	18/10/91	13	12	4	4	32	30	1	1	81	77
Liam Farrell	2/7/90	28	24	6	5	0	0	0	0	24	20
Callum Field	7/10/97	(5)	(4)	0	0	0	0	0	0	0	0
Ben Flower	19/10/87	13	12	0	0	0	0	0	0	0	0
Liam Forsyth	23/3/96	11(2)	10(2)	3	3	0	0	0	0	12	12
Josh Ganson	19/2/98	1(4)	1(3)	3	2	0	0	0	0	12	8
Anthony Gelling	18/10/90	24	20	8	8	0	0	0	0	32	32
Oliver Gildart	6/8/96	20	16	15	11	0	0	0	0	60	44
Nick Gregson	17/12/95	1(5)	(5)	1	0	0	0	0	0	4	0
Willie Isa	1/1/89	20(13)	18(11)	2	1	0	0	0	0	8	4
Thomas Leuluai	22/6/85	31	27	3	3	0	0	1	1	13	13
Liam Marshall	9/5/96	24	21	23	21	10	5	0	0	112	94
Michael McIlrorum	10/1/88	22(2)	18(2)	2	1	0	0	0	0	8	4
Romain Navarrete	30/6/94	(10)	(9)	0	0	0	0	0	0	0	0
Frank-Paul Nuuausala	13/2/87	34(1)	29(1)	2	2	0	0	0	0	8	8
Sean O'Loughlin	24/11/82	26	22	3	3	0	0	0	0	12	12
Sam Powell	3/7/92	14(17)	13(14)	2	2	7	6	0	0	22	20
Jake Shorrocks	26/10/95	(1)	(1)	0	0	0	0	0	0	0	0
Ryan Sutton	2/8/95	15(15)	13(12)	1	1	0	0	0	0	4	4
Taulima Tautai	3/4/88	1(32)	1(27)	0	0	0	0	0	0	0	0
Lewis Tierney	20/10/94	12	10	6	6	0	0	0	0	24	24
Joel Tomkins	21/3/87	15(7)	13(5)	2	1	0	0	0	0	8	4
Sam Tomkins	23/3/89	15	12	5	5	1	1	2	0	24	22
Jack Wells	21/9/97	5(8)	4(8)	1	1	0	0	0	0	4	4
George Williams	31/10/94	33	29	11	11	54	43	1	1	153	131
Josh Woods	13/12/97	2	2	0	0	3	3	0	0	6	6
James Worthington	21/5/99	1	1	2	2	0	0	0	0	8	8

'SL' totals include Super 8s; 'All' totals also include Challenge Cup & World Club Challenge

Liam Marshall

LEAGUE RECORD
P30-W14-D3-L13
(6th, SL)
F691, A668, Diff+23
31 points.

CHALLENGE CUP
Runners-Up

ATTENDANCES
Best - v St Helens (SL - 23,390)
Worst - v Huddersfield (S8 - 10,619)
Total (SL/S8s only) - 191,364
Average (SL/S8s only) - 13,669
(Up by 434 on 2016)

SUPER LEAGUE XXII
Round by Round

ROUND 1

Thursday 9th February 2017

ST HELENS 6 LEEDS RHINOS 4

SAINTS: 1 Jonny Lomax; 2 Tom Makinson; 3 Ryan Morgan (D); 4 Mark Percival; 5 Adam Swift; 6 Theo Fages; 24 Danny Richardson (D); 10 Kyle Amor; 17 Tommy Lee (D); 14 Luke Douglas (D); 11 Joe Greenwood; 18 Dominique Peyroux; 12 Jon Wilkin (C). Subs (all used): 8 Alex Walmsley; 9 James Roby; 16 Luke Thompson; 20 Morgan Knowles.
Try: Fages (43); **Goals:** Percival 1/1.
RHINOS: 1 Ashton Golding; 2 Tom Briscoe; 3 Kallum Watkins; 4 Joel Moon; 5 Ryan Hall; 14 Liam Sutcliffe; 7 Rob Burrow (C); 17 Mitch Garbutt; 9 Matt Parcell (D); 10 Adam Cuthbertson; 11 Jamie Jones-Buchanan; 12 Carl Ablett; 16 Brad Singleton. Subs (all used): 13 Stevie Ward; 18 Jimmy Keinhorst; 20 Anthony Mullally; 24 Jordan Baldwinson.
Try: Moon (22); **Goals:** L Sutcliffe 0/1.
Rugby Leaguer & League Express Men of the Match:
Saints: Theo Fages; *Rhinos:* Ashton Golding.
Penalty count: 6-10; **Half-time:** 0-4;
Referee: Phil Bentham; **Attendance:** 12,208.

Friday 10th February 2017

CASTLEFORD TIGERS 44 LEIGH CENTURIONS 16

TIGERS: 1 Zak Hardaker (D); 2 Greg Minikin; 3 Jake Webster; 4 Michael Shenton (C); 5 Greg Eden (D2); 6 Rangi Chase; 7 Luke Gale; 8 Andy Lynch; 9 Paul McShane; 19 Gadwin Springer; 15 Jesse Sene-Lefao (D); 12 Mike McMeeken; 14 Nathan Massey. Subs (all used): 10 Grant Millington; 17 Junior Moors; 18 Matt Cook; 16 Ben Roberts.
Tries: Gale (19, 58), Sene-Lefao (24), Minikin (30, 39), Moors (42), Eden (62); **Goals:** Gale 8/8.
CENTURIONS: 19 Ryan Hampshire (D); 2 Adam Higson; 3 Ben Crooks (D); 1 Mitch Brown; 5 Matty Dawson; 6 Martyn Ridyard; 7 Josh Drinkwater; 8 Gareth Hock; 21 Liam Hood; 15 Danny Tickle; 11 Cory Paterson; 12 Glenn Stewart (D); 13 Harrison Hansen (C). Subs (all used): 14 Eloi Pelissier (D); 17 Atelea Vea (D); 22 James Green (D); 10 Dayne Weston.
Tries: Hampshire (47), Dawson (70), Tickle (74);
Goals: Ridyard 2/3.
Rugby Leaguer & League Express Men of the Match:
Tigers: Luke Gale; *Centurions:* Josh Drinkwater.
Penalty count: 16-18; **Half-time:** 26-0;
Referee: Robert Hicks; **Attendance:** 8,722.

WIDNES VIKINGS 16 HUDDERSFIELD GIANTS 28

VIKINGS: 1 Rhys Hanbury; 2 Corey Thompson; 26 Tom Armstrong (D); 4 Charly Runciman; 17 Stefan Marsh; 3 Chris Bridge; 7 Tom Gilmore; 15 Gil Dudson; 9 Lloyd White; 23 Jay Chapelhow; 12 Matt Whitley; 11 Chris Houston (C); 19 Macgraff Leuluai. Subs (all used): 33 Aaron Heremaia; 13 Hep Cahill; 25 Tom Olbison (D); 22 Ted Chapelhow.
Tries: Runciman (5), Marsh (70), Hanbury (75);
Goals: Hanbury 2/3.
GIANTS: 4 Lee Gaskell (D); 2 Jermaine McGillvary; 3 Leroy Cudjoe (C); 30 Alex Mellor (D); 5 Aaron Murphy; 6 Danny Brough; 7 Ryan Brierley; 15 Sebastine Ikahihifo; 9 Ryan Hinchcliffe; 17 Ukuma Ta'ai; 11 Tom Symonds; 12 Dale Ferguson (D2); 13 Michael Lawrence. Subs (all used): 10 Shannon Wakeman (D); 14 Kruise Leeming; 16 Oliver Roberts; 18 Paul Clough (D).
Tries: McGillvary (13, 26), Gaskell (18), Symonds (30), Murphy (55), Cudjoe (78); **Goals:** Brough 2/6.
Rugby Leaguer & League Express Men of the Match:
Vikings: Aaron Heremaia; *Giants:* Dale Ferguson.
Penalty count: 6-8; **Half-time:** 6-20;
Referee: Jack Smith; **Attendance:** 5,031.

Saturday 11th February 2017

SALFORD RED DEVILS 16 WIGAN WARRIORS 26

RED DEVILS: 1 Gareth O'Brien; 21 Greg Johnson; 5 Niall Evalds; 4 Junior Sa'u; 2 Justin Carney; 6 Robert Lui; 7 Michael Dobson (C); 8 Craig Kopczak; 19 Josh Wood; 23 Lee Mossop (D); 3 Josh Jones; 10 George Griffin; 13 Mark Flanagan. Subs (all used): 20 Kriss Brining (D); 16 Olsi Krasniqi; 14 Lama Tasi (D2); 17 Adam Walne.
Tries: Brining (48), Sa'u (72), Dobson (76);
Goals: O'Brien 2/3.
WARRIORS: 22 Morgan Escare (D); 21 Lewis Tierney; 3 Anthony Gelling; 4 Oliver Gildart; 5 Joe Burgess (D2); 6 George Williams; 7 Thomas Leuluai (D2); 8 Frank-Paul Nuuausala; 16 Sam Powell; 10 Ben Flower; 20 Willie Isa; 12 Liam Farrell; 13 Sean O'Loughlin (C). Subs (all used): 11 Joel Tomkins; 15 Tony Clubb; 17 Taulima Tautai; 19 Ryan Sutton.
Tries: Gildart (3, 26), Burgess (13), Williams (31), J Tomkins (39); **Goals:** Escare 3/5.
On report: Gelling (9) - alleged high tackle on Sa'u.
Rugby Leaguer & League Express Men of the Match:
Red Devils: Michael Dobson; *Warriors:* George Williams.
Penalty count: 12-6; **Half-time:** 0-26;
Referee: Ben Thaler; **Attendance:** 6,527.

CATALANS DRAGONS 20 WARRINGTON WOLVES 12

DRAGONS: 4 Brayden Wiliame (D); 2 Jodie Broughton; 3 Krisnan Inu; 18 Vincent Duport; 5 Fouad Yaha; 6 Luke Walsh (D); 7 Richie Myler; 8 Sam Moa (D); 9 Paul Aiton; 10 Remi Casty (C); 12 Justin Horo; 15 Benjamin Garcia; 13 Greg Bird (D2). Subs (all used): 14 Julian Bousquet; 16 Thomas Bosc; 17 Jason Baitieri; 19 Mickael Simon (D2).
Tries: Myler (24), Bird (48), Wiliame (80);
Goals: Walsh 4/5.
WOLVES: 5 Matthew Russell; 3 Rhys Evans; 20 Toby King; 4 Ryan Atkins; 2 Tom Lineham; 22 Declan Patton; 7 Kurt Gidley (C); 14 Mike Cooper (D2); 9 Daryl Clark; 10 Ashton Sims; 18 Andre Savelio (D); 12 Jack Hughes; 13 Joe Westerman. Subs (all used): 15 Brad Dwyer; 17 Dominic Crosby (D); 28 Harvey Livett (D); 23 Joe Philbin.
Tries: Savelio (9), Evans (78); **Goals:** Patton 2/2.
Rugby Leaguer & League Express Men of the Match:
Dragons: Greg Bird; *Wolves:* Joe Westerman.
Penalty count: 12-8; **Half-time:** 6-6;
Referee: James Child; **Attendance:** 8,842.

Sunday 12th February 2017

WAKEFIELD TRINITY 8 HULL FC 12

TRINITY: 1 Scott Grix (D2); 5 Ben Jones-Bishop; 4 Reece Lyne; 3 Bill Tupou; 2 Tom Johnstone; 6 Jacob Miller; 14 Sam Williams (D); 8 Anthony England; 7 Liam Finn; 17 Craig Huby (D); 11 Matty Ashurst; 12 Danny Kirmond (C); 13 Michael Sio. Subs (all used): 9 Kyle Wood (D2); 16 Tinirau Arona; 20 David Fifita; 25 Anthony Walker.
Try: Grix (44); **Goals:** Williams 2/2.
HULL FC: 1 Jamie Shaul; 2 Mahe Fonua; 3 Carlos Tuimavave; 4 Josh Griffin (D); 5 Fetuli Talanoa; 6 Albert Kelly (D); 7 Marc Sneyd; 8 Scott Taylor; 9 Danny Houghton; 10 Liam Watts; 21 Sika Manu; 12 Mark Minichiello; 13 Gareth Ellis (C). Subs (all used): 14 Jake Connor (D); 15 Chris Green; 16 Jordan Thompson; 17 Danny Washbrook.
Try: Connor (68); **Goals:** Sneyd 4/4.
Rugby Leaguer & League Express Men of the Match:
Trinity: David Fifita; *Hull FC:* Gareth Ellis.
Penalty count: 7-8; **Half-time:** 2-6;
Referee: Chris Campbell; **Attendance:** 7,027.

ROUND 11

Thursday 16th February 2017

HUDDERSFIELD GIANTS 20 SALFORD RED DEVILS 30

GIANTS: 4 Lee Gaskell; 2 Jermaine McGillvary; 3 Leroy Cudjoe (C); 30 Alex Mellor; 5 Aaron Murphy; 6 Danny Brough; 7 Ryan Brierley; 15 Sebastine Ikahihifo; 9 Ryan Hinchcliffe; 17 Ukuma Ta'ai; 13 Michael Lawrence; 12 Dale Ferguson; 8 Sam Rapira. Subs (all used): 10 Shannon Wakeman; 14 Kruise Leeming; 16 Oliver Roberts; 18 Paul Clough.
Tries: McGillvary (18), Mellor (49, 51), Ta'ai (69);
Goals: Brough 2/4.
RED DEVILS: 1 Gareth O'Brien; 21 Greg Johnson; 22 Kris Welham (D); 4 Junior Sa'u; 2 Justin Carney; 6 Robert Lui; 7 Michael Dobson (C); 8 Craig Kopczak; 9 Logan Tomkins; 23 Lee Mossop; 3 Josh Jones; 10 George Griffin; 13 Mark Flanagan. Subs (all used): 19 Josh Wood; 16 Olsi Krasniqi; 14 Lama Tasi; 17 Adam Walne.
Tries: Sa'u (22), O'Brien (42, 63), Jones (75);
Goals: O'Brien 7/7.
Rugby Leaguer & League Express Men of the Match:
Giants: Sebastine Ikahihifo; *Red Devils:* Gareth O'Brien.
Penalty count: 6-8; **Half-time:** 4-10;
Referee: James Child; **Attendance:** 6,017.

Friday 17th February 2017

LEIGH CENTURIONS 14 LEEDS RHINOS 17

CENTURIONS: 1 Mitch Brown; 2 Adam Higson; 3 Ben Crooks; 4 Willie Tonga; 5 Matty Dawson; 20 Ben Reynolds; 7 Josh Drinkwater; 8 Gareth Hock; 14 Eloi Pelissier; 16 Antoni Maria (D); 11 Cory Paterson; 17 Atelea Vea; 13 Harrison Hansen (C). Subs (all used): 19 Ryan Hampshire; 23 Sam Hopkins; 24 Jamie Acton; 15 Danny Tickle.
Tries: Dawson (4), Brown (8), Crooks (68);
Goals: Reynolds 1/3.
Sin bin: Acton (55) - delaying restart.
RHINOS: 1 Ashton Golding; 2 Tom Briscoe; 3 Kallum Watkins; 18 Jimmy Keinhorst; 5 Ryan Hall; 14 Liam Sutcliffe; 7 Rob Burrow; 20 Anthony Mullally; 9 Matt Parcell; 16 Brad Singleton; 13 Stevie Ward; 12 Carl Ablett; 11 Jamie Jones-Buchanan. Subs (all used): 6 Danny McGuire (C); 10 Adam Cuthbertson; 21 Josh Walters; 23 Jack Ormondroyd (D).
Tries: Cuthbertson (12), Hall (15), Keinhorst (32);
Goals: L Sutcliffe 2/4; **Field goal:** L Sutcliffe (39).
Rugby Leaguer & League Express Men of the Match:
Centurions: Mitch Brown; *Rhinos:* Adam Cuthbertson.
Penalty count: 6-9; **Half-time:** 8-15;
Referee: Jack Smith; **Attendance:** 6,692.

ROUND 2

Thursday 23rd February 2017

HULL FC 14 CATALANS DRAGONS 16

HULL FC: 1 Jamie Shaul; 2 Mahe Fonua; 3 Carlos Tuimavave; 4 Josh Griffin; 5 Fetuli Talanoa; 14 Jake Connor; 7 Marc Sneyd; 8 Scott Taylor; 9 Danny Houghton; 10 Liam Watts; 21 Sika Manu; 12 Mark Minichiello; 13 Gareth Ellis (C). Subs (all used): 15 Chris Green; 16 Jordan Thompson; 17 Danny Washbrook; 22 Josh Bowden.
Tries: Tuimavave (37), Watts (61); **Goals:** Sneyd 3/3.
Sin bin: Watts (67) - dangerous challenge.
DRAGONS: 16 Thomas Bosc; 2 Jodie Broughton; 3 Krisnan Inu; 4 Brayden Wiliame; 21 Iain Thornley (D); 6 Luke Walsh; 7 Richie Myler; 8 Sam Moa; 9 Paul Aiton; 10 Remi Casty (C); 15 Benjamin Garcia; 12 Justin Horo; 13 Greg Bird. Subs (all used): 11 Louis Anderson; 14 Julian Bousquet; 17 Jason Baitieri; 23 Alrix Da Costa.
Try: Myler (41); **Goals:** Walsh 6/6.
Sin bin: Bird (22) - interference.
On report: Baitieri (58) - alleged contact with referee.
Rugby Leaguer & League Express Men of the Match:
Hull FC: Sika Manu; *Dragons:* Greg Bird.
Penalty count: 11-12; **Half-time:** 8-4;
Referee: Robert Hicks; **Attendance:** 13,544.

Friday 24th February 2017

HUDDERSFIELD GIANTS 24 WAKEFIELD TRINITY 16

GIANTS: 4 Lee Gaskell; 2 Jermaine McGillvary; 23 Sam Wood; 30 Alex Mellor; 5 Aaron Murphy; 6 Danny Brough (C); 7 Ryan Brierley; 8 Sam Rapira; 14 Kruise Leeming; 15 Sebastine Ikahihifo; 17 Ukuma Ta'ai; 12 Dale Ferguson; 9 Ryan Hinchcliffe. Subs (all used): 10 Shannon Wakeman; 16 Oliver Roberts; 18 Paul Clough; 20 Daniel Smith.
Tries: S Wood (4, 7), Ta'ai (62), Roberts (65), McGillvary (71); **Goals:** Brough 2/5.
TRINITY: 1 Scott Grix; 2 Tom Johnstone; 4 Reece Lyne; 3 Bill Tupou; 5 Ben Jones-Bishop; 6 Jacob Miller; 14 Sam Williams; 20 David Fifita; 7 Liam Finn; 8 Anthony England; 11 Matty Ashurst; 12 Danny Kirmond (C); 17 Craig Huby. Subs (all used): 9 Kyle Wood; 16 Tinirau Arona; 22 Jordan Crowther; 25 Anthony Walker.
Tries: Finn (13), Jones-Bishop (25, 38); **Goals:** Williams 2/4.
Rugby Leaguer & League Express Men of the Match:
Giants: Kruise Leeming; *Trinity:* Ben Jones-Bishop.
Penalty count: 9-8; **Half-time:** 8-16;
Referee: Chris Kendall; **Attendance:** 6,337.

LEEDS RHINOS 20 SALFORD RED DEVILS 14

RHINOS: 1 Ashton Golding; 2 Tom Briscoe; 3 Kallum Watkins; 18 Jimmy Keinhorst; 5 Ryan Hall; 6 Danny McGuire (C); 7 Rob Burrow; 17 Mitch Garbutt; 9 Matt Parcell; 16 Brad Singleton; 13 Stevie Ward; 12 Carl Ablett; 11 Jamie Jones-Buchanan. Subs (all used): 23 Jack Ormondroyd; 10 Adam Cuthbertson; 4 Joel Moon; 14 Liam Sutcliffe.
Tries: Hall (9), Keinhorst (43), L Sutcliffe (77);
Goals: Burrow 4/6.
RED DEVILS: 1 Gareth O'Brien; 21 Greg Johnson; 22 Kris Welham; 4 Junior Sa'u; 24 Jake Bibby; 6 Robert Lui; 7 Michael Dobson (C); 8 Craig Kopczak; 9 Logan Tomkins; 23 Lee Mossop; 3 Josh Jones; 10 George Griffin; 13 Mark Flanagan. Subs (all used): 14 Lama Tasi; 16 Olsi Krasniqi; 19 Josh Wood; 17 Adam Walne.
Tries: O'Brien (16), Welham (37), Tomkins (68);
Goals: O'Brien 1/4.
Rugby Leaguer & League Express Men of the Match:
Rhinos: Jimmy Keinhorst; *Red Devils:* Gareth O'Brien.
Penalty count: 10-9; **Half-time:** 6-8;
Referee: Chris Campbell; **Attendance:** 14,575.

LEIGH CENTURIONS 24 ST HELENS 16

CENTURIONS: 1 Mitch Brown; 2 Adam Higson; 3 Ben Crooks; 4 Willie Tonga; 5 Matty Dawson; 20 Ben Reynolds; 7 Josh Drinkwater; 8 Gareth Hock; 9 Micky Higham (C); 22 James Green; 11 Cory Paterson; 17 Atelea Vea; 13 Harrison Hansen. Subs (all used): 14 Eloi Pelissier; 15 Danny Tickle; 23 Sam Hopkins; 24 Jamie Acton.
Tries: Vea (5), Hock (10), Acton (27), Higham (67);
Goals: Reynolds 4/5.
Sin bin: Green (78) - shoulder charge on Walmsley.
SAINTS: 1 Jonny Lomax; 2 Tom Makinson; 3 Ryan Morgan; 4 Mark Percival; 5 Adam Swift; 6 Theo Fages; 24 Danny Richardson; 10 Kyle Amor; 17 Tommy Lee; 14 Luke Douglas; 13 Louie McCarthy-Scarsbrook; 18 Dominique Peyroux; 12 Jon Wilkin (C). Subs (all used): 8 Alex Walmsley; 9 James Roby; 16 Luke Thompson; 20 Morgan Knowles.

Tries: Swift (33), Roby (55), Walmsley (70);
Goals: Percival 2/3.
Rugby Leaguer & League Express Men of the Match:
Centurions: Harrison Hansen; *Saints:* James Roby.
Penalty count: 7-15; **Half-time:** 18-4;
Referee: Ben Thaler; **Attendance:** 9,012.

WARRINGTON WOLVES 22 CASTLEFORD TIGERS 30

WOLVES: 26 Jack Johnson; 5 Matthew Russell; 3 Rhys Evans; 4 Ryan Atkins; 2 Tom Lineham; 6 Kevin Brown; 22 Declan Patton; 14 Mike Cooper; 9 Daryl Clark; 10 Ashton Sims; 12 Jack Hughes (C); 18 Andre Savelio; 13 Joe Westerman. Subs (all used): 15 Brad Dwyer; 17 Dominic Crosby; 28 Harvey Livett; 34 Ben Westwood.
Tries: Savelio (6, 71), Lineham (37, 59);
Goals: Patton 2/3, Livett 1/1.
TIGERS: 1 Zak Hardaker; 2 Greg Minikin; 3 Jake Webster; 4 Michael Shenton (C); 5 Greg Eden; 6 Rangi Chase; 7 Luke Gale; 8 Andy Lynch; 13 Adam Milner; 19 Gadwin Springer; 15 Jesse Sene-Lefao; 12 Mike McMeeken; 14 Nathan Massey. Subs: 10 Grant Millington; 17 Junior Moors; 18 Matt Cook; 21 Joel Monaghan (not used).
Tries: Sene-Lefao (19), Hardaker (21), Eden (25, 75), Gale (27), Minikin (64); **Goals:** Gale 3/6.
Rugby Leaguer & League Express Men of the Match:
Wolves: Andre Savelio; *Tigers:* Zak Hardaker.
Penalty count: 9-4; **Half-time:** 10-22;
Referee: Phil Bentham; **Attendance:** 11,374.

WIDNES VIKINGS 26 WIGAN WARRIORS 28

VIKINGS: 1 Rhys Hanbury; 2 Corey Thompson; 26 Tom Armstrong; 4 Charly Runciman; 17 Stefan Marsh; 3 Chris Bridge; 32 Danny Craven; 15 Gil Dudson; 9 Lloyd White; 10 Jack Buchanan; 12 Matt Whitley; 11 Chris Houston (C); 19 Macgraff Leuluai. Subs (all used): 33 Aaron Heremaia; 13 Hep Cahill; 25 Tom Olbison; 18 Greg Burke.
Tries: White (22), Craven (29), Armstrong (38), Marsh (44);
Goals: Hanbury 5/6.
WARRIORS: 22 Morgan Escare; 21 Lewis Tierney; 3 Anthony Gelling; 4 Oliver Gildart; 5 Joe Burgess; 6 George Williams; 7 Thomas Leuluai; 8 Frank-Paul Nuuausala; 16 Sam Powell; 10 Ben Flower; 20 Willie Isa; 12 Liam Farrell; 13 Sean O'Loughlin (C). Subs (all used): 11 Joel Tomkins; 15 Tony Clubb; 17 Taulima Tautai; 25 Jake Shorrocks.
Tries: Leuluai (13), Gildart (32, 75), Burgess (60, 74), Tierney (67); **Goals:** Escare 2/5, Powell 0/1.
Rugby Leaguer & League Express Men of the Match:
Vikings: Lloyd White; *Warriors:* Sean O'Loughlin.
Penalty count: 10-9; **Half-time:** 18-12;
Referee: James Child; **Attendance:** 6,561.

ROUND 3

Thursday 2nd March 2017

CASTLEFORD TIGERS 66 LEEDS RHINOS 10

TIGERS: 1 Zak Hardaker; 2 Greg Minikin; 3 Jake Webster; 4 Michael Shenton (C); 5 Greg Eden; 9 Paul McShane; 7 Luke Gale; 8 Andy Lynch; 13 Adam Milner; 19 Gadwin Springer; 15 Jesse Sene-Lefao; 12 Mike McMeeken; 14 Nathan Massey. Subs: 10 Grant Millington; 17 Junior Moors; 18 Matt Cook; 22 Will Maher (not used).
Tries: Eden (3, 23, 70), Minikin (12, 16, 36), McMeeken (33), Hardaker (44), McShane (48), Webster (60), Gale (71), Shenton (74); **Goals:** Gale 9/12.
RHINOS: 1 Ashton Golding; 22 Ash Handley; 3 Kallum Watkins; 4 Joel Moon; 5 Ryan Hall; 6 Danny McGuire (C); 14 Liam Sutcliffe; 16 Brad Singleton; 9 Matt Parcell; 10 Adam Cuthbertson; 18 Jimmy Keinhorst; 15 Brett Delaney; 21 Josh Walters. Subs (all used): 23 Jack Ormondroyd; 20 Anthony Mullally; 24 Jordan Baldwinson; 25 Jordan Lilley.
Tries: Mullally (51), Moon (78);
Goals: L Sutcliffe 1/1, Lilley 0/1.
Rugby Leaguer & League Express Men of the Match:
Tigers: Luke Gale; *Rhinos:* Jimmy Keinhorst.
Penalty count: 7-6; **Half-time:** 30-0;
Referee: Ben Thaler; **Attendance:** 11,500.

HUDDERSFIELD GIANTS 8 HULL FC 48

GIANTS: 24 Darnell McIntosh (D); 21 Gene Ormsby; 30 Alex Mellor; 16 Oliver Roberts; 23 Sam Wood; 6 Danny Brough (C); 7 Ryan Brierley; 8 Sam Rapira; 14 Kruise Leeming; 15 Sebastine Ikahihifo; 9 Ryan Hinchcliffe; 20 Daniel Smith; 26 Mikey Wood. Subs (all used): 10 Shannon Wakeman; 19 Nathan Mason; 18 Paul Clough; 22 Tyler Dickinson.
Tries: S Wood (63), Roberts (80);
Goals: Brough 0/1, S Wood 0/1.
HULL FC: 1 Jamie Shaul; 2 Mahe Fonua; 3 Carlos Tuimavave; 4 Josh Griffin; 5 Fetuli Talanoa; 6 Albert Kelly; 7 Marc Sneyd; 8 Scott Taylor; 9 Danny Houghton (C); 22 Josh Bowden; 21 Sika Manu; 12 Mark Minichiello; 16 Jordan Thompson. Subs (all used): 14 Jake Connor; 15 Chris Green; 17 Danny Washbrook; 29 Masi Matongo.
Tries: Talanoa (5), Sneyd (10, 37, 75), Kelly (23, 50), Griffin (55), Tuimavave (68); **Goals:** Sneyd 8/8.
Rugby Leaguer & League Express Men of the Match:
Giants: Kruise Leeming; *Hull FC:* Marc Sneyd.
Penalty count: 6-10; **Half-time:** 0-24;
Referee: Phil Bentham; **Attendance:** 5,176.

Friday 3rd March 2017

ST HELENS 12 WAKEFIELD TRINITY 16

SAINTS: 2 Tom Makinson; 21 Jack Owens; 3 Ryan Morgan; 4 Mark Percival; 5 Adam Swift; 6 Theo Fages; 24 Danny Richardson; 8 Alex Walmsley; 9 James Roby; 16 Luke Thompson; 12 Jon Wilkin (C); 18 Dominique Peyroux; 20 Morgan Knowles. Subs (all used): 10 Kyle Amor; 13 Louie McCarthy-Scarsbrook; 15 Adam Walker (D); 36 Zeb Taia (D).
Tries: Morgan (36), Percival (49, 56); **Goals:** Percival 0/3.
TRINITY: 1 Scott Grix; 2 Tom Johnstone; 4 Reece Lyne; 3 Bill Tupou; 24 Mason Caton-Brown (D); 6 Jacob Miller; 14 Sam Williams; 16 Tinirau Arona; 9 Kyle Wood; 17 Craig Huby; 11 Matty Ashurst; 12 Danny Kirmond (C); 13 Michael Sio. Subs (all used): 7 Liam Finn; 25 Anthony Walker; 20 David Fifita; 27 James Batchelor.
Tries: Caton-Brown (21), Miller (74, pen);
Goals: Williams 4/4.
Rugby Leaguer & League Express Men of the Match:
Saints: Tom Makinson; *Trinity:* Sam Williams.
Penalty count: 8-5; **Half-time:** 4-10;
Referee: James Child; **Attendance:** 9,040.

WIGAN WARRIORS 20 LEIGH CENTURIONS 0

WARRIORS: 22 Morgan Escare; 21 Lewis Tierney; 3 Anthony Gelling; 5 Joe Burgess; 35 Liam Marshall (D); 6 George Williams; 7 Thomas Leuluai; 8 Frank-Paul Nuuausala; 16 Sam Powell; 10 Ben Flower; 20 Willie Isa; 12 Liam Farrell; 13 Sean O'Loughlin (C). Subs (all used): 11 Joel Tomkins; 15 Tony Clubb; 17 Taulima Tautai; 19 Ryan Sutton.
Tries: Gelling (7, 69), Williams (47); **Goals:** Escare 4/5.
CENTURIONS: 1 Mitch Brown; 5 Matty Dawson; 3 Ben Crooks; 4 Willie Tonga; 30 Curtis Naughton (D); 20 Ben Reynolds; 7 Josh Drinkwater; 8 Gareth Hock; 9 Micky Higham (C); 22 James Green; 15 Danny Tickle; 17 Atelea Vea; 13 Harrison Hansen. Subs (all used): 14 Eloi Pelissier; 23 Sam Hopkins; 24 Jamie Acton; 29 Lachlan Burr (D).
Rugby Leaguer & League Express Men of the Match:
Warriors: George Williams; *Centurions:* Micky Higham.
Penalty count: 9-7; **Half-time:** 6-0;
Referee: Robert Hicks; **Attendance:** 15,699.

Saturday 4th March 2017

SALFORD RED DEVILS 24 WARRINGTON WOLVES 14

RED DEVILS: 1 Gareth O'Brien; 21 Greg Johnson; 22 Kris Welham; 4 Junior Sa'u; 24 Jake Bibby; 6 Robert Lui; 7 Michael Dobson (C); 14 Lama Tasi; 9 Logan Tomkins; 23 Lee Mossop; 3 Josh Jones; 10 George Griffin; 13 Mark Flanagan. Subs (all used): 20 Kriss Brining; 16 Olsi Krasniqi; 8 Craig Kopczak; 15 Ryan Lannon.
Tries: Sa'u (5, 73), Griffin (35), Brining (42);
Goals: O'Brien 4/6.
WOLVES: 7 Kurt Gidley (C); 26 Jack Johnson; 3 Rhys Evans; 4 Ryan Atkins; 2 Tom Lineham; 6 Kevin Brown; 22 Declan Patton; 14 Mike Cooper; 9 Daryl Clark; 10 Ashton Sims; 12 Jack Hughes; 18 Andre Savelio; 13 Joe Westerman. Subs (all used): 15 Brad Dwyer; 21 Matty Blythe (D2); 28 Harvey Livett; 34 Ben Westwood.
Tries: Patton (25), Hughes (37), Johnson (62);
Goals: Patton 1/3.
Rugby Leaguer & League Express Men of the Match:
Red Devils: Michael Dobson; *Wolves:* Joe Westerman.
Penalty count: 9-6; **Half-time:** 8-10;
Referee: Jack Smith; **Attendance:** 5,492.

CATALANS DRAGONS 14 WIDNES VIKINGS 14

DRAGONS: 16 Thomas Bosc; 2 Jodie Broughton; 3 Krisnan Inu; 4 Brayden Wiliame; 21 Iain Thornley; 6 Luke Walsh; 7 Richie Myler; 20 Luke Burgess (D); 9 Paul Aiton; 10 Remi Casty (C); 12 Justin Horo; 15 Benjamin Garcia; 13 Greg Bird. Subs (all used): 11 Louis Anderson; 19 Mickael Simon; 23 Alrix Da Costa; 25 Thibaut Margalet.
Tries: Wiliame (7), Myler (12); **Goals:** Walsh 3/3.
VIKINGS: 1 Rhys Hanbury; 2 Corey Thompson; 26 Tom Armstrong; 4 Charly Runciman; 5 Patrick Ah Van; 3 Chris Bridge; 32 Danny Craven; 15 Gil Dudson; 9 Lloyd White; 10 Jack Buchanan; 12 Matt Whitley; 11 Chris Houston (C); 13 Hep Cahill. Subs (all used): 33 Aaron Heremaia; 19 Macgraff Leuluai; 25 Tom Olbison; 23 Jay Chapelhow.
Tries: Ah Van (36), Olbison (48), Hanbury (73);
Goals: Hanbury 1/3.
Rugby Leaguer & League Express Men of the Match:
Dragons: Remi Casty; *Vikings:* Aaron Heremaia.
Penalty count: 10-8; **Half-time:** 14-6;
Referee: Chris Kendall; **Attendance:** 7,254.

ROUND 4

Thursday 9th March 2017

WARRINGTON WOLVES 16 WIGAN WARRIORS 38

WOLVES: 7 Kurt Gidley (C); 5 Matthew Russell; 21 Matty Blythe; 4 Ryan Atkins; 2 Tom Lineham; 6 Kevin Brown; 28 Harvey Livett; 14 Mike Cooper; 9 Daryl Clark; 10 Ashton Sims; 12 Jack Hughes; 34 Ben Westwood; 13 Joe Westerman. Subs (all used): 15 Brad Dwyer; 23 Joe Philbin; 18 Andre Savelio; 3 Rhys Evans.
Tries: Atkins (39), Evans (65), Lineham (77);
Goals: Gidley 2/3.
WARRIORS: 22 Morgan Escare; 32 Liam Forsyth (D); 3 Anthony Gelling; 20 Willie Isa; 35 Liam Marshall; 6 George Williams; 7 Thomas Leuluai; 8 Frank-Paul Nuuausala; 16 Sam Powell; 10 Ben Flower; 11 Joel Tomkins; 12 Liam Farrell; 13 Sean O'Loughlin (C). Subs (all used): 15 Tony Clubb; 17 Taulima Tautai; 26 Romain Navarrete (D); 28 Jack Wells.
Tries: Marshall (6, 18, 48, 69), Gelling (14), Farrell (32), Wells (58); **Goals:** Escare 5/7.
Rugby Leaguer & League Express Men of the Match:
Wolves: Daryl Clark; *Warriors:* Liam Farrell.
Penalty count: 6-4; **Half-time:** 6-20;
Referee: Ben Thaler; **Attendance:** 11,250.

Friday 10th March 2017

HULL FC 24 ST HELENS 14

HULL FC: 1 Jamie Shaul; 2 Mahe Fonua; 3 Carlos Tuimavave; 4 Josh Griffin; 5 Fetuli Talanoa; 6 Albert Kelly; 7 Marc Sneyd; 8 Scott Taylor; 9 Danny Houghton (C); 22 Josh Bowden; 12 Mark Minichiello; 21 Sika Manu; 16 Jordan Thompson. Subs (all used): 15 Chris Green; 17 Danny Washbrook; 25 Jansin Turgut; 29 Masi Matongo.
Tries: Kelly (13, 80), Tuimavave (69); **Goals:** Sneyd 6/6.
Sin bin: Turgut (59) - use of the elbow on Walmsley.
SAINTS: 2 Tom Makinson; 21 Jack Owens; 3 Ryan Morgan; 4 Mark Percival; 5 Adam Swift; 6 Theo Fages; 12 Jon Wilkin (C); 8 Alex Walmsley; 9 James Roby; 14 Luke Douglas; 36 Zeb Taia; 18 Dominique Peyroux; 20 Morgan Knowles. Subs (all used): 10 Kyle Amor; 13 Louie McCarthy-Scarsbrook; 15 Adam Walker; 17 Tommy Lee.
Tries: Peyroux (24), Percival (62); **Goals:** Percival 3/4.
On report: Douglas (25) - alleged contact with referee.
Rugby Leaguer & League Express Men of the Match:
Hull FC: Albert Kelly; *Saints:* James Roby.
Penalty count: 12-6; **Half-time:** 6-8;
Referee: Phil Bentham; **Attendance:** 11,587.

LEEDS RHINOS 46 CATALANS DRAGONS 10

RHINOS: 1 Ashton Golding; 2 Tom Briscoe; 3 Kallum Watkins; 4 Joel Moon; 5 Ryan Hall; 6 Danny McGuire (C); 14 Liam Sutcliffe; 10 Adam Cuthbertson; 9 Matt Parcell; 16 Brad Singleton; 18 Jimmy Keinhorst; 12 Carl Ablett; 24 Jordan Baldwinson. Subs (all used): 7 Rob Burrow; 15 Brett Delaney; 20 Anthony Mullally; 21 Josh Walters.
Tries: Cuthbertson (7, 57), Parcell (36), Keinhorst (46), Burrow (65), McGuire (67), L Sutcliffe (76);
Goals: L Sutcliffe 9/9.
Sin bin: Cuthbertson (20) - professional foul; Keinhorst (29) - holding down.
On report: Singleton (10) - alleged use of the elbow on Bird.
DRAGONS: 16 Thomas Bosc; 2 Jodie Broughton; 18 Vincent Duport; 4 Brayden Wiliame; 21 Iain Thornley; 6 Luke Walsh; 7 Richie Myler; 20 Luke Burgess; 9 Paul Aiton; 10 Remi Casty (C); 15 Benjamin Garcia; 12 Justin Horo; 13 Greg Bird. Subs (all used): 14 Julian Bousquet; 11 Louis Anderson; 23 Alrix Da Costa; 17 Jason Baitieri.
Tries: Wiliame (30), Bousquet (50); **Goals:** Walsh 1/2.
Rugby Leaguer & League Express Men of the Match:
Rhinos: Matt Parcell; *Dragons:* Brayden Wiliame.
Penalty count: 9-10; **Half-time:** 14-4;
Referee: James Child; **Attendance:** 13,208.

LEIGH CENTURIONS 30 HUDDERSFIELD GIANTS 0

CENTURIONS: 19 Ryan Hampshire; 2 Adam Higson; 1 Mitch Brown; 3 Ben Crooks; 5 Matty Dawson; 20 Ben Reynolds; 7 Josh Drinkwater; 15 Danny Tickle; 9 Micky Higham (C); 24 Jamie Acton; 8 Gareth Hock; 17 Atelea Vea; 13 Harrison Hansen. Subs (all used): 14 Eloi Pelissier; 29 Lachlan Burr; 23 Sam Hopkins; 22 James Green.
Tries: Higson (12), Acton (36), Hansen (65), Reynolds (76), Hopkins (79); **Goals:** Reynolds 5/6.
Sin bin: Acton (59) - fighting.
On report: Higson (50) - alleged high tackle on Roberts.
GIANTS: 4 Lee Gaskell; 2 Jermaine McGillvary; 3 Leroy Cudjoe (C); 30 Alex Mellor; 5 Aaron Murphy; 6 Danny Brough; 7 Ryan Brierley; 8 Sam Rapira; 14 Kruise Leeming; 15 Sebastine Ikahihifo; 16 Oliver Roberts; 17 Ukuma Ta'ai; 9 Ryan Hinchcliffe. Subs (all used): 10 Shannon Wakeman; 18 Paul Clough; 20 Daniel Smith; 24 Darnell McIntosh.

Sin bin: Ikahihifo (59) - fighting.
Rugby Leaguer & League Express Men of the Match:
Centurions: Danny Tickle; *Giants:* Ukuma Ta'ai.
Penalty count: 10-11; **Half-time:** 12-0;
Referee: Chris Campbell; **Attendance:** 6,001.

Sunday 12th March 2017

WAKEFIELD TRINITY 24 SALFORD RED DEVILS 22

TRINITY: 1 Scott Grix; 24 Mason Caton-Brown; 4 Reece Lyne; 3 Bill Tupou; 2 Tom Johnstone; 6 Jacob Miller; 14 Sam Williams; 8 Anthony England; 9 Kyle Wood; 17 Craig Huby; 11 Matty Ashurst; 32 Dean Hadley (D); 16 Tinirau Arona. Subs (all used): 27 James Batchelor; 20 David Fifita; 10 Mitch Allgood (D); 7 Liam Finn (C).
Tries: Lyne (30, 78), Miller (37), Tupou (69);
Goals: Williams 4/6.
RED DEVILS: 1 Gareth O'Brien; 21 Greg Johnson; 22 Kris Welham; 5 Niall Evalds; 2 Justin Carney; 6 Robert Lui; 7 Michael Dobson (C); 23 Lee Mossop; 9 Logan Tomkins; 14 Lama Tasi; 3 Josh Jones; 11 Ben Murdoch-Masila; 13 Mark Flanagan. Subs (all used): 8 Craig Kopczak; 10 George Griffin; 16 Olsi Krasniqi; 20 Kriss Brining.
Tries: Murdoch-Masila (50), Welham (57), Johnson (60), Griffin (62); **Goals:** O'Brien 3/5.
Sin bin: Tasi (2) - dangerous challenge on England; Tomkins (26) - repeated team offences.
Rugby Leaguer & League Express Men of the Match:
Trinity: Reece Lyne; *Red Devils:* Robert Lui.
Penalty count: 11-6; **Half-time:** 12-2;
Referee: Robert Hicks; **Attendance:** 4,964.

WIDNES VIKINGS 0 CASTLEFORD TIGERS 34

VIKINGS: 1 Rhys Hanbury; 2 Corey Thompson; 26 Tom Armstrong; 4 Charly Runciman; 17 Stefan Marsh; 3 Chris Bridge; 32 Danny Craven; 23 Jay Chapelhow; 9 Lloyd White; 10 Jack Buchanan; 11 Chris Houston (C); 12 Matt Whitley; 13 Hep Cahill. Subs (all used): 33 Aaron Heremaia; 19 Macgraff Leuluai; 25 Tom Olbison; 18 Greg Burke.
TIGERS: 1 Zak Hardaker; 21 Joel Monaghan; 2 Greg Minikin; 4 Michael Shenton (C); 5 Greg Eden; 9 Paul McShane; 7 Luke Gale; 8 Andy Lynch; 13 Adam Milner; 19 Gadwin Springer; 15 Jesse Sene-Lefao; 12 Mike McMeeken; 14 Nathan Massey. Subs (all used): 17 Junior Moors; 10 Grant Millington; 18 Matt Cook; 16 Ben Roberts.
Tries: Minikin (22, 30), Shenton (32), Eden (35, 55), Cook (50); **Goals:** Gale 5/6.
Rugby Leaguer & League Express Men of the Match:
Vikings: Chris Houston; *Tigers:* Mike McMeeken.
Penalty count: 5-6; **Half-time:** 0-22;
Referee: Jack Smith; **Attendance:** 6,396.

ROUND 5

Thursday 16th March 2017

LEIGH CENTURIONS 22 WARRINGTON WOLVES 8

CENTURIONS: 19 Ryan Hampshire; 2 Adam Higson; 3 Ben Crooks; 1 Mitch Brown; 5 Matty Dawson; 20 Ben Reynolds; 7 Josh Drinkwater; 8 Gareth Hock; 9 Micky Higham (C); 24 Jamie Acton; 17 Atelea Vea; 12 Glenn Stewart; 13 Harrison Hansen. Subs (all used): 14 Eloi Pelissier; 15 Danny Tickle; 23 Sam Hopkins; 29 Lachlan Burr.
Tries: Hock (6, 67), Crooks (16), Higson (62);
Goals: Reynolds 3/6.
Sin bin: Stewart (47) - high tackle on Brown.
WOLVES: 26 Jack Johnson; 5 Matthew Russell; 3 Rhys Evans; 4 Ryan Atkins; 2 Tom Lineham; 6 Kevin Brown; 7 Kurt Gidley; 8 Chris Hill (C); 9 Daryl Clark; 14 Mike Cooper; 12 Jack Hughes; 34 Ben Westwood; 13 Joe Westerman. Subs (all used): 10 Ashton Sims; 15 Brad Dwyer; 18 Andre Savelio; 28 Harvey Livett.
Try: Lineham (70); **Goals:** Gidley 1/1, Livett 1/1.
Sin bin: Lineham (55) - use of the elbow on Hampshire.
Rugby Leaguer & League Express Men of the Match:
Centurions: Gareth Hock; *Wolves:* Mike Cooper.
Penalty count: 9-11; **Half-time:** 12-2;
Referee: Ben Thaler; **Attendance:** 7,011.

Friday 17th March 2017

HULL FC 32 WIDNES VIKINGS 12

HULL FC: 1 Jamie Shaul; 2 Mahe Fonua; 3 Carlos Tuimavave; 4 Josh Griffin; 19 Steve Michaels; 6 Albert Kelly; 7 Marc Sneyd; 8 Scott Taylor; 9 Danny Houghton; 22 Josh Bowden; 12 Mark Minichiello; 21 Sika Manu; 16 Jordan Thompson. Subs (all used): 15 Chris Green; 17 Danny Washbrook; 13 Gareth Ellis (C); 14 Jake Connor.
Tries: Kelly (7, 53), Fonua (32), Houghton (48), Shaul (50);
Goals: Sneyd 6/6.
VIKINGS: 2 Corey Thompson; 17 Stefan Marsh; 3 Chris Bridge; 4 Charly Runciman; 26 Tom Armstrong; 32 Danny Craven; 33 Aaron Heremaia; 23 Jay Chapelhow; 9 Lloyd White; 10 Jack Buchanan; 11 Chris Houston (C); 12 Matt Whitley; 13 Hep Cahill. Subs (all used): 19 Macgraff Leuluai; 22 Ted Chapelhow; 25 Tom Olbison; 31 Jordan Johnstone.
Tries: Heremaia (4), White (71); **Goals:** White 2/2.
Rugby Leaguer & League Express Men of the Match:
Hull FC: Albert Kelly; *Vikings:* Lloyd White.
Penalty count: 15-6; **Half-time:** 14-6;
Referee: Chris Campbell; **Attendance:** 10,814.

LEEDS RHINOS 38 WAKEFIELD TRINITY 14

RHINOS: 1 Ashton Golding; 2 Tom Briscoe; 3 Kallum Watkins; 18 Jimmy Keinhorst; 5 Ryan Hall; 6 Danny McGuire (C); 4 Joel Moon; 10 Adam Cuthbertson; 9 Matt Parcell; 24 Jordan Baldwinson; 12 Carl Ablett; 19 Brett Ferres; 15 Brett Delaney. Subs (all used): 17 Mitch Garbutt; 20 Anthony Mullally; 7 Rob Burrow; 21 Josh Walters.
Tries: Watkins (16, 39), Mullally (29), Hall (43), Cuthbertson (56), Parcell (61); **Goals:** Golding 7/7.
TRINITY: 1 Scott Grix; 2 Tom Johnstone; 3 Bill Tupou; 18 Joe Arundel; 5 Ben Jones-Bishop; 6 Jacob Miller; 14 Sam Williams; 10 Mitch Allgood; 9 Kyle Wood; 17 Craig Huby; 32 Dean Hadley; 11 Matty Ashurst; 16 Tinirau Arona. Subs (all used): 13 Michael Sio; 20 David Fifita; 25 Anthony Walker; 12 Danny Kirmond (C).
Tries: Johnstone (20, 79), Fifita (50); **Goals:** Williams 1/3.
Sin bin: Kirmond (59) - late challenge on Burrow.
Rugby Leaguer & League Express Men of the Match:
Rhinos: Mitch Garbutt; *Trinity:* Tinirau Arona.
Penalty count: 10-8; **Half-time:** 20-4;
Referee: Jack Smith; **Attendance:** 14,411.

Saturday 18th March 2017

CATALANS DRAGONS 24 ST HELENS 28

DRAGONS: 16 Thomas Bosc; 21 Iain Thornley; 3 Krisnan Inu; 4 Brayden Wiliame; 5 Fouad Yaha; 6 Luke Walsh; 7 Richie Myler; 8 Sam Moa; 9 Paul Aiton; 10 Remi Casty (C); 15 Benjamin Garcia; 12 Justin Horo; 17 Jason Baitieri. Subs (all used): 14 Julian Bousquet; 19 Mickael Simon; 20 Luke Burgess; 23 Alrix Da Costa.
Tries: Bosc (5), Bousquet (15), Thornley (34), Aiton (47);
Goals: Walsh 4/4.
SAINTS: 2 Tom Makinson; 21 Jack Owens; 3 Ryan Morgan; 4 Mark Percival; 5 Adam Swift; 6 Theo Fages; 12 Jon Wilkin (C); 8 Alex Walmsley; 9 James Roby; 14 Luke Douglas; 18 Dominique Peyroux; 36 Zeb Taia; 20 Morgan Knowles. Subs (all used): 10 Kyle Amor; 13 Louie McCarthy-Scarsbrook; 15 Adam Walker; 17 Tommy Lee.
Tries: Swift (2), Percival (11), Morgan (18), Walker (30), Owens (72); **Goals:** Percival 4/5.
Rugby Leaguer & League Express Men of the Match:
Dragons: Sam Moa; *Saints:* Theo Fages.
Penalty count: 6-6; **Half-time:** 18-22;
Referee: Robert Hicks; **Attendance:** 8,158.

Sunday 19th March 2017

SALFORD RED DEVILS 13 CASTLEFORD TIGERS 12

RED DEVILS: 1 Gareth O'Brien; 21 Greg Johnson; 22 Kris Welham; 4 Junior Sa'u; 2 Justin Carney; 6 Robert Lui; 7 Michael Dobson (C); 17 Adam Walne; 9 Logan Tomkins; 23 Lee Mossop; 11 Ben Murdoch-Masila; 10 George Griffin; 13 Mark Flanagan. Subs: 20 Kriss Brining; 16 Olsi Krasniqi; 8 Craig Kopczak; 29 Todd Carney (not used).
Tries: Murdoch-Masila (32, 54); **Goals:** O'Brien 2/3;
Field goal: O'Brien (76).
TIGERS: 1 Zak Hardaker; 2 Greg Minikin; 3 Jake Webster; 4 Michael Shenton (C); 5 Greg Eden; 16 Ben Roberts; 7 Luke Gale; 8 Andy Lynch; 9 Paul McShane; 14 Nathan Massey; 15 Jesse Sene-Lefao; 12 Mike McMeeken; 13 Adam Milner. Subs (all used): 10 Grant Millington; 17 Junior Moors; 18 Matt Cook; 19 Gadwin Springer.
Tries: Gale (5), Minikin (43); **Goals:** Gale 2/2.
Rugby Leaguer & League Express Men of the Match:
Red Devils: Ben Murdoch-Masila; *Tigers:* Adam Milner.
Penalty count: 6-4; **Half-time:** 4-6;
Referee: Phil Bentham; **Attendance:** 5,221.

WIGAN WARRIORS 16 HUDDERSFIELD GIANTS 16

WARRIORS: 22 Morgan Escare; 36 Tom Davies (D); 3 Anthony Gelling; 20 Willie Isa; 35 Liam Marshall; 6 George Williams; 7 Thomas Leuluai; 8 Frank-Paul Nuuausala; 16 Sam Powell; 10 Ben Flower; 11 Joel Tomkins; 28 Jack Wells; 13 Sean O'Loughlin (C). Subs (all used): 15 Tony Clubb; 17 Taulima Tautai; 26 Romain Navarrete; 32 Liam Forsyth.
Tries: Escare (12), Davies (30), Gelling (48);
Goals: Escare 2/4.
GIANTS: 24 Darnell McIntosh; 2 Jermaine McGillvary; 3 Leroy Cudjoe (C); 30 Alex Mellor; 5 Aaron Murphy; 6 Danny Brough; 4 Lee Gaskell; 8 Sam Rapira; 14 Kruise Leeming; 15 Sebastine Ikahihifo; 16 Oliver Roberts; 17 Ukuma Ta'ai; 18 Paul Clough. Subs (all used): 9 Ryan Hinchcliffe; 10 Shannon Wakeman; 20 Daniel Smith; 22 Tyler Dickinson.
Tries: Gaskell (3), McIntosh (19); **Goals:** Brough 4/5.
Sin bin: Leeming (66) - high tackle on Davies.
Rugby Leaguer & League Express Men of the Match:
Warriors: Joel Tomkins; *Giants:* Lee Gaskell.
Penalty count: 13-9; **Half-time:** 10-14;
Referee: Chris Kendall; **Attendance:** 12,704.

ROUND 6

Thursday 23rd March 2017

WAKEFIELD TRINITY 28 LEIGH CENTURIONS 24

TRINITY: 1 Scott Grix; 5 Ben Jones-Bishop; 18 Joe Arundel; 3 Bill Tupou; 2 Tom Johnstone; 14 Sam Williams; 7 Liam Finn; 10 Mitch Allgood; 32 Dean Hadley; 20 David Fifita; 11 Matty Ashurst; 12 Danny Kirmond (C); 16 Tinirau Arona. Subs (all used): 23 Keegan Hirst (D); 17 Craig Huby; 9 Kyle Wood; 6 Jacob Miller.
Tries: Arundel (19), Grix (22), Johnstone (48), Miller (58), Jones-Bishop (66); **Goals:** Williams 4/6.
CENTURIONS: 19 Ryan Hampshire; 2 Adam Higson; 3 Ben Crooks; 1 Mitch Brown; 5 Matty Dawson; 20 Ben Reynolds; 7 Josh Drinkwater; 8 Gareth Hock; 9 Micky Higham (C); 24 Jamie Acton; 15 Danny Tickle; 17 Atelea Vea; 13 Harrison Hansen. Subs (all used): 14 Eloi Pelissier; 22 James Green; 23 Sam Hopkins; 29 Lachlan Burr.
Tries: Reynolds (5), Higham (25), Hopkins (31), Crooks (34);
Goals: Reynolds 4/4.
Rugby Leaguer & League Express Men of the Match:
Trinity: David Fifita; *Centurions:* Gareth Hock.
Penalty count: 10-9; **Half-time:** 12-24;
Referee: Chris Campbell; **Attendance:** 4,592.

Friday 24th March 2017

HUDDERSFIELD GIANTS 12 LEEDS RHINOS 28

GIANTS: 24 Darnell McIntosh; 2 Jermaine McGillvary; 3 Leroy Cudjoe (C); 30 Alex Mellor; 5 Aaron Murphy; 6 Danny Brough; 4 Lee Gaskell; 8 Sam Rapira; 14 Kruise Leeming; 15 Sebastine Ikahihifo; 12 Dale Ferguson; 17 Ukuma Ta'ai; 18 Paul Clough. Subs (all used): 9 Ryan Hinchcliffe; 10 Shannon Wakeman; 16 Oliver Roberts; 20 Daniel Smith.
Tries: Ta'ai (18), McGillvary (21); **Goals:** Brough 2/2.
Sin bin: Brough (45) - fighting.
RHINOS: 1 Ashton Golding; 2 Tom Briscoe; 3 Kallum Watkins; 18 Jimmy Keinhorst; 5 Ryan Hall; 6 Danny McGuire (C); 4 Joel Moon; 24 Jordan Baldwinson; 9 Matt Parcell; 10 Adam Cuthbertson; 12 Carl Ablett; 19 Brett Ferres; 11 Jamie Jones-Buchanan. Subs (all used): 7 Rob Burrow; 14 Liam Sutcliffe; 17 Mitch Garbutt; 20 Anthony Mullally.
Tries: Briscoe (5), Hall (11), Ablett (25), Parcell (33), Baldwinson (79); **Goals:** Golding 2/5, L Sutcliffe 2/2.
Sin bin: Ablett (45) - fighting.
Rugby Leaguer & League Express Men of the Match:
Giants: Ukuma Ta'ai; *Rhinos:* Adam Cuthbertson.
Penalty count: 9-8; **Half-time:** 12-18;
Referee: Ben Thaler; **Attendance:** 8,666.

ST HELENS 31 WARRINGTON WOLVES 6

SAINTS: 2 Tom Makinson; 21 Jack Owens; 3 Ryan Morgan; 4 Mark Percival; 5 Adam Swift; 6 Theo Fages; 7 Matty Smith (D2); 8 Alex Walmsley; 17 Tommy Lee; 14 Luke Douglas; 36 Zeb Taia; 13 Louie McCarthy-Scarsbrook; 12 Jon Wilkin (C). Subs (all used): 9 James Roby; 10 Kyle Amor; 15 Adam Walker; 18 Dominique Peyroux.
Tries: Taia (30), Owens (34), Swift (36, 63), Walmsley (78);
Goals: Percival 5/7; **Field goal:** Smith (72).
WOLVES: 1 Stefan Ratchford; 5 Matthew Russell; 3 Rhys Evans; 20 Toby King; 26 Jack Johnson; 6 Kevin Brown; 7 Kurt Gidley; 8 Chris Hill (C); 9 Daryl Clark; 14 Mike Cooper; 34 Ben Westwood; 12 Jack Hughes; 13 Joe Westerman. Subs (all used): 10 Ashton Sims; 15 Brad Dwyer; 17 Dominic Crosby; 28 Harvey Livett.
Try: Gidley (43); **Goals:** Ratchford 1/1.
Rugby Leaguer & League Express Men of the Match:
Saints: Mark Percival; *Wolves:* Daryl Clark.
Penalty count: 9-5; **Half-time:** 18-0;
Referee: James Child; **Attendance:** 11,598.

WIDNES VIKINGS 10 SALFORD RED DEVILS 46

VIKINGS: 1 Rhys Hanbury; 2 Corey Thompson; 26 Tom Armstrong; 4 Charly Runciman; 17 Stefan Marsh; 33 Aaron Heremaia; 32 Danny Craven; 15 Gil Dudson; 31 Jordan Johnstone; 10 Jack Buchanan; 25 Tom Olbison; 12 Matt Whitley; 11 Chris Houston (C). Subs (all used): 3 Chris Bridge; 19 Macgraff Leuluai; 23 Jay Chapelhow; 22 Ted Chapelhow.
Tries: Thompson (43), Hanbury (76);
Goals: Hanbury 0/1, Bridge 1/1.
RED DEVILS: 1 Gareth O'Brien; 21 Greg Johnson; 22 Kris Welham; 4 Junior Sa'u; 2 Justin Carney; 6 Robert Lui; 7

Michael Dobson (C); 14 Lama Tasi; 9 Logan Tomkins; 17 Adam Walne; 10 George Griffin; 11 Ben Murdoch-Masila; 13 Mark Flanagan. Subs (all used): 8 Craig Kopczak; 16 Olsi Krasniqi; 20 Kriss Brining; 29 Todd Carney (D).
Tries: Tasi (13), Johnson (18), Griffin (21), Murdoch-Masila (24), Welham (37), J Carney (40), Dobson (55), Lui (66), O'Brien (68);
Goals: O'Brien 2/5, Dobson 3/4.
Rugby Leaguer & League Express Men of the Match:
Vikings: Chris Bridge; *Red Devils:* Robert Lui.
Penalty count: 6-6; **Half-time:** 0-30;
Referee: Chris Kendall; **Attendance:** 5,565.

WIGAN WARRIORS 20 HULL FC 22

WARRIORS: 22 Morgan Escare; 36 Tom Davies; 3 Anthony Gelling; 32 Liam Forsyth; 35 Liam Marshall; 6 George Williams; 7 Thomas Leuluai (C); 8 Frank-Paul Nuuausala; 16 Sam Powell; 10 Ben Flower; 11 Joel Tomkins; 20 Willie Isa; 15 Tony Clubb. Subs (all used): 17 Taulima Tautai; 23 Nick Gregson; 24 Joe Bretherton; 26 Romain Navarrete.
Tries: Forsyth (54), Williams (68), Davies (71), Marshall (75); **Goals:** Escare 2/4.
HULL FC: 1 Jamie Shaul; 2 Mahe Fonua; 14 Jake Connor; 4 Josh Griffin; 19 Steve Michaels; 6 Albert Kelly; 7 Marc Sneyd; 8 Scott Taylor; 9 Danny Houghton; 22 Josh Bowden; 12 Mark Minichiello; 21 Sika Manu; 13 Gareth Ellis (C). Subs (all used): 15 Chris Green; 16 Jordan Thompson; 17 Danny Washbrook; 29 Masi Matongo.
Tries: Michaels (12), Kelly (16), Connor (19), Shaul (41);
Goals: Sneyd 3/4.
Rugby Leaguer & League Express Men of the Match:
Warriors: Liam Marshall; *Hull FC:* Gareth Ellis.
Penalty count: 7-3; **Half-time:** 0-18;
Referee: Phil Bentham; **Attendance:** 12,319.

Sunday 26th March 2017

CASTLEFORD TIGERS 43 CATALANS DRAGONS 26

TIGERS: 1 Zak Hardaker; 21 Joel Monaghan; 3 Jake Webster; 4 Michael Shenton (C); 5 Greg Eden; 16 Ben Roberts; 7 Luke Gale; 8 Andy Lynch; 9 Paul McShane; 14 Nathan Massey; 10 Grant Millington; 12 Mike McMeeken; 13 Adam Milner. Subs (all used): 17 Junior Moors; 18 Matt Cook; 15 Jesse Sene-Lefao; 6 Rangi Chase.
Tries: Hardaker (13), Millington (26), Monaghan (31), Eden (39, 71), Moors (45), Shenton (61);
Goals: Gale 7/9; **Field goal:** Gale (65).
DRAGONS: 4 Brayden Wiliame; 5 Fouad Yaha; 3 Krisnan Inu; 18 Vincent Duport; 21 Iain Thornley; 6 Luke Walsh; 7 Richie Myler; 8 Sam Moa; 9 Paul Aiton; 10 Remi Casty (C); 14 Julian Bousquet; 15 Benjamin Garcia; 20 Luke Burgess. Subs (all used): 11 Louis Anderson; 17 Jason Baitieri; 23 Alrix Da Costa; 25 Thibaut Margalet.
Tries: Thornley (2), Myler (8), Anderson (42), Duport (76);
Goals: Walsh 5/5.
Rugby Leaguer & League Express Men of the Match:
Tigers: Junior Moors; *Dragons:* Paul Aiton.
Penalty count: 9-10; **Half-time:** 22-14;
Referee: Jack Smith; **Attendance:** 8,126.

ROUND 7

Thursday 30th March 2017

SALFORD RED DEVILS 22 ST HELENS 14

RED DEVILS: 1 Gareth O'Brien; 21 Greg Johnson; 22 Kris Welham; 3 Josh Jones; 2 Justin Carney; 6 Robert Lui; 7 Michael Dobson (C); 14 Lama Tasi; 9 Logan Tomkins; 23 Lee Mossop; 11 Ben Murdoch-Masila; 10 George Griffin; 13 Mark Flanagan. Subs (all used): 8 Craig Kopczak; 17 Adam Walne; 20 Kriss Brining; 29 Todd Carney.
Tries: Kopczak (35), Dobson (43, 75);
Goals: Dobson 4/4, O'Brien 1/1.
Sin bin: Lui (71) - delaying restart.
SAINTS: 1 Jonny Lomax; 21 Jack Owens; 3 Ryan Morgan; 4 Mark Percival; 2 Tom Makinson; 6 Theo Fages; 7 Matty Smith; 8 Alex Walmsley; 9 James Roby; 14 Luke Douglas; 36 Zeb Taia; 13 Louie McCarthy-Scarsbrook; 12 Jon Wilkin (C). Subs (all used): 10 Kyle Amor; 15 Adam Walker; 17 Tommy Lee; 18 Dominique Peyroux.
Tries: Walmsley (52), Morgan (59), Lomax (78);
Goals: Percival 1/3.
Rugby Leaguer & League Express Men of the Match:
Red Devils: Michael Dobson; *Saints:* Alex Walmsley.
Penalty count: 9-13; **Half-time:** 8-0;
Referee: James Child; **Attendance:** 3,686.

Friday 31st March 2017

CASTLEFORD TIGERS 52 HUDDERSFIELD GIANTS 16

TIGERS: 1 Zak Hardaker; 21 Joel Monaghan; 3 Jake Webster; 4 Michael Shenton (C); 5 Greg Eden; 16 Ben Roberts; 7 Luke Gale; 15 Jesse Sene-Lefao; 9 Paul McShane; 17 Junior Moors; 10 Grant Millington; 12 Mike McMeeken; 13 Adam Milner. Subs (all used): 18 Matt Cook; 19 Gadwin Springer; 6 Rangi Chase; 11 Oliver Holmes.
Tries: Roberts (19), Webster (22), McMeeken (27), Gale (41, 53, 57), Milner (43), Monaghan (56, 63, 77);
Goals: Gale 6/10.
GIANTS: 24 Darnell McIntosh; 2 Jermaine McGillvary; 3 Leroy Cudjoe (C); 30 Alex Mellor; 21 Gene Ormsby; 4 Lee Gaskell; 7 Ryan Brierley; 15 Sebastine Ikahihifo; 9 Ryan Hinchcliffe; 10 Shannon Wakeman; 17 Ukuma Ta'ai; 12 Dale Ferguson; 18 Paul Clough. Subs (all used): 8 Sam Rapira; 14 Kruise Leeming; 20 Daniel Smith; 22 Tyler Dickinson.
Tries: Hinchcliffe (7), Brierley (49), Gaskell (76);
Goals: Brierley 2/3.
Rugby Leaguer & League Express Men of the Match:
Tigers: Jake Webster; *Giants:* Ryan Brierley.
Penalty count: 9-5; **Half-time:** 16-4;
Referee: Chris Kendall; **Attendance:** 8,035.

LEEDS RHINOS 26 WIGAN WARRIORS 18

RHINOS: 1 Ashton Golding; 2 Tom Briscoe; 3 Kallum Watkins; 18 Jimmy Keinhorst; 5 Ryan Hall; 6 Danny McGuire (C); 4 Joel Moon; 10 Adam Cuthbertson; 9 Matt Parcell; 17 Mitch Garbutt; 12 Carl Ablett; 19 Brett Ferres; 11 Jamie Jones-Buchanan. Subs (all used): 20 Anthony Mullally; 7 Rob Burrow; 14 Liam Sutcliffe; 15 Brett Delaney.
Tries: Hall (21), Moon (24), Watkins (53), Ablett (77);
Goals: Golding 5/6.
Sin bin: Ferres (39) - dangerous challenge on Gildart.
WARRIORS: 22 Morgan Escare; 36 Tom Davies; 32 Liam Forsyth; 4 Oliver Gildart; 35 Liam Marshall; 6 George Williams; 7 Thomas Leuluai (C); 8 Frank-Paul Nuuausala; 16 Sam Powell; 10 Ben Flower; 11 Joel Tomkins; 20 Willie Isa; 15 Tony Clubb. Subs (all used): 17 Taulima Tautai; 19 Ryan Sutton; 23 Nick Gregson; 26 Romain Navarrete.
Tries: Williams (13, 32), Marshall (65); **Goals:** Escare 3/3.
Rugby Leaguer & League Express Men of the Match:
Rhinos: Carl Ablett; *Warriors:* George Williams.
Penalty count: 10-6; **Half-time:** 14-12;
Referee: Ben Thaler; **Attendance:** 17,030.

Saturday 1st April 2017

WARRINGTON WOLVES 22 HULL FC 22

WOLVES: 1 Stefan Ratchford; 5 Matthew Russell; 20 Toby King; 4 Ryan Atkins; 3 Rhys Evans; 6 Kevin Brown; 7 Kurt Gidley; 8 Chris Hill (C); 9 Daryl Clark; 14 Mike Cooper; 34 Ben Westwood; 12 Jack Hughes; 13 Joe Westerman. Subs (all used): 10 Ashton Sims; 15 Brad Dwyer; 16 George King; 23 Joe Philbin.
Tries: Russell (14, 39, 65), Clark (55); **Goals:** Gidley 3/5.
HULL FC: 1 Jamie Shaul; 2 Mahe Fonua; 14 Jake Connor; 4 Josh Griffin; 19 Steve Michaels; 6 Albert Kelly; 7 Marc Sneyd; 8 Scott Taylor; 17 Danny Washbrook; 22 Josh Bowden; 21 Sika Manu; 12 Mark Minichiello; 13 Gareth Ellis (C). Subs (all used): 25 Jansin Turgut; 30 Jez Litten (D); 16 Jordan Thompson; 10 Liam Watts.
Tries: Kelly (9), Connor (24), Shaul (36); **Goals:** Sneyd 5/6.
Rugby Leaguer & League Express Men of the Match:
Wolves: Daryl Clark; *Hull FC:* Albert Kelly.
Penalty count: 8-6; **Half-time:** 8-20;
Referee: Jack Smith; **Attendance:** 10,676.

LEIGH CENTURIONS 24 WIDNES VIKINGS 37

CENTURIONS: 19 Ryan Hampshire; 2 Adam Higson; 1 Mitch Brown; 3 Ben Crooks; 5 Matty Dawson; 6 Martyn Ridyard; 20 Ben Reynolds; 24 Jamie Acton; 9 Micky Higham (C); 10 Dayne Weston; 17 Atelea Vea; 15 Danny Tickle; 8 Gareth Hock. Subs (all used): 21 Liam Hood; 13 Harrison Hansen; 23 Sam Hopkins; 22 James Green.
Tries: Tickle (25), Crooks (30, 51), Hopkins (61);
Goals: Reynolds 4/4.
Sin bin: Crooks (75) - professional foul.
VIKINGS: 1 Rhys Hanbury; 26 Tom Armstrong; 3 Chris Bridge; 4 Charly Runciman; 17 Stefan Marsh; 32 Danny Craven; 7 Tom Gilmore; 23 Jay Chapelhow; 31 Jordan Johnstone; 18 Greg Burke; 25 Tom Olbison; 12 Matt Whitley; 11 Chris Houston (C). Subs (all used): 35 Danny Walker (D); 19 Macgraff Leuluai; 20 Manase Manuokafoa; 24 Sam Brooks.
Tries: Bridge (2), Craven (12, 37, 66), Brooks (42), Runciman (79); **Goals:** Gilmore 6/6, Marsh 0/1;
Field goal: Gilmore (47).
Rugby Leaguer & League Express Men of the Match:
Centurions: Harrison Hansen; *Vikings:* Tom Gilmore.
Penalty count: 6-9; **Half-time:** 12-18;
Referee: Robert Hicks; **Attendance:** 6,196.

CATALANS DRAGONS 18 WAKEFIELD TRINITY 38

DRAGONS: 16 Thomas Bosc; 5 Fouad Yaha; 3 Krisnan Inu; 18 Vincent Duport; 21 Iain Thornley; 6 Luke Walsh; 7 Richie Myler; 8 Sam Moa; 9 Paul Aiton; 10 Remi Casty (C); 11 Louis Anderson; 12 Justin Horo; 15 Benjamin Garcia. Subs (all used): 14 Julian Bousquet; 17 Jason Baitieri; 19 Mickael Simon; 23 Alrix Da Costa.
Tries: Garcia (38), Inu (46), Yaha (69); **Goals:** Walsh 3/3.
Sin bin: Thornley (60) - professional foul.
TRINITY: 1 Scott Grix; 5 Ben Jones-Bishop; 18 Joe Arundel; 3 Bill Tupou; 2 Tom Johnstone; 14 Sam Williams; 7 Liam Finn; 20 David Fifita; 9 Kyle Wood; 10 Mitch Allgood; 11 Matty Ashurst; 12 Danny Kirmond (C); 16 Tinirau Arona. Subs (all used): 6 Jacob Miller; 32 Dean Hadley; 23 Keegan Hirst; 17 Craig Huby.
Tries: Jones-Bishop (13, 16, 65), Johnstone (29, 71), Arundel (44), Ashurst (52); **Goals:** Williams 5/8.
Rugby Leaguer & League Express Men of the Match:
Dragons: Krisnan Inu; *Trinity:* Ben Jones-Bishop.
Penalty count: 8-6; **Half-time:** 6-16;
Referee: Gareth Hewer; **Attendance:** 7,931.

ROUND 8

Thursday 6th April 2017

WIGAN WARRIORS 10 CASTLEFORD TIGERS 27

WARRIORS: 22 Morgan Escare; 36 Tom Davies; 32 Liam Forsyth; 20 Willie Isa; 35 Liam Marshall; 6 George Williams; 7 Thomas Leuluai (C); 8 Frank-Paul Nuuausala; 16 Sam Powell; 10 Ben Flower; 11 Joel Tomkins; 12 Liam Farrell; 19 Ryan Sutton. Subs (all used): 15 Tony Clubb; 17 Taulima Tautai; 23 Nick Gregson; 24 Joe Bretherton.
Tries: Escare (36, 73); **Goals:** Escare 1/2.
TIGERS: 1 Zak Hardaker; 21 Joel Monaghan; 3 Jake Webster; 2 Greg Minikin; 5 Greg Eden; 16 Ben Roberts; 7 Luke Gale (C); 14 Nathan Massey; 9 Paul McShane; 18 Matt Cook; 11 Oliver Holmes; 12 Mike McMeeken; 13 Adam Milner. Subs (all used): 15 Jesse Sene-Lefao; 17 Junior Moors; 19 Gadwin Springer; 6 Rangi Chase.
Tries: Webster (24), Gale (26), Sene-Lefao (43), Eden (77); **Goals:** Gale 5/5; **Field goal:** Gale (79).
Rugby Leaguer & League Express Men of the Match:
Warriors: Taulima Tautai; *Tigers:* Junior Moors.
Penalty count: 8-8; **Half-time:** 4-14;
Referee: Robert Hicks; **Attendance:** 12,423.

Friday 7th April 2017

HULL FC 18 SALFORD RED DEVILS 54

HULL FC: 1 Jamie Shaul; 19 Steve Michaels; 2 Mahe Fonua; 4 Josh Griffin; 5 Fetuli Talanoa; 14 Jake Connor; 7 Marc Sneyd; 22 Josh Bowden; 17 Danny Washbrook; 10 Liam Watts; 12 Mark Minichiello (C); 21 Sika Manu; 25 Jansin Turgut. Subs (all used): 15 Chris Green; 16 Jordan Thompson; 28 Brad Fash; 30 Jez Litten.
Tries: Michaels (5, 51), Shaul (44);
Goals: Sneyd 2/3, Connor 1/1.
Sin bin: Sneyd (35) - interference;
Shaul (68) - professional foul.
RED DEVILS: 1 Gareth O'Brien; 2 Justin Carney; 4 Junior Sa'u; 22 Kris Welham; 21 Greg Johnson; 6 Robert Lui; 7 Michael Dobson (C); 23 Lee Mossop; 9 Logan Tomkins; 14 Lama Tasi; 11 Ben Murdoch-Masila; 3 Josh Jones; 13 Mark Flanagan. Subs (all used): 8 Craig Kopczak; 10 George Griffin; 17 Adam Walne; 29 Todd Carney.
Tries: Lui (12), Johnson (21, 36), Kopczak (26, 30), Sa'u (33), J Carney (40), Dobson (64), Griffin (72), Murdoch-Masila (78); **Goals:** Dobson 3/5, O'Brien 4/6.
Sin bin: J Carney (57) - interference.
Rugby Leaguer & League Express Men of the Match:
Hull FC: Sika Manu; *Red Devils:* Robert Lui.
Penalty count: 13-7; **Half-time:** 8-34;
Referee: Gareth Hewer; **Attendance:** 11,016.

LEIGH CENTURIONS 26 CATALANS DRAGONS 37

CENTURIONS: 18 Gregg McNally; 30 Curtis Naughton; 3 Ben Crooks; 1 Mitch Brown; 5 Matty Dawson; 20 Ben Reynolds; 6 Martyn Ridyard; 8 Gareth Hock; 9 Micky Higham (C); 23 Sam Hopkins; 17 Atelea Vea; 12 Glenn Stewart; 13 Harrison Hansen. Subs (all used): 14 Eloi Pelissier; 15 Danny Tickle; 10 Dayne Weston; 29 Lachlan Burr.
Tries: Naughton (33), Weston (44), McNally (74), Hopkins (79); **Goals:** Reynolds 5/5.
Sin bin: Hock (15) - dissent.
DRAGONS: 1 Tony Gigot; 21 Iain Thornley; 3 Krisnan Inu; 4 Brayden Wiliame; 18 Vincent Duport; 6 Luke Walsh; 7 Richie Myler; 8 Sam Moa; 9 Paul Aiton; 10 Remi Casty (C); 11 Louis Anderson; 15 Benjamin Garcia; 17 Jason Baitieri. Subs (all used): 14 Julian Bousquet; 19 Mickael Simon; 20 Luke Burgess; 23 Alrix Da Costa.
Tries: Thornley (7), Wiliame (9), Inu (13), Anderson (21), Myler (24), Gigot (65);
Goals: Walsh 6/7; **Field goal:** Walsh (77).
Rugby Leaguer & League Express Men of the Match:
Centurions: Micky Higham; *Dragons:* Tony Gigot.
Penalty count: 14-10; **Half-time:** 8-28;
Referee: Jack Smith; **Attendance:** 5,612.

ST HELENS 14 HUDDERSFIELD GIANTS 14

SAINTS: 1 Jonny Lomax; 2 Tom Makinson; 3 Ryan Morgan; 4 Mark Percival; 5 Adam Swift; 6 Theo Fages; 7 Matty Smith; 8 Alex Walmsley; 17 Tommy Lee; 14 Luke Douglas; 36 Zeb Taia; 13 Louie McCarthy-Scarsbrook; 12 Jon Wilkin (C). Subs (all used): 10 Kyle Amor; 15 Adam Walker; 18 Dominique Peyroux; 20 Morgan Knowles.
Tries: Fages (25, 33), Swift (37); **Goals:** Percival 1/3.
GIANTS: 24 Darnell McIntosh; 2 Jermaine McGillvary; 23 Sam Wood; 30 Alex Mellor; 5 Aaron Murphy; 6 Danny Brough (C); 4 Lee Gaskell; 15 Sebastine Ikahihifo; 9 Ryan Hinchcliffe; 10 Shannon Wakeman; 16 Oliver Roberts; 12 Dale Ferguson; 18 Paul Clough. Subs (all used): 8 Sam Rapira; 14 Kruise Leeming; 19 Nathan Mason; 22 Tyler Dickinson.
Tries: McIntosh (62, 72), S Wood (77); **Goals:** Brough 1/3.
Rugby Leaguer & League Express Men of the Match:
Saints: Alex Walmsley; *Giants:* Shannon Wakeman.
Penalty count: 4-3; **Half-time:** 14-0;
Referee: Chris Campbell; **Attendance:** 9,080.

WAKEFIELD TRINITY 30 WIDNES VIKINGS 4

TRINITY: 1 Scott Grix; 5 Ben Jones-Bishop; 18 Joe Arundel; 3 Bill Tupou; 2 Tom Johnstone; 14 Sam Williams; 7 Liam Finn; 10 Mitch Allgood; 9 Kyle Wood; 20 David Fifita; 11 Matty Ashurst; 12 Danny Kirmond (C); 16 Tinirau Arona. Subs (all used): 6 Jacob Miller; 17 Craig Huby; 32 Dean Hadley; 23 Keegan Hirst.
Tries: Tupou (2), Johnstone (16), Hadley (34, 58), Grix (50), Huby (62); **Goals:** Williams 0/3, Finn 3/3.
VIKINGS: 1 Rhys Hanbury; 2 Corey Thompson; 3 Chris Bridge; 4 Charly Runciman; 26 Tom Armstrong; 32 Danny Craven; 7 Tom Gilmore; 15 Gil Dudson; 31 Jordan Johnstone; 23 Jay Chapelhow; 25 Tom Olbison; 12 Matt Whitley; 11 Chris Houston (C). Subs (all used): 6 Joe Mellor (C); 16 Alex Gerrard; 20 Manase Manuokafoa; 22 Ted Chapelhow.
Try: Thompson (19); **Goals:** Gilmore 0/1.
Rugby Leaguer & League Express Men of the Match:
Trinity: David Fifita; *Vikings:* Rhys Hanbury.
Penalty count: 10-7; **Half-time:** 12-4;
Referee: Chris Kendall; **Attendance:** 4,214.

WARRINGTON WOLVES 25 LEEDS RHINOS 14

WOLVES: 1 Stefan Ratchford; 5 Matthew Russell; 20 Toby King; 4 Ryan Atkins; 2 Tom Lineham; 22 Declan Patton; 7 Kurt Gidley; 8 Chris Hill (C); 9 Daryl Clark; 10 Ashton Sims; 34 Ben Westwood; 12 Jack Hughes; 13 Joe Westerman. Subs (all used): 23 Joe Philbin; 15 Brad Dwyer; 16 George King; 3 Rhys Evans.
Tries: Atkins (14, 30), Lineham (44), Gidley (69);
Goals: Patton 4/4; **Field goal:** Patton (79).
Sin bin: Westwood (1) - late challenge on L Sutcliffe.
On report:
Sims (6) - alleged striking with the leg on Cuthbertson.
RHINOS: 1 Ashton Golding; 2 Tom Briscoe; 3 Kallum Watkins; 18 Jimmy Keinhorst; 5 Ryan Hall; 6 Danny McGuire (C); 4 Joel Moon; 17 Mitch Garbutt; 7 Rob Burrow; 10 Adam Cuthbertson; 14 Liam Sutcliffe; 12 Carl Ablett; 11 Jamie Jones-Buchanan. Subs (all used): 9 Matt Parcell; 15 Brett Delaney; 20 Anthony Mullally; 21 Josh Walters.
Tries: Briscoe (2), Parcell (54), Moon (61);
Goals: Golding 0/2, Watkins 1/1.
Rugby Leaguer & League Express Men of the Match:
Wolves: Declan Patton; *Rhinos:* Brett Delaney.
Penalty count: 7-8; **Half-time:** 12-4;
Referee: James Child; **Attendance:** 10,035.

ROUND 9

Wednesday 12th April 2017

HUDDERSFIELD GIANTS 22 CATALANS DRAGONS 29

GIANTS: 1 Jake Mamo (D); 2 Jermaine McGillvary; 23 Sam Wood; 5 Aaron Murphy; 24 Darnell McIntosh; 6 Danny Brough (C); 4 Lee Gaskell; 15 Sebastine Ikahihifo; 9 Ryan Hinchcliffe; 10 Shannon Wakeman; 11 Tom Symonds; 30 Alex Mellor; 18 Paul Clough. Subs (all used): 8 Sam Rapira; 14 Kruise Leeming; 16 Oliver Roberts; 19 Nathan Mason.
Tries: Murphy (13), Mamo (35), McGillvary (65), S Wood (80); **Goals:** Brough 3/4.
Sin bin: Brough (50) - dissent.
DRAGONS: 1 Tony Gigot; 21 Iain Thornley; 3 Krisnan Inu; 4 Brayden Wiliame; 18 Vincent Duport; 6 Luke Walsh; 7 Richie Myler; 8 Sam Moa; 9 Paul Aiton; 26 Lambert Belmas (D); 11 Louis Anderson; 15 Benjamin Garcia; 10 Remi Casty (C). Subs (all used): 14 Julian Bousquet; 16 Thomas Bosc; 19 Mickael Simon; 25 Thibaut Margalet.
Tries: Gigot (20), Wiliame (39), Myler (49), Duport (56), Walsh (60); **Goals:** Walsh 4/5; **Field goal:** Gigot (76).
Rugby Leaguer & League Express Men of the Match:
Giants: Sebastine Ikahihifo; *Dragons:* Tony Gigot.
Penalty count: 5-8; **Half-time:** 10-12;
Referee: Chris Campbell; **Attendance:** 4,973.

Thursday 13th April 2017

WIDNES VIKINGS 10 WARRINGTON WOLVES 19

VIKINGS: 1 Rhys Hanbury; 26 Tom Armstrong; 3 Chris Bridge; 4 Charly Runciman; 17 Stefan Marsh; 6 Joe Mellor (C); 32 Danny Craven; 15 Gil Dudson; 31 Jordan Johnstone; 23 Jay Chapelhow; 11 Chris Houston (C); 12 Matt Whitley; 24 Sam Brooks. Subs (all used): 14 Chris Dean; 16 Alex Gerrard; 25 Tom Olbison; 18 Greg Burke.
Tries: Marsh (2), Runciman (59); **Goals:** Bridge 1/2.
On report: Houston (76) - collision with referee.
WOLVES: 1 Stefan Ratchford; 5 Matthew Russell; 20 Toby King; 4 Ryan Atkins; 2 Tom Lineham; 22 Declan Patton; 7 Kurt Gidley; 8 Chris Hill (C); 15 Brad Dwyer; 10 Ashton Sims; 24 Benjamin Jullien; 12 Jack Hughes; 16 George King. Subs (all used): 3 Rhys Evans; 18 Andre Savelio; 23 Joe Philbin; 28 Harvey Livett.
Tries: Lineham (8), Hughes (14), Philbin (35);
Goals: Patton 3/4; **Field goal:** Patton (38).
Rugby Leaguer & League Express Men of the Match:
Vikings: Joe Mellor; *Wolves:* Stefan Ratchford.
Penalty count: 7-7; **Half-time:** 4-17;
Referee: Phil Bentham; **Attendance:** 8,279.

Friday 14th April 2017

WIGAN WARRIORS 29 ST HELENS 18

WARRIORS: 22 Morgan Escare; 36 Tom Davies; 3 Anthony Gelling; 5 Joe Burgess; 35 Liam Marshall; 6 George Williams; 7 Thomas Leuluai; 8 Frank-Paul Nuuausala; 16 Sam Powell; 10 Ben Flower; 11 Joel Tomkins; 12 Liam Farrell; 13 Sean O'Loughlin (C). Subs (all used): 9 Michael McIlorum; 17 Taulima Tautai; 19 Ryan Sutton; 20 Willie Isa.
Tries: Burgess (21, 66), Marshall (47, 62), Farrell (59);
Goals: Escare 4/6; **Field goal:** Escare (55).
SAINTS: 2 Tom Makinson; 28 Regan Grace (D); 3 Ryan Morgan; 4 Mark Percival; 5 Adam Swift; 6 Theo Fages; 7 Matty Smith; 10 Kyle Amor; 17 Tommy Lee; 14 Luke Douglas; 36 Zeb Taia; 12 Jon Wilkin (C); 13 Louie McCarthy-Scarsbrook. Subs (all used): 8 Alex Walmsley; 16 Luke Thompson; 19 Greg Richards; 20 Morgan Knowles.
Tries: Knowles (43), Grace (57), Makinson (72);
Goals: Percival 3/4.
Dismissal: Amor (13) - high tackle on Marshall.
Rugby Leaguer & League Express Men of the Match:
Warriors: George Williams; *Saints:* Regan Grace.
Penalty count: 9-5; **Half-time:** 8-2;
Referee: Ben Thaler; **Attendance:** 23,390.

CASTLEFORD TIGERS 42 WAKEFIELD TRINITY 24

TIGERS: 1 Zak Hardaker; 21 Joel Monaghan; 3 Jake Webster; 2 Greg Minikin; 5 Greg Eden; 16 Ben Roberts; 7 Luke Gale (C); 8 Andy Lynch; 9 Paul McShane; 19 Gadwin Springer; 11 Oliver Holmes; 12 Mike McMeeken; 13 Adam Milner. Subs (all used): 6 Rangi Chase; 15 Jesse Sene-Lefao; 17 Junior Moors; 10 Grant Millington.
Tries: Roberts (9), Webster (11, 37), O Holmes (19), Millington (28, 34), Eden (62); **Goals:** Gale 7/7.
TRINITY: 1 Scott Grix; 5 Ben Jones-Bishop; 18 Joe Arundel; 3 Bill Tupou; 2 Tom Johnstone; 6 Jacob Miller; 14 Sam Williams; 20 David Fifita; 9 Kyle Wood; 10 Mitch Allgood; 11 Matty Ashurst; 12 Danny Kirmond (C); 16 Tinirau Arona. Subs (all used): 7 Liam Finn; 32 Dean Hadley; 17 Craig Huby; 8 Anthony England.
Tries: Fifita (3, 54), Tupou (32), Jones-Bishop (76);
Goals: Williams 3/3, Finn 1/1.
Rugby Leaguer & League Express Men of the Match:
Tigers: Luke Gale; *Trinity:* Bill Tupou.
Penalty count: 10-8; **Half-time:** 36-12;
Referee: Chris Kendall; **Attendance:** 10,349.

HULL FC 24 LEEDS RHINOS 52

HULL FC: 1 Jamie Shaul; 19 Steve Michaels; 2 Mahe Fonua; 4 Josh Griffin; 5 Fetuli Talanoa; 6 Albert Kelly; 7 Marc Sneyd; 8 Scott Taylor; 17 Danny Washbrook; 22 Josh Bowden; 21 Sika Manu; 12 Mark Minichiello; 10 Liam Watts. Subs (all used): 28 Brad Fash; 14 Jake Connor; 13 Gareth Ellis (C); 16 Jordan Thompson.
Tries: Michaels (10), Taylor (24), Shaul (47), Minichiello (57); **Goals:** Sneyd 4/4.
Sin bin: Ellis (63) - interference; Manu (75) - dissent.
RHINOS: 1 Ashton Golding; 2 Tom Briscoe; 3 Kallum Watkins; 14 Liam Sutcliffe; 5 Ryan Hall; 6 Danny McGuire (C); 4 Joel Moon; 17 Mitch Garbutt; 9 Matt Parcell; 10 Adam Cuthbertson; 15 Brett Delaney; 11 Jamie Jones-Buchanan; 20 Anthony Mullally. Subs (all used): 8 Keith Galloway; 13 Stevie Ward; 24 Jordan Baldwinson; 7 Rob Burrow.
Tries: McGuire (5), Hall (16), Parcell (18), Moon (22, 36), Watkins (67), Garbutt (70), Mullally (77);
Goals: L Sutcliffe 9/11, Burrow 1/1.
Sin bin: McGuire (56) - holding down.
Rugby Leaguer & League Express Men of the Match:
Hull FC: Jamie Shaul; *Rhinos:* Joel Moon.
Penalty count: 9-12; **Half time:** 12-30;
Referee: James Child; **Attendance:** 15,487.

SALFORD RED DEVILS 12 LEIGH CENTURIONS 6

RED DEVILS: 1 Gareth O'Brien; 21 Greg Johnson; 22 Kris Welham; 4 Junior Sa'u; 2 Justin Carney; 6 Robert Lui; 7 Michael Dobson (C); 14 Lama Tasi; 9 Logan Tomkins; 23 Lee Mossop; 3 Josh Jones; 11 Ben Murdoch-Masila; 13 Mark Flanagan. Subs (all used): 8 Craig Kopczak; 10 George Griffin; 19 Josh Wood; 17 Adam Walne.
Tries: Welham (38), O'Brien (67);
Goals: O'Brien 1/1, Dobson 1/2.
CENTURIONS: 18 Gregg McNally; 2 Adam Higson; 3 Ben Crooks; 1 Mitch Brown; 5 Matty Dawson; 20 Ben Reynolds; 6 Martyn Ridyard; 24 Jamie Acton; 9 Micky Higham (C); 15 Danny Tickle; 17 Atelea Vea; 12 Glenn Stewart; 13 Harrison Hansen. Subs (all used): 14 Eloi Pelissier; 10 Dayne Weston; 23 Sam Hopkins; 29 Lachlan Burr.
Try: Brown (28); **Goals:** Reynolds 1/1.
Rugby Leaguer & League Express Men of the Match:
Red Devils: Michael Dobson; *Centurions:* Adam Higson.
Penalty count: 4-7; **Half-time:** 6-6;
Referee: Jack Smith; **Attendance:** 5,834.

ROUND 10

Monday 17th April 2017

WAKEFIELD TRINITY 10 WIGAN WARRIORS 16

TRINITY: 1 Scott Grix; 5 Ben Jones-Bishop; 24 Mason Caton-Brown; 15 Ashley Gibson; 2 Tom Johnstone; 6 Jacob Miller; 7 Liam Finn; 17 Craig Huby; 9 Kyle Wood; 8 Anthony England; 11 Matty Ashurst; 32 Dean Hadley; 16 Tinirau Arona. Subs (all used): 12 Danny Kirmond (C); 10 Mitch Allgood; 20 David Fifita; 23 Keegan Hirst.
Tries: Grix (9), Jones-Bishop (38); **Goals:** Finn 1/3.
WARRIORS: 22 Morgan Escare; 36 Tom Davies; 3 Anthony Gelling; 32 Liam Forsyth; 35 Liam Marshall; 6 George Williams; 7 Thomas Leuluai; 17 Taulima Tautai; 16 Sam Powell; 10 Ben Flower; 11 Joel Tomkins; 12 Liam Farrell; 13 Sean O'Loughlin (C). Subs (all used): 19 Ryan Sutton; 8 Frank-Paul Nuuausala; 26 Romain Navarrete; 23 Nick Gregson.
Tries: O'Loughlin (5), Escare (34), Marshall (78);
Goals: Escare 2/3.
Sin bin: Gelling (29) - dangerous challenge on Caton-Brown.
Rugby Leaguer & League Express Men of the Match:
Trinity: Jacob Miller; *Warriors:* Liam Marshall.
Penalty count: 11-7; **Half-time:** 10-12;
Referee: Jack Smith; **Attendance:** 4,640.

LEEDS RHINOS 42 WIDNES VIKINGS 22

RHINOS: 22 Ash Handley; 2 Tom Briscoe; 3 Kallum Watkins; 13 Stevie Ward; 5 Ryan Hall; 6 Danny McGuire (C); 4 Joel Moon; 8 Keith Galloway; 9 Matt Parcell; 10 Adam Cuthbertson; 11 Jamie Jones-Buchanan; 15 Brett Delaney; 20 Anthony Mullally. Subs (all used): 7 Rob Burrow; 21 Josh Walters; 17 Mitch Garbutt; 24 Jordan Baldwinson.
Tries: Watkins (6, 73), Parcell (9, 77), Moon (17, 28), Briscoe (36); **Goals:** Watkins 7/7.
VIKINGS: 2 Corey Thompson; 17 Stefan Marsh; 26 Tom Armstrong; 4 Charly Runciman; 5 Patrick Ah Van; 7 Tom Gilmore; 32 Danny Craven; 22 Ted Chapelhow; 9 Lloyd White; 10 Jack Buchanan; 11 Chris Houston (C); 14 Chris Dean; 34 Owen Farnworth (D). Subs (all used): 15 Gil Dudson; 18 Greg Burke; 31 Jordan Johnstone; 37 Liam Walsh (D).
Tries: Gilmore (25, 58), Houston (61), Thompson (65);
Goals: Gilmore 3/4.
Rugby Leaguer & League Express Men of the Match:
Rhinos: Joel Moon; *Vikings:* Tom Gilmore.
Penalty count: 9-9; **Half-time:** 30-6;
Referee: Scott Mikalauskas; **Attendance:** 15,408.

LEIGH CENTURIONS 10 HULL FC 24

CENTURIONS: 18 Gregg McNally; 19 Ryan Hampshire; 3 Ben Crooks; 5 Matty Dawson; 27 David Thompson (D); 20 Ben Reynolds; 7 Josh Drinkwater; 22 James Green; 21 Liam Hood; 23 Sam Hopkins; 17 Atelea Vea; 12 Glenn Stewart; 13 Harrison Hansen. Subs (all used): 9 Micky Higham (C); 10 Dayne Weston; 15 Danny Tickle; 29 Lachlan Burr.
Tries: Hood (64), Hampshire (73); **Goals:** Reynolds 1/2.
HULL FC: 1 Jamie Shaul; 2 Mahe Fonua; 14 Jake Connor; 3 Carlos Tuimavave; 19 Steve Michaels; 6 Albert Kelly; 7 Marc Sneyd; 8 Scott Taylor; 17 Danny Washbrook; 10 Liam Watts; 21 Sika Manu; 12 Mark Minichiello; 16 Jordan Thompson. Subs (all used): 13 Gareth Ellis (C); 28 Brad Fash; 30 Jez Litten; 25 Jansin Turgut.
Tries: Watts (18), Tuimavave (23, 52), Kelly (28);
Goals: Sneyd 4/4.

Rugby Leaguer & League Express Men of the Match: *Centurions:* Ryan Hampshire; *Hull FC:* Carlos Tuimavave.
Penalty count: 8-12; **Half-time:** 0-18;
Referee: Gareth Hewer; **Attendance:** 6,296.

ST HELENS 26 CASTLEFORD TIGERS 22

SAINTS: 2 Tom Makinson; 5 Adam Swift; 22 Matty Fleming; 4 Mark Percival; 28 Regan Grace; 6 Theo Fages; 7 Matty Smith; 10 Kyle Amor; 17 Tommy Lee; 8 Alex Walmsley; 36 Zeb Taia; 12 Jon Wilkin (C); 16 Luke Thompson. Subs (all used): 14 Luke Douglas; 15 Adam Walker; 18 Dominique Peyroux; 20 Morgan Knowles.
Tries: Fleming (24), Douglas (26), Percival (34), Grace (68);
Goals: Percival 5/5.
TIGERS: 1 Zak Hardaker; 2 Greg Minikin; 3 Jake Webster; 4 Michael Shenton (C); 5 Greg Eden; 16 Ben Roberts; 7 Luke Gale; 8 Andy Lynch; 9 Paul McShane; 17 Junior Moors; 10 Grant Millington; 12 Mike McMeeken; 14 Nathan Massey. Subs (all used): 11 Oliver Holmes; 13 Adam Milner; 15 Jesse Sene-Lefao; 18 Matt Cook.
Tries: Eden (7, 58), Roberts (45, 80); **Goals:** Gale 3/5.
Rugby Leaguer & League Express Men of the Match: *Saints:* Mark Percival; *Tigers:* Ben Roberts.
Penalty count: 3-8; **Half-time:** 20-8;
Referee: Chris Campbell; **Attendance:** 12,499.

WARRINGTON WOLVES 26 HUDDERSFIELD GIANTS 24

WOLVES: 1 Stefan Ratchford; 3 Rhys Evans; 20 Toby King; 28 Harvey Livett; 2 Tom Lineham; 22 Declan Patton; 7 Kurt Gidley; 8 Chris Hill (C); 9 Daryl Clark; 10 Ashton Sims; 24 Benjamin Jullien; 12 Jack Hughes; 14 Mike Cooper. Subs (all used): 18 Andre Savelio; 15 Brad Dwyer; 16 George King; 23 Joe Philbin.
Tries: Livett (3), Clark (12), Gidley (35), Evans (65), T King (69); **Goals:** Patton 3/5.
GIANTS: 1 Jake Mamo; 2 Jermaine McGillvary; 23 Sam Wood; 5 Aaron Murphy; 24 Darnell McIntosh; 6 Danny Brough (C); 4 Lee Gaskell; 15 Sebastine Ikahihifo; 9 Ryan Hinchcliffe; 10 Shannon Wakeman; 30 Alex Mellor; 16 Oliver Roberts; 18 Paul Clough. Subs (all used): 8 Sam Rapira; 14 Kruise Leeming; 19 Nathan Mason; 22 Tyler Dickinson.
Tries: McIntosh (6), Mamo (17), Brough (47), McGillvary (79); **Goals:** Brough 4/6.
Rugby Leaguer & League Express Men of the Match: *Wolves:* Stefan Ratchford; *Giants:* Sebastine Ikahihifo.
Penalty count: 4-9; **Half-time:** 16-12;
Referee: Ben Thaler; **Attendance:** 10,111.

CATALANS DRAGONS 38 SALFORD RED DEVILS 6

DRAGONS: 1 Tony Gigot; 18 Vincent Duport; 3 Krisnan Inu; 21 Iain Thornley; 5 Fouad Yaha; 6 Luke Walsh; 7 Richie Myler; 8 Sam Moa; 9 Paul Aiton; 10 Remi Casty (C); 11 Louis Anderson; 12 Justin Horo; 15 Benjamin Garcia. Subs (all used): 14 Julian Bousquet; 16 Thomas Bosc; 19 Mickael Simon; 25 Thibaut Margalet.
Tries: Duport (9, 30, 77), Inu (51), Myler (64), Gigot (67);
Goals: Walsh 5/6, Gigot 1/1; **Field goals:** Walsh (69, 71).
RED DEVILS: 1 Gareth O'Brien; 21 Greg Johnson; 22 Kris Welham; 4 Junior Sa'u; 2 Justin Carney; 29 Todd Carney; 7 Michael Dobson (C); 17 Adam Walne; 9 Logan Tomkins; 14 Lama Tasi; 3 Josh Jones; 13 Mark Flanagan; 16 Olsi Krasniqi. Subs (all used): 6 Robert Lui; 8 Craig Kopczak; 10 George Griffin; 15 Ryan Lannon.
Try: J Carney (58); **Goals:** O'Brien 1/1.
Rugby Leaguer & League Express Men of the Match: *Dragons:* Tony Gigot; *Red Devils:* Justin Carney.
Penalty count: 5-9; **Half-time:** 14-0;
Referee: Phil Bentham; **Attendance:** 10,804.

ROUND 11

Friday 21st April 2017

WIDNES VIKINGS 16 ST HELENS 14

VIKINGS: 1 Rhys Hanbury; 2 Corey Thompson; 17 Stefan Marsh; 4 Charly Runciman; 5 Patrick Ah Van; 6 Joe Mellor (C); 7 Tom Gilmore; 15 Gil Dudson; 31 Jordan Johnstone; 10 Jack Buchanan; 11 Chris Houston (C); 14 Chris Dean; 16 Alex Gerrard. Subs (all used): 12 Matt Whitley; 18 Greg Burke; 23 Jay Chapelhow; 35 Danny Walker.
Tries: Mellor (13), Ah Van (23, 71); **Goals:** Gilmore 2/4.
SAINTS: 25 Ricky Bailey; 5 Adam Swift; 22 Matty Fleming; 4 Mark Percival; 28 Regan Grace; 6 Theo Fages; 7 Matty Smith; 19 Greg Richards; 17 Tommy Lee; 10 Kyle Amor; 36 Zeb Taia; 12 Jon Wilkin (C); 16 Luke Thompson. Subs (all used): 8 Alex Walmsley; 13 Louie McCarthy-Scarsbrook; 18 Dominique Peyroux; 20 Morgan Knowles.
Tries: Fages (16), Smith (38); **Goals:** Percival 3/3.
Rugby Leaguer & League Express Men of the Match: *Vikings:* Tom Gilmore; *Saints:* Alex Walmsley.
Penalty count: 7-8; **Half-time:** 12-12;
Referee: Chris Kendall; **Attendance:** 6,171.

Saturday 22nd April 2017

WARRINGTON WOLVES 22 WAKEFIELD TRINITY 20

WOLVES: 1 Stefan Ratchford; 3 Rhys Evans; 28 Harvey Livett; 4 Ryan Atkins; 2 Tom Lineham; 22 Declan Patton; 7 Kurt Gidley; 8 Chris Hill (C); 15 Brad Dwyer; 10 Ashton Sims; 24 Benjamin Jullien; 12 Jack Hughes; 13 Joe Westerman. Subs (all used): 6 Kevin Brown; 16 George King; 18 Andre Savelio; 23 Joe Philbin.
Tries: Atkins (22), Hill (55), Brown (69), Lineham (77);
Goals: Patton 3/4.
TRINITY: 21 Max Jowitt; 5 Ben Jones-Bishop; 15 Ashley Gibson; 24 Mason Caton-Brown; 2 Tom Johnstone; 6 Jacob Miller; 7 Liam Finn; 8 Anthony England; 9 Kyle Wood; 20 David Fifita; 32 Dean Hadley; 12 Danny Kirmond (C); 16 Tinirau Arona. Subs (all used): 14 Sam Williams; 27 James Batchelor; 23 Keegan Hirst; 17 Craig Huby.
Tries: Gibson (8), Caton-Brown (10), Johnstone (46);
Goals: Finn 4/4.
Rugby Leaguer & League Express Men of the Match: *Wolves:* Chris Hill; *Trinity:* Jacob Miller.
Penalty count: 7-7; **Half-time:** 6-14;
Referee: Ben Thaler; **Attendance:** 9,152.

Sunday 23rd April 2017

HULL FC 26 CASTLEFORD TIGERS 24

HULL FC: 1 Jamie Shaul; 2 Mahe Fonua; 3 Carlos Tuimavave; 14 Jake Connor; 19 Steve Michaels; 6 Albert Kelly; 7 Marc Sneyd; 8 Scott Taylor; 17 Danny Washbrook; 10 Liam Watts; 21 Sika Manu; 12 Mark Minichiello; 13 Gareth Ellis (C). Subs (all used): 15 Chris Green; 16 Jordan Thompson; 25 Jansin Turgut; 28 Brad Fash.
Tries: Taylor (5), Fonua (7, 13), Tuimavave (26);
Goals: Sneyd 5/7.
Dismissal: Watts (22) - high tackle on Gale.
TIGERS: 1 Zak Hardaker; 2 Greg Minikin; 3 Jake Webster; 4 Michael Shenton (C); 5 Greg Eden; 16 Ben Roberts; 7 Luke Gale; 8 Andy Lynch; 9 Paul McShane; 19 Gadwin Springer; 11 Oliver Holmes; 12 Mike McMeeken; 13 Adam Milner. Subs (all used): 10 Grant Millington; 15 Jesse Sene-Lefao; 17 Junior Moors; 21 Joel Monaghan.
Tries: Minikin (23), Roberts (29, 58), Shenton (39), McMeeken (79); **Goals:** Roberts 0/2, McShane 2/3.
Rugby Leaguer & League Express Men of the Match: *Hull FC:* Albert Kelly; *Tigers:* Junior Moors.
Penalty count: 9-11; **Half-time:** 20-14;
Referee: Robert Hicks; **Attendance:** 12,801.

WIGAN WARRIORS 42 CATALANS DRAGONS 22

WARRIORS: 22 Morgan Escare; 36 Tom Davies; 32 Liam Forsyth; 5 Joe Burgess; 35 Liam Marshall; 6 George Williams; 7 Thomas Leuluai; 8 Frank-Paul Nuuausala; 16 Sam Powell; 10 Ben Flower; 20 Willie Isa; 12 Liam Farrell; 13 Sean O'Loughlin (C). Subs (all used): 9 Michael McIlorum; 17 Taulima Tautai; 19 Ryan Sutton; 26 Romain Navarrete.
Tries: Davies (14, 17), Burgess (20, 62), Forsyth (41, 60), Marshall (67), Farrell (79); **Goals:** Escare 2/5, Powell 3/3.
DRAGONS: 1 Tony Gigot; 5 Fouad Yaha; 21 Iain Thornley; 18 Vincent Duport; 16 Thomas Bosc; 6 Luke Walsh; 7 Richie Myler; 8 Sam Moa; 9 Paul Aiton; 26 Lambert Belmas; 11 Louis Anderson; 15 Benjamin Garcia; 10 Remi Casty (C). Subs (all used): 14 Julian Bousquet; 19 Mickael Simon; 23 Alrix Da Costa; 24 Thibaut Margalet.
Tries: Yaha (26), Gigot (35), Anderson (38, 47);
Goals: Walsh 3/4.
Rugby Leaguer & League Express Men of the Match: *Warriors:* Liam Forsyth; *Dragons:* Luke Walsh.
Penalty count: 8-5; **Half-time:** 16-16;
Referee: Gareth Hewer; **Attendance:** 11,637.

ROUND 12

Thursday 27th April 2017

LEEDS RHINOS 12 HUDDERSFIELD GIANTS 31

RHINOS: 31 Jack Walker; 2 Tom Briscoe; 3 Kallum Watkins; 22 Ash Handley; 5 Ryan Hall; 6 Danny McGuire (C); 4 Joel Moon; 8 Keith Galloway; 9 Matt Parcell; 20 Anthony Mullally; 11 Jamie Jones-Buchanan; 15 Brett Delaney; 10 Adam Cuthbertson. Subs (all used): 16 Brad Singleton; 17 Mitch Garbutt; 13 Stevie Ward; 7 Rob Burrow.
Tries: Parcell (13), Moon (31); **Goals:** Watkins 2/2.
GIANTS: 1 Jake Mamo; 2 Jermaine McGillvary; 30 Alex Mellor; 5 Aaron Murphy; 24 Darnell McIntosh; 6 Danny Brough (C); 23 Sam Wood; 15 Sebastine Ikahihifo; 14 Kruise Leeming; 10 Shannon Wakeman; 16 Oliver Roberts; 12 Dale Ferguson; 9 Ryan Hinchcliffe. Subs (all used): 18 Paul Clough; 20 Daniel Smith; 29 Matty English; 31 Adam O'Brien.
Tries: Mamo (18), Leeming (26), Ferguson (53), McIntosh (58), Roberts (70); **Goals:** Brough 5/5;
Field goal: Brough (67).

Rugby Leaguer & League Express Men of the Match: *Rhinos:* Jack Walker; *Giants:* Jermaine McGillvary.
Penalty count: 8-11; **Half time:** 12-12;
Referee: Chris Kendall; **Attendance:** 13,169.

Friday 28th April 2017

HULL FC 34 WARRINGTON WOLVES 10

HULL FC: 1 Jamie Shaul; 2 Mahe Fonua; 3 Carlos Tuimavave; 14 Jake Connor; 19 Steve Michaels; 6 Albert Kelly; 7 Marc Sneyd; 8 Scott Taylor; 17 Danny Washbrook; 15 Chris Green; 12 Mark Minichiello (C); 21 Sika Manu; 16 Jordan Thompson. Subs (all used): 4 Josh Griffin; 27 Jack Downs; 25 Jansin Turgut; 28 Brad Fash.
Tries: Connor (4), Fonua (10), Shaul (47), Kelly (56, 74);
Goals: Sneyd 7/7.
Sin bin: Manu (22) - dangerous challenge.
WOLVES: 1 Stefan Ratchford; 5 Matthew Russell; 3 Rhys Evans; 4 Ryan Atkins; 2 Tom Lineham; 6 Kevin Brown; 22 Declan Patton; 8 Chris Hill (C); 7 Kurt Gidley; 10 Ashton Sims; 24 Benjamin Jullien; 12 Jack Hughes; 13 Joe Westerman. Subs (all used): 14 Mike Cooper; 23 Joe Philbin; 15 Brad Dwyer; 18 Andre Savelio.
Tries: Russell (16), Westerman (22); **Goals:** Patton 1/2.
Rugby Leaguer & League Express Men of the Match: *Hull FC:* Marc Sneyd; *Wolves:* Chris Hill.
Penalty count: 8-7; **Half-time:** 14-10;
Referee: James Child; **Attendance:** 10,734.

ST HELENS 28 LEIGH CENTURIONS 6

SAINTS: 2 Tom Makinson; 5 Adam Swift; 3 Ryan Morgan; 4 Mark Percival; 28 Regan Grace; 6 Theo Fages; 7 Matty Smith; 8 Alex Walmsley; 17 Tommy Lee; 14 Luke Douglas; 36 Zeb Taia; 12 Jon Wilkin (C); 16 Luke Thompson. Subs (all used): 13 Louie McCarthy-Scarsbrook; 15 Adam Walker; 18 Dominique Peyroux; 20 Morgan Knowles.
Tries: Percival (20), Fages (26), Morgan (50), Grace (64), Walmsley (70); **Goals:** Percival 4/5.
Sin bin: Walker (78) - fighting.
CENTURIONS: 19 Ryan Hampshire; 2 Adam Higson; 5 Matty Dawson; 3 Ben Crooks; 30 Curtis Naughton; 20 Ben Reynolds; 7 Josh Drinkwater; 24 Jamie Acton; 21 Liam Hood; 10 Dayne Weston; 17 Atelea Vea; 12 Glenn Stewart; 13 Harrison Hansen (C). Subs (all used): 14 Eloi Pelissier; 15 Danny Tickle; 23 Sam Hopkins; 29 Lachlan Burr.
Try: Acton (7); **Goals:** Reynolds 1/1.
Sin bin: Pelissier (78) - fighting.
Rugby Leaguer & League Express Men of the Match: *Saints:* Alex Walmsley; *Centurions:* Glenn Stewart.
Penalty count: 8-7; **Half-time:** 12-6;
Referee: Gareth Hewer; **Attendance:** 10,268.

Saturday 29th April 2017

CASTLEFORD TIGERS 54 WIGAN WARRIORS 4

TIGERS: 1 Zak Hardaker; 2 Greg Minikin; 3 Jake Webster; 4 Michael Shenton (C); 5 Greg Eden; 16 Ben Roberts; 7 Luke Gale; 10 Grant Millington; 9 Paul McShane; 14 Nathan Massey; 15 Jesse Sene-Lefao; 12 Mike McMeeken; 13 Adam Milner. Subs (all used): 6 Rangi Chase; 17 Junior Moors; 18 Matt Cook; 21 Joel Monaghan.
Tries: Milner (1), Shenton (8), Cook (27), McMeeken (31), Minikin (46, 71), Gale (49), Millington (52), Webster (57);
Goals: Gale 8/9, McShane 1/1.
WARRIORS: 22 Morgan Escare; 36 Tom Davies; 3 Anthony Gelling; 5 Joe Burgess; 35 Liam Marshall; 6 George Williams; 16 Sam Powell; 8 Frank-Paul Nuuausala; 9 Michael McIlorum; 10 Ben Flower; 11 Joel Tomkins; 12 Liam Farrell; 13 Sean O'Loughlin (C). Subs (all used): 17 Taulima Tautai; 19 Ryan Sutton; 20 Willie Isa; 33 Josh Ganson (D).
Try: Powell (25); **Goals:** Escare 0/1.
Sin bin: Nuuausala (18) - dissent;
Escare (45) - high tackle on Gale.
Rugby Leaguer & League Express Men of the Match: *Tigers:* Luke Gale; *Warriors:* Morgan Escare.
Penalty count: 8-6; **Half-time:** 26-4;
Referee: Robert Hicks; **Attendance:** 9,333.

Sunday 30th April 2017

SALFORD RED DEVILS 30 WIDNES VIKINGS 10

RED DEVILS: 5 Niall Evalds; 21 Greg Johnson; 3 Josh Jones; 22 Kris Welham; 24 Jake Bibby; 6 Robert Lui; 7 Michael Dobson (C); 17 Adam Walne; 9 Logan Tomkins; 14 Lama Tasi; 11 Ben Murdoch-Masila; 13 Mark Flanagan; 16 Olsi Krasniqi. Subs (all used): 20 Kriss Brining; 8 Craig Kopczak; 26 Daniel Murray (D); 15 Ryan Lannon.
Tries: Murdoch-Masila (21, 73), Johnson (27), Evalds (48), Bibby (79); **Goals:** Dobson 5/6.
VIKINGS: 17 Stefan Marsh; 28 Ryan Ince; 14 Chris Dean; 4 Charly Runciman; 5 Patrick Ah Van; 6 Joe Mellor (C); 7 Tom Gilmore; 15 Gil Dudson; 31 Jordan Johnstone; 10

Salford's Kris Welham beats Wigan's Lewis Tierney and Joe Burgess to score

Jack Buchanan; 11 Chris Houston (C); 25 Tom Olbison; 16 Alex Gerrard. Subs (all used): 8 Eamon O'Carroll; 18 Greg Burke; 13 Hep Cahill; 12 Matt Whitley.
Tries: Gilmore (43), Ah Van (66); **Goals:** Gilmore 1/2.
Rugby Leaguer & League Express Men of the Match: *Red Devils:* Ben Murdoch-Masila; *Vikings:* Tom Gilmore.
Penalty count: 8-7; **Half-time:** 12-0;
Referee: Ben Thaler; **Attendance:** 3,127.

WAKEFIELD TRINITY 30 CATALANS DRAGONS 10

TRINITY: 1 Scott Grix; 5 Ben Jones-Bishop; 18 Joe Arundel; 24 Mason Caton-Brown; 2 Tom Johnstone; 6 Jacob Miller; 7 Liam Finn (C); 8 Anthony England; 9 Kyle Wood; 20 David Fifita; 11 Matty Ashurst; 32 Dean Hadley; 16 Tinirau Arona. Subs (all used): 27 James Batchelor; 17 Craig Huby; 23 Keegan Hirst; 4 Reece Lyne.
Tries: Caton-Brown (35, 43, 56), Jones-Bishop (38, 63), Huby (70); **Goals:** Finn 3/6.
DRAGONS: 1 Tony Gigot; 18 Vincent Duport; 3 Krisnan Inu; 21 Iain Thornley; 5 Fouad Yaha; 6 Luke Walsh; 7 Richie Myler; 8 Sam Moa; 9 Paul Aiton; 10 Remi Casty (C); 27 Ugo Perez; 15 Benjamin Garcia; 13 Greg Bird. Subs (all used): 14 Julian Bousquet; 16 Thomas Bosc; 19 Mickael Simon; 25 Thibaut Margalet.
Tries: Duport (15), Yaha (50); **Goals:** Walsh 1/2.
Sin bin: Yaha (35) - holding down; Walsh (56) - dissent; Duport (77) - interference.
Rugby Leaguer & League Express Men of the Match: *Trinity:* Joe Arundel; *Dragons:* Paul Aiton.
Penalty count: 10-10; **Half-time:** 8-6;
Referee: Phil Bentham; **Attendance:** 4,017.

ROUND 13

Thursday 4th May 2017

HUDDERSFIELD GIANTS 21 CASTLEFORD TIGERS 26

GIANTS: 1 Jake Mamo; 24 Darnell McIntosh; 5 Aaron Murphy; 30 Alex Mellor; 21 Gene Ormsby; 6 Danny Brough (C); 23 Sam Wood; 15 Sebastine Ikahihifo; 14 Kruise Leeming; 10 Shannon Wakeman; 16 Oliver Roberts; 12 Dale Ferguson; 9 Ryan Hinchcliffe. Subs (all used): 31 Adam O'Brien; 8 Sam Rapira; 20 Daniel Smith; 18 Paul Clough.
Tries: Mamo (19, 23, 36); **Goals:** Brough 4/5;
Field goal: Brough (56).
Sin bin: Brough (73) - dangerous challenge.

TIGERS: 5 Greg Eden; 2 Greg Minikin; 3 Jake Webster; 4 Michael Shenton (C); 21 Joel Monaghan; 6 Rangi Chase; 9 Paul McShane; 8 Andy Lynch; 13 Adam Milner; 10 Grant Millington; 15 Jesse Sene-Lefao; 34 Alex Foster (D); 14 Nathan Massey. Subs (all used): 23 Tom Holmes; 17 Junior Moors; 18 Matt Cook; 19 Gadwin Springer.
Tries: Monaghan (8), Minikin (27), Eden (47), Sene-Lefao (75); **Goals:** McShane 5/5.
Sin bin: Webster (70) - holding down.
Rugby Leaguer & League Express Men of the Match: *Giants:* Jake Mamo; *Tigers:* Matt Cook.
Penalty count: 8-5; **Half-time:** 18-12;
Referee: Ben Thaler; **Attendance:** 5,566.

Friday 5th May 2017

WARRINGTON WOLVES 40 ST HELENS 18

WOLVES: 7 Kurt Gidley (C); 5 Matthew Russell; 3 Rhys Evans; 4 Ryan Atkins; 2 Tom Lineham; 22 Declan Patton; 28 Harvey Livett; 14 Mike Cooper; 15 Brad Dwyer; 10 Ashton Sims; 24 Benjamin Jullien; 12 Jack Hughes; 34 Ben Westwood. Subs (all used): 23 Joe Philbin; 17 Dominic Crosby; 16 George King; 27 Morgan Smith.
Tries: Jullien (30), Cooper (35), Livett (45), Evans (51), Lineham (57), Atkins (59, 80); **Goals:** Livett 6/7.
SAINTS: 2 Tom Makinson; 5 Adam Swift; 26 Jake Spedding; 3 Ryan Morgan; 28 Regan Grace; 6 Theo Fages; 7 Matty Smith (C); 10 Kyle Amor; 17 Tommy Lee; 14 Luke Douglas; 36 Zeb Taia; 20 Morgan Knowles; 16 Luke Thompson. Subs (all used): 9 James Roby; 13 Louie McCarthy-Scarsbrook; 15 Adam Walker; 18 Dominique Peyroux.
Tries: Swift (1), Morgan (12), Peyroux (71);
Goals: Makinson 3/4.
Rugby Leaguer & League Express Men of the Match: *Wolves:* Harvey Livett; *Saints:* Morgan Knowles.
Penalty count: 8-6; **Half-time:** 12-14;
Referee: Phil Bentham; **Attendance:** 11,681.

WIGAN WARRIORS 16 SALFORD RED DEVILS 31

WARRIORS: 21 Lewis Tierney; 36 Tom Davies; 32 Liam Forsyth; 5 Joe Burgess; 35 Liam Marshall; 39 Josh Woods (D); 16 Sam Powell (C); 8 Frank-Paul Nuuausala; 33 Josh Ganson; 19 Ryan Sutton; 20 Willie Isa; 12 Liam Farrell; 11 Joel Tomkins. Subs (all used): 17 Taulima Tautai; 23 Nick Gregson; 24 Joe Bretherton; 26 Romain Navarrete.
Tries: Davies (53), Sutton (62), Tierney (72);
Goals: Woods 2/3.

RED DEVILS: 5 Niall Evalds; 21 Greg Johnson; 3 Josh Jones; 22 Kris Welham; 24 Jake Bibby; 6 Robert Lui; 7 Michael Dobson (C); 17 Adam Walne; 9 Logan Tomkins; 14 Lama Tasi; 11 Ben Murdoch-Masila; 15 Ryan Lannon; 16 Olsi Krasniqi. Subs (all used): 20 Kriss Brining; 8 Craig Kopczak; 26 Daniel Murray; 1 Gareth O'Brien.
Tries: Welham (4), Evalds (20, 43), Murdoch-Masila (24), Johnson (47); **Goals:** Dobson 4/5, O'Brien 1/1;
Field goal: O'Brien (75).
Rugby Leaguer & League Express Men of the Match: *Warriors:* Lewis Tierney; *Red Devils:* Robert Lui.
Penalty count: 9-6; **Half-time:** 0-16;
Referee: Chris Campbell; **Attendance:** 11,861.

Saturday 6th May 2017

CATALANS DRAGONS 24 LEEDS RHINOS 30

DRAGONS: 1 Tony Gigot; 5 Fouad Yaha; 21 Iain Thornley; 4 Brayden Wiliame; 18 Vincent Duport; 22 Lucas Albert; 7 Richie Myler; 8 Sam Moa; 9 Paul Aiton; 10 Remi Casty (C); 11 Louis Anderson; 15 Benjamin Garcia; 13 Greg Bird. Subs (all used): 14 Julian Bousquet; 16 Thomas Bosc; 19 Mickael Simon; 25 Thibaut Margalet.
Tries: Anderson (8), Wiliame (34), Casty (52); **Goals:** Gigot 4/5.
RHINOS: 1 Ashton Golding; 2 Tom Briscoe; 14 Liam Sutcliffe; 4 Joel Moon; 22 Ash Handley; 6 Danny McGuire (C); 7 Rob Burrow; 8 Keith Galloway; 9 Matt Parcell; 16 Brad Singleton; 11 Jamie Jones-Buchanan; 13 Stevie Ward; 10 Adam Cuthbertson. Subs: 15 Brett Delaney; 20 Anthony Mullally; 25 Jordan Lilley (not used); 28 Mikolaj Oledzki.
Tries: L Sutcliffe (5), Ward (40), Cuthbertson (65), Burrow (68), McGuire (76); **Goals:** L Sutcliffe 5/5.
Rugby Leaguer & League Express Men of the Match: *Dragons:* Richie Myler; *Rhinos:* Adam Cuthbertson.
Penalty count: 11-11; **Half-time:** 16-12;
Referee: Jack Smith; **Attendance:** 8,759.

LEIGH CENTURIONS 26 WAKEFIELD TRINITY 40

CENTURIONS: 18 Gregg McNally; 5 Matty Dawson; 3 Ben Crooks; 1 Mitch Brown; 30 Curtis Naughton; 19 Ryan Hampshire; 7 Josh Drinkwater; 8 Gareth Hock; 14 Eloi Pelissier; 22 James Green; 15 Danny Tickle; 13 Harrison Hansen (C); 12 Glenn Stewart. Subs (all used): 10 Dayne Weston; 21 Liam Hood; 24 Jamie Acton; 29 Lachlan Burr.
Tries: Naughton (17, 50), Acton (19), Dawson (38, 45);
Goals: Drinkwater 3/5.

Sin bin: Tickle (63) - professional foul.
On report:
Acton (28) - alleged dangerous challenge on Fifita.
TRINITY: 1 Scott Grix; 5 Ben Jones-Bishop; 4 Reece Lyne; 18 Joe Arundel; 24 Mason Caton-Brown; 6 Jacob Miller; 7 Liam Finn; 17 Craig Huby; 9 Kyle Wood; 20 David Fifita; 11 Matty Ashurst; 12 Danny Kirmond (C); 32 Dean Hadley. Subs (all used): 3 Bill Tupou; 13 Michael Sio; 16 Tinirau Arona; 23 Keegan Hirst.
Tries: Miller (2), Kirmond (7, 68), Lyne (15), Arundel (57), Caton-Brown (64); **Goals:** Finn 8/8.
Rugby Leaguer & League Express Men of the Match: *Centurions:* Jamie Acton; *Trinity:* Liam Finn.
Penalty count: 11-9; **Half-time:** 16-22;
Referee: Chris Kendall; **Attendance:** 4,938.

Sunday 7th May 2017

WIDNES VIKINGS 22 HULL FC 33

VIKINGS: 1 Rhys Hanbury; 17 Stefan Marsh; 3 Chris Bridge; 4 Charly Runciman; 5 Patrick Ah Van; 6 Joe Mellor (C); 7 Tom Gilmore; 15 Gil Dudson; 33 Aaron Heremaia; 10 Jack Buchanan; 11 Chris Houston (C); 14 Chris Dean; 13 Hep Cahill. Subs (all used): 12 Matt Whitley; 8 Eamon O'Carroll; 16 Alex Gerrard; 35 Danny Walker.
Tries: Houston (6), Hanbury (10), Ah Van (29, 36);
Goals: Gilmore 3/4.
HULL FC: 1 Jamie Shaul; 2 Mahe Fonua; 14 Jake Connor; 3 Carlos Tuimavave; 19 Steve Michaels; 6 Albert Kelly; 7 Marc Sneyd; 15 Chris Green; 9 Danny Houghton (C); 10 Liam Watts; 17 Danny Washbrook; 12 Mark Minichiello; 16 Jordan Thompson. Subs (all used): 28 Brad Fash; 25 Jansin Turgut; 4 Josh Griffin; 22 Josh Bowden.
Tries: Turgut (39), Shaul (41, 67), Tuimavave (58), Kelly (65), Washbrook (80); **Goals:** Sneyd 4/5, Griffin 0/1;
Field goal: Sneyd (70).
Rugby Leaguer & League Express Men of the Match: *Vikings:* Aaron Heremaia; *Hull FC:* Jamie Shaul.
Penalty count: 8-7; **Half-time:** 22-4;
Referee: Gareth Hewer; **Attendance:** 5,082.

ROUND 14 - MAGIC WEEKEND

Saturday 20th May 2017

WAKEFIELD TRINITY 34 WIDNES VIKINGS 12

TRINITY: 1 Scott Grix; 5 Ben Jones-Bishop; 4 Reece Lyne; 18 Joe Arundel; 24 Mason Caton-Brown; 6 Jacob Miller; 7 Liam Finn; 8 Anthony England; 9 Kyle Wood; 20 David Fifita; 11 Matty Ashurst; 12 Danny Kirmond (C); 16 Tinirau Arona. Subs (all used): 3 Bill Tupou; 17 Craig Huby; 23 Keegan Hirst; 27 James Batchelor.
Tries: Grix (19, 33), Lyne (22), Jones-Bishop (42, 68), Ashurst (74); **Goals:** Finn 5/7.
VIKINGS: 1 Rhys Hanbury; 28 Ryan Ince; 27 Ed Chamberlain; 4 Charly Runciman; 21 Jack Johnson (D); 31 Jordan Johnstone; 40 Rangi Chase (D); 10 Jack Buchanan; 33 Aaron Heremaia; 15 Gil Dudson; 11 Chris Houston (C); 39 Sam Wilde (D); 13 Hep Cahill. Subs (all used): 8 Eamon O'Carroll; 9 Lloyd White; 16 Alex Gerrard; 20 Manase Manuokafoa.
Tries: Ince (47), Cahill (76); **Goals:** Chamberlain 2/2.
Sin bin: White (38) - dangerous challenge.
Rugby Leaguer & League Express Men of the Match: *Trinity:* Scott Grix; *Vikings:* Ryan Ince.
Penalty count: 8-6; **Half-time:** 16-0;
Referee: Chris Kendall.

HULL FC 0 ST HELENS 45

HULL FC: 1 Jamie Shaul; 4 Josh Griffin; 3 Carlos Tuimavave; 25 Jansin Turgut; 19 Steve Michaels; 6 Albert Kelly; 7 Marc Sneyd; 8 Scott Taylor; 9 Danny Houghton (C); 10 Liam Watts; 21 Sika Manu; 12 Mark Minichiello; 15 Chris Green. Subs (all used): 22 Josh Bowden; 28 Brad Fash; 16 Jordan Thompson; 17 Danny Washbrook.
SAINTS: 2 Tom Makinson; 5 Adam Swift; 4 Mark Percival; 3 Ryan Morgan; 28 Regan Grace; 6 Theo Fages; 7 Matty Smith; 8 Alex Walmsley; 9 James Roby; 10 Kyle Amor; 36 Zeb Taia; 12 Jon Wilkin (C); 20 Morgan Knowles. Subs (all used): 14 Luke Douglas; 16 Luke Thompson; 13 Louie McCarthy-Scarsbrook; 17 Tommy Lee.
Tries: Walmsley (15, 46), Morgan (17), Knowles (23), McCarthy-Scarsbrook (54), Makinson (62), Grace (69, 77);
Goals: Percival 6/8; **Field goal:** Smith (39).
Rugby Leaguer & League Express Men of the Match: *Hull FC:* Danny Houghton; *Saints:* Alex Walmsley.
Penalty count: 8-7; **Half-time:** 0-19;
Referee: Robert Hicks.

WARRINGTON WOLVES 24 WIGAN WARRIORS 24

WOLVES: 1 Stefan Ratchford; 5 Matthew Russell; 12 Jack Hughes; 4 Ryan Atkins; 2 Tom Lineham; 6 Kevin Brown; 7 Kurt Gidley; 8 Chris Hill (C); 9 Daryl Clark; 14 Mike Cooper; 24 Benjamin Jullien; 34 Ben Westwood; 13 Joe Westerman. Subs (all used): 17 Dominic Crosby; 23 Joe Philbin; 15 Brad Dwyer; 16 George King.
Tries: Clark (14), Ratchford (52), Lineham (57), Hughes (76); **Goals:** Ratchford 4/5.
WARRIORS: 21 Lewis Tierney; 36 Tom Davies; 32 Liam Forsyth; 5 Joe Burgess; 35 Liam Marshall; 6 George Williams; 39 Josh Woods; 8 Frank-Paul Nuuausala; 9 Michael Mcllorum; 19 Ryan Sutton; 20 Willie Isa; 12 Liam Farrell; 13 Sean O'Loughlin (C). Subs (all used): 17 Taulima Tautai; 11 Joel Tomkins; 28 Jack Wells; 37 Callum Field.
Tries: Marshall (9, 26, 46), Burgess (79);
Goals: Woods 1/1, Williams 3/4.
Sin bin: Tierney (37) - professional foul.
Rugby Leaguer & League Express Men of the Match: *Wolves:* Stefan Ratchford; *Warriors:* Sean O'Loughlin.
Penalty count: 9-6; **Half-time:** 6-12; **Referee:** Ben Thaler.

Attendance: 35,361 *(at St James' Park, Newcastle)*.

Sunday 21st May 2017

CATALANS DRAGONS 10 HUDDERSFIELD GIANTS 18

DRAGONS: 1 Tony Gigot; 18 Vincent Duport; 3 Krisnan Inu; 21 Iain Thornley; 5 Fouad Yaha; 6 Luke Walsh; 7 Richie Myler; 8 Sam Moa; 9 Paul Aiton; 10 Remi Casty (C); 14 Julian Bousquet; 15 Benjamin Garcia; 13 Greg Bird. Subs (all used): 19 Mickael Simon; 23 Alrix Da Costa; 27 Ugo Perez; 28 Jordan Dezaria.
Tries: Myler (4), Thornley (48); **Goals:** Walsh 1/2.
GIANTS: 1 Jake Mamo; 2 Jermaine McGillvary; 3 Leroy Cudjoe (C); 5 Aaron Murphy; 24 Darnell McIntosh; 4 Lee Gaskell; 33 Martyn Ridyard (D); 15 Sebastine Ikahihifo; 14 Kruise Leeming; 10 Shannon Wakeman; 12 Dale Ferguson; 30 Alex Mellor; 9 Ryan Hinchcliffe. Subs (all used): 8 Sam Rapira; 18 Paul Clough; 31 Adam O'Brien; 16 Oliver Roberts.
Tries: Gaskell (13), Rapira (72), O'Brien (75);
Goals: Ridyard 3/4.
Rugby Leaguer & League Express Men of the Match: *Dragons:* Iain Thornley; *Giants:* Aaron Murphy.
Penalty count: 5-7; **Half-time:** 6-6;
Referee: Chris Campbell.

LEIGH CENTURIONS 22 SALFORD RED DEVILS 36

CENTURIONS: 1 Mitch Brown; 2 Adam Higson; 3 Ben Crooks; 31 Matty Fleming (D); 5 Matty Dawson; 19 Ryan Hampshire; 7 Josh Drinkwater; 29 Lachlan Burr; 21 Liam Hood; 13 Harrison Hansen (C); 11 Cory Paterson; 17 Atelea Vea; 12 Glenn Stewart. Subs (all used): 8 Gareth Hock; 14 Eloi Pelissier; 15 Danny Tickle; 23 Sam Hopkins.
Tries: Fleming (7), Brown (18), Crooks (48), Dawson (62);
Goals: Drinkwater 3/4.
Dismissal: Higson (55) - high tackle on O'Brien.
RED DEVILS: 1 Gareth O'Brien; 21 Greg Johnson; 22 Kris Welham; 4 Junior Sa'u; 5 Niall Evalds; 6 Robert Lui; 7 Michael Dobson (C); 8 Craig Kopczak; 9 Logan Tomkins; 14 Lama Tasi; 11 Ben Murdoch-Masila; 3 Josh Jones; 16 Olsi Krasniqi. Subs (all used): 12 Weller Hauraki; 13 Mark Flanagan; 15 Ryan Lannon; 20 Kriss Brining.
Tries: Murdoch-Masila (9, 22), Welham (25), Johnson (32, 66), Evalds (56);
Goals: O'Brien 1/1, Dobson 5/7.
Rugby Leaguer & League Express Men of the Match: *Centurions:* Josh Drinkwater; *Red Devils:* Ben Murdoch-Masila.
Penalty count: 7-9; **Half-time:** 12-24;
Referee: James Child.

CASTLEFORD TIGERS 29 LEEDS RHINOS 18

TIGERS: 1 Zak Hardaker; 2 Greg Minikin; 3 Jake Webster; 4 Michael Shenton (C); 5 Greg Eden; 23 Tom Holmes; 7 Luke Gale; 8 Andy Lynch; 9 Paul McShane; 10 Grant Millington; 15 Jesse Sene-Lefao; 12 Mike McMeeken; 13 Adam Milner. Subs (all used): 14 Nathan Massey; 17 Junior Moors; 18 Matt Cook; 34 Alex Foster.
Tries: Gale (3), Eden (46, 50, 63), T Holmes (57);
Goals: Gale 4/5; **Field goal:** Gale (72).
RHINOS: 1 Ashton Golding; 2 Tom Briscoe; 3 Kallum Watkins; 14 Liam Sutcliffe; 5 Ryan Hall; 6 Danny McGuire (C); 4 Joel Moon; 16 Brad Singleton; 9 Matt Parcell; 10 Adam Cuthbertson; 19 Brett Ferres; 13 Stevie Ward; 11 James Jones-Buchanan. Subs (all used): 7 Rob Burrow; 15 Brett Delaney; 22 Ash Handley; 20 Anthony Mullally.
Tries: Watkins (13), Moon (67), L Sutcliffe (76);
Goals: L Sutcliffe 3/3.
Rugby Leaguer & League Express Men of the Match: *Tigers:* Michael Shenton; *Rhinos:* Ashton Golding.
Penalty count: 3-5; **Half-time:** 6-6;
Referee: Phil Bentham.

Attendance: 30,046 *(at St James' Park, Newcastle)*.

ROUND 15

Thursday 25th May 2017

ST HELENS 22 WIGAN WARRIORS 19

SAINTS: 2 Tom Makinson; 5 Adam Swift; 4 Mark Percival; 3 Ryan Morgan; 28 Regan Grace; 6 Theo Fages; 7 Matty Smith; 8 Alex Walmsley; 9 James Roby; 10 Kyle Amor; 36 Zeb Taia; 12 Jon Wilkin (C); 20 Morgan Knowles. Subs (all used): 13 Louie McCarthy-Scarsbrook; 14 Luke Douglas; 16 Luke Thompson; 17 Tommy Lee.
Tries: Morgan (4), Taia (35), Percival (67, 77);
Goals: Percival 3/5.
WARRIORS: 21 Lewis Tierney; 36 Tom Davies; 32 Liam Forsyth; 5 Joe Burgess; 35 Liam Marshall; 6 George Williams; 7 Thomas Leuluai; 8 Frank-Paul Nuuausala; 9 Michael Mcllorum; 19 Ryan Sutton; 20 Willie Isa; 12 Liam Farrell; 13 Sean O'Loughlin (C). Subs (all used): 37 Callum Field; 16 Sam Powell; 17 Taulima Tautai; 28 Jack Wells.
Tries: Davies (14), Tierney (29), Burgess (60);
Goals: Williams 3/4; **Field goal:** Leuluai (72).
Rugby Leaguer & League Express Men of the Match: *Saints:* Mark Percival; *Warriors:* Sean O'Loughlin.
Penalty count: 5-5; **Half-time:** 12-14;
Referee: Phil Bentham; **Attendance:** 13,138.

Friday 26th May 2017

CASTLEFORD TIGERS 32 WIDNES VIKINGS 22

TIGERS: 1 Zak Hardaker; 21 Joel Monaghan; 2 Greg Minikin; 4 Michael Shenton (C); 5 Greg Eden; 16 Ben Roberts; 7 Luke Gale; 8 Andy Lynch; 9 Paul McShane; 10 Grant Millington; 15 Jesse Sene-Lefao; 12 Mike McMeeken; 14 Nathan Massey. Subs: 13 Adam Milner; 18 Matt Cook; 19 Gadwin Springer; 23 Tom Holmes (not used).
Tries: Eden (11, 58, 74), Springer (40), Minikin (54), Cook (78); **Goals:** Gale 4/6.
VIKINGS: 21 Jack Johnson; 28 Ryan Ince; 27 Ed Chamberlain; 4 Charly Runciman; 2 Corey Thompson; 33 Aaron Heremaia (C); 31 Jordan Johnstone; 18 Greg Burke; 9 Lloyd White; 16 Alex Gerrard; 29 Brad Walker; 25 Tom Olbison; 23 Jay Chapelhow. Subs (all used): 22 Ted Chapelhow; 13 Hep Cahill; 35 Danny Walker; 20 Manase Manuokafoa.
Tries: Ince (19), Johnson (27), Thompson (46), Johnstone (49); **Goals:** Chamberlain 3/4.
Rugby Leaguer & League Express Men of the Match: *Tigers:* Greg Eden; *Vikings:* Jack Johnson.
Penalty count: 6-3; **Half-time:** 10-12;
Referee: Chris Campbell; **Attendance:** 7,648.

HULL FC 22 LEIGH CENTURIONS 26

HULL FC: 1 Jamie Shaul; 19 Steve Michaels; 3 Carlos Tuimavave; 4 Josh Griffin; 23 Nick Rawsthorne (D); 6 Albert Kelly; 7 Marc Sneyd; 10 Liam Watts; 9 Danny Houghton (C); 22 Josh Bowden; 12 Mark Minichiello; 21 Sika Manu; 15 Chris Green. Subs (all used): 27 Jack Downs; 28 Brad Fash; 17 Danny Washbrook; 25 Jansin Turgut.
Tries: Shaul (20, 48), Tuimavave (39), Kelly (75);
Goals: Sneyd 3/4.
CENTURIONS: 18 Gregg McNally; 5 Matty Dawson; 31 Matty Fleming; 11 Cory Paterson; 1 Mitch Brown; 20 Ben Reynolds; 7 Josh Drinkwater; 10 Dayne Weston; 21 Liam Hood; 24 Jamie Acton; 17 Atelea Vea; 13 Harrison Hansen (C); 12 Glenn Stewart. Subs (all used): 14 Eloi Pelissier; 15 Danny Tickle; 23 Sam Hopkins; 29 Lachlan Burr.
Tries: Dawson (7, 24), Vea (36, 54), Reynolds (45);
Goals: Reynolds 3/5.
Rugby Leaguer & League Express Men of the Match: *Hull FC:* Albert Kelly; *Centurions:* Josh Drinkwater.
Penalty count: 9-8; **Half-time:** 10-14;
Referee: Ben Thaler; **Attendance:** 10,222.

LEEDS RHINOS 40 WARRINGTON WOLVES 0

RHINOS: 1 Ashton Golding; 2 Tom Briscoe; 3 Kallum Watkins; 14 Liam Sutcliffe; 5 Ryan Hall; 6 Danny McGuire (C); 4 Joel Moon; 16 Brad Singleton; 9 Matt Parcell; 10 Adam Cuthbertson; 19 Brett Ferres; 13 Stevie Ward; 11 Jamie Jones-Buchanan. Subs (all used): 15 Brett Delaney; 20 Anthony Mullally; 7 Rob Burrow; 24 Jordan Baldwinson.
Tries: Parcell (13, 44, 71), L Sutcliffe (29), Jones-Buchanan (49), Moon (61), Burrow (78);
Goals: L Sutcliffe 6/9.
Sin bin: Ward (60) - fighting.
WOLVES: 1 Stefan Ratchford; 5 Matthew Russell; 12 Jack Hughes; 4 Ryan Atkins; 2 Tom Lineham; 6 Kevin Brown; 7 Kurt Gidley; 8 Chris Hill (C); 9 Daryl Clark; 10 Ashton Sims; 24 Benjamin Jullien; 13 Joe Westerman; 14 Mike Cooper. Subs (all used): 23 Joe Philbin; 17 Dominic Crosby; 16 George King; 22 Declan Patton.
Sin bin: Clark (60) - fighting.

Rugby Leaguer & League Express Men of the Match: *Rhinos:* Jamie Jones-Buchanan; *Wolves:* Stefan Ratchford.
Penalty count: 7-6; **Half time:** 12-0;
Referee: James Child; **Attendance:** 14,974.

SALFORD RED DEVILS 50 CATALANS DRAGONS 12

RED DEVILS: 1 Gareth O'Brien; 21 Greg Johnson; 22 Kris Welham; 3 Josh Jones; 5 Niall Evalds; 6 Robert Lui; 7 Michael Dobson (C); 14 Lama Tasi; 9 Logan Tomkins; 30 James Hasson (D); 11 Ben Murdoch-Masila; 12 Weller Hauraki; 16 Olsi Krasniqi. Subs (all used): 20 Kriss Brining; 8 Craig Kopczak; 15 Ryan Lannon; 13 Mark Flanagan.
Tries: O'Brien (5), Jones (12), Welham (21), Evalds (30), Lannon (38), Brining (41), Lui (53), Krasniqi (62), Flanagan (69); **Goals:** Dobson 7/9.
Sin bin: Hasson (15) - high tackle on Gigot.
DRAGONS: 1 Tony Gigot; 21 Iain Thornley; 3 Krisnan Inu; 4 Brayden Wiliame; 5 Fouad Yaha; 6 Luke Walsh; 7 Richie Myler; 8 Sam Moa; 23 Alrix Da Costa; 19 Mickael Simon; 14 Julian Bousquet; 10 Remi Casty (C); 28 Jordan Dezaria. Subs (all used): 18 Vincent Duport; 22 Lucas Albert; 24 Paul Seguier; 27 Ugo Perez.
Tries: Duport (47), Yaha (78); **Goals:** Walsh 2/2.
Sin bin: Casty (3) - late challenge on O'Brien.
Rugby Leaguer & League Express Men of the Match: *Red Devils:* Robert Lui; *Dragons:* Tony Gigot.
Penalty count: 6-6; **Half-time:** 28-0;
Referee: Robert Hicks; **Attendance:** 4,957.

WAKEFIELD TRINITY 28 HUDDERSFIELD GIANTS 26

TRINITY: 1 Scott Grix; 5 Ben Jones-Bishop; 4 Reece Lyne; 18 Joe Arundel; 24 Mason Caton-Brown; 6 Jacob Miller; 7 Liam Finn; 8 Anthony England; 9 Kyle Wood; 20 David Fifita; 11 Matty Ashurst; 12 Danny Kirmond (C); 16 Tinirau Arona. Subs (all used): 14 Sam Williams; 27 James Batchelor; 17 Craig Huby; 23 Keegan Hirst.
Tries: Jones-Bishop (3, 71), Lyne (32, 56), Kirmond (38); **Goals:** Finn 3/4, Williams 1/1.
GIANTS: 1 Jake Mamo; 2 Jermaine McGillvary; 3 Leroy Cudjoe (C); 5 Aaron Murphy; 24 Darnell McIntosh; 4 Lee Gaskell; 33 Martyn Ridyard; 8 Sam Rapira; 14 Kruise Leeming; 15 Sebastine Ikahihifo; 30 Alex Mellor; 12 Dale Ferguson; 9 Ryan Hinchcliffe. Subs (all used): 31 Adam O'Brien; 10 Shannon Wakeman; 16 Oliver Roberts; 18 Paul Clough.
Tries: Mamo (10), McGillvary (15), Gaskell (21), Ferguson (45); **Goals:** Ridyard 5/5.
Rugby Leaguer & League Express Men of the Match: *Trinity:* Ben Jones-Bishop; *Giants:* Ryan Hinchcliffe.
Penalty count: 7-10; **Half-time:** 16-18;
Referee: Chris Kendall; **Attendance:** 4,642.

ROUND 16

Monday 29th May 2017

WARRINGTON WOLVES 12 SALFORD RED DEVILS 38

WOLVES: 1 Stefan Ratchford; 5 Matthew Russell; 12 Jack Hughes; 4 Ryan Atkins; 2 Tom Lineham; 6 Kevin Brown; 22 Declan Patton; 8 Chris Hill (C); 9 Daryl Clark; 14 Mike Cooper; 24 Benjamin Jullien; 23 Joe Philbin; 13 Joe Westerman. Subs (all used): 10 Ashton Sims; 15 Brad Dwyer; 16 George King; 18 Andre Savelio.
Tries: Dwyer (34), Lineham (64); **Goals:** Patton 2/2.
Sin bin: Jullien (26) - interference.
RED DEVILS: 1 Gareth O'Brien; 5 Niall Evalds; 4 Junior Sa'u; 24 Jake Bibby; 21 Greg Johnson; 6 Robert Lui; 29 Todd Carney; 14 Lama Tasi; 20 Kriss Brining; 30 James Hasson; 12 Weller Hauraki; 11 Ben Murdoch-Masila; 13 Mark Flanagan. Subs (all used): 8 Craig Kopczak (C); 19 Josh Wood; 16 Olsi Krasniqi; 26 Daniel Murray.
Tries: Bibby (15), Evalds (17, 50, 59), Sa'u (23, 38), Brining (75); **Goals:** O'Brien 5/7.
Sin bin: Hauraki (33) - professional foul.
Rugby Leaguer & League Express Men of the Match: *Wolves:* Matthew Russell; *Red Devils:* Todd Carney.
Penalty count: 3-5; **Half-time:** 6-22;
Referee: Phil Bentham; **Attendance:** 10,684.

WIDNES VIKINGS 28 LEEDS RHINOS 20

VIKINGS: 1 Rhys Hanbury; 2 Corey Thompson; 3 Chris Bridge; 4 Charly Runciman; 28 Ryan Ince; 9 Lloyd White; 40 Rangi Chase; 15 Gil Dudson; 31 Jordan Johnstone; 10 Jack Buchanan; 11 Chris Houston (C); 39 Sam Wilde; 13 Hep Cahill. Subs (all used): 33 Aaron Heremaia; 25 Tom Olbison; 23 Jay Chapelhow; 20 Manase Manuokafoa.
Tries: Hanbury (19), Ince (32, 72), Thompson (35, 75), Heremaia (61); **Goals:** Bridge 2/6.
RHINOS: 14 Liam Sutcliffe; 2 Tom Briscoe; 3 Kallum Watkins; 22 Ash Handley; 5 Ryan Hall; 4 Joel Moon; 7 Rob Burrow (C); 10 Adam Cuthbertson; 9 Matt Parcell; 16 Brad Singleton; 13 Stevie Ward; 19 Brett Ferres; 11 Jamie Jones-Buchanan. Subs (all used): 17 Mitch Garbutt; 20 Anthony Mullally; 24 Jordan Baldwinson; 21 Josh Walters.
Tries: Handley (10), Watkins (22), Ward (29), Cuthbertson (67); **Goals:** L Sutcliffe 2/4.
Rugby Leaguer & League Express Men of the Match: *Vikings:* Lloyd White; *Rhinos:* Joel Moon.
Penalty count: 7-10; **Half-time:** 12-14;
Referee: Scott Mikalauskas; **Attendance:** 5,518.

WIGAN WARRIORS 30 WAKEFIELD TRINITY 42

WARRIORS: 21 Lewis Tierney; 36 Tom Davies; 20 Willie Isa; 41 James Worthington (D); 35 Liam Marshall; 6 George Williams; 7 Thomas Leuluai; 8 Frank-Paul Nuuausala; 9 Michael McIlorum; 19 Ryan Sutton; 28 Jack Wells; 12 Liam Farrell; 13 Sean O'Loughlin (C). Subs (all used): 16 Sam Powell; 17 Taulima Tautai; 26 Romain Navarrete; 37 Callum Field.
Tries: Worthington (2, 59), Tierney (6), Marshall (14, 78), Leuluai (19); **Goals:** Williams 2/4, Marshall 1/2.
TRINITY: 1 Scott Grix; 3 Bill Tupou; 4 Reece Lyne; 15 Ashley Gibson; 24 Mason Caton-Brown; 6 Jacob Miller; 7 Liam Finn; 33 Adam Walker (D); 9 Kyle Wood; 17 Craig Huby; 11 Matty Ashurst; 12 Danny Kirmond (C); 13 Michael Sio. Subs (all used): 14 Sam Williams; 8 Anthony England; 16 Tinirau Arona; 20 David Fifita.
Tries: Tupou (25, 28, 36), Caton-Brown (34), Kirmond (45), England (56), Miller (70); **Goals:** Finn 7/8.
Rugby Leaguer & League Express Men of the Match: *Warriors:* George Williams; *Trinity:* Liam Finn.
Penalty count: 6-8; **Half-time:** 20-22;
Referee: Chris Campbell; **Attendance:** 13,110.

LEIGH CENTURIONS 0 CASTLEFORD TIGERS 38

CENTURIONS: 18 Gregg McNally; 5 Matty Dawson; 3 Ben Crooks; 31 Matty Fleming; 1 Mitch Brown; 20 Ben Reynolds; 7 Josh Drinkwater (C); 24 Jamie Acton; 21 Liam Hood; 29 Lachlan Burr; 11 Cory Paterson; 17 Atelea Vea; 12 Glenn Stewart. Subs (all used): 14 Eloi Pelissier; 15 Danny Tickle; 16 Antoni Maria; 23 Sam Hopkins.
TIGERS: 1 Zak Hardaker; 2 Greg Minikin; 3 Jake Webster; 4 Michael Shenton (C); 5 Greg Eden; 16 Ben Roberts; 7 Luke Gale; 10 Grant Millington; 9 Paul McShane; 14 Nathan Massey; 15 Jesse Sene-Lefao; 12 Mike McMeeken; 13 Adam Milner. Subs (all used): 17 Junior Moors; 18 Matt Cook; 23 Tom Holmes; 33 Kevin Larroyer (D).
Tries: Sene-Lefao (15, 23), Eden (33, 36, 38, 49), Webster (58); **Goals:** Gale 5/7.
Rugby Leaguer & League Express Men of the Match: *Centurions:* Sam Hopkins; *Tigers:* Michael Shenton.
Penalty count: 9-10; **Half-time:** 0-28;
Referee: Chris Kendall; **Attendance:** 5,905.

CATALANS DRAGONS 23 HULL FC 18

DRAGONS: 1 Tony Gigot; 18 Vincent Duport; 30 Arthur Romano; 21 Iain Thornley; 5 Fouad Yaha; 6 Luke Walsh; 7 Richie Myler; 28 Jordan Dezaria; 13 Greg Bird; 14 Julian Bousquet; 8 Sam Moa; 9 Paul Aiton; 10 Remi Casty (C). Subs (all used): 19 Mickael Simon; 23 Alrix Da Costa; 24 Paul Seguier; 27 Ugo Perez.
Tries: Moa (7), Yaha (70), Gigot (73); **Goals:** Walsh 5/5;
Field goal: Walsh (39).
Sin bin: Moa (16) - punching;
Romano (64) - professional foul.
HULL FC: 1 Jamie Shaul; 23 Nick Rawsthorne; 3 Carlos Tuimavave; 4 Josh Griffin; 19 Steve Michaels; 14 Jake Connor; 6 Albert Kelly; 22 Josh Bowden; 9 Danny Houghton (C); 10 Liam Watts; 21 Sika Manu; 12 Mark Minichiello; 17 Danny Washbrook. Subs (all used): 15 Chris Green; 25 Jansin Turgut; 27 Jack Downs; 28 Brad Fash.
Tries: Kelly (18), Rawsthorne (56, 67); **Goals:** Connor 3/3.
Dismissal: Watts (78) - dangerous challenge on Casty.
Rugby Leaguer & League Express Men of the Match: *Dragons:* Sam Moa; *Hull FC:* Jake Connor.
Penalty count: 13-15; **Half-time:** 9-6;
Referee: James Child; **Attendance:** 8,439.

ROUND 17

Friday 2nd June 2017

LEEDS RHINOS 22 LEIGH CENTURIONS 14

RHINOS: 14 Liam Sutcliffe; 2 Tom Briscoe; 3 Kallum Watkins; 4 Joel Moon; 5 Ryan Hall; 6 Danny McGuire (C); 7 Rob Burrow; 16 Brad Singleton; 9 Matt Parcell; 17 Mitch Garbutt; 19 Brett Ferres; 11 Jamie Jones-Buchanan; 10 Adam Cuthbertson. Subs (all used): 8 Keith Galloway; 20 Anthony Mullally; 12 Carl Ablett; 22 Ash Handley.
Tries: Cuthbertson (8, 57), Briscoe (14), Moon (34);
Goals: L Sutcliffe 3/6.
CENTURIONS: 18 Gregg McNally; 30 Curtis Naughton; 1 Mitch Brown; 31 Matty Fleming; 5 Matty Dawson; 19 Ryan Hampshire; 7 Josh Drinkwater (C); 24 Jamie Acton; 21 Liam Hood; 10 Dayne Weston; 17 Atelea Vea; 11 Cory Paterson; 29 Lachlan Burr. Subs (all used): 15 Danny Tickle; 23 Sam Hopkins; 16 Antoni Maria; 14 Eloi Pelissier.
Tries: Dawson (29, 39), Paterson (79);
Goals: Drinkwater 1/3.
Sin bin: Maria (42) - late challenge on McGuire;
Weston (68) - late challenge on McGuire.
Rugby Leaguer & League Express Men of the Match: *Rhinos:* Adam Cuthbertson; *Centurions:* Jamie Acton.
Penalty count: 14-12; **Half time:** 14-10;
Referee: James Child; **Attendance:** 13,445.

Saturday 3rd June 2017

HULL FC 39 WIGAN WARRIORS 26

HULL FC: 1 Jamie Shaul; 19 Steve Michaels; 5 Fetuli Talanoa; 3 Carlos Tuimavave; 23 Nick Rawsthorne; 6 Albert Kelly; 14 Jake Connor; 15 Chris Green; 9 Danny Houghton (C); 16 Jordan Thompson; 17 Danny Washbrook; 12 Mark Minichiello; 21 Sika Manu. Subs (all used): 25 Jansin Turgut; 27 Jack Downs; 28 Brad Fash; 29 Masi Matongo.
Tries: Michaels (3, 21), Minichiello (13), Houghton (29), Shaul (59), Kelly (66); **Goals:** Connor 5/7, Rawsthorne 2/2;
Field goal: Kelly (75).
WARRIORS: 21 Lewis Tierney; 36 Tom Davies; 32 Liam Forsyth; 5 Joe Burgess; 35 Liam Marshall; 6 George Williams; 7 Thomas Leuluai (C); 8 Frank-Paul Nuuausala; 9 Michael McIlorum; 19 Ryan Sutton; 28 Jack Wells; 12 Liam Farrell; 20 Willie Isa. Subs (all used): 11 Joel Tomkins; 16 Sam Powell; 17 Taulima Tautai; 37 Callum Field.
Tries: Davies (36, 80), Marshall (44, 76), Tierney (56), Burgess (70); **Goals:** Marshall 1/4, Williams 0/2.
Sin bin: Farrell (29) - dissent.
Rugby Leaguer & League Express Men of the Match: *Hull FC:* Mark Minichiello; *Warriors:* Michael McIlorum.
Penalty count: 12-4; **Half-time:** 26-4;
Referee: Phil Bentham; **Attendance:** 10,333.

Sunday 4th June 2017

HUDDERSFIELD GIANTS 44 WARRINGTON WOLVES 4

GIANTS: 1 Jake Mamo; 2 Jermaine McGillvary; 3 Leroy Cudjoe (C); 34 Jordan Turner (D); 5 Aaron Murphy; 6 Danny Brough; 4 Lee Gaskell; 15 Sebastine Ikahihifo; 14 Kruise Leeming; 8 Sam Rapira; 16 Oliver Roberts; 12 Dale Ferguson; 9 Ryan Hinchcliffe. Subs (all used): 10 Shannon Wakeman; 18 Paul Clough; 31 Adam O'Brien; 19 Nathan Mason.
Tries: Roberts (5), McGillvary (27, 62), Murphy (32, 75), Clough (44), Turner (49), Mamo (58); **Goals:** Brough 6/8.
WOLVES: 19 Kevin Penny; 5 Matthew Russell; 1 Stefan Ratchford; 4 Ryan Atkins; 2 Tom Lineham; 6 Kevin Brown; 22 Declan Patton; 8 Chris Hill (C); 15 Brad Dwyer; 14 Mike Cooper; 24 Benjamin Jullien; 12 Jack Hughes; 13 Joe Westerman. Subs (all used): 10 Ashton Sims; 18 Andre Savelio; 23 Joe Philbin; 27 Morgan Smith.
Try: Lineham (54); **Goals:** Patton 0/1.
Rugby Leaguer & League Express Men of the Match: *Giants:* Ryan Hinchcliffe; *Wolves:* Brad Dwyer.
Penalty count: 9-7; **Half-time:** 14-0;
Referee: Chris Kendall; **Attendance:** 5,362.

SALFORD RED DEVILS 24 WAKEFIELD TRINITY 34

RED DEVILS: 1 Gareth O'Brien; 5 Niall Evalds; 22 Kris Welham; 4 Junior Sa'u; 24 Jake Bibby; 6 Robert Lui; 7 Michael Dobson (C); 14 Lama Tasi; 9 Logan Tomkins; 30 James Hasson; 11 Ben Murdoch-Masila; 12 Weller Hauraki; 16 Olsi Krasniqi. Subs (all used): 20 Kriss Brining; 8 Craig Kopczak; 29 Todd Carney; 10 George Griffin.
Tries: Bibby (40, 54), Kopczak (51), Tasi (73);
Goals: Dobson 4/4.
TRINITY: 21 Max Jowitt; 5 Ben Jones-Bishop; 4 Reece Lyne; 15 Ashley Gibson; 24 Mason Caton-Brown; 14 Sam Williams; 7 Liam Finn (C); 8 Anthony England; 9 Kyle Wood; 23 Keegan Hirst; 11 Matty Ashurst; 27 James Batchelor; 13 Michael Sio. Subs (all used): 18 Joe Arundel; 20 David Fifita; 17 Craig Huby; 26 Chris Annakin.
Tries: Caton-Brown (6, 65, 77), Lyne (23, 34), Batchelor (79); **Goals:** Finn 5/6.
Rugby Leaguer & League Express Men of the Match: *Red Devils:* Craig Kopczak; *Trinity:* Mason Caton-Brown.
Penalty count: 7-3; **Half-time:** 6-16;
Referee: Robert Hicks; **Attendance:** 3,277.

WIDNES VIKINGS 26 CATALANS DRAGONS 6

VIKINGS: 1 Rhys Hanbury; 28 Ryan Ince; 3 Chris Bridge; 4 Charly Runciman; 2 Corey Thompson; 33 Aaron Heremaia; 40 Rangi Chase; 15 Gil Dudson; 31 Jordan Johnstone; 10 Jack Buchanan; 11 Chris Houston (C); 12 Matt Whitley; 13 Hep Cahill. Subs (all used): 20 Manase Manuokafoa; 23 Jay Chapelhow; 25 Tom Olbison; 35 Danny Walker.
Tries: Buchanan (15, 73), Hanbury (25), Thompson (46);
Goals: Hanbury 2/3, Thompson 3/3.
Sin bin: Bridge (4) - fighting.

Leigh's Liam Hood swamped by celebrating teammates after scoring against Wigan

DRAGONS: 1 Tony Gigot; 21 Iain Thornley; 3 Krisnan Inu; 30 Arthur Romano; 5 Fouad Yaha; 6 Luke Walsh; 7 Richie Myler; 8 Sam Moa; 9 Paul Aiton; 10 Remi Casty (C); 18 Vincent Duport; 13 Greg Bird; 28 Jordan Dezaria. Subs (all used): 19 Mickael Simon; 23 Alrix Da Costa; 24 Paul Seguier; 25 Thibaut Margalet.
Try: Moa (9); **Goals:** Walsh 1/1.
Sin bin: Thornley (4) - fighting; Myler (20) - holding down; Dezaria (57) - use of the knee;
Moa (65) - late challenge on Heremaia.
Rugby Leaguer & League Express Men of the Match:
Vikings: Rangi Chase; *Dragons:* Sam Moa.
Penalty count: 12-7; **Half-time:** 12-6;
Referee: Ben Thaler; **Attendance:** 4,253.

CASTLEFORD TIGERS 16 ST HELENS 12

TIGERS: 5 Greg Eden; 26 Kieran Gill (D); 3 Jake Webster (C); 21 Joel Monaghan; 2 Greg Minikin; 16 Ben Roberts; 23 Tom Holmes; 8 Andy Lynch; 9 Paul McShane; 14 Nathan Massey; 34 Alex Foster; 33 Kevin Larroyer; 15 Jesse Sene-Lefao. Subs (all used): 12 Mike McMeeken; 17 Junior Moors; 25 Jy Hitchcox; 35 Jake Trueman (D).
Tries: Gill (34), McMeeken (59), T Holmes (71);
Goals: McShane 2/3.
SAINTS: 2 Tom Makinson; 5 Adam Swift; 3 Ryan Morgan; 4 Mark Percival; 28 Regan Grace; 1 Jonny Lomax; 7 Matty Smith; 8 Alex Walmsley; 9 James Roby; 10 Kyle Amor; 36 Zeb Taia; 12 Jon Wilkin (C); 20 Morgan Knowles. Subs (all used): 17 Tommy Lee; 13 Louie McCarthy-Scarsbrook; 14 Luke Douglas; 16 Luke Thompson.

Tries: Percival (15), McCarthy-Scarsbrook (37);
Goals: Makinson 2/2.
Rugby Leaguer & League Express Men of the Match:
Tigers: Paul McShane; *Saints:* Alex Walmsley.
Penalty count: 9-8; **Half-time:** 4-12;
Referee: Chris Campbell; **Attendance:** 8,515.

ROUND 18

Thursday 8th June 2017

LEIGH CENTURIONS 50 WIGAN WARRIORS 34

CENTURIONS: 18 Gregg McNally; 5 Matty Dawson; 1 Mitch Brown; 11 Cory Paterson; 19 Ryan Hampshire; 20 Ben Reynolds; 7 Josh Drinkwater; 24 Jamie Acton; 14 Eloi Pelissier; 10 Dayne Weston; 15 Danny Tickle; 13 Harrison Hansen (C); 12 Glenn Stewart. Subs (all used): 21 Liam Hood; 16 Antoni Maria; 29 Lachlan Burr; 23 Sam Hopkins.
Tries: Hampshire (14), Tickle (20), Burr (24), Brown (48), Hood (54, 56), Paterson (63), Dawson (72);
Goals: Reynolds 9/9.
WARRIORS: 21 Lewis Tierney; 36 Tom Davies; 5 Joe Burgess; 4 Oliver Gildart; 35 Liam Marshall; 6 George Williams; 7 Thomas Leuluai (C); 8 Frank-Paul Nuuausala; 9 Michael McIlorum; 19 Ryan Sutton; 20 Willie Isa; 28 Jack Wells; 11 Joel Tomkins. Subs (all used): 17 Taulima Tautai; 26 Romain Navarrete; 33 Josh Ganson; 32 Liam Forsyth.
Tries: Marshall (4), Ganson (32, 78), Williams (34), Gildart (43), Nuuausala (59), Burgess (77);

Goals: Williams 0/2, Marshall 3/5.
Rugby Leaguer & League Express Men of the Match:
Centurions: Liam Hood; *Warriors:* Taulima Tautai.
Penalty count: 9-6; **Half-time:** 20-14;
Referee: Robert Hicks; **Attendance:** 7,080.

Friday 9th June 2017

SALFORD RED DEVILS 10 HULL FC 34

RED DEVILS: 1 Gareth O'Brien; 24 Jake Bibby; 22 Kris Welham; 4 Junior Sa'u; 5 Niall Evalds; 6 Robert Lui; 7 Michael Dobson (C); 14 Lama Tasi; 20 Kriss Brining; 30 James Hasson; 11 Ben Murdoch-Masila; 12 Weller Hauraki; 10 George Griffin. Subs (all used): 8 Craig Kopczak; 16 Olsi Krasniqi; 29 Todd Carney; 15 Ryan Lannon.
Tries: Evalds (43), Hauraki (64);
Goals: Dobson 1/1, O'Brien 0/1.
HULL FC: 1 Jamie Shaul; 19 Steve Michaels; 2 Mahe Fonua; 3 Carlos Tuimavave; 5 Fetuli Talanoa; 6 Albert Kelly; 14 Jake Connor; 10 Liam Watts; 17 Danny Washbrook (C); 22 Josh Bowden; 21 Sika Manu; 25 Jansin Turgut; 16 Jordan Thompson. Subs (all used): 27 Jack Downs; 28 Brad Fash; 29 Masi Matongo; 4 Josh Griffin.
Tries: Talanoa (7), Kelly (17, 27), Washbrook (35), Tuimavave (48), Shaul (60); **Goals:** Connor 5/6.
Rugby Leaguer & League Express Men of the Match:
Red Devils: Ben Murdoch-Masila; *Hull FC:* Albert Kelly.
Penalty count: 12-7; **Half-time:** 0-22;
Referee: Ben Thaler; **Attendance:** 2,678.

ST HELENS 26 WIDNES VIKINGS 10

SAINTS: 1 Jonny Lomax; 2 Tom Makinson; 3 Ryan Morgan; 4 Mark Percival; 28 Regan Grace; 6 Theo Fages; 7 Matty Smith; 8 Alex Walmsley; 9 James Roby; 10 Kyle Amor; 36 Zeb Taia; 12 Jon Wilkin (C); 13 Louie McCarthy-Scarsbrook. Subs (all used): 14 Luke Douglas; 16 Luke Thompson; 20 Morgan Knowles; 24 Danny Richardson.
Tries: Percival (22), Grace (26), Walmsley (56), Morgan (61), Fages (75); **Goals:** Percival 3/5.
VIKINGS: 21 Jack Johnson; 28 Ryan Ince; 17 Stefan Marsh; 4 Charly Runciman; 2 Corey Thompson; 40 Rangi Chase; 33 Aaron Heremaia; 15 Gil Dudson; 31 Jordan Johnstone; 10 Jack Buchanan; 12 Matt Whitley; 11 Chris Houston (C); 13 Hep Cahill. Subs (all used): 20 Manase Manuokafoa; 23 Jay Chapelhow; 25 Tom Olbison; 32 Danny Craven.
Tries: Ince (49), Craven (70); **Goals:** Craven 1/2.
Rugby Leaguer & League Express Men of the Match: *Saints:* Jonny Lomax; *Vikings:* Charly Runciman.
Penalty count: 11-9; **Half-time:** 10-0;
Referee: Scott Mikalauskas; **Attendance:** 10,474.

Saturday 10th June 2017

CATALANS DRAGONS 12 HUDDERSFIELD GIANTS 56

DRAGONS: 1 Tony Gigot; 18 Vincent Duport; 3 Krisnan Inu; 21 Iain Thornley; 5 Fouad Yaha; 6 Luke Walsh; 7 Richie Myler; 8 Sam Moa; 9 Paul Aiton; 10 Remi Casty (C); 31 Nabil Djalout (D); 14 Julian Bousquet; 25 Thibaut Margalet. Subs (all used): 11 Louis Anderson; 19 Mickael Simon; 23 Alrix Da Costa; 24 Paul Seguier.
Tries: Gigot (26), Moa (72); **Goals:** Walsh 2/2.
GIANTS: 1 Jake Mamo; 2 Jermaine McGillvary; 3 Leroy Cudjoe (C); 34 Jordan Turner; 5 Aaron Murphy; 6 Danny Brough; 33 Martyn Ridyard; 10 Shannon Wakeman; 14 Kruise Leeming; 15 Sebastine Ikahihifo; 12 Dale Ferguson; 16 Oliver Roberts; 9 Ryan Hinchcliffe. Subs (all used): 8 Sam Rapira; 18 Paul Clough; 30 Alex Mellor; 31 Adam O'Brien.
Tries: Murphy (13), Wakeman (16), Brough (18, 46), Mamo (38, 52, 63, 68), McGillvary (54, 75);
Goals: Brough 1/2, Ridyard 7/8.
Rugby Leaguer & League Express Men of the Match: *Dragons:* Richie Myler; *Giants:* Jake Mamo.
Penalty count: 5-7; **Half-time:** 6-22;
Referee: Chris Kendall; **Attendance:** 9,169.

WAKEFIELD TRINITY 16 LEEDS RHINOS 18

TRINITY: 1 Scott Grix; 5 Ben Jones-Bishop; 18 Joe Arundel; 3 Bill Tupou; 24 Mason Caton-Brown; 14 Sam Williams; 7 Liam Finn (C); 8 Anthony England; 9 Kyle Wood; 10 Mitch Allgood; 11 Matty Ashurst; 32 Dean Hadley; 13 Michael Sio. Subs (all used): 27 James Batchelor; 26 Chris Annakin; 23 Keegan Hirst; 20 David Fifita.
Tries: Caton-Brown (5), Wood (11), Jones-Bishop (72);
Goals: Finn 2/3.
RHINOS: 1 Ashton Golding; 2 Tom Briscoe; 3 Kallum Watkins; 14 Liam Sutcliffe; 5 Ryan Hall; 4 Joel Moon; 6 Danny McGuire (C); 16 Brad Singleton; 9 Matt Parcell; 10 Adam Cuthbertson; 13 Stevie Ward; 12 Carl Ablett; 11 Jamie Jones-Buchanan. Subs (all used): 19 Brett Ferres; 8 Keith Galloway; 17 Mitch Garbutt; 20 Anthony Mullally.
Tries: Ward (20), Briscoe (22, 58), Moon (61);
Goals: L Sutcliffe 1/4.
Rugby Leaguer & League Express Men of the Match: *Trinity:* Dean Hadley; *Rhinos:* Joel Moon.
Penalty count: 8-6; **Half-time:** 10-8;
Referee: Phil Bentham; **Attendance:** 7,183.

Sunday 11th June 2017

CASTLEFORD TIGERS 36 WARRINGTON WOLVES 16

TIGERS: 1 Zak Hardaker; 2 Greg Minikin; 21 Joel Monaghan; 4 Michael Shenton (C); 5 Greg Eden; 16 Ben Roberts; 7 Luke Gale; 8 Andy Lynch; 9 Paul McShane; 10 Grant Millington; 15 Jesse Sene-Lefao; 12 Mike McMeeken; 14 Nathan Massey. Subs (all used): 13 Adam Milner; 17 Junior Moors; 23 Tom Holmes; 34 Alex Foster.
Tries: Eden (3, 9, 28, 44, 52), Minikin (11), McMeeken (15);
Goals: Gale 4/7.
WOLVES: 32 Will Dagger (D); 19 Kevin Penny; 1 Stefan Ratchford; 21 Matty Blythe; 2 Tom Lineham; 22 Declan Patton; 13 Joe Westerman; 8 Chris Hill (C); 9 Daryl Clark; 10 Ashton Sims; 24 Benjamin Jullien; 12 Jack Hughes; 14 Mike Cooper. Subs (all used): 15 Brad Dwyer; 16 George King; 18 Andre Savelio; 23 Joe Philbin.
Tries: Lineham (23), Westerman (54), Hughes (74);
Goals: Patton 2/3.
Sin bin: Hill (7) - late challenge on Gale;
Lineham (70) - professional foul.
Rugby Leaguer & League Express Men of the Match: *Tigers:* Greg Eden; *Wolves:* Stefan Ratchford.
Penalty count: 8-8; **Half-time:** 26-6;
Referee: James Child; **Attendance:** 8,577.

ROUND 16

Friday 16th June 2017

HUDDERSFIELD GIANTS 24 ST HELENS 16

GIANTS: 1 Jake Mamo; 2 Jermaine McGillvary; 3 Leroy Cudjoe (C); 4 Lee Gaskell; 5 Aaron Murphy; 6 Danny Brough; 33 Martyn Ridyard; 10 Shannon Wakeman; 14 Kruise Leeming; 15 Sebastine Ikahihifo; 12 Dale Ferguson; 16 Oliver Roberts; 9 Ryan Hinchcliffe. Subs (all used): 8 Sam Rapira; 18 Paul Clough; 30 Alex Mellor; 31 Adam O'Brien.
Tries: Cudjoe (13), Ridyard (36), O'Brien (55), Gaskell (74);
Goals: Ridyard 4/5.
SAINTS: 1 Jonny Lomax; 2 Tom Makinson; 3 Ryan Morgan; 4 Mark Percival; 28 Regan Grace; 6 Theo Fages; 7 Matty Smith; 8 Alex Walmsley; 9 James Roby; 10 Kyle Amor; 36 Zeb Taia; 12 Jon Wilkin (C); 13 Louie McCarthy-Scarsbrook. Subs (all used): 14 Luke Douglas; 16 Luke Thompson; 17 Tommy Lee; 20 Morgan Knowles.
Tries: Thompson (39), Percival (43), Amor (66);
Goals: Percival 2/3.
Rugby Leaguer & League Express Men of the Match: *Giants:* Martyn Ridyard; *Saints:* Zeb Taia.
Penalty count: 5-2; **Half-time:** 12-6;
Referee: James Child; **Attendance:** 5,660.

ROUND 19

Thursday 22nd June 2017

WIDNES VIKINGS 36 LEIGH CENTURIONS 10

VIKINGS: 32 Danny Craven; 2 Corey Thompson; 3 Chris Bridge; 4 Charly Runciman; 28 Ryan Ince; 6 Joe Mellor (C); 40 Rangi Chase; 15 Gil Dudson; 33 Aaron Heremaia; 10 Jack Buchanan; 11 Chris Houston (C); 12 Matt Whitley; 13 Hep Cahill. Subs (all used): 8 Eamon O'Carroll; 9 Lloyd White; 16 Alex Gerrard; 25 Tom Olbison.
Tries: Bridge (3), Houston (6, 40), Thompson (33, 62), Ince (73), Whitley (80); **Goals:** Bridge 3/5, Craven 1/2.
CENTURIONS: 1 Mitch Brown; 5 Matty Dawson; 3 Ben Crooks; 11 Cory Paterson; 32 Nick Rawsthorne (D); 19 Ryan Hampshire; 7 Josh Drinkwater; 29 Lachlan Burr; 14 Eloi Pelissier; 10 Dayne Weston (C); 17 Atelea Vea; 13 Harrison Hansen; 12 Glenn Stewart. Subs (all used): 21 Liam Hood; 15 Danny Tickle; 16 Antoni Maria; 23 Sam Hopkins.
Tries: Rawsthorne (50), Vea (57); **Goals:** Drinkwater 1/2.
Rugby Leaguer & League Express Men of the Match: *Vikings:* Chris Houston; *Centurions:* Lachlan Burr.
Penalty count: 3-9; **Half-time:** 20-0;
Referee: James Child; **Attendance:** 5,604.

Friday 23rd June 2017

HUDDERSFIELD GIANTS 19 WIGAN WARRIORS 19

GIANTS: 24 Darnell McIntosh; 2 Jermaine McGillvary; 3 Leroy Cudjoe (C); 4 Lee Gaskell; 5 Aaron Murphy; 6 Danny Brough; 33 Martyn Ridyard; 15 Sebastine Ikahihifo; 14 Kruise Leeming; 10 Shannon Wakeman; 16 Oliver Roberts; 30 Alex Mellor; 9 Ryan Hinchcliffe. Subs (all used): 17 Ukuma Ta'ai; 18 Paul Clough; 19 Nathan Mason; 22 Tyler Dickinson.
Tries: Cudjoe (8), Gaskell (25), McGillvary (64);
Goals: Ridyard 1/1, Brough 2/2; **Field goal:** Brough (18).
WARRIORS: 1 Sam Tomkins; 36 Tom Davies; 5 Joe Burgess; 4 Oliver Gildart; 35 Liam Marshall; 6 George Williams; 7 Thomas Leuluai; 8 Frank-Paul Nuuausala; 9 Michael McIlorum; 11 Joel Tomkins; 14 John Bateman; 12 Liam Farrell; 13 Sean O'Loughlin (C). Subs (all used): 19 Ryan Sutton; 20 Willie Isa; 16 Sam Powell; 28 Jack Wells.
Tries: Bateman (30), Marshall (34, 43);
Goals: Williams 3/3; **Field goal:** Williams (68).
Rugby Leaguer & League Express Men of the Match: *Giants:* Sebastine Ikahihifo; *Warriors:* Liam Marshall.
Penalty count: 5-7; **Half-time:** 13-12;
Referee: Gareth Hewer; **Attendance:** 5,718.

HULL FC 40 WAKEFIELD TRINITY 18

HULL FC: 1 Jamie Shaul; 19 Steve Michaels; 2 Mahe Fonua; 3 Carlos Tuimavave; 5 Fetuli Talanoa; 14 Jake Connor; 7 Marc Sneyd; 10 Liam Watts; 9 Danny Houghton (C); 22 Josh Bowden; 25 Jansin Turgut; 17 Danny Washbrook; 21 Sika Manu. Subs (all used): 8 Scott Taylor; 28 Brad Fash; 16 Jordan Thompson; 4 Josh Griffin.
Tries: Shaul (16, 68), Talanoa (20), Connor (59), Sneyd (63), Fonua (75), Turgut (78); **Goals:** Sneyd 6/7.
Sin bin: Fonua (13) - fighting.
TRINITY: 1 Scott Grix; 5 Ben Jones-Bishop; 4 Reece Lyne; 3 Bill Tupou; 24 Mason Caton-Brown; 14 Sam Williams; 7 Liam Finn (C); 8 Anthony England; 9 Kyle Wood; 17 Craig Huby; 11 Matty Ashurst; 27 James Batchelor; 16 Tinirau Arona. Subs (all used): 18 Joe Arundel; 26 Chris Annakin; 23 Keegan Hirst; 33 Adam Walker.
Tries: Batchelor (28), Williams (31), Lyne (44);
Goals: Finn 3/3.
Sin bin: Huby (13) - fighting.
Rugby Leaguer & League Express Men of the Match: *Hull FC:* Liam Watts; *Trinity:* Scott Grix.
Penalty count: 7-5; **Half-time:** 10-12;
Referee: Chris Kendall; **Attendance:** 10,895.

LEEDS RHINOS 12 CASTLEFORD TIGERS 23

RHINOS: 14 Liam Sutcliffe; 2 Tom Briscoe; 3 Kallum Watkins; 5 Ryan Hall; 22 Ash Handley; 4 Joel Moon; 6 Danny McGuire (C); 16 Brad Singleton; 9 Matt Parcell; 8 Keith Galloway; 11 Jamie Jones-Buchanan; 13 Stevie Ward; 19 Brett Ferres. Subs: 10 Adam Cuthbertson; 17 Mitch Garbutt; 20 Anthony Mullally; 31 Jack Walker (not used).
Tries: Handley (8), Cuthbertson (60); **Goals:** L Sutcliffe 2/2.
Sin bin: McGuire (13) - dissent.
TIGERS: 1 Zak Hardaker; 25 Jy Hitchcox; 3 Jake Webster; 2 Greg Minikin; 5 Greg Eden; 16 Ben Roberts; 7 Luke Gale (C); 10 Grant Millington; 9 Paul McShane; 15 Jesse Sene-Lefao; 34 Alex Foster; 12 Mike McMeeken; 13 Adam Milner. Subs: 20 Larne Patrick; 14 Nathan Massey; 19 Gadwin Springer; 23 Tom Holmes (not used).
Tries: Eden (13), Hardaker (46), Millington (52);
Goals: Gale 5/5; **Field goal:** Gale (77).
Rugby Leaguer & League Express Men of the Match: *Rhinos:* Liam Sutcliffe; *Tigers:* Luke Gale.
Penalty count: 9-9; **Half time:** 6-8;
Referee: Robert Hicks; **Attendance:** 18,029.

ST HELENS 25 SALFORD RED DEVILS 24

SAINTS: 1 Jonny Lomax; 5 Adam Swift; 2 Tom Makinson; 4 Mark Percival; 28 Regan Grace; 6 Theo Fages; 7 Matty Smith; 8 Alex Walmsley; 9 James Roby; 10 Kyle Amor; 36 Zeb Taia; 12 Jon Wilkin (C); 20 Morgan Knowles. Subs (all used): 13 Louie McCarthy-Scarsbrook; 14 Luke Douglas; 16 Luke Thompson; 17 Tommy Lee.
Tries: Smith (25), Roby (72), Grace (75), Lomax (77);
Goals: Percival 4/5; **Field goal:** Smith (80).
RED DEVILS: 5 Niall Evalds; 24 Jake Bibby; 4 Junior Sa'u; 22 Kris Welham; 21 Greg Johnson; 6 Robert Lui; 29 Todd Carney; 8 Craig Kopczak (C); 9 Logan Tomkins; 14 Lama Tasi; 11 Ben Murdoch-Masila; 15 Ryan Lannon; 13 Mark Flanagan. Subs (all used): 3 Josh Jones; 16 Olsi Krasniqi; 20 Kriss Brining; 30 James Hasson.
Tries: Evalds (40, 66), Johnson (44), Lui (54);
Goals: T Carney 4/5.
Rugby Leaguer & League Express Men of the Match: *Saints:* Matty Smith; *Red Devils:* Niall Evalds.
Penalty count: 9-7; **Half-time:** 8-8;
Referee: Scott Mikalauskas; **Attendance:** 10,001.

Saturday 24th June 2017

WARRINGTON WOLVES 24 CATALANS DRAGONS 16

WOLVES: 32 Will Dagger; 26 Jack Johnson; 12 Jack Hughes; 4 Ryan Atkins; 19 Kevin Penny; 22 Declan Patton; 7 Kurt Gidley; 8 Chris Hill (C); 15 Brad Dwyer; 14 Mike Cooper; 24 Benjamin Jullien; 23 Joe Philbin; 13 Joe Westerman. Subs (all used): 9 Daryl Clark; 10 Ashton Sims; 18 Andre Savelio; 25 Sam Wilde.
Tries: Jullien (7), Atkins (21, 60), Savelio (79);
Goals: Gidley 4/6.
DRAGONS: 1 Tony Gigot; 2 Jodie Broughton; 21 Iain Thornley; 18 Vincent Duport; 5 Fouad Yaha; 6 Luke Walsh; 7 Richie Myler; 8 Sam Moa; 9 Paul Aiton; 10 Remi Casty (C); 11 Louis Anderson; 15 Benjamin Garcia; 17 Jason Baitieri. Subs (all used): 25 Thibaut Margalet; 14 Julian Bousquet; 19 Mickael Simon; 23 Alrix Da Costa.
Tries: Broughton (3), Myler (30, 71); **Goals:** Walsh 2/3.
Sin bin: Gigot (79) - dissent.
Rugby Leaguer & League Express Men of the Match: *Wolves:* Ryan Atkins; *Dragons:* Tony Gigot.
Penalty count: 11-6; **Half-time:** 12-10;
Referee: Phil Bentham; **Attendance:** 9,798.

ROUND 20

Thursday 29th June 2017

LEEDS RHINOS 24 ST HELENS 22

RHINOS: 31 Jack Walker; 2 Tom Briscoe; 3 Kallum Watkins (C); 14 Liam Sutcliffe; 5 Ryan Hall; 4 Joel Moon; 25 Jordan Lilley; 8 Keith Galloway; 9 Matt Parcell; 16 Brad Singleton; 12 Carl Ablett; 13 Stevie Ward; 10 Adam Cuthbertson. Subs: 17 Mitch Garbutt; 20 Anthony Mullally; 22 Ash Handley; 23 Jack Ormondroyd (not used).
Tries: Moon (18), Ward (43), Watkins (65), Hall (73);
Goals: Lilley 4/5.

SAINTS: 1 Jonny Lomax; 5 Adam Swift; 2 Tom Makinson; 3 Ryan Morgan; 28 Regan Grace; 6 Theo Fages; 7 Matty Smith; 16 Luke Thompson; 9 James Roby; 10 Kyle Amor; 36 Zeb Taia; 12 Jon Wilkin (C); 20 Morgan Knowles. Subs (all used): 18 Dominique Peyroux; 8 Alex Walmsley; 13 Louie McCarthy-Scarsbrook; 14 Luke Douglas.
Tries: Swift (15), Makinson (47), Roby (52), Walmsley (78);
Goals: Makinson 3/4.
Sin bin: Wilkin (62) - dangerous contact on Garbutt.
Rugby Leaguer & League Express Men of the Match:
Rhinos: Jack Walker; *Saints:* Theo Fages.
Penalty count: 10-3; **Half time:** 6-4;
Referee: James Child; **Attendance:** 13,262.

Friday 30th June 2017

CASTLEFORD TIGERS 24 HULL FC 22

TIGERS: 1 Zak Hardaker; 25 Jy Hitchcox; 3 Jake Webster; 4 Michael Shenton (C); 5 Greg Eden; 16 Ben Roberts; 7 Luke Gale; 14 Nathan Massey; 9 Paul McShane; 10 Grant Millington; 15 Jesse Sene-Lefao; 12 Mike McMeeken; 13 Adam Milner. Subs: 34 Alex Foster; 19 Gadwin Springer; 20 Larne Patrick; 23 Tom Holmes (not used).
Tries: Gale (11), McMeeken (22), Hardaker (39);
Goals: Gale 6/6.
On report: Webster (50) - alleged high tackle on Kelly.
HULL FC: 1 Jamie Shaul; 2 Mahe Fonua; 14 Jake Connor; 4 Josh Griffin; 5 Fetuli Talanoa; 6 Albert Kelly; 7 Marc Sneyd; 22 Josh Bowden; 9 Danny Houghton (C); 10 Liam Watts; 17 Danny Washbrook; 12 Mark Minichiello; 21 Sika Manu. Subs (all used): 28 Brad Fash; 16 Jordan Thompson; 8 Scott Taylor; 25 Jansin Turgut.
Tries: Fonua (6, 66), Talanoa (72, 77); **Goals:** Sneyd 3/4.
Rugby Leaguer & League Express Men of the Match:
Tigers: Luke Gale; *Hull FC:* Marc Sneyd.
Penalty count: 7-6; **Half-time:** 20-4;
Referee: Chris Kendall; **Attendance:** 8,371.

Saturday 1st July 2017

CATALANS DRAGONS 40 LEIGH CENTURIONS 36

DRAGONS: 1 Tony Gigot; 2 Jodie Broughton; 3 Krisnan Inu; 18 Vincent Duport; 5 Fouad Yaha; 6 Luke Walsh; 7 Richie Myler; 8 Sam Moa; 9 Paul Aiton; 10 Remi Casty (C); 12 Justin Horo; 13 Greg Bird; 17 Jason Baitieri. Subs (all used): 11 Louis Anderson; 14 Julian Bousquet; 15 Benjamin Garcia; 19 Mickael Simon.
Tries: Broughton (22), Simon (31), Yaha (47), Duport (49), Moa (59), Horo (70), Bousquet (80);
Goals: Walsh 6/7.
Sin bin: Bird (45) - fighting.
CENTURIONS: 1 Mitch Brown; 2 Adam Higson; 3 Ben Crooks; 31 Matty Fleming; 5 Matty Dawson; 20 Ben Reynolds; 7 Josh Drinkwater; 15 Danny Tickle; 21 Liam Hood; 24 Jamie Acton; 11 Cory Paterson; 13 Harrison Hansen (C); 12 Glenn Stewart. Subs (all used): 14 Eloi Pelissier; 16 Antoni Maria; 23 Sam Hopkins; 29 Lachlan Burr.
Tries: Dawson (6), Tickle (12), Reynolds (16, 54), Hopkins (36, 39); **Goals:** Reynolds 6/7.
Sin bin: Crooks (45) - fighting.
Rugby Leaguer & League Express Men of the Match:
Dragons: Tony Gigot; *Centurions:* Ben Reynolds.
Penalty count: 8-9; **Half-time:** 12-28;
Referee: Gareth Hewer; **Attendance:** 8,728.

WAKEFIELD TRINITY 26 WARRINGTON WOLVES 12

TRINITY: 1 Scott Grix; 5 Ben Jones-Bishop; 4 Reece Lyne; 3 Bill Tupou; 24 Mason Caton-Brown; 14 Sam Williams; 7 Liam Finn (C); 33 Adam Walker; 9 Kyle Wood; 17 Craig Huby; 11 Matty Ashurst; 32 Dean Hadley; 16 Tinirau Arona. Subs (all used): 8 Anthony England; 18 Joe Arundel; 26 Chris Annakin; 23 Keegan Hirst.
Tries: Tupou (21), Jones-Bishop (38), Wood (50), Caton-Brown (74); **Goals:** Finn 5/6.
Sin bin: Hirst (52) - dangerous contact on Clark.
WOLVES: 32 Will Dagger; 26 Jack Johnson; 35 Peta Hiku (D); 4 Ryan Atkins; 19 Kevin Penny; 1 Stefan Ratchford; 7 Kurt Gidley; 8 Chris Hill (C); 15 Brad Dwyer; 14 Mike Cooper; 24 Benjamin Jullien; 12 Jack Hughes; 23 Joe Philbin. Subs (all used): 9 Daryl Clark; 10 Ashton Sims; 18 Andre Savelio; 25 Sam Wilde.
Tries: Dwyer (12), Hill (55); **Goals:** Ratchford 2/2.
Rugby Leaguer & League Express Men of the Match:
Trinity: Kyle Wood; *Wolves:* Benjamin Jullien.
Penalty count: 12-11; **Half-time:** 14-6;
Referee: Robert Hicks; **Attendance:** 4,829.

Sunday 2nd July 2017

SALFORD RED DEVILS 36 HUDDERSFIELD GIANTS 20

RED DEVILS: 1 Gareth O'Brien; 21 Greg Johnson; 22 Kris Welham; 4 Junior Sa'u; 5 Niall Evalds; 6 Robert Lui; 7 Michael Dobson (C); 14 Lama Tasi; 9 Logan Tomkins; 8 Craig Kopczak; 11 Ben Murdoch-Masila; 3 Josh Jones; 13 Mark Flanagan. Subs (all used): 10 George Griffin; 20 Kriss Brining; 16 Olsi Krasniqi; 12 Weller Hauraki.
Tries: Sa'u (21, 50), Lui (26), Welham (28), O'Brien (46), Johnson (54), Murdoch-Masila (57); **Goals:** Dobson 4/8.
GIANTS: 35 Jordan Rankin (D); 24 Darnell McIntosh; 3 Leroy Cudjoe (C); 30 Alex Mellor; 5 Aaron Murphy; 4 Lee Gaskell; 6 Danny Brough; 10 Shannon Wakeman; 14 Kruise Leeming; 15 Sebastine Ikahihifo; 16 Oliver Roberts; 12 Dale Ferguson; 9 Ryan Hinchcliffe. Subs (all used): 8 Sam Rapira; 17 Ukuma Ta'ai; 18 Paul Clough; 19 Nathan Mason.
Tries: Cudjoe (6), Murphy (35), Leeming (66), McIntosh (77); **Goals:** Brough 2/4.
Rugby Leaguer & League Express Men of the Match:
Red Devils: Ben Murdoch-Masila; *Giants:* Danny Brough.
Penalty count: 5-5; **Half-time:** 18-10;
Referee: Phil Bentham; **Attendance:** 3,718.

WIGAN WARRIORS 28 WIDNES VIKINGS 12

WARRIORS: 1 Sam Tomkins; 21 Lewis Tierney; 3 Anthony Gelling; 4 Oliver Gildart; 5 Joe Burgess; 6 George Williams; 7 Thomas Leuluai; 8 Frank-Paul Nuuausala; 9 Michael McIlorum; 19 Ryan Sutton; 14 John Bateman; 12 Liam Farrell; 13 Sean O'Loughlin (C). Subs (all used): 15 Tony Clubb; 16 Sam Powell; 20 Willie Isa; 28 Jack Wells.
Tries: O'Loughlin (17), Clubb (32), Tierney (36), Burgess (73, 78); **Goals:** Williams 4/5.
VIKINGS: 32 Danny Craven; 17 Stefan Marsh; 3 Chris Bridge; 4 Charly Runciman; 2 Corey Thompson; 6 Joe Mellor (C); 7 Tom Gilmore; 15 Gil Dudson; 9 Lloyd White; 10 Jack Buchanan; 11 Chris Houston (C); 12 Matt Whitley; 13 Hep Cahill. Subs (all used): 8 Eamon O'Carroll; 16 Alex Gerrard; 25 Tom Olbison; 33 Aaron Heremaia.
Tries: White (39, 56); **Goals:** White 2/2.
Rugby Leaguer & League Express Men of the Match:
Warriors: Tony Clubb; *Vikings:* Lloyd White.
Penalty count: 10-9; **Half-time:** 16-6;
Referee: Scott Mikalauskas; **Attendance:** 12,758.

ROUND 21

Thursday 6th July 2017

WAKEFIELD TRINITY 24 CASTLEFORD TIGERS 25

TRINITY: 1 Scott Grix; 5 Ben Jones-Bishop; 18 Joe Arundel; 3 Bill Tupou; 24 Mason Caton-Brown; 14 Sam Williams; 7 Liam Finn (C); 17 Craig Huby; 9 Kyle Wood; 33 Adam Walker; 32 Dean Hadley; 11 Matty Ashurst; 16 Tinirau Arona. Subs (all used): 8 Anthony England; 20 David Fifita; 23 Keegan Hirst; 26 Chris Annakin.
Tries: Jones-Bishop (8), Wood (28), Fifita (69);
Goals: Finn 6/6.
TIGERS: 1 Zak Hardaker; 2 Greg Minikin; 3 Jake Webster; 4 Michael Shenton (C); 5 Greg Eden; 16 Ben Roberts; 7 Luke Gale; 10 Grant Millington; 9 Paul McShane; 14 Nathan Massey; 12 Mike McMeeken; 15 Jesse Sene-Lefao; 13 Adam Milner. Subs (all used): 8 Andy Lynch; 19 Gadwin Springer; 20 Larne Patrick; 34 Alex Foster.
Tries: Eden (42), Millington (46), McMeeken (55), Webster (76); **Goals:** Gale 4/4; **Field goal:** Gale (79).
Rugby Leaguer & League Express Men of the Match:
Trinity: Scott Grix; *Tigers:* Paul McShane.
Penalty count: 8-8; **Half-time:** 16-0;
Referee: Chris Kendall; **Attendance:** 6,430.

Friday 7th July 2017

HUDDERSFIELD GIANTS 40 WIDNES VIKINGS 0

GIANTS: 35 Jordan Rankin; 2 Jermaine McGillvary; 3 Leroy Cudjoe (C); 4 Lee Gaskell; 24 Darnell McIntosh; 6 Danny Brough; 33 Martyn Ridyard; 8 Sam Rapira; 14 Kruise Leeming; 10 Shannon Wakeman; 16 Oliver Roberts; 17 Ukuma Ta'ai; 9 Ryan Hinchcliffe. Subs (all used): 18 Paul Clough; 22 Tyler Dickinson; 30 Alex Mellor; 31 Adam O'Brien.
Tries: Wakeman (5), McGillvary (11, 70), Hinchcliffe (15), O'Brien (36), McIntosh (51), Ta'ai (77);
Goals: Ridyard 6/7.
VIKINGS: 2 Corey Thompson; 28 Ryan Ince; 3 Chris Bridge; 4 Charly Runciman; 17 Stefan Marsh; 6 Joe Mellor (C); 33 Aaron Heremaia; 15 Gil Dudson; 9 Lloyd White; 10 Jack Buchanan; 12 Matt Whitley; 11 Chris Houston (C); 13 Hep Cahill. Subs (all used): 18 Greg Burke; 20 Manase Manuokafoa; 29 Brad Walker; 31 Jordan Johnstone.
Rugby Leaguer & League Express Men of the Match:
Giants: Ryan Hinchcliffe; *Vikings:* Corey Thompson.
Penalty count: 16-8; **Half-time:** 24-0;
Referee: Tom Grant; **Attendance:** 5,253.

ST HELENS 19 HULL FC 12

SAINTS: 1 Jonny Lomax; 2 Tom Makinson; 3 Ryan Morgan; 4 Mark Percival; 28 Regan Grace; 6 Theo Fages; 24 Danny Richardson; 14 Luke Douglas; 9 James Roby (C); 16 Luke Thompson; 36 Zeb Taia; 18 Dominique Peyroux; 20 Morgan Knowles. Subs: 8 Alex Walmsley; 10 Kyle Amor; 13 Louie McCarthy-Scarsbrook; 17 Tommy Lee (not used).
Tries: Roby (30), Percival (47, 73); **Goals:** Percival 3/4;
Field goal: Richardson (77).
HULL FC: 1 Jamie Shaul; 2 Mahe Fonua; 4 Josh Griffin; 3 Carlos Tuimavave; 5 Fetuli Talanoa; 6 Albert Kelly; 7 Marc Sneyd; 8 Scott Taylor; 9 Danny Houghton (C); 22 Josh Bowden; 17 Danny Washbrook; 12 Mark Minichiello; 21 Sika Manu. Subs (all used): 10 Liam Watts; 14 Jake Connor; 16 Jordan Thompson; 29 Masi Matongo.
Tries: Shaul (25), Fonua (64); **Goals:** Sneyd 2/2.
Rugby Leaguer & League Express Men of the Match:
Saints: Mark Percival; *Hull FC:* Josh Griffin.
Penalty count: 7-3; **Half-time:** 8-6;
Referee: Phil Bentham; **Attendance:** 9,910.

WARRINGTON WOLVES 50 LEIGH CENTURIONS 10

WOLVES: 1 Stefan Ratchford; 35 Peta Hiku; 33 Ben Pomeroy (D); 4 Ryan Atkins; 2 Tom Lineham; 22 Declan Patton; 7 Kurt Gidley; 8 Chris Hill (C); 9 Daryl Clark; 10 Ashton Sims; 24 Benjamin Jullien; 12 Jack Hughes; 34 Ben Westwood. Subs (all used): 23 Joe Philbin; 16 George King; 18 Andre Savelio; 27 Morgan Smith.
Tries: Atkins (6), Sims (19), Lineham (27, 33, 67, 77), Pomeroy (48), Hughes (69), Patton (79);
Goals: Ratchford 6/9, Westwood 1/1.
Sin bin: Westwood (8) - dangerous challenge on Tickle.
CENTURIONS: 1 Mitch Brown; 5 Matty Dawson; 34 Samisoni Langi (D); 11 Cory Paterson; 2 Adam Higson; 20 Ben Reynolds; 33 Daniel Mortimer (D); 23 Sam Hopkins; 9 Micky Higham (C); 15 Danny Tickle; 17 Atelea Vea; 13 Harrison Hansen; 12 Glenn Stewart. Subs (all used): 21 Liam Hood; 16 Antoni Maria; 29 Lachlan Burr; 22 James Green.
Tries: Reynolds (40), Dawson (75); **Goals:** Reynolds 1/2.
Rugby Leaguer & League Express Men of the Match:
Wolves: Stefan Ratchford; *Centurions:* Cory Paterson.
Penalty count: 8-6; **Half-time:** 24-6;
Referee: Scott Mikalauskas; **Attendance:** 10,597.

Saturday 8th July 2017

CATALANS DRAGONS 10 WIGAN WARRIORS 32

DRAGONS: 1 Tony Gigot; 2 Jodie Broughton; 3 Krisnan Inu; 4 Brayden Wiliame; 18 Vincent Duport; 6 Luke Walsh; 22 Lucas Albert; 8 Sam Moa; 9 Paul Aiton; 10 Remi Casty (C); 11 Louis Anderson; 12 Justin Horo; 17 Jason Baitieri. Subs: 14 Julian Bousquet; 23 Alrix Da Costa (not used); 25 Thibaut Margalet; 26 Lambert Belmas.
Tries: Duport (25, 47); **Goals:** Walsh 1/2.
WARRIORS: 1 Sam Tomkins; 36 Tom Davies; 3 Anthony Gelling; 4 Oliver Gildart; 5 Joe Burgess; 6 George Williams; 7 Thomas Leuluai; 8 Frank-Paul Nuuausala; 9 Michael McIlorum; 19 Ryan Sutton; 12 Liam Farrell; 14 John Bateman; 13 Sean O'Loughlin (C). Subs (all used): 15 Tony Clubb; 16 Sam Powell; 17 Taulima Tautai; 20 Willie Isa.
Tries: Burgess (20, 60, 78), Williams (66), S Tomkins (74);
Goals: Williams 6/7.
Rugby Leaguer & League Express Men of the Match:
Dragons: Brayden Wiliame; *Warriors:* George Williams.
Penalty count: 5-7; **Half-time:** 4-8;
Referee: Robert Hicks; **Attendance:** 9,810.

Sunday 9th July 2017

SALFORD RED DEVILS 24 LEEDS RHINOS 50

RED DEVILS: 1 Gareth O'Brien; 21 Greg Johnson; 22 Kris Welham; 4 Junior Sa'u; 5 Niall Evalds; 6 Robert Lui; 7 Michael Dobson (C); 14 Lama Tasi; 19 Josh Wood; 8 Craig Kopczak; 11 Ben Murdoch-Masila; 3 Josh Jones; 12 Weller Hauraki. Subs (all used): 16 Olsi Krasniqi; 10 George Griffin; 20 Kriss Brining; 15 Ryan Lannon.
Tries: Wood (6), Murdoch-Masila (42, 73), Dobson (65);
Goals: Dobson 4/4.
Sin bin: Sa'u (29) - high tackle on Watkins.
RHINOS: 31 Jack Walker; 2 Tom Briscoe; 3 Kallum Watkins; 13 Stevie Ward; 5 Ryan Hall; 4 Joel Moon; 6 Danny McGuire (C); 8 Keith Galloway; 9 Matt Parcell; 16 Brad Singleton; 11 Jamie Jones-Buchanan; 12 Carl Ablett; 10 Adam Cuthbertson. Subs (all used): 25 Jordan Lilley; 17 Mitch Garbutt; 20 Anthony Mullally; 21 Josh Walters.
Tries: Hall (13), Briscoe (20, 37), Watkins (22), Parcell (25), Moon (30), Jones-Buchanan (35), Mullally (67), Walker (80); **Goals:** Watkins 3/4, Lilley 4/6.
Rugby Leaguer & League Express Men of the Match:
Red Devils: Ben Murdoch-Masila; *Rhinos:* Matt Parcell.
Penalty count: 7-12; **Half-time:** 6-36;
Referee: James Child; **Attendance:** 5,056.

ROUND 22

Thursday 13th July 2017

WIGAN WARRIORS 10 WARRINGTON WOLVES 16

WARRIORS: 1 Sam Tomkins; 35 Liam Marshall; 3 Anthony Gelling; 4 Oliver Gildart; 5 Joe Burgess; 6 George Williams; 7 Thomas Leuluai; 8 Frank-Paul Nuuausala; 9 Michael McIlorum; 19 Ryan Sutton; 14 John Bateman; 20 Willie Isa; 13 Sean O'Loughlin (C). Subs (all used): 15 Tony Clubb; 16 Sam Powell; 17 Taulima Tautai; 28 Jack Wells.
Tries: Gildart (2), Bateman (21); **Goals:** Williams 1/2.
WOLVES: 1 Stefan Ratchford; 35 Peta Hiku; 33 Ben Pomeroy; 4 Ryan Atkins; 2 Tom Lineham; 22 Declan Patton; 7 Kurt Gidley; 8 Chris Hill (C); 9 Daryl Clark; 10 Ashton Sims; 24 Benjamin Jullien; 12 Jack Hughes; 14 Mike Cooper. Subs (all used): 11 Ben Currie; 18 Andre Savelio; 23 Joe Philbin; 27 Morgan Smith.
Tries: Jullien (14), Atkins (38), Currie (57);
Goals: Ratchford 2/4.
Rugby Leaguer & League Express Men of the Match:
Warriors: Sean O'Loughlin; *Wolves:* Ben Currie.
Penalty count: 10-12; **Half-time:** 10-8;
Referee: James Child; **Attendance:** 12,790.

Friday 14th July 2017

CASTLEFORD TIGERS 38 SALFORD RED DEVILS 14

TIGERS: 1 Zak Hardaker; 25 Jy Hitchcox; 2 Greg Minikin; 4 Michael Shenton (C); 5 Greg Eden; 16 Ben Roberts; 7 Luke Gale; 10 Grant Millington; 9 Paul McShane; 15 Jesse Sene-Lefao; 34 Alex Foster; 12 Mike McMeeken; 14 Nathan Massey. Subs (all used): 8 Andy Lynch; 19 Gadwin Springer; 21 Joel Monaghan; 33 Kevin Larroyer.
Tries: Eden (3, 24), Roberts (21), Monaghan (47, 64), Hardaker (51); **Goals:** Gale 7/8.
RED DEVILS: 1 Gareth O'Brien; 24 Jake Bibby; 22 Kris Welham; 3 Josh Jones; 5 Niall Evalds; 29 Todd Carney; 7 Michael Dobson (C); 10 George Griffin; 9 Logan Tomkins; 26 Daniel Murray; 11 Ben Murdoch-Masila; 15 Ryan Lannon; 12 Weller Hauraki. Subs (all used): 6 Robert Lui; 18 Jordan Walne; 14 Lama Tasi; 16 Olsi Krasniqi.
Tries: O'Brien (8), Welham (33), Bibby (57);
Goals: Dobson 1/3.
Sin bin: Hauraki (76) - late challenge on Millington.
Rugby Leaguer & League Express Men of the Match:
Tigers: Luke Gale; *Red Devils:* Gareth O'Brien.
Penalty count: 12-4; **Half-time:** 18-10;
Referee: Phil Bentham; **Attendance:** 7,094.

HUDDERSFIELD GIANTS 26 LEIGH CENTURIONS 4

GIANTS: 35 Jordan Rankin; 2 Jermaine McGillvary; 3 Leroy Cudjoe (C); 23 Sam Wood; 24 Darnell McIntosh; 4 Lee Gaskell; 6 Danny Brough; 8 Sam Rapira; 14 Kruise Leeming; 15 Sebastine Ikahihifo; 16 Oliver Roberts; 12 Dale Ferguson; 9 Ryan Hinchcliffe. Subs (all used): 31 Adam O'Brien; 10 Shannon Wakeman; 18 Paul Clough; 17 Ukuma Ta'ai.
Tries: Gaskell (21, 47), Ta'ai (44), Cudjoe (74);
Goals: Brough 5/5.
CENTURIONS: 1 Mitch Brown; 2 Adam Higson; 3 Ben Crooks; 34 Samisoni Langi; 5 Matty Dawson; 33 Daniel Mortimer; 7 Josh Drinkwater; 8 Gareth Hock; 9 Micky Higham (C); 13 Harrison Hansen; 11 Cory Paterson; 17 Atelea Vea; 12 Glenn Stewart. Subs (all used): 14 Eloi Pelissier; 15 Danny Tickle; 23 Sam Hopkins; 29 Lachlan Burr.
Try: Drinkwater (57); **Goals:** Drinkwater 0/1.
Rugby Leaguer & League Express Men of the Match:
Giants: Ryan Hinchcliffe; *Centurions:* Daniel Mortimer.
Penalty count: 11-11; **Half-time:** 8-0;
Referee: Scott Mikalauskas; **Attendance:** 5,535.

LEEDS RHINOS 10 HULL FC 7

RHINOS: 1 Ashton Golding; 2 Tom Briscoe; 13 Stevie Ward; 18 Jimmy Keinhorst; 5 Ryan Hall; 4 Joel Moon; 6 Danny McGuire (C); 8 Keith Galloway; 9 Matt Parcell; 16 Brad Singleton; 11 Jamie Jones-Buchanan; 12 Carl Ablett; 10 Adam Cuthbertson. Subs (all used): 31 Jack Walker; 17 Mitch Garbutt; 20 Anthony Mullally; 25 Jordan Lilley.
Tries: Hall (46), Walker (56); **Goals:** Golding 0/1, Lilley 1/1.
HULL FC: 1 Jamie Shaul; 2 Mahe Fonua; 4 Josh Griffin; 3 Carlos Tuimavave; 5 Fetuli Talanoa; 14 Jake Connor; 7 Marc Sneyd; 8 Scott Taylor; 9 Danny Houghton (C); 10 Liam Watts; 16 Jordan Thompson; 12 Mark Minichiello; 21 Sika Manu. Subs (all used): 17 Danny Washbrook; 22 Josh Bowden; 27 Jack Downs; 29 Masi Matongo.
Try: Taylor (6); **Goals:** Sneyd 1/1; **Field goal:** Sneyd (40).
On report:
Connor (64) - alleged dangerous contact on Ablett.
Rugby Leaguer & League Express Men of the Match:
Rhinos: Ryan Hall; *Hull FC:* Liam Watts.
Penalty count: 7-5; **Half time:** 0-7;
Referee: Robert Hicks; **Attendance:** 16,938.

WIDNES VIKINGS 8 WAKEFIELD TRINITY 36

VIKINGS: 2 Corey Thompson; 28 Ryan Ince; 3 Chris Bridge; 4 Charly Runciman; 17 Stefan Marsh; 6 Joe Mellor (C); 40 Rangi Chase; 15 Gil Dudson; 33 Aaron Heremaia; 10 Jack Buchanan; 11 Chris Houston (C); 12 Matt Whitley; 13 Hep Cahill. Subs (all used): 31 Jordan Johnstone; 20 Manase Manuokafoa; 8 Eamon O'Carroll; 25 Tom Olbison.
Try: Mellor (6); **Goals:** Marsh 2/2.
Sin bin: Ince (26) - late challenge on Caton-Brown.
TRINITY: 1 Scott Grix; 5 Ben Jones-Bishop; 18 Joe Arundel; 3 Bill Tupou; 24 Mason Caton-Brown; 14 Sam Williams; 7 Liam Finn (C); 33 Adam Walker; 9 Kyle Wood; 17 Craig Huby; 11 Matty Ashurst; 32 Dean Hadley; 16 Tinirau Arona. Subs (all used): 26 Chris Annakin; 23 Keegan Hirst; 20 David Fifita; 8 Anthony England.
Tries: Caton-Brown (13, 70), Tupou (33, 72), Williams (37), Arona (62); **Goals:** Finn 6/7.
Rugby Leaguer & League Express Men of the Match:
Vikings: Chris Houston; *Trinity:* David Fifita.
Penalty count: 7-7; **Half-time:** 8-18;
Referee: Chris Kendall; **Attendance:** 4,977.

Sunday 16th July 2017

ST HELENS 46 CATALANS DRAGONS 28

SAINTS: 1 Jonny Lomax; 2 Tom Makinson; 3 Ryan Morgan; 4 Mark Percival; 28 Regan Grace; 6 Theo Fages; 24 Danny Richardson; 14 Luke Douglas; 9 James Roby; 16 Luke Thompson; 36 Zeb Taia; 18 Dominique Peyroux; 12 Jon Wilkin (C). Subs (all used): 8 Alex Walmsley; 13 Louie McCarthy-Scarsbrook; 17 Tommy Lee; 20 Morgan Knowles.
Tries: Fages (7), Walmsley (25), McCarthy-Scarsbrook (37), Lomax (60), Percival (73), Thompson (77), Morgan (80);
Goals: Percival 9/10.
DRAGONS: 1 Tony Gigot; 33 Lewis Tierney (D); 3 Krisnan Inu; 18 Vincent Duport; 5 Fouad Yaha; 6 Luke Walsh; 7 Richie Myler; 8 Sam Moa; 9 Paul Aiton; 14 Julian Bousquet; 11 Louis Anderson; 12 Justin Horo; 17 Jason Baitieri. Subs (all used): 10 Remi Casty (C); 13 Greg Bird; 23 Alrix Da Costa; 32 Romain Navarrete (D2).
Tries: Horo (4, 50), Walsh (17), Gigot (32), Myler (70);
Goals: Walsh 4/5.
Rugby Leaguer & League Express Men of the Match:
Saints: Mark Percival; *Dragons:* Krisnan Inu.
Penalty count: 12-4; **Half-time:** 20-18;
Referee: Ben Thaler; **Attendance:** 10,024.

ROUND 23

Thursday 20th July 2017

WARRINGTON WOLVES 22 WIDNES VIKINGS 6

WOLVES: 1 Stefan Ratchford (C); 5 Matthew Russell; 35 Peta Hiku; 4 Ryan Atkins; 2 Tom Lineham; 22 Declan Patton; 6 Kevin Brown; 14 Mike Cooper; 9 Daryl Clark; 10 Ashton Sims; 24 Benjamin Jullien; 12 Jack Hughes; 23 Joe Philbin. Subs (all used): 16 George King; 18 Andre Savelio; 11 Ben Currie; 27 Morgan Smith.
Tries: Russell (2, 63), Hiku (52), Brown (59);
Goals: Ratchford 3/4.
VIKINGS: 2 Corey Thompson; 26 Tom Armstrong; 27 Ed Chamberlain; 4 Charly Runciman; 17 Stefan Marsh; 6 Joe Mellor (C); 29 Brad Walker; 23 Jay Chapelhow; 31 Jordan Johnstone; 15 Gil Dudson; 12 Matt Whitley; 25 Tom Olbison; 13 Hep Cahill. Subs (all used): 16 Alex Gerrard; 18 Greg Burke; 35 Danny Walker; 22 Ted Chapelhow.
Try: Mellor (16); **Goals:** Marsh 1/1.
Rugby Leaguer & League Express Men of the Match:
Wolves: Peta Hiku; *Vikings:* Joe Mellor.
Penalty count: 7-7; **Half-time:** 4-6;
Referee: Robert Hicks; **Attendance:** 9,895.

Friday 21st July 2017

HULL FC 14 HUDDERSFIELD GIANTS 10

HULL FC: 1 Jamie Shaul; 2 Mahe Fonua; 4 Josh Griffin; 3 Carlos Tuimavave; 5 Fetuli Talanoa; 14 Jake Connor; 7 Marc Sneyd; 8 Scott Taylor; 9 Danny Houghton; 10 Liam Watts; 21 Sika Manu; 12 Mark Minichiello; 13 Gareth Ellis (C). Subs (all used): 15 Chris Green; 28 Brad Fash; 17 Danny Washbrook; 22 Josh Bowden.
Tries: Minichiello (14), Bowden (21); **Goals:** Sneyd 3/3.
GIANTS: 35 Jordan Rankin; 2 Jermaine McGillvary; 3 Leroy Cudjoe (C); 4 Lee Gaskell; 24 Darnell McIntosh; 6 Danny Brough; 33 Martyn Ridyard; 8 Sam Rapira; 14 Kruise Leeming; 15 Sebastine Ikahihifo; 16 Oliver Roberts; 12 Dale Ferguson; 9 Ryan Hinchcliffe. Subs (all used): 31 Adam O'Brien; 10 Shannon Wakeman; 18 Paul Clough; 17 Ukuma Ta'ai.
Tries: McIntosh (32), McGillvary (36); **Goals:** Brough 1/2.
Rugby Leaguer & League Express Men of the Match:
Hull FC: Gareth Ellis; *Giants:* Jermaine McGillvary.
Penalty count: 8-6; **Half-time:** 12-10;
Referee: Chris Kendall; **Attendance:** 11,467.

LEIGH CENTURIONS 25 SALFORD RED DEVILS 0

CENTURIONS: 18 Gregg McNally; 5 Matty Dawson; 3 Ben Crooks; 34 Samisoni Langi; 1 Mitch Brown; 33 Daniel Mortimer; 7 Josh Drinkwater; 8 Gareth Hock; 9 Micky Higham (C); 16 Antoni Maria; 11 Cory Paterson; 17 Atelea Vea; 29 Lachlan Burr. Subs (all used): 14 Eloi Pelissier; 15 Danny Tickle; 35 Greg Richards (D); 13 Harrison Hansen.
Tries: McNally (9, 79), Vea (19), Langi (36);
Goals: Drinkwater 4/5; **Field goal:** Drinkwater (75).
RED DEVILS: 5 Niall Evalds; 21 Greg Johnson; 22 Kris Welham; 4 Junior Sa'u; 24 Jake Bibby; 29 Todd Carney; 7 Michael Dobson (C); 10 George Griffin; 9 Logan Tomkins; 26 Daniel Murray; 11 Ben Murdoch-Masila; 15 Ryan Lannon; 12 Weller Hauraki. Subs (all used): 3 Josh Jones; 6 Robert Lui; 16 Olsi Krasniqi; 14 Lama Tasi.
Rugby Leaguer & League Express Men of the Match:
Centurions: Lachlan Burr; *Red Devils:* Todd Carney.
Penalty count: 8-6; **Half-time:** 18-0;
Referee: Jack Smith; **Attendance:** 7,002.

WIGAN WARRIORS 34 LEEDS RHINOS 0

WARRIORS: 1 Sam Tomkins; 36 Tom Davies; 3 Anthony Gelling; 4 Oliver Gildart; 5 Joe Burgess; 6 George Williams; 7 Thomas Leuluai; 8 Frank-Paul Nuuausala; 9 Michael McIlorum; 19 Ryan Sutton; 14 John Bateman; 20 Willie Isa; 13 Sean O'Loughlin (C). Subs (all used): 15 Tony Clubb; 16 Sam Powell; 17 Taulima Tautai; 28 Jack Wells.
Tries: McIlorum (11), S Tomkins (15), Williams (31, 74), Gildart (50, 55), Davies (72); **Goals:** Williams 2/6, Powell 1/1.
RHINOS: 31 Jack Walker; 2 Tom Briscoe; 18 Jimmy Keinhorst; 32 Alex Sutcliffe (D); 33 Harry Newman (D); 1 Ashton Golding; 25 Jordan Lilley; 17 Mitch Garbutt; 11 Jamie Jones-Buchanan (C); 24 Jordan Baldwinson; 23 Jack Ormondroyd; 12 Carl Ablett; 20 Anthony Mullally. Subs (all used): 27 Cameron Smith; 28 Mikolaj Oledzki; 29 Josh Jordan-Roberts; 34 Harvey Whiteley (D).
Rugby Leaguer & League Express Men of the Match:
Warriors: George Williams; *Rhinos:* Mitch Garbutt.
Penalty count: 7-8; **Half-time:** 14-0;
Referee: Ben Thaler; **Attendance:** 15,119.

Saturday 22nd July 2017

CATALANS DRAGONS 24 CASTLEFORD TIGERS 32

DRAGONS: 1 Tony Gigot; 33 Lewis Tierney; 3 Krisnan Inu; 18 Vincent Duport; 5 Fouad Yaha; 22 Lucas Albert; 7 Richie Myler; 8 Sam Moa; 9 Paul Aiton; 32 Romain Navarrete; 11 Louis Anderson; 12 Justin Horo; 13 Greg Bird (C). Subs (all used): 14 Julian Bousquet; 15 Benjamin Garcia; 17 Jason Baitieri; 25 Thibaut Margalet.
Tries: Albert (21), Gigot (27), Yaha (35), Duport (68);
Goals: Gigot 4/4.
TIGERS: 1 Zak Hardaker; 25 Jy Hitchcox; 2 Greg Minikin; 4 Michael Shenton (C); 21 Joel Monaghan; 16 Ben Roberts; 7 Luke Gale; 10 Grant Millington; 9 Paul McShane; 15 Jesse Sene-Lefao; 34 Alex Foster; 12 Mike McMeeken; 14 Nathan Massey. Subs: 8 Andy Lynch; 18 Matt Cook; 23 Tom Holmes (not used); 33 Kevin Larroyer.
Tries: Hitchcox (8, 74), Hardaker (19), Minikin (53), McShane (77); **Goals:** Gale 5/5, Hardaker 1/2.
Sin bin: Larroyer (59) - dangerous challenge on Duport; McMeeken (67) - holding down; Gale (78) - dissent.
Rugby Leaguer & League Express Men of the Match:
Dragons: Tony Gigot; *Tigers:* Zak Hardaker.
Penalty count: 13-9; **Half-time:** 18-16;
Referee: Phil Bentham; **Attendance:** 8,657.

Sunday 23rd July 2017

WAKEFIELD TRINITY 16 ST HELENS 41

TRINITY: 1 Scott Grix; 5 Ben Jones-Bishop; 4 Reece Lyne; 3 Bill Tupou; 24 Mason Caton-Brown; 14 Sam Williams; 7 Liam Finn; 33 Adam Walker; 9 Kyle Wood; 17 Craig Huby; 32 Dean Hadley; 11 Matty Ashurst; 16 Tinirau Arona. Subs (all used): 12 Danny Kirmond (C); 34 James Hasson (D); 20 David Fifita; 8 Anthony England.
Tries: Ashurst (12), Grix (43), Caton-Brown (61);
Goals: Finn 2/3.
SAINTS: 1 Jonny Lomax; 2 Tom Makinson; 3 Ryan Morgan; 4 Mark Percival; 28 Regan Grace; 6 Theo Fages; 24 Danny Richardson; 14 Luke Douglas; 9 James Roby; 16 Luke Thompson; 36 Zeb Taia; 18 Dominique Peyroux; 12 Jon Wilkin (C). Subs (all used): 8 Alex Walmsley; 10 Kyle Amor; 13 Louie McCarthy-Scarsbrook; 20 Morgan Knowles.
Tries: Richardson (9), Roby (18), Makinson (22), Grace (32), McCarthy-Scarsbrook (70), Taia (74);
Goals: Percival 8/8; **Field goal:** Richardson (80).
Rugby Leaguer & League Express Men of the Match:
Trinity: Matty Ashurst; *Saints:* Danny Richardson.
Penalty count: 9-4; **Half-time:** 6-24;
Referee: James Child; **Attendance:** 5,820.

SUPER 8s

ROUND 1

Thursday 3rd August 2017

CASTLEFORD TIGERS 12 ST HELENS 26

TIGERS: 1 Zak Hardaker; 21 Joel Monaghan; 2 Greg Minikin; 4 Michael Shenton (C); 25 Jy Hitchcox; 16 Ben Roberts; 7 Luke Gale; 10 Grant Millington; 9 Paul McShane; 15 Jesse Sene-Lefao; 34 Alex Foster; 12 Mike McMeeken; 14 Nathan Massey. Subs (all used): 11 Oliver Holmes; 13 Adam Milner; 18 Matt Cook; 20 Larne Patrick.
Tries: Milner (48), Monaghan (72); **Goals:** Gale 2/2.
SAINTS: 1 Jonny Lomax; 2 Tom Makinson; 3 Ryan Morgan; 4 Mark Percival; 28 Regan Grace; 6 Theo Fages; 24 Danny Richardson; 13 Louie McCarthy-Scarsbrook; 9 James Roby; 16 Luke Thompson; 36 Zeb Taia; 18 Dominique Peyroux; 12 Jon Wilkin (C). Subs (all used): 7 Matty Smith; 8 Alex Walmsley; 10 Kyle Amor; 20 Morgan Knowles.
Tries: Taia (17), Roby (54, 75), Lomax (67);
Goals: Percival 5/5.
Rugby Leaguer & League Express Men of the Match:
Tigers: Alex Foster; *Saints:* James Roby.
Penalty count: 9-6; **Half-time:** 0-8;
Referee: Robert Hicks; **Attendance:** 6,849.

Friday 4th August 2017

HUDDERSFIELD GIANTS 36 WAKEFIELD TRINITY 6

GIANTS: 35 Jordan Rankin; 2 Jermaine McGillvary; 3 Leroy Cudjoe (C); 34 Jordan Turner; 24 Darnell McIntosh; 4 Lee Gaskell; 6 Danny Brough; 8 Sam Rapira; 14 Kruise Leeming; 10 Shannon Wakeman; 17 Ukuma Ta'ai; 15 Sebastine Ikahihifo; 9 Ryan Hinchcliffe. Subs (all used): 18 Paul Clough; 20 Daniel Smith; 30 Alex Mellor; 31 Adam O'Brien.
Tries: Brough (7), McIntosh (11), Hinchcliffe (26), Cudjoe (61), McGillvary (67), Smith (78); **Goals:** Brough 6/8.
TRINITY: 1 Scott Grix; 5 Ben Jones-Bishop; 4 Reece Lyne; 3 Bill Tupou; 24 Mason Caton-Brown; 14 Sam Williams; 7 Liam Finn; 8 Anthony England; 9 Kyle Wood; 20 David Fifita; 12 Danny Kirmond (C); 11 Matty Ashurst; 32 Dean Hadley. Subs (all used): 16 Tinirau Arona; 23 Keegan Hirst; 26 Chris Annakin; 34 James Hasson.
Try: Williams (37); **Goals:** Finn 1/1.
Rugby Leaguer & League Express Men of the Match:
Giants: Danny Brough; *Trinity:* Keegan Hirst.
Penalty count: 9-11; **Half-time:** 18-6;
Referee: Tom Grant; **Attendance:** 5,429.

HULL FC 32 SALFORD RED DEVILS 18

HULL FC: 1 Jamie Shaul; 2 Mahe Fonua; 4 Josh Griffin; 3 Carlos Tuimavave; 5 Fetuli Talanoa; 6 Albert Kelly; 14 Jake Connor; 8 Scott Taylor; 9 Danny Houghton; 10 Liam Watts; 21 Sika Manu; 17 Danny Washbrook; 13 Gareth Ellis (C). Subs (all used): 15 Chris Green; 28 Brad Fash; 19 Steve Michaels; 16 Jordan Thompson.
Tries: Kelly (15), Tuimavave (18, 60), Talanoa (47), Connor (50); **Goals:** Connor 6/6.
RED DEVILS: 5 Niall Evalds; 21 Greg Johnson; 22 Kris Welham; 24 Jake Bibby; 31 Manu Vatuvei; 6 Robert Lui; 29 Todd Carney; 17 Adam Walne; 9 Logan Tomkins; 12 Weller Hauraki (C); 32 Tyrone McCarthy; 3 Josh Jones; 16 Olsi Krasniqi. Subs (all used): 1 Gareth O'Brien; 8 Craig Kopczak; 10 George Griffin; 11 Ben Murdoch-Masila.
Tries: Vatuvei (11, 67), Evalds (27), Lui (32);
Goals: T Carney 0/2, Lui 1/2.
Rugby Leaguer & League Express Men of the Match:
Hull FC: Jake Connor; *Red Devils:* Robert Lui.
Penalty count: 6-10; **Half-time:** 14-14;
Referee: Jack Smith; **Attendance:** 10,239.

LEEDS RHINOS 32 WIGAN WARRIORS 16

RHINOS: 1 Ashton Golding; 2 Tom Briscoe; 3 Kallum Watkins; 14 Liam Sutcliffe; 5 Ryan Hall; 4 Joel Moon; 6 Danny McGuire (C); 10 Adam Cuthbertson; 9 Matt Parcell; 16 Brad Singleton; 13 Stevie Ward; 12 Carl Ablett; 11 Jamie Jones-Buchanan. Subs (all used): 15 Brett Delaney; 20 Anthony Mullally; 18 Jimmy Keinhorst; 25 Jordan Lilley.
Tries: Ward (18, 68, 72), Golding (21, 43), Parcell (55);
Goals: Watkins 4/6.
WARRIORS: 1 Sam Tomkins; 36 Tom Davies; 3 Anthony Gelling; 4 Oliver Gildart; 5 Joe Burgess; 6 George Williams; 7 Thomas Leuluai; 8 Frank-Paul Nuuausala; 9 Michael McIlorum; 19 Ryan Sutton; 14 John Bateman; 12 Liam Farrell; 13 Sean O'Loughlin (C). Subs (all used): 15 Tony Clubb; 17 Taulima Tautai; 33 Josh Ganson; 20 Willie Isa.
Tries: Davies (24, 29), S Tomkins (74); **Goals:** Williams 2/3.
On report:
Tautai (35) - alleged use of the forearm on Parcell.
Rugby Leaguer & League Express Men of the Match:
Rhinos: Stevie Ward; *Warriors:* Tom Davies.
Penalty count: 8-6; **Half time:** 10-10;
Referee: Ben Thaler; **Attendance:** 13,579.

ROUND 2

Thursday 10th August 2017

WAKEFIELD TRINITY 38 LEEDS RHINOS 6

TRINITY: 1 Scott Grix; 5 Ben Jones-Bishop; 4 Reece Lyne; 18 Joe Arundel; 3 Bill Tupou; 6 Jacob Miller; 7 Liam Finn; 20 David Fifita; 9 Kyle Wood; 8 Anthony England; 12 Danny Kirmond (C); 11 Matty Ashurst; 16 Tinirau Arona. Subs (all used): 23 Keegan Hirst; 26 Chris Annakin; 32 Dean Hadley; 34 James Hasson.
Tries: Arundel (4), Jones-Bishop (25), Grix (28), Miller (40), Ashurst (51), Tupou (77); **Goals:** Finn 7/7.
RHINOS: 1 Ashton Golding; 2 Tom Briscoe; 3 Kallum Watkins; 14 Liam Sutcliffe; 5 Ryan Hall; 4 Joel Moon; 6 Danny McGuire (C); 16 Brad Singleton; 9 Matt Parcell; 10 Adam Cuthbertson; 11 Jamie Jones-Buchanan; 13 Stevie Ward; 12 Carl Ablett. Subs: 7 Rob Burrow; 15 Brett Delaney; 18 Jimmy Keinhorst (not used); 20 Anthony Mullally.
Try: Cuthbertson (11); **Goals:** Watkins 1/1.
Rugby Leaguer & League Express Men of the Match:
Trinity: Kyle Wood; *Rhinos:* Matt Parcell.
Penalty count: 9-8; **Half-time:** 26-6;
Referee: Ben Thaler; **Attendance:** 5,607.

Friday 11th August 2017

SALFORD RED DEVILS 4 CASTLEFORD TIGERS 23

RED DEVILS: 5 Niall Evalds; 21 Greg Johnson; 24 Jake Bibby; 3 Josh Jones; 31 Manu Vatuvei; 6 Robert Lui; 29 Todd Carney; 17 Adam Walne; 9 Logan Tomkins; 8 Craig Kopczak; 11 Ben Murdoch-Masila; 15 Ryan Lannon; 12 Weller Hauraki (C). Subs (all used): 10 George Griffin; 20 Kriss Brining; 16 Olsi Krasniqi; 26 Daniel Murray.
Try: Vatuvei (43); **Goals:** T Carney 0/1.
TIGERS: 1 Zak Hardaker; 21 Joel Monaghan; 3 Jake Webster; 2 Greg Minikin; 25 Jy Hitchcox; 16 Ben Roberts; 7 Luke Gale (C); 10 Grant Millington; 9 Paul McShane; 15 Jesse Sene-Lefao; 11 Oliver Holmes; 12 Mike McMeeken; 14 Nathan Massey. Subs (all used): 13 Adam Milner; 19 Gadwin Springer; 18 Matt Cook; 34 Alex Foster.
Tries: Hardaker (7, 26), McShane (59), Hitchcox (64);
Goals: Gale 3/4; **Field goal:** Gale (75).
Rugby Leaguer & League Express Men of the Match:
Red Devils: Manu Vatuvei; *Tigers:* Zak Hardaker.
Penalty count: 11-9; **Half-time:** 0-12;
Referee: Chris Kendall; **Attendance:** 2,811.

ST HELENS 6 HULL FC 8

SAINTS: 1 Jonny Lomax; 2 Tom Makinson; 3 Ryan Morgan; 4 Mark Percival; 28 Regan Grace; 6 Theo Fages; 24 Danny Richardson; 13 Louie McCarthy-Scarsbrook; 9 James Roby; 16 Luke Thompson; 36 Zeb Taia; 18 Dominique Peyroux; 12 Jon Wilkin (C). Subs (all used): 7 Matty Smith; 8 Alex Walmsley; 10 Kyle Amor; 20 Morgan Knowles.
Try: Grace (4); **Goals:** Percival 1/1.
HULL FC: 14 Jake Connor; 4 Josh Griffin; 16 Jordan Thompson; 3 Carlos Tuimavave; 19 Steve Michaels; 6 Albert Kelly; 7 Marc Sneyd; 8 Scott Taylor; 9 Danny Houghton; 10 Liam Watts; 25 Jansin Turgut; 21 Sika Manu; 13 Gareth Ellis (C). Subs (all used): 15 Chris Green; 17 Danny Washbrook; 28 Brad Fash; 29 Masi Matongo.
Try: Sneyd (34); **Goals:** Sneyd 2/2.
Rugby Leaguer & League Express Men of the Match:
Saints: Alex Walmsley; *Hull FC:* Marc Sneyd.
Penalty count: 10-7; **Half-time:** 6-6;
Referee: James Child; **Attendance:** 10,338.

WIGAN WARRIORS 18 HUDDERSFIELD GIANTS 4

WARRIORS: 1 Sam Tomkins; 36 Tom Davies; 3 Anthony Gelling; 4 Oliver Gildart; 5 Joe Burgess; 6 George Williams; 7 Thomas Leuluai; 8 Frank-Paul Nuuausala; 9 Michael McIlorum; 19 Ryan Sutton; 14 John Bateman; 12 Liam Farrell; 13 Sean O'Loughlin (C). Subs (all used): 15 Tony Clubb; 16 Sam Powell; 17 Taulima Tautai; 20 Willie Isa.
Tries: Gelling (13), Farrell (38), S Tomkins (80);
Goals: Williams 0/1, Powell 2/2, S Tomkins 1/1.
GIANTS: 35 Jordan Rankin; 2 Jermaine McGillvary; 30 Alex Mellor; 34 Jordan Turner; 24 Darnell McIntosh; 4 Lee Gaskell; 6 Danny Brough (C); 15 Sebastine Ikahihifo; 14 Kruise Leeming; 10 Shannon Wakeman; 17 Ukuma Ta'ai; 9 Ryan Hinchcliffe; 18 Paul Clough. Subs (all used): 13 Michael Lawrence; 20 Daniel Smith; 22 Tyler Dickinson; 31 Adam O'Brien.
Try: McGillvary (9); **Goals:** Brough 0/1.
Rugby Leaguer & League Express Men of the Match:
Warriors: Sam Tomkins; *Giants:* Sebastine Ikahihifo.
Penalty count: 14-7; **Half-time:** 10-4;
Referee: Phil Bentham; **Attendance:** 10,619.

ROUND 3

Thursday 17th August 2017

CASTLEFORD TIGERS 45 WAKEFIELD TRINITY 20

TIGERS: 1 Zak Hardaker; 2 Greg Minikin; 3 Jake Webster; 4 Michael Shenton (C); 5 Greg Eden; 16 Ben Roberts; 7 Luke Gale; 10 Grant Millington; 9 Paul McShane; 15 Jesse Sene-Lefao; 11 Oliver Holmes; 12 Mike McMeeken; 14 Nathan Massey. Subs (all used): 8 Andy Lynch; 13 Adam Milner; 17 Junior Moors; 34 Alex Foster.
Tries: Hardaker (10, 75), McMeeken (19), Webster (31, 55, 63, 70), Eden (52); **Goals:** Gale 6/8;
Field goal: Gale (65).
TRINITY: 21 Max Jowitt; 5 Ben Jones-Bishop; 4 Reece Lyne; 24 Mason Caton-Brown; 3 Bill Tupou; 6 Jacob Miller; 7 Liam Finn; 20 David Fifita; 32 Dean Hadley; 8 Anthony England; 11 Matty Ashurst; 12 Danny Kirmond (C); 16 Tinirau Arona. Subs (all used): 14 Sam Williams; 17 Craig Huby; 26 Chris Annakin; 23 Keegan Hirst.
Tries: Jones-Bishop (15), Caton-Brown (38), Kirmond (48), Jowitt (72); **Goals:** Finn 2/5.
Rugby Leaguer & League Express Men of the Match:
Tigers: Grant Millington; *Trinity:* Chris Annakin.
Penalty count: 6-8; **Half-time:** 18-10;
Referee: James Child; **Attendance:** 11,235.

Friday 18th August 2017

HULL FC 18 HUDDERSFIELD GIANTS 46

HULL FC: 14 Jake Connor; 19 Steve Michaels; 2 Mahe Fonua; 4 Josh Griffin; 5 Fetuli Talanoa; 3 Carlos Tuimavave; 7 Marc Sneyd; 22 Josh Bowden; 9 Danny Houghton; 10 Liam Watts; 12 Mark Minichiello; 25 Jansin Turgut; 13 Gareth Ellis (C). Subs (all used): 15 Chris Green; 21 Sika Manu; 17 Danny Washbrook; 16 Jordan Thompson.
Tries: Ellis (10), Connor (27), Griffin (64); **Goals:** Sneyd 3/3.
GIANTS: 35 Jordan Rankin; 2 Jermaine McGillvary; 30 Alex Mellor; 34 Jordan Turner; 24 Darnell McIntosh; 4 Lee Gaskell; 6 Danny Brough (C); 10 Shannon Wakeman; 14 Kruise Leeming; 15 Sebastine Ikahihifo; 9 Ryan Hinchcliffe; 17 Ukuma Ta'ai; 18 Paul Clough. Subs (all used): 31 Adam O'Brien; 13 Michael Lawrence; 20 Daniel Smith; 22 Tyler Dickinson.
Tries: McIntosh (18, 40), Gaskell (23, 57, 70), Mellor (31), Dickinson (51), Leeming (68);
Goals: Brough 4/5, Rankin 3/4.
Rugby Leaguer & League Express Men of the Match:
Hull FC: Josh Griffin; *Giants:* Lee Gaskell.
Penalty count: 7-9; **Half-time:** 12-22;
Referee: Scott Mikalauskas; **Attendance:** 10,535.

LEEDS RHINOS 16 ST HELENS 14

RHINOS: 31 Jack Walker; 2 Tom Briscoe; 3 Kallum Watkins; 14 Liam Sutcliffe; 5 Ryan Hall; 4 Joel Moon; 6 Danny McGuire (C); 10 Adam Cuthbertson; 9 Matt Parcell; 16 Brad Singleton; 13 Stevie Ward; 11 Jamie Jones-Buchanan; 12 Carl Ablett. Subs: 15 Brett Delaney; 20 Anthony Mullally; 18 Jimmy Keinhorst (not used); 7 Rob Burrow (not used).
Tries: Hall (49), Cuthbertson (64); **Goals:** Watkins 4/5.
SAINTS: 1 Jonny Lomax; 2 Tom Makinson; 3 Ryan Morgan; 4 Mark Percival; 28 Regan Grace; 6 Theo Fages; 7 Matty Smith; 10 Kyle Amor; 9 James Roby; 16 Luke Thompson; 36 Zeb Taia; 12 Jon Wilkin (C); 20 Morgan Knowles. Subs (all used): 8 Alex Walmsley; 18 Dominique Peyroux; 13 Louie McCarthy-Scarsbrook; 24 Danny Richardson.
Tries: Lomax (36), Richardson (74); **Goals:** Percival 3/4.
Rugby Leaguer & League Express Men of the Match:
Rhinos: Matt Parcell; *Saints:* James Roby.
Penalty count: 10-8; **Half-time:** 2-8;
Referee: Ben Thaler; **Attendance:** 16,326.

WIGAN WARRIORS 42 SALFORD RED DEVILS 6

WARRIORS: 1 Sam Tomkins; 35 Liam Marshall; 3 Anthony Gelling; 4 Oliver Gildart; 5 Joe Burgess; 6 George Williams; 7 Thomas Leuluai; 8 Frank-Paul Nuuausala; 9 Michael McIlorum; 15 Tony Clubb; 14 John Bateman; 12 Liam Farrell; 13 Sean O'Loughlin (C). Subs (all used): 16 Sam Powell; 17 Taulima Tautai; 19 Ryan Sutton; 20 Willie Isa.
Tries: O'Loughlin (7), Burgess (10, 24), Farrell (16), Powell (36), Williams (49), Nuuausala (54), Marshall (74);
Goals: Williams 5/8.
RED DEVILS: 5 Niall Evalds; 21 Greg Johnson; 24 Jake Bibby; 3 Josh Jones; 31 Manu Vatuvei; 29 Todd Carney; 7 Michael Dobson (C); 17 Adam Walne; 9 Logan Tomkins; 16 Olsi Krasniqi; 32 Tyrone McCarthy; 15 Ryan Lannon; 12 Weller Hauraki. Subs (all used): 1 Gareth O'Brien; 8 Craig Kopczak; 10 George Griffin; 20 Kriss Brining.
Try: Evalds (68); **Goals:** O'Brien 1/1.
Rugby Leaguer & League Express Men of the Match:
Warriors: Frank-Paul Nuuausala; *Red Devils:* Michael Dobson.
Penalty count: 8-5; **Half-time:** 26-0;
Referee: Chris Kendall; **Attendance:** 11,229.

ROUND 4

Thursday 31st August 2017

LEEDS RHINOS 38 HULL FC 26

RHINOS: 31 Jack Walker; 2 Tom Briscoe; 3 Kallum Watkins; 14 Liam Sutcliffe; 5 Ryan Hall; 6 Danny McGuire (C); 7 Rob Burrow; 10 Adam Cuthbertson; 9 Matt Parcell; 16 Brad Singleton; 13 Stevie Ward; 11 Jamie Jones-Buchanan; 12 Carl Ablett. Subs (all used): 17 Mitch Garbutt; 15 Brett Delaney; 20 Anthony Mullally; 18 Jimmy Keinhorst.
Tries: Burrow (7), Singleton (17), L Sutcliffe (30), Garbutt (37), Cuthbertson (49), Parcell (79);
Goals: Watkins 7/9.
HULL FC: 1 Jamie Shaul; 19 Steve Michaels; 2 Mahe Fonua; 3 Carlos Tuimavave; 5 Fetuli Talanoa; 6 Albert Kelly; 7 Marc Sneyd; 8 Scott Taylor; 9 Danny Houghton; 22 Josh Bowden; 25 Jansin Turgut; 21 Sika Manu; 13 Gareth Ellis (C). Subs (all used): 17 Danny Washbrook; 28 Brad Fash; 16 Jordan Thompson; 14 Jake Connor.
Tries: Michaels (13), Taylor (21), Washbrook (45), Bowden (62); **Goals:** Sneyd 5/5.
Sin bin: Ellis (25) - dangerous contact on Ward.
On report: Michaels (50) - alleged late challenge on Walker.
Rugby Leaguer & League Express Men of the Match: *Rhinos:* Matt Parcell; *Hull FC:* Jamie Shaul.
Penalty count: 12-8; **Half-time:** 24-14;
Referee: James Child; **Attendance:** 13,219.

Friday 1st September 2017

HUDDERSFIELD GIANTS 16 CASTLEFORD TIGERS 24

GIANTS: 35 Jordan Rankin; 2 Jermaine McGillvary; 3 Leroy Cudjoe (C); 34 Jordan Turner; 24 Darnell McIntosh; 4 Lee Gaskell; 6 Danny Brough; 15 Sebastine Ikahihifo; 14 Kruise Leeming; 10 Shannon Wakeman; 17 Ukuma Ta'ai; 16 Oliver Roberts; 9 Ryan Hinchcliffe. Subs (all used): 8 Sam Rapira; 13 Michael Lawrence; 18 Paul Clough; 30 Alex Mellor.
Tries: Roberts (22), Clough (34), McIntosh (77);
Goals: Brough 0/1, Rankin 2/3.
TIGERS: 1 Zak Hardaker; 25 Jy Hitchcox; 3 Jake Webster; 4 Michael Shenton (C); 5 Greg Eden; 16 Ben Roberts; 7 Luke Gale; 18 Matt Cook; 9 Paul McShane; 15 Jesse Sene-Lefao; 17 Junior Moors; 34 Alex Foster; 14 Nathan Massey. Subs (all used): 13 Adam Milner; 19 Gadwin Springer; 20 Larne Patrick; 33 Kevin Larroyer.
Tries: Webster (12), Roberts (44), Eden (51), Gale (62);
Goals: Gale 4/4.
Rugby Leaguer & League Express Men of the Match: *Giants:* Sebastine Ikahihifo; *Tigers:* Alex Foster.
Penalty count: 9-7; **Half-time:** 12-6;
Referee: Scott Mikalauskas; **Attendance:** 6,284.

SALFORD RED DEVILS 18 WAKEFIELD TRINITY 43

RED DEVILS: 1 Gareth O'Brien; 21 Greg Johnson; 22 Kris Welham; 4 Junior Sa'u; 31 Manu Vatuvei; 6 Robert Lui; 29 Todd Carney; 8 Craig Kopczak; 9 Logan Tomkins; 12 Weller Hauraki (C); 11 Ben Murdoch-Masila; 15 Ryan Lannon; 32 Tyrone McCarthy. Subs (all used): 10 George Griffin; 20 Kriss Brining; 16 Olsi Krasniqi; 3 Josh Jones.
Tries: Kopczak (3), Johnson (31), McCarthy (72);
Goals: T Carney 3/3.
TRINITY: 1 Scott Grix; 5 Ben Jones-Bishop; 4 Reece Lyne; 18 Joe Arundel; 3 Bill Tupou; 6 Jacob Miller; 7 Liam Finn; 8 Anthony England; 35 Tyler Randell (D); 23 Keegan Hirst; 11 Matty Ashurst; 12 Danny Kirmond (C); 16 Tinirau Arona. Subs (all used): 32 Dean Hadley; 20 David Fifita; 17 Craig Huby; 26 Chris Annakin.
Tries: Miller (13, 34), Arundel (22), Randell (47, 59), Tupou (51); **Goals:** Finn 9/9; **Field goal:** Miller (77).
Rugby Leaguer & League Express Men of the Match: *Red Devils:* Tyrone McCarthy; *Trinity:* Tyler Randell.
Penalty count: 8-8; **Half-time:** 12-22;
Referee: Phil Bentham; **Attendance:** 2,489.

ST HELENS 16 WIGAN WARRIORS 26

SAINTS: 37 Ben Barba (D); 2 Tom Makinson; 3 Ryan Morgan; 4 Mark Percival; 28 Regan Grace; 1 Jonny Lomax; 7 Matty Smith; 16 Luke Thompson; 9 James Roby; 10 Kyle Amor; 12 Jon Wilkin (C); 36 Zeb Taia; 20 Morgan Knowles. Subs (all used): 8 Alex Walmsley; 13 Louie McCarthy-Scarsbrook; 14 Luke Douglas; 18 Dominique Peyroux.
Tries: Barba (22), Taia (57), Makinson (61);
Goals: Percival 2/3.
WARRIORS: 1 Sam Tomkins; 35 Liam Marshall; 3 Anthony Gelling; 4 Oliver Gildart; 5 Joe Burgess; 6 George Williams; 7 Thomas Leuluai; 8 Frank-Paul Nuuausala; 9 Michael McIlorum; 15 Tony Clubb; 14 John Bateman; 12 Liam Farrell; 13 Sean O'Loughlin (C). Subs (all used): 16 Sam Powell; 17 Taulima Tautai; 20 Willie Isa; 28 Jack Wells.
Tries: Gildart (2, 5), Gelling (50), Williams (52);
Goals: Williams 5/6.
Sin bin: Isa (79) - pushing McCarthy-Scarsbrook.
On report: Isa (28) - alleged dangerous challenge on McCarthy-Scarsbrook.
Rugby Leaguer & League Express Men of the Match: *Saints:* Dominique Peyroux; *Warriors:* Sean O'Loughlin.
Penalty count: 4-7; **Half-time:** 4-14;
Referee: Robert Hicks; **Attendance:** 15,248.

ROUND 5

Thursday 7th September 2017

WAKEFIELD TRINITY 16 ST HELENS 18

TRINITY: 1 Scott Grix; 5 Ben Jones-Bishop; 4 Reece Lyne; 18 Joe Arundel; 3 Bill Tupou; 6 Jacob Miller; 7 Liam Finn; 8 Anthony England; 35 Tyler Randell; 23 Keegan Hirst; 12 Danny Kirmond (C); 11 Matty Ashurst; 16 Tinirau Arona. Subs (all used): 32 Dean Hadley; 26 Chris Annakin; 17 Craig Huby; 20 David Fifita.
Tries: Tupou (12, 31); **Goals:** Finn 4/6.
Sin bin: Hadley (44) - dangerous contact on Percival.
SAINTS: 37 Ben Barba; 2 Tom Makinson; 1 Jonny Lomax; 4 Mark Percival; 28 Regan Grace; 6 Theo Fages; 24 Danny Richardson; 14 Luke Douglas; 9 James Roby; 16 Luke Thompson; 36 Zeb Taia; 20 Morgan Knowles; 12 Jon Wilkin (C). Subs (all used): 8 Alex Walmsley; 13 Louie McCarthy-Scarsbrook; 18 Dominique Peyroux; 32 Matty Lees (D).
Tries: McCarthy-Scarsbrook (23), Fages (63), Lomax (78);
Goals: Percival 3/3.
Rugby Leaguer & League Express Men of the Match: *Trinity:* Jacob Miller; *Saints:* Alex Walmsley.
Penalty count: 7-5; **Half-time:** 12-6;
Referee: Ben Thaler; **Attendance:** 4,837.

Friday 8th September 2017

CASTLEFORD TIGERS 38 LEEDS RHINOS 24

TIGERS: 1 Zak Hardaker; 2 Greg Minikin; 3 Jake Webster; 4 Michael Shenton (C); 5 Greg Eden; 16 Ben Roberts; 7 Luke Gale; 14 Nathan Massey; 9 Paul McShane; 15 Jesse Sene-Lefao; 34 Alex Foster; 12 Mike McMeeken; 13 Adam Milner. Subs (all used): 10 Grant Millington; 19 Gadwin Springer; 17 Junior Moors; 20 Larne Patrick.
Tries: Eden (13), Roberts (24, 37), Webster (28), Foster (31), Minikin (48); **Goals:** Gale 7/7.
RHINOS: 31 Jack Walker; 2 Tom Briscoe; 3 Kallum Watkins; 14 Liam Sutcliffe; 5 Ryan Hall; 6 Danny McGuire (C); 25 Jordan Lilley; 16 Brad Singleton; 9 Matt Parcell; 17 Mitch Garbutt; 11 Jamie Jones-Buchanan; 13 Stevie Ward; 10 Adam Cuthbertson. Subs: 18 Jimmy Keinhorst; 12 Carl Ablett; 20 Anthony Mullally; 1 Ashton Golding (not used).
Tries: Watkins (6), Jones-Buchanan (44), Parcell (65), Garbutt (80); **Goals:** Watkins 4/4.
Rugby Leaguer & League Express Men of the Match: *Tigers:* Luke Gale; *Rhinos:* Jamie Jones-Buchanan.
Penalty count: 5-8; **Half-time:** 30-6;
Referee: Jack Smith; **Attendance:** 9,557.

HULL FC 22 WIGAN WARRIORS 30

HULL FC: 1 Jamie Shaul; 2 Mahe Fonua; 14 Jake Connor; 16 Jordan Thompson; 4 Josh Griffin; 6 Albert Kelly; 7 Marc Sneyd; 8 Scott Taylor; 9 Danny Houghton (C); 22 Josh Bowden; 12 Mark Minichiello; 21 Sika Manu; 10 Liam Watts. Subs (all used): 17 Danny Washbrook; 25 Jansin Turgut; 28 Brad Fash; 29 Masi Matongo.
Tries: Fonua (12, 70), Manu (60), Sneyd (65);
Goals: Sneyd 3/5.
Dismissal: Watts (22) - use of the elbow on McIlorum.
WARRIORS: 1 Sam Tomkins; 36 Tom Davies; 3 Anthony Gelling; 4 Oliver Gildart; 35 Liam Marshall; 6 George Williams; 7 Thomas Leuluai; 8 Frank-Paul Nuuausala; 9 Michael McIlorum; 15 Tony Clubb; 14 John Bateman; 12 Liam Farrell; 13 Sean O'Loughlin (C). Subs (all used): 19 Ryan Sutton; 17 Taulima Tautai; 16 Sam Powell; 20 Willie Isa.
Tries: Gildart (8), Gelling (42, 77), Davies (49), Bateman (80); **Goals:** Williams 5/7.
Rugby Leaguer & League Express Men of the Match: *Hull FC:* Albert Kelly; *Warriors:* Sean O'Loughlin.
Penalty count: 10-7; **Half-time:** 6-8;
Referee: Robert Hicks; **Attendance:** 11,291.

Saturday 9th September 2017

SALFORD RED DEVILS 52 HUDDERSFIELD GIANTS 14

RED DEVILS: 5 Niall Evalds; 24 Jake Bibby; 22 Kris Welham; 4 Junior Sa'u; 31 Manu Vatuvei; 6 Robert Lui; 1 Gareth O'Brien; 8 Craig Kopczak; 9 Logan Tomkins; 12 Weller Hauraki (C); 11 Ben Murdoch-Masila; 3 Josh Jones; 32 Tyrone McCarthy. Subs (all used): 17 Adam Walne; 20 Kriss Brining; 15 Ryan Lannon; 18 Jordan Walne.
Tries: Welham (5, 31), McCarthy (13), Vatuvei (27, 42), Evalds (34), Bibby (46), Murdoch-Masila (66), Jones (75);
Goals: O'Brien 8/11.
GIANTS: 35 Jordan Rankin; 2 Jermaine McGillvary; 30 Alex Mellor; 34 Jordan Turner; 21 Gene Ormsby; 4 Lee Gaskell; 6 Danny Brough (C); 15 Sebastine Ikahihifo; 14 Kruise Leeming; 17 Ukuma Ta'ai; 16 Oliver Roberts; 12 Dale Ferguson; 9 Ryan Hinchcliffe. Subs (all used): 31 Adam O'Brien; 8 Sam Rapira; 13 Michael Lawrence; 18 Paul Clough.
Tries: McGillvary (39), Roberts (50), Hinchcliffe (79);
Goals: Brough 1/3.
Rugby Leaguer & League Express Men of the Match: *Red Devils:* Robert Lui; *Giants:* Dale Ferguson.
Penalty count: 7-7; **Half-time:** 30-4;
Referee: James Child; **Attendance:** 1,405.

ROUND 6

Thursday 14th September 2017

HULL FC 19 WAKEFIELD TRINITY 18

HULL FC: 1 Jamie Shaul; 2 Mahe Fonua; 4 Josh Griffin; 3 Carlos Tuimavave; 19 Steve Michaels; 6 Albert Kelly; 7 Marc Sneyd; 8 Scott Taylor; 9 Danny Houghton; 10 Liam Watts; 12 Mark Minichiello; 17 Danny Washbrook; 13 Gareth Ellis (C). Subs (all used): 14 Jake Connor; 16 Jordan Thompson; 22 Josh Bowden; 28 Brad Fash.
Tries: Fonua (28), Sneyd (49), Ellis (71);
Goals: Sneyd 3/4; **Field goal:** Sneyd (75).
Sin bin: Shaul (38) - professional foul.
TRINITY: 1 Scott Grix; 5 Ben Jones-Bishop; 18 Joe Arundel; 3 Bill Tupou; 24 Mason Caton-Brown; 6 Jacob Miller; 7 Liam Finn; 8 Anthony England; 35 Tyler Randell; 17 Craig Huby; 11 Matty Ashurst; 12 Danny Kirmond (C); 16 Tinirau Arona. Subs (all used): 9 Kyle Wood; 20 David Fifita; 26 Chris Annakin; 34 James Hasson.
Tries: Arundel (11), Miller (21), Caton-Brown (77);
Goals: Finn 3/4.
Rugby Leaguer & League Express Men of the Match: *Hull FC:* Gareth Ellis; *Trinity:* Jacob Miller.
Penalty count: 4-5; **Half-time:** 6-12;
Referee: Phil Bentham; **Attendance:** 10,924.

Friday 15th September 2017

LEEDS RHINOS 44 SALFORD RED DEVILS 2

RHINOS: 1 Ashton Golding; 2 Tom Briscoe; 3 Kallum Watkins; 14 Liam Sutcliffe; 5 Ryan Hall; 4 Joel Moon; 6 Danny McGuire (C); 10 Adam Cuthbertson; 7 Rob Burrow; 17 Mitch Garbutt; 12 Mark Minichiello; 13 Stevie Ward; 11 Jamie Jones-Buchanan; 16 Brad Singleton. Subs (all used): 15 Brett Delaney; 20 Anthony Mullally; 19 Brett Ferres; 9 Matt Parcell.
Tries: L Sutcliffe (13), McGuire (15), Briscoe (33), Parcell (51, 59), Cuthbertson (57), Mullally (69), Ferres (71);
Goals: Watkins 6/8.
RED DEVILS: 5 Niall Evalds; 24 Jake Bibby; 11 Ben Murdoch-Masila; 4 Junior Sa'u; 31 Manu Vatuvei; 6 Robert Lui; 1 Gareth O'Brien; 8 Craig Kopczak; 9 Logan Tomkins; 12 Weller Hauraki (C); 3 Josh Jones; 10 George Griffin; 32 Tyrone McCarthy. Subs (all used): 20 Kriss Brining; 17 Adam Walne; 15 Ryan Lannon; 18 Jordan Walne.
Goals: O'Brien 1/1.
Rugby Leaguer & League Express Men of the Match: *Rhinos:* Tom Briscoe; *Red Devils:* Kriss Brining.
Penalty count: 8-9; **Half-time:** 16-2;
Referee: Liam Moore; **Attendance:** 13,094.

ST HELENS 40 HUDDERSFIELD GIANTS 16

SAINTS: 37 Ben Barba; 2 Tom Makinson; 3 Ryan Morgan; 4 Mark Percival; 28 Regan Grace; 1 Jonny Lomax; 24 Danny Richardson; 14 Luke Douglas; 9 James Roby; 16 Luke Thompson; 36 Zeb Taia; 20 Morgan Knowles; 12 Jon Wilkin (C). Subs (all used): 6 Theo Fages; 8 Alex Walmsley; 13 Louie McCarthy-Scarsbrook; 18 Dominique Peyroux.
Tries: Lomax (4, 34), Grace (9), Percival (37), Barba (47), Morgan (55), McCarthy-Scarsbrook (78);
Goals: Percival 6/7.
GIANTS: 35 Jordan Rankin; 2 Jermaine McGillvary; 30 Alex Mellor; 34 Jordan Turner; 24 Darnell McIntosh; 4 Lee Gaskell; 6 Danny Brough (C); 8 Sam Rapira; 31 Adam O'Brien; 17 Ukuma Ta'ai; 16 Oliver Roberts; 13 Michael Lawrence; 9 Ryan Hinchcliffe. Subs (all used): 14 Kruise Leeming; 18 Paul Clough; 20 Daniel Smith; 22 Tyler Dickinson.
Tries: Roberts (31), Hinchcliffe (65), Rankin (74);
Goals: Brough 2/3.
Rugby Leaguer & League Express Men of the Match: *Saints:* Ben Barba; *Giants:* Jordan Rankin.
Penalty count: 7-8; **Half-time:** 24-6;
Referee: Gareth Hewer; **Attendance:** 9,419.

Sunday 17th September 2017

WIGAN WARRIORS 20 CASTLEFORD TIGERS 38

WARRIORS: 1 Sam Tomkins (C); 36 Tom Davies; 3 Anthony Gelling; 4 Oliver Gildart; 5 Joe Burgess; 6 George Williams; 7 Thomas Leuluai; 8 Frank-Paul Nuuausala; 9 Michael McIlorum; 15 Tony Clubb; 14 John Bateman; 12 Liam Farrell; 11 Joel Tomkins. Subs (all used): 19 Ryan Sutton; 20 Willie Isa; 16 Sam Powell; 17 Taulima Tautai. **Tries:** Davies (53), S Tomkins (56), Leuluai (62), Isa (76); **Goals:** Williams 2/3, Powell 0/1.
On report: Clubb (14) - alleged late challenge.
TIGERS: 1 Zak Hardaker; 2 Greg Minikin; 3 Jake Webster; 4 Michael Shenton (C); 5 Greg Eden; 9 Paul McShane; 35 Jake Trueman; 10 Grant Millington; 13 Adam Milner; 34 Alex Foster; 11 Oliver Holmes; 12 Mike McMeeken; 14 Nathan Massey. Subs (all used): 15 Jesse Sene-Lefao; 18 Matt Cook; 19 Gadwin Springer; 23 Tom Holmes.
Tries: Eden (6), Trueman (16, 24, 33), Minikin (46, 80), Shenton (70); **Goals:** McShane 5/7.
Rugby Leaguer & League Express Men of the Match:
Warriors: Thomas Leuluai; *Tigers:* Michael Shenton.
Penalty count: 9-5; **Half-time:** 0-20;
Referee: Ben Thaler; **Attendance:** 15,706.

ROUND 7

Thursday 21st September 2017

SALFORD RED DEVILS 4 ST HELENS 30

RED DEVILS: 5 Niall Evalds; 24 Jake Bibby; 22 Kris Welham; 4 Junior Sa'u; 31 Manu Vatuvei; 6 Robert Lui; 1 Gareth O'Brien; 26 Daniel Murray; 9 Logan Tomkins; 12 Weller Hauraki (C); 11 Ben Murdoch-Masila; 3 Josh Jones; 32 Tyrone McCarthy. Subs (all used): 8 Craig Kopczak; 20 Kriss Brining; 15 Ryan Lannon; 18 Jordan Walne.
Try: Evalds (5); **Goals:** O'Brien 0/1.
Dismissal: Lannon (38) - late challenge on Fages.
SAINTS: 37 Ben Barba; 2 Tom Makinson; 3 Ryan Morgan; 4 Mark Percival; 28 Regan Grace; 6 Theo Fages; 24 Danny Richardson; 14 Luke Douglas; 9 James Roby; 16 Luke Thompson; 36 Zeb Taia; 20 Morgan Knowles; 12 Jon Wilkin (C). Subs (all used): 7 Matty Smith; 8 Alex Walmsley; 13 Louie McCarthy-Scarsbrook; 18 Dominique Peyroux.
Tries: Percival (17), Walmsley (33, 71), Taia (64), Barba (78); **Goals:** Percival 5/7.
On report:
Walmsley (34) - alleged use of the elbow on J Walne.
Rugby Leaguer & League Express Men of the Match:
Red Devils: Niall Evalds; *Saints:* Alex Walmsley.
Penalty count: 13-5; **Half-time:** 4-12;
Referee: James Child; **Attendance:** 2,840.

Friday 22nd September 2017

CASTLEFORD TIGERS 16 HULL FC 48

TIGERS: 5 Greg Eden; 27 Tuoyo Egodo (D); 3 Jake Webster; 21 Joel Monaghan; 25 Jy Hitchcox; 23 Tom Holmes; 35 Jake Trueman; 18 Matt Cook; 9 Paul McShane (C); 19 Gadwin Springer; 34 Alex Foster; 12 Mike McMeeken; 33 Kevin Larroyer. Subs (all used): 8 Andy Lynch; 15 Jesse Sene-Lefao; 16 Ben Roberts; 22 Will Maher.
Tries: Egodo (29, 44, 48); **Goals:** McShane 2/3.
HULL FC: 1 Jamie Shaul; 2 Mahe Fonua; 3 Carlos Tuimavave; 14 Jake Connor; 5 Fetuli Talanoa; 6 Albert Kelly; 7 Marc Sneyd; 8 Scott Taylor; 9 Danny Houghton; 10 Liam Watts; 21 Sika Manu; 12 Mark Minichiello; 13 Gareth Ellis (C). Subs (all used): 22 Josh Bowden; 28 Brad Fash; 15 Chris Green; 17 Danny Washbrook.
Tries: Kelly (9), Connor (11, 39, 52), Houghton (25), Shaul (34, 70), Tuimavave (64); **Goals:** Sneyd 8/9.
Rugby Leaguer & League Express Men of the Match:
Tigers: Tuoyo Egodo; *Hull FC:* Liam Watts.
Penalty count: 8-7; **Half-time:** 6-28;
Referee: Ben Thaler; **Attendance:** 7,974.

HUDDERSFIELD GIANTS 12 LEEDS RHINOS 36

GIANTS: 35 Jordan Rankin; 25 Jared Simpson; 30 Alex Mellor; 34 Jordan Turner; 24 Darnell McIntosh; 4 Lee Gaskell; 6 Danny Brough (C); 8 Sam Rapira; 14 Kruise Leeming; 15 Sebastine Ikahihifo; 13 Michael Lawrence; 9 Ryan Hinchcliffe; 17 Ukuma Ta'ai. Subs (all used): 18 Paul Clough; 19 Nathan Mason; 20 Daniel Smith; 31 Adam O'Brien.
Tries: Lawrence (25), Hinchcliffe (67); **Goals:** Brough 2/2.
RHINOS: 1 Ashton Golding; 2 Tom Briscoe; 3 Kallum Watkins; 18 Jimmy Keinhorst; 5 Ryan Hall; 4 Joel Moon; 6 Danny McGuire (C); 8 Mitch Garbutt; 9 Matt Parcell; 20 Anthony Mullally; 23 Jack Ormondroyd; 12 Carl Ablett; 15 Brett Delaney. Subs (all used): 7 Rob Burrow; 10 Adam Cuthbertson; 11 Jamie Jones-Buchanan; 14 Liam Sutcliffe.
Tries: Watkins (2), McGuire (17, 54), Keinhorst (21), Mullally (59), Burrow (70); **Goals:** Watkins 6/7.

Mike McMeeken tackled by Zeb Taia during a thrilling semi-final

Rugby Leaguer & League Express Men of the Match:
Giants: Ryan Hinchcliffe; *Rhinos:* Danny McGuire.
Penalty count: 3-6; **Half-time:** 6-16;
Referee: Scott Mikalauskas; **Attendance:** 6,247.

Saturday 23rd September 2017

WAKEFIELD TRINITY 32 WIGAN WARRIORS 0

TRINITY: 1 Scott Grix; 5 Ben Jones-Bishop; 18 Joe Arundel; 3 Bill Tupou; 24 Mason Caton-Brown; 6 Jacob Miller; 7 Liam Finn; 8 Anthony England; 9 Kyle Wood; 17 Craig Huby; 11 Matty Ashurst; 12 Danny Kirmond (C); 16 Tinirau Arona. Subs (all used): 14 Sam Williams; 32 Dean Hadley; 23 Keegan Hirst; 20 David Fifita.
Tries: Jones-Bishop (15), Miller (21), Williams (62), Grix (69), Hirst (78); **Goals:** Finn 6/6.
WARRIORS: 1 Sam Tomkins (C); 36 Tom Davies; 3 Anthony Gelling; 14 John Bateman; 4 Oliver Gildart; 6 George Williams; 7 Thomas Leuluai; 8 Frank-Paul Nuuausala; 9 Michael McIlorum; 15 Tony Clubb; 20 Willie Isa; 12 Liam Farrell; 11 Joel Tomkins. Subs (all used): 24 Joe Bretherton; 19 Ryan Sutton; 16 Sam Powell; 17 Taulima Tautai.
Rugby Leaguer & League Express Men of the Match:
Trinity: Liam Finn; *Warriors:* Taulima Tautai.
Penalty count: 10-7; **Half-time:** 12-0;
Referee: Robert Hicks; **Attendance:** 5,165.

SEMI-FINALS

Thursday 28th September 2017

CASTLEFORD TIGERS 23 ST HELENS 22
(after golden point extra-time)

TIGERS: 1 Zak Hardaker; 2 Greg Minikin; 3 Jake Webster; 4 Michael Shenton (C); 5 Greg Eden; 16 Ben Roberts; 7 Luke Gale; 14 Nathan Massey; 9 Paul McShane; 15 Jesse Sene-Lefao; 14 Mike McMeeken; 13 Adam Milner. Subs: 10 Grant Millington; 17 Junior Moors; 18 Matt Cook; 19 Gadwin Springer (not used).
Tries: Hardaker (1), Gale (57), Milner (64); **Goals:** Gale 5/5; **Field goal:** Gale (88).
SAINTS: 37 Ben Barba; 2 Tom Makinson; 3 Ryan Morgan; 4 Mark Percival; 28 Regan Grace; 1 Jonny Lomax; 7 Matty Smith; 14 Luke Douglas; 9 James Roby; 16 Luke Thompson; 20 Morgan Knowles; 36 Zeb Taia; 12 Jon Wilkin (C). Subs (all used): 8 Alex Walmsley; 13 Louie McCarthy-Scarsbrook; 18 Dominique Peyroux; 6 Theo Fages.
Tries: Grace (16), Knowles (37), Makinson (70), Percival (73), Morgan (77); **Goals:** Percival 1/5.
Rugby Leaguer & League Express Men of the Match:
Tigers: Adam Milner; *Saints:* Ben Barba.
Penalty count: 8-5; **Half-time:** 8-10;
Referee: James Child; **Attendance:** 11,235.

Friday 29th September 2017

LEEDS RHINOS 18 HULL FC 16

RHINOS: 31 Jack Walker; 2 Tom Briscoe; 3 Kallum Watkins; 14 Liam Sutcliffe; 5 Ryan Hall; 4 Joel Moon; 6 Danny McGuire (C); 16 Brad Singleton; 9 Matt Parcell; 17 Mitch Garbutt; 13 Stevie Ward; 11 Jamie Jones-Buchanan; 10 Adam Cuthbertson. Subs (all used): 20 Anthony Mullally; 12 Carl Ablett; 7 Rob Burrow; 19 Brett Ferres.
Tries: Ward (4), Mullally (17), L Sutcliffe (61); **Goals:** Watkins 3/3.
HULL FC: 1 Jamie Shaul; 2 Mahe Fonua; 14 Jake Connor; 3 Carlos Tuimavave; 5 Fetuli Talanoa; 6 Albert Kelly; 7 Marc Sneyd; 8 Scott Taylor; 9 Danny Houghton; 10 Liam Watts; 21 Sika Manu; 12 Mark Minichiello; 13 Gareth Ellis (C). Subs (all used): 22 Josh Bowden; 15 Chris Green; 28 Brad Fash; 4 Josh Griffin.
Tries: Ellis (27), Fonua (43), Manu (56); **Goals:** Sneyd 2/3.
Rugby Leaguer & League Express Men of the Match:
Rhinos: Brad Singleton; *Hull FC:* Gareth Ellis.
Penalty count: 4-5; **Half time:** 12-6;
Referee: Phil Bentham; **Attendance:** 12,500.

GRAND FINAL

Saturday 7th October 2017

CASTLEFORD TIGERS 6 LEEDS RHINOS 24

TIGERS: 5 Greg Eden; 2 Greg Minikin; 3 Jake Webster; 4 Michael Shenton (C); 25 Jy Hitchcox; 7 Luke Gale; 14 Nathan Massey; 9 Paul McShane; 15 Jesse Sene-Lefao; 11 Oliver Holmes; 12 Mike McMeeken; 13 Adam Milner. Subs (all used): 10 Grant Millington; 17 Junior Moors; 18 Matt Cook; 34 Alex Foster.
Try: Foster (79); **Goals:** Gale 1/1.
RHINOS: 31 Jack Walker; 2 Tom Briscoe; 3 Kallum Watkins; 14 Liam Sutcliffe; 5 Ryan Hall; 4 Joel Moon; 6 Danny McGuire (C); 16 Brad Singleton; 9 Matt Parcell; 17 Mitch Garbutt; 13 Stevie Ward; 11 Jamie Jones-Buchanan; 10 Adam Cuthbertson. Subs (all used): 20 Anthony Mullally; 12 Carl Ablett; 7 Rob Burrow; 19 Brett Ferres.
Tries: Briscoe (11, 59), McGuire (51, 70); **Goals:** Watkins 3/4; **Field goals:** McGuire (40, 77).
Rugby Leaguer & League Express Men of the Match:
Tigers: Matt Cook; *Rhinos:* Danny McGuire.
Penalty count: 5-1; **Half-time:** 0-7;
Referee: James Child; **Attendance:** 72,827
(at Old Trafford, Manchester).

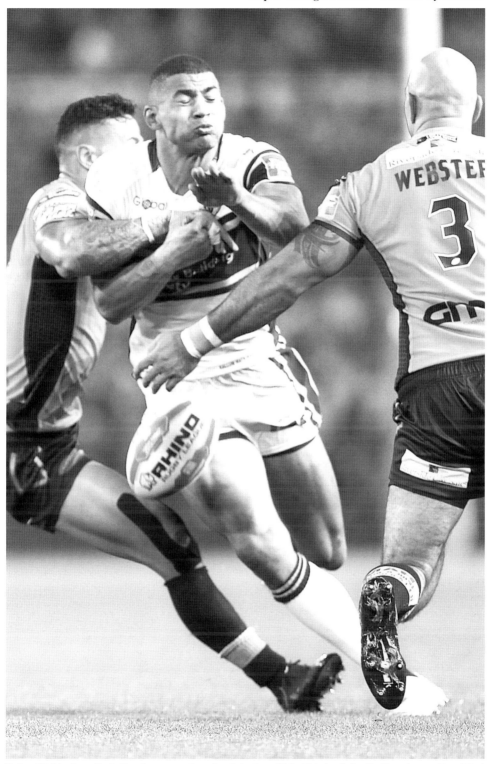

Kallum Watkins loses the ball under pressure from Ben Roberts and Jake Webster during the Super League Grand Final

SUPER 8s -
THE QUALIFIERS
2017 Round by Round

ROUND 1

Friday 4th August 2017

WIDNES VIKINGS 14 WARRINGTON WOLVES 28

VIKINGS: 1 Rhys Hanbury; 17 Stefan Marsh; 3 Chris Bridge; 4 Charly Runciman; 2 Corey Thompson; 6 Joe Mellor (C); 32 Danny Craven; 10 Jack Buchanan; 9 Lloyd White; 15 Gil Dudson; 11 Chris Houston (C); 12 Matt Whitley; 13 Hep Cahill. Subs (all used): 20 Manase Manuokafoa; 23 Jay Chapelhow; 25 Tom Olbison; 31 Jordan Johnstone.
Tries: Buchanan (14), Mellor (31); **Goals:** White 3/3.
WOLVES: 1 Stefan Ratchford; 5 Matthew Russell; 35 Peta Hiku; 4 Ryan Atkins; 2 Tom Lineham; 6 Kevin Brown; 22 Declan Patton; 8 Chris Hill (C); 9 Daryl Clark; 10 Ashton Sims; 24 Benjamin Jullien; 12 Jack Hughes; 14 Mike Cooper. Subs (all used): 16 George King; 18 Andre Savelio; 23 Joe Philbin; 27 Morgan Smith.
Tries: Hughes (4), Lineham (50), Patton (63), Russell (68), Hiku (74); **Goals:** Patton 4/6.
Rugby Leaguer & League Express Men of the Match:
Vikings: Lloyd White; *Wolves:* Stefan Ratchford.
Penalty count: 4-8; **Half-time:** 12-6;
Referee: Phil Bentham; **Attendance:** 6,202.

Saturday 5th August 2017

FEATHERSTONE ROVERS 12 LEIGH CENTURIONS 38

ROVERS: 1 Ian Hardman; 5 Luke Briscoe; 23 Josh Hardcastle; 4 Misi Taulapapa; 18 Scott Turner; 6 Kyle Briggs; 7 Anthony Thackeray; 13 Richard Moore; 9 Keal Carlile; 8 Darrell Griffin; 12 John Davies; 29 Connor Farrell; 21 James Lockwood. Subs (all used): 19 Matty Wildie; 10 Andrew Bostock; 14 Frankie Mariano; 28 Sam Brooks.
Tries: Griffin (18), Taulapapa (66); **Goals:** Hardman 2/2.
Sin bin: Moore (72) - shoulder charge on McNally.
CENTURIONS: 18 Gregg McNally; 5 Matty Dawson; 31 Matty Fleming; 34 Samisoni Langi; 1 Mitch Brown; 33 Daniel Mortimer; 7 Josh Drinkwater; 13 Harrison Hansen; 9 Micky Higham (C); 16 Antoni Maria; 11 Cory Paterson; 17 Atelea Vea; 29 Lachlan Burr. Subs (all used): 21 Liam Hood; 35 Greg Richards; 15 Danny Tickle; 12 Glenn Stewart.
Tries: Mortimer (3), McNally (6, 75), Brown (25), Hood (47), Dawson (57), Drinkwater (59); **Goals:** Drinkwater 5/7.
Rugby Leaguer & League Express Men of the Match:
Rovers: Misi Taulapapa; *Centurions:* Daniel Mortimer.
Penalty count: 9-10; **Half-time:** 6-16;
Referee: James Child; **Attendance:** 2,679.

CATALANS DRAGONS 20 LONDON BRONCOS 18

DRAGONS: 33 Lewis Tierney; 21 Iain Thornley; 3 Krisnan Inu; 4 Brayden Wiliame; 18 Vincent Duport; 6 Luke Walsh; 7 Richie Myler; 8 Sam Moa; 9 Paul Aiton; 10 Remi Casty (C); 11 Louis Anderson; 12 Justin Horo; 13 Greg Bird. Subs: 14 Julian Bousquet; 15 Benjamin Garcia; 17 Jason Baitieri; 25 Thibaut Margalet (not used).
Tries: Myler (13), Wiliame (40), Anderson (67);
Goals: Walsh 4/4.
BRONCOS: 24 Alex Walker; 2 Rhys Williams; 3 Ben Hellewell; 20 Michael Channing; 1 Elliot Kear; 6 Jarrod Sammut; 7 William Barthau; 18 Ben Evans; 14 Andy Ackers; 16 Junior Roqica; 36 Sam Wilde; 13 Jay Pitts; 22 Matt Davis. Subs (all used): 10 Mark Ioane; 15 Eddie Battye; 19 Api Pewhairangi; 23 Matty Gee.
Tries: Barthau (7), Williams (27), Ioane (80);
Goals: Sammut 3/4.
Rugby Leaguer & League Express Men of the Match:
Dragons: Richie Myler; *Broncos:* William Barthau.
Penalty count: 11-8; **Half-time:** 12-10;
Referee: Chris Kendall; **Attendance:** 7,102.

Sunday 6th August 2017

HULL KINGSTON ROVERS 26 HALIFAX 22

ROVERS: 32 Kieren Moss; 36 Justin Carney; 3 Thomas Minns; 22 Andrew Heffernan; 5 Ryan Shaw; 20 Matthew Marsh; 7 Jamie Ellis; 8 Nick Scruton; 9 Shaun Lunt; 37 Lee Jewitt; 11 Maurice Blair; 13 Danny Addy; 33 Ben Kavanagh. Subs (all used): 39 Mose Masoe; 19 George Lawler; 21 Rob Mulhern; 38 Chris Atkin.
Tries: Moss (1, 6), Marsh (15), Lawler (62), Scruton (72);
Goals: Ellis 3/5.
HALIFAX: 2 Will Sharp; 4 Ben Heaton; 16 Ed Barber; 3 Steve Tyrer; 23 Rob Worrincy; 6 Scott Murrell; 1 Ben Johnston; 26 Alex Mammone; 17 Brandon Moore; 14 Ryan Boyle; 11 Shane Grady; 8 Mitch Cahalane; 12 Simon Grix. Subs (all used): 9 Ben Kaye; 20 Elliot Morris; 29 Michael Sio; 37 Brandon Douglas.
Tries: Heaton (10, 23, 27, 52); **Goals:** Tyrer 3/4.
On report:
Boyle (60) - alleged dangerous challenge on Masoe.
Rugby Leaguer & League Express Men of the Match:
Rovers: Nick Scruton; *Halifax:* Ben Heaton.
Penalty count: 9-6; **Half-time:** 14-16;
Referee: Liam Moore; **Attendance:** 7,706.

ROUND 2

Saturday 12th August 2017

WARRINGTON WOLVES 52 CATALANS DRAGONS 24

WOLVES: 1 Stefan Ratchford; 5 Matthew Russell; 35 Peta Hiku; 4 Ryan Atkins; 2 Tom Lineham; 22 Declan Patton; 6 Kevin Brown; 8 Chris Hill (C); 9 Daryl Clark; 10 Ashton Sims; 24 Benjamin Jullien; 12 Jack Hughes; 34 Ben Westwood. Subs (all used): 16 George King; 18 Andre Savelio; 23 Joe Philbin; 27 Morgan Smith.
Tries: Ratchford (2, 34), Russell (9), Patton (15), Atkins (28, 50), Lineham (61, 79), Hiku (64);
Goals: Patton 8/9.
DRAGONS: 33 Lewis Tierney; 3 Krisnan Inu; 15 Benjamin Garcia; 4 Brayden Wiliame; 18 Vincent Duport; 6 Luke Walsh; 7 Richie Myler; 8 Sam Moa; 9 Paul Aiton; 10 Remi Casty (C); 11 Louis Anderson; 12 Justin Horo; 13 Greg Bird. Subs (all used): 5 Fouad Yaha; 14 Julian Bousquet; 17 Jason Baitieri; 25 Thibaut Margalet.
Tries: Casty (20), Inu (45, 69), Tierney (56);
Goals: Walsh 4/4.
Rugby Leaguer & League Express Men of the Match:
Wolves: Declan Patton; *Dragons:* Krisnan Inu.
Penalty count: 8-9; **Half-time:** 30-6;
Referee: Robert Hicks; **Attendance:** 8,595.

LEIGH CENTURIONS 16 HULL KINGSTON ROVERS 20

CENTURIONS: 18 Gregg McNally; 5 Matty Dawson; 31 Matty Fleming; 34 Samisoni Langi; 2 Adam Higson; 33 Daniel Mortimer; 7 Josh Drinkwater; 13 Harrison Hansen; 9 Micky Higham (C); 16 Antoni Maria; 17 Atelea Vea; 11 Cory Paterson; 29 Lachlan Burr. Subs (all used): 21 Liam Hood; 35 Greg Richards; 15 Danny Tickle; 12 Glenn Stewart.
Tries: Mortimer (12), Vea (68); **Goals:** Drinkwater 4/4.
ROVERS: 32 Kieren Moss; 36 Justin Carney; 11 Maurice Blair; 22 Andrew Heffernan; 5 Ryan Shaw; 20 Matthew Marsh; 7 Jamie Ellis; 8 Nick Scruton; 19 George Lawler; 37 Lee Jewitt; 13 Danny Addy; 10 Chris Clarkson; 33 Ben Kavanagh. Subs (all used): 9 Shaun Lunt; 12 James Greenwood; 38 Chris Atkin; 39 Mose Masoe.
Tries: Lunt (29, 75), Shaw (58); **Goals:** Ellis 4/4.
Rugby Leaguer & League Express Men of the Match:
Centurions: Daniel Mortimer; *Rovers:* Shaun Lunt.
Penalty count: 10-8; **Half-time:** 8-6;
Referee: Jack Smith; **Attendance:** 5,335.

Sunday 13th August 2017

HALIFAX 12 WIDNES VIKINGS 36

HALIFAX: 2 Will Sharp; 4 Ben Heaton; 16 Ed Barber; 3 Steve Tyrer; 23 Rob Worrincy; 6 Scott Murrell; 1 Ben Johnston; 20 Elliot Morris; 9 Ben Kaye; 13 Jacob Fairbank; 11 Shane Grady; 8 Mitch Cahalane; 12 Simon Grix. Subs (all used): 26 Alex Mammone; 29 Michael Sio; 17 Brandon Moore; 37 Brandon Douglas.
Tries: Heaton (52, 60); **Goals:** Tyrer 2/2.
VIKINGS: 1 Rhys Hanbury; 17 Stefan Marsh; 3 Chris Bridge; 4 Charly Runciman; 2 Corey Thompson; 32 Danny Craven; 6 Joe Mellor (C); 10 Jack Buchanan; 9 Lloyd White; 15 Gil Dudson; 11 Chris Houston (C); 12 Matt Whitley; 13 Hep Cahill. Subs (all used): 20 Manase Manuokafoa; 23 Jay Chapelhow; 25 Tom Olbison; 31 Jordan Johnstone.
Tries: Bridge (8), White (33), Runciman (37), Thompson (44, 47), Mellor (74), Craven (78);
Goals: White 4/7.
Rugby Leaguer & League Express Men of the Match:
Halifax: Ben Johnston; *Vikings:* Lloyd White.
Penalty count: 6-7; **Half-time:** 0-18;
Referee: Gareth Hewer; **Attendance:** 2,291.

LONDON BRONCOS 32 FEATHERSTONE ROVERS 32

BRONCOS: 24 Alex Walker; 2 Rhys Williams; 3 Ben Hellewell; 19 Api Pewhairangi; 1 Elliot Kear; 6 Jarrod Sammut; 7 William Barthau; 8 Tom Spencer; 14 Andy Ackers; 10 Mark Ioane; 36 Sam Wilde; 13 Jay Pitts; 22 Matt Davis. Subs (all used): 34 John Boudebza; 23 Matty Gee; 15 Eddie Battye; 31 Lewis Bienek.
Tries: Pitts (12), Kear (16), Barthau (18), Sammut (55), Ioane (57), Ackers (66); **Goals:** Sammut 4/6.
ROVERS: 1 Ian Hardman; 5 Luke Briscoe; 23 Josh Hardcastle; 3 Chris Ulugia; 4 Misi Taulapapa; 6 Kyle Briggs; 7 Anthony Thackeray; 8 Darrell Griffin; 9 Keal Carlile; 13 Richard Moore; 29 Connor Farrell; 12 John Davies; 32 Jordan Baldwinson. Subs (all used): 19 Matty Wildie; 10 Andrew Bostock; 14 Frankie Mariano; 28 Sam Brooks.
Tries: Farrell (24), Davies (36, 47), Briscoe (50, 69), Ulugia (79); **Goals:** Hardman 4/6.
Rugby Leaguer & League Express Men of the Match:
Broncos: Andy Ackers; *Rovers:* Kyle Briggs.
Penalty count: 8-10; **Half-time:** 14-10;
Referee: Liam Moore; **Attendance:** 926.

ROUND 3

Saturday 19th August 2017

WARRINGTON WOLVES 22 HALIFAX 8

WOLVES: 1 Stefan Ratchford; 5 Matthew Russell; 35 Peta Hiku; 4 Ryan Atkins; 2 Tom Lineham; 22 Declan Patton; 6 Kevin Brown; 8 Chris Hill (C); 27 Morgan Smith; 10 Ashton Sims; 24 Benjamin Jullien; 12 Jack Hughes; 34 Ben Westwood. Subs (all used): 16 George King; 18 Andre Savelio; 23 Joe Philbin; 15 Brad Dwyer.
Tries: Hiku (21), Hill (46), Russell (66), Savelio (79);
Goals: Patton 3/5.
HALIFAX: 5 James Saltonstall; 22 Chester Butler; 21 James Woodburn-Hall; 3 Steve Tyrer; 23 Rob Worrincy; 6 Scott Murrell; 1 Ben Johnston; 20 Elliot Morris; 9 Ben Kaye; 13 Jacob Fairbank; 11 Shane Grady; 16 Ed Barber; 12 Simon Grix. Subs (all used): 26 Alex Mammone; 39 Michael Sio; 17 Brandon Moore; 14 Ryan Boyle.
Tries: Butler (38, 55); **Goals:** Tyrer 0/2.
Rugby Leaguer & League Express Men of the Match:
Wolves: Chris Hill; *Halifax:* Chester Butler.
Penalty count: 12-7; **Half-time:** 4-4;
Referee: Robert Hicks; **Attendance:** 8,353.

CATALANS DRAGONS 6 LEIGH CENTURIONS 30

DRAGONS: 33 Lewis Tierney; 18 Vincent Duport; 3 Krisnan Inu; 4 Brayden Wiliame; 5 Fouad Yaha; 6 Luke Walsh; 7 Richie Myler; 8 Sam Moa; 9 Paul Aiton; 10 Remi Casty (C); 11 Louis Anderson; 12 Justin Horo; 13 Greg Bird. Subs (all used): 14 Julian Bousquet; 15 Benjamin Garcia; 17 Jason Baitieri; 25 Thibaut Margalet.
Try: Wiliame (70); **Goals:** Inu 1/1.
CENTURIONS: 18 Gregg McNally; 5 Matty Dawson; 1 Mitch Brown; 34 Samisoni Langi; 2 Adam Higson; 20 Ben Reynolds; 7 Josh Drinkwater; 13 Harrison Hansen; 33 Daniel Mortimer; 16 Antoni Maria; 11 Cory Paterson; 17 Atelea Vea; 29 Lachlan Burr. Subs (all used): 9 Micky Higham (C); 12 Glenn Stewart; 23 Sam Hopkins; 35 Greg Richards.
Tries: Higson (4, 20), Paterson (48, 77), Drinkwater (61);
Goals: Reynolds 5/6.
Rugby Leaguer & League Express Men of the Match:
Dragons: Brayden Wiliame; *Centurions:* Daniel Mortimer.
Penalty count: 7-7; **Half-time:** 0-10;
Referee: Phil Bentham; **Attendance:** 6,632.

Sunday 20th August 2017

HULL KINGSTON ROVERS 35 LONDON BRONCOS 30

ROVERS: 32 Kieren Moss; 5 Ryan Shaw; 22 Andrew Heffernan; 11 Maurice Blair; 36 Justin Carney; 38 Chris Atkin; 7 Jamie Ellis; 37 Lee Jewitt; 19 George Lawler; 39 Mose Masoe; 10 Chris Clarkson; 13 Danny Addy; 33 Ben Kavanagh. Subs (all used): 9 Shaun Lunt; 12 James Greenwood; 20 Matthew Marsh; 21 Rob Mulhern.
Tries: Addy (10), Moss (18), Mulhern (26), Shaw (31, 57);
Goals: Ellis 7/7; **Field goal:** Atkin (40).
BRONCOS: 24 Alex Walker; 2 Rhys Williams; 3 Ben Hellewell; 1 Elliot Kear; 5 Kieran Dixon; 6 Jarrod Sammut; 7 William Barthau; 8 Tom Spencer; 14 Andy Ackers; 10 Mark Ioane; 36 Sam Wilde; 13 Jay Pitts; 18 Ben Evans. Subs (all used): 9 James Cunningham; 22 Matt Davis; 23 Matty Gee; 16 Junior Roqica.
Tries: Ackers (4), Cunningham (54), Walker (64), Ioane (75), Kear (79); **Goals:** Sammut 5/6.
Rugby Leaguer & League Express Men of the Match:
Rovers: Lee Jewitt; *Broncos:* Andy Ackers.
Penalty count: 10-6; **Half-time:** 25-8;
Referee: Tom Grant; **Attendance:** 7,245.

WIDNES VIKINGS 58 FEATHERSTONE ROVERS 10

VIKINGS: 1 Rhys Hanbury; 17 Stefan Marsh; 3 Chris Bridge; 4 Charly Runciman; 2 Corey Thompson; 6 Joe Mellor (C); 32 Danny Craven; 10 Jack Buchanan; 9 Lloyd White; 15 Gil Dudson; 11 Chris Houston (C); 12 Matt Whitley; 13 Hep Cahill. Subs (all used): 16 Alex Gerrard; 18 Greg Burke; 35 Danny Walker; 25 Tom Olbison.
Tries: Hanbury (4, 11, 72), Runciman (14, 18), Bridge (33, 36, 53), Marsh (47, 61), Mellor (79);
Goals: White 5/6, Craven 1/1, Thompson 0/1, Hanbury 1/3.
ROVERS: 1 Ian Hardman; 5 Luke Briscoe; 23 Josh Hardcastle; 4 Misi Taulapapa; 18 Scott Turner; 6 Kyle Briggs; 7 Anthony Thackeray; 8 Darrell Griffin; 19 Matty Wildie; 13 Richard Moore; 12 John Davies; 21 James Lockwood; 32 Jordan Baldwinson. Subs (all used): 9 Keal Carlile; 28 Sam Brooks; 30 Jack Ormondroyd; 15 Bradley Knowles-Tagg.
Tries: Taulapapa (24), Lockwood (43); **Goals:** Hardman 1/2.

Rugby Leaguer & League Express Men of the Match: *Vikings:* Chris Bridge; *Rovers:* Ian Hardman.
Penalty count: 9-8; **Half-time:** 34-4;
Referee: Gareth Hewer; **Attendance:** 4,373.

ROUND 4

Saturday 2nd September 2017

LONDON BRONCOS 38 WARRINGTON WOLVES 40

BRONCOS: 24 Alex Walker; 2 Rhys Williams; 1 Elliot Kear; 19 Api Pewhairangi; 5 Kieran Dixon; 6 Jarrod Sammut; 7 William Barthau; 15 Eddie Battye; 14 Andy Ackers; 10 Mark Ioane; 23 Matty Gee; 13 Jay Pitts; 22 Matt Davis. Subs (all used): 9 James Cunningham; 12 Matt Garside; 18 Ben Evans; 8 Tom Spencer.
Tries: Dixon (2, 77), Williams (9), Sammut (16, 61, 72), Ackers (74); **Goals:** Sammut 5/7.
WOLVES: 1 Stefan Ratchford; 5 Matthew Russell; 35 Peta Hiku; 4 Ryan Atkins; 2 Tom Lineham; 22 Declan Patton; 6 Kevin Brown; 8 Chris Hill (C); 27 Morgan Smith; 10 Ashton Sims; 24 Benjamin Jullien; 12 Jack Hughes; 34 Ben Westwood. Subs (all used): 7 Kurt Gidley; 16 George King; 18 Andre Savelio; 23 Joe Philbin.
Tries: Lineham (29), G King (39), Hiku (45), Brown (51, 65), Patton (54), Westwood (58); **Goals:** Patton 6/7.
Rugby Leaguer & League Express Men of the Match: *Broncos:* Jarrod Sammut; *Wolves:* Kevin Brown.
Penalty count: 6-9; **Half-time:** 14-10;
Referee: Liam Moore; **Attendance:** 1,577.

Sunday 3rd September 2017

FEATHERSTONE ROVERS 18
HULL KINGSTON ROVERS 30

ROVERS: 1 Ian Hardman; 20 Kyran Johnson; 4 Misi Taulapapa; 23 Josh Hardcastle; 5 Luke Briscoe; 7 Anthony Thackeray; 19 Matty Wildie; 13 Richard Moore; 9 Keal Carlile; 30 Jack Ormondroyd; 12 John Davies; 29 Connor Farrell; 21 James Lockwood. Subs (all used): 28 Sam Brooks; 16 Luke Cooper; 14 Frankie Mariano; 6 Kyle Briggs.
Tries: Johnson (8, 78), Mariano (51); **Goals:** Hardman 3/3.
ROBINS: 1 Adam Quinlan; 5 Ryan Shaw; 22 Andrew Heffernan; 3 Thomas Minns; 36 Justin Carney; 38 Chris Atkin; 7 Jamie Ellis; 37 Lee Jewitt; 19 George Lawler; 8 Nick Scruton; 13 Danny Addy; 10 Chris Clarkson; 33 Ben Kavanagh. Subs (all used): 9 Shaun Lunt; 39 Mose Masoe; 12 James Greenwood; 11 Maurice Blair.
Tries: Shaw (13), Addy (22), Ellis (32), Minns (65), Heffernan (69); **Goals:** Ellis 5/5.
Rugby Leaguer & League Express Men of the Match: *Rovers:* Frankie Mariano; *Robins:* Andrew Heffernan.
Penalty count: 8-9; **Half-time:** 6-18;
Referee: Gareth Hewer; **Attendance:** 4,583.

HALIFAX 0 CATALANS DRAGONS 24

HALIFAX: 2 Will Sharp; 5 James Saltonstall; 22 Chester Butler; 16 Ed Barber; 4 Ben Heaton; 6 Scott Murrell; 1 Ben Johnston; 20 Elliot Morris; 9 Ben Kaye; 8 Mitch Cahalane; 11 Shane Grady; 10 Adam Tangata; 12 Simon Grix. Subs (all used): 14 Ryan Boyle; 29 Michael Sio; 17 Brandon Moore; 13 Jacob Fairbank.
Sin bin: Johnston (67) - punching Duport.
DRAGONS: 33 Lewis Tierney; 18 Vincent Duport; 3 Krisnan Inu; 4 Brayden Wiliame; 5 Fouad Yaha; 6 Luke Walsh; 7 Richie Myler; 8 Sam Moa; 23 Alrix Da Costa; 10 Remi Casty (C); 11 Louis Anderson; 12 Justin Horo; 15 Benjamin Garcia. Subs (all used): 13 Greg Bird; 14 Julian Bousquet; 17 Jason Baitieri; 22 Lucas Albert.
Tries: Anderson (29), Myler (35), Wiliame (44), Yaha (65); **Goals:** Walsh 4/5.
Sin bin: Bird (25) - dangerous challenge on Heaton; Duport (67) - unsportsmanlike conduct.
Rugby Leaguer & League Express Men of the Match: *Halifax:* Chester Butler; *Dragons:* Justin Horo.
Penalty count: 9-7; **Half-time:** 0-12;
Referee: Chris Kendall; **Attendance:** 1,853.

LEIGH CENTURIONS 8 WIDNES VIKINGS 24

CENTURIONS: 18 Gregg McNally; 28 James Clare (D); 1 Mitch Brown; 34 Samisoni Langi; 5 Matty Dawson; 20 Ben Reynolds; 7 Josh Drinkwater; 15 Danny Tickle; 33 Daniel Mortimer; 13 Harrison Hansen; 11 Cory Paterson; 17 Atelea Vea; 29 Lachlan Burr. Subs (all used): 9 Micky Higham (C); 23 Sam Hopkins; 12 Glenn Stewart; 35 Greg Richards.
Tries: Clare (55), Dawson (66); **Goals:** Reynolds 0/2.
VIKINGS: 1 Rhys Hanbury; 17 Stefan Marsh; 3 Chris Bridge; 4 Charly Runciman; 2 Corey Thompson; 6 Joe Mellor (C); 32 Danny Craven; 10 Jack Buchanan; 9 Lloyd White; 15 Gil Dudson; 12 Matt Whitley; 11 Chris Houston (C); 13 Hep Cahill. Subs (all used): 16 Alex Gerrard; 20 Manase Manuokafoa; 25 Tom Olbison; 35 Danny Walker.
Tries: White (4), Gerrard (25), Thompson (58);
Goals: Hanbury 3/4, Bridge 3/3.
Rugby Leaguer & League Express Men of the Match: *Centurions:* Samisoni Langi; *Vikings:* Corey Thompson.
Penalty count: 10-8; **Half-time:** 0-14;
Referee: Ben Thaler; **Attendance:** 6,209.

ROUND 5

Saturday 9th September 2017

WARRINGTON WOLVES 32 LEIGH CENTURIONS 30

WOLVES: 1 Stefan Ratchford; 5 Matthew Russell; 35 Peta Hiku; 28 Harvey Livett; 2 Tom Lineham; 22 Declan Patton; 6 Kevin Brown; 8 Chris Hill (C); 7 Kurt Gidley; 10 Ashton Sims; 24 Benjamin Jullien; 12 Jack Hughes; 34 Ben Westwood. Subs (all used): 13 Joe Westerman; 18 Andre Savelio; 15 Brad Dwyer; 14 Mike Cooper.
Tries: Russell (8), Westwood (12), Gidley (33), Brown (38), Hiku (54), Hill (65); **Goals:** Patton 2/5, Livett 2/2.
CENTURIONS: 18 Gregg McNally; 28 James Clare; 1 Mitch Brown; 34 Samisoni Langi; 5 Matty Dawson; 11 Cory Paterson; 7 Josh Drinkwater; 16 Antoni Maria; 21 Liam Hood; 15 Danny Tickle; 17 Atelea Vea; 29 Lachlan Burr; 12 Glenn Stewart. Subs (all used): 14 Eloi Pelissier; 35 Greg Richards; 23 Sam Hopkins; 13 Harrison Hansen (C).
Tries: Clare (4), Hood (15), Maria (18), Vea (45), Burr (59); **Goals:** Drinkwater 5/5.
Rugby Leaguer & League Express Men of the Match: *Wolves:* Peta Hiku; *Centurions:* Liam Hood.
Penalty count: 6-4; **Half-time:** 20-18;
Referee: Phil Bentham; **Attendance:** 9,787.

HULL KINGSTON ROVERS 12 WIDNES VIKINGS 6

ROVERS: 1 Adam Quinlan; 5 Ryan Shaw; 22 Andrew Heffernan; 3 Thomas Minns; 32 Kieren Moss; 16 Jordan Abdull; 7 Jamie Ellis; 8 Nick Scruton; 19 George Lawler; 37 Lee Jewitt; 13 Danny Addy; 10 Chris Clarkson; 33 Ben Kavanagh. Subs (all used): 12 James Greenwood; 9 Shaun Lunt; 39 Mose Masoe; 11 Maurice Blair.
Tries: Minns (39), Shaw (70); **Goals:** Ellis 2/4.
On report: Heffernan (49) - alleged use of the knees.
VIKINGS: 2 Corey Thompson; 17 Stefan Marsh; 14 Chris Dean; 4 Charly Runciman; 28 Ryan Ince; 6 Joe Mellor (C); 32 Danny Craven; 10 Jack Buchanan; 9 Lloyd White; 15 Gil Dudson; 12 Matt Whitley; 11 Chris Houston (C); 13 Hep Cahill. Subs (all used): 16 Alex Gerrard; 20 Manase Manuokafoa; 25 Tom Olbison; 35 Danny Walker.
Try: Cahill (22); **Goals:** White 1/1.
Rugby Leaguer & League Express Men of the Match: *Rovers:* Shaun Lunt; *Vikings:* Danny Craven.
Penalty count: 9-11; **Half-time:** 8-6;
Referee: Gareth Hewer; **Attendance:** 8,227.

CATALANS DRAGONS 26 FEATHERSTONE ROVERS 12

DRAGONS: 33 Lewis Tierney; 18 Vincent Duport; 3 Krisnan Inu; 4 Brayden Wiliame; 5 Fouad Yaha; 6 Luke Walsh; 7 Richie Myler; 8 Sam Moa; 23 Alrix Da Costa; 10 Remi Casty (C); 11 Louis Anderson; 12 Justin Horo; 15 Benjamin Garcia. Subs (all used): 14 Julian Bousquet; 17 Jason Baitieri; 22 Lucas Albert; 25 Thibaut Margalet.
Tries: Inu (6), Wiliame (24), Garcia (28), Moa (67);
Goals: Walsh 2/3, Inu 3/3.
Sin bin: Garcia (8) - dangerous challenge on Turner; Anderson (60) - fighting.
ROVERS: 20 Kyran Johnson; 5 Luke Briscoe; 23 Josh Hardcastle; 4 Misi Taulapapa; 18 Scott Turner; 7 Anthony Thackeray; 19 Matty Wildie; 28 Sam Brooks; 9 Keal Carlile; 14 Frankie Mariano; 29 Connor Farrell; 12 John Davies; 21 James Lockwood. Subs (all used): 15 Bradley Knowles-Tagg; 16 Luke Cooper; 25 Josh Walters; 27 Daniel Igbinedion.
Tries: Brooks (11), Thackeray (33); **Goals:** Johnson 2/2.
Sin bin: Briscoe (60) - fighting;
Carlile (64) - late challenge on Walsh.
Rugby Leaguer & League Express Men of the Match: *Dragons:* Krisnan Inu; *Rovers:* Anthony Thackeray.
Penalty count: 10-10; **Half-time:** 18-12;
Referee: Liam Moore; **Attendance:** 8,649.

Sunday 10th September 2017

LONDON BRONCOS 36 HALIFAX 14

BRONCOS: 24 Alex Walker; 2 Rhys Williams; 1 Elliot Kear; 19 Api Pewhairangi; 5 Kieran Dixon; 6 Jarrod Sammut; 7 William Barthau; 15 Eddie Battye; 14 Andy Ackers; 10 Mark Ioane; 23 Matty Gee; 22 Matt Davis; 13 Jay Pitts. Subs (all used): 9 James Cunningham; 12 Matt Garside; 18 Ben Evans; 31 Lewis Bienek.
Tries: Barthau (8), Walker (11), Ackers (17), Williams (54), Dixon (64), Kear (66); **Goals:** Sammut 5/5, Dixon 1/1.
Sin bin: Sammut (52) - fighting.
HALIFAX: 5 James Saltonstall; 23 Rob Worrincy; 3 Steve Tyrer; 16 Ed Barber; 22 Chester Butler; 6 Scott Murrell; 1 Ben Johnston; 20 Elliot Morris; 9 Ben Kaye; 10 Adam Tangata; 11 Shane Grady; 8 Mitch Cahalane; 12 Simon Grix. Subs (all used): 13 Jacob Fairbank; 37 Brandon Douglas; 17 Brandon Moore; 29 Michael Sio.
Tries: Tyrer (2), Cahalane (33), Worrincy (76);
Goals: Tyrer 1/3.
Sin bin: Worrincy (52) - fighting.
Rugby Leaguer & League Express Men of the Match: *Broncos:* Elliot Kear; *Halifax:* James Saltonstall.
Penalty count: 9-15; **Half-time:** 18-10;
Referee: Scott Mikalauskas; **Attendance:** 794.

ROUND 6

Friday 15th September 2017

HULL KINGSTON ROVERS 19 CATALANS DRAGONS 20

ROVERS: 2 Ben Cockayne; 32 Kieren Moss; 4 Liam Salter; 16 Jordan Abdull; 27 Will Oakes; 20 Matthew Marsh; 38 Chris Atkin; 33 Ben Kavanagh; 19 George Lawler; 21 Rob Mulhern; 14 Graeme Horne; 12 James Greenwood; 10 Chris Clarkson. Subs (all used): 30 Joe Cator; 26 Kieran Moran; 17 Mitch Clark; 18 Zach Dockar-Clay.
Tries: Oakes (48), Cockayne (55), Lawler (59);
Goals: Dockar-Clay 2/2, Atkin 1/1; **Field goal:** Atkin (66).
DRAGONS: 33 Lewis Tierney; 18 Vincent Duport; 3 Krisnan Inu; 4 Brayden Wiliame; 21 Iain Thornley; 6 Luke Walsh; 7 Richie Myler; 8 Sam Moa; 9 Paul Aiton; 14 Julian Bousquet; 11 Louis Anderson; 12 Justin Horo; 15 Benjamin Garcia. Subs (all used): 17 Jason Baitieri (C); 22 Lucas Albert; 25 Thibaut Margalet; 32 Romain Navarrete.
Tries: Myler (9), Thornley (71), Wiliame (76);
Goals: Walsh 4/5.
Rugby Leaguer & League Express Men of the Match: *Rovers:* George Lawler; *Dragons:* Luke Walsh.
Penalty count: 9-6; **Half-time:** 0-8;
Referee: Robert Hicks; **Attendance:** 7,405.

LEIGH CENTURIONS 40 HALIFAX 6

CENTURIONS: 18 Gregg McNally; 1 Mitch Brown; 3 Ben Crooks; 34 Samisoni Langi; 28 James Clare; 20 Ben Reynolds; 7 Josh Drinkwater; 16 Antoni Maria; 21 Liam Hood; 15 Danny Tickle; 11 Cory Paterson; 12 Glenn Stewart; 29 Lachlan Burr. Subs (all used): 14 Eloi Pelissier; 35 Greg Richards; 31 Matty Fleming; 13 Harrison Hansen (C).
Tries: Clare (4, 44), Reynolds (17), Brown (31, 40, 60), Hansen (50), McNally (62);
Goals: Reynolds 2/6, Drinkwater 2/2.
HALIFAX: 5 James Saltonstall; 22 Chester Butler; 4 Ben Heaton; 3 Steve Tyrer; 23 Rob Worrincy; 29 Michael Sio; 1 Ben Johnston; 37 Brandon Douglas; 17 Brandon Moore; 10 Adam Tangata; 11 Shane Grady; 8 Mitch Cahalane; 13 Jacob Fairbank. Subs (all used): 35 William Calcott; 36 Frazer Morris; 9 Ben Kaye; 14 Ryan Boyle.
Try: Cahalane (36); **Goals:** Tyrer 1/1.
Rugby Leaguer & League Express Men of the Match: *Centurions:* Samisoni Langi; *Halifax:* Mitch Cahalane.
Penalty count: 8-10; **Half-time:** 20-6;
Referee: Chris Kendall; **Attendance:** 4,341.

Saturday 16th September 2017

WIDNES VIKINGS 38 LONDON BRONCOS 16

VIKINGS: 32 Danny Craven; 27 Ed Chamberlain; 17 Stefan Marsh; 4 Charly Runciman; 28 Ryan Ince; 6 Joe Mellor (C); 7 Tom Gilmore; 10 Jack Buchanan; 9 Lloyd White; 15 Gil Dudson; 11 Chris Houston (C); 12 Matt Whitley; 18 Greg Burke. Subs (all used): 13 Hep Cahill; 16 Alex Gerrard; 25 Tom Olbison; 35 Danny Walker.
Tries: Whitley (22), White (26), Craven (33, 42), Runciman (40), Mellor (59, 80);
Goals: White 3/6, Gilmore 2/2.
Sin bin: Runciman (69) - repeated team offences.
BRONCOS: 24 Alex Walker; 2 Rhys Williams; 1 Elliot Kear; 19 Api Pewhairangi; 5 Kieran Dixon; 6 Jarrod Sammut; 7 William Barthau; 15 Eddie Battye; 14 Andy Ackers; 10 Mark Ioane; 23 Matty Gee; 13 Jay Pitts; 22 Matt Davis. Subs (all used): 9 James Cunningham; 12 Matt Garside; 8 Tom Spencer; 31 Lewis Bienek.
Tries: Ioane (11), Sammut (50), Dixon (67);
Goals: Sammut 2/3.
Sin bin: Gee (39) - late challenge on White; Cunningham (63) - repeated team offences.
Rugby Leaguer & League Express Men of the Match: *Vikings:* Joe Mellor; *Broncos:* Eddie Battye.
Penalty count: 13-9; **Half-time:** 22-6;
Referee: James Child; **Attendance:** 4,199.

Catalans' Iain Thornley scores against Leigh during the Million Pound Game

Sunday 17th September 2017

FEATHERSTONE ROVERS 0
WARRINGTON WOLVES 68

ROVERS: 20 Kyran Johnson; 18 Scott Turner; 4 Misi Taulapapa; 25 Josh Walters; 23 Josh Hardcastle; 7 Anthony Thackeray; 19 Matty Wildie; 8 Darrell Griffin; 9 Keal Carlile; 28 Sam Brooks; 12 John Davies; 29 Connor Farrell; 21 James Lockwood. Subs (all used): 6 Kyle Briggs; 13 Richard Moore; 15 Bradley Knowles-Tagg; 16 Luke Cooper.
WOLVES: 1 Stefan Ratchford; 33 Ben Pomeroy; 35 Peta Hiku; 28 Harvey Livett; 5 Matthew Russell; 6 Kevin Brown; 7 Kurt Gidley; 8 Chris Hill (C); 9 Daryl Clark; 10 Ashton Sims; 11 Ben Currie; 12 Jack Hughes; 14 Mike Cooper. Subs (all used): 16 George King; 18 Andre Savelio; 26 Jack Johnson; 27 Morgan Smith.
Tries: Hiku (2, 47, 73), Ratchford (4), Livett (8, 52), Hughes (16, 36), Pomeroy (22), Savelio (34), Johnson (62, 79); **Goals:** Livett 10/12.
Rugby Leaguer & League Express Men of the Match:
Rovers: Keal Carlile; *Wolves:* Peta Hiku.
Penalty count: 7-2; **Half-time:** 0-38;
Referee: Scott Mikalauskas; **Attendance:** 2,441.

ROUND 7

Friday 22nd September 2017

LONDON BRONCOS 4 LEIGH CENTURIONS 41

BRONCOS: 24 Alex Walker; 2 Rhys Williams; 3 Ben Hellewell; 20 Michael Channing; 1 Elliot Kear; 6 Jarrod Sammut; 7 William Barthau; 15 Eddie Battye; 9 James Cunningham; 18 Ben Evans; 23 Matty Gee; 13 Jay Pitts; 22 Matt Davis. Subs (all used): 34 John Boudebza; 12 Matt Garside; 8 Tom Spencer; 31 Lewis Bienek.
Try: Gee (63); **Goals:** Sammut 0/1.
CENTURIONS: 19 Ryan Hampshire; 5 Matty Dawson; 3 Ben Crooks; 31 Matty Fleming; 28 James Clare; 20 Ben Reynolds; 7 Josh Drinkwater; 16 Antoni Maria; 21 Liam Hood; 15 Danny Tickle; 17 Atelea Vea; 12 Glenn Stewart; 29 Lachlan Burr. Subs (all used): 14 Eloi Pelissier; 13 Harrison Hansen (C); 23 Sam Hopkins; 35 Greg Richards.
Tries: Fleming (12), Hansen (33), Hopkins (43), Clare (54), Reynolds (71), Drinkwater (73), Maria (76); **Goals:** Reynolds 6/7; **Field goal:** Drinkwater (80).
Rugby Leaguer & League Express Men of the Match:
Broncos: Elliot Kear; *Centurions:* Ben Reynolds.
Penalty count: 11-9; **Half-time:** 0-12;
Referee: Chris Kendall; **Attendance:** 1,234.

Saturday 23rd September 2017

WARRINGTON WOLVES 46
HULL KINGSTON ROVERS 24

WOLVES: 1 Stefan Ratchford; 5 Matthew Russell; 28 Harvey Livett; 35 Peta Hiku; 33 Ben Pomeroy; 6 Kevin Brown; 7 Kurt Gidley; 8 Chris Hill (C); 9 Daryl Clark; 10 Ashton Sims; 11 Ben Currie; 12 Jack Hughes; 14 Mike Cooper. Subs (all used): 34 John Boudebza; 18 Andre Savelio; 23 Joe Philbin; 24 Benjamin Jullien.
Tries: Pomeroy (19, 53), Ratchford (31), Dwyer (38), Savelio (48, 62), Hiku (69), Currie (73), Livett (78); **Goals:** Livett 5/8, Sims 0/1.
Sin bin: Hughes (50) - fighting.
ROVERS: 2 Ben Cockayne; 5 Ryan Shaw; 3 Thomas Minns; 20 Matthew Marsh; 27 Will Oakes; 38 Chris Atkin; 7 Jamie Ellis; 37 Lee Jewitt; 19 George Lawler; 21 Rob Mulhern; 12 James Greenwood; 11 Maurice Blair; 33 Ben Kavanagh. Subs (all used): 18 Zach Dockar-Clay; 10 Chris Clarkson; 17 Mitch Clark; 32 Kieren Moss.
Tries: Oakes (4, 58), Shaw (25, 27); **Goals:** Ellis 4/4.
Sin bin: Jewitt (50) - fighting.
Rugby Leaguer & League Express Men of the Match:
Wolves: Andre Savelio; *Rovers:* Ryan Shaw.
Penalty count: 11-9; **Half-time:** 16-18;
Referee: Gareth Hewer; **Attendance:** 10,466.

CATALANS DRAGONS 10 WIDNES VIKINGS 12

DRAGONS: 33 Lewis Tierney; 18 Vincent Duport; 3 Krisnan Inu; 4 Brayden Wiliame; 21 Iain Thornley; 6 Luke Walsh; 7 Richie Myler; 8 Sam Moa (C); 9 Paul Aiton; 14 Julian Bousquet; 11 Louis Anderson; 12 Justin Horo; 15 Benjamin Garcia. Subs (all used): 17 Jason Baitieri; 22 Lucas Albert; 25 Thibaut Margalet; 32 Romain Navarrete.
Try: Bousquet (71); **Goals:** Walsh 3/3.
VIKINGS: 32 Danny Craven; 2 Corey Thompson; 4 Charly Runciman; 17 Stefan Marsh; 28 Ryan Ince; 6 Joe Mellor (C); 7 Tom Gilmore; 15 Gil Dudson; 33 Aaron Heremaia; 10 Jack Buchanan; 12 Matt Whitley; 11 Chris Houston (C); 18 Greg Burke. Subs (all used): 13 Hep Cahill; 16 Alex Gerrard; 25 Tom Olbison; 35 Danny Walker.
Tries: Thompson (55), Marsh (62); **Goals:** Gilmore 2/4.
Sin bin: Houston (31) - high tackle on Margalet.
Rugby Leaguer & League Express Men of the Match:
Dragons: Sam Moa; *Vikings:* Danny Craven.
Penalty count: 6-4; **Half-time:** 4-4;
Referee: Phil Bentham; **Attendance:** 10,245.

Sunday 24th September 2017

HALIFAX 20 FEATHERSTONE ROVERS 26

HALIFAX: 2 Will Sharp; 4 Ben Heaton; 16 Ed Barber; 3 Steve Tyrer; 23 Rob Worrincy; 6 Scott Murrell; 1 Ben Johnston; 20 Elliot Morris; 17 Brandon Moore; 10 Adam Tangata; 11 Shane Grady; 8 Mitch Cahalane; 12 Simon Grix. Subs (all used): 9 Ben Kaye; 13 Jacob Fairbank; 29 Michael Sio; 35 William Calcott.
Tries: Kaye (37), Cahalane (45), Worrincy (67), Heaton (74); **Goals:** Tyrer 2/4.
Dismissal: Heaton (80) - fighting.
Sin bin: Fairbank (55) - professional foul.
ROVERS: 1 Ian Hardman; 4 Misi Taulapapa; 25 Josh Walters; 23 Josh Hardcastle; 5 Luke Briscoe; 19 Matty Wildie; 7 Anthony Thackeray; 8 Darrell Griffin; 9 Keal Carlile; 13 Richard Moore; 12 John Davies; 14 Frankie Mariano; 21 James Lockwood. Subs (all used): 6 Kyle Briggs; 16 Luke Cooper; 28 Sam Brooks; 32 Jordan Baldwinson.
Tries: Davies (8), Briscoe (44), Mariano (55), Taulapapa (65); **Goals:** Hardman 5/5.
Dismissal: Moore (80) - fighting.
Rugby Leaguer & League Express Men of the Match:
Halifax: Will Sharp; *Rovers:* Misi Taulapapa.
Penalty count: 13-8; **Half-time:** 6-8;
Referee: Tom Grant; **Attendance:** 2,057.

MILLION POUND GAME

Saturday 30th September 2017

LEIGH CENTURIONS 10 CATALANS DRAGONS 26

CENTURIONS: 19 Ryan Hampshire; 5 Matty Dawson; 3 Ben Crooks; 31 Matty Fleming; 28 James Clare; 20 Ben Reynolds; 7 Josh Drinkwater; 16 Antoni Maria; 9 Micky Higham (C); 15 Danny Tickle; 11 Cory Paterson; 12 Glenn Stewart; 29 Lachlan Burr. Subs (all used): 21 Liam Hood; 23 Sam Hopkins; 13 Harrison Hansen; 35 Greg Richards.
Tries: Dawson (7), Clare (45); **Goals:** Reynolds 1/2.
DRAGONS: 33 Lewis Tierney; 18 Vincent Duport; 21 Iain Thornley; 4 Brayden Wiliame; 5 Fouad Yaha; 6 Luke Walsh; 7 Richie Myler; 8 Sam Moa (C); 9 Paul Aiton; 14 Julian Bousquet; 11 Louis Anderson; 12 Justin Horo; 13 Greg Bird. Subs (all used): 15 Benjamin Garcia; 17 Jason Baitieri; 22 Lucas Albert; 25 Thibaut Margalet.
Tries: Thornley (35), Tierney (50, 59), Yaha (78); **Goals:** Walsh 5/7.
Rugby Leaguer & League Express Men of the Match:
Centurions: Micky Higham; *Dragons:* Lewis Tierney.
Penalty count: 6-10; **Half-time:** 6-4;
Referee: Ben Thaler; **Attendance:** 6,888.

SUPER LEAGUE XXII
Opta Analysis

SUPER LEAGUE XXII TOP PERFORMERS

TACKLES

Danny Houghton	Hull FC	1123
Jon Wilkin	St Helens	1072
Ryan Hinchcliffe	Huddersfield	1021
Matt Parcell	Leeds	1018
James Roby	St Helens	1000
Jamie Jones-Buchanan	Leeds	942
Kruise Leeming	Huddersfield	900
Paul McShane	Castleford	898
Adam Cuthbertson	Leeds	890
Kyle Wood	Wakefield	862

OFFLOADS

Adam Cuthbertson	Leeds	121
Sebastine Ikahihifo	Huddersfield	73
George Williams	Wigan	59
Zeb Taia	St Helens	52
Joel Moon	Leeds	51
Craig Huby	Wakefield	50
Jesse Sene-Lefao	Castleford	47
Anthony Gelling	Wigan	45
Mike McMeeken	Castleford	45
Mahe Fonua	Hull FC	43

CARRIES

Alex Walmsley	St Helens	525
Adam Cuthbertson	Leeds	500
Zeb Taia	St Helens	458
Jermaine McGillvary	Huddersfield	446
Ryan Hall	Leeds	428
Jesse Sene-Lefao	Castleford	414
Tommy Makinson	St Helens	403
Kris Welham	Salford	403
Liam Farrell	Wigan	397
Zak Hardaker	Castleford	393

CLEAN BREAKS

Greg Eden	Castleford	47
Mark Percival	St Helens	32
Ben Jones-Bishop	Wakefield	30
Liam Marshall	Wigan	28
Greg Minikin	Castleford	24
Jamie Shaul	Hull FC	24
Tom Davies	Wigan	23
Robert Lui	Salford	23
Jermaine McGillvary	Huddersfield	23
Mason Caton-Brown	Wakefield	22

4256 METRES -
Alex Walmsley

ERRORS

Mark Percival	St Helens	51
Albert Kelly	Hull FC	43
Greg Eden	Castleford	39
Mahe Fonua	Hull FC	37
Tom Briscoe	Leeds	36
Zeb Taia	St Helens	35
Ben Roberts	Castleford	33
Jake Connor	Hull FC	32
Scott Grix	Wakefield	32
Mason Caton-Brown	Wakefield	31

METRES

Alex Walmsley	St Helens	4256
Jermaine McGillvary	Huddersfield	3883
Adam Cuthbertson	Leeds	3446
Ryan Hall	Leeds	3398
Tom Davies	Wigan	3359
Zak Hardaker	Castleford	3257
Tommy Makinson	St Helens	3217
Jamie Shaul	Hull FC	3199
Mahe Fonua	Hull FC	3189
Zeb Taia	St Helens	3136

MISSED TACKLES

Adam Milner	Castleford	77
Kris Welham	Salford	76
Liam Finn	Wakefield	71
Albert Kelly	Hull FC	70
Jacob Miller	Wakefield	69
Mark Minichiello	Hull FC	69
Jon Wilkin	St Helens	69
Zeb Taia	St Helens	64
Robert Lui	Salford	62
Danny Washbrook	Hull FC	61

KICKS IN GENERAL PLAY

Danny Brough	Huddersfield	326
Marc Sneyd	Hull FC	287
Luke Gale	Castleford	278
Danny McGuire	Leeds	264
Matty Smith	St Helens	212
Michael Dobson	Salford	207
Luke Walsh	Catalans	193
Josh Drinkwater	Leigh	180
Liam Finn	Wakefield	157
Declan Patton	Warrington	156

QUICK PLAY-THE-BALLS

Jermaine McGillvary	Huddersfield	83
Tom Briscoe	Leeds	81
Ryan Hall	Leeds	76
Greg Johnson	Salford	76
Ryan Atkins	Warrington	68
David Fifita	Wakefield	67
Mahe Fonua	Hull FC	62
Alex Walmsley	St Helens	58
Liam Marshall	Wigan	56
Mason Caton-Brown	Wakefield	54

PENALTIES CONCEDED

Kruise Leeming	Huddersfield	37
Paul McShane	Castleford	28
David Fifita	Wakefield	27
Jon Wilkin	St Helens	27
Danny Brough	Huddersfield	26
Chris Houston	Widnes	26
Jamie Jones-Buchanan	Leeds	26
Liam Watts	Hull FC	24
Sika Manu	Hull FC	23
Mark Minichiello	Hull FC	23

TACKLE BUSTS

Sebastine Ikahihifo	Huddersfield	165
Mark Percival	St Helens	127
Zak Hardaker	Castleford	126
Jamie Shaul	Hull FC	124
Josh Jones	Salford	104
David Fifita	Wakefield	103
Ben Roberts	Castleford	101
Alex Walmsley	St Helens	80
George Williams	Wigan	79
Robert Lui	Salford	77

*All statistics in Opta Analysis include Super League regular season & Super 8s/Qualifiers.
(except pages 229-232 - Teams 1-8 include regular season and Super 8s;
teams 9-12 include regular season only) (Play-offs not included throughout)*

SUPER LEAGUE XXII TRIES SCORED/CONCEDED

TOTAL TRIES SCORED

Castleford Tigers	150
Warrington Wolves	127
Wigan Warriors	119
Wakefield Trinity	115
Leigh Centurions	113
Huddersfield Giants	110
Leeds Rhinos	110
Salford Red Devils	109
Catalans Dragons	101
Hull FC	100
St Helens	98
Widnes Vikings	99

TOTAL TRIES CONCEDED

Catalans Dragons	143
Widnes Vikings	141
Salford Red Devils	128
Leigh Centurions	127
Warrington Wolves	121
Huddersfield Giants	119
Hull FC	114
Wigan Warriors	113
Wakefield Trinity	112
Leeds Rhinos	109
Castleford Tigers	92
St Helens	86

SCORED FROM KICKS

Wigan Warriors	20
Catalans Dragons	18
Leeds Rhinos	18
Warrington Wolves	17
Wakefield Trinity	16
Castleford Tigers	13
Hull FC	13
Widnes Vikings	13
Huddersfield Giants	12
Leigh Centurions	12
St Helens	12
Salford Red Devils	8

Castleford's Greg Eden beats Wakefield's Scott Grix to score. The Tigers scored more tries than any other team in Super League XXII

CONCEDED FROM KICKS

Wigan Warriors	23
Salford Red Devils	17
Catalans Dragons	15
Warrington Wolves	14
Leeds Rhinos	13
Leigh Centurions	13
Hull FC	12
St Helens	12
Widnes Vikings	12
Castleford Tigers	11
Huddersfield Giants	10
Wakefield Trinity	8

TRIES SCORED FROM OWN HALF

Castleford Tigers	24
Hull FC	21
Wakefield Trinity	18
Wigan Warriors	17
Widnes Vikings	11
Catalans Dragons	10
Leeds Rhinos	10
St Helens	9
Leigh Centurions	8
Huddersfield Giants	7
Warrington Wolves	7
Salford Red Devils	5

TRIES CONCEDED FROM OVER 50M

Warrington Wolves	23
Catalans Dragons	19
Salford Red Devils	16
Huddersfield Giants	15
Leigh Centurions	15
Leeds Rhinos	13
Wigan Warriors	13
Widnes Vikings	12
Hull FC	8
Wakefield Trinity	8
St Helens	5
Castleford Tigers	4

TRIES SCORED FROM UNDER 10M

Huddersfield Giants	73
Castleford Tigers	64
Warrington Wolves	63
Salford Red Devils	61
Leeds Rhinos	59
Leigh Centurions	59
Wigan Warriors	56
Wakefield Trinity	52
Widnes Vikings	50
St Helens	49
Catalans Dragons	44
Hull FC	41

TRIES CONCEDED FROM UNDER 10M

Hull FC	66
Catalans Dragons	65
Leigh Centurions	65
Widnes Vikings	65
Wakefield Trinity	60
Wigan Warriors	59
Salford Red Devils	58
Huddersfield Giants	51
Leeds Rhinos	51
Warrington Wolves	50
St Helens	49
Castleford Tigers	45

SUPER LEAGUE XXII AVERAGES PER MATCH

TACKLES

Widnes Vikings	348.3
St Helens	341.8
Leigh Centurions	341.1
Salford Red Devils	341.0
Hull FC	340.8
Leeds Rhinos	332.6
Warrington Wolves	331.7
Huddersfield Giants	330.6
Wakefield Trinity	325.4
Wigan Warriors	315.1
Castleford Tigers	303.4
Catalans Dragons	297.0

MISSED TACKLES

Catalans Dragons	28.8
Hull FC	28.1
Leigh Centurions	27.4
Salford Red Devils	26.9
Widnes Vikings	26.7
Leeds Rhinos	24.8
Wakefield Trinity	24.7
Huddersfield Giants	23.8
Wigan Warriors	23.6
Castleford Tigers	22.7
St Helens	22.0
Warrington Wolves	20.8

OFFLOADS

Leeds Rhinos	14.2
Warrington Wolves	11.9
Wigan Warriors	11.6
Hull FC	10.8
Castleford Tigers	10.7
St Helens	10.6
Wakefield Trinity	9.8
Huddersfield Giants	9.2
Widnes Vikings	9.2
Leigh Centurions	8.4
Catalans Dragons	8.3
Salford Red Devils	8.1

METRES

St Helens	1301.8
Warrington Wolves	1286.7
Castleford Tigers	1286.0
Leeds Rhinos	1274.0
Huddersfield Giants	1257.9
Wigan Warriors	1255.2
Hull FC	1242.9
Wakefield Trinity	1240.0
Salford Red Devils	1211.5
Leigh Centurions	1149.0
Widnes Vikings	1148.5
Catalans Dragons	1134.8

CLEAN BREAKS

Castleford Tigers	6.9
Hull FC	6.0
Salford Red Devils	5.9
Wakefield Trinity	5.8
St Helens	5.5
Leeds Rhinos	5.3
Wigan Warriors	5.2
Leigh Centurions	5.1
Huddersfield Giants	4.8
Warrington Wolves	4.7
Widnes Vikings	4.6
Catalans Dragons	4.5

PASSES

St Helens	236.1
Huddersfield Giants	217.5
Wigan Warriors	216.4
Catalans Dragons	213.5
Castleford Tigers	211.2
Salford Red Devils	209.5
Leeds Rhinos	208.9
Wakefield Trinity	208.4
Warrington Wolves	201.8
Leigh Centurions	201.1
Hull FC	199.9
Widnes Vikings	197.9

ERRORS

Warrington Wolves	13.9
St Helens	13.5
Hull FC	13.0
Leigh Centurions	12.6
Widnes Vikings	12.6
Leeds Rhinos	12.0
Wigan Warriors	11.8
Wakefield Trinity	11.4
Huddersfield Giants	11.2
Castleford Tigers	11.1
Catalans Dragons	10.7
Salford Red Devils	10.5

KICKS IN GENERAL PLAY

Huddersfield Giants	18.9
Salford Red Devils	18.4
Hull FC	18.3
Leigh Centurions	18.1
St Helens	18.1
Warrington Wolves	18.1
Wigan Warriors	18.0
Leeds Rhinos	17.9
Wakefield Trinity	17.9
Catalans Dragons	17.6
Widnes Vikings	17.4
Castleford Tigers	16.5

SUPER LEAGUE XXII PENALTIES

TOTAL PENALTIES AWARDED
Leigh Centurions	267
Catalans Dragons	266
Leeds Rhinos	265
Warrington Wolves	247
Wakefield Trinity	243
Hull FC	240
Widnes Vikings	237
Huddersfield Giants	233
Wigan Warriors	232
St Helens	229
Castleford Tigers	227
Salford Red Devils	213

TOTAL PENALTIES CONCEDED
Leigh Centurions	282
Catalans Dragons	265
Widnes Vikings	258
Hull FC	252
Salford Red Devils	242
Wakefield Trinity	236
Castleford Tigers	233
Huddersfield Giants	228
Leeds Rhinos	227
Wigan Warriors	225
Warrington Wolves	221
St Helens	219

FOUL PLAY - AWARDED
Catalans Dragons	62
Wakefield Trinity	59
St Helens	56
Leigh Centurions	55
Huddersfield Giants	54
Widnes Vikings	50
Leeds Rhinos	49
Hull FC	47
Wigan Warriors	43
Warrington Wolves	41
Castleford Tigers	36
Salford Red Devils	34

FOUL PLAY - CONCEDED
Catalans Dragons	68
Hull FC	59
Salford Red Devils	53
Leigh Centurions	52
Widnes Vikings	52
Castleford Tigers	47
Wigan Warriors	47
Huddersfield Giants	46
Warrington Wolves	43
Wakefield Trinity	39
St Helens	37
Leeds Rhinos	35

OFFSIDE - AWARDED
Catalans Dragons	27
Leeds Rhinos	27
Wakefield Trinity	23
Huddersfield Giants	22
Leigh Centurions	21
Castleford Tigers	20
St Helens	20
Warrington Wolves	19
Wigan Warriors	18
Salford Red Devils	17
Hull FC	15
Widnes Vikings	11

OFFSIDE - CONCEDED
Huddersfield Giants	31
Wigan Warriors	26
Castleford Tigers	25
St Helens	23
Wakefield Trinity	21
Leigh Centurions	20
Leeds Rhinos	19
Salford Red Devils	19
Catalans Dragons	17
Hull FC	16
Warrington Wolves	10
Widnes Vikings	10

INTERFERENCE - AWARDED
Hull FC	120
Leigh Centurions	119
Warrington Wolves	118
Wigan Warriors	118
Leeds Rhinos	112
Widnes Vikings	110
St Helens	109
Castleford Tigers	105
Salford Red Devils	100
Wakefield Trinity	94
Catalans Dragons	92
Huddersfield Giants	87

INTERFERENCE - CONCEDED
Widnes Vikings	134
Leigh Centurions	121
Hull FC	117
Catalans Dragons	112
Leeds Rhinos	110
Wakefield Trinity	104
Huddersfield Giants	100
Salford Red Devils	98
Castleford Tigers	96
Wigan Warriors	95
Warrington Wolves	94
St Helens	90

OBSTRUCTION - AWARDED
Warrington Wolves	17
Wakefield Trinity	16
Leigh Centurions	15
Castleford Tigers	14
Catalans Dragons	14
Hull FC	14
Leeds Rhinos	13
Wigan Warriors	13
Salford Red Devils	11
St Helens	10
Widnes Vikings	9
Huddersfield Giants	8

OBSTRUCTION - CONCEDED
St Helens	21
Leigh Centurions	20
Catalans Dragons	18
Castleford Tigers	15
Salford Red Devils	15
Widnes Vikings	14
Warrington Wolves	13
Leeds Rhinos	11
Huddersfield Giants	10
Wakefield Trinity	8
Wigan Warriors	8
Hull FC	5

BALL STEALING - AWARDED
Catalans Dragons	34
Huddersfield Giants	21
Wakefield Trinity	19
Widnes Vikings	17
Salford Red Devils	16
Castleford Tigers	14
Hull FC	14
Leigh Centurions	14
Warrington Wolves	14
Wigan Warriors	11
Leeds Rhinos	10
St Helens	9

BALL STEALING - CONCEDED
Castleford Tigers	24
Leigh Centurions	22
Hull FC	21
Warrington Wolves	19
Wakefield Trinity	18
Widnes Vikings	17
Leeds Rhinos	16
Catalans Dragons	15
Huddersfield Giants	14
Salford Red Devils	12
Wigan Warriors	11
St Helens	6

OFFSIDE MARKERS - AWARDED
Huddersfield Giants	22
Catalans Dragons	18
Leeds Rhinos	17
Hull FC	15
Widnes Vikings	15
Castleford Tigers	14
Salford Red Devils	14
Warrington Wolves	13
Leigh Centurions	11
Wakefield Trinity	10
St Helens	8
Wigan Warriors	6

OFFSIDE MARKERS - CONCEDED
Leigh Centurions	23
Salford Red Devils	21
St Helens	19
Wigan Warriors	15
Huddersfield Giants	14
Catalans Dragons	13
Wakefield Trinity	12
Castleford Tigers	10
Warrington Wolves	10
Widnes Vikings	10
Leeds Rhinos	8
Hull FC	7

OFFSIDE FROM KICK - AWARDED
Leigh Centurions	7
Hull FC	6
Leeds Rhinos	6
Salford Red Devils	6
Widnes Vikings	6
Wigan Warriors	6
Warrington Wolves	5
St Helens	4
Wakefield Trinity	4
Castleford Tigers	3
Catalans Dragons	3
Huddersfield Giants	1

OFFSIDE FROM KICK - CONCEDED
Huddersfield Giants	7
Salford Red Devils	7
Hull FC	6
Wakefield Trinity	6
Warrington Wolves	6
Widnes Vikings	6
St Helens	5
Catalans Dragons	4
Leeds Rhinos	4
Castleford Tigers	3
Wigan Warriors	3
Leigh Centurions	2

DISSENT - AWARDED
Leigh Centurions	4
St Helens	4
Widnes Vikings	4
Hull FC	3
Leeds Rhinos	3
Wakefield Trinity	3
Catalans Dragons	2
Huddersfield Giants	1
Salford Red Devils	1
Warrington Wolves	1
Castleford Tigers	0
Wigan Warriors	0

DISSENT - CONCEDED
Hull FC	5
Warrington Wolves	4
Catalans Dragons	3
Leeds Rhinos	3
Salford Red Devils	3
Huddersfield Giants	2
Castleford Tigers	1
Leigh Centurions	1
St Helens	1
Widnes Vikings	1
Wigan Warriors	1
Wakefield Trinity	0

CASTLEFORD TIGERS
SUPER LEAGUE XXII LEADERS

CARRIES

Jesse Sene-Lefao	414
Zak Hardaker	393
Grant Millington	347
Mike McMeeken	345
Junior Moors	327

OFFLOADS

Jesse Sene-Lefao	47
Mike McMeeken	45
Zak Hardaker	25
Grant Millington	25
Junior Moors	23

METRES

Zak Hardaker	3257
Jesse Sene-Lefao	2779
Mike McMeeken	2717
Greg Minikin	2668
Greg Eden	2624

TACKLES

Paul McShane	898
Adam Milner	779
Grant Millington	732
Mike McMeeken	726
Jesse Sene-Lefao	679

CLEAN BREAKS

Greg Eden	47
Greg Minikin	24
Ben Roberts	20
Zak Hardaker	16
Jake Webster	15

TACKLE BUSTS

Zak Hardaker	126
Ben Roberts	101
Greg Eden	67
Mike McMeeken	67
Jesse Sene-Lefao	57

MARKER TACKLES

Paul McShane	165
Mike McMeeken	135
Adam Milner	134
Grant Millington	120
Matt Cook	111

TRY ASSISTS

Luke Gale	20
Paul McShane	19
Michael Shenton	19
Zak Hardaker	18
Ben Roberts	12

TOTAL OPTA INDEX

Zak Hardaker	16279
Mike McMeeken	14418
Greg Eden	13645
Jesse Sene-Lefao	13457
Paul McShane	13264

CATALANS DRAGONS
SUPER LEAGUE XXII LEADERS

CARRIES

Sam Moa	307
Vincent Duport	264
Remi Casty	249
Benjamin Garcia	222
Julian Bousquet	221

OFFLOADS

Krisnan Inu	21
Sam Moa	20
Julian Bousquet	19
Mickael Simon	16
Remi Casty	14

METRES

Sam Moa	2100
Remi Casty	1687
Vincent Duport	1590
Tony Gigot	1578
Julian Bousquet	1544

TACKLES

Paul Aiton	709
Remi Casty	623
Sam Moa	523
Julian Bousquet	501
Benjamin Garcia	463

CLEAN BREAKS

Richie Myler	19
Krisnan Inu	12
Vincent Duport	8
Luke Walsh	7
Brayden Wiliame	7

TACKLE BUSTS

Tony Gigot	66
Krisnan Inu	64
Richie Myler	48
Remi Casty	35
Brayden Wiliame	26

MARKER TACKLES

Remi Casty	126
Paul Aiton	105
Sam Moa	89
Julian Bousquet	73
Benjamin Garcia	73

TRY ASSISTS

Luke Walsh	20
Richie Myler	17
Tony Gigot	5
Paul Aiton	3
Thomas Bosc	3

TOTAL OPTA INDEX

Remi Casty	9565
Richie Myler	8890
Sam Moa	8701
Tony Gigot	8450
Paul Aiton	8220

HUDDERSFIELD GIANTS
SUPER LEAGUE XXII LEADERS

CARRIES

Jermaine McGillvary	446
Sebastine Ikahihifo	376
Alex Mellor	309
Ryan Hinchcliffe	308
Paul Clough	290

OFFLOADS

Sebastine Ikahihifo	73
Jermaine McGillvary	17
Lee Gaskell	16
Kruise Leeming	15
Alex Mellor	14

METRES

Jermaine McGillvary	3883
Sebastine Ikahihifo	2795
Darnell McIntosh	2296
Alex Mellor	2235
Paul Clough	2090

TACKLES

Ryan Hinchcliffe	1021
Kruise Leeming	900
Sebastine Ikahihifo	724
Paul Clough	693
Shannon Wakeman	671

CLEAN BREAKS

Jermaine McGillvary	23
Darnell McIntosh	15
Lee Gaskell	14
Ryan Hinchcliffe	10
Jake Mamo	10

TACKLE BUSTS

Sebastine Ikahihifo	165
Jermaine McGillvary	74
Leroy Cudjoe	54
Ryan Hinchcliffe	47
Darnell McIntosh	42

MARKER TACKLES

Ryan Hinchcliffe	187
Kruise Leeming	182
Sebastine Ikahihifo	137
Paul Clough	129
Shannon Wakeman	119

TRY ASSISTS

Danny Brough	22
Kruise Leeming	15
Jordan Rankin	9
Leroy Cudjoe	8
Lee Gaskell	7

TOTAL OPTA INDEX

Sebastine Ikahihifo	14976
Ryan Hinchcliffe	14341
Jermaine McGillvary	13353
Danny Brough	11828
Kruise Leeming	11351

229

HULL F.C.
SUPER LEAGUE XXII LEADERS

CARRIES
Mahe Fonua	381
Jamie Shaul	336
Liam Watts	324
Scott Taylor	315
Mark Minichiello	300

OFFLOADS
Mahe Fonua	43
Jake Connor	34
Liam Watts	32
Albert Kelly	24
Mark Minichiello	21

METRES
Jamie Shaul	3199
Mahe Fonua	3189
Scott Taylor	2606
Josh Griffin	2348
Liam Watts	2343

TACKLES
Danny Houghton	1123
Danny Washbrook	806
Sika Manu	750
Mark Minichiello	700
Liam Watts	697

CLEAN BREAKS
Jamie Shaul	24
Albert Kelly	18
Mahe Fonua	17
Josh Griffin	17
Jake Connor	16

TACKLE BUSTS
Jamie Shaul	124
Mahe Fonua	72
Mark Minichiello	70
Albert Kelly	66
Carlos Tuimavave	58

MARKER TACKLES
Danny Houghton	191
Danny Washbrook	133
Liam Watts	128
Sika Manu	99
Mark Minichiello	96

TRY ASSISTS
Marc Sneyd	18
Jake Connor	16
Albert Kelly	14
Danny Houghton	11
Josh Griffin	5

TOTAL OPTA INDEX
Jamie Shaul	15241
Danny Houghton	14489
Albert Kelly	13613
Marc Sneyd	11898
Sika Manu	11785

LEEDS RHINOS
SUPER LEAGUE XXII LEADERS

CARRIES
Adam Cuthbertson	500
Ryan Hall	428
Kallum Watkins	375
Tom Briscoe	364
Mitch Garbutt	358

OFFLOADS
Adam Cuthbertson	121
Joel Moon	51
Kallum Watkins	40
Matt Parcell	28
Jamie Jones-Buchanan	24

METRES
Adam Cuthbertson	3446
Ryan Hall	3398
Mitch Garbutt	2977
Tom Briscoe	2632
Kallum Watkins	2604

TACKLES
Matt Parcell	1018
Jamie Jones-Buchanan	942
Adam Cuthbertson	890
Brad Singleton	687
Stevie Ward	681

CLEAN BREAKS
Tom Briscoe	18
Ryan Hall	14
Joel Moon	12
Matt Parcell	12
Adam Cuthbertson	11

TACKLE BUSTS
Tom Briscoe	77
Kallum Watkins	60
Matt Parcell	59
Adam Cuthbertson	57
Mitch Garbutt	56

MARKER TACKLES
Jamie Jones-Buchanan	180
Matt Parcell	170
Adam Cuthbertson	154
Brad Singleton	138
Stevie Ward	123

TRY ASSISTS
Danny McGuire	24
Matt Parcell	16
Rob Burrow	10
Joel Moon	9
Kallum Watkins	8

TOTAL OPTA INDEX
Adam Cuthbertson	17082
Matt Parcell	16622
Kallum Watkins	14031
Jamie Jones-Buchanan	13045
Ryan Hall	11591

LEIGH CENTURIONS
SUPER LEAGUE XXII LEADERS

CARRIES
Mitch Brown	281
Danny Tickle	267
Harrison Hansen	248
Lachlan Burr	230
Matty Dawson	224

OFFLOADS
Lachlan Burr	28
Ben Crooks	21
Ryan Hampshire	16
Gareth Hock	14
Sam Hopkins	11

METRES
Mitch Brown	2202
Matty Dawson	1822
Danny Tickle	1749
Harrison Hansen	1631
Jamie Acton	1577

TACKLES
Danny Tickle	684
Atelea Vea	602
Sam Hopkins	547
Eloi Pelissier	546
Harrison Hansen	530

CLEAN BREAKS
Matty Dawson	19
Ben Crooks	13
Ryan Hampshire	8
Sam Hopkins	7
Ben Reynolds	6

TACKLE BUSTS
Ben Crooks	46
Matty Dawson	45
Atelea Vea	32
Mitch Brown	24
Sam Hopkins	24

MARKER TACKLES
Danny Tickle	130
Sam Hopkins	123
Eloi Pelissier	121
Lachlan Burr	93
Glenn Stewart	90

TRY ASSISTS
Josh Drinkwater	12
Ryan Hampshire	6
Micky Higham	6
Ben Reynolds	5
Ben Crooks	4

TOTAL OPTA INDEX
Danny Tickle	9521
Atelea Vea	8477
Harrison Hansen	7891
Mitch Brown	7875
Sam Hopkins	7804

SALFORD RED DEVILS
SUPER LEAGUE XXII LEADERS

CARRIES
Kris Welham	403
Greg Johnson	319
Josh Jones	319
Robert Lui	318
Craig Kopczak	316

OFFLOADS
Josh Jones	41
Greg Johnson	30
Robert Lui	26
Ben Murdoch-Masila	22
Kris Welham	19

METRES
Kris Welham	2869
Greg Johnson	2507
Junior Sa'u	2449
Craig Kopczak	2189
Robert Lui	2172

TACKLES
Craig Kopczak	772
Logan Tomkins	682
George Griffin	659
Lama Tasi	640
Olsi Krasniqi	621

CLEAN BREAKS
Robert Lui	23
Greg Johnson	21
Junior Sa'u	18
Kris Welham	16
Niall Evalds	13

TACKLE BUSTS
Josh Jones	104
Robert Lui	77
Greg Johnson	66
Ben Murdoch-Masila	55
Kris Welham	52

MARKER TACKLES
George Griffin	147
Craig Kopczak	128
Olsi Krasniqi	95
Ben Murdoch-Masila	94
Logan Tomkins	89

TRY ASSISTS
Robert Lui	23
Gareth O'Brien	14
Junior Sa'u	10
Michael Dobson	9
Todd Carney	8

TOTAL OPTA INDEX
Robert Lui	13590
Josh Jones	11490
Ben Murdoch-Masila	10792
Craig Kopczak	10745
Kris Welham	10148

ST HELENS
SUPER LEAGUE XXII LEADERS

CARRIES
Alex Walmsley	525
Zeb Taia	458
Tom Makinson	403
Mark Percival	368
Luke Thompson	307

OFFLOADS
Zeb Taia	52
Alex Walmsley	38
Mark Percival	30
Kyle Amor	26
Tom Makinson	23

METRES
Alex Walmsley	4256
Tom Makinson	3217
Zeb Taia	3136
Mark Percival	2879
Regan Grace	2488

TACKLES
Jon Wilkin	1072
James Roby	1000
Morgan Knowles	822
Zeb Taia	792
Luke Thompson	728

CLEAN BREAKS
Mark Percival	32
Theo Fages	21
Regan Grace	19
Tom Makinson	11
James Roby	11

TACKLE BUSTS
Mark Percival	127
Alex Walmsley	80
Tom Makinson	73
Regan Grace	66
Theo Fages	50

MARKER TACKLES
Jon Wilkin	229
James Roby	184
Morgan Knowles	178
Luke Thompson	149
Luke Douglas	135

TRY ASSISTS
Theo Fages	14
Mark Percival	13
Jonny Lomax	11
James Roby	11
Matty Smith	10

TOTAL OPTA INDEX
James Roby	17098
Alex Walmsley	15248
Mark Percival	14509
Zeb Taia	14469
Jon Wilkin	12683

WAKEFIELD TRINITY
SUPER LEAGUE XXII LEADERS

CARRIES
David Fifita	389
Mason Caton-Brown	335
Tinirau Arona	330
Ben Jones-Bishop	327
Bill Tupou	324

OFFLOADS
Craig Huby	50
David Fifita	26
Bill Tupou	26
Reece Lyne	19
Dean Hadley	17

METRES
David Fifita	3025
Bill Tupou	3025
Ben Jones-Bishop	2881
Mason Caton-Brown	2798
Craig Huby	2172

TACKLES
Tinirau Arona	850
Matty Ashurst	784
Danny Kirmond	611
Dean Hadley	600
David Fifita	598

CLEAN BREAKS
Ben Jones-Bishop	30
Mason Caton-Brown	22
Bill Tupou	21
Scott Grix	17
Sam Williams	8

TACKLE BUSTS
David Fifita	103
Jacob Miller	54
Mason Caton-Brown	53
Scott Grix	52
Bill Tupou	47

MARKER TACKLES
Matty Ashurst	175
Danny Kirmond	140
Tinirau Arona	132
Dean Hadley	117
Kyle Wood	114

TRY ASSISTS
Liam Finn	17
Sam Williams	17
Scott Grix	13
Jacob Miller	13
Kyle Wood	6

TOTAL OPTA INDEX
Matty Ashurst	13887
David Fifita	13504
Tinirau Arona	12083
Bill Tupou	11350
Scott Grix	11034

Super League XXII - Opta Analysis

WARRINGTON WOLVES
SUPER LEAGUE XXII LEADERS

WIDNES VIKINGS
SUPER LEAGUE XXII LEADERS

WIGAN WARRIORS
SUPER LEAGUE XXII LEADERS

CARRIES			CARRIES			CARRIES	
Jack Hughes	260		Charly Runciman	252		Liam Farrell	397
Chris Hill	258		Jack Buchanan	243		Tom Davies	384
Ashton Sims	251		Hep Cahill	238		George Williams	364
Tom Lineham	245		Chris Houston	201		Willie Isa	337
Matthew Russell	239		Corey Thompson	194		Anthony Gelling	335

OFFLOADS			OFFLOADS			OFFLOADS	
Ryan Atkins	38		Chris Bridge	24		George Williams	59
Ashton Sims	28		Charly Runciman	21		Anthony Gelling	45
Daryl Clark	22		Hep Cahill	20		John Bateman	40
Mike Cooper	22		Gil Dudson	17		Sean O'Loughlin	35
Stefan Ratchford	20		Corey Thompson	15		Liam Farrell	22

METRES			METRES			METRES	
Chris Hill	2058		Charly Runciman	1764		Tom Davies	3359
Matthew Russell	2020		Jack Buchanan	1673		Liam Farrell	3109
Ryan Atkins	1890		Corey Thompson	1628		Anthony Gelling	2627
Tom Lineham	1888		Hep Cahill	1626		Willie Isa	2282
Stefan Ratchford	1824		Chris Houston	1410		George Williams	2269

TACKLES			TACKLES			TACKLES	
Daryl Clark	642		Matt Whitley	691		Willie Isa	855
Jack Hughes	634		Chris Houston	684		Liam Farrell	772
Mike Cooper	615		Hep Cahill	616		Sam Powell	771
Ashton Sims	589		Gil Dudson	510		Ryan Sutton	674
Joe Westerman	557		Jack Buchanan	497		Taulima Tautai	655

CLEAN BREAKS			CLEAN BREAKS			CLEAN BREAKS	
Tom Lineham	16		Danny Craven	10		Liam Marshall	28
Ryan Atkins	10		Charly Runciman	10		Tom Davies	23
Rhys Evans	9		Corey Thompson	9		Joe Burgess	17
Stefan Ratchford	9		Rhys Hanbury	7		George Williams	15
Matthew Russell	8		Ryan Ince	7		Oliver Gildart	14

TACKLE BUSTS			TACKLE BUSTS			TACKLE BUSTS	
Stefan Ratchford	52		Corey Thompson	67		George Williams	79
Andre Savelio	52		Rhys Hanbury	41		Liam Marshall	65
Daryl Clark	49		Charly Runciman	32		Tom Davies	57
Joe Westerman	49		Joe Mellor	31		Liam Farrell	45
Ryan Atkins	45		Ryan Ince	30		Morgan Escare	44

MARKER TACKLES			MARKER TACKLES			MARKER TACKLES	
Ashton Sims	120		Hep Cahill	132		Willie Isa	171
Jack Hughes	110		Matt Whitley	127		Liam Farrell	151
Andre Savelio	95		Chris Houston	105		Sam Powell	141
Joe Westerman	91		Jay Chapelhow	99		Taulima Tautai	139
Chris Hill	90		Gil Dudson	91		Ryan Sutton	124

TRY ASSISTS			TRY ASSISTS			TRY ASSISTS	
Kurt Gidley	14		Tom Gilmore	8		George Williams	29
Declan Patton	12		Charly Runciman	7		Thomas Leuluai	11
Stefan Ratchford	12		Lloyd White	6		Sean O'Loughlin	7
Kevin Brown	6		Chris Bridge	5		Sam Powell	7
Ryan Atkins	2		Jordan Johnstone	5		Sam Tomkins	7

TOTAL OPTA INDEX			TOTAL OPTA INDEX			TOTAL OPTA INDEX	
Jack Hughes	9587		Hep Cahill	8488		Liam Farrell	14334
Daryl Clark	9087		Chris Houston	8450		George Williams	12464
Chris Hill	9018		Matt Whitley	8227		Willie Isa	11713
Ashton Sims	8689		Corey Thompson	7226		Tom Davies	10494
Kurt Gidley	8611		Jack Buchanan	7183		Liam Marshall	9938

CHAMPIONSHIP 2017
Club by Club

BATLEY BULLDOGS

DATE	FIXTURE	RESULT	SCORERS	LGE	ATT
4/2/17	Toulouse (a)	L44-6	t:Leak g:Walker	10th	1,623
12/2/17	Halifax (h)	W24-6	t:Smeaton,Bretherton,Manning,Chandler g:Walker(3),Southernwood	9th	900
19/2/17	Featherstone (h)	L6-32	t:Brambani g:Walker	10th	1,385
26/2/17	Sheffield (a)	W10-54	t:Leak,Day(2),Holmes(2),Reittie(2),Brambani,Hallett,Hayward g:Southernwood(7)	7th	662
5/3/17	Swinton (h)	W22-18	t:Scott(2),Hallett(2) g:Southernwood(3)	6th	726
12/3/17	Bradford (a)	L44-22	t:Leak,Farrell,Smeaton,Holmes g:Brambani(3)	7th	4,478
18/3/17	Toulouse (a) (CCR4) ●	W16-34	t:Smeaton(2),Cowling,Scott,Brown,Manning g:Walker(5)	N/A	150
26/3/17	Oldham (h)	W50-10	t:Scott,Leak(2),Hayward(2),Walker,Farrell,Smeaton,Gledhill g:Walker(7)	5th	761
2/4/17	Hull KR (a)	L50-16	t:Brown,Reittie,Manning g:Walker,Brambani	6th	6,815
9/4/17	Rochdale (h)	W38-36	t:Hallett(2),Smeaton(2),Maher,Ainscough(2),Lillycrop g:Brambani(3)	6th	718
14/4/17	Dewsbury (a)	L20-4	t:Hayward	6th	1,211
17/4/17	London Broncos (h)	L4-42	t:Day	6th	587
23/4/17	Dewsbury (a) (CCR5)	L23-22 (aet)	t:Hallett(2),Lillycrop,Brambani g:Southernwood(3)	N/A	962
30/4/17	Halifax (a)	L40-22	t:Cowling,Hitchcox,Rowe,Leak g:Southernwood(3)	6th	1,488
7/5/17	Hull KR (h)	L4-68	t:Hayward	7th	1,885
21/5/17	Oldham (a) ●●	W28-48	t:Cowling,Farrell,Leak,Gledhill,Reittie,Brambani,Harrison,Lillycrop g:Southernwood(8)	7th	578
28/5/17	Dewsbury (SB) ●●●	L12-13	t:Cowling,Reittie,Harrison	7th	N/A
4/6/17	Toulouse (h)	L20-28	t:Reittie(2),Ainscough g:Brambani(4)	7th	627
11/6/17	Swinton (a)	W12-26	t:Ainscough,Day,Leak,Cowling,Smeaton g:Walker(3)	7th	569
18/6/17	Sheffield (h)	W70-12	t:Reittie(4),Brambani(2),Scott,Walker(2),Farrell(2) g:Walker(13)	6th	2,106
25/6/17	Rochdale (a)	W14-24	t:Gledhill,Ainscough,Leak g:Walker(6)	6th	604
2/7/17	Featherstone (a)	L42-14	t:Day,Reittie,Ainscough g:Walker	6th	2,275
9/7/17	Dewsbury (h)	W36-20	t:Manning,Crookes,Reittie(2),Brambani,Farrell g:Walker(6)	6th	1,226
16/7/17	Bradford (h)	W23-16	t:Bretherton,Walker,Scott(2) g:Walker(3) fg:Brambani	6th	1,726
23/7/17	London Broncos (a)	L58-4	t:Brown	6th	879
6/8/17	Swinton (h) (CS)	W62-10	t:Bretherton(2),Reittie(2),Ainscough,Smeaton,Davey(2),Scott(2),Farrell,Brown g:Walker(7)	2nd(CS)	544
13/8/17	Rochdale (a) (CS)	W14-34	t:Scott(2),Ainscough,Bretherton(2),Crookes g:Walker(5)	2nd(CS)	453
20/8/17	Oldham (h) (CS)	D22-22	t:Crookes,Manning,Brambani,Scott g:Walker(3)	2nd(CS)	675
28/8/17	Bradford (a) (CS)	W18-44	t:Leak(3),Harrison(3),Day,Brambani g:Walker(6)	2nd(CS)	2,609
3/9/17	Dewsbury (h) (CS)	W38-0	t:Reittie(4),Manning,Rowe g:Walker(5)	2nd(CS)	906
9/9/17	Toulouse (a) (CS)	L56-14	t:Reittie,Hill,Harrison g:Brambani	2nd(CS)	868
17/9/17	Sheffield (h) (CS)	W34-18	t:Manning,Chandler,Ainscough,Leak(2),Bretherton g:Scott(5)	2nd(CS)	650
24/9/17	Sheffield (h) (CSSF)	L26-28	t:Manning,Harrison(2),Chandler,Brambani g:Walker(3)	N/A	550

● Played at Stade Arnaune ●● Played at Manchester Regional Arena ●●● Played at Bloomfield Road, Blackpool

		APP		TRIES		GOALS		FG		PTS	
	D.O.B.	ALL	Ch	ALL	Ch	ALL	Ch	ALL	Ch	ALL	Ch
Shaun Ainscough	27/11/89	24	15	9	6	0	0	0	0	36	24
Dominic Brambani	10/5/85	29	21	10	6	12	11	1	1	65	47
Alex Bretherton	5/12/82	12(9)	9(6)	7	2	0	0	0	0	28	8
James Brown	6/5/88	4(17)	3(14)	4	2	0	0	0	0	16	8
Joe Chandler	2/11/88	3(11)	1(7)	3	1	0	0	0	0	12	4
Danny Cowling	20/12/92	14(1)	11	5	4	0	0	0	0	20	16
Jason Crookes	21/4/90	13	6	3	1	0	0	0	0	12	4
James Davey	21/8/89	6(18)	5(12)	2	0	0	0	0	0	8	0
Brad Day	23/9/94	25(3)	20	6	5	0	0	0	0	24	20
Joel Farrell	15/3/94	21(5)	13(3)	7	6	0	0	0	0	28	24
Adam Gledhill	15/2/93	21(7)	14(4)	3	3	0	0	0	0	12	12
Macauley Hallett	27/11/95	13	12	7	5	0	0	0	0	28	20
James Harrison	15/6/96	11(11)	6(10)	8	2	0	0	0	0	32	8
Michael Hayward	2/9/88	12	10	5	5	0	0	0	0	20	20
Brad Hill	26/9/95	(5)	(3)	1	0	0	0	0	0	4	0
Jy Hitchcox	18/8/89	2	1	1	1	0	0	0	0	4	4
Tom Holmes	2/3/96	3(5)	3(5)	3	3	0	0	0	0	12	12
Alistair Leak	5/4/92	27(2)	17(2)	14	9	0	0	0	0	56	36
Tom Lillycrop	29/11/91	19(10)	13(8)	3	2	0	0	0	0	12	8
Will Maher	4/11/95	14(2)	9(2)	1	1	0	0	0	0	4	4
Dane Manning	15/4/89	31	21	9	3	0	0	0	0	36	12
Wayne Reittie	21/1/88	25	17	21	14	0	0	0	0	84	56
Alex Rowe	11/3/85	8(19)	7(12)	2	1	0	0	0	0	8	4
Dave Scott	8/6/93	31	21	12	6	5	0	0	0	58	24
Sam Smeaton	26/10/88	28	19	9	6	0	0	0	0	36	24
Cain Southernwood	4/5/92	12(5)	11(3)	0	0	25	22	0	0	50	44
Pat Walker	24/3/86	22	15	4	4	79	45	0	0	174	106

'Ch' totals include Championship regular season only; 'All' totals also include Championship Shield & Challenge Cup

Wayne Reittie

LEAGUE RECORD
Championship, before Super 8 split:
P23-W11-D0-L12 (6th)
F549, A663, Diff-114, 22 points.

After Championship Shield:
P30-W16-D1-L13 (2nd/Semi-Finalists)
F797, A801, Diff-4, 33 points.

CHALLENGE CUP
Round Five

ATTENDANCES
Best - v Sheffield (Ch - 2,106)
Worst - v Swinton (CS - 544)
Total (Championship/
Championship Shield only) - 15,972
Average (Championship/
Championship Shield only) - 998
(Down by 273 on 2016)

CLUB RECORDS
MATCH RECORDS

Highest score: 100-4 v Gateshead, 17/3/2010 **Highest score against:** 9-78 v Wakefield, 26/8/67 **Record attendance:** 23,989 v Leeds, 14/3/25
Tries: 5 Joe Oakland v Bramley, 19/12/1908; Tommy Brannan v Swinton, 17/1/20; Jim Wale v Bramley, 4/12/26; Jim Wale v Cottingham, 12/2/27;
Tommy Oldroyd v Highfield, 6/3/94; Ben Feehan v Halifax, 10/8/2008; Jermaine McGillvary v Whitehaven, 24/5/2009
Goals: 16 Gareth Moore v Gateshead, 17/3/2010 **Points:** 40 Gareth Moore v Gateshead, 17/3/2010

SEASON RECORDS
CAREER RECORDS

Tries: 30 Johnny Campbell 2010 **Goals:** 144 Barry Eaton 2004 **Points:** 308 Richard Price 1997
Tries: 142 Craig Lingard 1998-2008 **Goals:** 463 Wharton 'Wattie' Davies 1897-1912 **Points:** 1,297 Wharton 'Wattie' Davies 1897-1912
Appearances: 421 Wharton 'Wattie' Davies 1897-1912

BRADFORD BULLS

DATE	FIXTURE	RESULT	SCORERS	LGE	ATT
5/2/17	Hull KR (a)	L54-24	t:Kirk,Oakes,Ryan,Macani g:Thomas(4)	12th	8,817
12/2/17	Rochdale (h)	L14-22	t:Thomas,Bentley g:Thomas(3)	12th	4,051
19/2/17	Swinton (a)	W28-35	t:Ryan(3),Thomas,Oakes,Mendeika g:Thomas(5) fg:Thomas	12th	1,193
26/2/17	Toulouse (h)	W29-22	t:Macani,Bentley,Ryan,Moore,Oakes g:Thomas(4) fg:Thomas	12th	4,151
5/3/17	London Broncos (a)	L42-12	t:Larroyer,Roche g:Thomas(2)	12th	1,120
12/3/17	Batley (h)	W44-22	t:Oakes(2),Larroyer,Bentley,Ryan,Campbell(2),Thomas g:Thomas(6)	12th	4,478
19/3/17	Featherstone (h) (CCR4)	L13-21	t:Hodgson,Campbell g:Keyes(2) fg:Keyes	N/A	2,458
26/3/17	Dewsbury (h)	W56-18	t:Wilkinson,Murray,Caro,Macani(2),L Smith,Magrin(2),Roche,Oakes g:Keyes(5),Lilley(2),Caro	12th	4,136
2/4/17	Oldham (a)	L26-22	t:L Smith,Bentley,Ryan,Keyes g:Lilley(3)	12th	1,691
9/4/17	Sheffield (h)	W48-16	t:Ryan,Bentley(4),Oakes,Murray,Campbell g:Thomas(8)	12th	4,126
14/4/17	Halifax (h)	L12-22	t:Macani,Ryan g:Thomas(2)	12th	4,871
17/4/17	Featherstone (a)	L44-18	t:Oakes(2),Caro g:Thomas(3)	12th	3,112
29/4/17	Toulouse (a)	L60-4	t:Davies	12th	2,312
7/5/17	Sheffield (a)	L52-16	t:Thomas,Campbell,Hodgson g:Keyes(2)	12th	1,437
21/5/17	London Broncos (h)	L12-56	t:C Smith,Campbell g:Thomas(2)	12th	3,633
27/5/17	Hull KR (SB) ●	L19-20	t:Bentley,Chisholm,Ryan g:Thomas(3) fg:Chisholm	12th	N/A
4/6/17	Dewsbury (a)	L38-12	t:Macani,Bentley g:Thomas(2)	12th	1,975
11/6/17	Featherstone (h)	L12-36	t:Roche,Bentley g:Thomas(2)	12th	3,931
18/6/17	Rochdale (a)	L28-14	t:Bentley,Chapelhow g:Thomas(3)	12th	1,230
25/6/17	Oldham (h)	W47-12	t:Ryan(4),Bentley(2),Chamberlain(2),Mendeika g:Thomas(5) fg:Thomas	12th	3,708
2/7/17	Halifax (a)	L20-18	t:Halafihi,Ryan,Chapelhow g:Thomas(3)	12th	3,142
9/7/17	Hull KR (h)	L10-42	t:Kirk,Aston g:Thomas	12th	4,937
16/7/17	Batley (a)	L23-16	t:Keyes,Chamberlain,Macani g:Thomas(2)	12th	1,726
23/7/17	Swinton (a)	L6-16	t:Sironen g:Aston	12th	3,291
6/8/17	Toulouse (h) (CS)	L10-26	t:Macani,Peltier g:L Smith	8th(CS)	2,753
13/8/17	Oldham (a) (CS)	W16-20	t:Rickett,Moore,Bentley,Aston g:L Smith(2)	8th(CS)	853
20/8/17	Swinton (a) (CS)	W16-30	t:Bentley(2),Halafihi,Oledzki,Hallas g:Aston(5)	8th(CS)	660
28/8/17	Batley (h) (CS)	L18-44	t:Hallas,Kirk,Macani g:Aston(3)	8th(CS)	2,609
3/9/17	Sheffield (a) (CS)	W18-32	t:Halafihi,Caro(3),Macani,L Smith g:Aston(4)	8th(CS)	896
10/9/17	Dewsbury (a) (CS)	W12-16	t:Aston,Peltier,L Smith g:Aston(2)	8th(CS)	1,369
17/9/17	Rochdale (h) (CS)	W72-16	t:Bentley,Halafihi,Kirk,Hallas,Oakes,Ryan(2),Caro,Keyes,Peltier(2),Moore,Aston g:Aston(9),Caro	8th(CS)	3,604

● Played at Bloomfield Road, Blackpool

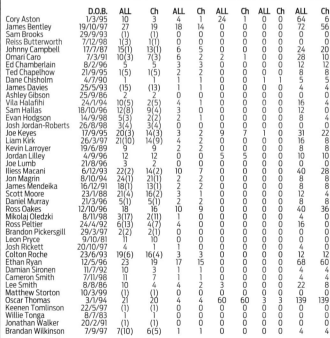

		APP		TRIES		GOALS		FG		PTS	
	D.O.B.	ALL	Ch	ALL	Ch	ALL	Ch	ALL	Ch	ALL	Ch
Cory Aston	1/3/95	10	3	4	1	24	1	0	0	64	6
James Bentley	19/10/97	27	19	18	14	0	0	0	0	72	56
Sam Brooks	29/9/93	(1)	(1)	0	0	0	0	0	0	0	0
Reiss Butterworth	7/12/98	1(3)	1(1)	0	0	0	0	0	0	0	0
Johnny Campbell	17/7/87	15(1)	13(1)	6	5	0	0	0	0	24	20
Omari Caro	7/3/91	10(3)	7(3)	6	2	2	1	0	0	28	10
Ed Chamberlain	8/2/96	5	5	3	3	0	0	0	0	12	12
Ted Chapelhow	21/9/95	1(5)	1(5)	2	2	0	0	0	0	8	8
Dane Chisholm	4/7/90	1	1	1	1	0	0	1	1	5	5
James Davies	25/5/93	(15)	(13)	1	1	0	0	0	0	4	4
Ashley Gibson	25/9/86	2	2	0	0	0	0	0	0	0	0
Vila Halafihi	24/1/94	10(5)	2(5)	4	1	0	0	0	0	16	4
Sam Hallas	18/10/96	12(8)	9(4)	3	0	0	0	0	0	12	0
Evan Hodgson	14/9/98	5(3)	2(2)	2	1	0	0	0	0	8	4
Josh Jordan-Roberts	26/8/98	3(4)	3(4)	0	0	0	0	0	0	0	0
Joe Keyes	17/9/95	20(3)	14(3)	3	2	9	7	1	0	31	22
Liam Kirk	26/3/97	21(10)	14(9)	4	2	0	0	0	0	16	8
Kevin Larroyer	19/6/89	9	9	2	2	0	0	0	0	8	8
Jordan Lilley	4/9/96	12	12	0	0	5	5	0	0	10	10
Joe Lumb	21/8/96	3	2	0	0	0	0	0	0	0	0
Iliess Macani	6/12/93	22(2)	14(2)	10	7	0	0	0	0	40	28
Jon Magrin	8/10/94	24(1)	21(1)	2	2	0	0	0	0	8	8
James Mendeika	16/12/91	18(1)	13(1)	2	2	0	0	0	0	8	8
Scott Moore	23/1/88	21(4)	16(2)	3	1	0	0	0	0	12	4
Daniel Murray	21/3/96	5(1)	5(1)	2	2	0	0	0	0	8	8
Ross Oakes	12/10/96	18	16	10	9	0	0	0	0	40	36
Mikolaj Oledzki	8/11/98	3(17)	2(11)	1	0	0	0	0	0	4	0
Ross Peltier	24/4/92	6(13)	4(7)	4	0	0	0	0	0	16	0
Brandon Pickersgill	29/3/97	2(2)	2(1)	0	0	0	0	0	0	0	0
Leon Pryce	9/10/81	11	10	0	0	0	0	0	0	0	0
Josh Rickett	20/10/97	4	1	1	0	0	0	0	0	4	0
Colton Roche	23/6/93	19(6)	16(4)	3	3	0	0	0	0	12	12
Ethan Ryan	12/5/96	23	19	17	15	0	0	0	0	68	60
Damian Sironen	11/7/92	10	3	1	1	0	0	0	0	4	4
Cameron Smith	7/11/98	11	7	1	1	0	0	0	0	4	4
Lee Smith	8/8/86	10	4	4	2	3	0	0	0	22	8
Matthew Storton	10/3/99	(1)	(1)	0	0	0	0	0	0	0	0
Oscar Thomas	3/1/94	21	20	4	4	60	60	3	3	139	139
Keenen Tomlinson	22/5/97	(1)	(1)	0	0	0	0	0	0	0	0
Willie Tonga	8/7/83	1	1	0	0	0	0	0	0	0	0
Jonathan Walker	20/2/91	(1)	(1)	0	0	0	0	0	0	0	0
Brandan Wilkinson	7/9/97	7(10)	6(5)	1	1	0	0	0	0	4	4

'Ch' totals include Championship regular season only; 'All' totals also include Championship Shield & Challenge Cup

Ethan Ryan

LEAGUE RECORD
Championship, before Super 8 split:
P23-W6-D0-L17 (12th)
F500, A719, Diff-219, 0 points.
(12 points deducted for entering administration)

After Championship Shield:
P30-W11-D0-L19 (8th)
F698, A867, Diff-169, 10 points.
(12 points deducted for entering administration)

CHALLENGE CUP
Round Four

ATTENDANCES
Best - v Hull KR (Ch - 4,937)
Worst - v Featherstone (CC - 2,458)
Total (Championship/
Championship Shield only) - 54,279
Average (Championship/
Championship Shield only) - 3,877
(Down by 301 on 2016)

CLUB RECORDS	
MATCH RECORDS	**Highest score:** 98-4 v Toulouse, 19/4/2008 **Highest score against:** 6-84 v Wigan, 21/4/2014 **Record attendance:** 69,429 v Huddersfield, 14/3/53 **Tries:** 6 Eric Batten v Leeds, 15/9/45; Trevor Foster v Wakefield, 10/4/48; Steve McGowan v Barrow, 8/11/92; Lesley Vainikolo v Hull, 2/9/2005 **Goals:** 15 Iestyn Harris v Toulouse, 15/4/2008 **Points:** 36 John Woods v Swinton, 13/10/85
SEASON RECORDS	**Tries:** 63 Jack McLean 1951-52 **Goals:** 213 *(inc 5fg)* Henry Paul 2001 **Points:** 457 Henry Paul 2001
CAREER RECORDS	**Tries:** 261 Jack McLean 1950-56 **Goals:** 1,165 *(inc 25fg)* Paul Deacon 1998-2009 **Points:** 2,605 Paul Deacon 1998-2009 **Appearances:** 588 Keith Mumby 1973-90; 1992-93

DEWSBURY RAMS

DATE	FIXTURE	RESULT	SCORERS	LGE	ATT
5/2/17	Rochdale (a)	L46-0		11th	718
12/2/17	Swinton (h)	L6-8	t:Glover g:Sykes	11th	802
18/2/17	Toulouse (a)	L56-2	g:Sykes	11th	1,438
26/2/17	London Broncos (h)	L6-20	t:Barnes g:Sykes	11th	678
12/3/17	Hull KR (h)	L6-48	t:Hirst g:Sykes	11th	2,477
17/3/17	Newcastle (h) (CCR4)	W36-8	t:Sykes,Ollett(2),Douglas,Morton,Glover g:Sykes(6)	N/A	425
26/3/17	Bradford (a)	L56-18	t:Crookes,Glover,Alex Brown g:Sykes(3)	11th	4,136
2/4/17	Featherstone (h)	L6-38	t:Teanby g:Sykes	11th	1,232
9/4/17	Halifax (a)	L34-6	t:Speakman g:Sykes	11th	1,218
14/4/17	Batley (h)	W20-4	t:Glover,Morton g:Glover(6)	11th	1,211
17/4/17	Sheffield (a)	L48-12	t:Aaron Brown,Douglas g:Glover(2)	11th	482
23/4/17	Batley (h) (CCR5)	W23-22		N/A	962
		(aet)	t:Guzdek(2),Sykes,Aaron Brown g:Sykes(3) fg:Fairhurst		
30/4/17	Oldham (h)	L24-28	t:Kain,Ward,Sykes,Glover g:Sykes(4)	11th	691
7/5/17	Halifax (h)	L18-36	t:Igbinedion,Day,Glover,Morton g:Glover	11th	718
12/5/17	Wakefield (h) (CCR6)	L6-54	t:Aaron Brown g:Glover	N/A	2,125
20/5/17	Featherstone (a)	L52-10	t:Fairhurst,Squires g:Glover	11th	2,038
28/5/17	Batley (SB) ●	W12-13	t:Aaron Brown g:Glover(4) fg:Sykes	11th	N/A
4/6/17	Bradford (h)	W38-12	t:Glover(2),Day,Squires(2),Walshaw,Hallett g:Glover(5)	11th	1,975
11/6/17	London Broncos (a)	L52-8	t:Potts,Glover	11th	854
18/6/17	Hull KR (a)	L64-11	t:Morton,Potts g:Sykes fg:Fairhurst	11th	6,772
21/6/17	Oldham (a)	W16-20	t:Morton,Ollett,Moore g:Sykes(4)	11th	575
25/6/17	Toulouse (h)	W34-22	t:Walshaw(2),Hallett,Aaron Brown,Sheriffe g:Sykes(7)	10th	626
2/7/17	Rochdale (h)	W40-10	t:Spicer(2),T Adamson,Morton,Hallett(2),Moore g:Sykes(6)	8th	775
9/7/17	Batley (a)	L36-20	t:Ward,Alex Brown,Morton,Moore g:Sykes(2)	9th	1,226
16/7/17	Swinton (a)	W20-42	t:Speakman,Moore(2),Aaron Brown(2),Sykes,Day g:Sykes(6),Morton	8th	1,002
23/7/17	Sheffield (h)	W28-18	t:Guzdek,Walshaw,Speakman,Glover g:Sykes(4),Glover(2)	8th	794
6/8/17	Rochdale (h) (CS)	W56-8	t:Glover(3),Potts(4),Hallett,Day(2),Guzdek g:Sykes(6)	4th(CS)	629
13/8/17	Toulouse (h) (CS)	W36-34	t:Sheriffe,Glover,Goudemand,Speakman,Ward,T Adamson g:Sykes(5),Glover	4th(CS)	628
20/8/17	Sheffield (a) (CS)	W28-35	t:Hallett,Glover,Speakman,Potts,Aaron Brown,Day g:Sykes(5) fg:Sykes	4th(CS)	363
28/8/17	Swinton (h) (CS)	L28-35	t:Potts,Speakman,Walshaw,Aaron Brown,Day g:Sykes(4)	4th(CS)	812
3/9/17	Batley (a) (CS)	L38-0		4th(CS)	906
10/9/17	Bradford (h) (CS)	L12-16	t:Speakman,Aaron Brown g:Sykes(2)	4th(CS)	1,369
17/9/17	Oldham (a) (CS)	W22-29	t:Squires(2),Day,Halliday g:Sykes(6) fg:Knowles	4th(CS)	429
23/9/17	Toulouse (a) (CSSF)	L36-22	t:Moore,Morton(2),Glover g:Sykes(3)	N/A	1,208

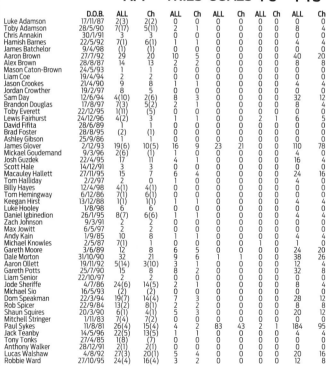

		APP		TRIES		GOALS		FG		PTS	
	D.O.B.	ALL	Ch	ALL	Ch	ALL	Ch	ALL	Ch	ALL	Ch
Luke Adamson	17/11/87	2(3)	2(2)	0	0	0	0	0	0	0	0
Toby Adamson	28/5/90	7(17)	5(11)	2	1	0	0	0	0	8	4
Chris Annakin	30/1/91	3	3	0	0	0	0	0	0	0	0
Hamish Barnes	22/5/92	7(1)	6(1)	1	1	0	0	0	0	4	4
James Batchelor	9/4/98	(1)	(1)	0	0	0	0	0	0	0	0
Aaron Brown	27/7/92	29	20	10	5	0	0	0	0	40	20
Alex Brown	28/8/87	14	13	2	2	0	0	0	0	8	8
Mason Caton-Brown	24/5/93	1	1	0	0	0	0	0	0	0	0
Liam Coe	19/4/94	2	2	0	0	0	0	0	0	0	0
Jason Crookes	21/4/90	9	8	1	1	0	0	0	0	4	4
Jordan Crowther	19/2/97	8	5	0	0	0	0	0	0	0	0
Sam Day	12/6/94	4(10)	2(6)	8	3	0	0	0	0	32	12
Brandon Douglas	17/8/97	7(3)	5(2)	2	1	0	0	0	0	8	4
Toby Everett	22/12/95	1(11)	(5)	0	0	0	0	0	0	0	0
Lewis Fairhurst	24/12/96	4(2)	3	1	1	0	0	0	2	1	6	5
David Fifita	28/6/89	1	1	0	0	0	0	0	0	0	0
Brad Foster	28/8/95	(2)	(1)	0	0	0	0	0	0	0	0
Ashley Gibson	25/9/86	1	1	0	0	0	0	0	0	0	0
James Glover	2/12/93	19(6)	10(5)	16	9	23	21	0	0	110	78
Mickael Goudemand	9/3/96	2(6)	(1)	1	0	0	0	0	0	4	0
Josh Guzdek	22/4/95	17	11	4	1	0	0	0	0	16	4
Scott Hale	14/12/91	3	3	0	0	0	0	0	0	0	0
Macauley Hallett	27/11/95	15	7	6	4	0	0	0	0	24	16
Tom Halliday	2/2/97	2	0	1	0	0	0	0	0	4	0
Billy Hayes	12/4/98	4(1)	4(1)	0	0	0	0	0	0	0	0
Tom Hemingway	6/12/86	7(1)	6(1)	0	0	0	0	0	0	0	0
Keegan Hirst	13/12/88	1(1)	1(1)	1	1	0	0	0	0	4	4
Luke Hooley	1/8/98	6	6	0	0	0	0	0	0	0	0
Daniel Igbinedion	26/1/95	8(7)	6(6)	1	1	0	0	0	0	4	4
Zach Johnson	9/3/91	2	2	0	0	0	0	0	0	0	0
Max Jowitt	6/5/97	2	2	0	0	0	0	0	0	0	0
Andy Kain	1/9/85	10	8	1	1	0	0	0	0	4	4
Michael Knowles	2/5/87	7(1)	1	0	0	0	0	1	0	1	0
Gareth Moore	3/6/89	12	8	6	5	0	0	0	0	24	20
Dale Morton	31/10/90	32	21	9	6	1	1	0	0	38	26
Aaron Ollett	19/11/92	5(14)	3(10)	3	1	0	0	0	0	12	4
Gareth Potts	25/7/90	15	8	8	2	0	0	0	0	32	8
Liam Senior	22/10/97	2	2	0	0	0	0	0	0	0	0
Jode Sheriffe	4/7/86	24(6)	14(5)	2	1	0	0	0	0	8	4
Michael Sio	16/5/93	(2)	(2)	0	0	0	0	0	0	0	0
Dom Speakman	22/3/94	19(7)	14(4)	7	3	0	0	0	0	28	12
Rob Spicer	22/9/84	13(2)	8(1)	2	2	0	0	0	0	8	8
Shaun Squires	20/3/90	6(1)	4(1)	5	3	0	0	0	0	20	12
Mitchell Stringer	1/11/83	7(4)	7(2)	0	0	0	0	0	0	0	0
Paul Sykes	11/8/81	26(4)	15(4)	4	2	83	43	2	1	184	95
Jack Teanby	14/5/96	22(5)	13(5)	1	1	0	0	0	0	4	4
Tony Tonks	27/4/85	1(8)	(7)	0	0	0	0	0	0	0	0
Anthony Walker	28/12/91	2(1)	2(1)	0	0	0	0	0	0	0	0
Lucas Walshaw	4/8/92	27(3)	20(1)	5	4	0	0	0	0	20	16
Robbie Ward	27/10/95	24(4)	16(4)	3	2	0	0	0	0	12	8

James Glover

LEAGUE RECORD
Championship, before Super 8 split:
P23-W8-D0-L15 (8th)
F388, A736, Diff-348, 16 points.

After Championship Shield:
P30-W12-D0-L18 (4th/Semi-Finalists)
F584, A917, Diff-333, 24 points.

CHALLENGE CUP
Round Six

ATTENDANCES
Best - v Hull KR (Ch - 2,477)
Worst - v Newcastle (CC - 425)
Total (Championship/
Championship Shield only) - 15,417
Average (Championship/
Championship Shield only) - 1,028
(Down by 54 on 2016)

● *Played at Bloomfield Road, Blackpool*

*'Ch' totals include Championship
regular season only; 'All' totals also include
Championship Shield & Challenge Cup*

CLUB RECORDS	
	Highest score: 90-5 v Blackpool, 4/4/93 **Highest score against:** 0-82 v Widnes, 30/11/86
MATCH RECORDS	**Record attendance:** 26,584 v Halifax, 30/10/20 *(Crown Flatt)*; 4,068 v Bradford, 6/4/2015 *(Tetley's Stadium)*
	Tries: 8 Dai Thomas v Liverpool, 13/4/1907
	Goals: 13 Greg Pearce v Blackpool Borough, 4/4/93; Francis Maloney v Hunslet, 25/3/2007 **Points:** 32 Les Holliday v Barrow, 11/9/94
SEASON RECORDS	**Tries:** 40 Dai Thomas 1906-07 **Goals:** 169 Barry Eaton 2000 **Points:** 394 Barry Eaton 2000
CAREER RECORDS	**Tries:** 144 Joe Lyman 1913-31 **Goals:** 863 Nigel Stephenson 1967-78; 1984-86 **Points:** 2,082 Nigel Stephenson 1967-78; 1984-86
	Appearances: 454 Joe Lyman 1913-31

FEATHERSTONE ROVERS

DATE	FIXTURE	RESULT	SCORERS	LGE	ATT
5/2/17	Halifax (a)	W26-32	t:Briscoe,Hardcastle(2),Handley,Briggs g:Hardman(2),Briggs(4)	5th	2,147
12/2/17	Oldham (h)	W8-6	t:Ulugia(2)	3rd	1,783
19/2/17	Batley (a)	W6-32	t:Hardman(2),Handley,Briscoe,Carlile g:Knowles(6)	2nd	1,385
26/2/17	Swinton (a)	W13-30	t:Wildie,Bostock,Walton,Handley g:Knowles(7)	2nd	850
5/3/17	Rochdale (h)	L9-10	t:Ulugia g:Knowles,Aston fg:Thackeray	2nd	1,839
12/3/17	Sheffield (a)	W22-47	t:Walton(2),Bostock,Handley,Ulugia,Thackeray(2),Briscoe g:Knowles(3),Briggs(2),Hardman(2) fg:Thackeray	2nd	1,017
19/3/17	Bradford (a) (CCR4)	W13-21	t:Hardcastle,Walton,Hardman g:Briggs(4) fg:Briggs	N/A	2,458
26/3/17	Toulouse (h)	L26-34	t:Mariano,Davies,Hardman,Ulugia(2) g:Hardman(3)	3rd	2,087
2/4/17	Dewsbury (a)	W6-38	t:Briscoe(2),Hardman,Wildie,Aston g:Aston(9)	3rd	1,232
9/4/17	London Broncos (h)	W38-18	t:Davies,Ulugia(2),Aston,Bostock,Briscoe g:Aston(7)	3rd	2,509
14/4/17	Hull KR (a)	L30-22	t:Davies,Duckworth,Thackeray g:Aston(5)	3rd	8,117
17/4/17	Bradford (h)	W44-18	t:Taulapapa,Hardcastle,Turner(2),Bostock,Aston(2),Griffin g:Aston(6)	3rd	3,112
23/4/17	Oldham (h) (CCR5)	W30-4	t:Hardcastle(2),Moore,Hardman,Lockwood,Davies g:Aston(3)	N/A	1,408
30/4/17	Sheffield (h)	W25-14	t:Wildie,Carlile,Turner,Ulugia g:Aston(4) fg:Aston	3rd	2,267
7/5/17	Rochdale (a)	W8-38	t:Hardcastle,Hardman(2),Knowles,Turner(2),Wildie,Taulapapa g:Aston(3)	2nd	766
11/5/17	Halifax (h) (CCR6)	W24-12	t:Davies,Turner(2),Hardcastle g:Aston(3) fg:Thackeray(2)	N/A	1,736
20/5/17	Dewsbury (h)	W52-10	t:Lockwood,Taulapapa,Hardcastle(2),Walton(2),Turner(2),Mariano,Ormondroyd g:Aston(6)	2nd	2,038
27/5/17	London Broncos (SB) ●	L16-42	t:Davies(2),Turner g:Aston(2)	4th	N/A
4/6/17	Hull KR (h)	D20-20	t:Taulapapa,Walton,Duckworth g:Knowles(2),Briggs(2)	4th	4,072
11/6/17	Bradford (h)	W12-36	t:Thackeray,Briggs,Hardcastle(2),Ormondroyd,Wildie g:Knowles(3),Briggs(3)	4th	3,931
16/6/17	Leeds (a) (CCQF)	L58-0		N/A	6,181
21/6/17	Swinton (a)	W36-2	t:Hardcastle(2),Wildie,Thackeray(2),Davies,Walton g:Johnson(2),Davies(2)	3rd	1,892
25/6/17	London Broncos (a)	L36-30	t:Baldwinson,Taulapapa,Mariano,Bostock,Wildie g:Hardman(5)	3rd	910
2/7/17	Batley (a)	W42-14	t:Turner(2),Baldwinson,Ormondroyd,Davies,Bostock,Hardman g:Hardman(7)	3rd	2,275
9/7/17	Oldham (a)	W14-32	t:Hardcastle,Ulugia,Lockwood,Turner,Briscoe,Thackeray g:Hardman(4)	3rd	851
16/7/17	Halifax (h)	L8-28	t:Taulapapa,Mariano	3rd	3,156
22/7/17	Toulouse (a)	L32-26	t:Thackeray,Briggs,Turner,Walton g:Hardman(5)	4th	2,417
5/8/17	Leigh (h) (S8-Q)	L12-38	t:Griffin,Taulapapa g:Hardman(2)	8th(S8-Q)	2,679
13/8/17	London Broncos (a) (S8-Q)	D32-32	t:Farrell,Davies(2),Briscoe(2),Ulugia g:Hardman(4)	7th(S8-Q)	926
20/8/17	Widnes (a) (S8-Q)	L58-10	t:Taulapapa,Lockwood g:Hardman	7th(S8-Q)	4,373
3/9/17	Hull KR (h) (S8-Q)	L18-30	t:Johnson(2),Mariano g:Hardman(3)	7th(S8-Q)	4,583
9/9/17	Catalans Dragons (a) (S8-Q)	L26-12	t:Brooks,Thackeray g:Johnson(2)	7th(S8-Q)	8,649
17/9/17	Warrington (h) (S8-Q)	L0-68		7th(S8-Q)	2,441
24/9/17	Halifax (a) (S8-Q)	W20-26	t:Davies,Briscoe,Mariano,Taulapapa g:Hardman(5)	7th(S8-Q)	2,057

● *Played at Bloomfield Road, Blackpool*

		APP		TRIES		GOALS		FG		PTS	
	D.O.B.	ALL	Ch	ALL	Ch	ALL	Ch	ALL	Ch	ALL	Ch
Cory Aston	1/3/95	11(1)	8(1)	4	4	49	43	1	1	115	103
Jordan Baldwinson	10/11/94	12(5)	10(4)	2	2	0	0	0	0	8	8
Andrew Bostock	25/2/85	13(8)	12(5)	6	6	0	0	0	0	24	24
Kyle Briggs	7/12/87	5(11)	(8)	3	3	15	11	1	0	43	34
Luke Briscoe	11/3/94	20	13	10	7	0	0	0	0	40	28
Sam Brooks	29/9/93	3(5)	1	1	0	0	0	0	0	4	0
Keal Carlile	20/3/90	31(2)	23	2	2	0	0	0	0	8	8
Luke Cooper	28/7/94	10(7)	6(3)	0	0	0	0	0	0	0	0
John Davies	8/1/91	31(2)	20(2)	12	7	2	2	0	0	52	32
Sam Day	12/6/94	(2)	0	0	0	0	0	0	0	0	0
Brett Delaney	26/10/85	(1)	(1)	0	0	0	0	0	0	0	0
James Duckworth	9/4/94	5	4	2	2	0	0	0	0	8	8
Connor Farrell	6/11/93	5		1		0		0		4	0
Darrell Griffin	19/6/81	11(19)	6(15)	2	1	0	0	0	0	8	4
Ash Handley	16/2/96	7	7	4	4	0	0	0	0	16	16
Josh Hardcastle	28/8/92	26(3)	16(2)	15	11	0	0	0	0	60	44
Ian Hardman	8/12/84	30	21	9	7	43	28	0	0	122	84
Daniel Igbinedion	26/1/95	(3)	(2)	0	0	0	0	0	0	0	0
Kyran Johnson	23/3/94	9	5	2	0	4	2	0	0	16	4
Michael Knowles	2/5/87	14	11	1	1	22	22	0	0	48	48
Bradley Knowles-Tagg	31/7/93	6(10)	5(4)	0	0	0	0	0	0	0	0
James Lockwood	21/3/86	23(4)	14(3)	4	2	0	0	0	0	16	8
Frankie Mariano	10/5/87	12(9)	9(5)	6	4	0	0	0	0	24	16
Richard Moore	2/2/81	16(13)	8(11)	1	0	0	0	0	0	4	0
Anthony Mullally	28/6/91	(1)	(1)	0	0	0	0	0	0	0	0
Mikolaj Oledzki	8/11/98	(2)	(2)	0	0	0	0	0	0	0	0
Jack Ormondroyd	7/11/91	3(13)	2(12)	3	3	0	0	0	0	12	12
Misi Taulapapa	25/1/82	23	13	9	6	0	0	0	0	36	24
Anthony Thackeray	19/2/86	30	22	9	8	0	0	4	2	40	34
Scott Turner	15/4/88	17	10	14	12	0	0	0	0	56	48
Chris Ulugia	15/1/92	22	18	11	10	0	0	0	0	44	40
Josh Walters	23/12/94	7(4)	5(3)	0	0	0	0	0	0	0	0
Jason Walton	13/6/90	16(1)	14(1)	9	8	0	0	0	0	36	32
Matty Wildie	25/10/90	24(10)	16(7)	7	7	0	0	0	0	28	28

Matty Wildie

'Ch' totals include Championship regular season only; 'All' totals also include Super 8s (Qualifiers) & Challenge Cup

LEAGUE RECORD
Championship, before Super 8 split:
P23-W15-D1-L7 (4th)
F687, A421, Diff+266, 31 points.

S8-Q: P7-W1-D1-L5 (7th)
F110, A272, Diff-162, 3 points.

CHALLENGE CUP
Quarter Finalists

ATTENDANCES
Best - v Hull KR (S8 - 4,583)
Worst - v Oldham (CC - 1,408)
Total (Championship/S8s only) - 36,733
Average (Championship/
S8s only) - 2,624
(Down by 31 on 2016)

CLUB RECORDS MATCH RECORDS	**Highest score:** 96-0 v Castleford Lock Lane, 8/2/2004 **Highest score against:** 14-80 v Bradford, 3/4/2005 **Record attendance:** 17,531 v St Helens, 21/3/59
	Tries: 6 Mike Smith v Doncaster, 13/4/68; Chris Bibb v Keighley, 17/9/89
	Goals: 13 Mark Knapper v Keighley, 17/9/89; Liam Finn v Hunslet Old Boys, 25/3/2012; Liam Finn v Swinton, 12/8/2012
	Points: 40 Martin Pearson v Whitehaven, 26/11/95
SEASON RECORDS	**Tries:** 48 Paul Newlove 1992-93 **Goals:** 183 *(inc 2fg)* Liam Finn 2012 **Points:** 436 Liam Finn 2012
CAREER RECORDS	**Tries:** 162 Don Fox 1953-66 **Goals:** 1,210 Steve Quinn 1975-88 **Points:** 2,654 Steve Quinn 1975-88 **Appearances:** 440 Jim Denton 1921-34

HALIFAX

DATE	FIXTURE	RESULT	SCORERS	LGE	ATT
5/2/17	Featherstone (h)	L26-32	t:Fairbank,Worrincy,Tangata,Murrell,Tyrer g:Tyrer(3)	8th	2,147
12/2/17	Batley (a)	L24-6	t:Saltonstall g:Tyrer	10th	900
19/2/17	Sheffield (h)	W42-16	t:O'Brien,Murrell,Johnston,Saltonstall(3),Ambler,Tyrer g:Tyrer(5)	7th	1,241
26/2/17	Rochdale (a)	W6-20	t:Barber,Tyrer,Worrincy g:Tyrer(4)	6th	854
5/3/17	Toulouse (h)	L10-12	g:Tyrer(3)	7th	1,271
12/3/17	London Broncos (h)	W19-6	t:Tyrer,Grix,G Moore g:Tyrer(3) fg:G Moore	6th	1,298
19/3/17	Hunslet (h) (CCR4)	W20-6	t:Barber,Butler,Worrincy g:Tyrer(4)	N/A	793
26/3/17	Hull KR (a)	L28-14	t:Grady,Saltonstall g:Tyrer(3)	7th	7,100
2/4/17	Swinton (h)	W38-28	t:Tyrer,Tangata,Saltonstall,E Morris,Grady,Fairbank g:Tyrer(7)	5th	1,501
9/4/17	Dewsbury (h)	W34-6	t:Saltonstall,Grix,Worrincy,Tyrer(2),Tangata g:Tyrer(5)	4th	1,218
14/4/17	Bradford (a)	W12-22	t:Saltonstall(2),Grady,Johnston g:Tyrer(3)	4th	4,871
17/4/17	Oldham (h)	W16-14	t:Johnston,Saltonstall g:Tyrer(4)	4th	1,341
23/4/17	Whitehaven (a) (CCR5)	W12-36	t:Tangata,Saltonstall,Woodburn-Hall,Grady,Kaye(2) g:Tyrer(6)	N/A	636
30/4/17	Batley (h)	W40-22	t:Saltonstall(2),Sharp(2),Murrell,Tyrer,B Moore,Woodburn-Hall g:Tyrer(4)	4th	1,488
7/5/17	Dewsbury (a)	W18-36	t:Tyrer(2),Saltonstall,Tangata,Heaton,Robinson,Barber g:Tyrer(4)	5th	718
11/5/17	Featherstone (a) (CCR6)	L24-12	t:Heaton,Johnston g:Tyrer(2)	N/A	1,736
21/5/17	Rochdale (h)	W28-2	t:Johnston,Tyrer,Sharp,Tangata,Grix g:Tyrer(4)	5th	1,424
28/5/17	Toulouse (SB) ●	L22-32	t:Tyrer(2),Worrincy,Woodburn-Hall g:Tyrer(3)	5th	N/A
4/6/17	London Broncos (a)	L34-6	t:Johnston g:Tyrer	5th	857
11/6/17	Sheffield (a)	W0-54	t:Woodburn-Hall(2),Tyrer,McGrath(3),Johnston,Wilkinson,E Morris,Douglas g:Tyrer(7)	5th	672
18/6/17	Oldham (a)	W12-30	t:Sharp(2),Douglas,B Moore,E Morris g:Tyrer(5)	5th	809
25/6/17	Swinton (a)	L13-12	t:Cahalane,Wood g:Tyrer(2)	5th	863
2/7/17	Bradford (h)	W20-18	t:Wood,Heaton,Murray g:Tyrer(4)	5th	3,142
8/7/17	Toulouse (a)	W8-16	t:Tyrer,Tangata,Johnston g:Tyrer(2)	4th	1,240
16/7/17	Featherstone (a)	W8-28	t:B Moore,Cahalane,Heaton,Worrincy g:Tyrer(6)	4th	3,156
23/7/17	Hull KR (h)	W28-6	t:Johnston,Heaton,Sharp,Sio g:Tyrer(6)	3rd	2,876
6/8/17	Hull KR (a) (S8-Q)	L26-22	t:Heaton(4) g:Tyrer(3)	6th(S8-Q)	7,706
13/8/17	Widnes (h) (S8-Q)	L12-36	t:Heaton(2) g:Tyrer(2)	8th(S8-Q)	2,291
19/8/17	Warrington (a) (S8-Q)	L22-8	t:Butler	8th(S8-Q)	8,353
3/9/17	Catalans Dragons (h) (S8-Q)	L0-24		8th(S8-Q)	1,853
10/9/17	London Broncos (a) (S8-Q)	L36-14	t:Tyrer,Cahalane,Worrincy g:Tyrer	8th(S8-Q)	794
15/9/17	Leigh (a) (S8-Q)	L40-6	t:Cahalane g:Tyrer	8th(S8-Q)	4,341
24/9/17	Featherstone (h) (S8-Q)	L20-26	t:Kaye,Cahalane,Worrincy,Heaton g:Tyrer(2)	8th(S8-Q)	2,057

● *Played at Bloomfield Road, Blackpool*

	D.O.B.	APP ALL	APP Ch	TRIES ALL	TRIES Ch	GOALS ALL	GOALS Ch	FG ALL	FG Ch	PTS ALL	PTS Ch
Luke Ambler	18/12/89	1(5)	1(4)	1	1	0	0	0	0	4	4
Ed Barber	26/4/90	18(10)	11(8)	3	2	0	0	0	0	12	8
Jake Bibby	17/6/96	3	3	0	0	0	0	0	0	0	0
Ryan Boyle	17/10/87	13(14)	11(10)	0	0	0	0	0	0	0	0
Chester Butler	10/3/95	7	2	3	0	0	0	0	0	12	0
Mitch Cahalane	5/5/89	32	23	5	2	0	0	0	0	20	8
William Calcott	16/12/97	(2)	0	0	0	0	0	0	0	0	0
Chris Cullimore	13/2/93	(1)	0	0	0	0	0	0	0	0	0
Brandon Douglas	17/8/97	2(9)	1(6)	2	2	0	0	0	0	8	8
Niall Evalds	26/8/93	1(1)	1(1)	0	0	0	0	0	0	0	0
Jacob Fairbank	4/3/90	20(5)	16(2)	2	2	0	0	0	0	8	8
Shane Grady	13/12/89	28	18	4	3	0	0	0	0	16	12
Simon Grix	28/9/85	26	20	3	3	0	0	0	0	12	12
Ben Heaton	12/3/90	17	11	12	4	0	0	0	0	48	16
Ben Johnston	8/3/92	25(4)	16(3)	9	8	0	0	0	0	36	32
Ben Kaye	19/12/88	16(8)	10(5)	3	0	0	0	0	0	12	0
Ryan Lannon	11/1/96	(4)	(4)	0	0	0	0	0	0	0	0
Alex Mammone	21/8/92	1(8)	(5)	0	0	0	0	0	0	0	0
Conor McGrath	14/8/96	4	4	3	3	0	0	0	0	12	12
Brandon Moore	27/7/96	14(10)	10(5)	3	3	0	0	0	0	12	12
Gareth Moore	3/6/89	4	3	1	1	0	0	1	1	5	5
Elliot Morris	4/1/96	9(21)	2(19)	3	0	0	0	0	0	12	12
Frazer Morris	22/2/97	(1)	0	0	0	0	0	0	0	0	0
Daniel Murray	21/3/96	6	6	1	1	0	0	0	0	4	4
Scott Murrell	5/9/85	31	23	3	3	0	0	0	0	12	12
Luke Nelmes	7/6/93	(2)	0	0	0	0	0	0	0	0	0
Adam O'Brien	11/7/93	2	2	1	1	0	0	0	0	4	4
Martyn Reilly	5/1/96	(2)	(1)	0	0	0	0	0	0	0	0
Connor Robinson	23/10/94	6(1)	4(1)	1	1	0	0	0	0	4	4
James Saltonstall	27/9/93	20	14	14	13	0	0	0	0	56	52
Will Sharp	12/5/86	27	21	6	6	0	0	0	0	24	24
Michael Sio	16/5/93	1(9)	(3)	1	1	0	0	0	0	4	4
Adam Tangata	17/3/91	16(6)	9(6)	7	6	0	0	0	0	28	24
Steve Tyrer	16/3/89	32	23	17	16	110	89	0	0	288	242
Jordan Walne	28/12/92	(2)	(2)	0	0	0	0	0	0	0	0
Matt Wilkinson	13/6/96	1(4)	1(4)	1	1	0	0	0	0	4	4
Connor Williams	29/8/98	1	0	0	0	0	0	0	0	0	0
Josh Wood	15/11/95	1(3)	1(3)	2	2	0	0	0	0	8	8
James Woodburn-Hall	2/2/95	17	13	5	4	0	0	0	0	20	16
Rob Worrincy	9/7/85	27	18	8	5	0	0	0	0	32	20

Steve Tyrer

LEAGUE RECORD
Championship, before Super 8 split:
P23-W16-D0-L7 (3rd)
F567, A357, Diff+210, 32 points.

S8-Q: P7-W0-D0-L7 (8th)
F82, A210, Diff-128, 0 points.

CHALLENGE CUP
Round Six

ATTENDANCES
Best - v Bradford (Ch - 3,142)
Worst - v Hunslet (CC - 793)
Total (Championship/S8s only) - 25,148
Average (Championship/
S8s only) - 1,796
(Up by 83 on 2016)

*'Ch' totals include Championship
regular season only; 'All' totals also include
Super 8s (Qualifiers) & Challenge Cup*

CLUB RECORDS	**Highest score:** 94-4 v Myton, 25/3/2012 **Highest score against:** 6-88 v Hull KR, 23/4/2006 **Record attendance:** 29,153 v Wigan, 21/3/59 *(Thrum Hall)*; 9,827 v Bradford, 12/3/2000 *(The Shay)*
MATCH RECORDS	**Tries:** 8 Keith Williams v Dewsbury, 9/11/57 **Goals:** 14 Bruce Burton v Hunslet, 27/8/72 **Points:** 32 John Schuster v Doncaster, 9/10/94; Steve Tyrer v Whitehaven, 7/2/2016
SEASON RECORDS	**Tries:** 48 Johnny Freeman 1956-57 **Goals:** 156 Graham Holroyd 2008 **Points:** 362 John Schuster 1994-95
CAREER RECORDS	**Tries:** 290 Johnny Freeman 1954-67 **Goals:** 1,028 Ronnie James 1961-71 **Points:** 2,191 Ronnie James 1961-71 **Appearances:** 482 Stan Kielty 1946-58

HULL KINGSTON ROVERS

DATE	FIXTURE	RESULT	SCORERS	LGE	ATT
5/2/17	Bradford (h)	W54-24	t:Heffernan(2),Scruton(2),Donaldson,Minns,Greenwood,Ellis,Quinlan g:Ellis(9)	3rd	8,817
12/2/17	London Broncos (a)	W22-28	t:Abdull,Ellis,Moss,Heffernan,Shaw g:Ellis(4)	2nd	1,250
19/2/17	Rochdale (a)	W18-28	t:Moss,Minns(2),Heffernan,Lunt g:Ellis(4)	1st	2,012
26/2/17	Oldham (h)	W48-0	t:Minns(2),Lunt,Donaldson,Scruton,Abdull,Ellis,Moss g:Ellis(8)	1st	7,268
5/3/17	Sheffield (h)	W50-10	t:Donaldson(2),Cockayne,Heffernan,Minns,Quinlan,Clarkson,Abdull g:Ellis(9)	1st	7,116
12/3/17	Dewsbury (a)	W6-48	t:Lunt,Greenwood,Heffernan(2),Blair,Mulhern,Donaldson,Horne g:Ellis(8)	1st	2,477
19/3/17	Sheffield (h) (CCR4)	W48-10	t:Minns,Lunt(2),Quinlan,Blair,Cockayne,Ellis,Greenwood g:Ellis(8)	N/A	3,408
26/3/17	Halifax (h)	W28-14	t:Blair,Greenwood,Abdull,Moss g:Ellis(6)	1st	7,100
2/4/17	Batley (h)	W50-16	t:Shaw(2),Moss,Heffernan,Minns,Salter(2),Clarkson,Donaldson g:Ellis(7)	1st	6,815
9/4/17	Swinton (a)	W18-52	t:Hodgson,Abdull,Ellis,Dockar-Clay,Donaldson(3),Oakes,Scruton,Shaw g:Ellis(6)	1st	1,375
14/4/17	Featherstone (h)	W30-22	t:Quinlan,Clarkson,Cockayne,Shaw,Hodgson,Blair g:Ellis(3)	1st	8,117
17/4/17	Toulouse (a)	L14-6	t:Heffernan g:Dockar-Clay	1st	4,107
22/4/17	Leigh (a) (CCR5)	W10-23	t:Shaw(2),Lawler,Greenwood g:Ellis(3) fg:Ellis	N/A	3,818
30/4/17	Rochdale (h)	W24-16	t:Lawler,Shaw,Lunt,Kavanagh g:Ellis(4)	1st	7,141
7/5/17	Batley (a)	W4-68	t:Mulhern,Shaw(3),Heffernan(2),Abdull,Dockar-Clay(2),Ellis,Butler-Fleming(2) g:Ellis(10)	1st	1,885
12/5/17	Salford (a) (CCR6)	L24-14	t:Lunt g:Ellis(3)	N/A	3,100
21/5/17	Swinton (h)	W42-18	t:Wardill,Abdull(2),Heffernan,Shaw(3) g:Dockar-Clay(7)	1st	7,236
27/5/17	Bradford (SB) ●	W19-20	t:Heffernan(2),Abdull g:Ellis(4)	1st	N/A
4/6/17	Featherstone (a)	D20-20	t:Moss(2),Abdull,Dockar-Clay g:Ellis(2)	1st	4,072
11/6/17	Oldham (a)	W24-32	t:Lunt,Abdull,Wardill(2),Shaw(2) g:Ellis(4)	1st	1,066
18/6/17	Dewsbury (h)	W64-11	t:Shaw(3),Heffernan(2),Salter(2),Ellis,Cockayne,Abdull,Cator,Addy g:Ellis(8)	1st	6,772
25/6/17	Sheffield (a)	W18-40	t:Carney(2),Clarkson,Butler-Fleming,Scruton,Shaw,Lunt,Dockar-Clay g:Ellis(4)	1st	1,619
2/7/17	London Broncos (h)	W40-22	t:Moss(2),Jewitt,Heffernan,Addy,Dockar-Clay,Mulhern g:Ellis(6)	1st	7,359
9/7/17	Bradford (a)	W10-42	t:Butler-Fleming,Carney,Addy(3),Clarkson,Mulhern g:Ellis(7)	1st	4,937
16/7/17	Toulouse (h)	L30-31	t:Addy,Lunt,Quinlan,Clarkson,Butler-Fleming g:Ellis(5)	1st	7,117
23/7/17	Halifax (h)	L28-6	t:Moss g:Ellis	1st	2,876
6/8/17	Halifax (h) (S8-Q)	W26-22	t:Moss(2),Marsh,Lawler,Scruton g:Ellis(3)	3rd(S8-Q)	7,706
12/8/17	Leigh (a) (S8-Q)	W16-20	t:Lunt(2),Shaw g:Ellis(4)	2nd(S8-Q)	5,335
20/8/17	London Broncos (h) (S8-Q)	W35-30	t:Addy,Moss,Mulhern,Shaw(2) g:Ellis(7) fg:Atkin	2nd(S8-Q)	7,245
3/9/17	Featherstone (a) (S8-Q)	W18-30	t:Shaw,Addy,Ellis,Minns,Heffernan g:Ellis(5)	2nd(S8-Q)	4,583
9/9/17	Widnes (h) (S8-Q)	W12-6	t:Minns,Shaw g:Ellis(2)	2nd(S8-Q)	8,227
15/9/17	Catalans Dragons (h) (S8-Q)	L19-20	t:Oakes,Cockayne,Lawler g:Dockar-Clay(2),Atkin fg:Atkin	2nd(S8-Q)	7,405
23/9/17	Warrington (a) (S8-Q)	L46-24	t:Oakes(2),Shaw(2) g:Ellis(4)	3rd(S8-Q)	10,466

● Played at Bloomfield Road, Blackpool

		APP		TRIES		GOALS		FG		PTS	
	D.O.B.	ALL	Ch	ALL	Ch	ALL	Ch	ALL	Ch	ALL	Ch
Jordan Abdull	5/2/96	23	18	12	12	0	0	0	0	48	48
Danny Addy	15/1/91	17(2)	12(2)	8	6	0	0	0	0	32	24
Chris Atkin	7/2/93	5(2)	1	0	0	1	0	2	0	4	0
Maurice Blair	16/10/84	26(2)	19	4	3	0	0	0	0	16	12
Jake Butler-Fleming	8/1/92	8(1)	7(1)	5	5	0	0	0	0	20	20
Justin Carney	16/6/88	7	3	3	3	0	0	0	0	12	12
Joe Cator	15/6/98	2(8)	2(7)	1	1	0	0	0	0	4	4
Mitch Clark	13/3/93	7(8)	7(6)	0	0	0	0	0	0	0	0
Chris Clarkson	7/4/90	14(11)	9(9)	6	6	0	0	0	0	24	24
Ben Cockayne	20/7/83	19(4)	16(3)	5	3	0	0	0	0	20	12
Zach Dockar-Clay	24/4/95	4(15)	4(11)	6	6	10	8	0	0	44	40
James Donaldson	14/9/91	8(3)	7(3)	9	9	0	0	0	0	36	36
Jamie Ellis	4/10/89	30	21	8	6	158	119	1	0	349	262
James Greenwood	17/6/91	14(5)	10	5	3	0	0	0	0	20	12
Liam Harris	20/4/97	1	1	0	0	0	0	0	0	0	0
Andrew Heffernan	24/1/95	24	16	18	17	0	0	0	0	72	68
David Hodgson	8/8/81	4(1)	3(1)	2	2	0	0	0	0	8	8
Graeme Horne	22/3/85	3(3)	2(2)	1	1	0	0	0	0	4	4
Lee Jewitt	14/2/87	11	5	1	1	0	0	0	0	4	4
Josh Johnson	25/7/94	9(4)	7(4)	0	0	0	0	0	0	0	0
Will Jubb	17/9/96	1(2)	1(2)	0	0	0	0	0	0	0	0
Ben Kavanagh	4/3/88	23(3)	14(2)	1	1	0	0	0	0	4	4
George Lawler	1/9/95	11(6)	4(4)	4	1	0	0	0	0	16	4
Shaun Lunt	15/4/86	23(4)	19	13	7	0	0	0	0	52	28
Matthew Marsh	21/4/95	4(2)	(1)	1	0	0	0	0	0	4	0
Mose Masoe	17/5/89	1(4)	0	0	0	0	0	0	0	0	0
George Milton	4/9/95	1(1)	1(1)	0	0	0	0	0	0	0	0
Thomas Minns	4/9/94	16	10	10	7	0	0	0	0	40	28
Kieran Moran	2/11/96	(2)	(1)	0	0	0	0	0	0	0	0
Kieren Moss	6/8/93	19(2)	13(1)	13	10	0	0	0	0	52	40
Rob Mulhern	18/10/94	6(21)	3(17)	5	4	0	0	0	0	20	16
Will Oakes	27/2/99	6(2)	4(2)	4	1	0	0	0	0	16	4
Adam Quinlan	13/11/92	13	9	5	4	0	0	0	0	20	16
Liam Salter	14/6/93	13(7)	11(6)	4	4	0	0	0	0	16	16
Nick Scruton	24/12/84	25	18	6	5	0	0	0	0	24	20
Ryan Shaw	27/2/92	31	22	27	18	0	0	0	0	108	72
Joe Wardill	26/11/97	(7)	(6)	3	3	0	0	0	0	12	12

'Ch' totals include Championship regular season only; 'All' totals also include Super 8s (Qualifiers) & Challenge Cup

Jamie Ellis

LEAGUE RECORD
Championship, before Super 8 split:
P23-W19-D1-L3 (1st)
F850, A385, Diff+465, 39 points.

S8-Q: P7-W5-D0-L2 (3rd)
F166, A158, Diff+8, 10 points.

CHALLENGE CUP
Round Six

ATTENDANCES
Best - v Bradford (Ch - 8,817)
Worst - v Sheffield (CC - 3,408)
Total (Championship/S8s only) - 111,441
Average (Championship/
S8s only) - 7,429
(Down by 181 on 2016, Super League)

CLUB RECORDS	
	Highest score: 100-6 v Nottingham City, 19/8/90 Highest score against: 6-84 v Wigan, 1/4/2013
	Record attendance: 27,670 v Hull FC, 3/4/53 *(Boothferry Park)*; 11,811 v Leeds, 8/2/2015 *(Craven Park)*
MATCH RECORDS	Tries: 11 George West v Brooklands Rovers, 4/3/1905 Goals: 14 Alf Carmichael v Merthyr, 8/10/1910; Mike Fletcher v Whitehaven, 18/3/90; Colin Armstrong v Nottingham City, 19/8/90; Damien Couturier v Halifax, 23/4/2006 Points: 53 George West v Brooklands Rovers, 4/3/1905
SEASON RECORDS	Tries: 45 Gary Prohm 1984-85 Goals: 199 Mike Fletcher 1989-90 Points: 450 Mike Fletcher 1989-90
CAREER RECORDS	Tries: 207 Roger Millward 1966-80 Goals: 1,268 Mike Fletcher 1987-98 Points: 2,760 Mike Fletcher 1987-98 Appearances: 489 Mike Smith 1975-91

LONDON BRONCOS

DATE	FIXTURE	RESULT	SCORERS	LGE	ATT
5/2/17	Swinton (a)	W23-26	t:Williams,Sammut,Barthau,Ioane,Harrison g:Sammut(3)	6th	603
12/2/17	Hull KR (h)	L22-28	t:Sammut(2),Dixon,Purtell g:Sammut(3)	8th	1,250
19/2/17	Oldham (a)	W18-20	t:Sammut,Ackers,Harrison,Williams g:Sammut(2)	5th	558
26/2/17	Dewsbury (a)	W6-20	t:Roqica,Sammut,Walker g:Sammut(4)	3rd	678
5/3/17	Bradford (h)	W42-12	t:Walker,Kear,Garside(2),Barthau,Sammut,Dixon g:Sammut(7)	3rd	1,120
12/3/17	Halifax (a)	L19-6	t:Hellewell g:Sammut	4th	1,298
17/3/17	Toronto (h) (CCR4)	L26-30	t:Sammut(2),Barthau,Kear,Dixon g:Sammut(3)	N/A	758
26/3/17	Rochdale (h)	W28-8	t:Pewhairangi,Harrison,Sammut,Purtell,Pitts g:Dixon,Sammut(3)	4th	650
2/4/17	Sheffield (a)	L32-20	t:Pitts,Evans,Dixon,Kear g:Sammut(2)	4th	319
9/4/17	Featherstone (a)	L38-18	t:Sammut,Roqica,Cunningham g:Sammut(3)	5th	2,509
14/4/17	Toulouse (h)	W30-16	t:Pitts,Barthau,Williams(2),Davis g:Pewhairangi(5)	5th	520
17/4/17	Batley (a)	W4-42	t:Kear,Pitts,Cunningham(2),Garside,Walker,Bienek,Pearce-Paul g:Pewhairangi(5)	4th	587
30/4/17	Swinton (h)	W38-28	t:Pitts,Garside,Cunningham,Pewhairangi(2),Ioane,Bienek g:Pewhairangi(5)	5th	618
7/5/17	Oldham (h)	W74-12	t:Dixon(2),Hellewell(2),Williams(2),Pewhairangi(2),Harrison(2),Sammut(2), Ioane,Pitts g:Dixon(9)	4th	500
21/5/17	Bradford (a)	W12-56	t:Dixon(3),Pitts,Williams,Roqica(2),Sammut(2),Garside g:Dixon(8)	4th	3,633
27/5/17	Featherstone (SB) ●	W16-42	t:Sammut,Williams,Ackers,Walker,Channing,Barthau,Dixon g:Dixon(7)	3rd	N/A
4/6/17	Halifax (h)	W34-6	t:Dixon(2),Barthau,Ackers,Williams,Pitts,Ioane g:Dixon(3)	3rd	857
11/6/17	Dewsbury (h)	W52-8	t:Barthau,Walker(2),Ackers,Hellewell,Channing,Pewhairangi(3) g:Dixon(8)	3rd	854
17/6/17	Toulouse (a)	W16-36	t:Ackers,Barthau,Harrison,Walker,Dixon(2),Pewhairangi g:Dixon(4)	2nd	2,548
25/6/17	Featherstone (h)	W36-30	t:Gee,Walker(2),Barthau,Sammut,Dixon,Kear g:Dixon(4)	2nd	910
2/7/17	Hull KR (a)	L40-22	t:Harrison(2),Sammut,Gee g:Sammut(3)	2nd	7,359
9/7/17	Sheffield (h)	W52-16	t:Sammut,Harrison,Hellewell(4),Pewhairangi(2),Ackers g:Sammut(8)	2nd	684
16/7/17	Rochdale (a)	W18-58	t:Ackers(2),Sammut(2),Walker(2),Davis,Bienek,Williams,Evans g:Sammut(9)	2nd	504
23/7/17	Batley (h)	W58-4	t:Kear(3),Channing,Pewhairangi(2),Williams(2),Roqica,Davis g:Sammut(9)	2nd	879
5/8/17	Catalans Dragons (a) (S8-Q)	L20-18	t:Barthau,Williams,Ioane g:Sammut(3)	5th(S8-Q)	7,102
13/8/17	Featherstone (h) (S8-Q)	D32-32	t:Pitts,Kear,Barthau,Sammut,Ioane,Ackers g:Sammut(4)	6th(S8-Q)	926
20/8/17	Hull KR (a) (S8-Q)	L35-30	t:Ackers,Cunningham,Walker,Ioane,Kear g:Sammut(5)	6th(S8-Q)	7,245
2/9/17	Warrington (h) (S8-Q)	L38-40	t:Dixon(2),Williams,Sammut(3),Ackers g:Sammut(5)	6th(S8-Q)	1,577
10/9/17	Halifax (a) (S8-Q)	W36-14	t:Barthau,Walker,Ackers,Williams,Dixon,Kear g:Sammut(5),Dixon	6th(S8-Q)	794
16/9/17	Widnes (a) (S8-Q)	L38-16	t:Ioane,Sammut,Dixon g:Sammut(2)	6th(S8-Q)	4,199
22/9/17	Leigh (h) (S8-Q)	L4-41	t:Gee	6th(S8-Q)	1,234

● *Played at Bloomfield Road, Blackpool*

		APP		TRIES		GOALS		FG		PTS	
	D.O.B.	ALL	Ch	ALL	Ch	ALL	Ch	ALL	Ch	ALL	Ch
Andy Ackers	25/12/93	19(1)	13(1)	12	8	0	0	0	0	48	32
Sadiq Adebiyi	8/1/97	(5)	(5)	0	0	0	0	0	0	0	0
William Barthau	30/1/90	26	18	12	8	0	0	0	0	48	32
Eddie Battye	24/7/91	7(7)	3(5)	0	0	0	0	0	0	0	0
Lewis Bienek	11/4/98	1(12)	1(8)	3	3	0	0	0	0	12	12
John Boudebza	13/6/90	(5)	(3)	0	0	0	0	0	0	0	0
Callum Bustin	12/8/97	(1)	(1)	0	0	0	0	0	0	0	0
Michael Channing	30/6/92	13	11	3	3	0	0	0	0	12	12
James Cunningham	3/4/94	10(4)	9	5	4	0	0	0	0	20	16
Matt Davis	5/7/96	14(2)	8(1)	3	3	0	0	0	0	12	12
Kieran Dixon	22/8/92	19(2)	14(2)	19	14	45	44	0	0	166	144
Ben Evans	30/10/92	18(7)	15(4)	2	2	0	0	0	0	8	8
Lewis Foster	21/12/93	1(5)	1(5)	0	0	0	0	0	0	0	0
Matt Garside	1/10/90	5(13)	5(8)	5	5	0	0	0	0	20	20
Matty Gee	12/12/94	9(16)	4(13)	3	2	0	0	0	0	12	8
Daniel Harrison	15/4/88	21	20	9	9	0	0	0	0	36	36
Ben Hellewell	30/1/92	24(1)	19(1)	8	8	0	0	0	0	32	32
Mark Ioane	3/2/90	23(4)	17(3)	8	4	0	0	0	0	32	16
Elliot Kear	29/11/88	29	21	11	7	0	0	0	0	44	28
Mark Offerdahl	15/10/87	9(8)	8(8)	0	0	0	0	0	0	0	0
Kameron Pearce-Paul	28/2/97	3	3	1	1	0	0	0	0	4	4
Api Pewhairangi	19/3/92	14(7)	10(5)	13	13	15	15	0	0	82	82
Jay Pitts	9/12/89	30(1)	22(1)	9	8	0	0	0	0	36	32
Ben Pointer	25/5/96	2(2)	1(2)	0	0	0	0	0	0	0	0
Adrian Purtell	31/1/85	10	9	2	2	0	0	0	0	8	8
Junior Roqica	13/2/91	5(15)	4(13)	5	5	0	0	0	0	20	20
Jarrod Sammut	15/2/87	26(2)	18(2)	25	18	84	57	0	0	268	186
Tom Spencer	2/1/91	6(3)	4	0	0	0	0	0	0	0	0
Alex Walker	4/9/95	25	18	13	11	0	0	0	0	52	44
Sam Wilde	8/9/95	3(1)	(1)	0	0	0	0	0	0	0	0
Rhys Williams	8/12/89	31	23	15	12	0	0	0	0	60	48

'Ch' totals include Championship regular season only; 'All' totals also include Super 8s (Qualifiers) & Challenge Cup

Jarrod Sammut

LEAGUE RECORD
Championship, before Super 8 split:
P23-W18-D0-L5 (2nd)
F832, A410, Diff+422, 36 points.

S8-Q: P7-W1-D1-L5 (6th)
F174, A220, Diff-46, 3 points.

CHALLENGE CUP
Round Four

ATTENDANCES
Best - v Warrington (S8 - 1,577)
Worst - v Oldham (Ch - 500)
Total (Championship/S8s only) - 13,373
Average (Championship/S8s only) - 891
(Up by 61 on 2016)

CLUB RECORDS	**Highest score:** 82-0 v Highfield, 12/11/95; 82-2 v Barrow, 20/5/2006 **Highest score against:** 6-82 v Warrington, 20/3/2011; 10-82 v Warrington, 8/6/2013
MATCH RECORDS	**Record attendance:** 15,013 v Wakefield, 15/2/81
	Tries: 5 Martin Offiah v Whitehaven, 14/3/99; Sean Morris v Batley, 13/9/2015
	Goals: 13 Rob Purdham v Barrow, 20/5/2006 **Points:** 34 Rob Purdham v Barrow, 20/5/2006
SEASON RECORDS	**Tries:** 43 Mark Johnson 1993-94 **Goals:** 159 John Gallagher 1993-94 **Points:** 384 John Gallagher 1993-94
CAREER RECORDS	**Tries:** 109 Luke Dorn 2005-2006; 2009-2013 **Goals:** 309 Steve Diamond 1981-84 **Points:** 772 Paul Sykes 2001-2007
	Appearances: 202 Steele Retchless 1998-2004

OLDHAM

DATE	FIXTURE	RESULT	SCORERS	LGE	ATT
5/2/17	Sheffield (h)	W26-10	t:Langtree(2),Clay,Hewitt g:Leatherbarrow(5)	4th	668
12/2/17	Featherstone (a)	L8-6	t:Turner g:Leatherbarrow	5th	1,783
19/2/17	London Broncos (h)	L18-20	t:S Wood(2) g:Leatherbarrow(3),Hewitt(2)	6th	558
26/2/17	Hull KR (a)	L48-0		9th	7,268
12/3/17	Rochdale (a)	D26-26	t:Walne,Clay,Egodo,Ward g:Leatherbarrow(5)	8th	1,087
18/3/17	Haydock (h) (CCR4)	W40-12	t:Lepori(2),Ward,Tyson,Grimshaw,Burke,Gill,Clay g:Leatherbarrow(4)	N/A	743
26/3/17	Batley (a)	L50-10	t:Ward,Lepori g:Leatherbarrow	9th	761
2/4/17	Bradford (h)	W26-22	t:Neal,Langtree,Egodo,Gill g:Leatherbarrow(5)	9th	1,691
8/4/17	Toulouse (a)	L58-18	t:Gill,Burke,Lepori g:Leatherbarrow(3)	9th	1,752
14/4/17	Swinton (h)	W22-18	t:Gee,Lepori,Ward g:Leatherbarrow(5)	9th	804
17/4/17	Halifax (a)	L16-14	t:Gill,Burke,Chisholm g:Leatherbarrow	9th	1,341
23/4/17	Featherstone (a) (CCR5)	L30-4	t:Turner	N/A	1,408
30/4/17	Dewsbury (a)	W24-28	t:Neal,Ward,Gill,Tyson,Burke g:Leatherbarrow(4)	8th	691
7/5/17	London Broncos (a)	L74-12	t:Tyson,Thompson g:Leatherbarrow(2)	8th	500
21/5/17	Batley (h) ●	L28-48	t:Clay(3),Neal,Grimshaw g:Leatherbarrow(4)	8th	578
27/5/17	Rochdale (SB) ●●	L28-38	t:Turner,Tyson,Lepori(2) g:Leatherbarrow(6)	9th	N/A
4/6/17	Swinton (a)	L26-4	t:Lepori	9th	628
11/6/17	Hull KR (h)	L24-32	t:Burke,Hewitt,S Wood,McIntosh g:Leatherbarrow(4)	9th	1,066
18/6/17	Halifax (a)	L12-30	t:Turner,Ward g:Leatherbarrow(2)	9th	809
21/6/17	Dewsbury (h)	L16-20	t:Grimshaw,Ward g:Leatherbarrow(4)	9th	575
25/6/17	Bradford (a)	L47-12	t:Langtree,Hewitt g:Hewitt(2)	11th	3,708
2/7/17	Toulouse (h)	W14-12	t:Nield,Tyson g:Hewitt(3)	10th	519
9/7/17	Featherstone (h)	L14-32	t:Wilkinson,Adebiyi,Tyson g:Hewitt	10th	851
16/7/17	Sheffield (a)	L42-28	t:Clay,Ward,Adamson,Tyson,Williams g:Hewitt(2),Leatherbarrow(2)	10th	329
23/7/17	Rochdale (h)	L24-34	t:Smith,Clay,Hewitt,Tyson g:Leatherbarrow(4)	11th	889
6/8/17	Sheffield (a) (CS)	L56-16	t:Wilkinson,Hewitt,Hughes g:Hooley(2)	7th(CS)	305
13/8/17	Bradford (h) (CS)	L16-20	t:Spencer,Grimshaw,Ward g:Hooley(2)	7th(CS)	853
20/8/17	Batley (a) (CS)	D22-22	t:Ward,Gee,Morris,Clay g:Hooley(3)	7th(CS)	675
28/8/17	Rochdale (a) (CS)	W24-30	t:Burke(2),Adamson,Clay,Hooley g:Hooley(5)	7th(CS)	927
3/9/17	Toulouse (a) (CS)	L18-24	t:Hughes(2) g:Hooley(5)	7th(CS)	581
10/9/17	Swinton (a) (CS)	L29-6	t:Tyson g:Hooley	7th(CS)	1,051
17/9/17	Dewsbury (h) (CS)	L22-29	t:Lepori,Burke,Grimshaw,Thompson g:Hewitt(3)	7th(CS)	429

● *Played at Manchester Regional Arena* ●● *Played at Bloomfield Road, Blackpool*

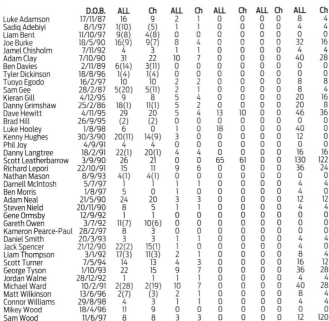

		APP		TRIES		GOALS		FG		PTS	
	D.O.B.	ALL	Ch	ALL	Ch	ALL	Ch	ALL	Ch	ALL	Ch
Luke Adamson	17/11/87	16	9	2	1	0	0	0	0	8	4
Sadiq Adebiyi	8/1/97	1(10)	(5)	1	1	0	0	0	0	4	4
Liam Bent	11/10/97	9(8)	4(8)	0	0	0	0	0	0	0	0
Joe Burke	18/5/90	16(9)	9(7)	8	4	0	0	0	0	32	16
Jamel Chisholm	7/11/92	4	3	1	1	0	0	0	0	4	4
Adam Clay	7/10/90	31	22	10	7	0	0	0	0	40	28
Ben Davies	2/11/89	6(14)	3(11)	0	0	0	0	0	0	0	0
Tyler Dickinson	18/8/96	1(4)	1(4)	0	0	0	0	0	0	0	0
Tuoyo Egodo	16/2/97	10	10	2	2	0	0	0	0	8	8
Sam Gee	28/2/87	5(20)	5(11)	2	1	0	0	0	0	8	4
Kieran Gill	4/12/95	9	8	5	4	0	0	0	0	20	16
Danny Grimshaw	25/2/86	18(1)	11(1)	5	2	0	0	0	0	20	8
Dave Hewitt	4/11/95	29	20	5	4	13	10	0	0	46	36
Brad Hill	26/9/95	(2)	(2)	0	0	0	0	0	0	0	0
Luke Hooley	1/8/98	6	0	1	0	18	0	0	0	40	0
Kenny Hughes	30/3/90	20(11)	14(9)	3	0	0	0	0	0	12	0
Phil Joy	4/9/91	4	4	0	0	0	0	0	0	0	0
Danny Langtree	18/2/91	22(1)	20(1)	4	4	0	0	0	0	16	16
Scott Leatherbarrow	3/9/90	26	21	0	0	65	61	0	0	130	122
Richard Lepori	22/10/91	15	11	9	6	0	0	0	0	36	24
Nathan Mason	8/9/93	4(1)	4(1)	0	0	0	0	0	0	0	0
Darnell McIntosh	5/7/97	1	1	1	1	0	0	0	0	4	4
Ben Morris	1/8/97	5	0	1	0	0	0	0	0	4	0
Adam Neal	21/5/90	24	20	3	3	0	0	0	0	12	12
Steven Nield	20/11/90	8	5	1	1	0	0	0	0	4	4
Gene Ormsby	12/9/92	1	1	0	0	0	0	0	0	0	0
Gareth Owen	3/7/92	11(7)	10(6)	0	0	0	0	0	0	0	0
Kameron Pearce-Paul	28/2/97	8	3	0	0	0	0	0	0	0	0
Daniel Smith	20/3/93	3	3	1	1	0	0	0	0	4	4
Jack Spencer	21/12/90	22(2)	15(1)	1	0	0	0	0	0	4	0
Liam Thompson	3/1/92	17(3)	11(3)	2	1	0	0	0	0	8	4
Scott Turner	7/5/94	14	13	4	3	0	0	0	0	16	12
George Tyson	1/10/93	22	15	9	7	0	0	0	0	36	28
Jordan Walne	28/12/92	1	1	1	1	0	0	0	0	4	4
Michael Ward	10/2/91	2(28)	2(19)	10	7	0	0	0	0	40	28
Matt Wilkinson	13/6/96	2(7)	(3)	2	1	0	0	0	0	8	4
Connor Williams	29/8/98	4	3	1	1	0	0	0	0	4	4
Mikey Wood	18/4/96	11	9	0	0	0	0	0	0	0	0
Sam Wood	11/6/97	8	8	3	3	0	0	0	0	12	120

'Ch' totals include Championship regular season only; 'All' totals also include Championship Shield & Challenge Cup

George Tyson

LEAGUE RECORD
Championship, before Super 8 split:
P23-W5-D1-L17 (11th)
F410, A735, Diff-325, 11 points.

After Championship Shield:
P30-W6-D2-L22 (7th)
F540, A939, Diff-399, 14 points.

CHALLENGE CUP
Round Five

ATTENDANCES
Best - v Bradford (Ch - 1,691)
Worst - v Dewsbury (CS - 429)
Total (Championship/
Championship Shield only) - 10,871
Average (Championship/
Championship Shield only) - 777
(Down by 54 on 2016)

CLUB RECORDS	Highest score: 80-6 v Blackwood, 7/3/2010 **Highest score against:** 0-84 v Widnes, 25/7/99
	Record attendance: 28,000 v Huddersfield, 24/2/1912 *(Watersheddings)*; 2,394 v Warrington, 7/5/2016 *(Bower Fold)*
MATCH RECORDS	Tries: 7 James Miller v Barry, 31/10/1908 Goals: 14 Bernard Ganley v Liverpool City, 4/4/59
	Points: 34 Andy Ballard v London Skolars, 2/5/2009; Chris Baines v Hunslet, 20/9/2009; Lewis Palfrey v Hemel, 9/8/2015
SEASON RECORDS	Tries: 49 Reg Farrar 1921-22 Goals: 200 Bernard Ganley 1957-58 Points: 412 Bernard Ganley 1957-58
CAREER RECORDS	Tries: 174 Alan Davies 1950-61 Goals: 1,358 Bernard Ganley 1951-61 Points: 2,761 Bernard Ganley 1951-61 Appearances: 627 Joe Ferguson 1899-1923

ROCHDALE HORNETS

DATE	FIXTURE	RESULT	SCORERS	LGE	ATT
5/2/17	Dewsbury (h)	W46-0	t:Tahraoui,Moores(2),Yates,Taira,Massam,Galbraith,Maneely g:Palfrey(7)	1st	718
12/2/17	Bradford (a)	W14-22	t:Greenwood,Tahraoui,Bridge g:Palfrey(5)	1st	4,051
19/2/17	Hull KR (h)	L18-28	t:Middlehurst,Yates,Moores g:Palfrey(3)	4th	2,012
26/2/17	Halifax (h)	L6-20	t:Massam g:Palfrey	5th	854
5/3/17	Featherstone (a)	W9-10	t:Bridge g:Palfrey(3)	5th	1,839
12/3/17	Oldham (h)	D26-26	t:Moores,Crowley,Holmes,Bennion,Maneely g:Palfrey(3)	5th	1,087
19/3/17	York (a) (CCR4)	L26-20	t:Greenwood,Riley(2),Massam g:Palfrey(2)	N/A	652
26/3/17	London Broncos (a)	L28-8	t:Massam(2)	6th	650
2/4/17	Toulouse (h)	L14-52	t:Moores,Middlehurst,Massam g:Yates	7th	609
9/4/17	Batley (a)	L38-36	t:Massam,Livett,Jullien,Galbraith,Hadden,Johnson g:Livett(6)	7th	718
14/4/17	Sheffield (h)	L18-42	t:Crowley,Tahraoui,Galbraith g:Palfrey(3)	8th	526
17/4/17	Swinton (a)	L23-22	t:Galbraith,Massam(2),Tahraoui g:Palfrey(3)	8th	538
30/4/17	Hull KR (a)	L24-16	t:Case(2),Massam g:Palfrey(2)	9th	7,141
7/5/17	Featherstone (h)	L8-38	t:Greenwood,Massam	9th	766
21/5/17	Halifax (a)	L28-2	g:Yates	9th	1,424
27/5/17	Oldham (SB) ●	W28-38	t:Greenwood,Eccleston(2),Massam,Moores,Case,Galbraith g:Yates(5)	8th	N/A
4/6/17	Sheffield (a)	L38-14	t:Smith,Massam(2) g:Palfrey	8th	341
10/6/17	Toulouse (a)	L56-16	t:Massam,Kay,Greenwood g:Whittaker(2)	8th	1,467
18/6/17	Bradford (h)	W28-14	t:Taira(2),Galbraith,Hadden g:Yates(5)	8th	1,230
25/6/17	Batley (h)	L14-24	t:Galbraith,Eccleston,Middlehurst g:Yates	8th	604
2/7/17	Dewsbury (a)	L40-10	t:Massam,Case g:Yates	9th	775
9/7/17	Swinton (h)	W33-28	t:Yates,Maneely,Crowley,Eccleston,Smith,Massam g:Yates(4) fg:Foster	8th	745
16/7/17	London Broncos (h)	L18-58	t:Eccleston,Foster,Massam g:Yates(3)	9th	504
23/7/17	Oldham (a)	W24-34	t:Penny(2),Kay(2),Eccleston,Case g:Yates(5)	9th	889
6/8/17	Dewsbury (a) (CS)	L56-8	t:Smith,Riley	5th(CS)	629
13/8/17	Batley (h) (CS)	L14-34	t:Eccleston,Penny,Yates g:Yates	5th(CS)	453
19/8/17	Toulouse (a) (CS)	L50-12	t:Yates,Middlehurst g:Palfrey(2)	5th(CS)	612
28/8/17	Oldham (h) (CS)	L24-30	t:Riley,Eccleston,Maneely,Massam,Taira g:Palfrey(2)	5th(CS)	927
3/9/17	Swinton (h) (CS)	W16-8	t:Kay,Foster g:Yates(4)	5th(CS)	606
10/9/17	Sheffield (a) (CS)	L26-22	t:Penny,Hadden,Holmes g:Yates(5)	5th(CS)	297
17/9/17	Bradford (a) (CS)	L72-16	t:Case,Riley,Holmes g:Yates(2)	5th(CS)	3,604

● *Played at Bloomfield Road, Blackpool*

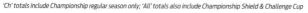

		APP		TRIES		GOALS		FG		PTS	
	D.O.B.	ALL	Ch	ALL	Ch	ALL	Ch	ALL	Ch	ALL	Ch
Gavin Bennion	31/12/93	18(10)	17(3)	1	1	0	0	0	0	4	4
Matty Blythe	20/11/88	2(1)	2(1)	0	0	0	0	0	0	0	0
Danny Bridge	4/1/93	5(2)	5(2)	2	2	0	0	0	0	8	8
Jordan Case	10/4/93	15(15)	10(12)	6	5	0	0	0	0	24	20
Josh Crowley	24/9/91	27(1)	20(1)	3	3	0	0	0	0	12	12
Jake Eccleston	24/4/95	24(1)	17(1)	8	6	0	0	0	0	32	24
Lewis Foster	21/12/93	9(2)	5(2)	2	1	0	0	1	1	9	5
Luke Fowden	1/9/96	(1)	(1)	0	0	0	0	0	0	0	0
Jack Francis	17/12/92	(1)	(1)	0	0	0	0	0	0	0	0
Lewis Galbraith	1/2/95	27(1)	19(1)	7	7	0	0	0	0	28	28
Miles Greenwood	30/7/87	15(3)	14(1)	5	4	0	0	0	0	20	16
Matty Hadden	7/6/90	3(28)	3(20)	3	2	0	0	0	0	12	8
Jordan Hand	13/5/93	4	4	0	0	0	0	0	0	0	0
Lewis Hatton	14/1/97	5(5)	2(2)	0	0	0	0	0	0	0	0
Jack Holmes	5/1/94	10(2)	6(1)	3	1	0	0	0	0	12	4
Jack Johnson	25/4/96	2	2	1	1	0	0	0	0	4	4
Benjamin Jullien	1/3/95	1	1	1	1	0	0	0	0	4	4
Declan Kay	24/11/96	11	5	4	3	0	0	0	0	16	12
Harvey Livett	4/1/97	1	1	1	1	6	6	0	0	16	16
Jay Lobwein	13/4/92	(2)	(2)	0	0	0	0	0	0	0	0
Ryan Maneely	19/10/94	9(15)	5(12)	4	3	0	0	0	0	16	12
Rob Massam	29/11/87	23(1)	22	19	17	0	0	0	0	76	68
Gary Middlehurst	24/10/83	21	19	4	3	0	0	0	0	16	12
Lee Mitchell	8/9/88	11(5)	5(5)	0	0	0	0	0	0	0	0
Ben Moores	6/12/93	21(4)	18(4)	6	6	0	0	0	0	24	24
Pat Moran	2/4/98	(1)	(1)	0	0	0	0	0	0	0	0
Lewis Palfrey	25/2/90	21	16	0	0	37	31	0	0	74	62
Kevin Penny	3/10/87	10	4	4	2	0	0	0	0	16	8
Taylor Prell	3/7/96	1	1	0	0	0	0	0	0	0	0
Danny Rasool	25/10/95	(1)	(1)	0	0	0	0	0	0	0	0
Chris Riley	22/2/88	23	16	5	0	0	0	0	0	20	0
Andre Savelio	21/3/95	1(1)	1(1)	0	0	0	0	0	0	0	0
Jono Smith	12/11/88	17(1)	13(1)	3	2	0	0	0	0	12	8
Samir Tahraoui	28/12/90	7(4)	6(4)	4	4	0	0	0	0	16	16
Jovili Taira	30/3/89	14(12)	8(11)	4	3	0	0	0	0	16	12
Anthony Walker	28/12/91	11	6	0	0	0	0	0	0	0	0
Tyler Whittaker	12/11/95	1	1	0	0	2	2	0	0	4	4
Sam Wilde	8/9/95	1(2)	1(2)	0	0	0	0	0	0	0	0
Danny Yates	28/5/94	31	23	5	3	39	27	0	0	98	66

'Ch' totals include Championship regular season only; 'All' totals also include Championship Shield & Challenge Cup

Danny Yates

LEAGUE RECORD
Championship, before Super 8 split:
P23-W7-D1-L15 (9th)
F457, A680, Diff-223, 15 points.

After Championship Shield:
P30-W8-D1-L21 (5th)
F569, A956, Diff-387, 17 points.

CHALLENGE CUP
Round Four

ATTENDANCES
Best - v Hull KR (Ch - 2,012)
Worst - v Batley (CS - 453)
Total (Championship/
Championship Shield only) - 11,641
Average (Championship/
Championship Shield only) - 832
(Up by 320 on 2016, League 1)

CLUB RECORDS	
	Highest score: 120-4 v Illingworth, 13/3/2005 **Highest score against:** 0-106 v Castleford, 9/9/2007
MATCH RECORDS	**Record attendance:** 26,664 v Oldham, 25/3/22 (*Athletic Grounds*); 8,061 v Oldham, 26/12/89 (*Spotland*)
	Tries: 5 Jack Corsi v Barrow, 31/12/21; Jack Corsi v Broughton Moor, 25/2/22; Jack Williams v St Helens, 4/4/33; Norman Brelsford v Whitehaven, 3/9/73; Marlon Billy v York, 8/4/2001 **Goals:** 18 Lee Birdseye v Illingworth, 13/3/2005 **Points:** 44 Lee Birdseye v Illingworth, 13/3/2005
SEASON RECORDS	**Tries:** 31 Marlon Billy 2001 **Goals:** 150 Martin Strett 1994-95 **Points:** 350 Mick Nanyn 2003
CAREER RECORDS	**Tries:** 103 Jack Williams 1931-37 **Goals:** 741 Walter Gowers 1922-36
	Points: 1,497 Walter Gowers 1922-36; Paul Crook 2010-2016 **Appearances:** 456 Walter Gowers 1922-36

SHEFFIELD EAGLES

DATE	FIXTURE	RESULT	SCORERS	LGE	ATT
5/2/17	Oldham (a)	L26-10	t:Fozard,Millar g:Brown	9th	668
12/2/17	Toulouse (h)	W32-14	t:Hopkins,James,Fozard,Yere,Lo g:Brown(4),Chisholm(2)	6th	442
19/2/17	Halifax (a)	L42-16	t:Wheeldon,Blackmore,Straugheir g:Brown(2)	9th	1,241
26/2/17	Batley (h)	L10-54	t:Minchella,Chisholm g:Brown	10th	662
5/3/17	Hull KR (a)	L50-10	t:Straugheir,Lo g:Chisholm	10th	7,116
12/3/17	Featherstone (h)	L22-47	t:Dean,Straugheir,Minchella,Lo g:Brown(3)	10th	1,017
19/3/17	Hull KR (a) (CCR4)	L48-10	t:Chisholm,Lo g:Brown	N/A	3,408
26/3/17	Swinton (a)	W24-28	t:Yere,Lo,James,Minchella,Scott g:Brown(4)	8th	479
2/4/17	London Broncos (h)	W32-20	t:Minchella(2),Lo,Yere,Straugheir g:Brown(6)	8th	319
9/4/17	Bradford (a)	L48-16	t:Hope,Blackmore(2) g:Brown(2)	8th	4,126
14/4/17	Rochdale (a)	W18-42	t:Lo(3),Minchella,Burns,Spedding,Straugheir g:Brown(7)	7th	526
17/4/17	Dewsbury (h)	W48-12	t:Yere,Blackmore,Lo(4),Burns,Scott g:Brown(8)	7th	482
30/4/17	Featherstone (a)	L25-14	t:Lo,Mexico g:Brown(3)	7th	2,267
7/5/17	Bradford (h)	W52-16	t:Millar,Scott(2),Wheeldon,Johnson,Fozard(2),Kelly,Trout g:Brown(8)	6th	1,437
20/5/17	Toulouse (a)	L45-20	t:Trout,Lo(2),Flynn g:Brown(2)	6th	2,413
28/5/17	Swinton (SB) ●	W30-24	t:Fozard(2),Hope,Yere,Lo g:Brown(5)	6th	N/A
4/6/17	Rochdale (h)	W38-14	t:Lo(5),Yere,Owens,Minchella g:Brown(3)	6th	341
11/6/17	Halifax (h)	L0-54		6th	672
18/6/17	Batley (a)	L70-12	t:Whiteley,Marginet g:Owens(2)	7th	2,106
25/6/17	Hull KR (h)	L18-40	t:Minchella,Trout,Johnson g:Brown(3)	7th	1,619
2/7/17	Swinton (h)	W42-34	t:James,Blackmore(3),Owens,Richardson,Lo g:Richardson(7)	7th	379
9/7/17	London Broncos (a)	L52-16	t:Fozard,James,Marginet g:Owens(2)	7th	684
16/7/17	Oldham (h)	W42-28	t:Wheeldon,Yere,Hope,Owens,Lo(3),Spedding g:Brown(5)	7th	329
23/7/17	Dewsbury (a)	L28-18	t:Lo(2),Yere,Marginet g:Owens	7th	794
6/8/17	Oldham (h) (CS)	W56-16	t:Flynn(2),Scott,Minchella(3),Fozard(2),Owens,Wheeldon g:Owens(8)	3rd(CS)	305
13/8/17	Swinton (a) (CS)	W30-32	t:Blackmore(2),Minchella(2),Flynn,Yere g:Owens(4)	3rd(CS)	434
20/8/17	Dewsbury (h) (CS)	L28-35	t:Fozard,Minchella,Lo,James,Milton g:Brown(4)	3rd(CS)	363
28/8/17	Toulouse (a) (CS)	L32-16	t:Lo,Straugheir,Blackmore g:Brown(2)	3rd(CS)	1,855
3/9/17	Bradford (h) (CS)	L18-32	t:Minchella,Fozard,Blackmore,Lo g:Brown	3rd(CS)	896
10/9/17	Rochdale (h) (CS)	W26-22	t:Fozard,Lo,Owens,Wheeldon,Yere g:Owens(3)	3rd(CS)	297
17/9/17	Batley (a) (CS)	L34-18	t:Flynn,Mexico,Straugheir,Yere g:Owens	3rd(CS)	650
24/9/17	Batley (a) (CSSF)	W26-28	t:Yere,Blackmore,Trout,Lo(2) g:Owens(4)	N/A	550
30/9/17	Toulouse (a) (CSF)	L44-14	t:Lo(3) g:Owens	N/A	1,528

● *Played at Bloomfield Road, Blackpool (All home games played at Beaumont Legal Stadium, Wakefield)*

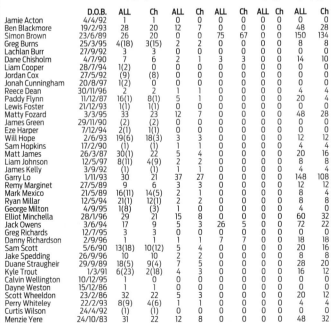

	D.O.B.	APP ALL	Ch	TRIES ALL	Ch	GOALS ALL	Ch	FG ALL	Ch	PTS ALL	Ch
Jamie Acton	4/4/92	1	1	0	0	0	0	0	0	0	0
Ben Blackmore	19/2/93	28	20	12	7	0	0	0	0	48	28
Simon Brown	23/6/89	26	20	0	0	75	67	0	0	150	134
Greg Burns	25/3/95	4(18)	3(15)	2	2	0	0	0	0	8	8
Lachlan Burr	27/9/92	3	3	0	0	0	0	0	0	0	0
Dane Chisholm	4/7/90	7	6	2	1	3	3	0	0	14	10
Liam Cooper	28/7/94	1(2)	0	0	0	0	0	0	0	0	0
Jordan Cox	27/5/92	(9)	(8)	0	0	0	0	0	0	0	0
Jonah Cunningham	20/8/97	1(2)	0	0	0	0	0	0	0	0	0
Reece Dean	30/11/96	2	2	1	1	0	0	0	0	4	4
Paddy Flynn	11/12/87	16(1)	8(1)	5	1	0	0	0	0	20	4
Lewis Foster	21/12/93	1(1)	1(1)	0	0	0	0	0	0	0	0
Matty Fozard	3/3/95	33	23	12	7	0	0	0	0	48	28
James Green	29/11/90	(2)	(2)	0	0	0	0	0	0	0	0
Eze Harper	7/12/94	2(1)	1(1)	0	0	0	0	0	0	0	0
Will Hope	2/6/93	19(6)	18(3)	3	3	0	0	0	0	12	12
Sam Hopkins	17/2/90	(1)	(1)	1	1	0	0	0	0	4	4
Matt James	26/3/87	30(1)	22	5	4	0	0	0	0	20	16
Liam Johnson	12/5/97	8(11)	4(9)	2	2	0	0	0	0	8	8
James Kelly	3/9/92	(1)	(1)	1	1	0	0	0	0	4	4
Garry Lo	1/11/93	30	21	37	27	0	0	0	0	148	108
Remy Marginet	27/5/89	9	6	3	3	0	0	0	0	12	12
Mark Mexico	21/5/93	16(11)	14(5)	2	1	0	0	0	0	8	4
Ryan Millar	12/5/94	21(1)	12(1)	2	2	0	0	0	0	8	8
George Milton	4/9/95	1(8)	(3)	1	0	0	0	0	0	4	0
Elliot Minchella	28/1/96	29	21	15	8	0	0	0	0	60	32
Jack Owens	3/6/94	17	9	5	3	26	5	0	0	72	22
Greg Richards	12/7/95	3	3	0	0	0	0	0	0	0	0
Danny Richardson	2/9/96	1	1	1	1	7	7	0	0	18	18
Sam Scott	5/6/90	13(18)	10(12)	5	4	0	0	0	0	20	16
Jake Spedding	26/9/96	10	10	2	2	0	0	0	0	8	8
Duane Straugheir	29/9/89	18(5)	9(4)	7	5	0	0	0	0	28	20
Kyle Trout	1/3/91	6(23)	2(18)	4	3	0	0	0	0	16	12
Calvin Wellington	10/12/95	1	0	0	0	0	0	0	0	0	0
Dayne Weston	15/12/86	1	1	0	0	0	0	0	0	0	0
Scott Wheeldon	23/2/86	32	22	5	3	0	0	0	0	20	12
Perry Whiteley	22/2/93	8(9)	4(6)	1	1	0	0	0	0	4	4
Curtis Wilson	24/4/92	(1)	(1)	0	0	0	0	0	0	0	0
Menzie Yere	24/10/83	31	22	12	8	0	0	0	0	48	32

'Ch' totals include Championship regular season only; 'All' totals also include Championship Shield & Challenge Cup

Garry Lo

LEAGUE RECORD
Championship, before Super 8 split:
P23-W10-D0-L13 (7th)
F568, A785, Diff-217, 20 points.

After Championship Shield:
P30-W13-D0-L17 (3rd/Runners-Up)
F762, A986, Diff-224, 26 points.

CHALLENGE CUP
Round Four

ATTENDANCES
Best - v Hull KR (Ch - 1,619)
Worst - v Rochdale (CS - 297)
Total (Championship/
Championship Shield only) - 9,560
Average (Championship/
Championship Shield only) - 637
(Up by 11 on 2016)

CLUB RECORDS	**Highest score:** 112-6 v Leigh East, 7/4/2013 **Highest score against:** 0-88 v Hull, 2/3/2003 **Record attendance:** 10,603 v Bradford, 16/8/97
MATCH RECORDS	**Tries:** 5 Daryl Powell v Mansfield, 2/1/89; Menzie Yere v Leigh East, 7/4/2013; Quentin Laulu-Togagae v Rochdale, 7/9/2014; Garry Lo v Rochdale, 4/6/2017
	Goals: 14 Dominic Brambani v Leigh East, 7/4/2013 **Points:** 32 Roy Rafferty v Fulham, 21/9/86
SEASON RECORDS	**Tries:** 46 Menzie Yere 2013 **Goals:** 169 *(inc 1fg)* Dominic Brambani 2013 **Points:** 361 Dominic Brambani 2013
CAREER RECORDS	**Tries:** 190 Menzie Yere 2009-2017 **Goals:** 986 Mark Aston 1986-2004 **Points:** 2,142 Mark Aston 1986-2004 **Appearances:** 389 Mark Aston 1986-2004

SWINTON LIONS

DATE	FIXTURE	RESULT	SCORERS	LGE	ATT
5/2/17	London Broncos (h)	L23-26	t:Robinson,Forsyth(2),T Davies g:Atkin(3) fg:Atkin	7th	603
12/2/17	Dewsbury (a)	W6-8	t:Forsyth g:Atkin(2)	7th	802
19/2/17	Bradford (h)	L28-35	t:Thornley(3),Robinson,Murphy g:Atkin(4)	8th	1,193
26/2/17	Featherstone (h)	L13-30	t:Thornley(2) g:Atkin(2) fg:Atkin	8th	850
5/3/17	Batley (a)	L22-18	t:Robinson,Murphy,Thornley g:Atkin(3)	8th	726
11/3/17	Toulouse (h)	L36-28	t:White(2),Hankinson,Butt,Murphy,Dwyer g:Atkin(2)	9th	2,377
18/3/17	London Skolars (h) (CCR4)	W40-8	t:Robinson(2),Butt,Gore(2),A Nicholson,Bracek g:Atkin(6)	N/A	200
26/3/17	Sheffield (h)	L24-28	t:Butt,Murphy,Kenny,Bate,Hankinson g:Atkin(2)	10th	479
2/4/17	Halifax (a)	L38-28	t:White,Butt(2),Atkin,Hankinson g:Hankinson(4)	10th	1,501
9/4/17	Hull KR (h)	L18-52	t:White(2),Butt,Bate g:Atkin	10th	1,375
14/4/17	Oldham (a)	L22-18	t:Robinson,Hankinson,Murphy g:Atkin(3)	10th	804
17/4/17	Rochdale (h)	W23-22	t:Butt,Dwyer,Bracek g:Atkin(5) fg:Atkin	10th	538
23/4/17	Huddersfield (a) (CCR5)	W24-28	t:Robinson,Lloyd,Butt,Dwyer,Waterworth g:Atkin(3),Hankinson	N/A	1,298
30/4/17	London Broncos (a)	L38-28	t:Butt(3),Bracek,Dwyer g:Atkin(4)	10th	618
7/5/17	Toulouse (a)	W27-20	t:Dwyer(3),Thornley g:Atkin(5) fg:Atkin	10th	601
14/5/17	Wigan (h) (CCR6)	L12-42	t:Gore,Butt g:Atkin(2)	N/A	2,003
21/5/17	Hull KR (a)	L42-18	t:Waterworth,Butt(2) g:Atkin(3)	10th	7,236
28/5/17	Sheffield (SB) ●	L30-24	t:Atkin,Robinson,C Farrell,Austin g:Atkin(4)	10th	N/A
4/6/17	Oldham (h)	W26-4	t:Lloyd,Hankinson(2),Murphy g:Atkin(5)	10th	628
11/6/17	Batley (h)	L12-26	t:Bate,Bracek g:Atkin,White	10th	569
21/6/17	Featherstone (a)	L36-2	g:Atkin	10th	1,892
25/6/17	Halifax (h)	W13-12	t:O Davies,Robinson g:Atkin(2) fg:Atkin	9th	863
2/7/17	Sheffield (a)	L42-34	t:Murphy(3),Robinson,Butt,Lloyd g:Atkin(5)	11th	379
9/7/17	Rochdale (a)	L33-28	t:Atkin,Butt(2),Murphy g:Atkin(6)	11th	745
16/7/17	Dewsbury (h)	L20-42	t:Butt,Forsyth,Paisley,White g:Hankinson(2)	11th	1,002
23/7/17	Bradford (a)	W6-16	t:Robinson,White,Forsyth g:Hankinson(2)	10th	3,291
6/8/17	Batley (a) (CS)	L62-10	t:Robinson,Austin g:Hankinson	6th(CS)	544
13/8/17	Sheffield (h) (CS)	L30-32	t:Bergal,Murphy,Lever(2),White g:Hankinson(5)	6th(CS)	434
20/8/17	Bradford (h) (CS)	L16-30	t:Bracek,Robinson,Waterworth g:Hankinson,I Farrell	6th(CS)	660
28/8/17	Dewsbury (a) (CS)	W28-35	t:Hankinson,White,Barlow,Bergal,Austin g:Hankinson(7) fg:White	6th(CS)	812
3/9/17	Rochdale (a) (CS)	L16-8	t:Bergal g:Hankinson(2)	6th(CS)	606
10/9/17	Oldham (h) (CS)	W29-6	t:Barnes,Bergal,Austin,O Davies,Lloyd g:Hankinson(4) fg:Woods	6th(CS)	1,051
16/9/17	Toulouse (a) (CS)	L38-34	t:Waterworth,Bergal,White,A Nicholson,Paisley,Butt,Hankinson g:Hankinson(3)	6th(CS)	1,073

● Played at Bloomfield Road, Blackpool

APP TRIES GOALS FG PTS

	D.O.B.	ALL	Ch	ALL	Ch	ALL	Ch	ALL	Ch	ALL	Ch
Chris Atkin	7/2/93	24	21	3	3	74	63	5	5	165	143
Ben Austin	3/5/95	15(12)	6(11)	4	1	0	0	0	0	16	4
Josh Barlow	15/5/91	12(13)	8(11)	1	0	0	0	0	0	4	0
Caine Barnes	22/2/99	2(5)	2(3)	1	0	0	0	0	0	4	0
Anthony Bate	28/4/93	6(13)	5(12)	3	3	0	0	0	0	12	12
Ilias Bergal	6/4/96	6	0	5	0	0	0	0	0	20	0
Andy Bracek	21/3/84	32(1)	22(1)	5	3	0	0	0	0	20	12
Joe Bretherton	5/10/95	1(1)	1(1)	0	0	0	0	0	0	0	0
Mike Butt	6/5/95	29	19	19	15	0	0	0	0	76	60
Liam Carberry	24/2/93	1(18)	1(10)	0	0	0	0	0	0	0	0
Thomas Coyle	10/5/88	2(1)	0	0	0	0	0	0	0	0	0
Olly Davies	30/11/95	15(7)	8(7)	2	1	0	0	0	0	8	4
Tom Davies	11/1/97	4	4	1	1	0	0	0	0	4	4
Connor Dwyer	29/12/93	16	13	7	6	0	0	0	0	28	24
Connor Farrell	6/11/93	3	3	1	1	0	0	0	0	4	4
Izaac Farrell	30/1/98	3	0	0	0	1	0	0	0	2	0
Callum Field	7/10/97	2(1)	2(1)	0	0	0	0	0	0	0	0
Liam Forsyth	23/3/96	6	6	5	5	0	0	0	0	20	20
Matt Gardner	24/8/84	1(1)	0	0	0	0	0	0	0	0	0
Grant Gore	21/11/91	15(1)	13	3	0	0	0	0	0	12	0
Nick Gregson	17/12/95	2	2	0	0	0	0	0	0	0	0
Jordan Hand	13/5/93	3	3	0	0	0	0	0	0	0	0
Chris Hankinson	30/11/93	31	21	8	6	32	8	0	0	96	40
Jack Hansen	12/1/97	1	0	0	0	0	0	0	0	0	0
Jack Higginson	4/4/97	1	0	0	0	0	0	0	0	0	0
Adam Jones	13/4/97	9(10)	6(4)	0	0	0	0	0	0	0	0
Sean Kenny	21/10/94	5(4)	5(3)	1	1	0	0	0	0	4	4
Rob Lever	13/7/95	19(11)	14(7)	2	0	0	0	0	0	8	0
Rhodri Lloyd	22/7/93	22	13	4	2	0	0	0	0	16	8
Jack Murphy	18/3/92	29	23	11	10	0	0	0	0	44	40
Romain Navarrete	30/6/94	1(1)	1(1)	0	0	0	0	0	0	0	0
Anthony Nicholson	28/11/90	9(18)	7(11)	2	0	0	0	0	0	8	0
Mark Nicholson	29/1/95	(4)	0	0	0	0	0	0	0	0	0
Dan Norman	8/9/97	1(1)	0	0	0	0	0	0	0	0	0
Liam Paisley	27/11/97	6	4	2	1	0	0	0	0	8	4
Shaun Robinson	13/7/89	30	22	13	8	0	0	0	0	52	32
Matt Sarsfield	10/9/91	2	2	0	0	0	0	0	0	0	0
Andy Thornley	1/3/89	11(2)	10(1)	7	7	0	0	0	0	28	28
Luke Waterworth	20/6/96	20(6)	11(6)	4	1	0	0	0	0	16	4
Ben White	27/10/94	25(1)	16(1)	10	7	1	1	1	1	43	30
Josh Woods	13/12/97	7	4	0	0	0	0	1	0	1	0

Mike Butt

'Ch' totals include Championship regular season only; 'All' totals also include Championship Shield & Challenge Cup

LEAGUE RECORD
Championship, before Super 8 split:
P23-W6-D0-L17 (10th)
F477, A648, Diff-171, 12 points.

After Championship Shield:
P30-W8-D0-L22 (6th)
F639, A860, Diff-221, 16 points.

CHALLENGE CUP
Round Six

ATTENDANCES
Best - v Wigan (CC - 2,003)
Worst - v London Skolars (CC - 200)
Total (Championship/
Championship Shield only) - 10,846
Average (Championship/
Championship Shield only) - 775
(Up by 8 on 2016)

CLUB RECORDS	
	Highest score: 96-4 v Oxford, 12/7/2015 **Highest score against:** 0-112 v Warrington, 20/5/2011
	Record attendance: 26,891 v Wigan, 12/2/64 *(Station Road)*; 2,003 v Wigan, 14/5/2017 *(Heywood Road)*
MATCH RECORDS	**Tries:** 6 Mark Riley v Prescot, 11/8/96 **Goals:** 14 Ian Mort v Oxford, 12/7/2015 **Points:** 48 Ian Mort v Oxford, 12/7/2015
SEASON RECORDS	**Tries:** 42 John Stopford 1963-64 **Goals:** 128 Albert Blan 1960-61 **Points:** 338 Ian Mort 2011
CAREER RECORDS	**Tries:** 197 Frank Evans 1921-31 **Goals:** 970 Ken Gowers 1954-73 **Points:** 2,105 Ken Gowers 1954-73 **Appearances:** 601 Ken Gowers 1954-73

TOULOUSE OLYMPIQUE

DATE	FIXTURE	RESULT	SCORERS	LGE	ATT
4/2/17	Batley (h)	W44-6	t:Marguerite(2),Minga(3),Hepi,Curran,Boyer,Maurel g:Kheirallah(4)	2nd	1,623
12/2/17	Sheffield (a)	L32-14	t:Curran,Ader,Leha g:Kheirallah	4th	442
18/2/17	Dewsbury (h)	W56-2	t:Maurel,Robin,Minga(3),Canet(2),Curran,Mika,Ader g:Kheirallah(8)	3rd	1,438
26/2/17	Bradford (a)	L29-22	t:Marguerite(3),Robin g:Maurel(3)	4th	4,151
5/3/17	Halifax (a)	W10-12	t:White,Ader g:Maurel(2)	4th	1,271
11/3/17	Swinton (h)	W36-28	t:Kheirallah,Canet,Minga,Kriouache,Maurel,Robin,Planas g:Maurel,Kheirallah(3)	3rd	2,377
18/3/17	Batley (h) (CCR4) ●	L16-34	t:Bianchini,Puech,Bouscayrol g:Maurel(2)	N/A	150
26/3/17	Featherstone (a)	W26-34	t:Kheirallah(3),Curran,Hepi,Robin g:Kheirallah(5)	2nd	2,087
2/4/17	Rochdale (a)	W14-52	t:Maurel(4),Marion,Marcon,Leha,Ader(2),Marguerite g:Kheirallah(6)	2nd	609
8/4/17	Oldham (h)	W58-18	t:Robin(2),White(2),Ford(2),Kheirallah,Marcon,Boyer,Canet g:Kheirallah(9)	2nd	1,752
14/4/17	London Broncos (a)	L30-16	t:Marguerite,Kriouache,Kheirallah g:Kheirallah(2)	2nd	520
17/4/17	Hull KR (h)	W14-6	t:Minga,Curran g:Kheirallah(3)	2nd	4,107
29/4/17	Bradford (h)	W60-4	t:Ford,Margerite,Marcon,Curran(2),Ader(2),Minga(3),Robin,Canet g:Maurel(6)	2nd	2,312
7/5/17	Swinton (a)	W27-20	t:Curran,Minga,Marcon,Marguerite g:Kheirallah(2)	3rd	601
20/5/17	Sheffield (h)	W45-20	t:Robin(2),K Bentley,Planas(2),Canet,Minga g:Kheirallah(8) fg:Kheirallah	3rd	2,413
28/5/17	Halifax (SB) ●●	W22-32	t:K Bentley,Maurel(2),Curran(2),Marion g:Kheirallah(4)	2nd	N/A
4/6/17	Batley (a)	W20-28	t:Robin,Marcon,Marion,Mika,K Bentley g:Kheirallah(4)	2nd	627
10/6/17	Rochdale (h)	W56-16	t:Mika,Ader(3),Robin,Kheirallah,Boyer,Marion,Marcon,Curran g:Kheirallah(8)	2nd	1,467
17/6/17	London Broncos (h)	L16-36	t:Canet(2),Leha g:Kheirallah(2)	3rd	2,548
25/6/17	Dewsbury (a)	L34-22	t:Marcon(3),Curran g:Kheirallah(3)	4th	626
2/7/17	Oldham (a)	L14-12	t:Planas,Bouzinac g:Kheirallah(2)	4th	519
8/7/17	Halifax (h)	L8-16	t:Boyer,Kheirallah	5th	1,240
16/7/17	Hull KR (a)	W30-31	t:Kheirallah,Ader(2),Robin(2) g:Kheirallah(5) fg:Robin	5th	7,117
22/7/17	Featherstone (h)	W32-26	t:Minga(2),Curran,Ader,Kheirallah(2) g:Kheirallah(4)	5th	2,417
6/8/17	Bradford (a) (CS)	W10-26	t:Curran(2),Marguerite(2),Maurel g:Kheirallah(3)	1st(CS)	2,753
13/8/17	Dewsbury (a) (CS)	L36-34	t:Marcon(3),Robin,Minga,Marguerite,Canet g:Kheirallah(3)	1st(CS)	628
19/8/17	Rochdale (a) (CS)	W50-12	t:Kheirallah(2),Marguerite,Minga(2),Mika,Bouzinac,Robin,Ader g:Kheirallah(7)	1st(CS)	612
28/8/17	Sheffield (h) (CS)	W32-16	t:Boyer,Ford,Kheirallah(2),Robin,Puech g:Kheirallah(4)	1st(CS)	1,855
3/9/17	Oldham (a) (CS)	W18-24	t:Curran,Marguerite,Mika,Hepi,Kheirallah g:Kheirallah(2)	1st(CS)	581
9/9/17	Batley (h) (CS)	W56-14	t:Ford,Robin(3),Kriouache(2),Marcon,Maurel,Kheirallah(2) g:Kheirallah(8)	1st(CS)	868
16/9/17	Swinton (a) (CS)	W38-34	t:Ader,Mika,Maurel,Leha,Curran,Minga,Boyer g:Bouzinac,Maurel(4)	1st(CS)	1,073
23/9/17	Dewsbury (h) (CSSF)	W36-22	t:Canet,Jouffret(2),Curran,Ford,Boyer g:Kheirallah(6)	N/A	1,208
30/9/17	Sheffield (h) (CSF)	W44-14	t:Kheirallah(2),Robin,Marguerite,Curran,Marcon,Marion,Mika,Maurel g:Kheirallah(4)	N/A	1,528

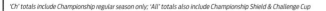
● *Played at Stade Arnaune* ●● *Played at Bloomfield Road, Blackpool*

		APP		TRIES		GOALS		FG		PTS	
	D.O.B.	ALL	Ch	ALL	Ch	ALL	Ch	ALL	Ch	ALL	Ch
Bastien Ader	6/6/91	30	21	15	13	0	0	0	0	60	52
Andrew Bentley	13/5/85	23(6)	18(4)	0	0	0	0	0	0	0	0
Kane Bentley	16/4/87	9(5)	6(4)	3	3	0	0	0	0	12	12
Nicolas Bianchini	14/9/91	1	0	1	0	0	0	0	0	4	0
Justin Bouscayrol	15/12/97	1	0	1	0	0	0	0	0	4	0
Charles Bouzinac	10/1/94	8(6)	2(4)	2	1	1	0	0	0	10	4
Clement Boyer	27/7/94	30(1)	23	7	4	0	0	0	0	28	16
Bastian Canet	26/6/93	26(3)	18(3)	10	8	0	0	0	0	40	32
Rhys Curran	7/7/89	29	22	19	13	0	0	0	0	76	52
Christopher Denis	6/11/96	(3)	(2)	0	0	0	0	0	0	0	0
Etienne Ferret	23/3/96	2	1	0	0	0	0	0	0	0	0
Johnathon Ford	17/8/89	15	9	6	3	0	0	0	0	24	12
Tyla Hepi	15/6/93	5(23)	5(16)	3	2	0	0	0	0	12	8
Louis Jouffret	24/5/95	6	3	2	0	0	0	0	0	8	0
Mark Kheirallah	15/2/90	28	20	20	11	120	83	1	1	321	211
Mourad Kriouache	10/5/91	2(20)	2(13)	4	2	0	0	0	0	16	8
Kalausa Leha	26/3/94	1(18)	(16)	4	3	0	0	0	0	16	12
Paul Marcon	10/7/95	24	15	14	9	0	0	0	0	56	36
Gavin Marguerite	12/8/96	23	14	15	9	0	0	0	0	60	36
Anthony Marion	12/1/94	31	22	5	4	0	0	0	0	20	16
Tony Maurel	21/4/93	29	20	13	9	18	12	0	0	88	60
Cedric Mazars	23/7/96	(1)	0	0	0	0	0	0	0	0	0
Constantine Mika	14/9/89	19(9)	13(7)	7	3	0	0	0	0	28	12
Kuni Minga	2/2/93	18	14	19	15	0	0	0	0	76	60
Levy Nzoungou	22/1/98	(8)	(3)	0	0	0	0	0	0	0	0
Ugo Perez	30/11/94	5	0	0	0	0	0	0	0	0	0
Sebastien Planas	5/5/84	23	22	4	4	0	0	0	0	16	16
Maxime Puech	16/3/94	6(20)	3(14)	2	0	0	0	0	0	8	0
Quentin Quemener	23/9/96	(1)	0	0	0	0	0	0	0	0	0
Stan Robin	21/10/90	26	20	20	13	0	0	1	1	81	53
Justin Sangare	7/3/98	3(8)	(6)	0	0	0	0	0	0	0	0
Gregory White	28/8/88	6	6	3	3	0	0	0	0	12	12

'Ch' totals include Championship regular season only; 'All' totals also include Championship Shield & Challenge Cup

Stan Robin

LEAGUE RECORD
Championship, before Super 8 split:
P23-W15-D0-L8 (5th)
F720, A466, Diff+254, 30 points.

After Championship Shield:
P30-W21-D0-L9 (1st/Winners)
F980, A606, Diff+374, 42 points.

CHALLENGE CUP
Round Four

ATTENDANCES
Best - v Hull KR (Ch - 4,107)
Worst - v Batley (CC - 150)
Total (Championship/
Championship Shield only) - 30,838
Average (Championship/
Championship Shield only) - 1,814
(Up by 301 on 2016, League 1)

CLUB RECORDS MATCH RECORDS	**Highest score:** 84-6 v Keighley, 18/6/2016 **Highest score against:** 10-90 v Featherstone, 3/7/2011 **Record attendance:** 4,107 v Hull KR, 17/4/2017 **Tries:** 4 Mark Kheirallah v Wath Brow, 27/2/2016; Danny Hulme v Coventry, 5/3/2016; Kuni Minga v South Wales, 10/4/2016; Mark Kheirallah v Keighley, 18/6/2016; Mark Kheirallah v London Skolars, 26/8/2016; Tony Maurel v Rochdale, 2/4/2017 **Goals:** 12 Mark Kheirallah v Keighley, 18/6/2016 **Points:** 40 Mark Kheirallah v Keighley, 18/6/2016
SEASON RECORDS CAREER RECORDS	**Tries:** 36 Kuni Minga 2016 **Goals:** 171 Mark Kheirallah 2016 **Points:** 466 Mark Kheirallah 2016 **Tries:** 55 Kuni Minga 2016-2017 **Goals:** 291 Mark Kheirallah 2016-2017 **Points:** 787 Mark Kheirallah 2016-2017 **Appearances:** 109 Sebastien Planas 2009-2011; 2016-2017

● *Records only include seasons when the club competed in the British game (2009-2011 & 2016-2017)*

CHAMPIONSHIP 2017
Round by Round

ROUND 1

Saturday 4th February 2017

TOULOUSE OLYMPIQUE 44 BATLEY BULLDOGS 6

OLYMPIQUE: 1 Mark Kheirallah; 2 Tony Maurel; 3 Bastien Ader; 21 Gavin Marguerite; 5 Kuni Minga; 6 Johnathon Ford; 7 Stan Robin; 8 Clement Boyer; 24 Anthony Marion; 16 Tyla Hepi; 11 Sebastien Planas; 12 Rhys Curran; 26 Constantine Mika. Subs (all used): - Christopher Denis; 17 Kalausa Leha; 23 Justin Sangare; 13 Andrew Bentley.
Tries: Marguerite (11, 80), Minga (13, 16, 29), Hepi (50), Curran (62), Boyer (64), Maurel (73); **Goals:** Kheirallah 4/9.
BULLDOGS: 1 Dave Scott; 2 Wayne Reittie; 3 Sam Smeaton; 4 Macauley Hallett; 5 Shaun Ainscough; 6 Cain Southernwood; 7 Dominic Brambani; 16 Tom Lillycrop; 9 Alistair Leak; 10 Alex Rowe; 11 Brad Day; 22 Dane Manning; 13 Pat Walker. Subs (all used): 14 James Davey; 18 James Harrison; 21 James Brown; 23 Brad Hill.
Try: Leak (5); **Goals:** Walker 1/1.
Rugby Leaguer & League Express Men of the Match: *Olympique:* Johnathon Ford; *Bulldogs:* Dave Scott.
Penalty count: 7-12; **Half-time:** 18-6;
Referee: Jack Smith; **Attendance:** 1,623.

Sunday 5th February 2017

HALIFAX 26 FEATHERSTONE ROVERS 32

HALIFAX: 19 Connor Robinson; 5 James Saltonstall; 3 Steve Tyrer; 4 Ben Heaton; 23 Rob Worrincy; 6 Scott Murrell; 1 Ben Johnston; 15 Luke Ambler; 9 Ben Kaye; 8 Mitch Cahalane; 11 Shane Grady; 12 Simon Grix; 13 Jacob Fairbank. Subs (all used): 10 Adam Tangata; 14 Ryan Boyle; 16 Ed Barber; 26 Alex Mammone.
Tries: Fairbank (27), Worrincy (39), Tangata (42), Murrell (46), Tyrer (66); **Goals:** Tyrer 3/5.
Sin bin: Cahalane (55) - high tackle on Ulugia.
ROVERS: 1 Ian Hardman; 24 Ash Handley; 5 Luke Briscoe; 3 Chris Ulugia; 23 Josh Hardcastle; 7 Anthony Thackeray; 19 Matty Wildie; 10 Andrew Bostock; 9 Keal Carlile; 32 Jordan Baldwinson; 12 John Davies; 14 Frankie Mariano; 15 Bradley Knowles-Tagg. Subs (all used): 6 Kyle Briggs; 8 Darrell Griffin; 25 Josh Walters; 30 Jack Ormondroyd.
Tries: Briscoe (7), Hardcastle (10, 49), Handley (21), Briggs (74); **Goals:** Hardman 2/5, Briggs 4/4.
Rugby Leaguer & League Express Men of the Match: *Halifax:* Ryan Boyle; *Rovers:* Andrew Bostock.
Penalty count: 8-11; **Half-time:** 10-16;
Referee: James Child; **Attendance:** 2,147.

HULL KINGSTON ROVERS 54 BRADFORD BULLS 24

ROVERS: 1 Adam Quinlan; 32 Kieren Moss; 3 Thomas Minns; 22 Andrew Heffernan; 5 Ryan Shaw; 16 Jordan Abdull; 7 Jamie Ellis; 8 Nick Scruton; 9 Shaun Lunt; 17 Mitch Clark; 11 Maurice Blair; 12 James Greenwood; 13 Danny Addy. Subs (all used): 15 James Donaldson; 10 Chris Clarkson; 19 George Lawler; 21 Rob Mulhern.
Tries: Heffernan (11, 69), Scruton (18, 21), Donaldson (36), Minns (39), Greenwood (46), Ellis (52), Quinlan (60); **Goals:** Ellis 9/9.
BULLS: 14 Oscar Thomas; 2 Ethan Ryan; 3 James Mendeika; 4 Ross Oakes; 5 Iliess Macani; 6 Leon Pryce; 28 Jordan Lilley; 8 Liam Kirk; 9 Joe Lumb; 17 Ross Peltier; 11 Colton Roche; 20 James Bentley; 21 Brandan Wilkinson. Subs (all used): 15 Jon Magrin; 29 Sam Hallas; 30 Josh Jordan-Roberts; 31 Mikolaj Oledzki.
Tries: Kirk (8), Oakes (25), Ryan (63), Macani (75); **Goals:** Thomas 4/4.
Rugby Leaguer & League Express Men of the Match: *Rovers:* Jamie Ellis; *Bulls:* Jordan Lilley.
Penalty count: 9-8; **Half-time:** 30-12;
Referee: Scott Mikalauskas; **Attendance:** 8,817.

OLDHAM 26 SHEFFIELD EAGLES 10

OLDHAM: 1 Scott Turner; 2 Adam Clay; 29 Tuoyo Egodo; 22 Danny Grimshaw; 25 Kieran Gill; 6 Scott Leatherbarrow; 7 Dave Hewitt; 8 Phil Joy; 20 Gareth Owen; 10 Adam Neal; - Mikey Wood; 12 Danny Langtree; 11 Jack Spencer. Subs (all used): 24 Michael Ward; 21 Kenny Hughes; 9 Sam Gee; - Tyler Dickinson.
Tries: Langtree (34, 77), Clay (42), Hewitt (51); **Goals:** Leatherbarrow 5/6.
Sin bin: Turner (40) - fighting.
EAGLES: 5 Ben Blackmore; 2 Garry Lo; 3 Menzie Yere; 4 Perry Whiteley; 18 Ryan Millar; 6 Simon Brown; 7 Dane Chisholm; 8 Scott Wheeldon; 9 Matty Fozard; 28 Lachlan Burr; 11 Matt James; 19 Will Hope; 13 Elliot Minchella. Subs (all used): 15 Kyle Trout; 10 Mark Mexico; 16 Sam Scott; 17 Jordan Cox.
Tries: Fozard (4), Millar (66); **Goals:** Brown 1/2.
Sin bin: Blackmore (40) - fighting.
Rugby Leaguer & League Express Men of the Match: *Oldham:* Adam Neal; *Eagles:* Elliot Minchella.
Penalty count: 13-6; **Half-time:** 4-6;
Referee: Chris Campbell; **Attendance:** 668.

ROCHDALE HORNETS 46 DEWSBURY RAMS 0

HORNETS: 2 Chris Riley; 1 Miles Greenwood; 3 Jake Eccleston; 4 Lewis Galbraith; 5 Rob Massam; 6 Lewis Palfrey; 7 Danny Yates; 8 Samir Tahraoui; 9 Ben Moores; 10 Gavin Bennion; 28 Danny Bridge; 12 Josh Crowley; 13 Gary Middlehurst. Subs (all used): 14 Ryan Maneely; 15 Jovili Taira; 16 Matty Hadden; 19 Jordan Case.
Tries: Tahraoui (15), Moores (20, 22), Yates (33), Taira (49), Massam (63), Galbraith (70), Maneely (73); **Goals:** Palfrey 7/10.
RAMS: 27 Max Jowitt; 5 Gareth Potts; 21 Hamish Barnes; 3 Jason Crookes; 28 Mason Caton-Brown; 6 Paul Sykes; 7 Andy Kain; 26 David Fifita; 17 Dom Speakman; 10 Mitchell Stringer; 11 Rob Spicer; 4 Lucas Walshaw; 13 Aaron Brown. Subs (all used): 29 Keegan Hirst; 15 Robbie Ward; 16 Toby Adamson; 24 Jode Sheriffe.
Rugby Leaguer & League Express Men of the Match: *Hornets:* Gary Middlehurst; *Rams:* Paul Sykes.
Penalty count: 12-5; **Half-time:** 22-0;
Referee: Ben Thaler; **Attendance:** 718.

SWINTON LIONS 23 LONDON BRONCOS 26

LIONS: 1 Jack Murphy; 2 Shaun Robinson; 3 Chris Hankinson; 26 Liam Forsyth; - Tom Davies; 6 Grant Gore; 7 Chris Atkin; 10 Jordan Hand; 20 Sean Kenny; 15 Andy Bracek; 11 Connor Dwyer; 12 Matt Sarsfield; 13 Andy Thornley. Subs (all used): 8 Rob Lever; 16 Anthony Bate; 18 Ben Austin; 19 Josh Barlow.
Tries: Robinson (3), Forsyth (8, 37), T Davies (45);
Goals: Atkin 3/6; **Field goal:** Atkin (70).
Sin bin: Dwyer (19) - holding down.
BRONCOS: 1 Elliot Kear; 2 Rhys Williams; 3 Ben Hellewell; 4 Adrian Purtell; 5 Kieran Dixon; 6 Jarrod Sammut; 7 William Barthau; 8 Tom Spencer; 14 Andy Ackers; 10 Mark Ioane; 11 Daniel Harrison; 13 Jay Pitts; 15 Eddie Battye. Subs (all used): 12 Matt Garside; 28 Sadiq Adebiyi; 17 Mark Offerdahl; 16 Junior Roqica.
Tries: Williams (15), Sammut (33), Barthau (48), Ioane (54), Harrison (74); **Goals:** Sammut 3/5.
Rugby Leaguer & League Express Men of the Match: *Lions:* Liam Forsyth; *Broncos:* Jarrod Sammut.
Penalty count: 7-7; **Half-time:** 16-10;
Referee: Chris Kendall; **Attendance:** 603.

ROUND 2

Sunday 12th February 2017

BATLEY BULLDOGS 24 HALIFAX 6

BULLDOGS: 1 Dave Scott; 25 Michael Hayward; 3 Sam Smeaton; 4 Macauley Hallett; 5 Shaun Ainscough; 13 Pat Walker; 7 Dominic Brambani; 16 Tom Lillycrop; 14 James Davey; 27 Will Maher; 19 Alex Bretherton; 22 Dane Manning; 11 Brad Day. Subs (all used): 6 Cain Southernwood; 21 James Brown; 17 Joe Chandler; 18 James Harrison.
Tries: Smeaton (2), Bretherton (21), Manning (35), Chandler (61); **Goals:** Walker 3/3, Southernwood 1/1.
HALIFAX: 19 Connor Robinson; 23 Rob Worrincy; 21 James Woodburn-Hall; 3 Steve Tyrer; 5 James Saltonstall; 6 Scott Murrell; 7 Gareth Moore; 14 Ryan Boyle; 27 Matt Wilkinson; 8 Mitch Cahalane; 10 Adam Tangata; 12 Simon Grix; 13 Jacob Fairbank. Subs (all used): 16 Ed Barber; 26 Alex Mammone; 1 Ben Johnston; 15 Luke Ambler.
Try: Saltonstall (75); **Goals:** Tyrer 1/1.
Rugby Leaguer & League Express Men of the Match: *Bulldogs:* Dominic Brambani; *Halifax:* James Saltonstall.
Penalty count: 11-6; **Half-time:** 18-0;
Referee: Chris Kendall; **Attendance:** 900.

BRADFORD BULLS 14 ROCHDALE HORNETS 22

BULLS: 14 Oscar Thomas; 2 Ethan Ryan; 3 James Mendeika; 4 Ross Oakes; 5 Iliess Macani; 6 Leon Pryce; 28 Jordan Lilley; 8 Liam Kirk; 9 Joe Lumb; 15 Jon Magrin; 11 Colton Roche; 20 James Bentley; 21 Brandan Wilkinson. Subs (all used): 17 Ross Peltier; 29 Sam Hallas; 30 Josh Jordan-Roberts; 31 Mikolaj Oledzki.
Tries: Thomas (2), Bentley (26); **Goals:** Thomas 3/4.
HORNETS: 1 Miles Greenwood; 2 Chris Riley; 3 Jake Eccleston; 4 Lewis Galbraith; 5 Rob Massam; 6 Lewis Palfrey; 7 Danny Yates; 8 Samir Tahraoui; 9 Ben Moores; 10 Gavin Bennion; 28 Danny Bridge; 12 Josh Crowley; 13 Gary Middlehurst. Subs (all used): 14 Ryan Maneely; 15 Jovili Taira; 16 Matty Hadden; 19 Jordan Case.
Tries: Greenwood (13), Tahraoui (52), Bridge (57); **Goals:** Palfrey 5/6.
Sin bin: Taira (35) - late challenge on Lilley.
Rugby Leaguer & League Express Men of the Match: *Bulls:* Jordan Lilley; *Hornets:* Miles Greenwood.
Penalty count: 12-10; **Half-time:** 12-8;
Referee: Jon Roberts; **Attendance:** 4,051.

DEWSBURY RAMS 6 SWINTON LIONS 8

RAMS: 6 Paul Sykes; 5 Gareth Potts; 21 Hamish Barnes; 3 Jason Crookes; 2 Dale Morton; 17 Dom Speakman; 7 Andy Kain; 24 Jode Sheriffe; 15 Robbie Ward; 10 Mitchell Stringer; 4 Lucas Walshaw; 12 Scott Hale; 13 Aaron Brown. Subs (all used): 23 James Glover; 18 Jack Teanby; 8 Tony Tonks; 16 Toby Adamson.
Try: Glover (54); **Goals:** Sykes 1/2.
LIONS: 1 Jack Murphy; 2 Shaun Robinson; 3 Chris Hankinson; 25 Liam Forsyth; - Tom Davies; 6 Grant Gore; 7 Chris Atkin; 15 Andy Bracek; 20 Sean Kenny; 10 Jordan Hand; 11 Connor Dwyer; 12 Matt Sarsfield; 13 Andy Thornley. Subs (all used): 8 Rob Lever; 16 Anthony Bate; 17 Olly Davies; 18 Ben Austin.
Try: Forsyth (77); **Goals:** Atkin 2/3.
Rugby Leaguer & League Express Men of the Match: *Rams:* Jode Sheriffe; *Lions:* Chris Atkin.
Penalty count: 10-9; **Half-time:** 0-2;
Referee: Callum Straw; **Attendance:** 802.

FEATHERSTONE ROVERS 8 OLDHAM 6

ROVERS: 1 Ian Hardman; 5 Luke Briscoe; 23 Josh Hardcastle; 3 Chris Ulugia; 24 Ash Handley; 7 Anthony Thackeray; 19 Matty Wildie; 10 Andrew Bostock; 9 Keal Carlile; 16 Luke Cooper; 12 John Davies; 22 Jason Walton; 15 Bradley Knowles-Tagg. Subs (all used): 6 Kyle Briggs; 25 Josh Walters; 30 Jack Ormondroyd; 8 Darrell Griffin.
Tries: Ulugia (26, 46); **Goals:** Handley 0/2.
OLDHAM: 1 Scott Turner; 2 Adam Clay; 29 Tuoyo Egodo; 22 Danny Grimshaw; 25 Kieran Gill; 6 Scott Leatherbarrow; 7 Dave Hewitt; 10 Adam Neal; 20 Gareth Owen; 8 Phil Joy; - Mikey Wood; 12 Danny Langtree; 11 Jack Spencer. Subs (all used): 24 Michael Ward; 30 Nathan Mason; 19 Joe Burke; 21 Kenny Hughes.
Try: Turner (8); **Goals:** Leatherbarrow 1/1.
Rugby Leaguer & League Express Men of the Match: *Rovers:* Chris Ulugia; *Oldham:* Scott Leatherbarrow.
Penalty count: 11-6; **Half-time:** 4-6;
Referee: Tom Grant; **Attendance:** 1,783.

LONDON BRONCOS 22 HULL KINGSTON ROVERS 28

BRONCOS: 1 Elliot Kear; 2 Rhys Williams; 3 Ben Hellewell; 4 Adrian Purtell; 5 Kieran Dixon; 6 Jarrod Sammut; 7 William Barthau; 8 Tom Spencer; 14 Andy Ackers; 15 Eddie Battye; 11 Daniel Harrison; 13 Jay Pitts; 23 Matty Gee. Subs (all used): 27 Ben Pointer; 12 Matt Garside; 10 Mark Ioane; 28 Sadiq Adebiyi.
Tries: Sammut (7, 48), Dixon (64), Purtell (68);
Goals: Sammut 3/4.
ROVERS: 1 Adam Quinlan; 32 Kieren Moss; 3 Thomas Minns; 22 Andrew Heffernan; 5 Ryan Shaw; 16 Jordan Abdull; 7 Jamie Ellis; 8 Nick Scruton; 9 Shaun Lunt; 17 Mitch Clark; 11 Maurice Blair; 12 James Greenwood; 13 Danny Addy. Subs (all used): 4 Liam Salter; 10 Chris Clarkson; 15 James Donaldson; 19 George Lawler.
Tries: Abdull (14), Ellis (25), Moss (28), Heffernan (56), Shaw (58); **Goals:** Ellis 4/6.
Rugby Leaguer & League Express Men of the Match: *Broncos:* Jarrod Sammut; *Rovers:* Jamie Ellis.
Penalty count: 8-11; **Half-time:** 6-16;
Referee: Scott Mikalauskas; **Attendance:** 1,250.

SHEFFIELD EAGLES 32 TOULOUSE OLYMPIQUE 14

EAGLES: 7 Dane Chisholm; 2 Garry Lo; 3 Menzie Yere; 4 Perry Whiteley; 5 Ben Blackmore; 6 Simon Brown; 13 Elliot Minchella; 8 Scott Wheeldon; 9 Matty Fozard; 26 Jamie Acton; 11 Matt James; 19 Will Hope; 28 Lachlan Burr. Subs (all used): 14 Greg Burns; 15 Kyle Trout; 16 Sam Scott; 29 Sam Hopkins.
Tries: Hopkins (23), James (26), Fozard (37), Yere (53), Lo (78); **Goals:** Brown 4/4, Chisholm 2/4.
OLYMPIQUE: 1 Mark Kheirallah; 2 Tony Maurel; 3 Bastien Ader; 21 Gavin Marguerite; 5 Kuni Minga; 19 Etienne Ferret; 7 Stan Robin; 8 Clement Boyer; 24 Anthony Marion; 16 Tyla Hepi; 11 Sebastien Planas; 12 Rhys Curran; 26 Constantine Mika. Subs (all used): - Christopher Denis; 13 Andrew Bentley; 23 Justin Sangare; 17 Kalausa Leha.
Tries: Curran (12), Ader (58), Leha (70);
Goals: Kheirallah 1/3.
Rugby Leaguer & League Express Men of the Match: *Eagles:* Dane Chisholm; *Olympique:* Rhys Curran.
Penalty count: 6-4; **Half-time:** 20-4;
Referee: Andrew Sweet; **Attendance:** 442.

ROUND 3

Saturday 18th February 2017

TOULOUSE OLYMPIQUE 56 DEWSBURY RAMS 2

OLYMPIQUE: 1 Mark Kheirallah; 2 Tony Maurel; 3 Bastien Ader; 4 Gregory White; 5 Kuni Minga; 26 Constantine

Mika; 7 Stan Robin; 8 Clement Boyer; 24 Anthony Marion; 16 Tyla Hepi; 11 Sebastien Planas; 12 Rhys Curran; 13 Andrew Bentley. Subs (all used): 9 Kane Bentley; 10 Bastian Canet; 15 Maxime Puech; 17 Kalausa Leha.
Tries: Maurel (16), Robin (30), Minga (35, 39, 44), Canet (47, 77), Curran (56), Mika (65), Ader (80);
Goals: Kheirallah 8/10.
RAMS: 23 James Glover; 5 Gareth Potts; 21 Hamish Barnes; 3 Jason Crookes; 2 Dale Morton; 6 Paul Sykes; 17 Dom Speakman; 24 Jode Sheriffe; 15 Robbie Ward; 10 Mitchell Stringer; 4 Lucas Walshaw; 12 Scott Hale; 13 Aaron Brown. Subs (all used): 8 Tony Tonks; 16 Toby Adamson; 18 Jack Teanby; 20 Aaron Ollett.
Goals: Sykes 1/2.
Sin bin: Sykes (75) - dissent.
Rugby Leaguer & League Express Men of the Match: *Olympique:* Rhys Curran; *Rams:* Mitchell Stringer.
Penalty count: 10-9; **Half-time:** 24-2;
Referee: Tom Grant; **Attendance:** 1,438.

Sunday 19th February 2017

BATLEY BULLDOGS 6 FEATHERSTONE ROVERS 32

BULLDOGS: 1 Dave Scott; 2 Wayne Reittie; 3 Sam Smeaton; 4 Macauley Hallett; 5 Shaun Ainscough; 13 Pat Walker; 7 Dominic Brambani; 16 Tom Lillycrop; 9 Alistair Leak; 21 James Brown; 19 Alex Bretherton; 22 Dane Manning; 11 Brad Day. Subs (all used): 14 James Davey; 27 Will Maher; 17 Joe Chandler; 10 Alex Rowe.
Try: Brambani (52); **Goals:** Walker 1/1.
ROVERS: 1 Ian Hardman; 5 Luke Briscoe; 22 Jason Walton; 3 Chris Ulugia; 24 Ash Handley; 7 Anthony Thackeray; 19 Matty Wildie; 10 Andrew Bostock; 9 Keal Carlile; 32 Jordan Baldwinson; 12 John Davies; 11 Michael Knowles; 15 Bradley Knowles-Tagg. Subs (all used): 6 Kyle Briggs; 23 Josh Hardcastle; 14 Frankie Mariano; 13 Richard Moore.
Tries: Hardman (13, 39), Handley (45), Briscoe (64), Carlile (70); **Goals:** Handley 0/1, Knowles 6/7.
Sin bin: Knowles (6) - punching Scott.
Rugby Leaguer & League Express Men of the Match: *Bulldogs:* Alistair Leak; *Rovers:* Keal Carlile.
Penalty count: 11-12; **Half-time:** 0-14;
Referee: Gareth Hewer; **Attendance:** 1,385.

HALIFAX 42 SHEFFIELD EAGLES 16

HALIFAX: 2 Will Sharp; 5 James Saltonstall; 3 Steve Tyrer; 21 James Woodburn-Hall; 23 Rob Worrincy; 6 Scott Murrell; 1 Ben Johnston; 14 Ryan Boyle; 28 Adam O'Brien; 8 Mitch Cahalane; 16 Ed Barber; 12 Simon Grix; 13 Jacob Fairbank. Subs (all used): 20 Elliot Morris; 27 Matt Wilkinson; 15 Luke Ambler; 29 Ryan Lannon.
Tries: O'Brien (3), Murrell (19), Johnston (23), Saltonstall (43, 56, 79), Ambler (48), Tyrer (61);
Goals: Tyrer 5/8.
EAGLES: 7 Dane Chisholm; 2 Garry Lo; 3 Menzie Yere; 4 Perry Whiteley; 5 Ben Blackmore; 6 Simon Brown; 13 Elliot Minchella; 8 Scott Wheeldon; 9 Matty Fozard; 30 Dayne Weston; 11 Matt James; 19 Will Hope; 28 Lachlan Burr. Subs (all used): 12 Duane Straugheir; 15 Kyle Trout; 16 Sam Scott; 21 Eze Harper.
Tries: Wheeldon (34), Blackmore (63), Straugheir (74);
Goals: Brown 2/3.
Sin bin: Wheeldon (19) - tripping; Weston (55) - holding down.
Rugby Leaguer & League Express Men of the Match: *Halifax:* Adam O'Brien; *Eagles:* Dane Chisholm.
Penalty count: 10-9; **Half-time:** 18-6;
Referee: Chris Kendall; **Attendance:** 1,241.

OLDHAM 18 LONDON BRONCOS 20

OLDHAM: 1 Scott Turner; 2 Adam Clay; - Sam Wood; 22 Danny Grimshaw; 25 Kieran Gill; 6 Scott Leatherbarrow; 7 Dave Hewitt; 8 Phil Joy; 20 Gareth Owen; 10 Adam Neal; 11 Jack Spencer; 12 Danny Langtree; 24 Michael Ward. Subs (all used): 19 Joe Burke; 21 Kenny Hughes; 9 Sam Gee; - Tyler Dickinson.
Tries: S Wood (1, 24); **Goals:** Leatherbarrow 3/3, Hewitt 2/3.
BRONCOS: 1 Elliot Kear; 2 Rhys Williams; 3 Ben Hellewell; 4 Adrian Purtell; 5 Kieran Dixon; 6 Jarrod Sammut; 7 William Barthau; 17 Mark Offerdahl; 14 Andy Ackers; 10 Mark Ioane; 11 Daniel Harrison; 13 Jay Pitts; 22 Matt Davis. Subs (all used): 23 Matty Gee; 12 Matt Garside; 18 Ben Evans; 16 Junior Roqica.
Tries: Sammut (9), Ackers (30), Harrison (67), Williams (75); **Goals:** Sammut 2/4.
Rugby Leaguer & League Express Men of the Match: *Oldham:* Dave Hewitt; *Broncos:* Jarrod Sammut.
Penalty count: 8-8; **Half-time:** 14-12;
Referee: Ben Thaler; **Attendance:** 558.

ROCHDALE HORNETS 18 HULL KINGSTON ROVERS 28

HORNETS: 1 Miles Greenwood; 2 Chris Riley; 3 Jake Eccleston; 4 Lewis Galbraith; 5 Rob Massam; 6 Lewis Palfrey; 7 Danny Yates; 8 Samir Tahraoui; 9 Ben Moores; 10 Gavin Bennion; 28 Danny Bridge; 12 Josh Crowley; 13 Gary Middlehurst. Subs (all used): 14 Ryan Maneely; 15 Jovili Taira; 16 Matty Hadden; 19 Jordan Case.
Tries: Middlehurst (5), Yates (44), Moores (61);
Goals: Palfrey 3/3.
ROVERS: 1 Adam Quinlan; 32 Kieren Moss; 3 Thomas Minns; 22 Andrew Heffernan; 5 Ryan Shaw; 16 Jordan Abdull; 7 Jamie Ellis; 8 Nick Scruton; 9 Shaun Lunt; 17 Mitch Clark; 11 Maurice Blair; 12 James Greenwood; 13 Danny Addy. Subs (all used): 10 Chris Clarkson; 15 James Donaldson; 33 Ben Kavanagh; 21 Rob Mulhern.
Tries: Moss (10), Minns (12, 15), Heffernan (35), Lunt (75);
Goals: Ellis 4/7.
Rugby Leaguer & League Express Men of the Match: *Hornets:* Gary Middlehurst; *Rovers:* Mitch Clark.
Penalty count: 7-10; **Half-time:** 6-18;
Referee: Chris Campbell; **Attendance:** 2,012.

SWINTON LIONS 28 BRADFORD BULLS 35

LIONS: 1 Jack Murphy; 2 Shaun Robinson; 25 Jack Higginson; 26 Liam Forsyth; - Tom Davies; 6 Grant Gore; 7 Chris Atkin; 10 Jordan Hand; 20 Sean Kenny; 15 Andy Bracek; 11 Connor Dwyer; 13 Andy Thornley; 8 Rob Lever. Subs (all used): 27 Romain Navarrete; 16 Anthony Bate; 17 Olly Davies; 18 Ben Austin.
Tries: Thornley (13, 44, 79), Robinson (28), Murphy (55);
Goals: Atkin 4/5.
Sin bin: Higginson (58) - high tackle; Bate (60) - fighting.
BULLS: 14 Oscar Thomas; 5 Iliess Macani; 4 Ross Oakes; 3 James Mendeika; 2 Ethan Ryan; 6 Leon Pryce; 7 Joe Keyes; 11 Colton Roche; 34 Scott Moore; 15 Jon Magrin; 16 Kevin Larroyer; 20 James Bentley; 30 Josh Jordan-Roberts. Subs: 8 Liam Kirk; 26 Vila Halafihi (not used); 31 Mikolaj Oledzki; 32 Jonathan Walker.
Tries: Ryan (5, 61, 66), Thomas (19), Oakes (32), Mendeika (39); **Goals:** Thomas 5/6;
Field goal: Thomas (69).
Sin bin: Roche (60) - fighting.
Rugby Leaguer & League Express Men of the Match: *Lions:* Andy Thornley; *Bulls:* Oscar Thomas.
Penalty count: 13-10; **Half-time:** 10-22;
Referee: Andrew Sweet; **Attendance:** 1,193.

ROUND 4

Sunday 26th February 2017

BRADFORD BULLS 29 TOULOUSE OLYMPIQUE 22

BULLS: 14 Oscar Thomas; 5 Iliess Macani; 3 James Mendeika; 4 Ross Oakes; 2 Ethan Ryan; 6 Leon Pryce; 28 Jordan Lilley; 11 Colton Roche; 34 Scott Moore; 15 Jon Magrin; 16 Kevin Larroyer; 20 James Bentley; 30 Josh Jordan-Roberts. Subs: 1 Lee Smith (not used); 22 Daniel Murray; 8 Liam Kirk; 31 Mikolaj Oledzki.
Tries: Macani (6), Bentley (10), Ryan (20), Moore (25), Oakes (53); **Goals:** Thomas 4/6; **Field goal:** Thomas (78).
OLYMPIQUE: 2 Tony Maurel; 21 Gavin Marguerite; 3 Bastien Ader; 4 Gregory White; 20 Paul Marcon; 26 Constantine Mika; 7 Stan Robin; 8 Clement Boyer; 9 Kane Bentley; 16 Tyla Hepi; 11 Sebastien Planas; 12 Rhys Curran; 13 Andrew Bentley. Subs (all used): 14 Mourad Kriouache; 15 Maxime Puech; 10 Bastian Canet; 17 Kalausa Leha.
Tries: Marguerite (2, 60, 67), Robin (64); **Goals:** Maurel 3/4.
Sin bin: Curran (8) - dangerous challenge.
Rugby Leaguer & League Express Men of the Match: *Bulls:* Jordan Lilley; *Olympique:* Constantine Mika.
Penalty count: 10-9; **Half-time:** 22-6;
Referee: Jack Smith; **Attendance:** 4,151.

DEWSBURY RAMS 6 LONDON BRONCOS 20

RAMS: 6 Paul Sykes; 5 Gareth Potts; 21 Hamish Barnes; 3 Jason Crookes; 2 Dale Morton; - Liam Coe; 7 Andy Kain; 16 Toby Adamson; 15 Robbie Ward; 24 Jode Sheriffe; 4 Lucas Walshaw; 12 Scott Hale; 28 Chris Annakin. Subs (all used): 23 James Glover; 11 Rob Spicer; 10 Mitchell Stringer; 29 Daniel Igbinedion.
Try: Barnes (13); **Goals:** Sykes 1/1.
BRONCOS: 24 Alex Walker; 2 Rhys Williams; 3 Ben Hellewell; 4 Adrian Purtell; 1 Elliot Kear; 6 Jarrod Sammut; 7 William Barthau; 16 Junior Roqica; 14 Andy Ackers; 10 Mark Ioane; 11 Daniel Harrison; 12 Matt Garside; 18 Ben Evans. Subs (all used): 13 Jay Pitts; 23 Matty Gee; 17 Mark Offerdahl; 30 Callum Bustin.
Tries: Roqica (7), Sammut (36), Walker (55);
Goals: Sammut 4/4.
Rugby Leaguer & League Express Men of the Match: *Rams:* Robbie Ward; *Broncos:* Jarrod Sammut.
Penalty count: 9-12; **Half-time:** 6-12;
Referee: Jon Roberts; **Attendance:** 678.

HULL KINGSTON ROVERS 48 OLDHAM 0

ROVERS: 1 Adam Quinlan; 32 Kieren Moss; 3 Thomas Minns; 22 Andrew Heffernan; 5 Ryan Shaw; 16 Jordan Abdull; 7 Jamie Ellis; 8 Nick Scruton; 9 Shaun Lunt; 17 Mitch Clark; 11 Maurice Blair; 12 James Greenwood; 15 James Donaldson. Subs (all used): 21 Rob Mulhern; 10 Chris Clarkson; 33 Ben Kavanagh; 2 Ben Cockayne.
Tries: Minns (4, 70), Lunt (8), Donaldson (11), Scruton (15), Abdull (24), Ellis (54), Moss (62); **Goals:** Ellis 8/8.
Sin bin: Scruton (62) - dangerous contact.
OLDHAM: 1 Scott Turner; 2 Adam Clay; 29 Tuoyo Egodo; 22 Danny Grimshaw; 25 Kieran Gill; 6 Scott Leatherbarrow; 7 Dave Hewitt; 19 Joe Burke; 20 Gareth Owen; 10 Adam Neal; 13 Liam Thompson; 12 Danny Langtree; 11 Jack Spencer. Subs (all used): 21 Kenny Hughes; 9 Sam Gee; 18 Ben Davies; 24 Michael Ward.
Rugby Leaguer & League Express Men of the Match: *Rovers:* James Donaldson; *Oldham:* Scott Leatherbarrow.
Penalty count: 12-8; **Half-time:** 30-0;
Referee: Gareth Hewer; **Attendance:** 7,268.

ROCHDALE HORNETS 6 HALIFAX 20

HORNETS: 2 Chris Riley; 3 Jake Eccleston; 27 Matty Blythe; 4 Lewis Galbraith; 5 Rob Massam; 6 Lewis Palfrey; 7 Danny Yates; 8 Samir Tahraoui; 9 Ben Moores; 10 Gavin Bennion; 28 Danny Bridge; 12 Josh Crowley; 13 Gary Middlehurst. Subs (all used): 14 Ryan Maneely; 15 Jovili Taira; 16 Matty Hadden; 19 Jordan Case.
Try: Massam (7); **Goals:** Palfrey 1/1.
Sin bin: Middlehurst (59) - high tackle; Moores (61) - dissent.
HALIFAX: 2 Will Sharp; 5 James Saltonstall; 3 Steve Tyrer; 21 James Woodburn-Hall; 23 Rob Worrincy; 6 Scott Murrell; 1 Ben Johnston; 14 Ryan Boyle; 28 Adam O'Brien; 8 Mitch Cahalane; 16 Ed Barber; 12 Simon Grix; 13 Jacob Fairbank. Subs (all used): 20 Elliot Morris; 9 Ben Kaye; 15 Luke Ambler; 10 Adam Tangata.
Tries: Barber (21), Tyrer (52), Worrincy (64);
Goals: Tyrer 4/5.
Rugby Leaguer & League Express Men of the Match: *Hornets:* Danny Bridge; *Halifax:* Scott Murrell.
Penalty count: 7-15; **Half-time:** 6-8;
Referee: Callum Straw; **Attendance:** 854.

SHEFFIELD EAGLES 10 BATLEY BULLDOGS 54

EAGLES: 7 Dane Chisholm; 2 Garry Lo; 3 Menzie Yere; 4 Perry Whiteley; 5 Ben Blackmore; 6 Simon Brown; 9 Matty Fozard; 8 Scott Wheeldon; 14 Greg Burns; 11 Matt James; 12 Duane Straugheir; 16 Sam Scott; 13 Elliot Minchella. Subs (all used): 18 Ryan Millar; 15 Kyle Trout; 19 Will Hope; 27 Lewis Foster.
Tries: Minchella (15), Chisholm (73);
Goals: Brown 1/1, Chisholm 0/1.
Sin bin: Hope (48) - shoulder charge.
BULLDOGS: 1 Dave Scott; 2 Wayne Reittie; 3 Sam Smeaton; 4 Macauley Hallett; 25 Michael Hayward; 6 Cain Southernwood; 7 Dominic Brambani; 8 Adam Gledhill; 9 Alistair Leak; 27 Will Maher; 22 Dane Manning; 11 Brad Day; 12 Joel Farrell. Subs (all used): 28 Tom Holmes; 17 Joe Chandler; 18 James Harrison; 10 Alex Rowe.
Tries: Leak (11), Day (21, 40), Holmes (31, 57), Reittie (34, 49), Brambani (46), Hallett (53), Hayward (63);
Goals: Southernwood 7/10.
Rugby Leaguer & League Express Men of the Match: *Eagles:* Dane Chisholm; *Bulldogs:* Tom Holmes.
Penalty count: 6-12; **Half-time:** 6-26;
Referee: Andrew Sweet; **Attendance:** 662.

SWINTON LIONS 13 FEATHERSTONE ROVERS 30

LIONS: 1 Jack Murphy; 2 Shaun Robinson; 14 Ben White; 13 Andy Thornley; 26 Tom Davies; 6 Grant Gore; 7 Chris Atkin; 15 Andy Bracek; 20 Sean Kenny; 27 Romain Navarrete; 11 Connor Dwyer; 17 Olly Davies; 8 Rob Lever. Subs (all used): 19 Josh Barlow; 16 Anthony Bate; 22 Luke Waterworth; 18 Ben Austin.
Tries: Thornley (18, 76); **Goals:** Atkin 2/3;
Field goal: Atkin (39).
Sin bin: Dwyer (65) - dissent.
ROVERS: 1 Ian Hardman; 5 Luke Briscoe; 22 Jason Walton; 3 Chris Ulugia; 24 Ash Handley; 7 Anthony Thackeray; 19 Matty Wildie; 10 Andrew Bostock; 9 Keal Carlile; 32 Jordan Baldwinson; 12 John Davies; 11 Michael Knowles; 15 Bradley Knowles-Tagg. Subs (all used): 33 Brett Delaney; 34 Anthony Mullally; 14 Frankie Mariano; 13 Richard Moore.
Tries: Wildie (34), Bostock (59), Walton (73), Handley (80);
Goals: Knowles 7/8.
Rugby Leaguer & League Express Men of the Match: *Lions:* Shaun Robinson; *Rovers:* Anthony Thackeray.
Penalty count: 11-14; **Half-time:** 7-6;
Referee: Brandon Robinson; **Attendance:** 850.

ROUND 5

Sunday 5th March 2017

BATLEY BULLDOGS 22 SWINTON LIONS 18

BULLDOGS: 1 Dave Scott; 2 Wayne Reittie; 3 Sam Smeaton; 4 Macauley Hallett; 25 Michael Hayward; 6 Cain Southernwood; 7 Dominic Brambani; 27 Will Maher; 13 Pat Walker; 8 Adam Gledhill; 22 Dane Manning; 11 Brad Day; 12 Joel Farrell. Subs (all used): 28 Tom Holmes; 10 Alex Rowe; 19 Alex Bretherton; 16 Tom Lillycrop.
Tries: Scott (21, 63), Hallett (58, 74);
Goals: Southernwood 3/5.
LIONS: 1 Jack Murphy; 2 Shaun Robinson; 3 Chris Hankinson; 13 Andy Thornley; 21 Mike Butt; 14 Ben White; 7 Chris Atkin; 15 Andy Bracek; 20 Sean Kenny; 8 Rob Lever; 11 Connor Dwyer; 17 Olly Davies; 16 Anthony Bate. Subs (all used): 18 Ben Austin; 9 Anthony Nicholson; 19 Josh Barlow; 5 Matt Gardner.
Tries: Robinson (5), Murphy (13), Thornley (42);
Goals: Atkin 3/5.
Rugby Leaguer & League Express Men of the Match: *Bulldogs:* Dane Manning; *Lions:* Jack Murphy.
Penalty count: 8-9; **Half-time:** 6-12;
Referee: Jon Roberts; **Attendance:** 726.

FEATHERSTONE ROVERS 9 ROCHDALE HORNETS 10

ROVERS: 1 Ian Hardman; 5 Luke Briscoe; 23 Josh Hardcastle; 3 Chris Ulugia; 18 Scott Turner; 7 Anthony Thackeray; 19 Matty Wildie; 14 Frankie Mariano; 9 Keal Carlile; 13 Richard Moore; 11 Michael Knowles; 22 Jason Walton; 12 John Davies. Subs (all used): 31 Cory Aston; 21 James Lockwood; 10 Andrew Bostock; 8 Darrell Griffin.
Try: Ulugia (54); **Goals:** Knowles 1/1, Aston 1/1;
Field goal: Thackeray (68).
HORNETS: 1 Miles Greenwood; 21 Jack Holmes; 19 Jordan Case; 3 Jake Eccleston; 5 Rob Massam; 6 Lewis Palfrey; 7 Danny Yates; 15 Jovili Taira; 9 Ben Moores; 10 Gavin Bennion; 27 Sam Wilde; 12 Josh Crowley; 13 Gary Middlehurst. Subs (all used): 22 Jay Lobwein; 20 Jack Francis; 16 Matty Hadden; 28 Danny Bridge.
Try: Bridge (35); **Goals:** Palfrey 3/4.
Sin bin: Yates (32) - interference.
Rugby Leaguer & League Express Men of the Match: *Rovers:* Anthony Thackeray; *Hornets:* Josh Crowley.
Penalty count: 15-8; **Half-time:** 2-8;
Referee: Gareth Hewer; **Attendance:** 1,839.

HALIFAX 10 TOULOUSE OLYMPIQUE 12

HALIFAX: 2 Will Sharp; 5 James Saltonstall; 3 Steve Tyrer; 22 Chester Butler; 21 James Woodburn-Hall; 6 Scott Murrell; 1 Ben Johnston; 14 Ryan Boyle; 9 Ben Kaye; 8 Mitch Cahalane; 10 Adam Tangata; 12 Simon Grix; 13 Jacob Fairbank. Subs (all used): 20 Elliot Morris; 26 Alex Mammone; 15 Luke Ambler; 19 Connor Robinson.
Try: Tyrer (7); **Goals:** Tyrer 3/3.
OLYMPIQUE: 2 Tony Maurel; 4 Gregory White; 3 Bastien Ader; 11 Sebastien Planas; 20 Paul Marcon; 6 Johnathon Ford; 7 Stan Robin; 8 Clement Boyer; 24 Anthony Marion; 10 Bastian Canet; 26 Constantine Mika; 12 Rhys Curran; 13 Andrew Bentley. Subs (all used): 14 Mourad Kriouache; 15 Maxime Puech; 16 Tyla Hepi; 17 Kalausa Leha.
Tries: White (25), Ader (39); **Goals:** Maurel 2/3.
Rugby Leaguer & League Express Men of the Match: *Halifax:* Will Sharp; *Olympique:* Johnathon Ford.
Penalty count: 10-10; **Half-time:** 8-10;
Referee: Chris Campbell; **Attendance:** 1,271.

HULL KINGSTON ROVERS 50 SHEFFIELD EAGLES 10

ROVERS: 1 Adam Quinlan; 2 Ben Cockayne; 3 Thomas Minns; 22 Andrew Heffernan; 5 Ryan Shaw; 16 Jordan Abdull; 7 Jamie Ellis; 8 Nick Scruton; 9 Shaun Lunt; 33 Ben Kavanagh; 11 Maurice Blair; 12 James Greenwood; 15 James Donaldson. Subs (all used): 21 Rob Mulhern; 10 Chris Clarkson; 14 Graeme Horne; 4 Liam Salter.
Tries: Donaldson (15, 71), Cockayne (36), Heffernan (38), Minns (42), Quinlan (45), Clarkson (51), Abdull (61);
Goals: Ellis 9/9.
EAGLES: 18 Ryan Millar; 2 Garry Lo; 3 Menzie Yere; 22 Liam Johnson; 21 Eze Harper; 27 Lewis Foster; 7 Dane Chisholm; 8 Scott Wheeldon; 9 Matty Fozard; 11 Matt James; 16 Sam Scott; 12 Duane Straugheir; 13 Elliot Minchella. Subs (all used): 14 Greg Burns; 4 Perry Whiteley; 19 Will Hope; 15 Kyle Trout.
Tries: Straugheir (25), Lo (28); **Goals:** Chisholm 1/2.
Sin bin: Yere (40) - dangerous challenge.
Rugby Leaguer & League Express Men of the Match: *Rovers:* James Donaldson; *Eagles:* Garry Lo.
Penalty count: 16-6; **Half-time:** 18-10;
Referee: Callum Straw; **Attendance:** 7,116.

LONDON BRONCOS 42 BRADFORD BULLS 12

BRONCOS: 24 Alex Walker; 2 Rhys Williams; 3 Ben Hellewell; 4 Adrian Purtell; 1 Elliot Kear; 6 Jarrod Sammut; 7 William Barthau; 10 Mark Ioane; 14 Andy Ackers; 16 Junior Roqica; 11 Daniel Harrison; 12 Matt Garside; 13 Jay Pitts. Subs (all used): 5 Kieran Dixon; 23 Matty Gee; 18 Ben Evans; 17 Mark Offerdahl.
Tries: Walker (5), Kear (17), Garside (24, 39), Barthau (33), Sammut (73), Dixon (75); **Goals:** Sammut 7/8.
BULLS: 14 Oscar Thomas; 5 Iliess Macani; 3 James Mendeika; 4 Ross Oakes; 2 Ethan Ryan; 1 Lee Smith; 7 Joe Keyes; 15 Jon Magrin; 34 Scott Moore; 22 Daniel Murray; 30 Josh Jordan-Roberts; 16 Kevin Larroyer; 20 James Bentley. Subs (all used): 19 Johnny Campbell; 8 Liam Kirk; 31 Mikolaj Oledzki; 11 Colton Roche.
Tries: Larroyer (22), Roche (57); **Goals:** Thomas 2/2.
Rugby Leaguer & League Express Men of the Match: *Broncos:* Jarrod Sammut; *Bulls:* James Bentley.
Penalty count: 9-8; **Half-time:** 30-6;
Referee: Tom Grant; **Attendance:** 1,120.

ROUND 6

Saturday 11th March 2017

TOULOUSE OLYMPIQUE 36 SWINTON LIONS 28

OLYMPIQUE: 1 Mark Kheirallah; 20 Paul Marcon; 5 Kuni Minga; 3 Bastien Ader; 2 Tony Maurel; 7 Stan Robin; 6 Johnathon Ford; 15 Maxime Puech; 24 Anthony Marion; 8 Clement Boyer; 11 Sebastien Planas; 10 Bastian Canet; 13 Andrew Bentley. Subs (all used): 14 Mourad Kriouache; 16 Tyla Hepi; 17 Kalausa Leha; 23 Justin Sangare.
Tries: Kheirallah (7), Canet (19), Minga (23), Kriouache (36), Maurel (43), Robin (46), Planas (69);
Goals: Maurel 1/3, Kheirallah 3/4.
LIONS: 1 Jack Murphy; 2 Shaun Robinson; 3 Chris Hankinson; 13 Andy Thornley; 21 Mike Butt; 14 Ben White; 7 Chris Atkin; 15 Andy Bracek; 9 Anthony Nicholson; 8 Rob Lever; 11 Connor Dwyer; 17 Olly Davies; 16 Anthony Bate. Subs (all used): 18 Ben Austin; 19 Josh Barlow; 24 Adam Jones; 20 Sean Kenny.
Tries: White (3, 64), Hankinson (26), Butt (32), Murphy (59), Dwyer (72); **Goals:** Atkin 2/6.
Rugby Leaguer & League Express Men of the Match: *Olympique:* Stan Robin; *Lions:* Jack Murphy.
Penalty count: 6-5; **Half-time:** 20-14;
Referee: Scott Mikalauskas; **Attendance:** 2,377.

Sunday 12th March 2017

BRADFORD BULLS 44 BATLEY BULLDOGS 22

BULLS: 14 Oscar Thomas; 19 Johnny Campbell; 3 James Mendeika; 4 Ross Oakes; 2 Ethan Ryan; 6 Leon Pryce; 1 Lee Smith; 22 Daniel Murray; 34 Scott Moore; 15 Jon Magrin; 11 Colton Roche; 16 Kevin Larroyer; 20 James Bentley. Subs: 5 Iliess Macani (not used); 8 Liam Kirk; 17 Ross Peltier; 31 Mikolaj Oledzki.
Tries: Oakes (4, 54), Larroyer (24), Bentley (30), Ryan (47), Campbell (68, 80), Thomas (71);
Goals: Thomas 6/8, Ryan 0/1.
BULLDOGS: 1 Dave Scott; 2 Wayne Reittie; 3 Sam Smeaton; 4 Macauley Hallett; 25 Michael Hayward; 28 Tom Holmes; 7 Dominic Brambani; 27 Will Maher; 9 Alistair Leak; 8 Adam Gledhill; 22 Dane Manning; 11 Brad Day; 12 Joel Farrell. Subs (all used): 6 Cain Southernwood; 10 Alex Rowe; 16 Tom Lillycrop; 19 Alex Bretherton.
Tries: Leak (7), Farrell (16), Smeaton (34), Holmes (42);
Goals: Brambani 3/4.
Sin bin: Smeaton (51) - interference;
Manning (77) - late challenge.
Rugby Leaguer & League Express Men of the Match: *Bulls:* Oscar Thomas; *Bulldogs:* Tom Lillycrop.
Penalty count: 12-10; **Half-time:** 18-18;
Referee: Andrew Sweet; **Attendance:** 4,478.

DEWSBURY RAMS 6 HULL KINGSTON ROVERS 48

RAMS: 1 Josh Guzdek; 31 Alex Brown; 21 Hamish Barnes; 3 Jason Crookes; 2 Dale Morton; 6 Paul Sykes; 25 Liam Coe; 29 Keegan Hirst; 15 Robbie Ward; 24 Jode Sheriffe; 4 Lucas Walshaw; 11 Rob Spicer; 26 Jordan Crowther. Subs (all used): 20 Aaron Ollett; 19 Brad Foster; 23 James Glover; 30 Daniel Igbinedion.
Try: Hirst (72); **Goals:** Sykes 1/1.
ROVERS: 1 Adam Quinlan; 2 Ben Cockayne; 3 Thomas Minns; 22 Andrew Heffernan; 32 Kieren Moss; 16 Jordan Abdull; 7 Jamie Ellis; 8 Nick Scruton; 9 Shaun Lunt; 33 Ben Kavanagh; 11 Maurice Blair; 12 James Greenwood; 15 James Donaldson. Subs (all used): 14 Graeme Horne; 21 Rob Mulhern; 4 Liam Salter; 10 Chris Clarkson.
Tries: Lunt (6), Greenwood (21), Heffernan (28, 62), Blair (34), Mulhern (55), Donaldson (67), Horne (76);
Goals: Ellis 8/8.
Rugby Leaguer & League Express Men of the Match: *Rams:* Josh Guzdek; *Rovers:* Shaun Lunt.
Penalty count: 6-9; **Half-time:** 0-24;
Referee: Tom Grant; **Attendance:** 2,477.

HALIFAX 19 LONDON BRONCOS 6

HALIFAX: 2 Will Sharp; 5 James Saltonstall; 3 Steve Tyrer; 21 James Woodburn-Hall; 30 Jake Bibby; 6 Scott Murrell; 7 Gareth Moore; 14 Ryan Boyle; 9 Ben Kaye; 8 Mitch Cahalane; 11 Shane Grady; 12 Simon Grix; 13 Jacob Fairbank. Subs (all used): 20 Elliot Morris; 10 Adam Tangata; 29 Ryan Lannon; 31 Josh Wood.
Tries: Tyrer (5), Grix (37), G Moore (59); **Goals:** Tyrer 3/5;
Field goal: G Moore (70).
On report: Boyle (49) - alleged high tackle on Barthau.
BRONCOS: 24 Alex Walker; 2 Rhys Williams; 3 Ben Hellewell; 4 Adrian Purtell; 1 Elliot Kear; 6 Jarrod Sammut; 7 William Barthau; 16 Junior Roqica; 27 Ben Pointer; 10 Mark Ioane; 11 Daniel Harrison; 12 Matt Garside; 13 Jay Pitts. Subs (all used): 5 Kieran Dixon; 28 Sadiq Adebiyi; 18 Ben Evans; 17 Mark Offerdahl.
Try: Hellewell (19); **Goals:** Sammut 1/1.
Rugby Leaguer & League Express Men of the Match: *Halifax:* Gareth Moore; *Broncos:* Ben Pointer.
Penalty count: 11-6; **Half-time:** 8-6;
Referee: Gareth Hewer; **Attendance:** 1,298.

ROCHDALE HORNETS 26 OLDHAM 26

HORNETS: 1 Miles Greenwood; 2 Chris Riley; 21 Jack Holmes; 4 Lewis Galbraith; 5 Rob Massam; 6 Lewis Palfrey; 7 Danny Yates; 15 Jovili Taira; 9 Ben Moores; 10 Gavin Bennion; 28 Danny Bridge; 12 Josh Crowley; 13 Gary Middlehurst. Subs (all used): 14 Ryan Maneely; 8 Samir Tahraoui; 16 Matty Hadden; 19 Jordan Case.
Tries: Moores (2), Crowley (37), Holmes (39), Bennion (75), Maneely (78); **Goals:** Palfrey 3/6.
OLDHAM: 1 Scott Turner; 2 Adam Clay; 3 George Tyson; 29 Tuoyo Egodo; 26 Richard Lepori; 6 Scott Leatherbarrow; 7 Dave Hewitt; 10 Adam Neal; 20 Gareth Owen; 14 Jordan Walne; 13 Liam Thompson; 12 Danny Langtree; 18 Ben Davies. Subs (all used): 19 Joe Burke; 24 Michael Ward; 21 Kenny Hughes; 9 Sam Gee.
Tries: Walne (7), Clay (44), Egodo (50), Ward (68);
Goals: Leatherbarrow 5/5.
Rugby Leaguer & League Express Men of the Match: *Hornets:* Josh Crowley; *Oldham:* Dave Hewitt.
Penalty count: 11-11; **Half-time:** 14-6;
Referee: Chris Kendall; **Attendance:** 1,087.

SHEFFIELD EAGLES 22 FEATHERSTONE ROVERS 47

EAGLES: 24 Reece Dean; 2 Garry Lo; 3 Menzie Yere; 22 Liam Johnson; 5 Ben Blackmore; 6 Simon Brown; 7 Dane Chisholm; 8 Scott Wheeldon; 9 Matty Fozard; 10 Mark Mexico; 11 Matt James; 12 Duane Straugheir; 13 Elliot Minchella. Subs (all used): 15 Kyle Trout; 16 Sam Scott; 17 Jordan Cox; 19 Will Hope.
Tries: Dean (2), Straugheir (21), Minchella (42), Lo (66);
Goals: Brown 3/4.
ROVERS: 1 Ian Hardman; 5 Luke Briscoe; 22 Jason Walton; 3 Chris Ulugia; 24 Ash Handley; 7 Anthony Thackeray; 19 Matty Wildie; 10 Andrew Bostock; 9 Keal Carlile; 30 Jack Ormondroyd; 12 John Davies; 11 Michael Knowles; 21 James Lockwood. Subs (all used): 14 Frankie Mariano; 13 Richard Moore; 8 Darrell Griffin; 6 Kyle Briggs.
Tries: Walton (10, 26), Bostock (16), Handley (29), Ulugia (37), Thackeray (52, 62), Briscoe (72);
Goals: Knowles 3/5, Briggs 2/2, Hardman 2/3;
Field goal: Thackeray (69).
Rugby Leaguer & League Express Men of the Match: *Eagles:* Dane Chisholm; *Rovers:* Jason Walton.
Penalty count: 4-7; **Half-time:** 12-26;
Referee: Jon Roberts; **Attendance:** 1,017.

ROUND 7

Sunday 26th March 2017

BATLEY BULLDOGS 50 OLDHAM 10

BULLDOGS: 1 Dave Scott; 25 Michael Hayward; 3 Sam Smeaton; 15 Danny Cowling; 5 Shaun Ainscough; 13 Pat Walker; 7 Dominic Brambani; 8 Adam Gledhill; 9 Alistair Leak; 10 Alex Rowe; 18 James Harrison; 12 Joel Farrell; 22 Dane Manning. Subs (all used): 14 James Davey; 16 Tom Lillycrop; 21 James Brown; 27 Will Maher.
Tries: Scott (9), Leak (23, 75), Hayward (29, 38), Walker (47), Farrell (63), Smeaton (66), Gledhill (78);
Goals: Walker 7/9.
OLDHAM: 14 Sam Wood; 2 Adam Clay; 3 George Tyson; 29 Tuoyo Egodo; - Richard Lepori; 6 Scott Leatherbarrow; 7 Dave Hewitt; 18 Ben Davies; 20 Gareth Owen; 10 Adam Neal; 17 Mikey Wood; 12 Danny Langtree; 13 Liam Thompson. Subs (all used): 15 Liam Bent; 21 Kenny Hughes; 24 Michael Ward; 11 Jack Spencer.

Sheffield's Elliot Minchella goes past London Broncos duo Jarrod Sammut and Jay Pitts

Tries: Ward (49), Lepori (59); **Goals:** Leatherbarrow 1/2.
Rugby Leaguer & League Express Men of the Match:
Bulldogs: Michael Hayward; *Oldham:* Liam Bent.
Penalty count: 12-7; **Half-time:** 24-0.
Referee: Callum Straw; **Attendance:** 761.

BRADFORD BULLS 56 DEWSBURY RAMS 18

BULLS: 19 Johnny Campbell; 5 Iliess Macani; 4 Ross Oakes; 1 Lee Smith; 2 Ethan Ryan; 7 Joe Keyes; 28 Jordan Lilley; 15 Jon Magrin; 34 Scott Moore; 22 Daniel Murray; 16 Kevin Larroyer; 11 Colton Roche; 21 Brandan Wilkinson. Subs (all used): 8 Liam Kirk; 18 Omari Caro; 26 Vila Halafihi; 30 Josh Jordan-Roberts.
Tries: Wilkinson (14), Murray (24), Caro (51), Macani (36), L Smith (59), Magrin (68, 75), Roche (73), Oakes (79); **Goals:** Keyes 5/7, Lilley 2/2, Caro 1/1.
RAMS: 1 Josh Guzdek; 31 Alex Brown; 21 Hamish Barnes; 3 Jason Crookes; 2 Dale Morton; 6 Paul Sykes; 7 Andy Kain; 28 Brandon Douglas; 15 Robbie Ward; 10 Mitchell Stringer; 11 Rob Spicer; 4 Lucas Walshaw; 20 Aaron Ollett. Subs (all used): 27 Michael Sio; 23 James Glover; 29 Anthony Walker; 18 Jack Teanby.
Tries: Crookes (5), Glover (34), Alex Brown (47); **Goals:** Sykes 3/4.
Rugby Leaguer & League Express Men of the Match:
Bulls: Johnny Campbell; *Rams:* Anthony Walker.
Penalty count: 12-7; **Half-time:** 12-14;
Referee: Gareth Hewer; **Attendance:** 4,136.

FEATHERSTONE ROVERS 26
TOULOUSE OLYMPIQUE 34

ROVERS: 1 Ian Hardman; 5 Luke Briscoe; 22 Jason Walton; 3 Chris Ulugia; 24 Ash Handley; 7 Anthony Thackeray; 19 Matty Wildie; 21 James Lockwood; 9 Keal Carlile; 10 Andrew Bostock; 14 Frankie Mariano; 12 John Davies; 15 Bradley Knowles-Tagg. Subs (all used): 13 Richard Moore; 8 Darrell Griffin; 25 Josh Walters; 23 Josh Hardcastle.
Tries: Mariano (26), Davies (37), Hardman (57), Ulugia (59, 69); **Goals:** Hardman 3/5.
Sin bin: Moore (79) - punching.
OLYMPIQUE: 1 Mark Kheirallah; 2 Tony Maurel; 21 Gavin Marguerite; 3 Bastien Ader; 5 Kuni Minga; 6 Johnathon Ford; 7 Stan Robin; 8 Clement Boyer; 24 Anthony Marion; 10 Bastian Canet; 11 Sebastien Planas; 12 Rhys Curran; 13 Andrew Bentley. Subs (all used): 14 Mourad Kriouache; 15 Maxime Puech; 16 Tyla Hepi; 17 Kalausa Leha.
Tries: Kheirallah (3, 16, 72), Curran (7), Hepi (31), Robin (45); **Goals:** Kheirallah 5/7.
Sin bin: Canet (68) - repeated team offences.
Rugby Leaguer & League Express Men of the Match:
Rovers: Ian Hardman; *Olympique:* Mark Kheirallah.
Penalty count: 15-6; **Half-time:** 12-22;
Referee: Scott Mikalauskas; **Attendance:** 2,087.

HULL KINGSTON ROVERS 28 HALIFAX 14

ROVERS: 2 Ben Cockayne; 32 Kieren Moss; 3 Thomas Minns; 22 Andrew Heffernan; 5 Ryan Shaw; 16 Jordan Abdull; 7 Jamie Ellis; 8 Nick Scruton; 9 Shaun Lunt; 33 Ben Kavanagh; 11 Maurice Blair; 12 James Greenwood; 15 James Donaldson. Subs (all used): 13 Danny Addy; 4 Liam Salter; 21 Rob Mulhern; 10 Chris Clarkson.
Tries: Blair (35), Greenwood (55), Abdull (65), Moss (77); **Goals:** Ellis 6/7.
HALIFAX: 2 Will Sharp; 5 James Saltonstall; 3 Steve Tyrer; 21 James Woodburn-Hall; 30 Jake Bibby; 6 Scott Murrell; 7 Gareth Moore; 14 Ryan Boyle; 9 Ben Kaye; 8 Mitch Cahalane; 11 Shane Grady; 12 Simon Grix; 13 Jacob Fairbank. Subs (all used): 16 Ed Barber; 20 Elliot Morris; 31 Josh Wood; 10 Adam Tangata.
Tries: Grady (30), Saltonstall (39); **Goals:** Tyrer 3/3.
Sin bin: Fairbank (70) - late challenge on Donaldson.
Rugby Leaguer & League Express Men of the Match:
Rovers: Jamie Ellis; *Halifax:* Will Sharp.
Penalty count: 11-7; **Half-time:** 8-14;
Referee: Robert Hicks; **Attendance:** 7,100.

LONDON BRONCOS 28 ROCHDALE HORNETS 8

BRONCOS: 24 Alex Walker; 2 Rhys Williams; 1 Elliot Kear; 4 Adrian Purtell; 5 Kieran Dixon; 19 Api Pewhairangi; 7 William Barthau; 17 Mark Offerdahl; 9 James Cunningham; 10 Mark Ioane; 11 Daniel Harrison; 13 Jay Pitts; 23 Matty Gee. Subs (all used): 6 Jarrod Sammut; 28 Sadiq Adebiyi; 16 Junior Roqica; 18 Ben Evans.
Tries: Pewhairangi (33), Harrison (61), Sammut (69), Purtell (74), Pitts (78); **Goals:** Dixon 1/2, Sammut 3/3.
Sin bin: Kear (38) - fighting.
HORNETS: 1 Miles Greenwood; 2 Chris Riley; 3 Jake Eccleston; 4 Lewis Galbraith; 5 Rob Massam; 6 Lewis Palfrey; 7 Danny Yates; 16 Matty Hadden; 9 Ben Moores; 10 Gavin Bennion; 11 Jono Smith; 12 Josh Crowley; 13 Gary Middlehurst. Subs (all used): 14 Ryan Maneely; 15 Jovili Taira; 8 Samir Tahraoui; 19 Jordan Case.
Tries: Massam (11, 29); **Goals:** Palfrey 0/3.
Sin bin: Middlehurst (38) - fighting;
Taira (73) - high tackle on Kear.
Rugby Leaguer & League Express Men of the Match:
Broncos: Daniel Harrison; *Hornets:* Lewis Palfrey.
Penalty count: 14-7; **Half-time:** 6-8;
Referee: John McMullen; **Attendance:** 650.

SWINTON LIONS 24 SHEFFIELD EAGLES 28

LIONS: 1 Jack Murphy; 2 Shaun Robinson; 3 Chris Hankinson; 13 Andy Thornley; 21 Mike Butt; 14 Ben White; 7 Chris Atkin; 15 Andy Bracek; 9 Anthony Nicholson; 8 Rob Lever; 11 Connor Dwyer; 17 Olly Davies; 16 Anthony Bate. Subs (all used): 19 Josh Barlow; 24 Adam Jones; 20 Sean Kenny; 18 Ben Austin.

Tries: Butt (9), Murphy (26), Kenny (65), Bate (73), Hankinson (75); **Goals:** Atkin 2/5.
Sin bin: Bate (60) - dissent.
EAGLES: 24 Reece Dean; 2 Garry Lo; 3 Menzie Yere; 23 Jake Spedding; 5 Ben Blackmore; 6 Simon Brown; 13 Elliot Minchella; 8 Scott Wheeldon; 9 Matty Fozard; 10 Mark Mexico; 11 Matt James; 12 Duane Straugheir; 19 Will Hope. Subs (all used): 14 Greg Burns; 15 Kyle Trout; 16 Sam Scott; 4 Perry Whiteley.
Tries: Yere (15), Lo (21), James (47), Minchella (49), Scott (67); **Goals:** Brown 4/5.
Rugby Leaguer & League Express Men of the Match:
Lions: Anthony Nicholson; *Eagles:* Simon Brown.
Penalty count: 10-7; **Half-time:** 8-10;
Referee: Tom Grant; **Attendance:** 479.

ROUND 8

Sunday 2nd April 2017

DEWSBURY RAMS 6 FEATHERSTONE ROVERS 38

RAMS: 1 Josh Guzdek; 5 Gareth Potts; 6 Paul Sykes; 3 Jason Crookes; 2 Dale Morton; 13 Aaron Brown; 7 Andy Kain; 28 Brandon Douglas; 15 Robbie Ward; 18 Jack Teanby; 20 Aaron Ollett. Subs (all used): 10 Mitchell Stringer; 27 Michael Sio; 21 Hamish Barnes; 30 Daniel Igbinedion.
Try: Teanby (5); **Goals:** Sykes 1/1.
Sin bin: Igbinedion (24) - professional foul;
Crookes (24) - fighting; Sykes (56) - dissent;
Potts (60) - shoulder charge.
ROVERS: 1 Ian Hardman; 5 Luke Briscoe; 22 Jason Walton; 3 Chris Ulugia; 24 Ash Handley; 7 Anthony Thackeray; 31 Cory Aston; 10 Andrew Bostock; 9 Keal Carlile; 32 Jordan Baldwinson; 21 James Lockwood; 12 John Davies; 25 Josh Walters. Subs (all used): 13 Richard Moore; 19 Matty Wildie; 8 Darrell Griffin; 16 Luke Cooper.
Tries: Briscoe (16, 32), Hardman (26), Wildie (44), Aston (77); **Goals:** Aston 9/9.
Dismissals: Moore (24) - fighting;
Briscoe (72) - dangerous challenge.
Rugby Leaguer & League Express Men of the Match:
Rams: Aaron Brown; *Rovers:* Cory Aston.
Penalty count: 10-16; **Half-time:** 6-22;
Referee: Brandon Robinson; **Attendance:** 1,232.

HALIFAX 38 SWINTON LIONS 28

HALIFAX: 2 Will Sharp; 5 James Saltonstall; 3 Steve Tyrer; 22 Chester Butler; 33 Niall Evalds; 6 Scott Murrell; 1 Ben Johnston; 10 Adam Tangata; 9 Ben Kaye; 8 Mitch Cahalane; 11 Shane Grady; 12 Simon Grix; 13 Jacob Fairbank. Subs (all used): 29 Ryan Lannon; 20 Elliot Morris; 27 Matt Wilkinson; 14 Ryan Boyle.

Tries: Tyrer (7), Tangata (10), Saltonstall (22), E Morris (35), Grady (46), Fairbank (66); **Goals:** Tyrer 7/8.
LIONS: 1 Jack Murphy; 2 Shaun Robinson; 3 Chris Hankinson; 14 Ben White; 21 Mike Butt; 6 Grant Gore; 7 Chris Atkin; 15 Andy Bracek; 9 Anthony Nicholson; 18 Ben Austin; 11 Connor Dwyer; 13 Andy Thornley; 8 Rob Lever. Subs (all used): 22 Luke Waterworth; 16 Anthony Bate; 19 Josh Barlow; 17 Olly Davies.
Tries: White (17), Butt (26, 80), Atkin (52), Hankinson (73); **Goals:** Hankinson 4/6.
Rugby Leaguer & League Express Men of the Match: *Halifax:* Simon Grix; *Lions:* Shaun Robinson.
Penalty count: 12-9; **Half-time:** 24-12;
Referee: Callum Straw; **Attendance:** 1,501.

HULL KINGSTON ROVERS 50 BATLEY BULLDOGS 16

ROVERS: 2 Ben Cockayne; 32 Kieren Moss; 3 Thomas Minns; 22 Andrew Heffernan; 5 Ryan Shaw; 16 Jordan Abdull; 7 Jamie Ellis; 8 Nick Scruton; 9 Shaun Lunt; 10 Chris Clarkson; 4 Liam Salter; 14 Graeme Horne; 15 James Donaldson. Subs (all used): 31 David Hodgson; 21 Rob Mulhern; 19 George Lawler; 35 Josh Johnson.
Tries: Shaw (5, 45), Moss (7), Heffernan (22), Minns (30), Salter (52, 65), Clarkson (56), Donaldson (77);
Goals: Ellis 7/9.
BULLDOGS: 1 Dave Scott; 2 Wayne Reittie; 15 Danny Cowling; 4 Macauley Hallett; 25 Michael Hayward; 13 Pat Walker; 7 Dominic Brambani; 8 Adam Gledhill; 14 James Davey; 27 Will Maher; 18 James Harrison; 19 Alex Bretherton; 22 Dane Manning. Subs (all used): 16 Tom Lillycrop; 17 Joe Chandler; 21 James Brown; 28 Tom Holmes.
Tries: Brown (26), Reittie (70), Manning (75);
Goals: Walker 1/1, Brambani 1/2.
Rugby Leaguer & League Express Men of the Match: *Rovers:* Liam Salter; *Bulldogs:* Dave Scott.
Penalty count: 6-10; **Half-time:** 24-6;
Referee: Chris Campbell; **Attendance:** 6,815.

OLDHAM 26 BRADFORD BULLS 22

OLDHAM: 17 Richard Lepori; 2 Adam Clay; 22 Danny Grimshaw; 25 Kieran Gill; 29 Tuoyo Egodo; 6 Scott Leatherbarrow; 7 Dave Hewitt; 10 Adam Neal; 9 Sam Gee; 30 Nathan Mason; 12 Danny Langtree; 13 Liam Thompson; 11 Jack Spencer. Subs (all used): 24 Michael Ward; 15 Liam Bent; 21 Kenny Hughes; 18 Ben Davies.
Tries: Neal (6), Langtree (39), Egodo (66), Gill (77);
Goals: Leatherbarrow 5/6.
BULLS: 19 Johnny Campbell; 5 Iliess Macani; 1 Lee Smith; 4 Ross Oakes; 2 Ethan Ryan; 28 Jordan Lilley; 7 Joe Keyes; 22 Daniel Murray; 34 Scott Moore; 15 Jon Magrin; 11 Colton Roche; 20 James Bentley; 21 Brandan Wilkinson. Subs (all used): 8 Liam Kirk; 18 Omari Caro; 26 Vila Halafihi; 30 Josh Jordan-Roberts.
Tries: L Smith (10), Bentley (13), Ryan (36), Keyes (63);
Goals: Lilley 3/5.
Rugby Leaguer & League Express Men of the Match: *Oldham:* Scott Leatherbarrow; *Bulls:* Johnny Campbell.
Penalty count: 8-7; **Half-time:** 12-14;
Referee: Scott Mikalauskas; **Attendance:** 1,691.

ROCHDALE HORNETS 14 TOULOUSE OLYMPIQUE 52

HORNETS: 1 Miles Greenwood; 2 Chris Riley; 3 Jake Eccleston; 4 Lewis Galbraith; 5 Rob Massam; 6 Lewis Palfrey; 7 Danny Yates; 16 Matty Hadden; 9 Ben Moores; 27 Andre Savelio; 11 Jono Smith; 12 Josh Crowley; 13 Gary Middlehurst. Subs (all used): 14 Ryan Maneely; 15 Jovili Taira; 28 Danny Bridge; 19 Jordan Case.
Tries: Moores (56), Middlehurst (71), Massam (79);
Goals: Yates 1/3.
Sin bin: Smith (14) - interference.
OLYMPIQUE: 1 Mark Kheirallah; 20 Paul Marcon; 21 Gavin Marguerite; 3 Bastien Ader; 2 Tony Maurel; 6 Johnathon Ford; 7 Stan Robin; 8 Clement Boyer; 24 Anthony Marion; 10 Bastian Canet; 11 Sebastien Planas; 12 Rhys Curran; 13 Andrew Bentley. Subs (all used): 14 Mourad Kriouache; 15 Maxime Puech; 16 Tyla Hepi; 17 Kalausa Leha.
Tries: Maurel (7, 26, 59, 67), Marion (14), Marcon (23), Leha (32), Ader (36, 40), Marguerite (53);
Goals: Kheirallah 6/10.
Rugby Leaguer & League Express Men of the Match: *Hornets:* Rob Massam; *Olympique:* Tony Maurel.
Penalty count: 3-8; **Half-time:** 0-36;
Referee: Phil Bentham; **Attendance:** 609.

SHEFFIELD EAGLES 32 LONDON BRONCOS 20

EAGLES: 18 Ryan Millar; 2 Garry Lo; 3 Menzie Yere; 23 Jake Spedding; 5 Ben Blackmore; 6 Simon Brown; 13 Elliot Minchella; 8 Scott Wheeldon; 9 Matty Fozard; 10 Mark Mexico; 11 Matt James; 12 Duane Straugheir; 19 Will Hope. Subs (all used): 15 Kyle Trout; 16 Sam Scott; 14 Greg Burns; 22 Liam Johnson.
Tries: Minchella (15, 23), Lo (33), Yere (43), Straugheir (68);
Goals: Brown 6/6.
BRONCOS: 1 Elliot Kear; 2 Rhys Williams; 3 Ben Hellewell; 4 Adrian Purtell; 5 Kieran Dixon; 6 Jarrod Sammut; 7 William Barthau; 18 Ben Evans; 33 Lewis Foster; 10 Mark Ioane; 11 Daniel Harrison; 13 Jay Pitts; 9 James Cunningham. Subs (all used): 19 Api Pewhairangi; 23 Matty Gee; 16 Junior Roqica; 28 Sadiq Adebiyi.
Tries: Pitts (8), Evans (48), Dixon (51), Kear (54);
Goals: Sammut 2/4.
Rugby Leaguer & League Express Men of the Match: *Eagles:* Elliot Minchella; *Broncos:* Elliot Kear.
Penalty count: 10-9; **Half-time:** 20-4;
Referee: Tom Crashley; **Attendance:** 319.

ROUND 9

Saturday 8th April 2017

TOULOUSE OLYMPIQUE 58 OLDHAM 18

OLYMPIQUE: 1 Mark Kheirallah; 2 Tony Maurel; 4 Gregory White; 21 Gavin Marguerite; 20 Paul Marcon; 7 Stan Robin; 6 Johnathon Ford; 8 Clement Boyer; 24 Anthony Marion; 10 Bastian Canet; 11 Sebastien Planas; 12 Rhys Curran; 13 Andrew Bentley. Subs (all used): 14 Mourad Kriouache; 15 Maxime Puech; 16 Tyla Hepi; 26 Constantine Mika.
Tries: Robin (1, 24), White (15, 59), Ford (19, 34), Kheirallah (27), Marcon (56), Boyer (67), Canet (74);
Goals: Kheirallah 9/10.
OLDHAM: 17 Richard Lepori; 2 Adam Clay; 22 Danny Grimshaw; 25 Kieran Gill; 29 Tuoyo Egodo; 6 Scott Leatherbarrow; 7 Dave Hewitt; 11 Jack Spencer; 9 Sam Gee; 10 Adam Neal; 14 Mikey Wood; 12 Danny Langtree; 15 Liam Bent. Subs (all used): 21 Kenny Hughes; 13 Liam Thompson; 19 Joe Burke; 24 Michael Ward.
Tries: Gill (47), Burke (52), Lepori (62);
Goals: Leatherbarrow 3/3.
Sin bin: Lepori (70) - interference;
Burke (72) - shoulder charge.
Rugby Leaguer & League Express Men of the Match: *Olympique:* Johnathon Ford; *Oldham:* Tuoyo Egodo.
Penalty count: 7-8; **Half-time:** 36-0;
Referee: Phil Bentham; **Attendance:** 1,752.

Sunday 9th April 2017

BATLEY BULLDOGS 38 ROCHDALE HORNETS 36

BULLDOGS: 25 Michael Hayward; 2 Wayne Reittie; 3 Sam Smeaton; 4 Macauley Hallett; 5 Shaun Ainscough; 28 Tom Holmes; 7 Dominic Brambani; 10 Alex Rowe; 9 Alistair Leak; 27 Will Maher; 11 Brad Day; 18 James Harrison; 17 Joe Chandler. Subs (all used): 14 James Davey; 16 Tom Lillycrop; 21 James Brown; 23 Brad Hill.
Tries: Hallett (23, 34), Smeaton (30, 59), Maher (62), Ainscough (74, 76), Lillycrop (77); **Goals:** Brambani 3/8.
Sin bin: Brown (52) - high tackle.
HORNETS: - Jack Johnson; 3 Jake Eccleston; - Benjamin Jullien; 4 Lewis Galbraith; 5 Rob Massam; - Harvey Livett; 7 Danny Yates; 15 Jovili Taira; 14 Ryan Maneely; 10 Gavin Bennion; 11 Jono Smith; 27 Andre Savelio; 13 Gary Middlehurst. Subs (all used): 9 Ben Moores; 8 Samir Tahraoui; 16 Matty Hadden; 19 Jordan Case.
Tries: Massam (9), Livett (13), Jullien (17), Galbraith (26), Hadden (44), Johnson (55); **Goals:** Livett 6/7.
Sin bin: Smith (33) - high tackle;
Hadden (72) - holding down.
Rugby Leaguer & League Express Men of the Match: *Bulldogs:* Tom Lillycrop; *Hornets:* Harvey Livett.
Penalty count: 19-7; **Half-time:** 12-22;
Referee: Callum Straw; **Attendance:** 718.

BRADFORD BULLS 48 SHEFFIELD EAGLES 16

BULLS: 14 Oscar Thomas; 18 Omari Caro; 4 Ross Oakes; 2 Ethan Ryan; 19 Johnny Campbell; 6 Leon Pryce; 28 Jordan Lilley; 15 Jon Magrin; 34 Scott Moore; 22 Daniel Murray; 16 Kevin Larroyer; 20 James Bentley; 11 Colton Roche. Subs (all used): 8 Liam Kirk; 21 Brandan Wilkinson; 36 James Davies; 7 Joe Keyes.
Tries: Ryan (4), Bentley (9, 33, 72, 76), Oakes (30), Murray (43), Campbell (78); **Goals:** Thomas 8/8.
EAGLES: 18 Ryan Millar; 2 Garry Lo; 3 Menzie Yere; 23 Jake Spedding; 5 Ben Blackmore; 6 Simon Brown; 13 Elliot Minchella; 8 Scott Wheeldon; 9 Matty Fozard; 10 Mark Mexico; 11 Matt James; 12 Duane Straugheir; 19 Will Hope. Subs (all used): 14 Greg Burns; 15 Kyle Trout; 16 Sam Scott; 22 Liam Johnson.
Tries: Hope (27), Blackmore (48, 60); **Goals:** Brown 2/3.
Sin bin: Yere (30) - dangerous challenge on Campbell.
Rugby Leaguer & League Express Men of the Match: *Bulls:* James Bentley; *Eagles:* Jake Spedding.
Penalty count: 14-12; **Half-time:** 24-6;
Referee: Liam Moore; **Attendance:** 4,126.

FEATHERSTONE ROVERS 38 LONDON BRONCOS 18

ROVERS: 1 Ian Hardman; 5 Luke Briscoe; 4 Misi Taulapapa; 3 Chris Ulugia; 2 James Duckworth; 7 Anthony Thackeray; 31 Cory Aston; 32 Jordan Baldwinson; 9 Keal Carlile; 10 Andrew Bostock; 11 Michael Knowles; 12 John Davies; 21 James Lockwood. Subs (all used): 8 Darrell Griffin; 19 Matty Wildie; 16 Luke Cooper; 33 Mikolaj Oledzki.
Tries: Davies (17), Ulugia (30, 58), Aston (39), Bostock (51), Briscoe (78); **Goals:** Aston 7/9.
Sin bin: Thackeray (6) - trip on Pewhairangi.
BRONCOS: 1 Elliot Kear; 2 Rhys Williams; 3 Ben Hellewell; 4 Adrian Purtell; 5 Kieran Dixon; 6 Jarrod Sammut; 19 Api Pewhairangi; 23 Matty Gee; 9 James Cunningham; 18 Ben Evans; 11 Daniel Harrison; 12 Matt Garside; 13 Jay Pitts. Subs (all used): 33 Lewis Foster; 22 Matt Davis; 10 Mark Ioane; 16 Junior Roqica.
Tries: Sammut (12), Roqica (42), Cunningham (69);
Goals: Sammut 3/3.
Sin bin: Foster (76) - high tackle on Briscoe.
Rugby Leaguer & League Express Men of the Match: *Rovers:* Andrew Bostock; *Broncos:* Elliot Kear.
Penalty count: 14-8; **Half-time:** 18-6;
Referee: Ben Thaler; **Attendance:** 2,509.

HALIFAX 34 DEWSBURY RAMS 6

HALIFAX: 2 Will Sharp; 5 James Saltonstall; 3 Steve Tyrer; 4 Ben Heaton; 23 Rob Worrincy; 6 Scott Murrell; 1 Ben Johnston; 10 Adam Tangata; 9 Ben Kaye; 8 Mitch Cahalane; 11 Shane Grady; 12 Simon Grix; 13 Jacob Fairbank. Subs (all used): 29 Ryan Lannon; 20 Elliot Morris; 17 Brandon Moore; 14 Ryan Boyle.
Tries: Saltonstall (40), Grix (43), Worrincy (55), Tyrer (59, 68), Tangata (72); **Goals:** Tyrer 5/7.
RAMS: 1 Josh Guzdek; 31 Alex Brown; 6 Paul Sykes; 25 Ashley Gibson; 2 Dale Morton; 13 Aaron Brown; 17 Dom Speakman; 26 Anthony Walker; 15 Robbie Ward; 28 Brandon Douglas; 4 Lucas Walshaw; 11 Rob Spicer; 27 Chris Annakin. Subs (all used): 9 Tom Hemingway; 20 Aaron Ollett; 29 James Batchelor; 8 Tony Tonks.
Try: Speakman (5); **Goals:** Sykes 1/1.
Rugby Leaguer & League Express Men of the Match: *Halifax:* Steve Tyrer; *Rams:* Anthony Walker.
Penalty count: 13-11; **Half-time:** 6-6;
Referee: Scott Mikalauskas; **Attendance:** 1,218.

SWINTON LIONS 18 HULL KINGSTON ROVERS 52

LIONS: 1 Jack Murphy; 2 Shaun Robinson; 3 Chris Hankinson; 14 Ben White; 21 Mike Butt; 6 Grant Gore; 7 Chris Atkin; 15 Andy Bracek; 9 Anthony Nicholson; 19 Josh Barlow; 11 Connor Dwyer; 17 Olly Davies; 13 Andy Thornley. Subs (all used): 16 Anthony Bate; 8 Rob Lever; 22 Luke Waterworth; 20 Sean Kenny.
Tries: White (15, 17), Butt (20), Bate (80);
Goals: Hankinson 0/3, Atkin 1/1.
ROVERS: 2 Ben Cockayne; 5 Ryan Shaw; 4 Liam Salter; 31 David Hodgson; 27 Will Oakes; 16 Jordan Abdull; 7 Jamie Ellis; 8 Nick Scruton; 9 Shaun Lunt; 35 Josh Johnson; 14 Graeme Horne; 15 James Donaldson; 19 George Lawler. Subs (all used): 18 Zach Dockar-Clay; 21 Rob Mulhern; 23 George Milton; 30 Joe Cator.
Tries: Hodgson (3), Abdull (8), Ellis (25), Dockar-Clay (36), Donaldson (38, 50, 77), Oakes (45), Scruton (47), Shaw (57); **Goals:** Ellis 6/10.
Rugby Leaguer & League Express Men of the Match: *Lions:* Chris Atkin; *Rovers:* Zach Dockar-Clay.
Penalty count: 9-11; **Half-time:** 12-26;
Referee: Andrew Sweet; **Attendance:** 1,375.

ROUND 10

Friday 14th April 2017

LONDON BRONCOS 30 TOULOUSE OLYMPIQUE 16

BRONCOS: 24 Alex Walker; 2 Rhys Williams; 3 Ben Hellewell; 1 Elliot Kear; 29 Kameron Pearce-Paul; 19 Api Pewhairangi; 7 William Barthau; 18 Ben Evans; 9 James Cunningham; 10 Mark Ioane; 11 Daniel Harrison; 13 Jay Pitts; 22 Matt Davis. Subs (all used): 33 Lewis Foster; 12 Matt Garside; 17 Mark Offerdahl; 31 Lewis Bienek.
Tries: Pitts (26), Barthau (28), Williams (46, 52), Davis (73);
Goals: Pewhairangi 5/6.
OLYMPIQUE: 1 Mark Kheirallah; 20 Paul Marcon; 21 Gavin Marguerite; 4 Gregory White; 2 Tony Maurel; 6 Johnathon Ford; 7 Stan Robin; 8 Clement Boyer; 24 Anthony Marion; 10 Bastian Canet; 11 Sebastien Planas; 12 Rhys Curran; 13 Andrew Bentley. Subs (all used): 14 Mourad Kriouache; 26 Constantine Mika; 16 Tyla Hepi; 17 Kalausa Leha.
Tries: Marguerite (32), Kriouache (37), Kheirallah (41);
Goals: Kheirallah 2/3.
Rugby Leaguer & League Express Men of the Match: *Broncos:* William Barthau; *Olympique:* Mark Kheirallah.
Penalty count: 9-10; **Half-time:** 12-10;
Referee: Tom Grant; **Attendance:** 520.

Championship 2017 - Round by Round

DEWSBURY RAMS 20 BATLEY BULLDOGS 4

RAMS: 1 Josh Guzdek; 31 Alex Brown; 13 Aaron Brown; 23 James Glover; 2 Dale Morton; 17 Dom Speakman; 7 Andy Kain; 10 Mitchell Stringer; 9 Tom Hemingway; 18 Jack Teanby; 4 Lucas Walshaw; 26 Liam Senior; 28 Brandon Douglas. Subs (all used): 15 Robbie Ward; 24 Jode Sheriffe; 30 Daniel Igbinedion; 8 Tony Tonks.
Tries: Glover (5), Morton (36); **Goals:** Glover 6/6.
Sin bin: Speakman (79) - fighting.
BULLDOGS: 1 Dave Scott; 25 Michael Hayward; 3 Sam Smeaton; 4 Macauley Hallett; 5 Shaun Ainscough; 13 Pat Walker; 28 Tom Holmes; 8 Adam Gledhill; 9 Alistair Leak; 10 Alex Rowe; 11 Brad Day; 12 Joel Farrell; 22 Dane Manning. Subs (all used): 14 James Davey; 16 Tom Lillycrop; 19 Alex Bretherton; 21 James Brown.
Tries: Hayward (26); **Goals:** Walker 0/1.
Sin bin: Gledhill (79) - fighting.
Rugby Leaguer & League Express Men of the Match:
Rams: Tom Hemingway; *Bulldogs:* Dane Manning.
Penalty count: 15-11; **Half-time:** 16-4;
Referee: Andrew Sweet; **Attendance:** 1,211.

**HULL KINGSTON ROVERS 30
FEATHERSTONE ROVERS 22**

ROBINS: 1 Adam Quinlan; 2 Ben Cockayne; 4 Liam Salter; 31 David Hodgson; 5 Ryan Shaw; 16 Jordan Abdull; 7 Jamie Ellis; 8 Nick Scruton; 18 Zach Dockar-Clay; 35 Josh Johnson; 11 Maurice Blair; 10 Chris Clarkson; 15 James Donaldson. Subs (all used): 21 Rob Mulhern; 19 George Lawler; 13 Danny Addy; 27 Will Oakes.
Tries: Quinlan (3), Clarkson (15), Cockayne (26), Shaw (42), Hodgson (66), Blair (75); **Goals:** Ellis 3/6.
ROVERS: 20 Kyran Johnson; 18 Scott Turner; 23 Josh Hardcastle; 3 Chris Ulugia; 2 James Duckworth; 7 Anthony Thackeray; 31 Cory Aston; 10 Andrew Bostock; 9 Keal Carlile; 16 Luke Cooper; 11 Michael Knowles; 12 John Davies; 21 James Lockwood. Subs (all used): 15 Bradley Knowles-Tagg; 6 Kyle Briggs; 19 Matty Wildie; 8 Darrell Griffin.
Tries: Davies (10), Duckworth (37), Thackeray (63);
Goals: Aston 5/7.
Rugby Leaguer & League Express Men of the Match:
Robins: Maurice Blair; *Rovers:* John Davies.
Penalty count: 14-11; **Half-time:** 14-14;
Referee: Scott Mikalauskas; **Attendance:** 8,117.

OLDHAM 22 SWINTON LIONS 18

OLDHAM: 17 Richard Lepori; 2 Adam Clay; 3 George Tyson; 22 Danny Grimshaw; 1 Scott Turner; 6 Scott Leatherbarrow; 7 Dave Hewitt; 10 Adam Neal; 20 Gareth Owen; 19 Joe Burke; 14 Mikey Wood; 12 Danny Langtree; 13 Liam Thompson. Subs (all used): 15 Liam Bent; 21 Kenny Hughes; 9 Sam Gee; 24 Michael Ward.
Tries: Gee (25), Lepori (28), Ward (42);
Goals: Leatherbarrow 5/5.
Sin bin: M Wood (78) - professional foul.
LIONS: 1 Jack Murphy; 2 Shaun Robinson; 3 Chris Hankinson; 14 Ben White; 21 Mike Butt; 6 Grant Gore; 7 Chris Atkin; 15 Andy Bracek; 9 Anthony Nicholson; 19 Josh Barlow; 11 Connor Dwyer; 17 Olly Davies; 13 Andy Thornley. Subs (all used): 16 Anthony Bate; 8 Rob Lever; 22 Luke Waterworth; 18 Ben Austin.
Tries: Robinson (46), Hankinson (60), Murphy (73);
Goals: Atkin 3/3.
Sin bin: Bate (34) - punching.
Rugby Leaguer & League Express Men of the Match:
Oldham: Adam Neal; *Lions:* Shaun Robinson.
Penalty count: 11-11; **Half-time:** 12-0;
Referee: Liam Moore; **Attendance:** 804.

ROCHDALE HORNETS 18 SHEFFIELD EAGLES 42

HORNETS: - Jack Johnson; - Taylor Prell; - Matty Blythe; 19 Jordan Case; 5 Rob Massam; 6 Lewis Palfrey; 7 Danny Yates; 17 Lee Mitchell; 14 Ryan Maneely; 10 Gavin Bennion; 11 Jono Smith; 12 Josh Crowley; 13 Gary Middlehurst. Subs (all used): 9 Ben Moores; 8 Samir Tahraoui; 16 Matty Hadden; 4 Lewis Galbraith.
Tries: Crowley (3), Tahraoui (30), Galbraith (58);
Goals: Palfrey 3/3.
EAGLES: 18 Ryan Millar; 2 Garry Lo; 3 Menzie Yere; 23 Jake Spedding; 5 Ben Blackmore; 6 Simon Brown; 13 Elliot Minchella; 8 Scott Wheeldon; 9 Matty Fozard; 10 Mark Mexico; 11 Matt James; 12 Duane Straugheir; 19 Will Hope. Subs (all used): 14 Greg Burns; 15 Kyle Trout; 16 Sam Scott; 22 Liam Johnson.
Tries: Lo (7, 35, 80), Minchella (9), Burns (27), Spedding (38), Straugheir (51); **Goals:** Brown 7/8.
Rugby Leaguer & League Express Men of the Match:
Hornets: Matty Hadden; *Eagles:* Garry Lo.
Penalty count: 13-9; **Half-time:** 12-30;
Referee: Gareth Hewer; **Attendance:** 526.

BRADFORD BULLS 12 HALIFAX 22

BULLS: 14 Oscar Thomas; 19 Johnny Campbell; 4 Ross Oakes; 2 Ethan Ryan; 18 Omari Caro; 6 Leon Pryce; 7 Joe Keyes; 15 Jon Magrin; 34 Scott Moore; 8 Liam Kirk; 20 James Bentley; 16 Kevin Larroyer; 21 Brandan Wilkinson. Subs (all used): 11 Colton Roche; 36 James Davies; 35 Evan Hodgson; 5 Iliess Macani.
Tries: Macani (66), Ryan (79); **Goals:** Thomas 2/2.
Sin bin: Campbell (28) - professional foul.
HALIFAX: 2 Will Sharp; 5 James Saltonstall; 3 Steve Tyrer; 4 Ben Heaton; 23 Rob Worrincy; 6 Scott Murrell; 1 Ben Johnston; 10 Adam Tangata; 9 Ben Kaye; 8 Mitch Cahalane; 11 Shane Grady; 12 Simon Grix; 13 Jacob Fairbank. Subs (all used): 16 Ed Barber; 20 Elliot Morris; 17 Brandon Moore; 14 Ryan Boyle.
Tries: Saltonstall (18, 68), Grady (29), Johnston (61);
Goals: Tyrer 3/5.
Sin bin: B Moore (52) - high tackle.
Rugby Leaguer & League Express Men of the Match:
Bulls: Ethan Ryan; *Halifax:* Scott Murrell.
Penalty count: 13-11; **Half-time:** 0-10;
Referee: Tom Crashley; **Attendance:** 4,871.

ROUND 11

Monday 17th April 2017

BATLEY BULLDOGS 4 LONDON BRONCOS 42

BULLDOGS: 1 Dave Scott; 25 Michael Hayward; 3 Sam Smeaton; 19 Alex Bretherton; 4 Macauley Hallett; 13 Pat Walker; 7 Dominic Brambani; 8 Adam Gledhill; 9 Alistair Leak; 10 Alex Rowe; 11 Brad Day; 12 Joel Farrell; 22 Dane Manning. Subs (all used): 16 Tom Lillycrop; 18 James Harrison; 21 James Brown; 28 Tom Holmes.
Try: Day (49); **Goals:** Brambani 0/1.
Sin bin: Bretherton (70) - dissent.
BRONCOS: 24 Alex Walker; 2 Rhys Williams; 3 Ben Hellewell; 1 Elliot Kear; 29 Kameron Pearce-Paul; 19 Api Pewhairangi; 7 William Barthau; 18 Ben Evans; 9 James Cunningham; 10 Mark Ioane; 11 Daniel Harrison; 13 Jay Pitts; 22 Matt Davis. Subs (all used): 33 Lewis Foster; 12 Matt Garside; 17 Mark Offerdahl; 31 Lewis Bienek.
Tries: Kear (5), Pitts (9), Cunningham (17, 73), Garside (45), Walker (60), Bienek (77), Pearce-Paul (79);
Goals: Pewhairangi 5/8.
Rugby Leaguer & League Express Men of the Match:
Bulldogs: Dane Manning; *Broncos:* James Cunningham.
Penalty count: 7-7; **Half-time:** 0-16;
Referee: Tom Crashley; **Attendance:** 587.

FEATHERSTONE ROVERS 44 BRADFORD BULLS 18

ROVERS: 1 Ian Hardman; 4 Misi Taulapapa; 3 Chris Ulugia; 23 Josh Hardcastle; 18 Scott Turner; 7 Anthony Thackeray; 31 Cory Aston; 16 Luke Cooper; 9 Keal Carlile; 13 Richard Moore; 11 Michael Knowles; 12 John Davies; 21 James Lockwood. Subs (all used): 8 Darrell Griffin; 19 Matty Wildie; 30 Jack Ormondroyd; 10 Andrew Bostock.
Tries: Taulapapa (2), Hardcastle (11), Turner (14, 35), Bostock (30), Aston (32, 38), Griffin (47); **Goals:** Aston 6/8.
Sin bin: Bostock (53) - professional foul;
Taulapapa (74) - high tackle.
BULLS: 19 Johnny Campbell; 5 Iliess Macani; 4 Ross Oakes; 2 Ethan Ryan; 18 Omari Caro; 14 Oscar Thomas; 7 Joe Keyes; 15 Jon Magrin; 34 Scott Moore; 8 Liam Kirk; 20 James Bentley; 16 Kevin Larroyer; 21 Brandan Wilkinson. Subs (all used): 26 Vila Halafihi; 36 James Davies; 35 Evan Hodgson; 25 Keenen Tomlinson.
Tries: Oakes (44, 66), Caro (77); **Goals:** Thomas 3/3.
Rugby Leaguer & League Express Men of the Match:
Rovers: Cory Aston; *Bulls:* Johnny Campbell.
Penalty count: 11-11; **Half-time:** 38-0;
Referee: Liam Moore; **Attendance:** 3,112.

SWINTON LIONS 23 ROCHDALE HORNETS 22

LIONS: 1 Jack Murphy; 2 Shaun Robinson; 3 Chris Hankinson; 14 Ben White; 21 Mike Butt; 6 Grant Gore; 7 Chris Atkin; 15 Andy Bracek; 22 Luke Waterworth; 19 Josh Barlow; 11 Connor Dwyer; 4 Rhodri Lloyd; 16 Anthony Bate. Subs (all used): 8 Rob Lever; 9 Anthony Nicholson; 24 Adam Jones; 17 Olly Davies.
Tries: Butt (1), Dwyer (57), Bracek (62); **Goals:** Atkin 5/5;
Field goal: Atkin (75).
Sin bin: Bracek (66) - retaliation.
HORNETS: 2 Chris Riley; 1 Miles Greenwood; 19 Jordan Case; 4 Lewis Galbraith; 5 Rob Massam; 6 Lewis Palfrey; 7 Danny Yates; 8 Samir Tahraoui; 9 Ben Moores; - Jordan Hand; 11 Jono Smith; 12 Josh Crowley; 13 Gary Middlehurst. Subs (all used): 14 Ryan Maneely; 15 Jovili Taira; 16 Matty Hadden; 17 Lee Mitchell.
Tries: Galbraith (18), Massam (55, 65), Tahraoui (70);
Goals: Palfrey 3/6.
Dismissal: Taira (66) - use of the elbow on Bracek.
Sin bin: Hand (56) - dangerous challenge.

Rugby Leaguer & League Express Men of the Match:
Lions: Chris Atkin; *Hornets:* Lewis Galbraith.
Penalty count: 9-13; **Half-time:** 10-8;
Referee: Tom Grant; **Attendance:** 538.

**TOULOUSE OLYMPIQUE 14
HULL KINGSTON ROVERS 6**

OLYMPIQUE: 1 Mark Kheirallah; 2 Tony Maurel; 3 Bastien Ader; 21 Gavin Marguerite; 5 Kuni Minga; 6 Johnathon Ford; 7 Stan Robin; 8 Clement Boyer; 24 Anthony Marion; 10 Bastian Canet; 11 Sebastien Planas; 12 Rhys Curran; 13 Andrew Bentley. Subs (all used): 9 Kane Bentley; 26 Constantine Mika; 17 Kalausa Leha; 16 Tyla Hepi.
Tries: Minga (4), Curran (77); **Goals:** Kheirallah 3/4.
ROVERS: 2 Ben Cockayne; 5 Ryan Shaw; 29 Jake Butler-Fleming; 22 Andrew Heffernan; 27 Will Oakes; 16 Jordan Abdull; 18 Zach Dockar-Clay; 17 Mitch Clark; 23 George Milton; 35 Josh Johnson; 10 Chris Clarkson; 19 George Lawler; 30 Joe Cator. Subs (all used): 25 Will Jubb; 26 Kieran Moran; 24 Joe Wardill; 21 Rob Mulhern.
Try: Heffernan (66); **Goals:** Dockar-Clay 1/1.
Rugby Leaguer & League Express Men of the Match:
Olympique: Rhys Curran; *Rovers:* Andrew Heffernan.
Penalty count: 11-9; **Half-time:** 8-0;
Referee: Chris Kendall; **Attendance:** 4,107.

HALIFAX 16 OLDHAM 14

HALIFAX: 2 Will Sharp; 5 James Saltonstall; 21 James Woodburn-Hall; 3 Steve Tyrer; 23 Rob Worrincy; 6 Scott Murrell; 1 Ben Johnston; 20 Elliot Morris; 9 Ben Kaye; 8 Mitch Cahalane; 11 Shane Grady; 10 Adam Tangata; 13 Jacob Fairbank. Subs (all used): 14 Ryan Boyle; 16 Ed Barber; 17 Brandon Moore; 33 Niall Evalds.
Tries: Johnston (8), Saltonstall (49); **Goals:** Tyrer 4/4.
OLDHAM: 1 Scott Turner; 2 Adam Clay; 29 Tuoyo Egodo; 25 Kieran Gill; 5 Jamel Chisholm; 6 Scott Leatherbarrow; 20 Gareth Owen; 19 Joe Burke; 21 Kenny Hughes; 10 Adam Neal; - Mikey Wood; 15 Liam Bent; 13 Liam Thompson. Subs (all used): 24 Michael Ward; 9 Sam Gee; 18 Ben Davies; 12 Danny Langtree.
Tries: Gill (56), Burke (67), Chisholm (75);
Goals: Leatherbarrow 1/3.
Rugby Leaguer & League Express Men of the Match:
Halifax: Mitch Cahalane; *Oldham:* Michael Ward.
Penalty count: 10-8; **Half-time:** 6-0;
Referee: Andrew Sweet; **Attendance:** 1,341.

SHEFFIELD EAGLES 48 DEWSBURY RAMS 12

EAGLES: 18 Ryan Millar; 2 Garry Lo; 3 Menzie Yere; 23 Jake Spedding; 5 Ben Blackmore; 6 Simon Brown; 13 Elliot Minchella; 11 Matt James; 9 Matty Fozard; 10 Mark Mexico; 16 Sam Scott; 12 Duane Straugheir; 19 Will Hope. Subs (all used): 15 Kyle Trout; 22 Liam Johnson; 14 Greg Burns; 4 Perry Whiteley.
Tries: Yere (28), Blackmore (30), Lo (33, 52, 63, 73), Burns (47), Scott (50); **Goals:** Brown 8/9.
RAMS: 1 Josh Guzdek; 31 Alex Brown; 4 Lucas Walshaw; 23 James Glover; 2 Dale Morton; 17 Dom Speakman; 9 Tom Hemingway; 10 Mitchell Stringer; 15 Robbie Ward; 18 Jack Teanby; 27 Liam Senior; 28 Brandon Douglas; 13 Aaron Brown. Subs (all used): 30 Daniel Igbinedion; 8 Tony Tonks; 14 Luke Adamson; 24 Jode Sheriffe.
Tries: Aaron Brown (36), Douglas (40); **Goals:** Glover 2/2.
Rugby Leaguer & League Express Men of the Match:
Eagles: Garry Lo; *Rams:* Brandon Douglas.
Penalty count: 11-15; **Half-time:** 16-12;
Referee: Jon Roberts; **Attendance:** 482.

ROUND 12

Saturday 29th April 2017

TOULOUSE OLYMPIQUE 60 BRADFORD BULLS 4

OLYMPIQUE: 2 Tony Maurel; 5 Kuni Minga; 3 Bastien Ader; 21 Gavin Marguerite; 20 Paul Marcon; 6 Johnathon Ford; 7 Stan Robin; 8 Clement Boyer; 24 Anthony Marion; 10 Bastian Canet; 11 Sebastien Planas; 12 Rhys Curran; 13 Andrew Bentley. Subs (all used): 9 Kane Bentley; 26 Constantine Mika; 16 Tyla Hepi; 17 Kalausa Leha.
Tries: Ford (4), Marguerite (13), Marcon (18), Curran (28, 78), Ader (33, 53), Minga (46, 70, 76), Robin (56), Canet (80); **Goals:** Maurel 6/11, Marion 0/1.
BULLS: 3 James Mendeika; 19 Johnny Campbell; 4 Ross Oakes; 2 Ethan Ryan; 18 Omari Caro; 14 Oscar Thomas; 6 Leon Pryce; 8 Liam Kirk; 34 Scott Moore; 15 Jon Magrin; 16 Kevin Larroyer; 35 Evan Hodgson; 11 Colton Roche. Subs (all used): 36 James Davies; 21 Brandan Wilkinson; 24 Brandon Pickersgill; - Matthew Storton.
Try: Davies (24); **Goals:** Thomas 0/1.
Rugby Leaguer & League Express Men of the Match:
Olympique: Gavin Marguerite; *Bulls:* Oscar Thomas.
Penalty count: 6-6; **Half-time:** 24-4;
Referee: Chris Campbell; **Attendance:** 2,312.

Sunday 30th April 2017

DEWSBURY RAMS 24 OLDHAM 28

RAMS: 1 Josh Guzdek; 2 Dale Morton; 3 Jason Crookes; 6 Paul Sykes; 31 Alex Brown; 17 Dom Speakman; 7 Andy Kain; 10 Mitchell Stringer; 15 Robbie Ward; 18 Jack Teanby; 16 Toby Adamson; 14 Luke Adamson; 13 Aaron Brown. Subs (all used): 26 Sam Day; 28 Brandon Douglas; 23 James Glover; 24 Jode Sheriffe.
Tries: Kain (9), Ward (12), Sykes (14), Glover (35);
Goals: Sykes 4/4.
OLDHAM: 1 Scott Turner; 2 Adam Clay; 3 George Tyson; 25 Kieran Gill; 17 Richard Lepori; 6 Scott Leatherbarrow; 7 Dave Hewitt; 10 Adam Neal; 21 Kenny Hughes; 19 Joe Burke; 14 Mikey Wood; 12 Danny Langtree; 11 Jack Spencer. Subs (all used): 20 Gareth Owen; 24 Michael Ward; 15 Liam Bent; 9 Sam Gee.
Tries: Neal (6), Ward (45), Gill (58), Tyson (69), Burke (73);
Goals: Leatherbarrow 4/5.
Rugby Leaguer & League Express Men of the Match:
Rams: Brandon Douglas; *Oldham:* Michael Ward.
Penalty count: 8-13; **Half-time:** 24-6;
Referee: Tom Crashley; **Attendance:** 691.

FEATHERSTONE ROVERS 25 SHEFFIELD EAGLES 14

ROVERS: 1 Ian Hardman; 18 Scott Turner; 3 Chris Ulugia; 23 Josh Hardcastle; 4 Misi Taulapapa; 19 Matty Wildie; 31 Cory Aston; 13 Richard Moore; 9 Keal Carlile; 32 Jordan Baldwinson; 25 Josh Walters; 12 John Davies; 21 James Lockwood. Subs (all used): 16 Luke Cooper; 8 Darrell Griffin; 33 Mikolaj Oledzki; 30 Jack Ormondroyd.
Tries: Wildie (7), Carlile (24), Turner (40), Ulugia (60);
Goals: Aston 4/6; **Field goal:** Aston (73).
EAGLES: 18 Ryan Millar; 2 Garry Lo; 3 Menzie Yere; 22 Liam Johnson; 5 Ben Blackmore; 13 Elliot Minchella; 6 Simon Brown; 8 Scott Wheeldon; 9 Matty Fozard; 10 Mark Mexico; 11 Matt James; 16 Sam Scott; 19 Will Hope. Subs (all used): 14 Greg Burns; 15 Kyle Trout; 4 Perry Whiteley; 17 Jordan Cox.
Tries: Lo (48), Mexico (56); **Goals:** Brown 3/3.
Sin bin: Burns (23) - repeated team offences.
Rugby Leaguer & League Express Men of the Match:
Rovers: Scott Turner; *Eagles:* Simon Brown.
Penalty count: 11-10; **Half-time:** 16-2;
Referee: Andrew Sweet; **Attendance:** 2,267.

HULL KINGSTON ROVERS 24 ROCHDALE HORNETS 16

ROVERS: 2 Ben Cockayne; 27 Will Oakes; 4 Liam Salter; 22 Andrew Heffernan; 5 Ryan Shaw; 16 Jordan Abdull; 7 Jamie Ellis; 33 Ben Kavanagh; 9 Shaun Lunt; 17 Mitch Clark; 11 Maurice Blair; 12 James Greenwood; 19 George Lawler. Subs (all used): 18 Zach Dockar-Clay; 24 Joe Wardill; 21 Rob Mulhern; 30 Joe Cator.
Tries: Lawler (25), Shaw (35), Lunt (49), Kavanagh (54);
Goals: Ellis 4/5.
Sin bin: Greenwood (20) - holding down.
HORNETS: 2 Chris Riley; 1 Miles Greenwood; 21 Jack Holmes; 4 Lewis Galbraith; 5 Rob Massam; 6 Lewis Palfrey; 7 Danny Yates; - Jordan Hand; 9 Ben Moores; 10 Gavin Bennion; 19 Jordan Case; 12 Josh Crowley; 13 Gary Middlehurst. Subs (all used): 11 Jono Smith; 3 Jake Eccleston; 16 Matty Hadden; - Sam Wilde.
Tries: Case (16, 77), Massam (59); **Goals:** Palfrey 2/4.
Sin bin: Galbraith (28) - holding down.
Rugby Leaguer & League Express Men of the Match:
Rovers: Maurice Blair; *Hornets:* Gary Middlehurst.
Penalty count: 16-9; **Half-time:** 10-6;
Referee: Scott Mikalauskas; **Attendance:** 7,141.

LONDON BRONCOS 38 SWINTON LIONS 28

BRONCOS: 24 Alex Walker; 2 Rhys Williams; 3 Ben Hellewell; 12 Matt Garside; 29 Kameron Pearce-Paul; 19 Api Pewhairangi; 7 William Barthau; 18 Ben Evans; 9 James Cunningham; 10 Mark Ioane; 11 Daniel Harrison; 13 Jay Pitts; 22 Matt Davis. Subs (all used): 23 Matty Gee; 33 Lewis Foster; 17 Mark Offerdahl; 31 Lewis Bienek.
Tries: Pitts (3), Garside (7), Cunningham (21), Pewhairangi (32, 51), Ioane (58), Bienek (80);
Goals: Pewhairangi 5/7.
Sin bin: Harrison (39) - professional foul.
LIONS: 1 Jack Murphy; 2 Shaun Robinson; 3 Chris Hankinson; 14 Ben White; 21 Mike Butt; 6 Grant Gore; 7 Chris Atkin; 15 Andy Bracek; 22 Luke Waterworth; 18 Ben Austin; 11 Connor Dwyer; 4 Rhodri Lloyd; 8 Rob Lever. Subs (all used): 27 Liam Carberry; 26 Callum Field; 9 Anthony Nicholson; 17 Olly Davies.
Tries: Butt (29, 48, 68), Bracek (54), Dwyer (61);
Goals: Atkin 4/5.
Rugby Leaguer & League Express Men of the Match:
Broncos: Api Pewhairangi; *Lions:* Chris Atkin.
Penalty count: 10-9; **Half-time:** 22-6;
Referee: Brandon Robinson; **Attendance:** 618.

HALIFAX 40 BATLEY BULLDOGS 22

HALIFAX: 2 Will Sharp; 5 James Saltonstall; 21 James Woodburn-Hall; 3 Steve Tyrer; 23 Rob Worrincy; 6 Scott Murrell; 19 Connor Robinson; 14 Ryan Boyle; 9 Ben Kaye; 8 Mitch Cahalane; 11 Shane Grady; 10 Adam Tangata; 13 Jacob Fairbank. Subs (all used): 16 Ed Barber; 17 Brandon Moore; 20 Elliot Morris; - Martyn Reilly.
Tries: Saltonstall (3, 69), Sharp (12, 79), Murrell (18), Tyrer (37), B Moore (45), Woodburn-Hall (50);
Goals: Tyrer 4/8.
BULLDOGS: 1 Dave Scott; 29 Jy Hitchcox; 3 Sam Smeaton; 15 Danny Cowling; 4 Macauley Hallett; 6 Cain Southernwood; 7 Dominic Brambani; 8 Adam Gledhill; 9 Alistair Leak; 10 Alex Rowe; 11 Brad Day; 12 Joel Farrell; 22 Dane Manning. Subs (all used): 16 Tom Lillycrop; 19 Alex Bretherton; 21 James Brown; 28 Tom Holmes.
Tries: Cowling (8), Hitchcox (32), Rowe (59), Leak (76);
Goals: Southernwood 3/4.
Rugby Leaguer & League Express Men of the Match:
Halifax: James Woodburn-Hall; *Bulldogs:* Joel Farrell.
Penalty count: 8-11; **Half-time:** 20-10;
Referee: Jack Smith; **Attendance:** 1,488.

ROUND 13

Sunday 7th May 2017

BATLEY BULLDOGS 4 HULL KINGSTON ROVERS 68

BULLDOGS: 1 Dave Scott; 25 Michael Hayward; 3 Sam Smeaton; 15 Danny Cowling; 4 Macauley Hallett; 6 Cain Southernwood; 7 Dominic Brambani; 16 Tom Lillycrop; 14 James Davey; 27 Will Maher; 22 Dane Manning; 12 Joel Farrell; 11 Brad Day. Subs (all used): 19 Alex Bretherton; 8 Adam Gledhill; 17 Joe Chandler; 18 James Harrison.
Try: Hayward (77); **Goals:** Southernwood 0/1.
ROVERS: 2 Ben Cockayne; 5 Ryan Shaw; 22 Andrew Heffernan; 16 Jordan Abdull; 29 Jake Butler-Fleming; 11 Maurice Blair; 7 Jamie Ellis; 21 Rob Mulhern; 9 Shaun Lunt; 33 Ben Kavanagh; 12 James Greenwood; 4 Liam Salter; 19 George Lawler. Subs (all used): 18 Zach Dockar-Clay; 17 Mitch Clark; 30 Joe Cator; 24 Joe Wardill.
Tries: Mulhern (3), Shaw (11, 34, 63), Heffernan (18, 36), Abdull (24), Dockar-Clay (29, 69), Ellis (47), Butler-Fleming (56, 79); **Goals:** Ellis 10/12.
Rugby Leaguer & League Express Men of the Match:
Bulldogs: James Davey; *Rovers:* Jamie Ellis.
Penalty count: 6-5; **Half-time:** 0-38;
Referee: Liam Moore; **Attendance:** 1,885.

DEWSBURY RAMS 18 HALIFAX 36

RAMS: 27 Max Jowitt; 2 Dale Morton; 32 Shaun Squires; 4 Lucas Walshaw; 31 Alex Brown; 23 James Glover; 17 Dom Speakman; 28 Anthony Walker; 9 Tom Hemingway; 18 Jack Teanby; 16 Toby Adamson; 14 Luke Adamson; 13 Aaron Brown. Subs (all used): 41 Sam Day; 26 Brandon Douglas; 24 Jode Sheriffe; 30 Daniel Igbinedion.
Tries: Igbinedion (22), Day (29), Glover (69), Morton (74);
Goals: Glover 1/4.
HALIFAX: 2 Will Sharp; 5 James Saltonstall; 3 Steve Tyrer; 4 Ben Heaton; 23 Rob Worrincy; 6 Scott Murrell; 19 Connor Robinson; 10 Adam Tangata; 9 Ben Kaye; 8 Mitch Cahalane; 11 Shane Grady; 16 Ed Barber; 13 Jacob Fairbank. Subs (all used): 20 Elliot Morris; 14 Ryan Boyle; 17 Brandon Moore; 1 Ben Johnston.
Tries: Tyrer (12, 48), Saltonstall (35), Tangata (43), Heaton (62), Robinson (67), Barber (72); **Goals:** Tyrer 4/7.
Sin bin: Heaton (39) - high tackle.
On report: Tangata (38) - alleged high tackle.
Rugby Leaguer & League Express Men of the Match:
Rams: Daniel Igbinedion; *Halifax:* Connor Robinson.
Penalty count: 7-6; **Half-time:** 10-12;
Referee: Andrew Sweet; **Attendance:** 718.

LONDON BRONCOS 74 OLDHAM 12

BRONCOS: 24 Alex Walker; 2 Rhys Williams; 3 Ben Hellewell; 20 Michael Channing; 5 Kieran Dixon; 19 Api Pewhairangi; 7 William Barthau; 17 Mark Offerdahl; 9 James Cunningham; 10 Mark Ioane; 11 Daniel Harrison; 13 Jay Pitts; 22 Matt Davis. Subs (all used): 6 Jarrod Sammut; 12 Matt Garside; 23 Matty Gee; 31 Lewis Bienek.
Tries: Dixon (7, 56), Hellewell (17, 30), Williams (22, 69), Pewhairangi (27, 37), Harrison (42, 50), Sammut (53, 79), Ioane (60), Pitts (64); **Goals:** Pewhairangi 0/3, Dixon 9/11.
OLDHAM: 17 Richard Lepori; 29 Tuoyo Egodo; 3 George Tyson; 22 Danny Grimshaw; 5 Jamel Chisholm; 6 Scott Leatherbarrow; 7 Dave Hewitt; 10 Adam Neal; 21 Kenny Hughes; 30 Nathan Mason; 13 Liam Thompson; 12 Danny Langtree; 18 Ben Davies. Subs (all used): 24 Michael Ward; 19 Joe Burke; 20 Gareth Owen; 9 Sam Gee.
Tries: Tyson (39), Thompson (76);
Goals: Leatherbarrow 2/2.
Rugby Leaguer & League Express Men of the Match:
Broncos: Alex Walker; *Oldham:* Scott Leatherbarrow.
Penalty count: 10-6; **Half-time:** 30-6;
Referee: Jon Roberts; **Attendance:** 500.

ROCHDALE HORNETS 8 FEATHERSTONE ROVERS 38

HORNETS: 2 Chris Riley; 1 Miles Greenwood; 21 Jack Holmes; 3 Jake Eccleston; 5 Rob Massam; 6 Lewis Palfrey; 7 Danny Yates; - Jordan Hand; 9 Ben Moores; 10 Gavin Bennion; 12 Josh Crowley; 19 Jordan Case; 13 Gary Middlehurst. Subs (all used): 22 Jay Lobwein; 15 Jovili Taira; 16 Matty Hadden; 17 Sam Wilde.
Tries: Greenwood (11), Massam (77); **Goals:** Yates 0/2.
ROVERS: 1 Ian Hardman; 4 Misi Taulapapa; 23 Josh Hardcastle; 3 Chris Ulugia; 18 Scott Turner; 7 Anthony Thackeray; 31 Cory Aston; 13 Richard Moore; 9 Keal Carlile; 16 Luke Cooper; 11 Michael Knowles; 12 John Davies; 21 James Lockwood. Subs (all used): 19 Matty Wildie; 8 Darrell Griffin; 32 Jordan Baldwinson; 15 Bradley Knowles-Tagg.
Tries: Hardcastle (5), Hardman (8, 18), Knowles (30), Turner (35, 39), Wildie (45), Taulapapa (53);
Goals: Aston 3/8.
Rugby Leaguer & League Express Men of the Match:
Hornets: Matty Hadden; *Rovers:* Anthony Thackeray.
Penalty count: 9-11; **Half-time:** 4-28;
Referee: John McMullen; **Attendance:** 766.

SHEFFIELD EAGLES 52 BRADFORD BULLS 16

EAGLES: 18 Ryan Millar; 2 Garry Lo; 3 Menzie Yere; 22 Liam Johnson; 5 Ben Blackmore; 6 Simon Brown; 9 Matty Fozard; 8 Scott Wheeldon; 14 Greg Burns; 10 Mark Mexico; 16 Sam Scott; 11 Matt James; 19 Will Hope. Subs (all used): 15 Kyle Trout; 17 Jordan Cox; 4 Perry Whiteley; 20 James Kelly.
Tries: Millar (10), Scott (12, 79), Wheeldon (29), Johnson (34), Fozard (44, 51), Kelly (60), Trout (63);
Goals: Brown 8/9.
BULLS: 14 Oscar Thomas; 19 Johnny Campbell; 4 Ross Oakes; 3 James Mendeika; 2 Ethan Ryan; 7 Joe Keyes; 6 Leon Pryce; 8 Liam Kirk; 34 Scott Moore; 15 Jon Magrin; 35 Evan Hodgson; 11 Colton Roche; 29 Sam Hallas. Subs (all used): - Sam Brooks; - Ted Chapelhow; 5 Iliess Macani; 36 James Davies.
Tries: Thomas (67), Campbell (70), Hodgson (74);
Goals: Keyes 2/3.
Rugby Leaguer & League Express Men of the Match:
Eagles: Matty Fozard; *Bulls:* Oscar Thomas.
Penalty count: 9-7; **Half-time:** 24-0;
Referee: Tom Grant; **Attendance:** 1,437.

SWINTON LIONS 27 TOULOUSE OLYMPIQUE 20

LIONS: 1 Jack Murphy; 2 Shaun Robinson; 3 Chris Hankinson; 14 Ben White; 21 Mike Butt; 6 Grant Gore; 7 Chris Atkin; 15 Andy Bracek; 22 Luke Waterworth; 18 Ben Austin; 11 Connor Dwyer; 4 Rhodri Lloyd; 8 Rob Lever. Subs: (all used): 9 Anthony Nicholson; 24 Adam Jones; 13 Andy Thornley; 27 Liam Carberry.
Tries: Dwyer (8, 13, 65), Thornley (72); **Goals:** Atkin 5/7;
Field goal: Atkin (77).
OLYMPIQUE: 2 Tony Maurel; 20 Paul Marcon; 21 Gavin Marguerite; 3 Bastien Ader; 5 Kuni Minga; 1 Mark Kheirallah; 7 Stan Robin; 8 Clement Boyer; 24 Anthony Marion; 10 Bastian Canet; 11 Sebastien Planas; 12 Rhys Curran; 13 Andrew Bentley. Subs (all used): 9 Kane Bentley; 15 Maxime Puech; 16 Tyla Hepi; 26 Constantine Mika.
Tries: Curran (36), Minga (41), Marcon (57), Marguerite (59);
Goals: Kheirallah 2/4.
Rugby Leaguer & League Express Men of the Match:
Lions: Chris Atkin; *Olympique:* Andrew Bentley.
Penalty count: 10-5; **Half-time:** 16-6;
Referee: Callum Straw; **Attendance:** 601.

ROUND 14

Saturday 20th May 2017

TOULOUSE OLYMPIQUE 45 SHEFFIELD EAGLES 20

OLYMPIQUE: 1 Mark Kheirallah; 2 Tony Maurel; 5 Kuni Minga; 3 Bastien Ader; 21 Gavin Marguerite; 24 Anthony Marion; 7 Stan Robin; 8 Clement Boyer; 9 Kane Bentley; 10 Bastian Canet; 11 Sebastien Planas; 12 Rhys Curran; 26 Constantine Mika. Subs (all used): 14 Mourad Kriouache; 13 Andrew Bentley; 16 Tyla Hepi; 17 Kalausa Leha.
Tries: Robin (11, 38), K Bentley (25), Planas (33, 58), Canet (49), Minga (66); **Goals:** Kheirallah 8/8;
Field goal: Kheirallah (79).
EAGLES: 18 Ryan Millar; 2 Garry Lo; 3 Menzie Yere; 24 Paddy Flynn; 5 Ben Blackmore; 6 Simon Brown; 13 Elliot Minchella; 8 Scott Wheeldon; 9 Matty Fozard; 10 Mark Mexico; 16 Sam Scott; 11 Matt James; 19 Will Hope. Subs (all used): 15 Kyle Trout; 17 Jordan Cox; 14 Greg Burns; 22 Liam Johnson.

Tries: Trout (15), Lo (45, 76), Flynn (52); **Goals:** Brown 2/4.
Rugby Leaguer & League Express Men of the Match: *Olympique:* Kane Bentley; *Eagles:* Simon Brown.
Penalty count: 10-9; **Half-time:** 26-6;
Referee: Liam Moore; **Attendance:** 2,413.

FEATHERSTONE ROVERS 52 DEWSBURY RAMS 10

ROVERS: 1 Ian Hardman; 18 Scott Turner; 22 Jason Walton; 23 Josh Hardcastle; 4 Misi Taulapapa; 31 Cory Aston; 7 Anthony Thackeray; 13 Richard Moore; 9 Keal Carlile; 16 Luke Cooper; 14 Frankie Mariano; 12 John Davies; 21 James Lockwood. Subs (all used): 19 Matty Wildie; 8 Darrell Griffin; 15 Bradley Knowles-Tagg; 30 Jack Ormondroyd.
Tries: Lockwood (8), Taulapapa (13), Hardcastle (17, 66), Walton (30, 46), Turner (32, 35), Mariano (49), Ormondroyd (74); **Goals:** Aston 6/10.
RAMS: 2 Dale Morton; 41 Lewis Fairhurst; 32 Shaun Squires; 4 Lucas Walshaw; 23 James Glover; 17 Dom Speakman; 7 Andy Kain; 24 Jode Sheriffe; 9 Tom Hemingway; 16 Toby Adamson; 30 Daniel Igbinedion; 20 Aaron Ollett; 13 Aaron Brown. Subs (all used): 14 Luke Adamson; 15 Robbie Ward; 26 Billy Hayes; 8 Tony Tonks.
Tries: Fairhurst (21), Squires (57); **Goals:** Glover 1/2.
Rugby Leaguer & League Express Men of the Match: *Rovers:* Jason Walton; *Rams:* Shaun Squires.
Penalty count: 12-9; **Half-time:** 32-4;
Referee: Tom Grant; **Attendance:** 2,038.

Sunday 21st May 2017

BRADFORD BULLS 12 LONDON BRONCOS 56

BULLS: 14 Oscar Thomas; 5 Iliess Macani; 2 Ethan Ryan; 26 Vila Halafihi; 19 Johnny Campbell; 6 Leon Pryce; 28 Jordan Lilley; 15 Jon Magrin; 29 Sam Hallas; 8 Liam Kirk; 11 Colton Roche; 37 Cameron Smith; - Ted Chapelhow. Subs (all used): 36 James Davies; 31 Mikolaj Oledzki; 17 Ross Peltier; 7 Joe Keyes.
Tries: C Smith (4), Campbell (61); **Goals:** Thomas 2/2.
BRONCOS: 24 Alex Walker; 2 Rhys Williams; 1 Elliot Kear; 20 Michael Channing; 5 Kieran Dixon; 6 Jarrod Sammut; 7 William Barthau; 18 Ben Evans; 9 James Cunningham; 10 Mark Ioane; 11 Daniel Harrison; 13 Jay Pitts; 17 Mark Offerdahl. Subs (all used): 33 Lewis Foster; 12 Matt Garside; 23 Matty Gee; 16 Junior Roqica.
Tries: Dixon (8, 38, 57), Pitts (14), Williams (18), Roqica (32, 47), Sammut (35, 67), Garside (80);
Goals: Dixon 8/10.
Sin bin: Harrison (78) - dangerous challenge.
Rugby Leaguer & League Express Men of the Match: *Bulls:* Johnny Campbell; *Broncos:* James Cunningham.
Penalty count: 12-9; **Half-time:** 6-34;
Referee: Jon Roberts; **Attendance:** 3,633.

HALIFAX 28 ROCHDALE HORNETS 2

HALIFAX: 2 Will Sharp; 4 Ben Heaton; 3 Steve Tyrer; 21 James Woodburn-Hall; 23 Rob Worrincy; 6 Scott Murrell; 1 Ben Johnston; 8 Mitch Cahalane; 17 Brandon Moore; 36 Daniel Murray; 11 Shane Grady; 12 Simon Grix; 13 Jacob Fairbank. Subs (all used): 20 Elliot Morris; 14 Ryan Boyle; 16 Ed Barber; 10 Adam Tangata.
Tries: Johnston (16), Tyrer (20), Sharp (51), Tangata (55), Grix (77); **Goals:** Tyrer 4/5.
HORNETS: 2 Chris Riley; - Kevin Penny; 21 Jack Holmes; 4 Lewis Galbraith; 5 Rob Massam; 6 Lewis Palfrey; 7 Danny Yates; 8 Samir Tahraoui; 14 Ryan Maneely; - Jordan Hand; 11 Jono Smith; 12 Josh Crowley; 13 Gary Middlehurst. Subs (all used): 1 Miles Greenwood; - Pat Moran; 16 Matty Hadden; 19 Jordan Case.
Goals: Yates 1/1.
Sin bin: Riley (34) - professional foul.
Rugby Leaguer & League Express Men of the Match: *Halifax:* Shane Grady; *Hornets:* Gary Middlehurst.
Penalty count: 9-5; **Half-time:** 10-2;
Referee: Gareth Hewer; **Attendance:** 1,424.

HULL KINGSTON ROVERS 42 SWINTON LIONS 18

ROVERS: 2 Ben Cockayne; 29 Jake Butler-Fleming; 3 Thomas Minns; 22 Andrew Heffernan; 5 Ryan Shaw; 16 Jordan Abdull; 18 Zach Dockar-Clay; 8 Nick Scruton; 9 Shaun Lunt; 35 Josh Johnson; 30 Joe Cator; 11 Maurice Blair; 33 Ben Kavanagh. Subs (all used): 27 Will Oakes; 24 Joe Wardill; 25 Will Jubb; 21 Rob Mulhern.
Tries: Wardill (25), Abdull (33, 44), Heffernan (56), Shaw (64, 73, 79); **Goals:** Dockar-Clay 7/8.
LIONS: 1 Jack Murphy; 2 Shaun Robinson; 3 Chris Hankinson; 4 Rhodri Lloyd; 21 Mike Butt; 6 Grant Gore; 7 Chris Atkin; 15 Andy Bracek; 22 Luke Waterworth; 18 Ben Austin; - Connor Farrell; 24 Adam Jones; 8 Rob Lever. Subs (all used): 27 Liam Carberry; 9 Anthony Nicholson; 16 Anthony Bate; 19 Josh Barlow.
Tries: Waterworth (3), Butt (67, 77); **Goals:** Atkin 3/4.
Rugby Leaguer & League Express Men of the Match: *Rovers:* Jordan Abdull; *Lions:* Chris Atkin.
Penalty count: 12-7; **Half-time:** 14-8;
Referee: Callum Straw; **Attendance:** 7,236.

OLDHAM 28 BATLEY BULLDOGS 48

OLDHAM: 17 Richard Lepori; 2 Adam Clay; 3 George Tyson; 22 Danny Grimshaw; 29 Tuoyo Egodo; 6 Scott Leatherbarrow; 20 Gareth Owen; 8 Phil Joy; 21 Kenny Hughes; 10 Adam Neal; 14 Mikey Wood; 12 Danny Langtree; 11 Jack Spencer. Subs (all used): 9 Sam Gee; 24 Michael Ward; 19 Joe Burke; 15 Liam Bent.
Tries: Clay (3, 16, 21), Neal (7), Grimshaw (80);
Goals: Leatherbarrow 4/6.
BULLDOGS: 1 Dave Scott; 2 Wayne Reittie; 19 Alex Bretherton; 15 Danny Cowling; 5 Shaun Ainscough; 6 Cain Southernwood; 7 Dominic Brambani; 27 Will Maher; 14 James Davey; 16 Tom Lillycrop; 22 Dane Manning; 12 Joel Farrell; 11 Brad Day. Subs (all used): 8 Adam Gledhill; 9 Alistair Leak; 17 Joe Chandler; 18 James Harrison.
Tries: Cowling (9), Farrell (12), Leak (27), Gledhill (32), Reittie (43), Brambani (51), Harrison (58), Lillycrop (65);
Goals: Southernwood 8/9.
Dismissal: Brambani (80) - dissent.
Sin bin: Brambani (39) - trip.
Rugby Leaguer & League Express Men of the Match: *Oldham:* Adam Clay; *Bulldogs:* Tom Lillycrop.
Penalty count: 14-12; **Half-time:** 22-22;
Referee: Andrew Sweet; **Attendance:** 578 *(at Manchester Regional Arena).*

ROUND 15 - SUMMER BASH

Saturday 27th May 2017

OLDHAM 28 ROCHDALE HORNETS 38

OLDHAM: 17 Richard Lepori; 2 Adam Clay; 3 George Tyson; 28 Sam Wood; 1 Scott Turner; 6 Scott Leatherbarrow; 20 Gareth Owen; 30 Nathan Mason; 21 Kenny Hughes; 10 Adam Neal; 14 Luke Adamson; 12 Danny Langtree; 11 Jack Spencer. Subs (all used): 9 Sam Gee; 13 Liam Thompson; 19 Joe Burke; 24 Michael Ward.
Tries: Turner (6), Tyson (23), Lepori (27, 32);
Goals: Leatherbarrow 6/7.
Dismissal: Gee (79) - fighting.
Sin bin: Lepori (13) - fighting.
HORNETS: 2 Chris Riley; 1 Miles Greenwood; 3 Jake Eccleston; 4 Lewis Galbraith; 5 Rob Massam; 6 Lewis Palfrey; 7 Danny Yates; 15 Jovili Taira; 14 Ryan Maneely; 10 Gavin Bennion; 11 Jono Smith; 12 Josh Crowley; 13 Gary Middlehurst. Subs (all used): 9 Ben Moores; 17 Lee Mitchell; 16 Matty Hadden; 19 Jordan Case.
Tries: Greenwood (8), Eccleston (20, 39), Massam (48), Moores (51), Case (57), Galbraith (63);
Goals: Yates 5/8, Palfrey 0/1.
Sin bin: Taira (13) - fighting; Yates (79) - fighting.
Rugby Leaguer & League Express Men of the Match: *Oldham:* Richard Lepori; *Hornets:* Lewis Palfrey.
Penalty count: 13-12; **Half-time:** 26-12;
Referee: Liam Moore.

FEATHERSTONE ROVERS 16 LONDON BRONCOS 42

ROVERS: 1 Ian Hardman; 5 Luke Briscoe; 4 Misi Taulapapa; 22 Jason Walton; 18 Scott Turner; 7 Anthony Thackeray; 31 Cory Aston; 13 Richard Moore; 9 Keal Carlile; 16 Luke Cooper; 14 Frankie Mariano; 12 John Davies; 21 James Lockwood. Subs (all used): 19 Matty Wildie; 8 Darrell Griffin; 15 Bradley Knowles-Tagg; 30 Jack Ormondroyd.
Tries: Davies (45, 66), Turner (64); **Goals:** Aston 2/3.
Sin bin: Hardman (57) - fighting.
BRONCOS: 24 Alex Walker; 2 Rhys Williams; 1 Elliot Kear; 20 Michael Channing; 5 Kieran Dixon; 6 Jarrod Sammut; 7 William Barthau; 18 Ben Evans; 9 James Cunningham; 10 Mark Ioane; 11 Daniel Harrison; 13 Jay Pitts; 17 Mark Offerdahl. Subs (all used): 14 Andy Ackers; 12 Matt Garside; 16 Junior Roqica; 31 Lewis Bienek.
Tries: Sammut (6), Williams (11), Ackers (49), Walker (52), Channing (60), Barthau (72), Dixon (77);
Goals: Dixon 7/9.
Sin bin: Kear (57) - fighting.
Rugby Leaguer & League Express Men of the Match: *Rovers:* John Davies; *Broncos:* Mark Ioane.
Penalty count: 7-9; **Half-time:** 0-14;
Referee: Gareth Hewer.

BRADFORD BULLS 19 HULL KINGSTON ROVERS 20

BULLS: 14 Oscar Thomas; 5 Iliess Macani; 2 Ethan Ryan; 20 James Bentley; 19 Johnny Campbell; 28 Jordan Lilley; 13 Dane Chisholm; 15 Jon Magrin; 29 Sam Hallas; 8 Liam Kirk; 37 Cameron Smith; 11 Colton Roche; 17 Ross Peltier. Subs (all used): 31 Mikolaj Oledzki; 34 Scott Moore; 7 Joe Keyes; 36 James Davies.
Tries: Bentley (2), Chisholm (54), Ryan (74);
Goals: Thomas 3/3; **Field goal:** Chisholm (34).
ROVERS: 2 Ben Cockayne; 32 Kieren Moss; 29 Jake Butler-Fleming; 22 Andrew Heffernan; 5 Ryan Shaw; 16 Jordan Abdull; 7 Jamie Ellis; 8 Nick Scruton; 9 Shaun Lunt; 35 Josh Johnson; 11 Maurice Blair; 13 Danny Addy; 33 Ben Kavanagh. Subs (all used): 21 Rob Mulhern; 4 Liam Salter; 18 Zach Dockar-Clay; 30 Joe Cator.
Tries: Heffernan (18, 59), Abdull (73); **Goals:** Ellis 4/6.
Rugby Leaguer & League Express Men of the Match: *Bulls:* Dane Chisholm; *Rovers:* Andrew Heffernan.
Penalty count: 7-14; **Half-time:** 7-8; **Referee:** Tom Grant.

Attendance: 11,557 *(at Bloomfield Road, Blackpool).*

Sunday 28th May 2017

SHEFFIELD EAGLES 30 SWINTON LIONS 24

EAGLES: 1 Jack Owens; 2 Garry Lo; 3 Menzie Yere; 24 Paddy Flynn; 5 Ben Blackmore; 6 Simon Brown; 13 Elliot Minchella; 8 Scott Wheeldon; 9 Matty Fozard; 10 Mark Mexico; 11 Matt James; 16 Sam Scott; 19 Will Hope. Subs (all used): 22 Liam Johnson; 15 Kyle Trout; 12 Duane Straugheir; 17 Jordan Cox.
Tries: Fozard (30, 62), Hope (49), Yere (54), Lo (59);
Goals: Brown 5/6.
LIONS: 1 Jack Murphy; 2 Shaun Robinson; 3 Chris Hankinson; 4 Rhodri Lloyd; 21 Mike Butt; 6 Grant Gore; 7 Chris Atkin; 15 Andy Bracek; 22 Luke Waterworth; 18 Ben Austin; 27 Connor Farrell; 24 Adam Jones; 8 Rob Lever. Subs (all used): 26 Caine Barnes; 9 Anthony Nicholson; 16 Anthony Bate; 19 Josh Barlow.
Tries: Atkin (23), Robinson (74), C Farrell (78), Austin (79);
Goals: Atkin 4/5.
Rugby Leaguer & League Express Men of the Match: *Eagles:* Matty Fozard; *Lions:* Adam Jones.
Penalty count: 8-8; **Half-time:** 6-8; **Referee:** Jack Smith.

HALIFAX 22 TOULOUSE OLYMPIQUE 32

HALIFAX: 2 Will Sharp; 5 James Saltonstall; 21 James Woodburn-Hall; 3 Steve Tyrer; 23 Rob Worrincy; 1 Ben Johnston; 6 Scott Murrell; 8 Mitch Cahalane; 17 Brandon Moore; 14 Ryan Boyle; 12 Simon Grix; 4 Ben Heaton; 13 Jacob Fairbank. Subs (all used): 10 Adam Tangata; 16 Ed Barber; 20 Elliot Morris; 37 Brandon Douglas.
Tries: Tyrer (19, 45), Worrincy (71), Woodburn-Hall (74);
Goals: Tyrer 3/4.
OLYMPIQUE: 1 Mark Kheirallah; 2 Tony Maurel; 11 Sebastien Planas; 3 Bastien Ader; 5 Kuni Minga; 24 Anthony Marion; 7 Stan Robin; 8 Clement Boyer; 9 Kane Bentley; 10 Bastian Canet; 26 Constantine Mika; 12 Rhys Curran; 13 Andrew Bentley. Subs (all used): 14 Mourad Kriouache; 15 Maxime Puech; 16 Tyla Hepi; 17 Kalausa Leha.
Tries: K Bentley (3), Maurel (7, 24), Curran (36, 50), Marion (63); **Goals:** Kheirallah 4/7.
Rugby Leaguer & League Express Men of the Match: *Halifax:* Steve Tyrer; *Olympique:* Rhys Curran.
Penalty count: 7-6; **Half-time:** 6-20;
Referee: Andrew Sweet.

BATLEY BULLDOGS 12 DEWSBURY RAMS 13

BULLDOGS: 1 Dave Scott; 2 Wayne Reittie; 3 Sam Smeaton; 15 Danny Cowling; 5 Shaun Ainscough; 6 Cain Southernwood; 7 Dominic Brambani; 27 Will Maher; 9 Alistair Leak; 16 Tom Lillycrop; 22 Dane Manning; 12 Joel Farrell; 11 Brad Day. Subs (all used): 10 Alex Rowe; 14 James Davey; 18 James Harrison; 8 Adam Gledhill.
Tries: Cowling (25), Reittie (35), Harrison (44);
Goals: Southernwood 0/3, Brambani 0/1.
Sin bin: Brambani (14) - dangerous challenge.
RAMS: 26 Luke Hooley; 2 Dale Morton; 23 James Glover; 4 Lucas Walshaw; 41 Lewis Fairhurst; 17 Dom Speakman; 9 Tom Hemingway; 24 Jode Sheriffe; 15 Robbie Ward; 18 Jack Teanby; 27 Billy Hayes; 30 Daniel Igbinedion; 13 Aaron Brown. Subs (all used): 6 Paul Sykes; 16 Toby Adamson; 20 Aaron Ollett; 8 Tony Tonks.
Try: Aaron Brown (48); **Goals:** Glover 4/4;
Field goal: Sykes (59).
Rugby Leaguer & League Express Men of the Match: *Bulldogs:* James Harrison; *Rams:* Aaron Brown.
Penalty count: 9-7; **Half-time:** 8-4; **Referee:** Jon Roberts.

Attendance: 4,887 *(at Bloomfield Road, Blackpool).*

ROUND 16

Sunday 4th June 2017

BATLEY BULLDOGS 20 TOULOUSE OLYMPIQUE 28

BULLDOGS: 1 Dave Scott; 2 Wayne Reittie; 3 Sam Smeaton; 15 Danny Cowling; 5 Shaun Ainscough; 6 Cain Southernwood; 7 Dominic Brambani; 8 Adam Gledhill; 9

Hull KR's Kieren Moss dives for a loose ball against Bradford at the Summer Bash

Alistair Leak; 16 Tom Lillycrop; 22 Dane Manning; 19 Alex Bretherton; 11 Brad Day. **Subs** (all used): 14 James Davey; 21 James Brown; 10 Alex Rowe; 18 James Harrison.
Tries: Reittie (22, 40), Ainscough (61); **Goals:** Brambani 4/5.
OLYMPIQUE: 1 Mark Kheirallah; 20 Paul Marcon; 11 Sebastien Planas; 3 Bastien Ader; 2 Tony Maurel; 24 Anthony Marion; 7 Stan Robin; 15 Maxime Puech; 9 Kane Bentley; 10 Bastian Canet; 26 Constantine Mika; 12 Rhys Curran; 8 Clement Boyer. **Subs** (all used): 14 Mourad Kriouache; 23 Justin Sangare; 13 Andrew Bentley; 17 Kalausa Leha.
Tries: Robin (16), Marcon (45), Marion (47), Mika (64), K Bentley (75); **Goals:** Kheirallah 4/5.
Rugby Leaguer & League Express Men of the Match:
Bulldogs: Wayne Reittie; *Olympique:* Constantine Mika.
Penalty count: 7-6; **Half-time:** 14-6;
Referee: Jack Smith; **Attendance:** 627.

DEWSBURY RAMS 38 BRADFORD BULLS 12

RAMS: 26 Luke Hooley; 2 Dale Morton; 29 Macauley Hallett; 23 James Glover; 32 Shaun Squires; 17 Dom Speakman; 41 Gareth Moore; 24 Jode Sheriff; 27 Sam Day; 18 Jack Teanby; 30 Daniel Igbinedion; 4 Lucas Walshaw; 15 Robbie Ward. **Subs:** 6 Paul Sykes; 20 Aaron Ollett; 16 Toby Adamson; 42 Billy Hayes (not used).
Tries: Glover (7, 75), Day (28), Squires (35, 67), Walshaw (43), Hallett (70); **Goals:** Glover 5/8.
Sin bin: Morton (52) - fighting.
BULLS: 14 Oscar Thomas; 5 Iliess Macani; 2 Ethan Ryan; 20 James Bentley; 18 Omari Caro; 28 Jordan Lilley; 7 Joe Keyes; 15 Jon Magrin; 29 Sam Hallas; 8 Liam Kirk; 26 Vila Halafihi; 11 Colton Roche; 17 Ross Peltier. **Subs** (all used): 34 Scott Moore; 36 James Davies; 38 Ted Chapelhow; 31 Mikolaj Oledzki.
Tries: Macani (16), Bentley (20); **Goals:** Thomas 2/2.
Sin bin: Thomas (52) - fighting.
Rugby Leaguer & League Express Men of the Match:
Rams: Gareth Moore; *Bulls:* James Davies.
Penalty count: 9-11; **Half-time:** 16-12;
Referee: Liam Moore; **Attendance:** 1,975.

FEATHERSTONE ROVERS 20
HULL KINGSTON ROVERS 20

ROVERS: 1 Ian Hardman; 2 James Duckworth; 22 Jason Walton; 23 Josh Hardcastle; 4 Misi Taulapapa; 7 Anthony Thackeray; 19 Matty Wildie; 13 Richard Moore; 9 Keal Carlile; 32 Jordan Baldwinson; 11 Michael Knowles; 12 John Davies; 21 James Lockwood. **Subs** (all used): 6 Kyle Briggs; 14 Frankie Mariano; 8 Darrell Griffin; 30 Jack Ormondroyd.
Tries: Taulapapa (11), Walton (25), Duckworth (40);
Goals: Knowles 2/4, Briggs 2/4.
ROBINS: 2 Ben Cockayne; 32 Kieren Moss; 22 Andrew Heffernan; 29 Jake Butler-Fleming; 5 Ryan Shaw; 16 Jordan Abdull; 7 Jamie Ellis; 8 Nick Scruton; 9 Shaun Lunt; 35 Josh Johnson; 11 Maurice Blair; 13 Danny Addy; 33 Ben Kavanagh. **Subs** (all used): 10 Chris Clarkson; 21 Rob Mulhern; 18 Zach Dockar-Clay; 4 Liam Salter.

Tries: Moss (42, 62), Abdull (48), Dockar-Clay (71);
Goals: Ellis 2/4.
Rugby Leaguer & League Express Men of the Match:
Rovers: Anthony Thackeray; *Robins:* Jordan Abdull.
Penalty count: 12-8; **Half-time:** 16-0;
Referee: Scott Mikalauskas; **Attendance:** 4,072.

LONDON BRONCOS 34 HALIFAX 6

BRONCOS: 24 Alex Walker; 2 Rhys Williams; 1 Elliot Kear; 20 Michael Channing; 5 Kieran Dixon; 6 Jarrod Sammut; 7 William Barthau; 18 Ben Evans; 14 Andy Ackers; 10 Mark Ioane; 13 Jay Pitts; 3 Ben Hellewell; 17 Mark Offerdahl. Subs (all used): 19 Api Pewhairangi; 23 Matty Gee; 16 Junior Roqica; 31 Lewis Bienek.
Tries: Dixon (12, 56), Barthau (16), Ackers (22), Williams (31), Pitts (34), Ioane (70); **Goals:** Dixon 3/7.
HALIFAX: 2 Will Sharp; 38 Conor McGrath; 16 Ed Barber; 3 Steve Tyrer; 23 Rob Worrincy; 21 James Woodburn-Hall; 6 Scott Murrell; 8 Mitch Cahalane; 17 Brandon Moore; 36 Daniel Murray; 11 Shane Grady; 12 Simon Grix; 13 Jacob Fairbank. Subs (all used): 1 Ben Johnston; 14 Ryan Boyle; 20 Elliot Morris; 37 Brandon Douglas.
Try: Johnston (43); **Goals:** Tyrer 1/1.
Rugby Leaguer & League Express Men of the Match:
Broncos: Kieran Dixon; *Halifax:* Shane Grady.
Penalty count: 6-10; **Half-time:** 22-0;
Referee: Tom Grant; **Attendance:** 857.

SHEFFIELD EAGLES 38 ROCHDALE HORNETS 14

EAGLES: 1 Jack Owens; 2 Garry Lo; 3 Menzie Yere; 24 Paddy Flynn; 5 Ben Blackmore; 6 Simon Brown; 13 Elliot Minchella; 8 Scott Wheeldon; 9 Matty Fozard; 10 Mark Mexico; 11 Matt James; 12 Duane Straugheir; 19 Will Hope. Subs (all used): 14 Greg Burns; 29 James Green; 16 Sam Scott; 17 Jordan Cox.
Tries: Lo (5, 17, 44, 75, 80), Yere (49), Owens (51), Minchella (62); **Goals:** Brown 3/8.
HORNETS: 2 Chris Riley; 1 Miles Greenwood; 3 Jake Eccleston; 4 Lewis Galbraith; 5 Rob Massam; 6 Lewis Palfrey; 7 Danny Yates; 15 Jovili Taira; 14 Ryan Maneely; 10 Gavin Bennion; 11 Jono Smith; 19 Jordan Case; 13 Gary Middlehurst. Subs (all used): 9 Ben Moores; 16 Matty Hadden; 17 Matty Blythe; - Lee Mitchell.
Tries: Smith (39), Massam (64, 70); **Goals:** Palfrey 1/3.
Rugby Leaguer & League Express Men of the Match:
Eagles: Garry Lo; *Hornets:* Jono Smith.
Penalty count: 9-11; **Half-time:** 8-6;
Referee: Jon Roberts; **Attendance:** 341.

SWINTON LIONS 26 OLDHAM 4

LIONS: 1 Jack Murphy; 2 Shaun Robinson; 3 Chris Hankinson; 4 Rhodri Lloyd; 21 Mike Butt; 14 Ben White; 7 Chris Atkin; 15 Josh Bracek; 22 Luke Waterworth; 19 Josh Barlow; 27 Connor Farrell; 24 Adam Jones; 8 Rob Lever. Subs (all used): 26 Caine Barnes; - Liam Carberry; 9 Anthony Nicholson; 16 Anthony Bate.

Tries: Lloyd (22), Hankinson (34, 69), Murphy (67);
Goals: Atkin 5/5.
Sin bin: Barlow (72) - punching;
Murphy (80) - holding down.
OLDHAM: 17 Richard Lepori; 2 Adam Clay; 3 George Tyson; 22 Danny Grimshaw; 1 Scott Turner; 6 Scott Leatherbarrow; 7 Dave Hewitt; 11 Jack Spencer; 21 Kenny Hughes; 10 Adam Neal; 14 Luke Adamson; 12 Danny Langtree; 13 Liam Thompson. Subs (all used): 27 Brad Hill; 15 Liam Bent; 20 Gareth Owen; 24 Michael Ward.
Try: Lepori (74); **Goals:** Leatherbarrow 0/1.
Rugby Leaguer & League Express Men of the Match:
Lions: Chris Hankinson; *Oldham:* Richard Lepori.
Penalty count: 8-11; **Half-time:** 12-0;
Referee: John McMullen; **Attendance:** 628.

ROUND 17

Saturday 10th June 2017

TOULOUSE OLYMPIQUE 56 ROCHDALE HORNETS 16

OLYMPIQUE: 1 Mark Kheirallah; 5 Kuni Minga; 3 Bastien Ader; 11 Sebastien Planas; 20 Paul Marcon; 24 Anthony Marion; 7 Stan Robin; 8 Clement Boyer; 14 Mourad Kriouache; 10 Bastian Canet; 26 Constantine Mika; 12 Rhys Curran; 13 Andrew Bentley. Subs (all used): 15 Maxime Puech; 17 Kalausa Leha; 22 Levy Nzoungou; 27 Charles Bouzinac.
Tries: Mika (2), Ader (12, 32, 37), Robin (30), Kheirallah (40), Boyer (42), Marion (49), Marcon (72), Curran (77); **Goals:** Kheirallah 8/10.
HORNETS: - Declan Kay; 1 Miles Greenwood; 3 Jake Eccleston; 4 Lewis Galbraith; 5 Rob Massam; - Tyler Whittaker; 7 Danny Yates; 16 Matty Hadden; 9 Ben Moores; 10 Gavin Bennion; 12 Josh Crowley; 19 Jordan Case; - Lewis Hatton. Subs (all used): - Lewis Foster; - Danny Rasool; 25 Luke Fowden; 21 Jack Holmes.
Tries: Massam (22), Kay (62), Greenwood (69);
Goals: Whittaker 2/3.
Rugby Leaguer & League Express Men of the Match:
Olympique: Stan Robin; *Hornets:* Jordan Case.
Penalty count: 5-6; **Half-time:** 34-4;
Referee: Gareth Hewer; **Attendance:** 1,467.

Sunday 11th June 2017

BRADFORD BULLS 12 FEATHERSTONE ROVERS 36

BULLS: 24 Brandon Pickersgill; 18 Omari Caro; 4 Ross Oakes; 3 James Mendeika; 5 Iliess Macani; 14 Oscar Thomas; 28 Jordan Lilley; 15 Jon Magrin; 34 Scott Moore; 8 Liam Kirk; 20 James Bentley; 11 Colton Roche; 29 Sam Hallas. Subs (all used): 17 Ross Peltier; 36 James Davies; 21 Brandan Wilkinson; 26 Vila Halafihi.
Tries: Roche (7), Bentley (24); **Goals:** Thomas 2/2.

ROVERS: 1 Ian Hardman; 2 James Duckworth; 20 Kyran Johnson; 23 Josh Hardcastle; 4 Misi Taulapapa; 7 Anthony Thackeray; 19 Matty Wildie; 13 Richard Moore; 9 Keal Carlile; 32 Jordan Baldwinson; 11 Michael Knowles; 12 John Davies; 21 James Lockwood. Subs (all used): 6 Kyle Briggs; 14 Frankie Mariano; 8 Darrell Griffin; 30 Jack Ormondroyd.
Tries: Thackeray (12), Briggs (33), Hardcastle (43, 77), Ormondroyd (50), Wildie (73);
Goals: Knowles 3/4, Briggs 3/3.
Rugby Leaguer & League Express Men of the Match: *Bulls:* Sam Hallas; *Rovers:* Kyle Briggs.
Penalty count: 7-9; **Half-time:** 12-10;
Referee: John McMullen; **Attendance:** 3,931.

LONDON BRONCOS 52 DEWSBURY RAMS 8

BRONCOS: 24 Alex Walker; 2 Rhys Williams; 1 Elliot Kear; 20 Michael Channing; 5 Kieran Dixon; 6 Jarrod Sammut; 7 William Barthau; 8 Tom Spencer; 14 Andy Ackers; 18 Ben Evans; 13 Jay Pitts; 3 Ben Hellewell; 17 Mark Offerdahl. Subs (all used): 19 Api Pewhairangi; 23 Matty Gee; 16 Junior Roqica; 15 Eddie Battye.
Tries: Barthau (6), Walker (17, 68), Ackers (20), Hellewell (26), Channing (34), Pewhairangi (54, 74, 80);
Goals: Dixon 8/9.
RAMS: 26 Luke Hooley; 2 Dale Morton; 29 Macauley Hallett; 23 James Glover; 5 Gareth Potts; 17 Dom Speakman; 41 Gareth Moore; 24 Jode Sheriffe; 15 Robbie Ward; 18 Jack Teanby; 30 Daniel Igbinedion; 4 Lucas Walshaw; 13 Aaron Brown. Subs (all used): 6 Paul Sykes; 27 Sam Day; 16 Toby Adamson; 20 Aaron Ollett.
Tries: Potts (58), Glover (63); **Goals:** Glover 0/1, Sykes 0/1.
Sin bin: Sykes (79) - high tackle.
Rugby Leaguer & League Express Men of the Match: *Broncos:* William Barthau; *Rams:* Gareth Moore.
Penalty count: 11-9; **Half-time:** 30-0;
Referee: Callum Straw; **Attendance:** 854.

OLDHAM 24 HULL KINGSTON ROVERS 32

OLDHAM: 1 Scott Turner; 2 Adam Clay; 3 George Tyson; 17 Sam Wood; 16 Darnell McIntosh; 6 Scott Leatherbarrow; 7 Dave Hewitt; 10 Adam Neal; 21 Kenny Hughes; 19 Joe Burke; 14 Luke Adamson; 12 Danny Langtree; 11 Jack Spencer. Subs (all used): 26 Tyler Dickinson; 20 Gareth Owen; 18 Ben Davies; 27 Brad Hill.
Tries: Burke (3), Hewitt (6), S Wood (9), McIntosh (70);
Goals: Leatherbarrow 4/4.
ROVERS: 2 Ben Cockayne; 5 Ryan Shaw; 4 Liam Salter; 16 Jordan Abdull; 31 David Hodgson; 13 Danny Addy; 7 Jamie Ellis; 21 Rob Mulhern; 9 Shaun Lunt; 35 Josh Johnson; 11 Maurice Blair; 10 Chris Clarkson; 33 Ben Kavanagh. Subs (all used): 17 Mitch Clark; 24 Joe Wardill; 30 Joe Cator; 18 Zach Dockar-Clay.
Tries: Lunt (33), Abdull (36), Wardill (40, 54), Shaw (44, 65); **Goals:** Ellis 4/6.
Rugby Leaguer & League Express Men of the Match: *Oldham:* Dave Hewitt; *Rovers:* Danny Addy.
Penalty count: 5-5; **Half-time:** 18-16;
Referee: Chris Campbell; **Attendance:** 1,066.

SHEFFIELD EAGLES 0 HALIFAX 54

EAGLES: 1 Jack Owens; 2 Garry Lo; 3 Menzie Yere; 24 Paddy Flynn; 18 Ryan Millar; 6 Simon Brown; 13 Elliot Minchella; 8 Scott Wheeldon; 9 Matty Fozard; 10 Mark Mexico; 11 Matt James; 16 Sam Scott; 19 Will Hope. Subs (all used): 29 James Green; 17 Jordan Cox; 14 Greg Burns; 22 Liam Johnson.
HALIFAX: 2 Will Sharp; 38 Conor McGrath; 3 Steve Tyrer; 21 James Woodburn-Hall; 23 Rob Worrincy; 6 Scott Murrell; 1 Ben Johnston; 8 Mitch Cahalane; 17 Brandon Moore; 36 Daniel Murray; 11 Shane Grady; 16 Ed Barber; 12 Simon Grix. Subs (all used): 20 Elliot Morris; 13 Jacob Fairbank; 37 Brandon Douglas; 27 Matt Wilkinson.
Tries: Woodburn-Hall (6, 16), Tyrer (13), McGrath (26, 33, 73), Johnston (29), Wilkinson (51), E Morris (64), Douglas (75); **Goals:** Tyrer 7/10.
Rugby Leaguer & League Express Men of the Match: *Eagles:* Scott Wheeldon; *Halifax:* James Woodburn-Hall.
Penalty count: 7-11; **Half-time:** 0-32;
Referee: Tom Grant; **Attendance:** 672.

SWINTON LIONS 12 BATLEY BULLDOGS 26

LIONS: 1 Jack Murphy; 2 Shaun Robinson; 3 Chris Hankinson; 14 Ben White; 21 Mike Butt; 6 Grant Gore; 7 Chris Atkin; 15 Andy Bracek; 22 Luke Waterworth; 19 Josh Barlow; 17 Olly Davies; 4 Rhodri Lloyd; 8 Rob Lever. Subs (all used): 18 Ben Austin; 27 Liam Carberry; 16 Anthony Bate; 9 Anthony Nicholson.
Tries: Bate (43), Bracek (74); **Goals:** Atkin 1/1, White 1/1.
Sin bin: Bate (77) - fighting.
BULLDOGS: 1 Dave Scott; 2 Wayne Reittie; 3 Sam Smeaton; 15 Danny Cowling; 5 Shaun Ainscough; 13 Pat Walker; 6 Cain Southernwood; 8 Adam Gledhill; 14 James Davey; 16 Tom Lillycrop; 22 Dane Manning; 19 Alex Bretherton; 11 Brad Day. Subs (all used): 9 Alistair Leak; 21 James Brown; 10 Alex Rowe; 18 James Harrison.
Tries: Ainscough (17), Day (32), Leak (40), Cowling (52), Smeaton (63); **Goals:** Walker 3/5.
Sin bin: Lillycrop (77) - fighting.
Rugby Leaguer & League Express Men of the Match: *Lions:* Andy Bracek; *Bulldogs:* Cain Southernwood.
Penalty count: 12-14; **Half-time:** 0-16;
Referee: Brandon Robinson; **Attendance:** 569.

ROUND 18

Saturday 17th June 2017

TOULOUSE OLYMPIQUE 16 LONDON BRONCOS 36

OLYMPIQUE: 1 Mark Kheirallah; 4 Gregory White; 3 Bastien Ader; 21 Gavin Marguerite; 2 Tony Maurel; 24 Anthony Marion; 20 Paul Marcon; 15 Maxime Puech; 14 Mourad Kriouache; 10 Bastian Canet; 26 Constantine Mika; 12 Rhys Curran; 8 Clement Boyer. Subs (all used): 16 Tyla Hepi; 17 Kalausa Leha; 22 Levy Nzoungou; 27 Charles Bouzinac.
Tries: Canet (60, 66), Leha (75); **Goals:** Kheirallah 2/3.
Sin bin: Marion (48) - biting.
BRONCOS: 24 Alex Walker; 2 Rhys Williams; 1 Elliot Kear; 20 Michael Channing; 5 Kieran Dixon; 6 Jarrod Sammut; 7 William Barthau; 18 Ben Evans; 14 Andy Ackers; 10 Mark Ioane; 11 Daniel Harrison; 13 Jay Pitts; 15 Eddie Battye. Subs (all used): 19 Api Pewhairangi; 3 Ben Hellewell; 23 Matty Gee; 16 Junior Roqica.
Tries: Ackers (15), Barthau (21), Harrison (27), Walker (45), Dixon (52, 68), Pewhairangi (73); **Goals:** Dixon 4/7.
Rugby Leaguer & League Express Men of the Match: *Olympique:* Charles Bouzinac; *Broncos:* William Barthau.
Penalty count: 7-7; **Half-time:** 0-16;
Referee: Scott Mikalauskas; **Attendance:** 2,548.

Sunday 18th June 2017

BATLEY BULLDOGS 70 SHEFFIELD EAGLES 12

BULLDOGS: 1 Dave Scott; 2 Wayne Reittie; 3 Sam Smeaton; 15 Danny Cowling; 30 Jason Crookes; 13 Pat Walker; 7 Dominic Brambani; 8 Adam Gledhill; 9 Alistair Leak; 16 Tom Lillycrop; 18 James Harrison; 22 Dane Manning; 11 Brad Day. Subs (all used): 10 Alex Rowe; 12 Joel Farrell; 14 James Davey; 21 James Brown.
Tries: Reittie (10, 23, 39, 73), Brambani (12, 60), Scott (18), Walker (31, 77), Farrell (49, 65); **Goals:** Walker 13/13.
EAGLES: 1 Jack Owens; 2 Garry Lo; 3 Menzie Yere; 24 Paddy Flynn; 5 Ben Blackmore; 6 Simon Brown; 27 Remy Marginet; 8 Scott Wheeldon; 9 Matty Fozard; 10 Mark Mexico; 16 Sam Scott; 11 Matt James; 13 Elliot Minchella. Subs (all used): 14 Greg Burns; 15 Kyle Trout; 4 Perry Whiteley; 25 George Milton.
Tries: Whiteley (45), Marginet (66); **Goals:** Owens 2/2.
Rugby Leaguer & League Express Men of the Match: *Bulldogs:* Wayne Reittie; *Eagles:* Perry Whiteley.
Penalty count: 8-2; **Half-time:** 38-0;
Referee: Gareth Hewer; **Attendance:** 2,106.

HULL KINGSTON ROVERS 64 DEWSBURY RAMS 11

ROVERS: 2 Ben Cockayne; 5 Ryan Shaw; 22 Andrew Heffernan; 4 Liam Salter; 27 Will Oakes; 16 Jordan Abdull; 7 Jamie Ellis; 21 Rob Mulhern; 25 Will Jubb; 37 Lee Jewitt; 13 Danny Addy; 10 Chris Clarkson; 11 Maurice Blair. Subs (all used): 18 Zach Dockar-Clay; 30 Joe Cator; 17 Mitch Clark; 24 Joe Wardill.
Tries: Shaw (5, 22, 38), Heffernan (12, 28), Salter (30, 74), Ellis (34), Cockayne (56), Abdull (66), Cator (69), Addy (72); **Goals:** Ellis 8/12.
RAMS: 2 Dale Morton; 5 Gareth Potts; 13 Aaron Brown; 26 Luke Hooley; 31 Alex Brown; 17 Dom Speakman; 25 Lewis Fairhurst; 28 Zach Johnson; 9 Tom Hemingway; 30 Daniel Igbinedion; 11 Rob Spicer; 42 Billy Hayes; 23 James Glover. Subs (all used): 6 Paul Sykes; 27 Sam Day; 15 Robbie Ward; 18 Jack Teanby.
Tries: Morton (46), Potts (52); **Goals:** Sykes 1/2;
Field goal: Fairhurst (9).
Rugby Leaguer & League Express Men of the Match: *Rovers:* Jamie Ellis; *Rams:* Daniel Igbinedion.
Penalty count: 7-9; **Half-time:** 36-1;
Referee: Tom Grant; **Attendance:** 6,772.

OLDHAM 12 HALIFAX 30

OLDHAM: 17 Richard Lepori; 2 Adam Clay; 3 George Tyson; 16 Sam Wood; 1 Scott Turner; 6 Scott Leatherbarrow; 7 Dave Hewitt; 10 Adam Neal; 21 Kenny Hughes; 19 Joe Burke; 14 Luke Adamson; 12 Danny Langtree; 11 Jack Spencer. Subs (all used): 26 Tyler Dickinson; 20 Gareth Owen; 18 Ben Davies; 24 Michael Ward.
Tries: Turner (45), Ward (51); **Goals:** Leatherbarrow 2/3.
HALIFAX: 2 Will Sharp; 38 Conor McGrath; 21 James Woodburn-Hall; 3 Steve Tyrer; 23 Rob Worrincy; 6 Scott Murrell; 1 Ben Johnston; 8 Mitch Cahalane; 17 Brandon Moore; 36 Daniel Murray; 11 Shane Grady; 16 Ed Barber; 12 Simon Grix. Subs (all used): 20 Elliot Morris; 14 Ryan Boyle; 37 Brandon Douglas; 27 Matt Wilkinson.
Tries: Sharp (23, 63), Douglas (31), B Moore (68), E Morris (77); **Goals:** Tyrer 5/6.
Rugby Leaguer & League Express Men of the Match: *Oldham:* Scott Turner; *Halifax:* Will Sharp.
Penalty count: 10-8; **Half-time:** 0-12;
Referee: John McMullen; **Attendance:** 809.

ROCHDALE HORNETS 28 BRADFORD BULLS 14

HORNETS: - Declan Kay; 3 Jake Eccleston; 19 Jordan Case; 4 Lewis Galbraith; 5 Rob Massam; 27 Lewis Foster; 7 Danny Yates; - Anthony Walker; 9 Ben Moores; 10 Gavin Bennion; 11 Jono Smith; 12 Josh Crowley; 13 Gary Middlehurst. Subs (all used): - Lewis Hatton; 15 Jovili Taira; 16 Matty Hadden; 17 Lee Mitchell.
Tries: Taira (27, 38), Galbraith (47), Hadden (76);
Goals: Yates 6/6.
BULLS: 14 Oscar Thomas; 19 Johnny Campbell; 4 Ross Oakes; 40 Ed Chamberlain; 18 Omari Caro; 28 Jordan Lilley; 7 Joe Keyes; 8 Liam Kirk; 34 Scott Moore; 17 Ross Peltier; 37 Cameron Smith; 20 James Bentley; 29 Sam Hallas. Subs (all used): 3 James Mendeika; 21 Brandan Wilkinson; 38 Ted Chapelhow; 36 James Davies.
Tries: Bentley (18), Chapelhow (21); **Goals:** Thomas 3/3.
Rugby Leaguer & League Express Men of the Match: *Hornets:* Danny Yates; *Bulls:* Ross Peltier.
Penalty count: 3-12; **Half-time:** 12-14;
Referee: Callum Straw; **Attendance:** 1,230.

Wednesday 21st June 2017

FEATHERSTONE ROVERS 36 SWINTON LIONS 2

ROVERS: 1 Ian Hardman; 20 Kyran Johnson; 3 Chris Ulugia; 23 Josh Hardcastle; 4 Misi Taulapapa; 7 Anthony Thackeray; 19 Matty Wildie; 32 Jordan Baldwinson; 9 Keal Carlile; 8 Darrell Griffin; 22 Jason Walton; 14 Frankie Mariano; 25 Josh Walters. Subs (all used): 12 John Davies; 13 Richard Moore; 10 Andrew Bostock; 30 Jack Ormondroyd.
Tries: Hardcastle (12, 54), Wildie (22), Thackeray (28, 47), Davies (40), Walton (76);
Goals: Johnson 2/6, Davies 2/2.
LIONS: 1 Jack Murphy; 3 Chris Hankinson; 25 Liam Forsyth; 4 Rhodri Lloyd; 21 Mike Butt; 14 Ben White; 7 Chris Atkin; 26 Caine Barnes; 9 Anthony Nicholson; 19 Josh Barlow; - Liam Paisley; 24 Adam Jones; 16 Anthony Bate. Subs (all used): 27 Liam Carberry; 15 Andy Bracek; 17 Olly Davies; 22 Luke Waterworth.
Goals: Atkin 1/1.
Rugby Leaguer & League Express Men of the Match: *Rovers:* Matty Wildie; *Lions:* Chris Atkin.
Penalty count: 14-9; **Half-time:** 20-2;
Referee: Liam Moore; **Attendance:** 1,892.

ROUND 5

Wednesday 21st June 2017

OLDHAM 16 DEWSBURY RAMS 20

OLDHAM: 1 Scott Turner; 2 Adam Clay; 3 George Tyson; 22 Danny Grimshaw; 5 Jamel Chisholm; 6 Scott Leatherbarrow; 7 Dave Hewitt; 10 Adam Neal; 21 Kenny Hughes; 19 Joe Burke; 14 Luke Adamson; 12 Danny Langtree; 11 Jack Spencer. Subs (all used): 13 Liam Thompson; 20 Gareth Owen; 18 Ben Davies; 24 Michael Ward.
Tries: Grimshaw (4), Ward (28); **Goals:** Leatherbarrow 4/5.
Sin bin: Neal (52) - late challenge.
RAMS: 26 Luke Hooley; 2 Dale Morton; 29 Macauley Hallett; 4 Lucas Walshaw; 31 Alex Brown; 6 Paul Sykes; 41 Gareth Moore; 28 Zach Johnson; 15 Robbie Ward; 24 Jode Sheriffe; 30 Daniel Igbinedion; 42 Billy Hayes; 13 Aaron Brown. Subs (all used): 20 Aaron Ollett; 27 Sam Day; 16 Toby Adamson; 18 Jack Teanby.
Tries: Morton (17), Ollett (53), Moore (75); **Goals:** Sykes 4/4.
Rugby Leaguer & League Express Men of the Match: *Oldham:* Danny Langtree; *Rams:* Gareth Moore.
Penalty count: 9-11; **Half-time:** 12-6;
Referee: Jon Roberts; **Attendance:** 575.

ROUND 19

Sunday 25th June 2017

BRADFORD BULLS 47 OLDHAM 12

BULLS: 14 Oscar Thomas; 40 Ed Chamberlain; 3 James Mendeika; 4 Ross Oakes; 2 Ethan Ryan; 28 Jordan Lilley; 7 Joe Keyes; 31 Mikolaj Oledzki; 34 Scott Moore; 15 Jon

Magrin; 20 James Bentley; 37 Cameron Smith; 29 Sam Hallas. Subs (all used): 17 Ross Peltier; 8 Liam Kirk; 36 James Davies; 11 Colton Roche.
Tries: Ryan (9, 17, 27, 53), Bentley (13, 76), Chamberlain (57, 77), Mendeika (63);
Goals: Thomas 5/9; **Field goal:** Thomas (40).
OLDHAM: 27 Steven Nield; 2 Adam Clay; 16 Sam Wood; 26 Kameron Pearce-Paul; 30 Gene Ormsby; 6 Scott Leatherbarrow; 7 Dave Hewitt; 24 Michael Ward; 21 Kenny Hughes; 10 Adam Neal; 13 Liam Thompson; 12 Danny Langtree; 11 Jack Spencer. Subs (all used): 9 Sam Gee; 28 Sadiq Adebiyi; 18 Ben Davies; 15 Liam Bent.
Tries: Langtree (69), Hewitt (72); **Goals:** Hewitt 2/2.
Rugby Leaguer & League Express Men of the Match: *Bulls:* Ethan Ryan; *Oldham:* Danny Langtree.
Penalty count: 9-5; **Half-time:** 21-0;
Referee: Jon Roberts; **Attendance:** 3,708.

DEWSBURY RAMS 34 TOULOUSE OLYMPIQUE 22

RAMS: 26 Luke Hooley; 2 Dale Morton; 29 Macauley Hallett; 4 Lucas Walshaw; 31 Alex Brown; 6 Paul Sykes; 41 Gareth Moore; 24 Jode Sheriffe; 15 Robbie Ward; 18 Jack Teanby; 43 Jordan Crowther; 42 Billy Hayes; 13 Aaron Brown. Subs (all used): 20 Aaron Ollett; 17 Dom Speakman; 16 Toby Adamson; 44 Toby Everett.
Tries: Walshaw (7, 58), Hallett (62), Aaron Brown (67), Sheriffe (71); **Goals:** Sykes 7/7.
OLYMPIQUE: 1 Mark Kheirallah; 20 Paul Marcon; 21 Gavin Marguerite; 3 Bastien Ader; 2 Tony Maurel; 24 Anthony Marion; 18 Louis Jouffret; 8 Clement Boyer; 27 Charles Bouzinac; 10 Bastian Canet; 11 Sebastien Planas; 12 Rhys Curran; 13 Andrew Bentley. Subs (all used): 14 Mourad Kriouache; 15 Maxime Puech; 16 Tyla Hepi; 26 Constantine Mika.
Tries: Marcon (17, 25, 77), Curran (56); **Goals:** Kheirallah 3/4.
Rugby Leaguer & League Express Men of the Match: *Rams:* Lucas Walshaw; *Olympique:* Paul Marcon.
Penalty count: 8-2; **Half-time:** 8-12;
Referee: John McMullen; **Attendance:** 626.

LONDON BRONCOS 36 FEATHERSTONE ROVERS 30

BRONCOS: 24 Alex Walker; 2 Rhys Williams; 1 Elliot Kear; 20 Michael Channing; 5 Kieran Dixon; 6 Jarrod Sammut; 7 William Barthau; 18 Ben Evans; 14 Andy Ackers; 10 Mark Ioane; 13 Jay Pitts; 3 Ben Hellewell; 23 Matty Gee. Subs (all used): 19 Api Pewhairangi; 17 Mark Offerdahl; 16 Junior Roqica; 15 Eddie Battye.
Tries: Gee (22), Walker (27, 77), Barthau (39), Sammut (57), Dixon (69), Kear (72); **Goals:** Dixon 4/7.
ROVERS: 1 Ian Hardman; 20 Kyran Johnson; 23 Josh Hardcastle; 3 Chris Ulugia; 4 Misi Taulapapa; 7 Anthony Thackeray; 19 Matty Wildie; 8 Darrell Griffin; 9 Keal Carlile; 32 Jordan Baldwinson; 14 Frankie Mariano; 22 Jason Walton; 25 Josh Walters. Subs (all used): 12 John Davies; 13 Richard Moore; 30 Jack Ormondroyd; 10 Andrew Bostock.
Tries: Baldwinson (11), Taulapapa (19), Mariano (33), Bostock (48), Wildie (79); **Goals:** Hardman 5/5.
Rugby Leaguer & League Express Men of the Match: *Broncos:* William Barthau; *Rovers:* Anthony Thackeray.
Penalty count: 5-6; **Half-time:** 16-18;
Referee: Jack Smith; **Attendance:** 910.

ROCHDALE HORNETS 14 BATLEY BULLDOGS 24

HORNETS: - Declan Kay; 3 Jake Eccleston; 19 Jordan Case; 4 Lewis Galbraith; 5 Rob Massam; 27 Lewis Foster; 7 Danny Yates; - Anthony Walker; 9 Ben Moores; 10 Gavin Bennion; 11 Jono Smith; 12 Josh Crowley; 13 Gary Middlehurst. Subs (all used): 14 Ryan Maneely; 15 Jovili Taira; 16 Matty Hadden; 17 Lee Mitchell.
Tries: Galbraith (1), Eccleston (28), Middlehurst (53);
Goals: Yates 1/2, Foster 0/1.
BULLDOGS: 1 Dave Scott; 2 Wayne Reittie; 15 Danny Cowling; 30 Jason Crookes; 5 Shaun Ainscough; 13 Pat Walker; 7 Dominic Brambani; 8 Adam Gledhill; 9 Alistair Leak; 16 Tom Lillycrop; 22 Dane Manning; 18 James Harrison; 11 Brad Day. Subs (all used): 10 Alex Rowe; 12 Joel Farrell; 14 James Davey; 21 James Brown.
Tries: Gledhill (12), Ainscough (20), Leak (78);
Goals: Walker 6/6.
Rugby Leaguer & League Express Men of the Match: *Hornets:* Gary Middlehurst; *Bulldogs:* Pat Walker.
Penalty count: 9-12; **Half-time:** 8-14;
Referee: Liam Moore; **Attendance:** 604.

SHEFFIELD EAGLES 18 HULL KINGSTON ROVERS 40

EAGLES: 1 Jack Owens; 18 Ryan Millar; 24 Paddy Flynn; 23 Jake Spedding; 5 Ben Blackmore; 6 Simon Brown; 27 Remy Marginet; 8 Scott Wheeldon; 9 Matty Fozard; 29 Greg Richards; 15 Kyle Trout; 19 Will Hope; 13 Elliot Minchella. Subs (all used): 14 Greg Burns; 10 Mark Mexico; 22 Liam Johnson; 26 Curtis Wilson.
Tries: Minchella (43), Trout (75), Johnson (79);
Goals: Brown 3/3.
ROVERS: 18 Zach Dockar-Clay; 2 Ben Cockayne; 5 Ryan Shaw; 4 Liam Salter; 36 Justin Carney; 28 Liam Harris; 7 Jamie Ellis; 8 Nick Scruton; 9 Shaun Lunt; 37 Lee Jewitt; 13 Danny Addy; 10 Chris Clarkson; 33 Ben Kavanagh. Subs (all used): 29 Jake Butler-Fleming; 35 Josh Johnson; 32 Kieren Moss; 17 Mitch Clark.
Tries: Carney (5, 52), Clarkson (8), Butler-Fleming (18), Scruton (33), Shaw (38), Lunt (48), Dockar-Clay (63);
Goals: Ellis 4/8.
Rugby Leaguer & League Express Men of the Match: *Eagles:* Mark Mexico; *Rovers:* Nick Scruton.
Penalty count: 8-8; **Half-time:** 0-24;
Referee: Nick Bennett; **Attendance:** 1,619.

SWINTON LIONS 13 HALIFAX 12

LIONS: 1 Jack Murphy; 2 Shaun Robinson; 3 Chris Hankinson; 4 Rhodri Lloyd; 21 Mike Butt; 14 Ben White; 7 Chris Atkin; 15 Andy Bracek; 22 Luke Waterworth; 26 Caine Barnes; - Liam Paisley; 17 Olly Davies; - Callum Field. Subs (all used): 27 Liam Carberry; 9 Anthony Nicholson; 16 Anthony Bate; 19 Josh Barlow.
Tries: O Davies (4), Robinson (32); **Goals:** Atkin 2/4;
Field goal: Atkin (72).
HALIFAX: 2 Will Sharp; 38 Conor McGrath; 4 Ben Heaton; 3 Steve Tyrer; 27 Connor Williams; 6 Scott Murrell; 1 Ben Johnston; 8 Mitch Cahalane; 17 Brandon Moore; 36 Daniel Murray; 11 Shane Grady; 16 Ed Barber; 12 Simon Grix. Subs (all used): 20 Elliot Morris; 39 Jordan Walne; 37 Brandon Douglas; 31 Josh Wood.
Tries: Cahalane (52), Wood (61); **Goals:** Tyrer 2/2.
Sin bin: B Moore (27) - punching.
Rugby Leaguer & League Express Men of the Match: *Lions:* Jack Murphy; *Halifax:* Will Sharp.
Penalty count: 3-5; **Half-time:** 10-0;
Referee: Callum Straw; **Attendance:** 863.

ROUND 20

Sunday 2nd July 2017

DEWSBURY RAMS 40 ROCHDALE HORNETS 10

RAMS: 1 Josh Guzdek; 2 Dale Morton; 29 Macauley Hallett; 4 Lucas Walshaw; 31 Alex Brown; 6 Paul Sykes; 41 Gareth Moore; 24 Jode Sheriffe; 27 Sam Day; 18 Jack Teanby; 43 Jordan Crowther; 11 Rob Spicer; 13 Aaron Brown. Subs (all used): 17 Dom Speakman; 20 Aaron Ollett; 44 Toby Everett; 16 Toby Adamson.
Tries: Spicer (14, 30), T Adamson (22), Morton (24), Hallett (35, 74), Moore (53); **Goals:** Sykes 6/8.
HORNETS: 1 Miles Greenwood; 2 Chris Riley; 19 Jordan Case; 4 Lewis Galbraith; 5 Rob Massam; 6 Lewis Palfrey; 7 Danny Yates; - Anthony Walker; 9 Ben Moores; 10 Gavin Bennion; 17 Lee Mitchell; 12 Josh Crowley; 13 Gary Middlehurst. Subs (all used): 27 Lewis Foster; 15 Jovili Taira; 16 Matty Hadden; - Lewis Hatton.
Tries: Massam (46), Case (78); **Goals:** Yates 1/2.
Sin bin: Galbraith (69) - dissent.
Rugby Leaguer & League Express Men of the Match: *Rams:* Gareth Moore; *Hornets:* Ben Moores.
Penalty count: 10-13; **Half-time:** 28-0;
Referee: Tom Grant; **Attendance:** 775.

FEATHERSTONE ROVERS 42 BATLEY BULLDOGS 14

ROVERS: 1 Ian Hardman; 4 Misi Taulapapa; 3 Chris Ulugia; 23 Josh Hardcastle; 18 Scott Turner; 7 Anthony Thackeray; 19 Matty Wildie; 10 Andrew Bostock; 9 Keal Carlile; 8 Darrell Griffin; 22 Jason Walton; 12 John Davies; 25 Josh Walters. Subs (all used): 21 James Lockwood; 13 Richard Moore; 32 Jordan Baldwinson; 30 Jack Ormondroyd.
Tries: Turner (9, 14), Baldwinson (20), Ormondroyd (46), Davies (55), Bostock (61), Hardman (75);
Goals: Hardman 7/8.
Sin bin: Ulugia (50) - interference.
BULLDOGS: 1 Dave Scott; 2 Wayne Reittie; 3 Sam Smeaton; 30 Jason Crookes; 5 Shaun Ainscough; 13 Pat Walker; 7 Dominic Brambani; 8 Adam Gledhill; 9 Alistair Leak; 16 Tom Lillycrop; 22 Dane Manning; 12 Joel Farrell; 11 Brad Day. Subs (all used): 6 Cain Southernwood; 10 Alex Rowe; 18 James Harrison; 21 James Brown.
Tries: Day (5), Reittie (34), Ainscough (44);
Goals: Walker 1/3.
Sin bin: Manning (65) - interference;
Lillycrop (74) - dissent.
Rugby Leaguer & League Express Men of the Match: *Rovers:* Anthony Thackeray; *Bulldogs:* Pat Walker.
Penalty count: 17-16; **Half-time:** 16-10;
Referee: Jon Roberts; **Attendance:** 2,275.

HALIFAX 20 BRADFORD BULLS 18

HALIFAX: 2 Will Sharp; 30 Jake Bibby; 3 Steve Tyrer; 4 Ben Heaton; 23 Rob Worrincy; 6 Scott Murrell; 31 Josh Wood; 8 Mitch Cahalane; 17 Brandon Moore; 36 Daniel Murray; 11 Shane Grady; 16 Ed Barber; 12 Simon Grix. Subs (all used): 20 Elliot Morris; 39 Jordan Walne; 14 Ryan Boyle; 9 Ben Kaye.
Tries: Wood (20), Heaton (23), Murray (66);
Goals: Tyrer 4/4.
BULLS: 14 Oscar Thomas; 40 Ed Chamberlain; 3 James Mendeika; 23 Ashley Gibson; 2 Ethan Ryan; 7 Joe Keyes; 33 Reiss Butterworth; 31 Mikolaj Oledzki; 29 Sam Hallas; 15 Jon Magrin; 20 James Bentley; 37 Cameron Smith; 11 Colton Roche. Subs (all used): 17 Ross Peltier; 8 Liam Kirk; 38 Ted Chapelhow; 26 Vila Halafihi.
Tries: Halafihi (55), Ryan (78), Chapelhow (80);
Goals: Thomas 3/3.
Rugby Leaguer & League Express Men of the Match: *Halifax:* Will Sharp; *Bulls:* Ethan Ryan.
Penalty count: 8-9; **Half-time:** 14-0;
Referee: Nick Bennett; **Attendance:** 3,142.

HULL KINGSTON ROVERS 40 LONDON BRONCOS 22

ROVERS: 32 Kieren Moss; 5 Ryan Shaw; 22 Andrew Heffernan; 4 Liam Salter; 36 Justin Carney; 13 Danny Addy; 7 Jamie Ellis; 8 Nick Scruton; 9 Shaun Lunt; 37 Lee Jewitt; 11 Maurice Blair; 10 Chris Clarkson; 33 Ben Kavanagh. Subs (all used): 21 Rob Mulhern; 17 Mitch Clark; 18 Zach Dockar-Clay; 30 Joe Cator.
Tries: Moss (3, 28), Jewitt (9), Heffernan (17), Addy (37), Dockar-Clay (51), Mulhern (77); **Goals:** Ellis 6/7.
BRONCOS: 24 Alex Walker; 2 Rhys Williams; 1 Elliot Kear; 20 Michael Channing; 5 Kieran Dixon; 19 Api Pewhairangi; 6 Jarrod Sammut; 18 Ben Evans; 14 Andy Ackers; 17 Mark Offerdahl; 11 Daniel Harrison; 3 Ben Hellewell; 13 Jay Pitts. Subs (all used): 27 Ben Pointer; 23 Matty Gee; 16 Junior Roqica; 31 Lewis Bienek.
Tries: Harrison (33, 65), Sammut (70), Gee (80);
Goals: Sammut 3/4.
Rugby Leaguer & League Express Men of the Match: *Rovers:* Kieren Moss; *Broncos:* Daniel Harrison.
Penalty count: 5-5; **Half-time:** 28-4;
Referee: Chris Campbell; **Attendance:** 7,359.

OLDHAM 14 TOULOUSE OLYMPIQUE 12

OLDHAM: 17 Steven Nield; 2 Adam Clay; 3 George Tyson; 9 Sam Gee; 26 Kameron Pearce-Paul; 16 Sam Wood; 7 Dave Hewitt; 10 Adam Neal; 21 Kenny Hughes; 30 Daniel Smith; 13 Liam Thompson; 12 Danny Langtree; 14 Luke Adamson. Subs (all used): 18 Ben Davies; 27 Matt Wilkinson; 15 Liam Bent; 28 Sadiq Adebiyi.
Tries: Nield (14), Tyson (49); **Goals:** Hewitt 3/4.
OLYMPIQUE: 1 Mark Kheirallah; 20 Paul Marcon; 21 Gavin Marguerite; 3 Bastien Ader; 2 Tony Maurel; 24 Anthony Marion; 18 Louis Jouffret; 8 Clement Boyer; 27 Charles Bouzinac; 16 Tyla Hepi; 11 Sebastien Planas; 12 Rhys Curran; 13 Andrew Bentley. Subs (all used): 14 Mourad Kriouache; 15 Maxime Puech; 10 Bastian Canet; 26 Constantine Mika.
Tries: Planas (23), Bouzinac (71); **Goals:** Kheirallah 2/2.
Rugby Leaguer & League Express Men of the Match: *Oldham:* George Tyson; *Olympique:* Constantine Mika.
Penalty count: 11-10; **Half-time:** 4-6;
Referee: Ben Thaler; **Attendance:** 519.

SHEFFIELD EAGLES 42 SWINTON LIONS 34

EAGLES: 1 Jack Owens; 2 Garry Lo; 3 Menzie Yere; 23 Jake Spedding; 5 Ben Blackmore; - Danny Richardson; 27 Remy Marginet; 8 Scott Wheeldon; 9 Matty Fozard; 29 Greg Richards; 19 Will Hope; 11 Matt James; 13 Elliot Minchella. Subs (all used): 24 Paddy Flynn; 10 Mark Mexico; 15 Kyle Trout; 16 Sam Scott.
Tries: James (3), Blackmore (15, 27, 44), Owens (21), Richardson (71), Lo (80); **Goals:** Richardson 7/8.
LIONS: 1 Jack Murphy; 2 Shaun Robinson; 3 Chris Hankinson; 4 Rhodri Lloyd; 21 Mike Butt; 26 Josh Woods; 7 Chris Atkin; 15 Andy Bracek; 22 Luke Waterworth; 19 Josh Barlow; 27 Liam Paisley; 24 Adam Jones; 18 Ben Austin. Subs (all used): - Caine Barnes; - Liam Carberry; 14 Ben White; 8 Rob Lever.
Tries: Murphy (28, 31, 33), Robinson (48), Butt (55), Lloyd (76); **Goals:** Atkin 5/8.
Rugby Leaguer & League Express Men of the Match: *Eagles:* Ben Blackmore; *Lions:* Jack Murphy.
Penalty count: 6-9; **Half-time:** 22-16;
Referee: Brandon Robinson; **Attendance:** 379.

ROUND 21

Saturday 8th July 2017

TOULOUSE OLYMPIQUE 8 HALIFAX 16

OLYMPIQUE: 1 Mark Kheirallah; 5 Kuni Minga; 3 Bastien Ader; 11 Sebastien Planas; 2 Tony Maurel; 18 Louis Jouffret; 7 Stan Robin; 8 Clement Boyer; 24 Anthony Marion; 10 Bastian Canet; 26 Constantine Mika; 12 Rhys Curran; 13 Andrew Bentley. Subs (all used): 14 Mourad Kriouache; 15 Maxime Puech; 16 Tyla Hepi; 22 Levy Nzoungou.

Batley's Joel Farrell shows his delight at scoring against Dewsbury

Tries: Boyer (3), Kheirallah (53); **Goals:** Kheirallah 0/2. **Sin bin:** Canet (78) – dissent.
HALIFAX: 2 Will Sharp; 4 Ben Heaton; 16 Ed Barber; 3 Steve Tyrer; 23 Rob Worrincy; 6 Scott Murrell; 1 Ben Johnston; 8 Mitch Cahalane; 17 Brandon Moore; 14 Ryan Boyle; 11 Shane Grady; 10 Adam Tangata; 12 Simon Grix. Subs (all used): 9 Ben Kaye; 39 Michael Sio; 20 Elliot Morris; 37 Brandon Douglas.
Tries: Tyrer (8), Tangata (33), Johnston (74);
Goals: Tyrer 2/4.
Rugby Leaguer & League Express Men of the Match: *Olympique:* Anthony Marion; *Halifax:* Ben Johnston.
Penalty count: 4-12; **Half-time:** 4-8;
Referee: Ben Thaler; **Attendance:** 1,240.

Sunday 9th July 2017

BATLEY BULLDOGS 36 DEWSBURY RAMS 20

BULLDOGS: 2 Wayne Reittie; 3 Sam Smeaton; 6 Cain Southernwood; 30 Jason Crookes; 5 Shaun Ainscough; 13 Pat Walker; 7 Dominic Brambani; 8 Adam Gledhill; 9 Alistair Leak; 16 Tom Lillycrop; 22 Dane Manning; 12 Joel Farrell; 11 Brad Day. Subs (all used): 10 Alex Rowe; 14 James Davey; 19 Alex Bretherton; 21 James Brown.
Tries: Manning (39), Crookes (56), Reittie (58, 73), Brambani (64), Farrell (70); **Goals:** Walker 6/6.
Sin bin: Brown (23) – dangerous challenge.
RAMS: 1 Josh Guzdek; 2 Dale Morton; 29 Macauley Hallett; 32 Shaun Squires; 31 Alex Brown; 6 Paul Sykes; 41 Gareth Moore; 24 Jode Sheriffe; 15 Robbie Ward; 18 Jack Teanby; 11 Rob Spicer; 43 Jordan Crowther; 13 Aaron Brown. Subs (all used): 4 Lucas Walshaw; 16 Toby Adamson; 17 Dom Speakman; 44 Toby Everett.
Tries: Ward (7), Alex Brown (14), Morton (48), Moore (78, pen); **Goals:** Sykes 2/4.
Dismissal: Hallett (76) – dissent.
Sin bin: Hallett (76) – dissent.
Rugby Leaguer & League Express Men of the Match: *Bulldogs:* Pat Walker; *Rams:* Josh Guzdek.
Penalty count: 6-8; **Half-time:** 6-8;
Referee: Tom Crashley; **Attendance:** 1,226.

BRADFORD BULLS 10 HULL KINGSTON ROVERS 42

BULLS: 14 Oscar Thomas; 40 Ed Chamberlain; 3 James

Mendeika; 23 Ashley Gibson; 2 Ethan Ryan; 7 Joe Keyes; 41 Cory Aston; 8 Liam Kirk; 29 Sam Hallas; 15 Jon Magrin; 20 James Bentley; 37 Cameron Smith; 10 Damian Sironen. Subs (all used): 31 Mikolaj Oledzki; 21 Brandan Wilkinson; 33 Reiss Butterworth; 36 James Davies.
Tries: Kirk (8), Aston (35); **Goals:** Thomas 1/2.
ROVERS: 32 Kieren Moss; 5 Ryan Shaw; 29 Jake Butler-Fleming; 4 Liam Salter; 36 Justin Carney; 13 Danny Addy; 7 Jamie Ellis; 8 Nick Scruton; 9 Shaun Lunt; 37 Lee Jewitt; 10 Chris Clarkson; 11 Maurice Blair; 33 Ben Kavanagh. Subs (all used): 21 Rob Mulhern; 17 Mitch Clark; 2 Ben Cockayne; 18 Zach Dockar-Clay.
Tries: Butler-Fleming (17), Carney (32), Addy (38, 50, 69), Clarkson (52), Mulhern (75); **Goals:** Ellis 7/7.
Rugby Leaguer & League Express Men of the Match: *Bulls:* Cory Aston; *Rovers:* Danny Addy.
Penalty count: 11-11; **Half-time:** 10-18;
Referee: Scott Mikalauskas; **Attendance:** 4,937.

LONDON BRONCOS 52 SHEFFIELD EAGLES 16

BRONCOS: 24 Alex Walker; 2 Rhys Williams; 3 Ben Hellewell; 20 Michael Channing; 1 Elliot Kear; 19 Api Pewhairangi; 6 Jarrod Sammut; 18 Ben Evans; 14 Andy Ackers; 31 Lewis Bienek; 11 Daniel Harrison; 13 Jay Pitts; 22 Matt Davis. Subs (all used): 34 John Boudebza; 23 Matty Gee; 16 Junior Roqica; 15 Eddie Battye.
Tries: Sammut (11), Harrison (15), Hellewell (19, 47, 61, 78), Pewhairangi (37, 67), Ackers (71); **Goals:** Sammut 8/9.
EAGLES: 1 Jack Owens; 18 Ryan Millar; 3 Menzie Yere; 23 Jake Spedding; 5 Ben Blackmore; 9 Matty Fozard; 27 Remy Marginet; 8 Scott Wheeldon; 14 Greg Burns; 29 Greg Richards; 11 Matt James; 24 Paddy Flynn; 19 Will Hope. Subs (all used): 22 Liam Johnson; 25 George Milton; 16 Sam Scott; 10 Mark Mexico.
Tries: Fozard (22), James (33), Marginet (54);
Goals: Owens 2/3.
Rugby Leaguer & League Express Men of the Match: *Broncos:* Ben Hellewell; *Eagles:* Remy Marginet.
Penalty count: 8-8; **Half-time:** 24-10;
Referee: Liam Moore; **Attendance:** 684.

OLDHAM 14 FEATHERSTONE ROVERS 32

OLDHAM: 17 Steven Nield; 2 Adam Clay; 3 George Tyson; 26 Kameron Pearce-Paul; - Connor Williams; 16 Sam

Wood; 7 Dave Hewitt; 19 Joe Burke; 21 Kenny Hughes; 30 Nathan Mason; 13 Liam Thompson; 12 Danny Langtree; 14 Luke Adamson. Subs (all used): 18 Ben Davies; 27 Matt Wilkinson; 28 Sadiq Adebiyi; 24 Michael Ward.
Tries: Wilkinson (34), Adebiyi (74), Tyson (79);
Goals: Hewitt 1/3.
ROVERS: 1 Ian Hardman; 5 Luke Briscoe; 23 Josh Hardcastle; 3 Chris Ulugia; 18 Scott Turner; 7 Anthony Thackeray; 19 Matty Wildie; 10 Andrew Bostock; 9 Keal Carlile; 8 Darrell Griffin; 12 John Davies; 11 Michael Knowles; 21 James Lockwood. Subs (all used): 13 Richard Moore; 32 Jordan Baldwinson; 30 Jack Ormondroyd; 27 Daniel Igbinedion.
Tries: Hardcastle (14), Ulugia (16), Lockwood (23), Turner (42), Briscoe (62), Thackeray (77);
Goals: Hardman 4/6.
Rugby Leaguer & League Express Men of the Match: *Oldham:* Sadiq Adebiyi; *Rovers:* Matty Wildie.
Penalty count: 7-7; **Half-time:** 4-16;
Referee: Nick Bennett; **Attendance:** 851.

ROCHDALE HORNETS 33 SWINTON LIONS 28

HORNETS: - Kevin Penny; 2 Chris Riley; 21 Jack Holmes; 3 Jake Eccleston; 5 Rob Massam; 27 Lewis Foster; 7 Danny Yates; 15 Jovili Taira; 9 Ben Moores; 17 Lee Mitchell; - Lewis Hatton; 11 Jono Smith; - Anthony Walker. Subs (all used): 14 Ryan Maneely; 10 Gavin Bennion; 16 Matty Hadden; 12 Josh Crowley.
Tries: Yates (7), Maneely (31), Crowley (45), Eccleston (54), Smith (60), Massam (77);
Goals: Yates 4/7; **Field goal:** Foster (74).
Sin bin: Smith (11) – late challenge on Atkin.
LIONS: 1 Jack Murphy; 2 Shaun Robinson; 3 Chris Hankinson; 4 Rhodri Lloyd; 21 Mike Butt; 26 Josh Woods; 7 Chris Atkin; 15 Andy Bracek; 22 Luke Waterworth; 19 Josh Barlow; 11 Nick Gregson; 24 Adam Jones; 8 Rob Lever. Subs (all used): - Joe Bretherton; 27 Liam Carberry; 9 Anthony Nicholson; 17 Olly Davies.
Tries: Atkin (11), Butt (27, 34), Murphy (56);
Goals: Atkin 6/8.
Sin bin: Barlow (11) – punching Smith; Bretherton (30) – dissent.
Rugby Leaguer & League Express Men of the Match: *Hornets:* Ben Moores; *Lions:* Jack Murphy.
Penalty count: 7-13; **Half-time:** 12-20;
Referee: Jack Smith; **Attendance:** 745.

ROUND 22

Sunday 16th July 2017

BATLEY BULLDOGS 23 BRADFORD BULLS 16

BULLDOGS: 1 Dave Scott; 2 Wayne Reittie; 3 Sam Smeaton; 30 Jason Crookes; 5 Shaun Ainscough; 13 Pat Walker; 7 Dominic Brambani; 21 James Brown; 9 Alistair Leak; 16 Tom Lillycrop; 22 Dane Manning; 19 Alex Bretherton; 11 Brad Day. Subs (all used): 8 Adam Gledhill; 10 Alex Rowe; 14 James Davey; 12 Joel Farrell.
Tries: Bretherton (17), Walker (56), Scott (60, 74);
Goals: Walker 3/4; **Field goal:** Brambani (79).
BULLS: 14 Oscar Thomas; 5 Iliess Macani; 3 James Mendeika; 40 Ed Chamberlain; 19 Johnny Campbell; 41 Cory Aston; 7 Joe Keyes; 8 Liam Kirk; 34 Scott Moore; 15 Jon Magrin; 20 James Bentley; 37 Cameron Smith; 10 Damian Sironen. Subs (all used): 31 Mikolaj Oledzki; 11 Colton Roche; 38 Ted Chapelhow; 29 Sam Hallas.
Tries: Keyes (6), Chamberlain (49), Macani (66);
Goals: Thomas 2/3.
Rugby Leaguer & League Express Men of the Match:
Bulldogs: James Brown; *Bulls:* Johnny Campbell.
Penalty count: 7-9; **Half-time:** 4-4;
Referee: Matt Rossleigh; **Attendance:** 1,726.

FEATHERSTONE ROVERS 8 HALIFAX 28

ROVERS: 20 Kyran Johnson; 4 Misi Taulapapa; 3 Chris Ulugia; 23 Josh Hardcastle; 5 Luke Briscoe; 7 Anthony Thackeray; 19 Matty Wildie; 10 Andrew Bostock; 9 Keal Carlile; 8 Darrell Griffin; 14 Frankie Mariano; 12 John Davies; 30 Jack Ormondroyd. Subs (all used): 22 Jason Walton; 21 James Lockwood; 13 Richard Moore; 32 Jordan Baldwinson.
Tries: Taulapapa (20), Mariano (74); **Goals:** Johnson 0/2.
HALIFAX: 2 Will Sharp; 4 Ben Heaton; 3 Steve Tyrer; 16 Ed Barber; 23 Rob Worrincy; 6 Scott Murrell; 1 Ben Johnston; 37 Brandon Douglas; 17 Brandon Moore; 14 Ryan Boyle; 11 Shane Grady; 8 Mitch Cahalane; 12 Simon Grix. Subs (all used): 20 Elliot Morris; 39 Michael Sio; 26 Alex Mammone; 9 Ben Kaye.
Tries: B Moore (7), Cahalane (14), Heaton (48), Worrincy (69); **Goals:** Tyrer 6/8.
Rugby Leaguer & League Express Men of the Match:
Rovers: John Davies; *Halifax:* Scott Murrell.
Penalty count: 11-12; **Half-time:** 4-16;
Referee: Liam Moore; **Attendance:** 3,156.

HULL KINGSTON ROVERS 30 TOULOUSE OLYMPIQUE 31

ROVERS: 1 Adam Quinlan; 32 Kieren Moss; 4 Liam Salter; 29 Jake Butler-Fleming; 5 Ryan Shaw; 13 Danny Addy; 7 Jamie Ellis; 8 Nick Scruton; 9 Shaun Lunt; 37 Lee Jewitt; 11 Maurice Blair; 10 Chris Clarkson; 33 Ben Kavanagh. Subs (all used): 21 Rob Mulhern; 18 Zach Dockar-Clay; 2 Ben Cockayne; 35 Josh Johnson.
Tries: Addy (13), Lunt (17), Quinlan (36), Clarkson (58), Butler-Fleming (80); **Goals:** Ellis 5/6.
Sin bin: Jewitt (49) - fighting.
OLYMPIQUE: 1 Mark Kheirallah; 20 Paul Marcon; 11 Sebastien Planas; 3 Bastien Ader; 5 Kuni Minga; 24 Anthony Marion; 7 Stan Robin; 8 Clement Boyer; 9 Kane Bentley; 10 Bastian Canet; 26 Constantine Mika; 12 Rhys Curran; 13 Andrew Bentley. Subs (all used): 27 Charles Bouzinac; 15 Maxime Puech; 16 Tyla Hepi; 23 Justin Sangare.
Tries: Kheirallah (8), Ader (45, 66), Robin (51, 72);
Goals: Kheirallah 5/5; **Field goal:** Robin (75).
Sin bin: Hepi (49) - fighting.
Rugby Leaguer & League Express Men of the Match:
Rovers: Danny Addy; *Olympique:* Stan Robin.
Penalty count: 5-5; **Half-time:** 20-6;
Referee: Jack Smith; **Attendance:** 7,117.

ROCHDALE HORNETS 18 LONDON BRONCOS 58

HORNETS: - Declan Kay; - Kevin Penny; 3 Jake Eccleston; 4 Lewis Galbraith; 5 Rob Massam; 27 Lewis Foster; 7 Danny Yates; 15 Jovili Taira; 9 Ben Moores; 17 Lee Mitchell; 11 Jono Smith; 12 Josh Crowley; - Anthony Walker. Subs (all used): 14 Ryan Maneely; 10 Gavin Bennion; 16 Matty Hadden; 19 Jordan Case.
Tries: Eccleston (18), Foster (22), Massam (27);
Goals: Yates 3/3.
BRONCOS: 24 Alex Walker; 2 Rhys Williams; 3 Ben Hellewell; 20 Michael Channing; 1 Elliot Kear; 19 Api Pewhairangi; 6 Jarrod Sammut; 18 Ben Evans; 14 Andy Ackers; 10 Mark Ioane; 11 Daniel Harrison; 13 Jay Pitts; 22 Matt Davis. Subs (all used): 34 John Boudebza; 23 Matty Gee; 15 Eddie Battye; 31 Lewis Bienek.
Tries: Ackers (3, 68), Sammut (8, 25), Walker (14, 70), Davis (31), Bienek (39), Williams (48), Evans (60);
Goals: Sammut 9/10.
Rugby Leaguer & League Express Men of the Match:
Hornets: Anthony Walker; *Broncos:* Jarrod Sammut.
Penalty count: 11-4; **Half-time:** 18-36;
Referee: John McMullen; **Attendance:** 504.

SHEFFIELD EAGLES 42 OLDHAM 28

EAGLES: 1 Jack Owens; 2 Garry Lo; 3 Menzie Yere; 23 Jake Spedding; 5 Ben Blackmore; 6 Simon Brown; 27 Remy Marginet; 8 Scott Wheeldon; 9 Matty Fozard; 10 Mark Mexico; 19 Will Hope; 11 Matt James; 13 Elliot Minchella. Subs (all used): 12 Duane Straugheir; 14 Greg Burns; 15 Kyle Trout; 16 Sam Scott.
Tries: Wheeldon (18), Yere (22), Hope (29), Owens (33), Lo (37, 49, 78), Spedding (45); **Goals:** Brown 5/8.
OLDHAM: 17 Steven Nield; 2 Adam Clay; 3 George Tyson; 9 Sam Gee; 16 Connor Williams; 6 Scott Leatherbarrow; 7 Dave Hewitt; 19 Joe Burke; 21 Kenny Hughes; 30 Daniel Smith; 26 Mikey Wood; 15 Liam Bent; 14 Luke Adamson. Subs (all used): 18 Ben Davies; 24 Michael Ward; 27 Matt Wilkinson; 28 Sadiq Adebiyi.
Tries: Clay (4), Ward (24), Adamson (58), Tyson (64), Williams (69); **Goals:** Hewitt 2/2, Leatherbarrow 2/3.
Rugby Leaguer & League Express Men of the Match:
Eagles: Garry Lo; *Oldham:* Sam Gee.
Penalty count: 7-8; **Half-time:** 28-12;
Referee: Greg Dolan; **Attendance:** 329.

SWINTON LIONS 20 DEWSBURY RAMS 42

LIONS: 1 Jack Murphy; 2 Shaun Robinson; 3 Chris Hankinson; - Liam Forsyth; 21 Mike Butt; 14 Ben White; 26 Josh Woods; 15 Andy Bracek; 9 Anthony Nicholson; 27 Liam Carberry; 4 Rhodri Lloyd; - Liam Paisley; - Callum Field. Subs (all used): 19 Josh Barlow; 22 Luke Waterworth; 18 Ben Austin; 8 Rob Lever.
Tries: Butt (9), Forsyth (29), Paisley (36), White (48);
Goals: Hankinson 2/4.
RAMS: 1 Josh Guzdek; 2 Dale Morton; 29 Macauley Hallett; 4 Lucas Walshaw; 31 Alex Brown; 6 Paul Sykes; 41 Gareth Moore; 24 Jode Sheriffe; 17 Dom Speakman; 18 Jack Teanby; 11 Rob Spicer; 43 Jordan Crowther; 13 Aaron Brown. Subs (all used): 27 Sam Day; 32 Shaun Squires; 44 Toby Everett; 16 Toby Adamson.
Tries: Speakman (17), Moore (19, 62), Aaron Brown (22, 44), Sykes (34), Day (76); **Goals:** Sykes 6/6, Morton 1/1.
Rugby Leaguer & League Express Men of the Match:
Lions: Josh Barlow; *Rams:* Aaron Brown.
Penalty count: 8-9; **Half-time:** 14-24;
Referee: Gareth Hewer; **Attendance:** 1,002.

ROUND 23

Saturday 22nd July 2017

TOULOUSE OLYMPIQUE 32 FEATHERSTONE ROVERS 26

OLYMPIQUE: 1 Mark Kheirallah; 20 Paul Marcon; 11 Sebastien Planas; 3 Bastien Ader; 5 Kuni Minga; 24 Anthony Marion; 7 Stan Robin; 8 Clement Boyer; 9 Kane Bentley; 10 Bastian Canet; 26 Constantine Mika; 12 Rhys Curran; 13 Andrew Bentley. Subs (all used): 27 Charles Bouzinac; 15 Maxime Puech; 16 Tyla Hepi; 23 Justin Sangare.
Tries: Minga (9, 79), Curran (17), Ader (22), Kheirallah (38, 65); **Goals:** Kheirallah 4/7.
ROVERS: 1 Ian Hardman; 18 Scott Turner; 4 Misi Taulapapa; 23 Josh Hardcastle; 5 Luke Briscoe; 7 Anthony Thackeray; 19 Matty Wildie; 28 Sam Brooks; 9 Keal Carlile; 8 Darrell Griffin; 22 Jason Walton; 14 Frankie Mariano; 21 James Lockwood. Subs (all used): 6 Kyle Briggs; 10 Andrew Bostock; 13 Richard Moore; 27 Daniel Igbinedion.
Tries: Thackeray (13), Briggs (35), Turner (40), Walton (45);
Goals: Hardman 5/5.
Rugby Leaguer & League Express Men of the Match:
Olympique: Stan Robin; *Rovers:* Anthony Thackeray.
Penalty count: 6-7; **Half-time:** 20-18;
Referee: Liam Moore; **Attendance:** 2,417.

Sunday 23rd July 2017

BRADFORD BULLS 6 SWINTON LIONS 16

BULLS: 24 Brandon Pickersgill; 5 Iliess Macani; 44 Willie Tonga; 27 Josh Rickett; 19 Johnny Campbell; 7 Joe Keyes; 41 Cory Aston; 8 Liam Kirk; 34 Scott Moore; 15 Jon Magrin; 20 James Bentley; 11 Colton Roche; 10 Damian Sironen. Subs (all used): 17 Ross Peltier; 18 Omari Caro; 29 Sam Hallas; 36 James Davies.
Try: Sironen (45); **Goals:** Aston 1/1.
Dismissal: Campbell (25) - dangerous challenge on Butt.
LIONS: 1 Jack Murphy; 2 Shaun Robinson; 3 Chris Hankinson; - Liam Forsyth; 21 Mike Butt; 14 Ben White; 26 Josh Woods; 15 Andy Bracek; 22 Luke Waterworth; - Joe Bretherton; - Nick Gregson; 4 Rhodri Lloyd; 8 Rob Lever. Subs (all used): 9 Anthony Nicholson; 18 Ben Austin; 19 Josh Barlow; 27 Liam Carberry.
Tries: Robinson (10), White (49), Forsyth (64);
Goals: Hankinson 2/4.
Rugby Leaguer & League Express Men of the Match:
Bulls: James Bentley; *Lions:* Liam Forsyth.
Penalty count: 8-13; **Half-time:** 0-6;
Referee: Greg Dolan; **Attendance:** 3,291.

DEWSBURY RAMS 28 SHEFFIELD EAGLES 18

RAMS: 1 Josh Guzdek; 5 Gareth Potts; 23 James Glover; 4 Lucas Walshaw; 31 Alex Brown; 6 Paul Sykes; 41 Gareth Moore; 24 Jode Sheriffe; 15 Robbie Ward; 18 Jack Teanby; 42 Michael Knowles; 16 Toby Adamson; 13 Aaron Brown. Subs (all used): 17 Dom Speakman; 20 Aaron Ollett; 44 Toby Everett; 26 Mickael Goudemand.
Tries: Guzdek (3), Walshaw (48), Speakman (53), Glover (75); **Goals:** Sykes 4/4, Glover 2/2.
Sin bin: Sykes (20) - dissent; Sheriffe (68) - high tackle.
EAGLES: 1 Jack Owens; 2 Garry Lo; 3 Menzie Yere; 23 Jake Spedding; 24 Paddy Flynn; 6 Simon Brown; 27 Remy Marginet; 8 Scott Wheeldon; 9 Matty Fozard; 11 Matt James; 16 Sam Scott; 15 Kyle Trout; 13 Elliot Minchella. Subs (all used): 14 Greg Burns; 10 Mark Mexico; 12 Duane Straugheir; 25 George Milton.
Tries: Lo (14, 28), Yere (39), Marginet (77);
Goals: Brown 0/3, Owens 1/1.
Rugby Leaguer & League Express Men of the Match:
Rams: James Glover; *Eagles:* Garry Lo.
Penalty count: 13-10; **Half-time:** 10-12;
Referee: Callum Straw; **Attendance:** 794.

HALIFAX 28 HULL KINGSTON ROVERS 6

HALIFAX: 2 Will Sharp; 4 Ben Heaton; 16 Ed Barber; 3 Steve Tyrer; 23 Rob Worrincy; 6 Scott Murrell; 1 Ben Johnston; 20 Elliot Morris; 17 Brandon Moore; 14 Ryan Boyle; 11 Shane Grady; 8 Mitch Cahalane; 12 Simon Grix. Subs (all used): 26 Alex Mammone; 29 Michael Sio; 13 Jacob Fairbank; 9 Ben Kaye.
Tries: Johnston (6), Heaton (31), Sharp (35), Sio (39);
Goals: Tyrer 6/7.
ROVERS: 1 Adam Quinlan; 32 Kieren Moss; 3 Thomas Minns; 2 Ben Cockayne; 5 Ryan Shaw; 7 Jamie Ellis; 38 Chris Atkin; 8 Nick Scruton; 13 Danny Addy; 12 James Greenwood; 11 Maurice Blair; 17 Mitch Clark; 33 Ben Kavanagh. Subs (all used): 18 Zach Dockar-Clay; 10 Chris Clarkson; 20 Matthew Marsh; 35 Josh Johnson.
Try: Moss (20); **Goals:** Ellis 1/1.
Rugby Leaguer & League Express Men of the Match:
Halifax: Ed Barber; *Rovers:* Mitch Clark.
Penalty count: 10-4; **Half-time:** 24-6;
Referee: Tom Grant; **Attendance:** 2,876.

LONDON BRONCOS 58 BATLEY BULLDOGS 4

BRONCOS: 24 Alex Walker; 2 Rhys Williams; 3 Ben Hellewell; 20 Michael Channing; 1 Elliot Kear; 19 Api Pewhairangi; 6 Jarrod Sammut; 8 Tom Spencer; 14 Andy Ackers; 16 Junior Roqica; 11 Daniel Harrison; 13 Jay Pitts; 22 Matt Davis. Subs (all used): 34 John Boudebza; 36 Sam Wilde; 10 Mark Ioane; 15 Eddie Battye.
Tries: Kear (5, 34, 45), Channing (22), Pewhairangi (41, 67), Williams (48, 70), Roqica (54), Davis (75);
Goals: Sammut 9/10.
BULLDOGS: 1 Dave Scott; 2 Wayne Reittie; 15 Danny Cowling; 30 Jason Crookes; 5 Shaun Ainscough; 6 Cain Southernwood; 7 Dominic Brambani; 10 Alex Rowe; 9 Alistair Leak; 21 James Brown; 19 Alex Bretherton; 12 Joel Farrell; 13 Pat Walker. Subs (all used): 14 James Davey; 17 Joe Chandler; 18 James Harrison; 23 Brad Hill.
Try: Brown (57); **Goals:** Walker 0/1.
Sin bin: Crookes (53) - dangerous challenge.
Rugby Leaguer & League Express Men of the Match:
Broncos: Elliot Kear; *Bulldogs:* Wayne Reittie.
Penalty count: 7-9; **Half-time:** 18-0;
Referee: Nick Bennett; **Attendance:** 879.

OLDHAM 24 ROCHDALE HORNETS 34

OLDHAM: 17 Steven Nield; 2 Adam Clay; 3 George Tyson; 9 Sam Gee; - Connor Williams; 6 Scott Leatherbarrow; 7 Dave Hewitt; 26 Tyler Dickinson; 21 Kenny Hughes; 30 Daniel Smith; 15 Liam Bent; 14 Luke Adamson; 11 Jack Spencer. Subs (all used): 18 Ben Davies; 22 Danny Grimshaw; 28 Sadiq Adebiyi; 24 Michael Ward.
Tries: Smith (25), Clay (38), Hewitt (44), Tyson (67);
Goals: Leatherbarrow 4/4.
HORNETS: - Declan Kay; - Kevin Penny; 3 Jake Eccleston; 4 Lewis Galbraith; 2 Chris Riley; - Lewis Foster; 7 Danny Yates; 15 Jovili Taira; 9 Ben Moores; 17 Lee Mitchell; 11 Jono Smith; 12 Josh Crowley; - Anthony Walker. Subs (all used): 14 Ryan Maneely; 10 Gavin Bennion; 16 Matty Hadden; 19 Jordan Case.
Tries: Penny (4, 71), Kay (13, 63), Eccleston (20), Case (50);
Goals: Yates 5/7.
Rugby Leaguer & League Express Men of the Match:
Oldham: Adam Clay; *Hornets:* Lewis Foster.
Penalty count: 7-9; **Half-time:** 12-20;
Referee: Gareth Hewer; **Attendance:** 889.

CHAMPIONSHIP SHIELD
2017 Round by Round

ROUND 1

Sunday 6th August 2017

BATLEY BULLDOGS 62 SWINTON LIONS 10

BULLDOGS: 1 Dave Scott; 2 Wayne Reittie; 3 Sam Smeaton; 30 Jason Crookes; 5 Shaun Ainscough; 13 Pat Walker; 7 Dominic Brambani; 8 Adam Gledhill; 9 Alistair Leak; 16 Tom Lillycrop; 22 Dane Manning; 19 Alex Bretherton; 11 Brad Day. Subs (all used): 21 James Brown; 10 Alex Rowe; 14 James Davey; 12 Joel Farrell.
Tries: Bretherton (6, 75), Reittie (10, 79), Ainscough (22), Smeaton (30), Davey (45, 61), Scott (48, 67), Farrell (73), Brown (77); **Goals:** Walker 7/12.
Sin bin: Brown (56) - high tackle.
On report: Brawl (56).
LIONS: 1 Jack Murphy; 2 Shaun Robinson; 3 Chris Hankinson; 4 Rhodri Lloyd; 21 Mike Butt; 14 Ben White; 26 Izaac Farrell; 15 Andy Bracek; 22 Luke Waterworth; 18 Ben Austin; 17 Olly Davies; - Dan Norman; 8 Rob Lever. Subs (all used): 19 Josh Barlow; 9 Anthony Nicholson; - Mark Nicholson; 27 Thomas Coyle.
Tries: Robinson (2), Austin (15); **Goals:** Hankinson 1/2.
Sin bin: Barlow (51) - dissent.
On report: Brawl (56).
Rugby Leaguer & League Express Men of the Match: *Bulldogs:* Dominic Brambani; *Lions:* Izaac Farrell.
Penalty count: 9-2; **Half-time:** 18-10;
Referee: Gareth Hewer; **Attendance:** 544.

BRADFORD BULLS 10 TOULOUSE OLYMPIQUE 26

BULLS: 1 Lee Smith; 5 Iliess Macani; 26 Vila Halafihi; 3 James Mendeika; 27 Josh Rickett; 41 Cory Aston; 7 Joe Keyes; 8 Liam Kirk; 34 Scott Moore; 11 Colton Roche; 37 Cameron Smith; 20 James Bentley; 10 Damian Sironen. Subs (all used): 17 Ross Peltier; 29 Sam Hallas; 31 Mikolaj Oledzki; 36 James Davies.
Tries: Macani (28), Peltier (37); **Goals:** L Smith 1/2.
OLYMPIQUE: 1 Mark Kheirallah; 20 Paul Marcon; 3 Bastien Ader; 21 Gavin Marguerite; 2 Tony Maurel; 24 Anthony Marion; 7 Stan Robin; 8 Clement Boyer; 27 Charles Bouzinac; 23 Justin Sangare; 26 Constantine Mika; 12 Rhys Curran; 13 Andrew Bentley. Subs (all used): 14 Mourad Kriouache; 15 Maxime Puech; 16 Tyla Hepi; 22 Levy Nzoungou.
Tries: Curran (3, 34), Marguerite (19, 42), Maurel (76);
Goals: Kheirallah 3/5.
Rugby Leaguer & League Express Men of the Match: *Bulls:* Ross Peltier; *Olympique:* Rhys Curran.
Penalty count: 11-8; **Half-time:** 10-18;
Referee: John McMullen; **Attendance:** 2,753.

DEWSBURY RAMS 56 ROCHDALE HORNETS 8

RAMS: 1 Josh Guzdek; 2 Dale Morton; 23 James Glover; 29 Macauley Hallett; 5 Gareth Potts; 6 Paul Sykes; 41 Gareth Moore; 44 Toby Everett; 15 Robbie Ward; 18 Jack Teanby; 42 Michael Knowles; 11 Rob Spicer; 13 Aaron Brown. Subs (all used): 27 Sam Day; 26 Mickael Goudemand; 16 Toby Adamson; 24 Jode Sheriffe.
Tries: Glover (4, 37, 77), Potts (9, 35, 43, 71), Hallett (17), Day (31, 75), Guzdek (61); **Goals:** Sykes 6/11.
HORNETS: 2 Chris Riley; - Kevin Penny; 3 Jake Eccleston; 4 Lewis Galbraith; 21 Jack Holmes; 27 Lewis Foster; 7 Danny Yates; - Lee Mitchell; 14 Ryan Maneely; 15 Jovili Taira; 11 Jono Smith; 12 Josh Crowley; 20 Anthony Walker. Subs (all used): 19 Jordan Case; 10 Gavin Bennion; 16 Matty Hadden; 28 Lewis Hatton.
Tries: Smith (27), Riley (64); **Goals:** Yates 0/2.
Rugby Leaguer & League Express Men of the Match: *Rams:* James Glover; *Hornets:* Jono Smith.
Penalty count: 6-7; **Half-time:** 28-4;
Referee: Chris Campbell; **Attendance:** 629.

SHEFFIELD EAGLES 56 OLDHAM 16

EAGLES: 18 Ryan Millar; 2 Garry Lo; 3 Menzie Yere; 32 Calvin Wellington; 24 Paddy Flynn; 1 Jack Owens; 27 Remy Marginet; 8 Scott Wheeldon; 9 Matty Fozard; 11 Matt James; 16 Sam Scott; 12 Duane Straugheir; 13 Elliot Minchella. Subs (all used): 14 Greg Burns; 15 Kyle Trout; 4 Perry Whiteley; 10 Mark Mexico.
Tries: Flynn (7, 52), Scott (19), Minchella (20, 60, 79), Fozard (24, 73), Owens (45), Wheeldon (55);
Goals: Owens 8/10.
OLDHAM: 15 Luke Hooley; 2 Adam Clay; 30 Ben Morris; 26 Kameron Pearce-Paul; 16 Connor Williams; 22 Danny Grimshaw; 7 Dave Hewitt; 28 Sadiq Adebiyi; 21 Kenny Hughes; 19 Joe Burke; 13 Liam Thompson; 11 Jack Spencer; 14 Luke Adamson. Subs (all used): 27 Matt Wilkinson; 9 Sam Gee; 18 Ben Davies; 24 Michael Ward.
Tries: Wilkinson (35), Hewitt (37), Hughes (78);
Goals: Hooley 2/3.
Sin bin: Davies (60) - shoulder charge.
Rugby Leaguer & League Express Men of the Match: *Eagles:* Jack Owens; *Oldham:* Matt Wilkinson.
Penalty count: 8-14; **Half-time:** 22-10;
Referee: Andrew Sweet; **Attendance:** 305.

ROUND 2

Sunday 13th August 2017

DEWSBURY RAMS 36 TOULOUSE OLYMPIQUE 34

RAMS: 1 Josh Guzdek; 2 Dale Morton; 23 James Glover; 29 Macauley Hallett; 5 Gareth Potts; 6 Paul Sykes; 41 Gareth Moore; 24 Jode Sheriffe; 15 Robbie Ward; 18 Jack Teanby; 42 Michael Knowles; 11 Rob Spicer; 13 Aaron Brown. Subs (all used): 17 Dom Speakman; 26 Mickael Goudemand; 16 Toby Adamson; 44 Toby Everett.
Tries: Sheriffe (9), Glover (20), Goudemand (37), Speakman (42), Ward (66), T Adamson (78);
Goals: Sykes 5/6, Glover 1/1.
Sin bin: Ward (79) - fighting.
OLYMPIQUE: 1 Mark Kheirallah; 20 Paul Marcon; 21 Gavin Marguerite; 3 Bastien Ader; 5 Kuni Minga; 24 Anthony Marion; 7 Stan Robin; 15 Maxime Puech; 9 Kane Bentley; 10 Bastian Canet; 11 Sebastien Planas; 28 Ugo Perez; 13 Andrew Bentley. Subs (all used): 27 Charles Bouzinac; 23 Justin Sangare; 16 Tyla Hepi; 26 Constantine Mika.
Tries: Marcon (15, 49, 57), Robin (31), Minga (34), Marguerite (47), Canet (72); **Goals:** Kheirallah 3/7.
Sin bin: Mika (77) - professional foul; Canet (79) - fighting.
Rugby Leaguer & League Express Men of the Match: *Rams:* Robbie Ward; *Olympique:* Tyla Hepi.
Penalty count: 11-9; **Half-time:** 18-14;
Referee: Scott Mikalauskas; **Attendance:** 628.

OLDHAM 16 BRADFORD BULLS 20

OLDHAM: 15 Luke Hooley; 2 Adam Clay; 30 Ben Morris; 26 Kameron Pearce-Paul; 17 Steven Nield; 22 Danny Grimshaw; 7 Dave Hewitt; 18 Ben Davies; 21 Kenny Hughes; 19 Joe Burke; 16 Mikey Wood; 14 Luke Adamson; 11 Jack Spencer. Subs (all used): 28 Sadiq Adebiyi; 9 Sam Gee; 27 Matt Wilkinson; 24 Michael Ward.
Tries: Spencer (29), Grimshaw (45), Ward (50);
Goals: Hooley 2/3.
BULLS: 1 Lee Smith; 5 Iliess Macani; 3 James Mendeika; 26 Vila Halafihi; 27 Josh Rickett; 7 Joe Keyes; 41 Cory Aston; 8 Liam Kirk; 34 Scott Moore; 11 Colton Roche; 37 Cameron Smith; 20 James Bentley; 10 Damian Sironen. Subs (all used): 17 Ross Peltier; 29 Sam Hallas; 31 Mikolaj Oledzki; 21 Brandan Wilkinson.
Tries: Rickett (7), Moore (15), Bentley (23), Aston (25);
Goals: L Smith 2/4.
Rugby Leaguer & League Express Men of the Match: *Oldham:* Michael Ward; *Bulls:* Damian Sironen.
Penalty count: 13-6; **Half-time:** 6-20;
Referee: John McMullen; **Attendance:** 853.

ROCHDALE HORNETS 14 BATLEY BULLDOGS 34

HORNETS: - Declan Kay; - Kevin Penny; 3 Jake Eccleston; 4 Lewis Galbraith; 2 Chris Riley; - Lewis Foster; 7 Danny Yates; 15 Jovili Taira; 9 Ben Moores; 20 Anthony Walker; 11 Jono Smith; 12 Josh Crowley; 13 Gary Middlehurst. Subs (all used): 14 Ryan Maneely; 10 Gavin Bennion; 16 Matty Hadden; 19 Jordan Case.
Tries: Eccleston (7), Penny (32), Yates (67);
Goals: Yates 1/3, Foster 0/1.
Dismissal: Middlehurst (60) - fighting.
Sin bin: Case (65) - punching; Moores (60) - punching.
BULLDOGS: 1 Dave Scott; 2 Wayne Reittie; 3 Sam Smeaton; 30 Jason Crookes; 5 Shaun Ainscough; 13 Pat Walker; 7 Dominic Brambani; 8 Adam Gledhill; 9 Alistair Leak; 16 Tom Lillycrop; 22 Dane Manning; 19 Alex Bretherton; 11 Brad Day. Subs (all used): 10 Alex Rowe; 12 Joel Farrell; 14 James Davey; 21 James Brown.
Tries: Scott (22, 79), Ainscough (36), Bretherton (57, 72), Crookes (60); **Goals:** Walker 5/6.
Dismissal: Crookes (60) - fighting.
Rugby Leaguer & League Express Men of the Match: *Hornets:* Danny Yates; *Bulldogs:* Alex Bretherton.
Penalty count: 6-12; **Half-time:** 10-12;
Referee: Tom Grant; **Attendance:** 453.

SWINTON LIONS 30 SHEFFIELD EAGLES 32

LIONS: 1 Jack Murphy; 2 Shaun Robinson; 3 Chris Hankinson; - Ilias Bergal; 21 Mike Butt; 14 Ben White; 26 Thomas Coyle; 15 Andy Bracek; 22 Luke Waterworth; 18 Ben Austin; 4 Rhodri Lloyd; 24 Adam Jones; 19 Josh Barlow. Subs (all used): 9 Anthony Nicholson; - Mark Nicholson; 27 Liam Carberry; 8 Rob Lever.
Tries: Bergal (2), Murphy (29), Lever (38, 44), White (76);
Goals: Hankinson 5/5.
EAGLES: 18 Ryan Millar; 2 Garry Lo; 3 Menzie Yere; 24 Paddy Flynn; 5 Ben Blackmore; 1 Jack Owens; 13 Elliot Minchella; 8 Scott Wheeldon; 9 Matty Fozard; 10 Mark Mexico; 15 Kyle Trout; 12 Duane Straugheir; 11 Matt James. Subs (all used): 14 Greg Burns; 22 Liam Johnson; 4 Perry Whiteley; 25 George Milton.
Tries: Blackmore (7, 70), Minchella (21, 53), Flynn (24), Yere (33); **Goals:** Owens 4/6.
Rugby Leaguer & League Express Men of the Match: *Lions:* Andy Bracek; *Eagles:* Ben Blackmore.
Penalty count: 9-4; **Half-time:** 18-20;
Referee: Chris Campbell; **Attendance:** 434.

ROUND 3

Saturday 19th August 2017

TOULOUSE OLYMPIQUE 50 ROCHDALE HORNETS 12

OLYMPIQUE: 1 Mark Kheirallah; 2 Tony Maurel; 21 Gavin Marguerite; 3 Bastien Ader; 5 Kuni Minga; 7 Stan Robin; 24 Anthony Marion; 8 Clement Boyer; 27 Charles Bouzinac; 10 Bastian Canet; 26 Constantine Mika; 28 Ugo Perez; 13 Andrew Bentley. Subs (all used): 14 Mourad Kriouache; 15 Maxime Puech; 16 Tyla Hepi; 22 Levy Nzoungou.
Tries: Kheirallah (5, 7), Marguerite (19), Minga (31, 73), Mika (62), Bouzinac (70), Robin (75), Ader (79);
Goals: Kheirallah 7/9.
HORNETS: - Declan Kay; 2 Chris Riley; 3 Jake Eccleston; 4 Lewis Galbraith; 21 Jack Holmes; 6 Lewis Palfrey; 7 Danny Yates; 17 Lee Mitchell; 9 Ben Moores; 20 Anthony Walker; 19 Jordan Case; 12 Josh Crowley; 13 Gary Middlehurst. Subs (all used): 10 Gavin Bennion; 14 Ryan Maneely; 16 Matty Hadden; - Lewis Hatton.
Tries: Yates (14), Middlehurst (34); **Goals:** Palfrey 2/2.
Sin bin: Middlehurst (68) - punching.
On report: Case (21) - alleged high tackle.
Rugby Leaguer & League Express Men of the Match: *Olympique:* Mark Kheirallah; *Hornets:* Danny Yates.
Penalty count: 12-9; **Half-time:** 22-12;
Referee: Liam Moore; **Attendance:** 612.

Sunday 20th August 2017

BATLEY BULLDOGS 22 OLDHAM 22

BULLDOGS: 1 Dave Scott; 2 Wayne Reittie; 15 Danny Cowling; 30 Jason Crookes; 5 Shaun Ainscough; 13 Pat Walker; 7 Dominic Brambani; 8 Adam Gledhill; 9 Alistair Leak; 27 Will Maher; 22 Dane Manning; 19 Alex Bretherton; 12 Joel Farrell. Subs (all used): 11 Brad Day; 16 Tom Lillycrop; 14 James Davey; 17 Joe Chandler.
Tries: Crookes (2), Manning (5), Brambani (17), Scott (21);
Goals: Walker 3/4.
Sin bin: Farrell (31) - high tackle.
OLDHAM: 15 Luke Hooley; 2 Adam Clay; 30 Ben Morris; 3 George Tyson; 17 Steven Nield; 6 Scott Leatherbarrow; 7 Dave Hewitt; 11 Jack Spencer; 27 Matt Wilkinson; 18 Ben Davies; 16 Mikey Wood; 26 Liam Bent; 14 Luke Adamson. Subs (all used): 24 Michael Ward; 28 Sadiq Adebiyi; 19 Joe Burke; 9 Sam Gee.
Tries: Ward (25), Gee (57), Morris (63), Clay (68);
Goals: Hooley 3/4.
Rugby Leaguer & League Express Men of the Match: *Bulldogs:* Dominic Brambani; *Oldham:* Luke Hooley.
Penalty count: 4-7; **Half-time:** 22-6;
Referee: Jack Smith; **Attendance:** 675.

SHEFFIELD EAGLES 28 DEWSBURY RAMS 35

EAGLES: 18 Ryan Millar; 2 Garry Lo; 3 Menzie Yere; 24 Paddy Flynn; 5 Ben Blackmore; 1 Jack Owens; 6 Simon Brown; 8 Scott Wheeldon; 9 Matty Fozard; 11 Matt James; 16 Sam Scott; 19 Will Hope; 13 Elliot Minchella. Subs (all used): 10 Mark Mexico; 12 Duane Straugheir; 22 Liam Johnson; 25 George Milton.
Tries: Fozard (17), Minchella (40), Lo (54), James (65), Milton (80); **Goals:** Brown 4/5.
RAMS: 1 Josh Guzdek; 2 Dale Morton; 23 James Glover; 29 Macauley Hallett; 5 Gareth Potts; 6 Paul Sykes; 17 Dom Speakman; 24 Jode Sheriffe; 15 Robbie Ward; 18 Jack Teanby; 4 Lucas Walshaw; 26 Mickael Goudemand; 13 Aaron Brown. Subs (all used): 16 Toby Adamson; 20 Aaron Ollett; 27 Sam Day; 44 Toby Everett.
Tries: Hallett (4), Glover (25), Speakman (30), Potts (45), Aaron Brown (60), Day (73);
Goals: Sykes 5/6; **Field goal:** Sykes (71).
Rugby Leaguer & League Express Men of the Match: *Eagles:* Matt James; *Rams:* Dom Speakman.
Penalty count: 8-8; **Half-time:** 10-18;
Referee: Nick Bennett; **Attendance:** 363.

SWINTON LIONS 16 BRADFORD BULLS 30

LIONS: - Jack Hansen; 2 Shaun Robinson; 3 Chris Hankinson; - Ilias Bergal; 21 Mike Butt; 25 Izaac Farrell; 26 Thomas Coyle; 15 Andy Bracek; 22 Luke Waterworth; 18 Ben Austin; 4 Rhodri Lloyd; 17 Olly Davies; 19 Josh Barlow. Subs (all used): 9 Anthony Nicholson; 27 Liam Carberry; 24 Adam Jones; 8 Rob Lever.

Championship Shield 2017 - Round by Round

Tries: Bracek (2), Robinson (39), Waterworth (59);
Goals: Hankinson 1/2, I Farrell 1/1.
Sin bin: Barlow (74) - holding down.
BULLS: 1 Lee Smith; 5 Iliess Macani; 3 James Mendeika; 26 Vila Halafihi; 19 Johnny Campbell; 14 Oscar Thomas; 41 Cory Aston; 8 Liam Kirk; 34 Scott Moore; 11 Colton Roche; 37 Cameron Smith; 20 James Bentley; 10 Damian Sironen. Subs (all used): 17 Ross Peltier; 29 Sam Hallas; 31 Mikolaj Oledzki; 21 Brandan Wilkinson.
Tries: Bentley (19, 68), Halafihi (21), Oledzki (47), Hallas (56); **Goals:** Aston 5/7.
Sin bin: Sironen (77) - dangerous challenge on I Farrell.
Rugby Leaguer & League Express Men of the Match: *Lions:* Andy Bracek; *Bulls:* James Bentley.
Penalty count: 16-13; **Half-time:** 10-10;
Referee: Andrew Sweet; **Attendance:** 660.

ROUND 4

Monday 28th August 2017

BRADFORD BULLS 18 BATLEY BULLDOGS 44

BULLS: 1 Lee Smith; 27 Josh Rickett; 26 Vila Halafihi; 3 James Mendeika; 5 Iliess Macani; 34 Scott Moore; 41 Cory Aston; 8 Liam Kirk; 29 Sam Hallas; 17 Ross Peltier; 37 Cameron Smith; 20 James Bentley; 10 Damian Sironen. Subs (all used): 31 Mikolaj Oledzki; 36 James Davies; 21 Brandan Wilkinson; 24 Brandon Pickersgill.
Tries: Hallas (2), Kirk (12), Macani (78); **Goals:** Aston 3/3.
BULLDOGS: 1 Dave Scott; 2 Wayne Reittie; 3 Sam Smeaton; 30 Jason Crookes; 5 Shaun Ainscough; 13 Pat Walker; 7 Dominic Brambani; 27 Will Maher; 9 Alistair Leak; 16 Tom Lillycrop; 22 Dane Manning; 18 James Harrison; 12 Joel Farrel. Subs (all used): 6 Cain Southernwood; 8 Adam Gledhill; 10 Alex Rowe; 11 Brad Day.
Tries: Leak (23, 36, 49), Harrison (25, 27, 34), Day (44), Brambani (48); **Goals:** Walker 6/8.
Rugby Leaguer & League Express Men of the Match: *Bulls:* Sam Hallas; *Bulldogs:* Alistair Leak.
Penalty count: 7-7; **Half-time:** 12-26;
Referee: Callum Straw; **Attendance:** 2,609.

DEWSBURY RAMS 28 SWINTON LIONS 35

RAMS: 1 Josh Guzdek; 2 Dale Morton; 23 James Glover; 29 Macauley Hallett; 5 Gareth Potts; 6 Paul Sykes; 17 Dom Speakman; 24 Jode Sheriffe; 27 Sam Day; 18 Jack Teanby; 42 Michael Knowles; 11 Rob Spicer; 13 Aaron Brown. Subs (all used): 26 Mickael Goudemand; 4 Lucas Walshaw; 16 Toby Adamson; 44 Toby Everett.
Tries: Potts (11), Speakman (39), Walshaw (65), Aaron Brown (74), Day (77); **Goals:** Sykes 4/5.
LIONS: 1 Jack Murphy; 2 Shaun Robinson; 3 Chris Hankinson; 26 Ilias Bergal; 21 Mike Butt; 14 Ben White; 25 Izaac Farrell; 15 Andy Bracek; 22 Luke Waterworth; 18 Ben Austin; 4 Rhodri Lloyd; 17 Olly Davies; 19 Josh Barlow. Subs (all used): 24 Adam Jones; 9 Anthony Nicholson; 8 Rob Lever; 27 Liam Carberry.
Tries: Hankinson (3), White (27), Barlow (33), Bergal (62), Austin (79); **Goals:** Hankinson 7/8;
Field goal: White (73).
Rugby Leaguer & League Express Men of the Match: *Rams:* Mickael Goudemand; *Lions:* Josh Barlow.
Penalty count: 11-10; **Half-time:** 12-22;
Referee: John McMullen; **Attendance:** 812.

ROCHDALE HORNETS 24 OLDHAM 30

HORNETS: - Declan Kay; - Kevin Penny; 3 Jake Eccleston; 4 Lewis Galbraith; 2 Chris Riley; 6 Lewis Palfrey; 7 Danny Yates; 17 Lee Mitchell; 14 Ryan Maneely; 15 Jovili Taira; 11 Jono Smith; 19 Jordan Case; 20 Anthony Walker. Subs (all used): 28 Lewis Hatton; 10 Gavin Bennion; 16 Matty Hadden; 5 Rob Massam.
Tries: Riley (12), Eccleston (18), Maneely (47), Massam (75), Taira (79); **Goals:** Palfrey 2/5.
Sin bin: Galbraith (30) - tripping.
OLDHAM: 15 Luke Hooley; 2 Adam Clay; 30 Ben Morris; 3 George Tyson; 26 Kameron Pearce-Paul; 6 Scott Leatherbarrow; 7 Dave Hewitt; 11 Jack Spencer; 27 Matt Wilkinson; 19 Joe Burke; 13 Liam Thompson; 16 Liam Bent; 14 Luke Adamson. Subs (all used): 21 Kenny Hughes; 28 Sadiq Adebiyi; 24 Michael Ward; 9 Sam Gee.
Tries: Burke (5, 69), Adamson (15), Clay (32), Hooley (78);
Goals: Hooley 5/5, Leatherbarrow 0/1.
Rugby Leaguer & League Express Men of the Match: *Hornets:* Danny Yates; *Oldham:* Dave Hewitt.
Penalty count: 7-5; **Half-time:** 8-18;
Referee: Gareth Hewer; **Attendance:** 927.

TOULOUSE OLYMPIQUE 32 SHEFFIELD EAGLES 16

OLYMPIQUE: 1 Mark Kheirallah; 2 Tony Maurel; 3 Bastien Ader; 21 Gavin Marguerite; 20 Paul Marcon; 7 Stan Robin; 6 Johnathon Ford; 24 Anthony Marion; 28 Ugo Perez; 12 Rhys Curran; 8 Clement Boyer; 27 Charles Bouzinac; 10 Bastian Canet. Subs (all used): 14 Mourad Kriouache; 15 Maxime Puech; 26 Constantine Mika; 22 Levy Nzoungou.
Tries: Boyer (11), Ford (13), Kheirallah (36, 52), Robin (43), Puech (62); **Goals:** Kheirallah 4/6.
EAGLES: 18 Ryan Millar; 2 Garry Lo; 4 Perry Whiteley; 24 Paddy Flynn; 5 Ben Blackmore; 6 Simon Brown; 27 Remy Marginet; 23 Jonah Cunningham; 12 Duane Straugheir; 16 Sam Scott; 15 Kyle Trout; 9 Matty Fozard; 8 Scott Wheeldon. Subs (all used): 14 Greg Burns; 25 George Milton; 21 Liam Cooper; 11 Matt James.
Tries: Lo (8), Straugheir (49), Blackmore (69);
Goals: Brown 2/3.
Rugby Leaguer & League Express Men of the Match: *Olympique:* Mark Kheirallah; *Eagles:* Simon Brown.
Penalty count: 8-9; **Half-time:** 16-6;
Referee: Steve Race; **Attendance:** 1,855.

ROUND 5

Sunday 3rd September 2017

BATLEY BULLDOGS 38 DEWSBURY RAMS 0

BULLDOGS: 1 Dave Scott; 2 Wayne Reittie; 3 Sam Smeaton; 30 Jason Crookes; 5 Shaun Ainscough; 13 Pat Walker; 7 Dominic Brambani; 27 Will Maher; 9 Alistair Leak; 16 Tom Lillycrop; 22 Dane Manning; 18 James Harrison; 12 Joel Farrell. Subs (all used): 6 Cain Southernwood; 8 Adam Gledhill; 10 Alex Rowe; 11 Brad Day.
Tries: Reittie (17, 21, 45, 54), Manning (39, 70), Rowe (75);
Goals: Walker 5/7.
RAMS: 23 James Glover; 2 Dale Morton; 29 Macauley Hallett; 4 Lucas Walshaw; 5 Gareth Potts; 6 Paul Sykes; 17 Dom Speakman; 24 Jode Sheriffe; 27 Sam Day; 18 Jack Teanby; 11 Rob Spicer; 42 Michael Knowles; 13 Aaron Brown. Subs (all used): 16 Toby Adamson; 20 Aaron Ollett; 26 Mickael Goudemand; 44 Toby Everett.
Rugby Leaguer & League Express Men of the Match: *Bulldogs:* Wayne Reittie; *Rams:* Dom Speakman.
Penalty count: 10-9; **Half-time:** 16-0;
Referee: John McMullen; **Attendance:** 906.

OLDHAM 18 TOULOUSE OLYMPIQUE 24

OLDHAM: 15 Luke Hooley; 2 Adam Clay; 30 Ben Morris; 3 George Tyson; 26 Kameron Pearce-Paul; 22 Danny Grimshaw; 7 Dave Hewitt; 19 Joe Burke; 21 Kenny Hughes; 11 Jack Spencer; 16 Liam Bent; 13 Liam Thompson; 14 Luke Adamson. Subs (all used): 27 Matt Wilkinson; 28 Sadiq Adebiyi; 24 Michael Ward; 9 Sam Gee.
Tries: Hughes (9, 75); **Goals:** Hooley 5/5.
OLYMPIQUE: 1 Mark Kheirallah; 20 Paul Marcon; 21 Gavin Marguerite; 3 Bastien Ader; 2 Tony Maurel; 6 Johnathon Ford; 18 Louis Jouffret; 23 Justin Sangare; 24 Anthony Marion; 10 Bastian Canet; 26 Constantine Mika; 12 Rhys Curran; 13 Andrew Bentley. Subs (all used): 27 Charles Bouzinac; 15 Maxime Puech; 16 Tyla Hepi; 22 Levy Nzoungou.
Tries: Curran (4), Marguerite (31), Mika (59), Hepi (63), Kheirallah (72); **Goals:** Kheirallah 2/5.
Sin bin: Canet (65) - shoulder charge.
Rugby Leaguer & League Express Men of the Match: *Oldham:* Luke Hooley; *Olympique:* Mark Kheirallah.
Penalty count: 6-8; **Half-time:** 10-8;
Referee: Andrew Sweet; **Attendance:** 581.

ROCHDALE HORNETS 16 SWINTON LIONS 8

HORNETS: - Declan Kay; 2 Chris Riley; 4 Lewis Galbraith; 3 Jake Eccleston; - Kevin Penny; 27 Lewis Foster; 7 Danny Yates; 15 Jovili Taira; 14 Ryan Maneely; 28 Lewis Hatton; 12 Josh Crowley; 17 Lee Mitchell; 20 Anthony Walker. Subs: 10 Gavin Bennion; 16 Matty Hadden; 19 Jordan Case; 21 Jack Holmes (not used).
Tries: Kay (47), Foster (67); **Goals:** Yates 4/4.
LIONS: 21 Mike Butt; 2 Shaun Robinson; 3 Chris Hankinson; 4 Rhodri Lloyd; 26 Ilias Bergal; 14 Ben White; 9 Anthony Nicholson; 15 Andy Bracek; 22 Luke Waterworth; 18 Ben Austin; 24 Adam Jones; 17 Olly Davies; 19 Josh Barlow. Subs (all used): 27 Liam Carberry; - Mark Nicholson; - Dan Norman; 8 Rob Lever.
Try: Bergal (55); **Goals:** Hankinson 2/2.
On report: Bracek (3) - alleged dangerous challenge.
Rugby Leaguer & League Express Men of the Match: *Hornets:* Lee Mitchell; *Lions:* Andy Bracek.
Penalty count: 10-8; **Half-time:** 2-2;
Referee: Jack Smith; **Attendance:** 606.

SHEFFIELD EAGLES 18 BRADFORD BULLS 32

EAGLES: 1 Jack Owens; 2 Garry Lo; 3 Menzie Yere; 24 Paddy Flynn; 5 Ben Blackmore; 6 Simon Brown; 27 Remy Marginet; 8 Scott Wheeldon; 9 Matty Fozard; 15 Kyle Trout; 11 Matt James; 12 Duane Straugheir; 13 Elliot Minchella. Subs (all used): 4 Perry Whiteley; 10 Mark Mexico; 16 Sam Scott; 25 George Milton.
Tries: Minchella (31), Fozard (34), Blackmore (43), Lo (47);
Goals: Brown 1/4.
BULLS: 2 Ethan Ryan; 5 Iliess Macani; 26 Vila Halafihi; 1 Lee Smith; 18 Omari Caro; 41 Cory Aston; 7 Joe Keyes; 15 Jon Magrin; 29 Sam Hallas; 8 Liam Kirk; 35 Evan Hodgson; 20 James Bentley; 10 Damian Sironen. Subs (all used): 17 Ross Peltier; 31 Mikolaj Oledzki; 21 Brandan Wilkinson; 33 Reiss Butterworth.
Tries: Halafihi (4), Caro (11, 39, 64), Macani (53), L Smith (77); **Goals:** Aston 4/6.
Rugby Leaguer & League Express Men of the Match: *Eagles:* Garry Lo; *Bulls:* Joe Keyes.
Penalty count: 9-13; **Half-time:** 10-16;
Referee: Tom Grant; **Attendance:** 896.

ROUND 6

Saturday 9th September 2017

TOULOUSE OLYMPIQUE 56 BATLEY BULLDOGS 14

OLYMPIQUE: 1 Mark Kheirallah; 2 Tony Maurel; 3 Bastien Ader; 21 Gavin Marguerite; 20 Paul Marcon; 6 Johnathon Ford; 7 Stan Robin; 23 Justine Sangare; 24 Anthony Marion; 10 Bastian Canet; 12 Rhys Curran; 28 Ugo Perez; 13 Andrew Bentley. Subs (all used): 8 Clement Boyer; 14 Mourad Kriouache; 17 Kalausa Leha; 9 Kane Bentley.
Tries: Ford (19), Robin (22, 40, 41), Kriouache (26, 54), Marcon (35), Maurel (46), Kheirallah (74, 76);
Goals: Kheirallah 8/10.
On report: Canet (28) - alleged dangerous challenge.
BULLDOGS: 1 Dave Scott; 2 Wayne Reittie; 3 Sam Smeaton; 30 Jason Crookes; 5 Shaun Ainscough; 11 Brad Day; 7 Dominic Brambani; 27 Will Maher; 9 Alistair Leak; 16 Tom Lillycrop; 22 Dane Manning; 18 James Harrison; 12 Joel Farrell. Subs (all used): 8 Adam Gledhill; 14 James Davey; 17 Joe Chandler; 23 Brad Hill.
Tries: Reittie (63), Hill (67), Harrison (80);
Goals: Brambani 1/3.
Rugby Leaguer & League Express Men of the Match: *Olympique:* Johnathon Ford; *Bulldogs:* Dane Manning.
Penalty count: 4-7; **Half-time:** 28-0;
Referee: Matt Rossleigh; **Attendance:** 868.

Sunday 10th September 2017

DEWSBURY RAMS 12 BRADFORD BULLS 16

RAMS: 23 James Glover; 2 Dale Morton; 29 Macauley Hallett; 4 Lucas Walshaw; 5 Gareth Potts; 6 Paul Sykes; 42 Michael Knowles; 24 Jode Sheriffe; 17 Dom Speakman; 18 Jack Teanby; 43 Jordan Crowther; 16 Toby Adamson; 13 Aaron Brown. Subs (all used): 27 Sam Day; 44 Toby Everett; 20 Aaron Ollett; 11 Rob Spicer.
Tries: Speakman (7), Aaron Brown (16); **Goals:** Sykes 2/2.
BULLS: 2 Ethan Ryan; 5 Iliess Macani; 26 Vila Halafihi; 1 Lee Smith; 18 Omari Caro; 7 Joe Keyes; 41 Cory Aston; 31 Mikolaj Oledzki; 29 Sam Hallas; 8 Liam Kirk; 20 James Bentley; 35 Evan Hodgson; 10 Damian Sironen. Subs (all used): 11 Colton Roche; 34 Scott Moore; 21 Brandan Wilkinson; 17 Ross Peltier.
Tries: Aston (4), Peltier (38), L Smith (57);
Goals: Aston 2/3.
Rugby Leaguer & League Express Men of the Match: *Rams:* Aaron Brown; *Bulls:* Joe Keyes.
Penalty count: 17-11; **Half-time:** 12-12;
Referee: Nick Bennett; **Attendance:** 1,369.

SHEFFIELD EAGLES 26 ROCHDALE HORNETS 22

EAGLES: 18 Ryan Millar; 2 Garry Lo; 3 Menzie Yere; 4 Perry Whiteley; 24 Paddy Flynn; 1 Jack Owens; 13 Elliot Minchella; 8 Scott Wheeldon; 9 Matty Fozard; 11 Matt James; 22 Liam Johnson; 12 Duane Straugheir; 25 George Milton. Subs (all used): 21 Liam Cooper; 15 Kyle Trout; 23 Jonah Cunningham; 16 Sam Scott.
Tries: Fozard (12), Lo (18), Owens (52), Wheeldon (58), Yere (77); **Goals:** Owens 3/5.
HORNETS: - Declan Kay; 21 Jack Holmes; 3 Jake Eccleston; 4 Lewis Galbraith; - Kevin Penny; 6 Lewis Palfrey; 7 Danny Yates; 15 Jovili Taira; 14 Ryan Maneely; - Lewis Hatton; 12 Josh Crowley; 17 Lee Mitchell; 19 Jordan Case. Subs: 2 Chris Riley (not used); 10 Gavin Bennion; 16 Matty Hadden; 1 Miles Greenwood.
Tries: Penny (4), Hadden (46), Holmes (48);
Goals: Yates 5/6.
Rugby Leaguer & League Express Men of the Match: *Eagles:* Perry Whiteley; *Hornets:* Matty Hadden.
Penalty count: 5-10; **Half-time:** 10-10;
Referee: Greg Dolan; **Attendance:** 297.

SWINTON LIONS 29 OLDHAM 6

LIONS: 1 Jack Murphy; - Ilias Bergal; 3 Chris Hankinson; 4 Rhodri Lloyd; 21 Mike Butt; 14 Ben White; 26 Josh Woods; 15 Andy Bracek; 22 Luke Waterworth; 18 Ben Austin; -

Liam Paisley; 17 Olly Davies; 8 Rob Lever. Subs (all used):
9 Anthony Nicholson; 24 Adam Jones; - Caine Barnes; 27
Liam Carberry.
Tries: Barnes (17), Bergal (37), Austin (63),
O Davies (73), Lloyd (75); **Goals:** Hankinson 4/5;
Field goal: Woods (58).
OLDHAM: 15 Luke Hooley; 2 Adam Clay; 3 George Tyson;
26 Kameron Pearce-Paul; 17 Richard Lepori; 22 Danny
Grimshaw; 7 Dave Hewitt; 10 Adam Neal; 21 Kenny
Hughes; 19 Joe Burke; 16 Liam Bent; 13 Liam Thompson;
14 Luke Adamson. Subs (all used): 9 Sam Gee; 28 Sadiq
Adebiyi; 24 Michael Ward; 11 Jack Spencer.
Try: Tyson (21); **Goals:** Hooley 1/1.
Rugby Leaguer & League Express Men of the Match:
Lions: Josh Woods; *Oldham:* George Tyson.
Penalty count: 8-7; **Half-time:** 12-6;
Referee: Chris Kendall; **Attendance:** 1,051.

ROUND 7

Saturday 16th September 2017

TOULOUSE OLYMPIQUE 38 SWINTON LIONS 34

OLYMPIQUE: 2 Tony Maurel; 5 Kuni Minga; 3 Bastien
Ader; 28 Ugo Perez; 20 Paul Marcon; 18 Louis Jouffret; 6
Johnathon Ford; 8 Clement Boyer; 27 Charles Bouzinac;
15 Maxime Puech; 26 Constantine Mika; 12 Rhys Curran;
9 Kane Bentley. Subs (all used): 14 Mourad Kriouache; 16
Tyla Hepi; 17 Kalausa Leha; 22 Levy Nzoungou.
Tries: Ader (2), Mika (5), Maurel (20), Leha (25),
Curran (38), Minga (49), Boyer (67);
Goals: Bouzinac 1/3, Maurel 4/4.
Sin bin: Mika (13) - punching; Ford (57) - obstruction.
LIONS: 1 Jack Murphy; - Ilias Bergal; 3 Chris Hankinson; 4
Rhodri Lloyd; 21 Mike Butt; 14 Ben White; 25 Josh Woods;
15 Andy Bracek; 22 Luke Waterworth; 18 Ben Austin; 17
Olly Davies; - Liam Paisley; 8 Rob Lever. Subs (all used):
27 Liam Carberry; 9 Anthony Nicholson; - Mark Nicholson;
24 Adam Jones.
Tries: Waterworth (16), Bergal (42), White (45),
A Nicholson (53), Paisley (58), Butt (63),
Hankinson (76); **Goals:** Hankinson 3/7.
Rugby Leaguer & League Express Men of the Match:
Olympique: Constantine Mika; *Lions:* Josh Woods.
Penalty count: 6-3; **Half-time:** 26-6;
Referee: Tom Crashley; **Attendance:** 1,073.

Sunday 17th September 2017

BATLEY BULLDOGS 34 SHEFFIELD EAGLES 18

BULLDOGS: 1 Dave Scott; 2 Wayne Reittie; 3 Sam
Smeaton; 15 Danny Cowling; 5 Shaun Ainscough; 17 Joe
Chandler; 14 James Davey; 27 Will Maher; 9 Alistair Leak;
8 Adam Gledhill; 22 Dane Manning; 18 James Harrison; 12
Joel Farrell. Subs: 30 Jason Crookes (not used); 19 Alex
Bretherton; 10 Alex Rowe; 23 Brad Hill.
Tries: Manning (14), Chandler (17), Ainscough (22),
Leak (46, 60), Bretherton (65); **Goals:** Scott 5/6.
Sin bin: Leak (28) - professional foul.
EAGLES: 18 Ryan Millar; 24 Paddy Flynn; 3 Menzie Yere; 4
Perry Whiteley; 5 Ben Blackmore; 1 Jack Owens; 9 Matty
Fozard; 8 Scott Wheeldon; 14 Greg Burns; 15 Kyle Trout; 22
Liam Johnson; 12 Duane Straugheir; 21 Liam Cooper. Subs
(all used): 23 Jonah Cunningham; 25 George Milton; 16
Sam Scott; 10 Mark Mexico.
Tries: Flynn (4), Mexico (31), Straugheir (51), Yere (57);
Goals: Owens 1/4.
Dismissal: Wheeldon (56) - headbutt.
Sin bin: Cunningham (49) - professional foul.
Rugby Leaguer & League Express Men of the Match:
Bulldogs: Alistair Leak; *Eagles:* Liam Johnson.
Penalty count: 12-12; **Half-time:** 16-10;
Referee: Steve Race; **Attendance:** 650.

BRADFORD BULLS 72 ROCHDALE HORNETS 16

BULLS: 2 Ethan Ryan; 5 Iliess Macani; 26 Vila Halafihi;
4 Ross Oakes; 18 Omari Caro; 41 Cory Aston; 7 Joe Keyes;
15 Jon Magrin; 34 Scott Moore; 8 Liam Kirk; 20 James
Bentley; 35 Evan Hodgson; 10 Damian Sironen. Subs (all
used): 29 Sam Hallas; 31 Mikolaj Oledzki; 17 Ross Peltier;
11 Colton Roche.
Tries: Bentley (5), Halafihi (8), Kirk (17), Hallas (19),
Oakes (22), Ryan (27, 54), Caro (36), Keyes (38),
Peltier (50, 78), Moore (70), Aston (80);
Goals: Aston 9/11, Caro 1/2.
Sin bin: Moore (15) - fighting.
HORNETS: - Declan Kay; 2 Chris Riley; 3 Jake Eccleston; 4
Lewis Galbraith; - Kevin Penny; 6 Lewis Palfrey; 7 Danny
Yates; 15 Jovili Taira; - Lewis Foster; - Lewis Hatton; 12
Josh Crowley; 17 Lee Mitchell; 19 Jordan Case. Subs (all
used): 1 Miles Greenwood; 10 Gavin Bennion; 16 Matty
Hadden; 21 Jack Holmes.
Tries: Case (30), Riley (64), Holmes (73); **Goals:** Yates 2/3.

Joe Chandler on the charge during Batley's semi-final defeat to Sheffield

Sin bin: Bennion (15) - late challenge;
Taira (15) - fighting; Foster (18) - dissent.
Rugby Leaguer & League Express Men of the Match:
Bulls: Ethan Ryan; *Hornets:* Matty Hadden.
Penalty count: 16-12; **Half-time:** 46-6;
Referee: Andrew Sweet; **Attendance:** 3,604.

OLDHAM 22 DEWSBURY RAMS 29

OLDHAM: 17 Richard Lepori; 2 Adam Clay; 3 George
Tyson; 22 Danny Grimshaw; 16 Steven Nield; 6 Scott
Leatherbarrow; 7 Dave Hewitt; 10 Adam Neal; 21 Kenny
Hughes; 19 Joe Burke; 11 Jack Spencer; 13 Liam Thompson;
14 Luke Adamson. Subs (all used): 27 Matt Wilkinson; 9
Sam Gee; 18 Ben Davies; 24 Michael Ward.
Tries: Lepori (4), Burke (19), Grimshaw (50),
Thompson (58); **Goals:** Hewitt 3/4.
RAMS: 32 Shaun Squires; 2 Dale Morton; 29 Macauley
Hallett; 4 Lucas Walshaw; 25 Tom Halliday; 6 Paul Sykes;
41 Gareth Moore; 24 Jode Sheriffe; 15 Robbie Ward; 18
Jack Teanby; 43 Jordan Crowther; 16 Toby Adamson; 26
Mickael Goudemand. Subs (all used): 44 Toby Everett; 27
Sam Day; 20 Aaron Ollett; 42 Michael Knowles.
Tries: Squires (9, 45), Day (31), Halliday (77);
Goals: Sykes 6/6; **Field goal:** Knowles (75).
Rugby Leaguer & League Express Men of the Match:
Oldham: Liam Thompson; *Rams:* Shaun Squires.
Penalty count: 12-12; **Half-time:** 12-14;
Referee: Greg Dolan; **Attendance:** 429.

SEMI-FINALS

Saturday 23rd September 2017

TOULOUSE OLYMPIQUE 36 DEWSBURY RAMS 22

OLYMPIQUE: 1 Mark Kheirallah; 2 Tony Maurel; 3 Bastien
Ader; 21 Gavin Marguerite; 20 Paul Marcon; 6 Johnathon
Ford; 7 Stan Robin; 8 Clement Boyer; 27 Charles
Bouzinac; 10 Bastian Canet; 26 Constantine Mika; 12
Rhys Curran; 24 Anthony Marion. Subs (all used): 14
Mourad Kriouache; 16 Tyla Hepi; 13
Andrew Bentley.
Tries: Canet (7), Jouffret (13, 33), Curran (24), Ford (59),
Boyer (64); **Goals:** Kheirallah 6/6.
Sin bin: Ford (71) - obstruction.
RAMS: 32 Shaun Squires; 25 Tom Halliday; 23 James
Glover; 29 Macauley Hallett; 2 Dale Morton; 6 Paul Sykes;
41 Gareth Moore; 24 Jode Sheriffe; 15 Robbie Ward; 18
Jack Teanby; 42 Michael Knowles; 43 Jordan Crowther; 13
Aaron Brown. Subs (all used): 4 Lucas Walshaw; 16 Toby
Adamson; 26 Mickael Goudemand; 17 Dom Speakman.
Tries: Moore (42), Morton (49, 76), Glover (74);
Goals: Sykes 3/4.
Sin bin: Moore (17) - professional foul.
On report: Halliday (59) - alleged high tackle.
Rugby Leaguer & League Express Men of the Match:
Olympique: Louis Jouffret; *Rams:* Gareth Moore.
Penalty count: 6-11; **Half-time:** 24-0;
Referee: Matt Rossleigh; **Attendance:** 1,208.

Sunday 24th September 2017

BATLEY BULLDOGS 26 SHEFFIELD EAGLES 28

BULLDOGS: 1 Dave Scott; 2 Wayne Reittie; 3 Sam
Smeaton; 30 Jason Crookes; 5 Shaun Ainscough; 13 Pat
Walker; 7 Dominic Brambani; 8 Adam Gledhill; 9 Alistair
Leak; 17 Joe Chandler; 22 Dane Manning; 18 James
Harrison; 12 Joel Farrell. Subs (all used): 10 Alex Rowe; 14
James Davey; 15 Danny Cowling; 19 Alex Bretherton.
Tries: Manning (9), Harrison (33, 62), Chandler (57),
Brambani (74); **Goals:** Walker 3/5.
Dismissal: Farrell (80) - shoulder charge on Hope.
Sin bin: Ainscough (7) - fighting.
EAGLES: 18 Ryan Millar; 2 Garry Lo; 3 Menzie Yere; 4
Perry Whiteley; 5 Ben Blackmore; 6 Simon Brown; 1 Jack
Owens; 8 Scott Wheeldon; 9 Matty Fozard; 11 Matt James;
22 Liam Johnson; 12 Duane Straugheir; 13 Elliot Minchella.
Subs (all used): 10 Mark Mexico; 15 Kyle Trout; 16 Sam
Scott; 19 Will Hope.
Tries: Yere (15), Blackmore (21), Trout (37), Lo (43, 46);
Goals: Owens 4/8.
Sin bin: Blackmore (7) - fighting; Lo (31) - punching Reittie.
Rugby Leaguer & League Express Men of the Match:
Bulldogs: James Harrison; *Eagles:* Garry Lo.
Penalty count: 14-14; **Half-time:** 10-18;
Referee: Jack Smith; **Attendance:** 550.

FINAL

Saturday 30th September 2017

TOULOUSE OLYMPIQUE 44 SHEFFIELD EAGLES 14

OLYMPIQUE: 1 Mark Kheirallah; 2 Tony Maurel; 3 Bastien
Ader; 21 Gavin Marguerite; 20 Paul Marcon; 6 Johnathon
Ford; 7 Stan Robin; 8 Clement Boyer; 27 Charles Bouzinac;
10 Bastian Canet; 26 Constantine Mika; 12 Rhys Curran; 24
Anthony Marion. Subs (all used): 14 Mourad Kriouache; 14
Mourad Kriouache; 15 Maxime Puech; 16 Tyla Hepi.
Tries: Kheirallah (23, 65), Robin (33), Marguerite (40),
Curran (42), Marcon (63), Marion (71), Mika (73),
Maurel (79); **Goals:** Kheirallah 4/9.
EAGLES: 18 Ryan Millar; 2 Garry Lo; 3 Menzie Yere; 24
Paddy Flynn; 5 Ben Blackmore; 6 Simon Brown; 1 Jack
Owens; 8 Scott Wheeldon; 9 Matty Fozard; 13 Matt James;
22 Liam Johnson; 12 Duane Straugheir; 13 Elliot Minchella.
Subs (all used): 10 Mark Mexico; 15 Kyle Trout; 16 Sam
Scott; 19 Will Hope.
Tries: Lo (7, 18, 28); **Goals:** Owens 1/3.
Rugby Leaguer & League Express Men of the Match:
Olympique: Mark Kheirallah; *Eagles:* Scott Wheeldon.
Penalty count: 7-3; **Half-time:** 16-14;
Referee: Gareth Hewer; **Attendance:** 1,528.

LEAGUE 1 2017
Club by Club

BARROW RAIDERS

DATE	FIXTURE	RESULT	SCORERS	LGE	ATT
18/2/17	Rochdale Mayfield (a) (L1CR1)	W18-46	t:Charnock,Wilkes,Cresswell,S Toal,Dallimore(3),Hulme g:Charnock(6),Dallimore	N/A	300
26/2/17	Rochdale Mayfield (h) (CCR3)	W60-6	t:Fieldhouse(4),Crellin,Hulme(2),Morrow,Stack(2),Charnock g:Charnock(8)	N/A	500
4/3/17	York (h)	W28-0	t:Morrow,Cresswell,Stack,S Toal(2),Charnock g:Charnock(2)	4th	799
12/3/17	Coventry (a)	W14-50	t:Stack(2),S Toal,Mossop,Litherland,Abram,Cresswell,Hulme,Bullock g:Charnock(7)	2nd	447
18/3/17	Keighley (h) (CCR4)	W20-0	t:Charnock(2),S Toal,Hulme g:Dallimore(2)	N/A	721
25/3/17	Hemel (h)	W82-0	t:Fieldhouse(3),Carter,Johnston(2),Walker,Hulme(2),Litherland(2),Marwood(2),Stack,Mossop g:Johnston(11)	1st	739
2/4/17	Keighley (h) (L1CQF)	W28-6	t:Cresswell,Dallimore,Fieldhouse,Hulme,Litherland g:Charnock(4)	N/A	828
8/4/17	Workington (h)	W26-10	t:Charnock,Litherland,Abram,Duerden g:Charnock(5)	2nd	1,284
14/4/17	Newcastle (a)	W6-50	t:Wilkes,Hulme,S Toal,Cresswell,Litherland,Duerden,Bullock,Fieldhouse g:Charnock(7)	2nd	1,073
23/4/17	York (a) (CCR5)	W28-50	t:Hulme,S Toal,D Toal(2),Cresswell(4),Mossop,Walker g:Charnock(5)	N/A	904
30/4/17	Oxford (h) (L1CSF)	W64-14	t:Fieldhouse,S Toal(3),Brennan,Walker,Duerden,Abram,Charnock(2),Bullock(2) g:Charnock(8)	N/A	962
6/5/17	South Wales (h)	W58-16	t:Fieldhouse(2),Loxam,Ashall,Johnston,Mossop(2),Duerden,Cresswell(2),Morrow g:Charnock(5),Johnston(2)	2nd	805
10/5/17	Keighley (a)	W42-58	t:Bullock,Charnock(4),S Toal(3),Cresswell,Fieldhouse g:Charnock(8),Ashall	2nd	728
14/5/17	Leeds (a) (CCR6)	L72-10	t:Cresswell,Stack g:Ashall	N/A	5,226
20/5/17	Toronto (a)	L70-2	g:Charnock	2nd	7,144
27/5/17	North Wales (L1CF) ●	W38-32	t:Mossop,Cresswell,Hulme,Morrow(2),S Toal,Bullock g:Charnock(2),Dallimore(3)	N/A	N/A
3/6/17	Hunslet (h)	W28-20	t:Harper,Dallimore,Fieldhouse(2) g:Charnock(6)	2nd	913
11/6/17	Doncaster (a) ●●	D24-24	t:Cresswell,Dallimore,Hulme,Harper g:Charnock(2),Dallimore(2)	3rd	673
17/6/17	North Wales (h)	W28-4	t:Marwood(2),Abram,Hulme,D Toal g:Dallimore(4)	3rd	835
24/6/17	London Skolars (a)	W10-20	t:Wilkes,Mossop g:Charnock(4),Dallimore(2)	3rd	374
1/7/17	Gloucestershire All Golds (h)	W36-6	t:Aspinwall,Hulme(2),S Toal(2),Mossop,Fieldhouse g:Charnock(4)	3rd	696
8/7/17	Oxford (h)	W80-10	t:Morrow(2),Marwood,Dallimore,S Toal,D Toal,Johnston,Harper(3),Carter,Wilkes,Bullock,Walker g:Charnock(12)	2nd	750
16/7/17	Whitehaven (a)	L32-6	t:Walker g:Charnock	3rd	1,502
30/7/17	Whitehaven (a) (S8)	W2-15	t:Stack,Fieldhouse g:Dallimore(3) fg:Dallimore	2nd	1,062
6/8/17	Doncaster (h) (S8)	W14-10	t:Dallimore,Carter g:Dallimore(3)	2nd	836
12/8/17	Newcastle (a) (S8)	W28-30	t:Harper(2),Fieldhouse,Hulme(2),Carter g:Charnock(3)	2nd	850
20/8/17	York (h) (S8)	W26-19	t:Carter(2),Ashall,Bullock g:Charnock(5)	2nd	977
3/9/17	Workington (h) (S8)	W36-14	t:S Toal(2),Mossop,Fieldhouse,Dallimore,Wilkes g:Charnock(5),Dallimore	2nd	1,021
9/9/17	Toronto (a) (S8)	L26-2	g:Charnock	2nd	7,972
17/9/17	Keighley (h) (S8)	W32-18	t:Mossop,S Toal,Walker,Bullock,Charnock g:Charnock(3),Dallimore(3)	2nd	1,007
24/9/17	Newcastle (h) (SF)	W60-0	t:Wilkes,S Toal(2),Dallimore(2),Carter,Fieldhouse,Marwood(2),Charnock g:Dallimore(9),Marwood	N/A	1,090
1/10/17	Whitehaven (h) (PF)	W10-6	t:S Toal(2) g:Dallimore	N/A	3,128

● Played at Bloomfield Road, Blackpool ●● Played at Keepmoat Athletics Ground

APP TRIES GOALS FG PTS

	D.O.B.	ALL	L1	ALL	L1	ALL	L1	ALL	L1	ALL	L1
Dan Abram	11/11/95	(14)	(7)	4	3	0	0	0	0	16	12
Karl Ashall	3/11/89	11(6)	10(6)	2	2	2	1	0	0	12	10
Martin Aspinwall	21/10/81	26	18	1	1	0	0	0	0	4	4
Brad Brennan	18/1/93	(8)	(4)	1	0	0	0	0	0	4	0
Joe Bullock	27/11/92	31	23	9	6	0	0	0	0	36	24
Brett Carter	9/7/88	15	15	7	7	0	0	0	0	28	28
Lewis Charnock	2/9/94	30	22	14	8	114	81	0	0	284	194
Bradd Crellin	2/7/89	15(2)	12(1)	1	0	0	0	0	0	4	0
Luke Cresswell	5/5/95	20	12	15	7	0	0	0	0	60	28
Jamie Dallimore	20/8/88	26	21	11	7	36	30	1	1	117	89
Andrew Dawson	12/3/89	(17)	(12)	0	0	0	0	0	0	0	0
James Duerden	9/10/91	2(25)	2(19)	4	3	0	0	0	0	16	12
Ryan Fieldhouse	10/4/88	29	21	20	14	0	0	0	0	80	56
Chris Fleming	11/1/91	2	1	0	0	0	0	0	0	0	0
Eze Harper	7/12/94	13	13	7	7	0	0	0	0	28	28
Declan Hulme	14/1/93	29	22	17	10	0	0	0	0	68	40
Ryan Johnston	16/3/98	4	4	4	4	13	13	0	0	42	42
Andy Litherland	15/5/90	11	5	6	5	0	0	0	0	24	20
Tom Loxam	27/1/92	7	6	1	1	0	0	0	0	4	4
Brad Marwood	4/11/93	6(2)	3(2)	7	7	1	1	0	0	30	30
Danny Morrow	30/4/90	14	10	7	4	0	0	0	0	28	16
Nathan Mossop	21/2/88	20(10)	13(9)	10	8	0	0	0	0	40	32
Jarrad Stack	13/2/88	30	23	8	5	0	0	0	0	32	20
Dan Toal	22/9/89	14(12)	10(11)	4	2	0	0	0	0	16	8
Shane Toal	11/11/95	25	18	24	17	0	0	0	0	96	68
Tom Walker	25/12/94	6(25)	5(19)	6	4	0	0	0	0	24	16
Matty While	25/11/96	2(6)	2(5)	0	0	0	0	0	0	0	0
Oliver Wilkes	2/5/80	27(1)	20(1)	6	5	0	0	0	0	24	20
Max Wiper	18/9/90	1	1	0	0	0	0	0	0	0	0

Shane Toal

LEAGUE RECORD
P22-W18-D1-L3
(2nd/Winners, Promotion Final)
F731, A381, Diff+350, 37 points.

LEAGUE 1 CUP
Winners

CHALLENGE CUP
Round Six

ATTENDANCES
Best - v Whitehaven (PF - 3,128)
Worst - v Rochdale Mayfield (CC - 500)
Total (excluding Challenge Cup) - 16,670
Average (excluding
Challenge Cup) - 1,042
(Up by 101 on 2016)

'L1' totals include Super 8s & play-offs; 'All' totals also include League 1 Cup & Challenge Cup

CLUB RECORDS
MATCH RECORDS

Highest score: 138-0 v Nottingham City, 27/11/94 **Highest score against:** 0-90 v Leeds, 11/2/90 **Record attendance:** 21,651 v Salford, 15/4/38
Tries: 6 Val Cumberbatch v Batley, 21/11/36; Jim Thornburrow v Maryport, 19/2/38; Steve Rowan v Nottingham City, 15/11/92
Goals: 17 Darren Carter v Nottingham City, 27/11/94 **Points:** 42 Darren Carter v Nottingham City, 27/11/94

SEASON RECORDS
CAREER RECORDS

Tries: 50 Jim Lewthwaite 1956-57 **Goals:** 135 Joe Ball 1956-57 **Points:** 323 Jamie Rooney 2010
Tries: 352 Jim Lewthwaite 1943-57 **Goals:** 1,099 *(inc 63fg)* Darren Holt 1998-2002; 2004-2009; 2012
Points: 2,403 Darren Holt 1998-2002; 2004-2009; 2012 **Appearances:** 500 Jim Lewthwaite 1943-57

COVENTRY BEARS

DATE	FIXTURE	RESULT	SCORERS	LGE	ATT
18/2/17	Oxford (a) (L1CR1)	L30-28	t:Morrison,Freeman,Reid(3) g:Roper(4)	N/A	121
26/2/17	Hunslet (a) (CCR3)	L34-0		N/A	249
5/3/17	Doncaster (a)	L26-4	t:Hunte	12th	545
12/3/17	Barrow (h)	L14-50	t:Freeman,Barratt,Russell g:Delaney	13th	447
25/3/17	London Skolars (a)	L42-16	t:Freeman,Delaney,Russell g:Delaney(2)	15th	287
9/4/17	Whitehaven (a)	L44-12	t:Medforth,Bass g:Delaney(2)	15th	413
14/4/17	Oxford (h)	W40-28	t:Morrison,Chapman,Hunte,Hughes(2),Johnson,Reid g:Delaney(6)	14th	303
7/5/17	Keighley (h)	L24-44	t:Chapman(2),Russell(3) g:Delaney(2)	14th	383
14/5/17	York (a)	L64-12	t:Freeman,Brierley g:Delaney(2)	14th	902
21/5/17	Gloucestershire All Golds (h)	L18-26	t:Geurtjens,Chapman,Barratt g:Delaney(3)	14th	323
3/6/17	Toronto (a)	L54-12	t:Hunte,Delaney g:Delaney(2)	14th	6,973
11/6/17	Hemel (h)	W28-24	t:Freeman,Hunte(2),Sherratt,Barratt g:Delaney(4)	14th	357
18/6/17	South Wales (a)	L24-22	t:Sherratt,Russell,Morrison,Reid g:Delaney(3)	14th	156
25/6/17	Workington (h)	L28-29	t:Delaney,Russell(2),Chapman,Freeman g:Delaney(4)	14th	571
2/7/17	Hunslet (a)	L56-24	t:Hunte(2),Beddows,Geurtjens g:Delaney(4)	14th	406
9/7/17	Newcastle (a)	L68-20	t:Barratt,Delaney,Russell,O'Mara g:Delaney(2)	14th	567
16/7/17	North Wales (h)	L13-36	t:Hunte,Reid g:Delaney(2) fg:Gale	14th	422
30/7/17	Hunslet (a) (L1S)	L56-10	t:P Jones,Freeman g:Delaney	6th(L1S)	384
6/8/17	Hemel (h) (L1S)	W29-26	t:Russell,Delaney(2),Kelly,Freeman g:Delaney(4) fg:Emanuelli	6th(L1S)	256
12/8/17	Gloucestershire All Golds (a) (L1S)	L30-28	t:Reid,Emanuelli,Barratt,Russell,Freeman g:Delaney(4)	6th(L1S)	178
20/8/17	London Skolars (h) (L1S)	L14-50	t:Sherratt,Russell,Bass g:Delaney	6th(L1S)	268
3/9/17	North Wales (a) (L1S)	W16-22	t:Hunte,Freeman,Delaney,S Davies g:Delaney,Emanuelli(2)	6th(L1S)	245
9/9/17	Oxford (a) (L1S)	L28-24	t:Freeman(2),Hunte,Reid,Delaney g:Emanuelli,Delaney	6th(L1S)	110
16/9/17	South Wales (h) (L1S)	W58-16	t:Brennan(2),Hunte(3),Freeman,Delaney,Reid,Emanuelli,Russell,Barratt g:Emanuelli(7)	6th(L1S)	332

APP   TRIES GOALS FG   PTS

	D.O.B.	ALL	L1	ALL	L1	ALL	L1	ALL	L1	ALL	L1
John Aldred	3/10/89	5(6)	4(3)	0	0	0	0	0	0	0	0
Chris Barratt	7/2/93	22	14	6	4	0	0	0	0	24	16
Jason Bass	10/5/96	13	5	2	1	0	0	0	0	8	4
Callan Beckett	24/3/93	2(1)	(1)	0	0	0	0	0	0	0	0
Alex Beddows	1/8/94	9(5)	5(4)	1	1	0	0	0	0	4	4
Brad Brennan	18/1/93	7(3)	1(3)	2	0	0	0	0	0	8	0
Tommy Brierley	8/9/96	5	5	1	1	0	0	0	0	4	4
Harry Chapman	15/7/97	11(1)	10(1)	5	5	0	0	0	0	20	20
Elliott Davies	15/9/91	2(1)	1(1)	0	0	0	0	0	0	0	0
Sam Davies	11/11/98	(1)	0	1	0	0	0	0	0	4	0
Brad Delaney	25/5/95	21	14	9	4	51	39	0	0	138	94
Paul Emanuelli	3/1/84	6(1)	0	2	0	10	0	1	0	29	0
Hayden Freeman	20/8/97	18(5)	9(5)	13	5	0	0	0	0	52	20
Luke Frixou	15/1/94	4	3	0	0	0	0	0	0	0	0
Jordan Gale	30/9/95	4	3	0	0	0	0	1	1	1	1
Billy Gaylor	30/4/97	22	13	0	0	0	0	0	0	0	0
James Geurtjens	28/4/86	9(13)	9(6)	2	2	0	0	0	0	8	8
Dan Gover	23/9/93	2(11)	2(9)	0	0	0	0	0	0	0	0
Richard Hughes	28/3/93	4(3)	4(3)	2	2	0	0	0	0	8	8
Jamahl Hunte	27/4/94	18	12	13	8	0	0	0	0	52	32
Joel James	17/2/95	1(1)	0	0	0	0	0	0	0	0	0
Zach Johnson	9/3/91	7(2)	6(1)	1	1	0	0	0	0	4	4
Jacob Jones	15/2/99	1(2)	0	0	0	0	0	0	0	0	0
Owen Jones	20/2/99	(1)	0	0	0	0	0	0	0	0	0
Paddy Jones	7/2/97	8(6)	4(3)	1	0	0	0	0	0	4	0
Harry Kaufman	20/12/91	(1)	(1)	0	0	0	0	0	0	0	0
James Kelly	3/9/92	(6)	(1)	1	0	0	0	0	0	4	0
Jay Lobwein	13/4/92	1	1	0	0	0	0	0	0	0	0
Lewis Lord	29/11/95	(1)	(1)	0	0	0	0	0	0	0	0
Rob Meadows	18/1/96	2(2)	2(2)	0	0	0	0	0	0	0	0
Eddie Medforth	30/3/95	10	9	1	1	0	0	0	0	4	4
Jack Morrison	16/9/92	8(14)	5(8)	3	2	0	0	0	0	12	8
Charlie O'Mara	11/9/96	7	5	1	1	0	0	0	0	4	4
Joe Prior	10/9/95	9(2)	7(2)	0	0	0	0	0	0	0	0
Matt Reid	16/9/92	24	15	9	3	0	0	0	0	36	12
Will Roper	6/10/93	3	2	0	0	4	0	0	0	8	0
Mikey Russell	29/8/94	19(2)	12(1)	13	9	0	0	0	0	52	36
Kieran Sherratt	15/11/95	20(1)	12	3	2	0	0	0	0	12	8
Liam Thompson	7/2/91	(3)	(3)	0	0	0	0	0	0	0	0
Cian Timmins	2/4/96	1	0	0	0	0	0	0	0	0	0
Zak Williams	17/9/96	7(1)	1(1)	0	0	0	0	0	0	0	0

'L1' totals include League 1 regular season only; 'All' totals also include League 1 Shield, League 1 Cup & Challenge Cup

Jack Morrison

LEAGUE RECORD
League 1, before Super 8 split:
P15-W2-D0-L13 (14th)
F287, A615, Diff-328, 4 points.

After League 1 Shield:
P22-W5-D0-L17 (6th)
F472, A837, Diff-365, 10 points.

LEAGUE 1 CUP
Round One

CHALLENGE CUP
Round Three

ATTENDANCES
Best - v Workington (L1 - 571)
Worst - v Hemel (L1S - 256)
Total (all home games
included) - 3,662
Average (all home games
included) - 366
(Down by 60 on 2016)

CLUB RECORDS	
MATCH RECORDS	**Highest score:** 58-16 v South Wales, 16/9/2017 **Highest score against:** 8-78 v Swinton, 14/6/2015 **Record attendance:** 1,097 v Keighley, 8/5/2016
SEASON RECORDS	**Tries:** 3 *(8 players)* **Goals:** 8 Connor Robinson v Hemel, 19/4/2015 **Points:** 22 Dan Parker v London Skolars, 7/6/2015
	Tries: 13 Jamahl Hunte 2015; Hayden Freeman 2017; Jamahl Hunte 2017; Mikey Russell 2017
	Goals: 60 *(inc 2fg)* Joel James 2016 **Points:** 138 Brad Delaney 2017
CAREER RECORDS	**Tries:** 30 Jamahl Hunte 2015-2017 **Goals:** 60 *(inc 2fg)* Joel James 2015-2017 **Points:** 138 Brad Delaney 2017 **Appearances:** 68 Chris Barratt 2015-2017

DONCASTER

DATE	FIXTURE	RESULT	SCORERS	LGE	ATT
19/2/17	Keighley (a) (L1CR1)	L30-22	t:Welham,Cross,Martin,Palea'aesina g:Howden(3)	N/A	520
26/2/17	Myton (h) (CCR3)	W34-6	t:Cross,Tali,Heil,Jones-Bishop,Welham,Carr g:Carr(5)	N/A	366
5/3/17	Coventry (h)	W26-4	t:Miller,Barnett,Cross,Tali g:Carr(5)	5th	545
12/3/17	North Wales (a)	W8-44	t:Barnett,Howden(2),Cross(2),Spiers,Tali(2),Sheriff g:Carr(3),Kesik	3rd	305
19/3/17	Gloucestershire All Golds (a) (CCR4) ●	W22-48	t:Welham(2),Cross(4),Sheriff(2) g:Miller(8)	N/A	280
2/4/17	Hunslet (h)	W29-24	t:Martin,Cross,Tonks,Wright,Tali g:Carr(4) fg:Carr	3rd	604
9/4/17	Toronto (h)	L6-82	t:Doherty g:Carr	5th	943
14/4/17	York (a)	L16-8	t:Palea'aesina g:Carr(2)	7th	1,012
21/4/17	Leeds (a) (CCR5)	L64-28	t:Cross,Wright,Sheriff(2),Martin,Kesik g:Carr(2)	N/A	5,097
7/5/17	London Skolars (h)	D28-28	t:Kesik,Tali(3),Sheriff g:Carr(3),Miller	7th	564
14/5/17	Hemel (a)	W24-50	t:Barnett(2),Kesik,Carr(2),Tali(2),Hedges,Doherty,Sheriff g;Carr(3),Miller(2)	4th	102
21/5/17	Keighley (h)	W28-14	t:Tali,Wright,Spiers,Howden g:Miller(6)	4th	516
4/6/17	Workington (a)	W26-30	t:Howden,Miller(2),Kesik,Spiers g:Miller(5)	4th	522
11/6/17	Barrow (h) ●	D24-24	t:Braham,Tali(2),Hedges g:Miller(4)	5th	673
25/6/17	Whitehaven (a)	L25-20	t:Sheriff(2),Logan(2) g:Miller(2)	6th	606
2/7/17	Newcastle (h) ●	L10-20	t:Barnett,Carr g:Miller	7th	550
5/7/17	Oxford (h) ●●	W34-16	t:Doherty(3),Cross,Miller(2),England g:Miller(3)	6th	334
9/7/17	South Wales (a)	W12-70	t:Spiers(2),Tali,Thackray,Palea'aesina,Dean,Doherty(2),Downs(2),Sheriff(2),Miller g:Miller(9)	6th	130
16/7/17	Gloucestershire All Golds (a)	W4-42	t:Castle,Palea'aesina,Doherty(2),Dean(2),England g:Miller(7)	5th	200
30/7/17	Keighley (h) (S8)	L24-32	t:Jones,Cross,Welham,Doherty,Rawsthorne g:Miller(2)	5th	501
6/8/17	Barrow (a) (S8)	L14-10	t:England,Miller g:Miller	5th	836
13/8/17	Whitehaven (h) (S8)	W30-22	t:Kesik,Palea'aesina,Doherty,Cross,Martin g:Miller(5)	5th	525
20/8/17	Workington (a) (S8)	L22-21	t:Palea'aesina,Tali,Cross g:Miller(4) fg:Miller	5th	441
3/9/17	York (a) (S8)	D21-21	t:Barnett,Rawsthorne,Miloudi(2) g:Miller(2) fg:Miller	5th	1,107
10/9/17	Newcastle (h) (S8)	L24-28	t:Green,Muranka,Tali,Cross g:Miller(3),Rawsthorne	5th	536
16/9/17	Toronto (a) (S8)	L26-14	t:Lane,Kesik g:Miller(3)	6th	8,456

● *Played at Keepmoat Athletics Ground*
●● *Played at LD Nutrition Stadium, Featherstone*

	D.O.B.	APP ALL	L1	TRIES ALL	L1	GOALS ALL	L1	FG ALL	L1	PTS ALL	L1
Makali Aizue	30/12/77	1(8)	1(5)	0	0	0	0	0	0	0	0
Richie Barnett	26/4/81	13	11	6	6	0	0	0	0	24	24
Zac Braham	14/1/95	11(5)	9(4)	1	1	0	0	0	0	4	4
Tom Carr	16/7/91	14	12	4	3	28	21	1	1	73	55
Mark Castle	19/2/86	11(6)	7(6)	1	1	0	0	0	0	4	4
Kieran Cross	18/2/95	14(6)	11(5)	16	9	0	0	0	0	64	36
Reece Dean	30/11/96	8	8	3	3	0	0	0	0	12	12
Sam Doherty	14/11/93	23	20	11	11	0	0	0	0	44	44
Jack Downs	10/11/95	4	4	2	2	0	0	0	0	8	8
Brad England	20/11/94	15(2)	12(2)	3	3	0	0	0	0	12	12
Peter Green	2/12/81	15	15	1	1	0	0	0	0	4	4
Jordie Hedges	4/8/95	7(11)	6(10)	2	2	0	0	0	0	8	8
Chris Heil	18/8/92	3	1	1	0	0	0	0	0	4	0
Jordan Howden	6/5/96	7	5	4	4	3	0	0	0	22	16
Ryan Jones	9/12/97	4	4	1	1	0	0	0	0	4	4
Aaron Jones-Bishop	18/1/90	5(1)	3(1)	1	0	0	0	0	0	4	0
Mike Kelly	23/5/89	(2)	(2)	0	0	0	0	0	0	0	0
Kyle Kesik	3/6/89	21	17	6	5	1	1	0	0	26	22
Jordan Lane	20/10/97	1	1	1	1	0	0	0	0	4	4
Jez Litten	10/3/98	(1)	(1)	0	0	0	0	0	0	0	0
Jack Logan	8/9/95	2	2	2	2	0	0	0	0	8	8
Charlie Martin	2/12/92	24(1)	21(1)	4	2	0	0	0	0	16	8
Jack Miller	28/11/94	21	19	7	7	68	60	2	2	166	150
Hakim Miloudi	26/6/93	5	5	2	2	0	0	0	0	8	8
Jason Muranka	4/8/89	10(6)	8(6)	1	1	0	0	0	0	4	4
Iafeta Palea'aesina	10/2/82	4(13)	4(10)	6	5	0	0	0	0	24	20
Nick Rawsthorne	30/9/95	8	8	2	2	1	1	0	0	10	10
Connor Scott	27/5/93	7(6)	6(4)	0	0	0	0	0	0	0	0
Louis Sheriff	6/9/92	17	13	11	7	0	0	0	0	44	44
Russ Spiers	28/4/91	17(5)	15(4)	5	5	0	0	0	0	20	20
Jason Tali	7/7/89	21	18	16	15	0	0	0	0	64	60
Jamie Thackray	30/9/79	5(11)	4(10)	1	1	0	0	0	0	4	4
Mason Tonks	11/10/94	1(1)	1(1)	1	1	0	0	0	0	4	4
Liam Welham	11/11/88	16(1)	13(1)	5	1	0	0	0	0	20	4
Michael Worriney	16/2/86	1	0	0	0	0	0	0	0	0	0
Ryan Wright	28/10/91	2(18)	2(15)	3	2	0	0	0	0	12	8

'L1' totals include Super 8s; 'All' totals also include League 1 Cup & Challenge Cup

Jason Tali

LEAGUE RECORD
P22-W10-D3-L9 (6th)
F593, A492, Diff+101, 23 points.

LEAGUE 1 CUP
Round One

CHALLENGE CUP
Round Five

ATTENDANCES
Best - v Toronto (L1 - 943)
Worst - v Gloucestershire All Golds (CC - 280)
Total (excluding Challenge Cup) - 6,291
Average (excluding Challenge Cup) - 572
(Down by 15 on 2016)

CLUB RECORDS	**Highest score:** 96-0 v Highfield, 20/3/94 **Highest score against:** 4-90 v Widnes, 10/6/2007
MATCH RECORDS	**Record attendance:** 10,000 v Bradford, 16/2/52 *(York Road)*; 6,528 v Castleford, 12/4/2007 *(Keepmoat Stadium)*
	Tries: 6 Kane Epati v Oldham, 30/7/2006; Lee Waterman v Sharlston, 24/3/2012
	Goals: 12 Tony Zelei v Nottingham City, 1/9/91; Robert Turner v Highfield, 20/3/94; Tom Carr v Hemel, 3/7/2016
	Points: 32 Tony Zelei v Nottingham City, 1/9/91; Lee Waterman v Sharlston, 24/3/2012
SEASON RECORDS	**Tries:** 36 Lee Waterman 2012 **Goals:** 129 Jonny Woodcock 2002 **Points:** 306 Jonny Woodcock 2002
CAREER RECORDS	**Tries:** 112 Mark Roache 1985-97 **Goals:** 850 David Noble 1976-77; 1980-89; 1992 **Points:** 1,751 David Noble 1976-77; 1980-89; 1992
	Appearances: 327 Audley Pennant 1980-83; 1985-97

GLOUCESTERSHIRE ALL GOLDS

DATE	FIXTURE	RESULT	SCORERS	LGE	ATT
19/2/17	Hemel (a) (L1CR1)	W12-48	t:Elliott,Kislingbury(2),Gaskell,Parry(2),Williams,Agoro,McClean g:Hyde(5),Stead	N/A	107
26/2/17	North Wales (h) (CCR3)	W36-18	t:Kislingbury(2),Gaskell,McClean,Kidd,Parry(2),Agoro g:Hyde(2)	N/A	87
5/3/17	Hunslet (a)	L10-6	t:Andrade g:Stead	10th	407
12/3/17	Keighley (h)	W46-22	t:Parry(2),Agoro(4),Mitchell,Elliott g:Hyde(5),Fallon(2)	6th	176
19/3/17	Doncaster (h) (CCR4) ●	L22-48	t:Barlow,Parry(2),Kislingbury g:Hyde(3)	N/A	280
26/3/17	Workington (a)	L54-22	t:Cowburn,McClean,Barlow,Agoro g:Hyde(3)	10th	509
1/4/17	Workington (h) (L1CQF) ●●	W30-22	t:Cowburn(2),Kidd,Parry,Barlow g:Hyde(5)	N/A	378
9/4/17	London Skolars (h)	L22-24	t:Parry,Agoro(2),McClean g:Hyde(3)	12th	179
14/4/17	South Wales (a)	W30-36	t:Agoro(3),Elliott,Cowburn,Kislingbury g:Hyde(6)	11th	351
30/4/17	North Wales (h) (L1CSF)	L28-37	t:Kislingbury,Agoro,Parry,Barlow,Kidd g:Hyde(2)	N/A	202
7/5/17	York (h)	L10-56	t:Parry,Kislingbury g:Ward	12th	180
13/5/17	North Wales (h)	W36-28	t:Reece(2),Agoro,Kidd(2),Brickhill g:Stead(6)	11th	201
21/5/17	Coventry (a)	W18-26	t:Mitchell,Agoro,Barlow,Nield,Kislingbury g:Stead(3)	10th	323
4/6/17	Newcastle (h)	L10-56	t:Kidd,Barlow g:Stead	11th	223
11/6/17	Whitehaven (a)	L62-6	t:Agoro g:Davies	13th	534
18/6/17	Hemel (a)	W20-32	t:Parry(2),Agoro,Kidd,Mitchell,Barlow g:Davies(4)	10th	102
25/6/17	Oxford (h)	W38-10	t:Agoro,Parry(2),Elliott,Barlow,Walter,Brickhill g:Davies(5)	9th	275
1/7/17	Barrow (a)	L36-6	t:Mitchell g:Davies	11th	696
8/7/17	Toronto (a)	L62-10	t:Parry,Reece g:Mitchell	11th	7,139
16/7/17	Doncaster (h)	L4-42	t:Agoro	12th	200
29/7/17	South Wales (a) (L1S) ●●●	L28-20	t:Kislingbury,Parry,Cowburn,McClean g:Stead(2)	4th(L1S)	212
5/8/17	North Wales (h) (L1S)	W40-22	t:Cowburn(2),Williams,Kidd,Barlow,Parry,Lloyd-Jones g:Mitchell(6)	4th(L1S)	211
12/8/17	Coventry (h) (L1S)	W30-28	t:Parry(2),Kidd,McClean,Mitchell g:Mitchell(5)	4th(L1S)	178
19/8/17	Hunslet (a) (L1S)	L32-18	t:Agoro,McClean,Parry g:Stead(3)	4th(L1S)	333
3/9/17	Oxford (h) (L1S)	L12-18	t:Cowburn,Kidd g:Stead(2)	4th(L1S)	202
9/9/17	London Skolars (a) (L1S)	L16-6	t:Kislingbury g:Stead	4th(L1S)	218
17/9/17	Hemel (h) (L1S)	W42-28	t:Elliott,Stead(2),Barlow,Cowburn,McClean,Parry g:Stead(7)	4th(L1S)	305

● *Played at Keepmoat Athletics Ground*
●● *Played at Derwent Park*
●●● *Played at Stebonheath Park, Llanelli*

APP TRIES GOALS FG PTS

	D.O.B.	ALL	L1	ALL	L1	ALL	L1	ALL	L1	ALL	L1
Mo Agoro	29/1/93	27	15	20	16	0	0	0	0	80	64
Jordan Andrade	24/1/92	(5)	(3)	1	1	0	0	0	0	4	4
Chris Barlow	24/10/95	24	13	11	5	0	0	0	0	44	20
Billy Brickhill	30/4/97	21(4)	11(4)	2	2	0	0	0	0	8	8
Errol Carter	22/1/96	2(2)	1(1)	0	0	0	0	0	0	0	0
Phil Cowburn	15/10/90	21	9	9	2	0	0	0	0	36	8
Courtney Davies	1/7/94	5	4	0	0	11	11	0	0	22	22
Harrison Elliott	16/3/92	19(7)	10(4)	5	3	0	0	0	0	20	12
Danny Fallon	26/7/95	13(3)	7(1)	0	0	2	2	0	0	4	4
Alex Gaskell	9/9/96	8(1)	2(1)	2	0	0	0	0	0	8	0
Brad Hargreaves	13/12/93	2(7)	1(5)	0	0	0	0	0	0	0	0
Josh Houghton	12/10/96	2(1)	1	0	0	0	0	0	0	0	0
Kieran Hyde	10/10/89	11	6	0	0	34	17	0	0	68	34
Adam Jones	13/4/97	1	1	0	0	0	0	0	0	0	0
Paddy Jones	7/2/97	(1)	(1)	0	0	0	0	0	0	0	0
Richard Jones	7/7/89	(7)	(5)	0	0	0	0	0	0	0	0
Harry Kidd	12/6/95	11(12)	6(5)	10	4	0	0	0	0	40	16
Brad Kislingbury	2/2/96	19	11	11	3	0	0	0	0	44	12
Malikhi Lloyd-Jones	29/8/94	5(18)	(12)	1	0	0	0	0	0	4	0
Jay Lobwein	13/4/92	(2)	(2)	0	0	0	0	0	0	0	0
James Mason	27/1/95	(2)		0	0	0	0	0	0	0	0
Joe McClean	10/8/89	24(2)	14	8	2	0	0	0	0	32	8
Jack Mitchell	16/3/95	19(2)	11(1)	5	4	12	1	0	0	44	18
Steven Nield	20/11/90	7	7	1	1	0	0	0	0	4	4
Graham O'Keeffe	13/5/91	1(3)	1(1)	0	0	0	0	0	0	0	0
Shaun Owens	29/11/88	2(1)	2(1)	0	0	0	0	0	0	0	0
Steve Parry	19/10/88	26(1)	15	23	9	0	0	0	0	92	36
Ross Price	14/12/92	(4)		0	0	0	0	0	0	0	0
Ollie Purslow	17/9/87	13(3)	9(2)	0	0	0	0	0	0	0	0
Lewis Reece	17/6/91	12(2)	8(1)	3	3	0	0	0	0	12	12
Ben Stead	13/10/92	10	4	2	0	27	11	0	0	62	22
Luke Stephens	21/11/96	1(5)	(3)	0	0	0	0	0	0	0	0
James Walter	11/9/91	12(7)	8(4)	1	1	0	0	0	0	4	4
Josh Ward	16/6/95	3(1)	2(1)	0	0	1	1	0	0	2	2
Kadeem Williams	23/3/95	7(4)	3(1)	2	0	0	0	0	0	8	0
Chris Worrall	11/10/96	24	14	0	0	0	0	0	0	0	0

'L1' totals include League 1 regular season only; 'All' totals also include League 1 Shield, League 1 Cup & Challenge Cup

Mo Agoro

LEAGUE RECORD
League 1, before Super 8 split:
P15-W6-D0-L9 (12th)
F310, A530, Diff-220, 12 points.

After League 1 Shield:
P22-W9-D0-L13 (4th)
F478, A702, Diff-224, 18 points.

LEAGUE 1 CUP
Semi-Finalists

CHALLENGE CUP
Round Four

ATTENDANCES
Best - v Hemel (L1S - 305)
Worst - v North Wales (CC - 87)
Total (excluding Challenge Cup) - 2,532
Average (excluding Challenge Cup) - 211
(Up by 77 on 2016)

CLUB RECORDS	
MATCH RECORDS	Highest score: 74-18 v Hemel, 14/8/2016 Highest score against: 6-82 v Salford, 21/4/2013 Record attendance: 867 v Salford, 21/4/2013
	Tries: 4 Joe McClean v Oxford, 10/7/2016; Brendon Newton v Hemel, 14/8/2016; Mo Agoro v Keighley, 12/3/2017
	Goals: 11 Kieran Hyde v Hemel, 14/8/2016 Points: 24 Matt Bradley v Coventry, 16/5/2015
SEASON RECORDS	Tries: 23 Steve Parry 2017 Goals: 76 Matt Bradley 2015 Points: 172 Matt Bradley 2015
CAREER RECORDS	Tries: 63 Steve Parry 2013-2017 Goals: 161 Matt Bradley 2013-2016 Points: 354 Matt Bradley 2013-2016 Appearances: 108 Phil Cowburn 2013-2017

HEMEL STAGS

DATE	FIXTURE	RESULT	SCORERS	LGE	ATT
19/2/17	Gloucestershire All Golds (h) (L1CR1)	L12-48	t:Burns,Jonas g:Coe(2)	N/A	107
26/2/17	London Skolars (h) (CCR3)	L12-22	t:Forde,Gregory g:Vincent(2)	N/A	112
5/3/17	Oxford (a)	L40-12	t:Richardson,Clavering g:Vincent(2)	13th	161
12/3/17	Hunslet (h)	L10-58	t:Burns,Forde g:Vincent	14th	155
25/3/17	Barrow (a)	L82-0		16th	739
9/4/17	Keighley (h)	L6-84	t:Elliott g:Vincent	16th	118
14/4/17	London Skolars (a)	L60-12	t:Vincent,Thornton g:Vincent(2)	16th	362
7/5/17	Workington (h)	L18-66	t:Nathaniel,Fairhurst,Whitehead g:Vincent(2),Fairhurst	16th	105
14/5/17	Doncaster (h)	L24-50	t:Whitehead,R Williams,Jowitt,Burns g:Vincent(4)	16th	102
21/5/17	Whitehaven (a)	L58-24	t:Burns(3),Whitehead g:Vincent(4)	16th	487
4/6/17	North Wales (h)	L20-26	t:A Williams,Whitehead,Tomlinson,Vincent g:Vincent,Barlow	16th	107
11/6/17	Coventry (a)	L28-24	t:Fairhurst(2),O'Brien,Jowitt g:Vincent(4)	16th	357
18/6/17	Gloucestershire All Golds (h)	L20-32	t:Elliott(2),Barlow g:Vincent(4)	16th	102
25/6/17	Newcastle (a)	L48-12	t:Casey,Burns g:Vincent(2)	16th	620
2/7/17	South Wales (h)	W25-18	t:Burns,Fairhurst,Fumhanda,Whitehead g:Vincent(4) fg:Vincent	16th	131
9/7/17	York (a)	L68-6	t:R Williams g:Vincent	16th	787
15/7/17	Toronto (a)	L74-16	t:Elliott,Barlow,O'Brien g:Vincent(2)	16th	7,247
30/7/17	Oxford (h) (L1S)	W32-26	t:Thornton,Hawksworth,Vincent,R Williams,O'Brien g:Vincent(6)	8th(L1S)	106
6/8/17	Coventry (a) (L1S)	L29-26	t:Welham,Vincent,Wray,Crowther,Bower g:Vincent(2),Fairhurst	8th(L1S)	256
13/8/17	South Wales (a) (L1S) ●	W4-22	t:A Williams,Vincent,Burns g:Lawton,Fairhurst(4)	7th(L1S)	192
20/8/17	North Wales (h) (L1S)	L18-38	t:R Williams,Burns,Welham g:Fairhurst(3)	7th(L1S)	114
3/9/17	London Skolars (a) (L1S)	L42-22	t:Barlow,Welham,Elliott,Thornton,A Williams g:Fairhurst	7th(L1S)	191
10/9/17	Hunslet (h) (L1S)	L16-60	t:Barlow(2),Welham g:Vincent(2)	7th(L1S)	135
17/9/17	Gloucestershire All Golds (a) (L1S)	L42-28	t:Fairhurst(2),O'Brien,Welham,Hawksworth g:Wray(4)	7th(L1S)	305

● *Played at Stebonheath Park, Llanelli*

		APP		TRIES		GOALS		FG		PTS	
	D.O.B.	ALL	L1	ALL	L1	ALL	L1	ALL	L1	ALL	L1
Rhys Allatt	1/1/98	2	2	0	0	0	0	0	0	0	0
Harley Axe	11/10/97	(3)	(3)	0	0	0	0	0	0	0	0
Mark Barlow	16/2/84	16(3)	9(2)	5	2	1	1	0	0	22	10
Mindu Bendikas	14/10/94	2	2	0	0	0	0	0	0	0	0
Connor Bower	18/1/97	6	0	1	0	0	0	0	0	4	0
Charlie Brown	15/9/97	1	1	0	0	0	0	0	0	0	0
Jono Burns	22/8/92	16(2)	12	10	7	0	0	0	0	40	28
Josh Casey	10/10/94	10	5	1	1	0	0	0	0	4	4
Brad Clavering	14/3/98	(1)	(1)	1	1	0	0	0	0	4	4
Liam Coe	19/4/94	1	0	0	0	2	0	0	0	4	0
Sam Crowther	21/10/86	(13)	(8)	1	0	0	0	0	0	4	0
Santino Decaro	2/2/95	(10)	(7)	0	0	0	0	0	0	0	0
Marcus Elliott	8/3/94	17(1)	12	5	4	0	0	0	0	20	16
Lewis Fairhurst	24/12/96	15	8	6	4	11	2	0	0	46	20
Darren Forde	8/1/96	18	14	2	1	0	0	0	0	8	4
Liam Frenneaux	17/2/93	1	0	0	0	0	0	0	0	0	0
Munashe Fumhanda	18/3/97	6(3)	4(2)	1	1	0	0	0	0	4	4
Declan Gregory	18/1/97	2(3)	2(2)	1	0	0	0	0	0	4	0
Josh Halliday	12/12/93	3	3	0	0	0	0	0	0	0	0
Corey Hanson	11/8/92	11(2)	10	0	0	0	0	0	0	0	0
Dan Hawksworth	22/6/91	14(1)	8(1)	2	0	0	0	0	0	8	0
Dom Horn	13/3/95	1(2)	1(1)	0	0	0	0	0	0	0	0
Aaron James	28/9/91	(4)	(3)	0	0	0	0	0	0	0	0
Casey Johnson	6/7/94	(1)	(1)	0	0	0	0	0	0	0	0
Roddy Jonas	8/4/90	4	2	1	0	0	0	0	0	4	0
Wayne Jowitt	13/2/84	8(14)	5(8)	2	2	0	0	0	0	8	8
Danny Lawton	10/3/90	12	6	0	0	1	0	0	0	2	0
Scott Lee	20/10/94	6(5)	6(2)	0	0	0	0	0	0	0	0
Ryan Matthews	12/7/92	2(1)	2(1)	0	0	0	0	0	0	0	0
George Milton	4/9/95	1	1	0	0	0	0	0	0	0	0
Josh Nathaniel	24/5/91	2	2	1	1	0	0	0	0	4	4
Jack O'Brien	9/2/93	15(4)	8(3)	4	2	0	0	0	0	16	8
Jorge Richardson	5/5/97	3	2	1	1	0	0	0	0	4	4
Danny Samuel	8/8/85	3(10)	2(6)	0	0	0	0	0	0	0	0
James Thornton	30/9/95	21(1)	13(1)	3	1	0	0	0	0	12	4
Declan Tomlinson	14/7/94	9(2)	7(2)	1	1	0	0	0	0	4	4
Mitch Vincent	14/3/94	20	14	5	2	45	33	1	1	111	75
Andy Walker	4/7/93	1	0	0	0	0	0	0	0	0	0
Matt Welham	1/2/93	6(1)	0	5	0	0	0	0	0	20	0
Ross White	7/8/90	5	3	0	0	0	0	0	0	0	0
Brett Whitehead	6/1/92	12(1)	10	5	5	0	0	0	0	20	20
Alex Williams	8/8/93	12(6)	7(4)	3	1	0	0	0	0	12	4
Reece Williams	28/2/95	21(2)	12(2)	4	2	0	0	0	0	16	8
Jack Wray	16/12/97	7	0	1	0	4	0	0	0	12	0

'L1' totals include League 1 regular season only; 'All' totals also include League 1 Shield, League 1 Cup & Challenge Cup

Mitch Vincent

LEAGUE RECORD
League 1, before Super 8 split:
P15-W1-D0-L14 (16th)
F229, A792, Diff-563, 2 points.

After League 1 Shield:
P22-W3-D0-L19 (7th)
F393, A1033, Diff-640, 6 points.

LEAGUE 1 CUP
Round One

CHALLENGE CUP
Round Three

ATTENDANCES
Best - v Hunslet (L1 - 155)
Worst - v Gloucestershire All Golds (L1 - 102)
Total (excluding Challenge Cup) - 1,282
Average (excluding Challenge Cup) - 116
(Down by 64 on 2016)

CLUB RECORDS MATCH RECORDS	Highest score: 52-24 v South Wales, 26/5/2013 Highest score against: 6-84 v Keighley, 9/4/2017 Record attendance: 679 v Oldham, 12/5/2013 Tries: 3 (4 players) Goals: 8 Mike Bishay v South Wales, 26/5/2013; Jy-mel Coleman v Oldham, 8/6/2014 Points: 16 Mike Bishay v South Wales, 26/5/2013; Jy-mel Coleman v Oldham, 8/6/2014; Mitch Vincent v Oxford, 30/7/2017
SEASON RECORDS CAREER RECORDS	Tries: 14 Alex Anthony 2015 Goals: 62 Barry-John Swindells 2014 Points: 160 Barry-John Swindells 2014 Tries: 19 Barry-John Swindells 2013-2016 Goals: 138 Barry-John Swindells 2013-2016 Points: 352 Barry-John Swindells 2013-2016 Appearances: 76 Barry-John Swindells 2013-2016

HUNSLET

DATE	FIXTURE	RESULT	SCORERS	LGE	ATT
19/2/17	Newcastle (h) (L1CR1)	L10-34	t:Normington,Mvududu g:Ansell	N/A	449
26/2/17	Coventry (h) (CCR3)	W34-0	t:Lee,Webb,Leeming(2),Gibson,Mackay g:Ansell(5)	N/A	249
5/3/17	Gloucestershire All Golds (h)	W10-6	t:Leeming,Ince g:Ansell	7th	407
12/3/17	Hemel (a)	W10-58	t:Ince(2),Walton,Leeming,Broughton,Flanagan(2),Watson,Webb,Wilson g:Ansell(9)	4th	155
19/3/17	Halifax (a) (CCR4)	L20-6	t:Ince g:Ansell	N/A	793
2/4/17	Doncaster (a)	L29-24	t:Duffy,Mvududu,Normington,Flanagan g:Ansell(4)	5th	604
9/4/17	South Wales (h)	W58-6	t:Webb,Mvududu,Normington(2),Wilson,Flanagan(3),Sanderson,Broughton g:Sanderson(9)	3rd	350
14/4/17	Keighley (a)	L20-12	t:Mvududu,Sanderson g:Sanderson(2)	3rd	744
30/4/17	Whitehaven (h)	L18-19	t:Normington,Flanagan,Webb g:Sanderson(3)	4th	382
7/5/17	North Wales (h)	W36-26	t:Watson,Tebb,Normington,Leeming,Flanagan(2),Ansell g:Sanderson(4)	4th	420
14/5/17	Oxford (a)	L24-22	t:Walker,Mackay,Leeming,Flanagan g:Sanderson(3)	6th	203
21/5/17	Workington (h)	W30-22	t:Watson,Flanagan,Leeming,Flynn,Reed g:Sanderson(5)	5th	388
3/6/17	Barrow (a)	L28-20	t:Hesketh,Ansell,Flanagan g:Ansell(4)	7th	913
11/6/17	York (h)	L20-52	t:Mackay,Hesketh,Hayward,Flanagan g:Gibson(2)	8th	589
24/6/17	Toronto (a)	L56-12	t:Mvududu,Flanagan g:Sanderson(2)	10th	6,042
2/7/17	Coventry (h)	W56-24	t:Flynn,Gibson,Mackay(2),Brierley,Flanagan(2),Mvududu,Lee,Coventry g:Sanderson(8)	9th	406
8/7/17	London Skolars (a)	L30-16	t:Coventry,Mvududu,Watson g:Sanderson(2)	10th	367
16/7/17	Newcastle (h)	W26-25	t:Cook,Watson,Flanagan(2) g:Sanderson(5)	10th	429
30/7/17	Coventry (h) (L1S)	W56-10	t:Teasdale,Mvududu(5),Watson,Duckworth,Flanagan,Williams g:Sanderson(8)	1st(L1S)	384
6/8/17	Oxford (a) (L1S)	W10-36	t:Nicholson(2),Flanagan,Leeming,Mackay,Normington g:Sanderson(6)	1st(L1S)	155
13/8/17	North Wales (a) (L1S)	L20-12	t:Sanderson,Mackay g:Sanderson(2)	1st(L1S)	306
19/8/17	Gloucestershire All Golds (h) (L1S)	W32-18	t:Sanderson(2),D Roberts,Watson(3) g:Sanderson(4)	1st(L1S)	333
3/9/17	South Wales (h) (L1S)	W64-7	t:Flynn,Mvududu(2),Reed,Flanagan(3),Gibson(2),Duckworth,Webb g:Sanderson(10)	2nd(L1S)	418
10/9/17	Hemel (a) (L1S)	W16-60	t:Reed,Leeming,Mackay(2),Mvududu(2),Walton,Nathaniel,Coventry,Flanagan g:Sanderson(10)	2nd(L1S)	135
17/9/17	London Skolars (h) (L1S)	W18-12	t:Webb,Sanderson,Flanagan g:Sanderson(3)	1st(L1S)	450
24/9/17	London Skolars (h) (L1SF)	W32-12	t:Mackay(2),Flanagan,Duckworth(2) g:Sanderson(6)	N/A	516

		APP		TRIES		GOALS		FG		PTS	
	D.O.B.	ALL	L1	ALL	L1	ALL	L1	ALL	L1	ALL	L1
Omar Alwari	31/8/89	1	0	0	0	0	0	0	0	0	0
Danny Ansell	9/10/91	15(3)	10(2)	2	2	25	18	0	0	58	44
Austin Bell	6/9/91	(1)	0	0	0	0	0	0	0	0	0
Tommy Brierley	8/9/96	4	4	1	1	0	0	0	0	4	4
Brooke Broughton	30/10/90	3(2)	3(2)	2	2	0	0	0	0	8	8
Matt Carbutt	3/10/85	9(4)	7(3)	0	0	0	0	0	0	0	0
Mathew Cook	28/6/94	4	3	1	1	0	0	0	0	4	4
Jack Coventry	5/3/94	5(12)	4(6)	3	2	0	0	0	0	12	8
James Duckworth	9/4/94	7	0	4	0	0	0	0	0	16	0
Gavin Duffy	9/4/87	4	3	1	1	0	0	0	0	4	4
George Flanagan	8/10/86	5(19)	(14)	26	18	0	0	0	0	104	72
Nyle Flynn	27/7/97	17(5)	9(3)	3	2	0	0	0	0	12	8
Luke Fowden	1/9/96	(1)	(1)	0	0	0	0	0	0	0	0
Joel Gibson	8/9/90	15(1)	8(1)	4	1	2	2	0	0	20	8
Michael Haley	19/9/87	7(11)	4(5)	0	0	0	0	0	0	0	0
Michael Hayward	2/9/88	2	2	1	1	0	0	0	0	4	4
Sean Hesketh	17/8/86	5(4)	3(4)	2	2	0	0	0	0	8	8
Ryan Ince	16/9/96	7	4	4	3	0	0	0	0	16	12
Jose Kenga	3/5/95	(11)	(6)	0	0	0	0	0	0	0	0
Jack Lee	1/11/88	13	11	2	1	0	0	0	0	8	4
Cameron Leeming	3/7/95	17(1)	9(1)	9	5	0	0	0	0	36	20
Liam Mackay	26/10/90	22(1)	11(1)	11	4	0	0	0	0	44	16
Mufaro Mvududu	29/8/91	22(1)	12(1)	16	6	0	0	0	0	64	24
Josh Nathaniel	24/5/91	5	4	1	0	0	0	0	0	4	0
Matt Nicholson	11/9/91	8(2)	1(2)	2	0	0	0	0	0	8	0
Jack Norfolk	14/10/96	2	1	0	0	0	0	0	0	0	0
Jake Normington	11/10/91	16	10	7	5	0	0	0	0	28	20
Trae O'Sullivan	7/9/96	2	2	0	0	0	0	0	0	0	0
Lewis Reed	24/3/91	19	12	3	1	0	0	0	0	12	4
Dean Roberts	19/8/96	1(6)	0	1	0	0	0	0	0	4	0
Shaun Roberts	26/2/93	3(1)	2	0	0	0	0	0	0	0	0
Joe Sanderson	17/3/97	19(1)	10	6	2	92	43	0	0	208	94
Luke Teasdale	8/6/94	4	0	1	0	0	0	0	0	4	0
Matthew Tebb	4/9/90	4(3)	4(1)	1	1	0	0	0	0	4	4
Danny Thomas	21/12/83	1	0	0	0	0	0	0	0	0	0
Niall Walker	21/4/97	1	1	1	1	0	0	0	0	4	4
Jack Walton	7/5/95	6(9)	4(4)	2	1	0	0	0	0	8	4
Jimmy Watson	9/9/91	25	15	9	5	0	0	0	0	36	20
Marcus Webb	11/1/97	18	9	6	3	0	0	0	0	24	12
Brett Whitehead	6/1/92	(1)	(1)	0	0	0	0	0	0	0	0
Daniel Williams	26/8/89	4(4)	(2)	1	0	0	0	0	0	4	0
Aston Wilson	23/10/90	16	13	2	2	0	0	0	0	8	8

George Flanagan

'L1' totals include League 1 regular season only; 'All' totals also include League 1 Shield, League 1 Cup & Challenge Cup

LEAGUE RECORD
League 1, before Super 8 split:
P15-W7-D0-L8 (10th)
F418, A377, Diff+41, 14 points.

After League 1 Shield:
P22-W13-D0-L9 (1st/Winners)
F696, A470, Diff+226, 26 points.

LEAGUE 1 CUP
Round One

CHALLENGE CUP
Round Four

ATTENDANCES
Best - v York (L1 - 589)
Worst - v Coventry (CC - 249)
Total (excluding Challenge Cup) - 5,921
Average (excluding Challenge Cup) - 423
(Down by 29 on 2016)

CLUB RECORDS
Highest score: 82-0 v Highfield, 21/1/96 **Highest score against:** 0-82 v Bradford, 2/3/2003
MATCH RECORDS **Record attendance:** 24,700 v Wigan, 15/3/24 *(Parkside)*; 2,454 v Wakefield, 13/4/98 *(South Leeds Stadium)*
Tries: 7 George Dennis v Bradford, 20/1/34 **Goals:** 12 Billy Langton v Keighley, 18/8/59 **Points:** 30 Simon Wilson v Highfield, 21/1/96
SEASON RECORDS **Tries:** 34 Alan Snowden 1956-57 **Goals:** 181 Billy Langton 1958-59 **Points:** 380 Billy Langton 1958-59
CAREER RECORDS **Tries:** 154 Fred Williamson 1943-55 **Goals:** 1,044 Billy Langton 1955-66 **Points:** 2,202 Billy Langton 1955-66 **Appearances:** 579 Geoff Gunney 1951-73

KEIGHLEY COUGARS

DATE	FIXTURE	RESULT	SCORERS	LGE	ATT
19/2/17	Doncaster (h) (L1CR1)	W30-22	t:Ryder,Gabriel(2),Welsh,Kelly,Whittel g:Beharrell(3)	N/A	520
25/2/17	Fryston (a) (CCR3) ●	W32-50	t:Feather,Tonks,Lawton,Kelly(2),Ryder,Rawlins,Gabriel,Hawkyard g:Beharrell(7)	N/A	739
5/3/17	North Wales (h)	W50-8	t:Gabriel(2),Ryder(2),Beharrell(2),Tonks,Finigan,Lawton g:Beharrell(2),Lawton(5)	2nd	752
12/3/17	Gloucestershire All Golds (a)	L46-22	t:Ryder,Tonks,Feather,Milner g:Lawton(3)	7th	176
18/3/17	Barrow (a) (CCR4)	L20-0		N/A	721
26/3/17	Toronto (h)	L21-48	t:Lynam(2),Beharrell g:Beharrell(4) fg:Beharrell	9th	1,128
2/4/17	Barrow (a) (L1CQF)	L28-6	t:Brook g:Beharrell	N/A	828
9/4/17	Hemel (a)	W6-84	t:Gabriel(3),Ryder(4),Tonks,Feather,Beharrell,Rawlins(3),Hawkyard,Nicholson, Emmett g:Beharrell(10)	6th	118
14/4/17	Hunslet (h)	W20-12	t:Ryder,Nicholson(2) g:Beharrell(4)	4th	744
7/5/17	Coventry (a)	W24-44	t:Emmett,Barnes,Gabriel,Nicholson,Aaronson,Law,Rawlins,Milner g:Beharrell(6)	5th	383
10/5/17	Barrow (h)	L42-58	t:Rawlins(2),Bailey,Whittel,Aaronson,Law,Emmett g:Beharrell(7)	7th	728
21/5/17	Doncaster (a)	L28-14	t:Conroy,Ryder(2) g:Beharrell	8th	516
3/6/17	South Wales (h)	W74-6	t:Gabriel(2),Darville(4),Ryder,Nicholson,Dixon(2),Tonks(2),Law g:Beharrell(11)	6th	532
11/6/17	Newcastle (a)	L36-12	t:Ryder,Finigan g:Beharrell(2)	7th	786
18/6/17	London Skolars (h)	W45-26	t:Dixon(2),Bailey,Aaronson,Emmett,Beharrell,Feather,Conroy g:Beharrell(6) fg:Beharrell	6th	457
25/6/17	York (h)	L18-25	t:Nicholson,Dixon(2),Gabriel g:Beharrell	7th	927
2/7/17	Whitehaven (a)	L28-22	t:Brook,Nicholson,Gabriel,Feather g:Beharrell(3)	8th	704
9/7/17	Workington (a)	D30-30	t:Gabriel(2),Hawkyard,Kelly(2),Ryder g:Beharrell(3)	8th	581
16/7/17	Oxford (h)	W92-6	t:Emmett,Rawlins,Feather,Barnes(4),Nicholson(2),Ryder,Lynam(2), Hawkyard(2),Aaronson(2) g:Beharrell(14)	7th	670
30/7/17	Doncaster (a) (S8)	W24-32	t:Bailey(2),Gabriel,Ryder,Beharrell g:Beharrell(6)	7th	501
6/8/17	York (h) (S8)	W22-20	t:Gabriel(2),Finigan,Feather g:Beharrell(3)	6th	1,362
13/8/17	Toronto (h) (S8)	D26-26	t:Barnes,Finigan(2),Hawkyard g:Beharrell(5)	6th	922
20/8/17	Whitehaven (a) (S8)	L36-4	t:Gabriel	6th	562
3/9/17	Newcastle (a) (S8)	L34-8	t:Rawlins,Ryder	6th	791
10/9/17	Workington (h) (S8)	W28-6	t:Feather,Bailey,Lynam,Tonks,Hawkyard g:Beharrell(4)	6th	661
17/9/17	Barrow (a) (S8)	L32-18	t:Cherryholme,Dixon,Gabriel g:Beharrell(3)	7th	1,007

● *Played at BigFellas Stadium, Featherstone*

		APP		TRIES		GOALS		FG		PTS	
	D.O.B.	ALL	L1	ALL	L1	ALL	L1	ALL	L1	ALL	L1
Harry Aaronson	28/3/98	8(7)	7(7)	5	5	0	0	0	0	20	20
Matthew Bailey	1/12/91	17(7)	16(6)	5	5	0	0	0	0	20	20
Hamish Barnes	22/5/92	11	11	6	6	0	0	0	0	24	24
Matty Beharrell	29/3/94	26	22	5	5	106	95	2	2	234	212
Adam Brook	29/9/94	10(4)	10(2)	2	1	0	0	0	0	8	4
James Brown	6/5/88	(1)	(1)	0	0	0	0	0	0	0	0
Josh Casey	10/10/94	1	1	0	0	0	0	0	0	0	0
Neil Cherryholme	20/12/86	9	9	1	1	0	0	0	0	4	4
Nathan Conroy	6/3/95	6(13)	6(13)	2	2	0	0	0	0	8	8
Liam Darville	7/7/94	6(1)	6(1)	4	4	0	0	0	0	16	16
Davey Dixon	31/5/97	19	16	7	7	0	0	0	0	28	28
Mike Emmett	13/5/87	24(2)	20(2)	5	5	0	0	0	0	20	20
James Feather	15/4/84	19(3)	15(3)	7	7	0	0	0	0	32	28
Vinny Finigan	4/8/89	14	12	5	5	0	0	0	0	20	20
Andy Gabriel	21/12/93	24	20	20	17	0	0	0	0	80	68
Ritchie Hawkyard	21/1/86	16(1)	13(1)	7	6	0	0	0	0	28	24
Sean Kelly	2/4/91	2(5)	2(3)	5	2	0	0	0	0	20	8
Nathan Kitson	11/12/88	(2)	(1)	0	0	0	0	0	0	0	0
Scott Law	19/2/85	11(4)	8(4)	3	3	0	0	0	0	12	12
Danny Lawton	10/3/90	5	2	2	1	8	8	0	0	24	20
Josh Lynam	16/2/93	13(6)	9(6)	5	5	0	0	0	0	20	20
Will Milner	28/10/94	13	9	2	2	0	0	0	0	8	8
Brad Nicholson	20/8/95	3(19)	3(16)	9	9	0	0	0	0	36	36
Trae O'Sullivan	7/9/96	2(4)	2(4)	0	0	0	0	0	0	0	0
Brendon Rawlins	28/1/86	14(11)	12(9)	10	9	0	0	0	0	40	36
Gavin Reed	12/11/94	(3)	(3)	0	0	0	0	0	0	0	0
Adam Ryder	20/10/89	26	22	18	16	0	0	0	0	72	64
Ben Sagar	19/12/89	10(2)	10(1)	0	0	0	0	0	0	0	0
Aidan Scully	16/5/92	1	1	0	0	0	0	0	0	0	0
Josh Tonks	14/8/91	20	16	7	6	0	0	0	0	28	24
Fran Welsh	9/11/92	3(3)	1(1)	1	0	0	0	0	0	4	0
Emmerson Whittel	13/9/94	5(6)	5(4)	2	1	0	0	0	0	8	4

'L1' totals include Super 8s; 'All' totals also include League 1 Cup & Challenge Cup

Andy Gabriel

LEAGUE RECORD
P22-W10-D2-L10 (7th)
F728, A565, Diff+163, 22 points.

LEAGUE 1 CUP
Quarter Finalists

CHALLENGE CUP
Round Four

ATTENDANCES
Best - v York (S8 - 1,362)
Worst - v London Skolars (L1 - 457)
Total (all home games included) - 9,403
Average (all home games included) - 784
(Up by 209 on 2016)

CLUB RECORDS MATCH RECORDS	**Highest score:** 104-4 v Highfield, 23/4/95 **Highest score against:** 2-92 v Leigh, 30/4/86 **Record attendance:** 14,500 v Halifax, 3/3/51 **Tries:** 6 Jason Critchley v Widnes, 18/8/96 **Goals:** 15 John Wasyliw v Nottingham City, 1/11/92; Martyn Wood v Lancashire Lynx, 1/5/2000 **Points:** 36 John Wasyliw v Nottingham City, 1/11/92
SEASON RECORDS CAREER RECORDS	**Tries:** 45 Nick Pinkney 1994-95 **Goals:** 187 John Wasyliw 1992-93 **Points:** 490 John Wasyliw 1992-93 **Tries:** 155 Sam Stacey 1904-20 **Goals:** 967 Brian Jefferson 1965-77 **Points:** 2,116 Brian Jefferson 1965-77 **Appearances:** 372 Hartley Tempest 1902-15; David McGoun 1925-38

LONDON SKOLARS

DATE	FIXTURE	RESULT	SCORERS	LGE	ATT
19/2/17	South Wales (a) (L1CR1)	W16-24	t:Mbaraga,Juma,Robinson,Nash g:C Lawrence(4)	N/A	122
26/2/17	Hemel (a) (CCR3)	W12-22	t:Bryan,Driver,Small,Martin g:C Lawrence(3)	N/A	112
4/3/17	Toronto (h)	L0-76		16th	1,524
12/3/17	Newcastle (a)	L24-22	t:Nash,Small,Bryan g:Lyon(4),Nash	15th	607
18/3/17	Swinton (a) (CCR4)	L40-8	t:Nash(2)	N/A	200
25/3/17	Coventry (h)	W42-16	t:Driver,Bryan,Mbaraga,Allison(2),Pointer,C Lawrence,Pickersgill g:C Lawrence(5)	12th	287
1/4/17	Oxford (a) (L1CQF)	L24-20	t:Allison,Mbaraga,Pointer,C Lawrence g:C Lawrence(2)	N/A	105
9/4/17	Gloucestershire All Golds (a)	W22-24	t:Brown(2),Robinson,Adebiyi g:C Lawrence(3) fg:C Lawrence(2)	10th	179
14/4/17	Hemel (h)	W60-12	t:Chester,Nash(4),Lyon,Bryan,Robinson,Pickersgill,Dollapi,Sykes,Mbaraga g:C Lawrence(6)	6th	362
7/5/17	Doncaster (a)	D28-28	t:Nash,Pointer,Adebiyi(2),D Williams g:Jy-mel Coleman(4)	6th	564
13/5/17	Whitehaven (h)	L14-28	t:Allison,Hill,Adebiyi g:Jy-mel Coleman	9th	335
21/5/17	North Wales (a)	L50-10	t:Pointer,Brown g:Jy-mel Coleman	11th	273
4/6/17	York (a)	L36-18	t:Sykes,Allison,Adebiyi g:Jy-mel Coleman(3)	13th	782
10/6/17	Oxford (h)	W31-18	t:Pointer(2),Adebiyi,Bishay,Bustin g:Jy-mel Coleman(5) fg:Jy-mel Coleman	10th	291
18/6/17	Keighley (a)	L45-26	t:D Williams,Driver(2),Bryan,Brown g:Jy-mel Coleman(3)	11th	457
24/6/17	Barrow (h)	L10-20	t:Bryan,Allison g:Jy-mel Coleman	12th	374
2/7/17	Workington (a)	L46-16	t:Robinson,Jy-mel Coleman,Winfield g:Jy-mel Coleman(2)	12th	479
8/7/17	Hunslet (h)	W30-16	t:Nash(2),Hill,Bishay,Bryan g:Jy-mel Coleman(5)	12th	367
16/7/17	South Wales (h)	W36-16	t:C Lawrence,Driver,D Williams(2),Allison(2),Bryan g:Jy-mel Coleman(2),C Lawrence(2)	11th	225
30/7/17	North Wales (a) (L1S)	W12-40	t:Mbaraga(2),Nash,Robinson,Jy-mel Coleman,Sykes,Lyon g:Jy-mel Coleman(6)	2nd(L1S)	268
12/8/17	Oxford (h) (L1S)	W66-0	t:Melling(3),Jy-mel Coleman,Mbaraga(2),Allison(2),Bishay(2),Faturoti g:Jy-mel Coleman(11)	2nd(L1S)	218
20/8/17	Coventry (a) (L1S)	W14-50	t:Sykes,Bishay(2),D Williams,Robinson,Mbaraga,Jermaine Coleman,Allison,Faturoti g:Jy-mel Coleman(7)	2nd(L1S)	268
25/8/17	South Wales (h) (L1S)	W32-4	t:Ogden(2),Robinson,Chester,Sykes,Allison g:Jy-mel Coleman(2),A Lawrence(2)	1st(L1S)	1,020
3/9/17	Hemel (h) (L1S)	W42-22	t:Allison,Chester,Pointer,Junor,Ogden,D Williams,Brown,Bishay g:Jy-mel Coleman(5)	1st(L1S)	191
9/9/17	Gloucestershire All Golds (h) (L1S)	W16-6	t:Bishay,Junor g:Jy-mel Coleman(4)	1st(L1S)	218
17/9/17	Hunslet (a) (L1S)	L18-12	t:Mbaraga,Ogden g:Jy-mel Coleman(2)	2nd(L1S)	450
24/9/17	Hunslet (a) (L1SF)	L32-12	t:Bryan,Brown g:Jy-mel Coleman(2)	N/A	516

		APP		TRIES		GOALS		FG		PTS	
	D.O.B.	ALL	L1	ALL	L1	ALL	L1	ALL	L1	ALL	L1
Sadiq Adebiyi	8/1/97	(8)	(7)	6	6	0	0	0	0	24	24
Josh Allison	5/4/93	21(1)	13	13	7	0	0	0	0	52	28
Mike Bishay	8/2/93	17	7	8	2	0	0	0	0	32	8
Michael Brown	9/9/86	23	14	6	4	0	0	0	0	24	16
Lamont Bryan	12/4/88	22(2)	12(1)	9	7	0	0	0	0	36	28
Callum Bustin	12/8/97	9(3)	7(2)	1	1	0	0	0	0	4	4
Rob Butler	15/5/98	3	0	0	0	0	0	0	0	0	0
Ryan Chester	19/3/92	23(1)	13	3	1	0	0	0	0	12	4
Jermaine Coleman	17/6/82	12(3)	6(1)	1	0	0	0	0	0	4	0
Jy-mel Coleman	13/10/88	18	10	3	1	66	27	1	1	145	59
Matt Davis	5/7/96	2(1)	2	0	0	0	0	0	0	0	0
Erjon Dollapi	16/3/93	3(5)	3(5)	1	1	0	0	0	0	4	4
Billy Driver	18/9/90	8(8)	4(8)	5	4	0	0	0	0	20	16
Kazeem Faturoti	22/10/93	(7)	(2)	2	0	0	0	0	0	8	0
Matty Gee	12/12/94	1	1	0	0	0	0	0	0	0	0
Mike Greenhalgh	8/6/94	7(11)	6(4)	0	0	0	0	0	0	0	0
James Hill	11/6/93	9	6	2	2	0	0	0	0	8	8
Josh I'Anson	7/9/94	1	0	0	0	0	0	0	0	0	0
Lameck Juma	6/12/90	15	9	1	0	0	0	0	0	4	0
Smokie Junor	15/4/90	5	0	2	0	0	0	0	0	8	0
Alfie Lawrence	5/10/97	(1)	0	0	0	2	0	0	0	4	0
Charlie Lawrence	6/10/94	23	12	3	2	25	16	2	2	64	42
Phil Lyon	21/3/92	5(7)	3(1)	2	1	4	4	0	0	16	12
Will Martin	28/12/93	1(3)	(2)	1	0	0	0	0	0	4	0
Eddie Mbaraga	9/9/87	16(4)	6(3)	10	2	0	0	0	0	40	8
Jake Melling	25/6/94	16(1)	10(1)	3	0	0	0	0	0	12	0
Sam Nash	1/5/89	19	13	12	8	1	1	0	0	50	34
Jake Ogden	23/1/98	5	0	4	0	0	0	0	0	16	0
John Paxton	20/4/85	2	2	0	0	0	0	0	0	0	0
Kameron Pearce-Paul	28/2/97	6	5	0	0	0	0	0	0	0	0
Brandon Pickersgill	29/3/97	4	2	2	2	0	0	0	0	8	8
Ben Pointer	25/5/96	5(6)	4(4)	7	5	0	0	0	0	28	20
Ollie Purslow	17/9/87	1(1)	0	0	0	0	0	0	0	0	0
Louis Robinson	9/1/91	(22)	(10)	7	3	0	0	0	0	28	12
Aaron Small	28/10/91	2	1	2	1	0	0	0	0	8	4
Michael Sykes	10/12/86	14(5)	6(3)	5	2	0	0	0	0	20	8
Keenen Tomlinson	22/5/97	2(1)	1	0	0	0	0	0	0	0	0
Simona Vavega	28/7/88	6(4)	4(3)	0	0	0	0	0	0	0	0
Dave Williams	29/1/87	21	11	6	4	0	0	0	0	24	16
Jordan Williams	4/6/97	(2)	(2)	0	0	0	0	0	0	0	0
Andy Winfield	8/7/91	4(1)	2(1)	1	1	0	0	0	0	4	4

Eddie Mbaraga

LEAGUE RECORD
League 1, before Super 8 split:
P15-W6-D1-L8 (11th)
F367, A453, Diff-86, 13 points.

After League 1 Shield:
P22-W12-D1-L9 (2nd/Runners-Up)
F625, A529, Diff+96, 25 points.

LEAGUE 1 CUP
Quarter Finalists

CHALLENGE CUP
Round Four

ATTENDANCES
Best - v Toronto (L1 - 1,524)
Worst - v Hemel (L1S - 191)
Total (all home games included) - 5,412
Average (all home games
included) - 451
(Up by 53 on 2016)

'L1' totals include League 1 regular season only; 'All' totals also include League 1 Shield, League 1 Cup & Challenge Cup

CLUB RECORDS	**Highest score:** 70-28 v St Albans, 19/3/2006 **Highest score against:** 4-98 v Sheffield, 3/8/2003 **Record attendance:** 1,524 v Toronto, 4/3/2017
MATCH RECORDS	**Tries:** 5 Mark Cantoni v Gateshead, 27/6/2004 **Goals:** 11 Jy-mel Coleman v Oxford, 12/8/2017 **Points:** 28 Dylan Skee v South Wales, 29/7/2012
SEASON RECORDS	**Tries:** 20 Mark Cantoni 2004; James Anthony 2013 **Goals:** 100 Dylan Skee 2013 **Points:** 248 Dylan Skee 2013
CAREER RECORDS	**Tries:** 57 Austen Aggrey 2004-2012 **Goals:** 230 *(inc 1fg)* Dylan Skee 2011-2013 **Points:** 579 Dylan Skee 2011-2013 **Appearances:** 198 Gareth Honor 2003-2011

NEWCASTLE THUNDER

DATE	FIXTURE	RESULT	SCORERS	LGE	ATT
19/2/17	Hunslet (a) (L1CR1)	W10-34	t:Blair,Craig,Olpherts,R Clarke,Young,Rennie,Simons g:Hardcastle(3)	N/A	449
25/2/17	Workington (h) (CCR3)	W18-16	t:Young,J Aldous,Olpherts g:Hardcastle(3)	N/A	400
5/3/17	Workington (a)	W20-24	t:Simons(2),Blair g:Hardcastle(6)	8th	660
12/3/17	London Skolars (h)	W24-22	t:Waller,Nicklas,Olpherts,Blair(2) g:Hardcastle(2)	5th	607
17/3/17	Dewsbury (a) (CCR4)	L36-8	t:Craig,Olpherts	N/A	425
26/3/17	South Wales (a)	W20-26	t:Rennie,Parker,Craig,Olpherts g:Hardcastle(5)	3rd	150
2/4/17	North Wales (h) (L1CQF)	L16-24	t:Olpherts(2),Nicklas g:Hardcastle(2)	N/A	345
9/4/17	North Wales (a)	L30-14	t:Young,Blair,Hardcastle g:Hardcastle	4th	323
14/4/17	Barrow (h)	L6-50	t:Shaw g:Hardcastle	8th	1,073
7/5/17	Whitehaven (a)	L34-20	t:Blair,R Clarke,Brown g:Hardcastle(4)	10th	425
12/5/17	Toronto (h)	L22-40	t:Z Clark,Nicklas,Young,Simons g:Hardcastle(3)	12th	1,087
19/5/17	York (h)	L18-22	t:Olpherts,Hardcastle(2) g:Hardcastle(3)	12th	2,111
4/6/17	Gloucestershire All Golds (a)	W10-56	t:Brown,Blair(2),Olpherts(3),Young,Nicklas,R Clarke,Luckley g:Hardcastle(7),Parker	9th	223
11/6/17	Keighley (h)	W36-12	t:Young(3),Blair(2),Brown,Hardcastle g:Hardcastle,Parker(3)	9th	786
18/6/17	Oxford (a)	W0-52	t:Young(3),Olpherts,Hardcastle(2),Teroi,Snitch g:Hardcastle(10)	7th	120
25/6/17	Hemel (h)	W48-12	t:Brown(2),Snitch,Young,Hardcastle,Simons,Blair,Barron,Olpherts g:Hardcastle(6)	5th	620
2/7/17	Doncaster (a) ●	W10-20	t:Parker,Olpherts,Young g:Hardcastle(3) fg:Hardcastle(2)	5th	550
9/7/17	Coventry (h)	W68-20	t:Craig,McAvoy,Nicklas(2),J Aldous,Parker,Young,Simons,Snitch,Hardcastle,R Clarke,Olpherts g:Hardcastle(10)	5th	567
16/7/17	Hunslet (a)	L26-25	t:Young(2),Snitch,Hardcastle g:Hardcastle(4) fg:Hardcastle	6th	429
30/7/17	Workington (h) (S8)	L14-30	t:Craig,Waller g:Hardcastle(3)	6th	655
6/8/17	Whitehaven (h) (S8)	L27-6	t:Simons g:Hardcastle	7th	539
12/8/17	Barrow (h) (S8)	L28-30	t:Hardcastle(2),Barron,Young,Brown g:Hardcastle(4)	7th	850
19/8/17	Toronto (a) (S8)	L50-0		8th	7,522
3/9/17	Keighley (h) (S8)	W34-8	t:Blair(2),Olpherts,McAvoy,Bielby g:Hardcastle(7)	7th	791
10/9/17	Doncaster (a) (S8)	W24-28	t:Olpherts,McAvoy,Rennie,Young,Simons g:Hardcastle(4)	7th	536
17/9/17	York (a) (S8)	W24-26	t:Simons,Shaw(2),Teroi,Olpherts g:Hardcastle(3)	5th	1,181
24/9/17	Barrow (a) (SF)	L60-0		N/A	1,090

● Played at Keepmoat Athletics Ground

		APP		TRIES		GOALS		FG		PTS	
	D.O.B.	ALL	L1	ALL	L1	ALL	L1	ALL	L1	ALL	L1
Harry Aldous	19/11/95	25	21	0	0	0	0	0	0	0	0
Jack Aldous	3/4/91	21(1)	17(1)	2	1	0	0	0	0	8	4
Matt Barron	17/11/86	2(13)	2(11)	2	2	0	0	0	0	8	8
Adam Bielby	13/10/98	1	1	1	1	0	0	0	0	4	4
Ali Blair	21/2/90	22	20	13	12	0	0	0	0	52	48
Joe Brown	24/4/87	26	22	6	6	0	0	0	0	24	24
Callum Bustin	12/8/97	5(6)	5(6)	0	0	0	0	0	0	0	0
Zach Clark	28/12/95	3	3	1	1	0	0	0	0	4	4
Rhys Clarke	12/3/91	21(4)	17(4)	4	3	0	0	0	0	16	12
Tyler Craig	4/7/93	12	10	5	3	0	0	0	0	20	12
Peter Fox	5/11/83	10	7	0	0	0	0	0	0	0	0
Benn Hardcastle	4/1/90	27	23	11	11	96	88	3	3	239	223
Corbyn Kilday	17/11/94	3(4)	1(2)	0	0	0	0	0	0	0	0
Sam Luckley	29/11/95	2(16)	2(15)	1	1	0	0	0	0	4	4
Liam McAvoy	24/9/93	24(1)	21(1)	3	3	0	0	0	0	12	12
George Milton	4/9/95	(2)	(2)	0	0	0	0	0	0	0	0
Danny Nicklas	29/6/91	12(4)	8(4)	6	5	0	0	0	0	24	20
Derrell Olpherts	7/1/92	24	20	18	13	0	0	0	0	72	52
Dan Parker	11/3/93	18(1)	17	3	3	4	4	0	0	20	20
Lee Paterson	5/7/81	3(2)	3(2)	0	0	0	0	0	0	0	0
Vincent Rennie	7/6/94	8(19)	7(16)	3	2	0	0	0	0	12	8
Tom Shaw	19/11/93	11	11	3	3	0	0	0	0	12	12
Evan Simons	11/10/91	24(2)	21(1)	9	8	0	0	0	0	36	32
Jared Simpson	4/1/96	2	2	0	0	0	0	0	0	0	0
Steve Snitch	22/2/83	12	12	4	4	0	0	0	0	16	16
Josh Stoker	26/7/92	(4)	(3)	0	0	0	0	0	0	0	0
Aaron Teroi	2/10/95	4(17)	3(14)	2	2	0	0	0	0	8	8
Dan Turland	11/1/94	1(1)	1(1)	0	0	0	0	0	0	0	0
Brett Waller	3/7/87	4(10)	2(9)	2	2	0	0	0	0	8	8
Mikey Wood	18/4/96	(1)	(1)	0	0	0	0	0	0	0	0
Lewis Young	1/7/95	24	21	18	16	0	0	0	0	72	64

'L1' totals include Super 8s & play-offs; 'All' totals also include League 1 Cup & Challenge Cup

Lewis Young

LEAGUE RECORD
P22-W12-D0-L10 (5th/Semi-Finalists)
F595, A521, Diff+74, 24 points.

LEAGUE 1 CUP
Quarter Finalists

CHALLENGE CUP
Round Four

ATTENDANCES
Best - v York (L1 - 2,111)
Worst - v North Wales (L1CQF - 345)
Total (excluding Challenge Cup) - 9,492
Average (excluding Challenge Cup) - 863
(Up to 53 on 2016)

CLUB RECORDS	**Highest score:** 68-20 v Coventry, 9/7/2017 **Highest score against:** 0-132 v Blackpool Panthers, 16/5/2010 **Record attendance:** 6,631 v Bradford, 16/5/99
MATCH RECORDS	**Tries:** 5 Andy Walker v London Skolars, 22/6/2003 **Goals:** 11 Ian Herron v Wakefield, 5/9/99 **Points:** 28 Benn Hardcastle v Oxford, 18/6/2017
SEASON RECORDS	**Tries:** 25 Matt Daylight 1999 **Goals:** 129 *(inc 1fg)* Dan Russell 2008 **Points:** 293 Dan Russell 2008
CAREER RECORDS	**Tries:** 74 Kevin Neighbour 2001-2006; 2008-2010 **Goals:** 283 *(inc 8fg)* Benn Hardcastle 2013-2017 **Points:** 682 Benn Hardcastle 2013-2017
	Appearances: 218 Robin Peers 2002-2012

NORTH WALES CRUSADERS

DATE	FIXTURE	RESULT	SCORERS	LGE	ATT
19/2/17	York (a) (L1CR1)	W16-17	t:Bloomfield,Johnson,Price g:Johnson(2) fg:Hansen	N/A	620
		(aet)			
26/2/17	Gloucestershire All Golds (a) (CCR3)	L36-18	t:Hurst,Dandy(2),Mulkeen g:Johnson	N/A	87
5/3/17	Keighley (a)	L50-8	t:Hurst,Johnson	15th	752
12/3/17	Doncaster (h)	L8-44	t:Bloomfield,Hurst	16th	305
26/3/17	York (a)	W22-26	t:Mulkeen,Davidson,Hurst,Smith,Bloomfield g:Johnson(3)	13th	702
2/4/17	Newcastle (a) (L1CQF)	W16-24	t:Lee,Houghton(2),Johnson g:Johnson(4)	N/A	345
9/4/17	Newcastle (h)	W30-14	t:A Thompson,Atherton,Johnson,Hudson,Houghton g:Johnson(5)	11th	323
14/4/17	Toronto (h)	L0-80		13th	590
30/4/17	Gloucestershire All Golds (a) (L1CSF)	W28-37	t:Davidson,Price(2),Warburton,Atherton,Johnson g:Johnson(6) fg:Smith	N/A	202
7/5/17	Hunslet (h)	L36-26	t:Smith,Price,Millington,Hurst,Hansen g:Johnson(3)	13th	420
13/5/17	Gloucestershire All Golds (a)	L36-28	t:Smith,Hurst(2),Dandy,A Thompson g:Johnson(4)	13th	201
21/5/17	London Skolars (h)	W50-10	t:Smith(3),Atherton,Moore(2),Warburton,Lee,Bloomfield g:Price(7)	13th	273
27/5/17	Barrow (L1CF) ●	L38-32	t:Houghton,Bloomfield,Hansen,Mulkeen,Smith g:Johnson(6)	N/A	N/A
4/6/17	Hemel (a)	W20-26	t:Atherton(2),Warburton,Hansen,Johnson g:Johnson(3)	12th	107
11/6/17	Workington (h)	L24-25	t:Lee,Baker,Johnson,Davidson g:Johnson(4)	12th	358
17/6/17	Barrow (a)	L28-4	t:Mulkeen	13th	835
25/6/17	South Wales (h)	W36-12	t:Atherton(2),Baker(2),Smith(2) g:Johnson(6)	11th	402
2/7/17	Oxford (a)	W20-52	t:Atherton,Houghton,Smith(2),Moulsdale,Bate,Walker,Mulkeen,Baker g:Johnson(8)	10th	140
9/7/17	Whitehaven (h)	D12-12	t:Bate,Prell g:Johnson(2)	9th	387
16/7/17	Coventry (a)	W13-36	t:Prell,Johnson,Bate,Hurst,Atherton,Price g:Johnson(6)	9th	422
30/7/17	London Skolars (h) (L1S)	L12-40	t:Price,Bate g:Johnson(2)	3rd(L1S)	268
5/8/17	Gloucestershire All Golds (a) (L1S)	L40-22	t:Millington,Whalley,Baker,Davies g:Price(3)	3rd(L1S)	211
13/8/17	Hunslet (h) (L1S)	W20-12	t:Atherton,Moore,Johnson g:Johnson(4)	3rd(L1S)	306
20/8/17	Hemel (a) (L1S)	W18-38	t:Bloomfield(2),Walker,Hudson,Baker(2),Moore g:Johnson(5)	3rd(L1S)	114
3/9/17	Coventry (h) (L1S)	L16-22	t:Millington,Moore,Johnson g:Johnson(2)	3rd(L1S)	245
9/9/17	South Wales (a) (L1S) ●●	W6-54	t:Hudson,Millington,Smith(3),Hudson,Davidson,Johnson(2),W Thompson g:Johnson(7)	3rd(L1S)	289
17/9/17	Oxford (h) (L1S)	W28-14	t:Hurst,Dandy(2),Bloomfield,Davidson g:Johnson(4)	3rd(L1S)	303

● Played at Bloomfield Road, Blackpool ●● Played at Stebonheath Park, Llanelli

		APP		TRIES		GOALS		FG		PTS	
	D.O.B.	ALL	L1	ALL	L1	ALL	L1	ALL	L1	ALL	L1
Simon Atherton	8/11/90	20	13	10	8	0	0	0	0	40	32
Kenny Baker	1/3/92	17(4)	8(3)	7	4	0	0	0	0	28	16
Joe Bate	24/10/92	(15)	(9)	4	3	0	0	0	0	16	12
Dale Bloomfield	24/10/87	21	12	8	3	0	0	0	0	32	12
John Cookson	12/12/84	3(5)	2(3)	0	0	0	0	0	0	0	0
James Dandy	23/5/90	20(2)	12	5	1	0	0	0	0	20	4
Alex Davidson	1/11/92	12(5)	4(4)	5	2	0	0	0	0	20	8
Matt Davies	18/6/96	(2)	0	1	0	0	0	0	0	4	0
Dave Eccleston	12/9/96	4	0	0	0	0	0	0	0	0	0
Jack Francis	17/12/92	(3)	(2)	0	0	0	0	0	0	0	0
Jack Hansen	12/1/97	14(1)	9(1)	3	2	0	0	1	0	13	8
Jack Houghton	10/1/97	24	14	5	2	0	0	0	0	20	8
Lee Hudson	28/9/90	15(1)	6	4	1	0	0	0	0	16	4
Earl Hurst	21/4/89	17	12	9	7	0	0	0	0	36	28
Tommy Johnson	19/4/91	25	14	12	5	87	44	0	0	222	108
Andrew Joy	7/2/94	(3)	(1)	0	0	0	0	0	0	0	0
Jonny Leather	29/7/89	(1)	(1)	0	0	0	0	0	0	0	0
Corey Lee	10/9/93	12	8	3	2	0	0	0	0	12	8
Ryan Millington	14/1/87	16(5)	6(4)	4	1	0	0	0	0	16	4
Aaron Moore	14/11/97	2(24)	1(13)	5	2	0	0	0	0	20	8
Andy Moulsdale	22/1/87	10(1)	4	1	1	0	0	0	0	4	4
Callum Mulkeen	10/12/90	18	11	5	3	0	0	0	0	20	12
Taylor Prell	3/7/96	4	4	2	2	0	0	0	0	8	8
Dan Price	5/10/92	16(2)	8(1)	6	2	10	7	0	0	44	22
Ryan Smith	25/9/89	27	15	14	10	0	0	1	0	57	40
Alex Thompson	11/2/90	4	3	2	2	0	0	0	0	8	8
Warren Thompson	24/2/90	11(6)	4(6)	1	0	0	0	0	0	4	0
Blake Turner	29/9/98	(7)	(6)	0	0	0	0	0	0	0	0
Andy Unsworth	14/9/92	(2)	(1)	0	0	0	0	0	0	0	0
Jonny Walker	26/9/86	17(6)	13(1)	2	1	0	0	0	0	8	4
Luke Warburton	4/8/94	21(3)	12	3	2	0	0	0	0	12	8
Alex Whalley	30/10/96	1(7)	(4)	1	0	0	0	0	0	4	0

'L1' totals include League 1 regular season only; 'All' totals also include League 1 Shield, League 1 Cup & Challenge Cup

Ryan Smith

LEAGUE RECORD
League 1, before Super 8 split:
P15-W7-D1-L7 (9th)
F366, A422, Diff-56, 15 points.

After League 1 Shield:
P22-W11-D1-L10 (3rd)
F556, A574, Diff-18, 23 points.

LEAGUE 1 CUP
Runners-Up

CHALLENGE CUP
Round Three

ATTENDANCES
Best - v Toronto (L1 - 590)
Worst - v Coventry (L1S - 245)
Total (all home games included) - 3,760
Average (all home games
included) - 342
(Down by 88 on 2016)

CLUB RECORDS
MATCH RECORDS

Highest score: 82-6 v West Hull, 6/4/2013 **Highest score against:** 4-98 v Wigan, 15/4/2012 **Record attendance:** 1,562 v South Wales, 1/9/2013
Tries: 5 Rob Massam v Rochdale, 30/6/2013; Jono Smith v Hemel, 16/5/2015
Goals: 11 Tommy Johnson v West Hull, 6/4/2013; Ian Mort v Hemel, 16/5/2015 **Points:** 30 Tommy Johnson v West Hull, 6/4/2013

SEASON RECORDS
CAREER RECORDS

Tries: 29 Rob Massam 2015 **Goals:** 109 Tommy Johnson 2015 **Points:** 266 Tommy Johnson 2015
Tries: 97 Rob Massam 2012-2016 **Goals:** 477 Tommy Johnson 2012-2017 **Points:** 1,154 Tommy Johnson 2012-2017
Appearances: 145 Tommy Johnson 2012-2017

OXFORD

DATE	FIXTURE	RESULT	SCORERS	LGE	ATT
18/2/17	Coventry (h) (L1CR1)	W30-28	t:Atkinson(2),Windley,Riley,Joynt,Fleming g:Cooke,Fleming(2)	N/A	121
26/2/17	South Wales (a) (CCR3)	W4-18	t:Canterbury,Cooke(2),McRae g:Gill	N/A	115
5/3/17	Hemel (h)	W40-12	t:Canterbury(3),Cooke,Bustin(2),Windley,McRae g:Burnett(4)	3rd	161
12/3/17	Workington (h)	L6-20	t:McDonald g:Burnett	8th	120
26/3/17	Whitehaven (a) (CCR4)	L46-14	t:McDonald,Moules,Atkinson g:Burnett	N/A	375
1/4/17	London Skolars (h) (L1CQF)	W24-20	t:McDonald,Atkinson(3),Gill g:Burnett(2)	N/A	105
9/4/17	York (h)	W35-28	t:Gill(3),Jowitt,Brooker,Siddons g:Jowitt(5) fg:Windley	9th	180
14/4/17	Coventry (a)	L40-28	t:Gill(2),Hoggins,McRae,Siddons g:Fleming(4)	10th	303
30/4/17	Barrow (a) (L1CSF)	L64-14	t:Canterbury,Gill,Fleming g:Fleming	N/A	962
6/5/17	Toronto (a)	L62-12	t:Brough(2) g:Burnett(2)	11th	6,281
14/5/17	Hunslet (h)	W24-22	t:Brough(2),Joynt,Atkinson,Burnett g:Burnett(2)	10th	203
20/5/17	South Wales (a)	W18-38	t:Riley,Atkinson(2),Canterbury,Biscomb,Hindmarsh-Takji,Windley,Brooker g:Fleming(3)	9th	128
4/6/17	Whitehaven (h)	L12-48	t:Burnett,Fleming g:Burnett(2)	10th	130
10/6/17	London Skolars (a)	L31-18	t:Canterbury,Windley,Fleming g:Burnett(3)	11th	291
18/6/17	Newcastle (h)	L0-52		12th	120
25/6/17	Gloucestershire All Golds (a)	L38-10	t:Brooker,Canterbury g:Burnett	13th	275
2/7/17	North Wales (h)	L20-52	t:Windley,Moules,Canterbury,Brough g:Burnett(2)	13th	140
5/7/17	Doncaster (a) ●	L34-16	t:Gill(2),Cooke,Brooker	13th	334
8/7/17	Barrow (a)	L80-10	t:Brough,Burnett g:Burnett	13th	750
16/7/17	Keighley (a)	L92-6	t:Newbould g:Kay	13th	670
30/7/17	Hemel (a) (L1S)	L32-26	t:Dent,Gill,Fleming,Kitson,Biscomb g:Burnett(3)	5th(L1S)	106
6/8/17	Hunslet (h) (L1S)	L10-36	t:Siddons,Gill g:Burnett	5th(L1S)	155
12/8/17	London Skolars (a) (L1S)	L66-0		5th(L1S)	218
20/8/17	South Wales (h) (L1S)	D22-22	t:Brough,Newbould,Moules,Gill(2) g:Burnett	5th(L1S)	65
3/9/17	Gloucestershire All Golds (a) (L1S)	W12-18	t:Gill,Davies,Canterbury g:Druce,Hyde(2)	5th(L1S)	202
9/9/17	Coventry (h) (L1S)	W28-24	t:Gill(4),Burnett,Canterbury g:Druce,Hyde	5th(L1S)	110
17/9/17	North Wales (a) (L1S)	L28-14	t:Davies,Gill,Cryer g:Hyde	5th(L1S)	303

● *Played at LD Nutrition Stadium, Featherstone*

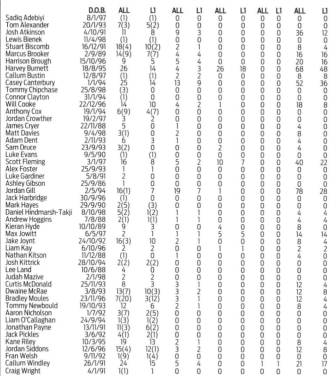

Harvey Burnett

		APP		TRIES		GOALS		FG		PTS	
	D.O.B.	ALL	L1	ALL	L1	ALL	L1	ALL	L1	ALL	L1
Sadiq Adebiyi	8/1/97	(1)	(1)	0	0	0	0	0	0	0	0
Tom Alexander	20/1/93	7(3)	5(2)	0	0	0	0	0	0	0	0
Josh Atkinson	4/10/91	11	8	9	3	0	0	0	0	36	12
Lewis Bienek	11/4/98	(1)	(1)	0	0	0	0	0	0	0	0
Stuart Biscomb	16/12/91	18(4)	10(2)	2	1	0	0	0	0	8	4
Marcus Brooker	2/9/89	14(9)	7(7)	4	4	0	0	0	0	16	16
Harrison Brough	15/10/96	9	5	5	4	0	0	0	0	20	16
Harvey Burnett	18/8/95	26	14	4	3	26	18	0	0	68	48
Callum Bustin	12/8/97	(1)	(1)	2	2	0	0	0	0	8	8
Casey Canterbury	1/1/94	25	14	13	9	0	0	0	0	52	36
Tommy Chipchase	25/8/98	(3)	0	0	0	0	0	0	0	0	0
Connor Clayton	31/1/94	(1)	0	0	0	0	0	0	0	0	0
Will Cooke	22/12/96	14	10	4	2	1	0	0	0	18	8
Anthony Cox	19/1/94	6(9)	4(7)	0	0	0	0	0	0	0	0
Jordan Crowther	19/2/97	3	2	0	0	0	0	0	0	0	0
James Cryer	22/11/88	5	0	1	0	0	0	0	0	4	0
Matt Davies	9/4/98	3(1)	0	2	0	0	0	0	0	8	0
Adam Dent	2/11/93	6	3	1	0	0	0	0	0	4	0
Sam Druce	23/9/93	3(2)	0	0	0	2	0	0	0	4	0
Luke Evans	9/5/90	(1)	(1)	0	0	0	0	0	0	0	0
Scott Fleming	3/1/97	16	8	5	2	10	7	0	0	40	22
Alex Foster	25/9/93	1	1	0	0	0	0	0	0	0	0
Luke Gardiner	5/8/91	2	0	0	0	0	0	0	0	0	0
Ashley Gibson	25/9/86	1	0	0	0	0	0	0	0	0	0
Jordan Gill	2/5/94	16(1)	7	19	7	1	0	0	0	78	28
Jack Harbridge	30/9/96	(1)	0	0	0	0	0	0	0	0	0
Mark Hayes	29/9/90	2(5)	(3)	0	0	0	0	0	0	0	0
Daniel Hindmarsh-Takji	8/10/98	5(2)	1(2)	1	1	0	0	0	0	4	4
Andrew Hoggins	7/8/88	2(1)	1(1)	1	1	0	0	0	0	4	4
Kieran Hyde	10/10/89	9	3	0	0	4	0	0	0	8	0
Max Jowitt	6/5/97	2	1	1	1	5	5	0	0	14	14
Jake Joynt	24/10/92	16(3)	10	2	1	0	0	0	0	8	4
Liam Kay	6/10/96	2	2	0	0	1	1	0	0	2	2
Nathan Kitson	11/12/88	(1)	0	1	0	0	0	0	0	4	0
Josh Kittrick	28/10/94	2(2)	2(2)	0	0	0	0	0	0	0	0
Lee Land	10/6/88	4	0	0	0	0	0	0	0	0	0
Judah Mazive	2/1/98	2	2	0	0	0	0	0	0	0	0
Curtis McDonald	25/11/93	8	3	3	1	0	0	0	0	12	4
Dwaine McRae	3/8/93	13(7)	10(3)	3	2	0	0	0	0	12	8
Bradley Moules	23/11/96	7(20)	3(12)	3	1	0	0	0	0	12	4
Tommy Newbould	19/10/93	12	6	2	1	0	0	0	0	8	4
Aaron Nicholson	1/7/92	3(7)	2(5)	0	0	0	0	0	0	0	0
Liam O'Callaghan	24/9/94	1(3)	1(2)	0	0	0	0	0	0	0	0
Jonathan Payne	13/11/91	11(3)	6(2)	0	0	0	0	0	0	0	0
Jack Pickles	3/6/92	4(1)	2(1)	0	0	0	0	0	0	0	0
Kane Riley	10/3/95	19	13	2	1	0	0	0	0	8	4
Jordan Siddons	12/6/96	15(4)	12(1)	3	2	0	0	0	0	12	8
Fran Welsh	9/11/92	1(9)	1(4)	0	0	0	0	0	0	0	0
Callum Windley	26/1/91	24	15	5	4	0	0	1	1	21	17
Craig Wright	4/1/91	1(1)	1	0	0	0	0	0	0	0	0

'L1' totals include League 1 regular season only; 'All' totals also include League 1 Shield, League 1 Cup & Challenge Cup

LEAGUE RECORD
League 1, before Super 8 split:
P15-W4-D0-L11 (13th)
F275, A629, Diff-354, 8 points.

After League 1 Shield:
P22-W6-D1-L15 (5th)
F393, A849, Diff-456, 13 points.

LEAGUE 1 CUP
Semi-Finalists

CHALLENGE CUP
Round Four

ATTENDANCES
Best - v Hunslet (L1 - 203)
Worst - v South Wales (L1S - 65)
Total (all home games included) - 1,610
Average (all home games included) - 134
(Down by 28 on 2016)

CLUB RECORDS	
MATCH RECORDS	**Highest score:** 46-10 v Hemel, 7/8/2016 **Highest score against:** 4-96 v Swinton, 12/7/2015 **Record attendance:** 502 v Coventry, 27/6/2015
	Tries: 4 Jordan Gill v Coventry, 10/9/2017 **Goals:** 6 Jonny Leather v Gloucestershire All Golds, 29/3/2013; Nathan Kitson v South Wales, 23/8/2015
	Points: 22 Nathan Kitson v Hemel, 7/8/2016
SEASON RECORDS	**Tries:** 19 Jordan Gill 2017 **Goals:** 46 *(inc 2fg)* Jimmy Rowland 2014 **Points:** 118 Jimmy Rowland 2014
CAREER RECORDS	**Tries:** 29 Sean Morris 2013-2016 **Goals:** 64 Nathan Kitson 2015-2017 **Points:** 208 Nathan Kitson 2015-2017 **Appearances:** 91 Marcus Brooker 2014-2017

SOUTH WALES IRONMEN

DATE	FIXTURE	RESULT	SCORERS	LGE	ATT
19/2/17	London Skolars (h) (L1CR1)	L16-24	t:Courtney Davies,Farrer,B Jones g:Courtney Davies(2)	N/A	122
26/2/17	Oxford (h) (CCR3)	L4-18	t:P Edwards	N/A	115
5/3/17	Whitehaven (h)	L10-27	t:Evans,Y Parker g:Emanuelli	11th	223
12/3/17	York (a)	L26-24	t:Gay(2),Chris Davies,Roets,Reece g:Emanuelli(2)	12th	752
26/3/17	Newcastle (h)	L20-26	t:P Edwards,R Jones,Reece,Hughes g:Emanuelli(2)	14th	150
9/4/17	Hunslet (a)	L58-6	t:C Parker g:Emanuelli	14th	350
14/4/17	Gloucestershire All Golds (h)	L30-36	t:Owens(3),Y Parker,Duffy g:Emanuelli(5)	15th	351
6/5/17	Barrow (a)	L58-16	t:S Jones,I'Anson,C Parker g:Emanuelli(2)	15th	805
14/5/17	Workington (a)	L56-0		15th	546
20/5/17	Oxford (h)	L18-38	t:Owens,Y Parker,Price g:Emanuelli(3)	15th	128
3/6/17	Keighley (a)	L74-6	t:Roets g:Emanuelli	15th	532
10/6/17	Toronto (h)	L0-66		15th	462
18/6/17	Coventry (h)	W24-22	t:Roets(2),Carter,B Phillips g:Emanuelli(4)	15th	156
25/6/17	North Wales (a)	L36-12	t:Farrer,C Parker g:Emanuelli(2)	15th	402
2/7/17	Hemel (a)	L25-18	t:Evans,B Phillips,Calcott g:B Jones(3)	15th	131
9/7/17	Doncaster (h)	L12-70	t:Nelmes,Farrer g:Punchard(2)	15th	130
16/7/17	London Skolars (a)	L36-16	t:Jeffries,I'Anson,Syme g:A Lewis(2)	15th	225
29/7/17	Gloucestershire All Golds (h) (L1S) ●	W28-20	t:Ford,Gay,Evans,B Jones,Tennant g:B Jones(4)	7th(L1S)	212
13/8/17	Hemel (h) (L1S) ●	L4-22	t:Roets	8th(L1S)	192
20/8/17	Oxford (a) (L1S)	D22-22	t:Breen,Tennant,C Parker g:B Jones(5)	8th(L1S)	65
25/8/17	London Skolars (a) (L1S)	L32-4	t:Breen	8th(L1S)	1,020
3/9/17	Hunslet (a) (L1S) ●	L64-7	t:H Davies g:B Jones fg:Gay	8th(L1S)	418
9/9/17	North Wales (h) (L1S) ●	L6-54	t:Green g:Stroud	8th(L1S)	289
16/9/17	Coventry (a) (L1S)	L58-16	t:Farrer,Uren,Roets g:B Jones(2)	8th(L1S)	332

		APP		TRIES		GOALS		FG		PTS	
	D.O.B.	ALL	L1	ALL	L1	ALL	L1	ALL	L1	ALL	L1
Kristian Baller	18/2/87	2(5)	2(4)	0	0	0	0	0	0	0	0
Josh Barden	21/5/98	(2)	(2)	0	0	0	0	0	0	0	0
Ashley Bateman	11/2/90	10	8	0	0	0	0	0	0	0	0
Dewi Billingham	9/11/98	(2)	0	0	0	0	0	0	0	0	0
Kade Breen	13/4/96	11(5)	4(5)	2	0	0	0	0	0	8	0
Sam Buckthought	10/8/98	(1)	(1)	0	0	0	0	0	0	0	0
Chester Butler	10/3/95	2	2	0	0	0	0	0	0	0	0
William Calcott	16/12/97	4	4	1	1	0	0	0	0	4	4
Errol Carter	22/1/96	5	5	1	1	0	0	0	0	4	4
Ethan Coombes	19/7/94	1	0	0	0	0	0	0	0	0	0
Liam Curnow	8/6/96	4(1)	1(1)	0	0	0	0	0	0	0	0
Chris Davies	24/12/91	1(2)	(2)	1	1	0	0	0	0	4	4
Connor Davies	17/1/97	(1)	(1)	0	0	0	0	0	0	0	0
Courtney Davies	1/7/94	4(1)	3(1)	1	0	2	0	0	0	8	0
Henry Davies	13/6/98	5	0	1	0	0	0	0	0	4	0
Izaak Duffy	16/2/89	3(2)	3(1)	1	1	0	0	0	0	4	4
Michael Edwards	7/9/94	2(5)	2(4)	0	0	0	0	0	0	0	0
Paul Edwards	18/5/96	8	6	2	1	0	0	0	0	8	4
Paul Emanuelli	3/1/84	12(2)	11(1)	0	0	23	23	0	0	46	46
Morgan Evans	23/3/92	15	8	3	2	0	0	0	0	12	8
Connor Farrer	6/6/95	16(2)	9(2)	4	2	0	0	0	0	16	8
Curtis Ford	3/6/98	3	0	1	0	0	0	0	0	4	0
Andrew Gay	5/10/89	24	15	3	2	0	0	1	0	13	8
Cobi Green	4/3/99	2(2)	(1)	1	0	0	0	0	0	4	0
Macauley Harris	27/2/99	(4)	(1)	0	0	0	0	0	0	0	0
Sam Hodge	19/3/98	9(2)	3(1)	0	0	0	0	0	0	0	0
Lewis Hughes	10/2/96	5	4	1	1	0	0	0	0	4	4
Jamie I'Anson	19/6/87	10(11)	6(7)	2	2	0	0	0	0	8	8
Morgan Jeffries	6/9/96	15(1)	8(1)	1	1	0	0	0	0	4	4
Ben Jones	7/9/96	16	8	2	0	15	3	0	0	38	6
Ieuan Jones	11/12/94	1(1)	1(1)	0	0	0	0	0	0	0	0
Richard Jones	7/7/89	3(4)	3(3)	1	1	0	0	0	0	4	4
Sion Jones	16/12/97	2(2)	2(2)	1	1	0	0	0	0	4	4
Aaron Lewis	18/2/92	1(1)	1	0	0	2	2	0	0	4	4
Craig Lewis	15/10/86	3	1	0	0	0	0	0	0	0	0
Dan Maiden	11/1/97	(1)	0	0	0	0	0	0	0	0	0
Conor McGrath	14/8/96	1	1	0	0	0	0	0	0	0	0
Luke Nelmes	7/6/93	3	3	1	1	0	0	0	0	4	4
Shaun Owens	29/11/88	7(1)	6(1)	4	4	0	0	0	0	16	16
Connor Parker	23/10/97	17(2)	10(2)	4	3	0	0	0	0	16	12
Yannic Parker	29/12/90	8	5	3	3	0	0	0	0	12	12
Huw Parkes	11/9/95	(3)	(2)	0	0	0	0	0	0	0	0
Tom Parks	19/3/90	1	0	0	0	0	0	0	0	0	0
Barrie Phillips	27/5/86	7(4)	3(1)	2	2	0	0	0	0	8	8
Dafydd Phillips	10/8/95	1(2)	1	0	0	0	0	0	0	0	0
Alan Pope	1/4/85	(1)	0	0	0	0	0	0	0	0	0
Ross Price	14/12/92	2(2)	2(2)	1	1	0	0	0	0	4	4
Morgan Punchard	26/1/99	1	1	0	0	2	2	0	0	4	4
Lewis Reece	17/6/91	5	4	2	2	0	0	0	0	8	8
Martyn Reilly	5/1/96	2(1)	2(1)	0	0	0	0	0	0	0	0
Christiaan Roets	5/9/80	17(1)	12	6	4	0	0	0	0	24	16
Archie Snook	26/3/99	3(3)	0	0	0	0	0	0	0	0	0
James Stringer	6/12/96	2	2	0	0	0	0	0	0	0	0
Fraser Stroud	12/4/99	3	0	0	0	1	0	0	0	2	0
Jordan Syme	14/11/96	2(1)	2(1)	1	1	0	0	0	0	4	4
Shaun Tennant	25/7/93	6	0	2	0	0	0	0	0	8	0
Jack Uren	3/1/98	13	6	1	0	0	0	0	0	4	0
Chris Vitalini	5/5/87	2(6)	2(4)	0	0	0	0	0	0	0	0
Zak Williams	17/9/96	14(1)	12(1)	0	0	0	0	0	0	0	0

Andrew Gay

LEAGUE RECORD
League 1, before Super 8 split:
P15-W1-D0-L14 (15th)
F212, A654, Diff-442, 2 points.

After League 1 Shield:
P22-W2-D1-L19 (8th)
F299, A926, Diff-627, 5 points.

LEAGUE 1 CUP
Round One

CHALLENGE CUP
Round Three

ATTENDANCES
Best - v Toronto (L1 - 462)
Worst - v Oxford (CC - 115)
Total (excluding Challenge Cup) - 2,415
Average (excluding Challenge Cup) - 219
(Down by 75 on 2016)

● Played at Stebonheath Park, Llanelli

'L1' totals include League 1 regular season only;
'All' totals also include League 1 Shield,
League 1 Cup & Challenge Cup

CLUB RECORDS — Highest score: 70-22 v London Skolars, 23/5/2010; 70-16 v Gateshead, 11/7/2010 **Highest score against:** 6-94 v Swinton, 13/9/2015
Record attendance: 1,025 v North Wales, 10/5/2015
MATCH RECORDS — **Tries:** 4 Dalton Grant v Gateshead, 22/5/2011 **Goals:** 11 Lewis Reece v Gateshead, 11/7/2010 **Points:** 30 Lewis Reece v Gateshead, 11/7/2010
SEASON RECORDS — **Tries:** 19 Steve Parry 2010 **Goals:** 55 Lewis Reece 2011 **Points:** 130 Lewis Reece 2011
CAREER RECORDS — **Tries:** 43 Steve Parry 2010-2013 **Goals:** 138 *(inc 2fg)* Paul Emanuelli 2014-2017 **Points:** 282 Paul Emanuelli 2014-2017
Appearances: 111 Ashley Bateman 2010-2014; 2017

TORONTO
WOLFPACK

TORONTO WOLFPACK

DATE	FIXTURE	RESULT	SCORERS	LGE	ATT
25/2/17	Siddal (a) (CCR3)	W6-14	t:Burroughs,Worthington,Sidlow g:Hall	N/A	1,023
4/3/17	London Skolars (a)	W0-76	t:Hall(2),Pownall,Moimoi(3),Beswick,Kay(2),Dixon,Worthington(2),Laulu-Togagae g:Hall(12)	1st	1,524
12/3/17	Whitehaven (a)	W10-24	t:Hall,Kay,Beswick,Pownall g:Hall(4)	1st	643
17/3/17	London Broncos (a) (CCR4)	W26-30	t:Hall,Kay,Bussey,Pownall,Jacks g:Hall(5)	N/A	758
26/3/17	Keighley (a)	W21-48	t:Pownall(3),Kay,Wallace,Hall,Sidlow(2),Dixon g:Hall(6)	2nd	1,128
9/4/17	Doncaster (a)	W6-82	t:Beswick,Moimoi(2),Bussey(3),Kay(2),Laulu-Togagae,Wallace(2),Worthington,Whiting,Jacks g:Hall(13)	1st	943
14/4/17	North Wales (a)	W0-80	t:Hall(3),Wheeler(2),Wallace,Penkywicz,Sidlow,Jacks,Moimoi,Kay,Laulu-Togagae g:Hall(12)	1st	590
23/4/17	Salford (a) (CCR5)	L29-22	t:Kay,Laulu-Togagae,Brierley,Moimoi g:Hall(3)	N/A	1,318
6/5/17	Oxford (h)	W62-12	t:Wallace,Dixon,Kay(2),Pownall(2),Whiting(2),Brierley(2),Hall,Worthington,Burroughs g:Hall(7)	1st	6,281
12/5/17	Newcastle (a)	W22-40	t:Brierley(2),Wallace,Pownall,Kay,Laulu-Togagae,Beswick g:Hall(6)	1st	1,087
20/5/17	Barrow (h)	W70-2	t:Wallace,Bailey,Laulu-Togagae(3),Dixon,Wheeler,Worthington,Brierley(2),Penkywicz,Pick g:Hall(11)	1st	7,144
3/6/17	Coventry (h)	W54-12	t:Dixon(2),Kay(3),Beswick,Brierley,Jacks,Moimoi(2) g:Hall(7)	1st	6,973
10/6/17	South Wales (a)	W0-66	t:Worthington(3),Whiting(2),Burroughs,Pownall,Bussey,Bailey,Hall(2),Brierley,Penkywicz g:Hall(7)	1st	462
18/6/17	Workington (a)	W12-58	t:Pownall(2),Worthington(2),Hall(2),Brierley(2),Bussey,Penkywicz g:Hall(9)	1st	835
24/6/17	Hunslet (h)	W56-12	t:Penkywicz,Brierley,Pownall(2),Laithwaite,Kay,Laulu-Togagae(3),Whiting,Hall g:Hall(6)	1st	6,042
1/7/17	York (h)	W64-22	t:Beswick,Pownall(2),Kay(5),Penkywicz,Bussey,Hall,Laulu-Togagae g:Hall(8)	1st	5,646
8/7/17	Gloucestershire All Golds (h)	W62-10	t:Burroughs,Hall(2),Pownall,Whiting,Jacks,Moimoi,Beswick,Worthington,Crossley,Laulu-Togagae g:Hall(9)	1st	7,139
15/7/17	Hemel (h)	W74-16	t:Hall(4),Wallace(3),Pownall,Kay,Beswick,Crossley,Moimoi,Fleming g:Hall(11)	1st	7,247
30/7/17	York (a) (S8)	L26-16	t:Brierley,Beswick,Hall g:Hall(2)	1st	2,602
6/8/17	Workington (a) (S8)	W0-68	t:Wallace(4),Laulu-Togagae,Pownall(2),Kay,Laithwaite,Hall(2),Emmitt g:Hall(10)	1st	592
13/8/17	Keighley (a) (S8)	D26-26	t:Pownall,Laulu-Togagae,Kay,Whiting,Worthington g:Hall(3)	1st	922
19/8/17	Newcastle (h) (S8)	W50-0	t:Kay(3),Jacks,Hall,Moimoi,Laulu-Togagae(2),Worthington g:Hall(7)	1st	7,522
2/9/17	Whitehaven (h) (S8)	W36-18	t:Whiting(2),Beswick,Pownall,Kay,Wheeler,Laulu-Togagae g:Hall(4)	1st	6,134
9/9/17	Barrow (h) (S8)	W26-2	t:Laulu-Togagae,Wallace(2),Whiting g:Hall(5)	1st	7,972
16/9/17	Doncaster (h) (S8)	W26-14	t:Pownall(3),Wallace,Kay g:Hall(3)	1st	8,456

		APP		TRIES		GOALS		FG		PTS	
	D.O.B.	ALL	L1	ALL	L1	ALL	L1	ALL	L1	ALL	L1
Ryan Bailey	11/11/83	5(3)	5(2)	2	2	0	0	0	0	8	8
Bob Beswick	8/12/84	22(1)	19(1)	10	10	0	0	0	0	40	40
Ryan Brierley	12/3/92	12	11	13	12	0	0	0	0	52	48
Ryan Burroughs	26/8/91	8(3)	7(3)	4	3	0	0	0	0	16	12
Jack Bussey	17/8/92	19(1)	16(1)	7	6	0	0	0	0	28	24
Steve Crossley	28/11/89	2(18)	1(17)	2	2	0	0	0	0	8	8
Tom Dempsey	3/4/94	(3)	(3)	0	0	0	0	0	0	0	0
Andrew Dixon	28/2/90	15	12	7	7	0	0	0	0	28	28
Joe Eichner	9/10/91	(1)	(1)	0	0	0	0	0	0	0	0
Jake Emmitt	4/10/88	19(2)	16(2)	1	1	0	0	0	0	4	4
Toby Everett	22/12/95	(3)	(2)	0	0	0	0	0	0	0	0
Daniel Fleming	8/7/92	6(9)	6(8)	1	1	0	0	0	0	4	4
Craig Hall	21/2/88	24(1)	22	25	24	171	162	0	0	442	420
Rhys Jacks	21/1/90	14(7)	12(6)	6	5	0	0	0	0	24	20
Liam Kay	17/12/91	21	19	27	25	0	0	0	0	108	100
James Laithwaite	23/9/91	16(1)	13(1)	2	2	0	0	0	0	8	8
Quentin Laulu-Togagae	1/12/84	22	19	20	19	0	0	0	0	80	76
Fuifui Moimoi	26/9/79	14(6)	13(5)	12	11	0	0	0	0	48	44
Quinn Ngawati	15/6/99	(2)	(2)	0	0	0	0	0	0	0	0
Sean Penkywicz	18/5/82	4(9)	4(9)	6	6	0	0	0	0	24	24
Shaun Pick	21/9/93	2(6)	2(5)	1	1	0	0	0	0	4	4
Jonny Pownall	22/8/91	24	21	25	24	0	0	0	0	100	96
Adam Sidlow	25/10/87	11(11)	10(9)	4	3	0	0	0	0	16	12
Blake Wallace	18/6/92	19	16	17	17	0	0	0	0	68	68
Gary Wheeler	30/9/89	7(6)	6(6)	4	4	0	0	0	0	16	16
Richard Whiting	20/12/84	17(6)	16(4)	11	11	0	0	0	0	44	44
Greg Worthington	17/7/90	22	20	15	14	0	0	0	0	60	56

'L1' totals include Super 8s; 'All' totals also include Challenge Cup

Craig Hall

LEAGUE RECORD
P22-W20-D1-L1 (1st/Champions)
F1164, A243, Diff+921, 41 points.

LEAGUE 1 CUP
Not entered

CHALLENGE CUP
Round Five

ATTENDANCES
Best - v Doncaster (S8 - 8,456)
Worst - v York (L1 - 5,646)
Total (all home games
included) - 76,556
Average (all home games
included) - 6,960

WHITEHAVEN

DATE	FIXTURE	RESULT	SCORERS	LGE	ATT
19/2/17	Workington (h) (L1CR1)	L6-22	t:Holland g:Crook	N/A	908
25/2/17	West Hull (a) (CCR3)	W16-18	t:Burns,Dalton,Pattinson(2) g:Crook	N/A	150
5/3/17	South Wales (a)	W10-27	t:Roper,Crook,Riley,Burns g:Crook(5) fg:Crook	6th	223
12/3/17	Toronto (h)	L10-24	t:Miller,Taylor g:Crook	10th	643
26/3/17	Oxford (h) (CCR4)	W46-14	t:Olstrum,Crook,Parker(2),Calvert,Burns,Newton,Taylor g:Crook(7)	N/A	375
9/4/17	Coventry (h)	W44-12	t:Riley,Calvert,McAvoy,Miller(2),Taylor,Crook,Parker g:Crook(6)	7th	413
14/4/17	Workington (a)	W20-24	t:McAvoy,Forster,Parker,Tilley g:Crook(4)	5th	1,103
23/4/17	Halifax (h) (CCR5)	L12-36	t:Miller,Parker g:Crook(2)	N/A	636
30/4/17	Hunslet (a)	W18-19	t:Shackley,Taylor,Roper g:Crook(3) fg:Roper	3rd	382
7/5/17	Newcastle (h)	W34-20	t:Miller,Burns,McAvoy(2),Forster,Riley g:Crook,Roper(4)	3rd	425
13/5/17	London Skolars (a)	W14-28	t:Forster(2),Parker,Newton g:Crook(6)	3rd	335
21/5/17	Hemel (h)	W58-24	t:Roper,Miller,Forster(3),Holland(2),Thompson(2),Newton,Parker g:Crook(7)	3rd	487
4/6/17	Oxford (a)	W12-48	t:McAvoy(2),Taylor(2),Forster(2),Burns(2),Calvert(2) g:Crook(4)	3rd	130
11/6/17	Gloucestershire All Golds (h)	W62-6	t:Burns,Forster,McAvoy,Miller(3),Calvert,Holland,Newton,Parker,Aiye g:Crook(9)	2nd	534
18/6/17	York (a)	W16-18	t:Calvert,Newton,Forster g:Crook(3)	2nd	1,150
25/6/17	Doncaster (h)	W25-20	t:Holland,Burns(2),Parker g:Crook(4) fg:Crook	2nd	606
2/7/17	Keighley (h)	W28-22	t:Aiye,Thompson,Roper,Burns,Worthington g:Crook(4)	2nd	704
9/7/17	North Wales (a)	D12-12	t:Burns(2),Aiye	3rd	387
16/7/17	Barrow (h)	W32-6	t:Thompson,Riley,Aiye,Roper,McAvoy g:Crook(6)	2nd	1,502
30/7/17	Barrow (h) (S8)	L2-15	g:Crook	3rd	1,062
6/8/17	Newcastle (h) (S8)	W27-6	t:Aiye(3),Miller,Parker g:Crook(3) fg:Crook	3rd	539
13/8/17	Doncaster (a) (S8)	L30-22	t:Parker(2),Holliday,Holland g:Crook(3)	3rd	525
20/8/17	Keighley (a) (S8)	W36-4	t:Parker,Holliday,Thompson,Forster,Burns,Olstrum g:Crook(6)	3rd	562
2/9/17	Toronto (a) (S8)	L36-18	t:Forster,Newton,Tilley g:Burns(3)	3rd	6,134
10/9/17	York (h) (S8)	W26-16	t:Miller(2),Aiye,Forster g:Crook(5)	3rd	605
17/9/17	Workington (a) (S8)	W6-56	t:Burns,Parker(2),Aiye(3),McAvoy,Forster,Riley,Calvert g:Crook(8)	3rd	927
24/9/17	York (h) (SF)	W21-20 *(aet)*	t:Parker(2),Holland g:Crook(4) fg:Roper	N/A	853
1/10/17	Barrow (a) (PF)	L10-6	t:Aiye g:Crook	N/A	3,128

		APP		TRIES		GOALS		FG		PTS	
	D.O.B.	ALL	L1	ALL	L1	ALL	L1	ALL	L1	ALL	L1
Shane Ackerley	19/11/91	(2)	0	0	0	0	0	0	0	0	0
Dion Aiye	6/11/87	15(2)	15(2)	12	12	0	0	0	0	48	48
Lewis Brown	29/11/98	2(7)	2(6)	0	0	0	0	0	0	0	0
Jordan Burns	2/9/95	27	23	14	12	3	3	0	0	62	54
Craig Calvert	10/2/84	16(3)	14(3)	7	6	0	0	0	0	28	24
Paul Crook	28/8/86	27	23	3	2	105	94	3	3	225	199
Tyrone Dalton	7/1/89	2(6)	1(4)	1	0	0	0	0	0	4	0
Carl Forster	4/6/92	22(4)	18(4)	15	15	0	0	0	0	60	60
Lewis Foster	21/12/93	(1)	(1)	0	0	0	0	0	0	0	0
Danny Green	21/6/92	2(2)	2(2)	0	0	0	0	0	0	0	0
Jordan Hand	13/5/93	1	1	0	0	0	0	0	0	0	0
Tommy Holland	28/8/95	6(22)	4(20)	7	6	0	0	0	0	28	24
Connor Holliday	9/6/95	17(8)	14(8)	2	2	0	0	0	0	8	8
Kurt Maudling	5/2/89	1(4)	1(2)	0	0	0	0	0	0	0	0
Scott McAvoy	9/4/86	25(1)	22(1)	9	9	0	0	0	0	36	36
Elliott Miller	14/9/90	23	21	12	11	0	0	0	0	48	44
Jake Moore	6/9/96	1	0	0	0	0	0	0	0	0	0
James Newton	20/12/91	12(16)	8(16)	6	5	0	0	0	0	24	20
Karl Olstrum	21/9/91	8(2)	6(2)	2	1	0	0	0	0	8	4
Jessie Joe Parker	22/8/85	27	23	17	14	0	0	0	0	68	56
Shane Pattinson	14/11/91	3	1	2	0	0	0	0	0	8	0
Glenn Morgan	21/9/92	13(10)	13(7)	5	5	0	0	0	0	20	20
Steve Roper	10/11/86	22(3)	19(3)	5	5	4	4	2	2	30	30
Marc Shackley	14/1/89	24	20	1	1	0	0	0	0	4	4
Chris Taylor	25/10/93	27	23	6	5	0	0	0	0	24	20
David Thompson	13/9/95	15(2)	15(2)	5	5	0	0	0	0	20	20
James Tilley	11/11/93	23(5)	20(4)	2	2	0	0	0	0	8	8
Aiden Worthington	18/5/85	3(8)	3(6)	1	1	0	0	0	0	4	4

'L1' totals include Super 8s & play-offs; 'All' totals also include League 1 Cup & Challenge Cup

Carl Forster

LEAGUE RECORD
P22-W17-D1-L4
(3rd/Losers, Promotion Final)
F656, A349, Diff+307, 35 points.

LEAGUE 1 CUP
Round One

CHALLENGE CUP
Round Five

ATTENDANCES
Best - v Barrow (L1 - 1,502)
Worst - v Oxford (CC - 375)
Total (excluding Challenge Cup) - 9,843
Average (excluding Challenge Cup) - 703
(Down by 13 on 2016, Championship)

CLUB RECORDS	Highest score: 86-6 v Highfield, 25/1/95 Highest score against: 8-106 v Wigan, 12/5/2008 Record attendance: 18,500 v Wakefield, 19/3/60
MATCH RECORDS	Tries: 6 Vince Gribbin v Doncaster, 18/11/84 Goals: 13 Lee Anderson v Highfield, 25/1/95 Points: 32 Mick Nanyn v Batley, 22/8/2004
SEASON RECORDS	Tries: 34 Mike Pechey 1994-95 Goals: 141 John McKeown 1956-57 Points: 398 Mick Nanyn 2004
CAREER RECORDS	Tries: 239 Craig Calvert 2004-2017 Goals: 1,050 John McKeown 1948-61 Points: 2,133 John McKeown 1948-61 Appearances: 417 John McKeown 1948-61

WORKINGTON TOWN

DATE	FIXTURE	RESULT	SCORERS	LGE	ATT
19/2/17	Whitehaven (a) (L1CR1)	W6-22	t:Forber(2),Ritson,Hambley g:Mewse(3)	N/A	908
25/2/17	Newcastle (a) (CCR3)	L18-16	t:Doran,Hambley,C Phillips g:Forber(2)	N/A	400
5/3/17	Newcastle (h)	L20-24	t:C Phillips,Joseph,Davies,Hambley g:Forber(2)	9th	660
12/3/17	Oxford (a)	W6-20	t:Chamberlain,Higginson,Hambley g:Forber(4)	9th	120
26/3/17	Gloucestershire All Golds (h)	W54-22	t:Curwen(2),Davies,Hambley,C Phillips,Mossop,Rooke,Forber,Scholey g:Forber(9)	6th	509
1/4/17	Gloucestershire All Golds (a) (L1CQF) ●	L30-22	t:B Phillips,Patrick,Hambley,Lister g:Forber(3)	N/A	378
8/4/17	Barrow (a)	L26-10	t:Doran,Chamberlain g:Forber	8th	1,284
14/4/17	Whitehaven (h)	L20-24	t:Rooke,Hambley(2),Mossop g:Forber(2)	9th	1,103
7/5/17	Hemel (a)	W18-66	t:Mossop(2),Rooke,Scholey,Forber,B Phillips,Maudling(3),Hambley,Singleton g:Forber(10),Mewse	8th	105
14/5/17	South Wales (h)	W56-0	t:Mossop,Hambley(3),Fell(2),Patrick,Rooke,Curwen,C Phillips g:Forber(8)	5th	546
21/5/17	Hunslet (a)	L30-22	t:Patrick,Mossop,C Phillips,Forber g:Forber(2),Mewse	7th	388
4/6/17	Doncaster (h)	L26-30	t:Fitzsimmons,Lister,Mossop,Joseph,Doran g:Forber(3)	8th	522
11/6/17	North Wales (a)	W24-25	t:Singleton(2),C Phillips,Hambley,Mossop g:Forber(2) fg:Forber	6th	358
18/6/17	Toronto (h)	L12-58	t:Maudling,Singleton g:Forber(2)	8th	835
25/6/17	Coventry (a)	W28-29	t:Hambley(2),Maudling,Doran,Rasool g:Forber(4) fg:Forber	8th	571
2/7/17	London Skolars (h)	W46-16	t:Ritson(4),Fell,B Phillips,Doran,Davies g:Forber(7)	6th	479
9/7/17	Keighley (h)	D30-30	t:Hambley(2),Fell,Doran,Ritson g:Forber(3)	7th	581
16/7/17	York (a)	L34-0		8th	1,011
30/7/17	Newcastle (a) (S8)	W14-30	t:Fell(2),Davies(2),Hambley(2) g:Doran(3)	8th	655
6/8/17	Toronto (h) (S8)	L0-68		8th	592
13/8/17	York (a) (S8)	L28-18	t:Lister,Davies,Hambley g:Forber(3)	8th	1,112
20/8/17	Doncaster (h) (S8)	W22-21	t:Fell(2),Davies,Fitzsimmons g:Forber(3)	7th	441
3/9/17	Barrow (a) (S8)	L36-14	t:Fell,B Philips,Ritson g:Forber	8th	1,021
10/9/17	Keighley (a) (S8)	L28-6	t:Hambley g:Forber	8th	661
17/9/17	Whitehaven (h) (S8)	L6-56	t:Maudling g:Forber	8th	927

● *Played at Derwent Park*

	D.O.B.	APP ALL	APP L1	TRIES ALL	TRIES L1	GOALS ALL	GOALS L1	FG ALL	FG L1	PTS ALL	PTS L1
Joe Bretherton	5/10/95	1	1	0	0	0	0	0	0	0	0
Liam Byrne	18/8/99	(5)	(5)	0	0	0	0	0	0	0	0
Ed Chamberlain	8/2/96	10	7	2	2	0	0	0	0	8	8
Kris Coward	1/10/81	7(6)	6(4)	0	0	0	0	0	0	0	0
Tom Curwen	15/8/89	17(2)	15(1)	3	3	0	0	0	0	12	12
Macauley Davies	4/9/96	13(3)	10(3)	7	7	0	0	0	0	28	28
Jamie Doran	8/12/94	19(3)	18(1)	7	6	3	3	0	0	34	30
Sam Dowsett	2/11/92	3(4)	3(2)	0	0	0	0	0	0	0	0
Gabriel Fell	12/9/95	12	12	9	9	0	0	0	0	36	36
Conor Fitzsimmons	7/5/98	6(16)	6(14)	2	2	0	0	0	0	8	8
Carl Forber	17/3/85	22(1)	20	5	3	73	68	2	2	168	150
Joe Hambley	2/12/95	23	20	21	18	0	0	0	0	84	72
Jack Higginson	4/4/97	2	2	1	1	0	0	0	0	4	4
Stuart Howarth	25/1/90	23(1)	20(1)	0	0	0	0	0	0	0	0
Phil Joseph	10/1/85	5(1)	4(1)	2	2	0	0	0	0	8	8
Phil Lister	28/11/87	6(3)	5(3)	3	2	0	0	0	0	12	8
Gordon Maudling	9/2/91	9(6)	9(6)	6	6	0	0	0	0	24	24
Kieran Mewse	6/5/98	7(3)	6(3)	0	0	5	2	0	0	10	4
Jake Moore	6/9/96	4(6)	4(6)	0	0	0	0	0	0	0	0
Jason Mossop	12/9/85	22	21	8	8	0	0	0	0	32	32
John Patrick	29/11/82	3(2)	2(2)	3	2	0	0	0	0	12	8
Brett Phillips	25/10/88	23	20	4	3	0	0	0	0	16	12
Callum Phillips	19/2/92	9(9)	6(9)	6	5	0	0	0	0	24	20
Joe Prior	10/9/95	1(5)	1(5)	0	0	0	0	0	0	0	0
Danny Rasool	25/10/95	10(1)	10(1)	1	1	0	0	0	0	4	4
Theerapol Ritson	7/1/96	12	10	7	6	0	0	0	0	28	24
Scott Rooke	3/11/94	10(2)	9(2)	4	4	0	0	0	0	16	16
Joe Ryan	27/9/95	4(1)	4(1)	0	0	0	0	0	0	0	0
Stevie Scholey	7/1/96	17	14	2	2	0	0	0	0	8	8
Kyle Shelford	13/9/96	2(8)	1(7)	0	0	0	0	0	0	0	0
Perry Singleton	5/1/94	21(1)	18(1)	4	4	0	0	0	0	16	16
Alex Szostak	4/3/86	2(11)	2(10)	0	0	0	0	0	0	0	0

'L1' totals include Super 8s; 'All' totals also include League 1 Cup & Challenge Cup

Joe Hambley

LEAGUE RECORD
P22-W9-D1-L12 (8th)
F532, A621, Diff-89, 19 points.

LEAGUE 1 CUP
Quarter Finalists

CHALLENGE CUP
Round Three

ATTENDANCES
Best - v Whitehaven (L1 - 1,103)
Worst - v Gloucestershire All Golds (L1CQF - 378)
Total (all home games included) - 7,573
Average (all home games included) - 631
(Down by 86 on 2016, Championship)

CLUB RECORDS
MATCH RECORDS
Highest score: 94-4 v Leigh, 26/2/95 Highest score against: 0-92 v Bradford, 14/2/99 Record attendance: 17,741 v Wigan, 3/3/65
Tries: 7 Ike Southward v Blackpool, 17/9/55 Goals: 14 Darren Holt v Gateshead, 12/6/2011
Points: 42 Dean Marwood v Highfield, 1/11/92; Dean Marwood v Leigh, 26/2/95
SEASON RECORDS
CAREER RECORDS
Tries: 49 Johnny Lawrenson 1951-52 Goals: 186 Lyn Hopkins 1981-82 Points: 438 Lyn Hopkins 1981-82
Tries: 274 Ike Southward 1952-68 Goals: 809 Iain MacCorquodale 1972-80 Points: 1,800 Iain MacCorquodale 1972-80
Appearances: 419 Paul Charlton 1961-69; 1975-80

YORK CITY KNIGHTS

DATE	FIXTURE	RESULT	SCORERS	LGE	ATT
19/2/17	North Wales (h) (L1CR1)	L16-17 *(aet)*	t:Morrison,P Smith,Robson g:H Tyson-Wilson(2)	N/A	620
26/2/17	Egremont (h) (CCR3)	W48-8	t:Robson(2),Carter,Foggin-Johnston(2),Morrison,Hey(2),Sowerby,Batchelor g:H Tyson-Wilson(4)	N/A	635
4/3/17	Barrow (a)	L28-0		14th	799
12/3/17	South Wales (h)	W26-24	t:Foggin-Johnston(2),Brierley,Ellis,H Tyson-Wilson g:H Tyson-Wilson(3)	11th	752
19/3/17	Rochdale (h) (CCR4)	W26-20	t:E Smith,Batchelor,Moran,B Tyson-Wilson g:H Tyson-Wilson(5)	N/A	652
26/3/17	North Wales (h)	L22-26	t:Dent,H Tyson-Wilson(2),Batchelor g:H Tyson-Wilson(3)	11th	702
9/4/17	Oxford (a)	L35-28	t:Carter,Rawsthorne,Presley,Hey,Jubb g:H Tyson-Wilson(4)	13th	180
14/4/17	Doncaster (h)	W16-8	t:E Smith,Ellis,Rawsthorne g:H Tyson-Wilson(2)	12th	1,012
23/4/17	Barrow (h) (CCR5)	L28-50	t:Foggin-Johnston,Morrison,Porter,Haynes(2) g:H Tyson-Wilson(4)	N/A	904
7/5/17	Gloucestershire All Golds (a)	W10-56	t:Batchelor,Dixon,Rawsthorne(3),Robson,Jubb,Foggin-Johnston,Harris,E Smith g:H Tyson-Wilson(3),Harris(5)	9th	180
14/5/17	Coventry (h)	W64-12	t:Harris,Haynes(2),Lancaster,E Smith,Porter,Batchelor(2),Rawsthorne,Carter,Presley,Hey g:Harris,Rawsthorne(7)	8th	902
19/5/17	Newcastle (a)	W18-22	t:Rawsthorne,Robson,A Robinson,E Smith g:Rawsthorne(3)	6th	2,111
4/6/17	London Skolars (h)	W36-18	t:Harris(2),Batchelor,Robson,Presley,Foggin-Johnston g:Harris(6)	5th	782
11/6/17	Hunslet (a)	W20-52	t:E Smith,Harris,Haynes,Siddons,Spears,Batchelor(2),Morrison,Jubb g:C Robinson(8)	4th	589
18/6/17	Whitehaven (h)	L16-18	t:Saxton,Hey,Spears g:C Robinson(2)	4th	1,150
25/6/17	Keighley (h)	W18-25	t:E Smith,Batchelor,Siddons g:C Robinson(6) fg:C Robinson	4th	927
1/7/17	Toronto (a)	L64-22	t:Harris,Foggin-Johnston(3) g:C Robinson(3)	4th	5,646
9/7/17	Hemel (a)	W68-6	t:Harris(4),Siddons,Foggin-Johnston(4),Batchelor(2),Hey,Mallinder g:Harris(8)	4th	787
16/7/17	Workington (h)	W34-0	t:Haynes(3),Jubb(2),Batchelor g:C Robinson(5)	4th	1,011
30/7/17	Toronto (h) (S8)	W26-16	t:Butler-Fleming,Harris(2),C Robinson g:C Robinson(5)	4th	2,602
6/8/17	Keighley (a) (S8)	L22-20	t:Moran,Batchelor,Saxton,Haynes g:C Robinson(2)	4th	1,362
13/8/17	Workington (h) (S8)	W28-18	t:Ellis(2),Cox,Morrison,C Robinson g:C Robinson(2)	4th	1,112
20/8/17	Barrow (a) (S8)	L26-19	t:Foggin-Johnston,Hey(2) g:C Robinson(3) fg:C Robinson	4th	977
3/9/17	Doncaster (h) (S8)	D21-21	t:Butler-Fleming,Harris(2),Morrison g:C Robinson(2) fg:C Robinson	4th	1,107
10/9/17	Whitehaven (a) (S8)	L26-16	t:Dent,Presley,Foggin-Johnston g:C Robinson(2)	4th	605
17/9/17	Newcastle (h) (S8)	L24-26	t:Ellis,Carter,Morrison,Swift g:C Robinson(4)	4th	1,181
24/9/17	Whitehaven (a) (SF)	L21-20 *(aet)*	t:Robson(2),Batchelor,Ellis g:C Robinson(2)	N/A	853

		APP		TRIES		GOALS		FG		PTS	
	D.O.B.	**ALL**	**L1**	**ALL**	**L1**	**ALL**	**L1**	**ALL**	**L1**	**ALL**	**L1**
Joe Batchelor	28/10/94	21	19	15	13	0	0	0	0	60	52
Tommy Brierley	8/9/96	5	3	1	1	0	0	0	0	4	4
Jake Butler-Fleming	8/1/92	3(11)	5	2	2	0	0	0	0	8	8
Harry Carter	10/2/94	4	2(9)	4	3	0	0	0	0	16	12
Mitch Clark	13/3/93	1	1	0	0	0	0	0	0	0	0
Brad Clavering	14/3/98	(2)	(1)	0	0	0	0	0	0	0	0
Jordan Cox	27/5/92	4	4	1	1	0	0	0	0	4	4
Ben Dent	27/9/91	7	5	2	2	0	0	0	0	8	8
Ronan Dixon	25/7/97	11(13)	9(11)	1	1	0	0	0	0	4	4
Tuoyo Egodo	16/2/97	2	2	0	0	0	0	0	0	0	0
Andy Ellis	15/12/84	12(3)	10(3)	6	6	0	0	0	0	24	24
David Foggin-Johnston	19/8/96	19	16	16	13	0	0	0	0	64	52
Liam Harris	20/4/97	18	16	14	14	20	20	0	0	96	96
James Haynes	22/3/89	17(1)	14(1)	9	7	0	0	0	0	36	28
Brad Hey	4/9/94	16(7)	13(7)	8	6	0	0	0	0	32	24
Graeme Horne	22/3/85	1(1)	1(1)	0	0	0	0	0	0	0	0
Will Jubb	17/9/96	10(6)	9(6)	5	5	0	0	0	0	20	20
Callum Lancaster	13/10/96	2	2	1	1	0	0	0	0	4	4
George Lawler	1/9/95	(1)	(1)	0	0	0	0	0	0	0	0
Ryan Mallinder	17/7/88	2(2)	2(2)	1	1	0	0	0	0	4	4
George Milton	4/9/95	(1)	(1)	0	0	0	0	0	0	0	0
Kieran Moran	2/11/96	8(10)	7(8)	2	1	0	0	0	0	8	4
Nev Morrison	27/5/90	22(1)	18(1)	7	4	0	0	0	0	28	16
Ross Osborne	7/7/97	1(1)	1(1)	0	0	0	0	0	0	0	0
Joe Porter	26/1/93	1(6)	(14)	2	1	0	0	0	0	8	4
Jon Presley	8/7/84	10	9	4	4	0	0	0	0	16	16
Nick Rawsthorne	30/9/95	5	5	7	7	10	10	0	0	48	48
Adam Robinson	8/4/87	13(7)	12(5)	1	1	0	0	0	0	4	4
Connor Robinson	23/10/94	14	14	2	2	48	48	3	3	107	107
Ash Robson	4/11/95	17	15	8	5	0	0	0	0	32	20
Tom Saxton	3/10/83	14	12	2	2	0	0	0	0	8	8
Chris Siddons	30/1/92	18(4)	15(4)	3	3	0	0	0	0	12	12
Zeus Silk	23/10/97	2	2	0	0	0	0	0	0	0	0
Ed Smith	12/11/92	18	15	7	6	0	0	0	0	28	24
Pat Smith	4/3/90	2(6)	2(4)	1	0	0	0	0	0	4	0
Danny Sowerby	13/9/96	4	2	1	0	0	0	0	0	4	0
Tim Spears	27/7/84	24	20	2	2	0	0	0	0	8	8
Adam Swift	7/3/96	3(1)	3(1)	1	1	0	0	0	0	4	4
Liam Thompson	7/2/91	2(4)	2(4)	0	0	0	0	0	0	0	0
Bobby Tyson-Wilson	6/11/94	3(8)	2(5)	1	0	0	0	0	0	4	0
Harry Tyson-Wilson	29/12/96	14(1)	10(1)	3	3	30	15	0	0	72	42

David Foggin-Johnston

LEAGUE RECORD
P22-W12-D1-L9 (4th/Semi-Finalists)
F641, A460, Diff+181, 25 points.

LEAGUE 1 CUP
Round One

CHALLENGE CUP
Round Five

ATTENDANCES
Best - v Toronto (S8 - 2,602)
Worst - v North Wales (L1C - 620)
Total (excluding Challenge Cup) - 13,720
Average (excluding Challenge Cup) - 1,055
(Up by 473 on 2016)

*'L1' totals include Super 8s & play-offs; 'All' totals
also include League 1 Cup & Challenge Cup*

CLUB RECORDS	**Highest score:** 132-0 v Northumbria University, 6/3/2011 **Highest score against:** 0-98 v Rochdale, 8/4/2001
MATCH RECORDS	**Record attendance:** 14,689 v Swinton, 10/2/34 *(Clarence Street)*; 2,602 v Toronto, 30/7/2017 *(Bootham Crescent)* **Tries:** 7 Brad Davis v Highfield, 17/9/95 **Goals:** 20 Chris Thorman v Northumbria University, 6/3/2011
	Points: 56 Chris Thorman v Northumbria University, 6/3/2011
SEASON RECORDS	**Tries:** 35 John Crossley 1980-81 **Goals:** 178 *(inc 4fg)* Danny Brough 2004 **Points:** 412 Danny Brough 2004
CAREER RECORDS	**Tries:** 167 Peter Foster 1955-67 **Goals:** 1,060 Vic Yorke 1954-67 **Points:** 2,159 Vic Yorke 1954-67 **Appearances:** 449 Willie Hargreaves 1952-67

LEAGUE 1 2017
Round by Round

ROUND 1

Saturday 4th March 2017

LONDON SKOLARS 0 TORONTO WOLFPACK 76

SKOLARS: 20 Jake Melling; 2 Sam Nash; 28 Kameron Pearce-Paul; 24 Michael Brown; 1 Andy Winfield; 9 Charlie Lawrence; 7 Mike Bishay; 25 Michael Sykes; 27 Ben Pointer; 10 Dave Williams; 11 Lamont Bryan; 30 Simona Vavega; 26 Matt Davis. Subs (all used): 8 Louis Robinson; 19 Erjon Dollapi; 12 Eddie Mbaraga; 14 Billy Driver.
WOLFPACK: 1 Quentin Laulu-Togagae; 2 Jonny Pownall; 3 Greg Worthington; 4 Craig Hall; 5 Liam Kay; 6 Blake Wallace; 7 Rhys Jacks; 8 Fuifui Moimoi; 9 Bob Beswick; 29 Jake Emmitt; 11 Andrew Dixon; 12 James Laithwaite; 13 Jack Bussey. Subs (all used): 14 Gary Wheeler; 19 Steve Crossley; 21 Adam Sidlow; 17 Richard Whiting.
Tries: Hall (7, 69), Pownall (12), Moimoi (16, 45, 73), Beswick (26), Kay (29, 49), Dixon (36), Worthington (56, 59), Laulu-Togagae (76); **Goals:** Hall 12/13.
Rugby Leaguer & League Express Men of the Match: *Skolars:* Louis Robinson; *Wolfpack:* Fuifui Moimoi.
Penalty count: 10-10; **Half-time:** 0-34;
Referee: John McMullen; **Attendance:** 1,524.

BARROW RAIDERS 28 YORK CITY KNIGHTS 0

RAIDERS: 1 Ryan Fieldhouse; 5 Shane Toal; 3 Declan Hulme; 20 Andy Litherland; 24 Luke Cresswell; 6 Jamie Dallimore; 7 Lewis Charnock; 8 Joe Bullock; 9 Nathan Mossop; 10 Oliver Wilkes; 18 Danny Morrow; 12 Jarrad Stack; 13 Martin Aspinwall. Subs (all used): 14 Dan Abram; 16 Andrew Dawson; 17 Tom Walker; 22 Bradd Crellin.
Tries: Morrow (10), Cresswell (17), Stack (21), S Toal (30, 72), Charnock (78); **Goals:** Charnock 2/6.
CITY KNIGHTS: 1 Ash Robson; 4 Tommy Brierley; 3 Nev Morrison; 11 Joe Batchelor; 2 David Foggin-Johnston; 7 Harry Tyson-Wilson; 6 Danny Sowerby; 20 Adam Robinson; 14 Harry Carter; 28 Kieran Moran; 17 Brad Hey; 12 Ed Smith; 13 Tim Spears. Subs (all used): 25 Joe Porter; 9 Pat Smith; 15 Liam Thompson; 16 Ronan Dixon.
Rugby Leaguer & League Express Men of the Match: *Raiders:* Jarrad Stack; *City Knights:* Harry Tyson-Wilson.
Penalty count: 10-11; **Half-time:** 20-0;
Referee: Andrew Sweet; **Attendance:** 799.

Sunday 5th March 2017

OXFORD 40 HEMEL STAGS 12

OXFORD: 1 Kane Riley; 2 Josh Atkinson; 3 Tommy Newbould; 4 Harvey Burnett; 5 Curtis McDonald; 6 Callum Windley; 7 Tom Alexander; 8 Jake Joynt; 9 Casey Canterbury; 10 Dwaine McRae; 11 Jordan Siddons; 12 Will Cooke; 13 Jack Pickles. Subs (all used): 14 Bradley Moules; 15 Liam O'Callaghan; 16 Callum Bustin; 17 Sadiq Adebiyi.
Tries: Canterbury (5, 25, 70), Cooke (17), Bustin (32, 60), Windley (37), McRae (65); **Goals:** Burnett 4/8.
STAGS: 1 Mitch Vincent; 2 Marcus Elliott; 3 Declan Tomlinson; 4 Mindu Bendikas; 5 Darren Forde; 6 Josh Halliday; 7 Jorge Richardson; 8 Danny Samuel; 9 Declan Gregory; 10 Wayne Jowitt; 11 Ross White; 12 James Thornton; 13 George Milton. Subs (all used): 14 Mark Barlow; 15 Reece Williams; 16 Alex Williams; 17 Brad Clavering.
Tries: Richardson (3), Clavering (74); **Goals:** Vincent 2/2.
Rugby Leaguer & League Express Men of the Match: *Oxford:* Casey Canterbury; *Stags:* Alex Williams.
Penalty count: 12-9; **Half-time:** 24-6;
Referee: Steve Race; **Attendance:** 161.

DONCASTER 26 COVENTRY BEARS 4

DONCASTER: 1 Tom Carr; 22 Louis Sheriff; 5 Sam Doherty; 4 Jason Tali; 24 Richie Barnett; 6 Jordan Howden; 15 Jack Miller; 8 Mark Castle; 9 Kyle Kesik; 14 Connor Scott; 13 Charlie Martin; 3 Liam Welham; 12 Jason Muranka. Subs (all used): 20 Kieran Cross; 16 Russ Spiers; 10 Iafeta Palea'aesina; 23 Jamie Thackray.
Tries: Miller (8), Barnett (15), Cross (51), Tali (58);
Goals: Carr 5/5.
BEARS: 1 Will Roper; 2 Hayden Freeman; 3 Jason Bass; 4 Eddie Medforth; 5 Jamahl Hunte; 6 Joe Prior; 7 Charlie O'Mara; 8 James Guertjens; 9 Billy Gaylor; 10 John Aldred; 11 Matt Reid; 12 Chris Barratt; 13 Kieran Sherratt. Subs (all used): 14 Mikey Russell; 15 Dan Gover; 16 Alex Beddows; 17 Zach Johnson.
Try: Hunte (42); **Goals:** Gaylor 0/1.
Rugby Leaguer & League Express Men of the Match: *Doncaster:* Liam Welham; *Bears:* Matt Reid.
Penalty count: 15-7; **Half-time:** 12-0;
Referee: Brandon Robinson; **Attendance:** 545.

HUNSLET 10 GLOUCESTERSHIRE ALL GOLDS 6

HUNSLET: 1 Jimmy Watson; 30 Ryan Ince; 12 Aston Wilson; 24 Cameron Leeming; 3 Marcus Webb; 18 Joel Gibson; 7 Danny Ansell; - Trae O'Sullivan; 9 Jack Lee; 19 Matt Carbutt; 11 Jake Normington; 22 Brooke Broughton; 13 Liam Mackay. Subs (all used): 25 Matthew Tebb; 23 Jose Kenga; 21 Jack Walton; 27 Brett Whitehead.
Tries: Leeming (5), Ince (25); **Goals:** Ansell 1/2.
ALL GOLDS: 1 Josh Houghton; 2 Mo Agoro; 3 Billy Brickhill; 4 Kadeem Williams; 5 Brad Kislingbury; 6 Ben Stead; 7 Kieran Hyde; 8 Ollie Purslow; 9 Steve Parry; 10 Harry Kidd; 11 Adam Jones; 12 Joe McClean; 13 Harrison Elliott. Subs (all used): 14 Jack Mitchell; 15 Jordan Andrade; 16 Malikhi Lloyd-Jones; 17 James Walter.
Try: Andrade (37); **Goals:** Stead 1/1.
Rugby Leaguer & League Express Men of the Match: *Hunslet:* Danny Ansell; *All Golds:* Ben Stead.
Penalty count: 6-11; **Half-time:** 10-6;
Referee: Tom Crashley; **Attendance:** 407.

KEIGHLEY COUGARS 50 NORTH WALES CRUSADERS 8

COUGARS: 22 Ritchie Hawkyard; 26 Vinny Finigan; 4 Danny Lawton; 32 Adam Ryder; 2 Andy Gabriel; 16 Will Milner; 7 Matty Beharrell; 8 Scott Law; 9 James Feather; 29 Brad Nicholson; 11 Josh Lynam; 18 Josh Tonks; 13 Mike Emmett. Subs (all used): 12 Brendon Rawlins; 17 Nathan Conroy; 19 Matthew Bailey; - James Brown.
Tries: Gabriel (4, 7), Ryder (13, 77), Beharrell (20, 23), Tonks (31), Finigan (37), Lawton (48);
Goals: Beharrell 2/4, Lawton 5/5.
CRUSADERS: 1 Tommy Johnson; 2 Corey Lee; 28 Callum Mulkeen; 4 Earl Hurst; 5 Dale Bloomfield; 26 Jack Hansen; 7 Ryan Smith; 8 Jonny Walker; 9 Lee Hudson; 17 Kenny Baker; 24 Jack Houghton; 16 Luke Warburton; 14 James Dandy. Subs (all used): 15 John Cookson; 19 Dan Price; 20 Andy Unsworth; 22 Andrew Joy.
Tries: Hurst (64), Johnson (69); **Goals:** Johnson 0/2.
Rugby Leaguer & League Express Men of the Match: *Cougars:* Danny Lawton; *Crusaders:* Tommy Johnson.
Penalty count: 8-7; **Half-time:** 38-0;
Referee: Nick Bennett; **Attendance:** 752.

SOUTH WALES IRONMEN 10 WHITEHAVEN 27

IRONMEN: 6 Andrew Gay; 2 Yannic Parker; 12 Lewis Reece; 4 Christiaan Roets; 3 Paul Edwards; 15 Shaun Owens; 5 Paul Emanuelli; 19 Jamie I'Anson; 14 Kristian Baller; 18 Morgan Evans; 24 Connor Parker; 17 Zak Williams; 16 Ashley Bateman. Subs (all used): 8 Chris Davies; 9 Connor Farrer; 11 Richard Jones; 13 Chris Vitalini.
Tries: Evans (60), Y Parker (65); **Goals:** Emanuelli 1/2.
WHITEHAVEN: 1 Elliott Miller; 5 Jordan Burns; 30 David Thompson; 3 Chris Taylor; 26 Shane Pattinson; 6 Steve Roper; 7 Paul Crook; 8 Marc Shackley; 9 James Newton; 17 Tommy Holland; 16 Connor Holliday; 12 Scott McAvoy; 10 Carl Forster. Subs (all used): 14 James Tilley; 18 Tyrone Dalton; 19 Glenn Riley; 24 Lewis Brown.
Tries: Roper (2), Crook (24), Riley (45), Burns (48);
Goals: Crook 5/5; **Field goal:** Crook (79).
Sin bin: Miller (64) - tripping; Brown (67) - high tackle.
Rugby Leaguer & League Express Men of the Match: *Ironmen:* Andrew Gay; *Whitehaven:* Paul Crook.
Penalty count: 8-9; **Half-time:** 0-12;
Referee: Greg Dolan; **Attendance:** 223.

WORKINGTON TOWN 20 NEWCASTLE THUNDER 24

TOWN: 3 Ed Chamberlain; 2 Joe Hambley; 22 Jack Higginson; 21 Macauley Davies; 4 Jason Mossop; 6 Carl Forber; 9 Callum Phillips; 10 Stevie Scholey; 14 Sam Dowsett; 16 Tom Curwen; 11 Brett Phillips; 23 Phil Joseph; 13 Stuart Howarth. Subs (all used): 7 Jamie Doran; 8 Kris Coward; 24 Conor Fitzsimmons; 12 Alex Szostak.
Tries: C Phillips (27), Joseph (31), Davies (55), Hambley (78);
Goals: Forber 2/4.
THUNDER: 1 Derrell Olpherts; 2 Ali Blair; 3 Joe Brown; 4 Tyler Craig; 5 Peter Fox; 6 Danny Nicklas; 7 Benn Hardcastle; 8 Liam McAvoy; 9 Evan Simons; 10 Rhys Clarke; 11 Harry Aldous; 12 Dan Parker; 13 Jack Aldous. Subs (all used): 14 Aaron Teroi; 15 Sam Luckley; 16 Vincent Rennie; 17 Brett Waller.
Tries: Simons (9, 65), Blair (37); **Goals:** Hardcastle 6/7.
Rugby Leaguer & League Express Men of the Match: *Town:* Phil Joseph; *Thunder:* Benn Hardcastle.
Penalty count: 13-17; **Half-time:** 12-12;
Referee: Liam Moore; **Attendance:** 660.

ROUND 2

Sunday 12th March 2017

HEMEL STAGS 10 HUNSLET 58

STAGS: 1 Mitch Vincent; 2 Darren Forde; 3 Declan Tomlinson; 4 Mindu Bendikas; 5 Marcus Elliott; 6 Josh Halliday; 7 Lewis Fairhurst; 8 Wayne Jowitt; 9 Jono Burns; 10 Reece Williams; 11 Ross White; 12 James Thornton; 13 Scott Lee. Subs (all used): 14 Declan Gregory; 15 Santino Decaro; 16 Jack O'Brien; 17 Danny Samuel.
Tries: Burns (18), Forde (51);
Goals: Vincent 1/1, Tomlinson 0/1.
HUNSLET: 1 Jimmy Watson; 3 Marcus Webb; 24 Cameron Leeming; 12 Aston Wilson; 30 Ryan Ince; 18 Joel Gibson; 7 Danny Ansell; - Trae O'Sullivan; 9 Jack Lee; 19 Matt Carbutt; 11 Jake Normington; 21 Jack Walton; 13 Liam Mackay. Subs (all used): 14 George Flanagan; 23 Jose Kenga; 4 Mufaro Mvududu; 22 Brooke Broughton.
Tries: Ince (14, 53), Walton (25), Leeming (30), Broughton (42), Flanagan (55, 66), Watson (67), Webb (76), Wilson (79); **Goals:** Ansell 9/10.
Sin bin: O'Sullivan (10) - dissent.
Rugby Leaguer & League Express Men of the Match: *Stags:* Reece Williams; *Hunslet:* Jimmy Watson.
Penalty count: 11-9; **Half-time:** 6-18;
Referee: Michael Mannifield; **Attendance:** 155.

OXFORD 6 WORKINGTON TOWN 20

OXFORD: 1 Kane Riley; 2 Josh Atkinson; 3 Curtis McDonald; 4 Harvey Burnett; 5 Andrew Hoggins; 6 Callum Windley; 7 Scott Fleming; 8 Jake Joynt; 9 Casey Canterbury; 10 Stuart Biscomb; 11 Alex Foster; 12 Will Cooke; 13 Jack Pickles. Subs (all used): 14 Bradley Moules; 15 Dwaine McRae; 16 Marcus Brooker; 17 Anthony Cox.
Try: McDonald (6); **Goals:** Burnett 1/1.
Sin bin: Pickles (80) - fighting.
TOWN: 3 Ed Chamberlain; 2 Joe Hambley; 22 Jack Higginson; 4 Jason Mossop; 20 Kieran Mewse; 6 Carl Forber; 9 Callum Phillips; 8 Kris Coward; 14 Sam Dowsett; 16 Tom Curwen; 11 Brett Phillips; 21 Macauley Davies; 13 Stuart Howarth. Subs (all used): 12 Alex Szostak; 15 Perry Singleton; 24 Conor Fitzsimmons; 17 Scott Rooke.
Tries: Chamberlain (38), Higginson (42), Hambley (61);
Goals: Forber 4/4.
Sin bin: Davies (80) - fighting.
Rugby Leaguer & League Express Men of the Match: *Oxford:* Josh Atkinson; *Town:* Carl Forber.
Penalty count: 10-15; **Half-time:** 6-6;
Referee: Brandon Robinson; **Attendance:** 120.

WHITEHAVEN 10 TORONTO WOLFPACK 24

WHITEHAVEN: 1 Elliott Miller; 30 David Thompson; 3 Chris Taylor; 4 Jessie Joe Parker; 5 Jordan Burns; 6 Steve Roper; 7 Paul Crook; 8 Marc Shackley; 9 James Newton; 17 Tommy Holland; 12 Scott McAvoy; 16 Connor Holliday; 13 Karl Olstrum. Subs (all used): 34 Lewis Foster; 19 Glenn Riley; 14 James Tilley; 10 Carl Forster.
Tries: Miller (61), Taylor (78); **Goals:** Crook 1/2.
WOLFPACK: 1 Quentin Laulu-Togagae; 2 Jonny Pownall; 3 Greg Worthington; 4 Craig Hall; 5 Liam Kay; 6 Blake Wallace; 7 Rhys Jacks; 29 Jake Emmitt; 9 Bob Beswick; 21 Adam Sidlow; 11 Andrew Dixon; 12 James Laithwaite; 13 Jack Bussey. Subs (all used): 14 Gary Wheeler; 19 Steve Crossley; 23 Toby Everett; 17 Richard Whiting.
Tries: Hall (20), Kay (38), Beswick (56), Pownall (68);
Goals: Hall 4/5.
Rugby Leaguer & League Express Men of the Match: *Whitehaven:* Elliott Miller; *Wolfpack:* Jake Emmitt.
Penalty count: 12-8; **Half-time:** 0-14;
Referee: Liam Moore; **Attendance:** 643.

COVENTRY BEARS 14 BARROW RAIDERS 50

BEARS: 1 Will Roper; 2 Hayden Freeman; 3 Jason Bass; 4 Eddie Medforth; 5 Mikey Russell; 6 Joe Prior; 7 Brad Delaney; 8 Zach Johnson; 9 Billy Gaylor; 10 John Aldred; 11 Matt Reid; 12 Chris Barratt; 13 Kieran Sherratt. Subs (all used): 14 Rob Meadows; 15 James Geurtjens; 16 Dan Gover; 17 Jack Morrison.
Tries: Freeman (32), Barratt (47), Russell (78);
Goals: Delaney 1/3.
RAIDERS: 1 Ryan Fieldhouse; 5 Shane Toal; 3 Declan Hulme; 20 Andy Litherland; 24 Luke Cresswell; 6 Jamie Dallimore; 7 Lewis Charnock; 8 Joe Bullock; 9 Nathan Mossop; 10 Oliver Wilkes; 22 Bradd Crellin; 12 Jarrad Stack; 13 Martin Aspinwall. Subs (all used): 14 Dan Abram; 21 James Duerden; 16 Andrew Dawson; 17 Tom Walker.
Tries: Stack (5, 56), S Toal (15), Mossop (16), Litherland (37), Abram (50), Cresswell (60), Hulme (70), Bullock (74); **Goals:** Charnock 7/9.
Rugby Leaguer & League Express Men of the Match: *Bears:* Chris Barratt; *Raiders:* Lewis Charnock.
Penalty count: 7-15; **Half-time:** 6-24;
Referee: Matt Rossleigh; **Attendance:** 447.

GLOUCESTERSHIRE ALL GOLDS 46 KEIGHLEY COUGARS 22

ALL GOLDS: 1 Alex Gaskell; 2 Mo Agoro; 3 Phil Cowburn; 4 Brad Kislingbury; 5 Chris Barlow; 6 Jack Mitchell; 7 Kieran Hyde; 8 Ollie Purslow; 9 Steve Parry; 10 Harry Kidd; 11 Chris Worrall; 12 Joe McClean; 13 Billy Brickhill. Subs (all used):

14 Kadeem Williams; 15 Harrison Elliott; 16 Danny Fallon; 17 James Walter.
Tries: Parry (9, 70), Agoro (14, 59, 68, 79), Mitchell (34), Elliott (43); **Goals:** Hyde 5/6, Fallon 2/4.
COUGARS: 22 Ritchie Hawkyard; 26 Vinny Finigan; 4 Danny Lawton; 32 Adam Ryder; 2 Andy Gabriel; 16 Will Milner; 7 Matty Beharrell; 13 Mike Emmett; 9 James Feather; 29 Brad Nicholson; 11 Josh Lynam; 18 Josh Tonks; 27 Sean Kelly. Subs (all used): 12 Brendon Rawlins; 17 Nathan Conroy; 19 Matthew Bailey; 23 Fran Welsh.
Tries: Ryder (1), Tonks (25), Feather (50), Milner (55); **Goals:** Lawton 3/4.
Rugby Leaguer & League Express Men of the Match: *All Golds:* Ollie Purslow; *Cougars:* Matty Beharrell.
Penalty count: 8-5; **Half-time:** 16-10; **Referee:** Marcus Griffiths; **Attendance:** 176.

NEWCASTLE THUNDER 24 LONDON SKOLARS 22

THUNDER: 1 Lewis Young; 2 Ali Blair; 3 Tyler Craig; 4 Derrell Olpherts; 5 Peter Fox; 6 Danny Nicklas; 7 Benn Hardcastle; 8 Matt Barron; 9 Evan Simons; 10 Corbyn Kilday; 11 Harry Aldous; 12 Rhys Clarke; 13 Liam McAvoy. Subs (all used): 14 Aaron Teroi; 15 Vincent Rennie; 16 Brett Waller; 17 Sam Luckley.
Tries: Waller (28), Nicklas (36), Olpherts (39), Blair (54, 80); **Goals:** Hardcastle 2/5.
Sin bin: Hardcastle (40) - fighting.
SKOLARS: 20 Jake Melling; 2 Sam Nash; 3 Aaron Small; 27 Kameron Pearce-Paul; 24 Michael Brown; - Jermaine Coleman; - Phil Lyon; 30 Simona Vavega; 26 Matt Davis; 28 Callum Bustin; 29 Matty Gee; 12 Eddie Mbaraga; 13 Ryan Chester. Subs (all used): 14 Billy Driver; 8 Louis Robinson; 19 Erjon Dollapi; 11 Lamont Bryan.
Tries: Nash (2), Small (19), Bryan (67); **Goals:** Lyon 4/4, Nash 1/1.
Dismissals: Vavega (80) - headbutt; Small (80) - dissent.
Sin bin: Small (40) - fighting.
Rugby Leaguer & League Express Men of the Match: *Thunder:* Benn Hardcastle; *Skolars:* Lamont Bryan.
Penalty count: 5-5; **Half-time:** 14-14; **Referee:** Nick Bennett; **Attendance:** 607.

NORTH WALES CRUSADERS 8 DONCASTER 44

CRUSADERS: 1 Tommy Johnson; 2 Corey Lee; 28 Callum Mulkeen; 4 Earl Hurst; 5 Dale Bloomfield; 19 Dan Price; 7 Ryan Smith; 8 Jonny Walker; 9 Lee Hudson; 17 Kenny Baker; 24 Jack Houghton; 16 Luke Warburton; 14 James Dandy. Subs (all used): 27 Aaron Moore; 15 John Cookson; 31 Blake Turner; 32 Warren Thompson.
Tries: Bloomfield (53), Hurst (72); **Goals:** Johnson 0/2.
DONCASTER: 1 Tom Carr; 22 Louis Sheriff; 3 Liam Welham; 4 Jason Tali; 24 Richie Barnett; 6 Jordan Howden; 20 Kieran Cross; 8 Mark Castle; 9 Kyle Kesik; 14 Connor Scott; 13 Charlie Martin; 34 Brad England; 12 Jason Muranka. Subs (all used): 18 Ryan Wright; 10 Iafeta Palea'aesina; 23 Jamie Thackray; 16 Russ Spiers.
Tries: Barnett (12), Howden (24, 29), Cross (32, 39), Spiers (36), Tali (48, 75), Sheriff (80); **Goals:** Carr 3/8, Kesik 1/1.
Rugby Leaguer & League Express Men of the Match: *Crusaders:* Blake Turner; *Doncaster:* Jordan Howden.
Penalty count: 10-8; **Half-time:** 0-30; **Referee:** John McMullen; **Attendance:** 305.

YORK CITY KNIGHTS 26 SOUTH WALES IRONMEN 24

CITY KNIGHTS: 1 Ash Robson; 4 Tommy Brierley; 3 Nev Morrison; 11 Joe Batchelor; 2 David Foggin-Johnston; 6 Danny Sowerby; 7 Harry Tyson-Wilson; 16 Ronan Dixon; 26 Andy Ellis; 20 Adam Robinson; 12 Ed Smith; 17 Brad Hey; 13 Tim Spears. Subs (all used): 14 Harry Carter; 29 George Milton; 25 Joe Porter; 8 Bobby Tyson-Wilson.
Tries: Foggin-Johnston (3, 10), Brierley (16), Ellis (27), H Tyson-Wilson (41); **Goals:** H Tyson-Wilson 3/5.
IRONMEN: 6 Andrew Gay; 2 Yannic Parker; 3 Paul Edwards; 12 Lewis Reece; 1 James Stringer; 15 Shaun Owens; 5 Paul Emanuelli; 18 Morgan Evans; 14 Kristian Baller; 13 Chris Vitalini; 11 Richard Jones; 4 Christiaan Roets; 16 Ashley Bateman. Subs (all used): 10 Izaak Duffy; 8 Chris Davies; 19 Jamie I'Anson; 17 Zak Williams.
Tries: Gay (13, 46), Chris Davies (40), Roets (51), Reece (60); **Goals:** Emanuelli 2/5.
Rugby Leaguer & League Express Men of the Match: *City Knights:* Adam Robinson; *Ironmen:* Andrew Gay.
Penalty count: 10-4; **Half-time:** 20-10; **Referee:** Liam Staveley; **Attendance:** 752.

ROUND 3

Saturday 25th March 2017

LONDON SKOLARS 42 COVENTRY BEARS 16

SKOLARS: 20 Jake Melling; 2 Sam Nash; 31 Josh Allison; 24 Michael Brown; 5 James Hill; 9 Charlie Lawrence; 27 Brandon Pickersgill; 25 Michael Sykes; 14 Billy Driver; 30 Callum Bustin; 29 Keenen Tomlinson; 12 Eddie Mbaraga; 11 Lamont Bryan. Subs (all used): 26 Ben Pointer; 28 Sadiq Adebiyi; 8 Louis Robinson; 18 Mike Greenhalgh.
Tries: Driver (7), Bryan (12), Mbaraga (19), Allison (21, 30), Pointer (40), C Lawrence (53), Pickersgill (62); **Goals:** C Lawrence 5/8.
BEARS: 1 Jason Bass; 2 Hayden Freeman; 3 Rob Meadows; 4 Eddie Medforth; 5 Mikey Russell; 6 Joe Prior; 7 Brad Delaney; 8 Zach Johnson; 9 Billy Gaylor; 10 James Geurtjens; 11 Matt Reid; 12 Chris Barratt; 13 Kieran Sherratt. Subs (all used): 14 Lewis Lord; 15 Jack Morrison; 16 Elliott Davies; 17 Dan Gover.
Tries: Freeman (50), Delaney (56), Russell (74); **Goals:** Delaney 2/3.
Rugby Leaguer & League Express Men of the Match: *Skolars:* Lamont Bryan; *Bears:* Jack Morrison.
Penalty count: 8-8; **Half-time:** 30-0; **Referee:** Matt Rossleigh; **Attendance:** 287.

BARROW RAIDERS 82 HEMEL STAGS 0

RAIDERS: 1 Ryan Fieldhouse; 45 Tom Loxam; 3 Declan Hulme; 20 Andy Litherland; 2 Brett Carter; 6 Jamie Dallimore; 27 Ryan Johnston; 8 Joe Bullock; 26 Brad Marwood; 10 Oliver Wilkes; 12 Jarrad Stack; 11 Dan Toal; 13 Martin Aspinwall. Subs (all used): 9 Nathan Mossop; 28 Brad Brennan; 17 Tom Walker; 25 Matty While.
Tries: Fieldhouse (5, 37, 41), Carter (10), Johnston (17, 20), Walker (24), Hulme (40, 45), Litherland (50, 79), Marwood (55, 76), Stack (70), Mossop (73); **Goals:** Johnston 11/15.
STAGS: 1 Mitch Vincent; 2 Charlie Brown; 3 Roddy Jonas; 4 Dom Horn; 5 Darren Forde; 6 Mark Barlow; 7 Jorge Richardson; 8 Wayne Jowitt; 9 Jono Burns; 10 Reece Williams; 11 Ross White; 12 James Thornton; 13 Scott Lee. Subs (all used): 14 Declan Gregory; 15 Declan Tomlinson; 16 Santino Decaro; 17 Jack O'Brien.
Rugby Leaguer & League Express Men of the Match: *Raiders:* Ryan Johnston; *Stags:* Reece Williams.
Penalty count: 9-7; **Half-time:** 38-0; **Referee:** Greg Dolan; **Attendance:** 739.

Sunday 26th March 2017

KEIGHLEY COUGARS 21 TORONTO WOLFPACK 48

COUGARS: 22 Ritchie Hawkyard; 26 Vinny Finigan; 3 Josh Casey; 32 Adam Ryder; 2 Andy Gabriel; 16 Will Milner; 7 Matty Beharrell; 8 Scott Law; 9 James Feather; 23 Fran Welsh; 11 Josh Lynam; 18 Josh Tonks; 13 Mike Emmett. Subs (all used): 12 Brendon Rawlins; 14 Adam Brook; 19 Matthew Bailey; 29 Brad Nicholson.
Tries: Lynam (28, 41), Beharrell (68); **Goals:** Beharrell 4/4; **Field goal:** Beharrell (38).
WOLFPACK: 1 Quentin Laulu-Togagae; 2 Jonny Pownall; 14 Gary Wheeler; 4 Craig Hall; 5 Liam Kay; 6 Blake Wallace; 7 Rhys Jacks; 21 Adam Sidlow; 9 Bob Beswick; 29 Jake Emmitt; 11 Andrew Dixon; 12 James Laithwaite; 10 Daniel Fleming. Subs (all used): 15 Ryan Burroughs; 17 Richard Whiting; 19 Steve Crossley; 23 Toby Everett.
Tries: Pownall (8, 49, 58), Kay (22), Wallace (46), Hall (52), Sidlow (71, 80), Dixon (73); **Goals:** Hall 6/9.
Sin bin: Fleming (15) - punching.
Rugby Leaguer & League Express Men of the Match: *Cougars:* Matty Beharrell; *Wolfpack:* Jonny Pownall.
Penalty count: 10-9; **Half-time:** 9-8; **Referee:** Andrew Sweet; **Attendance:** 1,128.

SOUTH WALES IRONMEN 20 NEWCASTLE THUNDER 26

IRONMEN: 6 Andrew Gay; 2 Yannic Parker; 3 Paul Edwards; 4 Christiaan Roets; 26 Lewis Hughes; 15 Shaun Owens; 5 Paul Emanuelli; 18 Morgan Evans; 17 Zak Williams; 10 Izaak Duffy; 24 Connor Parker; 12 Lewis Reece; 16 Ashley Bateman. Subs (all used): 11 Richard Jones; 13 Chris Vitalini; 14 Kristian Baller; 19 Jamie I'Anson.
Tries: P Edwards (18), R Jones (28), Reece (36), Hughes (39); **Goals:** Reece 0/2, Emanuelli 2/2.
Sin bin: Vitalini (77) - high tackle.
THUNDER: 1 Derrell Olpherts; 2 Ali Blair; 3 Tyler Craig; 4 Joe Brown; 5 Peter Fox; 6 Danny Nicklas; 7 Benn Hardcastle; 8 Vincent Rennie; 9 Evan Simons; 10 Rhys Clarke; 11 Dan Parker; 12 Harry Aldous; 13 Jack Aldous. Subs (all used): 14 Aaron Teroi; 15 Josh Stoker; 16 Matt Barron; 17 Brett Waller.
Tries: Rennie (5), Parker (24), Craig (49), Olpherts (55); **Goals:** Hardcastle 5/5.
Sin bin: Olpherts (21) - shoulder charge.
Rugby Leaguer & League Express Men of the Match: *Ironmen:* Lewis Reece; *Thunder:* Vincent Rennie.
Penalty count: 6-9; **Half-time:** 20-12; **Referee:** Steve Race; **Attendance:** 150.

WORKINGTON TOWN 54
GLOUCESTERSHIRE ALL GOLDS 22

TOWN: 3 Ed Chamberlain; 17 Scott Rooke; 2 Joe Hambley; 4 Jason Mossop; 20 Kieran Mewse; 6 Carl Forber; 13 Stuart Howarth; 10 Stevie Scholey; 9 Callum Phillips; 16 Tom Curwen; 11 Brett Phillips; 24 Conor Fitzsimmons; 15 Perry Singleton. Subs (all used): 14 Sam Dowsett; 12 Alex Szostak; 8 Kris Coward; 21 Macauley Davies.
Tries: Curwen (14, 20), Davies (43), Hambley (52), C Phillips (61), Mossop (69), Rooke (72), Forber (75), Scholey (77); **Goals:** Forber 9/9.
ALL GOLDS: 1 Alex Gaskell; 2 Mo Agoro; 3 Phil Cowburn; 4 Brad Kislingbury; 5 Chris Barlow; 6 Jack Mitchell; 7 Kieran Hyde; 8 Ollie Purslow; 9 Steve Parry; 10 Harrison Elliott; 11 Chris Worrall; 12 Joe McClean; 13 Billy Brickhill. Subs (all used): 14 Malikhi Lloyd-Jones; 15 James Walter; 16 Jordan Andrade; 17 Harry Kidd.
Tries: Cowburn (10), McClean (20), Barlow (47), Agoro (55); **Goals:** Hyde 3/4.
Rugby Leaguer & League Express Men of the Match: *Town:* Carl Forber; *All Golds:* Kieran Hyde.
Penalty count: 6-3; **Half-time:** 12-12; **Referee:** Liam Moore; **Attendance:** 509.

YORK CITY KNIGHTS 22
NORTH WALES CRUSADERS 26

CITY KNIGHTS: 31 Liam Harris; 21 Ben Dent; 3 Nev Morrison; 19 James Haynes; 5 Tom Saxton; 23 Jon Presley; 7 Harry Tyson-Wilson; 16 Ronan Dixon; 26 Andy Ellis; 20 Adam Robinson; 11 Joe Batchelor; 12 Ed Smith; 13 Tim Spears. Subs (all used): 14 Harry Carter; 28 Kieran Moran; 10 Chris Siddons; 8 Bobby Tyson-Wilson.
Tries: Dent (9), H Tyson-Wilson (16, 44), Batchelor (76); **Goals:** H Tyson-Wilson 3/5.
On report: E Smith (36) - alleged high tackle.
CRUSADERS: 1 Tommy Johnson; 2 Corey Lee; 28 Callum Mulkeen; 4 Earl Hurst; 5 Dale Bloomfield; 26 Jack Hansen; 7 Ryan Smith; 8 Jonny Walker; 9 Lee Hudson; 17 Kenny Baker; 24 Jack Houghton; 3 Simon Atherton; 16 Luke Warburton. Subs (all used): 27 Aaron Moore; 15 John Cookson; 31 Blake Turner; 10 Alex Davidson.
Tries: Mulkeen (26), Davidson (38), Hurst (53), Smith (66), Bloomfield (72); **Goals:** Johnson 3/5.
Rugby Leaguer & League Express Men of the Match: *City Knights:* Joe Batchelor; *Crusaders:* Tommy Johnson.
Penalty count: 9-9; **Half-time:** 12-10; **Referee:** Jon Roberts; **Attendance:** 702.

ROUND 11

Sunday 2nd April 2017

DONCASTER 29 HUNSLET 24

DONCASTER: 1 Tom Carr; 5 Sam Doherty; 3 Liam Welham; 4 Jason Tali; 24 Richie Barnett; 15 Jack Miller; 20 Kieran Cross; 8 Mark Castle; 9 Kyle Kesik; 14 Connor Scott; 34 Brad England; 13 Charlie Martin; 23 Jamie Thackray. Subs (all used): 18 Ryan Wright; 10 Iafeta Palea'aesina; 16 Russ Spiers; 11 Mason Tonks.
Tries: Martin (21), Cross (26), Tonks (35), Wright (62), Tali (80); **Goals:** Carr 4/6; **Field goal:** Carr (71).
Sin bin: England (27) - fighting.
HUNSLET: 1 Jimmy Watson; 5 Gavin Duffy; 12 Aston Wilson; 4 Mufaro Mvududu; 3 Marcus Webb; 7 Danny Ansell; 13 Liam Mackay; 10 Lewis Reed; 9 Jack Lee; 31 Sean Hesketh; 11 Jake Normington; 21 Jack Walton; 17 Nyle Flynn. Subs (all used): 18 Joel Gibson; 23 Jose Kenga; 19 Matt Carbutt; 14 George Flanagan.
Tries: Duffy (10), Mvududu (49), Normington (55), Flanagan (59); **Goals:** Ansell 4/6.
Sin bin: Normington (27) - fighting; Lee (79) - interference.
Rugby Leaguer & League Express Men of the Match: *Doncaster:* Kieran Cross; *Hunslet:* George Flanagan.
Penalty count: 10-13; **Half-time:** 16-6; **Referee:** Steve Race; **Attendance:** 604.

ROUND 4

Saturday 8th April 2017

BARROW RAIDERS 26 WORKINGTON TOWN 10

RAIDERS: 1 Ryan Fieldhouse; 5 Shane Toal; 3 Declan Hulme; 20 Andy Litherland; 24 Luke Cresswell; 6 Jamie Dallimore; 7 Lewis Charnock; 8 Joe Bullock; 9 Nathan Mossop; 10 Oliver Wilkes; 12 Jarrad Stack; 22 Bradd Crellin; 21 James Duerden. Subs (all used): 14 Dan Abram; 16 Andrew Dawson; 17 Tom Walker; 11 Dan Toal.
Tries: Charnock (6), Litherland (33), Abram (49), Duerden (65); **Goals:** Charnock 5/5.
Sin bin: Charnock (22) - repeated team offences.

TOWN: - Gabriel Fell; 2 Joe Hambley; 3 Ed Chamberlain; 4 Jason Mossop; 17 Scott Rooke; 6 Carl Forber; 7 Jamie Doran; 10 Stevie Scholey; 14 Sam Dowsett; 8 Kris Coward; 11 Brett Phillips; 21 Macauley Davies; 15 Perry Singleton. Subs (all used): 16 Tom Curwen; 12 Alex Szostak; 18 Conor Fitzsimmons; 9 Callum Phillips.
Tries: Doran (53), Chamberlain (58); **Goals:** Forber 1/2.
Rugby Leaguer & League Express Men of the Match: *Raiders:* Jamie Dallimore; *Town:* Brett Phillips.
Penalty count: 13-11; **Half-time:** 12-0;
Referee: Brandon Robinson; **Attendance:** 1,284.

Sunday 9th April 2017

DONCASTER 6 TORONTO WOLFPACK 82

DONCASTER: 1 Tom Carr; 5 Sam Doherty; 3 Liam Welham; 4 Jason Tali; 22 Louis Sheriff; 6 Jordan Howden; 20 Kieran Cross; 8 Mark Castle; 9 Kyle Kesik; 14 Connor Scott; 13 Charlie Martin; 11 Mason Tonks; 23 Jamie Thackray. Subs (all used): 18 Ryan Wright; 32 Makali Aizue; 7 Jordie Hedges; 16 Russ Spiers.
Try: Doherty (40); **Goals:** Carr 1/1.
Dismissal: Thackray (74) - punching.
WOLFPACK: 1 Quentin Laulu-Togagae; 2 Jonny Pownall; 3 Greg Worthington; 4 Craig Hall; 5 Liam Kay; 6 Blake Wallace; 7 Rhys Jacks; 8 Fuifui Moimoi; 9 Bob Beswick; 29 Jake Emmitt; 11 Andrew Dixon; 12 James Laithwaite; 13 Jake Bussey. Subs (all used): 14 Gary Wheeler; 17 Richard Whiting; 19 Steve Crossley; 21 Adam Sidlow.
Tries: Beswick (4), Moimoi (6, 47), Bussey (15, 73, 80), Kay (25, 53), Laulu-Togagae (31), Wallace (33, 67), Worthington (50), Whiting (60), Jacks (62);
Goals: Hall 13/14.
Rugby Leaguer & League Express Men of the Match: *Doncaster:* Jason Tali; *Wolfpack:* Blake Wallace.
Penalty count: 8-8; **Half-time:** 6-34;
Referee: Jon Roberts; **Attendance:** 943.

HEMEL STAGS 6 KEIGHLEY COUGARS 84

STAGS: 1 Mitch Vincent; 2 Marcus Elliott; 3 Declan Tomlinson; 4 Roddy Jonas; 5 Darren Forde; 6 Mark Barlow; 7 Lewis Fairhurst; 8 Wayne Jowitt; 9 Declan Gregory; 10 Reece Williams; 11 James Thornton; 12 Alex Williams; 13 Scott Lee. Subs (all used): 14 Aaron James; 15 Jack O'Brien; 16 Harley Axe; 17 Dom Horn.
Try: Elliott (16); **Goals:** Vincent 1/1.
Sin bin: A Williams (72) - fighting.
COUGARS: 22 Ritchie Hawkyard; 26 Vinny Finigan; 5 Davey Dixon; 32 Adam Ryder; 2 Andy Gabriel; 14 Adam Brook; 7 Matty Beharrell; 15 Neil Cherryholme; 9 James Feather; 19 Matthew Bailey; 25 Ben Sagar; 18 Josh Tonks; 13 Mike Emmett. Subs (all used): 12 Brendon Rawlins; 17 Nathan Conroy; 24 Liam Darville; 29 Brad Nicholson.
Tries: Gabriel (2, 32, 76), Ryder (5, 14, 42, 63), Tonks (8), Feather (19), Beharrell (26), Rawlins (37, 68, 74), Hawkyard (51), Nicholson (53), Emmett (78); **Goals:** Beharrell 10/16.
Sin bin: Hawkyard (72) - fighting.
Rugby Leaguer & League Express Men of the Match: *Stags:* Marcus Elliott; *Cougars:* Josh Tonks.
Penalty count: 4-6; **Half-time:** 6-42;
Referee: Matt Rossleigh; **Attendance:** 118.

OXFORD 35 YORK CITY KNIGHTS 28

OXFORD: 1 Max Jowitt; 2 Josh Atkinson; 3 Kane Riley; 4 Curtis McDonald; 5 Jordan Gill; 6 Callum Windley; 7 Scott Fleming; 8 Stuart Biscomb; 9 Casey Canterbury; 10 Dwaine McRae; 11 Harvey Burnett; 12 Will Cooke; 13 Jordan Crowther. Subs (all used): 14 Marcus Brooker; 15 Bradley Moules; 16 Anthony Cox; 17 Jordan Siddons.
Tries: Gill (15, 33, 66), Jowitt (21), Brooker (47), Siddons (76); **Goals:** Jowitt 5/6; **Field goal:** Windley (74).
CITY KNIGHTS: 31 Liam Harris; 4 Tommy Brierley; 24 Nick Rawsthorne; 19 James Haynes; 5 Tom Saxton; 7 Harry Tyson-Wilson; 23 Jon Presley; 8 Bobby Tyson-Wilson; 14 Harry Carter; 10 Chris Siddons; 12 Ed Smith; 17 Brad Hey; 13 Tim Spears. Subs (all used): 16 Ronan Dixon; - Will Jubb; 28 Kieran Moran; 3 Nev Morrison.
Tries: Carter (1), Rawsthorne (6), Presley (23), Hey (29), Jubb (39); **Goals:** H Tyson-Wilson 4/5.
Sin bin: E Smith (70) - high tackle.
Rugby Leaguer & League Express Men of the Match: *Oxford:* Max Jowitt; *City Knights:* Jon Presley.
Penalty count: 7-4; **Half-time:** 18-28;
Referee: Tom Crashley; **Attendance:** 180.

NORTH WALES CRUSADERS 30
NEWCASTLE THUNDER 14

CRUSADERS: 1 Tommy Johnson; 28 Callum Mulkeen; 11 Alex Thompson; 4 Earl Hurst; 5 Dale Bloomfield; 26 Jack Hansen; 7 Ryan Smith; 8 Jonny Walker; 9 Lee Hudson; 15 John Cookson; 24 Jack Houghton; 3 Simon Atherton; 16 Luke Warburton. Subs (all used): 27 Aaron Moore; 13 Ryan Millington; 23 Jack Francis; 10 Alex Davidson.
Tries: A Thompson (24), Atherton (44), Johnson (63), Hudson (75), Houghton (78); **Goals:** Johnson 5/5.
THUNDER: 1 Lewis Young; 2 Ali Blair; 3 Tyler Craig; 4 Joe Brown; 5 Peter Fox; 6 Benn Hardcastle; 7 Tom Shaw; 8 Brett Waller; 9 Aaron Teroi; 10 Liam McAvoy; 11 Harry Aldous; 12 Lee Paterson; 13 Jack Aldous. Subs (all used): 14 Danny Nicklas; 15 Vincent Rennie; 16 Matt Barron; 17 Corbyn Kilday.
Tries: Young (16), Blair (19), Hardcastle (67);
Goals: Hardcastle 1/3.
Rugby Leaguer & League Express Men of the Match: *Crusaders:* Simon Atherton; *Thunder:* Lewis Young.
Penalty count: 10-13; **Half-time:** 6-8;
Referee: Greg Dolan; **Attendance:** 323.

GLOUCESTERSHIRE ALL GOLDS 22
LONDON SKOLARS 24

ALL GOLDS: 1 Phil Cowburn; 2 Mo Agoro; 3 Billy Brickhill; 4 Steven Nield; 5 Chris Barlow; 6 Danny Fallon; 7 Kieran Hyde; 8 Harry Kidd; 9 Steve Parry; 10 James Walter; 11 Harrison Elliott; 12 Joe McClean; 13 Chris Worrall. Subs (all used): 14 Jay Lobwein; 15 Paddy Jones; 16 Ollie Purslow; 17 Malikhi Lloyd-Jones.
Tries: Parry (9), Agoro (14, 38), McClean (17);
Goals: Hyde 3/5.
SKOLARS: 20 Jake Melling; 2 Sam Nash; 31 Josh Allison; 26 Kameron Pearce-Paul; 24 Michael Brown; 6 Jermaine Coleman; 9 Charlie Lawrence; 29 Callum Bustin; 27 Ben Pointer; 30 Simona Vavega; 12 Eddie Mbaraga; 11 Lamont Bryan; 13 Ryan Chester. Subs (all used): 14 Billy Driver; 8 Louis Robinson; 25 Michael Sykes; 28 Sadiq Adebiyi.
Tries: Brown (3, 24), Robinson (54), Adebiyi (59);
Goals: C Lawrence 3/4; **Field goals:** C Lawrence (73, 78).
Rugby Leaguer & League Express Men of the Match: *All Golds:* Harry Kidd; *Skolars:* Charlie Lawrence.
Penalty count: 5-10; **Half-time:** 20-10;
Referee: Nick Bennett; **Attendance:** 179.

HUNSLET 58 SOUTH WALES IRONMEN 6

HUNSLET: 1 Jimmy Watson; 30 Ryan Ince; 12 Aston Wilson; 4 Mufaro Mvududu; 3 Marcus Webb; 18 Joel Gibson; 6 Joe Sanderson; 10 Lewis Reed; 25 Matthew Tebb; 19 Matt Carbutt; 22 Brooke Broughton; 11 Jake Normington; 13 Liam Mackay. Subs (all used): 31 Sean Hesketh; 14 George Flanagan; 17 Nyle Flynn; 7 Danny Ansell.
Tries: Webb (7), Mvududu (23), Normington (28, 80), Wilson (34), Flanagan (43, 61, 63), Sanderson (58), Broughton (73); **Goals:** Sanderson 9/10.
IRONMEN: 6 Andrew Gay; 2 Yannic Parker; 3 Paul Edwards; 4 Christiaan Roets; 26 Lewis Hughes; 5 Paul Emanuelli; 7 Courtney Davies; 19 Jamie I'Anson; 9 Connor Farrer; 10 Izaak Duffy; 11 Richard Jones; 17 Zak Williams; 16 Ashley Bateman. Subs (all used): 14 Kristian Baller; 13 Chris Vitalini; 24 Connor Parker; - Martyn Reilly.
Try: C Parker (39); **Goals:** Emanuelli 1/1.
Rugby Leaguer & League Express Men of the Match: *Hunslet:* Jake Normington; *Ironmen:* Andrew Gay.
Penalty count: 4-4; **Half-time:** 22-6;
Referee: John McMullen; **Attendance:** 350.

WHITEHAVEN 44 COVENTRY BEARS 12

WHITEHAVEN: 1 Elliott Miller; 30 David Thompson; 3 Chris Taylor; 4 Jessie Joe Parker; 2 Craig Calvert; 6 Steve Roper; 7 Paul Crook; 8 Marc Shackley; 9 James Newton; 19 Glenn Riley; 12 Scott McAvoy; 16 Connor Holliday; 10 Carl Forster. Subs (all used): 14 James Tilley; 18 Tyrone Dalton; 25 Aiden Worthington; 17 Tommy Holland.
Tries: Riley (3), Calvert (9), McAvoy (19), Miller (22, 59), Taylor (32), Crook (40), Parker (42); **Goals:** Crook 6/8.
BEARS: 1 Jason Bass; 2 Hayden Freeman; 3 Matt Reid; 4 Eddie Medforth; 5 Jamahl Hunte; 6 Joe Prior; 7 Brad Delaney; 8 Zach Johnson; 9 Billy Gaylor; 10 Jack Morrison; 11 Kieran Sherratt; 12 Chris Barratt; 13 Elliott Davies. Subs (all used): 14 Rob Meadows; 15 James Geurtjens; 16 Dan Gover; 17 Richard Hughes.
Tries: Medforth (12), Bass (71); **Goals:** Delaney 2/2.
Rugby Leaguer & League Express Men of the Match: *Whitehaven:* Craig Calvert; *Bears:* Brad Delaney.
Penalty count: 7-9; **Half-time:** 34-6;
Referee: Steve Race; **Attendance:** 413.

ROUND 5

Friday 14th April 2017

COVENTRY BEARS 40 OXFORD 28

BEARS: 1 Harry Chapman; 2 Hayden Freeman; 3 Rob Meadows; 4 Matt Reid; 5 Jamahl Hunte; 6 Joe Prior; 7 Brad Delaney; 8 John Aldred; 9 Billy Gaylor; 10 Jack Morrison; 11 Kieran Sherratt; 12 Chris Barratt; 13 Zach Johnson. Subs (all used): 14 Richard Hughes; 15 Alex Beddows; 16 James Guertjens; 17 Dan Gover.
Tries: Morrison (11), Chapman (26), Hunte (40), Hughes (42, 68), Johnson (63), Reid (66);
Goals: Delaney 6/7.
OXFORD: 1 Kane Riley; 2 Josh Atkinson; 3 Tommy Newbould; 4 Harvey Burnett; 5 Jordan Gill; 6 Callum Windley; 7 Scott Fleming; 8 Dwaine McRae; 9 Bradley Moules; 10 Stuart Biscomb; 11 Jordan Siddons; 12 Will Cooke; 13 Tom Alexander. Subs (all used): 14 Josh Kittrick; 15 Marcus Brooker; 16 Andrew Hoggins; 17 Jack Pickles.
Tries: Gill (4, 73), Hoggins (10), McRae (77), Siddons (79);
Goals: Fleming 4/5.
Rugby Leaguer & League Express Men of the Match: *Bears:* Richard Hughes; *Oxford:* Jordan Gill.
Penalty count: 15-19; **Half-time:** 16-10;
Referee: Michael Mannifield; **Attendance:** 303.

KEIGHLEY COUGARS 20 HUNSLET 12

COUGARS: 22 Ritchie Hawkyard; 26 Vinny Finigan; 5 Davey Dixon; 32 Adam Ryder; 2 Andy Gabriel; 16 Will Milner; 7 Matty Beharrell; 15 Neil Cherryholme; 9 James Feather; 19 Matthew Bailey; 11 Josh Lynam; 18 Josh Tonks; 13 Mike Emmett. Subs (all used): 12 Brendon Rawlins; 17 Nathan Conroy; 25 Ben Sagar; 29 Brad Nicholson.
Tries: Ryder (4), Nicholson (47, 79); **Goals:** Beharrell 4/4.
HUNSLET: 1 Jimmy Watson; 30 Ryan Ince; 12 Aston Wilson; 4 Mufaro Mvududu; 5 Gavin Duffy; 18 Joel Gibson; 6 Joe Sanderson; 10 Lewis Reed; 25 Matthew Tebb; 19 Matt Carbutt; 11 Jake Normington; 13 Liam Mackay; 17 Nyle Flynn. Subs (all used): 7 Danny Ansell; 14 George Flanagan; 23 Jose Kenga; 31 Sean Hesketh.
Tries: Mvududu (16), Sanderson (38);
Goals: Sanderson 2/3.
Rugby Leaguer & League Express Men of the Match: *Cougars:* Brad Nicholson; *Hunslet:* Joe Sanderson.
Penalty count: 11-6; **Half-time:** 6-12;
Referee: Matt Rossleigh; **Attendance:** 744.

NEWCASTLE THUNDER 6 BARROW RAIDERS 50

THUNDER: 1 Lewis Young; 2 Ali Blair; 3 Joe Brown; 4 Tyler Craig; 5 Peter Fox; 6 Tom Shaw; 7 Benn Hardcastle; 8 Vincent Rennie; 9 Evan Simons; 10 Liam McAvoy; 11 Harry Aldous; 12 Rhys Clarke; 13 Jack Aldous. Subs (all used): 14 Aaron Teroi; 15 Matt Barron; 16 Brett Waller; 17 Lee Paterson.
Try: Shaw (55); **Goals:** Hardcastle 1/1.
Dismissal: J Aldous (28) - punching Wilkes.
RAIDERS: 1 Ryan Fieldhouse; 5 Shane Toal; 3 Declan Hulme; 20 Andy Litherland; 24 Luke Cresswell; 6 Jamie Dallimore; 7 Lewis Charnock; 8 Joe Bullock; 9 Nathan Mossop; 10 Oliver Wilkes; 12 Jarrad Stack; 22 Bradd Crellin; 21 James Duerden. Subs (all used): 14 Dan Abram; 17 Tom Walker; 11 Dan Toal; 28 Brad Brennan.
Tries: Wilkes (9), Hulme (13), S Toal (35), Cresswell (40), Litherland (48), Duerden (64), Bullock (75), Fieldhouse (79); **Goals:** Charnock 7/7, Dallimore 2/2.
Rugby Leaguer & League Express Men of the Match: *Thunder:* Lewis Young; *Raiders:* Shane Toal.
Penalty count: 11-8; **Half-time:** 0-26;
Referee: Steve Race; **Attendance:** 1,073.

SOUTH WALES IRONMEN 30
GLOUCESTERSHIRE ALL GOLDS 36

IRONMEN: 6 Andrew Gay; 2 Yannic Parker; 3 Paul Edwards; 16 Ashley Bateman; 26 Lewis Hughes; 5 Paul Emanuelli; 15 Shaun Owens; 19 Jamie I'Anson; 9 Connor Farrer; 10 Izaak Duffy; 4 Christiaan Roets; 12 Lewis Reece; 17 Zak Williams. Subs (all used): 7 Courtney Davies; 24 Connor Parker; 11 Richard Jones; 13 Chris Vitalini.
Tries: Owens (16, 49, 63), Y Parker (30), Duffy (66);
Goals: Emanuelli 5/6, Courtney Davies 0/1.
Sin bin: Vitalini (45) - dissent.
ALL GOLDS: 1 Steven Nield; 2 Mo Agoro; 3 Phil Cowburn; 4 Brad Kislingbury; 5 Chris Barlow; 6 Josh Ward; 7 Kieran Hyde; 8 Harrison Elliott; 9 Steve Parry; 10 Ollie Purslow; 11 Chris Worrall; 12 Joe McClean; 13 Billy Brickhill. Subs (all used): 14 Jay Lobwein; 15 Graham O'Keeffe; 16 James Walter; 17 Jordan Andrade.
Tries: Agoro (2, 23, 69), Elliott (5), Cowburn (47), Kislingbury (54); **Goals:** Hyde 6/8.
Sin bin: Barlow (63) - high tackle.
Rugby Leaguer & League Express Men of the Match: *Ironmen:* Shaun Owens; *All Golds:* Mo Agoro.
Penalty count: 13-7; **Half-time:** 12-18;
Referee: Nick Bennett; **Attendance:** 351.

WORKINGTON TOWN 20 WHITEHAVEN 24

TOWN: 21 Gabriel Fell; 2 Joe Hambley; 3 Ed Chamberlain;

4 Jason Mossop; 17 Scott Rooke; 6 Carl Forber; 7 Jamie Doran; 10 Stevie Scholey; 9 Callum Phillips; 8 Kris Coward; 11 Brett Phillips; 18 Conor Fitzsimmons; 15 Perry Singleton. Subs (all used): 5 John Patrick; 12 Alex Szostak; 14 Sam Dowsett; 13 Stuart Howarth.
Tries: Rooke (44), Hambley (51, 71), Mossop (63);
Goals: Forber 2/4.
WHITEHAVEN: 1 Elliott Miller; 5 Jordan Burns; 3 Chris Taylor; 4 Jessie Joe Parker; 2 Craig Calvert; 6 Steve Roper; 7 Paul Crook; 8 Marc Shackley; 9 James Newton; 10 Carl Forster; 12 Scott McAvoy; 16 Connor Holliday; 14 James Tilley. Subs (all used): 19 Glenn Riley; 18 Tyrone Dalton; 25 Aiden Worthington; 17 Tommy Holland.
Tries: McAvoy (24), Forster (32), Parker (35), Tilley (75);
Goals: Crook 4/6.
Sin bin: Forster (20) - late challenge on Forber.
Rugby Leaguer & League Express Men of the Match:
Town: Kris Coward; *Whitehaven:* Connor Holliday.
Penalty count: 10-12; **Half-time:** 0-16;
Referee: Jon Roberts; **Attendance:** 1,103.

YORK CITY KNIGHTS 16 DONCASTER 8

CITY KNIGHTS: 1 Ash Robson; 2 David Foggin-Johnston; 24 Nick Rawsthorne; 19 James Haynes; 5 Tom Saxton; 7 Harry Tyson-Wilson; 23 Jon Presley; 10 Chris Siddons; 9 Pat Smith; 20 Adam Robinson; 12 Ed Smith; 17 Brad Hey; 13 Tim Spears. Subs (all used): 26 Andy Ellis; 16 Ronan Dixon; 25 Joe Porter; 27 Brad Clavering.
Tries: E Smith (16), Ellis (47), Rawsthorne (75);
Goals: H Tyson-Wilson 2/4.
DONCASTER: 1 Tom Carr; 22 Louis Sheriff; 5 Sam Doherty; 4 Jason Tali; 24 Richie Barnett; 20 Kieran Cross; 7 Jordie Hedges; 19 Zac Braham; 9 Kyle Kesik; 16 Russ Spiers; 21 Chris Heil; 13 Charlie Martin; 12 Jason Muranka. Subs (all used): 18 Ryan Wright; 14 Connor Scott; 10 Iafeta Palea'aesina; 23 Jamie Thackray.
Try: Palea'aesina (22); **Goals:** Carr 2/2.
Rugby Leaguer & League Express Men of the Match:
City Knights: Ash Robson; *Doncaster:* Iafeta Palea'aesina.
Penalty count: 15-12; **Half-time:** 6-8;
Referee: Greg Dolan; **Attendance:** 1,012.

LONDON SKOLARS 60 HEMEL STAGS 12

SKOLARS: 20 Jake Melling; 2 Sam Nash; 31 Josh Allison; 24 Michael Brown; 22 John Paxton; - Brandon Pickersgill; 9 Charlie Lawrence; 30 Simona Vavega; 14 Billy Driver; 19 Erjon Dollapi; 11 Lamont Bryan; 12 Eddie Mbaraga; 13 Ryan Chester. Subs (all used): 26 Phil Lyon; 8 Louis Robinson; 25 Michael Sykes; 15 Kazeem Faturoti.
Tries: Chester (7), Nash (19, 52, 61, 64), Lyon (31), Bryan (35), Robinson (45), Pickersgill (57), Dollapi (68), Sykes (74), Mbaraga (80);
Goals: C Lawrence 6/9, Lyon 0/3.
Sin bin: Bryan (75) - fighting.
STAGS: 1 Mitch Vincent; 2 Marcus Elliott; 3 Declan Tomlinson; 4 Josh Nathaniel; 5 Rhys Allatt; 6 Mark Barlow; 7 Josh Halliday; 8 Reece Williams; 9 Jono Burns; 10 Corey Hanson; 11 Brett Whitehead; 12 James Thornton; 13 Jack O'Brien. Subs (all used): 14 Danny Samuel; 15 Alex Williams; 16 Harley Axe; 17 Casey Johnson.
Tries: Vincent (2), Thornton (79); **Goals:** Vincent 2/2.
Dismissal: Samuel (40) - dissent.
Sin bin: R Williams (75) - fighting.
Rugby Leaguer & League Express Men of the Match:
Skolars: Sam Nash; *Stags:* Mitch Vincent.
Penalty count: 8-7; **Half-time:** 20-6;
Referee: Billy Pearson; **Attendance:** 362.

NORTH WALES CRUSADERS 0
TORONTO WOLFPACK 80

CRUSADERS: 1 Tommy Johnson; 2 Corey Lee; 11 Alex Thompson; 28 Callum Mulkeen; 5 Dale Bloomfield; 26 Jack Hansen; 7 Ryan Smith; 10 Alex Davidson; 14 James Dandy; 15 John Cookson; 24 Jack Houghton; 3 Simon Atherton; 16 Luke Warburton. Subs (all used): 27 Aaron Moore; 23 Jack Francis; 31 Blake Turner; 13 Ryan Millington.
WOLFPACK: 1 Quentin Laulu-Togagae; 15 Ryan Burroughs; 3 Greg Worthington; 4 Craig Hall; 5 Liam Kay; 14 Gary Wheeler; 6 Blake Wallace; 21 Adam Sidlow; 24 Sean Penkywicz; 25 Ryan Bailey; 17 Richard Whiting; 12 James Laithwaite; 13 Jack Bussey. Subs (all used): 8 Fuifui Moimoi; 10 Daniel Fleming; 7 Rhys Jacks; 19 Steve Crossley.
Tries: Hall (4, 31, 69), Wheeler (6, 11), Wallace (9), Penkywicz (14), Sidlow (23), Jacks (27), Moimoi (39), Kay (40), Laulu-Togagae (44, 46), Worthington (76);
Goals: Hall 12/14.
Rugby Leaguer & League Express Men of the Match:
Crusaders: Aaron Moore; *Wolfpack:* Gary Wheeler.
Penalty count: 6-10; **Half-time:** 0-60;
Referee: Brandon Robinson; **Attendance:** 590.

ROUND 3

Sunday 30th April 2017

HUNSLET 18 WHITEHAVEN 19

HUNSLET: 1 Jimmy Watson; 5 Gavin Duffy; 12 Aston Wilson; 24 Cameron Leeming; 3 Marcus Webb; 6 Joe Sanderson; 7 Danny Ansell; 10 Lewis Reed; 9 Jack Lee; 15 Jack Coventry; 11 Jake Normington; 17 Nyle Flynn; 19 Matt Carbutt. Subs (all used): 14 George Flanagan; 31 Sean Hesketh; 8 Michael Haley; 22 Brooke Broughton.
Tries: Normington (15), Flanagan (38), Webb (54);
Goals: Sanderson 3/3.
WHITEHAVEN: 1 Elliott Miller; 2 Craig Calvert; 3 Chris Taylor; 4 Jessie Joe Parker; 5 Jordan Burns; 6 Steve Roper; 7 Paul Crook; 8 Marc Shackley; 14 James Tilley; 10 Carl Forster; 16 Connor Holliday; 12 Scott McAvoy; 13 Karl Olstrum. Subs (all used): 30 David Thompson; 9 James Newton; 17 Tommy Holland; 19 Glenn Riley.
Tries: Shackley (12), Taylor (25), Roper (32);
Goals: Crook 3/4; **Field goal:** Roper (69).
Sin bin: Roper (37) - obstruction.
Rugby Leaguer & League Express Men of the Match:
Hunslet: Danny Ansell; *Whitehaven:* Steve Roper.
Penalty count: 10-14; **Half-time:** 12-16;
Referee: Tom Grant; **Attendance:** 382.

ROUND 6

Saturday 6th May 2017

BARROW RAIDERS 58 SOUTH WALES IRONMEN 16

RAIDERS: 1 Ryan Fieldhouse; 24 Luke Cresswell; 3 Declan Hulme; 12 Jarrad Stack; 45 Tom Loxam; 27 Ryan Johnston; 7 Lewis Charnock; 8 Joe Bullock; 15 Karl Ashall; 17 Tom Walker; 18 Danny Morrow; 11 Dan Toal; 25 Matty While. Subs (all used): 9 Nathan Mossop; 16 Andrew Dawson; 28 Brad Brennan; 21 James Duerden.
Tries: Fieldhouse (4, 60), Loxam (11), Ashall (18), Johnston (30), Mossop (36, 66), Duerden (40), Cresswell (57, 69), Morrow (63);
Goals: Charnock 5/7, Johnston 2/4.
IRONMEN: 6 Andrew Gay; - Conor McGrath; 28 Morgan Jeffries; 16 Ashley Bateman; 22 Ben Jones; 5 Paul Emanuelli; 15 Shaun Owens; 19 Jamie I'Anson; 9 Connor Farrer; 24 Connor Parker; 17 Zak Williams; 4 Christiaan Roets; 13 Chris Vitalini. Subs (all used): 14 Kristian Baller; - Sion Jones; - Jordan Syme; - Kade Breen.
Tries: S Jones (23), I'Anson (49), C Parker (74);
Goals: Emanuelli 2/3.
Sin bin: Emanuelli (78) - high tackle.
Rugby Leaguer & League Express Men of the Match:
Raiders: Dan Toal; *Ironmen:* Jamie I'Anson.
Penalty count: 5-7; **Half-time:** 34-6;
Referee: Liam Staveley; **Attendance:** 805.

TORONTO WOLFPACK 62 OXFORD 12

WOLFPACK: 4 Craig Hall; 2 Jonny Pownall; 3 Greg Worthington; 14 Gary Wheeler; 5 Liam Kay; 27 Ryan Brierley; 6 Blake Wallace; 21 Adam Sidlow; 24 Sean Penkywicz; 29 Jake Emmitt; 11 Andrew Dixon; 17 Richard Whiting; 10 Daniel Fleming. Subs (all used): 7 Rhys Jacks; 15 Ryan Burroughs; 16 Shaun Pick; 19 Steve Crossley.
Tries: Wallace (3), Dixon (10, 34), Pownall (16, 61), Whiting (20, 27), Brierley (23, 54), Hall (46), Worthington (51), Burroughs (75); **Goals:** Hall 7/12.
Dismissals: Emmitt (69) - fighting; Wallace (69) - fighting.
Sin bin: Kay (43) - punching; Emmitt (68) - interference; Penkywicz (76) - dissent.
OXFORD: 1 Jordan Gill; 2 Josh Atkinson; 3 Marcus Brooker; 4 Harvey Burnett; 5 Tommy Newbould; 6 Callum Windley; 7 Kane Riley; 8 Stuart Biscomb; 9 Casey Canterbury; 10 Dwaine McRae; 11 Jordan Siddons; 12 Anthony Cox; 13 Craig Wright. Subs (all used): 14 Bradley Moules; 15 Aaron Nicholson; 16 Mark Hayes; 17 Luke Evans.
Tries: Canterbury (31, 71); **Goals:** Burnett 2/2.
Dismissal: Windley (69) - fighting.
Rugby Leaguer & League Express Men of the Match:
Wolfpack: Craig Hall; *Oxford:* Casey Canterbury.
Penalty count: 11-10; **Half-time:** 40-6;
Referee: Brandon Robinson; **Attendance:** 6,281.

Sunday 7th May 2017

HEMEL STAGS 18 WORKINGTON TOWN 66

STAGS: 1 Mitch Vincent; 2 Darren Forde; 3 Josh Nathaniel; 4 Declan Tomlinson; 5 Rhys Allatt; 6 Ryan Matthews; 7 Lewis Fairhurst; 8 Corey Hanson; 9 Jono Burns; 10 Reece Williams; 11 Alex Williams; 12 James Thornton; 13 Brett Whitehead. Subs (all used): 14 Harley Axe; 15 Santino Decaro; 16 Dan Hawksworth; 17 Aaron James.
Tries: Nathaniel (18), Fairhurst (22), Whitehead (71);
Goals: Vincent 2/2, Fairhurst 1/1.
TOWN: 20 Kieran Mewse; 2 Joe Hambley; 3 Ed Chamberlain; 4 Jason Mossop; 17 Scott Rooke; 6 Carl Forber; 7 Jamie Doran; 10 Stevie Scholey; 13 Stuart Howarth; 16 Tom Curwen; 11 Brett Phillips; 25 Gordon Maudling; 15 Perry Singleton. Subs (all used): 12 Alex Szostak; 9 Callum Phillips; 18 Conor Fitzsimmons; 21 Kyle Shelford.
Tries: Mossop (4, 37), Rooke (10), Scholey (12), Forber (15), B Phillips (26), Maudling (52, 60, 63), Hambley (56), Singleton (66); **Goals:** Forber 10/10, Mewse 1/1.
Rugby Leaguer & League Express Men of the Match:
Stags: Lewis Fairhurst; *Town:* Gordon Maudling.
Penalty count: 6-7; **Half-time:** 12-36;
Referee: Matt Rossleigh; **Attendance:** 105.

WHITEHAVEN 34 NEWCASTLE THUNDER 20

WHITEHAVEN: 1 Elliott Miller; 5 Jordan Burns; 3 Chris Taylor; 4 Jessie Joe Parker; 2 Craig Calvert; 6 Steve Roper; 7 Paul Crook; 8 Marc Shackley; 18 Tyrone Dalton; 10 Carl Forster; 12 Scott McAvoy; 16 Connor Holliday; 14 James Tilley. Subs (all used): 9 James Newton; 19 Glenn Riley; 30 David Thompson; 17 Tommy Holland.
Tries: Miller (12), Burns (23), McAvoy (35, 49), Forster (68), Riley (74); **Goals:** Crook 1/2, Roper 4/5.
Sin bin: Shackley (74) - professional foul
THUNDER: 1 Derrell Olpherts; 2 Ali Blair; 3 Joe Brown; 4 Tyler Craig; 5 Peter Fox; 6 Lewis Young; 7 Benn Hardcastle; 8 Vincent Rennie; 9 Evan Simons; 10 Rhys Clarke; 11 Lee Paterson; 12 Dan Parker; 13 Liam McAvoy. Subs (all used): 14 Danny Nicklas; 15 Matt Barron; 16 Sam Luckley; 17 Josh Stoker.
Tries: Blair (20), R Clarke (38), Brown (58);
Goals: Hardcastle 4/4.
Sin bin: Simons (78) - punching.
Rugby Leaguer & League Express Men of the Match:
Whitehaven: Carl Forster; *Thunder:* Derrell Olpherts.
Penalty count: 10-7; **Half-time:** 14-12;
Referee: Steve Race; **Attendance:** 425.

COVENTRY BEARS 24 KEIGHLEY COUGARS 44

BEARS: 1 Harry Chapman; 2 Jamahl Hunte; 3 Eddie Medforth; 4 Matt Reid; 5 Mikey Russell; 6 Joe Prior; 7 Brad Delaney; 8 Alex Beddows; 9 Billy Gaylor; 10 Jack Morrison; 11 Kieran Sherratt; 12 Chris Barratt; 13 Zach Johnson. Subs (all used): 14 Richard Hughes; 15 James Geurtjens; 16 Dan Gover; 17 Callan Beckett.
Tries: Chapman (4, 66), Russell (13, 60, 73);
Goals: Delaney 2/5.
COUGARS: 1 Harry Aaronson; 26 Vinny Finigan; 34 Hamish Barnes; 32 Adam Ryder; 2 Andy Gabriel; 16 Will Milner; 7 Matty Beharrell; 15 Neil Cherryholme; 9 James Feather; 19 Matthew Bailey; 12 Brendon Rawlins; 18 Josh Tonks; 13 Mike Emmett. Subs (all used): 8 Scott Law; 14 Adam Brook; 17 Nathan Conroy; 29 Brad Nicholson.
Tries: Emmett (8), Barnes (15), Gabriel (18), Nicholson (30), Aaronson (32), Law (36), Rawlins (46), Milner (55);
Goals: Beharrell 6/8.
Sin bin: Aaronson (72) - professional foul.
Rugby Leaguer & League Express Men of the Match:
Bears: Harry Chapman; *Cougars:* Brendon Rawlins.
Penalty count: 12-5; **Half-time:** 8-34;
Referee: Billy Pearson; **Attendance:** 383.

DONCASTER 28 LONDON SKOLARS 28

DONCASTER: 1 Tom Carr; 5 Sam Doherty; 3 Liam Welham; 4 Jason Tali; 2 Aaron Jones-Bishop; 22 Louis Sheriff; 15 Jack Miller; 8 Mark Castle; 9 Kyle Kesik; 16 Russ Spiers; 34 Brad England; 13 Charlie Martin; 12 Jason Muranka. Subs (all used): 18 Ryan Wright; 10 Iafeta Palea'aesina; 14 Connor Scott; 7 Jordie Hedges.
Tries: Kesik (17), Tali (24, 40, 53), Sheriff (28);
Goals: Carr 3/4, Miller 1/1.
SKOLARS: 20 Jake Melling; 2 Sam Nash; 4 Lameck Juma; 31 Josh Allison; 24 Michael Brown; 6 Jy-mel Coleman; - Phil Lyon; 29 Callum Bustin; 9 Charlie Lawrence; 10 Dave Williams; 18 Mike Greenhalgh; 11 Lamont Bryan; 13 Ryan Chester. Subs (all used): 27 Ben Pointer; 30 Simona Vavega; 23 Will Martin; 28 Sadiq Adebiyi.
Tries: Nash (37), Pointer (43), Adebiyi (55, 69), D Williams (73); **Goals:** Jy-mel Coleman 4/6.
Sin bin: Vavega (53) - dissent.
Rugby Leaguer & League Express Men of the Match:
Doncaster: Jason Tali; *Skolars:* Ben Pointer.
Penalty count: 7-10; **Half-time:** 22-4;
Referee: Nick Bennett; **Attendance:** 564.

GLOUCESTERSHIRE ALL GOLDS 10
YORK CITY KNIGHTS 56

ALL GOLDS: 1 Steven Nield; 2 Mo Agoro; 3 Phil Cowburn; 4 Brad Kislingbury; 5 Chris Barlow; 6 Josh Ward; 7 Kieran Hyde; 8 Ollie Purslow; 9 Steve Parry; 10 Harrison Elliott; 11

Graham O'Keeffe; 12 Joe McClean; 13 Chris Worrall. Subs (all used): 14 Billy Brickhill; 15 Lewis Reece; 16 Harry Kidd; 17 Malikhi Lloyd-Jones.
Tries: Parry (17), Kislingbury (62); **Goals:** Ward 1/1, Hyde 0/1.
CITY KNIGHTS: 1 Ash Robson; 5 Tom Saxton; 3 Nev Morrison; 24 Nick Rawsthorne; 2 David Foggin-Johnston; 31 Liam Harris; 7 Harry Tyson-Wilson; 16 Ronan Dixon; 26 Andy Ellis; 10 Chris Siddons; 11 Joe Batchelor; 12 Ed Smith; 13 Tim Spears. Subs (all used): - Will Jubb; 17 Brad Hey; 8 Bobby Tyson-Wilson; 25 Joe Porter.
Tries: Batchelor (3), Dixon (8), Rawsthorne (11, 46, 57), Robson (28), Jubb (35), Foggin-Johnston (40), Harris (42), E Smith (54); **Goals:** H Tyson-Wilson 3/4, Harris 5/6.
Rugby Leaguer & League Express Men of the Match:
All Golds: Brad Kislingbury; *City Knights:* Nick Rawsthorne.
Penalty count: 5-9; **Half-time:** 6-32;
Referee: Greg Dolan; **Attendance:** 180.

HUNSLET 36 NORTH WALES CRUSADERS 26

HUNSLET: 1 Jimmy Watson; 24 Cameron Leeming; 4 Mufaro Mvududu; 12 Aston Wilson; 3 Marcus Webb; 6 Joe Sanderson; 7 Danny Ansell; 8 Michael Haley; 25 Matthew Tebb; 10 Lewis Reed; 22 Brooke Broughton; 11 Jake Normington; 13 Liam Mackay. Subs (all used): 23 Joe Kenga; 14 George Flanagan; 17 Nyle Flynn; 15 Jack Coventry.
Tries: Watson (1), Tebb (11), Normington (14), Leeming (28), Flanagan (34, 49), Ansell (52); **Goals:** Sanderson 4/7.
CRUSADERS: 1 Tommy Johnson; 19 Dan Price; 28 Callum Mulkeen; 4 Earl Hurst; 5 Dale Bloomfield; 26 Jack Hansen; 7 Ryan Smith; 8 Jonny Walker; 9 Lee Hudson; 10 Alex Davidson; 24 Jack Houghton; 3 Simon Atherton; 14 James Dandy. Subs (all used): 27 Aaron Moore; 13 Ryan Millington; 32 Warren Thompson; 31 Blake Turner.
Tries: Smith (18), Price (25), Millington (26), Hurst (44), Hansen (67); **Goals:** Johnson 3/5.
Rugby Leaguer & League Express Men of the Match:
Hunslet: George Flanagan; *Crusaders:* Ryan Smith.
Penalty count: 10-10; **Half-time:** 24-16;
Referee: Michael Mannifield; **Attendance:** 420.

ROUND 7

Wednesday 10th May 2017

KEIGHLEY COUGARS 42 BARROW RAIDERS 58

COUGARS: 1 Harry Aaronson; 26 Vinny Finigan; 5 Davey Dixon; 32 Adam Ryder; 2 Andy Gabriel; 16 Will Milner; 7 Matty Beharrell; 8 Scott Law; 17 Nathan Conroy; 15 Neil Cherryholme; 21 Emmerson Whittel; 12 Brendon Rawlins; 13 Mike Emmett. Subs (all used): 19 Matthew Bailey; 20 Nathan Kitson; 27 Sean Kelly; 29 Brad Nicholson.
Tries: Rawlins (8, 71), Bailey (37), Whittel (40), Aaronson (45), Law (59), Emmett (63);
Goals: Beharrell 7/7.
Dismissal: Kelly (77) - dangerous challenge on S Toal.
RAIDERS: 1 Ryan Fieldhouse; 5 Shane Toal; 3 Declan Hulme; 12 Jarrad Stack; 24 Luke Cresswell; 7 Lewis Charnock; 15 Karl Ashall; 8 Joe Bullock; 9 Nathan Mossop; 10 Oliver Wilkes; 18 Danny Morrow; 11 Dan Toal; 13 Martin Aspinwall. Subs (all used): 16 Andrew Dawson; 17 Tom Walker; 21 James Duerden; 26 Brad Marwood.
Tries: Bullock (3), Charnock (13, 17, 26, 79), S Toal (24, 50, 67), Cresswell (43), Fieldhouse (57);
Goals: Charnock 8/10, Ashall 1/1.
Rugby Leaguer & League Express Men of the Match:
Cougars: Harry Aaronson; *Raiders:* Lewis Charnock.
Penalty count: 9-9; **Half-time:** 18-30;
Referee: Andrew Sweet; **Attendance:** 728.

Friday 12th May 2017

NEWCASTLE THUNDER 22 TORONTO WOLFPACK 40

THUNDER: 1 Jared Simpson; 2 Ali Blair; 3 Joe Brown; 4 Derrell Olpherts; 5 Zach Clark; 6 Lewis Young; 7 Benn Hardcastle; 8 Vincent Rennie; 9 Evan Simons; 10 Sam Luckley; 11 Dan Parker; 12 Rhys Clarke; 13 Liam McAvoy. Subs (all used): 14 Danny Nicklas; 15 Brett Waller; 16 George Milton; 17 Matt Barron.
Tries: Z Clark (22), Nicklas (47), Young (68), Simons (74);
Goals: Hardcastle 3/4.
WOLFPACK: 4 Craig Hall; 2 Jonny Pownall; 3 Greg Worthington; 1 Quentin Laulu-Togagae; 5 Liam Kay; 6 Blake Wallace; 27 Ryan Brierley; 8 Fuifui Moimoi; 9 Bob Beswick; 29 Jake Emmitt; 16 Shaun Pick; 21 Adam Sidlow; 17 Richard Whiting. Subs (all used): 19 Steve Crossley; 25 Ryan Bailey; 24 Sean Penkywicz; 14 Gary Wheeler.
Tries: Brierley (6, 79), Wallace (12), Pownall (27), Kay (31), Laulu-Togagae (33), Beswick (53); **Goals:** Hall 6/7.
Rugby Leaguer & League Express Men of the Match:
Thunder: Lewis Young; *Wolfpack:* Ryan Brierley.
Penalty count: 7-5; **Half-time:** 4-28;
Referee: Steve Race; **Attendance:** 1,087.

Saturday 13th May 2017

GLOUCESTERSHIRE ALL GOLDS 36 NORTH WALES CRUSADERS 28

ALL GOLDS: 1 Jack Mitchell; 2 Mo Agoro; 3 Steven Nield; 4 Brad Kislingbury; 5 Chris Barlow; 6 Ben Stead; 7 Danny Fallon; 8 Ollie Purslow; 9 Steve Parry; 10 James Walter; 11 Lewis Reece; 12 Joe McClean; 13 Chris Worrall. Subs (all used): 14 Billy Brickhill; 15 Harrison Elliott; 16 Malikhi Lloyd-Jones; 17 Harry Kidd.
Tries: Reece (20, 77), Agoro (31), Kidd (39, 41), Brickhill (61);
Goals: Stead 6/6.
CRUSADERS: 1 Tommy Johnson; 19 Dan Price; 28 Callum Mulkeen; 4 Earl Hurst; 5 Dale Bloomfield; 26 Jack Hansen; 7 Ryan Smith; 8 Jonny Walker; 9 Lee Hudson; 32 Warren Thompson; 3 Simon Atherton; 11 Alex Thompson; 14 James Dandy. Subs (all used): 27 Aaron Moore; 10 Alex Davidson; 13 Ryan Millington; 22 Joe Bate.
Tries: Smith (9), Hurst (12, 25), Dandy (46), A Thompson (53); **Goals:** Johnson 4/5.
Rugby Leaguer & League Express Men of the Match:
All Golds: Mo Agoro; *Crusaders:* Earl Hurst.
Penalty count: 11-12; **Half-time:** 18-18;
Referee: Tom Grant; **Attendance:** 201.

LONDON SKOLARS 14 WHITEHAVEN 28

SKOLARS: 26 Kameron Pearce-Paul; 5 James Hill; 31 Josh Allison; 4 Lameck Juma; 24 Michael Brown; 6 Jy-mel Coleman; - Phil Lyon; 29 Callum Bustin; 9 Charlie Lawrence; 10 Dave Williams; 11 Lamont Bryan; 18 Mike Greenhalgh; 13 Ryan Chester. Subs (all used): 27 Ben Pointer; 28 Sadiq Adebiyi; 23 Will Martin; 30 Simona Vavega.
Tries: Allison (7), Hill (33), Adebiyi (74);
Goals: Jy-mel Coleman 1/3.
WHITEHAVEN: 1 Eliott Miller; 5 Jordan Burns; 4 Jessie Joe Parker; 3 Chris Taylor; 30 David Thompson; 6 Steve Roper; 7 Paul Crook; 19 Glenn Riley; 14 James Tilley; 10 Carl Forster; 16 Connor Holliday; 12 Scott McAvoy; 24 Lewis Brown. Subs (all used): 9 James Newton; 17 Tommy Holland; 22 Kurt Maudling; 15 Dion Aiye.
Tries: Forster (28, 44), Parker (66), Newton (79);
Goals: Crook 6/6.
Rugby Leaguer & League Express Men of the Match:
Skolars: Callum Bustin; *Whitehaven:* Carl Forster.
Penalty count: 7-8; **Half-time:** 8-6;
Referee: Matt Rossleigh; **Attendance:** 335.

Sunday 14th May 2017

HEMEL STAGS 24 DONCASTER 50

STAGS: 1 Mitch Vincent; 2 Marcus Elliott; 3 Declan Tomlinson; 4 Alex Williams; 5 Darren Forde; 6 Scott Lee; 7 Ryan Matthews; 8 Dan Hawksworth; 9 Jono Burns; 10 Reece Williams; 11 James Thornton; 12 Jack O'Brien; 13 Brett Whitehead. Subs (all used): 14 Danny Samuel; 15 Santino Decaro; 16 Sam Crowther; 17 Wayne Jowitt.
Tries: Whitehead (23), R Williams (33), Jowitt (35), Burns (69); **Goals:** Vincent 4/4.
DONCASTER: 22 Louis Sheriff; 24 Richie Barnett; 3 Liam Welham; 4 Jason Tali; 5 Sam Doherty; 1 Tom Carr; 15 Jack Miller; 16 Russ Spiers; 9 Kyle Kesik; 19 Zac Braham; 13 Charlie Martin; 34 Brad England; 27 Peter Green. Subs (all used): 18 Ryan Wright; 8 Mark Castle; 32 Makali Aizue; 7 Jordie Hedges.
Tries: Barnett (4, 57), Kesik (12), Carr (14, 28), Tali (19, 41), Hedges (51), Doherty (54), Sheriff (66);
Goals: Carr 3/5, Miller 2/5.
Rugby Leaguer & League Express Men of the Match:
Stags: Dan Hawksworth; *Doncaster:* Jason Tali.
Penalty count: 3-6; **Half-time:** 18-26;
Referee: Brandon Robinson; **Attendance:** 102.

OXFORD 24 HUNSLET 22

OXFORD: 1 Kane Riley; 2 Josh Atkinson; 3 Harvey Burnett; 4 Will Cooke; 5 Harrison Brough; 6 Callum Windley; 7 Josh Kittrick; 8 Dwaine McRae; 9 Casey Canterbury; 10 Anthony Cox; 11 Jordan Siddons; 12 Stuart Biscomb; 13 Jake Joynt. Subs (all used): 14 Bradley Moules; 15 Marcus Brooker; 16 Aaron Nicholson; 17 Daniel Hindmarsh-Takji.
Tries: Brough (13, 76), Joynt (18), Atkinson (26), Burnett (40); **Goals:** Burnett 2/5.
HUNSLET: 1 Jimmy Watson; 38 Niall Walker; 12 Aston Wilson; 24 Cameron Leeming; 39 Josh Nathaniel; 6 Joe Sanderson; 7 Danny Ansell; 8 Michael Haley; 25 Matthew Tebb; 10 Lewis Reed; 4 Mufaro Mvududu; 13 Liam Mackay; 17 Nyle Flynn. Subs (all used): 14 George Flanagan; 15 Jack Coventry; 19 Matt Carbutt; 21 Jack Walton.
Tries: Walker (7), Mackay (31), Leeming (45), Flanagan (50); **Goals:** Sanderson 3/5.
Rugby Leaguer & League Express Men of the Match:
Oxford: Harvey Burnett; *Hunslet:* George Flanagan.
Penalty count: 6-10; **Half-time:** 20-12;
Referee: Greg Dolan; **Attendance:** 203.

WORKINGTON TOWN 56 SOUTH WALES IRONMEN 0

TOWN: - Gabriel Fell; 2 Joe Hambley; 3 Ed Chamberlain; 4 Jason Mossop; 17 Scott Rooke; 6 Carl Forber; 7 Jamie Doran; 10 Stevie Scholey; 13 Stuart Howarth; 16 Tom Curwen; 11 Brett Phillips; 25 Gordon Maudling; 15 Perry Singleton. Subs (all used): 9 Callum Phillips; 12 Alex Szostak; 5 John Patrick; 21 Kyle Shelford.
Tries: Mossop (2), Hambley (14, 18, 69), Fell (41, 64), Patrick (50), Rooke (60), Curwen (62), C Phillips (71);
Goals: Forber 8/10.
IRONMEN: 6 Andrew Gay; 26 Lewis Hughes; 28 Morgan Jeffries; 16 Ashley Bateman; 22 Ben Jones; 5 Paul Emanuelli; 7 Courtney Davies; - Luke Nelmes; 9 Connor Farrer; 18 Morgan Evans; 17 Zak Williams; 24 Connor Parker; - William Calcott. Subs (all used): 15 Shaun Owens; 21 Ross Price; - Kade Breen; 19 Jamie l'Anson.
Rugby Leaguer & League Express Men of the Match:
Town: Jamie Doran; *Ironmen:* Andrew Gay.
Penalty count: 8-10; **Half-time:** 16-0;
Referee: John McMullen; **Attendance:** 546.

YORK CITY KNIGHTS 64 COVENTRY BEARS 12

CITY KNIGHTS: 1 Ash Robson; 32 Callum Lancaster; 19 James Haynes; 24 Nick Rawsthorne; 2 David Foggin-Johnston; 31 Liam Harris; 23 Jon Presley; 16 Ronan Dixon; 29 Will Jubb; 10 Chris Siddons; 11 Joe Batchelor; 12 Ed Smith; 13 Tim Spears. Subs (all used): 17 Brad Hey; 8 Bobby Tyson-Wilson; 25 Joe Porter; 14 Harry Carter.
Tries: Harris (2), Haynes (5, 71), Lancaster (14), E Smith (42), Porter (45), Batchelor (50, 68), Rawsthorne (55), Carter (58), Presley (63), Hey (76);
Goals: Harris 1/3, Rawsthorne 7/9.
BEARS: 1 Harry Chapman; 2 Hayden Freeman; 3 Tommy Brierley; 4 Eddie Medforth; 5 Mikey Russell; 6 Billy Gaylor; 7 Brad Delaney; 8 Zach Johnson; 9 Richard Hughes; 10 Alex Beddows; 11 Kieran Sherratt; 12 Chris Barratt; 13 Matt Reid. Subs (all used): 14 Joe Prior; 15 Jack Morrison; 16 James Geurtjens; 17 Dan Gover.
Tries: Freeman (25), Brierley (31); **Goals:** Delaney 2/2.
Rugby Leaguer & League Express Men of the Match:
City Knights: Joe Batchelor; *Bears:* Brad Delaney.
Penalty count: 7-9; **Half-time:** 14-12;
Referee: Callum Straw; **Attendance:** 902.

ROUND 8

Friday 19th May 2017

NEWCASTLE THUNDER 18 YORK CITY KNIGHTS 22

THUNDER: 1 Jared Simpson; 2 Ali Blair; 3 Joe Brown; 4 Derrell Olpherts; 5 Peter Fox; 6 Lewis Young; 7 Benn Hardcastle; 8 Brett Waller; 9 Evan Simons; 10 Liam McAvoy; 11 Dan Parker; 12 Harry Aldous; 13 Jack Aldous. Subs (all used): 14 Danny Nicklas; 15 Vincent Rennie; 16 Rhys Clarke; 17 George Milton.
Tries: Olpherts (6), Hardcastle (13, 72);
Goals: Hardcastle 3/3.
Sin bin: Nicklas (33) - late challenge on Presley; Fox (50) - late challenge on Lancaster; Brown (51) - fighting.
CITY KNIGHTS: 1 Ash Robson; 32 Callum Lancaster; 19 James Haynes; 24 Nick Rawsthorne; 5 Tom Saxton; 31 Liam Harris; 23 Jon Presley; 10 Chris Siddons; 26 Andy Ellis; 20 Adam Robinson; 12 Ed Smith; 11 Joe Batchelor; 13 Tim Spears. Subs (all used): 14 Harry Carter; 15 Liam Thompson; 17 Brad Hey; 28 Kieran Moran.
Tries: Rawsthorne (18), Robson (33), A Robinson (55), E Smith (62); **Goals:** Rawsthorne 3/5.
Sin bin: Robson (51) - fighting.
Rugby Leaguer & League Express Men of the Match:
Thunder: Benn Hardcastle; *City Knights:* Ash Robson.
Penalty count: 5-13; **Half-time:** 12-12;
Referee: Scott Mikalauskas; **Attendance:** 2,111.

Saturday 20th May 2017

SOUTH WALES IRONMEN 18 OXFORD 38

IRONMEN: 6 Andrew Gay; 2 Yannic Parker; 16 Ashley Bateman; 4 Christiaan Roets; 3 Paul Edwards; 5 Paul Emanuelli; 7 Courtney Davies; 18 Morgan Evans; 15 Shaun Owens; 30 Michael Edwards; 17 Zak Williams; 24 Connor Parker; 11 Richard Jones. Subs (all used): 9 Connor Farrer; - Kade Breen; 21 Ross Price; 28 Morgan Jeffries.
Tries: Owens (10), Y Parker (19), Price (35);
Goals: Emanuelli 3/3.
OXFORD: 1 Kane Riley; 2 Josh Atkinson; 3 Will Cooke; 4 Marcus Brooker; 5 Harrison Brough; 6 Callum Windley; 7 Scott Fleming; 8 Stuart Biscomb; 9 Casey Canterbury; 10 Anthony Cox; 11 Dwaine McRae; 12 Jordan Siddons; 13 Jake Joynt. Subs (all used): 14 Bradley Moules; 15 Aaron Nicholson; 16 Daniel Hindmarsh-Takji; 17 Jonathan Payne.
Tries: Riley (5), Atkinson (15, 46), Canterbury (25), Biscomb (31), Hindmarsh-Takji (50), Windley (64), Brooker (74); **Goals:** Fleming 3/8.

Rugby Leaguer & League Express Men of the Match: *Ironmen:* Shaun Owens; *Oxford:* Daniel Hindmarsh-Takji.
Penalty count: 12-8; **Half-time:** 18-18;
Referee: Billy Pearson; **Attendance:** 128.

TORONTO WOLFPACK 70 BARROW RAIDERS 2

WOLFPACK: 1 Quentin Laulu-Togagae; 2 Jonny Pownall; 3 Greg Worthington; 4 Craig Hall; 14 Gary Wheeler; 6 Blake Wallace; 27 Ryan Brierley; 8 Fuifui Moimoi; 9 Bob Beswick; 21 Adam Sidlow; 11 Andrew Dixon; 17 Richard Whiting; 25 Ryan Bailey. Subs (all used): 10 Daniel Fleming; 16 Shaun Pick; 19 Steve Crossley; 24 Sean Penkywicz.
Tries: Wallace (10), Bailey (16), Laulu-Togagae (28, 56, 70), Dixon (31), Wheeler (33), Worthington (35), Brierley (40, 59), Penkywicz (48), Pick (65);
Goals: Hall 11/12.
RAIDERS: 1 Ryan Fieldhouse; 5 Shane Toal; 3 Declan Hulme; 45 Tom Loxam; 24 Luke Cresswell; 27 Ryan Johnston; 7 Lewis Charnock; 8 Joe Bullock; 9 Nathan Mossop; 10 Oliver Wilkes; 23 Chris Fleming; 12 Jarrad Stack; 25 Matty While. Subs (all used): 15 Karl Ashall; 16 Andrew Dawson; 17 Tom Walker; 21 James Duerden.
Goals: Charnock 1/1.
Rugby Leaguer & League Express Men of the Match: *Wolfpack:* Quentin Laulu-Togagae; *Raiders:* Ryan Fieldhouse.
Penalty count: 12-13; **Half-time:** 40-2;
Referee: John McMullen; **Attendance:** 7,144.

Sunday 21st May 2017

WHITEHAVEN 58 HEMEL STAGS 24

WHITEHAVEN: 1 Elliott Miller; 5 Jordan Burns; 3 Chris Taylor; 4 Jessie Joe Parker; 30 David Thompson; 6 Steve Roper; 7 Paul Crook; 19 Glenn Riley; 14 James Tilley; 17 Tommy Holland; 22 Kurt Maudling; 16 Connor Holliday; 24 Lewis Brown. Subs (all used): 9 James Newton; 10 Carl Forster; 12 Scott McAvoy; 15 Dion Aiye.
Tries: Roper (16), Miller (19), Forster (22, 54, 67), Holland (29, 72), Thompson (33, 47), Newton (38), Parker (65); **Goals:** Crook 7/11.
STAGS: 1 Mitch Vincent; 2 Marcus Elliott; 3 Declan Tomlinson; 4 Danny Lawton; 5 Darren Forde; 6 Brett Whitehead; 7 Mark Barlow; 8 Dan Hawksworth; 9 Jono Burns; 10 Alex Williams; 11 James Thornton; 12 Jack O'Brien; 13 Corey Hanson. Subs (all used): 14 Reece Williams; 15 Wayne Jowitt; 16 Danny Samuel; 17 Sam Crowther.
Tries: Burns (26, 57, 78), Whitehead (60);
Goals: Vincent 4/4.
Rugby Leaguer & League Express Men of the Match: *Whitehaven:* David Thompson; *Stags:* Jono Burns.
Penalty count: 7-4; **Half-time:** 34-6;
Referee: Nick Bennett; **Attendance:** 487.

**NORTH WALES CRUSADERS 50
LONDON SKOLARS 10**

CRUSADERS: 2 Corey Lee; 19 Dan Price; 28 Callum Mulkeen; 16 Luke Warburton; 5 Dale Bloomfield; 26 Jack Hansen; 7 Ryan Smith; 8 Jonny Walker; 14 James Dandy; 10 Alex Davidson; 24 Jack Houghton; 3 Simon Atherton; 13 Ryan Millington. Subs (all used): 27 Aaron Moore; 17 Kenny Baker; 32 Warren Thompson; 22 Joe Bate.
Tries: Smith (7, 20, 72), Atherton (17), Moore (34, 71), Warburton (37), Lee (51), Bloomfield (57); **Goals:** Price 7/9.
SKOLARS: 20 Jake Melling; 5 James Hill; 31 Josh Allison; 4 Lameck Juma; 24 Michael Brown; 26 Jermaine Coleman; 6 Jy-mel Coleman; 28 Callum Bustin; 9 Charlie Lawrence; 10 Dave Williams; 18 Mike Greenhalgh; 12 Eddie Mbaraga; 13 Ryan Chester. Subs (all used): 27 Ben Pointer; 19 Erjon Dollapi; 25 Michael Sykes; 30 Simona Vavega.
Tries: Pointer (28), Brown (80); **Goals:** Jy-mel Coleman 1/2.
Rugby Leaguer & League Express Men of the Match: *Crusaders:* Ryan Smith; *Skolars:* Michael Brown.
Penalty count: 12-2; **Half-time:** 30-4;
Referee: Steve Race; **Attendance:** 273.

**COVENTRY BEARS 18
GLOUCESTERSHIRE ALL GOLDS 26**

BEARS: 1 Harry Chapman; 2 Mikey Russell; 3 Eddie Medforth; 4 Tommy Brierley; 5 Jamahl Hunte; 6 Billy Gaylor; 7 Brad Delaney; 8 James Geurtjens; 9 Richard Hughes; 10 Jack Morrison; 11 Kieran Sherratt; 12 Chris Barratt; 13 Matt Reid. Subs (all used): 14 Hayden Freeman; 15 Joe Prior; 16 Paddy Jones; 17 Dan Gover.
Tries: Geurtjens (13), Chapman (34), Barratt (73);
Goals: Delaney 3/3.
ALL GOLDS: 1 Jack Mitchell; 2 Mo Agoro; 3 Steven Nield; 4 Brad Kislingbury; 5 Chris Barlow; 6 Ben Stead; 7 Danny Fallon; 8 Ollie Purslow; 9 Steve Parry; 10 James Walter; 11 Lewis Reece; 12 Joe McClean; 13 Chris Worrall. Subs (all used): 14 Billy Brickhill; 15 Brad Hargreaves; 16 Harrison Elliott; 17 Harry Kidd.
Tries: Mitchell (4), Agoro (7), Barlow (58), Nield (62), Kislingbury (66); **Goals:** Stead 3/8.
Rugby Leaguer & League Express Men of the Match: *Bears:* Harry Chapman; *All Golds:* Brad Kislingbury.
Penalty count: 20-16; **Half-time:** 12-12;
Referee: Matt Rossleigh; **Attendance:** 323.

DONCASTER 28 KEIGHLEY COUGARS 14

DONCASTER: 7 Jordie Hedges; 5 Sam Doherty; 3 Liam Welham; 4 Jason Tali; 24 Richie Barnett; 6 Jordan Howden; 15 Jack Miller; 16 Russ Spiers; 9 Kyle Kesik; 19 Zac Braham; 13 Charlie Martin; 34 Brad England; 27 Peter Green. Subs (all used): 2 Aaron Jones-Bishop; 14 Connor Scott; 18 Ryan Wright; 32 Makali Aizue.
Tries: Tali (27), Wright (36), Spiers (49), Howden (54);
Goals: Miller 6/6.
COUGARS: 24 Liam Darville; 26 Vinny Finigan; 5 Davey Dixon; 32 Adam Ryder; 1 Harry Aaronson; 16 Will Milner; 7 Matty Beharrell; 8 Scott Law; 9 James Feather; 19 Matthew Bailey; 11 Josh Lynam; 18 Josh Tonks; 13 Mike Emmett. Subs (all used): 12 Brendon Rawlins; 17 Nathan Conroy; 21 Emmerson Whittel; 29 Brad Nicholson.
Tries: Conroy (30), Ryder (39, 45); **Goals:** Beharrell 1/3.
Rugby Leaguer & League Express Men of the Match: *Doncaster:* Jason Tali; *Cougars:* Will Milner.
Penalty count: 15-7; **Half-time:** 12-10;
Referee: Greg Dolan; **Attendance:** 516.

HUNSLET 30 WORKINGTON TOWN 22

HUNSLET: 1 Jimmy Watson; 3 Marcus Webb; 4 Mufaro Mvududu; 24 Cameron Leeming; 39 Josh Nathaniel; 6 Joe Sanderson; 7 Danny Ansell; 8 Michael Haley; 9 Jack Lee; 10 Lewis Reed; 12 Aston Wilson; 13 Liam Mackay; 19 Matt Carbutt. Subs (all used): 14 George Flanagan; 17 Nyle Flynn; 15 Jack Coventry; 31 Sean Hesketh.
Tries: Watson (15), Flanagan (42), Leeming (47), Flynn (55), Reed (75); **Goals:** Sanderson 5/5.
TOWN: - Gabriel Fell; 5 John Patrick; 2 Joe Hambley; 4 Jason Mossop; 24 Phil Lister; 6 Carl Forber; 7 Jamie Doran; 10 Stevie Scholey; 13 Stuart Howarth; 16 Tom Curwen; 11 Brett Phillips; 23 Phil Joseph; 15 Perry Singleton. Subs (all used): 9 Callum Phillips; 18 Conor Fitzsimmons; - Kyle Shelford; 20 Kieran Mewse.
Tries: Patrick (8), Mossop (28), C Phillips (41), Forber (64);
Goals: Forber 2/3, Mewse 1/1.
Rugby Leaguer & League Express Men of the Match: *Hunslet:* Mufaro Mvududu; *Town:* Carl Forber.
Penalty count: 1-7; **Half-time:** 6-10;
Referee: Tom Owen; **Attendance:** 388.

ROUND 9

Saturday 3rd June 2017

KEIGHLEY COUGARS 74 SOUTH WALES IRONMEN 6

COUGARS: 24 Liam Darville; 26 Vinny Finigan; 5 Davey Dixon; 32 Adam Ryder; 2 Andy Gabriel; 16 Will Milner; 7 Matty Beharrell; 8 Scott Law; 9 James Feather; 12 Brendon Rawlins; 11 Josh Lynam; 18 Josh Tonks; 21 Emmerson Whittel. Subs (all used): 13 Mike Emmett; 17 Nathan Conroy; 19 Matthew Bailey; 29 Brad Nicholson.
Tries: Gabriel (9, 79), Darville (13, 22, 50, 76), Ryder (18), Nicholson (29), Dixon (45, 56), Tonks (58, 73), Law (64);
Goals: Beharrell 11/13.
IRONMEN: 22 Ben Jones; - Jack Uren; - Errol Carter; 4 Christiaan Roets; 28 Morgan Jeffries; 6 Andrew Gay; 5 Paul Emanuelli; 19 Jamie I'Anson; 9 Connor Farrer; - Kade Breen; 17 Zak Williams; - Sion Jones; 21 Ross Price. Subs (all used): - Macauley Harris; - Sam Hodge; - Connor Davies; - Ieuan Jones.
Try: Roets (25); **Goals:** Emanuelli 1/1.
Rugby Leaguer & League Express Men of the Match: *Cougars:* Brendon Rawlins; *Ironmen:* Christiaan Roets.
Penalty count: 11-9; **Half-time:** 30-6;
Referee: Brandon Robinson; **Attendance:** 532.

BARROW RAIDERS 28 HUNSLET 20

RAIDERS: 1 Ryan Fieldhouse; 2 Brett Carter; 3 Declan Hulme; - Eze Harper; 24 Luke Cresswell; 6 Jamie Dallimore; 7 Lewis Charnock; 8 Joe Bullock; 9 Nathan Mossop; 17 Tom Walker; 18 Danny Morrow; 12 Jarrad Stack; 13 Martin Aspinwall. Subs (all used): 15 Karl Ashall; 16 Andrew Dawson; 11 Dan Toal; 21 James Duerden.
Tries: Harper (16), Dallimore (30), Fieldhouse (45, 78);
Goals: Charnock 6/6.
HUNSLET: 1 Jimmy Watson; 39 Josh Nathaniel; 4 Mufaro Mvududu; 24 Cameron Leeming; 3 Marcus Webb; 18 Joel Gibson; 7 Danny Ansell; 31 Sean Hesketh; 9 Jack Lee; 8 Michael Haley; 12 Aston Wilson; 13 Liam Mackay; 17 Nyle Flynn. Subs (all used): 14 George Flanagan; 19 Matt Carbutt; 21 Jack Walton; 15 Jack Coventry.
Tries: Hesketh (9), Ansell (19), Flanagan (37);
Goals: Ansell 4/5.
Dismissal: Hesketh (71) - high tackle.
Sin bin: Flanagan (78) - punching.
Rugby Leaguer & League Express Men of the Match: *Raiders:* Eze Harper; *Hunslet:* Mufaro Mvududu.
Penalty count: 11-9; **Half-time:** 12-18;
Referee: Callum Straw; **Attendance:** 913.

TORONTO WOLFPACK 54 COVENTRY BEARS 12

WOLFPACK: 2 Jonny Pownall; 15 Ryan Burroughs; 3 Greg Worthington; 4 Craig Hall; 5 Liam Kay; 27 Ryan Brierley; 7 Rhys Jacks; 25 Ryan Bailey; 9 Bob Beswick; 8 Fuifui Moimoi; 11 Andrew Dixon; 17 Richard Whiting; 21 Adam Sidlow. Subs (all used): 16 Shaun Pick; 20 Tom Dempsey; 24 Sean Penkywicz; 26 Joe Eichner.
Tries: Dixon (10, 34), Kay (12, 46, 55), Beswick (31), Brierley (36), Jacks (44), Moimoi (58, 79); **Goals:** Hall 7/10.
BEARS: 1 Harry Chapman; 2 Mikey Russell; 3 Tommy Brierley; 4 Eddie Medforth; 5 Jamahl Hunte; 6 Billy Gaylor; 7 Brad Delaney; 8 James Geurtjens; 9 Jay Lobwein; 10 Dan Gover; 11 Kieran Sherratt; 12 Chris Barratt; 13 Matt Reid. Subs (all used): 14 Liam Thompson; 15 Hayden Freeman; 16 Alex Beddows; 17 Paddy Jones.
Tries: Hunte (23), Delaney (50); **Goals:** Delaney 2/3.
Rugby Leaguer & League Express Men of the Match: *Wolfpack:* Liam Kay; *Bears:* Brad Delaney.
Penalty count: 8-12; **Half-time:** 24-6;
Referee: Nick Bennett; **Attendance:** 6,973.

Sunday 4th June 2017

HEMEL STAGS 20 NORTH WALES CRUSADERS 26

STAGS: 1 Mitch Vincent; 2 Darren Forde; 3 Alex Williams; 4 Danny Lawton; 5 Marcus Elliott; 6 Brett Whitehead; 7 Mark Barlow; 8 Dan Hawksworth; 9 Scott Lee; 10 Wayne Jowitt; 11 Jack O'Brien; 12 Munashe Fumhanda; 13 Corey Hanson. Subs (all used): 14 Santino Decaro; 15 Aaron James; 16 Sam Crowther; 17 Declan Tomlinson.
Tries: A Williams (8), Whitehead (16), Tomlinson (50), Vincent (73); **Goals:** Vincent 1/3, Barlow 1/1.
Sin bin: Hanson (59) - dissent.
CRUSADERS: 1 Tommy Johnson; 2 Corey Lee; 3 Simon Atherton; 16 Luke Warburton; 19 Dan Price; 26 Jack Hansen; 7 Ryan Smith; 8 Jonny Walker; 14 James Dandy; 10 Alex Davidson; 24 Jack Houghton; 17 Kenny Baker; 13 Ryan Millington. Subs (all used): 27 Aaron Moore; 31 Blake Turner; 22 Joe Bate; 32 Warren Thompson.
Tries: Atherton (20, 26), Warburton (33), Hansen (46), Johnson (62); **Goals:** Johnson 3/5.
Rugby Leaguer & League Express Men of the Match: *Stags:* Alex Williams; *Crusaders:* Tommy Johnson.
Penalty count: 5-8; **Half-time:** 10-16;
Referee: Billy Pearson; **Attendance:** 107.

OXFORD 12 WHITEHAVEN 48

OXFORD: 1 Kane Riley; 2 Harrison Brough; 3 Marcus Brooker; 4 Will Cooke; 5 Jordan Gill; 6 Callum Windley; 7 Scott Fleming; 8 Aaron Nicholson; 9 Casey Canterbury; 10 Jonathan Payne; 11 Jordan Siddons; 12 Harvey Burnett; 13 Jake Joynt. Subs (all used): 14 Bradley Moules; 15 Stuart Biscomb; 16 Anthony Cox; 17 Dwaine McRae.
Tries: Burnett (36), Fleming (71); **Goals:** Burnett 2/2.
Dismissal: Siddons (52) - high tackle.
WHITEHAVEN: 1 Elliot Miller; 5 Jordan Burns; 3 Chris Taylor; 4 Jessie Joe Parker; 2 Craig Calvert; 6 Steve Roper; 7 Paul Crook; 8 Marc Shackley; 14 James Tilley; 19 Glenn Riley; 15 Dion Aiye; 12 Scott McAvoy; 10 Carl Forster. Subs (all used, only three named): 9 James Newton; 16 Connor Holliday; 17 Tommy Holland.
Tries: McAvoy (4, 6), Taylor (9, 45), Forster (13, 75), Burns (53, 59), Calvert (66, 77); **Goals:** Crook 4/9, Roper 0/1.
Rugby Leaguer & League Express Men of the Match: *Oxford:* Harvey Burnett; *Whitehaven:* Carl Forster.
Penalty count: 4-8; **Half-time:** 6-22;
Referee: Andrew Sweet; **Attendance:** 130.

**GLOUCESTERSHIRE ALL GOLDS 10
NEWCASTLE THUNDER 56**

ALL GOLDS: 1 Jack Mitchell; 2 Mo Agoro; 3 Kadeem Williams; 4 Brad Kislingbury; 5 Chris Barlow; 6 Ben Stead; 7 Danny Fallon; 8 Ollie Purslow; 9 Steve Parry; 10 Harrison Elliott; 11 Lewis Reece; 12 Chris Worrall; 13 Billy Brickhill. Subs (all used): 14 Josh Ward; 15 Brad Hargreaves; 16 Malikhi Lloyd-Jones; 17 Harry Kidd.
Tries: Kidd (31), Barlow (38); **Goals:** Stead 1/2.
THUNDER: 1 Lewis Young; 2 Ali Blair; 3 Joe Brown; 4 Derrell Olpherts; 5 Dan Parker; 6 Danny Nicklas; 7 Benn Hardcastle; 8 Liam McAvoy; 9 Evan Simons; 10 Rhys Clarke; 11 Harry Aldous; 12 Steve Snitch; 13 Jack Aldous. Subs (all used): 14 Aaron Teroi; 15 Sam Luckley; 16 Vincent Rennie; 17 Brett Waller.

Tries: Brown (1), Blair (7, 77), Olpherts (26, 48, 71), Young (34), Nicklas (55), R Clarke (58), Luckley (64);
Goals: Hardcastle 7/9, Parker 1/1.
Rugby Leaguer & League Express Men of the Match: *All Golds:* Brad Hargreaves; *Thunder:* Derrell Olpherts.
Penalty count: 5-4; **Half-time:** 10-20;
Referee: Matt Rossleigh; **Attendance:** 223.

WORKINGTON TOWN 26 DONCASTER 30

TOWN: 17 Scott Rooke; 20 Kieran Mewse; 15 Perry Singleton; 4 Jason Mossop; 5 John Patrick; 6 Carl Forber; 7 Jamie Doran; 10 Stevie Scholey; 13 Stuart Howarth; 12 Alex Szostak; 11 Brett Phillips; 23 Phil Joseph; - Kyle Shelford. Subs (all used): 9 Callum Phillips; 18 Conor Fitzsimmons; 25 Gordon Maudling; 24 Phil Lister.
Tries: Fitzsimmons (8), Lister (16), Mossop (36), Joseph (49), Doran (69); **Goals:** Forber 3/5.
DONCASTER: 22 Louis Sheriff; 24 Richie Barnett; 3 Liam Welham; 4 Jason Tali; 5 Sam Doherty; 6 Jordan Howden; 15 Jack Miller; 19 Zac Braham; 9 Kyle Kesik; 16 Russ Spiers; 13 Charlie Martin; 34 Brad England; 27 Peter Green. Subs (all used): 7 Jordie Hedges; 18 Ryan Wright; 32 Makali Aizue; 12 Jason Muranka.
Tries: Howden (4), Miller (11, 23), Kesik (59), Spiers (79);
Goals: Miller 5/5.
Rugby Leaguer & League Express Men of the Match: *Town:* Phil Joseph; *Doncaster:* Brad England.
Penalty count: 17-6; **Half-time:** 14-18;
Referee: Greg Dolan; **Attendance:** 522.

YORK CITY KNIGHTS 36 LONDON SKOLARS 18

CITY KNIGHTS: 1 Ash Robson; 5 Tom Saxton; 19 James Haynes; 3 Nev Morrison; 2 David Foggin-Johnston; 31 Liam Harris; 23 Jon Presley; 20 Adam Robinson; 26 Andy Ellis; 10 Chris Siddons; 11 Joe Batchelor; 12 Ed Smith; 13 Tim Spears. Subs (all used): 14 Harry Carter; 16 Ronan Dixon; 17 Brad Hey; 8 Bobby Tyson-Wilson.
Tries: Harris (5, 65), Batchelor (43), Robson (47), Presley (69), Foggin-Johnston (74); **Goals:** Harris 6/7.
Sin bin: A Robinson (78) - retaliation.
SKOLARS: 20 Jake Melling; 2 Sam Nash; 31 Josh Allison; 4 Lameck Juma; 24 Michael Brown; 6 Jy-mel Coleman; 7 Mike Bishay; 25 Michael Sykes; 9 Charlie Lawrence; 10 Dave Williams; 12 Eddie Mbaraga; 18 Mike Greenhalgh; 13 Ryan Chester. Subs (all used): 14 Billy Driver; 15 Kazeem Faturoti; 29 Callum Bustin; 28 Sadiq Adebiyi.
Tries: Sykes (13), Allison (19), Adebiyi (40);
Goals: Jy-mel Coleman 3/3.
Dismissal: Juma (78) - dangerous challenge on A Robinson.
Sin bin: Brown (51) - obstruction.
Rugby Leaguer & League Express Men of the Match: *City Knights:* Liam Harris; *Skolars:* Jy-mel Coleman.
Penalty count: 14-4; **Half-time:** 6-18;
Referee: Steve Race; **Attendance:** 782.

ROUND 10

Saturday 10th June 2017

LONDON SKOLARS 31 OXFORD 18

SKOLARS: 20 Jake Melling; 2 Sam Nash; 31 Josh Allison; 4 Lameck Juma; 5 James Hill; 6 Jy-mel Coleman; 7 Mike Bishay; 25 Michael Sykes; 27 Ben Pointer; 10 Dave Williams; 11 Lamont Bryan; 18 Mike Greenhalgh; 13 Ryan Chester. Subs (all used): 14 Billy Driver; 29 Callum Bustin; 28 Sadiq Adebiyi; 19 Erjon Dollapi.
Tries: Pointer (8, 22), Adebiyi (36), Bishay (54), Bustin (75); **Goals:** Jy-mel Coleman 5/6;
Field goal: Jy-mel Coleman (66).
OXFORD: 1 Kane Riley; 2 Josh Atkinson; 3 Marcus Brooker; 4 Harvey Burnett; 5 Jordan Gill; 6 Callum Windley; 7 Scott Fleming; 8 Anthony Cox; 9 Casey Canterbury; 10 Jake Joynt; 11 Jordan Siddons; 12 Stuart Biscomb; 13 Jordan Crowther. Subs (all used): 14 Bradley Moules; 15 Tom Alexander; 16 Dwaine McRae; 17 Jonathan Payne.
Tries: Canterbury (5), Windley (15), Fleming (25);
Goals: Burnett 3/3.
Rugby Leaguer & League Express Men of the Match: *Skolars:* Ben Pointer; *Oxford:* Callum Windley.
Penalty count: 5-9; **Half-time:** 18-18;
Referee: Matt Rossleigh; **Attendance:** 291.

SOUTH WALES IRONMEN 0 TORONTO WOLFPACK 66

IRONMEN: - Jack Uren; - Ieuan Jones; 28 Morgan Jeffries; 4 Christiaan Roets; - Errol Carter; 6 Andrew Gay; 17 Zak Williams; 18 Morgan Evans; 9 Connor Farrer; - Luke Nelmes; 24 Connor Parker; - Chester Butler; - Sion Jones. Subs (all used): 5 Paul Emanuelli; 30 Michael Edwards; - Kade Breen; 29 Huw Parkes.
WOLFPACK: 2 Jonny Pownall; 4 Craig Hall; 3 Greg Worthington; 1 Quentin Laulu-Togagae; 15 Ryan Burroughs; 7 Rhys Jacks; 27 Ryan Brierley; 8 Fuifui Moimoi; 9 Bob Beswick; 10 Daniel Fleming; 11 Andrew Dixon; 17 Richard Whiting; 29 Jake Emmitt. Subs (all used): 24 Sean Penkywicz; 25 Ryan Bailey; 19 Steve Crossley; 13 Jack Bussey.
Tries: Worthington (15, 39, 57), Whiting (21, 44), Burroughs (30), Pownall (35), Bussey (48), Bailey (52), Hall (69, 80), Brierley (72), Penkywicz (75); **Goals:** Hall 7/13.
Rugby Leaguer & League Express Men of the Match: *Ironmen:* Andrew Gay; *Wolfpack:* Greg Worthington.
Penalty count: 5-6; **Half-time:** 0-24;
Referee: Geoffrey Poumes; **Attendance:** 462.

Sunday 11th June 2017

NORTH WALES CRUSADERS 24 WORKINGTON TOWN 25

CRUSADERS: 1 Tommy Johnson; 2 Corey Lee; 3 Simon Atherton; 4 Earl Hurst; 19 Dan Price; 26 Jack Hansen; 7 Ryan Smith; 8 Jonny Walker; 14 James Dandy; 17 Kenny Baker; 24 Jack Houghton; 16 Luke Warburton; 13 Ryan Millington. Subs (all used): 27 Aaron Moore; - Jonny Leather; 10 Alex Davidson; 22 Joe Bate.
Tries: Lee (9), Baker (13), Johnson (15), Davidson (72);
Goals: Johnson 4/4.
TOWN: 17 Scott Rooke; 2 Joe Hambley; 15 Perry Singleton; 4 Jason Mossop; 20 Kieran Mewse; 6 Carl Forber; 7 Jamie Doran; 19 Joe Ryan; 13 Stuart Howarth; 16 Tom Curwen; 11 Brett Phillips; 25 Gordon Maudling; 18 Conor Fitzsimmons. Subs (all used): 9 Callum Phillips; 21 Kyle Shelford; 23 Phil Joseph; - Liam Byrne.
Tries: Singleton (23, 37), C Phillips (35), Hambley (62), Mossop (64); **Goals:** Forber 2/5; **Field goal:** Forber (80).
Sin bin: Forber (8) - late challenge.
Rugby Leaguer & League Express Men of the Match: *Crusaders:* Kenny Baker; *Town:* Carl Forber.
Penalty count: 8-9; **Half-time:** 18-14;
Referee: Andrew Sweet; **Attendance:** 358.

COVENTRY BEARS 28 HEMEL STAGS 24

BEARS: 1 Harry Chapman; 2 Mikey Russell; 3 Tommy Brierley; 4 Hayden Freeman; 5 Jamahl Hunte; 6 Billy Gaylor; 7 Brad Delaney; 8 James Geurtjens; 9 Richard Hughes; 10 Dan Gover; 11 Kieran Sherratt; 12 Chris Barratt; 13 Matt Reid. Subs (all used): 14 Alex Beddows; 15 Paddy Jones; 16 Liam Thompson; 17 Jack Morrison.
Tries: Freeman (6), Hunte (9, 27), Sherratt (23), Barratt (68); **Goals:** Delaney 4/5.
STAGS: 1 Mitch Vincent; 2 Marcus Elliott; 3 Danny Lawton; 4 Alex Williams; 5 Darren Forde; 6 Brett Whitehead; 7 Lewis Fairhurst; 8 Corey Hanson; 9 Jono Burns; 10 Dan Hawksworth; 11 James Thornton; 12 Jack O'Brien; 13 Reece Williams. Subs (all used): 14 Munashe Fumhanda; 15 Danny Samuel; 16 Sam Crowther; 17 Wayne Jowitt.
Tries: Fairhurst (35, 51), O'Brien (45), Jowitt (47);
Goals: Vincent 4/4.
Rugby Leaguer & League Express Men of the Match: *Bears:* Jamahl Hunte; *Stags:* Lewis Fairhurst.
Penalty count: 17-16; **Half-time:** 22-6;
Referee: Marcus Griffiths; **Attendance:** 357.

DONCASTER 24 BARROW RAIDERS 24

DONCASTER: 22 Louis Sheriff; 26 Nick Rawsthorne; 3 Liam Welham; 4 Jason Tali; 5 Sam Doherty; 29 Reece Dean; 15 Jack Miller; 19 Zac Braham; 9 Kyle Kesik; 16 Russ Spiers; 13 Charlie Martin; 34 Brad England; 27 Peter Green. Subs (all used): 18 Ryan Wright; 23 Jamie Thackray; 32 Makali Aizue; 7 Jordie Hedges.
Tries: Braham (14), Tali (52, 77), Hedges (64);
Goals: Miller 4/5.
RAIDERS: 1 Ryan Fieldhouse; 24 Luke Cresswell; 3 Declan Hulme; - Eze Harper; 2 Brett Carter; 6 Jamie Dallimore; 7 Lewis Charnock; 8 Joe Bullock; 9 Nathan Mossop; 17 Tom Walker; 18 Danny Morrow; 12 Jarrad Stack; 13 Martin Aspinwall. Subs (all used): 15 Karl Ashall; 11 Dan Toal; 21 James Duerden; 16 Andrew Dawson.
Tries: Cresswell (4), Dallimore (8), Hulme (23), Harper (62);
Goals: Charnock 2/4, Dallimore 2/2.
Rugby Leaguer & League Express Men of the Match: *Doncaster:* Jason Tali; *Raiders:* Joe Bullock.
Penalty count: 6-5; **Half-time:** 6-16;
Referee: Steve Race; **Attendance:** 673
(at Keepmoat Athletics Ground).

HUNSLET 20 YORK CITY KNIGHTS 52

HUNSLET: 1 Jimmy Watson; - Michael Hayward; 4 Mufaro Mvududu; 24 Cameron Leeming; 3 Marcus Webb; 18 Joel Gibson; 7 Danny Ansell; 31 Sean Hesketh; 9 Jack Lee; 10 Lewis Reed; 11 Jake Normington; 13 Liam Mackay; 19 Matt Carbutt. Subs (all used): 14 George Flanagan; 8 Michael Haley; 15 Jack Coventry; 21 Jack Walton.
Tries: Mackay (50), Hesketh (54), Hayward (57), Flanagan (73); **Goals:** Ansell 0/3, Gibson 2/2.
CITY KNIGHTS: 1 Ash Robson; 5 Tom Saxton; 3 Nev Morrison; 19 James Haynes; 2 David Foggin-Johnston; 34 Connor Robinson; 31 Liam Harris; 20 Adam Robinson; 29 Will Jubb; 10 Chris Siddons; 12 Ed Smith; 11 Joe Batchelor; 13 Tim Spears. Subs (all used): 14 Harry Carter; 16 Ronan Dixon; 17 Brad Hey; 28 Kieran Moran.
Tries: E Smith (11), Harris (15), Haynes (21), Siddons (23), Spears (31), Batchelor (38, 42), Morrison (67), Jubb (75);
Goals: C Robinson 8/9.
Rugby Leaguer & League Express Men of the Match: *Hunslet:* Danny Ansell; *City Knights:* Liam Harris.
Penalty count: 9-8; **Half-time:** 0-36;
Referee: Greg Dolan; **Attendance:** 589.

NEWCASTLE THUNDER 36 KEIGHLEY COUGARS 12

THUNDER: 1 Lewis Young; 2 Ali Blair; 3 Dan Parker; 4 Derrell Olpherts; 5 Joe Brown; 6 Tom Shaw; 7 Benn Hardcastle; 8 Liam McAvoy; 9 Evan Simons; 10 Rhys Clarke; 11 Steve Snitch; 12 Harry Aldous; 13 Jack Aldous. Subs (all used): 14 Vincent Rennie; 15 Aaron Teroi; 16 Sam Luckley; 17 Mikey Wood.
Tries: Young (13, 62, 78), Blair (26, 51), Brown (33), Hardcastle (59); **Goals:** Hardcastle 1/5, Parker 3/3.
COUGARS: 24 Liam Darville; 26 Vinny Finigan; 34 Hamish Barnes; 32 Adam Ryder; 2 Andy Gabriel; 16 Will Milner; 7 Matty Beharrell; 8 Scott Law; 9 James Feather; 12 Brendon Rawlins; 11 Josh Lynam; 18 Josh Tonks; 21 Emmerson Whittel. Subs (all used): 13 Mike Emmett; 17 Nathan Conroy; 19 Matthew Bailey; 29 Brad Nicholson.
Tries: Ryder (4), Finigan (28); **Goals:** Beharrell 2/2.
Rugby Leaguer & League Express Men of the Match: *Thunder:* Lewis Young; *Cougars:* Andy Gabriel.
Penalty count: 10-6; **Half-time:** 14-12;
Referee: Jon Roberts; **Attendance:** 786.

WHITEHAVEN 62 GLOUCESTERSHIRE ALL GOLDS 6

WHITEHAVEN: 1 Elliott Miller; 5 Jordan Burns; 3 Chris Taylor; 4 Jessie Joe Parker; 2 Craig Calvert; 6 Steve Roper; 7 Paul Crook; 19 Glenn Riley; 14 James Tilley; 8 Marc Shackley; 15 Dion Aiye; 12 Scott McAvoy; 10 Carl Forster. Subs (all used): 9 James Newton; 17 Tommy Holland; 16 Connor Holliday; 25 Aiden Worthington.
Tries: Burns (8), Forster (13), McAvoy (18), Miller (21, 71, 77), Calvert (35), Holland (40), Newton (53), Parker (59), Aiye (68); **Goals:** Crook 9/11.
ALL GOLDS: 1 Jack Mitchell; 2 Mo Agoro; 3 Steven Nield; 4 Brad Kislingbury; 5 Chris Barlow; 6 Courtney Davies; 7 Steve Parry; 8 Ollie Purslow; 9 Billy Brickhill; 10 Harry Kidd; 11 Lewis Reece; 12 Joe McClean; 13 Chris Worrall. Subs (all used): 14 Harrison Elliott; 15 Brad Hargreaves; 16 Malikhi Lloyd-Jones; 17 Luke Stephens.
Try: Agoro (74); **Goals:** Davies 1/1.
Rugby Leaguer & League Express Men of the Match: *Whitehaven:* Steve Roper; *All Golds:* Courtney Davies.
Penalty count: 4-6; **Half-time:** 34-0;
Referee: Nick Bennett; **Attendance:** 534.

ROUND 11

Saturday 17th June 2017

BARROW RAIDERS 28 NORTH WALES CRUSADERS 4

RAIDERS: 1 Ryan Fieldhouse; 5 Shane Toal; 3 Declan Hulme; 33 Eze Harper; 24 Luke Cresswell; 6 Jamie Dallimore; 26 Brad Marwood; 8 Joe Bullock; 9 Nathan Mossop; 17 Tom Walker; 11 Dan Toal; 12 Jarrad Stack; 13 Martin Aspinwall. Subs (all used): 14 Dan Abram; 21 James Duerden; 10 Oliver Wilkes; 28 Brad Brennan.
Tries: Marwood (6, 20), Abram (38), Hulme (74), D Toal (76); **Goals:** Dallimore 4/6.
CRUSADERS: 1 Tommy Johnson; 2 Corey Lee; 28 Callum Mulkeen; 4 Earl Hurst; 19 Dan Price; 6 Andy Moulsdale; 7 Ryan Smith; 8 Jonny Walker; 14 James Dandy; 17 Kenny Baker; 24 Jack Houghton; 3 Simon Atherton; 16 Luke Warburton. Subs (all used): 27 Aaron Moore; 32 Warren Thompson; 31 Blake Turner; 22 Joe Bate.
Try: Mulkeen (28); **Goals:** Johnson 0/1.
Rugby Leaguer & League Express Men of the Match: *Raiders:* Nathan Mossop; *Crusaders:* Jonny Walker.
Penalty count: 3-7; **Half-time:** 16-4;
Referee: Brandon Robinson; **Attendance:** 835.

Sunday 18th June 2017

HEMEL STAGS 20 GLOUCESTERSHIRE ALL GOLDS 32

STAGS: 1 Mitch Vincent; 2 Darren Forde; 3 Danny Lawton; 4 Josh Casey; 5 Marcus Elliott; 6 Jack O'Brien; 7 Mark Barlow; 8 Dan Hawksworth; 9 Jono Burns; 10 Reece Williams; 11 Danny Samuel; 12 Munashe Fumhanda; 13 Corey Hansen. Subs (all used): 14 Ryan Matthews; 15 James Thornton; 16 Sam Crowther; 17 Wayne Jowitt.

Tries: Elliott (10, 24), Barlow (67); **Goals:** Vincent 4/6.
ALL GOLDS: 1 Steven Nield; 2 Mo Agoro; 3 Phil Cowburn; 4 Brad Kislingbury; 5 Chris Barlow; 6 Courtney Davies; 7 Jack Mitchell; 8 James Walter; 9 Steve Parry; 10 Harry Kidd; 11 Chris Worrall; 12 Joe McClean; 13 Billy Brickhill. Subs (all used): 14 Luke Stephens; 15 Brad Hargreaves; 16 Malikhi Lloyd-Jones; 17 Richard Jones.
Tries: Parry (4, 14), Agoro (53), Kidd (65), Mitchell (72), Barlow (80); **Goals:** Davies 4/6.
Rugby Leaguer & League Express Men of the Match: *Stags:* Mitch Vincent; *All Golds:* Jack Mitchell.
Penalty count: 7-8; **Half-time:** 16-8;
Referee: Tom Crashley; **Attendance:** 102.

OXFORD 0 NEWCASTLE THUNDER 52

OXFORD: 1 Scott Fleming; 2 Kane Riley; 3 Harvey Burnett; 4 Will Cooke; 5 Jordan Gill; 6 Callum Windley; 7 Josh Kittrick; 8 Dwaine McRae; 9 Casey Canterbury; 10 Jake Joynt; 11 Jordan Siddons; 12 Daniel Hindmarsh-Takji; 13 Tom Alexander. Subs (all used): 14 Bradley Moules; 15 Stuart Biscomb; 16 Lewis Bienek; 17 Marcus Brooker.
THUNDER: 1 Lewis Young; 2 Joe Brown; 3 Derrell Olpherts; 4 Dan Parker; 5 Ali Blair; 6 Tom Shaw; 7 Benn Hardcastle; 8 Liam McAvoy; 9 Evan Simons; 10 Rhys Clarke; 11 Harry Aldous; 12 Steve Snitch; 13 Jack Aldous. Subs (all used): 14 Aaron Teroi; 15 Vincent Rennie; 16 Sam Luckley; 17 Corbyn Kilday.
Tries: Young (15, 16, 75), Olpherts (25), Hardcastle (35, 60), Teroi (45), Snitch (50); **Goals:** Hardcastle 10/10.
Rugby Leaguer & League Express Men of the Match: *Oxford:* Daniel Hindmarsh-Takji; *Thunder:* Benn Hardcastle.
Penalty count: 7-7; **Half-time:** 0-26;
Referee: Billy Pearson; **Attendance:** 120.

KEIGHLEY COUGARS 45 LONDON SKOLARS 26

COUGARS: 1 Harry Aaronson; 5 Davey Dixon; 34 Hamish Barnes; 32 Adam Ryder; 2 Andy Gabriel; 14 Adam Brook; 7 Matty Beharrell; 8 Scott Law; 9 James Feather; 19 Matthew Bailey; 12 Brendon Rawlins; 18 Josh Tonks; 13 Mike Emmett. Subs (all used): 11 Josh Lynam; 17 Nathan Conroy; 21 Emmerson Whittel; 29 Brad Nicholson.
Tries: Dixon (4, 53), Bailey (8), Aaronson (14), Emmett (49), Beharrell (58), Feather (64), Conroy (78); **Goals:** Beharrell 6/8; **Field goal:** Beharrell (76).
SKOLARS: 1 Andy Winfield; 2 Sam Nash; 31 Josh Allison; - Kameron Pearce-Paul; 24 Michael Brown; 6 Jy-mel Coleman; 7 Mike Bishay; 25 Michael Sykes; 27 Ben Pointer; 29 Callum Bustin; 10 Dave Williams; 11 Lamont Bryan; 13 Ryan Chester. Subs (all used): 8 Louis Robinson; 14 Billy Driver; 20 Jake Melling; 28 Sadiq Adebiyi.
Tries: D Williams (26), Driver (33, 38), Bryan (69), Brown (79); **Goals:** Jy-mel Coleman 3/5.
Rugby Leaguer & League Express Men of the Match: *Cougars:* Harry Aaronson; *Skolars:* Billy Driver.
Penalty count: 2-6; **Half-time:** 14-18;
Referee: Nick Bennett; **Attendance:** 457.

SOUTH WALES IRONMEN 24 COVENTRY BEARS 22

IRONMEN: 22 Ben Jones; - Sam Hodge; 28 Morgan Jeffries; 4 Christiaan Roets; - Errol Carter; 6 Andrew Gay; 5 Paul Emanuelli; - William Calcott; 17 Zak Williams; - Kade Breen; 24 Connor Parker; - Jordan Syme; - Sion Jones. Subs (all used): 19 Jamie I'Anson; 30 Michael Edwards; 13 Barrie Phillips; 29 Huw Parkes.
Tries: Roets (9, 18), Carter (42), B Phillips (78); **Goals:** Emanuelli 4/6.
Sin bin: Syme (52) - repeated team offences.
BEARS: 1 Harry Chapman; 2 Mikey Russell; 3 Tommy Brierley; 4 Eddie Medforth; 5 Jamahl Hunte; 6 Billy Gaylor; 7 Brad Delaney; 8 James Geurtjens; 9 Joe Prior; 10 Alex Beddows; 11 Kieran Sherratt; 12 Chris Barratt; 13 Matt Reid. Subs (all used): 14 Hayden Freeman; 15 Liam Thompson; 16 Jack Morrison; 17 Dan Gover.
Tries: Sherratt (49), Russell (53), Morrison (66), Reid (72); **Goals:** Delaney 3/4.
Rugby Leaguer & League Express Men of the Match: *Ironmen:* Christiaan Roets; *Bears:* Matt Reid.
Penalty count: 9-8; **Half-time:** 12-0;
Referee: Andrew Sweet; **Attendance:** 156.

YORK CITY KNIGHTS 16 WHITEHAVEN 18

CITY KNIGHTS: 1 Ash Robson; 5 Tom Saxton; 19 James Haynes; 3 Nev Morrison; 2 David Foggin-Johnston; 31 Liam Harris; 34 Connor Robinson; 20 Adam Robinson; 9 Pat Smith; 10 Chris Siddons; 11 Joe Batchelor; 12 Ed Smith; 13 Tim Spears. Subs (all used): 14 Harry Carter; 17 Brad Hey; 16 Ronan Dixon; 28 Kieran Moran.
Tries: Saxton (5), Hey (70), Spears (76); **Goals:** C Robinson 2/6.
WHITEHAVEN: 1 Elliott Miller; 2 Craig Calvert; 4 Jessie Joe Parker; 3 Chris Taylor; 5 Jordan Burns; 6 Steve Roper; 7 Paul Crook; 25 Aiden Worthington; 14 James Tilley; 19 Glenn Riley; 15 Dion Aiye; 12 Scott McAvoy; 10 Carl Forster. Subs (all used): 9 James Newton; 16 Connor Holliday; 17 Tommy Holland; 24 Lewis Brown.
Tries: Calvert (20), Newton (45), Forster (66); **Goals:** Crook 3/4.
Rugby Leaguer & League Express Men of the Match: *City Knights:* Tim Spears; *Whitehaven:* Carl Forster.
Penalty count: 10-9; **Half-time:** 4-6;
Referee: Steve Race; **Attendance:** 1,150.

WORKINGTON TOWN 12 TORONTO WOLFPACK 58

TOWN: 21 Gabriel Fell; 20 Kieran Mewse; 2 Joe Hambley; 4 Jason Mossop; 17 Scott Rooke; 6 Carl Forber; 7 Jamie Doran; 12 Alex Szostak; 13 Stuart Howarth; 16 Tom Curwen; 11 Brett Phillips; 23 Phil Joseph; 15 Perry Singleton. Subs (all used): 19 Joe Ryan; 18 Conor Fitzsimmons; 25 Gordon Maudling; 24 Phil Lister.
Tries: Maudling (32), Singleton (50); **Goals:** Forber 2/2.
WOLFPACK: 15 Ryan Burroughs; 2 Jonny Pownall; 1 Quentin Laulu-Togagae; 4 Craig Hall; 3 Greg Worthington; 7 Rhys Jacks; 27 Ryan Brierley; 25 Ryan Bailey; 9 Bob Beswick; 13 Jack Bussey; 29 Jake Emmitt; 17 Richard Whiting; 10 Daniel Fleming. Subs (all used): 19 Steve Crossley; 24 Sean Penkywicz; 16 Shaun Pick; 8 Fuifui Moimoi.
Tries: Pownall (7, 79), Worthington (14, 47), Hall (19, 22), Brierley (38, 77), Bussey (44), Penkywicz (75); **Goals:** Hall 9/10.
Rugby Leaguer & League Express Men of the Match: *Town:* Perry Singleton; *Wolfpack:* Bob Beswick.
Penalty count: 12-12; **Half-time:** 6-28;
Referee: Greg Dolan; **Attendance:** 835.

ROUND 12

Saturday 24th June 2017

LONDON SKOLARS 10 BARROW RAIDERS 20

SKOLARS: 7 Mike Bishay; 2 Sam Nash; 24 Michael Brown; 4 Lameck Juma; 22 John Paxton; 6 Jy-mel Coleman; 29 Jermaine Coleman; 25 Michael Sykes; 9 Charlie Lawrence; 10 Dave Williams; 11 Lamont Bryan; 31 Josh Allison; 13 Ryan Chester. Subs (all used): 14 Billy Driver; 8 Louis Robinson; 32 Jordan Williams; 18 Mike Greenhalgh.
Tries: Bryan (15), Allison (27); **Goals:** Jy-mel Coleman 1/2.
Sin bin: Bryan (56) - dissent.
RAIDERS: 1 Ryan Fieldhouse; 2 Brett Carter; 3 Declan Hulme; - Eze Harper; 45 Tom Loxam; 6 Jamie Dallimore; 7 Lewis Charnock; 17 Tom Walker; 15 Karl Ashall; 10 Oliver Wilkes; 11 Dan Toal; 12 Jarrod Stack; 13 Martin Aspinwall. Subs (all used): 9 Nathan Mossop; 16 Andrew Dawson; 25 Matty While; 21 James Duerden.
Tries: Wilkes (21), Mossop (29); **Goals:** Charnock 4/4, Dallimore 2/2.
Rugby Leaguer & League Express Men of the Match: *Skolars:* Louis Robinson; *Raiders:* Jamie Dallimore.
Penalty count: 9-13; **Half-time:** 10-14;
Referee: Geoffrey Poumes; **Attendance:** 374.

TORONTO WOLFPACK 56 HUNSLET 12

WOLFPACK: 1 Quentin Laulu-Togagae; 2 Jonny Pownall; 3 Greg Worthington; 4 Craig Hall; 5 Liam Kay; 9 Bob Beswick; 27 Ryan Brierley; 25 Ryan Bailey; 24 Sean Penkywicz; 10 Daniel Fleming; 12 James Laithwaite; 17 Richard Whiting; 13 Jack Bussey. Subs (all used): 8 Fuifui Moimoi; 15 Ryan Burroughs; 19 Steve Crossley; 29 Jake Emmitt.
Tries: Penkywicz (16), Brierley (18), Pownall (24, 27), Laithwaite (36), Kay (44), Laulu-Togagae (52, 64, 77), Whiting (58), Hall (75); **Goals:** Hall 6/11.
Sin bin: Moimoi (72) - dissent.
HUNSLET: 1 Jimmy Watson; 34 Tommy Brierley; - Jack Norfolk; 4 Mufaro Mvududu; 39 Josh Nathaniel; 33 Shaun Roberts; 6 Joe Sanderson; 10 Lewis Reed; 9 Jack Lee; 15 Jack Coventry; 21 Jack Walton; 12 Aston Wilson; 17 Nyle Flynn. Subs (all used): 14 George Flanagan; 24 Cameron Leeming; 23 Jose Kenga; - Luke Fowden.
Tries: Mvududu (21), Flanagan (32); **Goals:** Sanderson 2/2.
Sin bin: Flanagan (42) - dangerous challenge on Moimoi.
Rugby Leaguer & League Express Men of the Match: *Wolfpack:* Quentin Laulu-Togagae; *Hunslet:* Mufaro Mvududu.
Penalty count: 16-12; **Half-time:** 22-12;
Referee: Tom Grant; **Attendance:** 6,042.

Sunday 25th June 2017

NORTH WALES CRUSADERS 36 SOUTH WALES IRONMEN 12

CRUSADERS: 1 Tommy Johnson; - Taylor Prell; 28 Callum Mulkeen; 4 Earl Hurst; 5 Dale Bloomfield; 6 Andy Moulsdale; 7 Ryan Smith; 8 Jonny Walker; 14 James Dandy; 17 Kenny Baker; 24 Jack Houghton; 3 Simon Atherton; 16 Luke Warburton. Subs (all used): 27 Aaron Moore; 32 Warren Thompson; - Alex Whalley; 22 Joe Bate.
Tries: Atherton (10, 44), Baker (49, 54), Smith (74, 75); **Goals:** Johnson 6/6.
IRONMEN: - Jack Uren; - Sam Hodge; 28 Morgan Jeffries; - Errol Carter; 22 Ben Jones; 6 Andrew Gay; 5 Paul Emanuelli; - William Calcott; 9 Connor Farrer; 24 Connor Parker; 17 Zak Williams; 4 Christiaan Roets; - Martyn Reilly. Subs (all used): - Kade Breen; 19 Jamie I'Anson; 30 Michael Edwards; - Cobi Green.
Tries: Farrer (1), C Parker (20); **Goals:** Emanuelli 2/2.
Rugby Leaguer & League Express Men of the Match: *Crusaders:* Warren Thompson; *Ironmen:* Paul Emanuelli.
Penalty count: 8-4; **Half-time:** 6-12;
Referee: Marcus Griffiths; **Attendance:** 402.

COVENTRY BEARS 28 WORKINGTON TOWN 29

BEARS: 1 Harry Chapman; 2 Mikey Russell; 3 Jason Bass; 4 Charlie O'Mara; 5 Jamahl Hunte; 6 Billy Gaylor; 7 Brad Delaney; 8 James Guertjens; 9 Richard Hughes; 10 Alex Beddows; 11 Kieran Sherratt; 12 Paddy Jones; 13 Matt Reid. Subs (all used): 14 Hayden Freeman; 15 John Aldred; 16 Brad Brennan; 17 Jack Morrison.
Tries: Delaney (24), Russell (36, 56), Chapman (43), Freeman (59); **Goals:** Delaney 4/5.
TOWN: - Gabriel Fell; 2 Joe Hambley; - Danny Rasool; 4 Jason Mossop; 17 Scott Rooke; 6 Carl Forber; 7 Jamie Doran; 16 Tom Curwen; 13 Stuart Howarth; 19 Joe Ryan; 11 Brett Phillips; 25 Gordon Maudling; 15 Perry Singleton. Subs (all used): - Joe Prior; - Liam Byrne; 18 Conor Fitzsimmons; - Jake Moore.
Tries: Hambley (4, 16), Maudling (9), Doran (20), Rasool (44); **Goals:** Forber 4/5; **Field goal:** Forber (77).
Sin bin: Rasool (52) - professional foul.
Rugby Leaguer & League Express Men of the Match: *Bears:* Mikey Russell; *Town:* Jamie Doran.
Penalty count: 7-9; **Half-time:** 10-22;
Referee: Craig Smith; **Attendance:** 571.

GLOUCESTERSHIRE ALL GOLDS 38 OXFORD 10

ALL GOLDS: 1 Phil Cowburn; 2 Mo Agoro; 3 Lewis Reece; 4 Brad Kislingbury; 5 Chris Barlow; 6 Courtney Davies; 7 Jack Mitchell; 8 James Walter; 9 Steve Parry; 10 Harry Kidd; 11 Chris Worrall; 12 Joe McClean; 13 Harrison Elliott. Subs (all used): 14 Billy Brickhill; 15 Brad Hargreaves; 16 Malikhi Lloyd-Jones; 17 Richard Jones.
Tries: Agoro (1), Parry (19, 62), Elliott (57), Barlow (65), Walter (71), Brickhill (76); **Goals:** Davies 5/7.
Sin bin: Reece (17) - interference.
OXFORD: 1 Scott Fleming; 2 Kane Riley; 3 Harvey Burnett; 4 Marcus Brooker; 5 Adam Dent; 6 Bradley Moules; 7 Callum Windley; 8 Jake Joynt; 9 Casey Canterbury; 10 Dwaine McRae; 11 Jordan Siddons; 12 Tom Alexander; 13 Jonathan Payne. Subs (all used): 14 Josh Kittrick; 15 Anthony Cox; 16 Fran Welsh; 17 Mark Hayes.
Tries: Brooker (8), Canterbury (13); **Goals:** Burnett 1/3.
Rugby Leaguer & League Express Men of the Match: *All Golds:* Steve Parry; *Oxford:* Callum Windley.
Penalty count: 10-8; **Half-time:** 10-8;
Referee: Michael Mannifield; **Attendance:** 275.

KEIGHLEY COUGARS 18 YORK CITY KNIGHTS 25

COUGARS: 1 Harry Aaronson; 5 Davey Dixon; 34 Hamish Barnes; 32 Adam Ryder; 2 Andy Gabriel; 14 Adam Brook; 7 Matty Beharrell; 15 Neil Cherryholme; 9 James Feather; 19 Matthew Bailey; 12 Brendon Rawlins; 18 Josh Tonks; 13 Mike Emmett. Subs (all used): 11 Josh Lynam; 17 Nathan Conroy; 21 Emmerson Whittel; 29 Brad Nicholson.
Tries: Nicholson (43), Dixon (46, 70), Gabriel (78); **Goals:** Beharrell 1/4.
Dismissal: Tonks (36) - late challenge on C Robinson.
CITY KNIGHTS: 1 Ash Robson; 5 Tom Saxton; 30 Tuoyo Egodo; 19 James Haynes; 2 David Foggin-Johnston; 34 Connor Robinson; 7 Harry Tyson-Wilson; 20 Adam Robinson; 29 Will Jubb; 10 Chris Siddons; 12 Ed Smith; 11 Joe Batchelor; 13 Tim Spears. Subs (all used): 28 Kieran Moran; 9 Pat Smith; 16 Ronan Dixon; 17 Brad Hey.
Tries: E Smith (3), Batchelor (16), Siddons (25); **Goals:** C Robinson 6/7; **Field goal:** C Robinson (72).
Sin bin: Moran (42) - late challenge.
Rugby Leaguer & League Express Men of the Match: *Cougars:* Davey Dixon; *City Knights:* Connor Robinson.
Penalty count: 7-14; **Half-time:** 0-22;
Referee: Tom Crashley; **Attendance:** 927.

NEWCASTLE THUNDER 48 HEMEL STAGS 12

THUNDER: 1 Lewis Young; 2 Ali Blair; 3 Dan Parker; 4 Derrell Olpherts; 5 Joe Brown; 6 Danny Nicklas; 7 Benn Hardcastle; 8 Vincent Rennie; 9 Aaron Teroi; 10 Matt Barron; 11 Harry Aldous; 12 Steve Snitch; 13 Sam Luckley. Subs (all used): 14 Jack Aldous; 15 Rhys Clarke; 16 Liam McAvoy; 17 Evan Simons.
Tries: Brown (7, 40), Snitch (24), Young (35), Hardcastle (39), Simons (49), Blair (67), Barron (70), Olpherts (79); **Goals:** Hardcastle 6/9.

STAGS: 1 Mitch Vincent; 2 Josh Casey; 3 Reece Williams; 4 Danny Lawton; 5 Darren Forde; 6 Mark Barlow; 7 Lewis Fairhurst; 8 Corey Hanson; 9 Jono Burns; 10 Dan Hawksworth; 11 James Thornton; 12 Jack O'Brien; 13 Brett Whitehead. Subs (all used): 14 Scott Lee; 15 Sam Crowther; 16 Munashe Fumhanda; 17 Wayne Jowitt.
Tries: Casey (14), Burns (54); **Goals:** Vincent 2/2.
Rugby Leaguer & League Express Men of the Match: *Thunder:* Joe Brown; *Stags:* Jono Burns.
Penalty count: 10-10; **Half-time:** 24-6;
Referee: Liam Staveley; **Attendance:** 620.

WHITEHAVEN 25 DONCASTER 20

WHITEHAVEN: 5 Jordan Burns; - Danny Green; 3 Chris Taylor; 4 Jessie Joe Parker; 2 Craig Calvert; 6 Steve Roper; 7 Paul Crook; 8 Marc Shackley; 9 James Newton; 17 Tommy Holland; 15 Dion Aiye; 12 Scott McAvoy; 14 James Tilley. Subs: 10 Carl Forster; 16 Connor Holliday; 22 Kurt Maudling (not used); 25 Aiden Worthington.
Tries: Holland (9), Burns (27, 50), Parker (60);
Goals: Crook 4/5; **Field goal:** Crook (48).
Sin bin: Taylor (39) - delaying restart.
DONCASTER: 1 Tom Carr; 22 Louis Sheriff; - Jack Logan; 4 Jason Tali; 24 Richie Barnett; 29 Reece Dean; 15 Jack Miller; 16 Russ Spiers; 9 Kyle Kesik; 14 Connor Scott; 13 Charlie Martin; - Jack Downs; 27 Peter Green. Subs (all used): 18 Ryan Wright; 10 Iafeta Palea'aesina; 23 Jamie Thackray; 12 Jason Muranka.
Tries: Sheriff (34, 70), Logan (63, 67); **Goals:** Miller 2/4.
Rugby Leaguer & League Express Men of the Match: *Whitehaven:* Scott McAvoy; *Doncaster:* Jack Logan.
Penalty count: 9-6; **Half time:** 14-6;
Referee: Andrew Sweet; **Attendance:** 606.

ROUND 13

Saturday 1st July 2017

BARROW RAIDERS 36 GLOUCESTERSHIRE ALL GOLDS 6

RAIDERS: 1 Ryan Fieldhouse; 2 Brett Carter; 12 Jarrad Stack; 3 Declan Hulme; 5 Shane Toal; 6 Jamie Dallimore; 7 Lewis Charnock; 8 Joe Bullock; 9 Nathan Mossop; 10 Oliver Wilkes; 11 Dan Toal; 22 Bradd Crellin; 13 Martin Aspinwall. Subs (all used): 15 Karl Ashall; 25 Matty While; 16 Andrew Dawson; 17 Tom Walker.
Tries: Aspinwall (7), Hulme (9, 71), S Toal (11, 36), Mossop (48), Fieldhouse (74); **Goals:** Charnock 4/8.
ALL GOLDS: 1 Jack Mitchell; 2 Mo Agoro; 3 Phil Cowburn; 4 Lewis Reece; 5 Chris Barlow; 6 Courtney Davies; 7 Danny Fallon; 8 Harrison Elliott; 9 Steve Parry; 10 James Walter; 11 Chris Worrall; 12 Joe McClean; 13 Billy Brickhill. Subs (all used): 14 Shaun Owens; 15 Brad Hargreaves; 16 Malikhi Lloyd-Jones; 17 Richard Jones.
Try: Mitchell (20); **Goals:** Davies 1/1.
Rugby Leaguer & League Express Men of the Match: *Raiders:* Nathan Mossop; *All Golds:* Lewis Reece.
Penalty count: 6-6; **Half-time:** 20-6;
Referee: Liam Moore; **Attendance:** 696.

TORONTO WOLFPACK 64 YORK CITY KNIGHTS 22

WOLFPACK: 1 Quentin Laulu-Togagae; 2 Jonny Pownall; 3 Greg Worthington; 4 Craig Hall; 5 Liam Kay; 27 Ryan Brierley; 14 Gary Wheeler; 8 Fuifui Moimoi; 9 Bob Beswick; 29 Jake Emmitt; 12 James Laithwaite; 17 Richard Whiting; 13 Jack Bussey. Subs (all used): 7 Rhys Jacks; 19 Steve Crossley; 21 Adam Sidlow; 24 Sean Penkywicz.
Tries: Beswick (21), Pownall (30, 49), Kay (33, 37, 42, 47, 52), Penkywicz (55), Bussey (58), Hall (60), Laulu-Togagae (67); **Goals:** Hall 8/12.
CITY KNIGHTS: 1 Ash Robson; 3 Nev Morrison; 17 Brad Hey; 24 Adam Swift; 2 David Foggin-Johnston; 34 Connor Robinson; 31 Liam Harris; 8 Bobby Tyson-Wilson; 29 Will Jubb; 28 Kieran Moran; 12 Ed Smith; 11 Joe Batchelor; 10 Chris Siddons. Subs (all used): 9 Pat Smith; 15 Liam Thompson; 16 Ronan Dixon; 19 James Haynes.
Tries: Harris (25), Foggin-Johnston (28, 75, 79);
Goals: C Robinson 3/4.
Rugby Leaguer & League Express Men of the Match: *Wolfpack:* Liam Kay; *City Knights:* David Foggin-Johnston.
Penalty count: 8-12; **Half-time:** 20-12;
Referee: John McMullen; **Attendance:** 5,646.

Sunday 2nd July 2017

HEMEL STAGS 25 SOUTH WALES IRONMEN 18

STAGS: 1 Mitch Vincent; 2 Marcus Elliott; 3 Corey Hanson; 4 Josh Casey; 5 Darren Forde; 6 Mark Barlow; 7 Lewis Fairhurst; 8 Dan Hawksworth; 9 Jono Burns; 10 Reece Williams; 11 James Thornton; 12 Munashe Fumhanda; 13 Brett Whitehead. Subs (all used): 14 Danny Samuel; 15 Wayne Jowitt; 16 Alex Williams; 17 Santino Decaro.
Tries: Burns (25), Fairhurst (38), Fumhanda (44), Whitehead (79); **Goals:** Vincent 4/5;
Field goal: Vincent (40).
IRONMEN: 27 Jack Uren; 23 Sam Hodge; - Errol Carter; - Chester Butler; 22 Ben Jones; 6 Andrew Gay; 17 Zak Williams; 18 Morgan Evans; 9 Connor Farrer; - Barrie Phillips; 24 Connor Parker; - Kade Breen; - William Calcott. Subs (all used): 30 Michael Edwards; 19 Jamie l'Anson; - Josh Barden; - Sam Buckthought.
Tries: Evans (20), B Phillips (58), Calcott (66);
Goals: B Jones 3/4.
Rugby Leaguer & League Express Men of the Match: *Stags:* Munashe Fumhanda; *Ironmen:* Ben Jones.
Penalty count: 10-10; **Half-time:** 13-6;
Referee: Cameron Worsley; **Attendance:** 131.

OXFORD 20 NORTH WALES CRUSADERS 52

OXFORD: 1 Adam Dent; 2 Judah Mazive; 3 Marcus Brooker; 4 Harvey Burnett; 5 Harrison Brough; 6 Callum Windley; 7 Casey Canterbury; 8 Aaron Nicholson; 9 Bradley Moules; 10 Dwaine McRae; 11 Jordan Siddons; 12 Jake Joynt; 13 Jonathan Payne. Subs (all used): 14 Liam O'Callaghan; 15 Fran Welsh; 16 Anthony Cox; 17 Tom Alexander.
Tries: Windley (40), Moules (49), Canterbury (57), Brough (60); **Goals:** Burnett 2/4.
CRUSADERS: 1 Tommy Johnson; - Taylor Prell; 28 Callum Mulkeen; 4 Earl Hurst; 5 Dale Bloomfield; 6 Andy Moulsdale; 7 Ryan Smith; 8 Jonny Walker; 27 Aaron Moore; 32 Warren Thompson; 24 Jack Houghton; 3 Simon Atherton; 13 Ryan Millington. Subs (all used): 26 Jack Hansen; - Alex Whalley; 17 Kenny Baker; 22 Joe Bate.
Tries: Atherton (1), Houghton (16), Smith (20, 80), Moulsdale (28), Bate (45), Walker (67), Mulkeen (73), Baker (78); **Goals:** Johnson 8/9.
Sin bin: Mulkeen (59) - dangerous challenge.
Rugby Leaguer & League Express Men of the Match: *Oxford:* Casey Canterbury; *Crusaders:* Ryan Smith.
Penalty count: 6-6; **Half-time:** 6-24;
Referee: Matt Rossleigh; **Attendance:** 140.

DONCASTER 10 NEWCASTLE THUNDER 20

DONCASTER: 1 Tom Carr; 5 Sam Doherty; - Jack Logan; 4 Jason Tali; 24 Richie Barnett; 29 Reece Dean; 15 Jack Miller; 16 Russ Spiers; 20 Kieran Cross; 14 Connor Scott; 13 Charlie Martin; - Jack Downs; 27 Peter Green. Subs (all used): 12 Jason Muranka; 23 Jamie Thackray; 18 Ryan Wright; 7 Jordie Hedges.
Tries: Barnett (65), Carr (80); **Goals:** Miller 1/2.
THUNDER: 1 Lewis Young; 2 Ali Blair; 3 Derrell Olpherts; 4 Dan Parker; 5 Joe Brown; 6 Aaron Teroi; 7 Benn Hardcastle; 8 Rhys Clarke; 9 Evan Simons; 10 Liam McAvoy; 11 Harry Aldous; 12 Steve Snitch; 13 Jack Aldous. Subs (all used): 14 Matt Barron; 15 Sam Luckley; 16 Vincent Rennie; 17 Callum Bustin.
Tries: Parker (13), Olpherts (17), Young (68);
Goals: Hardcastle 3/4; **Field goals:** Hardcastle (38, 40).
Rugby Leaguer & League Express Men of the Match: *Doncaster:* Richie Barnett; *Thunder:* Steve Snitch.
Penalty count: 11-12; **Half-time:** 0-12;
Referee: Greg Dolan; **Attendance:** 550
(at Keepmoat Athletics Ground).

HUNSLET 56 COVENTRY BEARS 24

HUNSLET: 1 Jimmy Watson; 18 Joel Gibson; 4 Mufaro Mvududu; 38 Mathew Cook; 34 Tommy Brierley; 6 Joe Sanderson; 7 Danny Ansell; 10 Lewis Reed; 9 Jack Lee; 15 Jack Coventry; 12 Aston Wilson; 11 Jake Normington; 17 Nyle Flynn. Subs (all used): 14 George Flanagan; 13 Liam Mackay; 8 Michael Haley; 35 Matt Nicholson.
Tries: Flynn (11), Gibson (18), Mackay (33, 58), Brierley (38), Flanagan (46, 62), Mvududu (72), Lee (78), Coventry (80); **Goals:** Sanderson 8/10.
BEARS: 1 Harry Chapman; 2 Jamahl Hunte; 3 Luke Frixou; 4 Charlie O'Mara; 5 Mikey Russell; 6 Jordan Gale; 7 Brad Delaney; 8 James Geurtjens; 9 Billy Gaylor; 10 Alex Beddows; 11 Matt Reid; 12 Chris Barratt; 13 Paddy Jones. Subs (all used): 14 Brad Brennan; 15 Hayden Freeman; 16 Jack Morrison; 17 John Aldred.
Tries: Hunte (24, 42), Beddows (27), Geurtjens (70);
Goals: Delaney 4/4.
Sin bin: Geurtjens (76) - high tackle.
Rugby Leaguer & League Express Men of the Match: *Hunslet:* Joe Sanderson; *Bears:* Brad Delaney.
Penalty count: 11-6; **Half-time:** 20-12;
Referee: Andrew Sweet; **Attendance:** 406.

WHITEHAVEN 28 KEIGHLEY COUGARS 22

WHITEHAVEN: 5 Jordan Burns; 30 David Thompson; 3 Chris Taylor; 4 Jessie Joe Parker; 2 Craig Calvert; 6 Steve Roper; 7 Paul Crook; 10 Carl Forster; 14 James Tilley; 8 Marc Shackley; 15 Dion Aiye; 12 Scott McAvoy; 25 Aiden Worthington. Subs (all used): 9 James Newton; 17 Tommy Holland; 16 Connor Holliday; 24 Lewis Brown.
Tries: Aiye (3), Thompson (41), Roper (56), Burns (60), Worthington (63); **Goals:** Crook 4/5.
COUGARS: 1 Harry Aaronson; 2 Andy Gabriel; 34 Hamish Barnes; 32 Adam Ryder; 5 Davey Dixon; 14 Adam Brook; 7 Matty Beharrell; 15 Neil Cherryholme; 9 James Feather; 19 Matthew Bailey; 25 Ben Sagar; 18 Josh Tonks; 13 Mike Emmett. Subs (all used): 11 Josh Lynam; 17 Nathan Conroy; 21 Emmerson Whittel; 29 Brad Nicholson.
Tries: Brook (20), Nicholson (32), Gabriel (44), Feather (76); **Goals:** Beharrell 3/4.
Rugby Leaguer & League Express Men of the Match: *Whitehaven:* Jordan Burns; *Cougars:* Adam Brook.
Penalty count: 11-7; **Half-time:** 6-12;
Referee: Marcus Griffiths; **Attendance:** 704.

WORKINGTON TOWN 46 LONDON SKOLARS 16

TOWN: 1 Theerapol Ritson; 2 Joe Hambley; - Danny Rasool; 4 Jason Mossop; 21 Gabriel Fell; 6 Carl Forber; 7 Jamie Doran; 19 Joe Ryan; 13 Stuart Howarth; 16 Tom Curwen; 11 Brett Phillips; 25 Gordon Maudling; 15 Perry Singleton. Subs (all used): - Macauley Davies; 22 Jake Moore; - Liam Byrne; 12 Alex Szostak.
Tries: Ritson (4, 29, 37, 59), Fell (16), B Phillips (32), Doran (44), Davies (52); **Goals:** Forber 7/8.
SKOLARS: 29 Jermaine Coleman; 2 Sam Nash; 24 Michael Brown; 4 Lameck Juma; 5 James Hill; 6 Jy-mel Coleman; 9 Charlie Lawrence; 18 Mike Greenhalgh; 14 Billy Driver; 11 Lamont Bryan; 10 Dave Williams; 31 Josh Allison; 13 Ryan Chester. Subs (all used): 1 Andy Winfield; 19 Erjon Dollapi; 32 Jordan Williams; 8 Louis Robinson.
Tries: Robinson (22), Jy-mel Coleman (48), Winfield (73);
Goals: Jy-mel Coleman 2/3.
Rugby Leaguer & League Express Men of the Match: *Town:* Theerapol Ritson; *Skolars:* Jy-mel Coleman.
Penalty count: 16-9; **Half-time:** 28-4;
Referee: Tom Crashley; **Attendance:** 479.

ROUND 3

Wednesday 5th July 2017

DONCASTER 34 OXFORD 16

DONCASTER: 29 Reece Dean; 5 Sam Doherty; 3 Liam Welham; 13 Charlie Martin; 24 Richie Barnett; 7 Jordie Hedges; 15 Jack Miller; 19 Zac Braham; 20 Kieran Cross; 16 Russ Spiers; 34 Brad England; - Jack Downs; 27 Peter Green. Subs (all used): 10 Iafeta Palea'aesina; 18 Ryan Wright; 12 Jason Muranka; 14 Connor Scott.
Tries: Doherty (1, 8, 69), Cross (4), Miller (11, 36), England (22); **Goals:** Miller 3/7.
OXFORD: 1 Kane Riley; 2 Adam Dent; 3 Will Cooke; 4 Tommy Newbould; 5 Jordan Gill; 6 Kieran Hyde; 7 Callum Windley; 8 Jordan Siddons; 9 Casey Canterbury; 10 Dwaine McRae; 11 Harvey Burnett; 12 Stuart Biscomb; 13 Jonathan Payne. Subs (all used): 14 Fran Welsh; 15 Bradley Moules; 16 Marcus Brooker; 17 Anthony Cox.
Tries: Gill (26, 74), Cooke (38), Brooker (79);
Goals: Burnett 0/2, Hyde 0/2.
Rugby Leaguer & League Express Men of the Match: *Doncaster:* Jack Miller; *Oxford:* Jordan Gill.
Penalty count: 11-8; **Half-time:** 30-8;
Referee: Billy Pearson; **Attendance:** 334
(at LD Nutrition Stadium, Featherstone).

ROUND 14

Saturday 8th July 2017

LONDON SKOLARS 30 HUNSLET 16

SKOLARS: 7 Mike Bishay; 2 Sam Nash; 24 Michael Brown; 4 Lameck Juma; 5 James Hill; 29 Jermaine Coleman; 6 Jy-mel Coleman; 11 Lamont Bryan; 9 Charlie Lawrence; 19 Erjon Dollapi; 10 Dave Williams; 31 Josh Allison; 13 Ryan Chester. Subs (all used): 14 Billy Driver; 8 Louis Robinson; 18 Mike Greenhalgh; 12 Eddie Mbaraga.
Tries: Nash (11, 53), Hill (50), Bishay (71), Bryan (80);
Goals: Jy-mel Coleman 5/6.
Dismissal: Juma (78) - fighting.
Sin bin: Bryan (38) - fighting; Greenhalgh (78) - fighting.
HUNSLET: 1 Jimmy Watson; 34 Tommy Brierley; 4 Mufaro Mvududu; 38 Mathew Cook; - Michael Hayward; 18 Joel Gibson; 6 Joe Sanderson; 15 Jack Coventry; 9 Jack Lee; 10 Lewis Reed; 11 Jake Normington; 12 Aston Wilson; 17 Nyle Flynn. Subs (all used): 14 George Flanagan; 8 Michael Haley; 35 Matt Nicholson; 39 Daniel Williams.
Tries: Coventry (45), Mvududu (58), Watson (79);
Goals: Sanderson 2/3.
Sin bin: Flanagan (38) – fighting; Reed (78) - fighting.
Rugby Leaguer & League Express Men of the Match: *Skolars:* Louis Robinson; *Hunslet:* George Flanagan.
Penalty count: 7-11; **Half-time:** 6-0;
Referee: Matt Rossleigh; **Attendance:** 367.

BARROW RAIDERS 80 OXFORD 10

RAIDERS: 27 Ryan Johnston; 2 Brett Carter; 12 Jarrad Stack; 33 Eze Harper; 5 Shane Toal; 6 Jamie Dallimore; 7 Lewis Charnock; 8 Joe Bullock; 26 Brad Marwood; 10 Oliver Wilkes; 18 Danny Morrow; 22 Bradd Crellin; 11 Dan Toal. Subs (all used): 14 Dan Abram; 25 Matty While; 17 Tom Walker; 21 James Duerden.
Tries: Morrow (2, 8), Marwood (6), Dallimore (12), S Toal (14), D Toal (17), Johnston (19), Harper (29, 34, 37), Carter (60), Wilkes (64), Bullock (74), Walker (78);
Goals: Charnock 12/14.
Dismissal: While (48) - fighting.
OXFORD: 1 Liam Kay; 2 Kane Riley; 3 Tommy Newbould; 4 Will Cooke; 5 Harrison Brough; 6 Callum Windley; 7 Kieran Hyde; 8 Stuart Biscomb; 9 Casey Canterbury; 10 Jonathan Payne; 11 Jordan Siddons; 12 Harvey Burnett; 13 Tom Alexander. Subs (all used): 14 Fran Welsh; 15 Marcus Brooker; 16 Bradley Moules; 17 Aaron Nicholson.
Tries: Brough (48), Burnett (58); **Goals:** Burnett 1/2.
Dismissal: Siddons (48) - fighting.
Rugby Leaguer & League Express Men of the Match: *Raiders:* Eze Harper; *Oxford:* Harvey Burnett.
Penalty count: 5-9; **Half-time:** 56-0;
Referee: John McMullen; **Attendance:** 750.

TORONTO WOLFPACK 62 GLOUCESTERSHIRE ALL GOLDS 10

WOLFPACK: 1 Quentin Laulu-Togagae; 15 Ryan Burroughs; 3 Greg Worthington; 5 Liam Kay; 2 Jonny Pownall; 4 Craig Hall; 7 Rhys Jacks; 10 Daniel Fleming; 9 Bob Beswick; 19 Steve Crossley; 17 Richard Whiting; 12 James Laithwaite; 13 Jack Bussey. Subs (all used): 8 Fuifui Moimoi; 29 Jake Emmitt; 21 Adam Sidlow; 28 Quinn Ngawati.
Tries: Burroughs (6), Hall (12, 34), Pownall (16), Whiting (27), Jacks (32), Moimoi (44), Beswick (61), Worthington (68), Crossley (71), Laulu-Togagae (78);
Goals: Hall 9/11.
ALL GOLDS: 1 Jack Mitchell; 2 Mo Agoro; 3 Phil Cowburn; 4 Lewis Reece; 5 Errol Carter; 6 Shaun Owens; 7 Danny Fallon; 8 James Walter; 9 Steve Parry; 10 Harrison Elliott; 11 Chris Worrall; 12 Joe McClean; 13 Billy Brickhill. Subs (all used): 14 Luke Stephens; 15 Alex Gaskell; 16 Malikhi Lloyd-Jones; 17 Richard Jones.
Tries: Parry (37), Reece (76); **Goals:** Mitchell 1/2.
Rugby Leaguer & League Express Men of the Match: *Wolfpack:* Craig Hall; *All Golds:* Steve Parry.
Penalty count: 10-6; **Half-time:** 34-6;
Referee: Brandon Robinson; **Attendance:** 7,139.

Sunday 9th July 2017

NORTH WALES CRUSADERS 12 WHITEHAVEN 12

CRUSADERS: 1 Tommy Johnson; - Taylor Prell; 3 Simon Atherton; 4 Earl Hurst; 5 Dale Bloomfield; 6 Andy Moulsdale; 7 Ryan Smith; 8 Jonny Walker; 14 James Dandy; 32 Warren Thompson; 24 Jack Houghton; 16 Luke Warburton; 13 Ryan Millington. Subs (all used): 27 Aaron Moore; 17 Kenny Baker; - Alex Whalley; 22 Joe Bate.
Tries: Bate (50), Prell (60); **Goals:** Johnson 2/3.
WHITEHAVEN: 1 Elliott Miller; 2 Craig Calvert; 4 Jessie Joe Parker; 30 David Thompson; 5 Jordan Burns; 6 Steve Roper; 7 Paul Crook; 8 Marc Shackley; 9 James Newton; 25 Aiden Worthington; 15 Dion Aiye; 12 Scott McAvoy; 14 James Tilley. Subs (all used): - Danny Green; 16 Connor Holliday; 17 Tommy Holland; 18 Tyrone Dalton.
Tries: Burns (2, 24), Aiye (67); **Goals:** Crook 0/3.
Rugby Leaguer & League Express Men of the Match: *Crusaders:* Taylor Prell; *Whitehaven:* Dion Aiye.
Penalty count: 12-7; **Half-time:** 0-8;
Referee: Andrew Sweet; **Attendance:** 387.

NEWCASTLE THUNDER 68 COVENTRY BEARS 20

THUNDER: 1 Lewis Young; 2 Dan Parker; 3 Derrell Olpherts; 4 Joe Brown; 5 Tyler Craig; 6 Danny Nicklas; 7 Benn Hardcastle; 8 Rhys Clarke; 9 Evan Simons; 10 Liam McAvoy; 11 Harry Aldous; 12 Steve Snitch; 13 Jack Aldous. Subs (all used): 14 Matt Barron; 15 Callum Bustin; 16 Vincent Rennie; 17 Brett Waller.
Tries: Craig (2), McAvoy (5), Nicklas (7, 55), J Aldous (12), Parker (15), Young (27), Simons (40), Snitch (47), Hardcastle (58), R Clarke (70), Olpherts (72);
Goals: Hardcastle 10/12.
BEARS: 1 Harry Chapman; 2 Hayden Freeman; 3 Luke Frixou; 4 Charlie O'Mara; 5 Jamahl Hunte; 6 Jordan Gale; 7 Brad Delaney; 8 James Geurtjens; 9 Mikey Russell; 10 John Aldred; 11 Matt Reid; 12 Chris Barratt; 13 Paddy Jones. Subs (all used): 14 Jack Morrison; 15 Brad Brennan; 16 Zak Williams; 17 Harry Kaufman.
Tries: Barratt (23), Delaney (41), Russell (52), O'Mara (78);
Goals: Delaney 2/4.
Rugby Leaguer & League Express Men of the Match: *Thunder:* Danny Nicklas; *Bears:* Brad Delaney.
Penalty count: 7-5; **Half-time:** 42-4;
Referee: Callum Straw; **Attendance:** 567.

SOUTH WALES IRONMEN 12 DONCASTER 70

IRONMEN: - Jack Uren; 1 James Stringer; - Dafydd Phillips; 28 Morgan Jeffries; 22 Ben Jones; 6 Andrew Gay; - Morgan Punchard; - Luke Nelmes; 9 Connor Farrer; - Barrie Phillips; - Craig Lewis; - Kade Breen; - Martyn Reilly. Subs (all used): 19 Jamie l'Anson; 14 Kristian Baller; - Josh Barden; - Liam Curnow.
Tries: Nelmes (15), Farrer (65); **Goals:** Punchard 2/2.
Sin bin: Breen (80) - dangerous challenge.
DONCASTER: 29 Reece Dean; 5 Sam Doherty; 3 Liam Welham; 4 Jason Tali; 22 Louis Sheriff; 7 Jordie Hedges; 15 Jack Miller; 16 Russ Spiers; 20 Kieran Cross; 19 Zac Braham; 13 Charlie Martin; - Jack Downs; 23 Jamie Thackray. Subs (all used): 8 Mark Castle; 34 Brad England; 10 Iafeta Palea'aesina; 18 Ryan Wright.
Tries: Spiers (2, 19), Tali (5), Thackray (11), Palea'aesina (26), Dean (30), Doherty (39, 73), Downs (49, 67), Sheriff (55, 76), Miller (78);
Goals: Miller 9/13.
Rugby Leaguer & League Express Men of the Match: *Ironmen:* Connor Farrer; *Doncaster:* Reece Dean.
Penalty count: 5-8; **Half-time:** 6-40;
Referee: Jon Roberts; **Attendance:** 130.

WORKINGTON TOWN 30 KEIGHLEY COUGARS 30

TOWN: 1 Theerapol Ritson; 2 Joe Hambley; - Danny Rasool; 4 Jason Mossop; 21 Gabriel Fell; 6 Carl Forber; 7 Jamie Doran; 19 Joe Ryan; 13 Stuart Howarth; 16 Tom Curwen; 11 Brett Phillips; 25 Gordon Maudling; 15 Perry Singleton. Subs (all used): - Macauley Davies; 22 Jake Moore; 18 Conor Fitzsimmons; 12 Alex Szostak.
Tries: Hambley (4, 67), Fell (13), Doran (23, 27), Ritson (76);
Goals: Forber 3/6.
Sin bin: Curwen (22) - fighting.
COUGARS: 1 Harry Aaronson; 5 Davey Dixon; 35 Aidan Scully; 32 Adam Ryder; 2 Andy Gabriel; 14 Adam Brook; 7 Matty Beharrell; 12 Brendon Rawlins; 27 Sean Kelly; 19 Matthew Bailey; 25 Ben Sagar; 21 Emmerson Whittel; 13 Mike Emmett. Subs (all used): 11 Josh Lynam; 17 Nathan Conroy; 22 Ritchie Hawkyard; 29 Brad Nicholson.
Tries: Gabriel (18, 79), Hawkyard (42), Kelly (61, 64), Ryder (71); **Goals:** Beharrell 3/6.
Dismissal: Nicholson (53) - punching.
Sin bin: Rawlins (22) - fighting.
Rugby Leaguer & League Express Men of the Match: *Town:* Jamie Doran; *Cougars:* Ritchie Hawkyard.
Penalty count: 11-10; **Half-time:** 22-4;
Referee: Steve Race; **Attendance:** 581.

YORK CITY KNIGHTS 68 HEMEL STAGS 6

CITY KNIGHTS: 1 Ash Robson; 3 Nev Morrison; 30 Tuoyo Egodo; 17 Brad Hey; 2 David Foggin-Johnston; 34 Connor Robinson; 31 Liam Harris; 20 Adam Robinson; 29 Will Jubb; 10 Chris Siddons; 12 Ed Smith; 11 Joe Batchelor; 35 Graeme Horne. Subs (all used): 9 Pat Smith; 16 Ronan Dixon; 27 Ryan Mallinder; 15 Liam Thompson.
Tries: Harris (3, 8, 20, 66), Siddons (12), Foggin-Johnston (15, 48, 54, 73), Batchelor (30, 64), Hey (68), Mallinder (77); **Goals:** Harris 8/13.
STAGS: 1 Marcus Elliott; 2 Josh Casey; 3 Brett Whitehead; 4 Corey Hanson; 5 Darren Forde; 6 Scott Lee; 7 Lewis Fairhurst; 8 Dan Hawksworth; 9 Jono Burns; 10 Reece Williams; 11 James Thornton; 12 Munashe Fumhanda; 13 Alex Williams. Subs (all used): 14 Wayne Jowitt; 15 Sam Crowther; 16 Santino Decaro; 17 Mark Barlow.
Try: R Williams (38); **Goals:** Fairhurst 1/1.
Dismissal: Elliott (53) - dangerous challenge on E Smith.
Rugby Leaguer & League Express Men of the Match: *City Knights:* Connor Robinson; *Stags:* Reece Williams.
Penalty count: 11-6; **Half-time:** 32-6;
Referee: Greg Dolan; **Attendance:** 787.

ROUND 15

Saturday 15th July 2017

TORONTO WOLFPACK 74 HEMEL STAGS 16

WOLFPACK: 2 Jonny Pownall; 15 Ryan Burroughs; 3 Greg Worthington; 4 Craig Hall; 5 Liam Kay; 6 Blake Wallace; 7 Rhys Jacks; 8 Fuifui Moimoi; 9 Bob Beswick; 29 Jake Emmitt; 13 Jack Bussey; 12 James Laithwaite; 21 Adam Sidlow. Subs (all used): 10 Daniel Fleming; 19 Steve Crossley; 20 Tom Dempsey; 28 Quinn Ngawati.
Tries: Hall (4, 6, 35, 54), Wallace (10, 51, 68), Pownall (15), Kay (28), Beswick (42), Crossley (59), Moimoi (73), Fleming (76); **Goals:** Hall 11/13.
Sin bin: Pownall (47) - dissent.
STAGS: 1 Mitch Vincent; 2 Marcus Elliott; 3 Josh Casey; 4 Danny Lawton; 5 Darren Forde; 6 Mark Barlow; 7 Lewis Fairhurst; 8 Corey Hanson; 9 Jono Burns; 10 Reece Williams; 11 James Thornton; 12 Jack O'Brien; 13 Brett Whitehead. Subs (all used): 14 Scott Lee; 15 Sam Crowther; 16 Wayne Jowitt; 17 Alex Williams.
Tries: Elliott (22), Barlow (38), O'Brien (46);
Goals: Vincent 2/3.
Rugby Leaguer & League Express Men of the Match: *Wolfpack:* Craig Hall; *Stags:* Mark Barlow.
Penalty count: 10-8; **Half-time:** 32-10;
Referee: Nick Bennett; **Attendance:** 7,247.

Sunday 16th July 2017

COVENTRY BEARS 13 NORTH WALES CRUSADERS 36

BEARS: 1 Charlie O'Mara; 2 Mikey Russell; 3 Hayden Freeman; 4 Luke Frixou; 5 Jamahl Hunte; 6 Jordan Gale; 7 Brad Delaney; 8 Brad Brennan; 9 Zak Williams; 10 Jack Morrison; 11 Matt Reid; 12 Chris Barratt; 13 Paddy Jones. Subs (all used): 14 Harry Chapman; 15 James Kelly; 16 John Aldred; 17 James Geurtjens.
Tries: Hunte (20), Reid (79); **Goals:** Delaney 2/2;
Field goal: Gale (30).
CRUSADERS: 1 Tommy Johnson; - Taylor Prell; 3 Simon Atherton; 4 Earl Hurst; 5 Dale Bloomfield; 19 Dan Price; 7 Ryan Smith; 17 Kenny Baker; 14 James Dandy; 32 Warren Thompson; 16 Luke Warburton; 24 Jack Houghton; 13 Ryan Millington. Subs (all used): 27 Aaron Moore; - Alex Whalley; 8 Jonny Walker; 22 Joe Bate.
Tries: Prell (6), Johnson (37), Bate (46), Hurst (56), Atherton (64), Price (68); **Goals:** Johnson 6/6.
Rugby Leaguer & League Express Men of the Match: *Bears:* Jamahl Hunte; *Crusaders:* Tommy Johnson.
Penalty count: 9-6; **Half-time:** 7-12;
Referee: Tom Crashley; **Attendance:** 422.

GLOUCESTERSHIRE ALL GOLDS 4 DONCASTER 42

ALL GOLDS: 1 Jack Mitchell; 2 Mo Agoro; 3 Kadeem Williams; 4 Lewis Reece; 5 Chris Barlow; 6 Shaun Owens; 7 Danny Fallon; 8 James Walter; 9 Steve Parry; 10 Harrison Elliott; 11 Chris Worrall; 12 Joe McClean; 13 Billy Brickhill. Subs (all used): 14 Errol Carter; 15 Ollie Purslow; 16 Malikhi Lloyd-Jones; 17 Richard Jones.
Try: Agoro (75); **Goals:** Mitchell 0/1.
DONCASTER: 29 Reece Dean; 5 Sam Doherty; 3 Liam Welham; 2 Aaron Jones-Bishop; 22 Louis Sheriff; 7 Jordie Hedges; 15 Jack Miller; 32 Makali Aizue; 18 Ryan Wright; 23 Jamie Thackray; 34 Brad England; 13 Charlie Martin; 27 Peter Green. Subs (all used): 8 Mark Castle; 20 Kieran Cross; 17 Mike Kelly; 10 Iafeta Palea'aesina.
Tries: Castle (25), Palea'aesina (42), Doherty (50, 54), Dean (66, 72), England (70); **Goals:** Miller 7/7.
Rugby Leaguer & League Express Men of the Match: *All Golds:* Kadeem Williams; *Doncaster:* Jack Miller.
Penalty count: 3-10; **Half-time:** 0-6;
Referee: Callum Straw; **Attendance:** 200.

HUNSLET 26 NEWCASTLE THUNDER 25

HUNSLET: 1 Jimmy Watson; 38 Mathew Cook; 4 Mufaro Mvududu; 24 Cameron Leeming; 34 Tommy Brierley; 33 Shaun Roberts; 6 Joe Sanderson; 10 Lewis Reed; 9 Jack Lee; 35 Matt Nicholson; 13 Liam Mackay; 21 Jack Walton; 17 Nyle Flynn. Subs (all used): 14 George Flanagan; 8 Michael Haley; 39 Daniel Williams; 15 Jack Coventry.
Tries: Cook (16), Watson (32), Flanagan (45, 73);
Goals: Sanderson 5/5.
THUNDER: 1 Lewis Young; 2 Joe Brown; 3 Dan Parker; 4 Derrell Olpherts; 5 Tyler Craig; 6 Danny Nicklas; 7 Benn Hardcastle; 8 Liam McAvoy; 9 Evan Simons; 10 Rhys Clarke; 11 Harry Aldous; 12 Steve Snitch; 13 Jack Aldous. Subs (all used): 14 Callum Bustin; 15 Sam Luckley; 16 Vincent Rennie; 17 Brett Waller.
Tries: Young (25, 56), Snitch (43), Hardcastle (50);
Goals: Hardcastle 4/4; **Field goal:** Hardcastle (78).
Rugby Leaguer & League Express Men of the Match: *Hunslet:* George Flanagan; *Thunder:* Benn Hardcastle.
Penalty count: 8-6; **Half-time:** 12-6;
Referee: Marcus Griffiths; **Attendance:** 429.

KEIGHLEY COUGARS 92 OXFORD 6

COUGARS: 22 Ritchie Hawkyard; 5 Davey Dixon; 34 Hamish Barnes; 32 Adam Ryder; 2 Andy Gabriel; 14 Adam Brook; 7 Matty Beharrell; - Trae O'Sullivan; 9 James Feather; 19 Matthew Bailey; 21 Emmerson Whittel; 12 Brendon Rawlins; 13 Mike Emmett. Subs (all used): 1 Harry Aaronson; 11 Josh Lynam; 17 Nathan Conroy; 29 Brad Nicholson.
Tries: Emmett (9), Rawlins (15), Feather (25), Barnes (30, 38, 67, 69), Nicholson (32, 42), Ryder (36), Lynam (48, 58), Hawkyard (62, 74), Aaronson (71, 76);
Goals: Beharrell 14/16.

OXFORD: 1 Liam Kay; 2 Tommy Newbould; 3 Harvey Burnett; 4 Marcus Brooker; 5 Judah Mazive; 6 Callum Windley; 7 Kieran Hyde; 8 Jake Joynt; 9 Casey Canterbury; 10 Fran Welsh; 11 Liam O'Callaghan; 12 Stuart Biscomb; 13 Jonathan Payne. Subs (all used): 14 Anthony Cox; 15 Bradley Moules; 16 Mark Hayes; 17 Aaron Nicholson.
Try: Newbould (3); **Goals:** Kay 1/1.
Rugby Leaguer & League Express Men of the Match: *Cougars:* Hamish Barnes; *Oxford:* Casey Canterbury.
Penalty count: 13-2; **Half-time:** 42-6;
Referee: Brandon Robinson; **Attendance:** 670.

LONDON SKOLARS 36 SOUTH WALES IRONMEN 16

SKOLARS: 7 Mike Bishay; 2 Sam Nash; 24 Michael Brown; 4 Lameck Juma; 20 Jake Melling; 9 Charlie Lawrence; 6 Jy-mel Coleman; 11 Lamont Bryan; 14 Billy Driver; 19 Erjon Dollapi; 10 Dave Williams; 31 Josh Allison; 13 Ryan Chester. Subs (all used): 29 Jermaine Coleman; 8 Louis Robinson; 12 Eddie Mbaraga; 18 Mike Greenhalgh.
Tries: C Lawrence (12), Driver (19), D Williams (31, 46), Allison (49, 53), Bryan (75);
Goals: Jy-mel Coleman 2/4, C Lawrence 2/3.
Dismissal: Dollapi (80) - dissent.
IRONMEN: 27 Jack Uren; - Liam Curnow; 28 Morgan Jeffries; 4 Christiaan Roets; - Aaron Lewis; 21 Ross Price; 22 Ben Jones; 18 Morgan Evans; 6 Andrew Gay; - Barrie Phillips; 30 Michael Edwards; - Jordan Syme; 19 Jamie I'Anson. (No subs named).
Tries: Jeffries (8), I'Anson (29), Syme (80);
Goals: A Lewis 2/3.
Rugby Leaguer & League Express Men of the Match: *Skolars:* Dave Williams; *Ironmen:* Jamie I'Anson.
Penalty count: 5-8; **Half-time:** 16-10;
Referee: Steve Race; **Attendance:** 225.

WHITEHAVEN 32 BARROW RAIDERS 6

WHITEHAVEN: 1 Elliott Miller; 30 David Thompson; 3 Chris Taylor; 4 Jessie Joe Parker; 5 Jordan Burns; 15 Dion Aiye; 7 Paul Crook; 8 Marc Shackley; 14 James Tilley; 19 Glenn Riley; 16 Connor Holliday; 12 Scott McAvoy; 10 Carl Forster. Subs (all used): 17 Tommy Holland; 9 James Newton; 6 Steve Roper; 25 Aiden Worthington.
Tries: Thompson (9), Riley (14), Aiye (60), Roper (69), McAvoy (72); **Goals:** Crook 6/7.
Sin bin: Newton (50) - head butt; Taylor (78) - fighting.
RAIDERS: 1 Ryan Fieldhouse; 2 Brett Carter; 12 Jarrad Stack; 3 Declan Hulme; 5 Shane Toal; 6 Jamie Dallimore; 7 Lewis Charnock; 8 Joe Bullock; 9 Nathan Mossop; 10 Oliver Wilkes; 18 Danny Morrow; 22 Bradd Crellin; 13 Martin Aspinwall. Subs (all used): 15 Karl Ashall; 21 James Duerden; 11 Dan Toal; 17 Tom Walker.
Try: Walker (27); **Goals:** Charnock 1/1.
Sin bin: Wilkes (7) - late challenge on Forster; Morrow (78) - fighting; Dallimore (79) - high tackle.
Rugby Leaguer & League Express Men of the Match: *Whitehaven:* Scott McAvoy; *Raiders:* Nathan Mossop.
Penalty count: 12-6; **Half time:** 12-6;
Referee: Jon Roberts; **Attendance:** 1,502.

YORK CITY KNIGHTS 34 WORKINGTON TOWN 0

CITY KNIGHTS: 1 Ash Robson; 3 Nev Morrison; 19 James Haynes; 17 Brad Hey; 2 David Foggin-Johnston; 34 Connor Robinson; 7 Harry Tyson-Wilson; 20 Adam Robinson; 29 Will Jubb; 27 Mitch Clark; 12 Ed Smith; 11 Joe Batchelor; 13 Tim Spears. Subs (all used): 26 Andy Ellis; 35 Graeme Horne; 30 George Lawler; 25 Joe Porter.
Tries: Haynes (7, 16, 18), Jubb (25, 66), Batchelor (34);
Goals: C Robinson 5/6.
TOWN: 1 Theerapol Ritson; 2 Joe Hambley; - Danny Rasool; 4 Jason Mossop; 24 Phil Lister; 6 Carl Forber; 7 Jamie Doran; 21 Joe Bretherton; 13 Stuart Howarth; 10 Stevie Scholey; 11 Brett Phillips; - Macauley Davies; 15 Perry Singleton. Subs (all used): 18 Conor Fitzsimmons; 25 Gordon Maudling; 22 Jake Moore; - Joe Prior.
Rugby Leaguer & League Express Men of the Match: *City Knights:* James Haynes; *Town:* Carl Forber.
Penalty count: 12-9; **Half-time:** 28-0;
Referee: Andrew Sweet; **Attendance:** 1,011.

SUPER 8s

ROUND 1

Sunday 30th July 2017

DONCASTER 24 KEIGHLEY COUGARS 32

DONCASTER: 1 Tom Carr; - Ryan Jones; 3 Liam Welham; 26 Nick Rawsthorne; 5 Sam Doherty; 29 Reece Dean; 15 Jack Miller; 19 Zac Braham; 9 Kyle Kesik; 16 Russ Spiers; 34 Brad England; 13 Charlie Martin; 27 Peter Green. Subs (all used): 10 Iafeta Palea'aesina; 23 Jamie Thackray; 12 Jason Muranka; 20 Kieran Cross.
Tries: Jones (8), Cross (40), Welham (59), Doherty (64), Rawsthorne (80); **Goals:** Miller 2/5.
COUGARS: 22 Ritchie Hawkyard; 5 Davey Dixon; 34 Hamish Barnes; 32 Adam Ryder; 2 Andy Gabriel; 14 Adam Brook; 7 Matty Beharrell; 36 Trae O'Sullivan; 17 Nathan Conroy; 19 Matthew Bailey; 25 Ben Sagar; 12 Brendon Rawlins; 13 Mike Emmett. Subs (all used): 1 Harry Aaronson; 8 Scott Law; 9 James Feather; 11 Josh Lynam.
Tries: Bailey (13, 22), Gabriel (32), Ryder (38), Rawlins (54);
Goals: Beharrell 6/6.
Sin bin: Lynam (64) - punching.
Rugby Leaguer & League Express Men of the Match: *Doncaster:* Peter Green; *Cougars:* Nathan Conroy.
Penalty count: 9-7; **Half-time:** 10-24;
Referee: Jon Roberts; **Attendance:** 501.

NEWCASTLE THUNDER 14 WORKINGTON TOWN 30

THUNDER: 1 Lewis Young; 2 Joe Brown; 3 Dan Parker; 4 Derrell Olpherts; 5 Tyler Craig; 6 Danny Nicklas; 7 Benn Hardcastle; 8 Liam McAvoy; 9 Evan Simons; 10 Rhys Clarke; 11 Harry Aldous; 12 Steve Snitch; 13 Jack Aldous. Subs (all used): 14 Callum Bustin; 15 Sam Luckley; 16 Vincent Rennie; 17 Brett Waller.
Tries: Craig (8), Waller (34); **Goals:** Hardcastle 3/3.
Dismissal: Young (57) - headbutt on Howarth.
Sin bin: Nicklas (28) - professional foul.
TOWN: 1 Theerapol Ritson; 2 Joe Hambley; 4 Jason Mossop; - Danny Rasool; 21 Gabriel Fell; 13 Stuart Howarth; 7 Jamie Doran; 18 Conor Fitzsimmons; 9 Callum Phillips; 10 Stevie Scholey; 11 Brett Phillips; - Macauley Davies; 15 Perry Singleton. Subs (all used): - Kyle Shelford; 8 Kris Coward; 22 Jake Moore; 25 Gordon Maudling.
Tries: Fell (9, 61), Davies (21, 48), Hambley (29, 64);
Goals: Doran 3/6.
Rugby Leaguer & League Express Men of the Match: *Thunder:* Danny Nicklas; *Town:* Joe Hambley.
Penalty count: 11-11; **Half-time:** 14-14;
Referee: Andrew Sweet; **Attendance:** 655.

WHITEHAVEN 2 BARROW RAIDERS 15

WHITEHAVEN: 1 Elliott Miller; 30 David Thompson; 3 Chris Taylor; 4 Jessie Joe Parker; 5 Jordan Burns; 15 Dion Aiye; 7 Paul Crook; 33 Jordan Hand; 14 James Tilley; 19 Glenn Riley; 16 Connor Holliday; 12 Scott McAvoy; 10 Carl Forster. Subs (all used): 17 Tommy Holland; 9 James Newton; 6 Steve Roper; 13 Karl Olstrum.
Goals: Crook 1/1.
Sin bin: Riley (72) - late challenge.
On report:
Forster (7) - alleged dangerous contact on Crellin.
RAIDERS: 1 Ryan Fieldhouse; 2 Brett Carter; 33 Eze Harper; 3 Declan Hulme; 5 Shane Toal; 6 Jamie Dallimore; 7 Lewis Charnock; 8 Joe Bullock; 15 Karl Ashall; 10 Oliver Wilkes; 12 Jarrad Stack; 22 Bradd Crellin; 13 Martin Aspinwall. Subs (all used): 9 Nathan Mossop; 21 James Duerden; 11 Dan Toal; 17 Tom Walker.
Tries: Stack (52), Fieldhouse (68); **Goals:** Dallimore 3/3;
Field goal: Dallimore (61).
Rugby Leaguer & League Express Men of the Match: *Whitehaven:* Dion Aiye; *Raiders:* Joe Bullock.
Penalty count: 11-9; **Half-time:** 0-0;
Referee: Gareth Hewer; **Attendance:** 1,062.

YORK CITY KNIGHTS 26 TORONTO WOLFPACK 16

CITY KNIGHTS: 1 Ash Robson; 3 Nev Morrison; 17 Brad Hey; 35 Jake Butler-Fleming; 2 David Foggin-Johnston; 31 Liam Harris; 34 Connor Robinson; 16 Ronan Dixon; 29 Will Jubb; 28 Kieran Moran; 30 Zeus Silk; 11 Joe Batchelor; 13 Tim Spears. Subs: 20 Adam Robinson; 10 Chris Siddons; 19 James Haynes (not used); 25 Joe Porter.
Tries: Butler-Fleming (13), Harris (19, 40), C Robinson (71);
Goals: C Robinson 5/5.
WOLFPACK: 1 Quentin Laulu-Togagae; 2 Jonny Pownall; 3 Greg Worthington; 4 Craig Hall; 5 Liam Kay; 6 Blake Wallace; 27 Ryan Brierley; 29 Jake Emmitt; 9 Bob Beswick; 21 Adam Sidlow; 17 Richard Whiting; 12 James Laithwaite; 13 Jack Bussey. Subs: 7 Rhys Jack (not used); 8 Fuifui Moimoi; 19 Steve Crossley; 16 Shaun Pick.
Tries: Brierley (41), Beswick (45), Hall (59); **Goals:** Hall 2/3.
Sin bin: Brierley (21) - dissent;
Bussey (62) - dangerous challenge on Silk.
On report:
Bussey (57) - alleged dangerous challenge on Robson.
Rugby Leaguer & League Express Men of the Match: *City Knights:* Liam Harris; *Wolfpack:* Craig Hall.
Penalty count: 8-5; **Half-time:** 18-0;
Referee: Tom Grant; **Attendance:** 2,602.

ROUND 2

Sunday 6th August 2017

BARROW RAIDERS 14 DONCASTER 10

RAIDERS: 1 Ryan Fieldhouse; 5 Shane Toal; 3 Declan Hulme; 33 Eze Harper; 2 Brett Carter; 6 Jamie Dallimore; 7 Lewis Charnock; 8 Joe Bullock; 15 Karl Ashall; 10 Oliver Wilkes; 12 Jarrad Stack; 11 Dan Toal; 13 Martin Aspinwall. Subs (all used): 17 Tom Walker; 9 Nathan Mossop; 16 Andrew Dawson; 21 James Duerden.
Tries: Dallimore (30), Carter (53); **Goals:** Dallimore 3/3.
DONCASTER: - Hakim Miloudi; - Ryan Jones; 26 Nick Rawsthorne; 4 Jason Tali; 5 Sam Doherty; 29 Reece Dean; 15 Jack Miller; 16 Russ Spiers; 9 Kyle Kesik; 8 Mark Castle; 13 Charlie Martin; 34 Brad England; 27 Peter Green. Subs (all used): 19 Zac Braham; 20 Kieran Cross; 3 Liam Welham; 23 Jamie Thackray.
Tries: England (7), Miller (70); **Goals:** Miller 1/2.
Rugby Leaguer & League Express Men of the Match: *Raiders:* Jamie Dallimore; *Doncaster:* Hakim Miloudi.
Penalty count: 13-8; **Half-time:** 6-6;
Referee: Greg Dolan; **Attendance:** 836.

KEIGHLEY COUGARS 22 YORK CITY KNIGHTS 20

COUGARS: 22 Ritchie Hawkyard; 26 Vinny Finigan; 34 Hamish Barnes; 32 Adam Ryder; 2 Andy Gabriel; 14 Adam Brook; 7 Matty Beharrell; 15 Neil Cherryholme; 17 Nathan Conroy; 19 Matthew Bailey; 25 Ben Sagar; 12 Brendon Rawlins; 13 Mike Emmett. Subs (all used): 8 Scott Law; 9 James Feather; 36 Trae O'Sullivan; 37 Gavin Reed.
Tries: Gabriel (34, 40), Finigan (58), Feather (77);
Goals: Beharrell 3/4.
CITY KNIGHTS: 19 James Haynes; 3 Nev Morrison; 35 Jake Butler-Fleming; 17 Brad Hey; 5 Tom Saxton; 31 Liam Harris; 34 Connor Robinson; 20 Adam Robinson; 29 Will Jubb; 28 Kieran Moran; 30 Zeus Silk; 11 Joe Batchelor; 13 Tim Spears. Subs (all used): 10 Chris Siddons; 16 Ronan Dixon; 25 Joe Porter; 26 Andy Ellis.
Tries: Moran (14), Batchelor (25), Saxton (52), Haynes (61);
Goals: C Robinson 2/4.
Rugby Leaguer & League Express Men of the Match: *Cougars:* Andy Gabriel; *City Knights:* Liam Harris.
Penalty count: 8-7; **Half-time:** 10-10;
Referee: Callum Straw; **Attendance:** 1,362.

WHITEHAVEN 27 NEWCASTLE THUNDER 6

WHITEHAVEN: 1 Elliott Miller; 30 David Thompson; 4 Jessie Joe Parker; 3 Chris Taylor; 5 Jordan Burns; 6 Steve Roper; 7 Paul Crook; 8 Marc Shackley; 14 James Tilley; 10 Carl Forster; 15 Dion Aiye; 12 Scott McAvoy; 13 Karl Olstrum. Subs (all used): 9 James Newton; 16 Connor Holliday; 19 Glenn Riley; 17 Tommy Holland.
Tries: Aiye (11, 70, 74), Miller (32), Parker (35);
Goals: Crook 3/5; **Field goal:** Crook (48).
THUNDER: 1 Lewis Young; 2 Joe Brown; 3 Tyler Craig; 4 Derrell Olpherts; 5 Ali Blair; 6 Tom Shaw; 7 Benn Hardcastle; 8 Liam McAvoy; 9 Evan Simons; 10 Rhys Clarke; 11 Harry Aldous; 12 Steve Snitch; 13 Jack Aldous. Subs (all used): 14 Callum Bustin; 15 Sam Luckley; 16 Vincent Rennie; 17 Aaron Teroi.
Try: Simons (79); **Goals:** Hardcastle 1/1.
Rugby Leaguer & League Express Men of the Match: *Whitehaven:* Dion Aiye; *Thunder:* Lewis Young.
Penalty count: 8-10; **Half-time:** 18-0;
Referee: Steve Race; **Attendance:** 539.

WORKINGTON TOWN 0 TORONTO WOLFPACK 68

TOWN: 1 Theerapol Ritson; 2 Joe Hambley; - Danny Rasool; 22 Jake Moore; 24 Phil Lister; 13 Stuart Howarth; 7 Jamie Doran; 16 Tom Curwen; 9 Callum Phillips; 10 Stevie Scholey; 11 Brett Phillips; - Macauley Davies; 25 Gordon Maudling. Subs (all used): 18 Conor Fitzsimmons; 12 Alex Szostak; 21 Kyle Shelford; - Joe Prior.
WOLFPACK: 1 Quentin Laulu-Togagae; 2 Jonny Pownall; 3 Greg Worthington; 4 Craig Hall; 5 Liam Kay; 6 Blake Wallace; 27 Ryan Brierley; 8 Fuifui Moimoi; 9 Bob Beswick; 29 Jake Emmitt; 12 James Laithwaite; 17 Richard Whiting; 13 Jack Bussey. Subs (all used): 7 Rhys Jacks; 10 Daniel Fleming; 21 Adam Sidlow; 19 Steve Crossley.
Tries: Wallace (21, 35, 47, 71), Laulu-Togagae (37), Pownall (40, 80), Kay (55), Laithwaite (59), Hall (61, 68), Emmitt (75); **Goals:** Hall 10/13.
Sin bin: Moimoi (9) - late challenge on C Phillips.
Rugby Leaguer & League Express Men of the Match: *Town:* Macauley Davies; *Wolfpack:* Bob Beswick.
Penalty count: 9-8; **Half-time:** 0-24;
Referee: Jon Roberts; **Attendance:** 592.

ROUND 3

Saturday 12th August 2017

NEWCASTLE THUNDER 28 BARROW RAIDERS 30

THUNDER: 1 Lewis Young; 2 Zach Clark; 3 Joe Brown; 4 Derrell Olpherts; 5 Ali Blair; 6 Tom Shaw; 7 Benn Hardcastle; 8 Vincent Rennie; 9 Evan Simons; 10 Rhys Clarke; 11 Harry Aldous; 12 Dan Turland; 13 Liam McAvoy. Subs (all used): 14 Matt Barron; 15 Callum Bustin; 16 Sam Luckley; 17 Aaron Teroi.
Tries: Hardcastle (40, 75), Barron (62), Young (67), Brown (74); **Goals:** Hardcastle 4/5.
RAIDERS: 1 Ryan Fieldhouse; 5 Shane Toal; 3 Declan Hulme; 33 Eze Harper; 2 Brett Carter; 6 Jamie Dallimore; 7 Lewis Charnock; 8 Joe Bullock; 15 Karl Ashall; 10 Oliver Wilkes; 12 Jarrad Stack; 11 Dan Toal; 13 Martin Aspinwall. Subs (all used): 9 Nathan Mossop; 21 James Duerden; 16 Andrew Dawson; 17 Tom Walker.
Tries: Harper (4, 7), Fieldhouse (21), Hulme (24, 28), Carter (45); **Goals:** Charnock 3/7.
Rugby Leaguer & League Express Men of the Match: *Thunder:* Lewis Young; *Raiders:* Eze Harper.
Penalty count: 7-7; **Half-time:** 6-26;
Referee: Callum Straw; **Attendance:** 850.

Sunday 13th August 2017

DONCASTER 30 WHITEHAVEN 22

DONCASTER: - Hakim Miloudi; 22 Louis Sheriff; 26 Nick Rawsthorne; 4 Jason Tali; 5 Sam Doherty; 20 Kieran Cross; 15 Jack Miller; 10 Iafeta Palea'aesina; 9 Kyle Kesik; 8 Mark Castle; 13 Charlie Martin; 12 Jason Muranka; 27 Peter Green. Subs (all used): 18 Ryan Wright; 19 Zac Braham; 23 Jamie Thackray; 7 Jordie Hedges.
Tries: Kesik (1), Palea'aesina (12), Doherty (46), Cross (75), Martin (78); **Goals:** Miller 5/6.
WHITEHAVEN: 1 Elliott Miller; 30 David Thompson; 4 Jessie Joe Parker; 3 Chris Taylor; 5 Jordan Burns; 6 Steve Roper; 7 Paul Crook; 8 Marc Shackley; 9 James Newton; 19 Glenn Riley; 16 Connor Holliday; 12 Scott McAvoy; 13 Karl Olstrum. Subs (all used): 2 Craig Calvert; 14 James Tilley; 17 Tommy Holland; 22 Kurt Maudling.
Tries: Parker (9, 65), Holliday (21), Holland (51);
Goals: Crook 3/4.
Rugby Leaguer & League Express Men of the Match: *Doncaster:* Hakim Miloudi; *Whitehaven:* Jessie Joe Parker.
Penalty count: 7-12; **Half-time:** 14-10;
Referee: Greg Dolan; **Attendance:** 525.

KEIGHLEY COUGARS 26 TORONTO WOLFPACK 26

COUGARS: 22 Ritchie Hawkyard; 5 Davey Dixon; 34 Hamish Barnes; 32 Adam Ryder; 26 Vinny Finigan; 14 Adam Brook; 7 Matty Beharrell; 8 Scott Law; 17 Nathan Conroy; 19 Matthew Bailey; 25 Ben Sagar; 12 Brendon Rawlins; 13 Mike Emmett. Subs (all used): 1 Harry Aaronson; 9 James Feather; 36 Trae O'Sullivan; 37 Gavin Reed.
Tries: Barnes (11), Finigan (17, 72), Hawkyard (48);
Goals: Beharrell 5/5.
WOLFPACK: 1 Quentin Laulu-Togagae; 2 Jonny Pownall; 3 Greg Worthington; 4 Craig Hall; 5 Liam Kay; 6 Blake Wallace; 27 Ryan Brierley; 8 Fuifui Moimoi; 9 Bob Beswick; 29 Jake Emmitt; 17 Richard Whiting; 12 James Laithwaite; 13 Jack Bussey. Subs (all used): 7 Rhys Jacks; 10 Daniel Fleming; 19 Steve Crossley; 21 Adam Sidlow.
Tries: Pownall (7), Laulu-Togagae (26), Kay (31), Whiting (36), Worthington (54); **Goals:** Hall 3/5.
Rugby Leaguer & League Express Men of the Match: *Cougars:* Ritchie Hawkyard; *Wolfpack:* Richard Whiting.
Penalty count: 10-12; **Half-time:** 12-22;
Referee: Andrew Sweet; **Attendance:** 922.

YORK CITY KNIGHTS 28 WORKINGTON TOWN 18

CITY KNIGHTS: 31 Liam Harris; 21 Ben Dent; 19 James Haynes; 17 Brad Hey; 3 Nev Morrison; 34 Connor Robinson; 7 Harry Tyson-Wilson; 10 Chris Siddons; 26 Andy Ellis; 28 Kieran Moran; - Jordan Cox; 11 Joe Batchelor; 13 Tim Spears. Subs (all used): 29 Will Jubb; - Ross Osborne; 25 Joe Porter; 20 Adam Robinson.
Tries: Ellis (9, 23), Cox (30), Morrison (47), C Robinson (65);
Goals: C Robinson 4/6.
TOWN: 1 Theerapol Ritson; 2 Joe Hambley; - Danny Rasool; 4 Jason Mossop; 24 Phil Lister; 6 Carl Forber; 7 Jamie Doran; 16 Tom Curwen; 13 Stuart Howarth; 10 Stevie Scholey; - Macauley Davies; 11 Brett Phillips; 15 Perry Singleton. Subs (all used): 9 Callum Phillips; 18 Conor Fitzsimmons; 22 Jake Moore; - Joe Prior.
Tries: Lister (14), Davies (42), Hambley (67);
Goals: Forber 3/3.
Rugby Leaguer & League Express Men of the Match: *City Knights:* Connor Robinson; *Town:* Jamie Doran.
Penalty count: 5-7; **Half-time:** 18-6;
Referee: Nick Bennett; **Attendance:** 1,112.

ROUND 4

Saturday 19th August 2017

TORONTO WOLFPACK 50 NEWCASTLE THUNDER 0

WOLFPACK: 1 Quentin Laulu-Togagae; 2 Jonny Pownall; 3 Greg Worthington; 4 Craig Hall; 5 Liam Kay; 6 Blake Wallace; 7 Rhys Jacks; 8 Fuifui Moimoi; 9 Bob Beswick; 29 Jake Emmitt; 13 Jack Bussey; 17 Richard Whiting; 11 Andrew Dixon. Subs (all used): 10 Daniel Fleming; 24 Sean Penkywicz; 12 James Laithwaite; 21 Adam Sidlow.
Tries: Kay (2, 24, 66), Jacks (33), Hall (35), Moimoi (55), Laulu-Togagae (66, 68), Worthington (69);
Goals: Hall 7/10.
THUNDER: 1 Lewis Young; 2 Dan Parker; 3 Zach Clark; 4 Joe Brown; 5 Ali Blair; 6 Tom Shaw; 7 Benn Hardcastle; 8 Vincent Rennie; 9 Evan Simons; 10 Callum Bustin; 11 Harry Aldous; 12 Steve Snitch; 13 Liam McAvoy. Subs (all used): 14 Sam Luckley; 15 Matt Barron; 16 Josh Stoker; 17 Aaron Teroi.
Sin bin: McAvoy (39) - dissent.
Rugby Leaguer & League Express Men of the Match: *Wolfpack:* Liam Kay; *Thunder:* Lewis Young.
Penalty count: 8-12; **Half-time:** 22-0;
Referee: Brandon Robinson; **Attendance:** 7,522.

Sunday 20th August 2017

BARROW RAIDERS 26 YORK CITY KNIGHTS 19

RAIDERS: 24 Luke Cresswell; 5 Shane Toal; 3 Declan Hulme; 33 Eze Harper; 2 Brett Carter; 6 Jamie Dallimore; 7 Lewis Charnock; 8 Joe Bullock; 15 Karl Ashall; 10 Oliver Wilkes; 12 Jarrad Stack; 22 Bradd Crellin; 13 Martin Aspinwall. Subs (all used): 17 Tom Walker; 21 James Duerden; 9 Nathan Mossop; 11 Dan Toal.
Tries: Carter (8, 50), Ashall (44), Bullock (75);
Goals: Charnock 5/5.
CITY KNIGHTS: 21 Ben Dent; 3 Nev Morrison; 35 Jake Butler-Fleming; 17 Brad Hey; 2 David Foggin-Johnston; 34 Connor Robinson; 23 Jon Presley; - Ross Osborne; 29 Will Jubb; 27 Ryan Mallinder; - Jordan Cox; 11 Joe Batchelor; 28 Kieran Moran. Subs (all used): 24 Adam Swift; 25 Joe Porter; 16 Ronan Dixon; 20 Adam Robinson.
Tries: Foggin-Johnston (5), Hey (69, 78);
Goals: C Robinson 3/4; **Field goal:** C Robinson (40).
Rugby Leaguer & League Express Men of the Match: *Raiders:* Lewis Charnock; *City Knights:* Jon Presley.
Penalty count: 6-8; **Half-time:** 6-7;
Referee: Jon Roberts; **Attendance:** 977.

WHITEHAVEN 36 KEIGHLEY COUGARS 4

WHITEHAVEN: 1 Elliott Miller; 30 David Thompson; 3 Chris Taylor; 4 Jessie Joe Parker; 5 Jordan Burns; 6 Steve Roper; 7 Paul Crook; 8 Marc Shackley; 14 James Tilley; 10 Carl Forster; 16 Connor Holliday; 15 Dion Aiye; 13 Karl Olstrum. Subs (all used): 2 Craig Calvert; 9 James Newton; 17 Tommy Holland; 25 Aiden Worthington.
Tries: Parker (23), Holliday (32), Thompson (39), Forster (47), Burns (64), Olstrum (74); **Goals:** Crook 6/8.
COUGARS: 22 Ritchie Hawkyard; 5 Davey Dixon; 34 Hamish Barnes; 32 Adam Ryder; 2 Andy Gabriel; 14 Adam Brook; 7 Matty Beharrell; 12 Brendon Rawlins; 17 Nathan Conroy; 19 Matthew Bailey; 25 Ben Sagar; 18 Josh Tonks; 13 Mike Emmett. Subs (all used): 1 Harry Aaronson; 29 Brad Nicholson; 36 Trae O'Sullivan; 37 Gavin Reed.
Try: Gabriel (58); **Goals:** Beharrell 0/1.
Rugby Leaguer & League Express Men of the Match: *Whitehaven:* David Thompson; *Cougars:* Ritchie Hawkyard.
Penalty count: 13-10; **Half-time:** 20-0;
Referee: Greg Dolan; **Attendance:** 562.

WORKINGTON TOWN 22 DONCASTER 21

TOWN: 1 Theerapol Ritson; - Danny Rasool; 22 Jake Moore; 4 Jason Mossop; 21 Gabriel Fell; 6 Carl Forber; 7 Jamie Doran; 16 Tom Curwen; 13 Stuart Howarth; 10 Stevie Scholey; 11 Brett Phillips; - Macauley Davies; 15 Perry Singleton. Subs (all used): 9 Callum Phillips; 8 Kris Coward; 18 Conor Fitzsimmons; 25 Gordon Maudling.
Tries: Fell (27, 32), Davies (35), Fitzsimmons (53);
Goals: Forber 3/5.
DONCASTER: 1 Tom Carr; 22 Louis Sheriff; 26 Nick Rawsthorne; 4 Jason Tali; 5 Sam Doherty; 20 Kieran Cross; 15 Jack Miller; 16 Russ Spiers; 18 Ryan Wright; 10 Iafeta Palea'aesina; 12 Jason Muranka; 13 Charlie Martin; 27 Peter Green. Subs (all used): 8 Mark Castle; 7 Jordie Hedges; 17 Mike Kelly; 23 Jamie Thackray.
Tries: Palea'aesina (4), Tali (47), Cross (79);
Goals: Miller 4/4; **Field goal:** Miller (40).
Sin bin: Sheriff (26) - high tackle on Ritson.
Rugby Leaguer & League Express Men of the Match: *Town:* Stevie Scholey; *Doncaster:* Jack Miller.
Penalty count: 15-8; **Half-time:** 14-9;
Referee: Tom Crashley; **Attendance:** 441.

ROUND 5

Saturday 2nd September 2017

TORONTO WOLFPACK 36 WHITEHAVEN 18

WOLFPACK: 1 Quentin Laulu-Togagae; 2 Jonny Pownall; 3 Greg Worthington; 4 Craig Hall; 5 Liam Kay; 6 Blake Wallace; 7 Rhys Jacks; 29 Jake Emmitt; 9 Bob Beswick; 8 Fuifui Moimoi; 11 Andrew Dixon; 17 Richard Whiting; 13 Jack Bussey. Subs (all used): 21 Adam Sidlow; 24 Sean Penkywicz; 14 Gary Wheeler; 10 Daniel Fleming.
Tries: Whiting (2, 14), Beswick (34), Pownall (51), Kay (63), Wheeler (66), Laulu-Togagae (72); **Goals:** Hall 4/7.
WHITEHAVEN: 1 Elliott Miller; 30 David Thompson; 3 Chris Taylor; 4 Jessie Joe Parker; 5 Jordan Burns; 15 Dion Aiye; 9 James Newton; 8 Marc Shackley; 14 James Tilley; 19 Glenn Riley; 16 Connor Holliday; 12 Scott McAvoy; 10 Carl Forster. Subs (all used): - Danny Green; 2 Craig Calvert; 17 Tommy Holland; 24 Lewis Brown.
Tries: Forster (32), Newton (47), Tilley (53);
Goals: Burns 3/3.
Rugby Leaguer & League Express Men of the Match: *Wolfpack:* Gary Wheeler; *Whitehaven:* Jordan Burns.
Penalty count: 9-12; **Half-time:** 16-6;
Referee: Nick Bennett; **Attendance:** 6,134.

Sunday 3rd September 2017

BARROW RAIDERS 36 WORKINGTON TOWN 14

RAIDERS: 1 Ryan Fieldhouse; 5 Shane Toal; 3 Declan Hulme; 33 Eze Harper; 2 Brett Carter; 6 Jamie Dallimore; 7 Lewis Charnock; 8 Joe Bullock; 9 Nathan Mossop; 10 Oliver Wilkes; 12 Jarrad Stack; 22 Bradd Crellin; 13 Martin Aspinwall. Subs (all used): 14 Dan Abram; 11 Dan Toal; 17 Tom Walker; 21 James Duerden.
Tries: S Toal (6, 76), Mossop (10), Fieldhouse (15), Dallimore (39), Wilkes (58);
Goals: Charnock 5/6, Dallimore 1/1.
Sin bin: Aspinwall (8) - fighting; Abram (56) - retaliation.
TOWN: 1 Theerapol Ritson; 2 Joe Hambley; 15 Perry Singleton; 4 Jason Mossop; - Gabriel Fell; 6 Carl Forber; 7 Jamie Doran; 16 Tom Curwen; 13 Stuart Howarth; 8 Kris Coward; 11 Brett Philips; - Macauley Davies; 25 Gordon Maudling. Subs (all used): - Kyle Shelford; 9 Callum Philips; - Danny Rasool; 18 Conor Fitzsimmons.
Tries: Fell (32), B Philips (61), Ritson (69); **Goals:** Forber 1/3.
Dismissal: Davies (56) - high tackle on Abram.
Sin bin: Singleton (8) - fighting;
B Philips (50) - late challenge.
Rugby Leaguer & League Express Men of the Match: *Raiders:* Nathan Mossop; *Town:* Theerapol Ritson.
Penalty count: 9-7; **Half-time:** 24-4;
Referee: Steve Race; **Attendance:** 1,021.

NEWCASTLE THUNDER 34 KEIGHLEY COUGARS 8

THUNDER: 1 Tom Shaw; 2 Joe Brown; 3 Derrell Olpherts; 4 Adam Bielby; 5 Ali Blair; 6 Lewis Young; 7 Benn Hardcastle; 8 Callum Bustin; 9 Evan Simons; 10 Liam McAvoy; 11 Harry Aldous; 12 Steve Snitch; 13 Jack Aldous. Subs (all used): 14 Vincent Rennie; 15 Rhys Clarke; 16 Aaron Teroi; 17 Sam Luckley.
Tries: Blair (7, 14), Olpherts (66), McAvoy (72), Bielby (77);
Goals: Hardcastle 7/7.
COUGARS: 22 Ritchie Hawkyard; 5 Davey Dixon; 25 Ben Sagar; 32 Adam Ryder; 2 Andy Gabriel; 24 Liam Darville; 7 Matty Beharrell; 29 Brad Nicholson; 17 Nathan Conroy; 19 Matthew Bailey; 11 Josh Lynam; 18 Josh Tonks; 13 Mike Emmett. Subs (all used): 1 Harry Aaronson; 12 Brendon Rawlins; 27 Sean Kelly; 36 Trae O'Sullivan.
Tries: Rawlins (46), Ryder (49); **Goals:** Beharrell 0/2.
Rugby Leaguer & League Express Men of the Match: *Thunder:* Ali Blair; *Cougars:* Josh Tonks.
Penalty count: 10-8; **Half-time:** 14-0;
Referee: Liam Staveley; **Attendance:** 791.

YORK CITY KNIGHTS 21 DONCASTER 21

CITY KNIGHTS: 31 Liam Harris; 3 Nev Morrison; 35 Jake Butler-Fleming; 17 Brad Hey; 2 David Foggin-Johnston; 34 Connor Robinson; 23 Jon Presley; 16 Ronan Dixon; 26 Andy Ellis; 28 Kieran Moran; 36 Jordan Cox; 11 Joe Batchelor; 13 Tim Spears. Subs (all used): 29 Will Jubb; 25 Joe Porter; 20 Adam Robinson; 10 Chris Siddons.
Tries: Butler-Fleming (18), Harris (25, 68), Morrison (58);
Goals: C Robinson 2/4; **Field goal:** C Robinson (79).
DONCASTER: - Hakim Miloudi; 24 Richie Barnett; 26 Nick Rawsthorne; 4 Jason Tali; 5 Sam Doherty; 20 Kieran Cross; 15 Jack Miller; 10 Iafeta Palea'aesina; 9 Kyle Kesik; 16 Russ Spiers; 13 Charlie Martin; 12 Jason Muranka; 27 Peter Green. Subs (all used): 19 Zac Braham; 8 Mark Castle; 7 Jordie Hedges; 18 Ryan Wright.
Tries: Barnett (21), Rawsthorne (34), Miloudi (54, 63);
Goals: Miller 2/4; **Field goal:** Miller (38).

Rugby Leaguer & League Express Men of the Match:
City Knights: Liam Harris; *Doncaster:* Hakim Miloudi.
Penalty count: 6-4; **Half-time:** 10-11;
Referee: Brandon Robinson; **Attendance:** 1,107.

ROUND 6

Saturday 9th September 2017

TORONTO WOLFPACK 26 BARROW RAIDERS 2

WOLFPACK: 1 Quentin Laulu-Togagae; 2 Jonny Pownall; 3 Greg Worthington; 4 Craig Hall; 5 Liam Kay; 6 Blake Wallace; 7 Rhys Jacks; 29 Jake Emmitt; 9 Bob Beswick; 8 Fuifui Moimoi; 11 Andrew Dixon; 17 Richard Whiting; 13 Jack Bussey. Subs (all used): 21 Adam Sidlow; 24 Sean Penkywicz; 14 Gary Wheeler; 10 Daniel Fleming.
Tries: Laulu-Togagae (15), Wallace (54, 62), Whiting (57);
Goals: Hall 5/5.
RAIDERS: 24 Luke Cresswell; 45 Tom Loxam; 4 Max Wiper; 12 Jarrad Stack; 33 Eze Harper; 6 Jamie Dallimore; 7 Lewis Charnock; 8 Joe Bullock; 15 Karl Ashall; 10 Oliver Wilkes; 18 Danny Morrow; 22 Bradd Crellin; 13 Martin Aspinwall. Subs (all used): 9 Nathan Mossop; 11 Dan Toal; 21 James Duerden; 17 Tom Walker.
Goals: Charnock 1/1.
Rugby Leaguer & League Express Men of the Match:
Wolfpack: Blake Wallace; *Raiders:* Luke Cresswell.
Penalty count: 8-10; **Half-time:** 8-0;
Referee: John McMullen; **Attendance:** 7,972.

Sunday 10th September 2017

DONCASTER 24 NEWCASTLE THUNDER 28

DONCASTER: - Hakim Miloudi; - Ryan Jones; 26 Nick Rawsthorne; 4 Jason Tali; 5 Sam Doherty; 20 Kieran Cross; 15 Jack Miller; 16 Russ Spiers; 9 Kyle Kesik; 10 Iafeta Palea'aesina; 13 Charlie Martin; 12 Jason Muranka; 27 Peter Green. Subs (all used): 34 Brad England; 19 Zac Braham; 8 Mark Castle; 7 Jordie Hedges.
Tries: Green (14), Muranka (34), Tali (40), Cross (61);
Goals: Miller 3/6, Rawsthorne 1/1.
Dismissal: Miloudi (78) - punching.
THUNDER: 1 Lewis Young; 24 Ali Blair; 3 Derrell Olpherts; 4 Joe Brown; 5 Dan Parker; 6 Tom Shaw; 7 Benn Hardcastle; 8 Callum Bustin; 9 Evan Simons; 10 Liam McAvoy; 11 Harry Aldous; 12 Steve Snitch; 13 Jack Aldous. Subs (all used): 14 Aaron Teroi; 15 Vincent Rennie; 16 Sam Luckley; 17 Rhys Clarke.
Tries: Olpherts (8), McAvoy (13), Rennie (28), Young (56), Simons (68); **Goals:** Hardcastle 4/5.
Rugby Leaguer & League Express Men of the Match:
Doncaster: Peter Green; *Thunder:* Benn Hardcastle.
Penalty count: 9-6; **Half-time:** 12-16;
Referee: Jon Roberts; **Attendance:** 536.

KEIGHLEY COUGARS 28 WORKINGTON TOWN 6

COUGARS: 22 Ritchie Hawkyard; 5 Davey Dixon; 25 Ben Sagar; 32 Adam Ryder; 2 Andy Gabriel; 24 Liam Darville; 7 Matty Beharrell; 15 Neil Cherryholme; 9 James Feather; 19 Matthew Bailey; 11 Josh Lynam; 18 Josh Tonks; 13 Mike Emmett. Subs (all used): 1 Harry Aaronson; 12 Brendon Rawlins; 27 Sean Kelly; 29 Brad Nicholson.
Tries: Feather (9), Bailey (17), Lynam (26), Tonks (61), Hawkyard (70); **Goals:** Beharrell 4/5.
TOWN: 1 Theerapol Ritson; 2 Joe Hambley; - Danny Rasool; 4 Jason Mossop; 24 Phil Lister; 6 Carl Forber; 7 Jamie Doran; 8 Kris Coward; 13 Stuart Howarth; 18 Conor Fitzsimmons; - Macauley Davies; 32 Jake Moore; 15 Perry Singleton. Subs (all used): - Liam Byrne; - Joe Prior; 20 Kieran Mewse; 25 Gordon Maudling.
Try: Hambley (22); **Goals:** Forber 1/1.
Rugby Leaguer & League Express Men of the Match:
Cougars: James Feather; *Town:* Joe Hambley.
Penalty count: 11-9; **Half-time:** 16-6;
Referee: Gareth Brent; **Attendance:** 661.

WHITEHAVEN 26 YORK CITY KNIGHTS 16

WHITEHAVEN: 1 Elliott Miller; 5 Jordan Burns; 3 Chris Taylor; 4 Jessie Joe Parker; 2 Craig Calvert; 6 Steve Roper; 7 Paul Crook; 8 Marc Shackley; 14 James Tilley; 19 Glenn Riley; 30 David Thompson; 12 Scott McAvoy; 15 Dion Aiye. Subs (all used): 9 James Newton; 10 Carl Forster; 17 Tommy Holland; 24 Lewis Brown.
Tries: Miller (4, 28), Aiye (65), Forster (75);
Goals: Crook 5/5.
CITY KNIGHTS: 21 Ben Dent; 3 Nev Morrison; 19 James Haynes; 24 Adam Swift; 2 David Foggin-Johnston; 34 Connor Robinson; 23 Jon Presley; 16 Ronan Dixon; 26 Andy Ellis; 10 Chris Siddons; 35 Jake Butler-Fleming; 15 Liam Thompson; 13 Tim Spears. Subs (all used): 29 Will Jubb; 25 Joe Porter; 28 Kieran Moran; 7 Harry Tyson-Wilson.

Tries: Dent (13), Presley (42), Foggin-Johnston (58);
Goals: C Robinson 2/4.
Rugby Leaguer & League Express Men of the Match:
Whitehaven: Lewis Brown; *City Knights:* Ben Dent.
Penalty count: 6-5; **Half-time:** 14-8;
Referee: Tom Crashley; **Attendance:** 605.

ROUND 7

Saturday 16th September 2017

TORONTO WOLFPACK 26 DONCASTER 14

WOLFPACK: 1 Quentin Laulu-Togagae; 2 Jonny Pownall; 5 Liam Kay; 4 Craig Hall; 15 Ryan Burroughs; 6 Blake Wallace; 14 Gary Wheeler; 16 Shaun Pick; 24 Sean Penkywicz; 21 Adam Sidlow; 11 Andrew Dixon; 12 James Laithwaite; 13 Jack Bussey. Subs (all used): 9 Bob Beswick; 19 Steve Crossley; 7 Rhys Jacks; 20 Tom Dempsey.
Tries: Pownall (15, 56, 66), Wallace (49), Kay (68);
Goals: Hall 3/5.
DONCASTER: 1 Tom Carr; - Ryan Jones; 2 Aaron Jones-Bishop; 26 Nick Rawsthorne; 5 Sam Doherty; - Hakim Miloudi; 15 Jack Miller; 27 Peter Green; 9 Kyle Kesik; 19 Zac Braham; 34 Brad England; 25 Jordan Lane; 7 Jordie Hedges. Subs (all used): - Jez Litten; 12 Jason Muranka; 13 Charlie Martin; 20 Kieran Cross.
Tries: Lane (10), Kesik (24); **Goals:** Miller 3/3.
Rugby Leaguer & League Express Men of the Match:
Wolfpack: Jonny Pownall; *Doncaster:* Hakim Miloudi.
Penalty count: 5-9; **Half-time:** 4-12;
Referee: Billy Pearson; **Attendance:** 8,456.

Sunday 17th September 2017

BARROW RAIDERS 32 KEIGHLEY COUGARS 18

RAIDERS: 1 Ryan Fieldhouse; 2 Brett Carter; 45 Tom Loxam; 3 Declan Hulme; 5 Shane Toal; 6 Jamie Dallimore; 7 Lewis Charnock; 8 Joe Bullock; 9 Nathan Mossop; 10 Oliver Wilkes; 22 Bradd Crellin; 18 Danny Morrow; 13 Martin Aspinwall. Subs (all used): 11 Dan Toal; 15 Karl Ashall; 17 Tom Walker; 21 James Duerden.
Tries: Mossop (2), S Toal (35), Walker (50), Bullock (62), Charnock (70); **Goals:** Charnock 3/4, Dallimore 3/3.
COUGARS: 22 Ritchie Hawkyard; 5 Davey Dixon; 34 Hamish Barnes; 32 Adam Ryder; 2 Andy Gabriel; 24 Liam Darville; 7 Matty Beharrell; 15 Neil Cherryholme; 9 James Feather; 19 Matthew Bailey; 25 Ben Sagar; 18 Josh Tonks; 13 Mike Emmett. Subs (all used): 1 Harry Aaronson; 8 Scott Law; 12 Brendon Rawlins; 29 Brad Nicholson.
Tries: Cherryholme (11), Dixon (52), Gabriel (78);
Goals: Beharrell 3/3.
Rugby Leaguer & League Express Men of the Match:
Raiders: Shane Toal; *Cougars:* Josh Tonks.
Penalty count: 9-5; **Half-time:** 14-6;
Referee: Nick Bennett; **Attendance:** 1,007.

WORKINGTON TOWN 6 WHITEHAVEN 56

TOWN: 1 Theerapol Ritson; 2 Joe Hambley; - Danny Rasool; 4 Jason Mossop; 21 Gabriel Fell; 6 Carl Forber; 13 Stuart Howarth; 8 Kris Coward; - Joe Prior; 10 Stevie Scholey; 32 Jake Moore; 25 Gordon Maudling; 18 Conor Fitzsimmons. Subs (all used): 17 Scott Rooke; - Liam Byrne; 20 Kieran Mewse; 24 Phil Lister.
Try: Maudling (20); **Goals:** Forber 1/1.
WHITEHAVEN: 5 Jordan Burns; - Danny Green; 3 Chris Taylor; 4 Jessie Joe Parker; 2 Craig Calvert; 15 Dion Aiye; 7 Paul Crook; 19 Glenn Riley; 14 James Tilley; 10 Carl Forster; 30 David Thompson; 12 Scott McAvoy; 8 Marc Shackley. Subs (all used): 9 James Newton; 16 Connor Holliday; 17 Tommy Holland; 24 Lewis Brown.
Tries: Burns (26), Parker (32, 45), Aiye (41, 72, 78), McAvoy (48), Forster (58), Riley (60), Calvert (68);
Goals: Crook 8/10.
Rugby Leaguer & League Express Men of the Match:
Town: Gordon Maudling; *Whitehaven:* Scott McAvoy.
Penalty count: 3-8; **Half-time:** 6-12;
Referee: Jack Smith; **Attendance:** 927.

YORK CITY KNIGHTS 24 NEWCASTLE THUNDER 26

CITY KNIGHTS: 31 Liam Harris; 3 Nev Morrison; 21 Ben Dent; 24 Adam Swift; 5 Tom Saxton; 34 Connor Robinson; 7 Harry Tyson-Wilson; 16 Ronan Dixon; 26 Andy Ellis; 10 Chris Siddons; 36 Jordan Cox; 15 Liam Thompson; 13 Tim Spears. Subs (all used): 14 Harry Carter; 27 Ryan Mallinder; 29 Will Jubb; 25 Joe Porter.
Tries: Ellis (19), Carter (51), Morrison (63), Swift (76);
Goals: C Robinson 4/4.
THUNDER: 1 Tom Shaw; 2 Dan Parker; 3 Derrell Olpherts; 4 Joe Brown; 5 Ali Blair; 6 Lewis Young; 7 Benn Hardcastle; 8 Liam McAvoy; 9 Evan Simons; 10 Callum Bustin; 11 Harry Aldous; 12 Rhys Clarke; 13 Jack Aldous. Subs (all used): 14 Sam Luckley; 15 Vincent Rennie; 16 Aaron Teroi; 17 Matt Barron.

Tries: Simons (12), Shaw (31, 72), Teroi (37), Olpherts (40);
Goals: Hardcastle 3/5.
Sin bin: Parker (62) - late challenge on Harris.
Rugby Leaguer & League Express Men of the Match:
City Knights: Tim Spears; *Thunder:* Benn Hardcastle.
Penalty count: 9-6; **Half-time:** 6-20;
Referee: John McMullen; **Attendance:** 1,181.

SEMI-FINALS

Sunday 24th September 2017

BARROW RAIDERS 60 NEWCASTLE THUNDER 0

RAIDERS: 1 Ryan Fieldhouse; 2 Brett Carter; 3 Declan Hulme; 33 Eze Harper; 5 Shane Toal; 6 Jamie Dallimore; 7 Lewis Charnock; 8 Joe Bullock; 15 Karl Ashall; 10 Oliver Wilkes; 18 Danny Morrow; 12 Jarrad Stack; 13 Martin Aspinwall. Subs (all used): 26 Brad Marwood; 17 Tom Walker; 25 Matty While; 21 James Duerden.
Tries: Wilkes (6), S Toal (11, 53), Dallimore (18, 72), Carter (40), Fieldhouse (51), Marwood (57, 78), Charnock (69); **Goals:** Dallimore 9/10, Marwood 1/1.
THUNDER: 1 Lewis Young; 2 Dan Parker; 3 Derrell Olpherts; 4 Joe Brown; 5 Ali Blair; 6 Tom Shaw; 7 Benn Hardcastle; 8 Liam McAvoy; 9 Evan Simons; 10 Callum Bustin; 11 Rhys Clarke; 12 Harry Aldous; 13 Jack Aldous. Subs (all used): 14 Matt Barron; 15 Dan Turland; 16 Vincent Rennie; 17 Aaron Teroi.
Rugby Leaguer & League Express Men of the Match:
Raiders: Jamie Dallimore; *Thunder:* Lewis Young.
Penalty count: 7-9; **Half-time:** 22-0;
Referee: Greg Dolan; **Attendance:** 1,090.

WHITEHAVEN 21 YORK CITY KNIGHTS 20
(after golden point extra-time)

WHITEHAVEN: 1 Elliott Miller; 5 Jordan Burns; 3 Chris Taylor; 4 Jessie Joe Parker; 2 Craig Calvert; 15 Dion Aiye; 7 Paul Crook; 8 Marc Shackley; 14 James Tilley; 19 Glenn Riley; 16 Connor Holliday; 12 Scott McAvoy; 10 Carl Forster. Subs (all used): 9 James Newton; 6 Steve Roper; 17 Tommy Holland; 13 Karl Olstrum.
Tries: Burns (31, 54), Holland (39); **Goals:** Crook 4/4;
Field goal: Roper (105).
Sin bin: Aiye (42) - trip on Carter.
CITY KNIGHTS: 1 Ash Robson; 3 Nev Morrison; 19 James Haynes; 17 Brad Hey; 5 Tom Saxton; 34 Connor Robinson; 31 Liam Harris; 16 Ronan Dixon; 26 Andy Ellis; 10 Chris Siddons; 11 Joe Batchelor; 27 Ryan Mallinder; 13 Tim Spears. Subs (all used): 14 Harry Carter; 28 Kieran Moran; 20 Adam Robinson; 25 Joe Porter.
Tries: Robson (5, 70), Batchelor (12), Ellis (64);
Goals: C Robinson 2/5.
Rugby Leaguer & League Express Men of the Match:
Whitehaven: Scott McAvoy; *City Knights:* Ash Robson.
Penalty count: 11-8; **Half-time:** 12-10;
Referee: John McMullen; **Attendance:** 853.

PROMOTION FINAL

Sunday 1st October 2017

BARROW RAIDERS 10 WHITEHAVEN 6

RAIDERS: 1 Ryan Fieldhouse; 2 Brett Carter; 33 Eze Harper; 3 Declan Hulme; 5 Shane Toal; 6 Jamie Dallimore; 7 Lewis Charnock; 8 Joe Bullock; 15 Karl Ashall; 10 Oliver Wilkes; 12 Jarrad Stack; 22 Bradd Crellin; 13 Martin Aspinwall. Subs (all used): 9 Nathan Mossop; 17 Tom Walker; 11 Dan Toal; 21 James Duerden.
Tries: S Toal (10, 71); **Goals:** Dallimore 1/3.
WHITEHAVEN: 1 Elliott Miller; 2 Craig Calvert; 4 Jessie Joe Parker; 3 Chris Taylor; 5 Jordan Burns; 15 Dion Aiye; 7 Paul Crook; 8 Marc Shackley; 14 James Tilley; 10 Carl Forster; 13 Karl Olstrum; 12 Scott McAvoy; 6 Steve Roper. Subs: 9 James Newton; 16 Connor Holliday (not used); 17 Tommy Holland; 19 Glenn Riley.
Try: Aiye (45); **Goals:** Crook 1/1.
Rugby Leaguer & League Express Men of the Match:
Raiders: Shane Toal; *Whitehaven:* James Newton.
Penalty count: 10-10; **Half-time:** 4-0;
Referee: Scott Mikalauskas; **Attendance:** 3,128.

LEAGUE 1 SHIELD 2017
Round by Round

ROUND 1

Saturday 29th July 2017

**SOUTH WALES IRONMEN 28
GLOUCESTERSHIRE ALL GOLDS 20**

IRONMEN: 1 Jack Uren; 2 Sam Hodge; 3 Morgan Jeffries; 4 Shaun Tennant; 5 Curtis Ford; 6 Andrew Gay; 7 Ben Jones; 8 Morgan Evans; 9 Connor Farrer; 10 Barrie Phillips; 11 Connor Parker; 12 Craig Lewis; 13 Kade Breen. Subs (all used): 14 Daffyd Phillips; 15 Aaron Lewis; 16 Archie Snook; 17 Henry Davies.
Tries: Ford (17), Gay (20), Evans (47), B Jones (70), Tennant (75); **Goals:** B Jones 4/6.
ALL GOLDS: 1 Phil Cowburn; 2 Mo Agoro; 3 Lewis Reece; 4 Brad Kislingbury; 5 Errol Carter; 6 Courtney Davies; 7 Ben Stead; 8 Harrison Elliott; 9 Steve Parry; 10 James Walter; 11 Chris Worrall; 12 Joe McClean; 13 Billy Brickhill. Subs (all used): 14 Ross Price; 15 Malikhi Lloyd-Jones; 16 Richard Jones; 17 Harry Kidd.
Tries: Kislingbury (13), Parry (28), Cowburn (58), McClean (65); **Goals:** Davies 0/2, Stead 2/2.
Rugby Leaguer & League Express Men of the Match: *Ironmen:* Andrew Gay; *All Golds:* Lewis Reece.
Penalty count: 7-6; **Half-time:** 10-8;
Referee: Chris Campbell; **Attendance:** 212
(at Stebonheath Park, Llanelli).

Sunday 30th July 2017

HEMEL STAGS 32 OXFORD 26

STAGS: 1 Mitch Vincent; 2 Jack Wray; 3 Connor Bower; 4 Danny Lawton; 5 Darren Forde; 6 Alex Williams; 7 Lewis Fairhurst; 8 Dan Hawksworth; 9 Jono Burns; 10 Reece Williams; 11 James Thornton; 12 Jack O'Brien; 13 Brett Whitehead. Subs (all used): 14 Mark Barlow; 15 Corey Hanson; 16 Matt Welham; 17 Wayne Jowitt.
Tries: Thornton (3), Hawksworth (23), Vincent (60), R Williams (65), O'Brien (68); **Goals:** Vincent 6/6.
OXFORD: 1 Kane Riley; 2 Jordan Gill; 3 Harvey Burnett; 4 James Cryer; 5 Adam Dent; 6 Callum Windley; 7 Scott Fleming; 8 Lee Land; 9 Bradley Moules; 10 Jake Joynt; 11 Dwaine McRae; 12 Stuart Biscomb; 13 Kieran Hyde. Subs (all used): 14 Nathan Kitson; 15 Jonathan Payne; 16 Aaron Nicholson; 17 Tom Alexander.
Tries: Dent (32), Gill (36), Fleming (38), Kitson (43), Biscomb (54); **Goals:** Burnett 3/5.
Sin bin: Land (22) - high tackle on Forde.
Rugby Leaguer & League Express Men of the Match: *Stags:* Mitch Vincent; *Oxford:* Scott Fleming.
Penalty count: 7-8; **Half-time:** 12-16;
Referee: Matt Rossleigh; **Attendance:** 106.

NORTH WALES CRUSADERS 12 LONDON SKOLARS 40

CRUSADERS: 1 Tommy Johnson; 19 Dan Price; 3 Simon Atherton; 28 Callum Mulkeen; 5 Dale Bloomfield; 6 Andy Moulsdale; 7 Ryan Smith; 17 Kenny Baker; 14 James Dandy; 32 Warren Thompson; 16 Luke Warburton; 24 Jack Houghton; 13 Ryan Millington. Subs (all used): 27 Aaron Moore; 22 Joe Bate; 8 Jonny Walker; - Alex Whalley.
Tries: Price (35), Bate (69); **Goals:** Johnson 2/2.
SKOLARS: 7 Mike Bishay; 2 Sam Nash; 31 Josh Allison; 20 Jake Melling; 5 James Hill; 29 Jermaine Coleman; 6 Jy-mel Coleman; 11 Lamont Bryan; 9 Charlie Lawrence; 25 Michael Sykes; 10 Dave Williams; 12 Eddie Mbaraga; 13 Ryan Chester. Subs (all used): 8 Louis Robinson; 15 Kazeem Faturoti; 26 Phil Lyon; 30 Ollie Purslow.
Tries: Mbaraga (13, 23), Nash (18), Robinson (26), Jy-mel Coleman (39), Sykes (60), Lyon (74);
Goals: Jy-mel Coleman 6/8.
Rugby Leaguer & League Express Men of the Match: *Crusaders:* Alex Whalley; *Skolars:* Eddie Mbaraga.
Penalty count: 5-5; **Half-time:** 6-28;
Referee: Brandon Robinson; **Attendance:** 268.

HUNSLET 56 COVENTRY BEARS 10

HUNSLET: 1 Jimmy Watson; 39 James Duckworth; 4 Mufaro Mvududu; 24 Cameron Leeming; 3 Marcus Webb; 33 Shaun Roberts; 6 Joe Sanderson; 31 Sean Hesketh; 38 Luke Teasdale; 35 Matt Nicholson; 13 Liam Mackay; - Dean Roberts; 17 Nyle Flynn. Subs (all used): 14 George Flanagan; 8 Michael Haley; 16 Daniel Williams; 23 Jose Kenga.
Tries: Teasdale (15), Mvududu (26, 34, 45, 58, 66), Watson (53), Duckworth (63), Flanagan (70), Williams (79);
Goals: Sanderson 8/10.
BEARS: 1 Billy Gaylor; 2 Mikey Russell; 3 Luke Frixou; 4 Jason Bass; 5 Hayden Freeman; 6 Jordan Gale; 7 Brad Delaney; 8 Brad Brennan; 9 Zak Williams; 10 Jack Morrison; 11 Matt Reid; 12 Chris Barratt; 13 Kieran Sherratt. Subs (all used): 14 John Aldred; 15 James Geurtjens; 16 Paddy Jones; 17 Paul Emanuelli.
Tries: P Jones (20), Freeman (32); **Goals:** Delaney 1/2.
Dismissal: Geurtjens (43) - use of the elbow.
Rugby Leaguer & League Express Men of the Match: *Hunslet:* Mufaro Mvududu; *Bears:* Brad Delaney.
Penalty count: 9-10; **Half-time:** 18-10;
Referee: Steve Race; **Attendance:** 384.

ROUND 2

Saturday 5th August 2017

**GLOUCESTERSHIRE ALL GOLDS 40
NORTH WALES CRUSADERS 22**

ALL GOLDS: 1 Phil Cowburn; 2 Mo Agoro; 3 Kadeem Williams; 4 Lewis Reece; 5 Chris Barlow; 6 Jack Mitchell; 7 Steve Parry; 8 Harrison Elliott; 9 Billy Brickhill; 10 Malikhi Lloyd-Jones; 11 Brad Hargreaves; 12 Joe McClean; 13 Chris Worrall. Subs (all used): 14 Danny Fallon; 15 Ross Price; 16 James Walter; 17 Harry Kidd.
Tries: Cowburn (21, 77), Williams (32), Kidd (38), Barlow (51), Parry (57), Lloyd-Jones (73); **Goals:** Mitchell 6/7.
CRUSADERS: - Dave Eccleston; 19 Dan Price; 10 Alex Davidson; 28 Callum Mulkeen; 27 Aaron Moore; 6 Andy Moulsdale; 7 Ryan Smith; 17 Kenny Baker; 14 James Dandy; 32 Warren Thompson; - Alex Whalley; 16 Luke Warburton; 13 Ryan Millington. Subs (only three named): 9 Lee Hudson; - Jonny Leather (not used); 25 Matt Davies.
Tries: Millington (19), Whalley (34), Baker (50), Davies (68);
Goals: Price 3/4.
Rugby Leaguer & League Express Men of the Match: *All Golds:* Phil Cowburn; *Crusaders:* Alex Whalley.
Penalty count: 6-5; **Half-time:** 18-12;
Referee: Matt Rossleigh; **Attendance:** 211.

Sunday 6th August 2017

OXFORD 10 HUNSLET 36

OXFORD: 1 Adam Dent; 2 Jordan Gill; 3 Harvey Burnett; 4 James Cryer; 5 Luke Gardiner; 6 Casey Canterbury; 7 Scott Fleming; 8 Lee Land; 9 Bradley Moules; 10 Jonathan Payne; 11 Jordan Siddons; 12 Kieran Hyde; 13 Stuart Biscomb. Subs (all used): 14 Sam Druce; 15 Marcus Brooker; 16 Dwaine McRae; 17 Fran Welsh.
Tries: Siddons (24), Gill (35); **Goals:** Burnett 1/2.
Dismissal: Land (72) - high tackle.
Sin bin: Cryer (30) - repeated team offences.
HUNSLET: 1 Jimmy Watson; 39 James Duckworth; 4 Mufaro Mvududu; 24 Cameron Leeming; 3 Marcus Webb; 6 Joe Sanderson; 7 Danny Ansell; 35 Matt Nicholson; 38 Luke Teasdale; 10 Lewis Reed; 11 Jake Normington; 13 Liam Mackay; 17 Nyle Flynn. Subs (all used): 8 Michael Haley; 14 George Flanagan; 15 Jack Coventry; 16 Daniel Williams.
Tries: Nicholson (10, 59), Flanagan (25), Leeming (27), Mackay (62), Normington (68); **Goals:** Sanderson 6/6.
Rugby Leaguer & League Express Men of the Match: *Oxford:* Jordan Siddons; *Hunslet:* Matt Nicholson.
Penalty count: 6-9; **Half-time:** 10-18;
Referee: James Jones; **Attendance:** 155.

COVENTRY BEARS 29 HEMEL STAGS 26

BEARS: 1 Harry Chapman; 2 Mikey Russell; 3 Jason Bass; 4 Matt Reid; 5 Hayden Freeman; 6 Paul Emanuelli; 7 Brad Delaney; 8 Brad Brennan; 9 Billy Gaylor; 10 Paddy Jones; 11 Kieran Sherratt; 12 Chris Barratt; 13 Zak Williams. Subs (all used): 14 James Kelly; 15 James Geurtjens; 16 John Aldred; 17 Jack Morrison.
Tries: Russell (16), Delaney (20, 28), Kelly (39), Freeman (49); **Goals:** Delaney 4/6;
Field goal: Emanuelli (68).
STAGS: 1 Mitch Vincent; 2 Matt Welham; 3 Connor Bower; 4 Danny Lawton; 5 Josh Casey; 6 Jack Wray; 7 Lewis Fairhurst; 8 Dan Hawksworth; 9 Jono Burns; 10 Reece Williams; 11 Jack O'Brien; 12 James Thornton; 13 Munashe Fumhanda. Subs (all used): 14 Wayne Jowitt; 15 Scott Lee; 16 Sam Crowther; 17 Alex Williams.
Tries: Welham (6), Vincent (18), Wray (55), Crowther (75), Bower (78); **Goals:** Vincent 2/3, Fairhurst 1/2.
Rugby Leaguer & League Express Men of the Match: *Bears:* Brad Delaney; *Stags:* Mitch Vincent.
Penalty count: 10-4; **Half-time:** 22-10;
Referee: Brandon Robinson; **Attendance:** 256.

ROUND 3

Saturday 12th August 2017

**GLOUCESTERSHIRE ALL GOLDS 30
COVENTRY BEARS 28**

ALL GOLDS: 1 Phil Cowburn; 2 Mo Agoro; 3 Kadeem Williams; 4 Lewis Reece; 5 Chris Barlow; 6 Jack Mitchell; 7 Danny Fallon; 8 Malikhi Lloyd-Jones; 9 Steve Parry; 10 James Walter; 11 Chris Worrall; 12 Joe McClean; 13 Billy Brickhill. Subs (all used): 14 Brad Hargreaves; 15 Ross Price; 16 Harry Kidd; 17 Harrison Elliott.
Tries: Parry (45, 64), Kidd (53), McClean (68), Mitchell (75); **Goals:** Mitchell 5/5.
BEARS: 1 Mikey Russell; 2 Jamahl Hunte; 3 Jason Bass; 4 Matt Reid; 5 Hayden Freeman; 6 Paul Emanuelli; 7 Brad Delaney; 8 Brad Brennan; 9 Billy Gaylor; 10 Paddy Jones; 11 Kieran Sherratt; 12 Chris Barratt; 13 Zak Williams. Subs (all used): 14 James Kelly; 15 Jack Morrison; 16 James Geurtjens; 17 Dan Gover.
Tries: Reid (18), Emanuelli (31), Barratt (37), Russell (49), Freeman (60); **Goals:** Delaney 4/6.
Rugby Leaguer & League Express Men of the Match: *All Golds:* Jack Mitchell; *Bears:* Brad Delaney.
Penalty count: 7-7; **Half-time:** 0-16;
Referee: Geoffrey Poumes; **Attendance:** 178.

LONDON SKOLARS 66 OXFORD 0

SKOLARS: 7 Mike Bishay; 2 Sam Nash; 31 Josh Allison; 20 Jake Melling; 5 James Hill; 29 Jermaine Coleman; 6 Jy-mel Coleman; 25 Michael Sykes; 9 Charlie Lawrence; 11 Lamont Bryan; 10 Dave Williams; 12 Eddie Mbaraga; 13 Ryan Chester. Subs (all used): 27 Phil Lyon; 8 Louis Robinson; 18 Mike Greenhalgh; 15 Kazeem Faturoti.
Tries: Melling (6, 10, 58), Jy-mel Coleman (13), Mbaraga (28, 64), Allison (34, 51), Bishay (47, 55), Faturoti (77); **Goals:** Jy-mel Coleman 11/12.
OXFORD: 1 Adam Dent; 2 Luke Gardiner; 3 Harvey Burnett; 4 Tommy Newbould; 5 Jordan Gill; 6 Casey Canterbury; 7 Scott Fleming; 8 Jake Joynt; 9 Bradley Moules; 10 Lee Land; 11 Dwaine McRae; 12 Kieran Hyde; 13 Stuart Biscomb. Subs (all used): 14 Sam Druce; 15 Fran Welsh; 16 Anthony Cox; 17 Jordan Siddons.
Rugby Leaguer & League Express Men of the Match: *Skolars:* Eddie Mbaraga; *Oxford:* Kieran Hyde.
Penalty count: 9-7; **Half-time:** 30-0;
Referee: Matt Rossleigh; **Attendance:** 218.

Sunday 13th August 2017

NORTH WALES CRUSADERS 20 HUNSLET 12

CRUSADERS: 1 Tommy Johnson; 19 Dan Price; 3 Simon Atherton; 17 Kenny Baker; - Dave Eccleston; 6 Andy Moulsdale; 7 Ryan Smith; 10 Alex Davidson; 9 Lee Hudson; 32 Warren Thompson; 14 James Dandy; 16 Luke Warburton; 13 Ryan Millington. Subs (all used): 27 Aaron Moore; - Alex Whalley; 8 Jonny Walker; 22 Joe Bate.
Tries: Atherton (5), Moore (38), Johnson (65);
Goals: Johnson 4/5.
HUNSLET: 1 Jimmy Watson; 39 James Duckworth; 4 Mufaro Mvududu; 36 Mathew Cook; 2 Omar Alwari; 7 Danny Ansell; 6 Joe Sanderson; 10 Lewis Reed; 38 Luke Teasdale; 35 Matt Nicholson; 11 Jake Normington; 13 Liam Mackay; 17 Nyle Flynn. Subs (all used): 14 George Flanagan; 8 Michael Haley; 15 Jack Coventry; 37 Dean Roberts.
Tries: Sanderson (17), Mackay (74); **Goals:** Sanderson 2/2.
Rugby Leaguer & League Express Men of the Match: *Crusaders:* Aaron Moore; *Hunslet:* Joe Sanderson.
Penalty count: 6-10; **Half-time:** 10-6;
Referee: Brandon Robinson; **Attendance:** 306.

SOUTH WALES IRONMEN 4 HEMEL STAGS 22

IRONMEN: 1 Jack Uren; 2 Sam Hodge; 3 Morgan Jeffries; 4 Shaun Tennant; 5 Curtis Ford; 6 Andrew Gay; 7 Ben Jones; 8 Morgan Evans; 9 Connor Farrer; 10 Barrie Phillips; 11 Jamie l'Anson; 12 Kade Breen; 13 Connor Parker. Subs (all used): 14 Dafydd Phillips; 15 Christiaan Roets; 16 Alan Pope; 17 Dan Maiden.
Try: Roets (52); **Goals:** B Jones 0/1.
STAGS: 1 Mitch Vincent; 2 Matt Welham; 3 Connor Bower; 4 Danny Lawton; 5 Josh Casey; 6 Jack Wray; 7 Lewis Fairhurst; 8 Dan Hawksworth; 9 Mark Barlow; 10 Reece Williams; 11 James Thornton; 12 Jack O'Brien; 13 Alex Williams. Subs (all used): 14 Santino Decaro; 15 Jono Burns; 16 Marcus Elliott; 17 Wayne Jowitt.
Tries: A Williams (4), Vincent (40), Burns (55);
Goals: Lawton 1/2, Fairhurst 4/4.
Rugby Leaguer & League Express Men of the Match: *Ironmen:* Christiaan Roets; *Stags:* Lewis Fairhurst.
Penalty count: 9-8; **Half-time:** 0-10;
Referee: Tom Crashley; **Attendance:** 192
(at Stebonheath Park, Llanelli).

ROUND 4

Saturday 19th August 2017

HUNSLET 32 GLOUCESTERSHIRE ALL GOLDS 18

HUNSLET: 1 Jimmy Watson; 39 James Duckworth; 4 Mufaro Mvududu; 24 Cameron Leeming; 3 Marcus Webb; 18 Joel Gibson; 6 Joe Sanderson; 10 Lewis Reed; 38 Luke Teasdale; 35 Matt Nicholson; 11 Jake Normington; 13 Liam Mackay; 17 Nyle Flynn. Subs (all used): 14 George Flanagan; 8 Michael Haley; 21 Jack Walton; - Dean Roberts.

League 1 Shield 2017 - Round by Round

Tries: Sanderson (15, 18), D Roberts (44), Watson (50, 60, 63); **Goals:** Sanderson 4/6.
Sin bin: Flanagan (40) - dissent.
ALL GOLDS: 1 Jack Mitchell; 2 Mo Agoro; 3 Phil Cowburn; 4 Brad Kislingbury; 5 Chris Barlow; 6 Danny Fallon; 7 Ben Stead; 8 Chris Worrall; 9 Steve Parry; 10 Malikhi Lloyd-Jones; 11 Harrison Elliott; 12 Joe McClean; 13 Billy Brickhill. Subs (all used): 14 Brad Hargreaves; 15 Lewis Reece; 16 Harry Kidd; 17 James Walter.
Tries: Agoro (7), McClean (31), Parry (70); **Goals:** Stead 3/5.
Rugby Leaguer & League Express Men of the Match: *Hunslet:* Jimmy Watson; *All Golds:* Ben Stead.
Penalty count: 6-10; **Half-time:** 10-12;
Referee: Callum Straw; **Attendance:** 333.

Sunday 20th August 2017

HEMEL STAGS 18 NORTH WALES CRUSADERS 38

STAGS: 1 Matt Welham; 2 Marcus Elliott; 3 Connor Bower; 4 Josh Casey; 5 Liam Frenneaux; 6 Jack Wray; 7 Lewis Fairhurst; 8 Wayne Jowitt; 9 Mark Barlow; 10 Reece Williams; 11 Danny Lawton; 12 Munashe Fumhanda; 13 James Thornton. Subs (all used): 14 Jono Burns; 15 Sam Crowther; 16 Santino Decaro; 17 Alex Williams.
Tries: R Williams (20), Burns (37), Welham (40);
Goals: Fairhurst 3/3.
Sin bin: Burns (67) - late challenge.
CRUSADERS: 1 Tommy Johnson; - Dave Eccleston; 3 Simon Atherton; 17 Kenny Baker; 5 Dale Bloomfield; 19 Dan Price; 7 Ryan Smith; 8 Jonny Walker; 9 Lee Hudson; 32 Warren Thompson; 24 Jack Houghton; 16 Luke Warburton; 13 Ryan Millington. Subs (all used): 27 Aaron Moore; 6 Andy Moulsdale; - Alex Whalley; 22 Joe Bate.
Tries: Bloomfield (3, 16), Walker (9), Hudson (56), Baker (68, 71), Moore (79); **Goals:** Johnson 5/7.
Sin bin: Bloomfield (41) - dissent.
Rugby Leaguer & League Express Men of the Match: *Stags:* Jack Wray; *Crusaders:* Ryan Smith.
Penalty count: 9-10; **Half-time:** 18-16;
Referee: Liam Staveley; **Attendance:** 114.

OXFORD 22 SOUTH WALES IRONMEN 22

OXFORD: 1 James Cryer; 2 Jordan Gill; 3 Marcus Brooker; 4 Tommy Newbould; 5 Harrison Brough; 6 Bradley Moules; 7 Scott Fleming; 8 Lee Land; 9 Casey Canterbury; 10 Jonathan Payne; 11 Jordan Siddons; 12 Daniel Hindmarsh-Takji; 13 Harvey Burnett. Subs (all used): 14 Matt Davies; 15 Jake Joynt; 16 Stuart Biscomb; 17 Fran Welsh.
Tries: Brough (9), Newbould (29), Moules (32), Gill (71, 74);
Goals: Burnett 1/5.
Dismissal: Newbould (34) - punching.
Sin bin: Siddons (25) - high tackle; Welsh (65) - fighting.
IRONMEN: 1 Jack Uren; 2 Sam Hodge; 3 Morgan Jeffries; 4 Shaun Tennant; 5 Tom Parks; 6 Andrew Gay; 7 Ben Jones; 8 Morgan Evans; 9 Connor Farrer; 10 Connor Parker; 11 Christiaan Roets; 12 Kade Breen; 13 Archie Snook. Subs (all used): 14 Barrie Phillips; 15 Macauley Harris; 16 Jamie I'Anson; 17 Henry Davies.
Tries: Breen (15), Tennant (21), C Parker (68);
Goals: B Jones 5/5.
Sin bin: Farrer (65) - fighting.
Rugby Leaguer & League Express Men of the Match: *Oxford:* Casey Canterbury; *Ironmen:* Ben Jones.
Penalty count: 8-7; **Half-time:** 14-12;
Referee: Matt Rossleigh; **Attendance:** 65.

COVENTRY BEARS 14 LONDON SKOLARS 50

BEARS: 1 Mikey Russell; 2 Hayden Freeman; 3 Jason Bass; 4 Matt Reid; 5 Jamahl Hunte; 6 Paul Emanuelli; 7 Brad Delaney; 8 Brad Brennan; 9 Billy Gaylor; 10 Paddy Jones; 11 Kieran Sherratt; 12 Chris Barratt; 13 Zak Williams. Subs (all used): 14 James Kelly; 15 Jack Morrison; 16 Alex Beddows; 17 James Geurtjens.
Tries: Sherratt (4), Russell (23), Bass (55);
Goals: Delaney 1/3.
Sin bin: Barratt (17) - high tackle on Lyon.
SKOLARS: 7 Mike Bishay; 27 Jake Ogden; 31 Josh Allison; 4 Lameck Juma; 24 Michael Brown; 29 Jermaine Coleman; 6 Jy-mel Coleman; 25 Michael Sykes; 9 Charlie Lawrence; 11 Lamont Bryan; 10 Dave Williams; 12 Eddie Mbaraga; 23 Will Martin. Subs (all used): 26 Phil Lyon; 15 Kazeem Faturoti; 8 Louis Robinson; 18 Mike Greenhalgh.
Tries: Sykes (18), Bishay (23, 69), D Williams (38), Robinson (47), Mbaraga (50), Jermaine Coleman (57), Allison (65), Faturoti (78); **Goals:** Jy-mel Coleman 7/9.
Rugby Leaguer & League Express Men of the Match: *Bears:* Brad Delaney; *Skolars:* Mike Bishay.
Penalty count: 12-6; **Half-time:** 10-18;
Referee: Steve Race; **Attendance:** 268.

ROUND 2

Friday 25th August 2017

LONDON SKOLARS 32 SOUTH WALES IRONMEN 4

SKOLARS: 7 Mike Bishay; 28 Smokie Junor; 31 Josh Allison; 24 Michael Brown; 27 Jake Ogden; 29 Jermaine Coleman; 6 Jy-mel Coleman; 25 Michael Sykes; 26 Phil Lyon; 11 Lamont Bryan; 10 Dave Williams; 12 Eddie Mbaraga; 13 Ryan Chester. Subs (all used): 8 Louis Robinson; 15 Kazeem Faturoti; 18 Mike Greenhalgh; 9 Alfie Lawrence.
Tries: Ogden (7, 50), Robinson (33), Chester (40), Sykes (65), Allison (70);
Goals: Jy-mel Coleman 2/4, A Lawrence 2/2.
IRONMEN: 1 Jack Uren; 2 Liam Curnow; 3 Morgan Jeffries; 4 Ben Jones; 5 Sam Hodge; 6 Fraser Stroud; 7 Cobi Green; 8 Morgan Evans; 9 Andrew Gay; 10 Jamie I'Anson; 11 Craig Lewis; 12 Kade Breen; 13 Archie Snook. Subs (all used): 14 Macauley Harris; 15 Barrie Phillips; 16 Dewi Billingham; 17 Henry Davies.
Try: Breen (57); **Goals:** B Jones 0/1.
Rugby Leaguer & League Express Men of the Match: *Skolars:* Ryan Chester; *Ironmen:* Sam Hodge.
Penalty count: 8-7; **Half-time:** 16-0;
Referee: Nick Bennett; **Attendance:** 1,020.

ROUND 5

Sunday 3rd September 2017

NORTH WALES CRUSADERS 16 COVENTRY BEARS 22

CRUSADERS: 1 Tommy Johnson; 19 Dan Price; 3 Simon Atherton; 17 Kenny Baker; 5 Dale Bloomfield; 6 Andy Moulsdale; 7 Ryan Smith; 10 Alex Davidson; 9 Lee Hudson; 32 Warren Thompson; 24 Jack Houghton; 14 James Dandy; 13 Ryan Millington. Subs (all used): 27 Aaron Moore; 22 Joe Bate; 8 Jonny Walker; 16 Luke Warburton.
Tries: Millington (28), Moore (44), Johnson (49);
Goals: Johnson 2/3.
BEARS: 1 Mikey Russell; 2 Hayden Freeman; 3 Jason Bass; 4 Matt Reid; 5 Jamahl Hunte; 6 Paul Emanuelli; 7 Brad Delaney; 8 Brad Brennan; 9 Billy Gaylor; 10 Alex Beddows; 11 Kieran Sherratt; 12 Zak Williams; 13 Paddy Jones. Subs (all used): 14 James Geurtjens; 15 Jack Morrison; 16 Sam Davies; 17 Jacob Jones.
Tries: Hunte (16), Freeman (21), Delaney (38), S Davies (55);
Goals: Delaney 1/2, Emanuelli 2/2.
Rugby Leaguer & League Express Men of the Match: *Crusaders:* Aaron Moore; *Bears:* Brad Delaney.
Penalty count: 7-7; **Half-time:** 6-16;
Referee: Greg Dolan; **Attendance:** 245.

GLOUCESTERSHIRE ALL GOLDS 12 OXFORD 18

ALL GOLDS: 1 Alex Gaskell; 2 Mo Agoro; 3 Phil Cowburn; 4 Lewis Reece; 5 Chris Barlow; 6 Danny Fallon; 7 Ben Stead; 8 Harry Kidd; 9 Steve Parry; 10 Malikhi Lloyd-Jones; 11 Chris Worrall; 12 Harrison Elliott; 13 Billy Brickhill. Subs (all used): 14 James Mason; 15 Ross Price; 16 Richard Jones; 17 Joe McClean.
Tries: Cowburn (46), Kidd (65); **Goals:** Stead 2/2.
On report: McClean (75) - alleged gouging.
OXFORD: 1 Jordan Gill; 2 James Cryer; 3 Marcus Brooker; 4 Harvey Burnett; 5 Harrison Brough; 6 Callum Windley; 7 Casey Canterbury; 8 Jonathan Payne; 9 Sam Druce; 10 Stuart Biscomb; 11 Daniel Hindmarsh-Takji; 12 Matt Davies; 13 Kieran Hyde. Subs: 14 Jack Harbridge (not used); 15 Jake Joynt; 16 Tommy Chipchase; 17 Bradley Moules.
Tries: Gill (23), Davies (59), Canterbury (63);
Goals: Druce 1/1, Hyde 2/2.
Rugby Leaguer & League Express Men of the Match: *All Golds:* Harry Kidd; *Oxford:* Kieran Hyde.
Penalty count: 7-6; **Half-time:** 0-6;
Referee: Matt Rossleigh; **Attendance:** 202.

HUNSLET 64 SOUTH WALES IRONMEN 7

HUNSLET: 1 Jimmy Watson; 39 James Duckworth; 4 Mufaro Mvududu; 24 Cameron Leeming; 3 Marcus Webb; 18 Joel Gibson; 6 Joe Sanderson; 35 Matt Nicholson; 14 George Flanagan; 10 Lewis Reed; 13 Liam Mackay; 16 Daniel Williams; 17 Nyle Flynn. Subs (all used): 8 Michael Haley; 21 Jack Walton; 40 Dean Roberts; 23 Jose Kenga.
Tries: Flynn (3), Mvududu (13, 79), Reed (17), Flanagan (21, 61, 65), Gibson (24, 44), Duckworth (39), Webb (52); **Goals:** Sanderson 10/11.
IRONMEN: 1 Jack Uren; 2 Liam Curnow; 3 Shaun Tennant; 4 Ben Jones; 5 Sam Hodge; 6 Fraser Stroud; 7 Cobi Green; 8 Morgan Evans; 9 Andrew Gay; 10 Barrie Phillips; 11 Morgan Jeffries; 12 Kade Breen; 13 Archie Snook. Subs (all used): 14 Macauley Harris; 15 Jamie I'Anson; 16 Henry Davies; 17 Dewi Billingham.
Try: H Davies (58); **Goals:** B Jones 1/1; **Field goal:** Gay (63).
Rugby Leaguer & League Express Men of the Match: *Hunslet:* George Flanagan; *Ironmen:* Henry Davies.
Penalty count: 8-5; **Half-time:** 36-0;
Referee: Jon Roberts; **Attendance:** 418.

LONDON SKOLARS 42 HEMEL STAGS 22

SKOLARS: 7 Mike Bishay; 27 Smokie Junor; 24 Michael Brown; 4 Lameck Juma; 28 Jake Ogden; 6 Jy-mel Coleman; 26 Phil Lyon; 25 Michael Sykes; 9 Charlie Lawrence; 30 Ollie Purslow; 10 Dave Williams; 31 Josh Allison; 13 Ryan Chester. Subs (all used): - Ben Pointer; 8 Louis Robinson; 18 Mike Greenhalgh; 12 Eddie Mbaraga.
Tries: Allison (8), Chester (20), Pointer (30), Junor (40), Ogden (44), D Williams (49), Brown (52), Bishay (76);
Goals: Jy-mel Coleman 5/8.
STAGS: 1 Matt Welham; 2 Marcus Elliott; 3 Josh Casey; 4 Danny Lawton; 5 Alex Williams; 6 Jack Wray; 7 Lewis Fairhurst; 8 Dan Hawksworth; 9 Mark Barlow; 10 Reece Williams; 11 James Thornton; 12 Jack O'Brien; 13 Corey Hanson. Subs (all used): 14 Munashe Fumhandha; 15 Danny Samuel; 16 Wayne Jowitt; 17 Sam Crowther.
Tries: Barlow (4), Welham (13), Elliott (57), Thornton (61), A Williams (70); **Goals:** Fairhurst 1/5.
Rugby Leaguer & League Express Men of the Match: *Skolars:* Mike Bishay; *Stags:* Marcus Elliott.
Penalty count: 10-10; **Half-time:** 24-8;
Referee: Tom Crashley; **Attendance:** 191.

ROUND 6

Saturday 9th September 2017

OXFORD 28 COVENTRY BEARS 24

OXFORD: 1 Kieran Hyde; 2 Harrison Brough; 3 Harvey Burnett; 4 Marcus Brooker; 5 Jordan Gill; 6 Callum Windley; 7 Matt Davies; 8 Mark Hayes; 9 Sam Druce; 10 Jonathan Payne; 11 Jake Joynt; 12 Daniel Hindmarsh-Takji; 13 Casey Canterbury. Subs (all used): 14 Bradley Moules; 15 Tommy Chipchase; 16 Jack Harbridge; 17 Fran Welsh.
Tries: Gill (2, 18, 26, 39), Burnett (34), Canterbury (52);
Goals: Druce 1/3, Hyde 1/3.
BEARS: 1 Mikey Russell; 2 Hayden Freeman; 3 Jason Bass; 4 Matt Reid; 5 Jamahl Hunte; 6 Paul Emanuelli; 7 Brad Delaney; 8 Alex Beddows; 9 Billy Gaylor; 10 Jack Morrison; 11 Jacob Jones; 12 Chris Barratt; 13 Kieran Sherratt. Subs (all used): 14 James Kelly; 15 James Geurtjens; 16 Owen Jones; 17 Paddy Jones.
Tries: Freeman (8, 41), Hunte (13), Reid (43), Delaney (76);
Goals: Emanuelli 1/3, Delaney 1/2.
Rugby Leaguer & League Express Men of the Match: *Oxford:* Jordan Gill; *Bears:* Matt Reid.
Penalty count: 5-6; **Half-time:** 24-8;
Referee: Steve Race; **Attendance:** 110.

LONDON SKOLARS 16 GLOUCESTERSHIRE ALL GOLDS 6

SKOLARS: 7 Mike Bishay; 27 Smokie Junor; 4 Lameck Juma; 24 Michael Brown; 28 Jake Ogden; 6 Jy-mel Coleman; 9 Charlie Lawrence; 29 Rob Butler; 26 Ben Pointer; 11 Lamont Bryan; 10 Dave Williams; 12 Eddie Mbaraga; 13 Ryan Chester. Subs (all used): - Phil Lyon; 8 Louis Robinson; 18 Mike Greenhalgh; 15 Kazeem Faturoti.
Tries: Bishay (22), Junor (43); **Goals:** Jy-mel Coleman 4/4.
All GOLDS: 1 Alex Gaskell; 2 Mo Agoro; 3 Phil Cowburn; 4 Brad Kislingbury; 5 Chris Barlow; 6 Jack Mitchell; 7 Ben Stead; 8 Malikhi Lloyd-Jones; 9 Luke Stephens; 10 Harrison Elliott; 11 Kadeem Williams; 12 Billy Brickhill; 13 Danny Fallon. Subs (all used): 14 Steve Parry; 15 James Mason; 16 Joe McClean; 17 Harry Kidd.
Try: Kislingbury (70); **Goals:** Stead 1/1.
Rugby Leaguer & League Express Men of the Match: *Skolars:* Mike Bishay; *All Golds:* Brad Kislingbury.
Penalty count: 8-7; **Half-time:** 6-0;
Referee: Brandon Robinson; **Attendance:** 218.

SOUTH WALES IRONMEN 6 NORTH WALES CRUSADERS 54

IRONMEN: 1 Jack Uren; 2 Sam Hodge; 3 Morgan Jeffries; 4 Yannic Parker; 5 Curtis Ford; 6 Andrew Gay; 7 Fraser Stroud; 8 Morgan Evans; 9 Connor Farrer; 10 Shaun Tennant; 11 Kade Breen; 12 Christiaan Roets; 13 Connor Parker. Subs (all used): 14 Archie Snook; 15 Barrie Phillips; 16 Jamie I'Anson; 17 Cobi Green.
Try: Green (77); **Goals:** Stroud 1/1.
Sin bin: Tennant (17) - persistent team offences; Evans (23) - high tackle.
CRUSADERS: 1 Tommy Johnson; - Dave Eccleston; 16 Luke Warburton; 4 Earl Hurst; 5 Dale Bloomfield; 6 Andy Moulsdale; 7 Ryan Smith; 32 Warren Thompson; 9 Lee Hudson; 10 Alex Davidson; 3 Simon Atherton; 24 Jack Houghton; 13 Ryan Millington. Subs (all used): 8 Jonny Walker; 17 Kenny Baker; 22 Joe Bate; 27 Aaron Moore.

Hunslet's Mufaro Mvududu takes on the London Skolars defence during the League 1 Shield Final

Tries: Hudson (2), Millington (7), Smith (18, 38, 63), Hudson (24), Davidson (27), Johnson (34, 72), W Thompson (80); **Goals:** Johnson 7/10.
Sin bin: Atherton (55) - persistent team offences.
Rugby Leaguer & League Express Men of the Match:
Ironmen: Cobi Green; Crusaders: Tommy Johnson.
Penalty count: 9-13; **Half-time:** 0-40;
Referee: Michael Mannifield; **Attendance:** 289
(at Stebonheath Park, Llanelli).

Sunday 10th September 2017

HEMEL STAGS 16 HUNSLET 60

STAGS: 1 Mitch Vincent; 2 Marcus Elliott; 3 Connor Bower; 4 Josh Casey; 5 Matt Welham; 6 Jack Wray; 7 Lewis Fairhurst; 8 Dan Hawksworth; 9 Mark Barlow; 10 Reece Williams; 11 James Thornton; 12 Jack O'Brien; 13 Danny Samuel. Subs (all used): 14 Sam Crowther; 15 Wayne Jowitt; 16 Brett Whitehead; 17 Corey Hanson.
Tries: Barlow (42, 48), Welham (74); **Goals:** Vincent 2/3.
HUNSLET: 1 Jimmy Watson; 32 Josh Nathaniel; 4 Mufaro Mvududu; 24 Cameron Leeming; 3 Marcus Webb; 18 Joel Gibson; 6 Joe Sanderson; 35 Matt Nicholson; 14 George Flanagan; 10 Lewis Reed; 13 Liam Mackay; 16 Daniel Williams; 17 Nyle Flynn. Subs (all used): 40 Dean Roberts; 33 Shaun Roberts; 15 Jack Coventry; 21 Jack Walton.
Tries: Reed (6), Leeming (8), Mackay (20, 39), Mvududu (23, 51), Walton (33), Nathaniel (46), Coventry (58); **Goals:** Sanderson 10/10.
Rugby Leaguer & League Express Men of the Match:
Stags: Mark Barlow; Hunslet: Jimmy Watson.
Penalty count: 6-9; **Half-time:** 0-36;
Referee: Andrew Sweet; **Attendance:** 135.

ROUND 7

Saturday 16th September 2017

COVENTRY BEARS 58 SOUTH WALES IRONMEN 16

BEARS: 1 Mikey Russell; 2 Hayden Freeman; 3 Jason Bass; 4 Matt Reid; 5 Jamahl Hunte; 6 Paul Emanuelli; 7 Brad Delaney; 8 Alex Beddows; 9 Billy Gaylor; 10 Brad Brennan; 11 Kieran Sherratt; 12 Chris Barratt; 13 Zak Williams. Subs (all used): 14 James Kelly; 15 Jack Morrison; 16 Jacob Jones; 17 Paddy Jones.
Tries: Brennan (2, 5), Hunte (8, 36, 42), Freeman (18), Delaney (24), Reid (27), Emanuelli (39), Russell (73), Barratt (76); **Goals:** Emanuelli 7/11.
IRONMEN: 1 Jack Uren; 2 Yannic Parker; 3 Morgan Jeffries; 4 Shaun Tennant; 5 Liam Curnow; 6 Andrew Gay; 7 Ben Jones; 8 Morgan Evans; 9 Connor Farrer; 10 Barrie Phillips; 11 Christiaan Roets; 12 Kade Breen; 13 Connor Parker. Subs

(all used): 14 Archie Snook; 15 Jamie I'Anson; 16 Sam Hodge; 17 Henry Davies.
Tries: Farrer (13), Uren (57), Roets (70); **Goals:** B Jones 2/3.
Rugby Leaguer & League Express Men of the Match:
Bears: Jamahl Hunte; Ironmen: Ben Jones.
Penalty count: 11-8; **Half-time:** 42-6;
Referee: Cameron Worsley; **Attendance:** 332.

Sunday 17th September 2017

NORTH WALES CRUSADERS 28 OXFORD 14

CRUSADERS: 1 Tommy Johnson; 19 Dan Price; 16 Luke Warburton; 4 Earl Hurst; 5 Dale Bloomfield; 6 Andy Moulsdale; 7 Ryan Smith; 10 Alex Davidson; 9 Lee Hudson; 32 Warren Thompson; 24 Jack Houghton; 3 Simon Atherton; 13 Ryan Millington. Subs (all used): 27 Aaron Moore; 22 Joe Bate; 8 Jonny Walker; 14 James Dandy.
Tries: Hurst (30), Dandy (43, 67), Bloomfield (51), Davidson (79); **Goals:** Johnson 4/5.
OXFORD: 1 Kieran Hyde; 2 Harrison Brough; 3 Marcus Brooker; 4 James Cryer; 5 Jordan Gill; 6 Callum Windley; 7 Matt Davies; 8 Jonathan Payne; 9 Sam Druce; 10 Stuart Biscomb; 11 Daniel Hindmarsh-Takji; 12 Harvey Burnett; 13 Casey Canterbury. Subs (all used): 14 Bradley Moules; 15 Jake Joynt; 16 Fran Welsh; 17 Tommy Chipchase.
Tries: Davies (5), Gill (37), Cryer (74);
Goals: Druce 0/1, Hyde 1/2.
Sin bin: Cryer (63) - dissent.
Rugby Leaguer & League Express Men of the Match:
Crusaders: Aaron Moore; Oxford: Matt Davies.
Penalty count: 7-9; **Half-time:** 6-10;
Referee: Jon Roberts; **Attendance:** 303.

GLOUCESTERSHIRE ALL GOLDS 42 HEMEL STAGS 28

ALL GOLDS: 1 Alex Gaskell; 2 Mo Agoro; 3 Phil Cowburn; 4 Brad Kislingbury; 5 Chris Barlow; 6 Jack Mitchell; 7 Ben Stead; 8 Harrison Elliott; 9 Steve Parry; 10 Harry Kidd; 11 Billy Brickhill; 12 Danny Fallon; 13 Joe McClean. Subs (all used): 14 Luke Stephens; 15 Errol Carter; 16 Kadeem Williams; 17 Malikhi Lloyd-Jones.
Tries: Elliott (5), Stead (8, 13), Barlow (38), Cowburn (42), McClean (64), Parry (79); **Goals:** Stead 7/7.
STAGS: 1 Matt Welham; 2 Connor Bower; 3 Alex Williams; 4 Danny Lawton; 5 Darren Forde; 6 Lewis Fairhurst; 7 Jack Wray; 8 Dan Hawksworth; 9 Mark Barlow; 10 Reece Williams; 11 Jack O'Brien; 12 James Thornton; 13 Brett Whitehead. Subs (all used): 14 Scott Lee; 15 Sam Crowther; 16 Danny Samuel; 17 Wayne Jowitt.
Tries: Fairhurst (23, 46), O'Brien (26), Welham (32), Hawksworth (76); **Goals:** Fairhurst 0/1, Wray 4/4.
Rugby Leaguer & League Express Men of the Match:
All Golds: Ben Stead; Stags: Matt Welham.

Penalty count: 11-6; **Half-time:** 24-16;
Referee: Brandon Robinson; **Attendance:** 305.

HUNSLET 18 LONDON SKOLARS 12

HUNSLET: 1 Jimmy Watson; 39 James Duckworth; 4 Mufaro Mvududu; 24 Cameron Leeming; 3 Marcus Webb; 18 Joel Gibson; 6 Joe Sanderson; 35 Matt Nicholson; 14 George Flanagan; 10 Lewis Reed; 13 Liam Mackay; 16 Daniel Williams; 17 Nyle Flynn. Subs (all used): 8 Michael Haley; 21 Jack Walton; - Dean Roberts; 15 Jack Coventry.
Tries: Webb (29), Sanderson (38), Flanagan (61);
Goals: Sanderson 3/6.
Sin bin:
Flanagan (34) - late challenge on Jermaine Coleman.
SKOLARS: 7 Mike Bishay; 28 Jake Ogden; 4 Lameck Juma; 24 Michael Brown; 27 Smokie Junor; 29 Jermaine Coleman; 6 Jy-mel Coleman; - Rob Butler; 9 Charlie Lawrence; 11 Lamont Bryan; 10 Dave Williams; 12 Eddie Mbaraga; 13 Ryan Chester. Subs (all used): 8 Louis Robinson; 18 Mike Greenhalgh; - Phil Lyon; 31 Josh Allison.
Tries: Mbaraga (18), Ogden (52);
Goals: Jy-mel Coleman 2/3.
Rugby Leaguer & League Express Men of the Match:
Hunslet: George Flanagan; Skolars: Jy-mel Coleman.
Penalty count: 11-5; **Half-time:** 8-8;
Referee: Tom Grant; **Attendance:** 450.

FINAL

Sunday 24th September 2017

HUNSLET 32 LONDON SKOLARS 12

HUNSLET: 1 Jimmy Watson; 39 James Duckworth; 4 Mufaro Mvududu; 24 Cameron Leeming; 3 Marcus Webb; 18 Joel Gibson; 6 Joe Sanderson; 8 Michael Haley; 14 George Flanagan; 10 Lewis Reed; 13 Liam Mackay; 16 Daniel Williams; 21 Jack Walton. Subs (all used): 7 Danny Ansell; 23 Jose Kenga; - Dean Roberts; 15 Jack Coventry.
Tries: Mackay (11, 42), Flanagan (27), Duckworth (39, 79); **Goals:** Sanderson 6/7.
Sin bin: Reed (68) - late challenge.
SKOLARS: 7 Mike Bishay; 27 Smokie Junor; 31 Josh Allison; 4 Lameck Juma; 24 Michael Brown; 29 Jermaine Coleman; 6 Jy-mel Coleman; 25 Michael Sykes; 9 Charlie Lawrence; 11 Lamont Bryan; 10 Dave Williams; 12 Eddie Mbaraga; - Rob Butler. Subs: 8 Louis Robinson; 18 Mike Greenhalgh; - Phil Lyon; 13 Ryan Chester.
Tries: Bryan (15), Brown (36); **Goals:** Jy-mel Coleman 2/2.
Rugby Leaguer & League Express Men of the Match:
Hunslet: Liam Mackay; Skolars: Jy-mel Coleman.
Penalty count: 9-5; **Half-time:** 18-12;
Referee: Nick Bennett; **Attendance:** 516.

LEAGUE 1 CUP 2017
Round by Round

Saturday 18th February 2017

ROCHDALE MAYFIELD 18 BARROW RAIDERS 46

MAYFIELD: 1 Lewis Sheridan; 2 Kieran Harmer; 3 Matthew Ashton; 4 Matthew Chrimes; 5 Ben Namulnatua; 6 Paul Brearley; 7 Zak Hartley; 8 James Shaw; 9 Callum Ogden; 10 Simon Moore; 11 Sean Watkins; 12 Callum Marriott; 13 Seta Tala. Subs (all used): 14 Declan Sheridan; 15 Cameron Connolly; 16 Nic Hargreaves; 17 Jimmy Connaughton.
Tries: Hartley (38, 65), L Sheridan (57); **Goals:** Hartley 3/3.
Sin bin: Watkins (45) - late challenge; Moore (46) - high tackle.
RAIDERS: 1 Ryan Fieldhouse; 5 Shane Toal; 20 Andy Litherland; 3 Declan Hulme; 24 Luke Cresswell; 6 Jamie Dallimore; 7 Lewis Charnock; 8 Joe Bullock; 9 Nathan Mossop; 10 Oliver Wilkes; 18 Danny Morrow; 12 Jarrad Stack; 13 Martin Aspinwall. Subs (all used): 14 Dan Abram; 21 James Duerden; 22 Bradd Crellin; 28 Brad Brennan.
Tries: Charnock (6), Wilkes (10), Cresswell (19), S Toal (26), Dallimore (28, 49, 62), Hulme (71);
Goals: Charnock 6/7, Dallimore 1/1.
Rugby Leaguer & League Express Men of the Match:
Mayfield: Lewis Sheridan; *Raiders:* Oliver Wilkes.
Penalty count: 8-12; **Half-time:** 6-30;
Referee: Tom Crashley; **Attendance:** 300.

OXFORD 30 COVENTRY BEARS 28

OXFORD: 1 Kane Riley; 2 Andrew Hoggins; 3 Harvey Burnett; 4 Josh Atkinson; 5 Curtis McDonald; 6 Callum Windley; 7 Scott Fleming; 8 Jake Joynt; 9 Casey Canterbury; 10 Stuart Biscomb; 11 Will Cooke; 12 Marcus Brooker; 13 Jack Pickles. Subs (all used): 14 Bradley Moules; 15 Mark Hayes; 16 Liam O'Callaghan; 17 Anthony Cox.
Tries: Atkinson (4, 67), Windley (25), Riley (45), Joynt (53), Fleming (57); **Goals:** Cooke 1/3, Fleming 2/3.
BEARS: 1 Will Roper; 2 Charlie O'Mara; 3 Eddie Medforth; 4 Callan Beckett; 5 Hayden Freeman; 6 Joe Prior; 7 Joel James; 8 Alex Beddows; 9 Billy Gaylor; 10 Elliott Davies; 11 Matt Reid; 12 Chris Barratt; 13 Zach Johnson. Subs (all used): 14 Mikey Russell; 15 Jack Morrison; 16 John Aldred; 17 Kieran Sherratt.
Tries: Morrison (33), Freeman (62), Reid (73, 77, 80);
Goals: Roper 4/5.
Rugby Leaguer & League Express Men of the Match:
Oxford: Jake Joynt; *Bears:* Matt Reid.
Penalty count: 8-12; **Half-time:** 10-6;
Referee: Greg Dolan; **Attendance:** 121.

Sunday 19th February 2017

HEMEL STAGS 12 GLOUCESTERSHIRE ALL GOLDS 48

STAGS: 1 Mitch Vincent; 2 Darren Forde; 3 Declan Tomlinson; 4 Roddy Jonas; 5 Marcus Elliott; 6 Mark Barlow; 7 Liam Coe; 8 Reece Williams; 9 Jono Burns; 10 Wayne Jowitt; 11 Ross White; 12 James Thornton; 13 Jack O'Brien. Subs (all used): 14 Scott Lee; 15 Aaron James; 16 Danny Samuel; 17 Dom Horn.
Tries: Burns (20), Jonas (80); **Goals:** Coe 2/3.
ALL GOLDS: 1 Alex Gaskell; 2 Mo Agoro; 3 Phil Cowburn; 4 Brad Kislingbury; 5 Chris Barlow; 6 Ben Stead; 7 Kieran Hyde; 8 Ollie Purslow; 9 Steve Parry; 10 James Walter; 11 Chris Worrall; 12 Joe McClean; 13 Harrison Elliott. Subs (all used): 14 Josh Houghton; 15 Kadeem Williams; 16 Malikhi Lloyd-Jones; 17 Harry Kidd.
Tries: Elliott (30), Kislingbury (35, 75), Gaskell (46), Parry (50, 63), Williams (52), Agoro (61), McClean (70);
Goals: Hyde 5/7, Stead 1/2.
Rugby Leaguer & League Express Men of the Match:
Stags: Mitch Vincent; *All Golds:* Steve Parry.
Penalty count: 10-4; **Half-time:** 8-10;
Referee: Matt Rossleigh; **Attendance:** 107.

WHITEHAVEN 6 WORKINGTON TOWN 22

WHITEHAVEN: 5 Jordan Burns; 4 Jessie Joe Parker; 21 Jake Moore; 3 Chris Taylor; 26 Shane Pattinson; 7 Paul Crook; 6 Steve Roper; 8 Marc Shackley; 9 James Newton; 17 Tommy Holland; 12 Scott McAvoy; 14 James Tilley; 10 Carl Forster. Subs (all used): 18 Tyrone Dalton; 19 Glenn Riley; 25 Aiden Worthington; 22 Kurt Maudling.
Try: Holland (74); **Goals:** Crook 1/1.
TOWN: 1 Theerapol Ritson; 2 Joe Hambley; 3 Ed Chamberlain; 21 Macauley Davies; 20 Kieran Mewse; 6 Carl Forber; 13 Stuart Howarth; 16 Tom Curwen; 9 Callum Phillips; 10 Stevie Scholey; 11 Brett Phillips; 23 Phil Joseph; 15 Perry Singleton. Subs (all used): 7 Jamie Doran; 14 Sam Dowsett; 8 Kris Coward; 22 Kyle Shelford.
Tries: Forber (25, 78), Ritson (28), Hambley (61);
Goals: Forber 0/2, Mewse 3/3.
Rugby Leaguer & League Express Men of the Match:
Whitehaven: Glenn Riley; *Town:* Phil Joseph.

Penalty count: 14-10; Half-time: 0-8;
Referee: Callum Straw; Attendance: 908.

SOUTH WALES IRONMEN 16 LONDON SKOLARS 24

IRONMEN: 6 Andrew Gay; 26 Lewis Hughes; 3 Paul Edwards; 4 Christiaan Roets; 22 Ben Jones; 5 Paul Emanuelli; 7 Courtney Davies; 19 Jamie I'Anson; 9 Connor Farrer; 23 Ethan Coombes; 24 Connor Parker; 17 Zak Williams; 16 Ashley Bateman. Subs (all used): 13 Chris Vitalini; 30 Michael Edwards; 29 Huw Parkes; 14 Kristian Baller.
Tries: Courtney Davies (20), Farrer (71), B Jones (78);
Goals: Courtney Davies 2/3.
SKOLARS: 20 Jake Melling; 2 Sam Nash; 26 Josh I'Anson; 4 Lameck Juma; 1 Andy Winfield; 7 Mike Bishay; 9 Charlie Lawrence; 25 Michael Sykes; 14 Billy Driver; 10 Dave Williams; 11 Lamont Bryan; 12 Eddie Mbaraga; 13 Ryan Chester. Subs (all used): 8 Louis Robinson; 30 Callum Bustin; 29 Sadiq Adebiyi; 28 Jermaine Coleman.
Tries: Mbaraga (5), Juma (11), Robinson (26), Nash (59);
Goals: C Lawrence 4/5.
Rugby Leaguer & League Express Men of the Match:
Ironmen: Connor Farrer; Skolars: Louis Robinson.
Penalty count: 8-11; Half-time: 6-20;
Referee: Liam Moore; Attendance: 122.

HUNSLET 10 NEWCASTLE THUNDER 34

HUNSLET: 20 Danny Thomas; 30 Ryan Ince; - Jack Norfolk; 4 Mufaro Mvududu; 5 Gavin Duffy; 6 Joe Sanderson; 7 Danny Ansell; 8 Michael Haley; 14 George Flanagan; 19 Matt Carbutt; 12 Aston Wilson; 11 Jake Normington; 13 Liam Mackay. Subs (all used): 25 Matthew Tebb; 26 Austin Bell; 15 Jack Coventry; 17 Nyle Flynn.
Tries: Normington (12), Mvududu (40);
Goals: Ansell 1/1, Sanderson 0/1.
Dismissal: Duffy (37) - punching.
THUNDER: 1 Lewis Young; 2 Tyler Craig; 3 Joe Brown; 4 Derrell Olpherts; 5 Ali Blair; 6 Danny Nicklas; 7 Benn Hardcastle; 8 Brett Waller; 9 Evan Simons; 10 Corbyn Kilday; 11 Harry Aldous; 12 Rhys Clarke; 13 Jack Aldous. Subs (all used): 14 Aaron Teroi; 15 Vincent Rennie; 16 Sam Luckley; 17 Lee Paterson.
Tries: Blair (8), Craig (19), Olpherts (23), R Clarke (37), Young (46), Rennie (72), Simons (79);
Goals: Hardcastle 3/7.
Rugby Leaguer & League Express Men of the Match:
Hunslet: George Flanagan; Thunder: Derrell Olpherts.
Penalty count: 7-8; Half-time: 10-18;
Referee: Brandon Robinson; Attendance: 449.

KEIGHLEY COUGARS 30 DONCASTER 22

COUGARS: 22 Ritchie Hawkyard; 5 Davey Dixon; 4 Danny Lawton; 32 Adam Ryder; 2 Andy Gabriel; 16 Will Milner; 7 Matty Beharrell; 8 Scott Law; 9 James Feather; 12 Brendon Rawlins; 11 Josh Lynam; 18 Josh Tonks; 13 Mike Emmett. Subs (all used): 21 Emmerson Whittel; 23 Fran Welsh; 27 Sean Kelly; 29 Brad Nicholson.
Tries: Ryder (22), Gabriel (43, 60), Welsh (48), Kelly (50), Whittell (80); Goals: Beharrell 3/6.
DONCASTER: 22 Louis Sheriff; 5 Sam Doherty; 3 Liam Welham; 4 Jason Tali; 24 Richie Barnett; 6 Jordan Howden; 7 Jordie Hedges; 8 Mark Castle; 9 Kyle Kesik; 16 Russ Spiers; 34 Brad England; 13 Charlie Martin; 23 Jamie Thackray. Subs (all used): 10 Iafeta Palea'aesina; 14 Connor Scott; 19 Zac Braham; 20 Kieran Cross.
Tries: Welham (16), Cross (36), Martin (67), Palea'aesina (75); Goals: Howden 3/4.
Sin bin: Martin (21) - shoulder charge on Milner; Hedges (42) - dangerous challenge.
Rugby Leaguer & League Express Men of the Match:
Cougars: Matty Beharrell; Doncaster: Zac Braham.
Penalty count: 12-12; Half-time: 4-12;
Referee: John McMullen; Attendance: 520.

YORK CITY KNIGHTS 16 NORTH WALES CRUSADERS 17

(after golden point extra-time)

CITY KNIGHTS: 1 Ash Robson; 4 Tommy Brierley; 19 James Haynes; 3 Nev Morrison; 2 David Foggin-Johnston; 6 Danny Sowerby; 7 Harry Tyson-Wilson; 8 Bobby Tyson-Wilson; 26 Will Jubb; 10 Chris Siddons; 12 Ed Smith; 17 Brad Hey; 13 Tim Spears. Subs (all used): 9 Pat Smith; 16 Ronan Dixon; 28 Kieran Moran; 20 Adam Robinson.
Tries: Morrison (32), P Smith (40), Robson (47);
Goals: H Tyson-Wilson 2/3.
Sin bin: Siddons (14) - holding down.
CRUSADERS: 1 Tommy Johnson; 19 Dan Price; 28 Callum Mulkeen; 4 Earl Hurst; 5 Dale Bloomfield; 26 Jack Hansen; 7 Ryan Smith; 17 Kenny Baker; 9 Lee Hudson; 10 Alex Davidson; 24 Jack Houghton; 14 James Dandy; 13 Ryan Millington. Subs (all used): 27 Aaron Moore; 15 John Cookson; 16 Luke Warburton; 22 Andrew Joy.
Tries: Bloomfield (27), Johnson (58), Price (79);
Goals: Johnson 2/3; Field goal: Hansen (82).

Rugby Leaguer & League Express Men of the Match:
City Knights: Brad Hey; Crusaders: Lee Hudson.
Penalty count: 9-7; Half-time: 12-4;
Referee: Nick Bennett; Attendance: 620.

QUARTER FINALS

Saturday 1st April 2017

GLOUCESTERSHIRE ALL GOLDS 30 WORKINGTON TOWN 22

ALL GOLDS: 1 Jack Mitchell; 2 Mo Agoro; 3 Kadeem Williams; 4 Phil Cowburn; 5 Chris Barlow; 6 Danny Fallon; 7 Kieran Hyde; 8 Harry Kidd; 9 Steve Parry; 10 James Walter; 11 Harrison Elliott; 12 Joe McClean; 13 Chris Worrall. Subs (all used): 14 Luke Stephens; 15 Graham O'Keeffe; 16 Ollie Purslow; 17 Malikhi Lloyd-Jones.
Tries: Cowburn (7, 78), Kidd (20), Parry (30), Barlow (67);
Goals: Hyde 5/5.
TOWN: 3 Ed Chamberlain; 24 Phil Lister; 22 Joe Hambley; 4 Jason Mossop; 5 John Patrick; 6 Carl Forber; 13 Stuart Howarth; 10 Stevie Scholey; 9 Callum Phillips; 16 Tom Curwen; 11 Brett Phillips; 21 Macauley Davies; 15 Perry Singleton. Subs (all used): 12 Alex Szostak; 8 Kris Coward; 18 Conor Fitzsimmons; 7 Jamie Doran.
Tries: B Phillips (26), Patrick (45), Hambley (49), Lister (55); Goals: Forber 3/4.
Rugby Leaguer & League Express Men of the Match:
All Golds: Kieran Hyde; Town: Stevie Scholey.
Penalty count: 3-5; Half-time: 18-6;
Referee: Matt Rossleigh; Attendance: 378
(at Derwent Park, Workington).

OXFORD 24 LONDON SKOLARS 20

OXFORD: 1 Max Jowitt; 2 Josh Atkinson; 3 Ashley Gibson; 4 Kane Riley; 5 Curtis McDonald; 6 Callum Windley; 7 Scott Fleming; 8 Anthony Cox; 9 Casey Canterbury; 10 Jack Pickles; 11 Harvey Burnett; 12 Tommy Newbould; 13 Jordan Crowther. Subs (all used): 14 Bradley Moules; 15 Marcus Brooker; 16 Dwaine McRae; 17 Jordan Gill.
Tries: McDonald (7), Atkinson (32, 47, 79), Gill (53);
Goals: Burnett 2/5.
Dismissal: McDonald (74) - dangerous challenge.
SKOLARS: 20 Jake Melling; 2 Sam Nash; 31 Josh Allison; 29 Kameron Pearce-Paul; 24 Michael Brown; 9 Charlie Lawrence; - Brandon Pickersgill; 28 Callum Bustin; 14 Billy Driver; 30 Simona Vavega; 11 Lamont Bryan; 12 Eddie Mbaraga; 13 Ryan Chester. Subs (all used): 8 Louis Robinson; 25 Michael Sykes; 27 Keenen Tomlinson; 26 Ben Pointer.
Tries: Allison (12), Mbaraga (19), Pointer (51), C Lawrence (74); Goals: C Lawrence 2/4.
Dismissal: Chester (70) - dangerous contact.
Rugby Leaguer & League Express Men of the Match:
Oxford: Josh Atkinson; Skolars: Ben Pointer.
Penalty count: 9-12; Half-time: 8-8;
Referee: Andrew Sweet; Attendance: 105.

Sunday 2nd April 2017

BARROW RAIDERS 28 KEIGHLEY COUGARS 6

RAIDERS: 1 Ryan Fieldhouse; 5 Shane Toal; 3 Declan Hulme; 20 Andy Litherland; 24 Luke Cresswell; 6 Jamie Dallimore; 7 Lewis Charnock; 8 Joe Bullock; 9 Nathan Mossop; 10 Oliver Wilkes; 12 Jarrad Stack; 22 Bradd Crellin; 13 Martin Aspinwall. Subs (all used): 14 Dan Abram; 16 Andrew Dawson; 17 Tom Walker; 11 Dan Toal.
Tries: Cresswell (2), Dallimore (6), Fieldhouse (40), Hulme (46), Litherland (78); Goals: Charnock 4/7.
Sin bin: D Toal (50) - late challenge.
COUGARS: 22 Ritchie Hawkyard; 26 Vinny Finigan; 5 Davey Dixon; 32 Adam Ryder; 2 Andy Gabriel; 16 Will Milner; 7 Matty Beharrell; 8 Scott Law; 9 James Feather; 23 Fran Welsh; 11 Josh Lynam; 18 Josh Tonks; 13 Mike Emmett. Subs (all used): 12 Brendon Rawlins; 14 Adam Brook; 19 Matthew Bailey; 29 Brad Nicholson.
Try: Brook (51); Goals: Beharrell 1/1.
Rugby Leaguer & League Express Men of the Match:
Raiders: Jarrad Stack; Cougars: Josh Lynam.
Penalty count: 12-9; Half-time: 16-0;
Referee: Nick Bennett; Attendance: 828.

NEWCASTLE THUNDER 16 NORTH WALES CRUSADERS 24

THUNDER: 1 Lewis Young; 2 Ali Blair; 3 Joe Brown; 4 Derrell Olpherts; 5 Peter Fox; 6 Danny Nicklas; 7 Benn Hardcastle; 8 Liam McAvoy; 9 Evan Simons; 10 Vincent Rennie; 11 Harry Aldous; 12 Rhys Clarke; 13 Jack Aldous. Subs (all used): 14 Aaron Teroi; 15 Matt Barron; 16 Corbyn Kilday; 17 Josh Stoker.
Tries: Olpherts (7, 38), Nicklas (55); Goals: Hardcastle 2/3.

CRUSADERS: 1 Tommy Johnson; 2 Corey Lee; 28 Callum Mulkeen; 4 Earl Hurst; 5 Dale Bloomfield; 26 Jack Hansen; 7 Ryan Smith; 17 Kenny Baker; 9 Lee Hudson; 15 John Cookson; 16 Luke Warburton; 24 Jack Houghton; 13 Ryan Millington. Subs (all used): 27 Aaron Moore; 10 Alex Davidson; 23 Jack Francis (not used).
Tries: Lee (22), Houghton (45, 52), Johnson (72);
Goals: Johnson 4/5.
Rugby Leaguer & League Express Men of the Match:
Thunder: Derrell Olpherts; Crusaders: Tommy Johnson.
Penalty count: 5-5; Half-time: 10-4;
Referee: John McMullen; Attendance: 345.

SEMI-FINALS

Sunday 30th April 2017

BARROW RAIDERS 64 OXFORD 14

RAIDERS: 1 Ryan Fieldhouse; 5 Shane Toal; 3 Declan Hulme; 20 Andy Litherland; 24 Luke Cresswell; 7 Lewis Charnock; 26 Brad Marwood; 8 Joe Bullock; 9 Nathan Mossop; 10 Oliver Wilkes; 11 Dan Toal; 12 Jarrad Stack; 13 Martin Aspinwall. Subs (all used): 14 Dan Abram; 28 Brad Brennan; 17 Tom Walker; 21 James Duerden.
Tries: Fieldhouse (3), S Toal (9, 31, 68), Brennan (38), Walker (45), Duerden (49), Abram (54), Charnock (62, 73), Bullock (65, 78); Goals: Charnock 8/12.
OXFORD: 1 Kane Riley; 2 Jordan Gill; 3 Curtis McDonald; 4 Marcus Brooker; 5 Tommy Newbould; 6 Callum Windley; 7 Scott Fleming; 8 Stuart Biscomb; 9 Casey Canterbury; 10 Dwaine McRae; 11 Harvey Burnett; 12 Will Cooke; 13 Anthony Cox. Subs (all used): 14 Bradley Moules; 15 Mark Hayes; 16 Aaron Nicholson; 17 Jordan Siddons.
Tries: Canterbury (7), Gill (24), Fleming (39);
Goals: Fleming 1/3.
Rugby Leaguer & League Express Men of the Match:
Raiders: Jarrad Stack; Oxford: Scott Fleming.
Penalty count: 12-6; Half-time: 20-14;
Referee: Liam Moore; Attendance: 962.

GLOUCESTERSHIRE ALL GOLDS 28 NORTH WALES CRUSADERS 37

ALL GOLDS: 1 Jack Mitchell; 2 Mo Agoro; 3 Phil Cowburn; 4 Brad Kislingbury; 5 Chris Barlow; 6 Josh Ward; 7 Kieran Hyde; 8 Harry Kidd; 9 Steve Parry; 10 Ollie Purslow; 11 Chris Worrall; 12 Joe McClean; 13 Billy Brickhill. Subs (all used): 14 Danny Fallon; 15 Graham O'Keeffe; 16 Harrison Elliott; 17 Malikhi Lloyd-Jones.
Tries: Kislingbury (8), Agoro (37), Parry (46), Barlow (60, 67), Kidd (77); Goals: Hyde 2/6.
CRUSADERS: 1 Tommy Johnson; 2 Corey Lee; 28 Callum Mulkeen; 16 Luke Warburton; 19 Dan Price; 26 Jack Hansen; 7 Ryan Smith; 8 Jonny Walker; 9 Lee Hudson; 10 Alex Davidson; 3 Simon Atherton; 24 Jack Houghton; 14 James Dandy. Subs: 27 Aaron Moore; 13 Ryan Millington; 25 Matt Davies; 6 Andy Moulsdale (not used).
Tries: Davidson (11), Price (22, 31), Warburton (28), Atherton (38), Johnson (43); Goals: Johnson 6/7;
Field goal: Smith (70).
Rugby Leaguer & League Express Men of the Match:
All Golds: Joe McClean; Crusaders: Tommy Johnson.
Penalty count: 8-10; Half-time: 10-30;
Referee: Jon Roberts; Attendance: 202.

FINAL

Saturday 27th May 2017

BARROW RAIDERS 38 NORTH WALES CRUSADERS 32

RAIDERS: 1 Ryan Fieldhouse; 5 Shane Toal; 3 Declan Hulme; 45 Tom Loxam; 24 Luke Cresswell; 6 Jamie Dallimore; 7 Lewis Charnock; 8 Joe Bullock; 9 Nathan Mossop; 10 Oliver Wilkes; 18 Danny Morrow; 11 Dan Toal; 13 Martin Aspinwall. Subs (all used): 14 Dan Abram; 17 Tom Walker; 21 James Duerden; 16 Andrew Dawson.
Tries: Mossop (2), Cresswell (30), Hulme (34), Morrow (39, 75), S Toal (64), Bullock (67);
Goals: Charnock 2/5, Dallimore 3/3.
CRUSADERS: 1 Tommy Johnson; 2 Corey Lee; 11 Alex Thompson; 28 Callum Mulkeen; 5 Dale Bloomfield; 26 Jack Hansen; 7 Ryan Smith; 8 Jonny Walker; 14 James Dandy; 10 Alex Davidson; 31 Blake Turner. Subs (all used): 27 Aaron Moore; 19 Dan Price; 24 Jack Houghton; 16 Luke Warburton.
Tries: Houghton (10), Bloomfield (21), Hansen (45), Mulkeen (54), Smith (56); Goals: Johnson 6/6.
Rugby Leaguer & League Express Men of the Match:
Raiders: Danny Morrow; Crusaders: Ryan Smith.
Penalty count: 9-9; Half-time: 20-12; Referee: Steve Race.
(at Bloomfield Road, Blackpool).

CHALLENGE CUP 2017
Round by Round

ROUND 3

Saturday 25th February 2017

SIDDAL 6 TORONTO WOLFPACK 14

SIDDAL: 1 Freddie Walker; 2 Gareth Blackburn; 3 Zack McComb; 4 Joe Martin; 5 Ben West; 6 Shaun Garrod; 7 Kyle Ackroyd; 8 Jack Georgiou; 9 Craig Sanderson; 10 George Ambler; 11 Tom Garratt; 12 Ben Hinsley; 13 Byron Smith. Subs (all used): 14 Sean McCormack; 15 Canaan Smithies; 16 Danny Williams; 17 Iain Davies.
Try: Blackburn (50); **Goals:** Blackburn 1/2.
WOLFPACK: 1 Quentin Laulu-Togagae; 2 Jonny Pownall; 3 Greg Worthington; 17 Richard Whiting; 15 Ryan Burroughs; 6 Blake Wallace; 7 Rhys Jacks; 29 Jake Emmitt; 9 Bob Beswick; 19 Steve Crossley; 11 Andrew Dixon; 12 James Laithwaite; 13 Jack Bussey. Subs (all used): 4 Craig Hall; 8 Fuifui Moimoi; 21 Adam Sidlow; 16 Shaun Pick.
Tries: Burroughs (36), Worthington (63), Sidlow (75);
Goals: Wallace 0/1, Hall 1/2.
Dismissal: Moimoi (77) - high tackle.
Rugby Leaguer & League Express Men of the Match:
Siddal: Craig Sanderson; *Wolfpack:* James Laithwaite.
Penalty count: 6-8; **Half-time:** 2-4;
Referee: Tom Grant; **Attendance:** 1,023.

WEST HULL 16 WHITEHAVEN 18

WEST HULL: 1 Craig Skelton; 2 Luke Foster; 3 Richard Squires; 4 Jordan Rowan; 5 Jamie Edwards; 6 Tommy Brett; 7 Ian Kerman; 8 Ryan Wilson; 9 Nathan Powley; 10 Scott Howlett; 11 Sam Cator; 12 Louis Crowther; 13 Ryan Steen. Subs (all used): 14 Elliott Windley; 15 Aaron Higginbotham; 16 Jon Eccles; 17 Richard Dougal.
Tries: Foster (10, 67), Wilson (30); **Goals:** Skelton 2/3.
WHITEHAVEN: 5 Jordan Burns; 16 Connor Holliday; 3 Chris Taylor; 4 Jessie Joe Parker; 26 Shane Pattinson; 18 Tyrone Dalton; 7 Paul Crook; 8 Marc Shackley; 9 James Newton; 17 Tommy Holland; 14 James Tilley; 12 Scott McAvoy; 10 Carl Forster. Subs (all used): 19 Glenn Riley; 22 Kurt Maudling; 24 Lewis Brown; 25 Aiden Worthington.
Tries: Burns (4), Dalton (21), Pattinson (44, 77);
Goals: Crook 1/4.
Rugby Leaguer & League Express Men of the Match:
West Hull: Ian Kerman; *Whitehaven:* James Newton.
Penalty count: 12-17; **Half-time:** 12-10;
Referee: Paul Marklove; **Attendance:** 150.

WESTS WARRIORS 12 HAYDOCK 26

WARRIORS: 1 Jarred Bassett; 2 David Dyer; 3 Adam Wilson; 4 Barry Dawson-Williams; 5 Brad Aird; 6 Daniel O'Brien; 7 Tom Zirbel; 8 Dario Esposito; 9 Jesse Walker; 10 Sebastian Taylor; 11 Hayden Nancarrow; 12 Brett Stratton; 13 Brenton Dean. Subs (all used): 14 Morgan Lundon; 15 Graham Harris; 16 Jason Kershaw; 17 Luke Donovan.
Tries: Kershaw (34), Wilson (62); **Goals:** O'Brien 2/2.
Sin bin: Walker (25) - dangerous contact.
HAYDOCK: 1 Steve Jones; 2 Alex James; 3 Dean Dollin; 4 Daryl Rotherham; 5 Danny Lee; 6 Jason Sibson; 7 Andrew Bacon; 8 Adam Brown; 9 Mike Sexton; 10 Gary Anderton; 11 Danny Gee; 12 Connor Smith; 13 Rob Sexton. Subs (all used): 14 Scott Johnson; 15 John Travena; 16 Carl Cheetham; 17 Kyle Braithwaite.
Tries: Sexton (18), Sibson (26), Bacon (30), Braithwaite (44); **Goals:** Dollin 5/5.
Rugby Leaguer & League Express Men of the Match:
Warriors: Daniel O'Brien; *Haydock:* Dean Dollin.
Penalty count: 23-9; **Half-time:** 6-18;
Referee: Matt Rossleigh; **Attendance:** 430
(at New River Stadium).

FRYSTON WARRIORS 32 KEIGHLEY COUGARS 50

WARRIORS: 1 Ben Strong; 2 Adam Rothwell; 3 Wayne McHugh; 4 Sean Gee; 5 Andy Matthews; 6 Paul Handforth; 7 Andy Speake; 8 Darren Fisher; 9 Jack Lee; 10 Lee Land; 11 Steve Scott; 12 Jack Smith; 13 Aaron Dobek. Subs (all used): 14 Dale Cogan; 15 Adam Withington; 16 Gaz Kear; 17 Craig Jones.
Tries: McHugh (11, 30), Matthews (27), Scott (48), Gee (64), Lee (72); **Goals:** Speake 3/4, Dobek 1/2.
Dismissal: Speake (55) - fighting.
Sin bin: Rothwell (55) - fighting.
COUGARS: 22 Ritchie Hawkyard; 5 Davey Dixon; 4 Danny Lawton; 32 Adam Ryder; 2 Andy Gabriel; 16 Will Milner; 7 Matty Beharrell; 8 Scott Law; 9 James Feather; 12 Brendon Rawlins; 18 Josh Tonks; 11 Josh Lynam; 13 Mike Emmett. Subs (all used): 21 Emmerson Whittel; 23 Fran Welsh; 27 Sean Kelly; 29 Brad Nicholson.
Tries: Feather (5), Tonks (14), Lawton (39), Kelly (45, 59), Ryder (57), Rawlins (61), Gabriel (68), Hawkyard (78);
Goals: Beharrell 7/9.
Dismissal: Whittel (55) - fighting.
Sin bin: Dixon (55) - fighting.
Rugby Leaguer & League Express Men of the Match:
Warriors: Paul Handforth; *Cougars:* Adam Ryder.
Penalty count: 14-12; **Half-time:** 16-16;
Referee: John McMullen; **Attendance:** 739
(at BigFellas Stadium, Featherstone).

NEWCASTLE THUNDER 18 WORKINGTON TOWN 16

THUNDER: 1 Lewis Young; 2 Joe Brown; 3 Dan Parker; 4 Derrell Olpherts; 5 Peter Fox; 6 Danny Nicklas; 7 Benn Hardcastle; 8 Corbyn Kilday; 9 Evan Simons; 10 Liam McAvoy; 11 Harry Aldous; 12 Rhys Clarke; 13 Jack Aldous. Subs (all used): 14 Aaron Teroi; 15 Vincent Rennie; 16 Brett Waller; 17 Matt Barron.
Tries: Young (27), J Aldous (42), Olpherts (60);
Goals: Hardcastle 3/4.
TOWN: 1 Theerapol Ritson; 2 Joe Hambley; 3 Ed Chamberlain; 21 Macauley Davies; 17 Scott Rooke; 7 Jamie Doran; 13 Stuart Howarth; 8 Kris Coward; 9 Callum Phillips; 10 Stevie Scholey; 11 Brett Phillips; 22 Kyle Shelford; 15 Perry Singleton. Subs (all used): 14 Sam Dowsett; 6 Carl Forber; 16 Tom Curwen; 24 Conor Fitzsimmons.
Tries: Doran (11), Hambley (17), C Phillips (20);
Goals: Forber 2/3.
Rugby Leaguer & League Express Men of the Match:
Thunder: Liam McAvoy; *Town:* Jamie Doran.
Penalty count: 10-12; **Half-time:** 6-16;
Referee: Michael Mannifield; **Attendance:** 400.

Sunday 26th February 2017

BARROW RAIDERS 60 ROCHDALE MAYFIELD 6

RAIDERS: 1 Ryan Fieldhouse; 5 Shane Toal; 3 Declan Hulme; 12 Jarrad Stack; 24 Luke Cresswell; 6 Jamie Dallimore; 7 Lewis Charnock; 8 Joe Bullock; 26 Brad Marwood; 10 Oliver Wilkes; 18 Danny Morrow; 22 Bradd Crellin; 13 Martin Aspinwall. Subs (all used): 9 Nathan Mossop; 16 Andrew Dawson; 17 Tom Walker; 25 Matty While.
Tries: Fieldhouse (8, 45, 47, 55), Crellin (25), Hulme (37, 67), Morrow (61), Stack (65, 79), Charnock (74);
Goals: Charnock 8/11.
MAYFIELD: 1 Lewis Sheridan; 2 Liam Riley; 3 Matthew Ashton; 4 Matthew Chrimes; 5 Lee Registe; 6 Zac Baher; 7 Zak Hartley; 8 James Shaw; 9 Callum Ogden; 10 Seta Tala; 11 Callum Marriott; 12 Chris Hough; 13 Paul Brearley. Subs (all used): 14 Declan Sheridan; 15 Jimmy Connaughton; 16 Simon Moore; 17 Sean Watkins.
Try: Tala (19); **Goals:** Hartley 1/1.
Rugby Leaguer & League Express Men of the Match:
Raiders: Danny Morrow; *Mayfield:* Chris Hough.
Penalty count: 10-6; **Half-time:** 14-6;
Referee: Marcus Griffiths; **Attendance:** 500.

HEMEL STAGS 12 LONDON SKOLARS 22

STAGS: 1 Mitch Vincent; 2 Darren Forde; 3 Roddy Jonas; 4 Andy Walker; 5 Marcus Elliott; 6 Jorge Richardson; 7 Mark Barlow; 8 Reece Williams; 9 Jono Burns; 10 Wayne Jowitt; 11 Ross White; 12 Alex Williams; 13 Declan Tomlinson. Subs (all used): 14 Declan Gregory; 15 Santino Decaro; 16 Danny Samuel; 17 Jack O'Brien.
Tries: Forde (69), Gregory (79); **Goals:** Vincent 2/2.
SKOLARS: 20 Jake Melling; 1 Andy Winfield; 3 Aaron Small; 24 Michael Brown; 2 Sam Nash; 9 Charlie Lawrence; 7 Mike Bishay; 25 Michael Sykes; 14 Billy Driver; 10 Dave Williams; 11 Lamont Bryan; 18 Mike Greenhalgh; 13 Ryan Chester. Subs (all used): 8 Louis Robinson; 28 Simona Vavega; 23 Will Martin; 26 Jermaine Coleman.
Tries: Bryan (9), Driver (25), Small (48), Martin (79);
Goals: C Lawrence 3/4.
Sin bin: Williams (60) - dissent.
Rugby Leaguer & League Express Men of the Match:
Stags: Mitch Vincent; *Skolars:* Lamont Bryan.
Penalty count: 19-16; **Half-time:** 0-16;
Referee: Steve Race; **Attendance:** 112.

DONCASTER 34 MYTON WARRIORS 6

DONCASTER: 1 Tom Carr; 22 Louis Sheriff; - Chris Heil; 4 Jason Tali; 2 Aaron Jones-Bishop; 20 Kieran Cross; 15 Jack Miller; 8 Mark Castle; 9 Kyle Kesik; 14 Connor Scott; 3 Liam Welham; 28 Michael Worrincy; 12 Jason Muranka. Subs (all used): 18 Ryan Wright; 16 Russ Spiers; 10 Iafeta Palea'aesina; 32 Makali Aizue.
Tries: Cross (5), Tali (9), Heil (16), Jones-Bishop (25), Welham (56), Carr (67); **Goals:** Carr 5/6.
WARRIORS: 1 Nathan Hill; 2 Anthony Wheeldon; 3 Jordan Precious; 4 Ash James; 5 Lee James; 6 Nathan Slater; 7 Kris Walker; 8 Aaron Pearce; 9 Wes Newton; 10 Liam Garnett; 11 Nick Halstead; 12 James Jennison; 13 Lee Fewlass. Subs (all used): 14 Liam Ward; 15 Ash Ward; 16 Dan Spencer; 17 James Johnson.
Try: Slater (2); **Goals:** A James 1/1.
Rugby Leaguer & League Express Men of the Match:
Doncaster: Jason Tali; *Warriors:* James Jennison.
Penalty count: 9-6; **Half-time:** 22-6;
Referee: Liam Moore; **Attendance:** 366.

GLOUCESTERSHIRE ALL GOLDS 36
NORTH WALES CRUSADERS 18

ALL GOLDS: 1 Alex Gaskell; 2 Mo Agoro; 3 Phil Cowburn; 4 Brad Kislingbury; 5 Chris Barlow; 6 Josh Houghton; 7 Kieran Hyde; 8 Ollie Purslow; 9 Steve Parry; 10 Harrison Elliott; 11 Chris Worrall; 12 Joe McClean; 13 Billy Brickhill. Subs (all used): 14 Jack Mitchell; 15 Jordan Andrade; 16 Malikhi Lloyd-Jones; 17 Harry Kidd.
Tries: Kislingbury (1, 62), Gaskell (11), McClean (19), Kidd (23), Parry (27, 45), Agoro (42);
Goals: Hyde 2/5, Mitchell 0/3.
CRUSADERS: 1 Tommy Johnson; 2 Corey Lee; 28 Callum Mulkeen; 4 Earl Hurst; 5 Dale Bloomfield; 26 Jack Hansen; 7 Ryan Smith; 17 Kenny Baker; 9 Lee Hudson; 8 Jonny Walker; 24 Jack Houghton; 14 James Dandy; 13 Ryan Millington. Subs (all used): 27 Aaron Moore; 15 John Cookson; 16 Luke Warburton; 22 Andrew Joy.
Tries: Hurst (35), Dandy (39, 49), Mulkeen (55);
Goals: Johnson 1/4.
Rugby Leaguer & League Express Men of the Match:
All Golds: Alex Gaskell; *Crusaders:* Ryan Smith.
Penalty count: 12-9; **Half-time:** 24-8;
Referee: Greg Dolan; **Attendance:** 87.

HUNSLET 34 COVENTRY BEARS 0

HUNSLET: 1 Jimmy Watson; 30 Ryan Ince; 12 Aston Wilson; 24 Cameron Leeming; 3 Marcus Webb; 18 Joel Gibson; 7 Danny Ansell; 8 Michael Haley; 9 Jack Lee; 15 Jack Coventry; 11 Jake Normington; 13 Liam Mackay; 17 Nyle Flynn. Subs (all used): 25 Matthew Tebb; 19 Matt Carbutt; 23 Jose Kenga; 21 Jack Walton.
Tries: Lee (8), Webb (23), Leeming (37, 80), Gibson (49), Mackay (78); **Goals:** Ansell 5/6.
BEARS: 1 Charlie O'Mara; 2 Jamahl Hunte; 3 Jason Bass; 4 Callan Beckett; 5 Hayden Freeman; 6 Joe Prior; 7 Cian Timmins; 8 John Aldred; 9 Billy Gaylor; 10 Jack Morrison; 11 Matt Reid; 12 Chris Barratt; 13 Kieran Sherratt. Subs (all used): 14 Joel James; 15 Dan Gover; 16 James Geurtjens; 17 Zach Johnson.
Rugby Leaguer & League Express Men of the Match:
Hunslet: Joel Gibson; *Bears:* Joe Prior.
Penalty count: 8-8; **Half-time:** 16-0;
Referee: Scott Mikalauskas; **Attendance:** 249.

SOUTH WALES IRONMEN 4 OXFORD 18

IRONMEN: 22 Ben Jones; 2 Yannic Parker; 12 Lewis Reece; 4 Christiaan Roets; 3 Paul Edwards; 6 Andrew Gay; 15 Shaun Owens; 8 Chris Davies; 9 Connor Farrer; 19 Jamie l'Anson; 17 Zak Williams; 24 Connor Parker; 16 Ashley Bateman. Subs (all used): 5 Paul Emanuelli; 11 Richard Jones; 13 Chris Vitalini; 10 Izaak Duffy.
Try: P Edwards (34); **Goals:** B Jones 0/1.
OXFORD: 1 Kane Riley; 2 Jordan Gill; 3 Tommy Newbould; 4 Harvey Burnett; 5 Curtis McDonald; 6 Callum Windley; 7 Scott Fleming; 8 Jake Joynt; 9 Casey Canterbury; 10 Mark Hayes; 11 Jordan Siddons; 12 Will Cooke; 13 Tom Alexander. Subs (all used): 14 Bradley Moules; 15 Stuart Biscomb; 16 Dwaine McRae; 17 Connor Clayton.
Tries: Canterbury (23), Cooke (31, 75), McRae (50);
Goals: Gill 1/4.
Rugby Leaguer & League Express Men of the Match:
Ironmen: Chris Vitalini; *Oxford:* Will Cooke.
Penalty count: 6-9; **Half-time:** 4-8;
Referee: Nick Bennett; **Attendance:** 115.

YORK CITY KNIGHTS 48 EGREMONT RANGERS 8

CITY KNIGHTS: 1 Ash Robson; 4 Tommy Brierley; 11 Joe Batchelor; 3 Nev Morrison; 2 David Foggin-Johnston; 6 Danny Sowerby; 7 Harry Tyson-Wilson; 16 Ronan Dixon; 14 Harry Carter; 10 Chris Siddons; 12 Ed Smith; 17 Brad Hey; 13 Tim Spears. Subs (all used): 9 Pat Smith; 8 Bobby Tyson-Wilson; 20 Adam Robinson; 25 Joe Porter.
Tries: Robson (4, 80), Carter (6), Foggin-Johnston (13, 65), Morrison (25), Hey (43, 73), Sowerby (50), Batchelor (52);
Goals: H Tyson-Wilson 4/10, Robson 0/1.
RANGERS: 1 Rhys Davies; 2 Callum Aitken; 3 Leon Crellin; 4 Jack Stainton; 5 James Newton; 6 John-Paul Brocklebank; 7 Joe Bold; 8 Tom Horner; 9 Matthew Henson; 10 Brad Hailes; 11 Matt Brewsher; 12 Kieran Glenn; 13 Quinn Wright. Subs (all used): 14 Daniel Telford; 15 Dean Laverick; 16 Anthony Leak; 17 Kevin Brown.
Tries: Brocklebank (32), Henson (61); **Goals:** Brewsher 0/2.
Dismissal: Crellin (69) - high tackle on Batchelor.
Sin bin: Glenn (63) - interference;
Davies (65) - late challenge on Foggin-Johnston.
Rugby Leaguer & League Express Men of the Match:
City Knights: Ash Robson; *Rangers:* Matt Brewsher.
Penalty count: 14-3; **Half-time:** 16-4;
Referee: Liam Staveley; **Attendance:** 635.

Challenge Cup 2017 - Round by Round

ROUND 4

Friday 17th March 2017

DEWSBURY RAMS 36 NEWCASTLE THUNDER 8

RAMS: 1 Josh Guzdek; 31 Alex Brown; 21 Hamish Barnes; 3 Jason Crookes; 2 Dale Morton; 6 Paul Sykes; 7 Andy Kain; 24 Jode Sheriffe; 15 Robbie Ward; 27 Brandon Douglas; 4 Lucas Walshaw; 11 Rob Spicer; 20 Aaron Ollett. Subs (all used): 23 James Glover; 10 Mitchell Stringer; 30 Daniel Igbinedion; 29 Lewis Fairhurst.
Tries: Sykes (11), Ollett (15, 56), Douglas (26), Morton (31), Glover (79); **Goals:** Sykes 6/7.
THUNDER: 1 Derrell Olpherts; 2 Joe Brown; 3 Aaron Teroi; 4 Tyler Craig; 5 Peter Fox; 6 Danny Nicklas; 7 Benn Hardcastle; 8 Brett Waller; 9 Lee Paterson; 10 Liam McAvoy; 11 Harry Aldous; 12 Rhys Clarke; 13 Jack Aldous. Subs (all used): 14 Evan Simons; 15 Vincent Rennie; 16 Corbyn Kilday; 17 Dan Parker.
Tries: Craig (38), Olpherts (59); **Goals:** Hardcastle 0/2.
Rugby Leaguer & League Express Men of the Match: *Rams:* Paul Sykes; *Thunder:* Derrell Olpherts.
Penalty count: 11-10; **Half-time:** 26-4;
Referee: John McMullen; **Attendance:** 425.

LONDON BRONCOS 26 TORONTO WOLFPACK 30

BRONCOS: 1 Elliot Kear; 2 Rhys Williams; 3 Ben Hellewell; 4 Adrian Purtell; 5 Kieran Dixon; 6 Jarrod Sammut; 7 William Barthau; 17 Mark Offerdahl; 27 Ben Pointer; 10 Mark Ioane; 11 Daniel Harrison; 13 Jay Pitts; 23 Matty Gee. Subs (all used): 19 Api Pewhairangi; 12 Matt Garside; 16 Junior Roqica; 18 Ben Evans.
Tries: Sammut (12, 72), Barthau (45), Kear (77), Dixon (80); **Goals:** Sammut 3/5.
WOLFPACK: 1 Quentin Laulu-Togagae; 2 Jonny Pownall; 14 Gary Wheeler; 4 Craig Hall; 5 Liam Kay; 6 Blake Wallace; 7 Rhys Jacks; 21 Adam Sidlow; 9 Bob Beswick; 29 Jake Emmitt; 11 Andrew Dixon; 12 James Laithwaite; 13 Jack Bussey. Subs (all used): 17 Richard Whiting; 10 Daniel Fleming; 19 Steve Crossley; 23 Toby Everett.
Tries: Hall (3), Kay (8), Bussey (30), Pownall (58), Jacks (68); **Goals:** Hall 5/6.
Rugby Leaguer & League Express Men of the Match: *Broncos:* Jarrod Sammut; *Wolfpack:* Ben Beswick.
Penalty count: 14-8; **Half-time:** 6-18;
Referee: Scott Mikalauskas; **Attendance:** 758.

Saturday 18th March 2017

OLDHAM 40 HAYDOCK 12

OLDHAM: - Richard Lepori; 2 Adam Clay; 22 Danny Grimshaw; 25 Kieran Gill; 5 Jamel Chisholm; 6 Scott Leatherbarrow; 7 Dave Hewitt; 10 Adam Neal; 20 Gareth Owen; 18 Ben Davies; 3 George Tyson; 12 Danny Langtree; 11 Jack Spencer. Subs (all used): 19 Joe Burke; 21 Kenny Hughes; 9 Sam Gee; 24 Michael Ward.
Tries: Lepori (20, 43), Ward (26), Tyson (33), Grimshaw (38), Burke (51), Gill (58), Clay (76);
Goals: Leatherbarrow 4/8.
HAYDOCK: 1 Steve Jones; 2 Alex James; 3 Dean Dollin; 4 John Travena; 5 Danny Lee; 6 Jordan Gibson; 7 Andrew Bacon; 8 Gary Anderton; 9 Mike Sexton; 10 Adam Brown; 11 Danny Gee; 12 Connor Smith; 13 Rob Sexton. Subs (all used): 14 Scott Johnson; 15 Carl Cheetham; 16 Kyle Braithwaite; 17 Danny Davies.
Tries: Gibson (4), Dollin (9), Jones (80);
Goals: Dollin 0/2, Gibson 0/1.
Sin bin: Gibson (29) - holding down.
Rugby Leaguer & League Express Men of the Match: *Oldham:* Scott Leatherbarrow; *Haydock:* Jordan Gibson.
Penalty count: 15-6; **Half-time:** 20-8;
Referee: Nick Bennett; **Attendance:** 743.

TOULOUSE OLYMPIQUE 16 BATLEY BULLDOGS 34

OLYMPIQUE: 2 Tony Maurel; 20 Paul Marcon; 21 Gavin Marguerite; 28 Nicolas Bianchini; 5 Kuni Minga; 19 Etienne Ferret; 18 Justin Bouscayrol; 15 Maxime Puech; 9 Kane Bentley; 17 Kalausa Leha; 10 Bastian Canet; 8 Clement Boyer; 24 Anthony Marion. Subs (all used): 23 Justin Sangare; 29 Cedric Mazars; 30 Quentin Quemener; 31 Christopher Denis.
Tries: Bianchini (12), Puech (56), Bouscayrol (69);
Goals: Maurel 2/3.
BULLDOGS: 1 Dave Scott; 25 Michael Hayward; 3 Sam Smeaton; 15 Danny Cowling; 5 Shaun Ainscough; 13 Pat Walker; 16 Tom Lillycrop; 8 Adam Gledhill; 9 Alistair Leak; 10 Alex Rowe; 11 Brad Day; 12 Joel Farrell; 22 Dane Manning. Subs (all used): 17 Joe Chandler; 18 James Harrison; 19 Alex Bretherton; 21 James Brown.
Tries: Smeaton (10, 76), Cowling (19), Scott (27), Brown (44), Manning (47); **Goals:** Walker 5/6.
Rugby Leaguer & League Express Men of the Match: *Olympique:* Tony Maurel; *Bulldogs:* Pat Walker.
Penalty count: 9-8; **Half-time:** 6-18;
Referee: James Child; **Attendance:** 150 *(at Stade Arnaune)*.

SWINTON LIONS 40 LONDON SKOLARS 8

LIONS: 7 Chris Atkin; 2 Shaun Robinson; 3 Chris Hankinson; 21 Mike Butt; 5 Matt Gardner; 14 Ben White; 6 Grant Gore; 15 Andy Bracek; 9 Anthony Nicholson; 16 Anthony Bate; 11 Connor Dwyer; 17 Olly Davies; 13 Andy Thornley. Subs (all used): 19 Josh Barlow; 24 Adam Jones; 20 Sean Kenny; 18 Ben Austin.
Tries: Robinson (2, 9), Butt (43), Gore (57, 68), A Nicholson (71), Bracek (74); **Goals:** Atkin 6/7.
SKOLARS: 20 Jake Melling; 2 Sam Nash; 31 Josh Allison; 24 Michael Brown; 5 James Hill; 27 Brandon Pickersgill; 9 Charlie Lawrence; 30 Simona Vavega; 14 Billy Driver; 29 Callum Bustin; 28 Keenen Tomlinson; 12 Eddie Mbaraga; 13 Ryan Chester. Subs (all used): 26 Matt Davis; 8 Louis Robinson; 25 Michael Sykes; 11 Lamont Bryan.
Tries: Nash (65, 78); **Goals:** C Lawrence 0/2.
Rugby Leaguer & League Express Men of the Match: *Lions:* Anthony Nicholson; *Skolars:* Brandon Pickersgill.
Penalty count: 15-7; **Half-time:** 10-0;
Referee: Greg Dolan; **Attendance:** 200.

BARROW RAIDERS 20 KEIGHLEY COUGARS 0

RAIDERS: 1 Ryan Fieldhouse; 5 Shane Toal; 3 Declan Hulme; 20 Andy Litherland; 24 Luke Cresswell; 6 Jamie Dallimore; 7 Lewis Charnock; 8 Joe Bullock; 9 Nathan Mossop; 10 Oliver Wilkes; 12 Jarrad Stack; 22 Bradd Crellin; 13 Martin Aspinwall. Subs (all used): 14 Dan Abram; 16 Andrew Dawson; 17 Tom Walker; 21 James Duerden.
Tries: Charnock (39, 44), S Toal (59), Hulme (64);
Goals: Dallimore 2/4.
COUGARS: 1 Harry Aaronson; 26 Vinny Finigan; 4 Danny Lawton; 32 Adam Ryder; 2 Andy Gabriel; 16 Will Milner; 7 Matty Beharrell; 19 Matthew Bailey; 9 James Feather; 23 Fran Welsh; 11 Josh Lynam; 18 Josh Tonks; 13 Mike Emmett. Subs (all used): 12 Brendon Rawlins; 14 Adam Brook; 20 Nathan Kitson; 25 Ben Sagar.
Rugby Leaguer & League Express Men of the Match: *Raiders:* Lewis Charnock; *Cougars:* Adam Ryder.
Penalty count: 11-6; **Half-time:** 6-0;
Referee: Gareth Hewer; **Attendance:** 721.

Sunday 19th March 2017

BRADFORD BULLS 13 FEATHERSTONE ROVERS 21

BULLS: 19 Johnny Campbell; 5 Iliess Macani; 3 James Mendeika; 4 Ross Oakes; 2 Ethan Ryan; 6 Leon Pryce; 7 Joe Keyes; 15 Jon Magrin; 9 Joe Lumb; 17 Ross Peltier; 21 Brandan Wilkinson; 20 James Bentley; 26 Vila Halafihi. Subs (all used): 34 Scott Moore; 8 Liam Kirk; 33 Reiss Butterworth; 35 Evan Hodgson.
Tries: Hodgson (48), Campbell (80); **Goals:** Keyes 2/2;
Field goal: Keyes (64).
ROVERS: 1 Ian Hardman; 18 Scott Turner; 22 Jason Walton; 3 Chris Ulugia; 2 James Duckworth; 6 Kyle Briggs; 19 Matty Wildie; 10 Andrew Bostock; 12 John Davies; 16 Luke Cooper; 14 Frankie Mariano; 23 Josh Hardcastle; 21 James Lockwood. Subs (all used): 15 Bradley Knowles-Tagg; 8 Darrell Griffin; 13 Richard Moore; 17 Sam Day.
Tries: Hardcastle (5), Walton (67), Hardman (75);
Goals: Briggs 4/4; **Field goal:** Briggs (55).
Rugby Leaguer & League Express Men of the Match: *Bulls:* Evan Hodgson; *Rovers:* Jason Walton.
Penalty count: 6-6; **Half-time:** 0-6;
Referee: Callum Straw; **Attendance:** 2,458.

GLOUCESTERSHIRE ALL GOLDS 22 DONCASTER 48

ALL GOLDS: 1 Alex Gaskell; 2 Mo Agoro; 3 Phil Cowburn; 4 Brad Kislingbury; 5 Chris Barlow; 6 Jack Mitchell; 7 Kieran Hyde; 8 Ollie Purslow; 9 Steve Parry; 10 Harry Kidd; 11 Chris Worrall; 12 Joe McClean; 13 Billy Brickhill. Subs (all used): 14 Kadeem Williams; 15 Harrison Elliott; 16 Jordan Andrade; 17 James Walter.
Tries: Barlow (16), Parry (36, 39), Kislingbury (58);
Goals: Hyde 3/4.
DONCASTER: 22 Louis Sheriff; 5 Sam Doherty; 3 Liam Welham; 21 Chris Heil; 24 Richie Barnett; 20 Kieran Cross; 15 Jack Miller; 19 Zac Braham; 9 Kyle Kesik; 8 Mark Castle; 34 Brad England; 13 Charlie Martin; 16 Russ Spiers. Subs (all used): 18 Ryan Wright; 10 Iafeta Palea'aesina; 32 Makali Aizue; 23 Jamie Thackray.
Tries: Welham (4, 80), Cross (29, 49, 69, 76), Sheriff (33, 65); **Goals:** Miller 8/9.
Rugby Leaguer & League Express Men of the Match: *All Golds:* Steve Parry; *Doncaster:* Kieran Cross.
Penalty count: 10-7; **Half-time:** 16-18;
Referee: Matt Rossleigh; **Attendance:** 280 *(at Keepmoat Athletics Ground, Doncaster)*.

HALIFAX 20 HUNSLET 6

HALIFAX: 2 Will Sharp; 22 Chester Butler; 3 Steve Tyrer; 21 James Woodburn-Hall; 23 Rob Worrincy; 1 Ben Johnston; 7 Gareth Moore; 10 Adam Tangata; 9 Ben Kaye; 8 Mitch Cahalane; 11 Shane Grady; 16 Ed Barber; 20 Elliot Morris. Subs (all used): 18 Luke Nelmes; 15 Luke Ambler; 26 Alex Mammone; 32 Chris Cullimore.
Tries: Barber (4), Butler (23), Worrincy (78);
Goals: Tyrer 4/5.
HUNSLET: 1 Jimmy Watson; 30 Ryan Ince; 12 Aston Wilson; 4 Mufaro Mvududu; 3 Marcus Webb; 18 Joel Gibson; 7 Danny Ansell; 31 Sean Hesketh; 9 Jack Lee; 19 Matt Carbutt; 21 Jack Walton; 11 Jake Normington; 13 Liam Mackay. Subs (all used): 14 George Flanagan; 6 Joe Sanderson; 17 Nyle Flynn; 23 Jose Kenga.
Try: Ince (70); **Goals:** Ansell 1/1.
Rugby Leaguer & League Express Men of the Match: *Halifax:* Shane Grady; *Hunslet:* Joe Sanderson.
Penalty count: 7-7; **Half-time:** 12-0;
Referee: Tom Grant; **Attendance:** 793.

HULL KINGSTON ROVERS 48 SHEFFIELD EAGLES 10

ROVERS: 1 Adam Quinlan; 32 Kieren Moss; 3 Thomas Minns; 22 Andrew Heffernan; 5 Ryan Shaw; 16 Jordan Abdull; 7 Jamie Ellis; 8 Nick Scruton; 9 Shaun Lunt; 21 Rob Mulhern; 11 Maurice Blair; 12 James Greenwood; 15 James Donaldson. Subs (all used): 2 Ben Cockayne; 14 Graeme Horne; 33 Ben Kavanagh; 10 Chris Clarkson.
Tries: Minns (10), Lunt (15, 44), Quinlan (28), Blair (58), Cockayne (61), Ellis (66), Greenwood (71); **Goals:** Ellis 8/8.
Sin bin: Cockayne (38) - high tackle on Cox.
EAGLES: 18 Ryan Millar; 2 Garry Lo; 3 Menzie Yere; 21 Eze Harper; 5 Ben Blackmore; 6 Simon Brown; 7 Dane Chisholm; 8 Scott Wheeldon; 9 Matty Fozard; 10 Mark Mexico; 11 Matt James; 12 Duane Straugheir; 13 Elliot Minchella. Subs (all used): 15 Kyle Trout; 16 Sam Scott; 17 Jordan Cox; 19 Will Hope.
Tries: Chisholm (22), Lo (40); **Goals:** Brown 1/2.
Rugby Leaguer & League Express Men of the Match: *Rovers:* Jordan Abdull; *Eagles:* Mark Mexico.
Penalty count: 11-7; **Half-time:** 18-10;
Referee: Jon Roberts; **Attendance:** 3,408.

YORK CITY KNIGHTS 26 ROCHDALE HORNETS 20

CITY KNIGHTS: 31 Liam Harris; 21 Ben Dent; 3 Nev Morrison; 19 James Haynes; 5 Tom Saxton; 23 Jon Presley; 7 Harry Tyson-Wilson; 16 Ronan Dixon; 26 Andy Ellis; 20 Adam Robinson; 11 Joe Batchelor; 12 Ed Smith; 13 Tim Spears. Subs (all used): 14 Harry Carter; 8 Bobby Tyson-Wilson; 28 Kieran Moran; 25 Joe Porter.
Tries: E Smith (4), Batchelor (18), Moran (40), B Tyson-Wilson (72); **Goals:** H Tyson-Wilson 5/5.
HORNETS: 1 Miles Greenwood; 2 Chris Riley; 21 Jack Holmes; 4 Lewis Galbraith; 5 Rob Massam; 6 Lewis Palfrey; 7 Danny Yates; 8 Samir Tahraoui; 9 Ben Moores; 10 Gavin Bennion; 11 Jono Smith; 12 Josh Crowley; 19 Jordan Case. Subs: 14 Ryan Maneely; 15 Jovili Taira; 16 Matty Hadden; 20 Jack Francis (not used).
Tries: Greenwood (30), Riley (33, 59), Massam (53);
Goals: Palfrey 2/4.
Rugby Leaguer & League Express Men of the Match: *City Knights:* Joe Batchelor; *Hornets:* Lewis Galbraith.
Penalty count: 9-5; **Half-time:** 20-12;
Referee: Brandon Robinson; **Attendance:** 652.

Sunday 26th March 2017

WHITEHAVEN 46 OXFORD 14

WHITEHAVEN: 1 Elliott Miller; 5 Jordan Burns; 3 Chris Taylor; 4 Jessie Joe Parker; 2 Craig Calvert; 6 Steve Roper; 7 Paul Crook; 8 Marc Shackley; 9 James Newton; 10 Carl Forster; 12 Scott McAvoy; 16 Connor Holliday; 13 Karl Olstrum. Subs (all used): 14 James Tilley; 19 Glenn Riley; - Shane Ackerley; 17 Tommy Holland.
Tries: Olstrum (2), Crook (6), Parker (17, 35), Calvert (26), Burns (47), Newton (50), Taylor (71); **Goals:** Crook 7/8.
Sin bin: Olstrum (77) - fighting.
OXFORD: 1 Kane Riley; 2 Josh Atkinson; 3 Tommy Newbould; 4 Harvey Burnett; 5 Curtis McDonald; 6 Callum Windley; 7 Tom Alexander; 8 Jake Joynt; 9 Casey Canterbury; 10 Aaron Nicholson; 11 Marcus Brooker; 12 Will Cooke; 13 Stuart Biscomb. Subs (all used): 14 Bradley Moules; 15 Dwaine McRae; 16 Craig Wright; 17 Jordan Siddons.
Tries: McDonald (31), Moules (54), Atkinson (67);
Goals: Burnett 1/3.
Sin bin: Siddons (77) - fighting.
Rugby Leaguer & League Express Men of the Match: *Whitehaven:* Karl Olstrum; *Oxford:* Callum Windley.
Penalty count: 10-7; **Half-time:** 30-4;
Referee: Tom Crashley; **Attendance:** 375.

ROUND 5

Friday 21st April 2017

LEEDS RHINOS 64 DONCASTER 28

RHINOS: 31 Jack Walker (D); 22 Ash Handley; 3 Kallum Watkins; 4 Joel Moon; 5 Ryan Hall; 6 Danny McGuire (C); 7 Rob Burrow; 8 Keith Galloway; 25 Jordan Lilley; 17 Mitch Garbutt; 16 Brad Singleton; 21 Josh Walters; 10 Adam Cuthbertson. Subs (all used): 23 Jack Ormondroyd; 24 Jordan Baldwinson; 30 Sam Hallas; 28 Mikolaj Oledzki (D).
Tries: Handley (2), Burrow (5, 63), Garbutt (10, 39), McGuire (13), Walker (21, 30, 37), Lilley (46), Oledzki (62), Moon (77); **Goals:** Watkins 6/9, Lilley 2/3.
DONCASTER: 1 Tom Carr; 5 Sam Doherty; 2 Aaron Jones-Bishop; 4 Jason Tali; 22 Louis Sheriff; 6 Jordan Howden; 20 Kieran Cross; 8 Mark Castle; 9 Kyle Kesik; 19 Zac Braham; 34 Brad England; 13 Charlie Martin; 12 Jason Muranka. Subs (all used): 14 Connor Scott; 32 Makali Aizue; 18 Ryan Wright; 7 Jordie Hedges.
Tries: Cross (15), Wright (48), Sheriff (55, 73), Martin (58), Kesik (69); **Goals:** Carr 2/6.
Rugby Leaguer & League Express Men of the Match: *Rhinos:* Jack Walker; *Doncaster:* Charlie Martin.
Penalty count: 6-7; **Half time:** 44-4;
Referee: Chris Campbell; **Attendance:** 5,097.

Saturday 22nd April 2017

LEIGH CENTURIONS 10 HULL KINGSTON ROVERS 23

CENTURIONS: 20 Ben Reynolds; 19 Ryan Hampshire; 3 Ben Crooks; 5 Matty Dawson; 30 Curtis Naughton; 6 Martyn Ridyard; 7 Josh Drinkwater; 24 Jamie Acton; 21 Liam Hood; 10 Dayne Weston; 17 Atelea Vea; 12 Glenn Stewart; 13 Harrison Hansen (C). Subs (all used): 14 Eloi Pelissier; 15 Danny Tickle; 23 Sam Hopkins; 29 Lachlan Burr.
Tries: Burr (20), Naughton (22); **Goals:** Reynolds 1/2.
ROVERS: 1 Adam Quinlan; 5 Ryan Shaw; 22 Andrew Heffernan; 4 Liam Salter; 31 David Hodgson; 16 Jordan Abdull; 7 Jamie Ellis; 8 Nick Scruton; 9 Shaun Lunt; 35 Josh Johnson; 19 George Lawler; 11 Maurice Blair; 33 Ben Kavanagh. Subs (all used): 12 James Greenwood; 18 Zach Dockar-Clay; 21 Rob Mulhern; 24 Joe Wardill.
Tries: Shaw (2, 78), Lawler (8), Greenwood (38); **Goals:** Ellis 3/4; **Field goal:** Ellis (71).
Rugby Leaguer & League Express Men of the Match: *Centurions:* Lachlan Burr; *Rovers:* Jordan Abdull.
Penalty count: 9-10; **Half-time:** 10-16;
Referee: James Child; **Attendance:** 3,818.

Sunday 23rd April 2017

SALFORD RED DEVILS 29 TORONTO WOLFPACK 22

RED DEVILS: 1 Gareth O'Brien; 21 Greg Johnson; 3 Josh Jones; 22 Kris Welham; 2 Justin Carney; 6 Robert Lui; 7 Michael Dobson (C); 23 Lee Mossop; 19 Josh Wood; 14 Lama Tasi; 10 George Griffin; 11 Ben Murdoch-Masila; 13 Mark Flanagan. Subs (all used): 20 Kriss Brining; 8 Craig Kopczak; 16 Olsi Krasniqi; 17 Adam Walne.
Tries: Welham (12), Johnson (22, 35), Dobson (45), O'Brien (67); **Goals:** Dobson 3/4, O'Brien 1/1;
Field goal: O'Brien (77).
Dismissal: J Carney (27) - verbal abuse.
WOLFPACK: 1 Quentin Laulu-Togagae; 2 Jonny Pownall; 3 Greg Worthington; 4 Craig Hall; 5 Liam Kay; 6 Blake Wallace; 27 Ryan Brierley; 8 Fuifui Moimoi; 9 Bob Beswick; 29 Jake Emmitt; 11 Andrew Dixon; 12 James Laithwaite; 13 Jack Bussey. Subs (all used): 7 Rhys Jacks; 17 Richard Whiting; 21 Adam Sidlow; 25 Ryan Bailey.
Tries: Kay (15), Laulu-Togagae (17), Brierley (27), Moimoi (80); **Goals:** Hall 3/4.
Rugby Leaguer & League Express Men of the Match: *Red Devils:* Michael Dobson; *Wolfpack:* Greg Worthington.
Penalty count: 11-7; **Half-time:** 18-16;
Referee: Jack Smith; **Attendance:** 1,318.

HUDDERSFIELD GIANTS 24 SWINTON LIONS 28

GIANTS: 24 Darnell McIntosh; 25 Jared Simpson; 23 Sam Wood; 30 Alex Mellor; 5 Aaron Murphy; 4 Lee Gaskell; 32 Izaac Farrell (D); 8 Sam Rapira (C); 14 Kruise Leeming; 19 Nathan Mason; 20 Daniel Smith; 16 Oliver Roberts; 22 Tyler Dickinson. Subs (all used): 10 Shannon Wakeman; 15 Sebastine Ikahihifo; 29 Matty English (D); 31 Adam O'Brien (D).
Tries: Murphy (9), S Wood (29), McIntosh (32), Roberts (67); **Goals:** Farrell 4/4.
Sin bin: Ikahihifo (50) - fighting.
LIONS: 14 Ben White; 2 Shaun Robinson; 3 Chris Hankinson; 4 Rhodri Lloyd; 21 Mike Butt; - Josh Woods; 7 Chris Atkin; 15 Andy Bracek; 22 Luke Waterworth; 8 Rob Lever; 11 Connor Dwyer; 24 Adam Jones; 18 Ben Austin. Subs (all used): 6 Grant Gore; 16 Anthony Bate; - Caine Barnes; - Liam Carberry.
Tries: Robinson (13), Lloyd (21), Butt (35), Dwyer (51), Waterworth (76); **Goals:** Atkin 3/4, Hankinson 1/1.
Sin bin: Bate (50) - fighting.
Rugby Leaguer & League Express Men of the Match: *Giants:* Shannon Wakeman; *Lions:* Connor Dwyer.
Penalty count: 6-8; **Half-time:** 18-16;
Referee: Scott Mikalauskas; **Attendance:** 1,298.

DEWSBURY RAMS 23 BATLEY BULLDOGS 22
(after golden point extra-time)

RAMS: 1 Josh Guzdek; 5 Gareth Potts; 6 Paul Sykes; 13 Aaron Brown; 2 Dale Morton; 23 James Glover; 7 Andy Kain; 24 Jode Sheriffe; 15 Robbie Ward; 18 Jack Teanby; 4 Lucas Walshaw; 30 Daniel Igbinedion; 28 Brandon Douglas. Subs (all used): 25 Lewis Fairhurst; 8 Tony Tonks; 14 Luke Adamson; 17 Dom Speakman.
Tries: Guzdek (10, 40), Sykes (31), Aaron Brown (55); **Goals:** Sykes 3/5; **Field goal:** Fairhurst (83).
BULLDOGS: 1 Dave Scott; 25 Michael Hayward; 3 Sam Smeaton; 4 Macauley Hallett; 29 Jy Hitchcox; 6 Cain Southernwood; 7 Dominic Brambani; 8 Adam Gledhill; 9 Alistair Leak; 21 James Brown; 11 Brad Day; 12 Joel Farrell; 22 Dane Manning. Subs (all used): 10 Alex Rowe; 14 James Davey; 16 Tom Lillycrop; 17 Joe Chandler.
Tries: Hallett (7, 22), Lillycrop (26), Brambani (63); **Goals:** Southernwood 3/4.
Sin bin: Smeaton (32) - interference.
Rugby Leaguer & League Express Men of the Match: *Rams:* Josh Guzdek; *Bulldogs:* James Brown.
Penalty count: 7-12; **Half-time:** 14-16;
Referee: Jon Roberts; **Attendance:** 962.

FEATHERSTONE ROVERS 30 OLDHAM 4

ROVERS: 1 Ian Hardman; 18 Scott Turner; 4 Misi Taulapapa; 3 Chris Ulugia; 23 Josh Hardcastle; 19 Matty Wildie; 31 Cory Aston; 13 Richard Moore; 9 Keal Carlile; 16 Luke Cooper; 11 Michael Knowles; 12 John Davies; 21 James Lockwood. Subs (all used): 17 Sam Day; 8 Darrell Griffin; 10 Andrew Bostock; 15 Bradley Knowles-Tagg.
Tries: Hardcastle (11, 63), Moore (18), Hardman (54), Lockwood (57), Davies (70); **Goals:** Aston 3/6.
Sin bin: Ulugia (28) - holding down.
OLDHAM: 17 Richard Lepori; 2 Adam Clay; 3 George Tyson; 22 Danny Grimshaw; 1 Scott Turner; 6 Scott Leatherbarrow; 7 Dave Hewitt; 10 Adam Neal; 21 Kenny Hughes; 19 Joe Burke; 15 Liam Bent; 12 Danny Langtree; 13 Liam Thompson. Subs (all used): 24 Michael Ward; 18 Ben Davies; 20 Gareth Owen; 9 Sam Gee.
Try: Turner (43); **Goals:** Leatherbarrow 0/1.
Rugby Leaguer & League Express Men of the Match: *Rovers:* John Davies; *Oldham:* Richard Lepori.
Penalty count: 10-9; **Half-time:** 10-0;
Referee: Tom Grant; **Attendance:** 1,408.

WHITEHAVEN 12 HALIFAX 36

WHITEHAVEN: 1 Elliott Miller; 5 Jordan Burns; 3 Chris Taylor; 4 Jessie Joe Parker; 2 Craig Calvert; 6 Steve Roper; 7 Paul Crook; 8 Marc Shackley; 9 James Newton; 10 Carl Forster; 14 James Tilley; 16 Connor Holliday; 13 Karl Olstrum. Subs: - Shane Ackerley; 18 Tyrone Dalton; 22 Kurt Maudling (not used); 17 Tommy Holland.
Tries: Miller (28), Parker (75); **Goals:** Crook 2/2.
HALIFAX: 19 Connor Robinson; 5 James Saltonstall; 3 Steve Tyrer; 21 James Woodburn-Hall; 23 Rob Worrincy; 6 Scott Murrell; 1 Ben Johnston; 14 Ryan Boyle; 9 Ben Kaye; 8 Mitch Cahalane; 11 Shane Grady; 10 Adam Tangata; 20 Elliot Morris. Subs (all used): 16 Ed Barber; - Martyn Reilly; 17 Brandon Moore; 18 Luke Nelmes.
Tries: Tangata (16), Saltonstall (20), Woodburn-Hall (35), Grady (39), Kaye (66, 78); **Goals:** Tyrer 6/6.
Rugby Leaguer & League Express Men of the Match: *Whitehaven:* Jessie Joe Parker; *Halifax:* Scott Murrell.
Penalty count: 10-8; **Half-time:** 6-24;
Referee: Liam Moore; **Attendance:** 636.

YORK CITY KNIGHTS 28 BARROW RAIDERS 50

CITY KNIGHTS: 21 Ben Dent; 2 David Foggin-Johnston; 3 Nev Morrison; 19 James Haynes; 5 Tom Saxton; 31 Liam Harris; 7 Harry Tyson-Wilson; 28 Kieran Moran; 26 Andy Ellis; 10 Chris Siddons; 17 Brad Hey; 25 Joe Porter; 13 Tim Spears. Subs (all used): 14 Harry Carter; 8 Bobby Tyson-Wilson; 16 Ronan Dixon; 27 Brad Clavering.
Tries: Foggin-Johnston (11), Morrison (24), Porter (32), Haynes (41, 50); **Goals:** H Tyson-Wilson 4/5.
Sin bin: H Tyson-Wilson (74) - punching.
RAIDERS: 1 Ryan Fieldhouse; 5 Shane Toal; 3 Declan Hulme; 20 Andy Litherland; 24 Luke Cresswell; 7 Lewis Charnock; 26 Brad Marwood; 8 Joe Bullock; 9 Nathan Mossop; 10 Oliver Wilkes; 11 Dan Toal; 12 Jarrad Stack; 13 Martin Aspinwall. Subs (all used): 14 Dan Abram; 17 Tom Walker; 21 James Duerden; 28 Brad Brennan.
Tries: Hulme (3), S Toal (14), D Toal (17, 66), Cresswell (28, 56, 69, 75), Mossop (79), Walker (80); **Goals:** Charnock 5/10.
Rugby Leaguer & League Express Men of the Match: *City Knights:* Bobby Tyson-Wilson; *Raiders:* Joe Bullock.
Penalty count: 1-7; **Half-time:** 18-20;
Referee: John McMullen; **Attendance:** 904.

ROUND 6

Thursday 11th May 2017

FEATHERSTONE ROVERS 24 HALIFAX 12

ROVERS: 1 Ian Hardman; 18 Scott Turner; 3 Chris Ulugia; 4 Misi Taulapapa; 5 Luke Briscoe; 31 Cory Aston; 7 Anthony Thackeray; 13 Richard Moore; 9 Keal Carlile; 16 Luke Cooper; 11 Michael Knowles; 12 John Davies; 21 James Lockwood. Subs (all used): 19 Matty Wildie; 8 Darrell Griffin; 15 Bradley Knowles-Tagg; 23 Josh Hardcastle.
Tries: Davies (22), Turner (28, 47), Hardcastle (73); **Goals:** Aston 3/5; **Field goals:** Thackeray (40, 68).
HALIFAX: 2 Will Sharp; 5 James Saltonstall; 21 James Woodburn-Hall; 3 Steve Tyrer; 23 Rob Worrincy; 6 Scott Murrell; 19 Connor Robinson; 10 Adam Tangata; 17 Brandon Moore; 8 Mitch Cahalane; 11 Shane Grady; 4 Ben Heaton; 13 Jacob Fairbank. Subs (all used): 20 Elliot Morris; 14 Ryan Boyle; 16 Ed Barber; 1 Ben Johnston.
Tries: Heaton (18), Johnston (61); **Goals:** Tyrer 2/2.
Sin bin: Grady (57) - trip on Taulapapa.
Rugby Leaguer & League Express Men of the Match: *Rovers:* John Davies; *Halifax:* Ben Heaton.
Penalty count: 11-8; **Half-time:** 13-6;
Referee: Chris Campbell; **Attendance:** 1,736.

Friday 12th May 2017

DEWSBURY RAMS 6 WAKEFIELD TRINITY 54

RAMS: 6 Paul Sykes; 2 Dale Morton; 4 Lucas Walshaw; 13 Aaron Brown; 23 James Glover; 17 Dom Speakman; 25 Lewis Fairhurst; 24 Jode Sheriffe; 9 Tom Hemingway; 8 Tony Tonks; 20 Aaron Ollett; 30 Daniel Igbinedion; 15 Robbie Ward. Subs: 10 Mitchell Stringer; 26 Brandon Douglas; 19 Brad Foster; 32 Shaun Squires (not used).
Try: Aaron Brown (42); **Goals:** Glover 1/1.
TRINITY: 1 Scott Grix; 3 Bill Tupou; 15 Ashley Gibson; 18 Joe Arundel; 24 Mason Caton-Brown; 14 Sam Williams; 7 Liam Finn (C); 8 Anthony England; 9 Kyle Wood; 20 David Fifita; 11 Matty Ashurst; 27 James Batchelor; 22 Jordan Crowther. Subs (all used): 13 Michael Sio; 16 Tinirau Arona; 23 Keegan Hirst; 25 Anthony Walker.
Tries: Caton-Brown (5, 51, 68, 70), Ashurst (15), Williams (31), Tupou (38, 61), Gibson (65); **Goals:** Finn 9/9.
Rugby Leaguer & League Express Men of the Match: *Rams:* Aaron Brown; *Trinity:* Mason Caton-Brown.
Penalty count: 12-14; **Half-time:** 0-24;
Referee: Scott Mikalauskas; **Attendance:** 2,125.

HULL FC 62 CATALANS DRAGONS 0

HULL FC: 1 Jamie Shaul; 2 Mahe Fonua; 14 Jake Connor; 4 Josh Griffin; 19 Steve Michaels; 6 Albert Kelly; 7 Marc Sneyd; 8 Scott Taylor; 9 Danny Houghton (C); 10 Liam Watts; 25 Jansin Turgut; 12 Mark Minichiello; 15 Chris Green. Subs (all used): 16 Jordan Thompson; 17 Danny Washbrook; 22 Josh Bowden; 28 Brad Fash.
Tries: Michaels (2, 35, 44), Griffin (7), Fonua (24), Watts (28), Taylor (40), Turgut (49), Thompson (56), Shaul (68, 77), Connor (80); **Goals:** Sneyd 2/8, Connor 5/5.
DRAGONS: 22 Lucas Albert; 18 Vincent Duport; 21 Iain Thornley; 30 Arthur Romano (D); 5 Fouad Yaha; 6 Luke Walsh; 7 Richie Myler; 8 Sam Moa; 23 Alrix Da Costa; 10 Remi Casty (C); 14 Julian Bousquet; 27 Ugo Perez; 26 Lambert Belmas. Subs (all used): 19 Mickael Simon; 24 Paul Seguier; 25 Thibaut Margalet; 29 Matthieu Khedimi (D).
Rugby Leaguer & League Express Men of the Match: *Hull FC:* Liam Watts; *Dragons:* Remi Casty.
Penalty count: 12-9; **Half-time:** 28-0;
Referee: Ben Thaler; **Attendance:** 6,470.

SALFORD RED DEVILS 24
HULL KINGSTON ROVERS 14

RED DEVILS: 5 Niall Evalds; 21 Greg Johnson; 3 Josh Jones; 22 Kris Welham; 4 Junior Sa'u; 6 Robert Lui; 7 Michael Dobson (C); 23 Lee Mossop; 9 Logan Tomkins; 14 Lama Tasi; 15 Ryan Lannon; 11 Ben Murdoch-Masila; 16 Olsi Krasniqi. Subs (all used): 20 Kriss Brining; 8 Craig Kopczak; 12 Weller Hauraki; 1 Gareth O'Brien.
Tries: Lannon (37), Kopczak (43), Brining (52), Murdoch-Masila (72); **Goals:** Dobson 4/4.
ROVERS: 2 Ben Cockayne; 5 Ryan Shaw; 22 Andrew Heffernan; 3 Thomas Minns; 29 Jake Butler-Fleming; 16 Jordan Abdull; 7 Jamie Ellis; 8 Nick Scruton; 9 Shaun Lunt; 35 Josh Johnson; 11 Maurice Blair; 12 James Greenwood; 33 Ben Kavanagh. Subs (all used): 18 Zach Dockar-Clay; 19 George Lawler; 4 Liam Salter; 21 Rob Mulhern.

Challenge Cup 2017 - Round by Round

Tries: Lunt (18, 23); **Goals:** Ellis 3/3.
Sin bin: Butler-Fleming (65) - professional foul.
Rugby Leaguer & League Express Men of the Match:
Red Devils: Michael Dobson; *Rovers:* Shaun Lunt.
Penalty count: 12-7; **Half-time:** 6-14;
Referee: Robert Hicks; **Attendance:** 3,100.

Saturday 13th May 2017

CASTLEFORD TIGERS 53 ST HELENS 10

TIGERS: 1 Zak Hardaker; 2 Greg Minikin; 3 Jake Webster; 4 Michael Shenton (C); 5 Greg Eden; 23 Tom Holmes; 7 Luke Gale; 8 Andy Lynch; 9 Paul McShane; 10 Grant Millington; 15 Jesse Sene-Lefao; 12 Mike McMeeken; 13 Adam Milner. Subs (all used): 16 Ben Roberts; 14 Nathan Massey; 17 Junior Moors; 18 Matt Cook.
Tries: Shenton (2), Webster (10, 32), McShane (34), Minikin (35, 67), Massey (39), Eden (44, 49, 63);
Goals: Gale 6/10; **Field goal:** Gale (39).
SAINTS: 2 Tom Makinson; 5 Adam Swift; 4 Mark Percival; 3 Ryan Morgan; 28 Regan Grace; 6 Theo Fages; 7 Matty Smith; 8 Alex Walmsley; 9 James Roby; 14 Luke Douglas; 36 Zeb Taia; 20 Morgan Knowles; 16 Luke Thompson. Subs (all used): 12 Jon Wilkin (C); 13 Louie McCarthy-Scarsbrook; 19 Greg Richards; 10 Kyle Amor.
Tries: Morgan (19), Douglas (73); **Goals:** Percival 1/2.
Rugby Leaguer & League Express Men of the Match:
Tigers: Luke Gale; *Saints:* James Roby.
Penalty count: 5-10; **Half-time:** 31-4;
Referee: Phil Bentham; **Attendance:** 5,216.

Sunday 14th May 2017

LEEDS RHINOS 72 BARROW RAIDERS 10

RHINOS: 1 Ashton Golding; 2 Tom Briscoe; 22 Ash Handley; 14 Liam Sutcliffe; 5 Ryan Hall; 6 Danny McGuire (C); 4 Joel Moon; 8 Keith Galloway; 9 Matt Parcell; 24 Jordan Baldwinson; 19 Brett Ferres; 13 Stevie Ward; 16 Brad Singleton. Subs (all used): 7 Rob Burrow; 11 Jamie Jones-Buchanan; 10 Adam Cuthbertson; 20 Anthony Mullally.
Tries: Moon (3, 16, 34), Parcell (6, 74), Handley (11, 45), Hall (38), Ward (48), L Sutcliffe (61), Burrow (65, 71), Galloway (77); **Goals:** L Sutcliffe 10/13.
Sin bin: Galloway (21) - late challenge.
RAIDERS: 1 Ryan Fieldhouse; 24 Luke Cresswell; 18 Danny Morrow; 20 Andy Litherland; 23 Chris Fleming; 7 Lewis Charnock; 15 Karl Ashall; 8 Joe Bullock; 9 Nathan Mossop; 17 Tom Walker; 11 Dan Toal; 12 Jarrad Stack; 13 Martin Aspinwall. Subs (all used): 14 Dan Abram; 16 Andrew Dawson; 21 James Duerden; 28 Brad Brennan.
Tries: Cresswell (21), Stack (68);
Goals: Charnock 0/1, Ashall 1/1.
Rugby Leaguer & League Express Men of the Match:
Rhinos: Matt Parcell; *Raiders:* Jarrad Stack.
Penalty count: 8-6; **Half-time:** 32-4;
Referee: Liam Moore; **Attendance:** 5,226.

SWINTON LIONS 12 WIGAN WARRIORS 42

LIONS: 1 Jack Murphy; 2 Shaun Robinson; 3 Chris Hankinson; 14 Ben White; 21 Mike Butt; 6 Grant Gore; 7 Chris Atkin; 15 Andy Bracek; 22 Luke Waterworth; 18 Ben Austin; 11 Connor Dwyer; 4 Rhodri Lloyd; 8 Rob Lever. Subs (all used): 27 Liam Carberry; 9 Anthony Nicholson; 13 Andy Thornley; 24 Adam Jones.
Tries: Gore (42), Butt (75); **Goals:** Atkin 2/2.
Sin bin: Butt (58) - fighting.
WARRIORS: 21 Lewis Tierney; 36 Tom Davies; 32 Liam Forsyth; 5 Joe Burgess; 35 Liam Marshall; 11 Joel Tomkins; 23 Nick Gregson; 8 Frank-Paul Nuuausala; 9 Michael McIlorum; 19 Ryan Sutton; 20 Willie Isa; 12 Liam Farrell (C); 28 Jack Wells. Subs (all used): 17 Taulima Tautai; 26 Romain Navarrete; 37 Callum Field (D); 33 Josh Ganson.
Tries: J Tomkins (8), Farrell (20), Burgess (24, 47), Marshall (30), Davies (52), Ganson (64), Gregson (67);
Goals: Marshall 5/8.
Sin bin: Isa (58) - fighting.
Rugby Leaguer & League Express Men of the Match:
Lions: Jack Murphy; *Warriors:* Liam Farrell.
Penalty count: 11-9; **Half-time:** 0-18;
Referee: Chris Kendall; **Attendance:** 2,003.

WARRINGTON WOLVES 34 WIDNES VIKINGS 20

WOLVES: 1 Stefan Ratchford; 5 Matthew Russell; 12 Jack Hughes; 4 Ryan Atkins; 2 Tom Lineham; 6 Kevin Brown; 22 Declan Patton; 8 Chris Hill (C); 7 Kurt Gidley; 10 Ashton Sims; 24 Benjamin Jullien; 34 Ben Westwood; 14 Mike Cooper. Subs (all used): 23 Joe Philbin; 17 Dominic Crosby; 27 Morgan Smith; 16 George King.
Tries: Atkins (21), Brown (28, 53, 69), Russell (73), Hill (76);
Goals: Ratchford 5/7.
VIKINGS: 1 Rhys Hanbury; 38 Lloyd Roby (D); 4 Charly Runciman; 37 Liam Walsh; 5 Patrick Ah Van; 6 Joe Mellor (C); 31 Jordan Johnstone; 10 Jack Buchanan; 33 Aaron Heremaia; 15 Gil Dudson; 13 Hep Cahill; 25 Tom Olbison; 18 Greg Burke. Subs (all used): 20 Manase Manuokafoa; 8 Eamon O'Carroll; 23 Jay Chapelhow; 35 Danny Walker.
Tries: Burke (15), J Chapelhow (46), Ah Van (64);
Goals: Ah Van 4/4.
Sin bin: Hanbury (26) - holding down.
Rugby Leaguer & League Express Men of the Match:
Wolves: Kevin Brown; *Vikings:* Greg Burke.
Penalty count: 8-8; **Half-time:** 12-6;
Referee: James Child; **Attendance:** 5,971.

QUARTER FINALS

Thursday 15th June 2017

SALFORD RED DEVILS 30 WAKEFIELD TRINITY 6

RED DEVILS: 5 Niall Evalds; 24 Jake Bibby; 22 Kris Welham; 4 Junior Sa'u; 21 Greg Johnson; 6 Robert Lui; 7 Michael Dobson (C); 14 Lama Tasi; 9 Logan Tomkins; 8 Craig Kopczak; 11 Ben Murdoch-Masila; 15 Ryan Lannon; 13 Mark Flanagan. Subs (all used): 12 Weller Hauraki; 29 Todd Carney; 10 George Griffin; 20 Kriss Brining.
Tries: Lannon (7), Murdoch-Masila (12), Evalds (37), Johnson (43), Kopczak (49); **Goals:** Dobson 5/6.
TRINITY: 1 Scott Grix; 15 Ashley Gibson; 4 Reece Lyne; 18 Joe Arundel; 24 Mason Caton-Brown; 14 Sam Williams; 7 Liam Finn (C); 8 Anthony England; 9 Kyle Wood; 33 Adam Walker; 32 Dean Hadley; 11 Matty Ashurst; 13 Michael Sio. Subs (all used): 22 Jordan Crowther; 26 Chris Annakin; 23 Keegan Hirst; 17 Craig Huby.
Try: Finn (72); **Goals:** Finn 1/1.
Rugby Leaguer & League Express Men of the Match:
Red Devils: Michael Dobson; *Trinity:* Joe Arundel.
Penalty count: 8-7; **Half-time:** 20-0;
Referee: Robert Hicks; **Attendance:** 2,808.

Friday 16th June 2017

LEEDS RHINOS 58 FEATHERSTONE ROVERS 0

RHINOS: 14 Liam Sutcliffe; 2 Tom Briscoe; 3 Kallum Watkins; 22 Ash Handley; 5 Ryan Hall; 4 Joel Moon; 6 Danny McGuire (C); 16 Brad Singleton; 9 Matt Parcell; 8 Keith Galloway; 13 Stevie Ward; 12 Carl Ablett; 19 Brett Ferres. Subs (all used): 17 Mitch Garbutt; 10 Adam Cuthbertson; 20 Anthony Mullally; 31 Jack Walker.
Tries: Ward (4), Ferres (12), Moon (14), Handley (38, 56), Ablett (51), L Sutcliffe (54), Singleton (61, 65), Hall (71);
Goals: L Sutcliffe 9/10.
ROVERS: 1 Ian Hardman; 4 Misi Taulapapa; 23 Josh Hardcastle; 22 Jason Walton; 20 Kyran Johnson; 6 Kyle Briggs; 31 Cory Aston; 13 Richard Moore; 19 Matty Wildie; 16 Luke Cooper; 11 Michael Knowles; 12 John Davies; 15 Bradley Knowles-Tagg. Subs (all used): 8 Darrell Griffin; 21 James Lockwood; 14 Frankie Mariano; 9 Keal Carlile.
Sin bin:
Lockwood (47) - dangerous contact on Cuthbertson.
Rugby Leaguer & League Express Men of the Match:
Rhinos: Stevie Ward; *Rovers:* Jason Walton.
Penalty count: 8-6; **Half-time:** 22-0;
Referee: Chris Campbell; **Attendance:** 6,181.

Saturday 17th June 2017

WARRINGTON WOLVES 26 WIGAN WARRIORS 27

WOLVES: 1 Stefan Ratchford; 32 Will Dagger; 12 Jack Hughes; 4 Ryan Atkins; 2 Tom Lineham; 22 Declan Patton; 7 Kurt Gidley (C); 14 Mike Cooper; 9 Daryl Clark; 10 Ashton Sims; 24 Benjamin Jullien; 23 Joe Philbin; 13 Joe Westerman. Subs (all used): 15 Brad Dwyer; 16 George King; 18 Andre Savelio; 25 Sam Wilde.
Tries: Atkins (27, 33), Savelio (56), Gidley (77);
Goals: Patton 5/5, Ratchford 0/1.
WARRIORS: 1 Sam Tomkins; 35 Liam Marshall; 3 Anthony Gelling; 4 Oliver Gildart; 5 Joe Burgess; 6 George Williams; 7 Thomas Leuluai; 8 Frank-Paul Nuuausala; 9 Michael McIlorum; 11 Joel Tomkins; 14 John Bateman; 12 Liam Farrell; 13 Sean O'Loughlin (C). Subs (all used): 20 Willie Isa; 19 Ryan Sutton; 16 Sam Powell; 17 Taulima Tautai.
Tries: Burgess (11, 21), Marshall (37), Bateman (65);
Goals: Williams 5/5; **Field goal:** S Tomkins (73).
Rugby Leaguer & League Express Men of the Match:
Wolves: Kurt Gidley; *Warriors:* Sam Tomkins.
Penalty count: 14-7; **Half-time:** 12-18;
Referee: Ben Thaler; **Attendance:** 7,312.

Sunday 18th June 2017

HULL FC 32 CASTLEFORD TIGERS 24

HULL FC: 1 Jamie Shaul; 19 Steve Michaels; 2 Mahe Fonua; 3 Carlos Tuimavave; 5 Fetuli Talanoa; 6 Albert Kelly; 14 Jake Connor; 22 Josh Bowden; 9 Danny Houghton (C); 10 Liam Watts; 17 Danny Washbrook; 12 Mark Minichiello; 21 Sika Manu. Subs (all used): 16 Jordan Thompson; 8 Scott Taylor; 25 Jansin Turgut; 28 Brad Fash.
Tries: Tuimavave (3), Talanoa (6), Fonua (64), Shaul (69);
Goals: Connor 8/9.
TIGERS: 1 Zak Hardaker; 2 Greg Minikin; 3 Jake Webster; 4 Michael Shenton (C); 5 Greg Eden; 16 Ben Roberts; 7 Luke Gale; 8 Andy Lynch; 9 Paul McShane; 14 Nathan Massey; 15 Jesse Sene-Lefao; 12 Mike McMeeken; 13 Adam Milner. Subs (all used): 10 Grant Millington; 20 Larne Patrick; 33 Kevin Larroyer; 34 Alex Foster.
Tries: Roberts (28, 47), Hardaker (30), Minikin (72);
Goals: Gale 4/4.
Rugby Leaguer & League Express Men of the Match:
Hull FC: Mahe Fonua; *Tigers:* Grant Millington.
Penalty count: 8-5; **Half-time:** 14-12;
Referee: Phil Bentham; **Attendance:** 11,944.

SEMI-FINALS

Saturday 29th July 2017

HULL FC 43 LEEDS RHINOS 24

HULL FC: 1 Jamie Shaul; 2 Mahe Fonua; 4 Josh Griffin; 3 Carlos Tuimavave; 5 Fetuli Talanoa; 6 Albert Kelly; 7 Marc Sneyd; 8 Scott Taylor; 9 Danny Houghton; 10 Liam Watts; 12 Mark Minichiello; 21 Sika Manu; 13 Gareth Ellis (C). Subs (all used): 15 Chris Green; 14 Jake Connor; 17 Danny Washbrook; 22 Josh Bowden.
Tries: Kelly (24), Tuimavave (34, 46), Green (39), Watts (65), Shaul (72), Taylor (75); **Goals:** Sneyd 7/7;
Field goal: Sneyd (55).
RHINOS: 1 Ashton Golding; 2 Tom Briscoe; 3 Kallum Watkins; 18 Jimmy Keinhorst; 5 Ryan Hall; 4 Joel Moon; 6 Danny McGuire (C); 10 Adam Cuthbertson; 9 Matt Parcell; 16 Brad Singleton; 13 Stevie Ward; 12 Carl Ablett; 11 Jamie Jones-Buchanan. Subs (all used): 17 Mitch Garbutt; 19 Brett Ferres; 20 Anthony Mullally; 25 Jordan Lilley.
Tries: Hall (20, 32), Watkins (60), Golding (79);
Goals: Watkins 3/3, Lilley 1/1.
Rugby Leaguer & League Express Men of the Match:
Hull FC: Albert Kelly; *Rhinos:* Kallum Watkins.
Penalty count: 6-3; **Half-time:** 18-12;
Referee: Phil Bentham; **Attendance:** 14,526
(at Keepmoat Stadium, Doncaster).

Sunday 30th July 2017

SALFORD RED DEVILS 14 WIGAN WARRIORS 27

RED DEVILS: 5 Niall Evalds; 21 Greg Johnson; 22 Kris Welham; 4 Junior Sa'u; 31 Manu Vatuvei (D); 29 Todd Carney; 7 Michael Dobson (C); 14 Lama Tasi; 9 Logan Tomkins; 8 Craig Kopczak; 11 Ben Murdoch-Masila; 3 Josh Jones; 12 Weller Hauraki. Subs (all used): 1 Gareth O'Brien; 16 Olsi Krasniqi; 32 Tyrone McCarthy (D); 10 George Griffin.
Tries: Johnson (24), McCarthy (26); **Goals:** Dobson 3/3.
WARRIORS: 1 Sam Tomkins; 36 Tom Davies; 3 Anthony Gelling; 4 Oliver Gildart; 5 Joe Burgess; 6 George Williams; 7 Thomas Leuluai; 8 Frank-Paul Nuuausala; 9 Michael McIlorum; 19 Ryan Sutton; 14 John Bateman; 20 Willie Isa; 13 Sean O'Loughlin (C). Subs (all used): 11 Joel Tomkins; 15 Tony Clubb; 16 Sam Powell; 17 Taulima Tautai.
Tries: Gildart (8, 79), Isa (16), McIlorum (61);
Goals: Williams 5/7; **Field goal:** S Tomkins (66).
Sin bin: S Tomkins (30) - professional foul;
Gelling (72) - delaying restart.
On report:
Powell (28) - alleged dangerous challenge on Tasi.
Rugby Leaguer & League Express Men of the Match:
Red Devils: Todd Carney; *Warriors:* Michael McIlorum.
Penalty count: 8-8; **Half-time:** 14-12;
Referee: James Child; **Attendance:** 10,796
(at Halliwell Jones Stadium, Warrington).

FINAL

Saturday 26th August 2017

HULL FC 18 WIGAN WARRIORS 14

HULL FC: 1 Jamie Shaul; 2 Mahe Fonua; 4 Josh Griffin; 3 Carlos Tuimavave; 5 Fetuli Talanoa; 6 Albert Kelly; 7 Marc Sneyd; 8 Scott Taylor; 9 Danny Houghton; 10 Liam Watts; 21 Sika Manu; 12 Mark Minichiello; 13 Gareth Ellis (C). Subs (all used): 14 Jake Connor; 22 Josh Bowden; 15 Chris Green; 17 Danny Washbrook.
Tries: Talanoa (13), Fonua (20, 49); **Goals:** Sneyd 3/3.
WARRIORS: 1 Sam Tomkins; 35 Liam Marshall; 3 Anthony Gelling; 4 Oliver Gildart; 5 Joe Burgess; 6 George Williams; 7 Thomas Leuluai; 8 Frank-Paul Nuuausala; 9 Michael McIlorum; 15 Tony Clubb; 12 Liam Farrell; 14 John Bateman; 13 Sean O'Loughlin (C). Subs (all used): 20 Willie Isa; 16 Sam Powell; 19 Ryan Sutton; 17 Taulima Tautai.
Tries: Bateman (5), Gildart (33), Burgess (73);
Goals: Williams 1/3.
Rugby Leaguer & League Express Men of the Match:
Hull FC: Marc Sneyd; *Warriors:* Sean O'Loughlin.
Penalty count: 6-7; **Half-time:** 12-10;
Referee: Phil Bentham; **Attendance:** 68,525
(at Wembley Stadium).

Hull FC's Albert Kelly jumps above Wigan's Liam Farrell to claim a high ball during the Challenge Cup Final

GRAND FINALS
1998-2016

Grand Finals 1998-2016

1998

DIVISION ONE GRAND FINAL

Saturday 26th September 1998

FEATHERSTONE ROVERS 22 WAKEFIELD TRINITY 24

ROVERS: 1 Steve Collins; 2 Carl Hall; 3 Shaun Irwin; 4 Danny Baker; 5 Karl Pratt; 6 Jamie Coventry; 7 Ty Fallins; 8 Chico Jackson; 9 Richard Chapman; 10 Stuart Dickens; 11 Gary Price; 12 Neil Lowe; 13 Richard Slater. Subs: 14 Paddy Handley for Coventry (70); 15 Asa Amone for Lowe (50); 16 Micky Clarkson for Jackson (50); 17 Steve Dooler (not used).
Tries: Baker (15), Jackson (45), Collins (49), Hall (69); **Goals:** Chapman 3.
TRINITY: 1 Martyn Holland; 2 Josh Bostock; 3 Adam Hughes; 4 Martin Law; 5 Kevin Gray; 6 Garen Casey; 7 Roger Kenworthy; 8 Francis Stephenson; 9 Roy Southernwood; 10 Gary Lord; 11 Ian Hughes; 12 Sonny Whakarau; 13 Matt Fuller. Subs: 14 Sean Richardson for I Hughes (32); 15 Andy Fisher for Lord (26); 16 David Mycoe (not used); 17 Wayne McDonald for Whakarau (70); Lord for Stephenson (40); Stephenson for Lord (70).
Tries: Southernwood (2), Bostock (7, 25), Casey (58), Stephenson (76); **Goals:** Casey 2.
League Express Men of the Match:
Rovers: Richard Chapman; *Trinity:* Garen Casey.
Penalty count: 8-3; **Half time:** 6-12;
Referee: Nick Oddy (Halifax); **Attendance:** 8,224 *(at McAlpine Stadium, Huddersfield).*

SUPER LEAGUE GRAND FINAL

Saturday 24th October 1998

LEEDS RHINOS 4 WIGAN WARRIORS 10

RHINOS: 1 Iestyn Harris (C); 22 Leroy Rivett; 3 Richie Blackmore; 4 Brad Godden; 5 Francis Cummins; 13 Daryl Powell; 7 Ryan Sheridan; 8 Martin Masella; 21 Terry Newton; 25 Darren Fleary; 11 Adrian Morley; 17 Anthony Farrell; 12 Marc Glanville. Subs: 20 Jamie Mathiou for Masella (25); 24 Marcus St Hilaire for Powell (40); 14 Graham Holroyd for Newton (49); 27 Andy Hay for Fleary (54); Powell for Godden (58); Masella for Mathiou (71).
Try: Blackmore (20).
WARRIORS: 1 Kris Radlinski; 2 Jason Robinson; 3 Danny Moore; 4 Gary Connolly; 5 Mark Bell; 6 Henry Paul; 7 Tony Smith; 16 Terry O'Connor; 9 Robbie McCormack; 10 Tony Mestrov; 20 Lee Gilmour; 17 Stephen Holgate; 13 Andy Farrell (C). Subs: 8 Neil Cowie for O'Connor (18BB, rev 48); 14 Mick Cassidy for McCormack (19BB, rev 27); 25 Paul Johnson for Moore (37); 12 Simon Haughton for Gilmour (27BB, rev 33); Haughton for Holgate (33); Cowie for Mestrov (54); Cassidy for Haughton (64); Holgate for Cowie (68); Haughton for Gilmour (71BB, rev 75); Mestrov for O'Connor (75BB).
Try: Robinson (37); **Goals:** Farrell 3.
League Express Men of the Match:
Rhinos: Iestyn Harris; *Warriors:* Jason Robinson.
Penalty count: 7-13; **Half-time:** 4-6;
Referee: Russell Smith (Castleford); **Attendance:** 43,553 *(at Old Trafford, Manchester).*

1999

NORTHERN FORD PREMIERSHIP GRAND FINAL

Saturday 25th September 1999

DEWSBURY RAMS 11 HUNSLET HAWKS 12

RAMS: 1 Nathan Graham; 2 Alex Godfrey; 3 Paul Evans; 4 Brendan O'Meara; 5 Adrian Flynn; 6 Richard Agar; 7 Barry Eaton; 8 Alan Boothroyd; 9 Paul Delaney; 10 Matthew Long; 11 Andy Spink; 12 Mark Haigh; 13 Damian Ball. Subs: 14 Brendan Williams for Eaton (5BB, rev 15); 15 Sean Richardson for Haigh (50); 16 Simon Hicks for Long (25); 17 Paul Medley for Spink (50); Williams for Evans (61); Long for Boothroyd (71); Spink for Long (78).
Tries: Flynn (27), Ball (54); **Goal:** Eaton; **Field goal:** Agar.
HAWKS: 1 Abraham Fatnowna; 2 Chris Ross; 3 Shaun Irwin; 4 Paul Cook; 5 Iain Higgins; 6 Marcus Vassilakopoulos; 7 Latham Tawhai; 8 Richard Hayes; 9 Richard Pachniuk; 10 Steve Pryce; 11 Rob Wilson; 12 Jamie Leighton; 13 Lee St Hilaire. Subs: 14 Mick Coyle for Wilson (57); 15 Phil Kennedy for Pryce (35); 16 Jamie Thackray for St Hilaire (25); 17 Richard Baker for Higgins (55); Higgins for Fatnowna (62); Pryce for Kennedy (65).
Tries: Cook (31), Higgins (46); **Goal:** Ross;
Field goals: Tawhai, Leighton.
League Express Men of the Match:
Rams: Barry Eaton; *Hawks:* Latham Tawhai.
Penalty count: 8-5; **Half-time:** 7-7;
Referee: Steve Ganson (St Helens); **Attendance:** 5,783 *(at Headingley Stadium, Leeds).*

SUPER LEAGUE GRAND FINAL

Saturday 9th October 1999

BRADFORD BULLS 6 ST HELENS 8

BULLS: 28 Stuart Spruce; 2 Tevita Vaikona; 20 Scott Naylor; 5 Michael Withers; 17 Leon Pryce; 6 Henry Paul; 1 Robbie Paul (C); 10 Paul Anderson; 9 James Lowes; 29 Stuart Fielden; 15 David Boyle; 23 Bernard Dwyer; 13 Steve McNamara. Subs: 14 Paul Deacon for R Paul (53); 4 Nathan McAvoy (not used); 12 Mike Forshaw for McNamara (18); 22 Brian McDermott for Anderson (18); Anderson for Fielden (61); Fielden for Dwyer (65); R Paul for Deacon (72).
Try: H Paul (18); **Goal:** H Paul.
SAINTS: 1 Paul Atcheson; 14 Chris Smith; 3 Kevin Iro; 4 Paul Newlove; 5 Anthony Sullivan; 13 Paul Sculthorpe; 20 Tommy Martyn; 8 Apollo Perelini; 9 Keiron Cunningham; 10 Julian O'Neill; 2 Fereti Tuilagi; 21 Sonny Nickle; 11 Chris Joynt (C). Subs: 26 Paul Wellens for Martyn (52); 6 Sean Hoppe for Newlove (43); 16 Vila Matautia for O'Neill (20); 7 Sean Long for Perelini (24); Perelini for Matautia (46); O'Neill for Perelini (69).
Tries: Iro (65); **Goals:** Long 2.
League Express Men of the Match:
Bulls: Henry Paul; *Saints:* Kevin Iro.
Penalty count: 4-7; **Half-time:** 6-2;
Referee: Stuart Cummings (Widnes);
Attendance: 50,717 *(at Old Trafford, Manchester).*

2000

NORTHERN FORD PREMIERSHIP GRAND FINAL

Saturday 29th July 2000

DEWSBURY RAMS 13 LEIGH CENTURIONS 12

RAMS: 1 Nathan Graham; 2 Richard Baker; 4 Dan Potter; 3 Brendan O'Meara; 5 Adrian Flynn; 6 Richard Agar; 7 Barry Eaton; 8 Shayne Williams; 9 David Mycoe; 10 Mark Haigh; 11 Sean Richardson; 12 Daniel Frame; 13 Damian Ball. Subs: 14 Gavin Wood (not used); 15 Paul Delaney for Mycoe (53); 16 Ryan McDonald for Haigh (30); 17 Matthew Long for Williams (23); Haigh for McDonald (64).
Tries: Eaton (2), Long (23); **Goals:** Eaton 2;
Field goal: Agar.
Sin bin: Williams (66) - use of the elbow.
On report: Richardson (20) - high tackle on Donlan.
CENTURIONS: 1 Stuart Donlan; 5 David Ingram; 3 Paul Anderson; 4 Andy Fairclough; 2 Alan Cross; 6 Liam Bretherton; 7 Kieron Purtill; 8 Tim Street; 9 Mick Higham; 10 Andy Leathem; 11 Simon Baldwin; 12 Heath Cruckshank; 13 Adam Bristow. Subs: 14 James Arkwright for Cross (68); 15 Paul Norman for Street (36); 16 Radney Bowker (not used); 17 David Whittle for Leathem (24); Street for Norman (62).
Tries: Higham (29, 69); **Goals:** Bretherton 2.
Sin bin: Whittle (66) - retaliation.
League Express Men of the Match:
Rams: Richard Agar; *Centurions:* Mick Higham.
Penalty count: 4-4; **Half-time:** 10-6;
Referee: Robert Connolly (Wigan); **Attendance:** 8,487 *(at Gigg Lane, Bury).*

SUPER LEAGUE GRAND FINAL

Saturday 14th October 2000

ST HELENS 29 WIGAN WARRIORS 16

SAINTS: 17 Paul Wellens; 24 Steve Hall; 3 Kevin Iro; 15 Sean Hoppe; 5 Anthony Sullivan; 20 Tommy Martyn; 7 Sean Long; 8 Apollo Perelini; 9 Keiron Cunningham; 10 Julian O'Neill; 11 Chris Joynt (C); 22 Tim Jonkers; 13 Paul Sculthorpe. Subs: 14 Fereti Tuilagi for O'Neill (20); 12 Sonny Nickle for Perelini (28); 26 John Stankevitch for Jonkers (50); 23 Scott Barrow (not used); Perelini for Nickle (52); Jonkers for Stankevitch (66); Stankevitch for Perelini (67BB); O'Neill for Hall (74).
Tries: Hoppe (7), Joynt (28, 50), Tuilagi (69), Jonkers (80); **Goals:** Long 4; **Field goal:** Sculthorpe.
WARRIORS: 5 Jason Robinson; 2 Brett Dallas; 1 Kris Radlinski; 3 Steve Renouf; 26 David Hodgson; 6 Tony Smith; 7 Willie Peters; 8 Terry O'Connor; 9 Terry Newton; 10 Neil Cowie; 11 Mick Cassidy; 12 Denis Betts; 13 Andy Farrell (C). Subs: 23 Brady Malam for Cowie (30); 17 Tony Mestrov for O'Connor (43); 19 Chris Chester for Cassidy (47BB, rev 69); 14 Lee Gilmour for Betts (51); O'Connor for Mestrov (61); Cowie for Malam (67); Chester for Newton (75).
Tries: Farrell (13), Hodgson (58), Smith (61);
Goals: Farrell 2.
League Express Men of the Match:
Saints: Chris Joynt; *Warriors:* Andy Farrell.
Penalty count: 10-6; **Half-time:** 11-4;
Referee: Russell Smith (Castleford); **Attendance:** 58,132 *(at Old Trafford, Manchester).*

2001

NORTHERN FORD PREMIERSHIP GRAND FINAL

Saturday 28th July 2001

OLDHAM 14 WIDNES VIKINGS 24

OLDHAM: 1 Mark Sibson; 2 Joey Hayes; 3 Anthony Gibbons; 4 Pat Rich; 5 Joe McNicholas; 6 David Gibbons; 7 Neil Roden; 8 Leo Casey; 9 Keith Brennan; 10 Paul Norton; 11 Phil Farrell; 12 Bryan Henare; 13 Kevin Mannion. Subs: 14 Mike Ford for Mannion (27); 15 Jason Clegg for Casey (18); 16 John Hough for Brennan (44); 17 Danny Guest for Norton (40BB, rev 54); Mannion for Henare (66); Guest for Clegg (73).
Tries: Brennan (9), Ford (74), Mannion (80); **Goal:** Rich.
VIKINGS: 1 Paul Atcheson; 2 Damian Munro; 3 Craig Weston; 4 Jason Demetriou; 5 Chris Percival; 6 Richard Agar; 7 Martin Crompton; 8 Simon Knox; 9 Phil Cantillon; 10 Stephen Holgate; 11 Steve Gee; 12 Sean Richardson; 13 Tommy Hodgkinson. Subs: 14 Andy Craig for Percival (65); 15 Chris McKinney for Gee (41); 16 Joe Faimalo for Knox (32); 17 Matthew Long for Holgate (23); Knox for Long (49BB, rev 61); Holgate for Long (74).
Tries: Gee (17), Demetriou (38, 60), Cantillon (50), Munro (69); **Goals:** Weston 2.
League Express Men of the Match:
Oldham: Jason Clegg; *Vikings:* Phil Cantillon.
Penalty count: 8-5; **Half-time:** 4-10;
Referee: Steve Ganson (St Helens); **Attendance:** 8,974 *(at Spotland, Rochdale).*

SUPER LEAGUE GRAND FINAL

Saturday 13th October 2001

BRADFORD BULLS 37 WIGAN WARRIORS 6

BULLS: 5 Michael Withers; 2 Tevita Vaikona; 20 Scott Naylor; 23 Graham Mackay; 3 Leon Pryce; 6 Henry Paul; 1 Robbie Paul (C); 8 Joe Vagana; 9 James Lowes; 22 Brian McDermott; 11 Daniel Gartner; 19 Jamie Peacock; 12 Mike Forshaw. Subs: 29 Stuart Fielden for McDermott (21BB, rev 65); 10 Paul Anderson for Vagana (22); 15 Shane Rigon for Pryce (40); 7 Paul Deacon for R Paul (69); Vagana for Anderson (53); Fielden for Gartner (72); Anderson for Vagana (74).
Tries: Lowes (9), Withers (11, 27, 31), Fielden (65), Mackay (72); **Goals:** H Paul 5, Mackay; **Field goal:** H Paul.
WARRIORS: 1 Kris Radlinski; 2 Brett Dallas; 4 Gary Connolly; 3 Steve Renouf; 5 Brian Carney; 6 Matthew Johns; 7 Adrian Lam; 8 Terry O'Connor; 9 Terry Newton; 20 Harvey Howard; 11 Mick Cassidy; 14 David Furner; 13 Andy Farrell (C). Subs: 15 Paul Johnson for Carney (12BB); 10 Neil Cowie for Howard (17); 12 Denis Betts for O'Connor (32); 19 Chris Chester for Farrell (59); O'Connor for Cowie (55); Howard for Newton (64); Cowie for Cassidy (72).
Try: Lam (63); **Goal:** Furner.
League Express Men of the Match:
Bulls: Michael Withers; *Warriors:* Adrian Lam.
Penalty count: 6-7; **Half-time:** 26-0;
Referee: Stuart Cummings (Widnes);
Attendance: 60,164 *(at Old Trafford, Manchester).*

2002

NORTHERN FORD PREMIERSHIP GRAND FINAL

Saturday 12th October 2002

HUDDERSFIELD GIANTS 38 LEIGH CENTURIONS 16

GIANTS: 1 Ben Cooper; 2 Hefin O'Hare; 3 Eorl Crabtree; 4 Graeme Hallas; 5 Marcus St Hilaire; 6 Stanley Gene; 7 Chris Thorman; 8 Michael Slicker; 9 Paul March; 10 Jeff Wittenberg; 11 David Atkins; 12 Robert Roberts; 13 Steve McNamara. Subs: 14 Heath Cruckshank for Roberts (24BB); 15 Chris Molyneux for Slicker (53); 16 Darren Turner for March (21); 17 Andy Rice for Cruckshank (57); Roberts for Wittenberg (34); Wittenberg for Roberts (74).
Tries: O'Hare (12, 78), St Hilaire (34, 53), Thorman (46), Gene (57); **Goals:** McNamara 7.
Sin bin: Roberts (47) - fighting.
CENTURIONS: 1 Neil Turley; 2 Leon Felton; 4 Jon Roper; 3 Dale Cardoza; 5 Oliver Marns; 6 Willie Swann; 7 Bobbie Goulding; 8 Vila Matautia; 9 Paul Rowley; 10 David Bradbury; 11 Simon Baldwin; 12 Andrew Isherwood; 13 Adam Bristow. Subs: 14 Gareth Price for Bradbury (24BB, rev 35); 15 John Duffy for Swann (32); 16 John Hamilton for Bristow (46BB, rev 57); 17 David Whittle for Matautia (22); Matautia for Bradbury (53BB); Swann for Goulding (58); Hamilton for Whittle (67); Bradbury for Turley (72); Goulding for Swann (75).
Tries: Cardoza (9), Marns (18), Hamilton (70);
Goals: Turley 2.

Sin bin: Whittle (47) - fighting; Bristow (74) - interference.
On report: Isherwood (66) - high tackle on Roberts.
Rugby Leaguer & League Express Men of the Match:
Giants: Chris Thorman; *Centurions:* Adam Bristow.
Penalty count: 11-11; **Half-time:** 14-10;
Referee: Karl Kirkpatrick (Warrington);
Attendance: 9,051 *(at Halton Stadium, Widnes)*.

SUPER LEAGUE GRAND FINAL

Saturday 19th October 2002

BRADFORD BULLS 18 ST HELENS 19

BULLS: 6 Michael Withers; 2 Tevita Vaikona; 20 Scott Naylor; 15 Brandon Costin; 5 Lesley Vainikolo; 1 Robbie Paul (C); 7 Paul Deacon; 8 Joe Vagana; 9 James Lowes; 29 Stuart Fielden; 11 Daniel Gartner; 12 Jamie Peacock; 13 Mike Forshaw. Subs: 14 Lee Gilmour for Gartner (21); 10 Paul Anderson for Vagana (25); 22 Brian McDermott for Fielden (34); 3 Leon Pryce for Vainikolo (53); Fielden for Anderson (55); Vainikolo for Paul (77).
Tries: Naylor (3), Paul (44), Withers (47); **Goals:** Deacon 3.
SAINTS: 1 Paul Wellens; 5 Darren Albert; 3 Martin Gleeson; 4 Paul Newlove; 19 Anthony Stewart; 13 Paul Sculthorpe; 7 Sean Long; 8 Darren Britt; 9 Keiron Cunningham; 10 Barry Ward; 23 Mike Bennett; 15 Tim Jonkers; 11 Chris Joynt (C). Subs: 2 Sean Hoppe for Wellens (3); 12 Peter Shiels for Ward (27); 14 John Stankevitch for Britt (31BB, rev 58); 17 Mick Higham for Joynt (54); Stankevitch for Shiels (58); Joynt for Britt (75); Shiels for Jonkers (77).
Tries: Bennett (24), Long (32), Gleeson (56);
Goals: Long 3; **Field goal:** Long.
Rugby Leaguer & League Express Men of the Match:
Bulls: Paul Deacon; *Saints:* Mike Bennett.
Penalty count: 5-4; **Half-time:** 12-8;
Referee: Russell Smith (Castleford); **Attendance:** 61,138 *(at Old Trafford, Manchester)*.

2003

NATIONAL LEAGUE TWO GRAND FINAL

Sunday 5th October 2003

KEIGHLEY COUGARS 13 SHEFFIELD EAGLES 11

COUGARS: 1 Matt Foster; 2 Max Tomlinson; 3 David Foster; 4 James Rushforth; 5 Andy Robinson; 6 Paul Ashton; 7 Matt Firth; 8 Phil Stephenson; 9 Simeon Hoyle; 10 Danny Ekis; 11 Oliver Wilkes; 12 Ian Sinfield; 13 Lee Patterson. Subs (all used): 14 Chris Wainwright; 15 Richard Mervill; 16 Mick Durham; 17 Jason Ramshaw.
Tries: M Foster (7), Robinson (74); **Goals:** Ashton 2;
Field goal: Firth.
EAGLES: 1 Andy Poynter; 2 Tony Weller; 3 Richard Goddard; 4 Tom O'Reilly; 5 Greg Hurst; 6 Gavin Brown; 7 Mark Aston; 8 Jack Howieson; 9 Gareth Stanley; 10 Dale Laughton; 11 Andy Raleigh; 12 Craig Brown; 13 Wayne Flynn. Subs (all used): 14 Peter Reilly; 15 Simon Tillyer; 16 Nick Turnbull; 17 Mitchell Stringer.
Try: O'Reilly (51); **Goals:** G Brown 3; **Field goal:** Reilly.
Rugby Leaguer & League Express Men of the Match:
Cougars: Simeon Hoyle; *Eagles:* Andy Raleigh.
Penalty count: 6-8; **Half-time:** 9-4;
Referee: Peter Taberner (Wigan).
(at Halton Stadium, Widnes).

NATIONAL LEAGUE ONE GRAND FINAL

Sunday 5th October 2003

LEIGH CENTURIONS 14 SALFORD CITY REDS 31

CENTURIONS: 1 Neil Turley; 2 Damian Munro; 3 Alan Hadcroft; 4 Danny Halliwell; 5 Leroy Rivett; 6 John Duffy; 7 Tommy Martyn; 8 Sonny Nickle; 9 Patrick Weisner; 10 Paul Norman; 11 Sean Richardson; 12 Willie Swann; 13 Adam Bristow. Subs (all used): 14 David Bradbury; 15 Lee Sanderson; 16 Bryan Henare; 17 Ricky Bibey.
Tries: Richardson (33), Halliwell (38), Swann (65);
Goal: Turley.
On report: Nickle (60) - late tackle on Clinch.
CITY REDS: 1 Jason Flowers; 2 Danny Arnold; 3 Stuart Littler; 4 Alan Hunte; 5 Andy Kirk; 6 Cliff Beverley; 7 Gavin Clinch; 8 Neil Baynes; 9 Malcolm Alker; 10 Andy Coley; 11 Simon Baldwin; 12 Paul Highton; 13 Chris Charles. Subs (all used): 14 Steve Blakeley; 15 David Highton; 16 Martin Moana; 17 Gareth Haggerty.
Tries: Hunte (3, 52), Beverley (23), Littler (73);
Goals: Charles 6, Blakeley; **Field goal:** Blakeley.
Rugby Leaguer & League Express Men of the Match:
Centurions: Willie Swann; *City Reds:* Gavin Clinch.
Penalty count: 10-10; **Half-time:** 10-16;
Referee: Richard Silverwood (Dewsbury);
Attendance: 9,186 *(at Halton Stadium, Widnes)*.

SUPER LEAGUE GRAND FINAL

Saturday 18th October 2003

BRADFORD BULLS 25 WIGAN WARRIORS 12

BULLS: 17 Stuart Reardon; 2 Tevita Vaikona; 6 Michael Withers; 4 Shontayne Hape; 5 Lesley Vainikolo; 15 Karl Pratt; 7 Paul Deacon; 8 Joe Vagana; 9 James Lowes; 29 Stuart Fielden; 11 Daniel Gartner; 12 Jamie Peacock; 13 Mike Forshaw. Subs (all used): 10 Paul Anderson; 18 Lee Radford; 3 Leon Pryce; 1 Robbie Paul (C).
Tries: Reardon (51), Hape (59), Lowes (75);
Goals: Deacon 6/6; **Field goal:** Deacon.
WARRIORS: 1 Kris Radlinski; 5 Brian Carney; 18 Martin Aspinwall; 14 David Hodgson; 2 Brett Dallas; 15 Sean O'Loughlin; 20 Luke Robinson; 30 Quentin Pongia; 9 Terry Newton; 10 Craig Smith; 11 Mick Cassidy; 12 Danny Tickle; 13 Andy Farrell (C). Subs (all used): 4 Paul Johnson; 8 Terry O'Connor; 23 Gareth Hock; 17 Mark Smith.
Tries: Tickle (17), Radlinski (72); **Goals:** Farrell 2/3.
Rugby Leaguer & League Express Men of the Match:
Bulls: Stuart Reardon; *Warriors:* Kris Radlinski.
Penalty count: 7-6; **Half-time:** 4-6;
Referee: Karl Kirkpatrick (Warrington);
Attendance: 65,537 *(at Old Trafford, Manchester)*.

2004

NATIONAL LEAGUE ONE GRAND FINAL

Sunday 10th October 2004

LEIGH CENTURIONS 32 WHITEHAVEN 16
(after extra-time)

CENTURIONS: 1 Neil Turley; 2 Rob Smyth; 3 Danny Halliwell; 4 Ben Cooper; 5 David Alstead; 6 John Duffy; 7 Tommy Martyn; 8 Simon Knox; 9 Paul Rowley; 10 Matt Sturm; 11 David Larder; 12 Oliver Wilkes; 13 Ian Knott. Subs (all used): 14 Dave McConnell; 15 Heath Cruckshank; 16 Richard Marshall; 17 Willie Swann.
Tries: Cooper (27, 83), Martyn (61), Turley (87);
Goals: Turley 6/8; **Field goals:** Turley 2, Rowley, Martyn.
WHITEHAVEN: 1 Gary Broadbent; 2 Craig Calvert; 3 David Seeds; 4 Mick Nanyn; 5 Wesley Wilson; 6 Leroy Joe; 7 Sam Obst; 8 Marc Jackson; 9 Aaron Lester; 10 David Fatialofa; 11 Paul Davidson; 12 Howard Hill; 13 Craig Walsh. Subs (all used): 14 Spencer Miller; 15 Carl Sice; 16 Chris McKinney; 17 Ryan Tandy.
Tries: Wilson (2, 71), Calvert (45); **Goals:** Nanyn 2/6.
Rugby Leaguer & League Express Men of the Match:
Centurions: Neil Turley; *Whitehaven:* Aaron Lester.
Penalty count: 5-9; **Half-time:** 7-6; **Full-time:** 16-16;
Referee: Ronnie Laughton (Barnsley);
Attendance: 11,005 *(at Halton Stadium, Widnes)*.

SUPER LEAGUE GRAND FINAL

Saturday 16th October 2004

BRADFORD BULLS 8 LEEDS RHINOS 16

BULLS: 6 Michael Withers; 17 Stuart Reardon; 16 Paul Johnson; 4 Shontayne Hape; 5 Lesley Vainikolo; 18 Iestyn Harris; 7 Paul Deacon; 8 Joe Vagana; 1 Robbie Paul (C); 29 Stuart Fielden; 12 Jamie Peacock; 13 Logan Swann; 11 Lee Radford. Subs: 10 Paul Anderson for Vagana (14); 15 Karl Pratt for Paul (23); 27 Rob Parker for Anderson (24); 19 Jamie Langley for Peacock (32); Paul for Withers (ht); Peacock for Radford (48); Radford for Swann (54); Vagana for Parker (56); Parker for Fielden (63); Fielden for Vagana (67); Swann for Langley (68).
Tries: Vainikolo (7), Hape (43); **Goals:** Deacon 0/2.
RHINOS: 21 Richard Mathers; 18 Mark Calderwood; 5 Chev Walker; 4 Keith Senior; 22 Marcus Bai; 13 Kevin Sinfield (C); 6 Danny McGuire; 19 Danny Ward; 9 Matt Diskin; 8 Ryan Bailey; 3 Chris McKenna; 29 Ali Lauitiiti; 11 David Furner. Subs: 16 Willie Poching for Furner (19); 10 Barrie McDermott for Ward (22); Ward for Bailey (29); 7 Rob Burrow for Lauitiiti (30); Bailey for McDermott (41); 20 Jamie Jones-Buchanan for McKenna (48); Lauitiiti for Ward (50); Furner for Sinfield (60); McKenna for Poching (63); Sinfield for Diskin (67); Poching for McKenna (72); Ward for Bailey (73).
Tries: Diskin (15), McGuire (75); **Goals:** Sinfield 4/4.
Rugby Leaguer & League Express Men of the Match:
Bulls: Lesley Vainikolo; *Rhinos:* Richard Mathers.
Penalty count: 5-5; **Half-time:** 4-10;
Referee: Steve Ganson (St Helens);
Attendance: 65,547 *(at Old Trafford, Manchester)*.

2005

NATIONAL LEAGUE ONE GRAND FINAL

Sunday 9th October 2005

CASTLEFORD TIGERS 36 WHITEHAVEN 8

TIGERS: 1 Michael Platt; 2 Waine Pryce; 3 Michael Shenton; 4 Jon Hepworth; 5 Damien Blanch; 6 Brad Davis; 7 Andrew Henderson; 8 Adam Watene; 9 Aaron Smith; 10 Richard Fletcher; 11 Tom Haughey; 12 Steve Crouch; 13 Deon Bird. Subs (all used): 14 Paul Handforth; 15 Craig Huby; 16 Adrian Vowles; 17 Frank Watene.
Tries: Huby (22), Crouch (24), Blanch (26), Davis (33, 45), Haughey (52); **Goals:** Fletcher 2/3, Huby 3/4, Hepworth 1/1.
WHITEHAVEN: 1 Gary Broadbent; 2 Craig Calvert; 3 David Seeds; 4 Mick Nanyn; 5 Wesley Wilson; 6 Leroy Joe; 7 Joel Penny; 8 Ryan Tandy; 9 Carl Sice; 10 David Fatialofa; 11 Spencer Miller; 12 Howard Hill; 13 Aaron Lester. Subs (all used): 14 Carl Rudd; 15 Aaron Summers; 16 Craig Chambers; 17 Marc Jackson.
Tries: Seeds (56), Calvert (78); **Goals:** Nanyn 0/2.
Sin bin: Joe (16) - late tackle on Davis.
On report: Joe (16) - late tackle on Davis;
Sice (40) - alleged biting.
Rugby Leaguer & League Express Men of the Match:
Tigers: Brad Davis; *Whitehaven:* Wesley Wilson.
Penalty count: 4-9; **Half-time:** 26-0;
Referee: Steve Ganson (St Helens);
Attendance: 13,300 *(at Halton Stadium, Widnes)*.

SUPER LEAGUE GRAND FINAL

Saturday 15th October 2005

BRADFORD BULLS 15 LEEDS RHINOS 6

BULLS: 6 Michael Withers; 3 Leon Pryce; 13 Ben Harris; 4 Shontayne Hape; 5 Lesley Vainikolo; 18 Iestyn Harris; 7 Paul Deacon; 12 Jamie Peacock (C); 9 Ian Henderson; 29 Stuart Fielden; 16 Paul Johnson; 10 Brad Meyers; 11 Lee Radford. Subs (all used): 24 Adrian Morley for Johnson (5); 19 Jamie Langley for Peacock (24); 8 Joe Vagana for Fielden (24); Johnson for Radford (24); 1 Robbie Paul for Henderson (31); Peacock for Vagana (45); Fielden for Morley (49); Henderson for Paul (54); Radford for Meyers (60); Morley for Peacock (62); Meyers for Langley (73); Peacock for Johnson (74).
Tries: L Pryce (29), Vainikolo (53); **Goals:** Deacon 3/5;
Field goal: I Harris.
RHINOS: 1 Richard Mathers; 2 Mark Calderwood; 3 Chev Walker; 12 Chris McKenna; 5 Marcus Bai; 6 Danny McGuire; 7 Rob Burrow; 8 Ryan Bailey; 14 Andrew Dunemann; 15 Danny Ward; 20 Gareth Ellis; 16 Willie Poching; 13 Kevin Sinfield (C). Subs (all used): 10 Barrie McDermott for Ward (17); 11 Ali Lauitiiti for Poching (21); 18 Jamie Jones-Buchanan for Bailey (31); Ward for McDermott (34); 9 Matt Diskin for Ellis (48); Poching for Lauitiiti (48); McDermott for Ward (54); Ellis for Poching (54); Lauitiiti for McDermott (61); Poching for Dunemann (65); Ward for Jones-Buchanan (68); Dunemann for Ellis (71).
Try: McGuire (22); **Goals:** Sinfield 1/2.
Rugby Leaguer & League Express Men of the Match:
Bulls: Leon Pryce; *Rhinos:* Danny McGuire.
Penalty count: 6-8; **Half-time:** 8-6;
Referee: Ashley Klein (Keighley); **Attendance:** 65,537 *(at Old Trafford, Manchester)*.

2006

NATIONAL LEAGUE TWO GRAND FINAL

Sunday 8th October 2006

SHEFFIELD EAGLES 35 SWINTON LIONS 10

EAGLES: 1 Johnny Woodcock; 5 Greg Hurst; 4 Jimmy Walker; 3 James Ford; 2 Rob Worrincy; 6 Brendon Lindsay; 7 Gavin Brown; 8 Jack Howieson; 9 Paul Pickering; 10 Mitchell Stringer; 11 Andy Hay; 12 Dale Holdstock; 13 Andy Smith. Subs (all used): 14 Craig Poucher; 15 Martin Ostler; 16 Sean Dickinson; 17 Waisale Sovatabua.
Tries: Worrincy (21, 43), Lindsay (38), Woodcock (39), Walker (51), Hay (60); **Goals:** Woodcock 5/6;
Field goal: G Brown.
LIONS: 1 Wayne English; 2 Andy Saywell; 3 Darren Woods; 4 David Alstead; 5 Marlon Billy; 6 Martin Moana; 7 Chris Hough; 8 Bruce Johnson; 9 Phil Wood; 10 Dave Newton; 11 Kris Smith; 12 Ian Sinfield; 13 Lee Marsh. Subs (all used): 14 Liam McGovern; 15 Chris Morley; 16 Danny Aboushakra; 17 Ian Parry.
Tries: Saywell (35), Alstead (74); **Goals:** McGovern 1/2.
Rugby Leaguer & League Express Men of the Match:
Eagles: Johnny Woodcock; *Lions:* Wayne English.
Penalty count: 3-4; **Half-time:** 16-4;
Referee: Peter Taberner (Wigan).
(at Halliwell Jones Stadium, Warrington).

Dewsbury Rams were National League Two Champions in 2006. This game was to determine who took the second promotion place.

Grand Finals 1998-2016

NATIONAL LEAGUE ONE GRAND FINAL

Sunday 8th October 2006

HULL KINGSTON ROVERS 29 WIDNES VIKINGS 16

ROVERS: 1 Ben Cockayne; 2 Leroy Rivett; 3 Gareth Morton; 4 Jon Goddard; 5 Byron Ford; 6 Scott Murrell; 7 James Webster; 8 Makali Aizue; 9 Ben Fisher; 10 David Tangata-Toa; 11 Iain Morrison; 12 Michael Smith; 13 Tommy Gallagher. Subs (all used): 14 Pat Weisner; 15 Dwayne Barker; 16 Jason Netherton; 17 Dave Wilson.
Tries: Ford (6), Goddard (18, 36), Murrell (24), Weisner (43); **Goals:** Morton 4/6; **Field goal:** Murrell.
VIKINGS: 1 Gavin Dodd; 2 Damien Blanch; 3 Sean Gleeson; 4 Daryl Cardiss; 5 John Kirkpatrick; 6 Dennis Moran; 7 Ian Watson; 8 Terry O'Connor; 9 Mark Smith; 10 Barrie McDermott; 11 Mick Cassidy; 12 David Allen; 13 Bob Beswick. Subs (all used): 14 Aaron Summers; 15 Oliver Wilkes; 16 Jordan James; 17 Ryan Tandy.
Tries: Dodd (32), Tandy (57), Blanch (70);.**Goals:** Dodd 2/3.
Rugby Leaguer & League Express Men of the Match:
Rovers: James Webster; *Vikings:* Mark Smith.
Penalty count: 8-5; **Half-time:** 22-4;
Referee: Phil Bentham (Warrington); **Attendance:** 13,024
(at Halliwell Jones Stadium, Warrington).

SUPER LEAGUE GRAND FINAL

Saturday 14th October 2006

HULL FC 4 ST HELENS 26

HULL: 1 Shaun Briscoe; 14 Motu Tony; 4 Sid Domic; 3 Kirk Yeaman; 5 Gareth Raynor; 13 Paul Cooke; 7 Richard Horne; 8 Ewan Dowes; 9 Richard Swain (C); 10 Garreth Carvell; 11 Lee Radford; 12 Shayne McMenemy; 24 Danny Washbrook. Subs: 15 Paul King for Carvell (17); 19 Graeme Horne for Radford (23); 26 Scott Wheeldon for Dowes (27); 6 Richard Whiting for McMenemy (29); Dowes for Wheeldon (49); Carvell for King (49); Radford for G Horne (51); McMenemy for Whiting (54); King for Carvell (68); Wheeldon for Dowes (73); Whiting for Tony (76); G Horne for Radford (77).
Try: Domic (24); **Goals:** Cooke 0/1.
SAINTS: 1 Paul Wellens; 2 Ade Gardner; 3 Jamie Lyon; 4 Willie Talau; 5 Francis Meli; 6 Leon Pryce; 7 Sean Long (C); 17 Paul Anderson; 9 Keiron Cunningham; 10 Jason Cayless; 11 Lee Gilmour; 12 Jon Wilkin; 16 Jason Hooper. Subs: 23 Maurie Fa'asavalu for P Anderson (12); 19 James Graham for Cayless (25); 15 Mike Bennett for Fa'asavalu (28); 14 James Roby for Cunningham (33); P Anderson for Wilkin (33); Cunningham for Gilmour (49); Cayless for P Anderson (52); Wilkin for Hooper (56); Fa'asavalu for Cayless (58); Gilmour for Graham (66); Cayless for Fa'asavalu (72); P Anderson for Wilkin (75).
Tries: Meli (17), Pryce (29), Talau (49), Gardner (52), Cunningham (62); **Goals:** Lyon 3/5.
Rugby Leaguer & League Express Men of the Match:
Hull: Shaun Briscoe; *Saints:* Paul Wellens.
Penalty count: 4-2; **Half-time:** 4-10;
Referee: Karl Kirkpatrick (Warrington);
Attendance: 72,582 (at Old Trafford, Manchester).

2007

NATIONAL LEAGUE TWO GRAND FINAL

Sunday 7th October 2007

FEATHERSTONE ROVERS 24 OLDHAM 6

ROVERS: 1 Loz Wildbore; 2 Danny Kirmond; 3 Jon Whittle; 4 Wayne McHugh; 5 Ade Adebisi; 6 Andy Kain; 7 Paul Handforth; 8 Gareth Handford; 9 Joe McLocklan; 10 Stuart Dickens; 11 Jamie Field; 12 Richard Blakeway; 13 Tom Haughey. Subs (all used): 14 Jamie Benn; 15 Ian Tonks; 16 James Houston; 17 Gavin Swinson.
Tries: McHugh (39, 49), Handforth (46);
Goals: Dickens 5/6; **Field goals:** Wildbore (66, 70).
Dismissal: Blakeway (64) – head butt on Roberts.
OLDHAM: 1 Gareth Langley; 2 Byron Ford; 3 Craig Littler; 4 Adam Hughes; 5 Lucas Onyango; 6 Neil Roden; 7 James Coyle; 8 Anthony Tonks; 9 Simeon Hoyle; 10 Richard Mervill; 11 Ian Sinfield; 12 Robert Roberts; 13 Geno Costin. Subs (all used): 14 Ian Hodson; 15 Alex Wilkinson; 16 Said Tamghart; 17 Matty Brooks.
Try: Hughes (31); **Goals:** Langley 1/2.
Rugby Leaguer & League Express Men of the Match:
Rovers: Paul Handforth; *Oldham:* Robert Roberts.
Penalty count: 9-5; **Half-time:** 10-6;
Referee: Gareth Hewer. (at Headingley Carnegie, Leeds).

Celtic Crusaders were National League Two Champions in 2007. This game was to determine who took the second promotion place.

NATIONAL LEAGUE ONE GRAND FINAL

Sunday 7th October 2007

CASTLEFORD TIGERS 42 WIDNES VIKINGS 10

TIGERS: 1 Stuart Donlan; 2 Danny Williams; 3 Michael Shenton; 4 Ryan McGoldrick; 5 Kirk Dixon; 6 Anthony Thackeray; 7 Danny Brough; 8 Liam Higgins; 9 Andrew Henderson; 10 Awen Guttenbeil; 11 Joe Westerman; 12 Ryan Clayton; 13 Peter Lupton. Subs (all used): 14 Mark Leafa; 15 Chris Charles; 16 Michael Wainwright; 17 Ryan Boyle.
Tries: Wainwright (20), McGoldrick (29), Guttenbeil (44, 76), M Shenton (52), Westerman (62), Clayton (66);
Goals: Brough 6/9; **Field goals:** Brough (25, 55).
VIKINGS: 1 Scott Grix; 2 Damien Blanch; 3 Toa Kohe-Love; 4 Mick Nanyn; 5 Gavin Dodd; 6 Dennis Moran; 7 Joel Penny; 8 Mick Cassidy; 9 Mark Smith; 10 Oliver Wilkes; 11 Joel Tomkins; 12 Paul Noone; 13 Bob Beswick. Subs (all used): 14 Aaron Summers; 15 Jordan James; 16 Ian Webster; 17 Lee Doran.
Tries: Nanyn (35), Wilkes (69); **Goals:** Nanyn 1/2.
Rugby Leaguer & League Express Men of the Match:
Tigers: Danny Brough; *Vikings:* Scott Grix.
Penalty count: 7-2; **Half-time:** 13-4;
Referee: Phil Bentham; **Attendance:** 20,814
(at Headingley Carnegie, Leeds).

SUPER LEAGUE GRAND FINAL

Saturday 13th October 2007

LEEDS RHINOS 33 ST HELENS 6

RHINOS: 1 Brent Webb; 5 Lee Smith; 3 Clinton Toopi; 4 Keith Senior; 2 Scott Donald; 6 Danny McGuire; 7 Rob Burrow; 8 Kylie Leuluai; 9 Matt Diskin; 10 Jamie Peacock; 11 Jamie Jones-Buchanan; 12 Gareth Ellis; 13 Kevin Sinfield (C). Subs (all used): 14 Ali Lauitiiti for Diskin (23); 16 Ryan Bailey for Leuluai (18); 18 Ian Kirke for Jones-Buchanan (33); 22 Carl Ablett for Kirke (57); Leuluai for Bailey (55); Jones-Buchanan for Lauitiiti (60); Diskin for Ablett (63); Kirke for Leuluai (65); Bailey for Kirke (76).
Tries: Webb (19), Lauitiiti (50), Donald (52), Smith (69), Jones-Buchanan (80); **Goals:** Sinfield 6/7;
Field goal: Burrow (55).
SAINTS: 1 Paul Wellens; 2 Ade Gardner; 3 Matt Gidley; 4 Willie Talau; 5 Francis Meli; 6 Leon Pryce; 7 Sean Long; 8 Nick Fozzard; 9 Keiron Cunningham (C); 10 Jason Cayless; 11 Lee Gilmour; 30 Chris Flannery; 12 Jon Wilkin. Subs (all used): 17 James Graham for Cayless (15); 14 James Roby for Cunningham (23); 23 Maurie Fa'asavalu for Fozzard (23); 15 Mike Bennett for Wilkin (31); Cayless for Fa'asavalu (34); Cunningham for Flannery (51); Wilkin for Bennett (55); Fa'asavalu for Cayless (55); Fozzard for Graham (57); Cayless for Fozzard (68); Graham for Fa'asavalu (68); Bennett for Gilmour (72).
Try: Roby (27); **Goals:** Long 1/2.
Rugby Leaguer & League Express Men of the Match:
Rhinos: Rob Burrow; *Saints:* Sean Long.
Penalty count: 4-5; **Half-time:** 8-6; **Referee:** Ashley Klein;
Attendance: 71,352 (at Old Trafford, Manchester).

2008

NATIONAL LEAGUE TWO GRAND FINAL

Sunday 28th September 2008

DONCASTER 18 OLDHAM 10

DONCASTER: 1 Zebastian Luisi; 2 Dean Colton; 3 Andreas Bauer; 4 Shaun Leaf; 5 Wayne Reittie; 6 Kyle Wood; 7 Luke Gale; 8 Nathan Freer; 9 Corey Lawrie; 10 Alex Benson; 11 Peter Green; 12 Craig Lawton; 13 Josh Weeden. Subs (all used): 14 Kyle Briggs; 15 Chris Buttery; 16 Michael Haley; 17 Mark Castle.
Tries: Buttery (44), Gale (49), Briggs (73); **Goals:** Gale 3/4.
OLDHAM: 1 Paul O'Connor; 2 Gareth Langley; 3 Marcus St Hilaire; 4 Mick Nanyn; 5 Daryl Cardiss; 6 Phil Joseph; 7 James Coyle; 8 Adam Robinson; 9 Matty Brooks; 10 Richard Mervill; 11 Tommy Goulden; 12 Danny Halliwell; 13 Robert Roberts. Subs (all used): 14 Ian Hodson; 15 Luke Menzies; 16 Chris Baines; 17 Said Tamghart.
Tries: Hodson (34), Nanyn (62); **Goals:** Nanyn 1/4.
Rugby Leaguer & League Express Men of the Match:
Doncaster: Luke Gale; *Oldham:* Adam Robinson.
Penalty count: 7-8; **Half-time:** 2-6;
Referee: Ronnie Laughton.
(at Halliwell Jones Stadium, Warrington).

Gateshead Thunder were National League Two Champions in 2008. This game was to determine who took the second promotion place.

NATIONAL LEAGUE ONE GRAND FINAL

Sunday 28th September 2008

CELTIC CRUSADERS 18 SALFORD CITY REDS 36

(after extra-time)

CRUSADERS: 1 Tony Duggan; 2 Luke Dyer; 3 Josh Hannay; 4 Mark Dalle Cort; 5 Anthony Blackwood; 6 Damien Quinn; 7 Jace Van Dijk; 8 Jordan James; 9 Neil Budworth; 10 David Tangata-Toa; 11 Chris Beasley; 12 Darren Mapp; 13 Terry Martin. Subs (all used): 14 Aaron Summers; 15 Ian Webster; 16 Mark Lennon; 17 Neale Wyatt.
Tries: Blackwood (38), Dyer (50), J James (54), Tangata-Toa (66); **Goals:** Hannay 0/1, Lennon 1/3.
CITY REDS: 1 Karl Fitzpatrick; 2 Matt Gardner; 3 Stuart Littler; 4 John Wilshere; 5 Paul White; 6 Robbie Paul; 7 Richard Myler; 8 Paul Highton; 9 Malcolm Alker; 10 Craig Stapleton; 11 Ian Sibbit; 12 Luke Adamson; 13 Jordan Turner. Subs (all used): 14 Stefan Ratchford; 15 Steve Bannister; 16 Lee Jewitt; 17 Phil Leuluai.
Tries: White (5, 86), Gardner (26), Fitzpatrick (63), Sibbit (83), Myler (99); **Goals:** Wilshere 6/7.
Rugby Leaguer & League Express Men of the Match:
Crusaders: Tony Duggan; *City Reds:* John Wilshere.
Penalty count: 5-5; **Half-time:** 4-10; **Full-time:** 18-18;
Referee: Ben Thaler; **Attendance:** 7,104
(at Halliwell Jones Stadium, Warrington).

SUPER LEAGUE GRAND FINAL

Saturday 4th October 2008

LEEDS RHINOS 24 ST HELENS 16

RHINOS: 5 Lee Smith; 22 Ryan Hall; 19 Carl Ablett; 4 Keith Senior; 2 Scott Donald; 6 Danny McGuire; 7 Rob Burrow; 8 Kylie Leuluai; 9 Matt Diskin; 10 Jamie Peacock; 11 Jamie Jones-Buchanan; 12 Gareth Ellis; 13 Kevin Sinfield (C). Subs (all used): 17 Nick Scruton; 14 Ali Lauitiiti; 18 Ian Kirke; 16 Ryan Bailey.
Tries: Smith (23), Hall (37), McGuire (49, 63);
Goals: Sinfield 4/4.
SAINTS: 1 Paul Wellens; 2 Ade Gardner; 3 Matt Gidley; 4 Willie Talau; 5 Francis Meli; 6 Leon Pryce; 7 Sean Long; 18 Bryn Hargreaves; 9 Keiron Cunningham (C); 17 James Graham; 11 Lee Gilmour; 12 Jon Wilkin; 16 Chris Flannery. Subs (all used): 8 Nick Fozzard; 21 Paul Clough; 14 James Roby; 23 Maurie Fa'asavalu.
Tries: Graham (6), Gidley (43), Gardner (59);
Goals: Long 2/3.
Rugby Leaguer & League Express Men of the Match:
Rhinos: Jamie Peacock; *Saints:* Sean Long.
Penalty count: 6-8; **Half-time:** 12-6;
Referee: Ashley Klein; **Attendance:** 68,810
(at Old Trafford, Manchester).

2009

CHAMPIONSHIP ONE GRAND FINAL

Sunday 4th October 2009

KEIGHLEY COUGARS 28 OLDHAM 26

COUGARS: 1 George Rayner; 2 Sam Gardner; 3 Dan Potter; 4 Oliver Pursglove; 5 Gavin Duffy; 6 Jon Presley; 7 Danny Jones; 17 Scott Law; 14 Jamaine Wray; 8 Andy Shickell; 11 Will Cartledge; 18 Greg Nicholson; 13 Carl Hughes. Subs (all used): 21 Ryan Smith; 28 Ryan Benjafield; 9 James Feather; 16 Brendan Rawlins.
Tries: Gardner (24), Jones (42, 50), Presley (63), Pursglove (67); **Goals:** Jones 4/5.
OLDHAM: 4 Paul Reilly; 21 Lucas Onyango; 24 Marcus St Hilaire; 22 Phil Joseph; 1 Paul O'Connor; 18 Neil Roden; 7 Thomas Coyle; 15 Jason Boults; 30 Martin Roden; 16 Wayne Kerr; 23 Chris Baines; 12 Tommy Goulden; 28 Craig Lawton. Subs (all used): 10 Jamie I'Anson; 25 Luke Menzies; 27 Matt Ashe; 29 Ben Heaton.
Tries: Menzies (35, 76), N Roden (54), St Hilaire (70), Kerr (78); **Goals:** Baines 3/4, Ashe 0/1.
Rugby Leaguer & League Express Men of the Match:
Cougars: Danny Jones; *Oldham:* Luke Menzies.
Penalty count: 9-2; **Half-time:** 4-6;
Referee: Ronnie Laughton.
(at Halliwell Jones Stadium, Warrington).

Dewsbury Rams were Championship One Champions in 2009. This game was to determine who took the second promotion place.

CHAMPIONSHIP GRAND FINAL

Sunday 4th October 2009

BARROW RAIDERS 26 HALIFAX 18

RAIDERS: 1 Gary Broadbent; 36 Andy Ballard; 32 Andreas Bauer; 4 Liam Harrison; 5 James Nixon; 24 Jamie Rooney; 31 James Coyle; 34 Rob Roberts; 9 Andy Ellis; 8 Brett McDermott; 33 Dave Allen; 22 Ned Catic; 26 Zebastian Luisi. Subs (all used): 15 Chris Young; 13 Andy Bracek; 35 Danny Halliwell; 14 Paul Noone.
Tries: Harrison (33), Ballard (37), Allen (61), Bauer (66, 78); **Goals:** Rooney 3/5.
HALIFAX: 4 Shad Royston; 5 James Haley; 15 Mark Roberts; 2 Lee Paterson; 23 Rob Worrincy; 19 Mick Govin; 7 Ben Black; 21 Neil Cherryholme; 9 Sean Penkywicz; 22 David Wrench; 11 David Larder; 27 Steve Bannister; 12 Paul Smith. Subs (all used): 13 Bob Beswick; 14 Mark Gleeson; 16 Said Tamghart; 26 Dominic Maloney.
Tries: Haley (12), Royston (31), Black (45), Govin (70); **Goals:** Paterson 1/5.
Rugby Leaguer & League Express Men of the Match: *Raiders:* Gary Broadbent; *Halifax:* Mick Govin.
Penalty count: 8-5; **Half-time:** 10-10;
Referee: Phil Bentham; **Attendance:** 11,398
(at Halliwell Jones Stadium, Warrington).

SUPER LEAGUE GRAND FINAL

Saturday 10th October 2009

LEEDS RHINOS 18 ST HELENS 10

RHINOS: 1 Brent Webb; 2 Scott Donald; 3 Lee Smith; 4 Keith Senior; 5 Ryan Hall; 6 Danny McGuire; 7 Rob Burrow; 8 Kylie Leuluai; 14 Matt Diskin; 10 Jamie Peacock; 11 Jamie Jones-Buchanan; 18 Carl Ablett; 13 Kevin Sinfield (C). Subs (all used): 16 Ryan Bailey for Leuluai (19); 19 Luke Burgess for Peacock (29); 17 Ian Kirke for Jones-Buchanan (29); 12 Ali Lauitiiti for Ablett (29); Jones-Buchanan for Lauitiiti (36); Peacock for Burgess (46); Leuluai for Bailey (53); Ablett for Kirke (57); Burgess for Diskin (62); Bailey for Leuluai (67); Diskin for Burgess (69); Kirke for Jones-Buchanan (76).
Tries: Diskin (30), Smith (37, 72); **Goals:** Sinfield 2/4;
Field goals: Sinfield (42), Burrow (78).
SAINTS: 1 Paul Wellens; 2 Ade Gardner; 3 Matt Gidley; 18 Kyle Eastmond; 5 Francis Meli; 6 Leon Pryce; 7 Sean Long; 10 James Graham; 9 Keiron Cunningham (C); 16 Tony Puletua; 12 Jon Wilkin; 11 Lee Gilmour; 13 Chris Flannery. Subs (all used): 14 James Roby for Cunningham (25); 15 Bryn Hargreaves for Puletua (24); 17 Paul Clough for Gilmour (31); 23 Maurie Fa'asavalu for Graham (31); Graham for Fa'asavalu (48); Puletua for Hargreaves (50); Gilmour for Wilkin (55); Cunningham for Clough (61); Wilkin for Roby (65); Roby for Flannery (73).
Try: Eastmond (13); **Goals:** Eastmond 3/3.
Rugby Leaguer & League Express Men of the Match: *Rhinos:* Kevin Sinfield; *Saints:* James Graham.
Penalty count: 8-7; **Half-time:** 8-8;
Referee: Steve Ganson; **Attendance:** 63,259
(at Old Trafford, Manchester).

2010

CHAMPIONSHIP ONE GRAND FINAL

Sunday 26th September 2010

OLDHAM 4 YORK CITY KNIGHTS 25

OLDHAM: 1 Paul O'Connor; 2 Lucas Onyango; 24 Marcus St Hilaire; 4 Mick Fogerty; 5 John Gillam; 6 Neil Roden; 28 Gregg McNally; 8 Jason Boults; 9 Martin Roden; 16 Wayne Kerr; 18 Chris Clarke; 13 Joe Chandler; 21 Valu Bentley. Subs (all used): 10 Dave Ellison; 19 Ben Heaton; 17 Danny Whitmore; 7 Matt Ashe.
Try: Fogerty (20); **Goals:** McNally 0/1.
CITY KNIGHTS: 31 James Haynes; 2 Wayne Reittie; 3 Mike Mitchell; 4 Lee Waterman; 28 Danny Wilson; 6 Chris Thorman; 1 Danny Ratcliffe; 17 Nathan Freer; 33 Jack Lee; 10 Alex Benson; 11 Jordan Ross; 29 Ryan Esders; 15 Luke Hardbottle. Subs (all used): 32 Paul Stamp; 36 Callum Dinsdale; 26 Steve Lewis; 30 Jack Stearman.
Tries: Reittie (7), Haynes (26), Thorman (64), Lewis (74);
Goals: Waterman 2/3, Thorman 2/2;
Field goal: Thorman (69).
Rugby Leaguer & League Express Men of the Match: *Oldham:* Neil Roden; *City Knights:* Chris Thorman.
Penalty count: 2-7; **Half-time:** 4-10;
Referee: Gareth Hewer.
(at Halliwell Jones Stadium, Warrington).

Hunslet Hawks were Championship One Champions in 2010. This game was to determine who took the second promotion place.

CHAMPIONSHIP GRAND FINAL

Sunday 26th September 2010

FEATHERSTONE ROVERS 22 HALIFAX 23
(after golden point extra-time)

ROVERS: 1 Ian Hardman; 26 Zak Hardaker; 3 Sam Smeaton; 4 Liam Welham; 2 Tom Saxton; 6 Kyle Briggs; 9 Liam Finn; 17 Tony Tonks; 31 Ben Kaye; 10 Stuart Dickens; 18 Tim Spears; 13 Jamie Field; 11 Matty Dale. Subs (all used): 19 Ross Divorty; 16 Dane Manning; 12 Jon Grayshon; 7 Andy Kain.
Tries: Briggs (28), Hardaker (30, 52), Dale (45);
Goals: Briggs 3/4.
HALIFAX: 4 Shad Royston; 2 Lee Paterson; 6 Luke Branighan; 18 Dylan Nash; 23 Rob Worrincy; 26 Graham Holroyd; 7 Ben Black; 10 Neil Cherryholme; 13 Bob Beswick; 8 Makali Aizue; 11 David Larder; 22 David Wrench; 27 Sam Barlow. Subs (all used): 9 Sean Penkywicz; 17 Frank Watene; 19 Dominic Maloney; 24 Steve Bannister.
Tries: Worrincy (20), Black (58), Branighan (60), Bannister (75); **Goals:** Paterson 3/4; **Field goal:** Black (82).
On report: Barlow (35) - alleged high tackle on Divorty.
Rugby Leaguer & League Express Men of the Match: *Rovers:* Tom Saxton; *Halifax:* Ben Black.
Penalty count: 6-3; **Half-time:** 12-4; **Full-time:** 22-22;
Referee: Robert Hicks; **Attendance:** 9,443
(at Halliwell Jones Stadium, Warrington).

SUPER LEAGUE GRAND FINAL

Saturday 2nd October 2010

ST HELENS 10 WIGAN WARRIORS 22

SAINTS: 1 Paul Wellens; 30 Jamie Foster; 3 Matt Gidley; 5 Francis Meli; 24 Jonny Lomax; 12 Jon Wilkin; 34 Matty Smith; 10 James Graham; 9 Keiron Cunningham (C); 15 Bryn Hargreaves; 4 Iosia Soliola; 13 Chris Flannery; 11 Tony Puletua. Subs (all used): 17 Paul Clough; 14 James Roby; 22 Andrew Dixon; 25 Jacob Emmitt.
Tries: Dixon (28), Meli (74); **Goals:** Foster 1/2.
WARRIORS: 6 Sam Tomkins; 24 Darrell Goulding; 3 Martin Gleeson; 4 George Carmont; 5 Pat Richards; 19 Paul Deacon; 7 Thomas Leuluai; 8 Stuart Fielden; 15 Michael Mcllorum; 10 Andy Coley; 11 Harrison Hansen; 12 Joel Tomkins; 13 Sean O'Loughlin (C). Subs (all used): 9 Mark Riddell; 17 Iafeta Palea'aesina; 25 Liam Farrell; 14 Paul Prescott.
Tries: Gleeson (4, 16), Goulding (20), S Tomkins (53);
Goals: Richards 2/3, Riddell 1/3, S Tomkins 0/1.
Rugby Leaguer & League Express Men of the Match: *Saints:* Tony Puletua; *Warriors:* Thomas Leuluai.
Penalty count: 6-11; **Half time:** 6-16;
Referee: Richard Silverwood; **Attendance:** 71,526
(at Old Trafford, Manchester).

2011

CHAMPIONSHIP ONE GRAND FINAL

Sunday 2nd October 2011

KEIGHLEY COUGARS 32 WORKINGTON TOWN 12

COUGARS: 18 James Haythornthwaite; 4 Danny Lawton; 22 Ben Sagar; 33 Jake Normington; 5 Gavin Duffy; 6 Jason Demetriou; 36 Jy-Mel Coleman; 17 Ryan Benjafield; 9 James Feather; 10 Scott Law; 11 Will Cartledge; 12 Oliver Pursglove; 21 Richard Jones. Subs (all used): 14 Jamaine Wray; 8 Andy Shickell; 16 Brendan Rawlins; 7 Ryan Smith.
Tries: Lawton (5), Feather (20), Rawlins (25), Pursglove (32), Normington (69, 77); **Goals:** Lawton 4/6.
TOWN: 1 Brett Carter; 2 Elliott Miller; 3 Jason Mossop; 4 Aaron Low; 5 Neil Frazer; 24 Darren Holt; 7 Scott Kaighan; 10 Kris Coward; 13 Karl Olstrum; 29 Dave Armitstead; 11 Mike Whitehead; 18 Joe McKenna; 12 Jarrad Stack. Subs (all used): 23 Marc Bainbridge; 15 Ruairi McGoff; 32 Chris Clough; 17 James Robinson.
Tries: Kaighan (65), Frazer (74); **Goals:** Holt 2/2.
Rugby Leaguer & League Express Men of the Match: *Cougars:* Jason Demetriou; *Town:* Jarrad Stack.
Penalty count: 7-5; **Half-time:** 22-0; **Referee:** Tim Roby.
(at Halliwell Jones Stadium, Warrington).

Swinton Lions were Championship One Champions in 2011. This game was to determine who took the second promotion place.

CHAMPIONSHIP GRAND FINAL

Sunday 2nd October 2011

FEATHERSTONE ROVERS 40 SHEFFIELD EAGLES 4

ROVERS: 1 Ian Hardman; 33 Ben Cockayne; 3 Sam Smeaton; 17 Greg Worthington; 5 Tom Saxton; 6 Andy Kain; 7 Liam Finn; 8 Tony Tonks; 9 Ben Kaye; 10 Stuart Dickens; 11 Jon Grayshon; 12 Tim Spears; 28 Jon Hepworth. Subs (all used): 18 Ross Divorty; 13 Matty Dale; 4 Andrew Bostock; 30 Kirk Netherton.
Tries: Spears (4), Finn (7, 39), Hardman (42), Cockayne (56), Hepworth (59), Saxton (79); **Goals:** Finn 6/7.
Sin bin: Netherton (54) - fighting.
EAGLES: 6 Quentin Laulu-Togagae; 5 Tim Bergin; 26 Corey Hanson; 1 Misi Taulapapa; 16 Vinny Finigan; 13 Dane McDonald; 7 Simon Brown; 8 Jack Howieson; 9 Andrew Henderson; 10 Mitchell Stringer; 11 Alex Szostak; 12 Peter Green; 19 Joe Hirst. Subs (all used): 22 Ryan Hepworth; 30 Sam Scott; 20 Pat Smith; 14 Jonny Woodcock.
Try: McDonald (12); **Goals:** Brown 0/1.
Sin bin: Hirst (54) - fighting.
Rugby Leaguer & League Express Men of the Match: *Rovers:* Liam Finn; *Eagles:* Joe Hirst.
Penalty count: 7-11; **Half-time:** 18-4;
Referee: Matthew Thomason; **Attendance:** 7,263
(at Halliwell Jones Stadium, Warrington).

SUPER LEAGUE GRAND FINAL

Saturday 8th October 2011

LEEDS RHINOS 32 ST HELENS 16

RHINOS: 1 Brent Webb; 23 Ben Jones-Bishop; 27 Zak Hardaker; 12 Carl Ablett; 5 Ryan Hall; 13 Kevin Sinfield (C); 6 Danny McGuire; 8 Kylie Leuluai; 9 Danny Buderus; 10 Jamie Peacock; 11 Jamie Jones-Buchanan; 3 Brett Delaney; 21 Chris Clarkson. Subs (all used): 7 Rob Burrow; 16 Ryan Bailey; 17 Ian Kirke; 14 Ali Lauitiiti.
Tries: Burrow (34), Webb (65), Hall (70), Ablett (74), Hardaker (80); **Goals:** Sinfield 6/7.
SAINTS: 1 Paul Wellens (C); 28 Tom Makinson; 3 Michael Shenton; 5 Francis Meli; 22 Jamie Foster; 25 Lee Gaskell; 20 Jonny Lomax; 10 James Graham (C); 9 James Roby; 11 Tony Puletua; 12 Jon Wilkin; 4 Iosia Soliola; 16 Paul Clough. Subs (all used): 19 Andrew Dixon; 14 Scott Moore; 15 Louie McCarthy-Scarsbrook; 17 Gary Wheeler.
Tries: Makinson (50), Shenton (55); **Goals:** Foster 4/5.
Rugby Leaguer & League Express Men of the Match: *Rhinos:* Rob Burrow; *Saints:* Lee Gaskell.
Penalty count: 5-7; **Half-time:** 8-2;
Referee: Phil Bentham; **Attendance:** 69,107
(at Old Trafford, Manchester).

2012

CHAMPIONSHIP ONE GRAND FINAL

Sunday 30th September 2012

BARROW RAIDERS 13 DONCASTER 16

RAIDERS: 1 Andy Ballard; 2 Lee Haney; 3 Chris Larkin; 4 Aaron Low; 5 James Nixon; 6 Scott Kaighan; 7 Liam Campbell; 8 Jamie Butler; 9 James Dandy; 10 Ryan Duffy; 11 Liam Harrison; 12 James Gordon; 13 Daniel Toal. Subs (all used): 14 Liam Finch; 15 Martin Ostler; 16 Ruairi McGoff; 17 Andrew Dawson.
Tries: Larkin (4), Low (77); **Goals:** Ballard 2/3;
Field goal: Kaighan (39).
DONCASTER: 1 Lee Waterman; 2 Tom Hodson; 3 Chris Spurr; 4 Danny Cowling; 5 Stewart Sanderson; 6 Kyle Kesik; 7 Craig Fawcett; 8 Mark Castle; 9 Mike Emmett; 10 Russ Spiers; 11 Lucas Walshaw; 12 Michael Kelly; 13 Carl Hughes. Subs (all used): 14 Nathan Powley; 15 Craig Robinson; 16 Grant Edwards; 17 Liam Cunningham.
Tries: Sanderson (11), Waterman (46), Fawcett (57);
Goals: Hodson 2/3.
Rugby Leaguer & League Express Men of the Match: *Raiders:* Liam Harrison; *Doncaster:* Craig Fawcett.
Penalty count: 4-5; **Half-time:** 7-4; **Referee:** Jamie Leahy.
(at Halliwell Jones Stadium, Warrington).

CHAMPIONSHIP GRAND FINAL

Sunday 30th September 2012

FEATHERSTONE ROVERS 16 SHEFFIELD EAGLES 20

ROVERS: 1 Ian Hardman; 2 Tangi Ropati; 3 Nathan Chappell; 4 Greg Worthington; 5 Tom Saxton; 6 Andy Kain; 7 Liam Finn; 8 Anthony England; 9 Ben Kaye; 10 James Lockwood; 11 Matty Dale; 12 Tim Spears; 13 Kyle Briggs. Subs (all used): 14 Dominic Maloney; 15 Stuart Dickens; 16 Andrew Bostock; 17 Jon Hepworth.
Tries: Hardman (17), Hepworth (51); **Goals:** Finn 4/4.
On report:
Maloney (57) - alleged use of the elbow on Turner.
EAGLES: 1 Quentin Laulu-Togagae; 2 Misi Taulapapa; 3 Duane Straugheir; 4 Menzie Yere; 5 Scott Turner; 6 Simon Brown; 7 Dominic Brambani; 8 Jack Howieson; 9 Andrew Henderson; 10 Mitchell Stringer; 11 Michael Knowles; 12 Sam Scott; 13 Alex Szostak. Subs (all used): 14 James Davey; 15 Peter Green; 16 Dane McDonald; 17 Liam Higgins.
Tries: Turner (9), Laulu-Togagae (32), McDonald (46), Taulapapa (57); **Goals:** Brown 2/5.
Rugby Leaguer & League Express Men of the Match: *Rovers:* Ian Hardman; *Eagles:* Michael Knowles.
Penalty count: 4-6; **Half-time:** 8-10; **Referee:** Tim Roby;
Attendance: 6,409
(at Halliwell Jones Stadium, Warrington).

SUPER LEAGUE GRAND FINAL

Saturday 6th October 2012

LEEDS RHINOS 26 WARRINGTON WOLVES 18

RHINOS: 4 Zak Hardaker; 2 Ben Jones-Bishop; 3 Kallum Watkins; 12 Carl Ablett; 5 Ryan Hall; 13 Kevin Sinfield (C); 6 Danny McGuire; 8 Kylie Leuluai; 7 Rob Burrow; 10 Jamie Peacock; 11 Jamie Jones-Buchanan; 15 Brett Delaney; 16 Ryan Bailey. Subs (all used): 17 Ian Kirke; 20 Darrell Griffin; 25 Stevie Ward; 31 Shaun Lunt.
Tries: Sinfield (19), Jones-Bishop (28), Ablett (59), Hall (72); **Goals:** Sinfield 5/5.
WOLVES: 1 Brett Hodgson; 5 Joel Monaghan; 19 Stefan Ratchford; 4 Ryan Atkins; 2 Chris Riley; 6 Lee Briers; 7 Richard Myler; 20 Chris Hill; 14 Mick Higham; 13 Ben Harrison; 12 Ben Westwood; 11 Trent Waterhouse; 15 Simon Grix. Subs (all used): 8 Adrian Morley (C); 9 Michael Monaghan; 16 Paul Wood; 17 Michael Cooper.
Tries: Myler (4), J Monaghan (38), Atkins (45);
Goals: Hodgson 3/4.
Rugby Leaguer & League Express Men of the Match:
Rhinos: Kevin Sinfield; *Wolves:* Richard Myler.
Penalty count: 6-5; **Half-time:** 14-14;
Referee: Richard Silverwood; **Attendance:** 70,676
(at Old Trafford, Manchester).

2013

CHAMPIONSHIP ONE GRAND FINAL

Sunday 29th September 2013

OLDHAM 18 ROCHDALE HORNETS 32

OLDHAM: 1 Richard Lepori; 2 Mo Agoro; 21 David Cookson; 25 Jonathan Ford; 5 Dale Bloomfield; 23 Lewis Palfrey; 16 Kenny Hughes; 18 Phil Joy; 9 Sam Gee; 10 Jason Boults; 11 Josh Crowley; 12 Danny Langtree; 13 Mark Hobson. Subs (all used): 14 Adam Files; 19 Michael Ward; 22 Liam Thompson; 28 Matthew Haggarty.
Tries: Ford (12), Hughes (38), Cookson (44);
Goals: Palfrey 3/3.
HORNETS: 1 Wayne English; 2 Gareth Langley; 20 Daniel Davies; 23 Dave Hull; 17 Martin Waring; 6 Paul Crook; 7 Steve Roper; 29 Carl Forster; 31 Chris Hough; 10 Warren Thompson; 26 Dave Llewellyn; 14 Alex Trumper; 18 Joe Greenwood. Subs (all used): 8 John Cookson; 9 Alex McClurg; 11 Chris Baines; 13 Jordan Case.
Tries: Llewellyn (5), Davies (20), Hull (58), Cookson (71), English (78); **Goals:** Crook 6/6.
Rugby Leaguer & League Express Men of the Match:
Oldham: Lewis Palfrey; *Hornets:* Paul Crook.
Penalty count: 1-2; **Half-time:** 12-12;
Referee: Chris Leatherbarrow. *(at Leigh Sports Village).*

North Wales Crusaders were Championship One Champions in 2013. This game was to determine who took the second promotion place.

CHAMPIONSHIP GRAND FINAL

Sunday 29th September 2013

BATLEY BULLDOGS 12 SHEFFIELD EAGLES 19

BULLDOGS: 1 Miles Greenwood; 5 Johnny Campbell; 3 Jason Walton; 4 Danny Maun; 21 Greg Johnson; 6 Ben Black; 7 Gareth Moore; 8 Byron Smith; 9 Paul Mennell; 28 Anthony Mullally; 11 Alex Bretherton; 16 John Davies; 13 Ashley Lindsay. Subs (all used): 14 George Flanagan; 15 Keegan Hirst; 19 Alex Rowe; 17 Liam Walmsley.
Try: Campbell (13); **Goals:** Moore 4/5.
EAGLES: 1 Quentin Laulu-Togagae; 5 Misi Taulapapa; 4 Tom Armstrong; 3 Menzie Yere; 2 Scott Turner; 6 Pat Walker; 7 Dominic Brambani; 25 Eddie Battye; 9 Andrew Henderson; 10 Mitchell Stringer; 11 Michael Knowles; 15 Alex Szostak; 13 Joe Hirst. Subs (all used): 14 James Davey; 12 Peter Green; 16 Duane Straugheir; 21 Matt Garside.
Tries: Turner (56, 67), Yere (61), Laulu-Togagae (70);
Goals: Brambani 1/5; **Field goal:** Walker (74).
Rugby Leaguer & League Express Men of the Match:
Bulldogs: Keegan Hirst; *Eagles:* Dominic Brambani.
Penalty count: 6-7; **Half-time:** 12-0;
Referee: Matthew Thomason; **Attendance:** 6,374
(at Leigh Sports Village).

SUPER LEAGUE GRAND FINAL

Saturday 5th October 2013

WARRINGTON WOLVES 16 WIGAN WARRIORS 30

WOLVES: 19 Stefan Ratchford; 5 Joel Monaghan; 3 Chris Bridge; 4 Ryan Atkins; 2 Chris Riley; 6 Lee Briers; 7 Richard Myler; 16 Paul Wood; 14 Mick Higham; 18 Chris Hill; 13 Ben Harrison; 12 Ben Westwood; 15 Simon Grix. Subs (all used): 9 Michael Monaghan; 8 Adrian Morley (C); 17 Michael Cooper; 10 Garreth Carvell.

Wigan's Willie Isa takes on Warrington's Kurt Gidley during the 2016 Super League Grand Final

Tries: J Monaghan (20), Grix (24), Westwood (27);
Goals: Ratchford 2/3.
On report: Westwood (2) - alleged punch on Green.
WARRIORS: 1 Sam Tomkins; 2 Josh Charnley; 3 Darrell Goulding; 17 Iain Thornley; 5 Pat Richards; 6 Blake Green; 7 Matty Smith; 10 Lee Mossop; 9 Michael McIlorum; 20 Gil Dudson; 11 Harrison Hansen; 12 Liam Farrell; 13 Sean O'Loughlin (C). Subs (all used): 15 Ben Flower; 4 Jack Hughes; 26 Dominic Crosby; 21 Scott Taylor.
Tries: Goulding (37), McIlorum (47), Charnley (53), Green (65), Richards (74); **Goals:** Richards 5/6.
Rugby Leaguer & League Express Men of the Match:
Wolves: Chris Hill; *Warriors:* Michael McIlorum.
Penalty count: 7-10; **Half-time:** 16-6;
Referee: Richard Silverwood; **Attendance:** 66,281
(at Old Trafford, Manchester).

2014

CHAMPIONSHIP ONE GRAND FINAL

Sunday 5th October 2014

HUNSLET HAWKS 17 OLDHAM 16
(after golden point extra-time)

HAWKS: 2 Jimmy Watson; 36 Gavin Duffy; 4 Danny Maun; 3 Lee Brickwood; 37 James Duckworth; 6 Thomas Coyle; 20 Danny Ansell; 38 Richard Moore; 9 David March; 10 James Houston; 11 John Oakes; 12 Aaron Lyons; 31 Luke Briscoe. Subs (all used): 27 Liam Hood; 8 Michael Haley; 1 Stuart Kain; 40 Luke Hardbottle.
Tries: Watson (22), Duckworth (45), T Coyle (53);
Goals: March 2/3; **Field goal:** T Coyle (85).
OLDHAM: 4 Steven Nield; 29 Adam Clay; 21 David Cookson; 25 Jonathan Ford; 5 Dale Bloomfield; 6 Lewis Palfrey; 26 Steve Roper; 8 Phil Joy; 30 Gareth Owen; 10 Jason Boults; 11 Josh Crowley; 12 Danny Langtree; 22 Liam Thompson. Subs (all used): 19 Michael Ward; 28 Nathan Mason; 16 Kenny Hughes; 20 George Tyson.
Tries: Roper (5), Bloomfield (31), Langtree (74);
Goals: Roper 2/3.
Rugby Leaguer & League Express Men of the Match:
Hawks: Liam Hood; *Oldham:* Jonathan Ford.
Penalty count: 4-3; **Half-time:** 6-10; **Referee:** Joe Cobb.
(at Headingley Carnegie, Leeds).

CHAMPIONSHIP GRAND FINAL

Sunday 5th October 2014

FEATHERSTONE ROVERS 12 LEIGH CENTURIONS 36

ROVERS: 2 Will Sharp; 35 Jason Crookes; 1 Ian Hardman; 18 Jamie Cording; 36 Ben Blackmore; 23 Andy Kain; 7 Gareth Moore; 8 Steve Crossley; 9 Andy Ellis; 13 Matt James; 31 Shaun Pick; 11 James Lockwood; 12 Tim Spears. Subs (all used): 30 Luke Teasdale; 6 Jack Bussey; 42 Chris Annakin; 10 Keegan Hirst.
Tries: Sharp (27, 51); **Goals:** Moore 2/2.
Sin bin: Crookes (68) - high tackle on Armstrong.

CENTURIONS

CENTURIONS: 1 Gregg McNally; 22 Adam Higson; 34 Michael Platt; 4 Tom Armstrong; 15 Liam Kay; 6 Martyn Ridyard; 7 Ryan Brierley; 29 Jake Emmitt; 14 Sean Penkywicz; 10 Oliver Wilkes; 11 Matt Sarsfield; 30 Kurt Haggerty; 13 Sam Barlow. Subs (all used): 9 Bob Beswick; 18 Jamie Acton; 16 Martin Aspinwall; 33 Jonathan Walker.
Tries: Sarsfield (5), McNally (17), Armstrong (22), Higson (65), Barlow (70), Brierley (80);
Goals: Ridyard 6/8.
Sin bin: Penkywicz (68) - retaliation.
Rugby Leaguer & League Express Men of the Match:
Rovers: Jack Bussey; *Centurions:* Tom Armstrong.
Penalty count: 6-8; **Half-time:** 6-20;
Referee: Matthew Thomason; **Attendance:** 9,164
(at Headingley Carnegie, Leeds).

SUPER LEAGUE GRAND FINAL

Saturday 11th October 2014

ST HELENS 14 WIGAN WARRIORS 6

SAINTS: 17 Paul Wellens (C); 2 Tom Makinson; 22 Mark Percival; 4 Josh Jones; 5 Adam Swift; 15 Mark Flanagan; 6 Lance Hohaia; 16 Kyle Amor; 9 James Roby; 8 Mose Masoe; 10 Louie McCarthy-Scarsbrook; 11 Iosia Soliola; 3 Jordan Turner. Subs (all used): 28 Luke Thompson; 13 Willie Manu; 18 Alex Walmsley; 27 Greg Richards.
Tries: Soliola (54), Makinson (69); **Goals:** Percival 3/3.
WARRIORS: 1 Matt Bowen; 2 Josh Charnley; 5 Anthony Gelling; 23 Dan Sarginson; 32 Joe Burgess; 6 Blake Green; 7 Matty Smith; 10 Ben Flower; 19 Sam Powell; 17 Dominic Crosby; 11 Joel Tomkins; 12 Liam Farrell; 13 Sean O'Loughlin (C). Subs (all used): 22 Eddy Pettybourne; 24 Tony Clubb; 25 John Bateman; 27 George Williams.
Try: Burgess (40); **Goals:** Smith 1/3.
Dismissal: Flower (2) - punching Hohaia.
Rugby Leaguer & League Express Men of the Match:
Saints: James Roby; *Warriors:* Liam Farrell.
Penalty count: 9-7; **Half-time:** 2-6;
Referee: Phil Bentham; **Attendance:** 70,102
(at Old Trafford, Manchester).

2015

SUPER LEAGUE GRAND FINAL

Saturday 10th October 2015

LEEDS RHINOS 22 WIGAN WARRIORS 20

RHINOS: 1 Zak Hardaker; 2 Tom Briscoe; 3 Kallum Watkins; 4 Joel Moon; 5 Ryan Hall; 13 Kevin Sinfield (C); 6 Danny McGuire; 30 Mitch Garbutt; 7 Rob Burrow; 10 Jamie Peacock; 12 Carl Ablett; 15 Brett Delaney; 19 Brad Singleton. Subs (all used): 8 Kylie Leuluai; 17 Adam Cuthbertson; 20 Jimmy Keinhorst; 21 Josh Walters.
Tries: McGuire (7, 35), Moon (27), Walters (64);
Goals: Sinfield 3/4.
WARRIORS: 1 Matt Bowen; 22 Dominic Manfredi; 14 John Bateman; 34 Oliver Gildart; 5 Joe Burgess; 6 George Williams; 7 Matty Smith; 8 Dominic Crosby; 9 Michael McIlorum; 10 Ben Flower; 11 Joel Tomkins; 12 Liam Farrell; 13 Sean O'Loughlin (C). Subs (all used): 16 Sam Powell; 17 Tony Clubb; 23 Lee Mossop; 25 Larne Patrick.
Tries: Burgess (4), Manfredi (46), Bowen (49);
Goals: Bowen 4/4.
Rugby Leaguer & League Express Men of the Match:
Rhinos: Danny McGuire; *Warriors:* Matt Bowen.
Penalty count: 5-4; **Half-time:** 16-6;
Referee: Ben Thaler; **Attendance:** 73,512
(at Old Trafford, Manchester).

2016

SUPER LEAGUE GRAND FINAL

Saturday 8th October 2016

WARRINGTON WOLVES 6 WIGAN WARRIORS 12

WOLVES: 6 Stefan Ratchford; 2 Tom Lineham; 3 Rhys Evans; 4 Ryan Atkins; 5 Matthew Russell; 1 Kurt Gidley; 26 Declan Patton; 8 Chris Hill (C); 9 Daryl Clark; 10 Ashton Sims; 27 Sam Wilde; 12 Jack Hughes; 14 Joe Westerman. Subs (all used): 24 Toby King; 18 George King; 7 Chris Sandow; 33 Ryan Bailey.
Try: Patton (21); **Goals:** Patton 1/1.
WARRIORS: 4 Dan Sarginson; 2 Josh Charnley; 3 Anthony Gelling; 20 Oliver Gildart; 22 Lewis Tierney; 6 George Williams; 7 Matty Smith; 24 Frank-Paul Nuuausala; 16 Sam Powell; 10 Ben Flower; 14 John Bateman; 12 Liam Farrell; 25 Willie Isa. Subs (all used): 8 Dominic Crosby; 9 Taulima Tautai; 21 Ryan Sutton; 13 Sean O'Loughlin (C).
Tries: Gildart (55), Charnley (63); **Goals:** Smith 2/4.
Rugby Leaguer & League Express Men of the Match:
Wolves: Kurt Gidley; *Warriors:* Liam Farrell.
Penalty count: 4-6; **Half-time:** 6-2;
Referee: Robert Hicks; **Attendance:** 70,202
(at Old Trafford, Manchester).

2017 SEASON
Stats round-up

SUPER LEAGUE CLUBS - AVERAGES

	2017 Avg	2016 Avg	Diff
Leeds Rhinos	14,573	15,478	-905
Wigan Warriors	13,669	13,235	+434
Hull FC	11,459	11,590	-131
St Helens	10,946	10,711	+235
Warrington Wolves	10,164	11,095	-931
Castleford Tigers	8,945	7,458	+1,487
Catalans Dragons	8,612	9,348	-736
Leigh Centurions	6,301	4,260	+2,041
		(Championship)	
Huddersfield Giants	5,873	5,271	+602
Widnes Vikings	5,587	5,471	+116
Wakefield Trinity	5,283	4,992	+291
Salford Red Devils	3,941	3,228	+713
2017 Average	8,779		
2016 Average	8,791		
Difference	-12		

CHAMPIONSHIP CLUBS - AVERAGES

	2017 Avg	2016 Avg	Diff
Hull Kingston Rovers	7,429	7,610	-181
		(Super League)	
Bradford Bulls	3,877	4,178	-301
Featherstone Rovers	2,624	2,655	-31
Toulouse Olympique	1,814	1,513	+301
		(League 1)	
Halifax	1,796	1,713	+83
Dewsbury Rams	1,028	1,082	-54
Batley Bulldogs	998	1,271	-273
London Broncos	891	830	+61
Rochdale Hornets	832	512	+320
		(League 1)	
Oldham	777	831	-54
Swinton Lions	775	767	+8
Sheffield Eagles	637	626	+11
2017 Average	1,957		
2016 Average	1,637		
Difference	+320		

LEAGUE 1 CLUBS - AVERAGES

	2017 Avg	2016 Avg	Diff
Toronto Wolfpack	6,960	N/A	N/A
York City Knights	1,055	582	+473
Barrow Raiders	1,042	941	+101
Newcastle Thunder	863	810	+53
Keighley Cougars	784	575	+209
Whitehaven	703	716	-13
		(Championship)	
Workington Town	631	717	-86
		(Championship)	
Doncaster	572	587	-15
London Skolars	451	398	+53
Hunslet	423	452	-29
Coventry Bears	366	426	-60
North Wales Crusaders	342	430	-88
South Wales Ironmen	219	294	-75
Gloucestershire All Golds	211	134	+77
Oxford	134	162	-28
Hemel Stags	116	180	-64
2017 Average	930		
2016 Average	533		
Difference	+397		

BEST ATTENDANCES

		Round	Date
72,827	Castleford v Leeds	SLGF	7/10/17
	(at Old Trafford, Manchester)		
68,525	Hull FC v Wigan	CCF	26/8/17
	(at Wembley Stadium)		
23,390	Wigan v St Helens	SLR9	14/4/17
21,011	Wigan v Cronulla	WCC	19/2/17
18,029	Leeds v Castleford	SLR19	23/6/17
17,030	Leeds v Wigan	SLR7	31/3/17
16,938	Leeds v Hull FC	SLR22	14/7/17
16,326	Leeds v St Helens	SLS8R3	18/8/17
15,706	Wigan v Castleford	SLS8R6	17/9/17
15,699	Wigan v Leigh	SLR3	3/3/17
15,487	Hull FC v Leeds	SLR9	14/4/17
15,408	Leeds v Widnes	SLR10	17/4/17
15,248	St Helens v Wigan	SLS8R4	1/9/17
15,119	Wigan v Leeds	SLR23	21/7/17
14,974	Leeds v Warrington	SLR15	26/5/17
14,575	Leeds v Salford	SLR2	24/2/17
14,526	Hull FC v Leeds	CCSF	29/7/17
	(at Keepmoat Stadium, Doncaster)		
14,411	Leeds v Wakefield	SLR5	17/3/17
13,579	Leeds v Wigan	SLS8R1	4/8/17
13,544	Hull FC v Catalans Dragons	SLR2	23/2/17

315

LEADING SCORERS

CHAMPIONSHIP *(Regular season only)*

TRIES

1	Garry Lo	Sheffield Eagles	27
2	Ryan Shaw	Hull Kingston Rovers	18
	Jarrod Sammut	London Broncos	18
4	Andrew Heffernan	Hull Kingston Rovers	17
	Rob Massam	Rochdale Hornets	17
6	Steve Tyrer	Halifax	16
7	Ethan Ryan	Bradford Bulls	15
	Mike Butt	Swinton Lions	15
	Kuni Minga	Toulouse Olympique	15
10	Wayne Reittie	Batley Bulldogs	14
	James Bentley	Bradford Bulls	14
	Kieran Dixon	London Broncos	14

GOALS

1	Jamie Ellis	Hull Kingston Rovers	119
2	Steve Tyrer	Halifax	89
3	Mark Kheirallah	Toulouse Olympique	83
4	Simon Brown	Sheffield Eagles	67
5	Chris Atkin	Swinton Lions	63
6	Scott Leatherbarrow	Oldham	61
7	Oscar Thomas	Bradford Bulls	60
8	Jarrod Sammut	London Broncos	57
9	Pat Walker	Batley Bulldogs	45
10	Cory Aston	Bradford Bulls/Featherstone Rovers	44
	Kieran Dixon	London Broncos	44

POINTS

			T	G	FG	Pts
1	Jamie Ellis	Hull Kingston Rovers	6	119	0	262
2	Steve Tyrer	Halifax	16	89	0	242
3	Mark Kheirallah	Toulouse Olympique	11	83	1	211
4	Jarrod Sammut	London Broncos	18	57	0	186
5	Kieran Dixon	London Broncos	14	44	0	144
6	Chris Atkin	Swinton Lions	3	63	5	143
7	Oscar Thomas	Bradford Bulls	4	60	3	139
8	Simon Brown	Sheffield Eagles	0	67	0	134
9	Scott Leatherbarrow	Oldham	0	61	0	122
10	Cory Aston	Bradford Bulls/Featherstone Rovers	5	44	1	109

CHALLENGE CUP

TRIES

1	Kieran Cross	Doncaster	6
2	Luke Cresswell	Barrow Raiders	5
	Ash Handley	Leeds Rhinos	5
	Joel Moon	Leeds Rhinos	5
	Joe Burgess	Wigan Warriors	5

GOALS

1	Liam Sutcliffe	Leeds Rhinos	19
2	Michael Dobson	Salford Red Devils	15
3	Jamie Ellis	Hull Kingston Rovers	14
4	Lewis Charnock	Barrow Raiders	13
	Jake Connor	Hull FC	13
	Harry Tyson-Wilson	York City Knights	13

POINTS

			T	G	FG	Pts
1	Liam Sutcliffe	Leeds Rhinos	2	19	0	46
2	Lewis Charnock	Barrow Raiders	3	13	0	38
3	Michael Dobson	Salford Red Devils	1	15	0	34
4	Jamie Ellis	Hull Kingston Rovers	1	14	1	33
5	Jake Connor	Hull FC	1	13	0	30

Garry Lo   Jamie Ellis   Mark Kheirallah

CHAMPIONSHIP SHIELD

TRIES

1	Garry Lo	Sheffield Eagles	9
	Mark Kheirallah	Toulouse Olympique	9
3	Wayne Reittie	Batley Bulldogs	7
	Elliot Minchella	Sheffield Eagles	7
	Stan Robin	Toulouse Olympique	7

GOALS

1	Mark Kheirallah	Toulouse Olympique	37
2	Paul Sykes	Dewsbury Rams	31
3	Pat Walker	Batley Bulldogs	29
4	Cory Aston	Bradford Bulls	23
	Chris Hankinson	Swinton Lions	23

POINTS

			T	G	FG	Pts
1	Mark Kheirallah	Toulouse Olympique	9	37	0	110
2	Paul Sykes	Dewsbury Rams	0	31	1	63
3	Cory Aston	Bradford Bulls	3	23	0	58
	Pat Walker	Batley Bulldogs	0	29	0	58
5	Chris Hankinson	Swinton Lions	2	23	0	54

LEAGUE 1 CUP

TRIES

1	Shane Toal	Barrow Raiders	5
	Josh Atkinson	Oxford	5
3	Jamie Dallimore	Barrow Raiders	4
	Steve Parry	Gloucestershire All Golds	4
	(11 players tied on 3)		

GOALS

1	Lewis Charnock	Barrow Raiders	20
2	Tommy Johnson	North Wales Crusaders	18
3	Kieran Hyde	Gloucestershire All Golds	12
4	Charlie Lawrence	London Skolars	6
5	Benn Hardcastle	Newcastle Thunder	5

POINTS

			T	G	FG	Pts
1	Lewis Charnock	Barrow Raiders	3	20	0	52
2	Tommy Johnson	North Wales Crusaders	3	18	0	48
3	Jamie Dallimore	Barrow Raiders	4	4	0	24
	Kieran Hyde	Gloucestershire All Golds	0	12	0	24
5	Josh Atkinson	Oxford	5	0	0	20
	Shane Toal	Barrow Raiders	5	0	0	20

LEADING SCORERS

SUPER LEAGUE

(Regular season, Super 8s, Semi-finals & Grand Final.
Super 8s (Qualifiers) not included)

TRIES

1	Greg Eden	Castleford Tigers	38
2	Liam Marshall	Wigan Warriors	21
3	Ben Jones-Bishop	Wakefield Trinity	20
4	Greg Minikin	Castleford Tigers	19
	Jermaine McGillvary	Huddersfield Giants	19
	Albert Kelly	Hull FC	19
7	Joe Burgess	Wigan Warriors	18
8	Jamie Shaul	Hull FC	17
	Matt Parcell	Leeds Rhinos	17
	Mark Percival	St Helens	17
	Mason Caton-Brown	Wakefield Trinity	17

GOALS

1	Luke Gale	Castleford Tigers	135
2	Marc Sneyd	Hull FC	105
3	Liam Finn	Wakefield Trinity	96
	Mark Percival	St Helens	96
5	Luke Walsh	Catalans Dragons	69
6	Danny Brough	Huddersfield Giants	61
7	Kallum Watkins	Leeds Rhinos	51
8	Ben Reynolds	Leigh Centurions	48
9	Michael Dobson	Salford Red Devils	46
10	Gareth O'Brien	Salford Red Devils	45
	Liam Sutcliffe	Leeds Rhinos	45

Greg Eden

Luke Gale

SUPER 8s - THE QUALIFIERS

TRIES

1	Peta Hiku	Warrington Wolves	9
2	Ben Heaton	Halifax	7
	Ryan Shaw	Hull Kingston Rovers	7
4	James Clare	Leigh Centurions	6
5	Brayden Wiliame	Catalans Dragons	5
	Jarrod Sammut	London Broncos	5
	Joe Mellor	Widnes Vikings	5

GOALS

1	Luke Walsh	Catalans Dragons	26
2	Jamie Ellis	Hull Kingston Rovers	25
3	Jarrod Sammut	London Broncos	24
4	Declan Patton	Warrington Wolves	23
5	Harvey Livett	Warrington Wolves	17

POINTS

			T	G	FG	Pts
1	Jarrod Sammut	London Broncos	5	24	0	68
2	Declan Patton	Warrington Wolves	3	23	0	58
3	Jamie Ellis	Hull Kingston Rovers	1	25	0	54
4	Luke Walsh	Catalans Dragons	0	26	0	52
5	Harvey Livett	Warrington Wolves	3	17	0	46

GOALS PERCENTAGE

			G	Att	%
1	Tony Gigot	Catalans Dragons	9	10	90.00
2	Marc Sneyd	Hull FC	105	119	88.23
3	Jake Connor	Hull FC	20	23	86.95
4	Luke Walsh	Catalans Dragons	69	81	85.18
5	Martyn Ridyard	Huddersfield Giants/ Leigh Centurions	28	33	84.84
6	Kallum Watkins	Leeds Rhinos	51	61	83.60
7	Luke Gale	Castleford Tigers	135	163	82.82
8	Liam Finn	Wakefield Trinity	96	116	82.75
9	Ben Reynolds	Leigh Centurions	48	60	80.00
	Tom Makinson	St Helens	8	10	80.00

(10 minimum attempts to qualify)

POINTS

			T	G	FG	Pts
1	Luke Gale	Castleford Tigers	14	135	8	334
2	Mark Percival	St Helens	17	96	0	260
3	Marc Sneyd	Hull FC	7	105	3	241
4	Liam Finn	Wakefield Trinity	1	96	0	196
5	Greg Eden	Castleford Tigers	38	0	0	152
6	Luke Walsh	Catalans Dragons	2	69	4	150
	Kallum Watkins	Leeds Rhinos	12	51	0	150
8	Danny Brough	Huddersfield Giants	4	61	3	141
9	George Williams	Wigan Warriors	11	43	1	131
10	Gareth O'Brien	Salford Red Devils	8	45	2	124

CONSECUTIVE APPEARANCES *(all club games included)*

1	Jack Hughes	Warrington Wolves	50
2	Frank-Paul Nuuausala	Wigan Warriors	44
3	Charly Runciman	Widnes Vikings	35
4	Jesse Sene-Lefao	Castleford Tigers	34
5	Paul McShane	Castleford Tigers	32
6	Kruise Leeming	Huddersfield Giants	31
7	Zeb Taia	St Helens	30
8	Sam Moa	Catalans Dragons	28
9	Vincent Duport	Catalans Dragons	27
	Liam Finn	Wakefield Trinity	27

Marc Sneyd

Jack Hughes

Peta Hiku

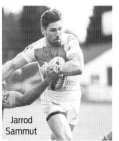
Jarrod Sammut

LEADING SCORERS

LEAGUE 1 *(Regular season, Super 8s & play-offs)*

TRIES

1	Liam Kay	Toronto Wolfpack	25
2	Craig Hall	Toronto Wolfpack	24
	Jonny Pownall	Toronto Wolfpack	24
4	Quentin Laulu-Togagae		
		Toronto Wolfpack	19
5	George Flanagan	Hunslet	18
	Joe Hambley	Workington Town	18
7	Shane Toal	Barrow Raiders	17
	Andy Gabriel	Keighley Cougars	17
	Blake Wallace	Toronto Wolfpack	17
10	Mo Agoro	Gloucestershire All Golds	16
	Adam Ryder	Keighley Cougars	16
	Lewis Young	Newcastle Thunder	16

GOALS

1	Craig Hall	Toronto Wolfpack	162
2	Matty Beharrell	Keighley Cougars	95
3	Paul Crook	Whitehaven	94
4	Benn Hardcastle	Newcastle Thunder	88
5	Lewis Charnock	Barrow Raiders	81
6	Carl Forber	Workington Town	68
7	Jack Miller	Doncaster	60
8	Connor Robinson	York City Knights	48
9	Tommy Johnson	North Wales Crusaders	44
10	Joe Sanderson	Hunslet	43

POINTS

			T	G	FG	Pts
1	Craig Hall	Toronto Wolfpack	24	162	0	420
2	Benn Hardcastle	Newcastle Thunder	11	88	3	223
3	Matty Beharrell	Keighley Cougars	5	95	2	212
4	Paul Crook	Whitehaven	2	94	3	199
5	Lewis Charnock	Barrow Raiders	8	81	0	194
6	Carl Forber	Workington Town	3	68	2	150
	Jack Miller	Doncaster	7	60	2	150
8	Tommy Johnson	North Wales Crusaders	5	44	0	108
9	Connor Robinson	York City Knights	2	48	3	107
10	Liam Kay	Toronto Wolfpack	25	0	0	100

LEAGUE 1 SHIELD

TRIES

1	Jordan Gill	Oxford	10
2	Mufaro Mvududu	Hunslet	9
3	George Flanagan	Hunslet	8
4	Hayden Freeman	Coventry Bears	7
5	Steve Parry	Gloucestershire All Golds	6
	Liam Mackay	Hunslet	6
	Mike Bishay	London Skolars	6
	Eddie Mbaraga	London Skolars	6

GOALS

1	Joe Sanderson	Hunslet	49
2	Jy-mel Coleman	London Skolars	39
3	Tommy Johnson	North Wales Crusaders	24
4	Ben Stead	Gloucestershire All Golds	15
5	Brad Delaney	Coventry Bears	12
	Ben Jones	South Wales Ironmen	12

POINTS

			T	G	FG	Pts
1	Joe Sanderson	Hunslet	4	49	0	114
2	Jy-mel Coleman	London Skolars	2	39	0	86
3	Tommy Johnson	North Wales Crusaders	4	24	0	64
4	Brad Delaney	Coventry Bears	5	12	0	44
5	Jordan Gill	Oxford	10	0	0	40

Greg Eden — Craig Hall

ALL COMPETITIONS

TRIES

1	Greg Eden	Castleford Tigers	41
2	Garry Lo	Sheffield Eagles	37
3	Ryan Shaw	Hull Kingston Rovers	27
	Liam Kay	Toronto Wolfpack	27
5	Joe Burgess	Wigan Warriors	26
	George Flanagan	Hunslet	26
7	Jarrod Sammut	London Broncos	25
	Craig Hall	Toronto Wolfpack	25
	Jonny Pownall	Toronto Wolfpack	25
10	Shane Toal	Barrow Raiders	24

GOALS

1	Craig Hall	Toronto Wolfpack	171
2	Jamie Ellis	Hull Kingston Rovers	158
3	Luke Gale	Castleford Tigers	145
4	Mark Kheirallah	Toulouse Olympique	120
5	Marc Sneyd	Hull FC	117
6	Lewis Charnock	Barrow Raiders	114
7	Steve Tyrer	Halifax	110
8	Liam Finn	Wakefield Trinity	106
	Matty Beharrell	Keighley Cougars	106
10	Paul Crook	Whitehaven	105

POINTS

			T	G	FG	Pts
1	Craig Hall	Toronto Wolfpack	25	171	0	442
2	Luke Gale	Castleford Tigers	14	145	9	355
3	Jamie Ellis	Hull Kingston Rovers	8	158	1	349
4	Mark Kheirallah	Toulouse Olympique	20	120	1	321
5	Steve Tyrer	Halifax	17	110	0	288
6	Lewis Charnock	Barrow Raiders	14	114	0	284
7	Jarrod Sammut	London Broncos	25	84	0	268
8	Marc Sneyd	Hull FC	7	117	4	266
9	Mark Percival	St Helens	17	97	0	262
10	Benn Hardcastle	Newcastle Thunder	11	96	3	239

FIELD GOALS

1	Luke Gale	Castleford Tigers	9
2	Chris Atkin	Hull Kingston Rovers/Swinton Lions	7
3	Marc Sneyd	Hull FC	4
	Luke Walsh	Catalans Dragons	4
	Anthony Thackeray	Featherstone Rovers	4

FINAL TABLES

SUPER LEAGUE - SUPER 8s

	P	W	D	L	F	A	D	Pts
Castleford Tigers	30	25	0	5	965	536	429	50
Leeds Rhinos	30	20	0	10	749	623	126	40
Hull FC	30	17	1	12	714	655	59	35
St Helens	30	16	1	13	663	518	145	33
Wakefield Trinity	30	16	0	14	745	648	97	32
Wigan Warriors	30	14	3	13	691	668	23	31
Salford Red Devils	30	14	0	16	680	728	-48	28
Huddersfield Giants	30	11	3	16	663	680	-17	25

SUPER 8s - THE QUALIFIERS

	P	W	D	L	F	A	D	Pts
Warrington Wolves	7	7	0	0	288	138	150	14
Widnes Vikings	7	5	0	2	188	96	92	10
Hull Kingston Rovers	7	5	0	2	166	158	8	10
Leigh Centurions	7	4	0	3	203	104	99	8
Catalans Dragons	7	4	0	3	130	143	-13	8
London Broncos	7	1	1	5	174	220	-46	3
Featherstone Rovers	7	1	1	5	110	272	-162	3
Halifax	7	0	0	7	82	210	-128	0

CHAMPIONSHIP SHIELD

	P	W	D	L	F	A	D	Pts
Toulouse Olympique	30	21	0	9	980	606	374	42
Batley Bulldogs	30	16	1	13	797	801	-4	33
Sheffield Eagles	30	13	0	17	762	986	-224	26
Dewsbury Rams	30	12	0	18	584	917	-333	24
Rochdale Hornets	30	8	1	21	569	956	-387	17
Swinton Lions	30	8	0	22	639	860	-221	16
Oldham	30	6	2	22	540	939	-399	14
Bradford Bulls *	30	11	0	19	698	867	-169	10

* Twelve points deducted for entering administration

LEAGUE 1 - SUPER 8s

	P	W	D	L	F	A	D	Pts
Toronto Wolfpack	22	20	1	1	1164	243	921	41
Barrow Raiders	22	18	1	3	731	381	350	37
Whitehaven	22	17	1	4	656	349	307	35
York City Knights	22	12	1	9	641	460	181	25
Newcastle Thunder	22	12	0	10	595	521	74	24
Doncaster	22	10	3	9	593	492	101	23
Keighley Cougars	22	10	2	10	728	565	163	22
Workington Town	22	9	1	12	532	621	-89	19

LEAGUE 1 SHIELD

	P	W	D	L	F	A	D	Pts
Hunslet	22	13	0	9	696	470	226	26
London Skolars	22	12	1	9	625	529	96	25
North Wales Crusaders	22	11	1	10	556	574	-18	23
Gloucestershire All Golds	22	9	0	13	478	702	-224	18
Oxford	22	6	1	15	393	849	-456	13
Coventry Bears	22	5	0	17	472	837	-365	10
Hemel Stags	22	3	0	19	393	1033	-640	6
South Wales Ironmen	22	2	1	19	299	926	-627	5

SUPER LEAGUE - REGULAR SEASON

	P	W	D	L	F	A	D	Pts
Castleford Tigers	23	20	0	3	769	378	391	40
Leeds Rhinos	23	15	0	8	553	477	76	30
Hull FC	23	13	1	9	541	483	58	27
Salford Red Devils	23	13	0	10	576	500	76	26
Wakefield Trinity	23	13	0	10	572	506	66	26
St Helens	23	12	1	10	513	420	93	25
Wigan Warriors	23	10	3	10	539	518	21	23
Huddersfield Giants	23	9	3	11	519	486	33	21
Warrington Wolves	23	9	2	12	422	557	-135	20
Catalans Dragons	23	7	1	15	469	689	-220	15
Leigh Centurions	23	6	0	17	425	615	-190	12
Widnes Vikings	23	5	1	17	359	628	-269	11

CHAMPIONSHIP - REGULAR SEASON

	P	W	D	L	F	A	D	Pts
Hull Kingston Rovers	23	19	1	3	850	385	465	39
London Broncos	23	18	0	5	832	410	422	36
Halifax	23	16	0	7	567	357	210	32
Featherstone Rovers	23	15	1	7	687	421	266	31
Toulouse Olympique	23	15	0	8	720	466	254	30
Batley Bulldogs	23	11	0	12	549	663	-114	22
Sheffield Eagles	23	10	0	13	568	785	-217	20
Dewsbury Rams	23	8	0	15	388	736	-348	16
Rochdale Hornets	23	7	1	15	457	680	-223	15
Swinton Lions	23	6	0	17	477	648	-171	12
Oldham	23	5	1	17	410	735	-325	11
Bradford Bulls *	23	6	0	17	500	719	-219	0

* Twelve points deducted for entering administration

LEAGUE 1 - REGULAR SEASON

	P	W	D	L	F	A	D	Pts
Toronto Wolfpack	15	15	0	0	916	157	759	30
Whitehaven	15	13	1	1	469	236	233	27
Barrow Raiders	15	12	1	2	576	264	312	25
York City Knights	15	10	0	5	487	305	182	20
Doncaster	15	9	2	4	449	327	122	20
Newcastle Thunder	15	9	0	6	459	328	131	18
Keighley Cougars	15	7	1	7	590	387	203	15
Workington Town	15	7	1	7	436	370	66	15
North Wales Crusaders	15	7	1	7	366	422	-56	15
Hunslet	15	7	0	8	418	377	41	14
London Skolars	15	6	1	8	367	453	-86	13
Gloucestershire All Golds	15	6	0	9	310	530	-220	12
Oxford	15	4	0	11	275	629	-354	8
Coventry Bears	15	2	0	13	287	615	-328	4
South Wales Ironmen	15	1	0	14	212	654	-442	2
Hemel Stags	15	1	0	14	229	792	-563	2